D1414495

CHRONOLOGY
OF THE MODERN WORLD

NEVILLE WILLIAMS
M.A., D.Phil., F.S.A., F.R. Hist. Soc.

Chronology of the Modern World

1763 to the present time

DAVID McKAY COMPANY, INC.
NEW YORK

FIRST AMERICAN EDITION 1967

LIBRARY OF CONGRESS CATALOG CARD NUMBER: 67–10887

Printed in Great Britain

TO
G. P. GOOCH

Contents

Introduction ix

Chronology 1

Index 711

Introduction

Chronology of the Modern World is a guide to the events and achievements in every walk of life of the past two centuries. The information is given chronologically, yet the volume incorporates a large-scale Index which readily provides specific references. Political and international events appear throughout on the left-hand page, year by year, in monthly paragraphs under precise calendar dates. The corresponding right-hand pages for each year are devoted to achievements in the Arts and Sciences, arranged under classified headings. Both the monthly paragraphs of the left-hand pages and the subject paragraphs of the right-hand pages bear individual letters, enabling speedy reference from the Index (A to N on the left; O to Z on the right). Thus the user will find the reference to Albert Schweitzer's death as '1965 Z', in fact the final paragraph in the volume.

1763 was chosen as the starting-point since the Treaty of Paris of that year, which concluded the Seven Years' War, marks the end of the long series of dynastic wars; the stage is set for the emergence of the New Europe and the New America. In 1763, too, we are on the threshold of the first great Industrial Revolution, and before long developments in science and technology come thick and fast. The tale has been carried forward from January 1763, year by year, with the increasing tempo of events in a gradually shrinking globe—and universe—to December 1965.

LEFT-HAND PAGES One or more of the chief events of the year have been selected to form head-lines. The January paragraph is given the reference 'A', February the reference 'B' and so on; but the letter 'I' has not been used to avoid possible confusion with 'J'. Those events for which no precise calendar date can be found have been placed at the end of the month in question, unless it is known that they took place early in the month. Beneath the December paragraph ('M') appears a final paragraph 'N', in which have been placed events that cannot be assigned to a particular month (e.g. a famine). Cross-references to the same or another year are included where appropriate; e.g. under 1807, Dec. 17th, 'Napoleon's Milan Decrees against British trade, extending Berlin Decrees (of Nov. 21st 1806).' To avoid unnecessary repetition in dates the convention —, has been used for indicating another event of the same date of the month as the previous entry. Each entry appears on a fresh line to make for clarity and quick reference.

RIGHT-HAND PAGES Here too, head-lines pick out the most significant achievements of the year. The paragraphs are classified under these headings:

- O Politics, Economics, Law and Education
- P Science, Technology, Discovery
- Q Scholarship (including archaeology and research in 'arts' subjects)
- R Philosophy and Religion
- S Art, Sculpture, Fine Arts and Architecture
- T Music
- U Literature (excluding plays)
- V The Press
- W Drama and Entertainment (including for the most modern period Films and Television programmes)
- X Sport
- Y Statistics (especially the populations of principal countries and cities, given at regular intervals, production figures for coal, steel and petroleum, the tonnage of merchant fleets, the size of armies and the demand for consumer goods)
- Z Births and Deaths of notabilities: exact calendar dates wherever known, including age at death and, if no longer living, adding death date in the birth entry, e.g. in paragraph 1792 Z under Aug. 4th we have 'Richard Arkwright d. (60) and Percy Bysshe Shelley b. (–1822)'

The titles of foreign works are given in translation whenever they have subsequently been translated into the English language. In works published anonymously the author's name is placed within square brackets, e.g. [A. and C. Tennyson], *Poems by Two Brothers*. Pseudonyms are noted and also works appearing posthumously.

On occasion an item might equally well have appeared in a different paragraph from the one in which it is placed; for example the first issue of the journal *The Musical Times* could be regarded as primarily a musical event or, alternatively, as a journalistic one. Again, comparative statistics for religious denominations could appear equally well under 'R' or under 'Y'. Any real problems raised by the choice of paragraphs for border-line cases and any unintentional oddities of arrangement that remain will be readily solved by means of the Index.

Though the selection of material for inclusion has not proved an easy task, the editor has throughout endeavoured to maintain a proper balance. In the last event the inclusion or omission of an item rested on personal choice; but he believes that though a score of different editors would all have included 95 per cent. of the same material, the final 5 per cent. would in each case have been very different. Nonetheless he holds that no major event has been omitted and no author, artist or musician of consequence has gone unrepresented. The editor and his assistants have always gone right to the sources to verify their facts and to resolve problems of inconsistency presented by different works of reference giving on occasion different dates for the same event. The number of common errors in various current works of reference has at times seemed alarming and every effort has been made to prevent their perpetuation in this volume. Opportunity has been taken in the long process of indexing of making further checks. In a work of this scope, however, it would be hypocritical to claim that no slips exist. Users of the *Chronology* are accordingly invited to inform the publisher of any entries in the text or index which they consider to be misleading or inaccurate and also to indicate any significant omissions. It is the aim of publisher and editor to provide the public with a work of reference of authority.

THE INDEX

Entries for Persons, Places and Subjects and titles of books are listed in one alphabetical sequence. Prefixes to surnames have been disregarded; e.g. de Gaulle appears under 'G'.

PERSONS The entries for Persons include full names and titles, dates of birth (and death), nationality and a brief description of their claim to fame (e.g. 'author', 'atomic physicist', 'soldier', 'Christian Democrat leader'). The nationality has been abbreviated: 'Am.' for American, 'B.' for British, 'F.' for French, 'G.' for German and 'R.' for Russian; for other countries abbreviations have been employed which avoid confusion—'Aus.' for Austrian and 'Austral.' for Australian. For important individuals there are classified sub-entries; in the case of a statesman, whose references are predominantly to the left-hand pages, these sub-entries are arranged chronologically and they give a conspectus of his entire career. For persons whose work features in right-hand pages the sub-entries are arranged by subjects (e.g. an important author's work will be subdivided 'as dramatist', 'as novelist' and 'as poet'). The entries for persons in fact form a Dictionary of Biography.

PLACES Places are assigned their country according to the current world map. Entries for major cities are for the sake of clarity divided into a series of sub-entries for events there, listed in date order, followed by a series for buildings and institutions in alphabetical order. For less important places there is only a chronological arrangement.

Prefixes such as 'New' or 'South' are taken as part of the place-name proper (e.g. New York appears under 'N' and South Africa under 'S'). Britain appears under 'B', and Russia under 'R'; but the United States of America appears under 'U'. The entries for countries are of two kinds. For minor states, such as Mexico or Poland, there is one chronological sequence of sub-entries; these show at a glance the country's history during these two centuries. For major states on the other hand, such as Britain, Russia and the United States, the sub-entries would be enormously bulky if the same system were followed. Accordingly, entries for major countries have been drastically pruned so that they relate to such topics as frontiers.

Someone primarily interested in the political history of a major country should turn to the classified Subject Entries mentioned below. For place-names the index entries provide a useful gazeteer.

SUBJECTS In this category the most important feature is the series in which political events are classified; these include entries for Administrations; Conferences and Congresses; Constitutions; Coup d'états; Elections; Legislation; Parliaments and other Elected Assemblies; Revolutions; Political Parties; Treaties. In each case the sub-entries are arranged by countries alphabetically and, within countries, chronologically. For example, to obtain the reference to the 20th amendment to the American Constitution the reader should turn to 'Constitutions, in US, Amendments to, 20th,' where he will see the reference = 1933 B. The entry 'Political Parties' lists all parties in each country from Algeria to Yugoslavia, alphabetically within the country. This approach forges a useful tool for the study of comparative history. In the same way there are general subject entries for such topics as Religious Denominations, and Wars.

TITLES OF WORKS All books and plays are indexed individually in the main alphabetical sequence; in each case the definite or indefinite article in the language of the title has been disregarded (e.g. *Importance of Being Earnest, The; Tale of Two Cities, A*. There are, however, general entries for Ballets; Films; Journals; Newspapers; Operas; and Overtures, within which these works are listed alphabetically.

OTHER SUBJECT ENTRIES such as Coal, Electricity, Epidemics, Photography and Universities are suitably subdivided. In the case of long entries this is by countries, otherwise it is alphabetical or chronological, as in each case seems most suitable.

CROSS-REFERENCES There are ample cross-references to guide the user, but without inflating the index unduly certain information is given in more than one place, to save the reader from unnecessary trouble (e.g. entries for the atomic bomb appear both under 'atom' and under 'bomb').

To sum up: the Index to the *Chronology* is almost an Encyclopaedia of Modern History. In not a few cases the user will find the index answers his problem without the necessity of turning to the text. (When did Goethe die? When was *Sunset Boulevard* filmed? What was Jerome K. Jerome's middle name? These and many kindred questions receive an immediate answer.) In many cases we predict that the user will be fascinated by the parallel entries in fields very different from his own and will become a happy browser.

* * *

The invitation to edit this *Chronology* came to me in April 1963 from Mr. Leopold Ullstein, who had for some time been pondering the possibilities of compiling a volume on the lines of Stein's *Kulturfahrplan* (first issued in Berlin in 1948). It at once became clear that to give adequate space both to political events and to all significant aspects of man's development in a single volume would mean concentrating on the last two centuries,

CHRONOLOGY

1763 Peace of Paris ends Seven Years' War

A **Jan:**

B **Feb:** 10th, the Peace of Paris between Britain, France and Spain ends the Seven Years' War (called in America the French and Indian War), the last of the series of dynastic wars; by its terms (1) Britain secures Canada, Nova Scotia, Cape Breton, St. Vincent, Tobago, Dominica, Grenada, Senegal and Minorca from France, and Florida from Spain; (2) France regains Martinique, Guadaloupe, St. Lucia and Goree and is guaranteed fishing rights off Newfoundland; (3) the French settlements in India are restored, but no fortifications are to be built there; (4) Spain acquires Louisiana from France, exchanges Florida for Havana and recovers Manila and the Philippines;
15th, peace treaty of Hubertusburg between Prussia and Austria restores the *status quo* with Austria restoring Glatz and Silesia to Prussia and Prussia evacuating Saxony, and by a secret article Frederick the Great of Prussia undertakes to support the election of Archduke Joseph of Austria as King of the Romans.

C **Mar:**

D **Apr:** 7th, Earl of Bute's ministry falls in Britain and,
16th, George Grenville becomes prime minister and chancellor of Exchequer;
18th, Henry Fox's refusal to give up the lucrative post of paymaster-general, on elevation to peerage, provokes bitter ministerial conflict;
23rd, John Wilkes attacks the King's Speech, commending the terms of peace, in No. 45 of the *North Briton* and
30th, he is arrested on a general warrant.

E **May:** 6th, chief justice Pratt discharges Wilkes on ground of Parliamentary privilege and declares general warrants illegal;
7th, rising of Indians under Pontiac near Detroit spreads rapidly east (–1766);
25th, internal free trade in corn in France (–1766).

F **Jun:**

G **Jul:** Mir Kasim of Murshidabad, defeated by Thomas Adams and deposed, takes refuge in Oudh;
Act to prevent fraudulent votes in British elections;
'Whiteboys' revolt against agrarian hardships in Ireland.

H **Aug:**

J **Sep:** 9th, the group of Whigs led by John Duke of Bedford joins the government and the Earl of Shelbourne retires from the ministry on personal grounds.

K **Oct:** 3rd, Augustus III, elective King of Poland, dies;
7th, British proclamation provides for government of the new colonies of Quebec, East and West Florida and Grenada, while assignment of region west of the Alleghenies as an Indian reserve halts westward expansion and imperial government takes over regulation of trade with the Indians.

L **Nov:** 23rd, in Wilkes affair the Commons resolve that Parliamentary privilege does not extend to seditious libels.

M **Dec:** Patrick Henry delivers radical speech in 'the parson's cause' in Virginia, brought by an incumbent for restitution of salary, in which he denies right of British crown to disallow acts of colonial legislatures.

N Hyder Ali, Indian adventurer in Mysore, conquers Kanara.

O **Politics, Economics, Law and Education**

J. J. Rousseau in *Lettres de la Montagne* attacks the constitution and council of Geneva for condemning his *Émile* (1762).

Frederick the Great establishes village schools in Prussia.

P **Science, Technology, Discovery, etc.**

J. G. Kölreuter's experiments on the fertilisation of plants by animal pollen-carriers.

Q **Scholarship**

David Hume, *History of Great Britain.*

Almanack de Gotha first issued.

R **Philosophy and Religion**

Voltaire, *Treatise on Tolerance.*

John Campbell, *Dissertation on Miracles.*

Justinus Febronius (von Hontheim, Bishop of Treves), *De Statu Ecclesiae*, urges the supremacy of general councils (it is to be condemned by Pope Clement XIII in 1766).

Henry Venn, *Complete Duty of Man.*

S **Art, Sculpture, Fine Arts and Architecture**

Francesco Guardi, *Election of a Doge* (painting).

Étienne Falconet, *Pygmalion and Galathea* (sculpture).

Horace Walpole, *Catalogue of Engravers born and resident in England.*

The Madeleine, Paris, completed.

T **Music**

U **Literature**

Giuseppi Parini, *Il Mattino.*

James Boswell meets Samuel Johnson (*May* 16th).

V **The Press**

St. James's Chronicle issued.

W **Drama and Entertainment**

Almack opens a gaming-house in London (later becoming Brooks').

X **Sport**

Y **Statistics**

Z **Births and Deaths**

Mar. 21st 'Jean Paul' (Frederick Richter) b. (–1825).

Oct. 10th Xavier de Maistre b. (–1852).

1764 Wilkes sentenced for seditious libel

A Jan: 19th, John Wilkes is expelled from Commons for having written seditious libel; riots in London in favour of Wilkes.

B Feb: 21st, court of King's Bench finds Wilkes guilty of reprinting No. 45 of the *North Briton* and printing the *Essay on Woman.*

C Mar:

D Apr: 11th, treaty between Russia and Prussia guarantees the present constitutions of Poland and Sweden, and provides for controlling election to Polish monarchy and joint action against Nationalists.

E May: 18th, British Parliament amends Sugar Act from a commercial to a fiscal measure, to tax American Colonists and establish a single Vice-Admiralty court for the thirteen colonies.

F Jun:

G Jul:

H Aug:

J Sep: 7th, Stanislas Poniatowski, the protégé of Russia, elected King of Poland.

K Oct: 23rd, Hector Munro defeats Nabwab of Oudh at Buxar, Bengal.

L Nov: 26th, suppression of Jesuits in France.

M Dec:

N Catharine II confiscates ecclesiastical lands in Russia, paying the clergy salaries, to deprive them of political power.
Hyder Ali usurps the throne of Mysore and takes Calcutta.
Réunion becomes a French crown colony.
De Bougainville claims Falkland Isles for France.

O Politics, Economics, Law and Education
C. Beccaria-Bonesana, *On Crimes and Punishments.*
Brown University, Providence, Rhode Island, founded.

P Science, Technology, Discovery, etc.
Joseph Black measures the latent heat of steam.
J. G. Zimmermann, *On Discovery in Medicine.*
James Hargreaves invents the spinning jenny.
P. M. J. Trésaguet develops three-tier method of road making in France.

Q Scholarship
J. A. Ernesti's edition of Polybius.
J. J. Winckelmann, *History of Ancient Art.*
The Dilettanti Society of London sends three members to Greece and Asia Minor to study antiquities.
Adam Anderson, *The Origins of Commerce.*

R Philosophy and Religion
Charles Bonnet, *Contemplation de la nature.*
Thomas Reid's *Inquiry in the Human Mind on the Principles of Common Sense* founds the philosophical school of natural realism.
F. M. A. de Voltaire, *Philosophical Dictionary.*
August Spangenberg reforms the Moravian Brethren.

S Art, Sculpture, Fine Arts and Architecture
J. A. Houdon, *St. Bruno* (sculpture).
Robert Adam, Kenwood House, Middlesex.
The Pantheon, Paris (–1790).

T Music
Joseph Haydn, 'The Philosopher' Symphony (No. 22 in E flat).
J. C. Bach gives recitals in London.

U Literature
Oliver Goldsmith, *The Traveller.*
Dr. Johnson founds The Literary Club, London, in which Edmund Burke, Edward Gibbon, Goldsmith and Joshua Reynolds are prominent.
Jeanne de Lespinasse and Suzanne Necker found salons in Paris.

V The Press

W Drama and Entertainment

X Sport

Y Statistics

Z Births and Deaths
Sept. 12th Jean Philippe Rameau d. (81).
Oct. 26th William Hogarth d. (67).
— John Kay d. (60).

1765 American colonists oppose Stamp Act—Clive's reforms in India

A Jan:

B Feb:

C Mar: 23rd, British Parliament passes Stamp Act, devised by Grenville for taxing the American colonies.

D Apr:

E May: 29th, In the Virginian assembly Patrick Henry challenges the right of Britain to tax the colonies;
Robert Clive begins administrative reforms in Bengal (–1767).

F Jun:

G Jul: 16th, Grenville resigns on collapse of ministry over a Regency bill, and Marquess of Rockingham forms a government.

H Aug: 13th, Archduke Leopold becomes ruler of Tuscany, and shortly abolishes the Inquisition in the duchy;
18th, Joseph II of Austria succeeds as Holy Roman Emperor on death of Francis I, but is co-regent with Maria Theresa in Bohemia and Hungary.

J Sep: British government acquires fiscal rights in Isle of Man from Duke of Atholl.

K Oct: 27th, delegates from nine colonies attend Stamp Act Congress in New York and, 19th, draw up a declaration of rights and liberties.

L Nov:

M Dec: on death of the Dauphin, his son, Louis Augustus (future Louis XVI) becomes heir to French throne.

N

O **Politics, Economics, Law and Education**
A. R. J. Turgot, *Réflexions sur la formation et la distribution des richesses.*
William Blackstone, *Commentaries on the Laws of England* (–1769).
The first gymnasium opened, Breslau.

P **Science, Technology, Discovery, etc.**
L. Spallanzani pioneers preserving through hermetic sealing and argues against spontaneous generation.
James Watt invents a condenser (which leads to his construction of a steam engine, 1775).

Q **Scholarship**

R **Philosophy and Religion**
A. Tucker, *The Light of Nature Pursued* (–1774).
C. F. Nicolai begins to edit the 'Universal German Library' as an organ for popular philosophy (–1792).

S **Art, Sculpture, Fine Arts and Architecture**
J. H. Fragonard, *Corésus et Callirhoé* (painting).
J. B. Greuze, *La Bonne Mère* and *Le Mauvais Fils Puni* (paintings).
F. Boucher is appointed court painter at Versailles and paints Mme de Pompadour.
A. J. Gabriel, Place de la Concorde, Paris.

T **Music**

U **Literature**
Henry Brooke, *The Fool of Quality; or The History of Henry Earl of Moreland* (–1770).
Thomas Chatterton forges the 'Rowley' poems.
Thomas Percy, aided by William Shenstone, *Reliquies of Ancient English Poetry.*
Horace Walpole's *The Castle of Otranto* founds the English romantic school of fiction.
C. M. Wieland, *Comic Tales.*

V **The Press**

W **Drama and Entertainment**
M. J. Sedaine, *Philosophe sans le savoir.*

X **Sport**

Y **Statistics**

Z **Births and Deaths**
Apr. 5th Edward Young d. (82).
Dec. 8th Eli Whitney b. (–1825).
— Robert Fulton b. (–1815).

1766 Britain declares its right to tax American colonies

A Jan:

B Feb: 23rd, on death of Stanislaus Leszczynski the duchy of Lorraine, then under his rule, is incorporated in France.

C Mar: 11th, British Parliament repeals the Stamp Act by 275–161 votes but, 18th, passes Declaratory Act, declaring Britain's right to tax the American colonies.

D Apr:

E May:

F Jun: Count Aranda becomes chief minister in Spain and introduces secular education.

G Jul: 12th, on Rockingham's dismissal by George III, Pitt, becoming Earl of Chatham, forms a ministry with Duke of Grafton; Henry Conway and Shelburne becoming secretaries of state and Charles Townshend chancellor of Exchequer (dubbed by Burke 'a tessellated pavement without cement').

H Aug:

J Sep:

K Oct:

L Nov: 12th, the Nizam Ali of Hyderabad cedes Northern Circars, Madras, to Britain.

M Dec:

N Russia and Prussia interfere in Polish affairs against the Nationalists.
Internal free trade in corn, in France, since 1763, abolished (re-introduced 1774).
John Byron, ignorant of de Bougainville's annexation in 1764, takes Falkland Isles for Britain and establishes Port Egmont.
Ali Bey assumes power in Egypt.

O Politics, Economics, Law and Education

Adam Ferguson, *Essay on the History of Civil Society*.

P Science, Technology, Discovery, etc.

Henry Cavendish discovers hydrogen is less dense than air and delivers papers to the Royal Society on the chemistry of gases.

John Byron returns (*May* 9th) from voyage of circumnavigation.

Louis de Bougainville's voyage of discovery in the Pacific (–*Mar.* 1769) on which he names the Navigators Islands.

Q Scholarship

G. E. Lessing, *Laocoön*.

R Philosophy and Religion

Francis Blackburne, *Confessional*.

The French clergy again required to observe the Gallican Articles, 1682, limiting papal authority.

Pope Clement XIII sanctions the celebration of the Sacred Heart (founded by Marguerite Alacoque, d. 1690).

Catherine the Great grants freedom of worship in Russia.

S Art, Sculpture, Fine Arts and Architecture

J. H. Fragonard, *The Swing* (painting).

E. M. Falconet, equestrian monument to Peter the Great, St. Petersburg (–1779).

Denis Diderot, *Essai sur la Peinture*.

T Music

J. Haydn, *Great Mass with Organ* (No. 4 in E flat).

U Literature

Heinrich Gerstenberg, *Letters on the Curiosities of Literature* (–1770), formulates the principles of *Sturm und Drang*.

Oliver Goldsmith, *Vicar of Wakefield*.

C. M. Wieland, *The Story of Agathon*.

V The Press

W Drama and Entertainment

X Sport

Y Statistics

Z Births and Deaths.

Feb. 17th T. R. Malthus b. (–1834).
Mar. 9th William Cobbett b. (–1835).
Apr. 22nd Mme de Staël b. (–1817).
Sep. 26th John Dalton b. (–1844).
Dec. 29th Charles Macintosh b. (–1843).

A **Jan:** Robert Clive leaves India, where chaos soon prevails, until the arrival of Warren Hastings in 1772.

B **Feb:** 29th, reduction of land tax in Britain from 4s. to 3s. in £ is forced on the government by back-benchers representing the landed interest.

C **Mar:** 1st, Charles III expels the Jesuits from Spain, later in year the Order is expelled from Parma and the Two Sicilies;
Chatham's illness prevents his attending Parliament until *Jan.* 1769.

D **Apr:** revised Russo-Prussian alliance, by which Frederick the Great undertakes to support the Polish Opposition factions, to enter Poland if Austria should invade it and to support Russia in the event of a war with Turkey.

E **May:** Townshend introduces taxes on imports of tea, glass, paper and dyestuffs in American colonies to provide revenue for colonial administration.

F **Jun:** New York Assembly is suspended for refusing to support the quartering of troops.

G **Jul:**

H **Aug:** Burmese invade Siam.

J **Sep:** at public meeting in Boston a non-importation agreement is framed in protest at the new taxes;
6th, Lord North becomes chancellorof Exchequer on Townshend's death.

K **Oct:**

L **Nov:** Polish Diet meets, under Russian sway.

M **Dec:**

N Russian agents agitate in Montenegro and Bosnia against Turkish rule.

O **Politics, Economics, Law and Education**

P **Science, Technology, Discovery, etc.**

P. S. Pallas, *Elenchus Zoophytorum*.

Nautical Almanac first issued, edited by Nevil Maskelyne, astronomer royal.

Joseph Priestley, *History of Electricity*.

Q **Scholarship**

C. Heyne, edits Vergil's *Opera*.

J. J. Winckelmann, *Monumenti antichi inediti* (–1768).

R **Philosophy and Religion**

Moses Mendelssohn, *Phaedon*.

J. F. Marmontel censured by Archbishop of Paris and the Sorbonne for dealing with religious toleration in his novel *Bélisaire*.

S **Art, Sculpture, Fine Arts and Architecture**

Allan Ramsay is appointed portrait painter to George III.

T **Music**

C. W. Gluck, *Alceste* (opera).

J.-J. Rousseau, *Dictionnaire de Musique*.

U **Literature**

Michael Bruce, *Elegy Written in Spring*.

J. K. Lavater, *Swiss Songs*.

H. Gerstenberg, *Ariadne auf Naxos*.

L. Sterne completes *Tristram Shandy*.

V **The Press**

W **Drama and Entertainment**

O. Goldsmith, *The Good Natur'd Man*.

G. E. Lessing, *Minna of Barnhelm* and *Hamburgische Dramaturgie* (–1768).

X **Sport**

Y **Statistics**

Z **Births and Deaths**

Mar. 15th Andrew Jackson b. (–1845).

July 11th John Quincy Adams b. (–1848).

Sept. 8th August Schlegel b. (–1845).

Oct. 25th Benjamin Constant b. (–1830).

1768 Turkey declares war on Russia

A **Jan**: 20th, a Secretary of State for the Colonies is first appointed in Britain.

B **Feb**:

C **Mar**: 28th, John Wilkes is elected M.P. for Middlesex.

D **Apr**:

E **May**: 10th, riots in Westminster in favour of Wilkes on assembling of Parliament (and in *June* when he is sentenced for seditious libel).

F **Jun**:

G **Jul**: Massachusetts Assembly is dissolved for refusing to assist collection of taxes;
France purchases Corsica from Genoa.

H **Aug**: Confederation founded in Poland at Bar, aided by France, to counter Russian designs; attempts are made by the Confederates to kidnap King Stanislas and Civil War breaks out.

J **Sep**: Boston citizens refuse to quarter troops sent to quell riot.

K **Oct**: 19th, Shelburne resigns from Grafton's ministry in Britain;
Austria finally renounces all claims to Silesia;
Turkey, instigated by France, declares war on Russia in defence of Polish liberties.

L **Nov**: 7th, Frederick the Great of Prussia completes Political Testament.

M **Dec**: 3rd, Prince von Kaunitz, Austrian Chancellor, suggests to Joseph II of Austria the practicability of partitioning Poland.

N Pope Clement XIII confiscates Parma in retaliation for the expulsion of the Jesuits, whereupon the King of Naples invades the Papal States and France seizes Avignon.
The Gurkhas conquer Nepal.

O **Politics, Economics, Law and Education**
Joseph Priestley, *Essay on the First Principles of Government.*

P **Science, Technology, Discovery, etc.**
P. S. Pallas travels through Russia to the Chinese frontier to observe (1769) the transit of Venus.
James Cook sails (*May* 25th) on first voyage of discovery, on which he explores the Society Islands and charts the coasts of New Zealand and W. Australia (returns *June* 1771).

Q **Scholarship**
J. A. Ernesti, *Archaeologia litteraria.*

R **Philosophy and Religion**
Abraham Booth, *Reign of Grace.*
Emanuel Swedenborg, *Delititiae Sapientiae.*

S **Art, Sculpture, Fine Arts and Architecture**
The Royal Academy is founded, with Joshua Reynolds as president, who begins delivering fifteen discourses on art (–1790).
Augustin Pajou undertakes decorative sculpture on Opera House, Versailles.

T **Music**
W. A. Mozart, *Bastien and Bastienne* (opera).

U **Literature**
James Boswell, *Account of Corsica, Journal of a Tour of that Island and Memoir of Pascal Paoli.*
Thomas Gray, *Poems.*
L. Sterne, *A Sentimental Journey.*
Jean de Saint-Lambert, *Les Saisons.*

V **The Press**
'Junius' first appears in *The Public Advertiser* (Oct.).

W **Drama and Entertainment**
M. J. Sedaine, *La Gageure Imprévue.*

X **Sport**

Y **Statistics**

Z **Births and Deaths**
Mar. 18th Laurence Sterne d. (55).
Mar. 22nd Bryan Donkin b. (–1855).
Sept. 4th. François Chateaubriand b. (–1848).

1769 Britain retains tax on tea in America

A **Jan**: John Wilkes is elected an alderman of London.
The Letters of Junius begin attacks on George III, Grafton, Lord Chief Justice Mansfield and other ministers.
The Bourbons demand the dissolution of the Jesuits.

B **Feb**: 2nd, death of Pope Clement XIII;
4th, Wilkes is expelled from Parliament and, though thrice re-elected for Middlesex, the Commons declare his opponent to be the successful candidate (*Apr.* 15th).
Chatham returns to Lords.
Austria occupies Lemberg and the Zips region of Poland.

C **Mar**:

D **Apr**: 22nd, Mme du Barry becomes official mistress of Louis XV.

E **May**: 1st, Privy Council decides to retain the tea duty in American colonies after weeks of argument;
19th, after three-month struggle between pro and anti Jesuit factions in the College of Cardinals, the latter's candidate, Lorenzo Ganganelli, is elected Pope Clement XIV.

F **Jun**: Hyder Ali of Mysore compels British at Madras to sign treaty of mutual assistance.

G **Jul**: The Virginia Assembly is dissolved after protesting about the practice of removing colonial treason trials to Westminster.

H **Aug**: France expels Pasquale Paoli, the Corsican patriot, from the island;
Frederick II and Joseph II meet in Neisse to discuss partition of Poland.

J **Sep**: Russian troops occupy Moldavia.

K **Oct**: Prusso-Russian alliance is renewed until 1780; Joseph II guaranteeing Frederick II the reversion of Ansbach and Bayreuth, while Prussia guarantees to uphold the Swedish constitution.

L **Nov**: Russian troops occupy Bucharest.

M **Dec**: Russia signs treaty with Denmark to prevent the overthrow of the Swedish constitution.

N Serious famine in Bengal (–1770).
Burma acknowledges suzerainty of China.

O **Politics, Economics, Law and Education**
E. Burke, *Observations on a late Publication on the Present State of the Nation.*
Richard Price's observations on population and the expectancy of life draw attention to inadequate calculations of British insurance and benefit societies.
The first crêche is opened, at Steintal, Alsace.

P **Science, Technology, Discovery, etc.**
Richard Arkwright's spinning machine.
Joseph Black's condenser.
Nicolas Cugnot's steam road carriage.
Josiah Wedgwood opens pottery works at Etruria, near Burslem.
First lightning conductors on high buildings.

Q **Scholarship**
E. Forcellini, *Totius Latinitatis Lexicon.*
W. Robertson, *History of Charles V.*
Museum Pio-Clementiano, Rome, opened.

R **Philosophy and Religion**
Charles Bonnet, *Palingénésie philosophique* (–1770).

S **Art, Sculpture, Fine Arts and Architecture**
Robert Adam and his brothers, The Adelphi, London.

T **Music**
C. P. E. Bach, *Passion Cantata.*

U **Literature**
J. G. Herder, *Kritische Wälder.*
G. E. Lessing, *Wie die Alten den Tod gebildet.*

V **The Press**
The Morning Chronicle, London, issued.

W **Drama and Entertainment**
J. F. Ducis produces his adaptation of Shakespeare's *Hamlet* in Paris.

X **Sport**

Y **Statistics**

Z **Births and Deaths**
Mar. 29th Nicholas Jean Soult b. (–1851).
May 1st Arthur Wellesley, later Duke of Wellington, b. (–1852).
May 4th Thomas Lawrence b. (–1830).
June 18th Robert Stewart, later Viscount Castlereagh b. (–1822).
Aug. 1st Napoleon b. (–1821).
Aug. 23rd G. L. P. C. Cuvier b. (–1832).
Sept. 14th Alexander von Humboldt b. (–1859).
— Giovanni Tiepolo d. (77).

1770 North becomes British prime minister—Struensee's government in Denmark

A Jan: 28th, North becomes prime minister on Grafton's resignation, forming the ministry of 'The King's Friends'.

B Feb:

C Mar: 3rd, brawl between civilians and troops in Boston (annually celebrated as Boston Massacre).

D Apr: British Parliament repeals duties on paper, glass and dyestuffs in American colonies, but retains tea duty.

E May: 16th, Dauphin of France marries Marie Antoinette, daughter of the Empress Maria Theresa of Austria.

F Jun: 13th, the printers and publishers of *The Letters of Junius* are tried for seditious libel.

G Jul: 5th (–6th), Russian fleet, officered by British sailors, defeats Turkish navy at Tchesme.

H Aug: duc de Choiseul's intervention prevents war between Spain and Britain over possession of Falkland Isles.

J Sep: Joseph II of Austria and Frederick II of Prussia meet at Neustadt to discuss plans for halting Russia's expansion;
13th, J. F. Struensee, favourite of Queen Caroline Matilda, secures fall of Count Bernstorff in Denmark.

K Oct:

L Nov:

M Dec: 5th, Struensee abolishes the Council in Denmark and becomes supreme; begins far-reaching programme of reforms, introducing freedom of worship and of press;
24th, Choiseul falls from power in France through intrigues of Mme du Barry and of duc D'Aiguillon, who succeeds him as minister of foreign affairs, aided by René Maupeou.

N Marathas bring Delhi under their sway.

O **Politics, Economics, Law and Education**
E. Burke, *Thoughts on the Cause of the Present Discontents.*
Ferdinando Galiani, in *Dialogues sur le Commerce des Blés*, attacks the Physiocrats.
Elementary education in the Austrian Empire is organised.
First public restaurant opened in Paris.

P **Science, Technology, Discovery, etc.**
John Hill introduces method of obtaining specimens for microscopic study.
Leonhard Euler, *Introduction to Algebra.*
Jesse Ramsden's screw-cutting lathe.
James Cook discovers Botany Bay (*Apr.* 28th).

Q **Scholarship**

R **Philosophy and Religion**
James Beattie, *Essay on the Nature and Immutability of Truth in opposition to Sophistry and Scepticism.*
Immanuel Kant, *De mundi sensibilis et intelligibilis forma et principiis.*
Paul Holbach, *Système de la Nature*, attacking Christianity, is refuted by Voltaire an by Frederick the Great.

S **Art, Sculpture, Fine Arts and Architecture**
T. Gainsborough, *The Blue Boy* (painting).

T **Music**
Handel's *Messiah* is first performed in New York.

U **Literature**
O. Goldsmith, *The Deserted Village.*
J. F. Marmontel, *Sylvain.*

V **The Press**
The Massachusetts Spy is issued.

W **Drama and Entertainment**
Johannes Ewald, *Rolf Krage*, the first Danish tragedy.

X **Sport**

Y **Statistics**

Z **Births and Deaths**
Mar. 11th William Huskisson b. (–1830).
Apr. 7th William Wordsworth b. (–1850).
Apr. 11th George Canning b. (–1827).
May 30th François Boucher d. (67).
Aug. 25th Thomas Chatterton d. (18).
Aug. 27th Georg Hegel b. (–1831).
Nov. 19th Bertil Thorwaldsen b. (–1857).
Dec. 17th Beethoven b. (–1827).

A **Jan**: 22nd, Spain agrees to cede the Falkland Isles to Britain, but makes no reparation for insult to British flag;

Prince Henry of Prussia visits Russia and proposes partition of Poland;

Maupeou overthrows the French Parlements, which he replaces by a simplified system of courts.

B **Feb**:

C **Mar**: 27th, Brass Crosby is taken into custody for breach of privilege over printing Parliamentary debates, the last attempt to prevent reporting of debates.

D **Apr**:

E **May**:

F **Jun**: Russia completes conquest of the Crimea.

G **Jul**: 6th, Austria and Turkey sign treaty with intention of forcing Russia to restore her conquests.

H **Aug**:

J **Sep**:

K **Oct**:

L **Nov**:

M **Dec**:

N

O **Politics, Economics, Law and Education**

Richard Price, *Appeal to the Public on the subject of the National Debt.*

Abolition of serfdom in Savoy.

P **Science, Technology, Discovery, etc.**

Luigi Galvani discovers electric nature of nervous impulse.

J. A. Deluc establishes rules for measuring heights by the barometer.

The Smeatonian Club, a society of engineers, is founded in Britain.

Q **Scholarship**

Jacopo Facciolati, aided by Egidio Forcellini, *Totius Latinitatis Lexicon.*

A. H. Anquetil Duperron translates *The Zenda Avesta.*

W. Robertson, *History of America.*

Encyclopædia Britannica, first edition.

R **Philosophy and Religion**

J. S. Semler, *Studies in the Free Investigation of the Canon* (–1775).

J. W. Fletcher publishes under John Wesley's stimulus *Five Checks to Antinomianism.*

Wesley disowns justification by works.

John Jebb and other divines become Unitarians on the failure of a Parliamentary petition to free English clergy from subscription to the 39 Articles.

S **Art, Sculpture, Fine Arts and Architecture**

Benjamin West, *The Death of Wolfe* (painting).

J. A. Houdon, bust of Diderot.

Horace Walpole completes *Anecdotes of Painting.*

T **Music**

J. Haydn, the 'Sun' quartets (Nos. 31–6).

N. Piccini, *Antigone* (opera).

U **Literature**

Matthias Claudius publishes essays and poems in *The Wandsbeck Messenger* (–1775).

F. Klopstock, *Odes.*

T. Smollett, *The Expedition of Humphry Clinker.*

C. M. Wieland, *Der neue Amadis.*

V **The Press**

W **Drama and Entertainment**

X **Sport**

Y **Statistics**

Z **Births and Deaths**

Apr. 13th Richard Trevithick b. (–1833).

May 14th Robert Owen b. (–1858).

June 3rd Sydney Smith b. (–1845).

July 7th Thomas Gray d. (55).

Aug. 15th Walter Scott b. (–1832).

Sept. 17th Tobias Smollet d. (51).

1772 First Partition of Poland

A Jan: 17th, Ove Guldberg secures arrest of Struensee in Denmark.

B Feb: 28th, Boston assembly threatens secession from Britain unless rights of colonies are maintained.

C Mar: 24th, following the marriages to commoners of the Dukes of Cumberland and Gloucester, Parliament places all descendants of George II under terms of Royal Marriage Act;
30th, Robert Clive defends his administration of Bengal in the Commons.

D Apr: 13th, Warren Hastings appointed governor of Bengal (–1785).

E May:

F Jun: 10th, mob in Rhode Island burns revenue cutter *Gaspée*.

G Jul: Britain refuses to allow French fleet to enter Baltic, to support Gustavus III against his Swedish subjects.

H Aug: 5th, Frederick the Great, fearing Austria's concern at Russian conquests in Turkey will lead to a general war, engineers First Partition of Poland, Prussia taking West Poland (except Danzig) and Ermland, Austria taking East Galicia and Lodomerica and Russia taking lands east of Dvina and Dnieper;
19th, Gustavus III re-establishes full authority of monarchy in Sweden.

J Sep:

K Oct:

L Nov: 2nd (–*Jan.* 1773), Committees of Correspondence for action against British are formed in Massachusetts under Samuel Adams.

M Dec:

N

O **Politics, Economics, Law and Education**

Comte de Mirabeau, *Essai sur le Despotisme*.

Lord Mansfield's decision that a slave is free on landing in England (Somerset's Case).

F. S. Sullivan, *Lectures on the Feudal and English Laws*.

P **Science, Technology, Discovery, etc.**

Daniel Rutherford discovers nitrogen.

Henry Cavendish, *Attempts to Explain some of the Phenomena of Electricity*.

J. Priestley discovers that plants give off oxygen.

L. Euler expounds the principles of mechanics, optics, acoustics and astronomy in *Lettres à une princesse d'Allemagne*.

Jean Rome de l'Isle, *Essai de Cristallographie*.

Thomas Coke begins reforms in animal husbandry at Holkham, Norfolk.

James Bruce explores Abyssinia and traces the Blue Nile to its confluence with the White Nile.

The Bromberg Canal, linking Rivers Oder and Vistula, begun (–1775).

First carriage-traffic on the Brenner Pass.

Q **Scholarship**

J. G. Herder's *On the Origins of Speech* begins the study of comparative philology.

R **Philosophy and Religion**

Albrecht von Haller, *Chief Truths of Revelation*.

S **Art, Sculpture, Fine Arts and Architecture**

T **Music**

J. Haydn, 'Farewell' Symphony (No. 45 in F sharp minor).

First German performance of Handel's *Messiah*.

U **Literature**

P. A. F. Choderlos de Laclos, *Les Liaisons Dangereuses*.

Hainbund, a society of young, patriotic poets, is formed at Göttingen.

V **The Press**

The Morning Post, London, issued (*Nov.* 2nd.).

W **Drama and Entertainment**

G. Bessenyei, *Tragedy of Agis*.

Lessing, *Emilia Galotti*.

X **Sport**

Y **Statistics**

British Textile Trade:

raw cotton imports	5·3 mill. lb.
exported linens	11·6 mill. yds.
exported silks	91,000 lb.

Z **Births and Deaths**

Mar. 29th Emanuel Swedenborg d. (84).

Apr. 11th Manuel Quintana b. (–1857).

Apr. 19th David Ricardo b. (–1823).

Sept. 30th James Brindley d. (56).

Oct. 21st S. T. Coleridge b. (–1834).

1773 Boston Tea Party

A **Jan:**

B **Feb:** Renewal of France's alliance with Sweden.

C **Mar:** 12th, Virginia House of Burgesses appoints a Provincial Committee of Correspondence for mutual action against British, and other colonies follow this lead.

D **Apr:**

E **May:** British East India Company Regulating Act provides for a governor-general and a council in India and officers are forbidden to trade for themselves.

F **Jun:**

G **Jul:** 21st, Pope Clement XIV by the bull *Dominus ac Redemptor* dissolves the Jesuits.

H **Aug:**

J **Sep:** Warren Hastings, first governor-general of India, makes alliance with the state of Oudh for campaign against the Mahrathas.

K **Oct:** 16th, Denmark cedes the duchy of Oldenburg to Russia.
Pugachoff, a pretender, leads revolt of Cossacks in S.E. Russia, which checks Russian advance in Turkey.

L **Nov:**

M **Dec:** 16th, Boston Tea Party.
France restores Avignon to Papacy.

N Spanish ordinance that an industrial occupation is not prejudicial to rank or prestige.

O **Politics, Economics, Law and Education**
John Erskine, *Institutes of the Law of Scotland.*

P **Science, Technology, Discovery, etc.**
Cast-iron bridge at Coalbrookdale, Shropshire (–1779).
Veterinary and Agricultural College, Copenhagen, founded.

Q **Scholarship**
James, Lord Monboddo, *Origin and Progress of Language* (–1792).
Philadelphia Museum, Pennsylvania, founded.

R **Philosophy and Religion**

S **Art, Sculpture, Fine Arts and Architecture**
Joshua Reynolds, *The Graces Decorating Hymen* (painting).

T **Music**
Charles Burney, *The Present State of Music in Germany, the Netherlands and the United Provinces.*

U **Literature**
G. A. Bürger, *Leonore.*
A. von Haller, *Alfred.*
J. G. Herder, *Von deutscher Art und Kunst.*
G. F. Klopstock, *Messiah.*

V **The Press**
Der Deutsche Mercur (–1810), edited by C. M. Wieland.

W **Drama and Entertainment**
J. W. Goethe, *Goetz von Berlichingen.*
O. Goldsmith, *She Stoops to Conquer.*
Swedish national theatre is established in Stockholm.

X **Sport**

Y **Statistics**

Z **Births and Deaths**
Mar. 24th Philip Stanhope, Earl of Chesterfield d. (78).
May 9th Sismondi b. (–1842).
May 15th Clemens Prince Metternich b. (–1859).
Oct. 6th Louis Philippe b. (–1850).
Nov. 22nd Robert Clive d. (48).

1774 Philadelphia Congress of American Colonies

A **Jan:** accession of Abdul Hamid I as Sultan of Turkey.

B **Feb:** petition from Massachusetts asking for removal of governor-general Thomas Hutchinson is refused by British House of Commons.

C **Mar:** 28th, British Parliament passes Coercive Acts against Massachusetts, which include act closing port of Boston from *June* 1st.

D **Apr:** Quebec Act, establishing Roman Catholicism and Roman law in Canada, to secure Canada's loyalty to Britain;
Hastings seizes Rohilkhand, N.W. India, from Rohilla tribe.

E **May:** 10th, accession of Louis XVI of France, who appoints Jean Maurepas premier and Vergennes foreign secretary;
27th, Virginia House of Burgesses adopt resolution for calling a continental congress.

F **Jun:**

G **Jul:** Russians rout Turks at battle of Shumla and
21st, the peace of Kutchuk-Kainardji is signed, by which Turkey cedes to Russia the Crimea and mouth of River Dnieper, grants her free navigation for trade in Turkish waters and promises to protect Christians in Constantinople.

H **Aug:** 12th, Russia signs secret alliance with Denmark;
Louis XVI recalls the Parlements and appoints Turgot controller-general of France;
Suffolk Convention in America resolves that the Coercive legislation of *Mar.* 28th be disregarded.

J **Sep:** 5th (–*Oct.* 26th), first Continental Congress of the thirteen American Colonies meets at Philadelphia with representatives from each colony except Georgia;
13th, Turgot re-introduces free trade in corn in France (suspended since 1766, but re-abolished 1776);
14th, the pretender Pugachoff is delivered by Cossacks to the Russian government, following a decisive defeat (executed *Jan.* 1775);
Austria occupies Bukovina.

K **Oct:**

L **Nov:** John Wilkes becomes lord mayor of London.

M **Dec:** 1st, by resolution of the Continental Congress non-importation of British goods comes into force in American colonies.

N With the insanity of Joseph I of Portugal, Pombal, the favourite of the Regent Queen Maria Anna, becomes all-powerful.
Rebellion in Shantung organised by the White Lotus Society.
Expulsion of the Jesuits from Poland.

O **Politics, Economics, Law and Education**

E. Burke, *On American Taxation.*
John Campbell, *A Political Survey of Great Britain.*
John Cartwright, *American Independence, the Glory and Interest of Great Britain.*
Charles, Earl of Stanhope, advocates Parliamentary Reform in pamphlets.
Arthur Young, *Political Arithmetic.*

P **Science, Technology, Discovery, etc.**

J. E. Bode founds *Astronomisches Jahrbuch*, Berlin.
J. Priestley discovers oxygen.
K. W. Scheele discovers chlorine and baryta.
T. Bergman's treatise on carbon dioxide and carbonic acid.
A. Lavoisier, *Opuscules physiques et chimiques.*
William Cullen, *First Lines of the Practice of Physics.*
William Hunter, *The Anatomy of the Gravid Uterus.*
N. Desmarest's essay on extinct volcanoes.
John Wilkinson builds boring mill which facilitates the manufacture of cylinders for steam engines.

Q **Scholarship**

O. Goldsmith, *The History of the Earth and Animated Nature.*

R **Philosophy and Religion**

Anne Lee of Manchester settles in New York city with a band of 'Shakers' to begin a spiritualists' revival.

S **Art, Sculpture, Fine Arts and Architecture**

T **Music**

C. W. Gluck, *Iphigenia in Aulis* (opera).

U **Literature**

Lord Chesterfield, *Letters to his Son.*
J. W. Goethe, *Clavigo* and *Sorrows of Werther.*
Thomas Warton, *History of English Poetry* (–1781).
C. M. Wieland, *Aberites.*

V **The Press**

W **Drama and Entertainment**

X **Sport**

Y **Statistics**

Z **Births and Deaths**

Mar. 16th Matthew Flinders b. (–1814).
Apr. 4th Oliver Goldsmith d. (46).
Aug. 12th Robert Southey b. (–1843).

1775 Beginning of War of American Independence

A **Jan:**

B **Feb:** 1st, Chatham introduces bill to conciliate American colonists, which is rejected, and repressive legislation follows;
Peasants in Bohemia revolt against servitude.

C **Mar:** 19th, Prusso-Polish commercial treaty.
Portuguese fleet is repulsed in attack on Monte Video.

D **Apr:** 19th, War of American Independence opens with defeat of British under Thomas Gage at Lexington and Concord.

E **May:** 7th, Turkey formally cedes Bukovina to Austria;
10th, Fort Ticonderoga, New York, and
12th, Crown Point fall to Americans;
10th, Second Continental Congress meets at Philadelphia;
31st, troops before Boston are adopted as the Continental Army.

F **Jun:** 15th, George Washington is appointed Commander-in-Chief of American forces (takes up command at Cambridge, Mass., *July* 3rd);
17th, British victory at Bunker Hill.

G **Jul:** 1st, failure of Spanish expedition to reduce pirate stronghold of Algiers leads to fall of d'Aranda;
6th, declaration of Philadelphia Congress under John Hancock sets out war aims;
19th, Chrétien Malesherbes appointed French minister of interior.

H **Aug:**

J **Sep:**

K **Oct:**

L **Nov:** 9th, Grafton resigns from North's ministry, disliking the war, and is succeeded as lord privy seal by Dartmouth, while Lord George Germain becomes colonial secretary.

M **Dec:** 31st, failure of Benedict Arnold's attack on Quebec.

N Nuncomar, who had accused Hastings of accepting bribes, is hanged at Calcutta.
Provincial administration in Russia is reformed.

Z **Births and Deaths**
Jan. 22nd André Ampère b. (–1836).
Jan. 30th W. S. Landor b. (–1864).
Feb. 10th Charles Lamb b. (–1834).
Apr. 23rd J. M. W. Turner b. (–1851).
Aug. 6th Daniel O'Connell b. (–1847).
Dec. 16th Jane Austen b. (–1817).

O **Politics, Economics, Law and Education**
E. Burke, *Speech on Conciliation with America.*
Thomas Spence advocates system of land nationalisation in England.
Justus Moser's *Patriotic Phantasies* plead for a national, organic state in Germany.
The study of Danish language and literature supplants German in Danish schools.
Pedro Campomanes, *Discourse on Popular Education.*

P **Science, Technology, Discovery, etc.**
K. W. Scheele, *Air and Fire.*
J. C. Fabricius classifies insects in *Systema Entomologiae.*
A. G. Werner inaugurates the modern study of geology.
James Watt perfects the invention of the steam engine at Matthew Boulton's Birmingham works.
James Cook returns to England (*July* 25th) after second voyage in South Seas, during which he discovered the Sandwich Islands and conquered scurvy.
Richard Chandler, *Travels in Asia Minor.*

Q **Scholarship**
J. J. Griesbach's critical edition of Greek New Testament.

R **Philosophy and Religion**
Louis St. Martin, *Des Erreurs et de la Verité.*

S **Art, Sculpture, Fine Arts and Architecture**
J. B. S. Chardin, self-portrait.
Ralph Earl, *Roger Sherman* (portrait).
Joshua Reynolds, *Miss Bowles* (portrait).
George Romney establishes himself in London as a portrait painter.
J. A. Houdon, busts of Turgot and Gluck.
Denis Diderot's accounts of the Salon, Paris, begin modern art criticism.
John Flaxman's neo-classical designs for friezes and medallion portraits for Josiah Wedgwood's pottery.

T **Music**
C. P. E. Bach, *The Israelites in the Wilderness* (oratorio).

U **Literature**
J. W. Goethe settles at Weimar and obtains a post at court for Herder.
S. Johnson, *A Journey to the Western Islands of Scotland.*

V **The Press**

W **Drama and Entertainment**
Vittorio Alfieri's first play, *Cleopatra*, produced in Turin.
P. A. C. Beaumarchais' *Barber of Seville* produced in Paris after two years' prohibition.
J. J. Eschenburg's German translation of Shakespeare's plays (–1781).
R. B. Sheridan, *The Rivals.*
Sarah Siddons's début at Drury Lane Theatre.

X **Sport**

Y **Statistics**

(*continued opposite*)

1776 American Declaration of Independence

A Jan: 6th, abolition of the *Corvée* (forced labour for repair of roads) in France (restored in *Aug.*).

B Feb: 5th, abolition of the *Jurandes*, or privileged corporations, by Turgot;
British Parliament passes Prohibitory Act placing colonies' external trade under interdict.

C Mar: 4th, Washington occupies Heights of Dorchester;
14th, Grafton unsuccessfully moves for suspension of Prohibitory Act in American Colonies in hope of peace;
15th, Congress resolves that the authority of the British Crown be suppressed;
17th, Washington forces British under William Howe to evacuate Boston;
American troops are driven from Canada.

D Apr: By treaty of Copenhagen with Denmark Russia cedes her claims to Holstein.

E May: 12th, Malesherbes resigns as French minister of the interior;
—, Turgot is dismissed by Louis XVI for attempting to make further financial reforms;
15th, Virginia convention instructs Richard Lee and other delegates to Congress to propose independence.

F Jun: 7th, Lee frames proposal that the United Colonies are of right independent states;
12th, Virginia publishes its Bill of Rights.

G Jul: 4th, American Declaration of Independence, drafted by Thomas Jefferson with revisions by Benjamin Franklin and Samuel Adams, is carried by Congress;
Silas Deane on mission to Paris obtains French loan of 1 mill. francs for America.

H Aug: Britain recruits Hessian mercenaries for American war.

J Sep: free trade in corn (re-introduced 1774) abolished in France;
15th, Howe takes New York and occupies Rhode Island.

K Oct: 11th (and 13th), Benedict Arnold is defeated in engagements on Lake Champlain;
Congress retires to Baltimore;
Jacques Necker is appointed finance minister in France;
The Rockingham Whigs cease to attend Parliament in protest at the continuation of the American War.

L Nov: 20th, Fort Lee surrenders to Britain;
28th, Washington retreats across New Jersey to Pennsylvania.

M Dec: 26th, Washington defeats Hessians at battle of Trenton.

N Unified administration for Portuguese S. American colonies under viceroyalty of River Plate, with capital in Rio de Janeiro.
Potemkin, favourite of Catherine II, organises Russian Black Sea fleet and begins construction of Sebastopol harbour.

O **Politics, Economics, Law and Education**

Jeremy Bentham, *A Fragment on Government.*

John Cartwright's *Take Your Choice* advocates Parliamentary Reform.

T. Paine, *Common-Sense* (pamphlet).

Richard Price, *Observations on Civil Liberty and the Justice and Policy of the War with America.*

Adam Smith, *An Inquiry into the Nature and Causes of the Wealth of Nations.*

U.S. Congress institutes a national lottery.

P **Science, Technology, Discovery, etc.**

The machine-plane is invented.

James Cook's third voyage of discovery in the Pacific (–1779).

Q **Scholarship**

Edward Gibbon, *Decline and Fall of the Roman Empire* (–1788).

B. Kennicott, *Vetus Testamentum hebraicum cum variis lectionibus.*

R **Philosophy and Religion**

Soame Jenyns, *View of the Internal Evidence of the Christian Religion.*

The sect of Illuminati is formed in Bavaria (suppressed in 1786).

S **Art, Sculpture, Fine Arts and Architecture**

J. H. Fragonard, *The Washerwoman* (painting).

William Chambers begins building the new Somerset House, London.

T **Music**

Charles Burney, *History of Music* (–1789).

John Hawkins, *The General History of the Science and Practice of Music.*

Lord Sandwich founds the Concert of Antient Music, London.

U **Literature**

V **The Press**

W **Drama and Entertainment**

V. Alfieri, *Antigone.*

F. M. von Klinger, *Sturm und Drang.*

J. M. R. Lenz, *Die Soldaten.*

X **Sport**

Col. St. Leger establishes the St. Leger at Doncaster Races.

Y **Statistics**

Z **Births and Deaths**

Jan. 24th Ernst Hoffmann b. (–1822).

June 11th John Constable b. (–1837).

Aug. 25th David Hume d. (65).

Aug. 27th B. Niebuhr b. (–1831).

1777 Burgoyne capitulates at Saratoga

A **Jan:** 3rd, Washington defeats British at Princeton, New Jersey.

B **Feb:** 24th, accession of Maria I of Portugal leads to Pombal's dismissal.

C **Mar:**

D **Apr:** Marquis de La Fayette's French volunteers arrive in America.

E **May:**

F **Jun:**

G **Jul:**

H **Aug:** 16th, Americans defeat British force at Bennington, Vermont.

J **Sep:** 11th, William Howe defeats Americans under Nathaniel Greene at Brandywine, Pennsylvania;
19th, General Burgoyne suffers heavy casualties at Bemis Heights, New York;
27th, Howe occupies Philadelphia.

K **Oct:** 4th, Washington is defeated at Germantown, Pennsylvania;
7th, Burgoyne loses second battle of Bemis Heights and
17th, capitulates to Americans under Horatio Gates at Saratoga, New York.

L **Nov:** 15th, Congress adopts Confederation Articles of perpetual union of United States of America, which are sent to states for ratification (completed 1781) as first U.S. constitution;
20th, British secure control of Delaware.

M **Dec:** suspension of Habeas Corpus act in England.
30th, on death of Maximilian III Bavaria passes to Charles Theodore, Elector Palatine, but Joseph II of Austria lays claim to Lower Bavaria.

N The Swiss Cantons fearing Austrian aggression sign alliance with France.
Spain and Portugal settle disputes arising from S. American Colonies.

O **Politics, Economics, Law and Education**

V. Alfieri, *La Tirannide.*

E. Burke, *A Letter to the Sheriffs of Bristol*, on Parliamentary representation, and *Address to the King.*

James Anderson, *Nature of the Corn Laws.*

John Howard, *The State of the Prisons of England and Wales.*

A co-operative workshop for tailors is formed at Birmingham to employ men on strike.

P **Science, Technology, Discovery, etc.**

K. W. Scheele prepares sulphuretted hydrogen.

K. F. Wenzel's work on atomic theory.

C. A. Coulomb invents the torsion balance.

David Bushnell invents the torpedo.

The Botanical Magazine founded.

Q **Scholarship**

R **Philosophy and Religion**

Joseph Priestley, *Disquisition relating to matter and spirit.*

Hugh Blair, *Sermons.*

Lessing in *Ernst und Falk* pleads for broad understanding in questions of religion and politics.

S **Art, Sculpture, Fine Arts and Architecture**

T. Gainsborough, *The Watering-Place* (painting).

J. B. Greuze, *La Cruche Cassée* (painting).

T **Music**

J. Haydn, 'La Roxolane' Symphony (No. 63 in C).

C. W. von Gluck, *Armide* (opera).

U **Literature**

V **The Press**

W **Drama and Entertainment**

X **Sport**

Y **Statistics**

Z **Births and Deaths**

Apr. 30th Karl Gauss b. (–1855).

July 9th Henry Hallam b. (–1859).

1778 France supports American Colonies—Beginning of War of Bavarian Succession

A Jan: 3rd, Palatinate recognises Austrian claim to Lower Bavaria.

B Feb: 6th, France and American Colonists sign offensive and defensive alliance and also a commercial treaty;
—, Britain declares war on France;
17th, North presents to Parliament his plan for conciliating the colonies.

C Mar:

D Apr: 5th, British commissioners are appointed to negotiate with Congress and in the meantime to suspend the obnoxious laws;
7th, Chatham delivers his last speech against continuing hostilities (he dies *May* 11th).

E May: 28th, Sir George Savile's act modifies British penal laws against Roman Catholics, while a further act relieves Protestant Dissenting ministers from making a declaration of faith.

F Jun: 17th, U.S. Congress rejects British peace offer;
18th, Henry Clinton evacuates British troops from Philadelphia;
28th, Washington defeats British at Monmouth, New Jersey.

G Jul: 3rd, Prussia declares war on Austria, with whom Saxony is allied, in the war of Bavarian Succession (lasting with minor skirmishes—*May* 1779);
3rd (–4th), Wyoming massacre by Indians in Pennsylvania;
8th, Comte d'Estaing's French fleet arrives off Delaware.

H Aug: 29th, Americans led by John Sullivan abandon siege of Newport, Rhode Island;
British force captures Savannah, Georgia.

J Sep: 4th, the States of Holland sign treaty of amity and commerce with American Colonies;
French seize Dominica, as a naval base.

K Oct:

L Nov: 11th, William Butler leads force of Indians to massacre the villagers of Cherry Valley in New York.
British force under Admiral Samuel Barrington takes St. Lucia, W. Indies, from the French.

M Dec:

N Warren Hastings takes Chandernagore, Bengal, and Hector Munro takes Pondichery from the French in India.
Jefferson champions the rights of slaves and secures passage of act prohibiting import of slaves into U.S.
Portugal cedes Fernando Po and Annobon Islands, Gulf of Guinea, to Spain.

O **Politics, Economics, Law and Education**

P **Science, Technology, Discovery, etc.**

Benjamin Thompson experiments on heat by friction and with the explosive force of gunpowder.

G. L. L. Buffon, *Époques de la nature.*

J. A. Deluc, *Lettres physiques et morales sur les montagnes.*

Friedrich Mesmer first practises 'mesmerism' in Paris.

Joseph Bramah's improved water closet.

James Cook surveys the coasts of Bering's Strait.

Q **Scholarship**

E. Malone's studies in Shakespearian controversy.

A. H. Anquetil Duperron, *Législation orientale.*

R **Philosophy and Religion**

Commission des Réguliers appointed to reform French religious houses, which leads to edict regulating admissions and the size of monasteries.

G. E. Lessing replies to the attacks of the orthodox J. M. Goeze in *Anti-Goeze.*

S **Art, Sculpture, Fine Arts and Architecture**

J. S. Copley, *Brook Watson and the Shark* (painting).

T **Music**

U **Literature**

Fanny Burney (pseud.), *Evelina.*

J. G. Herder's collection of folk songs (–1779) leads to study of folklore in Germany.

F. M. A. de Voltaire, *Irène.*

V **The Press**

W **Drama and Entertainment**

R. B. Sheridan, *The School for Scandal.*

X **Sport**

Y **Statistics**

Z **Births and Deaths**

Jan. 10th Carl Linnaeus d. (70).

Jan. 26th Ugo Foscolo b. (–1827).

Mar. 5th Thomas Arne d. (67).

Apr. 10th William Hazlitt b. (–1850).

Apr. – John Hargreaves d. (*c.* 55).

May 11th William Pitt, Earl of Chatham, d. (60).

May 30th Voltaire d. (83).

July 2nd J. J. Rousseau d. (66).

Dec. 6th J. L. Gay-Lussac b. (–1850).

Dec. 17th Humphry Davy b. (–1829).

—, Joseph Lancaster b. (–1838).

1779 Spain declares war on Britain

A Jan: France defends Senegal, W. Africa, against British attack.

B Feb: 25th, George Clark completes American conquest of the Old Northwest, forcing the British to surrender at Vincennes.

C Mar: the Irish Protestant Volunteer movement for the defence of Ireland from French invasion soon numbers 40,000.

D Apr:

E May: 13th, by Peace of Teschen, ending War of Bavarian Succession, Austria obtains the Inn Quarter of Bavaria and Prussia acquires the reversionary rights to Ansbach and Bayreuth (which fall to her in *Jan.* 1792);
France abandons Goree, W. Africa, to Britain.

F Jun: 16th, Spain declares war on Britain (after France has undertaken to assist her in recovering Gibraltar and Florida), and the siege of Gibraltar opens (–1783);
18th, French force takes St. Vincent, W. Indies.

G Jul: 4th, French force takes Grenada, W. Indies.

H Aug: British repulse American attack on Penobscot, Maine.
Congress despatches force into Wyoming Valley against the Indian tribes who had harried Pennsylvania in *July* 1778;
French fleet dominates the English Channel.

J Sep: 23rd, John Paul Jones in *Serapis* defeats H.M.S. *Countess of Scarborough.*

K Oct:

L Nov:

M Dec: Britain ends restrictions on Irish trade in answer to demands of Henry Flood and Henry Grattan.

N War against Mahrattas in India (–1782).
John Acton reforms Neapolitan Navy and British influence replaces French in Naples.

O **Politics, Economics, Law and Education**

P **Science, Technology, Discovery, etc.**

C. A. Coulomb investigates the laws of friction.
L. Spallanzani shows that semen is necessary to fertilisation.
Samuel Crompton's spinning mule.
A 'velocipede' is constructed in Paris.
Royal Academy of Sciences, Lisbon, founded.
James Rennel, *Bengal Atlas.*

Q **Scholarship**

R **Philosophy and Religion**

David Hume, *Dialogues of Natural Religion.*
William Cowper and John Newton, *Olney Hymns.*
Robert Lowth's new translation of *Isaiah.*
Selina, Countess of Huntingdon, builds Spa Fields Chapel, London, but in face of clerical opposition takes shelter under the Toleration Acts to register the chapel as a dissenting place of worship.

S **Art, Sculpture, Fine Arts and Architecture**

J. A. Houdon, bust of Molière.
Antonio Canova, *Daedalus and Icarus* (sculpture).
James Gillray's earliest satirical cartoon.

T **Music**

C. W. Gluck, *Iphigenia in Tauris* (opera).
Battles between Gluck's and Nicola Piccini's supporters in Paris.
J. C. Bach, *Amadis de Gaule* (opera).

U **Literature**

S. Johnson, *Lives of the Poets* (–1781).

V **The Press**

W **Drama and Entertainment**

G. E. Lessing, *Nathan the Wise.*
R. B. Sheridan, *The Critic.*

X **Sport**

The Derby is established at Epsom Racecourse, Surrey; first winner Sir C. Bunbury's 'Diomed'.

Y **Statistics**

Z **Births and Deaths**

Jan. 15th David Garrick d. (61).
Feb. 13th James Cook d. (50).
Feb. 21st Savigny b. (–1861).
May 15th William Lamb, Lord Melbourne, b. (–1848).
May 28th Thomas Moore b. (–1852).
—, Thomas Chippendale d. (*c.* 60).

A **Jan:** 16th, Admiral George Rodney defeats Spanish at Cape St. Vincent and temporarily relieves Gibraltar.

B **Feb:** 8th, Yorkshire petition for Parliamentary reform presented at Westminster.

C **Mar:** 10th, Russia's declaration of armed neutrality, to prevent British ships from searching neutral vessels for contraband of war, which is subsequently confirmed by France, Spain, Austria, Prussia, Denmark and Sweden.

D **Apr:** 17th, Rodney's indecisive action against the French at Martinique;
19th, Harry Grattan demands Home Rule for Ireland;
Dunning's resolution deploring the increased influence of the Crown leads Commons to affirm the principle of periodical scrutiny of the civil list.

E **May:** Charleston, Carolina, surrenders to the British under Sir Henry Clinton;
Burke introduces bill for economic reform, aiming at abolition of sinecures and redundant offices.

F **Jun:** 2nd, Duke of Richmond proposes manhood suffrage in England;
—, (–8th), Gordon riots in London, when Lord George Gordon heads procession for presenting petition to Parliament for repealing Catholic Relief act of 1778, and Roman Catholic chapels are pillaged;
Joseph II of Austria visits Catherine II of Russia for discussions leading to Austro-Russian treaty of 1781.

G **Jul:** French troops under Rochambeau arrive at Newport, Rhode Island.

H **Aug:** 16th, Cornwallis defeats American army under Horatio Gates at Camden;
18th, Sumpter's army is defeated by British under Tarleton.

J **Sep:** 10th, Hyder Ali of Mysore conquers the Carnatic;
23rd, John André, captured British agent, reveals Benedict Arnold's plot to surrender West Point to Clinton.

K **Oct:** 7th, British force under Ferguson is defeated at battle of King's Mountain, N. Carolina;
Serfdom in Bohemia and Hungary abolished.

L **Nov:** 20th, Britain declares war on Holland to prevent her joining the League of Armed Neutrality;
29th, Maria Theresa of Austria dies, succeeded by Joseph II (–1790).

M **Dec:** 13th, Ireland is granted free trade with Britain and is to enjoy advantages of the colonial trade.

N Abolition of British secretaryship for colonies and of Council of Trade and Plantations.
Jacques Necker abolishes farming of taxes in France.

O **Politics, Economics, Law and Education**
Gaetano Filangieri, *Science of Legislation.*

P **Science, Technology, Discovery, etc.**
A. Lavoisier concludes that respiration is a form of combustion.
L. Spallanzani, *Dissertation on Animal and Vegetable Science.*
Sébastien Erard makes the first pianoforte.
A circular saw is invented.
Oliver Evans invents a mechanical lift for a flour mill.
Steel pens are first used.

Q **Scholarship**

R **Philosophy and Religion**
James Bandinel delivers first Bampton Lectures at Oxford University.
Robert Raikes's Sunday School at Gloucester.

S **Art, Sculpture, Fine Arts and Architecture**
J. Reynolds' portrait of Mary Robinson as 'Perdita'.
J. S. Copley, *Death of Chatham* (painting).

T **Music**
Haydn, 'Toy' Symphony.
Giovanni Paisiello, *Barber of Seville* (opera).
Karl von Dittersdorf, *Job* (oratorio).

U **Literature**
Frederick the Great, *De la littérature allemande.*
C. M. Wieland, *Oberon.*

V **The Press**
The British Gazette and Sunday Monitor, the first Sunday newspaper issued (*Mar.* 26th).

W **Drama and Entertainment**

X **Sport**

Y **Statistics**
Roman Catholics in England, 70,000.

Z **Births and Deaths**
Feb. 14th William Blackstone d. (57).
Aug. 29th J. A. D. Ingres b. (–1867).
—, Robert Smirke b. (–1867).

A **Jan**: Daniel Morgan defeats Tarleton's British force at battle of the Cowpens, S. Carolina, and takes many prisoners, depriving Cornwallis of light troops.

B **Feb**: Conclusion of Russia's treaty with Austria, for driving the Turks out of Europe, restoring a Greek Empire under Catherine's grandson Constantine, forming a Kingdom of Dacia under an Orthodox prince and allocating Serbia and the western Balkans to Austria and the Morea, Candia and Cyprus to Venice.

C **Mar**: 15th, Cornwallis defeats Americans under Greene at battle of Guilford, Connecticut.

D **Apr**: 29th, de Grasse captures Tobago;
French fleet under Suffren prevents Britain from seizing Cape of Good Hope.

E **May**: 19th, Louis XVI of France dismisses Necker;
Prussia joins League of Armed Neutrality.

F **Jun**: Hastings deposes Rajah of Benares for refusing to contribute to war expenses.

G **Jul**: 1st, Eyre Coote defeats Hyder Ali at Porto Novo, saving Madras from destruction;
Spanish force takes Pensacola, Florida, from British.

H **Aug**: 30th, de Grasse occupies Chesapeake Bay.

J **Sep**: 8th, Cornwallis defeats Greene at Eutaw in N. Carolina;
30th, Washington and La Fayette cut Cornwallis's communications, beginning siege of Yorktown, Virginia.

K **Oct**: 13th, Joseph II grants patent of religious tolerance in Austrian Empire and freedom of the press;
19th, Cornwallis capitulates at Yorktown with 7,000 men; the British evacuate Charleston and Savannah and land operations are virtually over.

L **Nov**: 13th, Dutch settlement at Negapatam, Madras, is captured by British;
26th, British fleet takes St. Eustacius, W. Indies, from Holland;
—, Joseph II abolishes serfdom in Austria and
28th, makes monastic orders independent of Rome.

M **Dec**:

N Hastings plunders the treasure of the Nabob of Oudh.
Portuguese gain Delagoa Bay, E. Africa, from Austria.

O Politics, Economics, Law and Education
J. Necker, *Compte rendu.*
J. H. Pestalozzi expounds his educational theory in *Leonard and Gertrude.*

P Science, Technology, Discovery, etc.
F. W. Herschel discovers the planet Uranus (*Mar.* 13th).
K. W. Scheele discovers the composition of the mineral tungsten ('scheelite').
The Siberian highway is begun.

Q Scholarship
J. H. Voss, translation of Homer's *Odyssey.*
Clarendon Press, Oxford, founded.

R Philosophy and Religion
Immanuel Kant, *Critique of Pure Reason.*
G. J. Planck, *History of Protestant Dogma.*
Dissolution of a third of the monasteries of the Austrian Empire.
Moses Mendelssohn, *On the Civil Amelioration of the Condition of the Jews.*

S Art, Sculpture, Fine Arts and Architecture
John Opie, *The School* (painting).
J. A. Houdon, *Seated Voltaire* (sculpture).

T Music
J. Haydn, 'Russian' (or 'Maiden') string quartets (Nos. 37–42).
W. A. Mozart, *Idomeneo* (opera).
J. A. Hiller founds Gewandhaus concerts at Leipzig.

U Literature
G. Crabbe, *The Library.*
J.-J. Rousseau, *Confessions.*

V The Press

W Drama and Entertainment
F. Schiller, *Die Räuber*, produced at Mannheim.

X Sport
P. Beckford, *Thoughts on Hunting.*

Y Statistics

Z Births and Deaths
Feb. 13th Gotthold Ephraim Lessing d.(52).
Mar. 18th Anne Robert Jacques Turgot d. (53).
June 9th George Stephenson b. (–1848).
Oct. 17th Edward Hawke d. (76).

A Jan: 11th, Dutch surrender Trincomalee, Ceylon, to British.

B Feb: 5th, Spanish capture Minorca from British;
12th, indecisive battle of Sadras, Madras, between British and French;
13th, French take St. Christopher, W. Indies;
22nd, Motion against government, deprecating the continuation of the war in America, is defeated in British House of Commons by one vote.

C Mar: 15th, motion of lack of confidence in Lord North's administration is defeated in Commons by nine votes;
19th, Lord North resigns and, 27th, Marquess of Rockingham forms Whig Coalition ministry with C. J. Fox, E. Burke, Lord Shelburne and, on George III's insistence, Thurlow;
Pope Pius VI visits Vienna but fails to persuade Joseph II to rescind patent of tolerance.

D Apr: 12th, Admiral George Rodney defeats de Grasse at battle of The Saints, saving the West Indies;
Joseph II abrogates Barrier treaty of 1715 and requires Dutch to abandon garrisons in barrier towns in Austrian Netherlands which are evacuated, 18th;
Gratton makes Irish Declaration of Rights, demanding complete legislative freedom.

E May: 3rd, Commons vote the earlier resolution rejecting Wilkes as an M.P. to be subversive of the electors' rights;
9th, Thomas Grenville is sent to Paris to open negotiations with Count de Vergennes and Benjamin Franklin for a peace;
17th, Fox introduces repeal of Ireland Act, 1720, thus granting Ireland legislative independence (–1800), but Gratton's Parliament is elected solely by Protestants;
—, treaty of Salbai ends Mahratta War;
30th, Henry Dundas carries motion for recalling Warren Hastings from India.

F Jun: Spain completes conquest of Florida.

G Jul: 6th, naval battle of Cuddalore, off Madras, between Britain and France;
11th, Shelburne forms ministry, following Rockingham's death, (1st) with William Pitt the Younger, chancellor of Exchequer and leader of Commons, but Fox and Burke are excluded from office;
Portugal joins League of Armed Neutrality.

H Aug:

J Sep:

K Oct: Howe relieves Gibraltar.

L Nov: 30th, peace preliminaries, arranged by Franklin and Adams, are accepted by Britain and America.

M Dec: 7th, Tippoo Sahib succeeds Hyder Ali in Mysore.

N Rama I founds new dynasty in Siam, with capital at Bangkok.

O **Politics, Economics, Law and Education**
Royal Irish Academy, Dublin, founded.

P **Science, Technology, Discovery, etc.**

Q **Scholarship**
Girolamo Tiraboschi, *History of Italian Literature* completed.

R **Philosophy and Religion**
Dugald Stewart, *Elements of the Philosophy of the Human Mind.*
Joseph Priestley, *A History of the Corruptions of Christianity.*

S **Art, Sculpture, Fine Arts and Architecture**
H. Fuseli, *The Nightmare* (painting).
F. Guardi, *Fêtes for the Archduke Paul of Russia* and *The Concert* (paintings).
A. Canova begins monument to Pope Clement XIV in Rome.

T **Music**
W. A. Mozart, 'Haffner' Symphony (K.385 in D) and *Il Seraglio* (opera).

U **Literature**
Fanny Burney, *Cecilia.*
William Cowper, *Poems* and *Table Talk.*
J. G. Herder, *The Spirit of Hebrew Poetry* (–1783).

V **The Press**

W **Drama and Entertainment**

X **Sport**

Y **Statistics**
British Textiles Trade

raw cotton imports	11·8 mill. lb.
exported linens	5·6 mill. yds.
exported silks	60,000 lb.

Z **Births and Deaths**
Jan. 29th Daniel Auber b. (–1871).
Jan. – J. C. Bach d. (47).
Apr. 7th Francis Legatt Chantrey b. (–1841).
May 15th Richard Wilson d. (67).
June 19th H. F. R. de Lamennais b. (–1854).

1783 The Peace of Versailles

A Jan:

B Feb: 14th, British and
20th, American proclamations for cessation of arms;
24th, Lord Shelburne resigns, following resolution censuring the peace preliminaries and lengthy negotiations begin in which William Pitt and Lord North in turn decline to form ministry.

C Mar:

D Apr: 1st, Duke of Portland becomes nominal premier of a Fox-North coalition;
9th, Tippoo Sahib forces British to surrender Bednore.

E May: 7th, Pitt brings forward scheme for Parliamentary Reform, which is supported by Charles James Fox and opposed by Lord North.

F Jun: Joseph II enforces the German language in Bohemia and suppresses the permanent committee of the Diet.

G Jul: 17th, Besançon Parlement demands the calling of the French States-General;
Russia annexes Kuban on the plea of restoring order;
Britain and Austria persuade Turkey against declaring war on Russia.

H Aug:

J Sep: 3rd, by Peace of Versailles between Britain, France, Spain and U.S.A. Britain recognises independence of U.S.A. and recovers her West Indian possessions; France recovers St. Lucia, Tobago, Senegal, Goree and East Indian possessions; Spain retains Minorca and receives back Florida; France may fortify Dunkirk (a separate treaty between Britain and Holland is signed *May* 20th, 1784).

K Oct: Joseph II of Austria delivers Summary of Claims to States General of Holland, bringing to a head the question of the navigation of the Scheldt;
Following the sack of Tiflis by a Persian chief, Russia intervenes in Georgia, takes Baku and forces Heraclius of Georgia to recognise Russian sovereignty.

L Nov: 10th, Charles Calonne is appointed French controller-general and raises loans.

M Dec: 17th, Fox's India Bill is defeated in Lords and Fox-North coalition resigns;
19th, William Pitt forms ministry (–1801) and
27th, as chancellor of Exchequer is sole member of cabinet in Commons.

N Famine in Japan.

O **Politics, Economics, Law and Education**
Civil marriage and divorce established in Austrian Empire.

P **Science, Technology, Discovery, etc.**
William Herschel writes *Motion of the Solar System in Space.*
J. M. and J. E. Montgolfier ascend in a fire balloon at Annonay (*June* 5th).
Marquis Jouffroy d'Abbans sails a paddle-wheel steamboat on the R. Sâone.
Henry Bell's copper cylinder for calico printing.

Q **Scholarship**

R **Philosophy and Religion**
I. Kant in *Prolegomena to any Possible Metaphysic* answers attacks on his *Critique of Pure Reason.*
Moses Mendelssohn pleads for freedom of conscience in *Jerusalem.*
J. G. Eichhorn completes *Introduction to Old Testament.*
Charles Simeon starts evangelical movement in Cambridge.

S **Art, Sculpture, Fine Arts and Architecture**
J. Opie, *Age and Infancy* (painting).
J. L. David, *Grief of Andromache* (painting).
J. A. Houdon, *Girl Shivering* (sculpture).

T **Music**
W. A. Mozart, Mass in C Minor.
L. van Beethoven publishes first composition (Variations on a march of Dressler).

U **Literature**
William Blake, *Poetical Sketches.*
Thomas Crabbe, *The Village.*
Joseph Dobrovsky, *Scriptores rerum Bohemicarum.*

V **The Press**

W **Drama and Entertainment**

X **Sport**

Y **Statistics**

Z **Births and Deaths**
Jan. 23rd Marie Henri Beyle ('Stendhal') b. (–1842).
Apr. 3rd Washington Irving b. (–1859).
July 24th Simon Bolivar b. (–1830).
Sept. 18th Leonhard Euler d. (75).
Oct. 29th Jean D'Alembert d. (65).

1784 Pitt's India Act—The Scheldt Crisis

A **Jan**: 6th, by treaty of Constantinople Turkey acquiesces in Russia's annexation of the Crimea and Kuban.

B **Feb**:

C **Mar**: 8th, Parliamentary opposition to William Pitt dwindles to a majority of one;
11th, British sign peace treaty with Tippoo of Mysore;
20th, by Peace of Versailles Holland cedes Negapatam to Britain;
24th, Parliament is dissolved and in the ensuing election Pitt gains a large majority.

D **Apr**: 23rd, Thomas Jefferson's land ordinance passed, the basis of U.S. plan for colonisation.

E **May**: Andreas Bernstorff, recalled to office in Denmark, abolishes serfdom, permits a free press and begins educational reforms.

F **Jun**: 21st, Pitt reduces duties on tea and spirits.

G **Jul**: 4th, following revolution in Transylvania Joseph II abrogates the constitution; he subsequently rides roughshod over Hungarian sentiment by removing the Crown of Hungary to Vienna and suppressing feudal courts;
12th, Hovering Act checks smuggling round coasts of Britain.

H **Aug**: 13th, Pitt's India Act places East India Company under a government-appointed Board of Control (–1858) and forbids interference in native affairs, to check territorial expansion.

J **Sep**:

K **Oct**: Joseph II breaks off diplomatic relations with Holland when two Austrian vessels, ordered to navigate the Scheldt, are fired on by the Dutch, causing a European crisis, in which Louis XVI offers to mediate (leads to treaty of Fontainebleau, *Nov*. 8th, 1785).

L **Nov**:

M **Dec**:

N Financial depression in U.S.

O **Politics, Economics, Law and Education**
Gustav III founds Swedish Academy of Arts and Sciences.
Valentine Haüy founds in Paris the first school for the blind.

P **Science, Technology, Discovery, etc.**
Henry Cavendish discovers that water is a compound of hydrogen and oxygen.
George Attwood's machine for proving the laws of accelerated motion.
Rene Haüy, *Essai d'une théorie sur la structure des cristaux.*
Henry Cort's puddling process revolutionises the manufacture of wrought iron.
Andrew Meikle's threshing machine.
Joseph Bramah's patent lock.
River Eider linked by canal to the Baltic.

Q **Scholarship**
William Mitford's *History of Greece* (–1810).
William Jones founds the Bengal Asiatic Society and his discourses (–94) mark a turning-point in the study of Sanskrit.

R **Philosophy and Religion**
I. Kant. *Notion of a Universal History in a Cosmopolitan Sense.*
J. G. Herder, *Ideas towards a Philosophy of History* (–91).
Bernardin de Saint-Pierre, *Études de la Nature.*
John Wesley signs deed of declaration (*Feb.* 28th) as the charter of Wesleyan Methodism, and ordains two 'Presbyters' for the American Mission (*Sept.* 1st).

S **Art, Sculpture, Fine Arts and Architecture**
J. Reynolds' portraits of Mrs. Siddons as 'The Tragic Muse' and of T. Warton.
T. Rowlandson's first political cartoon.

T **Music**
André Gretry, *Richard Cœur de Lion* (opera).
Antonio Salieri, *Les Danaïdes* (opera).

U **Literature**

V **The Press**
The Boston Centinel (Mass.) founded.

W **Drama and Entertainment**
P. A. C. Beaumarchais, *Mariage de Figaro*
F. Schiller, *Kabale und Liebe.*

X **Sport**

Y **Statistics**

Z **Births and Deaths**
Feb. 18th Nicolò Paganini b. (–1840).
July 30th Denis Diderot d. (71).
Oct. 19th James Henry Leigh Hunt b. (–1859).
Oct. 20th Henry Temple, Viscount Palmerston b. (–1865).
Dec. 13th Samuel Johnson d. (74).

1785 The Bavarian Exchange

A **Jan**: Joseph II begins unsuccessful attempts to exchange Bavaria with Charles Theodore for the Austrian Netherlands, excepting Luxembourg and Namur.

B **Feb**:

C **Mar**:

D **Apr**: 18th, William Pitt's motion for Parliamentary reform is defeated.

E **May**:

F **Jun**: Hastings returns to England.

G **Jul**: 23rd, Frederick the Great forms Die Fürstenbund (League of German Princes) to oppose Joseph II's Bavarian exchange scheme.

H **Aug**: 15th, arrest of Cardinal de Rohan in Diamond Necklace Affair, which discredits Marie Antoinette.

J **Sep**: 10th, Prussia signs commercial treaty with U.S.

K **Oct**:

L **Nov**: 8th, by treaty of Fontainebleau, Holland recognises Joseph II's sovereignty over part of R. Scheldt, Joseph abandons his claim to Maestricht, renounces his right to free navigation of Scheldt outside his dominions and receives 10 mill. guilders;
10th, alliance between France and Holland, despite the efforts of the British envoy at The Hague.

M **Dec**:

N Parlement of Paris begins series of attacks on Charles de Calonne.

O **Politics, Economics, Law and Education**

J. H. Campe pioneers educational reforms in Germany.

P **Science, Technology, Discovery, etc.**

Henry Cavendish discovers the composition of nitric acid.

C. L. Berthollet uses chlorine ('eau de Javel') in bleaching.

C. A. Coulomb, *Recherches théoriques et expérimentales sur la force de torsion et sur l'élasticité des fils de métal.*

Steam engine with rotary motion installed by Matthew Boulton and James Watt in a cotton-spinning factory at Papplewick, Nottinghamshire.

Jean Blanchard and John Jeffries cross the English Channel in a balloon.

Russians settle in the Aleutian Isles, North Pacific.

Q **Scholarship**

R **Philosophy and Religion**

I. Kant, *Groundwork of the Metaphysic of Ethics.*

William Paley, *Principles of Moral and Political Philosophy.*

Samuel Johnson, *Prayers and Meditations* (posthm.).

London Society for the establishment of Sunday Schools is founded.

James Madison's religious freedom act (*Dec.* 26th) rescinds religious tests in Virginia.

S **Art, Sculpture, Fine Arts and Architecture**

J. Reynolds, *The Infant Hercules* (painting).

J. L. David, *Oath of the Horatii* (painting).

Alexander Cozens writes *New Methods of . . . Compositions of Landscape.*

J. A. Houdon visits U.S. to sculpt George Washington.

T **Music**

W. A. Mozart, six string quartets dedicated to J. Haydn.

Caecilian Society for the performance of sacred music founded in London (–1861).

U **Literature**

W. Cowper, *The Task* and *John Gilpin.*

C. F. D. Schubart, *Sämtliche Gedichte* (–86).

Moses Mendelssohn, *Morning Hours.*

V **The Press**

W **Drama and Entertainment**

X **Sport**

Y **Statistics**

Z **Births and Deaths**

Jan. 4th Jacob Grimm b. (–1863).

Mar. 7th Alessandro Manzoni b. (–1873).

Aug. 15th Thomas de Quincey b. (–1859).

Oct. 18th Thomas Love Peacock b. (–1866).

Nov. 18th David Wilkie b. (–1841).

1786 Pitt reduces taxation—Shays rebellion

A **Jan:**

B **Feb:** 24th, Charles Cornwallis is appointed Governor-General of India with power to override the council.

C **Mar:** 29th, William Pitt appoints commissioners for reducing the national debt through establishing a sinking fund (abolished 1828).

D **Apr:**

E **May:** Annapolis convention, under James Madison and Alexander Hamilton, attended by New York, Pennsylvania, Virginia, New Jersey and Delaware, draws attention to weakness of the Confederation.

F **Jun:** William Pitt establishes excise scheme and consolidates the militia.

G **Jul:**

H **Aug:** 11th, Penang ceded to Britain by Rajah of Kedah;
17th, Frederick the Great dies, succeeded by Frederick William II (–1797), brother of the Princess of Orange.

J **Sep:** 26th, Anglo-French commercial treaty, negotiated by William Eden, reduces many duties;
Rebellion of Daniel Shays in Massachusetts, aiming to prevent further judgments for debt until next state election; state troops are used to protect the arsenal and (*Nov.*) the revolt peters out.

K **Oct:** 16th, Joseph II's edict establishing a single seminary at Louvain for the entire Austrian Netherlands provokes wave of protest among clergy.

L **Nov:**

M **Dec:**

N Committee of Council of Trade is formed in Britain.
Dutch Patriot Party deprives William V of Orange of command of army.

O **Politics, Economics, Law and Education**
Thomas Clarkson, *Essay on Slavery*.

P **Science, Technology, Discovery, etc.**
W. Herschel's *Catalogue of Nebulae*.
E. F. F. Chladni founds the science of acoustics.
Edward Cartwright opens a cotton factory in Doncaster.
'Sea-island' cotton is planted in U.S.
Ezekiel Reed invents a nail-making machine in U.S.
Georges Buffon, *Histoire Naturelle des Oiseaux*.

Q **Scholarship**

R **Philosophy and Religion**
Lorenzo Ricci, Bishop of Pistoia and Prato, holds a diocesan synod, which adopts the Gallican articles of 1682, and celebrates the mass in Italian.
Leopold of Tuscany abolishes religious guilds.
German bishops, aiming at a national church, draw up the Punctation of Ems (*Aug.* 25th).
Members of the Mennonite sect from Central Europe settle in Canada.

S **Art, Sculpture, Fine Arts and Architecture**
John Hoppner, *Portrait of a Lady* (painting).

T **Music**
W. A. Mozart, *The Marriage of Figaro* (opera).
Karl von Dittersdorf, *Doctor und Apotheker* (opera).

U **Literature**
William Beckford, *An Arabian Tale, from an unpublished manuscript* (*The History of Caliph Vathek*).
Robert Burns, *Poems chiefly in the Scottish Dialect*.
G. A. Bürger, *Gedichte*.
J. K. A. Musäus's collection of stories, *Straussefedern*.
William Bilderdijck's *Elias* starts the Dutch Romantic Revival.

V **The Press**

W **Drama and Entertainment**
John Burgoyne's play, *The Heiress*.

X **Sport**

Y **Statistics**
British merchant shipping, 1,150,000 registered tonnage.

Z **Births and Deaths**
Jan. 26th Benjamin Robert Haydon b. (–1846).
Feb. 24th Wilhelm Grimm b. (–1859).
Apr. 16th John Franklin b. (–1847).
May 21st K. W. Scheele d. (44).
June (–) G. Hepplewhite d. (60).
Aug. 17th Frederick the Great d. (74).
Dec. 18th Carl Maria von Weber b. (–1826).

A **Jan**: Joseph II constitutes Austrian Netherlands as a province of the Austrian monarchy, provoking riots in Louvain and Brussels, led by Van der Noot;
Catherine II visits the Crimea where she is joined, *Feb.*, by Joseph II, with whom she forms a defensive alliance.

B **Feb**: 13th, on Comte de Vergenne's death Armand Comte de Montmorin is appointed French minister of foreign affairs;
22nd, French notables meet at Versailles (–*May* 25th) and reject Charles de Calonne's proposals for financial reform.

C **Mar**:

D **Apr**: 11th, New York assembly imposes duties on foreign goods;
17th, Calonne is banished to Lorraine, succeeded as minister of finance by Cardinal Étienne Brienne, Archbishop of Toulouse.

E **May**: 10th, Edmund Burke impeaches Warren Hastings;
14th, Philadelphia convention meets under Washington to frame a constitution.

F **Jun**: 28th, Dutch insurgents arrest Princess Wilhelmina of Holland near Gouda.

G **Jul**: 6th, Parlement of Paris opposes Étienne Brienne and demands the summoning of the States-General.
North-West ordinance in U.S., for creating five states out of old North-West Territory.

H **Aug**: 10th, Turkey declares war against Russia, fearing designs on Georgia;
14th, Parlement of Paris is banished by Louis XVI to Troyes (recalled to Paris *Sept.* 24th).

J **Sep**: 17th, U.S. constitution is signed;
Prussian troops assist restoration of William V of Orange (–*Oct.*).

K **Oct**: 27th, Comte de Montmorin declares that France has no intention of interfering in Dutch affairs.

L **Nov**: 20th, Louis XVI declares that the States-General will be summoned for *July* 1792

M **Dec**:

N France begins trade to Annam.
Rebellion in Formosa (suppressed by China in 1788).

O **Politics, Economics, Law and Education**

Jeremy Bentham, *Defence of Usury*.

John Adams, *A Defence of the Constitution of Government of the United States of America*. published in London, replies to Turgot's criticisms.

James Madison, *The Vices of the Political System of the United States*.

P **Science, Technology, Discovery, etc.**

A. L. Lavoisier, with collaborators, *Méthode de nomenclature chimique*.

Nicolas Leblanc's soda-making process.

John Fitch launches a steamboat on the Delaware.

Horace Saussure reaches the summit of Mt. Blanc (*Aug.* 2nd).

Q **Scholarship**

Jean Jacques Barthélemy completes his *Voyage du jeune Anacharsis en Grèce*.

Catharine II orders the compilation of an Imperial Dictionary, with 285 words translated into 200 languages.

R **Philosophy and Religion**

John Wesley's *Sermons*.

The Edict of Versailles grants religious freedom and legal status to French Protestants,

S **Art, Sculpture, Fine Arts and Architecture**

J. Reynolds' portrait of Lord Heathfield.

T **Music**

W. A. Mozart, *Don Giovanni*, 'Prague' Symphony and *Eine Kleine Nachtmusik*.

L. Boccherini's E major string quartet.

U **Literature**

Johann Heinse, *Ardinghello und die glückseligen Inseln*.

V **The Press**

W **Drama and Entertainment**

P. Beaumarchais, *Tarare*.

F. Schiller, *Don Carlos*.

J. W. Goethe, *Iphigenie auf Tauris*.

X **Sport**

M.C.C. move to Lord's cricket ground, in what is now Dorset Square, Marylebone.

Y **Statistics**

Z **Births and Deaths**

Mar. 10th William Etty b. (–1849).

Mar. 16th Georg Simon Ohm b. (–1854).

Mar. 17th Edmund Kean b. (–1833).

Oct. 4th François Pierre Guillaume Guizot b. (–1874).

Nov. 15th C. W. von Gluck d. (73).

Dec. 16th Mary Russell Mitford b. (–1855).

1788 Austria declares war on Turkey—Scandinavian War

A **Jan**: 20th, Parlement of Paris presents a list of grievances;
28th, first British penal settlement is founded at Botany Bay;
30th, death of Charles Edward Stuart, the Young Pretender, in Rome.

B **Feb**: 9th, Joseph II of Austria declares war on Turkey;
Trial of Warren Hastings, for high crimes and misdemeanours in India, begins (–1795).

C **Mar**:

D **Apr**: 15th, Anglo-Dutch alliance.

E **May**: 9th, British Parliamentary motion for abolition of Slave Trade.

F **Jun**: 9th, Joseph Banks founds Africa Association for arousing interest in exploration and trade;
21st, U.S. constitution comes into force, when ratified by the 9th state, New Hampshire;
Sweden declares war on Russia, invading Russian Finland.

G **Jul**: 17th, Russia destroys Swedish fleet.

H **Aug**: 8th, Louis XVI decides to summon the States-General for *May* 1789;
13th, Prussia joins the Anglo-Dutch alliance to form the Triple Alliance for preserving peace in Europe;
22nd, foundation of British settlement in Sierra Leone as an asylum for slaves;
25th, Loménie de Brienne, who has announced national bankruptcy, is dismissed and
27th, Jacques Necker is recalled as French minister of finance.

J **Sep**: 13th, New York is declared the federal capital of U.S.;
Denmark invades Sweden.

K **Oct**: Joseph II, having failed to take Belgrade, returns to Vienna;
6th, Last 4-years Diet meets in Poland.

L **Nov**: 6th, through the intervention of the Triple Alliance Denmark and Sweden sign the Convention of Uddevalla which provides for the evacuation of Danish troops;
George III's first derangement;
Louis XVI decides to summon the notables.

M **Dec**: 10th, Commons debate the Regency question;
17th, Russian army under Gregory Potemkin takes Ochákov.

N

O **Politics, Economics, Law and Education**

Hannah More, *Thoughts on the Importance of the Manners of the Great to General Society.*

P **Science, Technology, Discovery, etc.**

Pierre Laplace publishes his laws of the planetary system.

James Hutton expounds his dynamic theory of continual changes in the earth's features in *New Theory of the Earth.*

Linnean Society founded in London.

J. L. Lagrange, French mathematician, *Mécanique analytique.*

Q **Scholarship**

John Lemprière, *Classical Dictionary.*

F. Schiller, *History of the Revolt of the Netherlands under the Spanish Regime.*

R **Philosophy and Religion**

Thomas Reid, *Essays on the Active Powers of the Human Mind.*

I. Kant, *Critique of Practical Reason.*

Richard Porson's *Letters to Travis.*

Religious edict in Prussia imposes censorship in education and penalties for heresy (repealed 1797).

American Presbyterians revise the Westminster Catechism and introduce principles of religious liberty.

S **Art, Sculpture, Fine Arts and Architecture**

J. L. David, *Love of Paris and Helen* (painting).

T **Music**

J. Haydn, 'Oxford' Symphony (No. 92 in B).

W. A. Mozart, Symphonies 39 (E flat), 40 (C minor) and 41 ('Jupiter').

U **Literature**

V **The Press**

John Walter founds *The Times* (*Jan.* 1st).

W **Drama and Entertainment**

J. W. Goethe, *Egmont.*

X **Sport**

M.C.C. codifies the Laws of Cricket.

Y **Statistics**

Z **Births and Deaths**

Jan. 22nd George Lord Byron b. (–1824).
Feb. 5th Robert Peel b. (–1850).
Feb. 22nd Arthur Schopenhauer b. (–1860).
Apr. 15th George Louis Leclerk Buffon d. (80).
Aug. 2nd Thomas Gainsborough d. (61).
Dec. 14th Carl Philipp Emanuel Bach d. (74).

A **Jan**:

B **Feb**: 3rd, William Pitt introduces Regency bill, vesting Regency in Prince of Wales, but without power to create peers or grant offices;
19th, George III recovers;
20th, Gustavus III introduces act of Unity and Security in Sweden which grants him absolute powers (receives royal assent *Apr.* 3rd).

C **Mar**: 4th, first Congress meets at New York and during the session ten of the proposed twelve amendments to the constitution are made and sent to the states for ratification.

D **Apr**: 7th, accession of Selim III of Turkey (–1807);
30th, George Washington inaugurated as President of U.S. with John Adams vice-president, Thomas Jefferson secretary of state and Alexander Hamilton secretary of Treasury.

E **May**: 5th, States-General meet at Versailles.

F **Jun**: Spaniards attack British fishing vessels at Nootka Sound, W. Canada;
17th, third estate in France declares itself a National Assembly and undertakes to frame a constitution (–*Sept.* 30th, 1791);
20th, third estate takes tennis court oath, undertaking not to depart until a constitution is drawn up;
23rd, Honoré Mirabeau establishes his reputation in the Séance Royale;
27th, Union of the three estates in France.

G **Jul**: 4th, U.S. declare themselves to be an economic and customs union;
11th, Louis XVI's dismissal of Jacques Necker implies a royalist *coup d'état* and provokes the Paris mob
14th, to sack the Bastille;
17th, Jean Bailly becomes mayor of Paris and the Marquis de La Fayette commander of the National Guard;
31st, Austrian and Russian troops under Francis Duke of Coburg and Count Alexander Suvorov defeat Turks at Focshani.

H **Aug**: 4th, French feudal system is abolished;
27th, French National Assembly adopts Declaration of the Rights of Man.

J **Sep**: 22nd, Austrian and Russian troops under Duke of Coburg defeat Turks at Rimnik.

K **Oct**: 5th (–6th), march of women to Versailles to move Louis XVI and his court to Paris;
6th, Austrians take Belgrade;
9th, Coburg's army takes Bucharest;
Emigration of French royalists begins in earnest;
Revolution breaks out in Austrian Netherlands under Van der Noot, after Joseph II of Austria has revoked constitution of Brabant and Hainault.

L **Nov**: 2nd, nationalisation of property of church in France;
7th, National Assembly forbids any member to accept office under Louis XVI;
12th, France is divided into 80 administrative departments;
The Revolution Society, meeting in London, congratulates French National Assembly on fall of the Bastille.

M **Dec**: 13th, Austrian Netherlands declare independence as Belgium;
21st, issue of Assignats (paper money) in France;
29th, Tippoo of Mysore attacks the Rajah of Travancore.

N

o **Politics, Economics, Law and Education**

J. Bentham, *Introduction to the Principles of Morals and Legislation.*

E. J. Sièyes, *Qu'est-ce que le Tiers État?* and *Exposition des Droits de l'Homme.*

Pierre Malouet's *Considérations sur le Gouvernement* recommends a limited monarchy.

Journal des Débats founded in Paris.

Pierre Cabanis, *Observations sur les hôpitaux.*

P **Science, Technology, Discovery, etc.**

A. L. Lavoisier, *Traité élémentaire de chimie.*

Aloisio Galvani's observations on the muscular contraction of dead frogs, which he infers was caused electrically, prompts Alessandro Volta's assertion on the nature of electricity.

W. Herschel completes his reflecting telescope and discovers a seventh satellite ('Mimas') in the Saturnian system.

Antoine Jussieu begins the modern classification of plants in *Genera Plantarum.*

Gilbert White, *Natural History of Selborne.*

Q **Scholarship**

Jean Amiot, *Dictionnaire tartare-mantchou-français.*

Arabic studies in the western world come of age with Johann Reiske, *Adnotationes historicae* to his *Abulfeda* (posth.).

William Jones's translation of Kàlidàsa's drama, *Sakuntala.*

R **Philosophy and Religion**

Pope Pius VI admits the ninth-century decretals of Isidore, on which much papal authority was based, were forged.

The three ecclesiastical imperial electors recognise the Pope's right to send nuncios.

Pius VI refutes the Ems articles (of *Aug.* 1786).

S **Art, Sculpture, Fine Arts and Architecture**

François Gérard, *Joseph and his Brothers* (painting).

T **Music**

W. A. Mozart, *Così fan tutte* (opera).

U **Literature**

William Blake, *Songs of Innocence.*

William Bowles, *Fourteen Sonnets written chiefly on picturesque spots.*

J. H. B. de Saint-Pierre, *Paul et Virginie.*

F. Schiller, *Die Künstler.*

V **The Press**

W **Drama and Entertainment**

Joseph Chénier, *Charles IX.*

J. W. Goethe, *Tasso.*

X **Sport**

Y **Statistics**

Z **Births and Deaths**

Aug. 6th Friedrich List b. (–1846).

Sept. 15th James Fenimore Cooper b. (–1851).

— J. L. M. Daguerre b. (–1867).

A **Jan**: 9th, Britain, Prussia and Holland agree on a common policy over Belgium, but William Pitt subsequently refuses to recognise Belgian independence;
31st, Prussia withdraws from intervention in Russo-Turkish War.

B **Feb**: 20th, Leopold II of Austria becomes Holy Roman Emperor on Joseph II's death;
In British Parliament Edmund Burke condemns and Charles James Fox welcomes the developments in France;
French religious houses are suppressed and the municipality of Paris is reorganised;
Alexander Hamilton introduces Funding Bill in U.S.

C **Mar** 2nd, Edmund Burke secures defeat of C. J. Fox's bill for repeal of Test and Corporation Acts;
16th, Van der Noot drives the Democrats, or Vonckists, from power in Belgium;
29th, Poland cedes Thorn and Danzig to Prussia on the understanding that Prussia will obtain Austrian Galicia for her.

D **Apr**:

E **May**: Honoré Mirabeau becomes a secret agent of the Crown and begins series of Notes for the Court on proceedings in the National Assembly. The Assembly debates the right to declare war and make peace, which becomes a pertinent issue with the danger of war between Britain and Spain over Nootka Sound, in which France would be bound by the Family Compact to aid Spain.

F **Jun**: 1st, Britain forms alliance with Mahrathas in India;
At Reichenbach Conference Britain and Holland refuse to support Prussia, thus averting a war with Austria, and a treaty is signed between Austria and Prussia under which Frederick William II abandons his aggressive policy over Belgium, Sweden, Poland and Turkey.

G **Jul**: 4th, British alliance with the Nizam of Hyderabad;
12th, Civil constitution of the French clergy;
14th, festival of Champ de Mars, Paris; Louis XVI accepts the constitution.

H **Aug**: 14th, Treaty of Verela ends Swedish-Russian war, Russia acquiring part of Finland;
31st, mutiny is quelled in Nancy.

J **Sep**: 10th, Jacques Necker resigns.

K **Oct**: Wolfe Tone founds Society of United Irishmen as a political union of Roman Catholics and Protestants to further Irish Parliamentary reform;
28th, Spain yields to Britain's demands for reparation over Nootka Sound (see *June* 1789) and abandons claim to Vancouver Island.

L **Nov**: 27th, French clergy required to take oath to support the civil constitution;
William Pitt increases government majority in British election.

M **Dec**: 2nd, Austrians re-enter Brussels and suppress revolution;
10th, Austria renounces scheme for exchanging Bavaria for the Netherlands;
22nd, Alexander Suvorov captures Ismail from the Turks.

N Growing power of the Jacobins (Maximilien Robespierre), the Cordeliers (Georges Danton) and other political clubs in Paris.

O **Politics, Economics, Law and Education**

André de Chénier, *Avis au peuple français* and *Jeu de paume*.

E. Burke, *Reflections on the Revolution in France*.

Alexander Radistcheff's *Journey from St. Petersburg to Moscow* pleads for the emancipation of serfs.

P **Science, Technology, Discovery, etc.**

J. W. Goethe, *Versuch die Metamorphose der Pflanzen zu erklären*.

T. Clifford's nail-maker.

First steam-rolling-mill in England.

Firth-Clyde and Oxford-Birmingham canals begun.

George Vancouver explores the north-west coast of America.

First patent law in U.S.

James Bruce, *Travels to Discover the Source of the Nile, 1768–73*.

Q **Scholarship**

R **Philosophy and Religion**

I. Kant, *Critique of Judgment*.

Civil constitution of the clergy in France (July 12th). Jews in France are admitted to civil liberties.

John Carroll is consecrated as Roman Catholic bishop of Baltimore, the first bishop in America (becomes Archbishop of Baltimore in 1811).

S **Art, Sculpture, Fine Arts and Architecture**

Archibald Alison, *Essay on the Nature and Principles of Taste*.

T **Music**

U **Literature**

Robert Burns, *Tam O'Shanter*.

Karl Moritz completes *Anton Reiser*.

David Williams founds the Royal Literary Fund.

V **The Press**

W **Drama and Entertainment**

X **Sport**

Y **Statistics**

Z **Births and Deaths**

Apr. 17th Benjamin Franklin d. (84).

July 17th Adam Smith d. (63).

Sept. 26th Nassau William Senior b. (–1864).

Oct. 21st Alphonse de Lamartine b. (–1869).

— Théodore Géricault b. (–1824).

A **Jan**: 30th, Honoré Mirabeau elected President of French Assembly.

B **Feb**: Prussia and Austria guarantee a free constitution for Poland.

C **Mar**: 4th, Vermont becomes a state of U.S.;
28th, Britain increases navy, fearing a war with Russia over the Black Sea port of Ochákov, captured from the Turks.

D **Apr**: 2nd, death of Mirabeau;
18th, Louis XVI is prevented by riot from going to St. Cloud, which demonstrates he is a prisoner.

E **May**: 3rd, Polish constitution, converting an elective into a hereditary monarchy under the elector of Saxony, following the death of King Stanislas II;
6th, by Canada Constitution Act Canada is divided into two provinces, Upper (Ontario) and Lower (Quebec), with separate legislative assemblies;
14th, Lord Cornwallis overthrows Tippoo of Mysore at battle of Seringapatam.

F **Jun**: 20th (–25th), Louis XVI attempts to leave France, but is turned back at Varennes and taken to Paris.

G **Jul**: 5th, Frederick William II of Prussia dismisses Ewald Hertzberg;
6th, Leopold II of Austria issues letter calling on powers to support Louis XVI;
—, arrival of Comte d'Artois makes Coblenz the headquarters of French *émigrés*;
17th, massacre of Champ de Mars by Marquis de La Fayette restores order in Paris;
Rioters in Birmingham attack Joseph Priestley's house for his support of French Revolution.

H **Aug**: 4th, by peace of Sistova Turkey cedes Orsova to Austria, in defiance of treaty of Reichenbach (see *June* 1790);
22nd, Negro revolt in French part of San Domingo;
27th, by declaration of Pillnitz Austria and Prussia state they are ready to intervene in French affairs with consent of other powers, but William Pitt announces Britain will remain neutral; France interprets the declaration as a threat.

J **Sep**: 3rd, French Constitution is passed by National Assembly, making France a constitutional monarchy;
4th, France annexes Avignon;
30th, French National Assembly dissolves after decreeing that none of its members is eligible to serve in the Legislative Assembly.

K **Oct**: 1st, Legislative Assembly meets at Paris (–*Sept.* 1792); Jacques Brissot and others of the Girondist Party in France urge war against Austria.

L **Nov**: 9th, Louis XVI vetoes a decree of the Assembly demanding the return of the *émigrés* under pain of death.

M **Dec**: 15th, first ten amendments to U.S. constitution ratified;
Gustavus III of Sweden offers to head a crusade against France.

O Politics, Economics, Law and Education

E. Burke, *An Appeal from the New to the Old Whigs* and *Letter to a Member of the National Assembly.*

Thomas Paine, *The Rights of Man*, part I.

James Mackintosh, *Vindiciae Gallicae.*

K. W. von Humboldt, *Attempt to Determine the limits of the Frontier of the State.*

John Sinclair, *The Statistical Account of Scotland.*

Bank of North America founded (*July*).

Jeremy Bentham designs a 'panopticon' for the central inspection of convicts.

School for the Indigent Blind opened in Liverpool.

P Science, Technology, Discovery, etc.

Philippe Pinel, *Traité médico-philosophique de l'aliénation mentale.*

J. W. Goethe's optical studies (–92).

Ordnance Survey established in Britain.

Samuel Peel patents india-rubber cloth.

Q Scholarship

Constantin Volney's essay on the philosophy of history, *Les Ruines, ou méditations sur les révolutions des empires.*

George Martens, *Recueil des traités, 1671–1791* (–1801, Göttingen).

R Philosophy and Religion

Sulpicians found a Roman Catholic seminary in U.S.

Robert Hall, Baptist, *Sermons.*

S Art, Sculpture, Fine Arts and Architecture

George Morland, *The Stable* (painting).

Anguetin Pajou, *Psyche Abandoned* (sculpture).

Karl Langhans, Brandenburg Gate, Berlin.

T Music

W. A. Mozart, *Magic Flute* (opera) and Requiem.

J. Haydn, 'Surprise' Symphony.

Luigi Cherubini, *Lodoiska* (opera).

U Literature

Boswell, *Life of Johnson.*

V The Press

The Observer founded.

W Drama and Entertainment

Elizabeth Inchbald, *A Simple Story.*

Joseph Chénier's plays *Henry VIII* and *Jean Calas* produced in Paris.

Goethe becomes director of the Weimar theatre (–1817).

X Sport

Y Statistics

N Washington, D.C., is laid out.
Odessa is founded.

z **Births and Deaths**

Jan. 15th Franz Grillparzer b. (–1872).

Apr. 2nd Honoré Gabriel Riquetti Mirabeau d. (42).

Apr. 27th S. F. B. Morse b. (–1872).

Sept. 5th Giacomo Meyerbeer b. (–1864).

Sept. 22nd Michael Faraday b. (–1867).

Dec. 5th Wolfgang Amadeus Mozart d. (35).

1792 France declares war on Austria and Prussia

A **Jan**: 9th, Russia, deserted by Austria and concerned over Prussian intrigues in Poland, ends her war with Turkey by the peace of Jassy, obtaining Ochákov and a boundary on the R. Dniester, but surrendering her conquests in Moldavia and Bessarabia;
18th, Prussia gains Ansbach and Bayreuth by escheat, under Treaty of Teschen (*May* 1779).

B **Feb**: 5th, Tippoo of Mysore, defeated in his war with British and Hyderabad, cedes half Mysore to Britain;
7th, Austro-Prussian alliance against France.

C **Mar**: 1st, Francis II of Austria succeeds his brother Leopold II as Holy Roman Emperor (–1835);
24th, Girondins under Jean Roland and Charles Dumouriez form ministry in France;
29th, Gustavus III of Sweden is assassinated.

D **Apr**: 20th, France declares war on Austria (the War of the First Coalition).

E **May**: 19th, Russia invades Poland, where the constitution is abrogated.

F **Jun**: 1st, Kentucky becomes a U.S. state;
20th, mob invades Tuileries.

G **Jul**: 8th, France declares war on Prussia and
18th, on Sardinia;
25th, Duke of Brunswick's manifesto threatens destruction of Paris if French royal family is harmed.

H **Aug**: Prussian and Austrian troops invade France;
9th, revolutionary Commune established in Paris;
10th, mob invades Tuileries, massacring the Swiss guard; the Legislative Assembly is suspended;
13th, French royal family is imprisoned.

J **Sep**: 2nd, Prussians take Longwy and Verdun; but
20th, the invaders are stopped at battle of Valmy;
21st, French National Convention meets;
22nd, French Republic proclaimed; the Revolutionary Calendar comes into force.

K **Oct**: 19th, French troops take Mayence and cross Rhine.

L **Nov**: 6th, French under Charles Dumouriez defeat Austrians at Jemappes, take Brussels and conquer Austrian Netherlands;
19th, French Convention offers assistance to all peoples wishing to overthrow their government;
27th, France annexes Savoy and Nice and opens R. Scheldt to commerce;
The Jacobins, under G. J. Danton, wrest power from the Girondins.

M **Dec**: 5th, trial of Louis XVI before the Convention opens;
—, revolutionary *coup d'état* in Geneva;
12th, William Pitt introduces an Aliens bill;
15th, French decree compelling all lands occupied by French troops to accept their institutions;
18th, Paine is tried in his absence for publishing *The Rights of Man*.

O Politics, Economics, Law and Education

J. B. ('Anacharsis') Cloots, *La République universelle*.
T. Paine, *Rights of Man*, part II (*Feb.*).
Arthur Young, *Travels in France*.
William Cobbett attacks U.S. institutions in his 'Peter Porcupine' pamphlets.
Mary Wollstonecraft, *Vindication of the Rights of Women*.
Slave trade abolished in Denmark.
Dollar coinage introduced in U.S., with the opening of a mint at Philadelphia.
Libel Act in Britain.
William Tuke reforms the treatment of lunatics at the York Retreat.

P Science, Technology, Discovery, etc.

George Cartwright's *Journal of Transactions . . . on the Coast of Labrador*.
Cable-making machine invented.

Q Scholarship

D. Lysons, *The Environs of London*, Vol. I.
Joseph Eckhel, *Doctrina numorum veterum* (–98).

R Philosophy and Religion

Dugald Stewart, *Elements of the Philosophy of the Human Mind*, Vol. I (continued 1814 and 1827).
J. G. Fichte, *Critique of Revelation*.
In France the religious orders are dissolved and civil marriage and divorce is instituted.
A Swedenborgian church is founded in Baltimore.
Baptist Missionary Society founded in London.

S Art, Sculpture, Fine Arts and Architecture

James Hoban begins the White House, Washington.
Rafaello Morghen's engraving of Leonardo's *Last Supper*.

T Music

D. Cimarosa, *The Secret Marriage* (opera).
C. J. Rouget de Lisle, *La Marseillaise* ('Chant de guerre de l'armée du Rhin').

U Literature

Samuel Rogers, *The Pleasures of Memory*.

V The Press

W Drama and Entertainment

J. W. Goethe, *Der Grosskophta*.

X Sport

Y Statistics

1792

N Sierra Leone company formed.
Denmark becomes the first state to abolish Slave Trade.
Differences in U.S. arising from Alexander Hamilton's financial policy lead to formation of political parties, namely Republican (Thomas Jefferson) and Federal (Hamilton and John Adams).
Alvarez Godoy becomes a dictator in Spain, and John, Prince of Portugal, regent for his insane mother, represses revolutionary tendencies.

z **Births and Deaths**

Feb. 23rd Joshua Reynolds d. (69).

Feb. 29th Carl von Baer b. (–1876) and Gioacchino Rossini b. (–1868).

Mar. 3rd Robert Adam d. (64).

Apr. 25th John Keble b. (–1866).

May 13th Giovanni Mastai-Ferretti (later Pope Pius IX) b. (–1878).

Aug. 4th Richard Arkwright d. (60) and Percy Bysshe Shelley b. (–1822).

Aug. 18th Lord John Russell b. (–1878).

Oct. 28th John Smeaton d. (68).

1793 First Coalition against France—Louis XVI executed—Second Partition of Poland

A **Jan**: 21st, Louis XVI is executed;
23rd, Russia and Prussia agree on second partition of Poland (effected May 7th).

B **Feb**: 1st, France declares war on Britain and Holland;
13th, first Coalition against France is formed by Britain, Austria, Prussia, Holland, Spain and Sardinia.

C **Mar**: 7th, France declares war on Spain; the Spanish invade Roussillon and Navarre;
11th, William Pitt issues Exchequer bills to raise funds for defence and for subsidies to Britain's allies;
15th, Traitorous Correspondence Act is passed and Habeas Corpus Act suspended in Britain;
18th, Charles Dumouriez is defeated at Neerwinden, leading to the liberation of Belgium;
26th, Holy Roman Empire declares war on France; Royalist revolt in La Vendée;
France annexes the bishopric of Basle;
Britain and Russia sign convention to interdict all Baltic trade with France.

D **Apr**: 4th, Charles Dumouriez deserts to the allies;
6th, Committee of Public Safety established in France with dictatorial power, dominated by G. J. Danton;
23rd, U.S. proclaim their neutrality (despite the 1778 alliance with France).

E **May**: 7th, second partition of Poland effected, Russia taking Lithuania and W. Ukraine, and Prussia taking Danzig, Thorn, Posen, Gnesen and Kalisch.

F **Jun**: 2nd, final overthrow of Girondins and arrest of Jacques Brissot begins Reign of Terror;
24th, revised French constitution is framed.

G **Jul**: 13th, Jean Marat is murdered by Charlotte Corday;
23rd, allies recapture Mayence and drive French troops from Germany;
British force occupies Corsica;
Maximilien Robespierre and Antoine St. Just join Committee of Public Safety.

H **Aug**: 23rd, levy of entire male population capable of serving in France;
28th, Alexander Hood occupies Toulon (recaptured *Dec.* 19th).

J **Sep**: new French offensive in Netherlands, where British army under Duke of York is defeated at Hondschoote, and in Rhineland.
17th, French law fixes wages and maximum prices.

K **Oct**: 5th, Christianity is abolished in France;
16th, Marie Antoinette is executed;
20th, Vendéans are defeated at Cholet;
31st, prominent Girondins are executed by guillotine in Place de la Concorde, Paris.

L **Nov**: Philippe Égalité (Duke of Orléans) is executed.

M **Dec**: 12th, Vendéans are defeated at Le Mans;
19th, Bonaparte takes Toulon;
26th, French victory at Weissenburg forces allies to retreat across Rhine.

N Britain seizes French settlements in India.
Lord Cornwallis promulgates code of justice in India on British model, reorganises finances, and organises 'Permanent Settlement' of Bengal.
U.S. Law compelling return of fugitive slave to his master.

O **Politics, Economics, Law and Education**

J. B. ('Anacharsis') Cloots, *Base constitutionelle de la république du genre humain.*
M. J. Condorcet, *Tableau du Progrès de l'Esprit humain.*
William Godwin, *The Inquiry Concerning Political Justice.*
Compulsory public education in France from the age of six.

P **Science, Technology, Discovery, etc.**

Kurt Sprengel's investigations into plant fertility.
Claude Chappe invents semaphore.
Eli Whitney invents the cotton gin in U.S., which leads to the rapid growth of cotton exports from the southern states.
Samuel Bentham's woodworking machinery.
The Board of Agriculture established in Britain, with Arthur Young as Secretary.

Q **Scholarship**

Richard Porson is appointed Professor of Greek at Cambridge and, with Thomas Gaisford, leads a revival of classical scholarship.

R **Philosophy and Religion**

I. Kant, *Religion within the Boundaries of Reason.*
Jacques Hébert edits *Père Duchesne*, advocating atheism.
Hébert and Pierre Chaumette organise the Feast of Reason, celebrated in St. Eustache Church, Paris (*Nov.* 10th).

S **Art, Sculpture, Fine Arts and Architecture**

J. L. David, *Marat* (painting).
A. L. Girodet de Roussy, *Endymion* (painting).
A. Canova, *Cupid and Psyche* (sculpture).
Corner-stone of Capitol, Washington, laid (*Sept.* 18th), designed by William Thornton (completed 1830).
The Louvre, Paris, becomes a national art gallery.

T **Music**

N. Paganini makes his début as a virtuoso violinist.

U **Literature**

Jean Paul (pseud.), *Die Unsichtbare Loge.*
N. M. Karamzin (Russian short stories), *Poor Lisa* and *Natalia.*
Madame Jeanne Roland writes her *Appel à l'impartiale postérité* (published 1820).

V **The Press**

W **Drama and Entertainment**

X **Sport**

Y **Statistics**

Z **Births and Deaths**

June 26th Gilbert White d. (72).
July 3rd John Clare b. (–1864).
July 11th William Robertson d. (71).

1794 French invade Spain and Holland

A **Jan:**

B **Feb:**

C **Mar:** 5th, execution of partisans of Jacques Hébert (Hébertistes) in France;
Polish rising under T. A. Kosciuszko, which is suppressed by Russians (*Oct.*).

D **Apr:** 5th, execution of G. J. Danton and Camille Desmoulins;
19th, by treaty of The Hague Britain pays subsidies for 60,000 Prussian and Dutch troops in coalition against France.

E **May:** 18th, Charles Pichegru leads French to victory at Tourcoing.

F **Jun:** 1st, Lord Howe defeats French fleet in English Channel;
10th, power of revolutionary tribunals is increased by law of 22 Prairial, leading to mass executions;
25th, French troops take Charleroi;
26th, Austrians defeated by J. B. Jourdan at Fleurus; Duke of Coburg evacuates Belgium;
French force invades Spain.

G **Jul:** 11th, following the split of the Whig party on the issue of Parliamentary reform, Lord Portland and William Wyndham enter Pitt's cabinet, while C. J. Fox and Charles Grey lead a Whig rump of 40;
Lazare Hoche defeats *émigrés* at Quiberon Bay;
Conspiracy by Moderates of the Mountain and Dantonists against M. Robespierre, succeeds in abolishing the Commune of Paris (founded *Aug.* 1792) and
28th, Robespierre and A. St. Just are executed.

H **Aug:**

J **Sep:** 28th, alliance of St. Petersburg, of Britain, Russia and Austria against France.

K **Oct:** French troops reach the Rhine;
25th, Prussia withdraws her troops from the war.

L **Nov:** 9th, Russians enter Warsaw;
11th, Jacobin Club, Paris, is closed;
19th, following U.S. embargo on British shipping, John Jay negotiates treaty with Britain, by which Britain evacuates frontier posts in North-west and appoints commissioners to settle the boundary dispute.

M **Dec:** 8th, surviving Girondists are admitted to the Convention;
13th, in debate on the Address in British Parliament some members demand peace with France;
Prussia and Spain open separate negotiations for peace;
24th, a new issue of Assignats further depreciates the French currency;
27th, French troops under Charles Pichegru invade Holland.

N Britain takes the Seychelles, Martinique, St. Lucia and Guadaloupe, but Guadaloupe is later recaptured by the French.
Abolition of slavery in French colonies.
Whisky insurrections in Pennsylvania, occasioned by excise.
Eleventh amendment to U.S. constitution, closing federal courts to suits instituted against a state by citizens of another state or of foreign states.
Aga Mohammed founds Kajar dynasty in Persia.

O **Politics, Economics, Law and Education**
T. Paine, *The Age of Reason* (–95).
École Normale founded in France.
Stonyhurst College founded.

P **Science, Technology, Discovery, etc.**
Erasmus Darwin, *Zoonomia, or the laws of Organic Life* (–96).
John Hunter, *Treatise on the Blood, Inflammation and Gunshot Wounds* (posth.).
Adrien Legendre, *Éléments de Géométrie.*

Q **Scholarship**
James Stuart and Nicholas Revett, *The Antiquities of Athens, measured and delineated.*

R **Philosophy and Religion**
J. G. Fichte, *On the Notion of the Theory of Science* and *Vocation of a Scholar.*
W. Paley, *A View of the Evidences of Christianity.*
M. Robespierre presides over the Feast of the Supreme Being in Paris (*June* 8th).

S **Art, Sculpture, Fine Arts and Architecture**
J. H. Dannecker, bust of F. Schiller.

T **Music**
J. Haydn, 'Clock' Symphony.

U **Literature**
W. Blake, *Songs of Experience.*
Anne Radcliffe, *The Mysteries of Udolpho.*
W. Godwin, *Caleb Williams, or Things as They are.*
William Gifford's satirical *Baeviad.*
André de Chénier, *Jeune Captive* (poem).
Xavier de Maistre, *Voyage autour de ma chambre.*
J. W. Goethe, *Reinecke Fuchs.*
F. Schiller edits the *Horen* (–97).

V **The Press**

W **Drama and Entertainment**
S. T. Coleridge, R. Southey and R. Lovell collaborate in *The Fall of Robespierre.*

X **Sport**

Y **Statistics**

Z **Births and Deaths**
Jan. 16th Edward Gibbon d. (57).
Apr. 8th Marie Jean Antoine Condorcet d. (50).
May 8th Antoine Laurent Lavoisier d. (50).
July 17th John Roebuck d. (76).
Nov. 17th George Grote b. (–1871).

1795 Rule of the Directory in France—Third Partition of Poland

A **Jan**: 3rd, secret treaty between Russia and Austria for third partition of Poland;
19th, Charles Pichegru is received with open arms in Amsterdam, captures the Dutch fleet in Texel and French troops overrun Holland.

B **Feb**: 9th, Tuscany makes peace with France;
15th, by peace of La Jaunaie the Vendéans come to terms with the French government;
21st, freedom of worship in France;
The Dutch surrender Ceylon to Britain.

C **Mar**: 11th, the Mahrathas defeat Mogul at Kurdla.

D **Apr**: 1st, bread riots in Paris;
5th, by peace of Basle France cedes to Prussia her conquests on the right bank of the Rhine, Frederick William II defends the interests of the N. German princes and subsequently Saxony, Hanover, the Bavarian Palatinate and Hesse-Cassel make terms with France;
23rd, Warren Hastings is acquitted of high treason.

E **May**: 16th, Batavian Republic established in Holland;
20th, The White Terror in Paris (*–June*).

F **Jun**: 25th, Luxembourg capitulates to French;
27th, British force lands at Quiberon to aid revolt in Brittany (suppressed in *Oct.*);
French recapture St. Lucia.

G **Jul**: 27th, Spain signs peace with France, ceding her part of San Domingo.

H **Aug**: 23rd, third French constitution, vesting power in Directory (effective *Nov.* 3rd);
Prussia joins Austro-Russian agreement over Poland.

J **Sep**: 6th, C. J. Jourdan crosses the Rhine;
20th, Charles Pichegru occupies Mannheim;
Austria reconquers right bank of Rhine;
British force under James Craig occupies Cape of Good Hope as a colony for Prince William V of Orange, who has taken refuge in England on the French invasion of Holland.

K **Oct**: 1st, Belgium is incorporated with France;
5th, Napoleon Bonaparte's whiff of grapeshot puts down insurrection on the Day of the Sections;
24th, in third Partition of Poland Prussia takes Warsaw and land between R. Bug and R. Niemen, Austria takes Cracow and Galicia, and Russia the area between Galicia and R. Dvina;
27th, Thomas Pinckney negotiates treaty of San Lorenzo between U.S. and Spain, which settles boundary with Florida and grants U.S. right to navigate Mississippi.

L **Nov**: 3rd, Directory in France;
25th, Stanislaus II of Poland abdicates;
Austrians defeated at Loano, Piedmont, by Barthélemi Schérer;
Following attack on George III, Pitt introduces Treasonable Practices Bill and Seditious Meetings Bill, forbidding meetings of more than 50 persons held without notice to a magistrate.

M **Dec**: 19th, and 31st, Austria signs armistice with France.

N

O **Politics, Economics, Law and Education**

École Polytechnique, Paris.

Institut National, Paris, with sections for natural science, moral and political science and the arts, to replace the abolished Academies.

Joseph Lakanal's plans for *écoles centrales* in France.

'Speenhamland' Act for poor relief in Britain.

P **Science, Technology, Discovery, etc.**

Joseph Bramah invents a hydraulic press.

Mungo Park explores the course of the River Niger.

Q **Scholarship**

Charles François Dupuis, *Origine de tous les cultes*, arouses an interest in Upper Egypt.

Friedrich Wolf, *Prolegomena to Homer*.

R **Philosophy and Religion**

I. Kant, *Zum ewigen Frieden*.

Maynooth College, a Roman Catholic seminary, founded by Act of Irish Parliament to prevent priests from travelling for instruction to the Continent, whereby they might come under the influence of revolutionary ideas.

S **Art, Sculpture, Fine Arts and Architecture**

F. Goya, *The Duchess of Alba* (painting).

A. J. Carstens, *Night with Her Children* and *Battle of Rossbach* (paintings).

John Soane begins the Bank of England (–1827).

T **Music**

Haydn 'Drum Roll' Symphony and first performance of 'London' Symphony (composed '91).

Paris Conservatoire de Musique founded.

U **Literature**

M. G. Lewis, *The Monk*.

Ann Radcliffe, *The Italian*.

J. W. Goethe, *Wilhelm Meister*.

F. Schiller, *Letters Concerning the Aesthetic Education of Mankind*.

Jean Paul (pseud.), *Hesperus*.

Ludwig Tieck, *William Lovell* (–96).

J. H. Voss, *Luise*.

V **The Press**

W **Drama and Entertainment**

X **Sport**

Y **Statistics**

Z **Births and Deaths**

Jan. 3rd Josiah Wedgwood d. (65).

May 10th Augustin Thierry b. (–1856).

May 19th James Boswell d. (56).

June 13th Thomas Arnold b. (–1842).

Oct. 31st John Keats b. (–1821).

Dec. 3rd Rowland Hill b. (–1879).

Dec. 4th Thomas Carlyle b. (–1881).

Dec. 20th Leopold von Ranke b. (–1886).

1796 Bonaparte's Italian campaign

A **Jan:**

B **Feb:**

C **Mar:** 5th, final suppression of revolts in Vendée and Brittany;
9th, Napoleon Bonaparte marries Josephine de Beauharnais;
19th, freedom of the press in France;
William Pitt begins negotiations for peace with France through the Swiss Minister.

D **Apr:** Napoleon Bonaparte assumes command in Italy, 13th, defeating Austrians at Millesimo and, 22nd, the Piedmontese at Mondovi;
28th, Sardinia is forced to abandon the Austrian alliance.

E **May:** 10th, failure of François Babeuf's plot to restore French constitution of 1793;
—, Napoleon Bonaparte defeats Austrians at Lodi and
15th, enters Milan;
—, by peace of Cherasco Sardinia cedes Savoy and Nice to France;
16th, Lombardic Republic established.

F **Jun:** 1st, Tennessee becomes a U.S. state;
J. B. Jourdan invades Franconia, but is driven back;
Jean Moreau crosses the Rhine.

G **Jul:** Britain captures Elba.

H **Aug:** 5th, by treaty with France, Prussia yields lands on left bank of Rhine in exchange for Münster and other ecclesiastical territory;
15th, Napoleon Bonaparte defeats Wurmser at Castiglione delle Stiviere in his attempt to relieve Mantua;
19th, alliance of San Ildefonso between France and Spain against Britain, is virtually a renewal of the Family Compact;
J. B. Jourdan invades Germany, but Archduke Charles of Austria defeats him at Amberg.

J **Sep:** 3rd, Archduke Charles defeats J. B. Jourdan at Würzburg and Jourdan resigns his command;
18th, George Washington, who had refused to accept further nomination for election, delivers his farewell address.

K **Oct:** 5th, Spain declares war on Britain;
16th, Cispadane Republic is established from Bologna, Ferrara, Modena and Reggio.

L **Nov:** 15th (–17th), Napoleon Bonaparte defeats Austrians under Joseph Alvintzi at Arcole;
16th, Paul I succeeds as Emperor of Russia on Catherine II's death (–1801);
Royal Navy withdraws from Mediterranean;
John Adams defeats Thomas Jefferson in U.S. presidential election by 3 votes; Jefferson elected vice-president.

M **Dec:** 19th, Directory refuse further negotiations with Britain;
French expedition under Lazare Hoche to Bantry Bay fails through gales, but rumours of expedition cause run on provincial banks in England.

N Britain captures Demerara, Essequibo, Berbice, St. Lucia and Grenada, but abandons Corsica.
Aga Mohammed of Persia seizes Khorasan in Khuzistan.

O Politics, Economics, Law and Education

E. Burke, *Letters on a Regicide Peace*, and in *A Letter to a Noble Lord* castigates the Duke of Bedford for criticising him for accepting a pension.

Louis de Bonald, *Théorie du pouvoir politique et religieux.*

Joseph de Maistre, *Considérations sur la France.*

Jean Cambacérès *Projet de Code Civil* (taken as the basis for the Napoleonic Code in 1801).

J. G. Fichte, *Science of Rights.*

P Science, Technology, Discovery, etc.

Pierre Laplace enunciates the 'nebular hypothesis' in *Exposition du système du monde.*

Edward Jenner vaccinates against smallpox.

Drummond invents 'limelight'.

G. L. C. Cuvier's lectures at École Centrale du Panthéon found the science of comparative zoology.

Q Scholarship

Brockhaus, *Encyclopaedia* (first edition).

National Library, Lisbon, founded.

R Philosophy and Religion

Richard Watson, *An Apology for the Bible.*

S Art, Sculpture, Fine Arts and Architecture

F. Goya's *Los Capriccios*, which satirise the government and religion, are seized by the Inquisition.

J. Bacon sculpts Dr. Johnson's memorial in St. Paul's Cathedral.

T Music

J. Haydn, 'Kettledrum' Mass.

Benjamin Carr's opera *The Archers of Switzerland* given first performance in New York.

U Literature

Fanny Burney (pseud.), *Camilla.*

Jean Paul (pseud.), *Leben des Quintus Fixlein.*

V The Press

W Drama and Entertainment

August Iffland becomes director of the Prussian national theatre, Berlin.

X Sport

Y Statistics

Z Births and Deaths

Mar. 20th Edward Gibbon Wakefield b. (–1862).

May 4th William Hickling Prescott b. (–1859).

May 8th François Mignet b. (–1884).

June 25th Tsar Nicholas I b. (–1855).

July 26th Jean Baptiste Camille Corot b. (–1875).

July 31st Robert Burns d. (37).

1797 (Jan.–Nov.) Battle of Cape St. Vincent—Peace of Campo Formio

A **Jan**: 4th, Napoleon Bonaparte defeats Austrians under Joseph Alvintzi at Rivoli;
26th, final treaty of Polish partition.

B **Feb**: 2nd, Mantua surrenders to French;
14th, John Jervis and Horatio Nelson defeat Spanish fleet off Cape St. Vincent;
19th, Pius VI by treaty of Tolentino cedes the Romagna, Bologna and Ferrara to France, and Napoleon Bonaparte advances through Tyrol to Vienna;
Ralph Abercromby takes Trinidad;
Bank of England suspends cash payments.

C **Mar**: 4th, John Adams inaugurated President of U.S.;
Lord Lake quells rebellion in Ulster.

D **Apr**: 15th, naval mutiny at Spithead and
17th, government meets sailors' grievances;
18th, preliminary peace between Austria and France signed at Leoben.

E **May**: 2nd, naval mutiny at the Nore;
16th, Venetian constitution proclaimed;
Adam Duncan blockades the Texel.

F **Jun**: 6th, Napoleon Bonaparte founds the Ligurian Republic in Genoa;
28th, France occupies the Ionian Islands;
30th, suppression of the Nore mutiny.

G **Jul**: 9th, Cisalpine Republic proclaimed and
15th, Cispadane Republic is merged with it, comprising territories of Milan, Modena, Ferrara, Bologna and Romagna;
France puts forward peace-feelers to Britain;
Charles Talleyrand becomes French foreign minister (*–July* 1799).

H **Aug**:

J **Sep**: 4th, in *coup d'état* of 18 Fructidor a royalist reaction is prevented by Paul Barras; Lazare Carnot flees.

K **Oct**: 4th, following expulsion of U.S. minister to France commissioners reach Paris to negotiate with Directory for preserving peace, but on refusing to give bribes are returned to U.S. (the 'XYZ Affair');
11th, Adam Duncan defeats Dutch off Camperdown (the Batavian Republic had declared war on Britain in *Feb.* 1795);
14th, France annexes the Valtelline and Chiavenna, Switzerland, to the Cisalpine Republic;
17th, by Peace of Campo Formio between France and Austria, Austria cedes Belgium and Lombardy to France and obtains Istria, Dalmatia and Venice; and by a secret agreement Austria agrees to future cession of left bank of Rhine, from Basle to Andernach, to France and the free navigation of the Rhine in return for French help to acquire archbishopric of Salzburg and part of Bavaria;
Napoleon Bonaparte is appointed to command forces for invasion of England.

L **Nov**: 16th, Frederick William III succeeds as King of Prussia and continues policy of neutrality (–1840).

O **Politics, Economics, Law and Education**
F. R. Chateaubriand, *Essai historique, politique et moral sur les Révolutions.*
F. Genz's open letter to Frederick William III pleads for freedom of the press and free trade in Prussia.
Andrew Bell advocates teaching by the monitorial system.

P **Science, Technology, Discovery, etc.**
Heinrich Olbers publishes a method of calculating the orbits of comets.
J. L. Lagrange, *Théorie des fonctions analytiques.*
Nicolas de Saussure, *Recherches Chimiques sur la Végétation.*
Henry Maudslay invents carriage lathe.
Thomas Bewick, *British Birds* (–1804).

Q **Scholarship**
Karl Schlegel, *Die Griechen und Römer.*

R **Philosophy and Religion**
I. Kant, *Metaphysical Foundations of the Theory of Right.*
F. Schelling, *Philosophy of Nature.*
William Wilberforce, *Practical View of the Religious System.*
Methodist New Connexion leaves the Wesleyans.

S **Art, Sculpture, Fine Arts and Architecture**
J. M. W. Turner, *Millbank, Moonlight* (painting).
T. Girtin's first exhibition of water-colours.
Bertil Thorwaldsen settles in Rome.

T **Music**
J. Haydn, 'Emperor' quartet.
L. Cherubini, *Medea*, opera.

U **Literature**
S. T. Coleridge, *Kubla Khan* (published 1816).
Ludwig Tieck, *Tales of Peter Lebrecht.*
Johann Hölderlin, *Hyperion* (–99).
Wilhelm Wackenroden, *Outpourings of a Monk.*

V **The Press**

W **Drama and Entertainment**
George Colman, *The Heir at Law.*
August Kötzebue, *Menschenhass und Reue* (produced in London as *The Stranger*).
Ugo Foscolo, *Tieste.*

X **Sport**

Y **Statistics**

M Dec: 5th, Bonaparte arrives in Paris;
16th, peace conference to arrange terms between France and the Holy Roman Empire opens at Rastadt;
29th, French capture Mayence;
Ralph Abercromby arrives in Ireland as Commander-in-Chief.

N Paul I limits Russian peasants' work for their landlords to three days a week and decrees succession to property by strict seniority.

z **Births and Deaths**
Jan. 31st Franz Schubert b. (–1828).
Mar. 2nd Horace Walpole d. (80).
Mar. 27th Alfred de Vigny b. (–1863).
Apr. 16th Louis Adolphe Thiers b. (–1877).
July 8th Edmund Burke d. (68).
Aug. 30th Mary Wollstonecraft Shelley b. (–1851).
Oct. 16th James Brudenell, Earl of Cardigan, b. (–1868).
Dec. 13th Heinrich Heine b. (–1856).
Dec. 26th John Wilkes d. (70).

A **Jan**: 22nd, Directory established in Batavian Republic;
24th, Lemanic Republic proclaimed in Geneva;
Irish rebellion breaks out.

B **Feb**: 11th, French take Rome;
15th, Roman Republic proclaimed and Pius VI, refusing to surrender his temporal power, leaves Rome for Valence.

C **Mar**: 5th, France occupies Bern and
9th, annexes left bank of Rhine;
29th, Helvetian Republic proclaimed;
Alvarez Godoy is forced to resign in Spain, where the reforming party takes office.

D **Apr**: 26th, Geneva is annexed to France;
Publication in U.S. of the dispatches of the commissioners treating with the Directory in 1797 (the 'XYZ affair'), arouses war fever in U.S.

E **May**: Income tax is introduced in Britain, as a tax of 10 per cent. on all incomes over £200;
19th, French expedition to Egypt sails from Toulon;
Marquess of Wellesley appointed governor-general of India.

F **Jun**: 12th, French force takes Malta;
21st, Lord Lake defeats Irish rebels at Vinegar Hill and enters Wexford, ending the Irish Rebellion.

G **Jul**: Napoleon Bonaparte occupies Alexandria and, 21st, at battle of the Pyramids becomes master of Egypt.
Navy Department created in U.S. to fit out squadrons to attack French shipping and possessions in West Indies.

H **Aug**: 1st, Horatio Nelson destroys French fleet off Aboukir (battle of the Nile), cutting Bonaparte's communications with Europe;
19th, French alliance with Helvetian Republic;
22nd, French force lands in Ireland (fails, *Oct.*).

J **Sep**: 1st, treaty of Hyderabad between Britain and the Nizam;
5th, new law of conscription in France;
Turkey declares war on France.

K **Oct**: 27th, failure of French attempt to invade Ireland.

L **Nov**: Barthélemy Joubert occupies Piedmont;
29th, Ferdinand IV of Naples declares war against France and enters Rome;
Britain captures Minorca.

M **Dec**: 4th, France declares war on Naples;
9th, Charles Emmanuel of Sardinia is forced by Barthélemy Joubert to abdicate;
15th, French recapture Rome, and overrun the Kingdom of Naples;
24th, Anglo-Russian alliance, the foundation of a Second Coalition against France, is signed.

N Britain takes Honduras from Spain.
Following the passage of the Aliens and Seditions Acts, the Virginia and Kentucky legislatures pass resolutions, framed by James Madison and Thomas Jefferson respectively, to nullify any act of Congress in any state which considers it to be unconstitutional.

O **Politics, Economics, Law and Education**

T. R. Malthus, *Essay on the Principle of Population.*
Anton Thibaut, *Versuche über einzelne Theile der Theorie des Rechts.*

P **Science, Technology, Discovery, etc.**

Henry Cavendish determines the mean density of the earth.
Count Rumford discovers heat is generated by friction.
The Voltaic pile is invented.
Charles Tennant improves the manufacture of chloride of lime.
N. L. Robert's paper-making machine.
Philippe Lebon's patent for systems of heating and lighting from coal-gas.
Alois Senefelder invents lithography.
George Bass proves Tasmania is an island.

Q **Scholarship**

K. W. F. Schlegel, *Geschichte der Poesie der Griechen und Römer.*

R **Philosophy and Religion**

J. G. Fichte, *System der Sittenlehre.*
I. Kant, *Strife of the Faculties.*
J. F. Saint-Lambert, *Principe des mœurs chez toutes les nations ou catéchisme universel.*

S **Art, Sculpture, Fine Arts and Architecture**

T **Music**

J. Haydn, *The Creation* (oratorio).

U **Literature**

Charles Brockden Brown, *Wieland: or the Transformation.*
Ugo Foscolo, *Letters of Jacopo Ortis.*
W. S. Landor, *Gebir.*
W. Wordsworth and S. T. Coleridge, *Lyrical Ballads* (including *The Rime of the Ancient Mariner*).

V **The Press**

William Pitt increases the tax on British newspapers from 1½d. to 2½d. per copy and prohibits the import of foreign newspapers.
Johann Cotta founds *Allgemeine Zeitung* in Leipzig.

W **Drama and Entertainment**

X **Sport**

Y **Statistics**

Z **Births and Deaths**

Jan. 19th Auguste Comte b. (–1857).
Apr. 26th Ferdinand Delacroix b. (–1863).
June 29th Giacomo Leopardi b. (–1837).
Aug. 21st Jules Michelet b. (–1874).
Dec. 4th Luigi Galvani d. (61).

1799 Pitt forms second Coalition against France—Napoleon becomes First Consul

A **Jan**: 2nd, Britain joins the Russo-Turkish alliance;
—, Napoleon Bonaparte advances into Syria;
23rd (–*June* 19th), the Parthenopean Republic established in Piedmont.

B **Feb**:

C **Mar**: 1st, Turks and Russians complete the conquest of the Ionian Islands, which are organised as a Republic under Turkish protection;
12th, Austria declares war on France;
19th, Bonaparte begins siege of Acre, defended by Turks aided by Sidney Smith;
25th, Austrians under Archduke Charles defeat J. B. Jourdan's army at Stockach;
25th, French troops occupy Tuscany.

D **Apr**: 5th, French under B. Schérer defeated at Magnano by Austrians under Paul Kray;
8th, Conference of Rastadt (opened *Dec.* 1797), for settlement between France and the Holy Roman Empire, is dissolved;
27th, success of Austrians and Russians at battle of Cassano ends Cisalpine Republic;
—, Russians under A. Suvorov occupy Turin.

E **May**: 4th, Tippoo of Mysore is killed at Seringapatam and his kingdom is divided between Britain and the Nizam of Hyderabad;
20th, Napoleon Bonaparte abandons siege of Acre.

F **Jun**: 1st, William Pitt concludes formation of Second Coalition of Britain, Russia, Austria, Turkey, Portugal and Naples against France;
4th, Archduke Charles defeats André Masséna at Zürich;
17th (–19th), A. Suvorov recaptures Naples from the French in the battle of The Trebbia.

G **Jul**: 12th, political associations are forbidden in Britain;
20th, Charles Talleyrand retires from ministry of foreign affairs in France (reappointed *Nov.* 10th);
24th, Napoleon Bonaparte defeats the Turks at Aboukir.

H **Aug**: 15th, French are defeated at Novi by A. Suvorov, who then crosses the Alps;
22nd, Bonaparte leaves Egypt.

J **Sep**: 13th, Duke of York takes command of British army in Holland;
19th, Austro-Russian army is defeated at Bergen-op-Zoom;
25th (–27th), Russians under A. Korsakov are defeated by A. Masséna at Zürich; the main Russian army under A. Suvorov arrives too late and is forced to retreat across the Alps; Archduke Charles falls back on the River Danube.

K **Oct**: 9th, Napoleon Bonaparte lands at Fréjus;
18th, Duke of York capitulates at Alkmaar and Britain surrenders prisoners of war;
21st, Britain declares the entire coast of Holland under blockade;
22nd, Russia, disgusted with Austria, leaves Coalition.

L **Nov**: 9th, Bonaparte overthrows the Directory and
10th, appoints C. Talleyrand foreign minister (–1807);
13th, Austria occupies Ancona.

M **Dec**: 24th, Constitution of Year VIII establishes the Consulate, with Napoleon Bonaparte First Consul for ten years; Britain and Austria reject French offers of peace.

N James Madison's further Virginia Resolution, to reduce effects of acts of Congress in states.
The Carnatic, Mysore, is placed under British administration.

O **Politics, Economics, Law and Education**

James Mackintosh, *Introduction to the Law of Nature and Nations.*

Russian government grants the Russia-American company the monopoly of trade in Alaska.

P **Science, Technology, Discovery, etc.**

Count Rumford procures a charter for the Royal Institution, with Joseph Banks as first president.

Mungo Park, *Travels in the Interior of Africa.*

Q **Scholarship**

Sharon Turner, *History of England from the Earliest Period to the Norman Conquest* (–1805).

R **Philosophy and Religion**

J. G. Herder in *Metakritik* attacks the critical philosophy of I. Kant and J. G. Fichte.

F. Schleiermacher, *Reden über die Religion.*

Church Missionary Society and Religious Tract Society founded in London.

S **Art, Sculpture, Fine Arts and Architecture**

J. L. David, *Rape of the Sabine Women* (painting).

F. Goya, *Caprichos.*

T **Music**

L. van Beethoven, 'Pathétique' Sonata in C Minor (op. 13).

F. Boïeldieu, *The Caliph of Baghdad* (opera).

U **Literature**

Thomas Campbell, *The Pleasures of Hope.*

Novalis (pseud.), *Heinrich von Ofterdingen.*

K. W. F. von Schlegel, *Lucinde.*

V **The Press**

W **Drama and Entertainment**

F. Schiller, *Wallenstein.*

X **Sport**

Y **Statistics**

Z **Births and Deaths**

Feb. 28th Ignaz von Döllinger b. (–1890).

May 18th Pierre Augustin Caron de Beaumarchais d. (67).

May 20th Honoré de Balzac b. (–1850).

June 7th Alexander Pushkin b. (–1837).

Oct. 18th Christian Friedrich Schönbein b. (–1868).

Dec. 14th George Washington d. (67).

A Jan: 17th, treaty of Montluçon ends disaffection in La Vendée, releasing troops for new French offensive in Europe.

B Feb: 19th, Napoleon Bonaparte as First Consul establishes himself in the Tuileries.

C Mar: 14th, election of Luigi Chiaramonti, the candidate of the French Cardinal Jean Maury, as Pope Pius VII (–1823);
20th, French army under J. B. Kléber defeats Turks at Heliopolis and advances to Cairo (where he is assassinated *June* 14th);
28th, Act of Union with England passes Irish Parliament.

D Apr: Paul von Kray succeeds Archduke Charles as commander of Austrian army.

E May: 9th, Jean Moreau defeats Austrians at Biberach;
15th (–20th), Napoleon Bonaparte's army crosses the Great St. Bernard Pass;
Alvarez Godoy returns to power in Spain.

F Jun: 2nd, Joachim Murat occupies Milan;
4th, Genoa capitulates;
14th, Napoleon Bonaparte defeats Austrians at battle of Marengo and reconquers Italy;
19th, Moreau defeats Austrians at Höchstedt;
U.S. Departments of State are moved from Philadelphia to Washington, the new seat of government.

G Jul:

H Aug:

J Sep: 5th, Britain captures Malta;
30th, William Pitt advocates Catholic Emancipation in Britain.

K Oct: 1st, by secret treaty of San Ildefonso Spain sells Louisiana to France;
Napoleon Bonaparte promises Tuscany, with the title of King, to the Duke of Parma, son-in-law of Charles IV of Spain.

L Nov: 7th, Paul I imposes embargo on British vessels in Russian ports until Britain restores Malta to the Knights of St. John;
In U.S. presidential election Thomas Jefferson and James Madison (Republican) each secure 73 votes against John Adams, 65 and Charles Pinckney 64 (Federalist) and House of Representatives determines election of Jefferson; downfall of Federalist Party.

O **Politics, Economics, Law and Education**

Paul Feuerbach, and others, *Encyclopaedia of Penal Jurisprudence.*

Arnold Heeren, *European Political Systems.*

J. G. Fichte, *Exclusive Commercial State.*

Robert Owen's model factory at New Lanark.

Combination Acts forbid trade associations in Britain.

Letter post is introduced in Berlin.

P **Science, Technology, Discovery, etc.**

Humphry Davy, *Researches, Chemical and Philosophical, Chiefly Concerning Nitrous Oxide.*

William Herschel discovers the existence of infra-red solar rays.

Alessandro Volta produces electricity from his cell.

Thomas Young, *Outlines and Experiments respecting Sound and Light.*

Richard Trevithick's light-pressure steam engine.

Earl of Stanhope's iron printing press.

Eli Whitney makes muskets with interchangeable parts.

Henry Maudslay's precision screw-cutting lathe.

Royal College of Surgeons, London, founded.

French engineers begin carriage road over the Simplon Pass (–06).

Q **Scholarship**

Hervás y Panduro collects philological peculiarities of 300 languages and compiles grammars to 40 tongues in *Catalogue for the Languages of the Nations* (–05).

R **Philosophy and Religion**

F. W. Schelling, *System of Transcendental Idealism.*

Church of United Brethren in Christ founded in U.S.

S **Art, Sculpture, Fine Arts and Architecture**

J. L. David, *Portrait of Mme Récamier.*

Thomas Girtin, *White House at Chelsea* (painting).

F. Goya, *Portrait of a Woman.*

T **Music**

L. van Beethoven, 1st Symphony in C major (op.21), and 3rd Piano Concerto in C minor (op.37).

M. L. C. Cherubini, *The Water-Carrier* (opera).

U **Literature**

Robert Bloomfield, *The Farmer's Boy*, with Thomas Bewick's woodcuts, becomes first best seller of English verse.

Maria Edgeworth, *Castle Rackrent.*

Novalis (pseud.), *To the Night.*

Jean Paul (pseud.), *Titan* (–03).

Anne de Staël, *On Literature.*

William Wordsworth's manifesto of romanticism as preface to 2nd edition of *Lyrical Ballads.*

V **The Press**

Many newspapers are suppressed in France.

M Dec: 3rd, J. Moreau defeats Austrians at Hohenlinden and advances on Vienna;
16th, Second Armed Neutrality of the North agreed between Russia, Sweden, Denmark and Prussia and St. Petersburg, to counter British right of search, imposes new criteria for a valid blockade;
24th, discovery in Paris of plot to assassinate Bonaparte enables him to deport democratic republicans to Guiana.

N

W **Drama and Entertainment**

F. Schiller, *Mary Stuart*.

Joseph Fouché establishes theatrical censorship in France.

X **Sport**

Y **Statistics**

Z **Births and Deaths**

Jan. 24th Edwin Chadwick b. (–1890).
Feb. 11th William Henry Fox Talbot b. (–1877).
Apr. 25th William Cowper d. (68).
May 9th John Brown b. (–1859).
July 31st Friedrich Wöhler b. (–1882).
Oct. 25th Thomas Babington Macaulay b. (–1859).
Oct. 26th Helmuth von Moltke b. (–1891).
Nov. 5th Jesse Ramsden d. (65).

A **Jan**: 1st, Act of Union of England and Ireland comes into force;
14th, Britain places embargo on vessels of Armed Neutrality of the North;
29th, Convention between France and Spain to issue an ultimatum to Portugal to break that country's traditional allegiance to Britain which, if not accepted, will lead to war (promulgated by the Treaty of Aranjuez, *Mar.* 21st, when Spain also agrees to cede Louisiana to France).

B **Feb**: 9th, Peace of Lunéville between Austria and France marks virtual destruction of Holy Roman Empire; France gains the left bank of the Rhine, Tuscany is ceded to Parma to form the new kingdom of Etruria, and recognition is given to Batavian, Cisalpine, Helvetian, and Ligurian Republics.

C **Mar**: 2nd, War of the Oranges with Portugal is declared by Spain;
4th Thomas Jefferson inaugurated as President of U.S. in new capital of Washington;
14th, William Pitt (having first tendered resignation *Feb.* 5th) resigns over question of Catholic Emancipation, and is replaced by Henry Addington;
21st, French defeated near Alexandria by Ralph Abercromby;
23rd, Assassination of Tsar Paul I who is succeeded by Alexander I (–1825);
28th, Peace of Florence between France and Naples, by which British vessels to be excluded from Neapolitan ports;
29th, embargo on British vessels in Danish ports; the Danes enter Hamburg in order to close the Elbe (and subsequently enter Lübeck);
Britain seizes Danish and Swedish islands in West Indies;
Prussia finally decides to join Armed Neutrality of North.

D **Apr**: 2nd, because of Danish actions on the Elbe, a British fleet is sent to Denmark where Horatio Nelson is victorious off Copenhagen and the Danes are forced, 9th, to consent to a truce;
3rd, Hanover is overrun by the Prussians;
14th, suspension of Habeas Corpus Act (previously suspended 1794) to allow detention in Britain of political suspects without trial; to continue during war and for first month of peace.

E **May**:

F **Jun**: 6th, by Treaty of Badajoz with Spain, Portugal cedes Olivenza, and agrees to shut ports to British ships;
17th, the Armed Neutrality of the North breaks up with the signing with Britain of Treaty of St. Petersburg, which recognises British right of search (Denmark signs *Oct.* 23rd, 1801, and Sweden, *Mar.* 30th, 1802);
19th, formal reconciliation between Russia and Britain;
23rd, Horne Tooke Act whereby clergy not eligible to sit in Parliament, although Tooke is allowed to retain seat until end of session;
27th, Cairo falls to English force.

G **Jul**: 15th, under French Concordat with Papacy French ecclesiastics are to be appointed by government and merely confirmed by Pope, who is allowed to keep the Papal States, with exception of Ferrara, Bologna, and Romagna (ratified by Napoleon 28th *Sept.*, but not fully ratified by France until *Apr.* 18th, 1802).

H **Aug**:

O **Politics, Economics, Law and Education**

J. H. Pestalozzi, *How Gertrude teaches her children.*

Foundation of the Bank of France.

P **Science, Technology, Discovery, etc.**

Giuseppe Piazzi discovers the first asteroid, Ceres (*Jan.* 1st).

Heinrich Olbers discovers Pallas (*Mar.* 28th).

K. F. Gauss, *Disquisitiones arithmeticae.*

Marie Bichat, *Anatomie générale.*

Robert Fulton constructs first submarine, *Nautilus*, at Brest.

Iron tram-road from Croydon to Wandsworth.

Q **Scholarship**

R **Philosophy and Religion**

G. W. F. Hegel and F. W. J. Schelling found *Critical Journal of Philosophy.*

Episcopal Church in U.S. adopts 39 Articles of Religion.

S **Art, Sculpture, Fine Arts and Architecture**

J. L. David, *Napoléon au Grand Saint-Bernard* (painting).

J. M. W. Turner, *Calais Pier* (painting).

Elgin marbles brought from Athens to London.

T **Music**

J. Haydn, *The Seasons.*

L. van Beethoven, 1st (op.15) and 2nd (op.19) Piano Concertos, and six string quartets (op.18).

U **Literature**

Vicomte de Chateaubriand, *Atala.*

R. Southey, *Thalaba the Destroyer.*

V **The Press**

New York *Evening Post* issued.

W **Drama and Entertainment**

F. Schiller, *The Maid of Orleans.*

X **Sport**

Y **Statistics**

First accurate censuses taken in 1800 and 1801 provide population statistics for Italy, 17·2 mill.; Spain 10·5 mill.; Great Britain, 10·4 mill.; Ireland 5·2 mill.; and U.S., 5·3 mill.; London, 864,000; Paris, 547,756; Vienna, 231,050; Berlin, 183,294, and New York, 60,515.

1801 (Sep.–Dec.)

J **Sep:** 12th, Alexander I of Russia announces annexation of Georgia and George XIII (Regent of Georgia since *Jan.* 15th) recognises Russian decision instead of accepting traditional suzerainty of Persia;
29th, Treaty of Madrid between France and Portugal confirming Treaty of Badajoz;
France obtains part of Guiana;
French troops evacuate Egypt.

K **Oct:** 1st, peace preliminaries between Britain and France signed whereby Britain to restore all maritime conquests, except Trinidad and Ceylon, to France, Spain and Holland; France agrees to evacuate Naples; the integrity of Portugal is recognised; the independence of the Ionian Islands is agreed upon; both French and English armies are to evacuate Egypt which is to be restored to Turkey, and Malta is to be restored to the Knights by Britain (see Peace of Amiens, *Mar.* 27th, 1802);
9th, by treaty with France, Turkey formally recovers Egypt.

L **Nov:**

M **Dec:**

N

z **Births and Deaths**

Feb. 21st John Henry Newman b. (–1890).

Mar. 25th Friedrich von Hardenberg ('Novalis') d. (29).

Nov. 1st Vincenzo Bellini b. (–1835).

1802 Peace of Amiens

A **Jan:** 26th, Napoleon Bonaparte becomes President of Italian Republic (the former Cisalpine Republic).

B **Feb:**

C **Mar:** 27th, Peace of Amiens between Britain and France which achieves the complete pacification of Europe (for terms, see Preliminaries, *Oct.* 1st, 1801).

D **Apr:**

E **May:** 19th, Creation of Napoleon's Order of Legion of Honour.

F **Jun:**

G **Jul:**

H **Aug:** 2nd, Napoleon Bonaparte becomes First Consul for life, with right to appoint his successor;

4th, Introduction of Fifth Constitution in France in which the Senate, which is ruled by Napoleon, is enlarged, whereas the Tribunate and the legislative bodies lose influence.

J **Sep:** 21st, Napoleon Bonaparte annexes Piedmont.

K **Oct:** 23rd, in India Maharaja Holkar of Indore defeats both Peshaw of Poona and Sindhia of Gwalior at Poona;

Napoleon annexes the duchies of Parma and Piacenza.

L **Nov:**

M **Dec:** 31st, by Treaty of Bassein, Peshaw of Poona surrenders independence to East India Company.

N

O **Politics, Economics, Law and Education**

Jeremy Bentham's *Civil and Penal Legislation* introduces the theory of utilitarianism.
Daniel Webster, *The Rights of Neutral Nations in Time of War.*
Health and Morals of Apprentices Act in Britain pioneers the prevention of injury and the protection of labour in factories.
Dorpat University founded.

P **Science, Technology, Discovery, etc.**

William Herschel discovers that some stars revolve round one another.
Gottfried Treviranus first uses the term 'biology'.
Thomas Wedgwood makes the first photograph in copying paintings on glass.
Thomas Telford begins constructing roads in the Scottish Highlands.
John Truter and William Somerville explore Bechuanaland, penetrating almost to Lake Ngami.

Q **Scholarship**

Richard Porson's revised edition of the *Hecuba* of Euripides.

R **Philosophy and Religion**

William Paley, *Natural Theology.*
F. Schelling, *Bruno.*

S **Art, Sculpture, Fine Arts and Architecture**

Antonio Canova, *Napoleon Bonaparte* (sculpture).
Thomas Girtin completes *The Eidometropolis.*

T **Music**

L. van Beethoven, 'Moonlight' Sonata (op. 27, no. 2); and 2nd Symphony (D major, op 36).

U **Literature**

Vicomte de Chateaubriand, *Le Génie du Christianisme.*
Anne de Staël, *Delphine.*

V **The Press**

William Cobbet's *Weekly Political Register* (*Jan.*).
Edinburgh Review (*Oct.* –1929).

W **Drama and Entertainment**

To celebrate the Peace of Amiens, William Murdock illuminates the Soho foundry, Birmingham, with gas-burners.

X **Sport**

Duke of Richmond establishes horse-racing at Goodwood.

Y **Statistics**

Raw cotton imports	56 mill. lb.
Linen exports	15·7 mill. yds.
Silk exports	78,000 lb.

Z **Births and Deaths**

Feb. 26th Victor Hugo b. (–1885).
Apr. 18th Erasmus Darwin d. (71).
July 22nd M. F. X. Bichat d. (31).
July 24th 'Alexandre Dumas' (pseud. of Alexandre Davy de la Pailleterie) b. (–1870)
Aug. 2nd Nicholas Wiseman b. (–1865).

1803 U.S.A. purchases Louisiana from France—Britain declares war on France

A **Jan:**

B **Feb:** 19th, Act of Mediation in Switzerland, whereby Cantons regain independence;
25th, Enactment of Delegates of the Empire at Diet of Ratisbon, which reconstructs German States under influence of France and Russia; most of the ecclesiastical estates and the free imperial cities are abolished and four new electorates are created.

C **Mar:** 1st, Ohio becomes a state of the Union (Congress having extended Federal laws to Ohio, *Feb.* 19th).

D **Apr:** 30th, U.S. purchases Louisiana and New Orleans from the French.

E **May:** 17th, by Orders-in-Council Britain places her first embargo on all French and Dutch ships in British ports;
18th, renewal of hostilities between Britain and France because of Napoleon's interference in Italian and Swiss affairs, and because of Britain's refusal to part with Malta immediately.

F **Jun:** 10th, French occupation of Hanover completed;
Britain obtains St. Lucia and Tobago.

G **Jul:** 23rd, rebellion of Robert Emmet in Ireland, influenced by the French.

H **Aug:** 3rd, second Mahratha War against Sindhia of Gwalior begins when British troops open offensive.

J **Sep:** 23rd, Arthur Wellesley defeats Sindhia at Assaye; Britain takes Dutch Guiana.

K **Oct:** 19th, by convention with France, Spain is declared neutral and is to enforce Portugal's neutrality.

L **Nov:**

M **Dec:** 30th, Sindhia of Gwalior finally submits to the British.

N

O Politics, Economics, Law and Education

A. Coräes publishes *Present conditions of Civilisation in Greece* to interest the great powers in the cause of Greek independence.

J. B. Say, *Traité d'Économique politique.*

Joseph Lancaster, *Improvements in Education as it respects the industrious Classes.*

P Science, Technology, Discovery, etc.

John Dalton formulates the law of partial pressure in gases and compiles tables of atomic weights, leading to the atomic theory of chemistry.

Claude Berthollet, *Essai de Statique Chimique.*

J. B. A. Lamarck, *Recherches.*

Lazare Carnot, *Principes fondamentaux de l'équilibre et du mouvement.*

Robert Fulton propels a boat by steam power.

Caledonian Canal begun.

Henry Shrapnel invents his shell.

Q Scholarship

J. L. Tieck's translation of *Minnelieder* leads to the study of old Germanic literature.

R Philosophy and Religion

S Art, Sculpture, Fine Arts and Architecture

J. S. Cotman and J. B. Crome found Norwich School of artists.

Henry Raeburn, *The Macnab* (portrait).

Benjamin West, *Christ Healing the Sick* (painting).

John Soane, Governor's Court, Bank of England.

T Music

L. van Beethoven, 'Kreutzer' Sonata for piano and violin (op. 47).

U Literature

F. Schiller, *Die Braut von Messina.*

V The Press

The Globe founded.

W Drama and Entertainment

X Sport

Y Statistics

Z Births and Deaths

May 12th Justus von Liebig b. (–1873).

May 25th Edward George Bulwer Lytton, Lord Lytton, b. (–1873); and Ralph Waldo Emerson b. (–1882).

June 2nd Michael Ivanovich Glinka b. (–1857).

July 5th George Borrow b. (–1881).

July 20th Thomas Lovell Beddoes b. (–1849).

Aug. 3rd. Joseph Paxton b. (–1865).

Sept. 28th Prosper Mérimée b. (–1870).

Oct. 8th Vittoria Alfieri d. (54).

Dec. 11th Hector Berlioz b. (–1869).

Dec. 18th Johann Gottfried von Herder d. (59).

1804 Napoleon Bonaparte crowned Napoleon I

A **Jan:**

B **Feb:** 16th, discovery of conspiracy against Napoleon.

C **Mar:** 20th, Duc d'Enghien, implicated in February plot, is executed.

D **Apr:** 16th, war between East India Company and Holkar of Indore opens;
26th, Henry Addington tenders resignation after the Irish Militia bill which shows William Pitt's opposition to the Ministry (his resignation is accepted, 29th).

E **May:** 10th, William Pitt forms Cabinet, but finds it necessary to exclude C. J. Fox;
16th, Napoleon proclaimed Emperor by Senate and Tribunate (–1815).

F **Jun:**

G **Jul:**

H **Aug:** 11th, Francis II assumes title of hereditary Emperor of Austrian possessions (though he still maintains title of Holy Roman Emperor).

J **Sep:** 25th, Twelfth Amendment added to American Constitution which provides for separate ballots for the Presidency and the Vice-Presidency.

K **Oct:** 9th, Hobart, Tasmania, founded;
27th, Heinrich Baron Stein appointed Prussian Minister of Trade.

L **Nov:** 13th–17th, defeats of Holkar's forces;
Austria and Russia make a declaration to maintain the Ottoman Empire against French expansion.

M **Dec:** 2nd, Napoleon Bonaparte is crowned Emperor as Napoleon I by Pope Pius VII in Paris;
12th, Spain declares war on Britain at instigation of France.

N

O Politics, Economics, Law and Education
Code Napoléon promulgated in France.

P Science, Technology, Discovery, etc.
W. H. Wollaston finds palladium in platinum.
J. Leslie, *Experimental Inquiry into the Nature and Properties of Heat.*
François Appert opens canning factory.

Q Scholarship
F. Hoelderlin's translations of the tragedies of Sophocles into German.

R Philosophy and Religion
Thomas Brown, *Inquiry into the Relation of Cause and Effect.*
K. C. F. Kreuse, *Philosophical Systems.*
British and Foreign Bible Society founded.

S Art, Sculpture, Fine Arts and Architecture
English Water Colour Society founded.
St. Petersburg Bourse built.

T Music
L. van Beethoven, 3rd ('Eroica') Symphony (op. 55).

U Literature
Jean Paul (pseud.), *Flegeljahre* (–05).
William Blake, *Jerusalem.*

V The Press

W Drama and Entertainment
F. Schiller, *Wilhelm Tell.*

X Sport

Y Statistics

Z Births and Deaths
Feb. 6th Joseph Priestley, d. (71).
Feb. 12th Immanuel Kant d. (80).
Apr. 5th Matthias Schleiden b. (–1881).
Apr. (–) Jacques Necker d. (72).
June 3rd Richard Cobden b. (–1865).
July 1st 'George Sand' (pseud. of Amandine Dupin, later Dudevant) b. (–1876).
July 4th Nathaniel Hawthorne b. (–1864).
Dec. 21st Benjamin Disraeli, Earl of Beaconsfield, b. (–1881).
Dec. 23rd C. A. Sainte-Beuve b. (–1869).

1805 Battles of Trafalgar and Austerlitz

A **Jan:**

B **Feb:** 24th, Arthur Wellesley resigns civil and military positions in India.

C **Mar:** 4th, Thomas Jefferson begins second term as President of U.S.

D **Apr:** 11th, by treaty of St. Petersburg, Britain and Russia agree to form a European league for the liberation of the northern German states, the Third Coalition against France.

E **May:** 26th, Napoleon is crowned King of Italy in Milan Cathedral.

F **Jun:** 4th, the Ligurian Republic is united with France, which thus gains Genoa.

G **Jul:**

H **Aug:** 9th, Austria joins signatories of Treaty of St. Petersburg.

J **Sep:**

K **Oct:** 20th, Austrians under Karl Mack are defeated by French at Ulm;
21st, Lord Nelson defeats combined Franco-Spanish fleet at Trafalgar, and is mortally wounded in the action.

L **Nov:** 23rd, peace treaty between East India Company and Sindhia.

M **Dec:** 2nd, Napoleon defeats combined Russo-Austrian forces at Austerlitz;
15th, by treaty of Schönbrunn with France, Prussia cedes Cleves, Neuchâtel and Ansbach, and is allowed to occupy Hanover in order to prevent her joining the coalition against Napoleon;
26th, by Peace of Pressburg between Austria and France, the Austrians give up the Tyrol and all possessions in Italy and in Dalmatia and, in addition, give up all possessions and influence in Southern Germany so that Bavaria and Württemberg become kingdoms, and Baden becomes a Grand Duchy.

N After *May*, England closes down on the American trade with the West Indies, resulting in loss of friendship with the U.S. practically leading to war.

O **Politics, Economics, Law and Education**
Lord Liverpool, *Treatise on the Coins of the Realm.*
Internal customs duties in Prussia are abolished.

P **Science, Technology, Discovery, etc.**
Artillery rocket is invented.
Thomas Telford's iron aqueduct over the Ellesmere Canal.
Mungo Park undertakes expedition to the Niger River.

Q **Scholarship**
H. T. Colebrooke, *Essay on the Vedas* and *Sanskrit Grammar*.

R **Philosophy and Religion**
Hosea Ballou, *A Treatise on Atonement.*

S **Art, Sculpture, Fine Arts and Architecture**
F. Goya, *Doña Isabel Cobos de Porcal* (portrait).
Philipp Runge, *The Morning* (painting).
J. M. W. Turner, *Shipwreck* (painting).
British Institution for the development of the Fine Arts.

T **Music**
L. van Beethoven, 4th Piano Concerto in G (op. 58); and *Fidelio* (opera).
Nicolò Paganini begins to tour Europe as a virtuoso violinist.

U **Literature**
Vicomte Chateaubriand, *René.*
Walter Scott, *The Lay of the Last Minstrel.*
Robert Southey, *Madoc.*
William Wordsworth completes *The Prelude.*

V **The Press**

W **Drama and Entertainment**

X **Sport**

Y **Statistics**
U.K. total state expenditure, £62·8 mill.

Z **Births and Deaths**
Mar. 4th Jean Baptiste Greuze d. (80).
Apr. 2nd Hans Christian Andersen b. (–1875).
June 22nd Giuseppe Mazzini b. (–1872).
July 29th Charles Alexis de Tocqueville b. (–1859).

A **Jan**: 8th, Britain finally occupies Cape of Good Hope;
23rd, death of William Pitt.

B **Feb**: 10th, Formation of 'Ministry of all the Talents' with Lord Grenville as Prime Minister and C. J. Fox as Foreign Secretary;
15th, French troops enter Naples;
—, Franco-Prussian Treaty against Britain, whereby Prussia is to close her ports to British ships.

C **Mar**: 30th, Joseph Bonaparte becomes King of Naples.

D **Apr**: 1st, Britain declares war on Prussia after the seizure of Hanover;
Britain begins blockade of French coast.

E **May**:

F **Jun**: 5th, Louis Bonaparte becomes King of Holland;
27th, Buenos Aires surrenders to a small British force (but is retaken by the Spanish in *Aug*.).

G **Jul**: 12th, establishment of Confederation of Rhine under protection of France, uniting Bavaria, Württemberg, Mainz, Baden, and eight lesser principalities.

H **Aug**: 6th, The Holy Roman Empire ends; Francis II formally resigns the Imperial Dignity and becomes Francis I, Emperor of Austria.

J **Sep**: 13th, death of Fox.

K **Oct**: 1st, Prussian ultimatum to France for retaining Hanover, which Napoleon intends to restore to Britain;
9th, Prussia declares war on France;

14th, Napoleon defeats Prussia at Jena and Saxony at Auerstädt;
16th, war between Turkey and Russia at instigation of French emissary at Constantinople, with Russia's occupation of Danubian Provinces;
24th, British Parliament dissolved in order to acquire more pro-Grenville supporters into Parliament by means of patronage;
27th, Napoleon occupies Berlin.

L **Nov**: 21st, by the Berlin Decrees, Napoleon begins the 'Continental System', closing continental ports to British vessels and declaring all British ports to be in a state of blockade;
28th, Joachim Murat leads a French force into Warsaw.

M **Dec**: 11th, by Peace of Posen with France, Saxony is made a kingdom and enters the Confederation of the Rhine;
15th, Napoleon enters Warsaw;
—, new British Parliament, in which Lord Grenville's ministry is returned with considerable majority.

N Burr Plot in the U.S., when Aaron Burr, having collected men at Blennerhasset's Island, after *Aug*., forms an expedition to march into Louisiana (he is subsequently arrested, tried, and acquitted in 1807).

O **Politics, Economics, Law and Education**

Ernst Arndt, *Spirit of the Age* (–18) inspires the German national revival.

James Madison, *An Examination of the British Doctrine which subjects to Capture a Neutral Trade not open in Time of Peace.*

K. Zacharies von Lingerthel, *Legislation.*

J. F. Herbert, *German Education.*

P **Science, Technology, Discovery, etc.**

Humphry Davy's electrical preparation of potassium and sodium.

P. A. Latreille, *Genera Crustaceorum et Insectorum.*

A nail-cutting machine is invented.

Q **Scholarship**

J. C. Adelung, *Mithridates*, a history of languages and dialects.

Wilhelm De Wette, *Introduction to the Old Testament.*

R **Philosophy and Religion**

J. G. Fichte, *Bericht über die Wissenschaftslehre.*

Napoleon convokes a Sanhedrin and establishes a consistorial organisation for Jews in France.

S **Art, Sculpture, Fine Arts and Architecture**

David Wilkie, *Village Politicians* (painting).

Brera Gallery, Milan, opened.

Claude Clodion begins Arc de Triomphe, Paris.

T **Music**

L. van Beethoven, 'Rasoumoffsky' string quartets (op. 59), 4th Symphony in B flat (op. 60) and Violin Concerto (op. 61).

U **Literature**

V **The Press**

W **Drama and Entertainment**

X **Sport**

Y **Statistics**

U.K. registered tonnage of merchant shipping, 2,080,000.

U.K. iron production, 243,851 tons.

U.K. cotton industry employs 90,000 factory workers and 184,000 handloom weavers.

Z **Births and Deaths**

Mar. 6th Elizabeth Barrett Browning b. (–1861).

Apr. 9th Isambard Kingdom Brunel b. (–1859).

May 20th John Stuart Mill b. (–1873).

Aug. 22nd Jean Honoré Fragonard d. (73).

1807 (Jan.–Oct.) Treaty of Tilsit leaves Britain alone against Napoleon

A **Jan**: 4th, dismissal of Baron Stein by Frederick William III of Prussia;
7th, Britain declares a blockade of coasts of France and of Napoleon's allies, and all ships trading in ports where Britain is excluded are liable to capture.

B **Feb**: 8th, indecisive battle of Eylau between France and combined Russo-Prussian army;
19th, British fleet forces way through Dardanelles, to support Russia in war against Turkey (but is forced to withdraw *Mar*. 2nd., suffering severe damage).

C **Mar**: 24th, fall of 'Ministry of all the Talents' over Lord Grenville's refusal to grant Catholic Emancipation at a future date, and the Whigs surrender seals of office, never to take office again under George III;
31st, Duke of Portland becomes Prime Minister with George Canning and Lord Castlereagh as Secretaries of State.

D **Apr**: 26th, by Convention of Bartenstein, Russia and Prussia form an alliance to drive France out of German States;
27th, Duke of Portland dissolves Parliament to test support for new Ministry.

E **May**: 29th, Sultan Selim III of Turkey is deposed by Mustapha IV.

F **Jun**: 14th, at the battle of Friedland France defeats combined Russian and Prussian force;
22nd, the new British Parliament assembles with a majority for the new ministry (as a result of the 'No-Popery' general election);
22nd, U.S. frigate *Chesapeake* is stopped by British vessel *Leopard*, and demands are made to hand over British deserters, which nearly causes war, averted by Thomas Jefferson's pacific policy;
27th, Britain joins Convention of Bartenstein (see *Apr*.).

G **Jul**: 7th, Napoleon meets Tsar Alexander and Frederick William II on the R. Niemen, and by Treaty of Tilsit with France, Russia agrees to establishment of Duchy of Warsaw, recognises Confederation of Rhine, agrees to close all ports to British ships, and, by a secret agreement, the Tsar agrees to coerce Denmark, Sweden, and Portugal into joining alliance against Britain, and is given a free hand in Finland;
9th, by a separate Treaty of Tilsit with France, Prussia loses all possessions west of Elbe and all Polish territories, which are to form Duchy of Warsaw under King of Saxony, and by a secret agreement, agrees to join the 'Continental System' and to exclude British ships from Prussian ports;
10th, Baron Stein becomes Prussia's principal minister.

H **Aug**: Jerome Bonaparte is created King of Westphalia (formed from former Prussian possessions west of R. Elbe), and Erfurt is incorporated in France.

J **Sep**: 2nd–5th, British bombardment of Copenhagen because of Napoleon's plan to use Danish fleet against Britain;
7th, the Danes surrender;
—, France obtains Hither Pomerania from Sweden;
Napoleon suppresses Tribunate, thus ensuring his dictatorship.

K **Oct**: 9th, Emancipation of Prussian serfs;
27th, by Treaty of Fontainebleau, Spain and France agree to conquer Portugal;
29th, Denmark joins France against Britain.

O Politics, Economics, Law and Education

Gottlieb Hufeland, *New Foundations of Political Economy.*
Comte de Saint-Simon, *Introduction aux Travaux Scientifiques du xix Siècle.*
Napoleon introduces Commercial Law Code in France.

P Science, Technology, Discovery, etc.

J. L. Gay-Lussac, *Observations on Magnetism.*
Alexander von Humboldt and Aimé Bonpland, in *Voyage aux régions équinoxiales du Nouveau Continent, 1799–1804*, study climate, volcanoes, etc., of Spanish America.
Charles Bell, *System of Comparative Surgery.*
Rolbert Fulton's steamboat *Clermont*, built by Boulton and Watt, plies on Hudson River.
Thomson patents aerated waters.

Q Scholarship

J. C. L. Sismondi, *History of the Italian Republics in the Middle Ages.*
Friedrich Wolf, *Science of Antiquity.*

R Philosophy and Religion

G. W. F. Hegel, *Phenomenology of Spirit.*
First Convention of U.S. Evangelical Association, or 'New Methodists', founded by Jacob Albright.

S Art, Sculpture, Fine Arts and Architecture

J. M. W. Turner, *Sun Rising in a Mist* (painting).
J. L. David completes *Coronation of Napoleon* (painting).

T Music

L. van Beethoven, *Leonora No. 3* and *Coriolanus* overtures; 'Appassionata' sonata.
G. L. P. Spontini, *The Vestal Virgin* (opera).
Étienne Méhul, *Joseph* (opera).
Thomas Moore's *Irish Melodies* with music by John Stevenson (–34).

U Literature

Lord Byron, *Hours of Idleness.*
B. Constant, *Adolphe* (published 1815).
Anne de Staël, *Corinne.*
Charles and Mary Lamb, *Tales from Shakespeare.*
Ugo Foscolo, *Carme sui sepolcri.*
Jean Paul, *Levana.*
William Wordsworth, *Ode on Intimations of Immortality.*

V The Press

W Drama and Entertainment

X Sport

Horse-racing: Ascot Gold Cup first given.

Y Statistics

L Nov: 7th, Russia breaks off relations with Britain, amounting to declaration of war (as result of Treaty of Tilsit of *July* 7th);
11th, further British Orders-in-Council declaring blockade of Continental ports (extended *Nov.* 25th);
19th, France invades Portugal for refusing to enter 'Continental System';
29th, the Portuguese royal family, the Braganzas, flee to Brazil.

M Dec: 17th, Napoleon's Milan Decrees against British trade, extending Berlin Decrees (of *Nov.* 21st 1806);
22nd, U.S. Embargo Act as reprisal for French and British restrictions and for the *Chesapeake* Incident, by which the U.S. withholds raw materials and finished products with idea of forcing belligerents to end the wars.

N Buenos Aires is attacked by the British at the end of *June* but they are forced to withdraw *July*.
Military reforms in Prussia after Scharnhorst's Manifesto of *July*.

z Births and Deaths

Feb. 27th Henry Wadsworth Longfellow b. (–1882).
May 28th Jean Louis Rodolphe Agassiz d. (73).
July 4th Giuseppe Garibaldi b. (–1882).

1808 Napoleon's 'Continental System' at its height—British expedition to Portugal

A **Jan**: 1st, Sierra Leone becomes a British Crown Colony;
—, U.S. prohibits import of slaves from Africa.

B **Feb**: 2nd, a French force occupies Rome after Pope Pius VII refuses to recognise Kingdom of Naples and to join alliance against Britain;
16th, France invades Spain;
28th, Austria joins Napoleon's 'Continental System';
29th, French take Barcelona.

C **Mar**: 3rd, Joachim Murat occupies Madrid;
16th, Tsar Alexander I proclaims Finland to be a province conquered by Russia.

D **Apr**:

E **May**: 2nd, Spanish rising against the French begins in Madrid;
6th, Charles IV of Spain and Crown Prince Ferdinand renounce the Spanish throne;
30th, Napoleon annexes Tuscany, allowing it seats in the French Senate and legislature.

F **Jun**: 9th, Creation of Austrian *Landwehr*;
15th, Joseph of Naples becomes King of Spain (subsequently Joachim Murat becomes King of Naples);
17th, Tsar Alexander I, suspecting French intentions against Russia, promises to restore privileges in Finland.

G **Jul**: Mahamud II succeeds Mustapha IV, who is dethroned as Sultan of Turkey.

H **Aug**: 1st, British expedition is sent to Portugal;
—, King Joseph flees from Madrid, fearing Spanish rebels;
21st, Arthur Wellesley defeats French at Vimiero and subsequently returns to England;
30th, by convention of Cintra with the British commander Hew Dalrymple, Andache Junot withdraws French troops from Portugal.

J **Sep**: 8th, Napoleon forces Prussia to limit its army to 42,000 men.

K **Oct**: 12th, Napoleon holds Erfurt Congress with his vassals and Tsar Alexander to strengthen Franco-Russian alliance, particularly regarding the Eastern Question.

L **Nov**: 19th, Municipal Councils are introduced in Prussia.

M **Dec**: 13th, Madrid capitulates to Napoleon;
16th, fall of Baron Stein in Prussia, following Napoleon's criticisms of him.

N

O **Politics, Economics, Law and Education**

J. G. Fichte, *Addresses to the German Nation.*

Foundation of Tugendbund (Society of Virtue) in Königsberg.

Royal Lancasterian Institution for promoting education of the poor, on the model of Joseph Lancaster.

P **Science, Technology, Discovery, etc.**

John Dalton, *New System of Chemical Philosophy* (–27).

J. L. Gay-Lussac, *The Combination of Gases.*

Q **Scholarship**

K. F. Eichhorn, *History of German Law* (–23).

F. Schlegel, *Language and Wisdom of the Indians.*

R **Philosophy and Religion**

J. F. Fries, *New Critique of Reason.*

Alexander Humboldt, *Opinions of Nature.*

Napoleon abolishes the Inquisition in Spain and Italy.

Sydney Smith, *Peter Plymley's Letters*, attacks disabilities of Roman Catholics in Britain.

S **Art, Sculpture, Fine Arts and Architecture**

Antonio Canova, *Pauline Bonaparte Borghese as Venus* (sculpture).

Kaspar Friedrich, *The Cross on the Mountains* (painting).

F. Goya, *Execution of the Citizens of Madrid* (painting).

J. D. Ingres, *La Grande Baigneuse* (painting).

T **Music**

L. van Beethoven, 5th Symphony (op. 67) and 6th, 'Pastoral' Symphony (op. 68).

U **Literature**

Vicomte de Chateaubriand, *Les Aventures du dernier Abencérage* (published 1826).

W. Scott, *Marmion.*

V **The Press**

The Examiner founded with Leigh Hunt as editor.

The Times sends Henry Crabb Robinson as special correspondent to the Peninsular Campaign.

W **Drama and Entertainment**

J. W. Goethe, *Faust*, pt. 1.

Bernd Kleist, *Das Kätchen von Heilbronn.*

X **Sport**

Y **Statistics**

Z **Births and Deaths**

Apr. 20th Charles Louis Napoleon Bonaparte (Napoleon III) b. (–1873).

— Honoré Daumier b. (–1879).

1809 (Jan.–Sep.) Death of Sir John Moore—Napoleon imprisons Pope Pius VII

A **Jan**: 5th, Britain concludes Treaty of Dardanelles with Turkey;
16th, Sir John Moore is killed at Corunna, having created diversion to distract Napoleon;
The Spanish Supreme Junta and Britain agree not to make separate peace with Napoleon.

B **Feb**: 8th, Francis I of Austria decides on war with France, fearing Napoleon will overrun Austria.

C **Mar**: 1st, The Non-Intercourse Act comes into force whereby U.S. refuses to trade with Britain and France, but will begin trade with the one which removes restrictions;
4th, James Madison becomes the fourth President of U.S.;
15th, U.S. Embargo Act (of *Dec.* 22nd 1807) expires;
29th, Gustavus IV of Sweden is forced to abdicate after military defeats in war with Denmark; is succeeded (*June* 5th) by Charles XIII (–1818).

D **Apr**: 22nd, Arthur Wellesley lands at Lisbon to take command in Portugal;
—, Austrian forces occupy Warsaw (but compelled to withdraw *June* 3rd);
25th, British conclude treaty of friendship with Sikhs at Amritsar;
26th, Britain restricts limits of blockade to Holland, France, and Italian states;
Britain agrees to provide Austria with a monthly subsidy of £150,000 and to send an expedition to the Scheldt.

E **May**: 12th, Arthur Wellesley defeats French under Soult at Oporto and forces them to retreat from Portugal;
13th, French army takes Vienna;
17th, Napoleon issues Imperial Decree annexing Papal States;
21st–22nd, after the battle of Aspern against Austrians, Napoleon is forced to recross the R. Danube. France calls on Russian support against Austria which is given ineffectively;
Russian offensive against the Turks is renewed.

F **Jun**: 19th, Curwen's Act is passed to prevent sale of Parliamentary seats, thus decreasing number of seats which British government can manipulate for its regular supporters.

G **Jul**: 5th (–6th), Napoleon defeats Austrians at Wagram;
6th, Pope Pius VII, having excommunicated Napoleon, is taken prisoner by the French;
16th, revolt in Upper Peru against Spanish authority;
28th, Arthur Wellesley is victorious at Talavera and is subsequently created Duke of Wellington;
—, (–*Dec.* 23rd), British expedition to Walcheren, to help Austrians by diverting Napoleon's attention from Danube, fails.

H **Aug**: 4th, Prince Metternich becomes Chief Minister of Austria.

J **Sep**: 6th, Duke of Portland resigns because of ill health;
17th, by Peace of Frederikshavn with Sweden, Russia obtains Finland, although Napoleon refuses to recognise this treaty;
21st, Castlereagh and Canning fight a duel over the latter's attempts to have Castlereagh removed from the War Office due to alleged incompetency, with particular regard to the Walcheren expedition;
26th, Turkey is defeated by Russians at Brailoff (and subsequently at Silestria).

O **Politics, Economics, Law and Education**
Joseph de Maistre, *Principe Générateur des Constitutions Politiques.*
David Ricardo, *The High Price of Bullion or Proof of the Depreciation of Bank Notes.*

P **Science, Technology, Discovery, etc.**
K. F. Gauss, *Theoria motus corporum coelestium.*
Étienne Malus discovers polarisation of light by reflection.
W. Maclure, *Observations on the Geology of the U.S.*
Chevalier de Lamarck, *Système des animaux sans vertèbres.*
S. T. Sömmering invents water voltameter telegraph.
John Heathcoat's bobbin net machine.
Pall Mall, London, is lit by gas.

Q **Scholarship**

R **Philosophy and Religion**
Evangelical revival begins in Germany.
Theological Seminary, St. Petersburg, founded.
Elizabeth Seton founds Sisters of Charity of St. Joseph in U.S.

S **Art, Sculpture, Fine Arts and Architecture**
John Constable, *Malvern Hall* (painting).
Kaspar Friedrich, *Mönch am Meer* (painting).
Henry Raeburn, *Mrs. Spiers* (portrait).

T **Music**
L. van Beethoven, 5th Piano Concerto, 'Emperor' in E flat (op. 73).
G. L. P. Spontini, *Ferdinand Cortez* (opera).

U **Literature**
Lord Byron, *English Bards and Scots Reviewers.*
Thomas Campbell, *Gertrude of Wyoming.*
Vicomte de Chateaubriand, *Les Martyrs.*
J. W. Goethe, *The Elective Affinities.*
Washington Irving, *Knickerbocker's History of New York* and *Rip Van Winkle.*
Ivan Kriloff, *Fables* (–1811).
Hannah More, *Coelebs in Search of a Wife.*
August Schlegel, *Lectures on Dramatic Art and Literature.*

V **The Press**
Quarterly Review founded (*Feb.*) by Walter Scott and other Tories.

W **Drama and Entertainment**

X **Sport**
2,000 Guineas established at Newmarket Races.

Y **Statistics**

1809 (Oct.–Dec.)

K Oct: 4th, Spencer Perceval forms an administration in Britain;
14th, by Peace of Schönbrunn, Austria cedes Trieste and Illyria to France, Galicia to Saxony and Russia, Salzburg and Inn District to Bavaria, and joins the Continental System.

L Nov: 19th, Spanish defeated at Ocana; French overrun all Andalusia, apart from Cadiz.

M Dec: 16th, Napoleon is divorced from Josephine by an act of Senate.

N Britain captures Martinique and Cayenne from the French.

z **Births and Deaths**

Jan. 15th Pierre Joseph Proudhon b. (–1865).
Jan. 19th Edgar Allan Poe b. (–1849).
Feb. 12th Charles Darwin b. (–1882) and Abraham Lincoln b. (–1865).
Mar. 31st Edward Fitzgerald b. (–1883) and Nicolai Gogol b. (–1852).
May 31st Joseph Haydn d. (77).
June 8th Thomas Paine d. (72).
June 14th Henry Keppel b. (–1904).
July 9th Friedrich Henle b. (–1885).
Aug. 6th Alfred Lord Tennyson b. (–1892).
Aug. 29th Oliver Wendell Holmes b. (–1894).
Nov. 3rd Felix Mendelssohn-Bartholdy b. (–1847).
Dec. 29th William Ewart Gladstone b. (–1898).

1810 Napoleon annexes Holland

A **Jan**: 6th, by Treaty of Paris, Sweden agrees to join 'Continental System' in return for Napoleon's recognition of Treaty of Frederikshavn (*Sept.* 17 1809), and recovers Pomerania.

B **Feb**: 11th, Napoleon marries Marie-Louise of Austria.

C **Mar**: 23rd, by the Rambouillet Decrees (kept secret until *May*) Napoleon orders sale of all U.S. ships which have been seized for violation of French decrees.

D **Apr**: 19th, under influence of Simon Bolivar, the Junta in Venezuela breaks from Spain, refusing to recognise Joseph Bonaparte, and proclaiming allegiance to Ferdinand VII.

E **May**: 1st, U.S. reopens commerce with Britain and France with various provisos;
21st, Whig Reform Bill, to provide for triennial parliaments and for extension of franchise, is defeated;
22nd, revolt in New Grenada against Spanish authority;
25th, revolt in Rio de la Plata, against Joseph Bonaparte's régime.

F **Jun**: K. A. von Hardenberg succeeds Stein in Prussia.

G **Jul**: 1st, Louis, King of Holland abdicates after pressure from Napoleon;
9th, Napoleon annexes Holland;
10th, Michel Ney takes Ciudad Rodrigo after long siege; British force takes Île de Bourbon and Mauritius in Indian Ocean.

H **Aug**: 5th, Trianon Tariff, whereby Napoleon places tax on all colonial imports into France;
18th, Charles XIII of Sweden adopts General Jean Bernadotte as heir.

J **Sep**: 16th, Revolt in Mexico in favour of independence from Spain;
18th, Junta in Chile revolts against Joseph Bonaparte and assumes authority;
20th, report of Bullion Committee in Britain, suggesting return to cash payments within two years, is not accepted.

K **Oct**: 18th and 25th, by Decrees of Fontainebleau Napoleon orders confiscation and burning of British goods found within Napoleonic states and establishes tribunals to try persons accused of introducing illicit wares;
Duke of Wellington holds the lines of Torres Vedras throughout the month, forcing the French to withdraw.

L **Nov**: 1st, Napoleon revokes Berlin and Milan Decrees with regard to U.S. trade (not published until *May* 11th 1812).

M **Dec**: 10th, Napoleon annexes northern Hanover, Bremen, Hamburg, Lauenburg, and Lübeck, in order to strengthen blockade to prevent smuggling of British goods;
31st, Tsar Alexander introduces new tariffs aimed at French goods, in violation of Treaty of Tilsit (*July* 1807).

N Obstinate fighting in Danubian Provinces between Turkey and Russia.
Guadaloupe, the last French colony in West Indies, is taken by the British.

O Politics, Economics, Law and Education

Lazare Carnot, *De la défense de places fortes.*

K. W. von Humboldt as Prussian minister of education reforms the gymnasia and institutes pre-university matriculation.

Berlin University founded with J. G. Fichte as rector.

P Science, Technology, Discovery, etc.

J. W. Goethe, *Theory of Colours.*

Samuel Hahnemann's *Organon of Therapeutics* founds homoeopathy.

Franz Gall and Johann Spurzheim, *Anatomie et physiologie du système nerveux.*

Krupps works opened at Essen.

Q Scholarship

G. F. Creuser, *Symbolism of the Ancients* (–12).

R Philosophy and Religion

John Milner opposes the right of the British government to veto the appointment of Roman Catholic bishops.

Protestant revivalists in Geneva form *Société des Amis.*

The Cumberland Presbytery, Kentucky, excluded from the Presbyterian Church.

S Art, Sculpture, Fine Arts and Architecture

Francisco Goya engraves *Los Desastres de la Guerra* (–13).

J. F. Overbeck founds the 'Nazarenes' to regenerate German religious art.

San Carlo Opera House, Naples (–12).

T Music

L. van Beethoven, incidental music to *Egmont.*

G. Rossini, *La Cenerentola* (opera).

U Literature

Anne de Staël, *De l'Allemagne.*

F. H. von der Hagen edits *Nibelungenlied* (–42).

Walter Scott, *The Lady of the Lake.*

V The Press

F. C. Perthes edits *Das deutsche Museum.*

W Drama and Entertainment

X Sport

Y Statistics

Z Births and Deaths

Feb. 22nd Frédéric Chopin b. (–1849).
Feb. 24th Henry Cavendish d. (79).
Mar. 15th Charles de Montalembert b. (–1870).
June 8th Robert Schumann b. (–1856);
Aug. 10th Camillo Count Cavour b. (–1861).
Sept. 29th Elizabeth Cleghorn Gaskell (*née* Stevenson) b. (–1865).
Dec. 7th Theodor Schwann b. (–1882).
Dec. 11th Alfred de Musset b. (–1857).

1811 British victories in Portugal—Prince of Wales becomes Prince Regent

A **Jan**: 22nd, by annexing Oldenburg, Napoleon virtually alienates Tsar Alexander, since the heir apparent to that Duchy is his brother-in-law, and the annexation violates Treaty of Tilsit (*July* 1807).

B **Feb**: 2nd, U.S. renews Non-Intercourse Act against British commerce;
5th, George III's insanity necessitates Regency Act, whereby Prince of Wales becomes Prince Regent, but with limited powers for twelve months;
10th, Russians take Belgrade and capture Turkish army;
20th, Austria declares itself bankrupt.

C **Mar**: 1st, Mehemet Ali massacres Mamelukes at Cairo;
20th, birth of François-Charles-Joseph, heir to Napoleon's throne; he is given the title of King of Rome.

D **Apr**:

E **May**: 8th, Duke of Wellington defeats French at Fuentes d'Onoro;
16th, British check French under Nicolas Soult at Albuhera.

F **Jun**: 17th, National Council meets in Paris to settle disputes between Napoleon and Pope Pius VII (but is dissolved *July* 6th, when it refuses to support Napoleon's orders unless the Pope is freed).

G **Jul**: 5th, Venezuela becomes independent and adopts constitution under influence of Simon Bolivar and Francisco de Miranda, having disavowed allegiance to Ferdinand VII of Spain (lasts until *July* 1812).

H **Aug**: 14th, Paraguay declares itself independent of Spain (and later of Buenos Aires *Oct.* 12th);
British occupy Java in East Indies.

J **Sep**: 7th, K. von. Hardenberg's Edict in Prussia provides for peasant proprietorship.

K **Oct**: 29th, Napoleon threatens to invade Berlin unless Prussia cancels her military plans for rapprochement with Russia, and the French state the terms of proposed alliance with Prussia.

L **Nov**: 5th, James Madison recommends Congress to prepare U.S. for hostilities against Britain, in view of the British Orders-in-Council on trade and violation of the 30-mile limit.

M **Dec**:

N

Z **Births and Deaths**

Mar. 31st R. W. von Bunsen b. (–1899).
June 4th Harriet Beecher Stowe b. (–1896).
June 7th James Young Simpson b. (–1870).
July 18th W. M. Thackeray b. (–1863).
Aug. 31st Théophile Gautier b. (–1872).
Sept. 30th Thomas Percy d. (81).
Oct. 22nd Franz Liszt b. (–1886).
Oct. 29th Louis Blanc b. (–1882).
Nov. 16th John Bright b. (–1889).

O **Politics, Economics, Law and Education**

'Luddites' destroy machinery in Nottingham and Yorkshire towns (*Mar.*).

Hampden Clubs are formed in England to agitate against the government, particularly for extending the franchise.

Civil Code is introduced into Austrian Empire, excepting Hungary, after 50 years of preparation.

Joshua Watson founds National Society for Educating the Poor in the Principles of the Established Church.

University of Christiana, Oslo, founded.

P **Science, Technology, Discovery, etc.**

Charles Bell, *New Idea of the Anatomy of the Brain.*

Amadeo Avogadro states his hypothesis on the composition of gases.

Courtois isolates iodine from kelp.

S. O. Poisson, *Traité de Mécanique* (–33).

Steam power is used at Leeds for conveying coal on a railway.

J. R. Meyer climbs the Jungfrau.

Q **Scholarship**

Berthold Niebuhr, *Roman History* (–32).

R. C. Rask, *Icelandic and Old Norse Grammar.*

J. P. A. Récusat, *Essai sur la langue et la littérature chinoises.*

K. A. Böttiger, *Kunstmythologie.*

R **Philosophy and Religion**

Large numbers of Welsh Protestants leave Anglican Church in 'the Great Schism'.

S **Art, Sculpture, Fine Arts and Architecture**

T. Lawrence, *Benjamin West* (painting).

B. Thorwaldsen, *Procession of Alexander the Great* (sculpture).

J. Rennie, *Waterloo Bridge* (–17).

J. Nash begins Regent Street.

T **Music**

L. van Beethoven, piano sonata 'Les Adieux' (*op.* 81a).

Carl von Weber, *Abu Hassan* (opera).

U **Literature**

Jane Austen, *Sense and Sensibility.*

Friedrich Fouqué, *Undine.*

J. W. Goethe, *My Life, Poetry and Truth.*

Heinrich Kleist, *The Broken Pitcher.*

V **The Press**

W **Drama and Entertainment**

X **Sport**

Y **Statistics**

Population of Great Britain 12·5 mill., an increase of 2·1 mill. in a decade. London's population exceeds 1 mill.

(*Continued opposite*)

1812 (Jan.–Sep.) U.S. declares war on Britain—Napoleon's retreat from Moscow

A **Jan**: 19th, Duke of Wellington takes Ciudad Rodrigo; French re-occupy Swedish Pomerania and Rügen to put pressure on Sweden to end clandestine trade and to prevent Russo-Swedish alliance.

B **Feb**: 11th, British Act of Parliament removes the restrictions on the Prince Regent (of *Feb.* 5th 1811);

24th, by alliance with France, Prussia agrees to allow free passage for French troops, to provide troops in event of war with Russia and to adhere to the 'Continental System'; August Scharnhorst and Gerhard von Gneisenau resign in disgust.

C **Mar**: 4th, Marquess Wellesley resigns as foreign secretary because of lack of support for the Peninsular campaign and is replaced by Lord Castlereagh;

16th, by alliance with France, Austria agrees to provide army for Napoleon, who guarantees integrity of Turkey and promises to restore Illyrian Provinces to Austria;

19th, Spanish Cortes passes liberal constitution under a hereditary monarch;

20th, by Act of Parliament frame-breaking becomes a capital offence in Britain.

D **Apr**: 4th, U.S. introduces ninety-day embargo to ensure that all U.S. ships are safely in port when war begins with Britain;

6th, British capture Badajoz (after siege since *March* 16th);

9th, by secret Treaty of Abo, Sweden agrees to aid Russia by creating diversion against the French in North Germany, while in return Tsar suggests Swedish annexation of Norway as compensation for loss of Finland (*Sept.* 17th 1809);

14th, Louisiana becomes a state of the U.S.

E **May**: 11th, Spencer Perceval is assassinated in House of Commons, and Lord Liverpool agrees to form an administration;

21st, Lord Liverpool resigns after vote of no confidence;

28th, by Treaty of Bucharest with Turkey, Russia obtains Bessarabia and withdraws demand for Moldavia and Wallachia, and the peace enables the Tsar to act against Napoleon.

F **Jun**: 8th, Tory administration under Liverpool resumes office;

18th, U.S. Congress approves war against Britain (the formal declaration is made 19th);

23rd, British Orders-in-Council of *Apr.* 26th 1809 restricting trade of U.S. are revoked;

24th, Napoleon crosses the R. Niemen and enters Russian territory;

26th, Polish Diet declares Poland independent (but Napoleon refuses to acknowledge Polish decision *July* 14th);

28th, Napoleon crosses the R. Vilna after Tsar's retreat.

G **Jul**: Britain makes peace with Russia and Sweden, and

18th, by Alliance of Orebro, Britain joins Sweden and Russia;

22nd, Wellington defeats French under Marshal Marmont at Salamanca;

31st, Venezuelan Republic falls to Spanish force and Francisco de Miranda is arrested.

H **Aug**: 12th, Duke of Wellington enters Madrid;

16th, Governor of Detroit surrenders that state to British forces, thus postponing U.S. plan to invade Canada;

17th (–18th), Russia is defeated at Smolensk, which is occupied by the French.

J **Sep**: 7th, following their defeat at Borodino the Russians are obliged to retreat, and abandon Moscow;

14th, Napoleon enters Moscow, which burns until 19th (occupation lasts until *Oct.* 18th);

19th (–*Oct.* 19th), British are forced to withdraw from Burgos.

O **Politics, Economics, Law and Education**

W. M. Leake's *Greece* arouses interest in England in the political state of that country.

P **Science, Technology, Discovery, etc.**

Humphry Davy, *Elements of Chemical Philosophy*.
Pierre Laplace, *Théorie Analytique* (theory of probability).
Georges Cuvier, *Recherches sur les ossements fossiles de quadrupèdes*.
Henry Bell's steamship *Comet* (25 tons) plies on the Clyde, maximum speed 7 knots.
Main streets of London lit by gas.
Philippe Girard invents machine for spinning flax.

Q **Scholarship**

H. F. Gesenius, *Hebrew and Chaldaic Dictionary*.

R **Philosophy and Religion**

G. W. Hegel, *Logic*.
J. G. Fichte, *Transcendental Philosophy*.
Repeal of Conventicle Act eases position of Protestant dissenters in England.
Baptist Union of Great Britain formed.
Jews in Prussia emancipated.

S **Art, Sculpture, Fine Arts and Architecture**

Francisco Goya, *Duke of Wellington* (painting).

T **Music**

L. van Beethoven, 7th (op. 92) and 8th Symphonies (op. 93).
G. Rossini, *La Pietra del Paragone* (opera).

U **Literature**

Lord Byron, *Childe Harold's Pilgrimage* (–18).
J. and W. Grimm, *Fairy Tales*.

V **The Press**

W **Drama and Entertainment**

The Waltz is introduced to English ballrooms.
Mrs. Siddons's last appearance.

X **Sport**

Y **Statistics**

U.K. textile trade: raw cotton imports, 73 mill. lb.
linen exports, 15,275,000 yds.

1812 (Oct.–Dec.)

K Oct: 13th, British under Isaac Brock defeat U.S. at Queenston Heights, preventing further attempted invasion of Canada;
19th, Napoleon's retreat from Moscow begins;
23rd, Malet's conspiracy to dethrone Napoleon, install Louis XVIII and end the wars, begins, but he is arrested and, 29th, executed.

L Nov: 26th (–28th), disaster for the French army retreating across the Beresina;
In U.S. presidential election James Madison (128 electoral votes) defeats De Witt Clinton (89 votes).

M Dec: 5th, Napoleon leaves his troops under command of Joachim Murat and sets out for Paris (where he arrives, 18th);
30th, by Convention of Tauroggen with Russia, unknown to Frederick William III, the Prussian General von York breaks away from French alliance and becomes temporarily neutral.

N

z **Births and Deaths**

Feb. 7th Charles Dickens b. (–1870).
Apr. 26th Alfred Krupp b. (–1887).
May 7th Robert Browning b. (–1889).
Dec. 23rd Samuel Smiles b. (1904).

1813 (Jan.–Sep.) Wellington's army enters France—Napoleon's defeat at Battle of Leipzig

A **Jan:**

B **Feb:** 28th, Prussia agrees, by Alliance of Kalisch with Russia, to conduct joint campaign in Saxony and Silesia against Napoleon and the Confederation of the Rhine.

C **Mar:** 3rd, Britain concludes Treaty of Stockholm with Sweden who agrees to supply army in return for British subsidies and for promise not to oppose union with Norway;
17th, Frederick William III of Prussia declares war against the French, appeals to the people to support the campaign, and begins formation of *Landwehr* and *Landsturm*;
18th, after patriotic outbreak in Hamburg against the French, the city is occupied by the Russians;
27th, combined Russo-Prussian force occupies Dresden, forcing King of Saxony to flee.

D **Apr:** 27th, U.S. force in search of British ships captures York (now Toronto).

E **May:** 2nd, Napoleon defeats the Prussian and Russian armies at Lützen (Gross-Gorschen);
20th (–21st), indecisive battle of Bautzen is fought with heavy losses on both sides;
24th, Catholic Relief Bill is abandoned in Parliament when the Speaker has the clause allowing Catholics to sit and vote in Parliament deleted, thus rendering the Bill ineffective;
27th, U.S. force occupies Fort St. George, and British abandon entire Niagara frontier.

F **Jun:** 1st, U.S. frigate *Chesapeake* is captured by H.M.S. *Shannon*;
4th, Armistice of Poischwitz between Prussia and France through the mediation of Prince Metternich (*Aug.* 10th);
14th (–15th), Britain undertakes to pay subsidies to Russia and Prussia;
21st, Wellington completely routs the French at Vittoria, forcing Joseph Bonaparte to flee from Spain to France;
26th, Metternich agrees to peace congress at interview with Napoleon at Dresden, though he is fully aware of Austria's impending alliances with Russia and Prussia;
27th, by Treaty of Reichenbach with Prussia and Russia, Austria agrees to declare war on *July* 20th, if the French refuse the conditions of peace.

G **Jul:** 28th, Congress of Prague between France, Prussia and Austria begins but is dissolved (*Aug.* 10th) with nothing achieved;
Venezuela becomes independent for second time with Simon Bolivar as virtual dictator.

H **Aug:** 12th, Austria declares war against Napoleon;
23rd, the French defeat by Friedrich von Bülow at Grossbeeren prevents march on Berlin;
26th, French are defeated at Katzbach by Gebhard von Blücher;
26th (–27th), in battle of Dresden, Napoleon defeats the allied army from Bohemia.

J **Sep:** 6th, Michel Ney is defeated by von Bülow at Dennewitz;
9th, Treaty of Teplitz confirms Reichenbach agreement (of *June* 27th) uniting Russia, Prussia and Austria against France;
—, San Sebastian finally capitulates to Wellington, after siege lasting since *Aug.* 31st;
10th, U.S. successes on Lake Erie;
29th, Detroit is re-occupied by U.S.

O **Politics, Economics, Law and Education**

Benjamin Constant, *De l'esprit de conquête et de l'usurpation dans les rapports avec la civilisation européene.*
Robert Owen, *A New View of Society.*
Elizabeth Fry begins to visit Newgate Prison.
East India Company's trade monopoly in India abolished, but its monopoly in China continues.

P **Science, Technology, Discovery, etc.**

Augustin de Candolle's agricultural and botanical survey of France.
'Puffing Billy' steam engine installed at Wylam colliery.
George Clymer's 'Columbia' printing-press eliminates the screw process.
David Brewster discovers crystals with two axes of double refraction.
John Leslie, *Experiments and Instruments depending on the relations of air to heat and moisture.*

Q **Scholarship**

R. Southey, *Life of Nelson.*

R **Philosophy and Religion**

J. F. Herbart, *Introduction to Philosophy.*
Methodist Missionary Society founded.

S **Art, Sculpture, Fine Arts and Architecture**

J. M. W. Turner, *Frosty Morning* (painting).
David Cox, *Treatise on Landscape Painting and Effect in Water Colours* (–14).

T **Music**

G. Rossini, *Tancredi* and *The Italian Girl in Algiers* (operas).
Philharmonic Society founded in London, with regular concerts in the Argyll Rooms.

U **Literature**

Ernst Arndt, *Was ist das deutsche Vaterland?* and other patriotic songs.
Jane Austen, *Pride and Prejudice.*
Lord Byron, *The Giaour* and *Bride of Abydos.*
A. von Chamisso, *Peter Schlemihl.*
Alessandro Manzoni, *Inni Sacri.*
P. B. Shelley, *Queen Mab.*

V **The Press**

W **Drama and Entertainment**

X **Sport**

Y **Statistics**

K Oct: 5th, U.S. victory at Battle of Thames River (Ontario);
8th, Wellington crosses Bidassoa and enters France;
—, Bavaria joins allies by Treaty of Ried with Austria, and leaves Confederation of Rhine (formal declaration of war against France, 14th);
12th, by Peace of Gulistan with Russia, Persia cedes Caucasus region;
16th (–19th), Napoleon's defeat in the 'Battle of the Nations' at Leipzig and retreat leads to dissolution of Confederation of the Rhine and of Kingdom of Westphalia;
26th, after a rising in Italian States the Austrians defeat Eugene de Beauharnais at Valsarno, thus regaining foothold in Italy;
31st, Pampeluna finally surrenders to British force.

L Nov: 6th, Mexico declares itself independent;
8th, Allies offer Frankfurt peace proposals to Napoleon by which France would be left with the boundaries of the Alps and the Pyrenees (but he replies evasively 16th);
10th, Wellington defeats Nicolas Soult in France and goes on to invest Bayonne (*Dec.* 10th);
11th, U.S. forces are defeated by an inferior British force at Chrysler's Farm, Montreal;
15th (–17th), French expelled from Holland after risings by Dutch people, and
30th, William of Orange returns to Holland.

M Dec: 1st, by Declaration of Frankfurt the allies resolve to invade France because of vague reply to peace terms by Napoleon;
10th, U.S. forces burn Newark;
11th, Napoleon agrees to restore Ferdinand VII of Spain, by Treaty of Valençay;
19th, British force takes Fort Niagara from U.S.;
21st, Karl Schwarzenberg's Austrian forces enter France through Switzerland;
29th, Swiss Diet votes restoration of old constitution and revokes Act of Mediation;
29th (–31st), British forces burn Buffalo as reprisal for U.S. attack on Newark;
31st, Prussians under Gebhard von Blücher cross the Rhine.

N

z **Births and Deaths**

Jan. 19th Henry Bessemer b. (–1898).
Mar. 19th David Livingstone b. (–1873).
Apr. 8th Joseph Lagrange d. (78).
May 5th Søren Kierkegaard b. (–1855).
May 22nd Richard Wagner b. (–1883).
July 12th Claude Bernard b. (–1878).
Oct. 10th Giuseppe Verdi b. (–1901).

A **Jan:** 11th, Joachim Murat deserts Napoleon and joins allies;
14th, by Treaty of Kiel with Sweden, Denmark cedes Norway in return for Western Pomerania and Rügen;
—, in separate treaty with Britain, Denmark regains her lost territories, with exception of Heligoland.

B **Feb:** 1st, in battle of La Rothière, Blücher first attacks the French and the Russians complete the victory;
5th, (– *Mar.* 19th), peace negotiations at Chatillon are futile as Napoleon refuses to accept 1792 frontier of France;
27th, Karl Schwarzenberg defeats French forces at Bar-sur-Aube.

C **Mar:** 9th, by Treaty of Chaumont, the allies agree not to negotiate separate peace with Napoleon;
9th (–10th), at battle of Laon the combined allied army compels Napoleon to withdraw;
12th, Wellington captures Bordeaux;
30th (–31st), allies triumphantly enter Paris.

D **Apr:** 1st, Senate, influenced by Talleyrand, names provisional French government in Paris;
8th, National Assembly in Norway meets to discuss constitution, as Norway has declared itself independent, in defiance of Treaty of Kiel (*Jan.* 14th), and decides on limited monarchy (Christian Frederick of Denmark is elected King on *May* 17th);
11th, by Treaty of Fontainebleau, Napoleon abdicates unconditionally and is banished to Elba.

E **May:** 3rd, Louis XVIII enters Paris;
4th, Ferdinand of Spain annuls Constitution of the Cortes;
30th, by First Peace of Paris, the French recognise frontier of 1792 and agree to recognise independence of the Netherlands and the Italian and the German States.

F **Jun:** 4th, Louis XVIII issues Constitutional Charter, taking up throne on his hereditary right, not by a contract with the people.

G **Jul:** 5th, a British force is compelled to retire after a defeat by the U.S. forces at Chippewa.

H **Aug:** 13th, Cape of Good Hope Province becomes a British Colony while other former Dutch colonies are restored, apart from Demerara, Essequibo and Berbice;
14th, by Convention of Moss, Sweden recognises Norwegian Constitution, with provision that King Frederick Christian must renounce his throne;
24th, a British force takes Washington and burns main buildings.

J **Sep:** 11th, U.S. force capture British flotilla on Lake Champlain.

K **Oct:** 26th, Hanover is proclaimed a kingdom by the Prince Regent in the name of George III;
Governor-General of India declares war on the Gurkhas of Nepal.

L **Nov:** 1st, Congress of Vienna formally opens;
4th, Norwegian constitution is established, and
11th, Charles XIII of Sweden is elected to the throne;
13th, Russia hands over Saxony to Prussia, an action opposed by Austria, the German States, and France, as the Tsar wishes to obtain Poland in exchange.

M **Dec:** 24th, Treaty of Ghent ends the war between Britain and U.S., the latter abandoning the main demands for an end to impressment and compensation for commercial losses.

N

O **Politics, Economics, Law and Education**

Vicomte de Chateaubriand, *Bonaparte et les Bourbons.*

Berthold Niebuhr, *Prussia's Right to Saxony.*

F. K. von Savigny, *The Claim of Our Age on Legislation.*

English Statute of Apprentices, 1563, repealed.

P **Science, Technology, Discovery, etc.**

J. J. Berzelius, *Theory of Chemical Proportions and the Chemical Action of Electricity.*

M. J. B. Orfila, *Toxicologie générale.*

George Stephenson constructs the first effective steam locomotive (*July* 25th).

Q **Scholarship**

R **Philosophy and Religion**

Pope Pius VII on returning to Rome (*May*) restores the Inquisition and revives the Index and the Jesuits.

First Anglican Bishop in India (Calcutta).

S **Art, Sculpture, Fine Arts and Architecture**

Francisco Goya, *2 May* and *3 May 1808* (paintings).

Dulwich Gallery is opened, the first collection accessible to the public in Britain.

T **Music**

John Field, *Nocturnes.*

Franz Schubert, *Gretchen am Spinnrade.*

L. van Beethoven, *Fidelio*, final two-act form.

J. N. Mälzel invents the metronome.

U **Literature**

Jane Austen, *Mansfield Park.*

Lord Byron, *The Corsair.*

Friedrich Rückert, *Poems.*

[Walter Scott], *Waverley.*

R. Southey, *Vision of Judgment* (published -21).

William Wordsworth, *The Excursion.*

V **The Press**

John Walter II begins to print *The Times* by steam.

W **Drama and Entertainment**

Edmund Kean's début at Drury Lane as Shylock.

X **Sport**

M.C.C. move to Lord's Ground.

Y **Statistics**

Z **Births and Deaths**

Jan. 27th Johann Gottlieb Fichte d. (52).

Apr. 15th John Lothrop Motley b. (-1877).

Oct. 4th Jean François Millet b. (-1875).

Oct. 29th Joanna Southcott d. (65).

— Michael Bakunin b. (-1876).

1815 (Jan.–Sep.) Napoleon's 'Hundred Days' end in Battle of Waterloo— The Congress of Vienna settles the map of Europe

A Jan: 3rd, by secret treaty, Austria, Britain and France form defensive alliance against Prusso-Russian plans to solve the Saxon and Polish problems;
8th, before news of peace of Ghent, the battle of New Orleans is fought and the British are defeated within half an hour;
10th, Britain declares war against King of Kandy, Ceylon.

B Feb:

C Mar: 1st, Napoleon lands in France forcing Louis XVIII to flee (19th);
2nd, Dominion of Kandyan Provinces is vested in the Sovereign of the British Empire, and exercised through Governor of Ceylon;
20th, Napoleon enters Paris and the 'Hundred Days' begin (until *June* 29th);
23rd, Corn Law is passed, prohibiting imports of foreign corn into Britain when average home price of wheat is below 80 shillings per quarter, but allowing duty-free imports when that price is exceeded;
25th, Austria, Britain, Prussia, and Russia form new alliance against Napoleon in order to maintain the established order in Europe.

D Apr: 10th, Austria sends a note to Joachim Murat, King of Naples, declaring war against him for occupying Rome, Florence and Bologna (although formal declaration not made until 12th).

E May: 3rd, Murat is defeated at Tolentino by the Austrians;
18th, Treaty of peace concluded by Prussia, Russia and Austria with King of Saxony;
25th, Frederick William III promises constitution in Prussia.

F Jun: 2nd, Napoleon issues the liberal constitution of 'Le Champ de Mai';
4th, Denmark cedes Pomerania and Rügen to Prussia in return for part of Duchy of Lauenburg;
9th, Congress of Vienna closes after Final Act is passed; Holland, Belgium and Luxembourg are united to form the Netherlands (by Act of *May* 31st), Switzerland is to be neutral, East Poland is ceded to Russia and the Western Provinces of Poland to Prussia, Cracow becomes an independent republic, Lombardy and Venetia are restored to Austria, Prussia gains the Rhineland and the northern region of Saxony, Hanover obtains East Friesland and Hildesheim, the German Confederation is established under Presidency of Austria (by Act of 8th *June*), the Bourbon monarch Ferdinand VII is restored in Spain, the Braganza dynasty returns to the Portuguese throne, Ferdinand IV is recognised as King of Two Sicilies, the Pope and the minor Italian princes are restored, and Britain retains the majority of her overseas conquests, including Malta and Heligoland;
18th, Duke of Wellington and Gebhard von Blücher defeat Napoleon at Waterloo;
22nd, Napoleon abdicates for second time, after being given choice of resignation or deposition by the French Chambers.

G Jul: 7th, Allies enter Paris, enabling Louis XVIII to return, 8th, to Tuileries;
White Terror begins in Southern France by fanatical royalists against revolutionary elements, Bonapartists and Protestants.

H Aug: 2nd, by agreement between Prussia, Austria, Britain and Russia, the imprisonment of Napoleon is left to the British decision and he is banished to St. Helena (where he arrives 17th).

J Sep: 26th, anti-Liberal Holy Alliance is formed between Austria, Russia and Prussia to maintain Vienna settlement.

O **Politics, Economics, Law and Education**
T. R. Malthus, *An Inquiry into the Nature and Progress of Rent.*
David Ricardo, *The Influence of a Low Price of Corn on the Profits of Stock.*
Apothecaries Act in Britain forbids unqualified doctors practising medicine.

P **Science, Technology, Discovery, etc.**
L. J. Prout's hypothesis on relation between specific gravity and atomic weight.
Augustin Fresnel's researches on the diffraction of light.
Jean Lamarck, *Histoire naturelle des animaux* (–22).
Humphry Davy invents miner's arc lamp.
John Macadam as surveyor general of Bristol roads constructs roads of broken stone.
U.S.N. *Fulton*, first steam warship (38 tons).
William Smith's geological map of England and Wales.

Q **Scholarship**
F. K. von Savigny, *History of Roman Law in the Middle Ages.*
G. J. Thorkelin's edition of *Beowulf.*

R **Philosophy and Religion**
Dugald Stewart, *Progress of Metaphysical, Ethical and Political Philosophy.*
Julius Wegschneider, *Institutiones theologicae dogmaticae.*

S **Art, Sculpture, Fine Arts and Architecture**
Francisco Goya, *Tauromaquia* (engravings).
J. M. W. Turner, *Crossing the Brook* (painting).
Antonio Canova, *Three Graces* (sculpture).
Pius VII sends Canova to Paris to secure the return to Rome of works of art looted by Napoleon.
John Nash, Brighton Pavilion (–23).

T **Music**

U **Literature**
Pierre Béranger, *Chansons* I.
Ernst Hoffmann, *Die Elixiere des Teufels.*
Walter Scott, *Guy Mannering.*
William Wordsworth, *White Doe of Rylstone.*

V **The Press**

W **Drama and Entertainment**
The quadrille is first danced in England.

X **Sport**

Y **Statistics**
U.K. total state expenditure, £112·9 mill.

K **Oct**: 6th, Prince Regent supports principles of Holy Alliance but avoids any commitments involving Britain;
13th, Joachim Murat is shot after abortive attempt to regain Naples;
British occupy Ascension Island.

L **Nov**: 5th, by treaty with Russia, Austria and Prussia, Britain establishes protectorate over Ionian Islands;
20th, by Second Peace of Paris, France yields territory to Savoy and to Switzerland, and agrees to restore captured art treasures, while the Quadruple Alliance between Austria, Prussia, Russia, and Britain is renewed;
27th, Alexander I issues a Polish Constitution (having proclaimed Poland to be part of Russia, *May* 25th).

M **Dec**: 2nd, treaty of peace between Britain and Rajah of Nepal, but war is soon resumed;
7th, Michel Ney is shot, following trial for treason in aiding Napoleon at Waterloo.

N

z **Births and Deaths**

Mar. 5th Franz Mesmer d. (81).
Apr. 1st Otto von Bismarck b. (–1898).
Apr. 24th Anthony Trollope b. (–1882).
Dec. 8th Adolf Menzel b. (–1905).

1816 Argentina declares independence from Spain—Spa Fields Riots in London

A **Jan**: 16th, Brazil made an Empire under John, Prince Regent of Portugal.

B **Feb**: 7th, Simon Bolivar is entrusted by the Congress of New Grenada with political and military control in invasion of Venezuela from Haiti, but is subsequently defeated by the royalist Pablo Morillo.

C **Mar**: 20th, Maria I, the insane Queen of Portugal, dies, and is succeeded by her son, John VI (–1826).

D **Apr**:

E **May**: 5th, Carl August of Saxe-Weimar grants first German Constitution.

F **Jun**: 20th, George Canning returns to Cabinet as President of Board of Control for India; 21st, United Netherlands accedes to Holy Alliance.

G **Jul**: 9th, at Congress of Tucuman, independence of United Provinces of La Plata (Argentina) is declared.

H **Aug**: 8th, Bavaria joins the Holy Alliance.

J **Sep**: 5th, Louis XVIII dissolves the Chamber and reduces number of members so that Moderates obtained majority in ensuing election.

K **Oct**:

L **Nov**: 5th, Diet of German Confederation opened at Frankfurt-am-Main under Prince Metternich.

M **Dec**: 2nd, Spa Fields Riots take place when crowd, which assembles to hear demands for political reform, marches on London;
11th, Indiana becomes an American state.
Britain restores Java to the Netherlands.

N

O **Politics, Economics, Law and Education**
Protective tariff in U.S.
Distress in England causes large-scale emigration to Canada and U.S.
Friedrich Froebel starts an educational community at Keilhau, Thuringia.
Ghent university founded.

P **Science, Technology, Discovery, etc.**
David Brewster invents kaleidoscope.

Q **Scholarship**
Franz Bopp, *System of Conjugation.*
Nikolai Karamzin, *History of the Russian Empire.*
Berthold Niebuhr discovers the Institutes of Gaius in Verona.

R **Philosophy and Religion**
American Bible Society founded.

S **Art, Sculpture, Fine Arts and Architecture**
Francisco Goya, *Duke of Osuna.*
Leo Klenze, Glyptothek, Munich (–30).
Through the success of B. R. Haydon's campaign for public patronage of the arts the Elgin Marbles are bought for the British Museum.

T **Music**
L. van Beethoven, *Liederkreis* (op. 98).
Franz Schubert, *Erl King* and 5th Symphony in B flat.
G. Rossini, *Barber of Seville* (opera).

U **Literature**
Jane Austen, *Emma.*
Lord Byron, *The Siege of Corinth.*
S. T. Coleridge, *Kubla Khan* (written 1797).
Leigh Hunt, *The Story of Rimini.*
Count Leopardi, *Alle Pressamente alle Morte.*
T. L. Peacock, *Headlong Hall.*
Walter Scott, *The Antiquary* and *Old Mortality.*
P. B. Shelley, *Alastor.*

V **The Press**
William Cobbett's *Political Register*, published at 2d., the first cheap periodical.

W **Drama and Entertainment**

X **Sport**

Y **Statistics**
U.K. registered tonnage of merchant shipping, 2,504,000 (steamships 1,000).

Z **Births and Deaths**
Apr. 21st Charlotte Brontë b. (–1855).
July 17th R. B. Sheridan d. (65).
Dec. 13th E. W. Siemens b. (–1892).

1817 Unrest in Britain provokes repressive legislation—Independence of Venezuela under Bolivar

A Jan: 28th, Prince Regent is fired at on return from opening of Parliament.

B Feb: 5th, new electoral law, limiting franchise, is introduced in France;
10th, Britain, Prussia, Austria and Russia agree to first decrease in army of occupation in France.

C Mar: 4th, James Monroe is inaugurated fifth President of U.S.;
4th, Habeas Corpus Act is suspended after secret Parliamentary committee's report that insurrection is imminent (extended by Act of Parliament, *June* 30th to last until *March* 1st 1818);
10th, 'March of the Blanketeers' begins in Manchester to present petition in London in protest against suspension of Habeas Corpus Act, but majority are halted, 11th, at Stockport;
17th, Act of Parliament for protection of King and Prince Regent, that any acts against them will amount to treason;
31st, Act to prevent seditious meetings is passed;
—, Lord Sidmouth's 'Circular' sent to magistrates advising them to suppress seditious publications;
Establishment of Councils of State in Prussia to supervise separate provinces.

D Apr: 28th, Rush-Bagot Agreement is concluded between Britain and U.S. to limit naval forces on the Great Lakes.

E May: Sweden accedes to Holy Alliance.

F Jun: 9th, riots in Derbyshire against low wages and local unemployment.

G Jul:

H Aug:

J Sep: 23rd, by treaty with Britain, Spain agrees to end slave trade;
Ultra-Royalists lose ground in French election.

K Oct: 1st, Bank of England makes partial resumption of cash payments;
18th, Wartburg Festival reveals revolutionary tendencies of German students who meet at Jena to celebrate anniversaries of Luther's death and of Battle of Leipzig;
30th, Simon Bolivar organises independent government of Venezuela, but not on liberal lines.

L Nov: 5th, Third Mahratta War against the British in India with attacks at Poona, Nagpur and Indore;
Sultan of Turkey grants partial autonomy to Serbs after lengthy struggle for independence.

M Dec: 10th, Mississippi is admitted to the Union as an American state.

N

O **Politics, Economics, Law and Education**

David Ricardo, *Principles of Political Economy and Taxation.*

P **Science, Technology, Discovery, etc.**

Karl Ritter, *Geography in its relation to Nature and History* (–18).

Q **Scholarship**

Philipp Böckh, *The Public Economy of Athens.*

R **Philosophy and Religion**

G. W. F. Hegel, *Encyclopaedia of Philosophy.*

Joseph de Maistre, *Du Pape.*

H. F. R. de Lamennais, *Essai sur l'indifférence.*

Lutheran and Reformed Churches in Prussia unite in an Evangelical Union, which spreads to other states.

Juan Llorentz, late secretary of the Inquisition, publishes *History of the Inquisition in Spain.*

S **Art, Sculpture, Fine Arts and Architecture**

John Constable, *Flatford Mill* (painting).

Francis Chantrey, *Sleeping Children* (sculpture).

Braccio Nuova, Vatican Museum, Rome (–21).

St. Isaac's cathedral, St. Petersburg (–51).

T. Jefferson, University of Virginia, Charlottesville (–26).

T **Music**

M. Clementi, *Gradus ad Parnassum.*

G. Rossini, *La Gazza Ladra* (opera).

U **Literature**

W. C. Bryant, *Thanatopsis.*

Lord Byron, *Manfred.*

S. T. Coleridge, *Sybilline Leaves.*

G. Crabbe, *Tales of the Hall.*

Franz Grillparzer, *Die Ahnfrau.*

P. B. Shelley, *The Revolt of Islam.*

V **The Press**

Thomas Barnes edits *The Times* (–41).

The Scotsman founded (*Jan.*).

Blackwood's Magazine with John Wilson (under the pseudonym of 'Christopher North'), editor.

W **Drama and Entertainment**

X **Sport**

Y **Statistics**

Z **Births and Deaths**

Feb. 23rd George Frederick Watts b. (–1904).

July 12th Henry David Thoreau b. (–1862).

July 14th Madame de Staël d. (51).

July 18th Jane Austen d. (41).

Aug. 29th John Leech b. (–1864).

Nov. 22nd John Thadeus Delane b. (–1879).

Nov. 30th Theodor Mommsen b. (–1903).

A **Jan:** 6th, by Treaty of Mundoseer, the dominions of Holkar of Indore are annexed with the Rajput States and come under British protection;
31st, Act suspending Habeas Corpus is repealed, and suspension is never again introduced in Britain.

B **Feb:** 5th, on the death of Charles XIII of Sweden, Bernadotte succeeds to throne as Charles XIV, founding a new dynasty;
12th, Independence of Chile proclaimed in Santiago (and is safeguarded by defeat of Spanish Royalist forces, *April* 5th).

C **Mar:**

D **Apr:**

E **May:** 19th, defeat of Bill to repeal Septennial Act, in attempt to shorten duration of British Parliament from seven years;
26th, Bavarian Constitution, providing for Diet of two Chambers, for comparative freedom of speech and for legal equality, is proclaimed;
28th, Prussian Tariff Reform Act abolishes internal customs.

F **Jun:** 2nd, Francis Burdett's motion for parliamentary reform with annual parliaments and universal suffrage is overwhelmingly defeated;
3rd, Baji Rao, Peshwa of Poona and his dominions come under British control in Bombay presidency.
10th, Parliament is dissolved and in ensuing election (*July* 1st–25th) the Whig opposition increases its seats.

G **Jul:**

H **Aug:** 22nd, liberal Constitution introduced in Baden, providing for Diet of two Chambers, legal equality and fiscal reforms.

J **Sep:** 27th (–*Nov.* 21st), Conference at Aix-la-Chapelle is held between Austria, Prussia, Russia, France, and Britain to discuss French indemnity.

K **Oct:** 9th, Allies agree to evacuate their troops from France by *Nov.* 30th, as the indemnity is being paid;
20th, by convention between U.S. and Britain, the border between Canada and U.S. is defined as the 49th Parallel, and a joint occupation of Oregon is to take place for 10 years.

L **Nov:** 15th, France is invited to join European Concert;
15th, at same time the Quadruple Alliance between Russia, Austria, Prussia and Britain is renewed to watch over France in order to protect her against revolution; Britain refuses to make a formal alliance with her allies and with France;
20th, Simon Bolivar formally declares Venezuela independent of Spain.

M **Dec:** 3rd, Illinois becomes U.S. state, with population of approximately 40,000;
21st, Duc de Richelieu resigns in France and is succeeded by Élie Decazes, after October elections show increasing influence of the Left.

N

O **Politics, Economics, Law and Education**

Anne de Staël, *Considérations sur la Révolution.*

Bonn University founded.

P **Science, Technology, Discovery, etc.**

F. W. Bessel's *Fundamenta Astronomiae* codifies 3,222 stars on the basis of James Bradley's observations.

J. F. Encke discovers the circulation of 'Encke's comet'.

F. Stromeyer and K. S. L. Hermann discover the metallic element cadmium.

First steamship, *Savannah*, crosses the Atlantic in 26 days.

John Ross's expedition to discover North-West Passage.

Q **Scholarship**

Henry Hallam, *The View of the State of Europe in the Middle Ages.*

Joseph Dobrovsky, *History of the Czech Language.*

R **Philosophy and Religion**

G. W. Hegel succeeds J. G. Fichte as professor of philosophy at Berlin.

S **Art, Sculpture, Fine Arts and Architecture**

Edwin Landseer, *Fighting Dogs getting Wind* (painting).

Prado Museum, Madrid.

Piazza Vittorio Veneto, Turin.

T **Music**

G. Rossini, *Moses in Egypt.*

Franz Schubert, 6th Symphony in C.

U **Literature**

Jane Austen, *Northanger Abbey* and *Persuasion* (posth.).

Lord Byron, *Don Juan* (–23).

Jean Delavigne, *Les Messéniennes.*

F. Grillparzer, *Sappho.*

William Hazlitt, *Lectures on the English Poets* (–19).

John Keats, *Endymion.*

T. L. Peacock, *Nightmare Abbey.*

Walter Scott, *Heart of Midlothian* and *Rob Roy.*

Mary Wollstonecraft Shelley, *Frankenstein.*

V **The Press**

W **Drama and Entertainment**

X **Sport**

First professional horse-racing in U.S.

Y **Statistics**

U.K. iron production 325,000 tons.

Z **Births and Deaths**

Apr. 23rd James Anthony Froude b. (–1894).

May 5th Karl Marx b. (–1883).

May 25th Jacob Burckhardt b. (–1897).

June 17th Charles François Gounod b. (–1893).

July 11th William Edward Forster b. (–1886).

Dec. 24th J. P. Joule b. (–1889).

– Ivan Turgeniev b. (–1883).

1819 British settlement at Singapore—U.S. obtains Florida—Carlsbad Decrees and Six Acts

A **Jan:**

B **Feb:** 6th, East India Company, represented by Stamford Raffles, establishes a settlement at Singapore by treaty with local ruler (preliminary treaty having been concluded, 30th *Jan.*);

22nd, U.S. obtains Florida from Spain by Adams–Onis Treaty (ratified by Congress, *July*).

C **Mar:** 23rd, August von Kötzebue, a reactionary and an alleged Russian agent, is assassinated by a student in Mannheim.

D **Apr:** 24th, after lengthy negotiations with Britain, Turkey obtains Parga from Ionian Islands.

E **May:** 1st, liberty of press introduced in France.

F **Jun:**

G **Jul:** 2nd, Robert Peel's Act for gradual resumption of cash payments, which must be totally resumed by *May* 1st 1823, is passed.

H **Aug:** 16th, 'Peterloo' Massacre takes place when a crowd which has gathered in St. Peter's Fields, Manchester, to listen to speeches on parliamentary reform and on repeal of Corn Laws, is charged on by the militia.

J **Sep:** 20th, after A. von Kötzebue's murder the Frankfurt Diet, instigated by Prince Metternich, sanctions the Carlsbad Decrees, whereby freedom of press is abolished, universities are placed under State supervision, all political agitation is to be suppressed, and a meeting to investigate rumours of conspiracy is to take place in attempt to check revolutionary and liberal movements in the German Confederation;

25th, Württemberg is given constitution similar to those recently established in other German States.

K **Oct:** first step towards *Zollverein* (Customs Union) taken when Prussia concludes tariff treaty with Schwarzburg-Sonderhausen.

L **Nov:** Prince Metternich uses influence to begin conference in Vienna to modify the Federal Act of the German States in order to fix the functions of the Diet, with idea of eliminating all elements of constitutional control in German States.

M **Dec:** 7th, Hanover given Constitution with two Chambers by Ordinance of Prince Regent of Britain;

14th, Alabama is admitted as a U.S. state;

—, Lord John Russell begins his parliamentary reform campaign after evidence of corruption at an earlier election;

17th, Simon Bolivar becomes President of newly-formed Republic of Colombia, created from Venezuela and New Granada;

British Parliament passes the 'Six Acts' to deal with disorders and provide for the speedy trial of offenders, for wider powers to enable magistrates to search for arms, for the increase in penalties for seditious libel, for the prohibition in the training in the use of weapons, for the greater curtailment of public meetings and for the introduction of stamp duty on newspapers.

N

O Politics, Economics, Law and Education

Simon Bolivar, *Discourse Before the Congress of Angostura.*

Jean Sismondi, *Nouveaux Principes d'Économie Politique.*

Twelve-hour day for juveniles in England.

In McCulloch *v.* Maryland, Chief Justice John Marshall gives judicial sanction to doctrine of centralisation of power, at expense of states.

P Science, Technology, Discovery, etc.

H. C. Oersted discovers electro-magnetism.

E. Mitscherlich propounds the theory of isomorphism from observations on the crystallisation of phosphates and arsenates.

Thomas Telford begins Menai suspension bridge (–21).

John Barrow enters 'Barrow's Straits' in N. Arctic (*Aug.*).

Q Scholarship

Angelo Mai discovers Cicero's *De Republica* in Vatican Library.

Jakob Grimm's *German Grammar* establishes the permutation of consonants.

Horace Wilson, *Sanskrit Dictionary.*

R Philosophy and Religion

Arthur Schopenhauer, *World as Will and Idea.*

Georg Hermes, *Philosophical Introduction to Christian Theology* (–29).

S Art, Sculpture, Fine Arts and Architecture

Théodore Géricault, *Raft of the Medusa* (painting).

Francisco Goya, *Doña Antonia Zárate* (painting).

J. M. W. Turner, *Childe Harold's Pilgrimage* (painting).

Bertel Thorwaldsen, *Christ and the Apostles* (–38) (sculpture).

William Inwood, St. Pancras Church, London (–22).

K. F. Schinkel, Schauspielhaus, Berlin (–23).

T Music

Franz Schubert, 'Trout' Quintet (op. 114).

U Literature

Lord Byron, *Mazeppa.*

J. W. Goethe, *West-östlicher Divan.*

Victor Hugo, *Odes.*

John Keats, *Hyperion* (published 1856).

V The Press

W Drama and Entertainment

X Sport

Y Statistics

z **Births and Deaths**

Feb. 8th John Ruskin b. (–1900).
Feb. 22nd James Russell Lowell b. (–1891).
May 24th Princess Alexandrina Victoria (Queen Victoria) b. (–1901).
May 27th Julia Ward Howe b. (–1910).
May 31st Walt Whitman b. (–1892).
June 10th Gustave Courbet b. (–1877).
June 12th Charles Kingsley b. (–1875).
June 21st Jacques Offenbach b. (–1880).
July 19th Gottfried Keller b. (–1890).
Aug. 1st Herman Melville b. (–1891).
Aug. 19th James Watt d. (83).
Aug. 26th Albert, Prince Consort b. (–1861).
Nov. 22nd 'George Eliot' (pseud. of Mary Ann Evans) b. (–1880).

1820 (Jan.–Oct.) The Missouri Compromise—The Cato Street Conspiracy

A **Jan:** 1st, Revolution in Spain begins due to Ferdinand VII's failure to adhere to Constitution of 1812, also his sending troops to Spanish America to put down risings with which Spanish rebels are in sympathy;
29th, George III dies and is succeeded by Prince Regent as George IV (–1830).

B **Feb:** 13th, Duc de Berry, heir presumptive to French throne, is assassinated when proposals to modify Louis XVIII's Charter are being discussed;
20th, Duc de Decazes is dismissed after Berry's death, and succeeded by Duc de Richelieu;
23rd, Cato Street Conspiracy to murder Cabinet ministers is discovered and leaders later executed;
28th, following the accession of George IV Parliament is dissolved (resulting elections of *March* 6th–*April* 14th are mainly favourable to the Tory government).

C **Mar:** 3rd, Maine enters the Union as a free state to counteract impending entrance of Missouri as slave state;
6th, 'The Missouri Compromise' is decided by Congress, whereby Missouri to enter Union as slave state, but slavery is to be abolished in the remainder of Louisiana purchase;
7th, Ferdinand VII of Spain is forced to restore the Constitution of 1812 and to abolish Inquisition;
26th, liberty of the individual curtailed in France;
30th, Duc de Richelieu re-establishes censorship of French press.

D **Apr:** 4th, U.S. Land Law abolishes credit system, and establishes minimum price of land at $1·25 per acre.

E **May:** 15th, Final Act of the Conference at Vienna under Metternich (meeting since *Nov.* 1819) is passed authorising the German Confederation to interfere in the affairs of those states unable to maintain public order and the principles of despotic government (this is passed as law by Frankfurt Diet, *June* 8th).

F **Jun:** 6th, Caroline, Princess of Wales, whom George IV wishes to divorce, triumphantly enters London, demanding her recognition as Queen;
New electoral law in France regulates electoral colleges and introduces system of 'double-voting', resulting in increased strength of the Right.

G **Jul:** 2nd, revolt begins in Naples, due to misrule of Ferdinand IV, at the instigation of the Carbonari and other secret societies, resulting in promise of Constitution similar to that in Spain (by royal decree, 7th);
5th, Bill of Pains and Penalties against Princess Caroline, to deprive her of titles and to dissolve her marriage to King George IV, is introduced in Parliament.

H **Aug:** 24th, revolution in Portugal begins in Oporto and spreads to Lisbon (29th), caused by discontent at King John VI living in Brazil and at the Regency under English influence; the leaders demand a constitution.

J **Sep:** 29th, birth of Comte de Chambord as heir to French throne (son of late Duc de Berry).

K **Oct:** 23rd, Conference at Troppau begins to discuss policy against revolutionary tendencies in Europe and is attended by Austria, Russia, and Prussia, and by plenipotentiaries from France and Britain.

O **Politics, Economics, Law and Education**
J. R. Malthus, *Principles of Political Economy.*
J. J. von Görres, *Germany and the Revolution.*

P **Science, Technology, Discovery, etc.**
André Ampère's laws of electro-dynamic action.
Regent's Canal, London.
Rich deposits of platinum discovered in Urals.
First iron steamship.

Q **Scholarship**

R **Philosophy and Religion**
Thomas Brown, *Lectures on the Philosophy of the Human Mind.*
Thomas Erskine, *Internal Evidence for the Truth of Revealed Religion.*

S **Art, Sculpture, Fine Arts and Architecture**
William Blake's illustrations to the Book of Job.
John Constable, *Harwich Lighthouse* (painting).
Bertel Thorwaldsen, *The Lion of Lucerne* (sculpture).
The Vénus de Milo is discovered.

T **Music**
Franz Schubert, Wanderer fantasia.
G. Meyerbeer, *Margherita d'Anjou* (opera).

U **Literature**
Washington Irving, *The Sketch Book of Geoffrey Cravon Gent.*
John Keats, *The Eve of St. Agnes* and *Ode to a Nightingale.*
Alphonse de Lamartine, *Méditations poétiques.*
C. Lamb, *Essays of Elia* (–23).
Alexander Pushkin, *Ruslan and Ludmila.*
P. B. Shelley, *Prometheus Unbound* and *Ode to the West Wind.*
Walter Scott, *Ivanhoe.*

V **The Press**
John Bull founded.

W **Drama and Entertainment**
Edmund Kean acts Richard III in New York (revisits U.S. in 1825–6).

X **Sport**

Y **Statistics**

1820 (Nov.–Dec.)

L **Nov**: 10th, Bill against Queen Caroline is dropped and inquiry into her conduct also ends, due in part to popular sympathy for her;

19th, Preliminary Protocol issued by Austria, Russia and Prussia at Troppau, expelling those nations undergoing revolutions from the Concert of Europe and allowing other States to intervene to crush revolts by force if necessary (an agreement repudiated by Britain, *Dec.* 16th);

23rd, to avoid embarrassing discussions over Queen Caroline, Parliament is prorogued;

25th, temporary truce is concluded between Spain and Colombia as Ferdinand VII is faced with revolution, but he still refuses to uphold Colombian independence under Simon Bolivar so that war is soon resumed.

M **Dec**: 17th, Conference at Troppau is adjourned until *Jan.* 1821 when the powers are to meet at Laibach.

George Canning resigns from Lord Liverpool's Cabinet, after disagreeing with treatment of Queen Caroline.

N

z **Births and Deaths**

Feb. 28th John Tenniel b. (–1914).
Apr. 27th Herbert Spencer b. (–1900).
May 12th Florence Nightingale b. (–1910).
Sept. 16th Francis Parkman b. (–1893).
— Friedrich Engels b. (–1895).

1821 (Jan.–Jun.) Greek War of Independence begins—Independence of Mexico and Peru—First Free-Trade Legislation in Britain

A **Jan:** 12th, European powers meet at Laibach (–*May* 12th);
23rd, when Parliament reopens Queen Caroline is granted annuity of £50,000 and a house;
26th, Portuguese Cortes are established and discuss basis of Constitution whereby feudalism and the Inquisition are to be abolished; a single elective Chamber is to be established and the King is to have only a suspensory vote (this basis is decreed *May* 9th).

B **Feb:** 13th, at Laibach, Austria agrees to Ferdinand IV's request to send army into Naples to suppress revolt;
24th, John VI of Portugal promises to introduce equitable clauses of Portuguese Constitution into Brazil;
24th, proposals for independence of Mexico from Spain, and for the future of its government, are drawn up under Vicente Guerrero.

C **Mar:** 5th, James Monroe begins second term as U.S. President;
6th, revolt in Moldavia (after earlier outbreak in Wallachia in *Feb.*) against oppressive rule of the Turks; the rebels appeal to Tsar Alexander I for help, thus beginning Greek War of Independence;
7th, Neapolitan rebels are crushed at Rieti by the Austrians (who enter Naples, 23rd, and restore Ferdinand IV to the throne);
10th, Revolution, influenced by the Carbonari, begins in Piedmont to put Charles Albert Carignan on the throne;
13th, Victor Emmanuel of Piedmont abdicates and proclaims his brother Charles Felix, not Charles Albert, as his successor;
16th, Charles Felix issues decree forcing Charles Albert to renounce claim to throne of Piedmont.

D **Apr:** 8th, Austrian army intervenes in Piedmont and defeats supporters of Charles Albert at Novara;
17th, Roman Catholic Removal of Disability Bill is defeated in House of Lords on second reading;
22nd, John VI of Portugal issues decree in Brazil (confirming earlier decree of *Mar.* 27th) to agree to Regency there under his son and to remove the main government to Lisbon.
22nd, after several outbreaks in the Morea, in which the Greeks massacre Turks, the Greek Patriarch of Constantinople is murdered by the Turks as a reprisal, and a reign of terror begins.

E **May:** 7th, by Act of Parliament the Bank of England resumes cash payments two years earlier than previously stipulated, to avoid making drain on gold supplies of other countries;
7th, Africa Company is dissolved because of heavy expenses incurred, and Sierra Leone, Gambia, and Gold Coast are taken over by the British government to form British West Africa;
9th, Lord John Russell's motion for parliamentary reform is rejected;
28th, repeal of customs duties on certain timber imports begins British free trade legislation.

F **Jun:** 19th, Turks defeat Greek rebels at Dragashan;
24th, Simon Bolivar ensures independence of Venezuela by defeating Spanish army at Carabobo, but the subsequent Constitution of the Cortes severely curtails power of the President.

O **Politics, Economics, Law and Education**

George Grote, *Statement of the Question of Parliamentary Reform.*
J. J. von Görres, *Europe and the Revolution.*
James Mill, *Elements of Political Economy.*
Comte de St.-Simon, *Du Système industriel.*

P **Science, Technology, Discovery, etc.**

Michael Faraday discovers electromagnetic rotation.
T. J. Seebeck discovers thermo-electricity.
First international congress on biology.

Q **Scholarship**

École des Chartes, Paris, founded for the study of historical documents.

R **Philosophy and Religion**

G. W. Hegel, *Philosophy of Right.*
B. Neibuhr brings about a concordat between Prussia and the Papacy.

S **Art, Sculpture, Fine Arts and Architecture**

John Constable, *Hay Wain* (painting).

T **Music**

C. M. von Weber, *Der Freischütz* (opera).

U **Literature**

James Fenimore Cooper, *The Spy.*
Thomas de Quincey, *Confessions of an English Opium Eater.*
John Galt, *Annals of the Parish.*
J. W. Goethe, *Wilhelm Meisters Wanderjahre.*
W. Hazlitt, *Table Talk* (–22).
Heinrich Heine, *Poems.*
Alessandro Manzoni, *Il Cinque Maggio.*
Walter Scott, *Kenilworth.*
P. B. Shelley, *Adonais.*
John Bowring's *Specimens of the Russian Poets* introduces Russian literature to England.

V **The Press**

Manchester Guardian founded.

W **Drama and Entertainment**

X **Sport**

Y **Statistics**

Populations (in millions): France, 30·4; Great Britain, 20·8 (of which Ireland, 6·8); Italian states, 18; Austria, 12; U.S. 9·6; combined populations of Prussia, Bavaria, Saxony, the duchies, principalities and free cities of Germany, 26·1.
Coal Production: U.K. 8 mill. tons; U.S. 3,650 tons.

1821 (Jul.–Dec.)

G Jul: 19th, Coronation of George IV, but Queen Caroline not admitted to ceremony;
26th, relations severed between Turkey and Russia, after Turks' refusal to protect Christian subjects;
28th, Independence of Peru from Spain formally proclaimed.

H Aug: 7th, Queen Caroline dies;
10th, Missouri finally becomes member of the Union as a slave state (see *Mar.* 6th 1820).

J Sep: 15th, Guatemala is declared independent of Spain and aligns itself with Mexico;
29th, Portuguese Cortes decrees that King John's earlier acts with regard to Brazil are repealed and recalls the Regent in an attempt to reintroduce old colonial system.

K Oct: 5th, Greeks take Tripolitza in the Morea and massacre the Turkish population there.

L Nov: 28th, Panama is declared independent of Spain and joins Republic of Colombia.

M Dec: 1st, Republic of San Domingo is established independent of Spain;
12th, Duc de Richelieu succeeded by Jean Villèle in France, ending the rule of the Right Centre, and leading to a period of reaction under the Ultra-Conservatives.

N

z **Births and Deaths**

Feb. 23rd John Keats d. (26).
Feb. 26th Joseph de Maistre d. (66).
Apr. 9th Charles Pierre Baudelaire b. (–1867).
May 5th Napoleon I d. (52).
July 16th Mary Baker Eddy b. (–1910).
Aug. 31st Hermann Helmholtz b. (–1894).
Oct. 30th Feodor Dostoievsky b. (–1881).
Nov. 21st Henry Thomas Buckle b. (–1862).
Dec. 12th Gustave Flaubert b. (–1880).

1822 Brazil becomes independent of Portugal—Turks massacre Greeks at Chios

A **Jan:** 13th, liberal republican Constitution is adopted in Greece;
17th, Robert Peel enters Lord Liverpool's Cabinet as home secretary.
27th, Greek independence formally proclaimed.

B **Feb:** 5th, the assassination of Ali of Janina enables the Porte to concentrate forces against Greeks.

C **Mar:** 17th, in France new press law prohibits sale of newspapers unless they are approved by government, requiring offenders to be tried in royal courts, where magistrates take orders from government officials.

D **Apr:** 22nd, Turkish fleet captures island of Chios and massacres Christian inhabitants or sells them as slaves.

E **May:** 19th, Augustus de Iturbide is elected Emperor of Mexico by the Constitutional Congress.

F **Jun:** 18th, Greeks set fire to Turkish admiral's vessel, as reprisal for atrocities in Chios, and the rest of the fleet scatters;
24th, partial repeal of British Navigation Acts allows foreign ships to bring goods from European ports, provided that the ship is registered in the port in question; also opens up West Indies trade with the U.S.;
President of Council of French universities placed in charge of all education and of all teachers, a notable victory for Clerical party.

G **Jul:** 15th, Corn Law is amended, reducing price at which foreign wheat may enter Britain from 80 shillings to 70 shillings per quarter and fixing a sliding scale of duties (this Act never becomes effective).
Turkish invasion of Greece begins; the Turks overrun peninsula north of Gulf of Corinth (but are later forced to retreat).

H **Aug:** 12th, Lord Castlereagh commits suicide (aged 82).

J **Sep:** 16th, George Canning succeeds Castlereagh as Foreign Secretary and as leader of the House of Commons;
23rd, Portuguese Constitution is decreed, providing for liberty, legal equality, a single Chamber which the King may not dissolve until its period of four years has expired, and a constitutional monarchy.

K **Oct:** 12th, Brazil becomes formally independent of Portugal and Dom Pedro is proclaimed Emperor.
20th, Congress of Verona opens, attended by representatives of Austria, Prussia, France, Russia and Britain, for whom the Duke of Wellington is plenipotentiary, to discuss European problems.

L **Nov:** 19th, French plan for intervention in Spain is tentatively accepted by other powers at Verona after opposition from Austria, Prussia and Britain to an outright invasion by Louis XVIII; France may intervene in Spain if attacked or if the Spanish rebels depose Ferdinand VII.

M **Dec:** 2nd, San Salvador, Bahamas, not wishing to be united with Mexico, asks for incorporation with U.S.;
14th, Congress of Verona ends, having ignored Greek War of Independence;
—, Bottle Riots in Dublin, where Viceroy of Ireland is attacked by Orangemen, the violent element of Irish Protestants.

N Liberia is founded as a colony for freed American slaves.

O Politics, Economics, Law and Education

Francis Place, *Illustrations . . . of the Principles of Population*, advocates birth control.

P Science, Technology, Discovery, etc.

F. Fournier de Pescay, *Théorie Analytique de la Chaleur*.
J. V. Poncelet, *Traité des Propriétés projectives les figures*.
German Association for Science, founded by Oken, meets at Leipzig.
A. J. Fresnel perfects lenses for lighthouses.
Beaumont begins study of digestion in exposed human stomach.
Streets of Boston, Mass., lit by gas.

Q Scholarship

H. T. Colebrooke founds Royal Asiatic Society for study of eastern languages.

R Philosophy and Religion

S Art, Sculpture, Fine Arts and Architecture

F. Delacroix, *Dante and Virgil Crossing the Styx* (painting).
John Martin, *Destruction of Herculaneum* (painting).

T Music

L. van Beethoven, Mass in D (op. 123).
Franz Schubert, Symphony No. 8 in B minor ('Unfinished').
Royal Academy of Music, London, founded.
Franz Liszt, aged eleven, makes début as pianist in Vienna.

U Literature

Washington Irving, *Bracebridge Hall, or the Humourist*.
Alexander Pushkin, *Eugenie Onegin* (–32).
Esias Tegner, *Axel*.
Alfred de Vigny, *Poèmes*.
Stendhal (pseud.), *De l'amour*, which sells only 17 copies in 11 years.

V The Press

The *Sunday Times* founded.

W Drama and Entertainment

X Sport

Y Statistics

U.K. Textiles trade:

raw cotton imports	145 mill. lb.
exports of cottons	304 mill. yds.
exports of woollens	1·7 mill. pieces.
exports of linen	33·8 mill. yds.
exports of silks	287,000 lb.

Z Births and Deaths

Mar. 24th Henri Murger b. (–1861).
Apr. 27th Ulysses Grant b. (–1885).
May 26th Edmond de Goncourt b. (–1896).
July 8th Percy Bysshe Shelley d. (29).
July 24th Ernst Hoffmann d. (46).
Aug. 25th William Herschel d. (88).
Oct. 13th Antonio Canova d. (64).
Dec. 10th César Franck b. (–1895).
Dec. 24th Matthew Arnold b. (–1888).

A Jan: 31st, William Huskisson enters British Cabinet as President of Board of Trade;
Russia, Austria, France, and Prussia demand abolition of Spanish Constitution of 1812, but Cortes refuses so that ambassadors of those countries leave Madrid.

B Feb:

C Mar: 19th, Augustus de Iturbide forced to abdicate in Mexico (and Mexico becomes a republic, *Oct.* 1824);
25th, British government recognises Greeks as belligerents in war with Turkey.

D Apr: 6th, French army crosses the Bidassoa and war with Spain begins.

E May: 12th, Warehousing of Goods Act allows foreigners to deposit goods for import in British warehouses without payment of duty, a victory for free trade principles;
12th, Catholic Association established in Ireland by Daniel O'Connell, virtually taking over government.

F Jun: 11th, Ferdinand VII of Spain refuses to leave Madrid in the face of French invasion and is declared to be temporarily incapacitated, a provisional Regency of the Cortes being established;
18th, John VI annuls Portuguese Constitution of 1822 after risings against his rule and against the loss of Brazil.

G Jul: 1st, Guatemala, San Salvador, Nicaragua, Honduras and Costa Rica form the Confederation of United Provinces of Central America;
4th, Robert Peel allows employment of transported convicts in colonies instead of placing them in hulks;
10th, British Act, due largely to Peel, sets pattern for prison reform;
14th, Switzerland refuses to grant asylum to foreign refugees;
18th, further British duties are repealed to modify Navigation Acts, providing equality of rights for all nations reciprocating these concessions, in order to develop trade.

H Aug: 31st, the French storm the Trocadero, and enter Cadiz.

J Sep: 10th, Simon Bolivar, having landed in Peru, is recognised as dictator and prepares to meet Royalist forces (he is formally proclaimed Emperor *Feb.* 10th 1824).

K Oct: 1st, Ferdinand VII of Spain, having been restored by the French who have crushed Spanish rebellion, issues Decree for execution of his enemies and reign of tyranny begins.

L Nov: 13th, Dom Pedro dissolves Brazilian Assembly after several conspiracies against him, and a Council of State is subsequently established to draw up a Constitution for Brazil.

M Dec: 2nd, Monroe Doctrine excludes European powers from interfering in politics of American Republics and closes American continent to colonial settlements by them.

N Provincial Diets are established in Prussia.

O **Politics, Economics, Law and Education**
William Huskisson begins to reduce British tariff.
Death penalty abolished for over 100 crimes in Britain.
Comte de St.-Simon, *Catéchisme des Industriels* (–24).
George Birkbeck founds Mechanics' Institute.

P **Science, Technology, Discovery, etc.**
Michael Faraday liquefies chlorine.
G. Amici observes pollen approaching plant ovary.
The Lancet first issued.
Charles Babbage begins construction of calculating machine.
Charles Macintosh invents waterproof fabric.
Lake Chad, Central Africa, discovered by Walter Oudney on an expedition from Tripoli.

Q **Scholarship**
George IV presents his father's library to British Museum.
Louis Thiers, *Histoire de la Révolution française* (–27).

R **Philosophy and Religion**
Friedrich Schleiermacher, *Christian Dogma*.

S **Art, Sculpture, Fine Arts and Architecture**
Jean Ingres, *La Source* (painting).
Louis Lebas, Notre Dame-de-Lorette, Paris.
Robert Smirke, General Post Office, St. Martin's-le-Grand, and British Museum (–47).

T **Music**
Franz Schubert, incidental music to *Rosamunde*.
Carl von Weber, *Euryanthe* (opera).
Sébastien Érard makes a grand piano with double escapement.

U **Literature**
James Fenimore Cooper, *The Pioneers* (first of the 'Leather-stocking' novels).
Alphonse de Lamartine, *Nouvelles Méditations Poétiques*.
Stendhal (pseud.), *Racine et Shakespeare* (–25).
The *Forget-me-not*, the first English illustrated annual.

V **The Press**

W **Drama and Entertainment**
Oxford Union Society founded.

X **Sport**

Y **Statistics**

Z **Births and Deaths**
Feb. 27th Ernest Renan b. (–1892).
Aug. 2nd Edward Augustus Freeman b. (–1892).
Aug. 11th Charlotte M. Yonge b. (–1901).

1824 Anglo-Burmese War

A Jan:

B Feb: 24th, Governor-General of India declares war against Burmese after the latter have violated territory of East India Company by capturing island of Shahpuri.

C Mar: 27th, Decree in Brazil for election of deputies to legislative assembly.

D Apr: 17th, frontier treaty, between Russia and U.S., defining respective rights in Pacific Ocean and on north-west coast of America;
19th, Lord Byron dies at Missolonghi (aged 36) aiding Greeks against Turkey;
30th, garrison of Lisbon revolts against John VI and recognises his younger son, Dom Miguel, as ruler;
Crete is captured by Egyptians.

E May: 3rd, John VI of Portugal sanctions son's actions but
9th, boards British warship, repudiates this decree and re-asserts his authority;
11th, British take Rangoon.

F Jun:

G Jul: in war with the Greeks, Turkey captures island of Ipsara.

H Aug: 6th, Simon Bolivar defeats Spanish forces at Junin in Peru.

J Sep: 16th, Louis XVIII dies and is succeeded by Charles X (–1830).
29th, Press Law, censoring French press (of *Mar.* 30th, 1820) suspended, but Charles' policy is generally illiberal.

K Oct: Greeks nearly annihilate Turks at Mitylene.

L Nov: in U.S. presidential election none of the four candidates has a majority; House of Representatives elect John Adams as president.

M Dec: 9th, at Battle of Ayacucho, Peru, the Spanish army is defeated and agrees to leave South America, 12th;
31st, George Canning recognises the independence of Buenos Aires, Mexico and Colombia, thus countering the Monroe Doctrine (of *Dec.* 2nd 1823).

N

O Politics, Economics, Law and Education

Repeal of the Combinations Acts of 1799–1800, due largely to Francis Place and Joseph Hume (*June* 21st), permits British workers to combine.

P Science, Technology, Discovery, etc.

Nicolas Carnot, *Puissance motrice du Feu*, a pioneer study of thermodynamics.
C. Prevost and J. B. Dumas show that the sperm is essential to fertilisation.
Joseph Aspdin makes Portland cement.

Q Scholarship

Philip Böckh edits *Corpus Inscriptionum Graecum* (–59).
Leopold von Ranke's *History of the Roman and Teutonic People, 1494–1514*, founds modern historiography.
Carlo Botta, *History of Italy*.
Sequoyah invents the Cherokee alphabet.

R Philosophy and Religion

J. F. Herbart, *Psychology as a Science* (–25).
American Sunday School Union founded.

S Art, Sculpture, Fine Arts and Architecture

Eugène Delacroix, *Les Massacres de Chios* (painting).
Jean Ingres, *Vow of Louis XIII* (painting).
John Flaxman, *Pastoral Apollo* (sculpture).
J. F. Overbeck, *Entry of Christ into Jerusalem* (painting).
National Gallery, London, founded with the collection of J. J. Angerstein.
Jeffry Wyatville, royal apartments, Windsor Castle (–28).
K. F. Schinkel, Atlas Museum, Berlin.

T Music

L. van Beethoven's 9th ('Choral') Symphony performed in Vienna; quartets (op. 127, 130, 131 and 135).

U Literature

W. S. Landor, *Imaginary Conversations* (–37).
Count Leopardi, *Canzoni e Versi*.
Mary Mitford, *Our Village* (–32).
Walter Scott, *Redgauntlet*.

V The Press

Westminster Review founded by J. Bentham.
Le Globe, Paris, issued.

W Drama and Entertainment

X Sport

Y Statistics

Z Births and Deaths

Mar. 2nd Friedrich Smetana b. (–1884).
June 26th William Thomson, Lord Kelvin b. (–1907).
Aug. 8th Friedrich August Wolf d. (65).
Sept. 4th Anton Bruckner b. (–1896).

1825 Independence of Bolivia and Uruguay—British Navigation Acts are modified

A **Jan:** 4th, Ferdinand I (IV) of Naples dies and is succeeded by Francis I.

B **Feb:** 24th, Egyptian forces land in the Morea, after call for help from Porte, and begin to subdue peninsula;
28th, Anglo-Russian Treaty over the latter's territory on north-west coast of America, and over respective rights in Pacific Ocean (similar to U.S.-Russian Treaty *Apr.* 17th 1824).

C **Mar:** 4th, John Quincy Adams is inaugurated sixth President of U.S.

D **Apr:** 15th, French law makes sacrilege a capital offence;
27th, French law of indemnity compensates nobles for losses in French Revolution.

E **May:** 17th, Roman Catholic Relief Bill rejected by House of Lords on second reading.

F **Jun:** 22nd, Act to regulate Cotton Mills and Factories, with particular regard to young people, is passed, whereby no one under sixteen years is to work more than twelve-hour day, excluding time for meals;
Greeks put forward proposals to place themselves under British protection (which are passed by Greek Provisional government, *July* 24th, but subsequently rejected by British government).

G **Jul:** 5th, Acts of Parliament passed modifying Navigation Acts permitting European goods to enter Britain in ships of country of origin;
6th, because of strikes and industrial disorder, the legislation repealing Anti-Combination Acts (*June* 21st 1824) is amended so that, although trade unions are still recognised as legal, violence is prohibited, which has effect of prohibiting strike action.

H **Aug:** 6th, Bolivia (Upper Peru) becomes independent of Peru;
25th, Uruguay becomes independent of Brazil;
29th, Portugal recognises Brazilian independence under Dom Pedro.

J **Sep:** 19th, Hungarian Diet reopened after 13 years, and Austrian Emperor, in face of discontent in Hungary, agrees to triennial meetings.

K **Oct:**

L **Nov:**

M **Dec:** 1st, Tsar Alexander I dies (aged 47) and is succeeded by Nicholas I, his younger son (–1855).
10th, Brazil declares war against Argentina over question of Uruguay;
26th, Decembrist Rising in Russian army, aiming at assembly of national representatives, is easily crushed.

N

O **Politics, Economics, Law and Education**

Rapid expansion of trade unions in Britain.

Hungarian Academy of Sciences, Budapest, founded.

P **Science, Technology, Discovery, etc.**

Michael Faraday isolates benzene.

J. F. Herschel invents actinometer for measuring the heat of the sun's rays.

W. E. and E. H. Weber, *Treatise on Magnetic Waves.*

Stockton and Darlington railway is opened.

Q **Scholarship**

Lord Macaulay's 'Essay on Milton' in *Edinburgh Review.*

Augustin Thierry, *Histoire de la Conquête d'Angleterre par les Normands.*

R **Philosophy and Religion**

Joe Smith, founder of Mormons, claims he had his vision.

Comte de St.-Simon, *Nouveau Christianisme.*

S **Art, Sculpture, Fine Arts and Architecture**

Samuel Morse, *Lafayette* (painting).

Thomas Cole founds Hudson River School of landscape painting, New York.

Cornelius's frescoes in Ludwigskirche, Munich.

John Nash, Buckingham Palace.

T **Music**

L. van Beethoven, *Grosse Fuge*; 9th Symphony first performed in England by Philharmonic Society who commissioned it.

Franz Schubert, 'Death and the Maiden' quartet (–26).

U **Literature**

W. Hazlitt, *The Spirit of the Age: or Contemporary Portraits*

Alessandro Manzoni, *I Promessi Sposi.*

Alexander Pushkin, *Boris Godunov.*

Esias Tegner, *Frithjofs Saga.*

V **The Press**

W **Drama and Entertainment**

X **Sport**

Y **Statistics**

U.K. total state expenditure, £55·5 mill.

U.K. iron production, 581,367 tons.

Z **Births and Deaths**

Apr. 11th Ferdinand Lassalle b. (–1864).

May 4th Thomas Henry Huxley b. (–1895).

June 21st William Stubbs b. (–1901).

Oct. 10th Stephanis Johannes Paulus Kruger b. (–1904).

Oct. 25th Johann Strauss b. (–1899).

Nov. 14th Jean Paul Friedrich Richter ('Jean Paul'), d. (62).

Nov. 29th Jean Martin Charcot b. (–1893).

Dec. 29th Jacques Louis David d. (76).

1826 St. Petersburg Protocol for Autonomy of Greece—Russo-Persian war begins

A Jan:

B Feb: 24th, by treaty of Yandabu, ending Burmese War, Burmese pay indemnity and British resident is established at Ava.

C Mar: 10th, John VI of Portugal dies, succeeded by Dom Pedro of Brazil as Peter IV;
25th, promulgation of Brazilian Constitution with hereditary monarchy and general assembly of two chambers (which convenes *May* 6th).

D Apr: 4th, St. Petersburg Protocol between Britain and Russia respecting Greek problem, on the basis of complete autonomy of Greece under Turkish suzerainty (but does not become treaty until *July* 6th 1827 when France also joins);
5th, Russian ultimatum to Turkey over Serbia and Danubian Provinces;
22nd, Ibrahim, son of Mohammed Ali of Egypt, takes Missolonghi after long siege;
29th, liberal Constitution promulgated in Portugal for a hereditary monarchy with legislative power in hands of Cortes of two Chambers (which meets *Oct.* 30th).

E May: 2nd, Peter IV waives right of accession to Portuguese throne, in order to remain in Brazil; his daughter Maria is to become queen, provided Dom Miguel, his brother, marries her.

F Jun: 19th, Decree by Mahmud II, Sultan of Turkey, for dissolution of corps of janissaries after week of rioting;
20th, treaty of commerce between Siam and Britain, whereby Perak and Selangor are independent, Kedah becomes Siamese territory and Britain obtains Isle of Pangkor and Sembilan Islands;
22nd, Pan-American Congress meets in Panama under influence of Simon Bolivar in effort to unite American Republics (ends without effect *July* 15th).

G Jul:

H Aug:

J Sep: 28th, Russia declares war against Persia over latter's encroachment in Transcaucasia.

K Oct: 7th, Akkerman Convention (as result of Tsar's ultimatum to Sultan in *Apr.*) settles problem of Danubian Provinces and of Serbia to the advantage of Russia.

L Nov:

M Dec: George Canning's agreement to send troops to Portugal, to counteract Spanish threat of invasion in support of Dom Miguel, who is trying to obtain throne from Maria;
19th, treaty of commerce between Prussia and Mecklenburg-Schwerin develops the idea of the *Zollverein*.

N Secret authorisation from Charles X allows Jesuits to return to France and teach in State seminaries.

O **Politics, Economics, Law and Education**
University College, London, and Munich University founded.

P **Science, Technology, Discovery, etc.**
André Ampère, *Electrodynamics.*
Alcohol is synthesised.
Leopoldo Nobili invents galvanometer.
Stamford Raffles founds Royal Zoological Society, London.
First railway tunnel (Liverpool-Manchester railway).

Q **Scholarship**
G. H. Pertz, under H. F. K. Stein's direction, edits *Monumenta Germaniae Historica.*

R **Philosophy and Religion**

S **Art, Sculpture, Fine Arts and Architecture**
F. W. Schadow becomes director of Düsseldorf Art Gallery.
U.S. National Academy of Design founded.

T **Music**
C. von Weber, *Oberon* (opera).
F. Mendelssohn, music for *A Midsummer Night's Dream.*

U **Literature**
E. B. Browning, *Essay on Mind, with Other Poems.*
James Fenimore Cooper, *The Last of the Mohicans.*
Alfred De Vigny, *Cinq Mars.*
Benjamin Disraeli, *Vivian Grey* (–27).
Heinrich Heine, *Pictures of Travel*, I.
Walter Scott, *Woodstock.*

V **The Press**

W **Drama and Entertainment**

X **Sport**

Y **Statistics**
U.K. registered tonnage of merchant shipping 2,411,000 tons (24,000 tons steamships).

Z **Births and Deaths**
Feb. 3rd Walter Bagehot b. (–1877).
Mar. 29th Johann H. Voss d. (75).
Apr. 6th Gustave Moreau b. (–1898).
June 5th Carl von Weber d. (39).
July 4th Thomas Jefferson d. (73).

A **Jan:** 26th, Peru secedes from Colombia in protest against Simon Bolivar's alleged tyranny;
British forces arrive at Lisbon in support of Portuguese Queen Maria.

B **Feb:** 17th, Lord Liverpool suffers a stroke and is forced to resign as Prime Minister;
20th, Brazilian forces defeated at battle of Ituziango by combined army of Uruguay and Argentina.

C **Mar:**

D **Apr:** 4th, Note from Russia, France and Britain to Sultan urging a truce in war with Greece;
10th, George Canning forms ministry of liberal Tories and moderate Whigs;
17th, French law to censor press is rejected by Peers;
29th, dissolution of French National Guard by decree of Charles X after unrest, a decision unpopular among the middle classes who dominated those forces;
Count Capo d'Istria elected President of Greece.

E **May:**

F **Jun:** 5th, Turks capture the Acropolis and enter Athens;
9th, Turkish Manifesto rejects allied Note (of *Apr.* 4th) for truce with Greece;
18th, Concordat between Netherlands and Pope Leo XII allowing the Dutch a preponderance in church affairs;
21st, Robert Peel reforms criminal law, by reducing number of capital offences, abolishing immunity of clergy from arrest in cases of felony, and by defining law of offences against property in a simplified form;
24th, Jean Villèle secures royal ordinance to censor French press.

G **Jul:** 3rd, Decree of Brazilian Emperor appointing Dom Miguel lieutenant of Portugal;
6th, Treaty of London whereby Russia, Britain, and France agree to recognise autonomy of Greece and to force truce on Sultan.

H **Aug:** 8th, death of George Canning (aged 56);
16th, Sultan rejects Note of Russian, French and British ambassadors demanding truce and power to negotiate is now placed in hands of admirals of the respective allied fleets;
31st, Lord Goderich forms Tory administration in Britain.

J **Sep:**

K **Oct:** 1st, Russia defeats Persian forces and takes Erivan in Armenia;
20th, Turkish and Egyptian fleets are destroyed at Battle of Navarino by allied squadrons (the Egyptians having arrived *Sept.*).

L **Nov:** 17th and 24th, in the French elections the Ultra-Conservatives are defeated by Liberal opposition.

M **Dec:** 8th (–12th), allied ambassadors leave Constantinople;
26th, Sultan Mahmud II rejects right of allies to mediate in war with Greece.

N

O **Politics, Economics, Law and Education**
Henry Brougham founds Society for the Diffusion of Useful Knowledge.

P **Science, Technology, Discovery, etc.**
George Ohm formulates Ohm's Law.
Friedrich Wöhler obtains metallic aluminium.
Joseph Niepce produces photographs on a metal plate.
Karl von Baer, *Epistola de Ova Mammalium et Hominis Generis.*
Joseph Ressel invents the ship's screw.
Friction matches ('Lucifers') introduced.

Q **Scholarship**
Henry Hallam, *Constitutional History of England.*

R **Philosophy and Religion**
John Keble, *The Christian Year.*
John Darby secedes from Church of England to found Plymouth Brethren.

S **Art, Sculpture, Fine Arts and Architecture**
John Constable, *The Cornfield* (painting).
J. M. W. Turner, *Ulysses Deriding Polyphemus* (painting).

T **Music**
Franz Schubert, *Die Winterreise.*
G. Bellini, *Il Pirata* (opera).

U **Literature**
John Clare, *The Shepherd's Calendar.*
Heinrich Heine, *Buch der Lieder.*
Giacomo Leopardi, *Operette morali.*
[E. A. Poe], *Tamerlane.*
[A. and C. Tennyson], *Poems by Two Brothers.*

V **The Press**
The Evening Standard, London, founded.

W **Drama and Entertainment**

X **Sport**

Y **Statistics**

Z **Births and Deaths**
Mar. 5th Pierre Simon Laplace d. (77), and Alessandro Volta d. (82).
Mar. 26th Ludwig van Beethoven d. (56).
Apr. 2nd William Holman Hunt b. (–1910).
Apr. 5th Joseph Lister b. (–1912).
Oct. 10th Ugo Foscolo d. (49).
Oct. 16th Arnold Böcklin b. (–1901).

1828 Repeal of British Test and Corporation Acts—Russo-Turkish War begins

A Jan: 3rd, Jean Villèle resigns as French Prime Minister after election defeats (*Nov.* 1827) and Vicomte de Martignac succeeds, 5th, forming administration of moderates;
18th, commercial treaty between Bavaria and Württemberg abolishes customs duties on their common frontier;
25th, Duke of Wellington forms Tory administration, following resignation of Goderich, 8th, on question of appointing chairman of finance committee.

B Feb: 22nd, Peace of Turkmanchai by which Persia cedes part of Armenia, including Erivan, to Russia;
26th, Dom Miguel takes oath as Regent of Portugal.

C Mar: 3rd, Peter IV abdicates as King of Portugal.

D Apr: 14th, new press law in France suppresses censorship, but press trials are still held in government-influenced tribunals and are not conducted by juries;
26th, Russia declares war on Turkey;
British troops recalled by Duke of Wellington from Portugal.

E May: 9th, repeal of British Test and Corporation Acts so that Catholic and Protestant Nonconformists now allowed to hold public office in Britain;
29th, William Huskisson resigns as Secretary of State for War and the Colonies after friction with Wellington;
—, 'Tariff of Abominations' passed by Congress in attempt to make U.S. economically self-sufficient by obstructing and prohibiting entry of foreign goods and materials.

F Jun: 16th, attack on French Jesuits by Vicomte de Martignac, who prohibits religious orders from teaching unless sanctioned by State;
23rd, Dom Miguel is proclaimed King of Portugal, following peaceful *coup d'état*;
30th, in the Clare Election Daniel O'Connell stands as a Roman Catholic candidate (and is elected *July* 4th).

G Jul: 15th, new Corn Law allowing imports of corn at any price and using sliding scale;
19th, London Protocol issued by Britain, Russia, and France, allowing France to intervene in the Morea to evacuate hostile troops in order to secure Greek independence;
Union of Clerical and Liberal Parties in Belgium after King William I has estranged Clericals by concluding Concordat of 1827.

H Aug: 6th, Mehemet Ali agrees to British admiral's demand to quit Greece;
27th, Uruguay formally proclaimed independent at preliminary peace between Brazil and Argentina.

J Sep:

K Oct: 11th, Russians occupy Varna in war against Turkey.

L Nov: 16th, London Protocol, issued by France, Britain, and Russia, recognises independence of Greece when Morea and Cyclades Isles are guaranteed by those powers;
In U.S. presidential election, Andrew Jackson (178 electoral votes) defeats John Quincy Adams (83 votes).

M Dec:

N Working Men's Party founded in New York.
Prussia forms customs union with Hesse-Darmstadt.

O **Politics, Economics, Law and Education**

Thomas Arnold is appointed headmaster of Rugby School (–41).

P **Science, Technology, Discovery, etc.**

Friedrich Wöhler's synthesis of urea founds organic chemistry.

Niels Abel begins the study of elliptic functions.

Von Baer, *Ueber die Entwickelungsgeschichte der Thiere* (–37), establishes science of comparative embryology.

Q **Scholarship**

J. G. Grimm, *German Legal Antiquities.*

Noah Webster's *Dictionary.*

W. F. P. Napier, *History of Peninsular War* (–40).

R **Philosophy and Religion**

Dugald Stewart, *Philosophy of the Active and Moral Powers of Man.*

S. T. Coleridge, *Constitution of Church and State.*

S **Art, Sculpture, Fine Arts and Architecture**

John Constable, *Dedham Vale* (painting).

William Dyce's *Madonna* introduces ideas of 'Nazarener' artists to Britain.

T **Music**

Franz Schubert, C. Major Symphony ('Great') and Klavierstücke.

Daniel Auber, *Masaniello* (opera).

G. Rossini, *Le Comte Ory* (opera).

U **Literature**

Thomas Carlyle's *Essay on Goethe* draws attention of English readers to German literature.

Alexander Pushkin, *Poltava.*

V **The Press**

The Spectator and *Athenaeum* are issued.

W **Drama and Entertainment**

X **Sport**

Y **Statistics**

Z **Births and Deaths**

Feb. 12th George Meredith b. (–1909).
Mar. 20th Henrik Ibsen b. (–1906).
Apr. 13th Josephine Butler b. (–1906).
Apr. 16th Francisco Goya y Lucientes d. (81).
Apr. 21st Hippolyte Taine b. (–1893).
May 12th Dante Gabriel Rossetti b. (–1882).
Aug. 28th Leo Tolstoy b. (–1910).
Nov. 19th Franz Schubert d. (31).

1829 Catholic Emancipation in Britain—Independence of Serbia and Danubian Provinces

A **Jan:**

B **Feb:**

C **Mar:** 4th, Andrew Jackson is inaugurated President of U.S.;
21st, Duke of Wellington challenges Earl of Winchilsea to a duel after latter's criticism of his support for Catholic Relief;
22nd, London Protocol on Greece modifies Protocol of *Nov.* 1828, extending guarantee of powers to include Continental Greece and Island of Euboea.

D **Apr:** 13th, Roman Catholic Relief Bill passes Lords (having passed Commons, *Mar.* 5th) allowing Catholics to sit and vote in Parliament, giving them right of suffrage and making them eligible for all military, civil and corporate offices except those of Regent, Lord Chancellor of England, and Lord Lieutenant of Ireland; they are to take an oath denying the Pope has power to interfere in domestic affairs and recognising Protestant succession.

E **May:** 27th, Prussia finally obtains support for commercial policy from Bavaria and Württemberg.

F **Jun:** 19th, Robert Peel's Act to establish new police force in London and its suburbs.

G **Jul:**

H **Aug:** 6th, dismissal of Vicomte de Martignac in France after alienating both extreme parties by proposals to change electoral law;
8th, Charles X appoints Prince de Polignac Prime Minister in France, an Ultra-Conservative who does not possess the confidence of the Chamber, which constitutes a departure from ministerial responsibility.

J **Sep:** 14th, treaty of Adrianople ends Russo-Turkish War and Sultan Mahmud II recognises London Protocol (*Mar.* 1829) which guarantees territory of Greece, the independence of Danubian Provinces and of Serbia, while Tsar Nicholas I obtains land south of Caucasus.

K **Oct:**

L **Nov:**

M **Dec:**

N

O Politics, Economics, Law and Education

Earl of Surrey, elected for Horsham (*May* 4th), becomes first Roman Catholic M.P.

Robert Peel founds the Metropolitan Police force.

Governor-General Lord Bentinck secures abolition of 'Suttee' in Bengal (extended to Bombay and Madras in 1830).

P Science, Technology, Discovery, etc.

Thomas Graham formulates law on diffusion of gases.

James Nelson invents process for pre-heating the blast air in blast furnaces, to produce very high temperatures.

George Stephenson's *Rocket* wins Liverpool and Manchester Railway competition (*Oct.*).

First steam locomotive runs in U.S. (Baltimore-Ohio, *Aug.* 9th).

Horse-drawn omnibus runs in London.

Q Scholarship

Archaeological Institute, Rome, founded.

F. Guizot, *Histoire de la Civilisation en France*.

H. H. Milman, *History of the Jews*.

R Philosophy and Religion

James Mill, *Analysis of the Human Mind*.

S Art, Sculpture, Fine Arts and Architecture

E. Delacroix, *Sardanapalus* (painting).

T Music

G. Rossini, *William Tell* (opera).

F. Mendelssohn revives interest in Bach's *St. Matthew Passion* through Berlin performance.

F. Damian invents the mouth organ and Charles Wheatstone the concertina.

U Literature

Honoré de Balzac, *Les Chouans* and *La Comédie Humaine* (–48).

William Cobbett, *Advice to a Young Man*.

Alfred de Musset, *Contes d'Espagne et d'Italie*.

Victor Hugo, *Les Orientales*.

[Charles Ste-Beuve], *Joseph Delorme*.

V The Press

Revue des Deux Mondes first issued (re-founded 1831).

W Drama and Entertainment

X Sport

Oxford and Cambridge boat race first rowed.

Y Statistics

Z Births and Deaths

Apr. 10th William Booth b. (–1912).

May 29th Humphry Davy d. (50).

June 8th John Everett Millais b. (–1896).

Sept. 7th Friedrich August Kekulé b. (–1897).

Dec. 18th Jean de Lamarck d. (63).

A Jan: Debate in U.S. Congress between Daniel Webster and Robert Y. Hayne on the nature of the Union, with Hayne supporting state rights.

B Feb: 3rd, at London Conference, Greece is declared independent under the protection of France, Russia and Britain.

C Mar: 18th, Charles X's appointment of Polignac is opposed by French Chambers in the answer to the address from the throne;
29th, Ferdinand VII of Spain publishes law of 1789 which abrogates Salic Law, thus allowing females to be heirs to throne.

D Apr: 27th, Simon Bolivar abdicates as President of Colombia.

E May: 16th, Charles X of France dissolves Chambers and calls for elections;
28th, U.S. act settles controversy between Georgia and Cherokee Indians in order ultimately to settle Indians on land west of the Missouri, if they give up lands east of that river.

F Jun: 26th, George IV dies and is succeeded by William IV (–1837).

G Jul: 5th, French begin invasion of Algeria and take Algiers;
19th, French elections finally held, after delays caused by Charles X, and the Liberal opposition obtains majority;
25th, Charles X issues five ordinances, for controlling press, dissolving Chambers and changing electoral system;
27th (–29th), Revolution in Paris and other areas of France on news of Charles's law;
31st, Louis Philippe is appointed Lieutenant-General of France.

H Aug: 2nd, abdication of Charles X;
7th, Louis Philippe is elected King of France by Chambers, and, 9th, accepts throne (–1848);
14th, Constitutional Charter in France, based on an elective monarchy, allowing for initiation of legislation in Chambers, for the permanent suppression of press censorship, and for end to Catholicism as State religion of France;
25th, Revolution in Belgium, against union with Dutch.

J Sep: 11th, Republic of Ecuador established and granted Constitution by Colombia under which it is to be part of Confederation of Colombia;
15th, William Huskisson killed by train at opening of Liverpool-Manchester Railway;
22nd, Venezuela secedes from Colombia and becomes an independent sovereign state;
Revolts in Saxony, Hesse and Brunswick where rulers are dethroned and constitution granted.

K Oct:

L Nov: 8th, accession of Ferdinand II of Naples on death of Francis I;
15th, Duke of Wellington resigns over the civil list and Lord Grey is asked to form a Liberal-Whig ministry, with Lord Palmerston as Foreign Secretary;
18th, National Congress in Belgium decrees independence;
22nd, Belgian Congress votes for monarchy (but excludes House of Orange, 24th *Nov.*);
29th, insurrection in Poland against Russian domination is brought to a head by intention of Tsar Nicholas to use Polish forces to march into France and Belgium to crush revolts there.

M Dec: 20th, London Conference of Britain, France, Austria, Prussia and Russia agree with Belgium on separation from Holland.

N

O **Politics, Economics, Law and Education**
H. F. R. de Lamennais advocates a free press and religious toleration in France.
F. J. Stahl, *Philosophy of Law*.
Count Mikhail Speranski codifies Russian law (45 vols. with commentaries).
King's College, London, founded.
First epidemic of cholera in Europe.

P **Science, Technology, Discovery, etc.**
Charles Lyell, *Principles of Geology* (–33).
Charles Bell, *The Nervous System of the Human Body*.
Nitrates first shipped from Chile and Peru.
Liverpool-Manchester Railway opened.
Richard and John Lander explore lower course of R. Niger.
Royal Geographic Society, London.
J. J. Audubon, *Birds of America*.

Q **Scholarship**

R **Philosophy and Religion**
Auguste Comte, *Course of Positive Philosophy* (–42).
Roman Catholicism no longer the State religion of France.
Joseph Smith, *Book of Mormon*; a Mormon church is established at Fayette, New York.

S **Art, Sculpture, Fine Arts and Architecture**
Franz Klenze, the Walhalla near Regensburg.
Honoré Daumier's drawings in *La Caricature*.

T **Music**
Hector Berlioz, *Symphonie Fantastique*.
Daniel Auber, *Fra Diavolo* (opera).

U **Literature**
William Cobbett, *Rural Rides*.
Victor Hugo, *Hernani*.
Stendhal (pseud.), *Le Rouge et le Noir*.
Alfred Lord Tennyson, *Poems chiefly Lyrical*.

V **The Press**

W **Drama and Entertainment**

X **Sport**

Y **Statistics**
Emigration from Great Britain to U.S., 1820–30, totals 27,489, and from Ireland to U.S., 54,338.

Z **Births and Deaths**
Jan. 7th Thomas Lawrence d.(60).
Feb. 3rd Robert Cecil, Marquess of Salisbury b. (–1903).
Sept. 8th Frédéric Mistral b. (–1914).
Sept. 18th William Hazlitt d. (51).
Dec. 8th Benjamin Constant d. (63).
Dec. 17th Simon Bolivar d. (47).

1831 (Jan.–Nov.) Separation of Belgium from Holland—Russia suppresses Polish revolt—Britain annexes Mysore

A **Jan**: 5th, a Constitution is granted in Hesse-Cassel;
20th (and 27th), two Protocols by powers in London for separation of Belgium and Holland and for limit of their boundaries, which is accepted by Holland but rejected by Belgium;
25th, Polish Diet declares independence of Poland, dethrones Nicholas and deposes Romanovs.

B **Feb**: 3rd, revolutionary outbreaks in Modena, Parma and Papal States influenced by French Revolution (of *July* 1830), and crisis worsens after election of a reactionary Pope, Gregory XVI;
3rd, Belgians elect French Duc de Nemours King (but this is subsequently rejected by Louis Philippe to prevent outcry in Britain);
7th, Belgian Constitution proclaimed assigning executive power to hereditary king who governs through Ministers, responsible to legislative body, with judiciary independent, and freedom of worship, of education and of the press.

C **Mar**: 8th, Constitution proclaimed in Hanover after unrest since revolution in France (*July* 1830);
21st, First Reform Bill, initiated by Lord John Russell, to redistribute seats and to extend franchise is defeated during committee stage;
Austrian troops enter Italian Peninsula to put down revolts.

D **Apr**: 7th, Pedro I of Brazil abdicates in favour of son, in order to return to Portugal to aid Maria I;
22nd, Dissolution of Parliament by Lord Grey after defeat of Reform Bill. Subsequent election, fought on question of support for whole Bill, gives majority to Whigs.

E **May**: 26th, Polish forces are defeated by Russian army at Ostrolenke.

F **Jun**: 4th, Belgian Congress proclaims Leopold of Saxe-Coburg King;
26th, London Conference issues Eighteen Articles for peace preliminaries between Belgium and Holland as substitute for January Protocols, but these are rejected by Dutch.

G **Jul**:

H **Aug**: 2nd, Dutch troops invade Belgium, but are forced to withdraw, 20th, when French army enters Belgian territory.

J **Sep**: 4th, Saxony is granted Constitution after revolt (of *Sept.* 1830);
8th, Russia takes Warsaw after two-day battle and Polish revolt collapses (Tsar proclaims peace *Oct.* 18th);
21st, Second Reform Bill passes House of Commons (but is rejected by Lords *Oct.* 7th).

K **Oct**: 9th, assassination of Count Capo d'Istria after hostility to his bureaucratic methods in Greece;
14th, London Conference issues Twenty-four Articles, which are rejected by Dutch as too advantageous to Belgians;
Bristol Riots after rejection of Reform Bill.

L **Nov**: 15th, treaty incorporating Twenty-four Articles for separation of Holland and Belgium is accepted by Austria, France, Britain, Prussia, Russia and Belgium (ratified 31 *Jan.* 1832).

O **Politics, Economics, Law and Education**

Ebenezer Elliott, *Corn Law Rhymes*.

William L. Garrison begins publishing *The Liberator*, an abolitionist periodical, in Boston.

P **Science, Technology, Discovery, etc.**

Michael Faraday's electric transformer.

M. Melloni's discoveries in radiant heat through the thermomultiplier.

British Association for the Advancement of Science established.

R. Brown discovers nucleus in plant cells.

Charles Darwin's voyage on the *Beagle* (–36).

Q **Scholarship**

R **Philosophy and Religion**

Alexander Campbell deposed by General Assembly of Church of Scotland for teaching against atonement.

William Miller founds Second Adventists in U.S., predicting the end of the world in 1843.

S **Art, Sculpture, Fine Arts and Architecture**

E. Delacroix, *The Barricade* (painting).

H. Delaroche, *Princes in the Tower* (painting).

'Barbizon School' of artists, including Jean Millet and Pierre Rousseau, first exhibit in the salon.

T **Music**

L. J. F. Hérold, *Zampa* (opera).

V. Bellini, *La Sonnambula* and *Norma* (operas).

U **Literature**

Honoré de Balzac, *Peau de Chagrin* and *Le Chef-d'œuvre inconnu*.

Henri Barbier, *Les Iambes*.

V. Hugo, *Notre-Dame de Paris*.

T. L. Peacock, *Crotchet Castle*.

V **The Press**

W **Drama and Entertainment**

Catharine Gore, *School for Coquettes*.

X **Sport**

Y **Statistics**

Populations (in millions): Great Britain, 12·2; Ireland, 7·7; U.S., 12·8.

Coal production: U.K. 30,000,000 tons; France, 2,571,000 tons.

L Nov: 17th, Venezuela, Ecuador and New Granada dissolve Union of Colombia (of 1819) and New Granada becomes an independent state;
Riot of silk-weavers in Lyons, due mainly to low wages.

M Dec: 12th, Third Reform Bill introduced in House of Commons.

N East India Company annexes Mysore, after suppression of a peasants' revolt.

z **Births and Deaths:**

Jan. 2nd Berthold Niebuhr d. (54).
Mar. 21st Dorothea Beale b. (–1906).
June 8th Sarah Siddons d. (75).
July 4th James Monroe d. (73).
Nov. 9th Henry Labouchere b. (–1912).
Nov. 13th J. Clerk-Maxwell b. (–1879).
Nov. 14th Georg Wilhelm Friedrich Hegel d. (61).
— Camille Pissarro b. (–1903).

A **Jan**: 19th, Austrian troops, under Count Radetzky, occupy Ancona after fresh risings in Papal States (at end of 1831) and remain until 1838.

B **Feb**: 26th, Polish Constitution abolished and new organic statute imposed by Tsar Nicholas I allowing for partial autonomy which, however, remains a dead letter;
29th, New Granada's constitution is proclaimed providing for republican system of government with Congress of two Chambers.

C **Mar**: 23rd, Reform Bill passes Commons.

D **Apr**: 10th, French law excludes families of Charles X and of Napoleon from France;
Turkey declares war on Mohammed Ali, Khedive of Egypt, who demands Syria as reward for aid against Greece.

E **May**: 9th, William IV, having lost confidence in Grey over Reform Bill, forces him to resign, but he is recalled within a week as the Duke of Wellington is unable to form administration;
27th, Hambach Festival of South German Democrats advocates armed revolt;
—, Ibrahim, son of Mohammed Ali, takes Acre.

F **Jun**: 5th, Insurrection in Paris by Republicans attending funeral of their late leader, General Lamarque;
7th, Reform Bill becomes law (after King has agreed to create sufficient Whig Peers to out-vote Tory opposition in Lords if necessary). Over 140 seats redistributed, and in the boroughs all antiquated forms of franchise are eliminated and the franchise is extended to include leaseholders paying minimum of £10 rent per annum, while in counties the 40-shilling freehold qualification is retained and certain lease-holders acquire the vote;
28th, Prince Metternich's Six Articles to maintain despotic government in face of opposition within the German Confederation.

G **Jul**: 9th, Dom Pedro, with aid of France and Britain, takes Oporto and Dom Miguel's forces are defeated;
14th, U.S. Tariff Act (less rigid than that of *May* 1828) but subsequently rejected in South Carolina (*Nov.* 24th);
17th, Act for amendment of representation in Scotland extends Reform Act across border.

H **Aug**: 7th, Irish Reform Act passed;
8th, Greek National Assembly elects Prince Otto of Bavaria King as Otto I (–1862);
East India Company, under William Bentinck, annexes Cathar after residents ask for British protection.

J **Sep**:

K **Oct**: 11th, Marshal Soult forms ministry in France.

L **Nov**: 7th, Duchesse de Berry, a leading Legitimist conspirator in France, is arrested;
In U.S. presidential election, Andrew Jackson, who was nominated as candidate at the first Democratic Convention to be held, defeats Henry Clay (219 electoral votes to 49).

O **Politics, Economics, Law and Education**
Giuseppe Mazzini founds 'Young Italy' movement.
Slavery Abolition Society founded in Boston, Mass.
Silvio Pellico, *My Imprisonment.*
Zürich University founded.

P **Science, Technology, Discovery, etc.**
Diastase, the first enzyme, is separated from barley.
Justus Liebig investigates constitution of ether-alcohol.
Marshall Hall discovers reflex action of nerve centres.
Jakob Steiner founds synthetic geometry.
Samuel Morse invents telegraph.
First railway in Europe (Budweis-Linz) is completed.
Göta Canal completed.

Q **Scholarship**

R **Philosophy and Religion**
Gregory XVI's encyclical condemning freedom of conscience and of the press.
Gustavus Adolphus Society founded to combat Roman Catholicism.
T. Arnold's *Essay on Church Reform.*

S **Art, Sculpture, Fine Arts and Architecture**
William Wilkins, National Gallery, London.

T **Music**
F. Chopin, Mazurkas (op. 6).
G. Donizetti, *L'Elisir d'Amore* (opera).

U **Literature**
Carl Almqvist, *Book of the Thorn and the Rose.*
Honoré de Balzac, *Contes Drôlatiques.*
Washington Irving, *A Town of the Prairie.*
Alexander Pushkin, *Eugenie Onegin* completed.
George Sand (pseud.), *Indiana.*
Lord Tennyson, *The Lotus-Eaters* and *The Lady of Shalott.*

V **The Press**
Penny Magazine started.

W **Drama and Entertainment**
Goethe, *Faust*, pt. ii.
V. Hugo, *Le Roi s'amuse.*

X **Sport**

Y **Statistics**
U.K. Textiles trade:

Raw cotton imports	277 mill. lb.
Cotton exports	461 mill. yds.
Woollen exports	2,297,000 pieces.
Linen exports	49,531,000 yds.

1832 (Dec.)

M Dec: 21st, at Battle of Konieh Egyptian forces rout Turkish army;
23rd, French take Antwerp, forcing Holland to recognise independence of Belgium (after siege since late *Nov.*).

N

z **Births and Deaths**

Jan. 23rd Édouard Manet b. (–1883).
Jan. 27th C. L. Dodgson ('Lewis Carroll') b. (–1898).
Feb. 3rd George Crabbe d. (78).
Mar. 22nd Johann Wolfgang Goethe d. (82).
May 13th G. L. P. C. Cuvier d. (62).
June 6th Jeremy Bentham d. (84).
June 17th William Crookes b. (–1919).
Aug. 16th Wilhelm Wundt b. (–1920).
Sept. 21st. Walter Scott d. (61).
Sept. 30th Frederick, Lord Roberts b. (–1914).
Nov. 28th Leslie Stephen b. (–1904).
Dec. 8th G. A. Henty b. (–1902).

1833 Prussia establishes *Zollverein*—Turkey recognises independence of Egypt—Factory inspection in Britain

A **Jan:** 1st, Britain proclaims sovereignty over Falkland Islands;
16th, Andrew Jackson asks Congress for legislation to enforce tariff (of *July* 14th 1832) in South Carolina.

B **Feb:** 20th, Russian ships enter Bosphorus on way to Constantinople to aid Turkey against Egypt (after conference with Porte *Dec.* 1832–*Feb.* 1833).

C **Mar:** 1st, Clay Tariff passed by U.S. Congress to amend tariff of *July* 1832 in order to appease South Carolina; Congress also passes Force Act, authorising President to use armed force to collect revenues if necessary;
4th, Jackson begins second term as U.S. President;
23rd, Prussia establishes *Zollverein* (customs union) in Germany by a series of treaties, but Austria is excluded.

D **Apr:** 3rd, attempt by revolutionaries in Germany to take over Frankfurt Diet in protest against articles of *June* 1832 is easily crushed.

E **May:** 3rd, Turkey recognises independence of Egypt and cedes Syria and Aden to Mehemet Ali;
21st, Dutch conclude armistice of indefinite length with Belgium;
22nd, constitution in Chile gives greater power to president and establishes Roman Catholicism as State religion.

F **Jun:** 28th, Primary Education Law in France gives effective control to Church.

G **Jul:** 8th, by treaty of Unkiar-Skelessi, a defensive alliance between Turkey and Russia, Sultan agrees to close Dardanelles to all but Russian warships;
24th, Lisbon evacuated by Miguelist forces and occupied by supporters of Dom Pedro and Queen Maria (who returns *Sept.* 22nd).

H **Aug:** 29th, British Factory Act passed, whereby no children under nine to work in factories, those between nine and 13 not to work more than nine-hour day and inspectors are to be appointed to ensure that regulations are carried out;
29th, Bank Charter Act allows Bank of England to retain exclusive possession of government balances, monopoly of limited liability, and to be only Joint-Stock Bank allowed to issue own notes within 65-mile radius of London.

J **Sep:** 10th (–20th), Conference at Münchengrätz between Russia, Prussia and Austria to discuss European problems, particularly with regard to Turkey;
26th, new liberal Constitution granted in Hanover by William IV;
29th, death of Ferdinand VII of Spain, who is succeeded by Queen Isabella II (–1868).

K **Oct:** 15th, at Berlin, Prussia, Russia and Austria agree to support the integrity of the Ottoman Empire and to further the Holy Alliance by promising to aid one another in the event of attack.

L **Nov:**

M **Dec:**

N General Trades Union in New York links all unions in one organisation (collapses 1837).
Beginning of Whig Party in U.S. which absorbs the National Republican Party, the former opposition, and attacks Andrew Jackson's democratic policies.

O **Politics, Economics, Law and Education**
End of East India Company's monopoly of China trade.
First State grant for education in England.
Académie des Sciences Morales et Politiques revived in France.
The charity bazaar becomes popular in England.

P **Science, Technology, Discovery, etc.**
W. E. Weber and K. F. Gauss construct an electric telegraph at Göttingen.

Q **Scholarship**
Franz Bopp, *Comparative Grammar* (–52).
J. M. Kemble's edition of Beowulf.
Jules Michelet, *Histoire de France* (–67).

R **Philosophy and Religion**
John Keble, *National Apostasy* (Assize sermon at Oxford) begins Oxford Movement.
Tracts for the Times (–41).
Nonconformists allowed to celebrate marriages in chapels in Britain.
Orson Pratt begins Mormon mission in Canada.

S **Art, Sculpture, Fine Arts and Architecture**

T **Music**
F. Mendelssohn, 4th Symphony in A ('Italian').
F. Chopin, 12 Études (op. 10).

U **Literature**
Robert Browning, *Pauline.*
Thomas Carlyle, *Sartor Resartus.*
Alfred de Musset, *André del Sarto* and *Les Caprices de Marianne.*
Nicolai Gogol, *The Government Inspector.*
George Sand (pseud.), *Lelia.*

V **The Press**
Knickerbocker Magazine.

W **Drama and Entertainment**
Edmund Kean's last appearance (*Mar.*) as Othello.

X **Sport**

Y **Statistics**

Z **Births and Deaths**
May 7th Johannes Brahms b. (–1897).
June 4th Garnet Wolseley b. (–1913).
Aug. 20th Benjamin Harrison b. (–1901).
Aug. 28th Edward Burne-Jones b. (–1898).
Oct. 21st Alfred Nobel b. (–1896).

1834 The Tolpuddle Martyrs—Slavery abolished in British Empire—Civil war in Spain

A **Jan:** formation of Grand National Consolidated Trades Union, led by Robert Owen, to organise general strike for eight-hour day (but collapses *Oct.*).

B **Feb:** Attempt by 'Young Italy' followers of Giuseppe Mazzini on Savoy fails.

C **Mar:** 18th, Tolpuddle labourers in Dorset sentenced to be transported for making illegal oath in forming lodge of Owen's Union.

D **Apr:** 9th, revolt of silk-weavers in Lyons, lasting four days, after attempts by French government to suppress trade union activities;
12th, 150 Republicans arrested in Paris from fear of insurrection and, 14th, rising crushed by army under Adolphe Thiers;
22nd, Britain, France, Spain and Portugal form Quadruple Alliance in support of liberal constitutions in Iberian Peninsula.

E **May:** 26th, Dom Miguel of Portugal finally surrenders and abdicates, allowing for restoration of Maria II;
Sikhs capture Peshawar.

F **Jun:**

G **Jul:** 9th, Lord Grey resigns over problem of tithes and coercion act in Ireland, and is succeeded, 16th, by Melbourne;
Beginning of civil war in Spain when Don Carlos, brother of late Ferdinand VII of Spain, claims throne (the Carlists are finally defeated, *Aug.* 1839).

H **Aug:** 15th, South Australia Act is passed allowing for establishment of colony there.

J **Sep:** 24th, Peter IV of Portugal dies, succeeded by Maria II.

K **Oct:** 16th, British Houses of Parliament practically destroyed by fire.

L **Nov:** Lord Melbourne resigns after King's refusal to allow Lord Russell to become leader of House of Commons and Robert Peel is asked to form Tory administration (he accepts, *Dec.* 9th).

M **Dec:** 17th, Robert Peel issues Tamworth Manifesto giving Tory Party a policy of liberal Conservatism, accepting Reform Act of 1832 and agreeing to pass more equitable reforms.

N

Z **Births and Deaths** (*cont.*)
July 10th James Whistler b. (–1903).
July 19th Edgar Degas b. (–1917).
July 25th Samuel Taylor Coleridge d. (61).
Sept. 15th Heinrich Treitschke b. (–1896).
Nov. 12th Alexander Borodin b. (–1887).
Dec. 23rd T. R. Malthus d. (68).
Dec. 27th Charles Lamb d. (59).
— Edwin Klebs b. (–1913).

O **Politics, Economics, Law and Education**

J. Bentham, *Deontology; or the Science of Morality* (posth.).
Poor Law Amendment Act forbids outdoor relief in Britain and establishes workhouses.
Abolition of slavery in British Empire (*Aug.* 1st).
Chimney Sweeps Act in Britain.
Liverpool Mechanics Institute is founded.

P **Science, Technology, Discovery, etc.**

J. F. Herschel begins astronomical observations at Cape of Good Hope.
Michael Faraday discovers electrical self-induction.
Jean Dumas formulates Law of Substitution.
Louis Braille perfects system of characters for the blind to read.
Cyrus McCormick's reaping machine.
'Hansom' cabs are introduced to London.

Q **Scholarship**

L. von Ranke, *History of the Popes* (–36).
George Bancroft, *History of the United States* (–74).

R **Philosophy and Religion**

H. F. R. Lamennais, *Paroles d'un croyant.*
Portuguese monasteries suppressed.

S **Art, Sculpture, Fine Arts and Architecture**

William Dunlap, *Rise and Progress of the Arts of Design in the United States.*

T **Music**

H. Berlioz, *Harold in Italy.*
R. Schumann, *Carnaval* (op. 9).

U **Literature**

Honoré de Balzac, *La Recherche de l'Absolu* and *Le Père Goriot.*
Franz Grillparzer, *Der Traum, ein Leben.*
Francesco Guerrazzi, *L'Assedio di Firenze.*
Edward Bulwer Lytton, *Last Days of Pompeii.*
Leopold Schefer, *Laienbrever* (–35).

V **The Press**

Lloyd's Register of Shipping.

W **Drama and Entertainment**

X **Sport**

Royal and Ancient Golf Club, St. Andrews, is patronised by William IV.

Y **Statistics**

Z **Births and Deaths**

Jan. 10th John Dalberg Acton, Lord Acton b. (–1902).
Feb. 7th Dimitry Mendeléev b. (–1907).
Feb. 16th Ernst Haeckel b. (–1919).
Mar. 24th William Morris b. (–1896).

(*Continued opposite*)

1835 September Laws in France suppress radicalism—British Municipal Corporations reformed

A **Jan:**

B **Feb:**

C **Mar:** 2nd, Francis I of Austria dies, succeeded by Ferdinand I (–1848);
'Lichfield House Compact', a tacit agreement between Daniel O'Connell, leader of Irish Nationalists, and Whig opposition, whereby the Irish promise Parliamentary support provided Whigs vote against coercion acts.

D **Apr:** 8th, Robert Peel resigns after defeat when voting against resolution to appropriate surplus revenues of Irish Church for non-ecclesiastical objects and
18th, Lord Melbourne forms Whig ministry.

E **May:** 12th, Baden joins *Zollverein.*

F **Jun:**

G **Jul:** 28th, assassination attempt on Louis Philippe by the Corsican, Giuseppe Fieschi.

H **Aug:**

J **Sep:** 9th, British Municipal Corporations Act abolishes all old Charter privileges and establishes new governing body of councillors elected by ratepayers with aldermen elected by councillors, and a mayor elected for one year;
'September Laws' in France severely censor the press and suppress the radical movement.

K **Oct:**

L **Nov:**

M **Dec:**

N Juan de Rosas becomes Dictator in Argentina (–1852).
Milosh is forced to grant Constitution in Serbia but soon withdraws it at the Sultan's demand.

Z **Births and Deaths**

Feb. 4th Albert Venn Dicey b. (–1922).
June 16th William Cobbett d. (72).
Sept. 24th Vincenzo Bellini d. (33).
Oct. 3rd Charles Camille Saint-Saëns b. (–1921).
Nov. 25th Andrew Carnegie b. (–1919).
Nov. 30th 'Mark Twain' (pseud. of Samuel Langhorne Clemens) b. (–1910).
Dec. 4th Samuel Butler b. (–1902).

O **Politics, Economics, Law and Education**

A. de Tocqueville, *De la Démocratie en Amérique* (–40).

Richard Cobden's free trade pamphlet *England, Ireland and America* and, to combat Russophobia, *Russia.*

P **Science, Technology, Discovery, etc.**

S. D. Poisson, *Théorie mathématique de la Chaleur.*

L. A. J. Quetalet, *Sur l'homme et le développement de ses facultés*, suggests the physique and intellect of the 'average man'.

Samuel Colt's revolver.

William Hooker establishes a botanical laboratory at Kew.

Q **Scholarship**

C. A. Brandis, *Handbook to the History of Graeco-Roman Philosophy* (–66).

Connor Thirlwall, *History of Greece* (–44).

J. Grimm, *German Mythology.*

R **Philosophy and Religion**

D. F. Strauss, *Life of Jesus.*

Revival of Sabbatarianism in England.

Papal Bull condemns rationalist teaching of Georg Hermes.

S **Art, Sculpture, Fine Arts and Architecture**

Casper Friedrich, *Rest during the Harvest* (painting).

T **Music**

G. Donizetti, *Lucy of Lammermoor* (opera).

U **Literature**

Hans Andersen, *Fairy Tales* (–72).

R. Browning, *Paracelsus.*

Georg Büchner, *Danton's Death.*

T. Gautier, *Mademoiselle de Maupin.*

N. Gogol, *Dead Souls.*

Bulwer Lytton, *Rienzi.*

A. de Vigny, *Servitude et grandeur militaires.*

W. Wordsworth, *Yarrow Revisited.*

V **The Press**

New York Herald (*May*), founded as a 1-cent popular paper.

W **Drama and Entertainment**

The polka first danced in Prague.

X **Sport**

Y **Statistics**

U.K. total State expenditure, £48·9 mill.

U.K. iron production, 1 mill. tons.

(*Continued opposite*)

1836 Origins of Chartism—Texas becomes independent of Mexico

A Jan:

B Feb: 22nd, first ministry of Adolphe Thiers in France (–*Sept.*).

C Mar: 2nd, Texas declares itself independent of Mexico and
17th, proclaims republican constitution.

D Apr: 21st, Texan independence is ensured by defeat of Mexico at battle of San Jacinto.

E May:

F Jun: 15th, Arkansas becomes U.S. state;
16th, formation of London Working Men's Association begins Chartist Movement.

G Jul:

H Aug: 13th, Tithe Commutation Act commutes tithes for money payment equal to between 60 and 75 per cent of nominal value;
13th, British Stamp Duties are reduced from 4d. to 1d.;
17th, Parliament provides for registration of births, marriages and deaths in Britain.

J Sep: 6th, Adolphe Thiers is forced to resign in France after proposing invasion of Spain.

K Oct: 28th, Federation of Peru and Bolivia proclaimed (Constitution is promulgated *May* 1st 1837);
30th, Louis Napoleon fails to create a revolt among the garrison of Strasbourg as a first step to seizing power and is subsequently exiled to U.S.

L Nov: 11th, Chile declares war on Peru-Bolivian Federation.

M Dec:

N

O **Politics, Economics, Law and Education**
Communist league formed in Paris.
Victor Considérant, *Destinée sociale* (–38).
London University founded as an examining body.
Adelaide becomes capital of S. Australia.

P **Science, Technology, Discovery, etc.**
J. N. von Dreyse invents needle-gun.
Acetylene is made.
First railway in Canada opened and first train in London.

Q **Scholarship**
F. C. Diez, *Grammar of the Romance Languages* (–44).

R **Philosophy and Religion**
R. W. Emerson's *Nature* founds Transcendentalism.
Johann Görres, *Christian Mysticism* (–42).
E. B. Pusey's tract *On the Holy Eucharist*.
In England the Ecclesiastical Commissioners are incorporated.

S **Art, Sculpture, Fine Arts and Architecture**
Arc de Triomphe, Paris, completed.

T **Music**
M. I. Glinka, *A Life for the Czar* (opera).
G. Meyerbeer, *The Huguenots* (opera).

U **Literature**
Charles Dickens, *Sketches by Boz* and *Pickwick Papers* (–37).
A. Garcia-Gutiérrez, *El Trovador*.
Karl Immermann, *Epigonen*.
A. de Lamartine, *Jocelyn*.
Nikolas Lenau (*pseud.*), *Faust*.
F. Marryat, *Mr. Midshipman Easy*.

V **The Press**
Beginnings of cheap press in France with *La Presse* and *Le Siècle*.

W **Drama and Entertainment**
'The Lancers' is first danced in Paris.

X **Sport**
Prix du Jockey Club, France, first run.

Y **Statistics**
U.K. registered tonnage of merchant shipping 2,350,000 tons (60,000 tons of steamships).

Z **Births and Deaths**
Jan. 21st Léo Délibes b. (–1891).
Apr. 7th T. H. Greene b. (–1882).
May 24th Joseph Rowntree b. (–1925).
June 9th Elizabeth Garrett Anderson b. (–1917).
June 10th André Ampère d. (61).
June 20th Emmanuel Joseph Sieyès d. (78).
July 8th Joseph Chamberlain b. (–1914).
Sept. 7th Henry Campbell-Bannerman b. (–1908).
Nov. 18th W. S. Gilbert b. (–1911).

1837 Natal Republic founded—Rebellions in Canada

A **Jan:** 26th, Michigan becomes a U.S. state.

B **Feb:**

C **Mar:** 4th, Martin Van Buren is inaugurated President of U.S.

D **Apr:**

E **May:**

F **Jun:** 18th, liberal Constitution is proclaimed in Spain providing for national sovereignty, House of two Chambers, absolute veto of crown and restricted suffrage;
20th, on death of William IV Queen Victoria succeeds to British throne (–1901);
—, Hanover is automatically separated from Britain, as Salic Law forbids female succession, and the throne is taken up by Ernest Augustus, Duke of Cumberland, eldest surviving son of George III (–1851);
Natal Republic founded by Dutch settlers and a Constitution is proclaimed.

G **Jul:** Ernest Augustus suppresses the Constitution in Hanover.

H **Aug:**

J **Sep:**

K **Oct:**

L **Nov:** Louis Joseph Papineau's rebellion in Lower Canada, result of conflicts between governor and legislative councils, and the popularly-elected assemblies, and also due to opposition between French and British elements; the rebels are successful, 22nd, at St. Denis, but are routed, 24th, at St. Charles.

M **Dec:** 5th, similar revolt in Upper Canada under William Lyon Mackenzie;
13th, W. L. Mackenzie sets up provisional government for Upper Canada from headquarters on Navy Island in Niagara River and prepares for invasion of Canada;
29th, Canadian government forces burn U.S. steamer *Caroline* which is helping rebels;
King of Hanover dismisses seven professors of Göttingen University, including the brothers Grimm, who oppose his revocation of Constitution.

N

O Politics, Economics, Law and Education

F. W. A. Froebel opens first kindergarten near Blankenburg.

Horace Mann begins educational reforms in Massachusetts.

P Science, Technology, Discovery, etc.

René Dutrochet recognises that chlorophyll is necessary to photosynthesis.

F. G. W. Struve publishes micrometric measurements of 2,714 double stars.

K. F. Mohr's theory of conservation of energy.

James Dana, *System of Mineralogy.*

J. L. G. Agassiz's work on fossils.

Isaac Pitman invents shorthand.

Q Scholarship

Georg Grotefend deciphers cuneiform inscriptions in Persia.

Thomas Carlyle, *French Revolution.*

W. H. Prescott, *Ferdinand and Isabella.*

R Philosophy and Religion

Immanuel Fichte founds *Zeitschrift für Philosophie.*

Archbishops of Cologne, Gnesen and Posen imprisoned for refusing to compromise over mixed marriages in Prussia.

American Presbyterians split into 'old' and 'new' schools.

S Art, Sculpture, Fine Arts and Architecture

Fitzwilliam Museum, Cambridge.

T Music

Hector Berlioz, *Benvenuto Cellini* and *Requiem.*

U Literature

Hendrik Conscience, *In't Wonderjaar, 1566.*

C. Dickens, *Oliver Twist* (–38).

M. Y. Lermontov, *Elegy on the Death of Pushkin.*

N. Lenau (pseud.), *Savonarola.*

V The Press

W Drama and Entertainment

X Sport

Y Statistics

Methodists: in U.S., 650,678; in U.K., 318,716.

Z Births and Deaths

Feb. 10th Alexander Pushkin d. (37).

Mar. 1st William Dean Howells b. (–1920).

Mar. 18th Stephen Grover Cleveland b. (–1908).

Mar. 31st John Constable d. (59).

Apr. 5th Algernon C. Swinburne b. (–1909).

Apr. 17th J. Pierpont Morgan b. (–1913).

Dec. 25th E. T. Gerry b. (–1927).

1838 Anti-Corn Law League founded—Anglo-Afghan war

A **Jan:** 13th, W. L. Mackenzie is arrested in U.S.

B **Feb:** 10th, temporary provision made by British government for Lower Canada after collapse of Constitution, forbidding meeting of legislative assembly.

C **Mar:**

D **Apr:**

E **May:** 29th, Lord Durham arrives in Quebec as Governor-in-Chief of all British North America.

F **Jun:**

G **Jul:** 31st, first Irish Poor Law based on English Act (*Aug.* 14th 1834).

H **Aug:**

J **Sep:** 18th, Anti-Corn Law League is established in Manchester by Richard Cobden.

K **Oct:** 1st, Britain's First Afghan War, to prevent increased influence of Russia, which constitutes threat to British position in India;
9th, Lord Durham resigns position in Canada after criticism of him for leniency towards rebels;
Austrian troops evacuate Papal States except for Ferrara (after occupation since *Jan.* 19th 1832).

L **Nov:** 30th, Mexico declares war on France after French occupation of Vera Cruz (*Nov.* 27th) in attempt to obtain compensation for French victims of civil disturbances in Mexico.

M **Dec:** 16th, Boers defeat Zulus on Blood River, Natal;
24th, Sultan of Turkey, supported by Russia, limits authority of Milosh in Serbia.

N

Y **Statistics**
Navies: Britain, 90 ships of the line; France, 49; Russia, 50; U.S., 15.

Z **Births and Deaths**
Feb. 6th Henry Irving b. (–1917).
Mar. 26th W. E. H. Lecky b. (–1903).
Apr. 2nd Léon Gambetta b. (–1882).
May 10th James Bryce b. (–1922).
May 17th Charles de Talleyrand-Périgord d. (84).
July 8th Ferdinand Zeppelin b. (–1905).
Oct. 24th Joseph Lancaster d. (60).
Oct. 25th Georges Bizet b. (–1875).
Dec. 3rd Octavia Hill b. (–1912).
Dec. 24th John Morley b. (–1923).

O **Politics, Economics, Law and Education**

Antoine Cournot, *The Mathematics of Commerce.*

F. Lieber, *Political Ethics.*

The Working Men's Association, led by F. O'Connor, draw up the People's Charter, demanding reform, including manhood suffrage, vote by ballot, annual parliaments and payment of members (*May* 8th).

Foundation of the Public Record Office, London, the first central national archives repository.

P **Science, Technology, Discovery, etc.**

Hugh Miller, *Crystallography.*

Mathias Schleiden's cellular theory of plants.

H. G. Dyer and J. Hemming invent ammonia process for making soda.

J. Liebig demonstrates that animal heat is due to respiration, founding the science of biochemistry.

Bruce's type-casting machine.

Great Western and *Sirius* cross the Atlantic to inaugurate regular steamship communication between U.K. and U.S.

Q **Scholarship**

T. Arnold, *History of Rome* (-43).

Camden Society for publishing historical documents founded in London.

R **Philosophy and Religion**

J. B. H. Lacordaire revives the Dominican Order in France.

S **Art, Sculpture, Fine Arts and Architecture**

National Gallery, London, opened.

The Kremlin, Moscow, begun (-49).

T **Music**

R. Schumann, *Nouvelletten* (piano).

H. Berlioz, dramatic symphony *Romeo and Juliet.*

U **Literature**

C. Dickens, *Nicholas Nickleby* (-39).

V. Hugo, *Ruy Blas.*

Karl Immermann, *Münchhausen.*

E. F. Mörike, *Poems.*

E. A. Poe, *Arthur Gordon Pym.*

R. S. Surtees, *Jorrocks' Jaunts and Jollities.*

W. M. Thackeray, *The Yellowplush Correspondence*, in *Frazer's Magazine.*

V **The Press**

Times of India founded.

Northern Star, edited by Feargus O'Connor, as a Chartist manifesto.

W **Drama and Entertainment**

Jenny Lind's début as Agathe in C. M. Weber's *Der Freischütz* in Stockholm.

Elisa Rachel's début as Camille in Corneille's *Horace* at the Théatre Français begins the revival of French classical drama.

X **Sport**

(*Continued opposite*)

1839 Turkey invades Syria—Anglo-Chinese Opium War—Chartist riots in Britain

A **Jan:** 20th, Battle of Yungay, resulting in victory for Chile against Peru-Bolivian Federation, leads to dissolution of that union;
The Times declares in favour of free trade.

B **Feb:** 4th, National Convention of Chartists begins in London;
11th, Durham Report on North America debated in House of Lords;
24th, Uruguay declares war against Argentina.

C **Mar:** 9th, French forces withdraw from Mexico, whose government agrees to compensate French victims of civil riots;
Establishment of National Anti-Corn Law League in London.

D **Apr:** 19th, treaty of London whereby territorial arrangements between Belgium and Holland are finally accepted by King William I of Holland, so that Belgium is independent, Luxembourg becomes an independent Grand Duchy, and R. Scheldt is opened to commerce of both Dutch and Belgian nations;
21st, Turkish army invades Syria in opposition to Mehemet Ali (war continues until *Feb.* 1841).

E **May:** 6th, Bill to suspend Jamaican Constitution after riots due to emancipation of slaves, passes Commons by narrow majority;
7th, Lord Melbourne resigns because of small majority for Jamaican Bill and Robert Peel is asked to form Conservative administration, but he fails to do so because of 'Bedchamber Question' when Queen Victoria refuses to dismiss certain of her Whig ladies-in-waiting, so that, 13th, Melbourne's Whig administration returns.

F **Jun:** 13th, abdication of Milosh in Serbia who is succeeded by his son, Milan (who dies *July* 9th, and is succeeded by younger brother, Michael (–1842));
24th, at battle of Nezib, Ibrahim routs Turkish forces.

G **Jul:** 1st, death of Sultan Mahmud II who is succeeded by a boy, Abdul Mejid (–1861);
—, Turkish fleet voluntarily surrenders to Mehemet Ali at Alexandria;
12th, Chartist petition rejected by Parliament;
27th, note from the Powers to the Sultan of Turkey reserving their right to deal with Mehemet Ali;
Chartist riots in Birmingham and elsewhere throughout month;
Beginning of Opium War between China and Britain after Chinese authorities seize and burn British cargoes of opium.

H **Aug:** 17th, British Parliament establishes special council to make laws for Lower Canada;
23rd, Hong Kong taken by British in war with China.

J **Sep:**

K **Oct:**

L **Nov:** 3rd, Opium War flares up when British frigate sinks Chinese fleet of junks;
3rd, Reform Decree in Ottoman Empire guarantees life, liberty and property of all subjects;
4th, Chartist rising in Newport, Mon., in attempt to break open jail is easily crushed.

M **Dec:** 3rd, death of Frederick VI of Denmark who is succeeded by nephew Christian VIII (–1848).

N

O **Politics, Economics, Law and Education**

Louis Blanc, *L'Organisation du travail*, proposes system of national workshops.

Institute of Physiology founded in Breslau.

P **Science, Technology, Discovery, etc.**

Theodor Schwann, *Microscopic Investigations on the Accordance in the Structure and Growth of Plants and Animals*, founds modern cell theory.

Michael Faraday, *Researches in Electricity* (–1855).

W. H. Fox Talbot produces a photographic negative (*Jan.* 25th), and Louis Daguerre perfects process for producing a silver image on a copper plate (*Mar.*)—the 'daguerreotype'.

K. G. Mosander discovers the metallic element Lanthanum.

James Nasmyth's steam hammer.

Charles Goodyear vulcanises rubber.

First tunnel kiln is made in Denmark.

S.S. *Great Britain* becomes first screw steamer to cross the Atlantic.

Robert Murchison's geological treatise, *The Silurian System.*

Charles Darwin, *Voyage of the 'Beagle'.*

Q **Scholarship**

L. von Ranke, *History of the Reformation in Germany* (–43).

Lowell Institute, Boston founded by John Lowell, junior, to provide free public lectures by eminent scholars.

R **Philosophy and Religion**

S **Art, Sculpture, Fine Arts and Architecture**

J. M. W. Turner, *Fighting Téméraire* (painting).

Thomas V. Walter, State Capitol, Columbus, Ohio (–61).

T **Music**

F. Chopin, 24 Preludes (op. 28).

F. Mendelssohn conducts F. Schubert's C Major Symphony ('Great') at Leipzig.

U **Literature**

M. Y. Lermontov, *A Hero of Our Time.*

H. W. Longfellow, *Voices of the Night.*

Stendhal (pseud.), *La Chartreuse de Parme.*

Rodolphe Töpffer, *Nouvelles genevoises.*

V **The Press**

W **Drama and Entertainment**

X **Sport**

Henley Royal Regatta instituted.

Grand National first run at Aintree and Cesarewitch at Newmarket.

Baseball first played (probably at Cooperstown, New York).

Y **Statistics**

Z **Births and Deaths**

Jan. 19th Paul Cézanne b. (–1906).

Mar. 16th M. P. Moussorgsky b. (–1881).

July 8th John D. Rockefeller b. (–1937).

Aug. 4th Walter Pater b. (–1894).

Sept. 19th George Cadbury b. (–1922).

1840 Quadruple Alliance aids Turkey against Mehemet Ali

A **Jan:**

B **Feb:** 5th, by treaty of Waitangi, Maori chiefs surrender sovereignty to British;
10th, marriage of Queen Victoria to Prince Albert of Saxe-Coburg-Gotha;
26th, Adolphe Thiers forms second ministry in France (–*Oct.* 28th).

C **Mar:**

D **Apr:**

E **May:**

F **Jun:** 6th, Carlist Wars in Spain end when Carlist forces finally surrender, due mainly to negotiations of General Espartero;
7th, death of Frederick William III of Prussia, who is succeeded by Frederick William IV (–1861).

G **Jul:** 15th, Russia, Britain, Prussia and Austria form Quadruple Alliance in support of Turkey and by treaty of London offer Mehemet Ali Egypt, as hereditary possession, and southern Syria for life, provided he gives up Crete and northern Syria (but he refuses in hope of French aid);
23rd, act of Parliament for union of Upper and Lower Canada with equal representation for both of these former provinces.

H **Aug:** 6th, Louis Napoleon's attempted rising at Boulogne fails and he is subsequently sentenced to life imprisonment in Ham;
6th, Ernest Augustus of Hanover imposes new Constitution with increased powers for monarch;
10th, Municipal Act for Ireland gives right to vote to all paying £10 annual rent.

J **Sep:** 11th, bombardment of Beirut by British to force Mehemet Ali to submit.

K **Oct:** 7th, William I of Holland abdicates in favour of his son, William II (–1849);
12th, Queen Regent Cristina of Spain resigns after revolts and Espartero's influence increases;
28th, Adolphe Thiers forced to resign after attempting to obtain French aid for Mehemet Ali.

L **Nov:** 3rd, bombardment and capture of Acre by British forces Ibrahim to evacuate all Syria;
5th, by convention of Alexandria, Mehemet Ali agrees to terms of treaty of London (*July* 15th);
—, end of Afghan War when Afghan forces surrender to British.

M **Dec:** 15th, Napoleon I's remains brought to Les Invalides in Paris.

N

O **Politics, Economics, Law and Education**

P. J. Proudhon, *Qu'est-ce-que la Propriété?*
Rowland Hill introduces penny post in Britain (*Jan.* 10th).
P. Shuttleworth founds first teachers' training college.

P **Science, Technology, Discovery, etc.**

J. E. Purkinje first uses the term 'protoplasm'.
J. P. Joule begins work on heat.
P. J. Liebig, *The Chemistry of Diet.*
J. L. G. Agassiz, *Études sur les glaciers.*
Botanical Gardens, Kew, opened.
R. Kölliker identifies spermatozoa as cells.
W. Whewell, *Philosophy of Inductive Sciences.*
J. W. Draper photographs the moon.

Q **Scholarship**

Augustin Thierry, *Récits des temps mérovingiens.*
J. Y. Akerman, *Numismatic Manual.*

R **Philosophy and Religion**

R. W. Emerson and Margaret Fuller edit *The Dial* as an organ of Transcendentalism.

S **Art, Sculpture, Fine Art and Architecture**

Charles Barry, Houses of Parliament (-52).
Heinrich Hübach, Trinkhalle, Baden-Baden.
George Kemp, Scott Museum, Edinburgh.

T **Music**

F. Chopin, two nocturnes (op. 37) and two polonaises (op. 40).
G. Donizetti, *La Fille du Régiment* (opera).
R. Schumann, *Dichterliebe* song cycle.
A. Sax invents saxophone.
R. Wagner, *Faust* overture.

U **Literature**

R. H. Barham, *Ingoldsby Legends* (-47).
J. F. Cooper, *The Pathfinder.*
C. Dickens, *Old Curiosity Shop.*
P. Mérimée, *Colomba.*
E. A. Poe, *Tales of the Grotesque and Arabesque.*
C. Sainte-Beuve, *Histoire de Port-Royal* (-60).

V **The Press**

The Tablet.

W **Drama and Entertainment**

X **Sport**

Y **Statistics**

Religions in U.S.: Roman Catholics, 1,000,000; Baptists, 850,000; Methodists, 870,000; Presbyterians, 228,600.
Railways in operation: U.S. 2,816 miles; U.K. 1,331 miles.

Y **Statistics** (*cont.*)

Industry: cotton textiles become leading U.S. industry with 1,778,000 spindles and 75,000 workers.

Emigration: 75,810 leave Great Britain for U.S., 1831–40, and 207,381 leave Ireland for U.S.

Z **Births and Deaths**

Jan. 6th Fanny Burney (Frances D'Arblay) d. (87).
Apr. 2nd Émile Zola b. (–1902).
Apr. 27th Edward Whymper b. (–1911).
May 7th Peter Iljitch Tchaikovsky b. (–1893).
May 13th Alphonse Daudet b. (–1897).
June 2nd Thomas Hardy b. (–1928).
June 10th H. M. Stanley b. (–1904).
Sept. 2nd Austin Dobson b. (–1921).
Sept. 27th A. T. Mahan b. (–1914).
Nov. 14th Claude Oscar Monet b. (–1926), and Auguste Rodin b. (–1917).

1841 British sovereignty in New Zealand and Hong Kong—The Dardanelles are closed to warships

A **Jan:** 26th, British sovereignty proclaimed over Hong Kong.

B **Feb:** 13th, Sultan finally accepts treaty with regard to Mehemet Ali who obtains Egypt as a hereditary possession.

C **Mar:** 4th, W. H. Harrison inaugurated President of U.S.

D **Apr:** 4th, on Harrison's death, John Tyler becomes President of U.S.

E **May:** 3rd, New Zealand is formally proclaimed as British colony;
8th, Baldomero Espartero is appointed Regent of Spain.

F **Jun:**

G **Jul:** 13th, France joins Quadruple Alliance of *July* 1840 with regard to Turkey;
13th, by Convention of the Straits the powers guarantee Ottoman independence and the Dardanelles and Bosphorus are closed to warships of all nations in peacetime (thus overthrowing treaty of Unkiar Skelessi, 1833).

H **Aug:** 30th, Robert Peel forms Conservative ministry when Lord Melbourne resigns after defeat over amendment to Address.

J **Sep:**

K **Oct:** Dorr Rebellion in Rhode Island, against decrepit form of government, fails (but new Constitution is granted 1842).

L **Nov:** 2nd, beginning of Second Afghan War when Afghans rise and massacre British army officers;
9th, birth of Prince of Wales, heir to British throne;
U.S. slave ship *Creole* is taken over by slaves who murder crew and put into port in British West Indies where slavery is not recognised; U.S. demands for their return are ignored by Britain.

M **Dec:**

N Pre-Emption Distribution Act in U.S. gives rights to squatters who take up locations on surveyed public lands.

X **Sport**
Tom Hyer becomes first recognised boxing champion in U.S. (–48).

Y **Statistics**
Populations: Great Britain, 18,534,000; Ireland, 8,175,000; U.S. 17,063,353.
Principal cities: London, 2,235,344; Paris, 935,261; Vienna, 356,870; New York, 312,710; Berlin, 300,000.
Coal production: Great Britain, 40,000,000 tons; France, 4,078,500 tons.
Iron production: Great Britain, 1,350,000 tons; France, 1,247,000 tons.

Z **Births and Deaths**
Jan. 25th John, Lord Fisher b. (–1920).
Feb. 26th Evelyn Baring, Lord Cromer b. (–1917).
May 14th Squire Bancroft b. (–1926).
Sept. 2nd Hirobumi Ito b. (–1909).
Sept. 8th Anton Dvořák b. (–1904).
Sept. 28th Georges Clémenceau b. (–1929).
Nov. 20th Wilfrid Laurier b. (–1919).
— Firmin Auguste Renoir b. (–1919).

O **Politics, Economics, Law and Education**

Louis Blanc attacks July monarchy in *Histoire de dix ans.*

Friedrich List, *National System of Political Economy.*

Degrees are granted to women in U.S.

P **Science, Technology, Discovery, etc.**

R. W. Bunsen invents carbon-zinc battery.

H. R. Worthington's direct-action steam pump.

Steam machinery applied to biscuit manufacture at Reading factory.

Demonstration of arc lamps for Paris streets.

J. B. Elie de Beaumont and Ours Dufrénoy, geological map of France.

David Livingstone discovers Lake Ngami.

James Ross discovers the Great Southern Continent.

William Hooker reforms Kew Gardens.

British Pharmaceutical Society founded.

Q **Scholarship**

L. van Ranke is appointed historiographer of Prussia.

London Library opened (*May*) as a private subscription circulating library.

R **Philosophy and Religion**

Rudolf Lotze, *Metaphysics.*

J. H. Newman is censured in Oxford for the doctrine of Tract 90 in which he explained the 39 Articles in a Catholic sense.

Ludwig Feuerbach, *Essence of Christianity.*

Oratory of St. Francis de Sales founded in Italy for work among poor youths.

David Livingstone begins missionary work in Africa.

S **Art, Sculpture, Fine Arts and Architecture**

H. Daumier's lithographs *Physionomies tragico-classiques.*

F. Chantrey's bequest to Royal Academy.

T **Music**

R. Schumann, Piano Concerto in A minor (op. 54; completed 1845).

Daniel Auber, *The Crown Diamonds* (opera).

G. Rossini, *Stabat Mater* (oratorio).

A. H. Hoffman, *Deutschland, Deutschland über Alles.*

U **Literature**

Honoré de Balzac, *Une Ténébreuse Affaire.*

T. Carlyle, *On Heroes and Hero-Worship.*

Charles Lever, *Charles O'Malley.*

Hugh Miller, *Old Red Sandstone.*

V **The Press**

Punch is issued, with Mark Lemon editor and John Leech chief illustrator.

New York Tribune founded.

J. T. Delane appointed editor of *The Times* (–77).

George Bradshaw's first *Railway Guide* (*Dec.*).

W **Drama and Entertainment**

Catherine Gore, *Cecil, or the Adventures of a Coxcomb.*

Thomas Cook leads first travel tour to Europe.

(*Continued opposite*)

1842 Canadian-U.S. frontier settled—Chinese ports opened to British trade

A **Jan:** 1st, British forces capitulate at Kabul in war with Afghans and agree to withdraw to India, but majority are killed fighting on journey.

B **Feb:**

C **Mar:**

D **Apr:** 29th, Robert Peel's Budget modifies sliding scale to encourage imports of corn, reduces many duties and revives income tax.

E **May:** 3rd, Parliament rejects Chartist Petition.

F **Jun:**

G **Jul:**

H **Aug:** 9th, Webster-Ashburton Treaty between Britain and U.S. defines frontier between Canada and U.S.;
10th, Lord Ashley's Mines Act prevents women, and children below 10 years, working underground;
29th, by treaty of Nanking ending Anglo-Chinese War, Canton, Shanghai and Chinese ports are opened to British commerce with consular facilities, and Britain obtains large indemnity;
Chartist risings in manufacturing areas of England.

J **Sep:**

K **Oct:** 10th, Second Afghan War ends with British proclamation of victory;
Rising against Baldomero Espartero in Barcelona.

L **Nov:**

M **Dec:** 4th, Espartero bombards Barcelona and revolts are soon crushed;
19th, U.S. recognises independence of Hawaii.

N New Whig Tariff in U.S. replaces Compromise Tariff (1833) (but is itself replaced by Walker Tariff 1846).
War between the Boers and British in Natal (–43).

Z **Births and Deaths** (*cont.*)
Mar. 7th Henry Mayers Hyndman b. (–1921).
Mar. 18th Stéphane Mallarmé b. (–1898).
Mar. 20th Antonio Fogazzaro b. (–1911).
Mar. 23rd 'Stendhal' (Marie Henri Beyle), d. (59).
May 12th Jules Massenet b. (–1912).
May 13th Arthur Sullivan b. (–1900).
June 12th Thomas Arnold d. (46).
July 25th Charles Jean Sismondi d. (69).
July 26th Alfred Marshall b. (–1924).
Aug. 13th Albert Sorel b. (–1906).

O Politics, Economics, Law and Education

Étienne Cabet, *Voyage en Icarie*.

Edwin Chadwick's commission reports on the sanitary condition of the labouring population.

Act for inspection of asylums.

C. E. Mudie's circulating library.

P Science, Technology, Discovery, etc.

Crawford Long uses ether as an anaesthetic for minor operation in U.S.

Justus Mayer, *Law of Conservation of Energy*.

James Braid studies 'hypnotism'.

Great Western Railway converts some rails to standard gauge in Britain.

Q Scholarship

Bibliographical Society, London, founded.

R Philosophy and Religion

William Miller, *Evidence from Scripture of the Second Coming of Christ*.

Hippolytus, *Refutation of all Heresies*, is discovered at Mount Athos.

S Art, Sculpture, Fine Arts and Architecture

J. D. Ingres begins studies for 'Golden Age' wall-paintings.

F. W. Schadow, *Wise and Foolish Virgins* (painting).

T Music

F. Mendelssohn, Symphony in A minor ('Scottish', op. 36).

R. Wagner, *Rienzi* (opera).

M. Glinka, *Russlan and Ludmilla* (opera).

Philharmonic Society of New York founded under Ureli Hill.

U Literature

Théodore de Banville, *Les Cariatides*.

H. W. Longfellow, *Ballads and Other Poems*.

Lord Macaulay, *Lays of Ancient Rome*.

Lord Tennyson, *Morte d'Arthur and other Idylls*.

V The Press

Illustrated London News (*May*).

W Drama and Entertainment

X Sport

Ruff's *Guide to the Turf* first issued.

Y Statistics

British Textiles trade:

imports of raw cotton	435 mill. lb.
cotton exports	734 mill. yds.
woollen exports	75·3 mill. yds.
linen exports	69·2 mill. yds.
silk exports	369,000 lb.

Z Births and Deaths

Jan. 11th William James b. (–1910).

Feb. 4th Georg Brandes b. (–1927).

(*Continued opposite*)

A Jan: (–*Apr.*), British forces under Charles Napier conquer Sind, in lower valley of Indus (but war not declared until after Indian attack on British Residency, *Feb.* 15th).

B Feb:

C Mar:

D Apr: 11th, British Act of Parliament separates Gambia from Sierra Leone as Crown Colony.

E May: 4th, Natal is proclaimed a British Colony.

F Jun: 17th, Maori revolts against British in New Zealand.

G Jul: 15th, General Narvaez defeats Baldomero Espartero, who leaves Spain.

H Aug: Britain formally annexes Sind.

J Sep: 15th Otto I of Greece convokes National Assembly after popular rising against his misrule.

K Oct: 8th, Anglo-Chinese commercial treaties confirm Treaty of Nanking (of *Aug.* 1842).

L Nov: 8th, Queen Isabella II of Spain is declared of age;
28th, Britain and France recognise independence of Hawaii.

M Dec: 13th, Basutoland becomes a native state under British protection.

N

X Sport

Y Statistics

Z Births and Deaths
Jan. 20th Paul Cambon b. (–1924).
Feb. 19th Adelina Patti, b. (–1919).
Mar. 21st Robert Southey d. (68).
Apr. 15th Henry James b. (–1916).
June 15th Edvard Grieg b. (–1907).
Aug. 19th C. M. Doughty b. (–1926).

O **Politics, Economics, Law and Education**

August Haxthausen undertakes survey of land laws in Russia at invitation of Tsar Nicholas I.

Ethnological Society is founded.

P **Science, Technology, Discovery, etc.**

Michael Faraday coats metals with nickel by electrical process.

J. P. Joule, *Production of Heat by Voltaic Electricity*.

Georg Ohm analyses harmonic vibrations.

An aerostat is made.

J. B. Lawes and J. H. Gilbert at Rothamsted establish that nitrogen, potassium and phosphorus are necessary for plant growth, and Lawes opens superphosphate factory at Deptford Creek.

I. K. Brunel's Thames Tunnel opened.

Zola arched dam near Aix-en-Provence.

The export of machinery from Britain is legalised.

Charles Thurber invents 'chirographer' typewriter.

Q **Scholarship**

H. G. Liddell and R. Scott, *Greek-English Lexicon*.

R **Philosophy and Religion**

J. S. Mill, *Logic*.

S. Kierkegaard, *Either-or*.

Thomas Chalmers leads Scottish Disruption (*May* 18th), when 474 clergy withdraw from general assembly to form United Free Church of Scotland on the issue of lay patronage.

Joseph Smith authorises polygamy among Mormons.

Babist sect is founded in Persia.

S **Art, Sculpture, Fine Art and Architecture**

J. M. W. Turner, *The Sun of Venice Going to Sea* (painting).

J. Ruskin, *Modern Painters* (–60).

T **Music**

M. W. Balfe, *The Bohemian Girl* (opera).

G. Donizetti, *Don Pasquale* (opera).

R. Wagner, *Flying Dutchman* (opera).

F. Mendelssohn establishes Leipzig Conservatoire.

U **Literature**

George Borrow, *The Bible in Spain*.

Thomas Carlyle, *Past and Present*.

C. Dickens, *A Christmas Carol*.

J. R. Lowell, *Poems*.

Bulwer Lytton, *Last of the Barons*.

William Wordsworth is appointed poet laureate on Robert Southey's death.

V **The Press**

The Economist and *The News of the World* are first issued.

W **Drama and Entertainment**

Theatres Act ends monopoly of London managements.

(*Continued opposite*)

1844 French war in Morocco

A **Jan:**

B **Feb:**

C **Mar:** 8th, accession of Oscar I in Sweden on death of Charles XIV (–1859);
16th, Greek Constitution with two Chambers, the Senate and the Deputies.

D **Apr:** 12th, J. C. Calhoun's treaty for annexation of Texas by U.S. is signed (but defeated in Senate, *June* 8th).

E **May:** Natal is combined with Cape Colony for administrative purposes.

F **Jun:** 6th, Factory Act in Britain restricts female workers to twelve-hour day and children between eight and 13 years limited to six-and-a-half hours;
Tsar Nicholas I visits London and suggests partition of Ottoman Empire based on memorandum of Count Karl Nesselrode.

G **Jul:** 19th, Bank Charter Act separates banking and note-issuing departments of Bank of England, note-issuing is to be covered by coin and bullion except for fiduciary sum of £14 mill.

H **Aug:** 6th, French, under Duc de Joinville, begin hostilities against Morocco.

J **Sep:** 10th, French War in Morocco ends with treaty of Tangier.

K **Oct:**

L **Nov:** 23rd, Holstein Estates resolve on independence of Duchies of Schleswig and Holstein from Denmark.
James K. Polk (Democrat) wins U.S. presidential election with 170 electoral votes over Henry Clay (Whig), 105 votes.

M **Dec:**

N

O Politics, Economics, Law and Education

J. S. Mill, *Unsettled Questions of Political Economy*.

Edward Miall founds Anti-State Church Association (later the Liberation Society) to increase number of Dissenters in Parliament.

'Ragged School' Union.

Rochdale pioneers found Co-operative Society (*Dec.*).

First public baths and wash-houses opened at Liverpool.

British Royal Commission on the health of towns.

P Science, Technology, Discovery, etc.

Robert Chambers, *The Vestiges of the Natural History of Creation*.

Samuel Morse transmits first message on U.S. telegraph line (Washington-Baltimore, *May* 24th).

Q Scholarship

Lobegott Tischendorf discovers part of the *Codex Sinaiticus* of the New Testament.

R Philosophy and Religion

John Thomas founds the Christadelphians.

Y.M.C.A. is founded.

S Art, Sculpture, Fine Arts and Architecture

T Music

F. Mendelssohn, violin concerto in E minor (op. 64).

G. Verdi, *Ernani* (opera).

J. Joachim's début in London, playing Beethoven's Violin Concerto under Mendelssohn.

H. Berlioz, *Traité de l'Instrumentation*.

The Musical Times is first issued.

U Literature

B. Disraeli, *Coningsby*.

Alexandre Dumas, *The Three Musketeers* and *The Count of Monte Cristo*.

H. Heine, *Deutschland, ein Wintermärchen*.

A. W. Kinglake, *Eothen*.

E. Sue, *The Wandering Jew* (–45).

José Zorilla y Moral, *Don Juan Tenorio*.

V The Press

Society of Women Journalists is founded in London.

W Drama and Entertainment

X Sport

Y Statistics

Z Births and Deaths

Mar. 18th Nicolai Rimsky-Korsakov b. (–1908).
Mar. 24th Bertel Thorwaldsen d. (73).
Mar. 30th Paul Verlaine b. (–1896).
Apr. 16th Anatole France b. (–1924).
July 27th John Dalton d. (77).
Oct. 15th Friedrich Wilhelm Nietzsche b. (–1900).
Oct. 23rd Robert Bridges b. (–1930).
Dec. 2nd Francis Carruthers Gould b. (–1925).

1845 U.S. annexes Texas—Anglo-Sikh war

A Jan:

B Feb:

C Mar: 1st, U.S. Congress agrees to annexation of Texas and admission into the Union;
3rd, Florida becomes U.S. state;
4th, James K. Polk is inaugurated U.S. President;
11th, further Maori risings against British rule in New Zealand.

D Apr: Robert Peel's second 'Free-Trade' Budget repeals export duties entirely, and duties on many imports are limited or abolished.

E May: 23rd, new Spanish Constitution.

F Jun: 30th, Maynooth Grant increased to aid education in Ireland;
Anglo-French expedition sent to Madagascar against local ruler.

G Jul:

H Aug:

J Sep:

K Oct:

L Nov: 22nd, Whig leader, Lord John Russell, announces conversion to free trade in the 'Edinburgh Letter'.

M Dec: 6th, Robert Peel resigns, as Conservatives are not in favour of free trade, but he returns, 20th, as Russell is unable to form government;
11th, outbreak of Anglo-Sikh war when Sikhs cross Sutlej and surprise British;
—, the *Sonderbund*, a league of the seven Catholic Cantons in Switzerland, is formally established to protect Catholic interests;
29th, Texas becomes U.S. state.

N

O **Politics, Economics, Law and Education**

F. Engels, *The Condition of the Working Classes in England* (Leipzig).

College of Chemistry founded in London.

P **Science, Technology, Discovery, etc.**

A. von Humboldt, *Cosmos* (–58).

Arthur Cayley, *Theory of Linear Transformations.*

Adolphe Kolbe synthesises acetic acid.

William McNaught's compound steam engine.

Josué Heilmann's machine comb for combing cotton and wool.

E. B. Bigelow of Massachusetts invents Brussels power loom for making carpets.

W. G. Armstrong's hydraulic crane.

John Franklin leads expedition to discover North-West Passage.

Q **Scholarship**

A. H. Layard begins excavations at Nineveh.

Louis Thiers, *History of the Consulate and Empire* (–65).

T. Carlyle, *Cromwell's Letters and Speeches.*

R **Philosophy and Religion**

J. H. Newman is received into the Roman Catholic Church (*Oct.* 9th) and explains his step in *Essay on the Development of Christian Doctrine.*

S **Art, Sculpture, Fine Arts and Architecture**

British Museum (Robert Smirke).

The Madeleine, Paris, is completed by J. T. Huvé.

Restoration of Notre-Dame, Paris, revives Gothic style.

T **Music**

F. Chopin, Piano Sonata in B minor (op. 58).

F. Liszt, *Les Préludes.*

R. Wagner, *Tannhäuser* (opera).

U **Literature**

Honoré de Balzac, *Les Paysans.*

B. Disraeli, *Sybil, or the Two Nations.*

V **The Press**

W **Drama and Entertainment**

Henrick Hertz, *King René's Daughter.*

X **Sport**

Knickerbocker Club codifies rules of baseball.

Y **Statistics**

U.K. total State expenditure, £54·8 mill.

Z **Births and Deaths**

Feb. 15th Elihu Root b. (–1937).

Mar. 27th Wilhelm von Röntgen b. (–1923).

May 10th Benito Pérez Galdós b. (–1920).

June 18th Andrew Jackson d. (78).

Oct. 23rd Sarah Bernhardt b. (–1923).

Dec. 10th Frederick Pollock b. (–1937).

A Jan: 2nd, French troops defeat Algerian rebels but sustain heavy losses;
28th, East India Company's forces under Harry Smith defeat Sikhs at Aliwal.

B Feb: 10th, Hugh Gough defeats Sikhs at Sobrahan;
14th, rising in Cracow Republic swiftly spreads throughout Poland.

C Mar: 9th, by Treaty of Lahore ending First Sikh War Britain gains territory beyond the Sutlej River;
12th, Austrian and Russian troops occupy Cracow.

D Apr: 12th, on failure of U.S. negotiations with Mexico for purchasing New Mexico, President Polk sends troops into the disputed area;
23rd, U.S. Senate resolves to end British joint occupation of Oregon under the Convention of *Aug.* 1827.

E May: 8th, U.S. forces under Zachary Taylor defeat Mexicans at Palo Alto and, 9th, at Resaca de la Palma;
13th, formal declaration of war by U.S. against Mexico;
16th, Dom Miguel's supporters force Costa Cabral, the effective ruler of Portugal, into exile and Britain, under the terms of the Quadruple Alliance, 1834, sends a squadron to Oporto to suppress the rising;
25th, Louis Napoleon escapes from Ham to London;
26th, Robert Peel repeals the Corn Laws (royal assent given *June* 26th), splitting the Conservative Party;
German Professors meet at Frankfurt ('The Intellectual Diet of the German People') to discuss German reunification.

F Jun: 12th, mammoth meeting of Liberals in Brussels demands reforms;
14th, Treaty of Washington declares 49th Parallel the boundary between Oregon and Canada;
15th, election of Cardinal Mastai-Ferretti as Pope Pius IX (–1878);
30th, Robert Peel resigns on failing to secure passage of Coercion bill for preserving public order in Ireland, and Lord John Russell forms Liberal government, with Lord Palmerston as Foreign Secretary;
Mormons under Brigham Young leave Nauvoo City on trail for the Great Salt Lake.

G Jul: 8th, Christian VIII of Denmark declares the Danish State indivisible and heritable by females, thus excluding the Duchies of Schleswig-Holstein from becoming a separate province, with resultant tension in Germany.

H Aug: 8th, David Wilmot's proviso, that slavery should be excluded in any territory acquired from Mexico, introduced in House of Representatives but fails to pass U.S. Senate through opposition of South;
18th, U.S. forces capture Santa Fé;
22nd, U.S. annexes New Mexico;
28th, British Possessions Act gives Canada the right to fix tariffs.

J Sep: 17th, Germanic Confederation reserves its right in Schleswig-Holstein.

K Oct: 10th, Princess Luisa Fernanda, sister of Isabella II of Spain, marries Duc de Montpensier, Louis Philippe's youngest son, contrary to François Guizot's undertaking to Lord Aberdeen in 1843, which threatens Anglo-French relations and weakens the Orléanist monarchy in France.

O Politics, Economics, Law and Education

Massino D'Azeglio attacks the Papacy in *Degli ultimi casa de Romagna* and is expelled from Tuscany.

P. J. Proudhon, *Philosophie de la misère*.

Smithsonian Institution, Washington, founded.

P Science, Technology, Discovery, etc.

John Galle discovers the planet Neptune (*Sept.* 23rd) on the basis of Urbain Leverrier's calculations.

R. Owen, *British Fossils* (–1884).

E. Galois's research on the resolubility of algebraic equations published posth.

H. von Mohl discovers protoplasm, overthrowing Mathias Schleiden's theory of free-cell formation.

G. B. Amici establishes circulation of the sap in plants.

A. Sobrero prepares nitroglycerine.

Auguste Laurent obtains carbolic acid through distillation of pit coal.

Christian Schönbein invents gun-cotton.

Morton uses ether as an anaesthetic.

F. G. J. Henle, *Manual of Rational Pathology*.

Zeiss optical factory opened at Jena.

Elias Howe patents sewing machine in U.S.

John Deere makes plough with steel mould board.

Rapid development of railways in Britain on introduction of a standard gauge.

Q Scholarship

F. C. Baur traces the composition of the synoptic Gospels.

Henry Rawlinson opens up Assyrian history by deciphering Persian cuneiform inscriptions at Behistan.

George Grote, *History of Greece*.

W. H. Prescott completes *The Conquest of Peru*.

R Philosophy and Religion

William Whewell, *Elements of Systematic Morality*.

Friedrich Vischer, *Aesthetics*.

Theodor Waitz, *Foundations of Psychology*.

Evangelical Alliance founded in London to oppose Romanism.

British Presbyterian mission to Nigerian coast.

S Art, Sculpture, Fine Arts and Architecture

F. Delacroix decorates library of the Luxembourg, Paris.

J. F. Millet, *Oedipus Unbound* (painting).

G. F. Watts, *Paolo and Francesca* (painting).

Franz Klenze, Propylaea, Munich (–62).

J. B. Bunning, London Coal Exchange.

T Music

H. Berlioz, *Damnation of Faust*.

F. Liszt, 1st Hungarian Rhapsody.

F. Mendelssohn, *Elijah* (oratorio, in Birmingham).

R. Schumann, 2nd Symphony (C major).

U Literature

Ferdinand Freiligrath's revolutionary poetic cycle, *Ça Ira*.

Gottfried Keller, *Poems*.

1846 (Nov.–Dec.)

L Nov: 6th, Austria annexes Cracow Republic in violation of Treaty of Vienna, provoking protests from Britain, France, Sweden and Turkey.

M Dec: 28th, Iowa becomes a state of U.S.

Duke of Lucca, forced to grant administrative reforms, decides to sell his duchy to Leopold of Tuscany.

N The Irish potato crop again fails and famine increases despite organised relief.

Agricultural and industrial depression in France causes widespread distress.

Beginnings of native segregation in Natal where the first location commission sets up preserves for immigrant Zulus.

Commodore James Biddle of U.S. visits Edo Bay, Japan, but is refused facilities for trade.

U **Literature** (*cont.*)

Edward Lear, *Book of Nonsense.*
H. W. Longfellow, *The Belfry of Bruges.*
J. G. Whittier, *Voices of Freedom.*
Honoré de Balzac, *La Cousine Bette.*
George Sand (pseud.), *La Marc au diable.*
F. Dostoievsky, *Poor Folk.*
M. Jokai, *Working Days.*
H. Melville, *Typee; a Peep at Polynesian Life.*

V **The Press**

Daily News, first cheap English newspaper founded (*Jan.* 21st), with C. Dickens as editor.

W **Drama and Entertainment**

X **Sport**

Y **Statistics**

U.K. registered tonnage of merchant shipping 3,200,000 tons (131,000 steamships).

Z **Births and Deaths**

Jan. 30th F. H. Bradley b. (–1924).
Mar. 17th Friedrich Wilhelm Bessel d. (61).
Oct. 6th George Westinghouse b. (–1914).
Nov. 4th Felix Mendelssohn-Bartholdy d. (38).
Nov. 30th Friedrich List d. (57).

1847 Liberia becomes independent republic

A **Jan:**

B **Feb:** 3rd, United Diet summoned in Prussia by Frederick William IV.

C **Mar:** Liberals in Hungary obtain majority to the Table of Deputies, and March laws provide for a ten-point programme of responsible government.

D **Apr:**

E **May:**

F **Jun:** 8th, Factory Act providing for ten-hour day for women and for young people between ages of 13 and 18.

G **Jul:** 4th, Adolphe Thiers holds first reform banquet held in Paris, demanding wider franchise;
17th, Austrian troops occupy Ferrara after unrest caused by disappointment at Pius IX not undertaking reforms;
24th, Convention of Gramido ends war in Portugal.

H **Aug:** 26th, Liberia is proclaimed independent republic.

J **Sep:** 3rd, Baldomero Espartero is recalled to Spain;
14th, U.S. forces capture Mexico City;
François Guizot becomes French premier at critical time when France is subjected to severe political and economic unrest.

K **Oct:** 21st, *Sonderbund* War begins in Switzerland after Catholic Cantons refuse to dissolve union in face of liberal majority in Diet (*July* 20th), the *Sonderbund* is dissolved after defeat of Catholic Cantons (*Nov.* 29th);
Charles Albert of Piedmont dismisses reactionary ministers and proceeds with more liberal policy.

L **Nov:**

M **Dec:**

N

Z **Births and Deaths** (*cont.*)
Mar. 3rd Alexander Graham Bell b. (–1922).
May 7th Archibald Philip Primrose, Lord Rosebery b. (–1929).
May 15th Daniel O'Connell d. (71).
June 11th Millicent Garrett Fawcett b. (–1929).
Oct. 2nd Paul von Hindenburg b. (–1934).

O **Politics, Economics, Law and Education**

Louis Blanc's partisan *History of the French Revolution* (–62).

Karl Marx attacks P. J. Proudhon in *The Poverty of Philosophy*.

P **Science, Technology, Discovery, etc.**

H. Helmholtz, *On the Conservation of Energy*.

George Boole, *Mathematical Logic*.

Sir James Simpson uses chloroform as an anaesthetic.

Evaporated milk first made.

Gold is discovered in California (*Sept.*) and leads to the first 'gold rush'.

Improvements to the St. Lawrence completed, Lake Ontario to Montreal.

Q **Scholarship**

Jules Michelet, *Histoire de la Révolution française* (–53).

L. von Ranke, *Neun Bücher preussischer Geschichte* (–1848).

R **Philosophy and Religion**

Giuseppe Ferrari, *Philosophy of History*.

United Presbyterian Church of Scotland is formed from the United Secession Church of 1733 and the Relief Church of 1752.

H. Ward Beecher begins ministry at Plymouth Congregational Church, Brooklyn, making its pulpit a national platform.

The Mormons found Salt Lake City.

First Roman Catholic working-men's club, at Cologne.

S **Art, Sculpture, Fine Arts and Architecture**

Thomas Couture, *Romans of the Decadence*.

T **Music**

G. Verdi, *Macbeth* (opera).

Friedrich von Flotow, *Martha* (opera).

U **Literature**

Charlotte Brontë, *Jane Eyre*.

Emily Brontë, *Wuthering Heights*.

A. H. Hoffmann, *Struwwelpeter*.

G. Sand (pseud.), *Le Péché de M. Antoine*.

W. M. Thackeray, *Vanity Fair* (–48).

V **The Press**

W **Drama and Entertainment**

P. Mérimée, *Carmen*.

N. Ostrovsky, *The Bankrupt* (for which he is dismissed the Russian government service and the play is prohibited).

X **Sport**

Y **Statistics**

Z **Births and Deaths**

Jan. 14th Wilson Carlile b. (–1942).

Feb. 11th Joseph Alva Edison b. (–1931).

(*Continued opposite*)

1848 (Jan.–May) Year of Revolutions—Louis Napoleon elected French President

A Jan: 12th, Earl of Dalhousie becomes Governor-General of India;
—, revolt in Palermo, Sicily, against corruption of Bourbons; is completely successful by end of month;
20th, Christian VIII of Denmark dies, succeeded by Frederick VII (–1863).

B Feb: 2nd, treaty of Guadaloupe Hidalgo ends Mexican-U.S. War;
3rd, Harry Smith annexes country between Orange and Vaal rivers;
10th, constitution in Naples proclaimed by Ferdinand II (after demonstration against him over loss of Sicily);
15th, decree for constitution in Tuscany published;
22nd (–24th), revolt in Paris due to failure of Louis Philippe's reign, the economic depression and prohibition of reform banquets;
24th, Louis Philippe abdicates in favour of grandson, Comte de Paris, but Republican Provisional government is proclaimed under Alphonse de Lamartine;
27th, National Workshops are erected in France on Louis Blanc's plan to provide relief in Paris.

C Mar: 4th, Constitution in Piedmont and Sardinia, proclaimed by Charles Albert;
12th (–15th), revolution in Vienna begins with university demonstrations; 13th, Prince Metternich resigns and calling of States-General is promised;
14th, Constitution in Rome promulgated by Pope Pius IX;
15th, Hungarian Diet adopts reforms of *Mar.* 1847;
17th, revolution in Venice under Daniele Manin, after knowledge of success of Italian, French and Viennese Revolts, and Republic is proclaimed (22nd);
—, William II of Holland appoints committee to revise Constitution (power of Parliament is increased by Constitutional amendment, *Nov.*);
—, (–19th), in revolution in Berlin, Frederick William IV agrees to grant constitution, but, 21st, is forced to parade in streets of Berlin;
18th (–22nd), five-day revolution in Milan (*Cinque Giornate*) against Austrian rule, and Joseph Radetzky forced to abandon city;
20th, revolt in Parma;
—, Second Sikh War begins, arising out of Sikh aristocracy's discontent at British administration and murder of two British officers;
21st, Frederick VII of Denmark announces decision to incorporate Schleswig;
24th, German elements in Duchies of Schleswig and Holstein form government and Prussia recognises autonomy of Duchies;
—, Sardinia declares war on Austria;
31st, German Ante-Parliament (*Vorparlement*) meets at Frankfurt (–*Apr.* 4th).

D Apr: 8th, Austrians defeated by Piedmontese (Sardinian) troops at first battle of Goito;
10th, Chartist Petition to Parliament fails;
13th, Sicily is declared independent of Naples;
25th, Constitution in Austria with responsible government (repealed *May* 15th);
—, Papacy joins Sardinia against Austria;
—, Austrians suppress revolt in Cracow;
29th, Pius IX disassociates himself from Italian National Movement;
30th, Austrians are defeated at Pastrengo and Radetzky retreats.

E May: 2nd, Prussians invade Denmark over position of Schleswig-Holstein;
4th, French National Assembly meets, after elections based on universal male suffrage, with majority for moderate Republicans;
7th, Polish rebels surrender after Prussian troops put down insurrection in Warsaw;

O **Politics, Economics, Law and Education**

Karl Marx and Friedrich Engels issue *Communist Manifesto* (*Feb.*).
Marx's pamphlet, *Wage, Labour and Capital.*
J. S. Mill, *Principles of Political Economy.*
Public Health Act inaugurates sanitary legislation in Britain.

P **Science, Technology, Discovery, etc.**

Richard Owen, *On the Archetypes and Homologies of the Vertebrate Skeleton.*
Foundation of American Association for the Advancement of Science at Philadelphia (*Sept.* 20th).

Q **Scholarship**

Jakob Grimm, *History of the German Language.*
Lord Macaulay, *History of England* (–61).
J. C. Hart in *The Romance of Yachting* inaugurates the Shakespeare-Bacon controversy.

R **Philosophy and Religion**

J. A. Froude, *Nemesis of Faith.*
Frédéric Monod founds the *Église Libre* seceding from the French National Church.
Spiritualism gains ground in U.S.

S **Art, Sculpture, Fine Arts and Architecture**

H. Holman Hunt, J. Millais and D. G. Rossetti found the Pre-Raphaelite Brotherhood.
J. E. Millais, *Ophelia* (painting).
J. F. Millet, *The Winnower* (painting).

T **Music**

Carl Nicolai, *The Merry Wives of Windsor* (opera).
Friedrich Smetana opens music school in Prague.

U **Literature**

Vicomte de Chateaubriand, *Mémoires d'Outre-tombe.*
Alexandre Dumas, *La Dame aux Camélias.*
Elizabeth Gaskell, *Mary Barton.*
J. R. Lowell, *The Biglow Papers.*
H. Merger, *Scènes de la Vie de Bohème.*
Juan Valera, *Pepita Jimenez.*

V **The Press**

W **Drama and Entertainment**

X **Sport**

Y **Statistics**

Z **Births and Deaths**

Feb. 5th Joris Karl Huysmans b. (–1907).
Feb. 27th Ellen Terry b. (–1928), and C. H. H. Parry b. (–1918).
Mar. 31st William Waldorf, Viscount Astor b. (–).
Apr. 7th Randall Davidson b. (–1930).
Apr. 8th G. Donizetti d. (51).
June 14th Bernard Bosanquet b. (–1923).

E May: 15th, Communist rising in Paris, after news of suppression of Polish revolt; workmen overturn government and set up provisional administration which immediately collapses;
—, second rising in Vienna against new Austrian Constitution which is thereupon repealed;
—, collapse of Naples revolt;
17th, Ferdinand I of Austria flees from Vienna to Innsbruck;
18th, German National Assembly meets at Frankfurt and suspends German Confederation;
22nd, Prussian National Assembly meets in Berlin;
29th, Wisconsin becomes U.S. state;
—, Austrian victory at Curtatone against Tuscany;
30th, delay caused by Tuscan forces, however, allows Sardinian troops to defeat Austrians at second battle of Goito;
—, Treaty of Guadaloupe Hidalgo (*Feb.* 2nd) ratified by Mexico so that U.S. obtains Texas, New Mexico, California, Nevada, Utah, Arizona, parts of Colorado and of Wyoming from Mexico in return for large indemnity.

F Jun: 2nd, Pan-Slav Congress meets at Prague under Presidency of Francis Palacky;
10th, Austrians victorious at Vicenza, despite vigorous defence;
17th, Austrian troops under Prince Windischgrätz suppress Czech revolt in Prague;
23rd (–24th), 'June Days' in France, when Louis Cavaignac suppresses Paris workmen in effort to close workshops, killing thousands;
29th, Archduke John of Austria is elected Regent of the Reich which is to replace German Confederation.

G Jul: 22nd, Austrian Reichstag (Constituent Assembly) meets;
25th, Austrian army under Joseph Radetzky victorious at Custozza, enabling him to drive Sardinian forces from Milan and rest of Lombardy (*Aug.* 4th–5th);
—, Habeas Corpus Act suspended in Ireland, which leads to insurrection in Tipperary, led by Smith O'Brien;
27th, formal union of Venice, Sardinia and Lombardy;
Russians invade Danubian Principalities at request of Turkey to put down revolts there.

H Aug: 9th, Armistice between Austria and Sardinia is concluded at Vigevano, by which Sardinia gives up Lombardy and recognises *status quo* in Italy apart from in Venice before revolutions;
11th, Sardinian troops are expelled from Venice;
12th, Ferdinand I returns to Vienna;
26th, Truce of Malmö between Denmark and Prussia;
29th, Boers defeated at Boomplatz by British forces, and retire across the Vaal, thus ensuring Orange River sovereignty.

J Sep: 7th, abolition of serfdom in Austria;
11th, Bourbons of Naples accept armistice with Sicily at instigation of British and French admirals;
12th, new constitution by which Switzerland becomes federal union with strong central government;
24th, Louis Kossuth proclaimed president of committee for national defence of Hungary.

(*Continued opposite*)

Z **Births and Deaths** (*cont.*)

July 4th François de Chateaubriand d. (79).
July 18th W. G. Grace b. (–1915).
July 25th A. J. Balbour b. (–1930).
Aug. 12th George Stephenson d. (67).
Nov. 24th William Lamb, Viscount Melbourne, d. (69).
Dec. 8th Joel Chandler Harris ('Uncle Remus') b. (–1908).
— Paul Gauguin b. (–1903).

K Oct: 6th, third revolution in Vienna at news that government is to crush revolt in Hungary;
13th, Nasir Ud-Din becomes Shah of Persia;
31st, Prince Windischgrätz takes Vienna.

L Nov: 4th, Republican Constitution in France is promulgated with single Chamber, strong President and direct election under universal suffrage;
10th, Ibrahim, Viceroy of Egypt, dies and is succeeded by Abbas (–1854);
15th, Count Rossi, Papal Premier, assassinated by fanatical democrat;
16th, popular insurrection in Rome;
24th, Pius IX flees to Gaeta.

M Dec: 2nd, Emperor Ferdinand I of Austria abdicates in favour of nephew Franz Joseph I (–1916);
5th, Prussian National Assembly is dissolved and Constitution granted, but ultimate authority of King maintained;
10th, Louis Napoleon is elected President of France by a massive majority;
27th, German National Assembly proclaims fundamental rights.

N

1849 (Jan.–Jul.) Austrians defeat Sardinians at Novara—Britain annexes Punjab—Failure of German reunification by parliamentary means

A Jan: 13th, Sikhs defeated at Chillianwalla, but British lose many troops;
23rd, Prussian dispatch suggests German Union without Austria;
29th, French National Assembly announces own dissolution (but lingers on till end of *May*).

B Feb: 7th, Grand Duke of Tuscany flees to Gaeta;
9th, Rome proclaimed Republic under Giuseppe Mazzini;
21st, British defeat Sikhs at Gujerat;
22nd, Benjamin Disraeli becomes leader of Conservative Party (following death of Lord George Bentinck, *Sept.* 1848).

C Mar: 4th, proclamation of Austrian Constitution whereby all national groups to have own rights and Reichstag of two Chambers to be established, but this is immediately replaced by Constitution in which territories are indivisible and, 7th, Assembly is dissolved;
4th, Zachary Taylor inaugurated President of U.S.;
12th, Sardinia ends truce with Austria (of *Aug.* 9th, 1848);
—, Sikhs surrender at Rawalpindi;
13th, Neapolitan Parliament finally dissolved;
23rd, on Austrian victory at Novara, Charles Albert of Sardinia abdicates in favour of Victor Emmanuel II;
27th, German National Assembly passes Constitution and
28th, elects Frederick William IV of Prussia 'Emperor of the Germans';
29th, Britain annexes Punjab by treaty with Maharajah of Lahore.

D Apr: 3rd, Frederick William IV is unwilling to take crown from the people but wishes to receive it from the German Princes, and his vague reply is taken by German National Assembly as a refusal;
12th, Tuscany recalls Grand Duke Leopold;
14th, Hungarian Diet proclaims independence, with Louis Kossuth as Governor-President;
25th, French expedition lands in Papal States;
Rebellion in Montreal against British rule.

E May: 1st, Convention of Balta Liman by which joint Russo-Turkish occupation of Danubian Principalities is established for seven years;
3rd (–8th), revolts in Dresden, suppressed by Prussians;
11th (–13th), military revolt in Baden which causes Grand Duke to flee;
15th, Palermo is entered by Neapolitan forces and Sicily is forced to submit to Naples;
26th, 'Three-Kings' League' of Prussia, Saxony and Hanover to promote closer unity (but not recognised by Austria; and Saxony withdraws *Oct.* 19th).

F Jun: 5th, liberal Constitution in Denmark provides for limited monarchy, and civil liberties are guaranteed;
6th, German National Assembly (a 'rump') moves to Stuttgart and, 18th, is dissolved by troops; marks failure of attempt at German unification under a Parliamentary system;
13th, Communist riots in Paris are easily defeated and lead to repressive legislation;
26th, British Navigation Acts finally repealed.

G Jul: 3rd, French enter Rome, despite heroic resistance by Giuseppe Garibaldi, and restore Pope Pius IX;

O **Politics, Economics, Law and Education**
Agricultural co-operative land banks are founded in Germany.
Bedford College for Women, London, founded.
Amelia Bloomer begins to reform women's dress.

P **Science, Technology, Discovery, etc.**
Armand Fizeau measures the velocity of light.
Edward Frankland isolates amyl.
Joseph Monier's reinforced concrete.
C. E. Minié's rifle.
Krupps's steel gun bursts during tests.
Tubular railway bridge over Menai Straits (–50).

Q **Scholarship**
J. M. Kemble, *The Saxons in England.*

R **Philosophy and Religion**
Papal encyclical condemns socialism and communism.
Charles Kingsley and F. D. Maurice teach Christian Socialism.
F. W. Faber founds the Oratory, London.

S **Art, Sculpture, Fine Arts and Architecture**
Gustave Courbet, *After Dinner at Ornans* (painting).
E. Delacroix paints ceiling of Salon d'Apollon in the Louvre.
Alfred Rethel's wood-engravings, *The Dance of Death.*
John Ruskin, *The Seven Lamps of Architecture.*

T **Music**
G. Meyerbeer, *The Prophet* (oratorio).
F. Liszt, *Tasso.*
R. Schumann, music for *Manfred.*

U **Literature**
Matthew Arnold, *The Strayed Reveller.*
C. Dickens, *David Copperfield* (–50).
Charles Kingsley, *Alton Locke.*
Charles Saint-Beuve begins his 'Causeries du Lundi' series in *Le Constitutionnel.*

V **The Press**

W **Drama and Entertainment**

X **Sport**

Y **Statistics**

1849 (Jul.–Dec.)

G Jul: 10th, peace preliminaries between Denmark and Prussia;
23rd, Baden insurgents capitulate to Prussian troops.

H Aug: 2nd, death of Mehemet Ali;
6th, Peace of Milan ends war between Sardinia and Austria;
13th, Hungarian army capitulates at Vilagos when Russians aid Austria;
28th, Venice submits to Austria after long siege (which began *July* 20th).

J Sep:

K Oct: *October Manifesto* by Canadians in support of union with U.S. after repeal of Navigation Act (*June* 26th) increases economic depression.

L Nov: 22nd, Cape Colony forbids landing of convicts and forces ship from Britain to sail to Tasmania.

M Dec:

N Beginning of Russian advance into Persia.

z Births and Deaths

Jan. 22nd August Strindberg b. (–1912).
Mar. 19th Alfred von Tirpitz b. (–1930).
May 22nd Aston Webb b. (–1930).
July 5th W. T. Stead b. (–1912).
Oct. 7th Edgar Allan Poe d. (40).
Oct. 17th Frédéric Chopin d. (39).

1850 (Jan.–Oct.) Anglo-Kaffir War—French troops restore Pius IX to Rome

A Jan: 15th, British fleet blockades the Piraeus to force Greece to compensate Don Pacifico, a Moorish Jew who was a British subject, for damages sustained in Athens;
29th, Henry Clay's compromise resolutions about slavery, boundaries, California and Texas laid before U.S. Senate;
31st, liberal Constitution granted in Prussia.

B Feb: 23rd, Hanover follows the lead of Saxony in leaving the Three Kings' alliance with Prussia;
27th, Austria, Bavaria, Saxony and Württemberg agree to uphold German union.

C Mar: 20th, a German Parliament is summoned by Frederick William IV of Prussia to Erfurt to form a new confederation in opposition to Austria;
Further Anglo-Kaffir war breaks out (–1853);
Improvement in Anglo-Spanish relations.

D Apr: 12th, French troops restore Pius IX and garrison Rome; Pius revokes the Constitution;
19th, Clayton-Bulwer agreement by which Britain and U.S. agree not to obtain exclusive control of a proposed Panama canal;
27th, the Greek Government submits to British demands for compensation;
29th, Erfurt Parliament is prorogued.

E May: 10th, Austria revives the old Bundestag at Frankfurt under Prince Félix Schwarzenberg to counter Prussian attempts at German unification;
31st, universal suffrage in France is abolished.

F Jun: Lord Palmerston survives a Parliamentary attack on his conduct of foreign affairs with the *Civis Romanus sum* speech;
Tenant Right league is founded in Ireland.

G Jul: 2nd, peace of Berlin between Prussia and Denmark; Schleswig to be governed by Denmark while Holstein to be ruled by an administrator;
9th, death of U.S. President Zachary Taylor who is succeeded by Millard Fillmore;
24th, Schleswig-Holstein insurgents defeated at Idstedt.

H Aug: 2nd, Treaty of London between Britain, France, Russia, Denmark and Sweden on Schleswig-Holstein;
5th, Australia Government act grants representative government to South Australia, Tasmania and Victoria (which is separated from New South Wales);
9th, Texas surrenders her claim to New Mexico;
12th, California is admitted to the Union as a free state;
17th, Britain buys forts on the Gold Coast from Denmark;
26th, bill for the more effective recovery of fugitive slaves in U.S.;
Death of Louis Philippe; Orléanist claim to French throne is now upheld by Comte de Paris.

J Sep: 12th, rising in Hesse-Cassel in which Austria supports the Elector, Prussia the insurgents;
16th, the slave trade is forbidden in the District of Columbia;
26th, liberty of the press is restricted in France.

K Oct: 11th, Camillo Cavour is appointed minister in Piedmont where he begins economic reforms;

O **Politics, Economics, Law and Education**

Herbert Spencer, *Social Studies*, founds sociology.
Austro-Hungarian customs union.
Single coinage in Switzerland.
Mines Inspection Act in U.K.
Sunday rest introduced in Austria, and old-age insurance in France.
William Ewart's Public Libraries Act in Britain; first public libraries in Berlin.
School of Mines, London, founded (origin of Imperial College of Science and Technology).
Natural Science Honours School established at Oxford.
University extension lectures begin in New York.
Secondary education in Belgium.
Frances Buss founds North London Collegiate School.

P **Science, Technology, Discovery, etc.**

Rudolf Clausius enunciates the second law of thermodynamics and founds the kinetic theory of gases.
M. Melloni discovers that heat rays vary.
R. W. von Bunsen's burner.
P. L. Chebichev, *On Primary Numbers.*
R. Remak, *Development of the Frog.*
H. Helmholtz establishes speed of nervous impulse.
Claude Bernard demonstrates glycogenic function of the liver.
E. C. Carré invents vacuum freezing machine.
George Stephenson's cast-iron railway bridge at Newcastle upon Tyne opened.
J. W. Brett lays first submarine cable between Dover and Calais.
Royal Meteorological Society founded.
Heinrich Barth undertakes expedition to Central Africa.
Francis Galton explores Damaraland.
Arctic expedition under Erasmus Ommanney to search for John Franklin (–51); subsequent expeditions make known the north coast of Canada.

Q **Scholarship**

A. F. F. Mariette discovers the ruins of the Serapeum and the catacombs of the Apis bulls.
Karl Lachmann's edition of Lucretius.

R **Philosophy and Religion**

Re-establishment of the Roman Catholic hierarchy in Britain (*Sept.*).
Privy Council's judgment in George Gorham's case, denying the regenerative power of baptism, leads H. E. Manning and others to join Roman Church.
Abolition of the Church's jurisdiction in matters of heresy and sacrilege in Victor Emmanuel's dominions.
Frederick William IV entrusts the management of Prussian evangelical churches to a church council.
Civita Cattolica founded in Rome as the organ of the Curia and the Jesuits.

S **Art, Sculpture, Fine Arts and Architecture**

J. B. Corot, *Une Matinée* (painting).
Gustave Courbet, *The Stone-Breakers* (painting).
J. E. Millais, *Christ in the House of his Parents* (painting).

1850 (Oct.–Dec.)

K Oct: 26th, Russian intervention in Germany in Austria's favour;
Taiping rebellion in China under Hung Siu-tsuen, who takes Nanking and Shanghai, proclaims himself emperor and attacks Peking.

L Nov: 1st, Austrian and Bavarian troops occupy Hanau in Hesse-Cassel while Prussia prepares for war;
28th, as a result of Russian mediation, Prince Schwarzenberg of Austria and Otto von Manteuffel of Prussia sign the Punctation of Olmütz, by which Prussia subordinates herself to Austria and recognises the Frankfurt Diet;
29th, Austria and Prussia unite to restore order in Hesse-Cassel.

M Dec: 23rd (*–Mar.* 1851), Dresden conference, to settle the constitutional problems of Germany, proves fruitless.

N

s **Art, Sculpture, Fine Arts and Architecture** (*cont.*)
F. Goya's *Proverbios* engravings (posth.).
Joseph Paxton, Crystal Palace (–51).

T **Music**
F. Liszt produces R. Wagner's opera *Lohengrin.*
R. Schumann, 3rd Symphony ('The Rhenish') in E flat.

U **Literature**
E. B. Browning, *Sonnets from the Portuguese.*
R. W. Emerson, *Representative Men.*
N. Hawthorne, *The Scarlet Letter.*
Alexander Hertzen, *From Another Shore.*
Lord Tennyson publishes *In Memoriam* and succeeds William Wordsworth as poet laureate.
W. M. Thackeray, *Pendennis* completed.

V **The Press**
Reynolds Weekly News (*May*).

W **Drama and Entertainment**
H. Ibsen, *Catalina.*
Otto Ludwig, *Die Erbförster,*
P. T. Barnum persuades Jenny Lind to tour U.S.

X **Sport**

Y **Statistics**
Railways in operation: U.S. 9,015 miles; U.K. 6,635 miles.
Emigration to U.S. (1841–50): From Britain, 267,044; from Ireland, 780,719.

Z **Births and Deaths**
Jan. 14th 'Pierre Loti' (Julien Viaud) b. (–1923).
Jan. 29th Ebenezer Howard b. (–1928).
Mar. 7th Thomas Masaryk b. (–1937).
Apr. 23rd William Wordsworth d. (80).
May 9th J. L. Gay-Lussac d. (71).
May 28th F. W. Maitland b. (–1906).
June 24th Horatio, Lord Kitchener b. (–1916).
July 2nd Robert Peel d.(62).
Aug. 5th Guy de Maupassant b. (–1893).
Aug. 17th Honoré de Balzac d. (51).
Aug. 26th Louis Philippe d. (76).
Nov. 13th R. L. Stevenson b. (–1894).

1851 Louis Napoleon's *coup d'état*

A Jan:

B Feb: 22nd, Lord John Russell resigns after defeat, 20th, when voting against motion to assimilate county and borough franchises, but as Lord Stanley is unable to form Conservative administration, he returns on same day.

C Mar: 16th, Spanish Concordat with Papacy by which Catholicism becomes sole faith in Spain and Church gains control of education and the press.

D Apr:

E May: 16th, Prussia again recognises German Confederation at Conference at Dresden; Censorship of Prussian press is revived.

F Jun:

G Jul: 1st, Victoria proclaimed separate colony;
24th, abolition of British window-tax encourages construction of windows in buildings.

H Aug: 1st, Ecclesiastical Titles Act prevents Roman Catholic bishops taking titles from territory within Britain.

J Sep: 7th, Prussia concludes commercial treaty with Hanover.

K Oct:

L Nov: 18th, death of Ernest Augustus of Hanover; succeeded by George V (–1866).

M Dec: 2nd, Louis Napoleon carries out *coup d'état* in order to change constitution of France, risings break out 3rd (–4th), but are easily suppressed;
19th, Lord Palmerston resigns as Foreign Secretary, after his unauthorised approval of Louis Napoleon's actions, and is succeeded, 26th, by Lord Granville;
21st, result of plebiscite in France supports new constitution to be drawn up by Louis Napoleon;
31st, Austrian Constitution is abolished.

N German Diet appoints Reaction Committee to control small states and abolishes Fundamental Rights.

Y Statistics

Populations (in millions): China, 430; German States and free cities, 34; France, 33; Great Britain, 20·8; Ireland, 6·5; Italy, 24; U.S. 23; Austria, 16.
Coal production (in million tons): Great Britain, 60; France, 11·8; U.S. 7; German States, 1·7.
Iron production: Great Britain, 3 million tons; France, 2,414,000 tons; Russia, 400,000 tons.

Z Births and Deaths

May 27th Vincent D'Indy b. (–1931).
May 29th Léon Bourgeois b. (–1925).
June 11th Mrs. Humphrey Ward (Mary Augusta Arnold) b. (–1920).
July 8th Arthur Evans b. (–1941).
July 12th Louis Daguerre d. (62).
Sept. 14th James Fenimore Cooper d. (61).
Oct. 2nd Ferdinand Foch b. (–1929).
Nov. 21st Leslie Ward ('Spy') b. (–1922).
Nov. 26th Nicolas Jean Soult d. (82).
Dec. 19th J. M. W. Turner d. (76).

O **Politics, Economics, Law and Education**
Vincenzo Gioberti, *Il Rinnovamento Civile d'Italia.*
French government begins transportation of convicts to French colonies.
Illinois follows Maine in enforcing Prohibition, but Ohio abandons liquor licensing.
Owens College, Manchester, founded.
Mary Carpenter, *Reformatory Schools for . . . Juvenile Offenders.*

P **Science, Technology, Discovery, etc.**
Franz Neumann states the mathematical laws of magnetic-electric induction.
William Thomson's papers on the laws of conservation and dissipation of energy.
George Bond photographs the moon at Cambridge, Mass.
William Kelly's steel-making converter.
James Bogardus constructs a cast-iron-frame building.
Isaac Singer's sewing machine.
Hermann Helmholtz's ophthalmoscope.
Gold is found in Australia.

Q **Scholarship**
Francis Parkman, *The Conspiracy of Pontiac.*

R **Philosophy and Religion**
Philip Schaff, *History of the Apostolic Church.*

S **Art, Sculpture, Fine Arts and Architecture**
J. B. Corot, *Danse des Nymphes* (painting).
C. D. Rauch and K. F. Schinkel complete equestrian monument to Frederick the Great, Berlin.
J. Tenniel draws for *Punch.*
J. Ruskin, *The Stones of Venice* (–53).
Joseph Cubitt, King's Cross Station, London (–52).
Thomas Walter begins building wings and dome of the Capitol, Washington (–65).

T **Music**
G. Verdi, *Rigoletto* (opera).
R. Wagner attacks G. Meyerbeer in *Opera and Drama.*

U **Literature**
G. Borrow, *Lavengro.*
N. Hawthorne, *The House of Seven Gables.*
H. Heine, *Romanzero.*
G. Keller, *Der grüne Heinrich* (–53).
H. Melville, *Moby Dick.*
H. W. Longfellow, *Golden Legend.*

V **The Press**
New York Times (*Sept.*).

W **Drama and Entertainment**
The Great Exhibition, Hyde Park.
William Macready retires from the London stage.

X **Sport**

(*Continued opposite*)

1852 Beginning of Second Empire in France

A **Jan:** 14th, French Constitution gives President monarchical power;
17th, Sand River Convention establishes South African Republic (Transvaal);
22nd, Orléans family is banished from France by Presidential decree.

B **Feb:** 3rd, Juan de Rosas is overthrown in Argentina at battle of Caseros;
17th, repressive measures in France, including censorship of press;
23rd, Lord John Russell resigns, after defeat on amendment to Militia Bill and, 27th, a Conservative administration is formed under Lord Derby, with B. Disraeli chancellor of Exchequer (–*Dec.* 20th).

C **Mar:**

D **Apr:** 1st, Second Burmese War breaks out after British ultimatum to King of Burma, for compensation following outrages.

E **May** 6th, Leopold II of Tuscany abolishes Constitution;
8th, treaty of London by Britain, France, Russia, Prussia, Austria and Sweden guarantees integrity of Denmark.

F **Jun:** 30th, British Act of Parliament gives new Constitution providing for representative government for New Zealand.

G **Jul:**

H **Aug:**

J **Sep:**

K **Oct:**

L **Nov:** 4th, Count Cavour becomes Prime Minister of Piedmont;
21st, plebiscite is held in France in support of revival of French Empire;
In U.S. presidential election Franklin Pierce (Democrat) defeats Winfield Scott (Whig) by 254 electoral votes to 42.

M **Dec:** 2nd, French (Second) Empire is proclaimed with Napoleon III Emperor;
16th, B. Disraeli's first budget is defeated and
20th, Derby's government resigns, when a Coalition of Whigs and Peelites is formed under Lord Aberdeen, with W. E. Gladstone as chancellor of Exchequer;
—, British forces annex Pegu (Lower Burma) in war with Burmese.

N Russia obtains territory at mouth of River Amur; expansion in this coastal area of Pacific continues (–1860).

Z **Births and Deaths** (*cont.*)
Mar. 3rd Nicolai Gogol d. (41).
Sept. 5th Paul Bourget b. (–1935).
Sept. 12th Herbert Henry Asquith b. (–1928).
Sept. 14th Arthur Wellesley, Duke of Wellington, d. (83).
Sept. 30th Charles Villiers Stanford b. (–1924).
Oct. 9th Emil Fischer b. (–1919).
Dec. 15th Henri Becquerel b. (–1908).

O **Politics, Economics, Law and Education**

P **Science, Technology, Discovery, etc.**

C. F. Gerhardt formulates new theory of organic compounds.
James Sylvester discusses the calculus of forms.
Herbert Spencer coins the term 'evolution' in *The Development Hypothesis.*
Heinrich Barth explores Lake Chad.
David Livingstone embarks on expedition to explore Zambesi (–56).
Niagara Falls Suspension Bridge.

Q **Scholarship**

Léopold Delisle begins the modern study of palaeography at the Bibliothèque Impériale, Paris.
L. von Ranke, *History of France, Principally in the Sixteenth and Seventeenth Centuries.*

R **Philosophy and Religion**

Kuno Fischer, *History of Modern Philosophy* (–93).
Convocation of the Church of England, dormant since 1741, is revived through the efforts of Bishops Wilberforce and Phillpotts.
First biennial (later annual) Conference at Eisenach of Protestants from each German state.
First Plenary Council of Roman Catholics in U.S., held at Baltimore.

S **Art, Sculpture, Fine Arts and Architecture**

F. M. Brown, *The Last of England* (painting).
Charles Méryon's series of etchings 'Eaux-fortes sur Paris'.
I. K. Brunel and T. H. Wyatt, Paddington Station (–54).

T **Music**

U **Literature**

M. Arnold, *Empedocles on Etna.*
H. Beecher Stowe, *Uncle Tom's Cabin.*
T. Gautier, *Émaux et Camées.*
W. M. Thackeray, *History of Henry Esmond.*
Ivan Turgeniev, *A Sportsman's Sketches.*

V **The Press**

W **Drama and Entertainment**

Charles Reade, *Masks and Faces.*

X **Sport**

Y **Statistics**

British Textiles trade:

imports of raw cotton	740 mill. lb.
exports of cottons	1,524 mill. yds.
exports of woollens	165,527,000 yds.
exports of linens	133,193,000 yds.
exports of silks	1,131,000 lb.

Z **Births and Deaths**

Jan. 4th Joseph Joffre b. (–1931).
Feb. 24th George Augustus Moore b. (–1933).
Feb. 25th Thomas Moore d. (72).
Mar. 1st Théophile Delcassé b. (–1923).

(*Continued opposite*)

1853 Russia occupies Danubian Principalities—Gladstone's Free Trade Budget

A Jan: 29th, Napoleon III marries Eugénie de Montijo at Tuileries.

B Feb: 19th, commercial treaty between Prussia and Austria.

C Mar: 4th, Franklin Pierce inaugurated President of U.S.

D Apr: 4th, Oldenburg and Hanover join *Zollverein*;
18th, W. E. Gladstone introduces first Budget which abolishes most of duties on partially manufactured goods and foodstuffs and halves most duties on manufactured products;
19th, Prince Alexander Menshikov, Russian emissary to Turkey, claims protectorate for Russia over Christian subjects of Ottoman Empire.

E May: 1st, new Constitution in Argentina is not accepted by Buenos Aires;
21st, Turks reject Russian ultimatum (of *Apr*. 19th) and Menshikov leaves Constantinople.
31st, Tsar Nicholas I orders occupation of the Danubian Principalities.

F Jun: 2nd, British fleet ordered to assemble off Dardanelles (arriving there 13th, and is joined by French squadron 14th);
20th, peace between Britain and Burma, but Burmese King refuses to sign a treaty.

G Jul: 1st, Cape Colony obtains Constitution with elective Legislative Council (first Parliament meets *June* 30th 1854);
2nd, Russian army crosses the Pruth and invades Danubian Provinces;
28th, Vienna Note to solve Eastern Question, drawn up by French ambassador, is submitted to Russia by Austria (and subsequently is approved by Russia *Aug*. 3rd, amended by Turkey *Aug*. 19th, the amendments being rejected by Russia, *Sept*. 7th).

H Aug:

J Sep: 24th, France annexes New Caledonia.

K Oct: 4th, Turkey declares war on Russia.

L Nov: 15th, death of Maria II of Portugal who is succeeded by Pedro V;
30th, Turkish fleet destroyed by Russia off Sinope.

M Dec: 11th, Britain annexes Nagpur, one of leading Mahratha States.

N German Navy of 1848 is sold by auction.
Britain discontinues transportation of convicts to Tasmania.

Z **Births and Deaths**
Feb. 9th Leander Starr Jameson b. (–1917).
May 14th Hall Caine b. (–1931).
June 3rd William Flinders Petrie b. (–1942).
July 5th Cecil Rhodes b. (–1902).
Nov. 5th Marcus Samuel b. (–1927).
Nov. 27th Frank Dicksee b. (–1928).
Dec. 17th Herbert Beerbohm Tree b. (–1917).
— Vincent Van Gogh b. (–1890).

O **Politics, Economics, Law and Education**

Repeal of advertisement tax in Britain.

The Mayor of Mulhausen sponsors an 'artisan's town' of 1,200 model dwellings intended for owner-occupiers.

P **Science, Technology, Discovery, etc.**

Samuel Colt opens armoury at Hartford, Connecticut, with 1,400 machine tools, which revolutionises the manufacture of small arms.

I. K. Brunel, Saltash Bridge (–59).

Vienna-Trieste railway through the Alps.

Destruction of Turkish wooden frigates by Russian shells at Sinope emphasises the need for armour plating.

The *Wellingtonia gigantea*, the largest tree in the world, is discovered in California.

Q **Scholarship**

T. Mommsen, *History of Rome* (–56).

H. von Sybel, *History of the French Revolution.*

H. Taine, *La Fontaine et ses Fables* (–60).

R **Philosophy and Religion**

Johann Herzog, *Encyclopaedia of Protestant Theology* (–68).

F. D. Maurice is expelled from his professorship at King's College, London, for questioning the doctrine of eternal punishment in *Theological Essays.*

C. H. Spurgeon begins preaching at Exeter Hall, London.

Roman Catholic hierarchy is established in Holland.

W. A. Muhlenberg's memorial urging the Episcopal Church in U.S. to widen its activities in social work.

S **Art, Sculpture, Fine Arts and Architecture**

Georges Haussmann begins reconstruction of Paris and lays out the Bois de Boulogne.

T **Music**

G. Verdi, *Il Trovatore* and *La Traviata* (operas).

Johannes Brahms, Piano Sonata in C (op. 1).

R. Schumann's article 'New Paths'.

R. Wagner issues his text of *The Ring.*

William Steinway begins to make pianos in New York.

U **Literature**

M. Arnold, *The Scholar Gipsy* and *Sohrab and Rustum.*

Elizabeth Gaskell, *Cranford.*

N. Hawthorne, *Tanglewood Tales.*

Charles Kingsley, *Hypatia.*

Leconte de Lisle's *Poèmes Antiques* founds the 'Parnassus School' of poets.

C. M. Yonge, *The Heir of Redclyffe.*

V **The Press**

The Field, London.

W **Drama and Entertainment**

Gustave Freytag, *The Journalist.*

X **Sport**

Y **Statistics**

(*Continued opposite*)

A Jan: 3rd, British ambassador in Constantinople, Stratford Canning, receives order to send British fleet into Black Sea, which is subsequently carried out.

B Feb: 23rd, at Convention of Bloemfontein, British agree to leave territory north of Orange River which allows for establishment of Constitution for Orange Free State.

C Mar: 12th, Britain and France conclude alliance with Turkey against Russia;
26th, Charles III, Duke of Parma, is murdered;
27th, France and, 28th, Britain declare war on Russia;
31st, U.S. makes first treaty with Japan, negotiated by Commodore Perry.

D Apr: 12th, Buenos Aires adopts separate Constitution from Argentina;
20th, Austria and Prussia conclude defensive alliance against Russia;
25th, U.S. possessions in Far West are completed when Senate ratifies Gadsden Purchase (of *Dec.* 1853) which comprises area which is now New Mexico and southern part of Arizona.

E May: 26th, France and Britain occupy the Piraeus after declaring blockade of Greece for attempting to attack Turkey, and Greece subsequently promises neutrality;
30th, Kansas-Nebraska Act repeals Missouri Compromise (of 1820) and provides for settlement of these territories under popular sovereignty, a situation which immediately leads to 'War for Bleeding Kansas' between free-states and pro-slavery elements;
Britain declares Monroe Doctrine not binding on European countries.

F Jun: 3rd, Austrian ultimatum to Russia against carrying the war across the Balkans;
5th, Elgin Treaty between Britain and U.S. establishes reciprocity for trade between U.S. and Canada (and is made act of Canadian Legislature *Sept.* 23rd);
14th, Austro-Turkish treaty, for Austria to occupy the Danubian Principalities until the end of the war;
Colonial Secretaryship is separated from the Secretaryship for War in Britain.

G Jul: 6th, Republican Party formally established in U.S. in opposition to Kansas-Nebraska Act (title having first been adopted *Feb.* 28th);
7th, manifesto is published in Spain which begins liberal revolt led by General O'Donnell;
13th, Abbas I, Viceroy of Egypt, is murdered; succeeded by Mohammed Said (–1863).

H Aug: 3rd, B. Espartero becomes premier of Spain (and Regent Maria Christina is exiled, 28th);
8th, Vienna Four Points by Britain, Austria and France state conditions of peace to be Russia's abandonment of claim to protectorate over Sultan's Christian subjects, revision of Straits settlement in interests of European powers, free passage of mouths of Danube and guarantee of integrity of Danubian principalities and of Serbia;
22nd, Austria occupies Danubian Principalities after Russians withdraw.

J Sep: 14th, allied powers land unopposed in Crimea;
20th, at the battle of the Alma British and French troops are victorious but do not press advantage to its conclusion.

K Oct: 17th, English and French forces begin siege of Sebastopol but assault is postponed after ineffective allied bombardment;
18th, Ostend Manifesto, signed by U.S. ambassadors to Britain, France and Spain, is dispatched to Washington advising acquisition of Cuba by force if Spain refuses to cede it to U.S.;

O **Politics, Economics, Law and Education**

Report by Stafford Northcote and Charles Trevelyan leads to foundation of Civil Service Commission.

Juvenile Offenders Act in U.K.

John Bowring's *The Decimal System* leads to the introduction of the florin in U.K.

F. D. Maurice founds the Working Men's College, London.

University College, Dublin, founded.

P **Science, Technology, Discovery, etc.**

Christian Ehrenberg, *Microgeology.*

Georg Riemann, *On the Hypotheses forming the Foundation of Geometry.*

H. J. S. Smith investigates the theory of numbers (–64).

Claude Bernard makes known the function of the vasodilator nerves.

Abraham Gesner manufactures kerosene.

Richard Burton and John Speke travel to the interior of Somaliland.

Q **Scholarship**

J. Grimm, *German Dictionary*, vol. 1.

R **Philosophy and Religion**

George Boole, *The Laws of Thought on which are founded the Mathematical Theories of Logic and Probabilities.*

Pius IX declares the dogma of Immaculate Conception of Blessed Virgin Mary to be an article of faith (*Dec.* 8th).

Jewish seminary founded at Breslau.

S **Art, Sculpture, Fine Arts and Architecture**

Moritz Schwind's frescoes at Wartburg Castle depicting the life of St. Elisabeth of Hungary.

T **Music**

F. Liszt, *Mazeppa.*

H. Berlioz, *The Childhood of Christ* (oratorio).

U **Literature**

F. D. Guerazzi, *Beatrice Cenci.*

C. Kingsley, *Westward Ho!*

Frédéric Mistral founds the Félibrige Society for the revival of Provençal culture.

G. de Nerval, *Les Filles du feu.*

Coventry Patmore, *Angel in the House.*

H. D. Thoreau, *Walden, or Life in the Woods.*

M. Tompa, *Legends or Flowers.*

V **The Press**

Le Figaro, Paris, issued.

W **Drama and Entertainment**

G. V. Angier and L. S. J. Sandeau, *Le Gendre de M. Poirier.*

X **Sport**

Y **Statistics**

K Oct: 25th, battle of Balaclava is begun by Russians and results in allied victory at great loss after Charges of the Heavy Brigade and of the Light Brigade;
Prussian Upper House reconstituted with increased influence of great landowners and repressive legislation is subsequently carried out.

L Nov: 5th, at battle of Inkerman allies defeat Russians who suffer heavy losses;
14th, storm bursts over Sebastopol wrecking allied supply ships, leading to chaos and loss of life.

M Dec: 2nd, Austria concludes alliance with Britain and France whereby her Italian possessions are guaranteed during war in return for Austrian defence of Danubian Principalities.

N

Z **Births and Deaths**

Jan. 1st James George Frazer b. (–1941).
Feb. 9th Edward Carson b. (–1935).
Feb. 27th H. F. R. de Lamennais d. (71).
Mar. 23rd Alfred Milner b. (–1925).
Apr. 28th Johann Ludwig Tieck d. (80).
June 10th G. E. Buckle b. (–1935).
July 12th George Eastman b. (–1932).
Aug. 20th Friedrich Schelling d. (79).
Sept. 1st Engelbert Humperdinck b. (–1921).
Oct. 20th Arthur Rimbaud b. (–1891).

1855 Fall of Sebastopol

A Jan: 26th, Piedmont joins allies against Russia.

B Feb: 6th, Lord Palmerston undertakes to form Liberal ministry after resignation of Lord Aberdeen (1st), due to popular dissatisfaction with war policy;
Panama given federal status by constitutional amendment.

C Mar: 2nd, Tsar Nicholas I of Russia dies (aged 58) and is succeeded by Alexander II (–1881);
30th, by treaty of Peshawar Britain and Afghanistan form alliance against Persia;
End of Taiping Rebellion in China.

D Apr:

E May: King George V of Hanover abolishes liberal institutions at demand of Federal Diet.

F Jun: 15th, abolition of stamp duty on newspapers in Britain.

G Jul: 16th, British Parliament establishes responsible government throughout Australian States, except for Western Australia.

H Aug: 18th, Austrian Concordat with Pope gives clergy control of education, censorship and of matrimonial law (revoked 1867).

J Sep: 11th, Sebastopol entered by allies after capitulation of Russians.

K Oct:

L Nov: 21st, Swedish alliance with Britain, France and Turkey against Russia;
28th, Kars, on Asiatic front, is taken by Russian forces.

M Dec: 29th, Austrian ultimatum to Russia threatens war unless Russia accepts 'Vienna Points' (of *Aug.* 8th 1854), with addition of neutrality of Black Sea and cession of Bessarabia.

N Victoria government restricts Chinese immigration.

X **Sport**

Y **Statistics**
U.K. total State expenditure, £69·1 mill.

Z **Births and Deaths**
Feb. 23rd K. F. Gauss d. (77).
Mar. 31st Charlotte Brontë d. (39).
May 17th Timothy Healy b. (–1931).
May 24th Arthur Wing Pinero b. (–1934).
Aug. 7th Stanley J. Weyman b. (–1928).
Nov. 5th Eugene Debs b. (–1926).
Nov. 11th Søren Kierkegaard d. (42).
— 'Marie Corelli' (pseud. of Mary Mackay) b. (–1924).

O **Politics, Economics, Law and Education**

Administrative Reform Association founded in London (*May* 5th), as protest against the muddles and disasters of the Crimean War.

Pierre Le Play, *Les Ouvriers européens*, the first comparative study of working-class incomes.

Chair of Technology founded at Edinburgh University.

P **Science, Technology, Discovery, etc.**

Franz Köller makes tungsten-steel.

E. St. Claire Deville's process for making aluminium.

R. S. Lawrence constructs turret lathe.

Powdered milk.

Electric telegraph between London and Balaclava is completed (*Apr.*).

Matthew Mauray, *Physical Geography of the Sea.*

D. Livingstone discovers Victoria Falls of the Zambesi River (*Nov.*).

Q **Scholarship**

Johann Droysen, *History of Prussian Policy* (-86).

H. Milman, *History of Latin Christianity.*

W. H. Prescott, *Philip II.*

R **Philosophy and Religion**

Alexander Bain, *Sense and the Intellect.*

H. Spencer, *Principles of Psychology.*

Auguste Gratry, *Connaissance de Dieu*, opposing Positivism.

Religious Worship Act in U.K.

Sardinian Monastic Law dissolves all contemplative orders.

S **Art, Sculpture, Fine Arts and Architecture**

G. Courbet's *Pavillon du Réalisme* at Paris World Fair, including his *L'Atelier* (painting).

Jacob Burckhardt's treatise on art history, *Der Cicerone.*

T **Music**

H. Berlioz, *Sicilian Vespers*, and *Te Deum.*

George Bristow, *Rip Van Winkle* (opera).

R. Wagner conducts orchestral concerts in London, where the Crystal Palace concerts are also established.

U **Literature**

H. W. Longfellow, *The Song of Hiawatha.*

G. de Nerval's *La Rêve et la Vie* (posth.) begins the Symbolist Movement.

Lord Tennyson, *Maud and Other Poems.*

W. M. Thackeray, *The Rose and the Ring.*

Anthony Trollope, *The Warden.*

Ivan Turgeniev, *Rudin.*

Walt Whitman, *Leaves of Grass.*

V **The Press**

Newspaper tax abolished in Britain.

Foundation of *The Daily Telegraph* (June 29th) and *The Saturday Review.*

W **Drama and Entertainment**

Adelaide Ristori takes Paris by storm in S. Pellico's *Francesca da Rimini.*

Paris World Fair.

(*Continued opposite*)

1856 (Jan.–Nov.) Treaty of Paris ends Crimean War—Second Anglo-Chinese War

A Jan: 29th, Queen Victoria institutes the Victoria Cross.

B Feb: 13th, Britain annexes Oudh, which increases hostility of India to British rule;
18th, Reform Edict in Turkish Empire guarantees life, honour and property of all subjects, abolishes civil power of heads of Christian Churches, ends torture and provides for large-scale reform of prisons, and for religious freedom;
25th, Peace conference at Paris (–*Mar.* 30th) attended by representatives of Britain, France, Austria, Turkey, Sardinia and Russia (Prussian delegate is allowed to attend later).

C Mar: 16th, birth of Prince Imperial in France (Eugène Louis Jean Joseph) ensures succession to throne;
30th, the integrity of Turkey is recognised by the powers in the Treaty of Paris who guarantee Danubian Principalities, Russia cedes Bessarabia, the Black Sea is to be neutral, and the R. Danube is to be free.

D Apr: 15th, Britain, France and Austria guarantee integrity and independence of Turkey in a further treaty;
16th, Declaration of Paris abolishes privateering, defines nature of contraband and blockade and recognises principle of 'free ships, free goods'.

E May: 24th, Massacre of Pottawatomie Creek by John Brown in war for 'Bleeding Kansas' in which pro-slavers are murdered by free-staters;
27th, Tsar Alexander II grants amnesty for Polish insurgents.

F Jun:

G Jul: 12th, Austria grants amnesty for Hungarian insurgents of 1848–9;
—, Natal is established as a separate British Crown Colony with an elected assembly.

H Aug:

J Sep: 3rd, unsuccessful rising of Prussian royalists in Neufchâtel Canton, Switzerland, a possession of the King of Prussia, which had proclaimed a republic in 1848;
15th, re-establishment of Spanish Constitution of 1845 with additional provision for annual assembly of Cortes, by Leopold O'Donnell (who replaced Baldomero Espartero, *July*).

K Oct: 8th, *Arrow* Incident, when ship flying British flag is boarded by Chinese, who arrest members of crew; provokes second Anglo-Chinese War (–1858);
14th, Spanish Constitutional amendment annulled after O'Donnell's dismissal.

L Nov: 1st, war between Britain and Persia after latter occupies Herat (–1857);
3rd (–4th), British fleet bombards Canton;
James Buchanan (Democrat) wins U.S. presidential election (174 electoral votes) over John C. Frémont (Republican, 114 votes) and Millard Fillmore (Whig, 8 votes).

O **Politics, Economics, Law and Education**

Christian von Bunsen's *Signs of the Times* revives Liberal movement in Prussia.

P **Science, Technology, Discovery, etc.**

Hermann Helmholtz, *Physiological Optics* (–66).

Nathaniel Pringsheim observes sperm entering ovum.

Henry Bessemer's process for making steel brings down prices.

William Siemens makes ductile steel for boiler plating.

W. H. Perkins prepares first aniline dye ('mauve').

Richard Burton and John Speke set out to find source of the Nile and (1858) discover Lake Tanganyika and Lake Victoria Nyanza.

Q **Scholarship**

Neanderthal skull found in Quaternary bed in Feldhofen Cave near Hochdal.

J. A. Froude, *History of England from the Death of Wolsey to the Defeat of the Armada* (–70).

J. R. Motley, *Rise of the Dutch Republic.*

C. A. de Tocqueville, *L'Ancien Régime et la Révolution.*

Theodor Goldstücker, *Sanskrit Dictionary.*

R **Philosophy and Religion**

Friedrich Schelling's Berlin lectures on philosophy published posth. (–58).

Rudolf Lotze, *Mikrokosmus* (–64).

H. Taine, *Les Philosophes Français du XIX siècle* (serially).

G. A. Denison is acquitted by the Judicial Committee of the Privy Council, after condemnation by the Court of Arches, for favouring the Real Presence.

Wilhelm Ketteler, Bishop of Mainz, founds *The Catholic*, an Ultramontane journal, to oppose Ignaz von Döllinger and the Munich School.

S **Art, Sculpture, Fine Arts and Architecture**

J. D. Ingres completes *La Source* (painting).

H. von Ferstel, Votivkirche, Vienna (–79).

T **Music**

Alexander Dargomijsky, *Russalka* (opera).

U **Literature**

Gustave Flaubert, *Madame Bovary* (–57).

Victor Hugo, *Les Contemplations.*

Charles Reade, *It Is Never Too Late to Mend.*

V **The Press**

Harper's Weekly, New York.

Frankfurter Zeitung.

W **Drama and Entertainment**

Henry Irving's début on the London stage.

X **Sport**

Y **Statistics**

U.K. registered tonnage of merchant shipping 4,367,000 (387,000 steamships).

U.K. cotton industry employs 379,000 factory workers and 23,000 handloom weavers.

M Dec: 2nd, frontier between France and Spain is defined;
16th, The South African Republic (Transvaal) is organised under Marthinius Pretorius.

N During the year Britain grants self-government to Tasmania and allows responsible government in New Zealand.

z **Births and Deaths**

Jan. 12th J. S. Sargent b. (–1925).
Feb. 17th Heinrich Heine d. (58).
Apr. 26th W. F. Massey b. (–1925) and Henry Morgenthau b. (–1946).
May 6th Sigmund Freud b. (–1939) and Robert Edwin Peary b. (–1920).
May 22nd Augustin Thierry d. (61).
June 22nd H. Rider Haggard b. (–1925).
July 26th George Bernard Shaw b. (–1950).
July 29th Robert Schumann d. (46).
Aug. 15th Keir Hardie b. (–1915).
Oct. 15th Oscar Wilde b. (–1900).
Dec. 18th J. J. Thomson b. (–1940).
Dec. 22nd Frank Billings Kellogg b. (–1937).
Dec. 28th Woodrow Wilson b. (–1924).

1857 Indian Mutiny begins—Garibaldi founds Italian National Association

A **Jan:**

B **Feb:**

C **Mar:** 4th, Peace of Paris ends Anglo-Persian War and Shah recognises independence of Afghanistan;
4th, James Buchanan inaugurated President of U.S.;
7th, the decision of the Supreme Court in the Dred Scott case in connection with position of a slave in a free state renders the Missouri compromise unconstitutional.

D **Apr:**

E **May:** 10th, Revolt of Sepoys at Meerut begins Indian Mutiny against British rule (–1858);
26th, Prussia renounces sovereignty over Neufchâtel.

F **Jun:** 1st, Royal Navy destroys Chinese fleet;
14th, commercial treaty between France and Russia (promulgated by France, 30th *July*);
27th, Massacre of Cawnpore when British soldiers and male residents are executed after promise of safe-conduct.

G **Jul:** 15th, women and children, taken by Indians at Cawnpore, are brutally murdered.

H **Aug:** Italian National Association formed by Giuseppe Garibaldi for unification under Piedmont.

J **Sep:** 20th, Delhi is captured by British after siege since June;
25th, Henry Havelock and James Outram temporarily relieve Lucknow.

K **Oct:** Irish Republican Brotherhood (Fenians) founded in New York; soon spreads to Ireland;
Frederick William IV of Prussia suffers a stroke.

L **Nov:** 17th, Colin Campbell relieves Lucknow;
20th, Tsar Alexander II appoints committee to study the problem of emancipation of serfs (Emancipation Edict is approved *Mar.* 1861).

M **Dec:** 6th, British forces recapture Cawnpore;
29th, British and French forces take Canton.

N

Z **Births and Deaths** (*cont.*)
Sept. 5th Auguste Comte d. (59).
Sept. 15th William Howard Taft b. (–1930).
Sept. 30th Hermann Sudermann b. (–1938).
Dec. 3rd. Joseph Conrad b. (–1924).
— Max Klinger b. (–1920).

O **Politics, Economics, Law and Education**
Matrimonial Causes Act establishes divorce courts in England and Wales.
Science Museum, South Kensington, is founded.
Widespread cattle disease in Europe.

P **Science, Technology, Discovery, etc.**
Louis Pasteur demonstrates that lactic fermentation is due to a living organism.
E. G. Otis installs first safety elevator which, with the development of cheaper steel, makes possible the skyscraper.
Transatlantic cable is laid (–65).

Q **Scholarship**
C. T. Newton discovers remains of the mausoleum of Halicarnassus.
'Rolls Series' of edited texts of chronicles and memorials of the Middle Ages is begun.
H. T. Buckle, *History of Civilisation* (–61).

R **Philosophy and Religion**
Ernest Renan, *Études d'histoire religieuse.*
First ritualistic cases in English church courts.

S **Art, Sculpture, Fine Arts and Architecture**
J. F. Millet, *The Gleaners* (painting).
E. Delacroix, decorations for S. Sulpice, Paris (–60).
Gavarni (pseud.), *Masques et Visages* (lithographs –58).
National Portrait Gallery, London, opened.

T **Music**
F. Liszt, *A Faust Symphony.*

U **Literature**
Charles Baudelaire, *Les Fleurs du Mal.*
B. Björnson, *Synnöve Solbakken.*
George Borrow, *The Romany Rye.*
E. B. Browning, *Aurora Leigh.*
George Eliot (pseud.), *Scenes from Clerical Life* in *Blackwood's Magazine.*
Thomas Hughes, *Tom Brown's Schooldays.*
Dinah Muloch (later Mrs. Craik), *John Halifax Gentleman.*
W. M. Thackeray, *The Virginians* (serially).
Anthony Trollope, *Barchester Towers.*

V **The Press**
Birmingham Post.
Atlantic Monthly founded, with J. R. Lowell as editor.

W **Drama and Entertainment**

X **Sport**

Y **Statistics**

Z **Births and Deaths**
Feb. 2nd Michael Ivanovich Glinka d. (54).
Feb. 22nd Robert Baden-Powell b. (–1941).
Feb. 26th Émile Coué (–1926).
Mar. 2nd Alfred de Musset d. (47), and Paul Doumer b. (–1932).
Mar. 18th Rudolf Diesel b. (–1913).
May 13th Ronald Ross b. (–1932).
June 2nd Edward Elgar b. (–1934).

(*Continued opposite*)

1858 British Crown takes over powers of East India Company—Napoleon III and Cavour plan unification of Italy

A **Jan**: 14th, Felice Orsini's plot to assassinate Napoleon III.

B **Feb**: 19th, Lord Palmerston resigns after defeat on Conspiracy to Murder bill following Orsini plot and
26th, Lord Derby forms Conservative administration.

C **Mar**:

D **Apr**: 1st, Granadian Confederation formed from provinces in former Colombian Federation (Republican Constitution promulgated *May* 22nd).

E **May**: 12th, Minnesota becomes U.S. state.

F **Jun**: 26th, Treaty of Tientsin ends Anglo-Chinese War; China opens further ports to British commerce and legalises opium trade (similar treaty with France by Chinese *June* 27th).

G **Jul**: 8th, proclamation of peace in India by British;
20th, Napoleon III and Cavour begin meetings at Plombières to plan unification of Italy;
23rd, Act of Parliament removes disabilities of Jews;
O'Donnell returns to power in Spain.

H **Aug**: 2nd, British Columbia organised as Colony;
2nd, powers of East India Company are transferred to the British Crown;
19th, Austria, Prussia, France, Britain, Russia, Turkey and Sardinia decide to unite Moldavia with Wallachia;
21st (–*Oct.* 15th), debates between Abraham Lincoln and Stephen Douglas in Senatorial campaign, which Douglas ultimately wins;
26th, Anglo-Japanese commercial treaty providing for unsupervised trade and for setting up British residency.

J **Sep**:

K **Oct**: 7th, William, Prince of Prussia, declared Regent for the insane King Frederick William IV.

L **Nov**: 8th, boundaries of Montenegro fixed by France, Britain, Prussia, Russia and Turkey, after friction between Montenegro and Turkish Empire.

M **Dec**: 7th, notification of Franco-Spanish blockade of Cochin-China (–1862);
23rd, Serbian Diet deposes Alexander Karageorgevitch and declares Milosh Obrenovitch (who abdicated in *June* 1839) King again.

N

Z **Births and Deaths** (*cont.*)
Sept. 16th Andrew Bonar Law b. (–1923).
Oct. 20th John Burns b. (–1943).
Nov. 4th F. R. Benson b. (–1939).
Nov. 17th Robert Owen d. (87).
Nov. 20th Selma Lagerlöf b. (–1940).
Dec. 23rd Giacomo Puccini b. (–1924).

O **Politics, Economics, Law and Education**

Abolition of property qualification for Members of British Parliament. Lionel de Rothschild becomes first Jewish M.P.

Henry Carey, *Principles of Social Science.*

Alexander II begins emancipation of Russian serfs.

Prussian army is entirely equipped with needle-guns.

Ottawa is appointed the capital of Canada.

P **Science, Technology, Discovery, etc.**

Hermann Helmholtz propounds vortex motion theory.

William Thomson invents the mirror galvanometer (patented '67).

Charles Darwin and Alfred Wallace contribute joint paper on variation of species to Linnean Society.

T. H. Huxley lectures to Royal Society on the theory of vertebrate skulls.

Göransson improves Bessemer steel-making process.

South Foreland lighthouse is lit by electricity.

Q **Scholarship**

Henry Rawlinson, *The History of Herodotus* (–60).

Thomas Carlyle, *Frederick the Great* (–65).

R **Philosophy and Religion**

Blessed Virgin Mary is reputed to have appeared to Bernadette Soubirous at Lourdes, which becomes a centre of pilgrimage.

Stundist Sect, on Lutheran lines, is founded in Russia.

Isaac Hecker founds the Paulist Fathers in U.S.

S **Art, Sculpture, Fine Arts and Architecture**

Édouard Manet, *Le Concert aux Tuileries* (painting).

W. P. Frith, *Derby Day* (painting).

Alfred Stevens begins monument to Wellington.

Covent Garden Opera House built by Charles Barry.

Ringstrasse, Vienna, is begun.

T **Music**

Peter von Cornelius, *The Barber of Baghdad* (opera).

Jacques Offenbach, *Orpheus in the Underworld* (opera).

César Franck, *Messe Solennelle.*

U **Literature**

Octave Feuillet, *Roman d'un jeune homme pauvre.*

O. W. Holmes, *The Autocrat of the Breakfast Table.*

William Morris, *The Defence of Guenevere.*

V **The Press**

W **Drama and Entertainment**

X **Sport**

Y **Statistics**

Z **Births and Deaths**

Jan. 22nd Beatrice Webb (*née* Potter), Lady Passfield, b. (–1943), and Frederick Lugard b. (–1945).

May 8th Ruggiero Leoncavallo b. (–1919).

May 31st Graham Wallas b. (–1932).

July 26th Edward Mandell House b. (–1938).

(*Continued opposite*)

1859 John Brown raids Harper's Ferry—Austrian defeats in Italy

A **Jan**: 19th, treaty of alliance between France and Sardinia.

B **Feb**: 14th, Oregon becomes a U.S. state.

C **Mar**: 31st, Lord Derby's ministry is defeated over B. Disraeli's Reform Bill.

D **Apr**: 17th, French decree for amnesty for political offenders and extension of political rights;
19th, Austrian ultimatum to Sardinia to disarm (rejected by Count Cavour, 26th);
27th, peaceful revolution in Tuscany demanding that House of Lorraine choose between Austria and Italy (followed by similar peaceful risings in Modena and Parma);
29th, Austrian forces cross Sardinian frontier.

E **May**: 3rd, France declares war on Austria;
22nd, death of Ferdinand II of the Two Sicilies, succeeded by Francis II.

F **Jun**: 4th, Austrians defeated at Magenta by French who free Milan;
10th, Lord Derby resigns after further defeat and Lord Palmerston subsequently forms Liberal administration;
14th, Prussia begins to mobilise against France;
24th, Austrians defeated at Solferino by French and Sardinian forces.

G **Jul**: 8th, death of Oscar I in Sweden; succeeded by Charles XV (–1872);
8th, Franco-Austrian armistice;
11th, preliminary Peace of Villafranca (confirmed *Nov.*) by which Austria is to cede Parma and Lombardy to France, for subsequent cession to Sardinia; Tuscany and Modena are to be restored and Venice is to remain Austrian, a treaty which causes Count Cavour to resign in disgust.

H **Aug**:

J **Sep**: Formation of German National Association by Rudolf von Bennigsen to work for German unity under Prussia.

K **Oct**: 16th (–18th), John Brown, American abolitionist, makes abortive raid on Harper's Ferry, site of a federal arsenal (he is hanged *Dec.* 2nd);
22nd, Spain declares war against the Moors in Morocco (–1860);
—, Buenos Aires, having seceded from the Argentine Confederation 1853–4, is defeated by federal troops (and agrees to reunion *Nov.* 10th).

L **Nov**: 10th, Treaty of Zürich confirms the preliminary peace of Villafranca (*July*).

M **Dec**: Albert von Roon is appointed Minister of War in Prussia to carry out military reforms.

N Queensland is separated from New South Wales and Brisbane becomes its capital.

O **Politics, Economics, Law and Education**

Carlo Passaglia, under Cavour's influence, attacks Pope's temporal power in *Epistola ad Episcopos Catholicos pro causa Italica.*

F. Lassalle, *Italian War and the Mission of Prussia.*

J. S. Mill, *On Liberty.*

K. Marx, *Criticism of Political Economy.*

Reforms of curriculum in Prussian secondary schools.

P **Science, Technology, Discovery, etc.**

R. L. G. Planté invents electric accumulator.

R. W. von Bunsen and G. R. Kirchhoff by elaborating the spectrum analysis forge a vital weapon for the chemist and astronomer.

Charles Darwin, *The Origin of Species by Natural Selection.*

Edwin Drake drills the first oil well, at Titusville, Pennsylvania.

S. S. *Great Eastern* completed.

The steam-roller is invented.

Q **Scholarship**

L. von Ranke, *History of England Principally in the Seventeenth Century* (–68).

Pasquale Villari, *Life of Savonarola.*

L. Tischendorf, with the Tsar's support, gains access to the remainder of the *Codex Sinaiticus.*

R **Philosophy and Religion**

E. Renan, *Essais de monde et de critique.*

Moritz Lazarus and Heymann Steinthal found a journal of comparative psychology.

S **Art, Sculpture, Fine Arts and Architecture**

J. B. Corot, *Macbeth* (painting).

J. A. Ingres, *Le Bain Turc* (painting).

É Manet, *Absinthe Drinker* (painting).

J. F. Millet, *L'Angélus* (painting).

Wilhelm Busch invents the captionless strip cartoon.

Parliament House, Ottawa (–67).

T **Music**

C. F. Gounod, *Faust* (opera).

R. Wagner, *Tristan und Isolde* (opera).

U **Literature**

Pedro Alarcón, *Diary of a Witness of the War in Africa.*

Charles Dickens, *A Tale of Two Cities.*

George Eliot (pseud.), *Adam Bede.*

Edward Fitzgerald, *Rubaiyat of Omar Khayyam.*

Ivan Goncharov, *Oblomov.*

Victor Hugo, *La Légende des siècles* (–1883).

George Meredith, *The Ordeal of Richard Feverel.*

George Sand (pseud.), *Elle et Lui.*

Lord Tennyson, *Idylls of the King.*

V **The Press**

W **Drama and Entertainment**

Adelina Patti's début in New York as Lucia in Donizetti's *Bride of Lammermoor.*

Blondin (pseud.) crosses Niagara Falls on a tightrope (*June* 30th).

x **Sport**

y **Statistics**

z **Births and Deaths**

Jan. 6th Samuel Alexander b. (–1938).
Jan. 21st Henry Hallam d. (81).
Jan. 27th William Hickling Prescott d. (62).
Feb. 21st George Lansbury b. (–1940).
Apr. 3rd Washington Irving d. (76).
Apr. 16th Charles Alexis de Tocqueville d. (53).
May 2nd Jerome K. Jerome b. (–1927).
May 6th Alexander von Humboldt d. (89).
May 22nd Arthur Conan Doyle b. (–1930).
May 26th A. E. Housman b. (–1936).
June 11th Clemens, Prince Metternich d. (86).
Aug. 28th Leigh Hunt d. (74).
Sept. 3rd Jean Léon Jaurès b. (–1914).
Sept. 7th Isambard Kingdom Brunel d. (53).
Oct. 18th Henri Bergson b. (–1941).
Oct. 27th Theodore Roosevelt b. (–1919).
Nov. 24th Cass Gilbert b. (–1934).
Dec. 5th Sidney Lee b. (–1926).
Dec. 8th Thomas de Quincey d. (74).
Dec. 28th Thomas, Lord Macaulay d. (59).

1860 Garibaldi proclaims Victor Emmanuel King of Italy—Abraham Lincoln elected U.S. President

A **Jan**: 20th, Count Cavour is recalled as Prime Minister in Sardinia;
23rd, Cobden-Chevalier Treaty establishes substantial degree of free trade between Britain and France.

B **Feb**: 2nd, Jefferson Davis introduces Resolutions, in favour of federal slave trade, in U.S. Congress.

C **Mar**: 5th, size of Austrian Imperial Council (*Reichsrat*) increased by March Patent;
11th (–15th), Plebiscites in Tuscany, Emilia, Parma, Modena and Romagna in favour of union with Sardinia;
17th, Second Maori War breaks out in New Zealand (–1870);
24th, Sardinia cedes Nice and Savoy to France by treaty of Turin.

D **Apr**: 2nd, first Italian Parliament meets in Turin;
3rd, Pretoria becomes capital of Transvaal;
26th, peace between Spain and Morocco.

E **May**: 5th, G. Garibaldi and Redshirts sail for Genoa, land, 11th, and, 27th, take Palermo.

F **Jun**: 6th, formal reunion of Argentina and Buenos Aires.

G **Jul**: Russians found Vladivostok in vicinity of Korean border.

H **Aug**: 22nd, Garibaldi crosses the Straits, with British connivance;
25th, Anglo-French troops take Tientsin in war with China.

J **Sep**: 5th, treaty between Britain, Austria, France, Prussia, Russia and Turkey, to restore order in Syria after massacre of Christians by Druses;
7th, G. Garibaldi enters Naples; Francis II of Naples flees;
11th, Victor Emmanuel, King of Sardinia, invades Papal States, after rising of 8th;
18th, Cavour defeats Papal troops at Castelfidardo;
21st, Anglo-French troops defeat Chinese at Pa-li-Chau.

K **Oct**: 20th, October Diploma amends Austrian Constitution, providing for federation with wide autonomy for separate territories;
21st (–22nd), plebiscites in Naples and Sicily in support of union with Sardinia;
24th, treaty of Peking by which Chinese ratify Treaty of Tientsin with Britain (of *June* 26th 1858) and recognise treaty with France (of *June* 27th 1858);
26th, G. Garibaldi meets Victor Emmanuel and proclaims him King of Italy.

L **Nov**: 4th (–5th), plebiscites in Umbria and Legations for union with Sardinia;
6th, in U.S. presidential election, Abraham Lincoln (Republican) opposing further extension of slavery secures a majority of popular votes, but only 180 out of 303 electoral votes; John C. Breckinidge (Southern Democrat) has 72 votes, John Bell (Constitutional Union), 39, and Stephen A. Douglas (Northern Democrat), 12 votes;
24th, Napoleon III extends power of French legislature.

M **Dec**: 20th, South Carolina secedes from Union, in protest at Abraham Lincoln's election.

N

O **Politics, Economics, Law and Education**
J. S. Mill, *Treatise on Representative Government.*
Russians found Vladivostok.
Food and Drugs Act in U.K.
Degrees in Science are established at London University.

P **Science, Technology, Discovery, etc.**
Chemical congress at Karlsruhe settles problem of atomic weights.
G. T. Fechner, *Elements of Psycho-Physics.*
Rhinoscope invented.
Exploitation of potassium deposits at Stassfurt, near Magdeburg.

Q **Scholarship**
Charles de Montalembert, *Moines d'Occident.*
J. L. Motley, *History of the United Netherlands* (–67).

R **Philosophy and Religion**
Frederick Temple, Mark Pattison and others contribute to *Essays and Reviews*, which is condemned by Convocation.
English Church Union is founded to counter the High Church movement in England.
Russian Orthodox Church establishes monastery and hospice at Jerusalem.

S **Art, Sculpture, Fine Arts and Architecture**
É Manet, *The Guitarist* (painting).
W. Holman Hunt, *The Discovery of Our Saviour in the Temple* (painting).
J. Burckhardt, *The Culture of the Renaissance in Italy.*

T **Music**

U **Literature**
Wilkie Collins, *The Woman in White.*
George Eliot (pseud.), *The Mill on the Floss.*
Ivan Turgeniev, *On the Eve.*

V **The Press**
The Cornhill Magazine founded under W. M. Thackeray's editorship.
Charles Bradlaugh founds and edits *The National Reformer.*
The Catholic Times first issued.

W **Drama and Entertainment**
Dion Boucicault, *The Colleen Bawn.*
Eugène Labiche, *Le Voyage de M. Perrichon.*
Alexander Ostrovsky, *The Tempest.*

X **Sport**
Open Golf Championship started (first won by W. Park).
Prize fight at Farnborough (*Apr.*) between Tom Sayers (U.K.) and John C. Heenan (U.S.), the last contest with bare fists in England.

Y **Statistics**
Railway mileage in operation: U.S. 30,600; U.K. 10,410; Russia, 900.
Oil production: U.S., 500,000 barrels; Rumania, 8,542 barrels.
Emigration to U.S. (1851–60): from Britain, 423,964; from Ireland, 914,119.
Pig-iron production (in mill. tons): Gt. Britain, 3·9; France, 0·9; U.S., 0·8.

z **Births and Deaths**

Jan. 17th Anton Chekhov b. (–1904).
Mar. 13th Hugo Wolf b. (–1903).
May 9th J. M. Barrie b. (–1937).
July 7th Gustave Mahler b. (–1911).
July 20th Margaret McMillan b. (–1931).
Aug. 20th Raymond Poincaré b. (–1934).
Sept. 21st Arthur Schopenhauer d. (72).
Nov. 6th Ignaz Paderewski b. (–1941).
Dec. 14th George Hamilton Gordon, Earl of Aberdeen, d. (76).
Dec. 28th Philip Wilson Steer b. (–1942).

1861 (Jan.–Nov.) Outbreak of American Civil War—Death of Prince Consort

A **Jan**: 2nd, Frederick William IV of Prussia dies and is succeeded by William I (–88); 29th, Kansas is created U.S. state.

B **Feb**: 4th, Peace Convention at Washington in effort to preserve Union;
4th, Congress of Montgomery at which South Carolina, Georgia, Alabama, Mississippi, Florida, and Louisiana decide, 8th, to elect Jefferson Davis as President of Confederate States of America which is formed 9th (five more states join—*Apr.–May*);
13th, Francis II of Naples surrenders at Gaeta to Garibaldi;
18th, Italian Parliament proclaims Victor Emmanuel King (and Kingdom of Italy proclaimed *Mar.* 17th);
26th, Austrian constitution centralised by 'February Patent' which is unpopular in Hungary;
27th, Warsaw Massacre when crowd fired on by Russian troops during demonstration against Russian rule.

C **Mar**: 2nd, Morrill Tariff, precipitated by panic in 1857, is beginning of several tariff increases in U.S.;
3rd, emancipation of Russian serfs proclaimed (*Feb.* 19th, old style);
4th, Abraham Lincoln inaugurated President of U.S.;
18th, Spain annexes San Domingo at latter's request;
19th, end of Maori War in New Zealand.

D **Apr**: 10th, Finland obtains constitution from Russia;
12th (–13th), Confederates take Fort Sumter, Charleston, S. Carolina after 40-hour bombardment, marking outbreak of American Civil War;
15th, A. Lincoln calls for Militia to suppress Confederacy;
19th, blockade of Confederate forts decreed (and extended, 27th).

E **May**:

F **Jun**: 6th, Count Cavour dies in Italy (aged 50);
25th, Sultan Abdul Mejid dies and is succeeded as Sultan of Turkey by brother Abdul Aziz.

G **Jul**: 21st, indecisive victory of Confederates at Bull Run.

H **Aug**: 21st, Hungarian Diet is dissolved after opposition to 'February Patent', and government carried out by Imperial Commission;
28th (–29th), Unionists capture Forts Clark and Hatteras on North Carolina coast.

J **Sep**: 2nd, Prussia concludes commercial treaty with China at Tientsin.

K **Oct**: 31st, London Convention of Britain, Spain and France to protect their interests on Mexico's suspension of payments of foreign debts.

L **Nov**: 8th, *Trent* affair, when Confederate Commissioners to Great Britain and France are taken off British ship by Unionists, but given up when Britain subsequently protests;
11th, Pedro V of Portugal dies and succeeded by Louis I;
Financial powers of French legislature extended.

O **Politics, Economics, Law and Education**

F. Lassalle, *System of Assigned Rights.*

H. Spencer, *Education, Moral, Intellectual, Physical.*

Paper duties in U.K. are repealed.

P **Science, Technology, Discovery, etc.**

R. W. von Bunsen isolates caesium and rubidium, elements of the alkali group, by means of spectrum analysis.

William Crookes discovers thallium.

Louis Pasteur develops the germ theory of disease.

William Thomson persuades British Association to appoint committee to determine electrical standards.

William Siemens in U.K. and Pierre and Émile Martin in France simultaneously develop the open-hearth process for making steel with a regenerative gas-fired furnace, which effects a rapid rise in steel production and a reduction in the coal used.

Ernest Solvay's soda-making process.

Philipp Reis makes first practical instrument capable of transmitting speech.

First machine-chilled cold store built by T. S. Mort at Sydney.

H.M.S. *Warrior*, the first all-iron warship, is completed (steam screw, but also rigged for sail).

Q **Scholarship**

A. P. Stanley, *Lectures on the Eastern Church.*

H. Maine, *Ancient Law.*

Vladimir Dahl, *Dictionary of the Living Russian Tongue.*

R **Philosophy and Religion**

Ignaz von Döllinger, in *The Church and the Churches*, declares war on Ultramontane party.

S **Art, Sculpture, Fine Arts and Architecture**

Jean Garnier builds Paris Opera House (–75).

T. Hansen, Heinrichshof, Vienna (–63).

William Morris begins to make wallpapers and tapestries.

T **Music**

Johannes Brahms, Piano Concerto no. 1 in D minor (op. 15).

Royal Academy of Music, London, founded.

U **Literature**

Charles Dickens, *Great Expectations.*

George Eliot (pseud.), *Silas Marner.*

O. W. Holmes, *Elsie Venner* (or *The Professor*).

Charles Reade, *The Cloister and the Hearth.*

Mrs. Henry Wood, *East Lynne.*

V **The Press**

W **Drama and Entertainment**

X **Sport**

M Dec: 14th, death of Prince Consort (aged 42);
23rd, Sultan of Turkey agrees to unification of Moldavia and Wallachia as Rumania (and assemblies meet in Bucharest, *Feb*. 5th 1862).

N

Y **Statistics**

Populations (in millions): Russia, 76; U.S., 32; Great Britain, 23·1; Ireland, 5·7; Italy, 25.

Coal production (in mill. tons): Great Britain, 83·6; France, 6·8; Russia, 0·3.

Iron production (in mill. tons): Great Britain, 3·7; France, 3; U.S., 2·8; Germany, 0·2.

Z **Births and Deaths**

Jan. 28th Henri Murger d. (38).
Feb. 15th A. N. Whitehead b. (–1947).
Apr. 23rd Edmund Allenby b. (–1936).
May 6th Rabindranath Tagore b. (–1941).
May 19th Nellie Melba b. (–1931).
June 19th Douglas, Earl Haig, b. (–1928).
June 30th Elizabeth Barrett Browning d. (55).
Oct. 10th Fridtjof Nansen b. (–1930).
Oct. 16th J. B. Bury b. (–1927).
— Elmer Ambrose Sperry b. (–1930).

1862 Lincoln declares all slaves to be free—Bismarck's 'Blood and Iron' speech

A **Jan**:

B **Feb**: 6th, Ulysses S. Grant captures Fort Henry on Tennessee River from Confederates;
8th, Unionists take Roanoke Isle and, 10th, Elizabeth City, North Carolina;
15th (–16th), U. S. Grant captures Fort Donelson;
France purchases Mentone and Roquebrune from Monaco.

C **Mar**: 3rd (–4th), Unionists take Amelia Island, Florida;
8th, Confederate frigate *Merrimack* sinks *Cumberland* in Hampton Roads, Virginia, but, 9th, is forced to withdraw by Unionist vessel *Monitor*;
10th, Britain and France recognise independence of Zanzibar;
12th, Jacksonville, Florida, is taken by Unionists.
14th, New Berne, N. Carolina, is captured by Unionists.

D **Apr**: 7th, Confederates forced to withdraw after initial success at Shilton, Tennessee;
24th (–25th), Unionists lay siege to New Orleans, Louisiana (taken *May* 1st).

E **May**:

F **Jun**: 5th, treaty of Saigon between France and Annam; France annexes Cochin-China;
15th, Turks bombard Belgrade after Serb rising there;
25th (–*July* 1st), Seven Days battle results in withdrawal of Federal troops from the Peninsula;
U.S. recognises independence of Liberia.

G **Jul**: *Alabama* case after British fail to stop new vessel sailing to aid Confederates, which causes considerable damage to Unionist fleets (settled 1872).

H **Aug**: 2nd, commercial treaty between France and Prussia;
18th, Sioux rising begins in Minnesota but is subsequently defeated;
29th, G. Garibaldi plans to take Rome but is captured by Royalist troops at Aspromonte;
—, (–30th), second battle of Bull Run, where Thomas ('Stonewall') Jackson defeats Union Army.

J **Sep**: 17th, indecisive battle of Antietam, Maryland, but Confederates forced to withdraw;
22nd, A. Lincoln declares all slaves to be free from *Jan.* 1st 1863;
—, Otto von Bismarck becomes Prussian premier;
29th, Bismarck's 'Blood and Iron' speech.

K **Oct**: 7th, Prussian Diet rejects increase in military budget, but subsequently passed by Peers, and Diet is adjourned so that Bismarck rules without budget for four years;
8th, indecisive battle of Perryville, Kentucky, in American Civil War;
22nd, garrison in Athens revolts and forces King Otto I to resign, 24th.

L **Nov**:

M **Dec**: 13th, Confederate army under Robert E. Lee gains victory over Ambrose Burnside, at Fredericksburg.

N

O **Politics, Economics, Law and Education**

J. S. Mill, *Utilitarianism.*

John Ruskin, *Unto this Last.*

Herbet Spencer, *First Principles.*

F. Lassalle's Working-Class Programme advocates a system of State socialism.

Foundation of colleges in each U.S. state in which science and technology is placed on a par with arts subjects.

P **Science, Technology, Discovery, etc.**

Julius Sachs proves that starch is produced by photosynthesis.

F. Wöhler finds that water decomposes calcium carbonate into lime and acetylene.

F. W. A. Argelander completes the Bonn catalogue of stars visible in the Northern Hemisphere.

Johann von Lamont discovers earth current.

H. Helmholtz, *Sensations of Tones.*

Joseph Brown constructs a universal milling machine.

Richard Gatling's ten-barrel gun.

Q **Scholarship**

August Potthast, *Bibliotheca Historia Medii Aevi.*

Henry Rawlinson, *The Five Great Monarchies of the Ancient Eastern World* (–67).

R **Philosophy and Religion**

J. W. Colenso, Bishop of Natal, denies authenticity of The Pentateuch.

Joseph Lyne (Fr. Ignatius) forms a monastic community in Suffolk, preparatory to founding Llanthony Abbey, first post-Reformation religious house in England.

S **Art, Sculpture, Fine Arts and Architecture**

É. Manet, *Lola de Valence* (painting).

Gilbert Scott designs Albert Memorial.

T **Music**

G. Verdi, *La Forza del Destino* (opera).

U **Literature**

G. Flaubert, *Salammbô.*

V. Hugo, *Les Misérables.*

George Meredith, *Modern Love* and *Poems of the English Roadside.*

Ivan Turgeniev, *Fathers and Sons.*

[C. F. Browne], *Artemus Ward, His Book.*

J. G. Whittier, *Snow-Bound.*

V **The Press**

W **Drama and Entertainment**

Sarah Bernhardt's début at Comédie Française.

International Exhibition, London.

X **Sport**

An English cricket team tours Australia.

Y **Statistics**

British Textile trade:

imports of raw cotton	452 mill. lb.
exports of cottons	1,681 mill. yds.
exports of woollens	167 mill. yds.
exports of linens	156·8 mill. yds.
exports of silks	2·6 mill. yds.

Z **Births and Deaths**

Apr. 25th Edward Grey b. (–1933).
May 6th Henry David Thoreau d. (44).
May 16th Edward Gibbon Wakefield d. (66).
May 28th Henry Thomas Buckle d. (40).
June 6th Henry Newbolt b. (–1938).
July 2nd William Bragg b. (–1942).
Aug. 17th Maurice Barrès b. (–1923).
Aug. 22nd Claude Debussy b. (–1918).
Aug. 29th Maurice Maeterlinck b. (–1949).
Sept. 22nd Louis Botha b. (–1919).
Nov. 15th Gerhart Hauptmann b. (–1946).
— Aristide Briand b. (–1932).
— Edith Wharton (*née* Jones) b. (–1937).

1863 (Jan.–Nov.) Confederates defeated at Gettysburg—Denmark incorporates Schleswig

A **Jan**: 22nd, Polish insurrection begins when National Committee publishes manifesto; On death of Mohammed Said, Ismail becomes Khedive of Egypt (–79).

B **Feb**: 3rd, Greek Assembly elects Prince Alfred, second son of Queen Victoria, King, but British government rejects decision;
8th, Prussia allies with Russia to suppress Polish Revolt at Convention made by Count Alvensleben;
24th, Arizona organised as territory of U.S.;
25th, National Banking Act in U.S. to provide uniform system and to create market for State Bonds (revised *June* 3rd 1864).

C **Mar**: 3rd, Idaho organised as territory of U.S.;
30th, William, Prince of Denmark, recognised as King of Greece and takes title of George I (–1919);
—, Denmark incorporates Schleswig by March Patent;
Poland divided into provinces by Russia.

D **Apr**:

E **May**: 4th, new Maori risings in New Zealand;
5th, Confederate victory at Chancellorsville, Virginia, after five-day battle, but 'Stonewall' Jackson dies of wounds, 10th.

F **Jun**: 20th, West Virginia created U.S. state;
Civil War in Afghanistan after death of Dost Mohammed.

G **Jul**: 1st (–3rd), Robert E. Lee's Confederate army defeated by General Meade's force at Gettysburg, Pennsylvania;
4th, Confederate defeat at Vicksburg, Missouri;
9th, Confederates surrender Fort Hudson, Missouri, to Unionists, which cuts off Texas, Arkansas and Louisiana from rest of Confederacy.

H **Aug**: 11th, French protectorate established over Cambodia;
16th, Frankfurt meeting of German princes to reform Confederation, but Prussia opposes this and meeting ends *Sept.* with nothing achieved.

J **Sep**:

K **Oct**: 1st, German Diet votes for federal action against Denmark.

L **Nov**: 13th, Schleswig incorporated in New Danish Constitution;
14th, conference between Britain, France, Austria, Russia and Prussia to decide on position of Ionian Islands (see *Mar*. 29th 1864);
15th, Frederick VII of Denmark dies and is succeeded by Christian IX;
18th, Christian IX of Denmark signs new constitution;
23rd (–25th), Confederates defeated at Chattanooga, Tennessee;
A. Thiers forms opposition Third Party in France.

O **Politics, Economics, Law and Education**

P **Science, Technology, Discovery, etc.**

T. H. Huxley, *Man's Place in Nature.*

Charles Lyell, *The Antiquity of Man.*

Max Schultze propounds cell theory.

Thomas Graham's process for separating gases by atmolysis.

A. Nader makes ascents (*Oct.*) in his balloon '*Le Géant*', in Paris and starts a newspaper, *L'Aéronaute*, devoted to aeronautics.

Q **Scholarship**

T. Mommsen issues first part of *Corpus Inscriptionum Latinum.*

S. R. Gardiner, *History of England, 1603–56* (–1903).

Paul Littré, *Dictionnaire de la langue française* (–72).

A. W. Kinglake, *History of the Crimean War* (–87).

R **Philosophy and Religion**

E. Renan, *Vie de Jésus* and *Histoire des origines du christianisme.*

Church of England congress at Manchester.

J. W. Colenso, Bishop of Natal, is deposed by South African bishops in conclave for denying doctrine of eternal punishment and condoning polygamy (*Dec.*); on his appeal the Privy Council decides his deposition was *ultra vires.*

S **Art, Sculpture, Fine Arts and Architecture**

É. Manet, *Luncheon on the Grass* (painting).

Napoleon III orders a special exhibition of works refused by the Academy ('the Salon des Refusés).

C. Baudelaire's essay on Constantin Guy, 'Le Peintre de la vie moderne'.

D. G. Rossetti, *Beata Beatrix* (painting).

James Whistler, *Symphony in White* (painting).

T **Music**

H. Berlioz, *The Trojans*, pt. i—*The Trojans at Carthage* (opera).

G. Bizet, *The Pearl Fishers* (opera).

W. H. Fry, *Notre Dame de Paris* (opera).

U **Literature**

Charles Kingsley, *The Water Babies.*

V **The Press**

Le Petit Journal, first cheap newspaper in France issued.

W **Drama and Entertainment**

X **Sport**

Football Association founded.

Grand Prix de Paris is first run at Longchamp.

Y **Statistics**

U.S. crude petroleum production, 2,611,000 barrels.

M Dec: 24th, Saxon and Hanoverian federal troops enter Holstein.

N

z **Births and Deaths**

Jan. 18th Constantin Stanislavsky b. (–1938).
Jan. 19th Werner Sombart b. (–1941).
Jan. 29th Frederick Delius b. (–1934).
Feb. 9th Anthony Hope Hawkins (A. Hope) b. (–1933).
Feb. 20th Lucien Pissarro b. (–1944).
Mar. 12th Gabriele D'Annunzio b. (–1938).
Mar. 27th Frederick Henry Royce b. (–1933).
May 31st Francis Younghusband b. (–1942).
July 17th David Lloyd George b. (–1945).
Aug. 13th Eugène Delacroix d. (64).
Aug. 14th Colin Campbell, Lord Clyde, d. (70).
Sept. 17th Alfred de Vigny d. (66).
Sept. 20th Jacob Grimm d. (78).
Nov. 21st Arthur Quiller-Couch ('Q') b. (–1944).
Dec. 12th Edvard Munch b. (–1944).
Dec. 23rd W. M. Thackeray d. (52).

1864 (Jan.–Nov.) W. Sherman marches Union Army through Georgia—Austria and Prussia declare war on Denmark over Schleswig and Holstein

A **Jan:** 13th, Zemstvo Law in Russia establishing provincial councils (*Jan.* 1st, old style);
16th, Austria and Prussia send ultimatum to Denmark for repeal of constitution for the incorporation of Schleswig and form alliance in case of its rejection.

B **Feb:** 1st, Austro-Prussian troops enter Schleswig.

C **Mar:** 29th, Ionian Islands ceded by Britain to Greece.

D **Apr:** 10th, Archduke Maximilian of Austria accepts title of Emperor of Mexico;
18th, Danish forces defeated at Düppel and German troops invade Denmark;
25th, Lord John Russell calls London Conference of Britain, Russia, France, Austria and Prussia to solve Danish Question.

E **May:** 5th, William Sherman leaves Chattanooga, Tennessee, to march army through Georgia;
5th (–6th), U. S. Grant and R. E. Lee fight indecisive battle of the Wilderness, Virginia, in American Civil War;
8th (–21st), at battle of Sportsylvania Courthouse in Civil War, Grant is unable to defeat Lee;
26th, territory of Montana organised in U.S.

F **Jun:** 3rd, revised National Banking Act in U.S.;
25th, through Bismarck's astuteness London Conference on Denmark ends with nothing achieved and, 26th, war resumes.

G **Jul:** 22nd, Sherman defeats Confederate army of John Hood at Atlanta.

H **Aug:**

J **Sep:** 1st, Confederates abandon Atlanta, Georgia, which is occupied, 2nd, by Sherman;
5th (–8th), British, French and Dutch fleets attack Japan in Shimonoseki Straits in reprisal for closing ports and expelling foreigners (a truce, 14th, is followed by peace convention, *Oct.* 22nd, when Japan pays indemnity);
15th, Franco-Italian Treaty whereby Italy renounces claim to Rome and Florence becomes Italian capital (–1870) in place of Turin;
The reactionary Ramon Narvaez becomes premier of Spain.

K **Oct:** 30th, Peace of Vienna by which Denmark cedes Schleswig, Holstein and Lauenburg to Austria and Prussia;
31st, Nevada created U.S. state.

L **Nov:** 8th, re-election of Abraham Lincoln as U.S. President;
Andrew Johnson elected Vice-President;
28th, new democratic Constitution, with one Chamber of Deputies, in Greece;
29th, massacre of Cheyenne and Arapahoe Indians at Sand Creek, Colorado, by Col. Chivington's troops.

O **Politics, Economics, Law and Education**

Geneva Convention prescribes immunity for the Red Cross League, founded by Henri Dunant, in time of war.

Le Play, *La Réforme Sociale.*

Octavia Hill begins reform of tenement dwellings in St. Marylebone.

International Working-Men's Association founded in London.

Universities of Belgrade and Bucharest founded.

P **Science, Technology, Discovery, etc.**

Louis Pasteur invents pasteurisation (for wine).

Joseph Bertrand, *Treatise on Differential and Integral Calculus.*

Robert Whitehead constructs torpedo.

Metropolitan Railway, London, opened.

Q **Scholarship**

James Bryce, *The Holy Roman Empire.*

N. Fustel de Coulanges, *La Cité Antique.*

Michele de Rossi begins exploration of the Catacombs, Rome.

R **Philosophy and Religion**

J. H. Newman, *Apologia pro vita sua.*

Pius IX issues Syllabus of Errors, claiming the Church's control over culture, science and education (*Dec.* 8th), and provokes a discussion of papal infallibility.

Episcopally ordained Scottish ministers are permitted to hold English benefices.

S **Art, Sculpture, Fine Arts and Architecture**

Arnold Böcklin, *Villa at the Sea* (painting).

Auguste Rodin, *Man With the Broken Nose* (sculpture).

T **Music**

Anton Bruckner, Mass No. 1 in D minor.

P. I. Tchaikovsky, Overture *Romeo and Juliet.*

U **Literature**

Charles Dickens, *Our Mutual Friend.*

J. Goncourt, *Renée Mauperin.*

Wilhelm Raabe, *Der Hungerpastor.*

Leo Tolstoy, *War and Peace* (–69).

A. Trollope, *The Small House at Allington.*

A. de Vigny, *Les Destinées* (posth.).

V **The Press**

Neue Freie Presse, Vienna.

W **Drama and Entertainment**

H. Ibsen, *The Pretenders.*

X **Sport**

Y **Statistics**

1864 (Dec.)

M Dec: 1st, Russian judiciary reformed (*Nov.* 20th, old style);
22nd, W. T. Sherman occupies Savannah, Georgia, after its surrender to Union army.

N

z Births and Deaths

Feb. 14th Israel Zangwill b. (–1926).
Apr. 9th Sebastian de Ferranti b. (–1930).
May 2nd Giacomo Meyerbeer d. (73).
May 19th Nathaniel Hawthorne d. (59).
May 20th John Clare d. (71).
June 4th Nassau William Senior d. (74).
July 15th Marie Tempest b. (–1942).
July 24th Frank Wedekind b. (–1918).
Aug. 28th Ferdinand Lassalle d. (39).
Sept. 17th Walter Savage Landor d. (89).
Oct. 28th John Leech d. (47).
— Henri Toulouse-Lautrec b. (–1901).

1865 Assassination of Lincoln—End of U.S. Civil War—Bismarck meets Napoleon III at Biarritz

A Jan: 27th, treaty between Spain and Peru virtually recognises Peruvian independence.

B Feb: 17th, Unionists take Columbia, South Carolina;
18th, Unionist fleet takes Charleston after long siege.

C Mar: 18th, Paraguay begins war against Argentina, Brazil and Uruguay (–*Mar.* 1st 1870);
27th, the independent British Colony of Kaffaria is incorporated with Cape Colony.

D Apr: 3rd, Richmond, Virginia, surrenders to Grant;
9th, Lee, Confederate C.-in-C., capitulates to U. S. Grant at Appomattox;
14th, Abraham Lincoln assassinated by J. W. Booth and is succeeded by Andrew Johnson as President of U.S.;
26th, Confederate force under Joseph E. Johnston surrenders at Durham, North Carolina.

E May: 5th, revolt in San Domingo forces Spain to renounce sovereignty;
10th, Jefferson Davis, president of the Confederacy, is captured near Florida border and imprisoned;
26th, surrender of last Confederate army at Shreveport, near New Orleans, ends U.S. Civil War;
30th, commercial treaty between Britain and *Zollverein.*

F Jun: 29th, Ramon Narvaez dismissed in Spain and replaced by Leopold O'Donnell.

G Jul:

H Aug: 14th, Convention of Gastein by which Austria receives Holstein, whereas Prussia obtains Schleswig and Kiel, and purchases Lauenburg.

J Sep: 2nd, end of Maori War in New Zealand when Governor issues proclamation of peace;
20th, Austrian constitution temporarily annulled.

K Oct: 4th (and 11th), Otto von Bismarck and Napoleon III meet at Biarritz when the French Emperor agrees to Prussian supremacy in Germany, and to a united Italy;
18th, Lord Palmerston dies (aged 80) and Lord John Russell becomes Prime Minister, with W. E. Gladstone leader of House of Commons;
U.S. demands recall of French troops from Mexico.

L Nov:

M Dec: 10th, Leopold I of Belgium dies and is succeeded by his son, Leopold II (–1909);
18th, 13th Amendment to U.S. Constitution abolishes slavery;
Kolozsvár Diet, dominated by Hungarians, decrees for the incorporation of Transylvania in Hungary (completed 1868);
New constitution in Sweden abolishing traditional four Estates which are replaced by two Chambers.

N Capital of New Zealand is moved from Auckland to Wellington.

O **Politics, Economics, Law and Education**

Henri Baudrillant, *La Liberté du travail.*

W. S. Jevons, *The Coal Question.*

Commons Preservation Society founded in U.K.

Foundation of Massachusetts Institute of Technology and of Odessa University.

Jean Duruy organises French secondary education.

P **Science, Technology, Discovery, etc.**

Julius Plückner invents line geometry.

Friedrich Kekulé propounds ring theory of the structure of benzene.

Joseph Lister begins antiseptic surgery by using carbolic acid on a compound wound.

Karl Ludwig devises the kymograph for recording blood pressure.

Paul Schutzenberger invents 'celanese' acetate rayon (not commercially produced until 1904).

Pierre Lallement constructs the 'bone-shaker' pedalled bicycle.

First carpet sweeper and first mechanical dish-washer.

Atlantic cable finally successful.

Q **Scholarship**

F. Parkman, *France and England in the New World* (–92).

W. E. H. Lecky, *A History of the Rise and Influence of Rationalism in Europe.*

R **Philosophy and Religion**

J. S.Mill, *Auguste Comte and Positivism.*

E. B. Pusey in *Eirenicon* trys to find a basis for reunion with Rome.

William Booth founds Salvation Army.

China Inland Mission founded.

S **Art, Sculpture, Fine Arts and Architecture**

Winslow Homer, *Prisoners from the Front* (painting).

É. Manet, *Olympia* (painting).

H. Taine, *La Philosophie de l'art* (–69).

T **Music**

Nicholas Rimsky-Korsakov, 1st Symphony in E minor.

R. Wagner's opera *Tristan und Isolde* is performed in Munich.

U **Literature**

M. Arnold, *Essays in Criticism.*

Lewis Carroll (pseud.), *Alice's Adventures in Wonderland.*

John Ruskin, *Sesame and Lilies.*

A. C. Swinburne, *Atalanta in Calydon.*

V **The Press**

Pall Mall Gazette.

Fortnightly Review.

W **Drama and Entertainment**

X **Sport**

W. G. Grace's début as cricketer in Gentlemen *v.* Players.

Edward Whymper climbs the Matterhorn (*July* 13th).

Y **Statistics**

U.K. total State expenditure £70·3 mill.

Z **Births and Deaths**

Jan. 16th Pierre Joseph Proudhon d. (56).
Feb. 9th Beatrice Tanner (Mrs. Patrick Campbell) b. (–1940).
Feb. 15th Nicholas Wiseman, Cardinal d. (62).
Mar. 21st Richard Cobden d. (60), and H. A. L. Fisher b. (–1940).
Apr. 9th Erich Ludendorff b. (–1937).
Apr. 15th Abraham Lincoln d. (56).
June 8th Joseph Paxton d. (59).
June 13th W. B. Yeats b. (–1939).
July 15th Alfred Harmsworth, Viscount Northcliffe, b. (–1922).
Aug. 10th Alexander Glazounov b. (–1936).
Oct. 1st Paul Dukas b. (–1935).
Nov. 2nd Warren Gamaliel Harding b. (–1923).
Nov. 12th Elizabeth Gaskell d. (55).
Dec. 30th Rudyard Kipling b. (–1936).

 Prussia defeats Austria at Sadowa—War between Austria and Italy

A **Jan**: 14th, Peru declares war on Spain in resentment at clauses in the treaty (of *Jan.* 1865).

B **Feb**: 17th, Habeas Corpus Act suspended in Ireland after unrest;
23rd, Alexander Cuss, Prince of Rumania, dethroned, succeeded by Charles, Prince of Hohenzollern, as Carol I (–1914) (who is recognised by Sultan of Turkey *Oct.* 24th).

C **Mar**:

D **Apr**: 8th, Italy concludes offensive and defensive alliance with Prussia against Austria with promise of Venezia as reward.

E **May**: 27th, Sultan grants rights of primogeniture to Ismail, Khedive of Egypt.

F **Jun**: 7th, Prussian troops march into Holstein and
8th, annex that Duchy;
12th, secret treaty between Austria and France, whereby Napoleon III promises French neutrality provided that Austria cedes Venezia, which France will in turn hand over to Italy;
13th, U.S. 14th Amendment incorporates Civil Rights Act and gives states the choice of Negro enfranchisement or reduced representation in Congress;
14th, Federal Diet in Germany votes for mobilisation against Prussian intervention in Holstein, at which Prussian delegates declare the German Confederation at an end;
15th (–16th), Prussia invades Saxony, Hanover and Hesse during the night;
20th, Italy declares war on Austria;
24th, Austrian forces under Archduke Albert defeat Italians at Custozza, northern Italy;
25th, Japan concludes tariff convention with Britain, France, Holland and U.S.;
26th, Russell's ministry resigns after defeat on Reform Bill;
29th, Prussians defeat Hanoverian army at Langensalza.

G **Jul**: 3rd, Prussians defeat Austrians at Sadowa (Königgrätz);
4th, Napoleon III announces cession of Venezia by Austria;
6th, Lord Derby forms Conservative administration, with B. Disraeli leader of the House of Commons;
20th, Italian fleet destroyed by Austrians off Lissa;
26th, preliminary peace treaty between Prussia and Austria at Nikolsburg;
28th, Danish constitution altered in favour of King and Upper House.

H **Aug**: 10th, treaty between Bolivia and Chile whereby territory between Andes and the Pacific is ceded to Chile;
12th, Austro-Italian armistice;
13th, Prussia concludes treaty of peace with Württemberg, with secret military alliance against France, and similar treaties are made, 7th, with Baden, and 22nd, with Bavaria;
23rd, Peace of Prague confirms preliminary peace of Nikolsburg (*July* 26th), whereby Austria to be excluded from Germany, while Hanover, Hesse, Nassau and Frankfurt are to be incorporated with Prussia, South German States to be independent, but States north of the Main to form Confederation under Prussia, which also obtains Austrian Silesia and territory from Saxony and from South German States.

J **Sep**: 2nd, after long discontent against Turkish authority Crete revolts and decrees union with Greece;

O **Politics, Economics, Law and Education**

Cobden Club, London, founded by Thomas Potter.

'Black Friday' (*May* 11th) scenes of commercial panic in London following the stoppage of Overend and Gurney.

People's Bank, Milan, is founded.

Gottenberg system of State control of sales of spirits in Sweden.

Elizabeth Garrett Anderson opens dispensary for women and children in Euston Road, London.

Dr. T. J. Barnardo opens home for waifs in Stepney.

P **Science, Technology, Discovery, etc.**

Gregor Mendel's papers (–1869) establish the laws of heredity.

Alfred Nobel invents dynamite.

French army is equipped with Chassepot rifle.

Q **Scholarship**

William Stubbs is appointed Professor at Oxford and founds the study of medieval English history.

Pierre Larousse, *Grand Dictionnaire Universel du XIX siècle* (–1876).

Charles Wilson begins to excavate environs of Jerusalem.

R **Philosophy and Religion**

Friedrich Lange, *History of Materialism* (neo-Kantian).

J. R. Seeley, *Ecce Homo.*

American Evangelical Alliance founded.

S **Art, Sculpture, Fine Arts and Architecture**

Claude Monet, *Camille* (painting).

Gustave Moreau, *Head of Orpheus* (sculpture).

Edgar Degas begins to paint scenes of ballet dancers.

Act to facilitate public exhibitions in Britain.

Joseph Poelaert, Palace of Justice, Brussels (–83).

T **Music**

Friedrich Smetana, *The Bartered Bride* (opera).

Ambrose Thomas, *Mignon* (opera).

U **Literature**

Charles Baudelaire, *Les Épaves.*

Alphonse Daudet, *Lettres de Mon Moulin.*

Fyodor Dostoievsky, *Crime and Punishment.*

Victor Hugo, *Les Travailleurs de la Mer.*

J. H. Newman, *Dream of Gerontius.*

A. C. Swinburne, *Poems and Ballads.*

P. Verlaine, *Poèmes saturniens.*

Walt Whitman, *Drum Taps.*

V **The Press**

W **Drama and Entertainment**

H. Ibsen, *Brand.*

Squire Bancroft and Henry Irving act on the London stage.

1866 (Sep.–Dec.)

J Sep: 3rd, Bismarck obtains indemnity from Prussian Diet for having ruled unconstitutionally with regard to Budget;
20th, Prussia annexes Hanover, Hesse, Nassau and Frankfurt (as agreed at Prague *Aug.* 23rd).

K Oct: 3rd, war between Austria and Italy ended by treaty of Vienna;
21st (–22nd), plebiscites in Venezia result in support for union with Italy;
—, peace between Prussia and Saxony.

L Nov: after split in North German Liberal Party, Rudolf von Bennigsen forms a new National Liberal Party.

M Dec: 24th, Schleswig-Holstein is incorporated in Prussia.

N

x **Sport**

J. G. Chambers founds Amateur Athletic Club.
The Marquess of Queensberry codifies boxing rules.

y **Statistics**

U.K. registered tonnage of merchant shipping, 5,779,000 (876,000 steamships).

z **Births and Deaths**

Jan. 15th Massimo d'Azeglio d. (67).
Jan. 23rd Thomas Love Peacock d. (80).
Jan. 29th Romain Rolland b. (–1944).
Mar. 29th John Keble d. (73).
Apr. 3rd James Hertzog b. (–1942).
Sept. 21st H. G. Wells b. (–1946).
Oct. 12th James Ramsay MacDonald b. (–1937).
Nov. 8th Herbert, Lord Austin b. (–1941).
Dec. 14th Roger Fry b. (–1934).

1867 (Jan.–Nov.) Canada becomes a Dominion—Formation of North German Confederation—Garibaldi's march on Rome—Fenian outrages

A **Jan:**

B **Feb:** 13th, Fenian outrages occur in Kerry, and a separate attempt is made at Chester Castle;
17th, Hungarian Diet is opened, and subsequently the Constitution of 1848 is restored so that *Ausgleich* (Compromise) takes place allowing for Dual Monarchy, whereby Magyars dominate Hungary and German element dominates rest of Austrian territories, though to be single foreign and war policies.

C **Mar:** 1st, Nebraska becomes a U.S. state;
2nd, Basic Reconstruction Act in U.S. dividing southern states into five military districts; to re-enter Union these districts are to draw up constitutions passed by Congress, and they must recognise 14th Amendment (of *June* 1866);
—, Tenure-of-Office Act passed in U.S., over President's veto, to restrict powers of the President to dismiss and appoint;
5th, abortive Fenian risings in Ireland;
12th, Napoleon III withdraws French support for Maximilian of Mexico;
29th, British North America Act establishes Dominion of Canada comprising Quebec, Ontario, Nova Scotia and New Brunswick;
30th, U.S. purchases Alaska from Russia;
Last French troops quit Mexico.

D **Apr:** 1st, end of rule of East India Company in Straits Settlements which now become Crown Colony;
16th, formation of North German Confederation with Prussia at head.

E **May:** 11th, London Conference guarantees neutrality of Luxembourg which Napoleon III was trying to buy from the King of the Netherlands (treaty signed *Sept.* 9th) and Prussia is to forgo her right to garrison the Luxembourg fortresses.

F **Jun:** 8th, Francis Joseph I of Austria is crowned King of Hungary at Budapest;
19th, Emperor Maximilian executed in Mexico.

G **Jul:** 23rd, Russia forms governor-generalship over Turkestan.

H **Aug:** 15th, Parliamentary Reform Act in Britain extends suffrage in boroughs to all householders paying rates and all lodgers paying £10 rent annually, in counties to landowners with land at value of £5 p.a. and tenants paying £12 rent annually; redistribution of seats takes place;
15th, British Factory Act, whereby terms of previous acts extended to cover other premises, manufactures or processes;
21st, Act of Parliament regulates hours and conditions of work for children, young persons and women in workshops;
First Socialist, Ferdinand Bebel, elected to North German Reichstag.

J **Sep:** 18th, Fenian outrage in Manchester when prison van attacked and policeman killed.

K **Oct:** 27th, G. Garibaldi begins march on Rome;
28th, French force lands at Civita Vecchia.

L **Nov:** 3rd, G. Garibaldi, defeated by French and Papal troops at Mentana, is sent as captive to Caprera;
5th, death of General O'Donnell in Spain.

O **Politics, Economics, Law and Education**

Walter Bagehot, *The English Constitution.*

Karl Marx, *Das Kapital*, vol. I.

W. T. Torrens secures passage of Artisans' Dwellings Act in Britain.

J. S. Mill and Mark Pattison urge reform of English education.

P **Science, Technology, Discovery, etc.**

William Thomson invents siphon recorder.

Pierre Michaux manufactures bicycles.

Gold is discovered in Wyoming.

Q **Scholarship**

E. A. Freeman, *History of the Norman Conquest* (–76).

Von Sickel, *Acta Karolinorum.*

R **Philosophy and Religion**

Archbishop A. C. Tait holds first Pan Anglican Synod (*Sept.*).

Holders of civil office in U.K. no longer required to make declarations against transubstantiation.

Pius IX celebrates 18th centenary of death of SS. Peter and Paul and announces intention of holding a Council.

S **Art, Sculpture, Fine Arts and Architecture**

Paul Cézanne, *Rape* (painting).

É. Manet and G. Courbet hold one-man shows at Paris World Fair in defiance of the Salon.

The Paris World Fair introduces Japanese art to the West.

T **Music**

Georges Bizet, *Fair Maid of Perth* (opera).

G. Verdi, *Don Carlos* (opera).

J. Strauss, The 'Blue Danube' Waltz.

U **Literature**

Charles de Coster, *Légende d'Uylenspiegel.*

Adam Lindsey Gordon, *Sea Spray and Smoke Drift* introduces the first Australian poet.

O. W. Holmes, *The Guardian Angel.*

Ouida (pseud.), *Under Two Flags.*

Anthony Trollope, *Last Chronicle of Barset.*

Ivan Turgeniev, *Smoke.*

Émile Zola, *Thérèse Raquin.*

V **The Press**

W **Drama and Entertainment**

H. Ibsen, *Peer Gynt.*

Paris World Fair.

X **Sport**

Y **Statistics**

1867 (Dec.)

M Dec: 13th, Fenian outrage at Clerkenwell kills 12 people;
21st, new Austrian Constitution accepts Dual System with regard to Hungary.

N

z Births and Deaths

Jan. 17th Jean Dominique Ingres d. (87).
Apr. 10th G. W. Russell ('A.E.') b. (–1935).
Apr. 18th Robert Smirke d. (86).
May 26th Princess Mary of Teck (Queen Mary) b. (–1953).
May 27th Arnold Bennett b. (–1931).
June 28th Luigi Pirandello b. (–1936).
Aug. 3rd Philipp August Böckh d. (81), and Stanley, Earl Baldwin, b. (–1947).
Aug. 14th John Galsworthy b. (–1933).
Aug. 25th Michael Faraday d. (76).
Aug. 31st Charles Pierre Baudelaire d. (46).
Nov. 7th Marie Sklodowska (Marie Curie) b. (–1934).
— Sun Yat-Sen b. (–1925).

1868 Revolution in Spain—Britain annexes Basutoland

A **Jan**: 2nd, British expedition to Ethiopia, led by Sir Robert Napier, after ruler has imprisoned British consul;
3rd, Shogunate abolished in Japan and restoration of Meiji dynasty.

B **Feb**: 4th, President A. Johnson is impeached for violating the Tenure-of-Office Act of *Mar.* 1867;
25th, Lord Derby resigns through ill health and
28th, B. Disraeli replaces him as Prime Minister.

C **Mar**: 12th, Britain annexes Basutoland;
Prussia confiscates territory of King of Hanover.

D **Apr**: 13th, Robert Napier captures Magdala in Ethiopia.

E **May**: 11th, freedom of press granted in France;
12th, Samarkand is occupied by Russians;
16th, President A. Johnson is acquitted by Senate.

F **Jun**: 10th, Michael III, King of Serbia, is murdered; succeeded by Milan IV (–1889);
11th, limited right of public meeting allowed in France.

G **Jul**: 28th, 14th Amendment to U.S. Constitution, concerned with civil rights;
Third Maori War breaks out in New Zealand (–1870).

H **Aug**: 8th, France concludes commercial treaty with Madagascar.

J **Sep**: 17th, Liberal revolution against Queen Isabella II in Spain under Marshal Juan Prim and, 18th, Admiral Topete issues a Liberal manifesto in Cadiz;
30th, Queen Isabella of Spain flees to France, and is declared deposed.

K **Oct**:

L **Nov**: In U.S. presidential election U. S. Grant (Republican) has 214 electoral votes over Horatio Seymour (Democrat), with 80 votes.

M **Dec**: 2nd, following Liberal victory (387 seats) over Conservatives (272 seats) in British general election, B. Disraeli resigns without waiting for Parliament's re-assembly. W. E. Gladstone, who lost his seat in south-west Lancashire, forms a Liberal ministry with Lord Clarendon as Foreign Secretary and Robert Lowe as chancellor of Exchequer;
11th, Turkish ultimatum to Greeks to leave Crete (accepted *Feb.* 1869);
22nd, W. E. Gladstone is elected M.P. for Greenwich.

N

O **Politics, Economics, Law and Education**

Alexander Hamilton Stephens, *A Constitutional View of the War Between the States* (–70).

Hospital for epileptics founded near Bielefeld, Germany.

Austrian schools are freed from clerical control.

P **Science, Technology, Discovery, etc.**

Charles Darwin, *Variations of Animals and Plants under Domesticisation.*

Ernst Haeckel, *The History of Creation.*

George Westinghouse's brake.

P. D. Armour's meat-packing factory at Chicago opened.

Q **Scholarship**

Royal Historical Society and Cambridge Philological Society are founded.

R **Philosophy and Religion**

Abolition of compulsory church rates in England and Wales.

S **Art, Sculpture, Fine Arts and Architecture**

E. Degas, *L'Orchestre* (painting).

É. Manet, *Zola* (painting).

P. A. Renoir, *Lise* (painting).

Renoir and Manet begin to paint continually out of doors.

George Street, The Law Courts, London (–82).

T **Music**

J. Brahms, *A German Requiem*, op. 45 (additions made, 1872).

E. Grieg, Piano Concerto in A minor (op. 16).

R. Wagner, *The Mastersingers of Nuremberg* (opera).

U **Literature**

L. A. Alcott, *Little Women.*

G. Brandes, *Aesthetic Studies.*

R. Browning, *The Ring and the Book* (–69).

W. Collins, *The Moonstone.*

F. Dostoievsky, *The Idiot.*

W. Morris, *The Early Paradise.*

V **The Press**

The Overland Monthly (San Francisco), with Bret Harte as editor.

W **Drama and Entertainment**

X **Sport**

The Cincinnati Red Stockings, first U.S. professional baseball club, founded.

Y **Statistics**

Z **Births and Deaths**

Mar. 14th Maxim Gorki b. (–1936).
Apr. 1st Edmond Rostand b. (–1918).
Apr. 12th J. L. Garvin b. (–1947).
Apr. 26th Harold Harmsworth, Lord Rothermere, b. (–1940).
May 7th Henry, Lord Brougham, d. (89).
June 6th Robert Falcon Scott b. (–1912).
July 12th Stefan George b. (–1933).
July 14th Gertrude Bell b. (–1926).
Aug. 29th Christian Friedrich Schönbein d. (68).
Nov. 13th Gioacchino Rossini d. (76).

1869 Red River rebellion in Canada—Suez Canal opened

A **Jan:**

B **Feb:** 6th, Greece agrees to leave Crete (after Turkish ultimatum of *Dec.* 1868).

C **Mar:** 4th, General U. S. Grant, Republican, is inaugurated President of U.S.

D **Apr:**

E **May:**

F **Jun:** 1st, new Spanish Constitution promulgated, providing for continuation of monarchical form of government.

G **Jul:** 12th, Parliamentary system adopted by Napoleon III, based on programme of Third Party;
26th, Disestablishment of Irish Church whereby Episcopal Church to end its existence from beginning of 1871.

H **Aug:**

J **Sep:** National Prohibition Party formed in Chicago to agitate for temperance.

K **Oct:** 11th, Red River Rebellion begins in Canada when half-breeds, led by Louis Riel, stop survey team near Winnipeg.

L **Nov:** 17th, opening of Suez Canal;
19th, Canadian Government purchases territories in north-west belonging to Hudson Bay Company.

M **Dec:**

N Tunis accepts control by Britain, Italy and France because of bankruptcy.

Y **Statistics**

Roman Catholics in Britain number 950,000, of whom 750,000 are Irish immigrants.

Z **Births and Deaths**

Feb. 28th Alphonse de Lamartine d. (79).
Mar. 9th Hector Berlioz d. (66).
Mar. 20th Neville Chamberlain b. (–1940).
Mar. 26th Edwin Lutyens b. (–1944).
Mar. 31st Henry J. Wood b. (–1944).
June 8th Frank Lloyd Wright b. (–).
Oct. 2nd Gandhi b. (–1948).
Oct. 13th Charles Augustin Sainte-Beuve d. (65).
Oct. 23rd Edward Stanley, Earl of Derby, d. (70).
Dec. 30th Stephen Leacock b. (–1944).
Dec. 31st Henri Matisse b. (–1954).
— André Gide b. (–).

O **Politics, Economics, Law and Education**

Walter Bagehot, *Physics and Politics*.

J. S. Mill, *The Subjection of Women*.

The State of Wyoming enfranchises women and gives them the right to hold office.

M. Bakunin founds the Social Democratic Alliance.

W. T. Thornton, *On Labour*.

Uriah Stephens founds Knights of Labor.

M. Arnold, *Culture and Anarchy*.

Girton College, Cambridge, founded.

P **Science, Technology, Discovery, etc.**

Dimitry Mendeleeff's periodic law for the classification of the elements.

Francis Galton, *Hereditary Genius, its Laws and Consequences*, founds the science of eugenics.

H. Mège-Mouries invents margarine.

Hyatt invents celluloid.

Alizarin, synthetic dye, is prepared.

'Cup and cone' ball-bearings are invented.

The first electric washing-machine.

Gustave Nachtigal explores the Sahara and the Sudan.

Q **Scholarship**

W. E. H. Lecky, *A History of European Morals from Augustus to Charlemagne*.

Karl Lehr's edition of *Horace's Odes*.

R **Philosophy and Religion**

Eduard Hardtmann, *The Philosophy of the Unconscious*.

James Knowles founds the Philosophical Society, London.

The Vatican Council meets (*Dec.*) and H. E. Manning advocates a definition of papal infallibility.

I. Döllinger, J. N. Huber and J. Friedrich, in the *Letters of Janus*, oppose the doctrine and the tendencies of the Syllabus of Errors.

The Church of England revives suffragan bishops.

The Irish Church is disestablished.

S **Art, Sculpture, Fine Arts and Architecture**

Claude Monet, *The Balcony* (painting).

Joseph Boehm, marble statue of Queen Victoria at Windsor Castle.

T **Music**

J. Brahms, *Hungarian Dances* Nos. 1 and 2 (as piano duets).

R. Wagner, *The Rhinegold* (opera).

U **Literature**

R. D. Blackmore, *Lorna Doone*.

G. Flaubert, *L'Éducation sentimentale*.

Bret Harte, *The Outcasts of Poker Flat*.

V. Hugo, *L'Homme qui rit*.

M. Twain, *The Innocents Abroad*.

P. Verlaine, *Fêtes galantes*.

Jules Verne, *Twenty Thousand Leagues Under the Sea*.

V **The Press**

W **Drama and Entertainment**

W. Halévy, *Frou-frou*.

X **Sport**

(*Continued opposite*)

1870 (Jan.–Sep.) Franco-Prussian War begins—Napoleon III capitulates at Sedan

A **Jan:** 2nd, Olivier Ollivier becomes French premier;
Baden decides to seek entry to North German Confederation.

B **Feb:**

C **Mar:** 1st, end of war between Paraguay and combined forces of Brazil, Argentina and Uruguay;
30th, 15th Amendment in U.S. ratified, whereby suffrage not to be revoked, particularly Negro suffrage.

D **Apr:** 20th, Senate in France made an Upper House, sharing legislative powers with Assembly.

E **May:** 12th, Manitoba made Canadian province, which helps to end Red River Rebellion;
Fenian attack from Vermont, U.S., on Quebec, Canada, fails.

F **Jun:** 4th, Order-in-Council reforms British Civil Service so that most departments, apart from Foreign Office, open to competitive examination;
20th, British War Office Act subordinates Commander-in-Chief to Secretary of State;
25th, Isabella of Spain abdicates in Paris in favour of Alfonso XII;
28th, decree in Russia for reform of municipal government.

G **Jul:** 2nd, news reaches France of acceptance of Spanish throne by Leopold, Prince of Hohenzollern;
12th, Leopold's acceptance is withdrawn by his father;
13th, French ultimatum to Prussia not to renew Spanish candidature results in 'Ems Telegram';
19th, France declares war on Prussia;
30th, Austria revokes Concordat with Papacy (of 1855) after decree of Papal Infallibility (18th).

H **Aug:** 1st, Irish Land Act provides for loans to peasants to buy land and for compensation for eviction and for improvements;
4th, French, led by Marie MacMahon, are defeated at Weissenberg by Crown Prince Frederick;
6th, further French defeats at Worth and Spicheren;
9th, Married Women's Property Act in Britain gives wives greater power over own property;
—, Prussia guarantees Belgian neutrality in war with France and, 11th, Britain and France also guarantee this;
16th, Prussian forces victorious at Vionville and Mars-la-Tour;
18th, French defeated at Gravelotte and St. Privat;
Western Australia granted representative government.

J **Sep:** 1st, French defeated at battle of Sedan, France;
2nd, Napoleon III capitulates at Sedan;
4th, defeat leads to revolt in Paris, provisional government of national defence is set up and a Republic proclaimed;
19th, Siege of Paris by Prussian forces begins;
20th, Italians enter Rome.

O **Politics, Economics, Law and Education**

W. E. Forster's education act establishes board schools.
Benjamin Jowett becomes Master of Balliol.
Keble College, Oxford, founded.
University Extension Lectures at Cambridge.
Royal Commission on Science under Duke of Devonshire.

P **Science, Technology, Discovery, etc.**

T. H. Huxley's address to British Association on spontaneous generation.
Z. T. Gramme invents dynamo with ring armature.
Walter Weldon's process for making bleaching powder increases output fourfold.
Adolf Nordenskjöld explores interior of Greenland.
J. D. Rockefeller founds Standard Oil Company.

Q **Scholarship**

Heinrich Schliemann begins to excavate Troy.
Dictionary of American Biography begun.

R **Philosophy and Religion**

Vatican Council declares (*July* 18th) dogma of papal infallibility in matters of faith and morals by 533 votes to 2.
Convocation of Church of England appoints committees (*May*) to revise the Old and New Testaments, which lead to the 'Revised Version'.
J. H. Newman, *Grammar of Assent*.
I. D. Sankey joins D. L. Moody in Chicago mission.

S **Art, Sculpture, Fine Arts and Architecture**

Jean Corot, *Femme à la Perle* (painting).
H. Fantin-Latour, *Hommage à Manet* (painting).

T **Music**

Clément Delibes, *Coppélia* (opera).
R. Wagner, *Die Walküre* (opera).
R. Wagner's *Essay on Beethoven* studies the metaphysics of music in terms of A. Schopenhauer's philosophy.

U **Literature**

C. Dickens, *Mystery of Edwin Drood* (unfinished).
B. Disraeli, *Lothair*.
F. Dostoievsky, *The House of the Dead*.
Ivan Goncharov, *The Precipice*.
D. G. Rossetti, *Poems*.

V **The Press**

W **Drama and Entertainment**

X **Sport**

W. G. Grace and his brothers found Gloucestershire Cricket Club.

Y **Statistics**

Coal production (in mill. tons): U.K. 110·4; U.S. 35; Germany, 29·4; Austria, 13; France, 12.
Iron production (in mill. tons): U.K. 5·9; U.S. 1·6; Germany, 1·3; France, 1·2; Russia, 0·4.

1870 (Oct.–Dec.)

K Oct: 2nd, Rome made capital of Italy by Decree of 9th, and King of Italy formally incorporates Rome and Roman provinces in Italy;
27th, French troops surrender Metz, France;
28th, Strasbourg surrenders to Prussian forces.

L Nov: 16th, Amadeus, Duke of Aosta, elected King of Spain;
23rd, alliance treaty between North German Confederation and Bavaria (following similar North German treaty with Württemberg, *Nov.* 15th).

M Dec: 30th, Marshal Prim dies in Spain, after being wounded by assassin;
German Centre Party (Catholic) is established.

N Diamonds discovered in Orange Free State.

Y **Statistics** (*cont.*)

World Steel production: 560,000 tons (half by U.K.).
Railway mileage: U.K., 15,310.
Emigration to U.S. (1861–70): from Britain, 606,896; from Ireland, 435,779.
436,000 tons of shipping use Suez Canal, 71 per cent British.
Defence Estimates in £ mill.: Great Britain, 23·4; France, 22; Russia 22; Germany, 10·8; Austria-Hungary, 8·2; Italy, 7·8.

Z **Births and Deaths**

Feb. 12th 'Marie Lloyd' (pseud. of Matilda Wood) b. (–1922).
Mar. 4th Thomas Sturge Moore b. (–1944).
Mar. 13th Charles, Count de Montalembert d. (60).
Apr. 9th Nikolai Lenin b. (–1924).
May 6th James Young Simpson d. (59).
May 24th J. C. Smuts b. (–1950).
June 9th Charles Dickens d. (58).
Aug. 4th Harry Lauder b. (–1950).
Sept. 23rd Prosper Mérimée d. (66).
Oct. 27th Roscoe Pound b. (–1965).
Nov. 6th Herbert, Viscount Samuel b. (–1963).
Dec. 5th Alexandre Dumas d. (67).

1871 German Empire is incorporated—Rising of Commune in Paris

A **Jan:** 18th, William I of Prussia proclaimed German Emperor at Versailles;
19th, French defeated at St. Quentin;
28th, Paris capitulates and armistice with Germany is signed.

B **Feb:** 1st, French Eastern Army crosses Swiss frontier and is disarmed;
13th, French National Assembly meets at Bordeaux;
17th, L. A. Thiers becomes head of French executive;
26th, preliminary peace of Versailles between France and Germany.

C **Mar:** 13th, London Conference between great powers repudiates Black Sea clauses of 1856 (after Russian repudiation of clauses, *Oct.* 1870);
18th, rising of Commune begins in Paris;
26th, Commune is formally set up.

D **Apr:** 16th, German Empire receives Constitution remodelled from that of North German Confederation.

E **May:** 8th, Treaty of Washington settles existing difficulties between Britain and U.S., over the north-west boundary, the fisheries and the *Alabama* claims;
10th, Franco-German Peace of Frankfurt by which France cedes Alsace-Lorraine, pays indemnity of 5 milliards of francs, and is to be subjected to army of occupation until payment completed;
13th, Law of Guarantees in Italy declares the Pope's person inviolable and allows him the possession of the Vatican;
21st (–28th), 'Bloody Week' in Paris ends with defeat of the Commune.

F **Jun:** 16th, University Test Acts allow students to enter Oxford and Cambridge without religious tests;
29th, British Act of Parliament for legalising trade unions.

G **Jul:** 20th, British Columbia joins Dominion of Canada (after Imperial Order-in-Council of *May*);
31st, discovery that William Tweed's Ring in New York has systematically defrauded City treasury;
Germany begins *Kulturkampf* (cultural struggle) with Catholic Church, when Otto von Bismarck suppresses the Roman Catholic Department for spiritual affairs.

H **Aug:** 14th, Local government boards created in England;
17th, Edward Cardwell's Army reforms reorganise British army and the introduction of short service provides for trained reserve forces;
31st, L. A. Thiers elected French President;
Basutoland is united with Cape Colony.

J **Sep:**

K **Oct:** 27th, Britain annexes diamond fields of Kimberley, Griqualand West.

L **Nov:**

M **Dec:**

N

O **Politics, Economics, Law and Education**

W. S. Jevons, *Theory of Political Economy.*

John Ruskin, *Fors Claveriga.*

Germany adopts gold standard (*Dec.* 4th).

Purchase of commissions in British Army abolished.

Adolph Wagner, *The Social Question.*

Anne Clough provides house of residence for first women students at Cambridge which becomes (1880) Newnham College.

P **Science, Technology, Discovery, etc.**

Charles Darwin, *The Descent of Man.*

Discovery of the element gallium.

Chair of experimental physics is founded at Cambridge University.

Mt. Cenis tunnel opened (*Sept.* 17th).

H. M. Stanley meets D. Livingstone at Ujiji (*Nov.* 10th).

Q **Scholarship**

T. Mommsen, *Roman Constitutional Law* (–88).

R **Philosophy and Religion**

Ignaz Döllinger is excommunicated by Archbishop of Munich for refusing to accept Vatican decrees.

First Congress of Old Catholics meets at Munich.

Repeal of Ecclesiastical Titles Act of 1851 against 'papal aggression'.

Jehovah's Witnesses founded.

S **Art, Sculpture, Fine Arts and Architecture**

James Whistler, *The Artist's Mother* (painting).

T **Music**

Anton Bruckner, 2nd Symphony.

G. Verdi *Aïda* (opera).

Camille Saint-Saëns, symphonic poem *Le Rouet D'Omphale* (op. 35).

U **Literature**

L. Carroll (pseud.), *Through the Looking-Glass.*

George Eliot (pseud.), *Middlemarch* (–72).

Walt Whitman, *Democratic Vistas.*

É. Zola, *Les Rougon-Macquart* series of novels (–93).

V **The Press**

W **Drama and Entertainment**

Bank holidays introduced in England and Wales.

P. T. Barnum and J. A. Bailey open their circus at Brooklyn as the 'greatest show on earth'.

X **Sport**

F.A. Cup established.

Y **Statistics**

Populations (in millions): Germany, 41; U.S., 39; France, 36·1; Japan, 33; Great Britain, 26, and Ireland, 5·4; Italy, 26·8.

Y **Statistics** (*cont.*)

Coal production (in mill. tons): Great Britain, 117·4; U.S., 35; Germany, 29·4; France, 13·3; Austria, 12·5.

Iron production (in mill. tons): Great Britain, 6·6; France, 2·5; Germany, 1·4.

Z **Births and Deaths**

Jan. 17th David, Earl Beatty, b. (–1936).
Feb. 4th Friedrich Ebert b. (–1925).
May 11th John Herschel d. (79).
May 14th Daniel Auber d. (89).
June 18th George Grote d. (76).
July 10th Marcel Proust b. (–1922).
Aug. 27th Theodore Dreiser b. (–1945).
Aug. 30th Ernest Rutherford b. (–1937).
Sept. 6th Montagu Norman b. (–1950).
Oct. 2nd Cordell Hull b. (–1955).
Nov. 1st Stephen Crane b. (–1900).
— Paul Valéry b. (–1945).

A **Jan:** 6th, assassination of Fick, the 'Eire Ring' speculator, in New York, draws attention to corruption under the Grant régime;
25th, Henri Comte de Chambord's Antwerp Declaration, countering the suggestions of 'a Revolution Monarchy'.

B **Feb:** 2nd, Holland sells trading posts on the Gold Coast to Britain;
8th, murder of Earl of Mayo, Viceroy of India;

C **Mar:** 19th, Charles Dilke, declaring himself a Republican, moves for an inquiry into Queen Victoria's expenditure.

D **Apr:** 26th, proclamation of Don Carlos as Charles VII of Spain leads to civil war.

E **May:** 4th, defeat of Carlist forces and Don Carlos escapes to France;
Liberal Democrats at the Cincinnati Convention decide to run Horace Greeley, editor of the *New York Tribune*, as presidential candidate against U. Grant.

F **Jun:** 25th, the Jesuits are expelled from Germany.

G **Jul:** 1st, T. F. Burgers is elected President of Transvaal Republic;
18th, Ballot Act in Britain introduces voting by secret ballot;
28th, France adopts conscription.

H **Aug:**

J **Sep:** 7th, meeting of the three emperors in Berlin leads to an *entente* between Germany, Russia and Austria-Hungary;
14th, Geneva court of arbitration finds Britain legally responsible for depredations of the *Alabama* and other Confederate cruisers, awarding U.S. $15,500,000 damages.

K **Oct:** 21st, German emperor, called on to adjudicate between Britain and U.S. over disputed ownership of St. Juan, decides in favour of U.S.;
Responsible government in Cape Colony, with J. C. Molteno first premier;
George Berkeley, governor of Cape Colony, annexes Griqualand West.

L **Nov:** 5th, Anglo-French commercial treaty, modifies the treaty of 1860;
5th, re-election of Ulysses Grant, the Republican candidate (286 electoral votes) as President, over Horace Greeley, Liberal Democrat (62 votes), who dies, 30th;
22nd, Comte de Paris accepts compensation for confiscation of his estates.

M **Dec:** 9th, Otto von Bismarck's County Organisation bill, for remodelling local government in Prussia at expense of nobles' powers, passes Upper House after special creation of 25 peers.

N Compulsory military service in Japan.
First rebellion against Spain in Philippines.

O **Politics, Economics, Law and Education**

M. Bakunin is expelled from the International at the Hague Conference.
National Agricultural Labourers' Union founded in Britain by Joseph Arch.
German Criminal Code in force.
Strasbourg University founded.

P **Science, Technology, Discovery, etc.**

Albert Billroth makes first resection of the oesophagus.
Thomas Edison perfects the 'duplex' telegraph.
William Thomson's sounding-machine (the 'Kelvin') for determining depth at sea.
The Challenger undertakes world oceanographic survey (–76).
New York-Brooklyn bridge opened (*July*).
Electric filament lighting installed in St. Petersburg docks.

Q **Scholarship**

T. Mommsen edits *Corpus Juris Civilis.*
G. Brandes, *Main Streams of XIXth Century Literature* (–75).

R **Philosophy and Religion**

D. F. Strauss, *The Old Faith and the New.*
Père Hyacinthe attempts to found national church in France.
General Assembly of French Protestants holds first meeting since 1659.

S **Art, Sculpture, Fine Arts and Architecture**

A. Böcklin, *Battle of the Centaurs* (painting).
E. Degas, *Le Foyer de la Danse* (painting).
P. Cézanne and C. Pissarro paint at Pontoise.

T **Music**

G. Bizet's incidental music to Alphonse Daudet's *L'Arlésienne.*
C. Franck, *Les Béatitudes* (oratorio).
Alexandre Lecocq, *Madame Angot's Daughter* (opera).

U **Literature**

Samuel Butler, *Erewhon, or Over the Range.*
Charles Stuart Calverley, *Fly Leaves.*
Alphonse Daudet, *Aventures Prodigieuses de Tartarin de Tarascon.*
Thomas Hardy, *Under the Greenwood Tree.*
Ivan Turgeniev, *A Month in the Country.*
Jules Verne, *Around the World in 80 Days*, appears in *Le Temps.*

V **The Press**

C. P. Scott edits *Manchester Guardian* (–1929).

W **Drama and Entertainment**

Eleanora Duse's début.
Royal Albert Hall, London, opened.
Alexandre Ostrovsky, *The Snow Maiden.*

X **Sport**

1st International Association football match, England *v.* Scotland (*Nov.* 30th).

Y Statistics

British Textiles trade:

imported raw cotton	1,181 mill. lb.
cottons exported	3,538 mill. yds.
woollens exported	412,541,000 yds.
linens exported	245,019,000 yds.
silks exported	4,417,000 yds.

Z Births and Deaths

Jan. 10th Alexander Scriabin b. (–1915).
Jan. 21st Franz Grillparzer d. (81).
Mar. 10th Giuseppe Mazzini d. (66).
Mar. 19th Serge Diaghilev b. (–1929).
Apr. 9th Léon Blum b. (–1950).
May 18th Bertrand Russell b. (–).
May 31st Heath Robinson b. (–1944).
July 1st Louis Blériot b. (–1936).
July 4th Calvin Coolidge b. (–1933).
July 12th F. E. Smith, Lord Birkenhead b. (–1930).
July 16th Roald Amundsen b. (–1928).
Aug. 24th Max Beerbohm b. (–1956).
Oct. 4th Roger Keyes b. (–1945).
Dec. 23rd Théophile Gautier d. (61).

A **Jan**: 9th, Napoleon III dies at Chislehurst, England (aged 64) leaving an only son aged 17.

B **Feb**: 11th, abdication of Amadeo I of Spain;
16th, Republic proclaimed in Spain.

C **Mar**: 13th, W. E. Gladstone resigns following defeat of Irish University bill in which forty-three Liberals vote against government, but as B. Disraeli refuses to take office with a minority administration Gladstone returns;
Judicature Act reforms system of central courts in England by establishing a Supreme Court of Judicature with its separate divisions, and a Court of Appeal.

D **Apr**: 2nd, reform of Austrian franchise in favour of Germans;
23rd, massive monarchist demonstrations in Madrid;
Ashanti War breaks out;
Dutch War against Sultan of Achin in north-west Sumatra.

E **May**: 6th, military convention between Germany and Russia;
11th (–14th), Paul Falk, Prussian minister of public worship, introduces the May Laws, subjecting the clergy to State control;
24th, L. A. Thiers falls and M. MacMahon is elected French president;
Financial crisis begins in Vienna, spreading to other European capitals and leading to withdrawal of foreign investments from U.S.A.

F **Jun**: 5th, abolition of slave markets and export of slaves by Sultan of Zanzibar, under pressure from Sir John Kirk.

G **Jul**: 1st, Prince Edward Island joins the Dominion of Canada;
Dissolution of monasteries in Italy.

H **Aug**: 5th, reconciliation of Comte de Chambord and Comte de Paris;
12th, Russia assumes suzerainty of Khiva and Bokhara;
W. E. Gladstone reforms his ministry, himself becoming chancellor of Exchequer.

J **Sep**: 8th, during Carlist risings Emilio Castelar is made ruler of Spain to restore order under a centralised republic;
15th, Germans evacuate France;
Marco Minghetti forms ministry in Italy following break-up of Giovanni Lanza's government;
Financial panic in U.S. caused by speculation, over-production and withdrawal of foreign capital.

K **Oct**: 17th, Comte de Chambord's Frohsdorf letter of uncompromising Legitimism;
20th, Ecuador becomes a theocracy (–75).
22nd, alliance of the emperors of Germany, Russia and Austria-Hungary;
27th, Comte de Chambord ends hope of restoration of French monarchy by refusing to accept tricolour.

L **Nov**: 20th, French monarchists confer M. MacMahon with presidential powers for seven years;
Croats are granted internal self-government;
Rival cities of Buda and Pesth are statutorily united to form capital of Hungary.

M **Dec**: Papal nuncio is expelled from Switzerland.

N The Flemish language is admitted in courts of Flanders.
Abolition of the Office of Statholder (or King of Sweden's lieutenant) in Norway.
Andrew Clarke, governor of Straits Settlements, places British residents in the several Malay states.
Famine in Bengal.

O **Politics, Economics, Law and Education**
H. Taine, *Les Origines de la France contemporaine.*
H. Spencer, *The Study of Sociology.*
National Federation of Employers founded in Britain.
Economic crises in Europe, U.S. and Australia.
Germany adopts the Mark coinage and U.S. adopts the gold standard.

P **Science, Technology, Discovery, etc.**
W. K. Clifford, *Preliminary Sketch of Bi-quaternions.*
Jean Charcot, *Le cours sur les maladies du système nerveux.*
J. Clerk-Maxwell, *A Treatise on Electricity and Magnetism.*
W. Thomson reforms the mariner's compass.
G. Drayton's oil engine.
First oil well sunk in Baku.
Philo Remington's company produce typewriter designed by C. L. Scholes.
Julius Payer and Karl Weyprecht discover Franz Joseph Land (*Aug.* 13th).
Introduction of colour sensitising makes possible colour photography.

Q **Scholarship**
Walter Pater, *Studies in the History of the Renaissance.*

R **Philosophy and Religion**
Christoph Sigwart, *Logic.*
D. L. Moody and I. Sankey begin revivalist meetings in England (–75).

S **Art, Sculpture, Fine Arts and Architecture**
Paul Cézanne, *Straw Hat* (painting).
Jean Corot, *Souvenir d'Italie* (painting).
É. Manet, *Le Bon Bock* (painting).

T **Music**
N. Rimsky-Korsakov, *Ivan the Terrible* (opera).

U **Literature**
Paul Heyse, *Kinder der Welt.*
J. S. Mill, *Autobiography.*
Arthur Rimbaud, *Une Saison en Enfer.*
Leo Tolstoy, *Anna Karenina* (–75).

V **The Press**

W **Drama and Entertainment**

X **Sport**

Y **Statistics**
U.S. Petroleum production: 9,894,000 barrels.
Crime: 14,893 convictions for offences in England and Wales (of which 123 for murder and 943 for manslaughter); 2,721 convictions in Scotland.

Z **Births and Deaths**
Jan. 15th Edward Bulwer Lytton, Lord Lytton, d. (69).
Feb. 1st Clara Butt b. (–1936), and Fedor Chaliapin b. (–1938).
Feb. 10th Justus von Liebig d. (69).
Feb. 28th John Simon b. (–1954).
Mar. 26th Gerald du Maurier b. (–1934).
Apr. 1st Sergei Rachmaninoff b. (–1943).
May 8th John Stuart Mill d. (67).
Dec. 17th Ford Maddox Hueffer (F. M. Ford) b. (–1939).

1874 (Jan.–Oct.) *Kulturkampf* in Germany—Conservatives win British General Election

A Jan: 2nd, Emilio Castelar retires in Spain and
3rd, Marshal Francisco Serrano becomes dictator;
13th, conscription is introduced in Russia;
23rd, Prince Alfred, Duke of Edinburgh, marries Princess Marie Alexandrovna in St. Petersburg;
In Reichstag elections the Ultramontane Catholic Centre increases its seats through hatred of the May Laws.

B Feb: 2nd, in British general election W. E. Gladstone holds out the promise of abolition of income tax; election riots at Dudley, Hanley and Wolverhampton, Staffs.;
4th, Garnet Wolseley burns Kumasi, ending Ashanti War and, 13th, by treaty of Fommenah King Koffee of Ashanti promises free trade, an open road to Kumasi and undertakes to pay indemnity to Britain and stop human sacrifices;
17th, British general election results in Conservative majority of 83 (the first clear Conservative majority since 1841), W. E. Gladstone resigns and
18th, B. Disraeli forms ministry, with Stafford Northcote chancellor of Exchequer, 15th Earl of Derby as foreign secretary and Richard Cross as home secretary;
Strike of agricultural workers in eastern England (–*Aug.* 10th).

C Mar: 15th, France assumes protectorate over Annam, which breaks off its vassalage to China.

D Apr:

E May: 20th, end of civil disturbances in Arkansas caused by disputed election of governorship;
23rd, G. O. Trevelyan's bill for extension of household suffrage to the counties is defeated;
25th, Marco Minghetti resigns in Italy, following the defeat of Quintino Sella's financial proposals, but the King refuses to accept his resignation;
Further May Laws in Germany against Ultramontane clergy (which provoke Pius IX's bull *Quod Nunquam* annulling them, in *Mar.* 1875);
At the Gotha Conference German Marxians and Lassalleans unite to form Socialist Working-Men's Party;
The Swiss Constitution is revised to centralise authority and the federal court receives more power.

F Jun: Federal forces reinstate U. P. Kellogg, Republican governor of Louisiana, after S. D. McEnery, Democrat, claimed to be installed as rival governor.

G Jul: Denmark grants Iceland self-government with a representative Althing.

H Aug: Bolivia-Chile boundary is fixed as parallel 24°S.

J Sep: 15th, Prince of Wales visits France.

K Oct: 4th, Count Arnim, lately German ambassador in Paris, is arrested in Germany, on charge of embezzling State papers, but in reality because of his attacks on the French Republic, and subsequently a Conservative plot is uncovered in Germany for replacing Bismarck by Arnim;
25th, Britain annexes the Fiji Islands.

O Politics, Economics, Law and Education

Union Générale des Postes established at Berne.

Building Societies Act in Britain protects small investors and encourages home ownership.

E. T. Gerry founds Society for the Prevention of Cruelty to Children in New York.

Civil marriage made compulsory in Germany.

Arthur Orton, the Tichborne Claimant, found guilty of perjury (*Feb.* 28th).

Yorkshire College (later Leeds University) founded.

P Science, Technology, Discovery, etc.

Ernst Haeckel, *Anthropogenia.*

W. S. Jevons constructs an 'abecedarium' (or logical machine).

Solomon introduces pressure-cooking method for canning foods.

Q Scholarship

J. R. Green, *Short History of the English People.*

W. Stubbs, *Constitutional History of England* (–78).

Augustus Pitt-Rivers exhibits his collections relating to primitive peoples at Bethnal Green Museum (he presents them to Oxford University in 1883).

R Philosophy and Religion

Henry Sidgwick, *Methods of Ethics.*

Wilhelm Wundt, *Physiological Psychology.*

Disraeli's Public Worship Regulation Act aims at curbing ritualistic practices.

W. E. Gladstone attacks papal infallibility in his pamphlet, *The Vatican Decrees.*

The Old Catholics permit the use of the vernacular and the marriage of priests.

S Art, Sculpture, Fine Arts and Architecture

First Impressionist Exhibition, Paris, includes works by P. Cézanne, E. Degas, C. Pissarro and A. Sisley.

C. Monet's painting, *Impression: Sunrise* gives rise to the derisive title 'Impressionism'.

A. Renoir, *La Loge* (painting).

T Music

M. P. Moussorgsky, *Boris Godunov* (opera), and *Pictures from an Exhibition.*

J. Strauss, *Die Fledermaus* (opera).

R. Wagner completes *Götterdämmerung.*

G. Verdi, *Requiem.*

F. Smetana, symphonic poem *My Fatherland.*

U Literature

P. Alarcón, *The Three-cornered Hat.*

G. Flaubert, *La Tentation de Saint Antoine.*

A. Fogazzaro, *Miranda.*

T. Hardy, *Far from the Madding Crowd.*

V. Hugo, *Ninety-Three.*

P. Verlaine, *Romances sans Paroles.*

V The Press

W Drama and Entertainment

X Sport

Wingfield invents lawn tennis ('Sphairistike').

L Nov: 2nd (–3rd), Democrats make sweeping gains in U.S. state elections;
24th, Alfonso, son of Queen Isabella, comes of age and declares for a constitutional monarchy in Spain.

M Dec: 29th (–31st), Spanish generals rally to Alfonso who is proclaimed King as Alfonso XII (–85).

N Financial collapse of Turkey through heavy borrowing abroad.
Canada adopts voting by ballot on a single day.

Y **Statistics**

Z **Births and Deaths**

Jan. 25th W. Somerset Maugham b. (–1965).
Feb. 3rd Gertrude Stein b. (–1946).
Feb. 9th Jules Michelet d. (75).
Feb. 15th Ernest Shackleton b. (–1922).
Mar. 26th Robert Frost b. (–1964).
Apr. 25th Guglielmo Marconi b. (–1937).
May 29th Gilbert Keith Chesterton b. (–1936).
Aug. 10th Herbert Hoover b. (–).
Sept. 12th François Guizot d. (86).
Sept. 13th Arnold Schönberg b. (–1951).
Sept. 21st Gustav Holst b. (–1934).
Oct. 25th Geoffrey Dawson b. (–1944).
Nov. 27th Chaim Weizmann b. (–1953).
Nov. 30th Winston Churchill b. (–1965).
Dec. 17th William Mackenzie King b. (–1950).

1875 Revised Constitution in France—Britain buys Suez Canal Shares —Risings in Bosnia and Herzegovina

A **Jan**: 9th, Alfonso XII lands at Barcelona, but Carlist War continues;
12th, Kwang-su becomes Emperor of China (–1908);
13th, W. E. Gladstone resigns Liberal leadership in House of Commons;
30th, Republican Constitution in France, with Wallon amendment, is passed by one vote.

B **Feb**: 3rd, Marquess of Hartington is elected Liberal leader as Gladstone's successor;
24th (–25th), enactment of laws on the organisation of the Public Powers and of the Senate of France;
In the face of deteriorating relations with France Otto von Bismarck endeavours to preserve Germany's *entente* with Russia.

C **Mar**: Kálmár Tisza, leader of the Left, forms ministry in Hungary on break-up of Deak party.

D **Apr**: 8th, article 'Is War Safe?' in *Berlin Post* starts war scare;
Louis Decazes, French foreign minister, appeals to Britain and Russia for support against Bismarck, and war is averted;
14th, reforms of Japanese courts of law;
House of Commons decides to exclude strangers by majority vote of the House alone.

E **May**: 10th, Tsar Alexander and his foreign minister, Prince Gorchakov, visit Berlin;
Religious orders abolished in Prussia.

F **Jun**:

G **Jul**: 16th, law on the relation of the Public Powers completes the French Constitution of 1875;
Risings in Bosnia and Herzegovina against Turkish rule.

H **Aug**: Prince of Wales visits India;
Public Health Act in Britain;
Lord Carnarvon holds informal conversations in London on South African federation.

J **Sep**: 29th, B. Disraeli overrules Admiralty ruling requiring the restitution of fugitive slaves within territorial waters;
Rebellion in Cuba leads to deterioration of U.S.-Spanish relations.

K **Oct**: 12th, in New Zealand provincial governments are abolished and the government centralised, through efforts of Julius Vogel.

L **Nov**: 25th, Britain buys 176,602 shares in Suez Canal from the Khedive of Egypt.

M **Dec**: 12th, the Sultan of Turkey promises reforms throughout the Ottoman Empire to meet the rebels' demands;
Julius Andrássy, on behalf of the Eastern powers, calls for religious freedom in Bosnia and Herzegovina, which Disraeli accepts as the basis for reform;
Stanley Cave is sent to Egypt to inquire into its finances.

O **Politics, Economics, Law and Education**
Labourers' Dwellings Act.
Agricultural Holdings Act, allowing compensation for unexhausted improvements.
Food and Drugs Act.
S. Plimsoll's Merchant Shipping Act in Britain.
Reichsbank founded in Germany.
London Medical School for Women founded.

P **Science, Technology, Discovery, etc.**
Caton begins experiments on electrical responses of brain.
H. M. Stanley traces the Congo to the Atlantic.
London's main-drainage system completed.

Q **Scholarship**
F. Max Müller edits *The Sacred Books of the East* (51 vols. –1903).
Dictionary of German Biography is begun.

R **Philosophy and Religion**
Émile Laveleye, *L'Avenir des Peuples Catholiques.*
Helena Blavatsky founds Theosophical Society in New York.
Mary Baker Eddy, *Science and Health.*

S **Art, Sculpture, Fine Arts and Architecture**
Adolf Menzel, *The Forge* (painting).
Claude Monet, *Boating at Argenteuil* (painting).
The *Hermes* of Praxiteles is found at Olympia.

T **Music**
P. I. Tchaikovsky, 1st Piano Concerto in B flat minor (op. 23).
G. Bizet, *Carmen* (opera).
Karl Goldmark, *Queen of Sheba* (opera).
Trial by Jury begins W. S. Gilbert and A. Sullivan partnership.

U **Literature**
M. Twain (pseud.), *The Adventures of Tom Sawyer.*

V **The Press**

W **Drama and Entertainment**
Gabrielle Réjane's début in Paris.

X **Sport**

Y **Statistics**
Production of pig iron (in thousand tons): Great Britain, 6,365; Germany, 2,029; France, 1,416.
Production of steel (in thousand tons): Great Britain, 536; Germany, 370; France, 258.
Strength of armies: Russia, 3,360,000; Germany, 2,800,000; France, 412,000; Great Britain, 113,649.
U.K. State expenditure: £73 mill.

1875

N President MacMahon arbitrates in the Delagoa Bay dispute, recognising Portuguese claims against Britain.
Treaty of friendship between Japan and Korea, after various incidents.

z **Births and Deaths**

Jan. 14th Albert Schweitzer b. (–1965).
Jan. 20th J. F. Millet d. (60).
Jan. 23rd Charles Kingsley d. (55).
Feb. 22nd Jean-Baptiste Camille Corot d. (78).
Mar. 7th Maurice Ravel b. (–1937).
June 3rd Georges Bizet d. (36).
Aug. 4th Hans Christian Andersen d. (70).
Aug. 13th Samuel Coleridge-Taylor b. (–1912),
Aug. 26th John Buchan, Lord Tweedsmuir, b. (–1940).
Dec. 4th Rainer Maria Rilke b. (–1926).
— M. I. Kalinin b. (–1946).

1876 (Jan.–Nov.) Turks massacre Bulgarians—Franco-British Control in Egypt

A **Jan:** 31st, Sultan Abdul Aziz agrees to adopt reform programme of Andrássy Note (of *Dec.* 1875) in Ottoman Empire, but this is rejected by the insurgents;
Cortes adopt new Constitution in Spain providing for two-chamber legislature, elected on limited suffrage.

B **Feb:** 26th, China declares Korea to be an independent state;
28th, end of Carlist War with flight of Don Carlos.

C **Mar:** 5th (–7th), Egyptians defeated at Gura by Ethiopians;
8th, rule of National Assembly in France ends with summoning of a new Senate (Conservative) and a Chamber (overwhelmingly Republican);
9th (–16th), Turkish troops massacre Bulgarians;
28th, Agostino Depretis forms ministry of the Left in Italy, following Marco Minghetti's fall;
Stephen Cave's report on Egyptian finances published.

D **Apr:**

E **May:** 10th, the Liberal Midhat Pasha forms ministry in Constantinople;
13th, Berlin Memorandum of Germany, Russia and Austria to Turkey, calling for an armistice, the re-establishment of the insurgents and the supervision of Turkish reforms by the powers, but Britain refuses to approve;
30th, deposition of Sultan Abdul Aziz, whose nephew is proclaimed as Murad V.

F **Jun:** 15th, several members of Ottoman government assassinated;
30th, Serbia, under the nationalist Jovan Ristich, declares war on Turkey.

G **Jul:** 2nd, Montenegro declares war on Turkey.

H **Aug:** 1st, Colorado becomes a U.S. state;
12th, Disraeli leaves the Commons on being created Earl of Beaconsfield;
31st, Murad V of Turkey, Sultan since *May*, is deposed on plea of insanity, succeeded by Abdul Hamid II (–1909).

J **Sep:** 1st, Serbs defeated at Alexinatz;
6th, W. E. Gladstone's *The Bulgarian Horrors and the Question of the East.*

K **Oct:** 31st, Turkey agrees to 6-week armistice as result of a Russian ultimatum.

L **Nov:** 1st, Appellate Jurisdictions Act in Britain restores jurisdiction of House of Lords and of Judicial Committee of the Privy Council;
7th, in U.S. Presidential election S. J. Tilden, Democrat, secures 184 out of the 185 electoral votes required, against R. B. Hayes, Republican, with 165, but 20 votes are in dispute (settled by electoral commission, *Jan*, 1877);
G. J. Goschen and Joubert visit Egypt to establish dual control;
Russia prepares for war against Turkey.

O **Politics, Economics, Law and Education**

First International (International Working Men's Association) dissolved at Philadelphia Congress (*July*),

M. Bakunin organises 'Land and Liberty', a secret society in Russia, which becomes spearhead of the Populist Movement.

German Conservative Party founded.

Industrial and Provident Societies Act in Britain.

Lembroso, *The Criminal*, founds criminology.

Z. R. Brockway founds reformatory at Elmire, New York, for juvenile offenders.

Reichsbank opened (*Jan.*).

Johns Hopkins University, Baltimore, founded, the first graduate school in U.S.

P **Science, Technology, Discovery, etc.**

A. G. Bell invents the telephone.

Formation of chromosomes first observed.

T. A. Edison invents the phonograph.

Rich deposits of nickel ores are found in New Caledonia.

Q **Scholarship**

R **Philosophy and Religion**

F. H. Bradley, *Ethical Studies*.

Felix Adler founds Society for Ethical Culture, New York.

A. Bain founds *Mind*.

Presbyterian Churches in England unite with the English congregations of United Presbyterian Church of Scotland to form the Presbyterian Church of England.

S **Art, Sculpture, Fine Arts and Architecture**

A. Renoir, *Au Théâtre* and *Le Moulin de la Galette* (paintings).

P. Gauguin exhibits landscapes at the Salon, Paris.

T **Music**

J. Brahms, 1st Symphony in C Minor (op. 68).

P. I. Tchaikovsky, *Francesca da Rimini*.

R. Wagner, *Siegfried* (opera).

Bayreuth Festspielhaus opens for first complete performance of Wagner's *The Ring*.

Léo Delibes, *Sylvia* (opera).

Hans Richter conducts concerts in London.

Purcell Society is founded.

U **Literature**

Julius Dahn, *Ein Kampf*.

Henry James, *Roderick Hudson*.

S. Mallarmé, *L'Après-midi d'un faune*.

B. Pérez-Galdós, *Doña Perfecta*.

W. Morris, *Sigurd the Volsung*.

V **The Press**

W **Drama and Entertainment**

X **Sport**

W. G. Grace scores two triple centuries in successive county cricket matches.

U.S. National Baseball League is founded.

M Dec: 5th, Ulysses Grant's last message to Congress;
12th (–*Jan.* 20th 1877), Constantinople Conference, called at Britain's suggestion, to consider Turkish problem;
23rd, proclamation of Ottoman Constitution, embodying parliamentary government, freedom of worship and a free press.

N New Zealand Constitution sweeps away provincial councils.
Coup d'état in Bolivia leads to Hilarión Daza's presidency.

Y **Statistics**

U.K. Merchant Shipping tonnage: 6,263,000 (2,005,000 steamships).

Z **Births and Deaths**

Jan. 5th Konrad Adenauer b. (–).
Feb. 16th G. M. Trevelyan b. (–1964).
June 8th 'George Sand' (Amandine Dudevant, *née* Dupin) d. (71).
Nov. 28th Carl von Baer d. (84).
Dec. 30th Pablo Casals b. (–)
— Michael Bakunin d. (62).

1877 (Jan.–Nov.) Russia declares war on Turkey—Britain annexes Transvaal

A **Jan**: 1st, Queen Victoria proclaimed Empress of India;
15th, by Budapest convention Austria undertakes to remain neutral in event of a Russo-Turkish War, and is to occupy Bosnia and Herzegovina when she sees fit, thereafter Serbia, Montenegro and Herzegovina are to form a neutral zone;
20th, failure of the powers at the Constantinople Conference to effect accord between Russia and Turkey in the Balkans;
29th, U.S. electoral commission decides in favour of R. B. Hayes, the Republican candidate.

B **Feb**: 5th, dismissal of Midhat Pasha, leader of the Turkish Liberals;
28th, peace signed between Turkey and Serbia.

C **Mar**: 3rd, U.S. Desert Land bill;
4th, R. B. Hayes inaugurated U.S. President;
12th, Britain annexes Walvis Bay on south-west African coast;
18th, additional Russo-Austrian convention that no large state be erected in the Balkans;
19th, first Turkish Parliament meets;
31st, London Protocol of great powers demands Turkey to undertake reforms;
Bartle Frere appointed High Commissioner of South Africa with instructions to work towards federation.

D **Apr**: 12th, Sultan of Turkey refuses London Protocol;
—, Theophilus Shepstone annexes South African Republic of Transvaal for Britain on grounds of bankruptcy and danger from Basutos and Zulus, but annexation violates Sand River convention of 1852;
24th, Russia declares war on Turkey and invades Roumania.

E **May**: 2nd, Porfirio Diaz becomes President of Mexico (–1911);
6th, British note to Russia warning her against attempted blockade of Suez or occupation of Egypt;
16th, crisis of *Seize Mai* in France when M. MacMahon, annoyed at Jules Simon's failure to stand up to the anti-clerical Left, dismisses him, appointing de Broglie to form a Monarchist ministry, which, 19th, is given a vote of no confidence in the Chamber;
Roumania enters war against Turkey.

F **Jun**: 27th, Russians cross the Danube.

G **Jul**: 20th, first Russian reverses;
21st, British Cabinet decides to declare war on Russia if she were to occupy Constantinople.

H **Aug**: first Kaffir War (–78).

J **Sep**: suppression of Satsuma Rebellion in Japan.

K **Oct**: Britain signs treaty of commerce with Madagascar, which agrees to liberate slaves.

L **Nov**: 18th, Russians storm Kars;
19th, Duc de Broglie's ministry forced to resign and is succeeded by General Rochebouet's, which also fails to enjoy confidence of the Chamber.

O **Politics, Economics, Law and Education**
Protection for patents in Germany.
Compulsory education in Italy, six–nine years.

P **Science, Technology, Discovery, etc.**
Asaph Hall discovers two satellites of Mars at Washington (*Aug.* 11th and 18th).
Lord Rayleigh, *Treatise on Sound.*
Koch demonstrates techniques of fixing and straining bacteria.
Joseph Monier's reinforced concrete beams.
Carl Laval invents cream separator.
First public telephone.
Frozen meat is shipped from Argentina to France.

Q **Scholarship**

R **Philosophy and Religion**
Truth first issued.

S **Art, Sculpture, Fine Arts and Architecture**
P. Cézanne shows 16 pictures at 3rd Impressionist Exhibition.
É. Manet's painting *Nana* is rejected by the Salon.
Winslow Homer, *The Cotton-Pickers* (painting).
A. Rodin, *The Bronze Age* (sculpture).
Society for the Protection of Ancient Buildings from Injudicious Restoration founded in London.
P. J. H. Cuyper, Rijksmuseum, Amsterdam.

T **Music**
Alexander Borodin, Symphony No. 1 in B minor.
J. Brahms, Symphony No. 2 in D (op. 75).
P. I. Tchaikovsky, Symphony No. 4 in F minor (op. 36).
C. Saint-Saëns, *Samson and Delilah* (opera).

U **Literature**
Henry James, *The American.*
Sarah Jewett, *Deephaven.*
É. Zola, *L'Assommoir.*

V **The Press**
The Nineteenth Century issued (edited by J. Knowles).

W **Drama and Entertainment**
H. Ibsen, *The Pillars of Society.*

X **Sport**
All-England Lawn Tennis championships first played at Wimbledon; 1st champion, Spencer Gore.

Y **Statistics**

M Dec: 10th, fall of Plevna, Bulgaria, to Russian army;
12th, Turks appeal to powers to mediate, but Bismarck declines and the British cabinet is divided;
13th, Jules Dufaure forms ministry in France;
14th, Serbia, siding with Russia, declares war on Turkey.

N Famine in India.

z **Births and Deaths**

Jan. 22nd Hjalmar Schacht b. (–).
Feb. 17th André Maginot b. (–1932).
Mar. 24th Walter Bagehot d. (51).
May 29th John Lothrop Motley d. (63).
July 27th Ernest Dohnányi b. (–).
Sept. 3rd Louis Adolphe Thiers d. (80).
Sept. 11th James Jeans b. (–1946).
Nov. 25th Harley Granville-Barker b. (–1946).
Dec. 31st Gustave Courbet d. (58).
— Lev Trotsky b. (–1940).

1878 (Jan.–Jul.) Congress of Berlin settles Eastern Question—Anti-Socialist legislation in Germany

A **Jan**: 9th, on Victor Emmanuel's death, Humbert I succeeds as King of Italy (–1900);
9th, Turks capitulate at Shipka Pass and appeal to Russia for an armistice;
16th, U.S. signs treaty of friendship with Samoa;
20th, Russians take Adrianople;
23rd, British cabinet sends fleet to Constantinople at Sultan Abdul Hamid II's request, Lord Derby resigns in protest but later withdraws as fleet is recalled; 'Jingoist' war fever in Britain;
28th, risings in Thessaly;
28th, Count Andrássy proposes calling a European conference, meanwhile, 31st, Turkey signs armistice with Russia.

B **Feb**: 2nd, Greece declares war on Turkey;
7th, election of Cardinal Joachim Pecci as Pope Leo XIII, who soon opens negotiations with Germany for abrogation of May Laws of 1873 and 1874;
8th, Britain again decides to send fleet to Constantinople, but Sultan, under Russian pressure, refuses permission to enter the Straits (notwithstanding the fleet arrives, 15th);
10th, by convention of El Zanjóu, ending the Ten Years War, Spain promises reforms in Cuba;
28th, Bland-Allison bill reintroduces silver standard in U.S.

C **Mar**: 3rd, by preliminary treaty of San Stefano between Russia and Turkey, Montenegro to be enlarged, with port of Antivari; Roumania, Montenegro and Serbia to be independent; reforms to be undertaken in Bosnia and Herzegovina; Bulgaria to be enlarged with a seaboard on Aegean and most of Macedonia; Russia to receive Ardaham, Kars and Batum, while Turkey to pay Russia a huge indemnity;
25th, Nikolai Ignatiev, Russian diplomat, on mission to Vienna fails to reconcile Austria to treaty of San Stefano;
27th, fearing further Russian aggression British cabinet calls out reserves and drafts Indian troops to Malta.

D **Apr**: 2nd, Derby resigns and is succeeded as foreign minister by Lord Salisbury;
8th, Austria evades Salisbury's suggestions for common action against Russia.

E **May**: 8th, Peter Shuvalov, Russian ambassador in London, undertakes mission to St. Petersburg to divide Bulgaria;
11th (and *June* 2nd), radical attempt to assassinate Emperor William I of Germany;
18th, Colombia grants French company a nine-year concession to build Panama Canal;
24th, Reichstag rejects Bismarck's proposed repressive legislation against radicals;
30th, secret Anglo-Russian agreement to reduce the size of Bulgaria.

F **Jun**: 4th, secret Anglo-Turkish agreement to check Russian advance in Asia Minor, by which Britain promises to defend Turkey against further attack and Britain is allowed to occupy Cyprus;
6th, Anglo-Austrian agreement on Bulgaria;
13th (*July* 13th), Berlin Congress attended by Count Andrássy, Otto von Bismarck, Peter Shuvalov, W. H. Waddington, L. Corti, B. Disraeli and Lord Salisbury to discuss Eastern Question.

G **Jul**: 13th, by Treaty of Berlin Bulgaria is split into (a) autonomous Bulgaria, north of Balkans, (b) Eastern Rumelia with a special organisation under Turkey and (c) Macedonia where reforms are to be undertaken; Austria is given mandate to occupy Bosnia and Herzegovina; Roumania is awarded Dobrudja but has to hand over South

O Politics, Economics, Law and Education

H. Treitschke draws attention to growth of Jewish influence in Germany.

Flemish becomes the official language in Flanders.

P Science, Technology, Discovery, etc.

The sphygmograph is invented.

Sidney Thomas and Percy Gilchrist perfect the 'basic' process for steel production by lining the Bessemer furnace with dolomite.

Swan's carbon filament lamp.

David Hughes invents the microphone.

New Eddystone Lighthouse.

Earliest electric street lighting in London.

A. A. Pope manufactures first American bicycles.

Q Scholarship

W. E. H. Lecky, *History of England in the XVIIIth Century* (–90).

R Philosophy and Religion

William Booth founds Salvation Army in Britain.

F. Max Müller delivers first Hibbert Lectures on Comparative Religion.

Georges Romanes, *A Candid Examination of Theism.*

Roman Catholic hierarchy is restored in Scotland.

S Art, Sculpture, Fine Arts and Architecture

Albert Bierstadt, *Sierra Nevada.*

Pierre Puvis de Chavannes, *Life of St. Geneviève.*

James Whistler awarded ¼d. damages in libel action with John Ruskin for disparaging remarks on his painting, *Nocturne in Black and Gold.*

Cleopatra's Needle from Heliopolis, given to England in 1819, is removed from Alexandria to London.

T Music

Anton Dvořák, *Three Slavonic Rhapsodies* (op. 56).

A. Sullivan, *H.M.S. Pinafore.*

George Grove edits *Dictionary of Music and Musicians* (–79).

P. I. Tschaikovsky *Swan-Lake* (ballet).

U Literature

Theodor Fontane, *Vor dem Sturm.*

T. Hardy, *The Return of the Native.*

H. James, *Daisy Miller.*

René Sully-Prudhomme, *La Justice.*

A. C. Swinburne, *Poems and Ballads.*

V The Press

W Drama and Entertainment

Ellen Terry joins Irving's Company at the Lyceum Theatre.

X Sport

Bicycle Touring Club founded in England.

Y Statistics

G **Jul**: 13th, Bessarabia to Russia; Montenegro is given Antivari; Montenegro, Roumani and Serbia become independent states; Russia receives Batum, Kars and Ardaham; British occupation of Cyprus is confirmed; Italian and Greek demands are shelved; promises for reforms in Macedonia and Asia Minor lead to agitation;
30th, in Reichstag elections Conservatives gain seats at expense of National Liberals.

H **Aug**: 15th, Nubar Pasha forms ministry in Egypt, with Rivers Wilson as minister of finance.

J **Sep**:

K **Oct**: 11th, Germany and Austria annul clause in Peace of Prague, 1866, over plebiscite in North Schleswig;
17th, J. A. MacDonald becomes premier of Canada on Conservatives winning general election on protectionist platform;
18th, anti-Socialist law in Germany (–1890), prohibits public meetings, publications and collections, thus driving Socialism underground;
21st, Irish National Land League founded with C. S. Parnell as president.

L **Nov**: 25th, Comité d'Études du Haut-Congo formed to organise Belgian advance in Congo.

M **Dec**: 11th, Bartle Frere, British High Commissioner in South Africa, delivers ultimatum to Zulus;
Franco-British dual control in Egypt is suspended on the Khedive's introduction of ministerial government.

N Beginning of Irredentist agitation in Italy to obtain Trieste and other Italian-speaking areas.

z **Births and Deaths**

Jan. 23rd Rutland Boughton b. (–1963).
Feb. 7th Pope Pius IX d. (85).
Feb. 10th Claude Bernard d. (64).
May 10th Gustav Stresemann b. (–1929).
May 28th Lord John Russell, Earl Russell d. (85).
Sept. 20th Upton Sinclair b. (–).
Oct. 8th A. J. Munnings b. (–1959).
Oct. 19th Paul Reynaud b. (–).
Nov. 27th William Orpen b. (–1931).
— John Masefield b. (–).
— Martin Buber b. (–).

1879 Zulu War

A **Jan**: 1st, resumption of specie payments in U.S., suspended since 1873;
5th, Republicans gain in French senatorial elections;
12th, British-Zulu War (*–July*);
22nd, Zulus massacre British troops at Isandhlwana, Zululand;
24th, Germany signs commercial treaty with Samoa;
30th, on M. MacMahon's resignation, Jules Grévy, a Conservative Republican, is elected President of France.

B **Feb**: 4th, W. H. Waddington becomes French premier;
18th, fall of Nubar ministry in Egypt after army demonstration;
22nd, constitution granted in Bulgaria, with a national assembly.

C **Mar**:

D **Apr**: 29th, Alexander of Battenberg is elected Prince Alexander I of Bulgaria (–1866).

E **May**: 26th, by treaty of Gandamak Britain occupies the Khyber Pass and pays the Amir of Afghanistan an annual subsidy.

F **Jun**: 25th, Ismael Khedive of Egypt is deposed by the Sultan, succeeded by Tewfik (–1892);
Law against Jesuits in France.

G **Jul**: 1st, primary education in Belgium is secularised;
12th, protectionist laws for industry and agriculture in Germany split the Liberal Party.

H **Aug**: 4th, Alsace-Lorraine is declared an integral part of the German *Reich* under a governor-general;
17th, French Panama Canal Company is organised under Ferdinand de Lesseps;
28th, in Zulu War British troops capture Cetywayo;
Count Taaffe forms Austrian ministry (–1893) and ends German predominance in Austria-Hungary in favour of Slavs.

J **Sep**: 1st, Britain signs peace with Zulu chiefs;
3rd, Afghan troops massacre the British legation at Kabul;
4th, Anglo-French dual control of Egypt re-established (suspended in *Dec.* 1878);
15th, treaty of Livadia between Russia and China gives Russia key points in Ili Valley.

K **Oct**: 7th, Austro-German dual alliance for five years (renewed until 1918);
Britain invades Afghanistan and, 19th, Yakub the Amir abdicates and surrenders to Britain;
P. A. Saburov's mission to Berlin for renewal of Russo-German alliance fails.

L **Nov**: 24th (*–Dec.* 9th), W. E. Gladstone in Midlothian Campaign denounces Conservative government for imperialism and mishandling of domestic affairs;
27th, French Chamber is moved from Versailles to Paris.

M **Dec**: 16th, Transvaal Republic is proclaimed.

N

O **Politics, Economics, Law and Education**

Henry George, *Progress and Poverty.*
Robert Giffen, *Essay on Finance.*
W. L. Blackley proposes scheme for old-age pensions.
The radical, terrorist, Will of the People Society is founded in Russia.
Afrikander Bond is founded in South Africa to work for the recognition of the Dutch language.

P **Science, Technology, Discovery, etc.**

The element scandium is discovered.
Researches of the Hon. Henry Cavendish (posth., ed. J. Clerk Maxwell.)
Dugald Clark uses an electric arc to heat steel furnace.
W. E. Ayrton pioneers electricity as a motive power, and W. E. Siemens exhibits an electric railway in Berlin.
London's first telephone exchange.
First Pullman dining-car.
Australian frozen meat is on sale in London.

Q **Scholarship**

W. W. Skeat, *Etymological English Dictionary* (–82).
H. Treitschke, *History of Germany in the XIXth Century* (–95).

R **Philosophy and Religion**

A. J. Balfour, *Defence of Philosophic Doubt.*
H. Spencer, *Principles of Ethics* (–93).
Papal Encyclical (*Aug.* 4th) protesting against modern metaphysics.
Mary Baker Eddy becomes pastor of a Church of Christ, Scientist, Boston.

S **Art, Sculpture, Fine Arts and Architecture**

J. Bastien-Lepage, *Portrait of Sarah Bernhardt.*
A. Renoir, *Mme Charpentier and her children.*
A. Rodin, *John the Baptist* (sculpture).

T **Music**

J. Brahms, Violin Concerto in D (op. 77) played by H. Joachim.
P. I. Tchaikovsky, *Eugen Onegin* (opera).
A. Bruckner, 6th Symphony.

U **Literature**

G. Meredith, *The Egoist.*
B. Pérez-Galdós, *Episodios Nacionales* (–83).
R. L. Stevenson, *Travels with a Donkey.*
Juan Valera, *Doña Luz.*

V **The Press**

W **Drama and Entertainment**

H. Ibsen, *The Doll's House.*
A. Strindberg, *The Red Room.*
The public granted unrestricted admission to the galleries of the British Museum.

X **Sport**

Y **Statistics**

O Politics, Economics, Law and Education
Henry George, *Progress and Poverty*.
Robert Giffen, *Essays in Finance*.
W. L. Blackley proposes scheme for old-age pensions.
The radical, terrorist wing of the Populist Society is founded in Russia.
Afrikaner Bond is founded in South Africa to work for the recognition of the Dutch language.

P Science, Technology, Discovery, etc.
The element scandium is discovered.
Papers of the Hon. Henry Cavendish (publ., ed. J. Clerk Maxwell).
Dugald Clerk uses an electric arc to heat steel furnace.
W. E. Ayrton proposes electricity as a motive power, and W. E. Siemens exhibits an electric railway at Berlin.
London's first telephone exchange.
First Pullman dining car.
Australian frozen meat is on sale in London.

Q Scholarship
W. W. Skeat, *Etymological English Dictionary* (-1882).
H. Treitschke, *History of Germany in the 19th Century* (-95).

R Philosophy and Religion
A. J. Balfour, *Defence of Philosophic Doubt*.
H. Spencer, *Principles of Ethics* (-93).
Papal Encyclical (Aug. 4th) protesting against modern metaphysics.
Mary Baker Eddy becomes pastor of a Church of Christ, Scientist, Boston.

S Art, Sculpture, Fine Arts and Architecture
J. Bastien-Lepage, *Portrait of Sarah Bernhardt*.
A. Renoir, *Mme Charpentier and her children*.
A. Rodin, *John the Baptist* (sculpture).

T Music
J. Brahms, Violin Concerto in D (op. 77) played by J. Joachim.
P. I. Tchaikovsky, *Eugene Onegin* (opera).
A. Bruckner, 6th symphony.

U Literature
G. Meredith, *The Egoist*.
B. Pérez Galdós, *Episodios Nacionales* (-79).
R. L. Stevenson, *Travels with a Donkey*.
Jules Vallès, *Jacques Vingtras*.

V The Press

W Drama and Entertainment
H. Ibsen, *The Doll's House*.
A. Strindberg, *The New Kingdom*.
The public granted unrestricted admission to the galleries of the British Museum.

X Sport

Y Statistics

z **Births and Deaths**

Jan. 13th William Reid Dick b. (–).
Mar. 14th Albert Einstein b. (–1955).
May 5th William Beveridge b. (–1963).
May 25th William Maxwell Aitken, Lord Beaverbrook, b. (–1964).
Aug. 27th Rowland Hill d. (83).
Nov. 5th James Clerk Maxwell d. (48).
Nov. 22nd John Thadeus Delane d. (59).
Dec. 21st Joseph Stalin b. (–1953).
— Honoré Daumier d. (71).
— Edward Morgan Forster b. (–).

1880 Liberals in power in Britain—Transvaal declares itself an independent republic

A **Jan:**

B **Feb:**

C **Mar:** 8th, Lord Beaconsfield appeals to electorate on issue of Irish Home Rule;
24th, Britain, U.S. and Germany recognise the King of Samoa and provide for an executive with European representation;
29th (–30th), decrees in France for non-authorised religious associations to regularise their positions and for dispersal of Jesuits.

D **Apr:** 18th, in British elections Liberals secure majority of 137 over Conservatives and Irish Nationalists win 65 seats, so Beaconsfield resigns;
28th, W. E. Gladstone forms Liberal ministry in which he is also chancellor of Exchequer, with Lord Granville foreign secretary, William Harcourt home secretary and Joseph Chamberlain president of Board of Trade.

E **May:** 3rd, Charles Bradlaugh, M.P. for Northampton, claims rights to affirm at swearing-in of Commons, instead of taking oath (for persistent refusal to take oath he is taken into custody, *June* 23rd, and is subsequently excluded from the House); during the Bradlaugh affair Henry Wolff, John Gorst, Lord Randolph Churchill and sometimes H. H. Asquith associate as a group independent of the Conservative leadership, nicknamed the Fourth Party;
Acute rivalry between France and Italy begins in Tunis;
Michael Loris-Melikov becomes Russian minister of interior, with wide powers for dealing with Nihilists; the problem of constitutional reform is shelved.

F **Jun:** 25th, Cape Parliament rejects scheme for South African federation;
29th, France annexes Tahiti;
—, Papal nuncio is expelled from Belgium during crisis over educational policy;
Clericals defeat Liberals in Belgian elections and begin long era of power (–1914).
France, alarmed at Stanley's advance in Congo for Leopold II of Belgium, sends de Brazza to treat with chiefs on north side of river.

G **Jul:** 11th, French law grants amnesty to Marquis de Rochefort and other Communards of 1871;
17th, Egyptian finances are reorganised;
New penal code in Japan, based on that of France.

H **Aug:** 2nd, Relief of Distress Act for Ireland.

J **Sep:**

K **Oct:** 13th, Transvaal declares itself independent of Britain.

L **Nov:** 2nd, Irish Land League is prosecuted (results in acquittal of Parnellites in *Jan.* 1881 through disagreement of jury);
8th, civil war in Samoa;
26th, Turkey yields to the powers and permits Montenegro to occupy Dulcigno, in place of the territory assigned by the Berlin Congress of 1878.

M **Dec:** 30th, Transvaal Boers under Kruger declare a Republic.

O **Politics, Economics, Law and Education**

Employers' Liability Act grants workmen compensation for accidents caused by employers' negligence.

Walter Bagehot, *Economic Studies* (posth.).

Parcel post introduced in England.

Owens College becomes Manchester University.

First girls' high schools in England.

De Beers Mining Corporation is formed by Cecil Rhodes.

P **Science, Technology, Discovery, etc.**

Louis Pasteur discovers streptococcus.

Laveran observes the malarian parasite.

Andrew Carnegie's first large steel furnace.

Adolf von Beyer makes synthetic indigo.

T. A. Edison and J. W. Swan independently make the first practical electric light.

Beginning of street lighting by electricity in New York.

Tinned salmon, meat and fruit are available.

Q **Scholarship**

R **Philosophy and Religion**

John Caird, *Philosophy of Religion.*

Jesuits in France disbanded and military chaplains are abolished.

Burials Bill enables dissenters to hold services in parish churchyards in Britain.

S **Art, Sculpture, Fine Arts and Architecture**

Cologne Cathedral completed.

T **Music**

A. Dvořák, Symphony No. 1 in D (op. 60).

P. I. Tchaikovsky, *1812 Overture* and *Italian Capriccio.*

C. Franck, piano quintet.

A. Sullivan, *Pirates of Penzance* (opera).

U **Literature**

B. Disraeli, *Endymion.*

F. Dostoievsky, *The Brothers Karamazov* (–81).

Jens Jacobsen, *Niels Lyhne.*

H. W. Longfellow, *Ultima Thule.*

G. de Maupassant, *Boule de Suif.*

J. H. Shorthouse, *John Inglesant.*

Francis Thompson, *The City of Dreadful Night.*

Lewis Wallace, *Ben Hur.*

É. Zola, *Nana.*

V **The Press**

Half-tone block used in *New York Daily Graphic.*

W **Drama and Entertainment**

X **Sport**

First test match between England and Australia.

Society of American Wheelmen founded.

N Captain C. C. Boycott, land agent in Mayo, is 'boycotted' for refusing to take rents at the figures fixed by tenants.

War of the Pacific, Chile against Bolivia and Peru (–1884).

First federal confederation assembly meets at Sydney, New South Wales, under Henry Parkes.

Y **Statistics**

Coal production (in mill. tons): Great Britain, 149; U.S., 64·9; Germany, 59; France, 19·4; Russia, 3·2.

Pig-iron production (in mill. tons): Great Britain, 7·8; U.S., 3·9; Germany, 2·5; France, 0·5; Russia, 0·4.

Railway mileage in operation: U.S., 87,801; Great Britain, 17,935; France, 16,430; Russia, 12,200.

Emigration to U.S. (1871–80): from U.K., 548,043; from Ireland, 436,871.

Suez Canal: used by 4,344,000 tons of shipping, 70 per cent British.

Telephones: 50,000 private telephones in use in U.S.

Z **Births and Deaths**

Jan. 26th Douglas MacArthur b. (–1964).
Mar. 1st Giles Lytton Strachey b. (–1932).
May 8th Gustave Flaubert d. (58).
July 24th Ernest Bloch b. (–).
Oct. 5th Jacques Offenbach d. (61).
Dec. 22nd 'George Eliot' (Mary Ann Evans) d. (61).
Dec. 28th St. John Irvine b. (–).
— R. H. Tawney b. (–1962).
— Jacob Epstein b. (–1959).

1881 (Jan.–Nov.) Repressive legislation for Ireland—France occupies Tunis—Three Emperors' league formed

A **Jan**: 28th, Transvaal Boers in their revolt repulse a British force under George Colley at Laing's Nek;

31st (–*Feb.* 2nd), Irish members at Westminster obstruct passage of repressive Coercion bill for Ireland in Commons, which sits for 41 hours continuously when, *Feb.* 2nd, Speaker, H. B. W. Brand, takes division on first reading.

B **Feb**: 1st, first signs of nationalist movement in Egypt with rising of officers;

24th, by treaty of St. Petersburg China pays indemnity to Russia for return of Ili Valley;

27th, Boers defeat British under G. Colley at Majuba Hill.

C **Mar**: 2nd, suspension of Habeas Corpus Act in Ireland;

4th, James A. Garfield, Republican, is inaugurated U.S. President;

12th, following raids of Krumir tribes into Algiers, France occupies Tunis;

13th, Alexander II signs Ukase calling an assembly of Russian nobles and the same day is assassinated by terrorists. Alexander III succeeds (–1894).

D **Apr**: 5th, Britain concludes treaty of Pretoria with Boers, recognising independence of South African Republic of Transvaal;

19th, on death of Lord Beaconsfield, Lord Salisbury becomes leader of Conservatives in Lords, Stafford Northcote in Commons;

30th, French navy seizes Bizerta and troops invade Tunis from Algeria.

E **May**: 12th, by treaty of Bardo with the Bey Tunis accepts French protectorate.

F **Jun**: 18th, Three Emperors' League, a secret alliance between Germany, Austria and Russia for three years;

28th, Austro-Serbian alliance;

Immigration Act in New Zealand restricts Japanese immigration.

G **Jul**: 2nd, President Garfield is shot; he dies *Sept.* 19th, and is succeeded by Chester Arthur;

3rd, Britain persuades Turkey to sign convention with Greece, granting Greece Thessaly and part of Epirus, as was promised at Berlin Congress;

13th, constitution revised in Bulgaria, where a new ministry of Russian officers is formed;

28th, Serbia becomes virtual protectorate of Austria by secret treaty;

Rising against the French in Algeria (–83).

H **Aug**: 16th, W. E. Gladstone's Irish Land Act fixes tenures, and establishes a land court to deal with excessive rents.

J **Sep**: 9th, Nationalist rising in Egypt under Arabi Pasha.

K **Oct**: 13th, C. S. Parnell is imprisoned for inciting Irish to intimidate tenants taking advantage of Land Act.

L **Nov**: 14th, Léon Gambetta forms ministry in France (–*Jan.* 1882), following Jules Ferry's resignation on attack of his Tunisian policy.

O **Politics, Economics, Law and Education**

Natural History Museum, South Kensington, opened (*Apr.*).
Freedom of press in France.
American Federation of Labor founded at Pittsburgh.
Flogging is abolished in Royal Navy and British Army.
University College, Liverpool, founded.

P **Science, Technology, Discovery, etc.**

L. Pasteur attenuates anthrax virus by vaccine.
S. P. Langley invents bolometer for determining minute changes of temperature.
Edward Tylor, *Anthropology*.
A. A. Common in England and H. Draper in U.S. each photograph a comet (*June* 24th).

Q **Scholarship**

B. F. Westcott and F. J. A. Hort, *Greek New Testament*.

R **Philosophy and Religion**

Revised Version of New Testament.
Anti-papal demonstrations on the removal of the remains of Pius IX.
C. P. Pobédonostsev, procurator of the Holy Synod, persecutes Jews in Russia.

S **Art, Sculpture, Fine Arts and Architecture**

Max Liebermann, *An Asylum for Old Men* (painting).
C. Monet, *Sunshine and Snow* (painting).

T **Music**

J. Brahms, *Academic Festival* (op. 80) and *Tragic* (op. 81) overtures.
Jacques Offenbach, *The Tales of Hoffmann* (opera).

U **Literature**

G. Flaubert, *Bouvard et Pécuchet*.
A. France (pseud.), *Le Crime de Sylvestre Bonnard*.
H. James, *Portrait of a Lady*.
G. de Maupassant, *La Maison Tellier*.
D. G. Rossetti, *Ballads and Sonnets*.
S. C. F. Schandorph, *The History of Thomas Friis*.
R. L. Stevenson, *Virginibus Puerisque*.
P. Verlaine, *Sagesse*.

V **The Press**

Evening News issued.

W **Drama and Entertainment**

H. Ibsen, *Ghosts*.
Édouard Pailleron, *Le Monde ou l'on s'ennuie*.
Sarah Bernhardt leaves the *Comédie Française*.
D'Oyly Carte builds the Savoy Theatre, the first public building in England lit by electricity.

X **Sport**

First U.S. lawn tennis championships (R. D. Sears champion until 1888).

1881 (Dec.)

M **Dec:** Canadian Pacific Railway Company founded.

N Moderate extension of Italian franchise.
Foundation of political parties in Japan, following imperial decree that an assembly will be convened in 1890.

Y **Statistics**

Population (in millions): U.S., 53; Germany, 45·2; France, 37·6; Italy, 28·4; Great Britain, 29·7; Ireland, 5·1.

Populations of chief cities: London, 3·3; Paris, 2·2; New York, 1·2; Berlin, 1·1; Vienna, 1·0; Tokio, 0·8; St. Petersburg, 0·6; Brussels, 0·1.

Z **Births and Deaths**

Feb. 4th Thomas Carlyle d. (86).
Feb. 9th Feodor Dostoievsky d. (60).
Mar. 9th Ernest Bevin b. (–1951).
Mar. 16th M. P. Moussorgsky d. (42).
Apr. 19th Benjamin Disraeli, Earl of Beaconsfield, d. (77).
May 25th Béla Bartók b. (–1945).
July 26th George Borrow d. (78).
Aug. 2nd Ethel M. Dell (Savage) b. (–1939).
Aug. 6th Alexander Fleming b. (–1955).
Oct. 15th William Temple b. (–1944), and P. G. Wodehouse b. (–).
Oct. 25th Pablo Picasso b. (–).
— Clive Bell b. (–1964).
— Kemel Atatürk b. (–1938).

1882 Phoenix Park Murders—Italy joins German-Austrian Alliance—Battle of Tel-el-Kebir

A **Jan**: 8th, Léon Gambetta's note to Egypt by France and Britain, to strengthen Khedive's hands against Nationalists;
22nd, Italian electoral reform lowers tax requirements and age limit of electors;
27th, Léon Gambetta falls and Charles Freycinet forms ministry in France.

B **Feb**: 5th, Khedive is forced to appoint a Nationalist ministry in Egypt;
Pan Slav speech by Russian General M. D. Skobelev in Paris alarms Germany.

C **Mar**: 6th, Prince Milan proclaims himself King of Serbia, with Austrian support;
29th, primary education in France to be free, compulsory and non-sectarian.

D **Apr**: 4th, the Prussian legation at the Vatican is restored.

E **May**: 2nd, Kilmainham 'treaty' between C. S. Parnell and British government for an amnesty on condition that Parnell seeks to end disorders; Lord Cowper, Lord Lieutenant of Ireland, and his chief secretary resign;
6th, Fenians murder new Irish chief secretary, Lord Frederick Cavendish, and T. H. Burke, Irish under-secretary, in Phoenix Park, Dublin;
—, U.S. bans Chinese immigrants for ten years;
20th, Italy joins Austro-German alliance, which becomes Triple Alliance, for five years (renewed until 1915); this assures Italy of support in event of French attack, but secures no guarantee of her possession of Rome;
22nd, U.S. secures trading rights in Korea.

F **Jun**: 6th, Hague convention fixes three-mile limit for territorial waters;
12th, anti-foreign riots in Alexandria led by Arabi Pasha;
28th, Anglo-French agreement on boundaries of Sierra Leone and French Guinea.

G **Jul**: 9th, Royal Navy bombards Alexandria and John Bright resigns from Gladstone's cabinet in protest;
23rd, Koreans attack Japanese legation in Seoul, provoking Chinese intervention;
Repressive Prevention of Crimes bill for Ireland suspends trial by jury and grants police wide powers of search and arrest.

H **Aug**: 17th, Massacre of Irish family at Maamtrasna, by the 'Invincibles', a secret Irish terrorist society.

J **Sep**: 13th, Garnet Wolseley defeats Egyptians at Tel-el-Kebir, Lower Egypt, and proceeds to occupy Egypt and the Sudan;
15th, British force occupies Cairo; Arabi surrenders and is banished to Ceylon.

K **Oct**:

L **Nov**: 9th, Franco-British dual control of Egypt established.

M **Dec**: Italy takes over Assab Bay in Red Sea and establishes colony of Eritrea.

N During the year there are 2,590 agrarian outrages in Ireland and 10,457 families are evicted.

O **Politics, Economics, Law and Education**

M. Bakunin, *Dieu et l'État* (posth.).
W. Besant, *All Sorts and Conditions of Men.*
W. S. Jevons, *The State in Relation to Labour.*
Primrose League is founded in Britain to foster Conservative Party principles.
Married Women's Property Act in Britain gives married women the right of separate ownership of property of all kinds.
Republican Party is founded in Portugal.
American Colonial Society founded.
London Chamber of Commerce first meets (*Jan.* 25th).
Cotton duties abolished in India.
Bank of Japan founded.
Bohemian National University, Prague.
Regent Street Polytechnic opened in London.

P **Science, Technology, Discovery, etc.**

Ralph Copeland observes transit of Venus in Jamaica.
George Kynoch's brass cartridge-case.
Gottlieb Daimler builds petrol engine.
T. A. Edison's generating station at Pearl Street, New York, and the first hydro-electric plant at Appleton, Wisconsin.
Society for Psychical Research founded, with Henry Sidgwick president.
The idea of a Channel Tunnel is first discussed in Britain, but military authorities disapprove.

Q **Scholarship**

R **Philosophy and Religion**

Leslie Stephen, *Science of Ethics.*
Wilson Carlile founds Church Army.

S **Art, Sculpture, Fine Arts and Architecture**

É. Manet, *Le Bar aux Folies-Bergères* (painting).
J. S. Sargent, *El Jaleo* (painting).
O. Wilde's *Lectures on the Decorative Arts* explains the aesthetic movement.

T **Music**

J. Brahms, Piano Concerto No. 2 in B flat (op. 83).
F. Gounod, *The Redemption* (oratorio).
N. Rimsky-Korsakov, *The Snow Maiden* (opera).
A. Sullivan, *Iolanthe* (opera).
R. Wagner, *Parsifal* (opera).
Berlin Philharmonic Orchestra founded.

U **Literature**

W. D. Howells, *A Modern Instance.*
F. Nietzsche, *Die fröhliche Wissenschaft.*

V **The Press**

Berliner Tageblatt.

W **Drama and Entertainment**

H. F. Becque, *Les Corbeaux.*
H. Ibsen, *An Enemy of the People.*

W **Drama and Entertainment** (*cont.*)
H. A. Jones, *The Silver King.*
V. Sardou, *Féodora.*

X **Sport**
American Baseball Association founded.

Y **Statistics**
British Textiles trade:

imports of raw cotton	1,458 mill. lb.
exports of cotton	4,349 mill. yds.
exports of woollens	265,211,000 yds.
exports of linens	176,451,000 yds.
exports of silks	7,662,000 yds.

Z **Births and Deaths**
Jan. 11th Theodor Schwann d. (72).
Jan. 25th Virginia Woolf b. (–1941).
Jan. 26th Léon Gambetta d. (43).
Jan. 30th F. D. Roosevelt b. (–1945).
Feb. 2nd James Joyce b. (–1941).
Feb. 22nd Eric Gill b. (–1940).
Mar. 24th Henry Wadsworth Longfellow d. (75).
Mar. 26th T. H. Green d. (46).
Apr. 9th D. G. Rossetti d. (54).
Apr. 19th Charles Darwin d. (71).
Apr. 27th Ralph Waldo Emerson d. (78).
June 1st John Drinkwater b. (–1937).
June 2nd Giuseppe Garibaldi d. (74).
June 5th Igor Stravinsky b. (–).
Aug. 27th Samuel Goldwyn b. (–).
Sept. 23rd Friedrich Wöhler d. (82).
Oct. 14th Eamon de Valéra b. (–).
Dec. 6th Louis Blanc d. (71) and Anthony Trollope d. (67).
Dec. 16th J. B. Hobbs b. (–1964).
Dec. 28th Arthur Stanley Eddington b. (–1944).
— Georges Braque b. (1963).

1883 Paul Kruger becomes President of Transvaal—French protectorate over Annam and Tonkin

A **Jan:** 3rd, Lord Granville's circular to the powers on Britain's desire to withdraw forces from Egypt as soon as the state of the country permits;
16th, Pendleton act begins reform of U.S. civil service (completed 1901);
30th, Clement Fallières forms ministry in France, lasting three weeks.

B **Feb:** 21st, Jules Ferry forms second ministry in France (–1885).

C **Mar:** 15th, Irish-American terrorists attempt to blow up *The Times* office and the Local Government Board, London.

D **Apr:** 16th, Paul Kruger becomes President of South African Republic;
24th, Germany begins settlements in South-West Africa and Angra Pequeña, which prompts Britain to state that any claims to sovereignty in territory between Cape Colony and Angola will be regarded as an infringement of her rights.

E **May:** 1st, Otto von Bismarck introduces sickness insurance schemes in Germany;
—, the Organic Law in Egypt, based on Lord Dufferin's report of *Feb.* 6th, establishes a legislative Council and a general assembly, though authority remains vested in the British agent.

F **Jun:** 1st (–*Dec.* 1885), French war with Madagascar;
8th, by convention of Marsa with the Bey of Tunis, France gains effective control of Tunisia.

G **Jul:**

H **Aug:** 18th, Corrupt and Illegal Practices Act limits spending of all parties in a British general election to £800,000 and limits spending of individual candidates;
24th, Comte de Chambord, French pretender, dies without heir;
25th, France acquires protectorate over Annam and Tonkin, Indo-China.

J **Sep:** 11th, Evelyn Baring lands in Egypt as British agent;
30th, Alexander of Bulgaria restores the constitution of 1879, alienating Russia;
Boer republic of Stellaland founded in Bechuanaland.

K **Oct:** 20th, by peace of Ancór Peru cedes territory to Chile, who is to occupy Tacna and Arica for ten years, when a plebiscite is to be held;
30th, secret Austro-Rumanian alliance (–1914), through Rumanian fear of Russia.

L **Nov:** 5th, the Madhi defeats Egyptian force under William Hicks at El Obeid and Britain decides to evacuate the Sudan;
Nationalist Radical party revolts against Serbian government.

M **Dec:** 14th, Portuguese government grants concession for a railway from Delagoa Bay to Transvaal to a U.S. promoter.

N French troops begin conquest of the Upper Niger.
Queensland's request to annex New Guinea is declined by Britain.

O **Politics, Economics, Law and Education**
Lester Ward, *Dynamic Sociology.*
Boys' Brigade founded.

P **Science, Technology, Discovery, etc.**
W. Thomson's discourse to Royal Institution on the size of atoms.
R. Koch discovers preventive inoculation against anthrax.
L. A. Bertillon, *Ethnographie moderne des races sauvages.*
Electrical exhibition, Munich.
Northern Pacific Railroad constructed.
First skyscraper, Chicago.
Sydney-Melbourne railway opened.
Orient Express first runs (*Oct.* 4th).

Q **Scholarship**
Heinrich Brugsch, *Inscriptiones Aegypticae.*
J. R. Seeley, *The Expansion of England.*

R **Philosophy and Religion**
F. H. Bradley, *The Principles of Logic.*
F. Nietzsche, *Thus Spake Zarathustra.*
Franz Reusch, *History of the Index of Forbidden Books.*

S **Art, Sculpture, Fine Arts and Architecture**
P. Cézanne, *Rocky Landscape* (painting).
A. Renoir, *Dance at Bougival* and *Umbrellas* (paintings).

T **Music**
J. Brahms, Symphony No. 3 in F (op. 90).
A. E. Chabrier, *España* Rhapsody.
A. Dvořák, *Stabat Mater* (oratorio).
Metropolitan Opera, New York, founded.
Royal College of Music, London, founded under George Grove.

U **Literature**
H. F. Amial, *Journal Intime* (posth.) (trans. 1885 by Mrs. Humphry Ward).
B. Björnson, *Beyond Human Endurance.*
Paul Bourget, *Essais de Psychologie contemporaine.*
G. de Maupassant, *Une Vie.*
E. Renan, *Souvenirs d'enfance et de jeunesse.*
R. L. Stevenson, *Treasure Island.*
E. Verhaeren, *Les Flamandes.*

V **The Press**
La Tribune.

W **Drama and Entertainment**

X **Sport**

Y **Statistics**
U.S. petroleum production, 23,450,000 barrels.

z **Births and Deaths**

Jan. 3rd Clement, Lord Attlee, b. (–).
Jan. 17th Compton Mackenzie b. (–).
Feb. 18th Richard Wagner d. (70).
Feb. 23rd Karl Jaspers b. (–).
Mar. 14th Karl Marx d. (65).
May 5th Archibald, Lord Wavell, b. (–1950).
May 18th Walter Gropius b. (–).
June 5th John Maynard Keynes b. (–1946).
June 14th Edward Fitzgerald d. (74).
July 19th Benito Mussolini b. (–1945).
Sept. 4th Ivan Turgeniev d. (65).
— Pierre Laval b. (–1945).

1884 The Mahdi takes Omdurman—Germany occupies S.W. Africa and Cameroons—Third British Reform Bill

A **Jan**: 31st, Russians take Merv from the Amir of Afghanistan;
Poll tax, a relic of serfdom, is abolished in Russia.

B **Feb**: 18th, C. G. Gordon reaches Khartoum, but the Mahdi rejects his offer of negotiations;
26th, Britain recognises Portugal's right to territory at mouth of Congo, in order to frustrate Belgian designs but, in the face of protests from France and Germany, Britain abandons the treaty (*June* 26th);
27th, London convention regulates the status of Transvaal.

C **Mar**: 17th, Germany, Austria and Russia renew Three Emperors' Alliance (of *June* 1881);
21st, trades unions in France are legalised.

D **Apr**: 4th, Bolivia cedes Atacama to Chile by treaty of Valparaiso;
German occupation of South-West Africa, Togoland and Cameroons (*–Aug.*).

E **May**: 17th, Organic Act applies laws of Oregon to Alaska after interim term of government under U.S. war department.

F **Jun**: 6th, by treaty of Hué the Emperor of Annam recognises French protectorate;
28th (*–Aug.* 2nd), international conference on Egyptian finance in London, at which Otto von Bismarck and Jules Ferry oppose Britain's attempts to use Egyptian revenues for paying costs of Sudanese campaign.

G **Jul**: 27th, divorce (abolished in 1816) is re-established in France.

H **Aug**: 5th, in France members of former dynasties are excluded from the presidency and life senatorships are abolished.

J **Sep**:

K **Oct**: 13th, the Mahdi takes Omdurman.

L **Nov**: In U.S. presidential election Stephen G. Cleveland, Democrat, wins 219 electoral votes against James G. Blair, Republican, with 182, who is deserted by the Mugwumps, the reformist Republicans;
Britain annexes St. Lucia Bay to Natal, to prevent the Boers in Zululand gaining access to the east coast;
15th, Berlin conference of 14 nations on African affairs, organised by Otto von Bismarck and Jules Ferry, provides for free trade on Congo river and the abolition of slavery and the slave trade.

M **Dec**: 10th, Porfirio Diaz becomes President of Mexico (–1911);
British Franchise bill passes, after W. E. Gladstone undertakes to meet Conservative demands to introduce a further measure for redistributing seats, with uniform male suffrage in counties and boroughs for householders and lodgers, increasing the electorate to 5 million;
16th, Britain, following earlier recognition by U.S. and Germany, recognises International Association of the Congo.

N The Norwegian Constitution is reformed.
Britain establishes protectorate over section of Somali coast from the port of Zeila.

Z **Births and Deaths** (*cont.*)
May 12th Friedrich Smetana d. (60).
June 30th Georges Duhamel b. (–1915).
Nov. 5th J. E. Flecker b. (–1915).
— Damon Runyon b. (–1946).

O **Politics, Economics, Law and Education**

P. A. Kropotkin, *Paroles d'un Revolté*.
H. Spencer, *The Man versus the State*.
Fabian Society founded.
Royal Commission on the housing of the working classes (Dilke chairman).
Imperial Federation League founded in Canada.
Charlottenburg Technical High School, Berlin.

P **Science, Technology, Discovery, etc.**

Nikolaier discovers tetanus bacillus.
Cocaine is used as an anaesthetic.
Charles Parsons constructs first practical steam turbine for making electricity.
Oliver Lodge discovers electrical precipitation.
Hiram Maxim's recoil-operated gun.
Edwin Lankester founds Marine Biological Association.

Q **Scholarship**

Oxford English Dictionary (ed. James Murray –1928).

R **Philosophy and Religion**

S **Art, Sculpture, Fine Arts and Architecture**

'Les Vingt' exhibiting society founded by James Ensor in Brussels, supported by Georges Seurat, Paul Gauguin, Paul Cézanne and Vincent van Gogh (–94).
G. Seurat, *Bathers at Asnières* (painting).
E. Burne-Jones, *King Cophetua and the Beggar Maid* (painting).
A. Rodin, *Burghers of Calais* (sculpture) (–95).

T **Music**

A. Bruckner, Symphony No. 7, and *Te Deum*.
C. Franck, *Les Djinns* (opera).
J. Massenet, *Manon* (opera).
C. V. Stanford, *Savonarola* (opera).

U **Literature**

E. Amicis, *An Italian Schoolboy's Journal*.
G. D'Annunzio, *Il Libro delle Vergini*.
C. M. Leconte de Lisle, *Poèmes tragiques*.
Jean Moréas, *Les Syrtes*.
Mark Twain (pseud.), *Huckleberry Finn*.
P. Verlaine, *Jadis et naguère*.

V **The Press**

Le Matin issued.

W **Drama and Entertainment**

H. Ibsen, *The Wild Duck*.

X **Sport**

Y **Statistics**

Z **Births and Deaths**

Jan. 19th Ivan Maisky b. (–).
Feb. 1st Hugo von Hofmannsthal b. (–1929).
Mar. 24th François Mignet d. (88).
Mar. 31st Sean O'Casey b. (–1964).
May 8th Harry S. Truman b. (–).

(*Continued opposite*)

1885 (Jan.–Nov.) Death of Gordon at Khartoum—Leopold II establishes Congo State—Germany annexes Tanganyika and Zanzibar

A **Jan**: 9th, Spain proclaims protectorate over Spanish Guinea;
22nd, treaty of friendship between Germany and South African Republic;
26th, the Mahdi takes Khartoum and General Charles Gordon dies;
28th, British relief force arrives at Khartoum; the Sudan is evacuated.

B **Feb**: 5th, Congo State is established under Leopold II of Belgium, as a personal possession;
6th, Italy occupies Massawa, Eritrea;
12th, German East Africa Company is chartered;
25th, Germany annexes Tanganyika and Zanzibar.

C **Mar**: 4th, Grover Cleveland, Democrat, is inaugurated U.S. President;
30th, Russian occupation of Penjdeh, Afghanistan, provokes crisis in Anglo-Russian relations;
31st, fall of Jules Ferry's ministry in France, following French reverse at Hanoi in war with China;
Britain proclaims protectorate over North Bechuanaland, ending the Stellaland Republic.

D **Apr**: 26th, Britain occupies Port Hamilton, Korea (–*Feb.* 1887).

E **May**: 17th, Germany annexes Northern New Guinea and the Bismarck Archipelago.

F **Jun**: 5th, British establish protectorate over Niger River region;
9th, treaty of Tientsin between France and China recognises French protectorate in Annam;
—, W. E. Gladstone resigns, following hostile amendment to budget;
21st, death of Mahdi;
25th, Lord Salisbury forms Conservative ministry (–*Jan.* 1886), himself taking foreign secretaryship, with Michael Hicks Beach chancellor of Exchequer and Richard Cross home secretary;
British Redistribution of Seats Bill, introduced in *Feb.*, enacted, providing London with 37 additional seats, Liverpool 6 and Yorkshire industrial towns 16 and merging boroughs with population of under 15,000 with counties.

G **Jul**: 30th, Dervishes take Kassala, extending their control to the whole Sudan except Red Sea forts.

H **Aug**: 14th, a secretary of state for Scotland is appointed;
—, Lord Ashburne's Act authorises loans for Irish tenants to buy holdings on easy terms.

J **Sep**: 10th, Britain makes compromise settlement with Russia over Afghanistan frontier;
18th, disturbances in Eastern Rumelia in favour of union with Bulgaria.

K **Oct**: 22nd, Britain sends ultimatum to King Thibaw of Burma concerning his interference with trade and his refusal to comply leads to Third Burmese War.

L **Nov**: 11th, boundary between Sierra Leone and Liberia is defined;
13th, Serbia invades Bulgaria, following the union with Eastern Rumelia;
17th, Serbs defeated at Slivnitza, but Austrian intervention saves Serbia from invasion;
21st, C. S. Parnell calls on Irish in Britain to vote Conservative;
23rd, in British general election Liberals win 335 seats, Conservatives 249, Irish Home-Rulers 86; Lord Salisbury remains premier;

O **Politics, Economics, Law and Education**

Henry Maine, *Popular Government.*
Karl Marx, *Das Kapital*, vol. 2.
Gustav Cohn, *Foundations of Political Economy.*
The Pope excommunicates the Knights of Labor, but later withdraws his censure.

P **Science, Technology, Discovery, etc.**

Louis Pasteur cures hydrophobia.
F. Galton proves permanence and individuality of fingerprints.
Gottlieb Daimler invents internal combustion engine and Karl Benz builds single-cylinder engine for motor-car.
Starley's 'Rover' safety bicycle.
George Eastman's machine for manufacturing coated photographic paper.
Ney Elias crosses the Pamirs from east to west.
Gold is discovered in Transvaal.

Q **Scholarship**

Dictionary of National Biography is begun under Leslie Stephen.
Albert Sorel, *Europe and the French Revolution* (–1904).

R **Philosophy and Religion**

Leo Tolstoy, *My Religion.*
The Mormons split into polygamic and monogamic sections.

S **Art, Sculpture, Fine Arts and Architecture**

E. Degas, *Woman Bathing* (pastel).

T **Music**

J. Brahms, Symphony No. 4 in E minor (op. 98).
César Franck, *Symphonic Variations.*
A. Sullivan, *The Mikado* (opera).

U **Literature**

Paul Bourget, *Cruelle Énigme.*
Richard Burton, *The Arabian Nights* (–88).
A. Daudet, *Tartarin the Mountaineer.*
Jules Laforgue, *Complaintes.*
G. de Maupassant, *Bel Ami.*
George Meredith, *Diana of the Crossways.*
George Moore, *A Mummer's Wife.*
Walter Pater, *Marius the Epicurean.*
Leo Tolstoy, *The Power of Darkness.*
Émile Zola, *Germinal.*

V **The Press**

W **Drama and Entertainment**

H. F. Becque, *La Parisienne.*

X **Sport**

Y **Statistics**

U.K. total State expenditure: £88·5 mill.
Steel production (in mill. tons): Great Britain, 2·4; Germany, 1·2; France, 0·5.

L Nov: 27th, Bulgarians take Pirot, but are forced to withdraw from Serbia;
28th, British troops occupy Mandalay;
—, Cape railway reaches to Kimberley.

M Dec: 17th, France acquires control of Madagascar's foreign relations;
19th, Jules Grévy is re-elected President of France;
Germany's dispute with Spain over the Carolines is settled by papal arbitration in favour of Spain.

N British protectorate over Southern New Guinea is proclaimed, following German annexation in the north.
Belgian Labour Party is founded, with demand for universal suffrage.

z **Births and Deaths**

Feb. 7th Alban Berg b. (–1935).
May 13th Friedrich Henle d. (74).
May 22nd Victor Hugo d. (83).
July 23rd Ulysses Grant d. (63).
Aug. 23rd Henry Tizard b. (–1959).
Sept. 11th D. H. Lawrence b. (–1930).
Nov. 11th George Smith Patton b. (–1945).
— Ezra Pound b. (–).

1886 (Jan.–Nov.) Liberals defeated on Irish Home Rule Bill—Revolution in Eastern Rumelia

A **Jan**: 1st, Britain annexes Upper Burma, though guerilla warfare continues;
7th, General Georges Boulanger, who embodies French revenge on Germany for the Franco-Prussian War, becomes war minister in Charles Freycinet's cabinet;
13th, Lagos becomes separate British colony from Nigeria;
27th, Lord Salisbury resigns, after defeat on 'three acres and a cow' amendment of Jesse Collings to Address.

B **Feb**: 1st, W. E. Gladstone forms third Liberal ministry (*–Jul.* 20th), with Lord Rosebery foreign minister and W. V. Harcourt chancellor of Exchequer;
7th, H. M. Hyndman holds rally of Social Democratic Federation in Trafalgar Square.

C **Mar**: 3rd, peace of Bucharest between Serbia and Bulgaria.

D **Apr**: 5th, Abdul Hamid II, Sultan of Turkey, appoints Alexander of Bulgaria governor of Eastern Rumelia;
8th, Gladstone introduces Home Rule bill for Ireland;
26th, the major powers send ultimatum to Greece to stop support for revolution in Eastern Rumelia;
—, Prussian government expropriates Polish land-owners in West Prussia and Posen;
27th, de Brazza is appointed commissioner-general of French Congo.

E **May**: 1st (*–July* 1887), Japanese foreign minister calls conference in Tokio, but fails to abolish extra-territorial concessions;
4th, Knights of Labor riot in Chicago;
8th (*–June*), the powers blockade Greece, compelling her to maintain *status quo* in Eastern Rumelia;
Presidential Succession law in U.S., providing for succession to presidency in the event of the deaths of both the President and the Vice-President.

F **Jun**: 8th, W. E. Gladstone's Liberal government is defeated on second reading of Irish Home Rule bill, with 93 Liberals, including John Bright, Joseph Chamberlain and the Marquess of Hartington, voting with the Opposition;
23rd, Bonaparte and Orléans families are banished from France.

G **Jul**: 10th, British Royal Niger Company is chartered;
14th, Anglo-German agreement on frontiers of Gold Coast and Togoland;
24th, Anglo-Chinese agreement recognises British position in Burma;
In British general election Conservatives win 316 seats, dissident Liberals 78; Liberals 191 and Irish Nationalists 85; and 26th Lord Salisbury forms Conservative ministry (*–Aug.* 1892).

H **Aug**: 20th (–21st), military *coup d'état* in Sofia.

J **Sep**: 4th, Alexander of Bulgaria abdicates and Stephen Stambulov becomes Regent.

K **Oct**: 2nd, Lord Randolph Churchill's speech at Dartford outlines bold programme of domestic reform.

L **Nov**: 1st, Anglo-German agreement delimiting respective spheres of influence in East Africa;
10th, Prince Waldemar of Denmark is elected King of Bulgaria, but refuses to serve;
20th, 'Plan of Campaign', drawn up by William O'Brien and John Dillon, calls on Irish tenants to organise themselves.

O **Politics, Economics, Law and Education**

A. Carnegie, *Triumphant Democracy*.
Karl Marx, *Capital* (first English edition of vol. 1).
American Federation of Labor founded (*Dec.* 8th).
A. V. Dicey, *The Law of the Constitution*.
Charles Dilke appears as co-respondent (*Feb.* 12th) in sensational divorce suit.

P **Science, Technology, Discovery, etc.**

The element germanium discovered.
Henri Moissan prepares fluorine.
The synthetic drugs pyramidon and antifebrin discovered.
R. Krafft-Ebling, *Psychopathia Sexualis*.
C. A. von Welsbach invents gas mantle.
Canadian Pacific Railway completed (*Nov.* 7th).
The Severn Tunnel opened.
Niagara Falls hydro-electric installations begun.
The French army is equipped with the Lebel rifle, using smokeless powder.

Q **Scholarship**

English Historical Review founded under Mandell Creighton's editorship.
British School of Archaeology, Athens, opened (*Nov.*).

R **Philosophy and Religion**

A. Harnack, *History of Dogma*.

S **Art, Sculpture, Fine Arts and Architecture**

J. S. Sargent, *Carnation, Lily, Lily, Rose* (painting).
G. Seurat, *Sunday on the Island of Grande Jatte* (painting).
Eighth and last Impressionist Exhibition.
J. Whistler, P. W. Steer and W. Sickert found New English Art Club.
Statue of Liberty.

T **Music**

U **Literature**

George Gissing, *Demos*.
H. Rider Haggard, *King Solomon's Mines*.
Henry James, *The Bostonians* and *The Princess Casamassina*.
Pierre Loti (pseud.), *Pêcheurs d'Islande*.
F. Nietzsche, *Beyond Good and Evil*.
A. Rimbaud, *Les Illuminations*.
R. L. Stevenson, *Dr. Jekyll and Mr. Hyde*.
A. Strindberg, *The Son of a Servant* (–87).
E. Vogüé, *Le Roman Russe*.

V **The Press**

Jean Moréas and Gustave Kahn found *Le Symboliste*, a literary review of the Symbolist Movement.
Linotype is first used by the *New York Tribune*.

W **Drama and Entertainment**

H. Ibsen, *Rosmersholm*.
Stephens of San Francisco completes world trip on a 'penny-farthing' cycle.

M Dec: 15th, René Goblet forms ministry in France on C. Freycinet's fall;
23rd, Lord Randolph Churchill resigns through faltering support of cabinet for his budget, calling for army and naval economies;
30th, German-Portuguese agreement on boundaries between Angola and German South-West Africa;
Conflict in Reichstag over army bill (–*Mar.* 1887), with Liberals attempting to secure control over appropriations.

N First Indian National Congress meets, but lacks Moslem support.

X **Sport**

Amateur Golf Championship started; Horace Hutchinson first champion.

Y **Statistics**

U.K. merchant shipping tonnage 7,362,000 (3,965,000 steamships).

Z **Births and Deaths**

Feb. 15th Edward Cardwell d. (72).
Mar. 1st Oskar Kokoschka b. (–).
Apr. 5th William Edward Forster d. (67).
May 10th Karl Barth b. (1965).
May 23rd Leopold von Ranke d. (91).
July 23rd Salvador de Madariaga b. (–).
July 31st Franz Liszt d. (75).
Oct. 16th David Ben-Gurion b. (–).
— Mily Alexeivich Balakirev b. (–1910).

1887 (Jan.–Nov.) Britain annexes Zululand and holds first Colonial Conference

A **Jan**: 11th, Otto von Bismarck advocates a larger German army;
14th, G. J. Goschen is appointed chancellor of the Exchequer in succession to Lord Randolph Churchill, and W. H. Smith, leader of House;
A drastic Irish Crimes Act is introduced; its passage is aided by articles in *The Times* on 'Parnellism and Crime' (see *July* 1888);
20th, New Zealand annexes Kermadec Isles, Pacific.

B **Feb**: 4th, U.S. Interstate Commerce Act regulates railways;
8th, H. L. Dawes's Act empowers U.S. President to terminate tribal government and divide lands amongst Indians;
12th, Anglo-Italian agreement to maintain *status quo* in Mediterranean;
20th, Triple Alliance between Germany, Austria and Italy renewed for three years.

C **Mar**: 24th, Austria becomes signatory to Anglo-Italian agreement on Mediterranean.

D **Apr**: 4th, first Colonial Conference in London opens;
20th, tension between France and Germany following a German court's conviction of Schnaebele, a French frontier official, for espionage.

E **May**: 4th, Spain supports Anglo-Italian agreement on Mediterranean;
16th, René Goblet's cabinet falls in France and,
18th, Maurice Rouvier forms ministry from which Georges Boulanger is excluded;
22nd, Henry Drummond Wolff signs convention with Egypt, by which Britain agrees to evacuate Egypt in three years, with the right to return if there are further disorders, an agreement nullified by French opposition;
26th, British East Africa Company is chartered.

F **Jun**: 17th, reform of suffrage in Holland;
18th, Germano-Russo Reinsurance treaty (–1890) to replace expiring Three Emperors' Alliance, which Russia had refused to renew;
21st, Queen Victoria's Golden Jubilee;
—, Britain annexes Zululand, blocking the attempt of Transvaal to gain communication with coast;
25th (–*July* 26th), U.S., Britain and Germany confer in Washington on Samoa.

G **Jul**: 4th, Bulgaria elects Prince Ferdinand of Saxe-Coburg King (–1918) but he is not immediately recognised by the powers;
Anglo-Russian agreement on Afghanistan;
31st, Francesco Crispi forms ministry in Italy (–1891) on A. Depreti's death.

H **Aug**:

J **Sep**:

K **Oct**: 1st, Baluchistan is united with India;
G. Boulanger's *coup d'état* fails in France, but his popularity increases with revelations of scandals connected with President Grévy's family.

L **Nov**: 13th, 'Bloody Sunday' with casualties and arrests in Trafalgar Square at Socialist meeting attended by Irish agitators;
16th, Anglo-French condominium over New Hebrides.

O **Politics, Economics, Law and Education**

Allotments and Copyhold Acts in England.

First Congress of criminal anthropologists, held at Rome.

L. Zamenhof founds 'Esperanto'.

P **Science, Technology, Discovery, etc.**

Joseph Lockyer, *The Chemistry of the Sun.*

Phenacetin, an analgesic drug, is discovered.

Emil Fischer and Tafel synthesise fructose.

Aluminium is produced electrolytically in Switzerland,

Cyanide process for extracting gold and silver.

Rudolf Hertz shows that electromagnetic waves are reflected in a manner similar to light waves.

Hilaire Comte de Chardonnet invents artificial silk.

Emil Berliner invents his version of the gramophone.

Carl Laval's turbine.

H. M. Stanley discovers the Lake Albert Edward Nyanza (*Dec.* 13th).

Q **Scholarship**

F. W. Maitland, *Bracton's Notebook.*

R **Philosophy and Religion**

Canonisation of Sir Thomas More, John Fisher and other English Roman Catholic martyrs.

S **Art, Sculpture, Fine Arts and Architecture**

T **Music**

J. Brahms, Concerto in A minor (op. 102) for violin and 'cello.

A. Borodin, *Prince Igor* (opera—unfinished).

G. Verdi, *Otello* (opera).

A. Sullivan, *Ruddigore* (opera).

I. Paderewski gives first recitals in Vienna.

U **Literature**

T. Hardy, *The Woodlanders.*

Konrad Meyer, *Temptation of Pescara.*

Herman Sudermann, *Frau Sorge.*

V **The Press**

W **Drama and Entertainment**

Victorien Sardou, *La Tosca.*

André Antoine founds Théâtre Libre in Paris for production of plays by H. F. Becque.

X **Sport**

Y **Statistics**

M **Dec**: 1st, Portugal secures cession of Macao from China;

2nd, Jules Grévy resigns presidency of France owing to financial scandals connected with his son-in-law, Wilson, who trafficked in medals of the Legion of Honour; Marie Sadi-Carnot is elected President;

12th, Britain, Austria and Italy sign treaty for maintenance of *status quo* in Near East.

N Central American states, under leadership of Guatemala, sign treaty of amity and consider draft federal constitution.

France organises Cochin China, Cambodia, Annam and Tonkin as Union Indo-Chinoise.

z Births and Deaths

Feb. 20th Vincent Massey b. (–).
Feb. 28th Alexander Borodin d. (53).
June 22nd Julian Huxley b. (–).
July 14th Alfred Krupp d. (75).
Oct. 6th Charles Édouard Jeanneret ('Le Corbusier') b. (–1965).
Oct. 31st Chiang Kai-shek b. (–).
Nov. 17th Bernard, Viscount Montgomery, b. (–).

1888 Turkey's concession to Germany for first stage of Baghdad Railway

A **Jan**: 28th, military agreement between Germany and Italy provides for use of Italian troops against France in the event of a Franco-German war.

B **Feb**: 3rd, Bismarck publishes the Germano-Austrian alliance of 1879, as a warning to Russia, and, 6th, speaks in Reichstag on Russian designs;
11th, King Lobengula of Matabele accepts British protection;
Tension in Franco-Italian relations, Italy fearing the French fleet will attack Spezia.

C **Mar**: 9th, Frederick III succeeds as Emperor of Germany on William I's death;
17th, British protectorate over Sarawak;
27th, Boulanger is retired from French army, becoming eligible for election to Chamber.

D **Apr**: 15th, on election to French Chamber G. Boulanger begins campaign for revision of constitution. Charles Floquet forms French cabinet (*–Feb.* 1889);
G. J. Goschen reduces interest on Britain's national debt;
Agrarian rising in Rumania.

E **May**: 12th, British protectorate over North Borneo and Brunei;
13th, serfdom abolished in Brazil.

F **Jun**: 15th, William II becomes Emperor of Germany, on death of his father, Frederick I.

G **Jul**: 2nd, *The Times* is sued by a former Irish Nationalist M.P. over publication of letters of C. S. Parnell, later proved as forgeries (settled by a special commission in *Feb.* 1890).

H **Aug**: 9th, Local Government Act establishes county councils in Britain.

J **Sep**: Arab rising in German East Africa.

K **Oct**: 6th, Turkey grants concession to Germany to build a railway to Ankara, the first stage of Baghdad Railway;
14th, Hamburg and Bremen join German customs union;
29th, by Suez Canal convention, signed at Constantinople, the powers declare the canal open to all nations in war as in peace;
30th, King Lobengula grants Rhodes mining rights in Matabeleland;
France floats Russian loan, the beginnings of a Franco-Russian *entente*.

L **Nov**: In U.S. presidential election, fought on tariff issue, Benjamin Harrison, Republican, wins 233 electoral votes, Grover Cleveland, Democrat, 168 and Cleveland's loss is ascribed to treachery of Tammany Hall, the Democratic organisation in New York.

M **Dec**: 11th, French colony of Gabon united with French Congo;
Italy supports Menelek of Shoa in his revolt against Johannes IV of Ethiopia.

N Protective tariffs in New Zealand and Sweden.

O **Politics, Economics, Law and Education**

James Bryce, *American Commonwealth.*

Cecil Rhodes amalgamates Kimberley diamond companies.

P **Science, Technology, Discovery, etc.**

The word 'chromosome' is first used.

Pasteur Institute, Paris, founded.

N. Tesla invents A.C. electric motor which is manufactured by George Westinghouse.

E. J. Marey's *chambre chronophotographique*, forerunner of the cinematograph.

George Eastman's 'Kodak' box camera.

J. B. Dunlop invents pneumatic tyre.

First refrigerated railway truck; first railway in China.

Aeronautical exhibition, Vienna (*Apr.*).

F. Nansen crosses Greenland.

C. M. Doughty, *Travels in Arabia Deserta.*

Q **Scholarship**

University of Pennsylvania equips expedition to excavate Babylonian remains at Nippu, Iraq.

R **Philosophy and Religion**

Bernard Bosanquet, *Logic or the Morphology of Thought.*

G. J. Romanes, *Mental Evolution in Man.*

James Martineau, *A Study of Religion.*

S **Art, Sculpture, Fine Arts and Architecture**

James Ensor, *Entry of Christ into Brussels* (painting).

V. van Gogh, *Sunflowers* and *The Yellow Chair* (paintings).

T **Music**

N. Rimsky-Korsakov, symphonic suite *Scheherezade* (op. 35).

Richard Strauss, tone poem *Don Juan.*

Hugo Wolf, *Der Gärtner* and other lieder.

Gustav Mahler directs the Budapest opera.

U **Literature**

Maurice Barrès, *Sous l'Œil des Barbares.*

Edward Bellamy, *Looking Backwards, 2000–1887.*

Rolf Boldrewood (pseud.), *Robbery under Arms.*

A. France (pseud.), *La Vie littéraire* begins.

R. Kipling, *Plain Tales from the Hills.*

G. de Maupassant, *Pierre et Jean.*

A. Quiller-Couch, *Astonishing History of Troy Town.*

Mark Rutherford (pseud.), *The Revolution in Tanner's Lane.*

P. Verlaine, *Amour.*

É. Zola, *La Terre.*

V **The Press**

The Financial Times, *The Star* (ed. O'Connor –1960), and *Collier's Weekly* are first issued.

W **Drama and Entertainment**

A. W. Pinero, *Sweet Lavender.*

A. Strindberg, *Miss Julie.*

First beauty contest, at Spa, Belgium (*Sept.*).

X **Sport**

Football League founded.
Lawn Tennis Association established.

Y **Statistics**

Value of World Production: percentages contributed by U.S., 31·8; Great Britain, 17·8; Germany, 13·3; France, 10·7; Russia, 8·1; Austro-Hungary, 5·6; Italy, 2·7; Belgium, 2·2; Spain, 1·9; other countries, 5·9.

Z **Births and Deaths**

Apr. 15th Matthew Arnold d. (65).
May 11th Irving Berlin b. (–).
July 30th Werner Jaeger b. (–).
Aug. 13th J. L. Baird, b. (–1946).
Aug. 15th T. E. Lawrence b. (–1935).
Sept 12th Maurice Chevalier b. (–).
Oct. 14th Katherine Mansfield (*née* Beauchamp, pseud. of Kathleen Murray) b. (–1923).
Nov. 18th Frank Dobson b. (–).
— T. S. Eliot b. (–1965).

1889 French protectorate over Ivory Coast—Italy claims protectorate over Ethiopia

A **Jan:** 10th, France establishes protectorate over Ivory Coast;
27th, Georges Boulanger is rumoured to be about to make himself the master of Paris, but fails to seize his opportunity;
30th, Crown Prince Archduke Rudolf of Austria commits suicide at Mayerling.

B **Feb:** 11th, Constitution granted in Japan, with two-chamber Diet, but Emperor retains extensive powers;
22nd, North and South Dakota, Montana and Washington are created U.S. states;
Pierre Tirard forms ministry in France (–*Mar.* 1890).

C **Mar:** 4th, Benjamin Harrison, Republican, inaugurated as U.S. President;
6th, Milan of Serbia abdicates in favour of his son and Jovan Ristich acts as Regent.

D **Apr:** 8th, G. Boulanger, fearing trial for treason, flees from France and in the subsequent elections the Republicans triumph;
22nd, Oklahoma is opened to settlement.

E **May:** 2nd, by treaty of Ucciali with Menelek of Ethiopia, Italy claims protectorate over Ethiopia;
31st, Naval Defence Act in Britain inaugurates extensive naval building programme;
German old-age insurance law.

F **Jun:** Brussels Conference for abolition of slave trade and suppression of traffic in arms and liquor to undeveloped peoples.

G **Jul:** 17th, French law forbidding multiple candidates in elections;
23rd, British Board of Agriculture founded;
Crisis in Italian-Vatican relations.

H **Aug:** 19th (–*Sept.* 14th), London dock strike.

J **Sep:**

K **Oct:** 2nd, first Pan-American conference at Washington rejects J. G. Blaine's plan for reciprocity;
29th, British South Africa Company, headed by Cecil Rhodes, is granted royal charter with extensive powers for expanding its territory at the expense of Transvaal;
Antonio Blanco, President since 1870, is deprived of office in Venezuela, while absent in Europe.

L **Nov:** 15th, on Pedro II's abdication Brazil is proclaimed a republic;
Menelek, through Italian support, becomes King of Ethiopia, following disputed succession on death (*Mar.* 12th) of Johannes IV.

M **Dec:** 6th, Calvinist-Catholic coalition in Holland, following fall of Liberals.

N Manhood suffrage in New Zealand.

Z **Births and Deaths** (*cont.*)
May 11th Paul Nash b. (–1946).
July 5th Jean Cocteau b. (–1963).
Oct. 11th J. P. Joule d. (71).
Nov. 16th George S. Kaufman b. (–).
Dec. 12th Robert Browning d. (77).
Dec. 18th Gladys Cooper b. (–).

O **Politics, Economics, Law and Education**

G. B. Shaw, *Fabian Essays.*

London County Council is formed (–1965). Lord Rosebery is elected first chairman (*Feb.* 12th).

Welsh Intermediate Education Act founds secondary education in Wales.

Catholic University, Washington, founded.

P **Science, Technology, Discovery, etc.**

G. V. Schiaparelli determines the synchronous rotation of the planet Mercury.

Frederick Abel invents cordite.

George Eastman produces a celluloid roll-film.

Institution of Electrical Engineers is founded in London.

Q **Scholarship**

H. Bresslau, *Handbuch der Urkundenlehre für Deutschland und Italien.*

R **Philosophy and Religion**

S. Alexander, *Moral Order and Progress.*

H. Bergson, *Les Données immédiates et la conscience.*

T. H. Huxley, *Agnosticism.*

S **Art, Sculpture, Fine Arts and Architecture**

V. van Gogh, *Landscape with Cypress Tree* (painting).

P. Puvis de Chavannes decorates Hôtel de Ville, Paris (–93).

Eiffel Tower, Paris, built.

T **Music**

A. Dvořák, Symphony No. 4 in G (op. 88).

C. Franck, Symphony in D minor.

R. Strauss, symphonic poem *Death and Transfiguration* (op. 31).

P. I. Tchaikovsky, Symphony No. 5 in E minor (op. 64).

A. Sullivan, *The Gondoliers* (opera).

The 'Red Flag' is written in London after a dock strike.

U **Literature**

J. M. Barrie, *A Window in Thrums.*

B. Björnson, *In God's Way.*

A. Gide begins *Journal* (–1949).

Gerhardt Hauptmann, *Before Dawn.*

J. K. Jerome, *Three Men in a Boat.*

D. von Liliencron, *Poems.*

M. Maeterlinck, *Serres chaudes.*

W. B. Yeats, *The Wanderings of Oisin.*

W **Drama and Entertainment**

P. T. Barnum and J. A. Bailey's show at Olympia (*Nov.*).

X **Sport**

Y **Statistics**

Z **Births and Deaths**

Mar. 27th John Bright d. (76).

Apr. 14th Arnold Toynbee b. (–).

Apr. 16th Charles Chaplin b. (–).

Apr. 20th Adolf Hitler b. (–1945).

Apr. 24th Stafford Cripps b. (–1952).

Apr. 28th Antonio Salazar b. (–).

(*Continued opposite*)

1890 (Jan.–Nov.) William II dismisses Bismarck—Anti-Trust Laws in U.S.—Bechuanaland and Uganda come under British control

A **Jan:**

B **Feb:**

C **Mar:** 15th (–28th), international congress for Protection of Workers held in Berlin;
20th, Otto von Bismarck is dismissed by William II and Georg Caprivi becomes German chancellor (–94);
27th, universal suffrage in Spain.

D **Apr:** Conservatives defeated in New Zealand elections by Labour and Liberal parties.

E **May:** 24th, by Mackinnon treaty between Leopold of Belgium and British East Africa Company, the latter recognises Leopold's rights on the west bank of the Upper Nile in return for territory near Lake Tanganyika;
Italy reorganises her Red Sea territories as the Colony of Eritrea.

F **Jun:** 18th, Germany allows Reinsurance treaty (see *June* 1887) with Russia to lapse, despite Russian attempts to open negotiations for a renewal;
19th, U.S. Force bill, for federal control of elections, especially to protect Negro voters in the South, passes House of Representatives but is not adopted by Senate;
Swiss federal government introduces social insurance.

G **Jul:** 1st, by Anglo-German convention Britain exchanges Heligoland for Zanzibar and Pemba;
1st, Idaho becomes a U.S. state;
2nd, John Sherman's anti-trust law enacted in U.S.;
—, Brussels act passed by international conference to eradicate African slave trade and liquor traffic with primitive peoples;
8th, Wyoming becomes a U.S. state;
17th, Cecil Rhodes becomes premier of Cape Colony;
29th, industrial courts established in Germany to adjust wage disputes;
First general election in Japan.

H **Aug:** 5th, Anglo-French convention defines spheres of influence in Nigeria, the British Protectorate in Zanzibar and Pemba and the French Protectorate in Madagascar;
17th, Tsar Alexander III fails to persuade Germany to make an *entente* with Russia at his meeting with the Emperor William II at Narva.

J **Sep:** 12th, British South Africa Company founds Salisbury in Mashonaland.

K **Oct:** 1st, German anti-socialist law of 1878 expires and, 21st, Social Democrats adopt Marxist programme at Erfurt congress;
22nd, responsible government in Western Australia;
28th, German East Africa Company cedes its territorial rights to Germany;
Following McKinley tariff, Liberals in Canada urge reciprocity with U.S.

L **Nov:** 12th, Cardinal Charles Lavigerie's 'Algiers Toast', calling on all Frenchmen to rally to the constitution, an attempt to reconcile the Roman Catholic Church with the Republic;
14th, Anglo-Portuguese agreement on Zambesi and the Congo grants Britain the control of the Lower Zambesi and the right to colonise central territory up to the Congo;
23rd, on accession of Queen Wilhelmina the Grand Duchy of Luxembourg is separated from the Netherlands;
29th, first Japanese Diet opened.

O **Politics, Economics, Law and Education**

Alfred Marshall, *Principles of Economics.*

William Booth, *In Darkest England and the Way Out.*

Act for the housing of the working classes in Britain.

First May Day labour celebrations in Germany.

Failure of Baring's Bank, London.

L. A. Bertillon describes identification of criminals in *Photographie judiciare.*

Free elementary education in England.

W. H. O'Shea is granted a decree nisi against C. S. Parnell (*Nov.* 17th).

Daughters of the American Revolution founded in Washington.

P **Science, Technology, Discovery, etc.**

T. Curtius obtains azoimide (compound of hydrogen and nitrogen) from organic sources.

First English electrical power station, at Deptford.

First 'tube' railway, City and South London Railway, passing beneath River Thames.

Earliest corridor-train.

Forth Bridge completed.

Building entirely steel-framed erected in Chicago.

Q **Scholarship**

J. G. Frazer, *The Golden Bough* (–1914).

A. T. Mahan, *The Influence of Sea Power on History, 1660–1783.*

R **Philosophy and Religion**

William James, *The Principles of Psychology.*

Lux Mundi, edited by Charles Gore.

Privy Council upholds judgment of the Archbishop of Canterbury's court against Bishop Edward King of Lincoln for ritualistic practices.

S **Art, Sculpture, Fine Arts and Architecture**

P. Cézanne, *The Cardplayers* (painting).

Frederick Leighton, *The Bath of Psyche* (painting).

P. Puvis de Chavannes leads secession of artists from the Salon to exhibit in the Champ de Mars.

William Morris founds Kelmscott Press.

T **Music**

A. Borodin, *Prince Igor* (opera).

P. Mascagni, *Cavalleria Rusticana* (opera).

P. I. Tchaikovsky, *Queen of Spades* (opera).

U **Literature**

Knut Hamsun (pseud.), *Hunger.*

Leo Tolstoy, *The Kreutzer Sonata.*

J. G. Whittier, *At Sundown.*

V **The Press**

W. T. Stead edits *Review of Reviews.*

Daily Graphic, first fully-illustrated English newspaper (*Jan.* 4th).

Stefan George founds *Blätter fur die Kunst.*

W **Drama and Entertainment**

H. Ibsen, *Hedda Gabler.*

1890 (Dec.)

M Dec: 12th, C. S. Parnell resigns and is succeeded as leader of Irish Nationalists by Justin McCarthy;
18th, Frederick Lugard occupies Uganda for the British East Africa Company.

N Bechuanaland is placed under a British governor.
Beginnings of Armenian nationalist revolutionary movement.

X **Sport**

English county cricket clubs officially classified, with seven 1st-class counties.

Y **Statistics**

Railway mileage in operation: U.S., 125,000; France, 20,800; Great Britain, 20,073; Russia, 19,000.

Coal production (in mill. tons): Great Britain, 184; U.S., 143; Germany, 89; France, 26·1; Austro-Hungary, 26; Russia, 6.

Steel production (in mill. tons): U.S., 4·3; Great Britain, 3·6; Germany, 2·3; France, 0·7; Austro-Hungary, 0·5; Russia, 0·4.

Emigration to U.S. (1881–90): from Great Britain, 807,357; from Ireland, 655,482.

Z **Births and Deaths**

Jan. 9th Karel Čapek b. (–1938).
Jan. 14th Ignaz von Döllinger d. (91).
Mar. 9th Vyacheslav Molotov b. (–).
Mar. 29th Harold Spencer Jones b. (–).
Apr. 6th Anthony Fokker b. (–1939).
July 15th Gottfried Keller d. (71).
Aug. 11th John Henry Newman d. (89).
Sept. 24th A. P. Herbert b. (–).
Oct. 14th Dwight D. Eisenhower b. (–).
Nov. 8th César Franck d. (67).
Nov. 10th Arthur Rimbaud d. (37).
Nov. 22nd Charles de Gaulle b. (–).
— Harry L. Hopkins b. (–1946).
— Vincent van Gogh d. (37).

1891 British Liberals adopt 'Newcastle Programme'—Renewal of Triple Alliance

A Jan: 31st, Marquis de Rudin, of the Right, forms coalition in Italy on F. Crispi's resignation; Civil War in Chile.

B Feb: 9th, Menelek, Emperor of Ethiopia, denounces Italian claims to a protectorate; 24th, federal Constitution in Brazil.

C Mar: 24th, Anglo-Italian agreement over Ethiopia, defining the frontiers of their Red Sea colonies (further convention, *Apr.* 15th);
Sydney Convention under Henry Parkes draws up a federal Constitution for Australia (*–July*), but the scheme is dropped through opposition of New South Wales.

D Apr: 15th, The Katanga Company is formed under Leopold of Belgium's direction to exploit copper deposits.

E May: 6th, Triple Alliance of Germany, Austria and Italy is renewed for twelve years.

F Jun: 1st, thorough factory inspection in force in Germany;
10th, L. Starr Jameson becomes administrator of South Africa Company's territories;
11th, further Anglo-Portuguese convention on territories north and south of Zambesi: Portugal assigns Barotseland to Britain. Nyasaland is subsequently proclaimed a British Protectorate;
16th, John Abbot becomes premier of Canada on Macdonald's death (premier since 1878);
20th, Britain and Holland define their boundaries in Borneo.

G Jul: 4th, William II visits London, hoping Britain might accede to Triple Alliance;
23rd, French squadron visits Kronstadt and a French loan is floated to finance Trans-Siberian railway.

H Aug: 27th, Franco-Russian *entente*.

J Sep: 19th, José Balmaceda driven from office in Chile;
30th, Georges Boulanger commits suicide in exile in Brussels.

K Oct: British Liberal party adopts the 'Newcastle Programme', advocating Irish Home Rule, Disestablishment of Welsh Church, reform of Lords, triennial parliaments, abolition of plural franchise and local veto on sales of liquor.

L Nov: 23rd, Deodoroda Fonseca, first President, driven from office in Brazil by naval revolt, is succeeded by Florians Peixoto who governs dictatorially.

M Dec: Joseph Chamberlain becomes leader of Liberal Unionists in Commons on Lord Hartington's succession to the dukedom of Devonshire.

N Felix Méline introduces rigid Protection in France.
Social legislation in Denmark.

O Politics, Economics, Law and Education

Charles Booth, *Life and Labour of the People in London* (–1903).
Goldwin Smith, *The Canadian Question.*
Public Health Act in Britain.
Pan-German League is founded (*Apr.*).
The Prince of Wales, giving evidence in libel action Gordon-Cumming *v.* Lycett Green, concerning cheating at cards at Tranby Croft, admits he played baccarat for high stakes.

P Science, Technology, Discovery, etc.

Johnstone Stoney introduces the term 'electron'.
Trans-Siberian Railway begun (–1904).

Q Scholarship

R Philosophy and Religion

R. W. Church (posth.), *History of the Oxford Movement.*
Cardinal R. W. Vaughan denies the validity of Anglican Orders (*Oct.* 5th).
Papal encyclical *Rerum novarum* on condition of working classes (*May* 15th), earns Leo XIII the name of 'the working man's Pope'.
Union of General and Particular Baptists in England under John Clifford.

S Art, Sculpture, Fine Arts and Architecture

P. Gauguin settles in Tahiti.
Retrospective Vincent van Gogh exhibition at *Salon des Indépendents.*
Henri Toulouse-Lautrec's first posters for Montmartre music halls.
Giovanni Segantini, *Ploughing of the Engadine* (painting).
William Richmond undertakes interior decorations and glass mosaics for St. Paul's Cathedral.

T Music

P. I. Tchaikovsky's *Casse-Noisette* ballet music.
Carnegie Music Hall, New York, opened.

U Literature

M. Barrès, *Le Jardin de Bérénice.*
J. M. Barrie, *The Little Minister.*
A. C. Doyle's *Adventures of Sherlock Holmes* begin in *Strand Magazine.*
G. Gissing, *New Grub Street.*
T. Hardy, *Tess of the D'Urbervilles.*
J. K. Huysmans, *Là-bas.*
F. Wedekind, *Spring's Awakening.*
O. Wilde, *The Picture of Dorian Gray.*

V The Press

Il Mattino issued.

W Drama and Entertainment

V. Sardou, *Thermidor.*
J. T. Grein founds the Independent Theatre Society, London, for introducing plays by Henrik Ibsen and other continental dramatists to the English stage.
E. Duse's début in Vienna.

X Sport

Y **Statistics**

Populations (in mills.): U.S. 65; Germany, 49·4; Japan, 40·7; France, 38·3; Great Britain, 33; Ireland, 4·7; Italy, 30·3; Austria, 23·8.

Z **Births and Deaths**

Jan. 16th Léo Delibes d. (55).
Mar. 19th Earl Warren b. (–).
Mar. 29th Georges Seurat d. (32).
Apr. 7th David Low b. (–1964).
June 20th John H. Costello b. (–).
Aug. 2nd Arthur Bliss b. (–).
Aug. 12th James Russell Lowell d. (72).
Sept. 28th Herman Melville d. (72).
Oct. 26th Helmuth Count von Moltke d. (90).
Nov. 15th Averell Harriman b. (–).
—Ilya Ehrenburg b. (–).

A **Jan**: 7th, Abbas, aged 18, succeeds Tewfik as Khedive of Egypt (–1914) and is hostile to British influence.

B **Feb**: 1st, Germany signs commercial treaties with Austria-Hungary, Italy, Switzerland and Belgium;
22nd, U.S. Populist party is organised at St. Louis;
29th, Anglo-U.S. treaty on Bering Sea seal fishery.

C **Mar**: 26th, Labour Department formed in Germany;
In Prussia a bill for religious education of children by the clergy is withdrawn after acrimonious debate.

D **Apr**:

E **May**: Giovanni Giolitti replaces Marquis di Rudin as premier of Italy.

F **Jun**: 30th, iron and steel workers begin strike in U.S.;
Prince Ito becomes premier of Japan.

G **Jul**: in British general election Liberals win 273 seats, Irish Home Rulers 81, Labour 1 against Conservatives 269, and Liberal Unionists 46, but Lord Salisbury awaits Parliament's re-assembly before resigning;
At Omaha the Populist Party convention nominates James B. Weaver for presidency.

H **Aug**: 11th, Lord Salisbury resigns and W. E. Gladstone forms Liberal ministry (–*Mar.* 9th), with Lord Rosebery foreign secretary, W. V. Harcourt chancellor of exchequer and H. H. Asquith home secretary;
17th, Franco-Russian military convention.

Sep: Sergei Witte becomes Russian finance minister;
First trains arrive at Johannesburg from the Cape.

K **Oct**: 15th, Anglo-German convention over Cameroons.

L **Nov**: 8th, Grover Cleveland, Democrat, wins U.S. presidential election with 277 electoral votes, on platform opposing the McKinley tariff and the Force bill, against Benjamin Harrison, Republican, 145, and James B. Weaver, Populist, 22;
10th, the Panama scandal breaks in France and Ferdinand de Lesseps and associates are committed for trial for corruption and mismanagement;
22nd, Belgians suppress rising of Arab slave-holders in Upper Congo.

M **Dec**: 5th, John Thompson becomes premier of Canada on John Abbott's resignation (–*Dec.* 1894);
12th, Pan-Slav conference at Cracow.

N French War against King Dahomey in West Africa.
Serious famine in Russia.

Z **Births and Deaths** (*cont.*)
May 16th Edward Augustus Freeman d. (68).
May 25th Josip Broz Tito b. (–).
July 23rd Haile Selassie b. (–).
Oct. 4th Engelbert Dolfuss b. (–1934).
Oct. 6th Alfred Lord Tennyson d. (83).
Oct. 12th Ernest Renan d. (69).
Oct. 14th Sumner Wells b. (–).
Nov. 6th J. W. Alcock b. (–1919).
Dec. 6th E. W. Siemens d. (76).

O **Politics, Economics, Law and Education**

Émile Faguet, *Politiques et Moralistes français du XIX siècle.*
California earthquake disaster (*Apr.* 19th).
Age of marriage for Italian girls raised to twelve.
Pioneer Club for Ladies founded in London.
Pan-Slav Conference at Cracow (*Dec.*).

P **Science, Technology, Discovery, etc.**

Auriga, a new star, observed in Milky Way (*Feb.* 1st).
C. F. Cross discovers viscose, making possible the manufacture of rayon.
Rudolf Diesel patents a petrol engine.
First automatic telephone switchboard.
Pineapples are canned.

Q **Scholarship**

James Darmesteter edits the Zend-Avesta (–93).
W. E. Gladstone delivers first Romanes Lecture at Oxford.

R **Philosophy and Religion**

G. J. Romanes, *Darwin and After Darwinism.*
Charles Gore founds the Community of the Resurrection.

S **Art, Sculpture, Fine Arts and Architecture**

Claude Monet begins pictures of Rouen Cathedral (–95).
Henri Toulouse-Lautrec, *At the Moulin Rouge* (painting).

T **Music**

A. Bruckner, *Psalm 150.*
C. H. H. Parry, *Job* (oratorio).
R. Leoncavallo, *I Pagliacci* (opera).
A. Dvořák becomes director of New York National Conservatory.

U **Literature**

R. Kipling, *Barrack Room Ballads.*
I. Zangwill, *The Children of the Ghetto.*
É. Zola, *La Débâcle.*

V **The Press**

W **Drama and Entertainment**

M. Maeterlinck, *Pelléas et Mélisande*, with C. Debussy's music.
G. B. Shaw, *Widower's Houses.*
O. Wilde, *Lady Windermere's Fan.*
Lottie Collins sings Ta-ra-ra-boom-de-ay in London.

X **Sport**

Y **Statistics**

U.K. Textiles trade:

Imports of raw cotton	1,548 mill. lb.
Exports of cottons	4,873 mill. yds.
Exports of woollens	203,376,000 yds.
Exports of linens	171,303,000 yds.
Exports of silks	5,952,000 yds.

U.K. Trades union membership, 1,576,000.

Z **Births and Deaths**

Jan. 14th Martin Niemöller b. (–).
Feb. 18th Wendell Wilkie b. (–1944).
Mar. 27th Walt Whitman d. (72).
Apr. 13th Robert Watson-Watt b. (–).

(*Continued opposite*)

A **Jan**: 13th, Independent Labour Party formed at conference in Bradford under Keir Hardie;
17th, Hawaii proclaimed a republic with the connivance of the resident U.S. minister;
Franco-Russian alliance is signed;
Abbas Khedive of Egypt dismisses pro-British ministers, but Lord Cromer asserts his authority.

B **Feb**: 14th, Hawaii is annexed by treaty to U.S. (but the treaty is withdrawn by President Grover Cleveland, *Mar*. 9th, in hope of restoring the monarchy and James Blount is sent to investigate the affair).

C **Mar**: 8th, trial of Ferdinand de Lesseps and associates for corruption over Panama Canal opens in Paris (the sentences, 21st, are set aside, *June* 15th, by *cour de cassation* under the statute of limitations);
10th, French colonies of French Guinea and Ivory Coast formally established;
Anarchist outrages in Paris;
Gerald Portal hoists British flag in Uganda, which British East Africa Company evacuates.

D **Apr**: 14th, Alexander I of Serbia, now eighteen, declares himself of age and dissolves Regency Council;
22nd, Paul Kruger is re-elected in Transvaal for third time;
General strike in Belgium.

E **May**: 10th, Natal is granted self-government.

F **Jun**: Franco-Russian commercial treaty;
Alarmed at Belgian advance in the Congo, France sends an occupying force to forestall further annexations.

G **Jul**: 13th, army bill increases size of German army but reduces military service to two years;
15th, French note to Siam provokes crisis in Franco-British relations, and 31st, France agrees to maintain Siam as buffer state;
Matabeles rise against rule of British South Africa Company.

H **Aug**:

J **Sep**: 1st, the Second Irish Home Rule bill, proposing that 80 Irish representatives should sit at Westminster, passes the Commons but is rejected, 8th, by the Lords.

K **Oct**: 13th (–29th), Russian fleet visits Toulon;
29th, Count Taaffe, premier of Austria-Hungary, resigns when the question of universal suffrage splits his coalition.

L **Nov**: 1st, Grover Cleveland repeals Sherman bill on compulsory silver purchase;
13th, by Pretoria convention Britain agrees to the annexation of Swaziland by the Transvaal;
15th, Anglo-German agreement defines Nigeria-Cameroons boundary, and leases territory east of Lake Chad to within 100 miles of the Nile to Germany;
17th, Dahomey becomes a French protectorate;
L. Starr Jameson crushes Matabele revolt and occupies Bulawayo.

O **Politics, Economics, Law and Education**

C. H. Pearson, *National Life and Character, a Forecast.*
Imperial Institute, South Kensington, and the University of Wales are founded.
Franchise in New Zealand is extended to women.
Universal suffrage in Belgium with plural voting, on basis of wealth and education.

P **Science, Technology, Discovery, etc.**

Robert Armstrong-Jones begins modern treatment of mental diseases at London County Council's Claybury Asylum.
Karl Benz's four-wheel car.
Automatic signals are installed at Liverpool.
Manchester Ship Canal completed.
New Crotoun aqueduct tunnel, New York, completed.
Egbert Judson invents zip fastener.
F. Nansen leads expedition to North Pole (–96).
Corinth Canal is opened (*Aug.* 6th).

Q **Scholarship**

R **Philosophy and Religion**

F. H. Bradley, *Appearance and Reality.*
W. T. Stead, *If Christ Came to Chicago.*
Leslie Stephen, *Agnostic's Apology.*

S **Art, Sculpture, Fine Arts and Architecture**

The Studio, with Aubrey Beardsley's drawings, spreads the ideas of *art nouveau* in architecture and interior decoration.
Copenhagen Town Hall (–1902).

T **Music**

A. Dvořák, Symphony no. 5 ('From the New World', op. 95).
J. Sibelius, *Karelia Suite* (op. 10).
P. I. Tchaikovsky, Symphony no. 6 in B minor ('Pathétique', op. 74).
E. Humperdinck, *Hansel and Gretel* (opera).
G. Puccini, *Manon Lescaut* (opera).
G. Verdi, *Falstaff* (opera).

U **Literature**

A. France (pseud.), *La Rôtisserie de la Reine Pédauque.*
José de Heredia, *Les Trophées.*
M. Rutherford (pseud.), *Catherine Furze.*

V **The Press**

The Sketch issued.

W **Drama and Entertainment**

Georges Courteline, *Boubouroche.*
A. W. Pinero, *The Second Mrs. Tanqueray.*
O. Wilde, *A Woman of No Importance.*
Chicago World Exhibition.

X **Sport**

M **Dec**: 4th, Anglo-French agreement on Siam, but Britain's concessions to French designs dismay Germany;

9th, the anarchist, Auguste Vailland, explodes bomb in the Paris Chamber of Deputies;

10th, on fall of G. Giolitti's ministry through bank scandals, F. Crispi forms cabinet in Italy (–*Mar*. 96);

Italians defeat Mahdists in attack on Eritrea.

N France acquires protectorate over Laos.

Tariff war between France and Switzerland.

Germany signs further commercial treaties with Balkan states.

Internal Macedonia Revolutionary Organisation founded in Bulgaria to work for independence for Macedonia.

Anti-Saloon League founded in U.S. to further the cause of Prohibition.

Y **Statistics**

U.S. crude petroleum production: 48,431,000 barrels.

Z **Births and Deaths**

Jan. 12th Hermann Goering b. (–1946).
Mar. 5th Ivon Hitchens b. (–); and Hippolyte Taine d. (65).
Apr. 8th Mary Pickford b. (–).
Apr. 11th Dean Acheson b. (–).
Apr. 29th Harold Clayton Urey b. (–).
June 9th Cole Porter b. (–).
June 30th Harold Laski b. (–1950).
July 6th Guy de Maupassant d. (43).
Aug. 16th J. M. Charcot d. (67).
Aug. 30th Huey Pierce Long b. (–1935).
Oct. 18th Charles François Gounod d. (75).
Nov. 6th Peter Iljich Tchaikovsky d. (53).
Nov. 8th Francis Parkman d. (73).
Dec. 1st Ernst Toller b. (–1939).

A **Jan**: L. Starr Jameson completes occupation of Matabeleland.

B **Feb**: 10th, Germany signs commercial treaty with Russia;
W. E. Gladstone withdraws Employers' Liability bill on Lords' amendments.

C **Mar**: 3rd, W. E. Gladstone resigns, having split Liberal Party over Home Rule, and Lord Rosebery, a Liberal Unionist, becomes prime minister, with W. V. Harcourt as leader of the Commons;
15th, Franco-German agreement on boundaries between French Congo and the Cameroons.

D **Apr**: 11th, Uganda is declared a British protectorate;
H. V. Harcourt introduces death duties in budget.

E **May**: 5th, Anglo-Italian agreement over East Africa, by which Italy is assigned Harar;
12th, Anglo-Belgian agreement assigning Leopold territory on the left bank of the Upper Nile;
21st, restoration of Serbian constitution of 1869;
G. Cleveland repeals McKinley tariff (of *Oct.* 1891).

F **Jun**: 22nd, Dahomey proclaimed a French Colony;
23rd, Colonial Conference in Ottawa (–*July* 10th);
24th, President M. F. Sadi-Carnot of France is assassinated by an Italian anarchist at Lyons; succeeded by Jean Casimir-Périer;
Germany thwarts Lord Rosebery's attempts to draw Britain closer to the Triple Alliance.

G **Jul**: 11th, laws suppressing anarchist and socialist organisations in Italy;
17th, Italians take Kassala, Sudan, from the Dervishes;
23rd, Japanese troops seize the palace in Seoul, Korea;
27th, Regent of Korea declares war on China.

H **Aug**: 1st, Japan declares war on China over question of Korea;
14th, on protest from France, Leopold II of Belgium abandons claims to Upper Nile territory;
18th, Carey Act in U.S. grants lands in Colorado, Idaho and six other states to encourage irrigation;
27th, Wilson-Gorman tariff, embodying a 2 per cent income tax, becomes law in U.S. without President Cleveland's signature;
Glen Grey act in Cape Colony embarks on a new natives policy.

J **Sep**: 25th Britain annexes Pondoland, connecting Cape Colony with Natal.

K **Oct**: 15th, Alfred Dreyfus is arrested on treason charge;
26th, Prince Hohenlohe succeeds Count Caprivi as German chancellor; the unpopularity of the commercial treaty with Russia (*Feb.*) contributes to Caprivi's fall.

L **Nov**: On Alexander III's death Nicholas II becomes Tsar (–1917);
10th, French troops begin conquest of Madagascar (–*Jan.* 96);
21st, Japanese victory over Chinese at Port Arthur;
Banks in Newfoundland fail.

O **Politics, Economics, Law and Education**
Benjamin Kidd, *Social Revolution.*
S. and B. Webb, *History of Trade Unionism.*
Parish Councils are established in England.
Dutch Labour Party is founded.

P **Science, Technology, Discovery, etc.**
Lord Rayleigh and William Ramsay discover argon.
James Dewar liquefies oxygen.
H. Y. Castner's electrolytic process for making caustic soda.
First railway over the Andes.
Gold is discovered in Transvaal.

Q **Scholarship**
F. Pollock and F. W. Maitland, *History of English Law.*

R **Philosophy and Religion**
Lord Halifax opens discussions on reunion of Anglican Church with Rome.
Freedom of worship in Austria, where civil marriage becomes compulsory.

S **Art, Sculpture, Fine Arts and Architecture**
Matthew Corbett, *Morning Glory* (painting).
Gustave Caillebotte collection of Impressionist paintings is rejected by Luxembourg Museum, Paris.
The Yellow Book, with Aubrey Beardsley as art editor.
Ashendene Press is established by Charles St. John Hornby.

T **Music**
Claude Debussy, *L'Après-midi d'un Faune.*
Jules Massenet, *Thaïs* (opera).
Hugo Wolf, *Italian Serenade.*

U **Literature**
Hall Caine, *The Manxman.*
Anthony Hope (pseud.), *Prisoner of Zenda.*
R. Kipling, *The Jungle Book.*
G. Moore, *Esther Waters.*
S. Weyman, *Under the Red Robe.*
É. Zola, *Les Trois Villes* (–98).

V **The Press**

W **Drama and Entertainment**
G. B. Shaw, *Arms and the Man.*
T. A. Edison's Kinetoscope Parlour, New York.

X **Sport**
Paris-Rouen trial run for motor-cars.
New York Jockey Club founded.

Y **Statistics**

M **Dec:** 21st, MacKenzie Bowell becomes Canadian premier, following John Thompson's death;
22nd, A. Dreyfus is convicted by a court martial *in camera*, and imprisoned in Devil's Island, French Guiana.

N Lord Spencer's naval programme in England.
Standing Committee of Commons appointed to consider measures for Scotland.
Riots in Sicily.
Risings of Christians against Turks in Crete (–97).
Revolts in Dutch East Indies.

z Births and Deaths

Feb. 10th Harold Macmillan b. (–).
Apr. 10th Ben Nicholson b. (–).
Apr. 17th Nikita Khrushchev b. (–).
Apr. 30th Herbert Evatt b. (–).
May 6th Alan Cobham b. (–).
July 9th Dorothy Thompson b. (–).
July 26th Aldous Huxley b. (–1963).
July 30th Walter Pater d. (55).
Sept. 8th Hermann Helmholtz d. (73).
Oct. 7th Oliver Wendell Holmes d. (85).
Oct. 20th James Anthony Froude d. (76).
Dec. 3rd Robert Louis Stevenson d. (44).
Dec. 8th James Thurber b. (–1963).
Dec. 20th Robert Menzies b. (–).
— J. B. Priestley b. (–).

A **Jan**: 1st, British Niger Company proclaims protectorate over Busa, on middle Niger, and Nikki, near Dahomey;
French Trades Union Congress at Nantes adopts principle of general strike and
13th, President Casimir-Périer resigns in disgust;
17th, succeeded by Jules Faure (–99) and Alexandre Ribot forms ministry.

B **Feb**: 12th, resounding Japanese victory at Wei-hai-We.

C **Mar**: 25th, Italian troops advance into Ethiopia;
28th, Edward Grey announces that Britain would regard a French occupation of Upper Nile as an unfriendly act.

D **Apr**: 17th, by treaty of Shimonoseki China and Japan recognise independence of Korea, China opens seven new ports and cedes Formosa, Port Arthur and the Liao Tung peninsula to Japan;
23rd, Russia, France and Germany (with Britain at last moment abstaining) protest against cession of mainland to Japan.

E **May**: 2nd, British South Africa Company territory South of Zambesi is organised as Rhodesia;
8th, by revised treaty Japan surrenders Liao Tung peninsula and Port Arthur to China in return for huge indemnity;
15th, Agenor Goluchowski becomes Austrian foreign secretary;
20th, U.S. income tax declared unconstitutional.

F **Jun**: 10th, Henry Campbell-Bannerman, British War Secretary, forces Queen Victoria to accept the resignation of Duke of Cambridge as Commander-in-Chief;
11th, Lord Rosebery is defeated on a vote relating to cordite supply;
—, Britain annexes Togoland to block Transvaal's access to sea;
25th, Lord Salisbury forms Unionist ministry, with Joseph Chamberlain as colonial secretary (–*July* 1902);
28th, union of Nicaragua, Honduras and El Salvador (ended in 1898 by El Salvador's opposition);
Raids from Bulgaria into Macedonia are made following foundation of External Macedonian Revolutionary Organisation at Sofia.

G **Jul**: 1st, East African Protectorate organised on dissolution of British East Africa Company;
8th, opening of Delagoa Bay railway gives Transvaal an outlet;
15th, Stephen Stambulov, Bulgarian premier, murdered;
20th, U.S. note to Britain that a modification by force of British Guiana's boundary with Venezuela would be a violation of the Monroe doctrine;
British general election confirms Lord Salisbury's majority, with Unionists majority of 152 (Conservatives 340; Liberal Unionists 71; Liberals 177; Irish Nationalists 82).

H **Aug**: 1st (–8th), Kaiser William II's conversations at Cowes with Lord Salisbury, who proposes the partition of Turkey, but there is misunderstanding and, subsequently, profound mutual distrust;
30th, compulsory Roman Catholic instruction in Belgian State schools.

J **Sep**: Leopold II of Belgium agrees to co-operate with French on Upper Nile;
Casimir Badeni forms ministry in Austro-Hungary and attempts to pacify Czechs.

O Politics, Economics, Law and Education

T. G. Masaryk, *The Czech Question.*
K. Marx, *Das Kapital*, volume 3.
London School of Economics and Political Science founded.
National Trust founded.
Oscar Wilde brings unsuccessful libel action against Marquess of Queensberry and in a sensational trial (*May*) is found guilty of homosexual charges.

P Science, Technology, Discovery, etc.

W. Röntgen discovers X-rays.
J. H. Northrop's automatic loom.
G. Marconi invents wireless telegraphy.
Auguste and Louis Lumière invent the cinematograph.
First main-line railway is electrified.
Kiel Canal opened (*June* 20th).

Q Scholarship

American Historical Review issued.

R Philosophy and Religion

Sigmund Freud in *Studien über Hysterie* founds psychoanalysis.
A. J. Balfour, *The Foundations of Belief.*
Bible Conference of conservative evangelicals at Niagara defines 'fundamentalism'.
World Student Christian Federation founded.
Cardinal Herbert Vaughan lays foundation stone of Westminster Cathedral.

S Art, Sculpture, Fine Arts and Architecture

T Music

G. Mahler, Symphony no. 2.
R. Strauss, *Till Eulenspiegel's Merry Pranks* (symphonic poem).
Robert Newman arranges first series of Promenade Concerts at Queen's Hall, under Henry J. Wood.

U Literature

Hilaire Belloc, *Verses and Sonnets.*
Joseph Conrad, *Almayer's Folly.*
J. K. Huysmans, *En Route.*
Henry James, *The Middle Years* (autobiography).
George Moore, *The Celibates.*
A. Rimbaud, *Le Bateau Ivre.*
Henry Sienkiewicz, *Quo Vadis?*
H. G. Wells, *The Time Machine.*
W. B. Yeats, *Poems.*

V The Press

W Drama and Entertainment

O. Wilde, *The Importance of Being Earnest.*

X Sport

Peter Latham becomes world champion of both lawn tennis and racquets.

1895 (Oct.–Dec.)

K Oct: 1st, massacre of Armenians in Constantinople;
8th, assassination of Queen of Korea with Japanese connivance;
17th, Sultan Abdul Hamid II of Turkey is forced by the powers to agree to undertake reforms, yet the massacres continue;
Britain sends a squadron to the Dardanelles and Austria recommends international naval action against Turkey.

L Nov: 7th, Russia plans to seize Constantinople but, owing to France being unwilling to risk a general war, postpones action;
11th, 'British' Bechuanaland is annexed to Cape Colony;
26th, Lord Salisbury rejects U.S. plan for arbitration in British Guiana–Venezuela boundary dispute;
Léon Bourgeois forms Radical ministry in France on defeat of Alexandre Ribot.

M Dec: 7th, Ethiopians defeat Italians at Amba Alagi;
17th, President Cleveland asks Congress to appoint commission to obtain facts in Venezuelan boundary question;
29th, L. Starr Jameson's Raid into Transvaal from Bechuanaland.

N Native risings in Mozambique (–99).
Risings in Cuba against Spain, aiming at independence.

Y **Statistics**

Coal production (in mill. tons): Great Britain, 190; U.S., 179; Germany, 120; France, 28.

Iron production (in mill. tons): U.S., 11·3; Great Britain, 8·9; Germany, 5·7; France, 2·0.

U.K. total State expenditure: £100·9 mill.

Z **Births and Deaths**

Feb. 18th Semyon Timoshenko b. (–).
Mar. 28th Christian Herter b. (–).
June 29th T. H. Huxley d. (70).
July 12th Oscar Hammerstein b. (–).
Sept. 18th John Diefenbaker b. (–).
Sept. 28th Louis Pasteur d. (73).
Oct. 19th Lewis Mumford b. (–).
Nov. 16th Paul Hindemith b. (–).
Dec. 1st Henry Williamson b. (–).
— Nikolai Bulganin b. (–).
—Friedrich Engels d. (75).

A **Jan**: 2nd, L. Starr Jameson surrenders at Doornkop;
3rd, William II sends 'Kruger telegram', congratulating Transvaal leader on suppressing the Raid, which provokes crisis in Anglo-German relations;
4th, Utah becomes a U.S. state;
6th, Cecil Rhodes resigns premiership of Cape Colony; a committee of Cape Assembly reports, subsequently, that Rhodes engineered the Jameson Raid. Transvaal orders munitions from Europe and fortifies Pretoria and Johannesburg;
15th, Anglo-French agreement over Siam;
18th, Francis Scott takes Coomassie in Britain's 4th Ashanti War, imprisoning King Prempeh.

B **Feb**: Beginning of Cretan revolution against Turkey, inspired by Greeks;
Reconciliation of Russia and Bulgaria when Crown Prince Boris is converted to Orthodox faith;
19th, Ferdinand I of Bulgaria is recognised by Russia, subsequently by the other powers.

C **Mar**: 1st, Ethiopians defeat Italians at Adowa, forcing Italy to sue for peace;
5th, F. Crispi's ministry falls in Italy, through indignation at failure of Ethiopian War, and Antonio Rudini forms ministry with support from Radicals under Felice Cavalotti;
12th, Britain decides on re-conquest of Sudan, to protect the Nile from French advance;
17th, Transvaal and Orange Free State conclude offensive and defensive alliance;
Further Matabele rising in Rhodesia (*–Oct.*);
New evidence favourable to Dreyfus is suppressed in France.

D **Apr**: Félix Méline, Progressive, forms ministry in France.

E **May**: 1st, murder of Nasr-ed-Din, Shah of Persia.

F **Jun**: 3rd, treaty signed in Moscow by which China and Russia form defensive alliance for 15 years and China grants Russia the right to operate railway in North Manchuria;
9th, Russo-Japanese agreement recognises Russia's position in Korea;
29th, Liberal government in Holland widens the franchise, but leaves working-class dissatisfied;
Expedition under Major Marchand leaves France to advance to Fashoda and claim Sudan.

G **Jul**: 1st, treaty of federation of Straits Settlements;
3rd, Abdul Hamid II, Sultan of Turkey, agrees to introduce self-government in Crete and as Greek support of insurgents continues, Austria proposes international blockade of the island which, 29th, is rejected by Britain;
11th, Wilfred Laurier forms Liberal ministry in Canada;
Land bill for Ireland extends tenants' rights with regard to improvements.

H **Aug**: 16th, British protectorate in Ashanti proclaimed;
18th, France annexes Madagascar whose external treaties with other states are annulled;
25th, ambassadors of the powers draw up revised scheme for Crete under a Christian governor, approved by Turkey (which is accepted by insurgents *Sept.* 12th);
26th, native insurrection in Philippines;
—, Armenian revolutionaries attack Ottoman Bank, Constantinople, which provokes a three-day massacre.

O **Politics, Economics, Law and Education**
Nobel Prizes established.

P **Science, Technology, Discovery, etc.**
William Ramsay discovers helium.
Ernest Rutherford's magnetic detection of electrical waves.
S. P. Langley's flying machine makes successful flights (*May* 6th, *Nov.* 28th).
Power plant at Niagara Falls opened.
An electric submarine is constructed in France.
Martin Conway crosses Spitzbergen.

Q **Scholarship**

R **Philosophy and Religion**
Henri Bergson, *Matière et Mémoire*.

S **Art, Sculpture, Fine Arts and Architecture**
Frederic Leighton, *Clytie* (painting).
W. Morris and E. Burne-Jones make designs for *Kelmscott Chaucer*.
National Portrait Gallery moved from Bethnal Green to permanent home in Westminster.

T **Music**
J. Brahms, *Four Serious Songs* (op. 121).
R. Strauss, tone poem *Thus Spake Zarathustra*.
G. Puccini, *La Bohème* (opera).
H. Wolf, *The Corregidor* (opera).
The Grand Duke ends Gilbert and Sullivan partnership of 'Savoy' operas.

U **Literature**
A. France (pseud.), *L'Histoire contemporaine* (–1901).
T. Hardy, *Jude the Obscure*.
A. E. Housman, *A Shropshire Lad*.
R. L. Stevenson, *Weir of Hermiston* (unfinished).

V **The Press**
Alfred Harmsworth founds the *Daily Mail*, selling at ½d.
Phil May joins *Punch*.

W **Drama and Entertainment**
H. Ibsen, *John Gabriel Borkman*.
A. Chekhov, *The Seagull*.

X **Sport**
First Olympiad of modern era held at Athens.
Persimmon, owned by Prince of Wales, wins the Derby.

Y **Statistics**
Steel production (in mill. tons): U.S., 5·2; Germany, 4·7; Great Britain, 4·1; France, 1·1.
U.K. merchant shipping tonnage: 9,020,000 (of which 284,000 steamships).

J Sep: 21st, Horatio Kitchener takes Dongola in Sudan;
24th, W. E. Gladstone's last speech, at Liverpool, on Armenian massacres, pleads for isolated action by Britain;
30th, Russia and China sign convention over Manchuria;
—, Franco-Italian convention over Tunis, by which Italy surrenders many claims.

K Oct: 4th, Lord Rosebery resigns Liberal leadership on account of party's view of Armenian question, being succeeded in Lords by Lord Kimberley and in Commons by W. V. Harcourt;
24th, Otto von Bismarck publishes the secret Russo-German Re-insurance treaty of 1887, which was unknown to Austria;
26th, by treaty of Addis Ababa Italian protectorate of Ethiopia is withdrawn;
Robert Baden-Powell puts down Matabele rising;
Tsar Nicholas II visits Paris and London.

L Nov: In U.S. presidential election William McKinley, Republican, on gold-standard platform, gains 271 electoral votes against William Jennings Bryan, Democratic and Populist candidate, standing for policy of free silver coinage, with 176 votes;
26th, Aliens Immigration Act in Transvaal restricts liberty of press and public meetings (it is repealed in 1897 on Joseph Chamberlain's protest that it violates convention of 1884);
Russia plans to seize Constantinople if Britain intervenes in Crete.

M Dec:

N Revival of Young Turk movement.

z **Births and Deaths**

Jan. 8th Paul Verlaine d. (51).
Jan. 14th John Dos Passos b. (–).
July 1st Harriet Beecher Stowe d. (85).
July 16th Edmond de Goncourt d. (74); and Trygve Lie b. (–).
Aug. 13th John E. Millais d. (67).
Oct. 3rd William Morris d. (62).
Oct. 11th Anton Bruckner d. (72).
Nov. 16th Oswald Mosley b. (–).
Dec. 10th Alfred Nobel d. (63).

1897 (Jan.–Oct.) War between Turkey and Greece

A **Jan:** Federal convention, with representatives from each Australian colony except Queensland, meets at Hobart to discuss draft federal constitution.

B **Feb:** 2nd, Cretan insurrection resumed;
6th, Crete proclaims union with Greece;
15th, the powers land troops in the island but
17th, Britain rejects Austro-Russian proposal for blockade of Piraeus.

C **Mar:** 4th, William McKinley inaugurated president of U.S. (–1901);
18th, blockade of Crete by the powers begins on Greece's refusal to withdraw troops;
20th, France, now preponderant influence in Addis Ababa, obtains treaty with Ethiopia defining Somali frontier;
28th, Japan adopts gold standard.

D **Apr:** 5th, the Czech language is granted equality with German in Bohemia;
6th, Sultan of Zanzibar abolishes slavery;
7th, Turkey declares war on Greece;
30th, Austro-Russian agreement to maintain *status quo* in the Balkans.

E **May:** 8th, Greece begs powers to intervene; intervention follows Turkish defeat of Greeks, 12th, in Thessaly;
14th, by treaty with Ethiopia Britain abandons certain claims in Somaliland but Emperor Menelek refuses to surrender his claims to lands near the Nile;
19th, armistice in Graeco-Turkish war.

F **Jun:** 15th, Alfred von Tirpitz appointed German naval secretary;
Second Colonial Conference, London, presided over by Joseph Chamberlain (–*July*).

G **Jul:** 10th, French force under Marchand occupies Fashoda;
24th, Nelson Dingley's tariff increases U.S. protection;
Britain denounces treaties with Belgium and Germany which would prevent Canadian preference;
Report of Parliamentary committee into Jameson Raid censures Cecil Rhodes, but acquits Joseph Chamberlain and the Colonial Office.

H **Aug:** 7th, Egyptian force takes Abu Hamed in Sudan;
Franco-Russian alliance extended;
French expedition to Sudan under Marchand reaches River Bahr-el-Ghazal;
Alfred Milner becomes high commissioner for South Africa.

J **Sep:** Rising of Batetelas on Upper Congo;
Mutiny of Sudanese troops in Uganda (–98).

K **Oct:** 20th, Prince Bernhard von Bülow becomes German foreign secretary;
King of Korea proclaims himself emperor and Russia and Japan intervene to preserve order, but leave the emperor independent.

O **Politics, Economics, Law and Education**

S. & B. Webb, *Industrial Democracy*.
Workmen's Compensation Act in Britain.

P **Science, Technology, Discovery, etc.**

Ronald Ross discovers malaria bacillus.
W. Thomson's experiments with cathode rays.
Monotype type-setting machine.
Julius Hann, *Handbook of Climatology*.
The discovery of gold at Bonanza Creek, Yukon, Canada, leads to Klondike Gold Rush.

Q **Scholarship**

R **Philosophy and Religion**

Havelock Ellis, *Studies in the Psychology of Sex* (–1900).
Zionist Conference held at Basle, under Theodor Herzl and Max Nordau.

S **Art, Sculpture, Fine Arts and Architecture**

P. Gauguin, *Where do we come from? What are we? Where are we going?* (painting).
M. Klinger, *Christus in Olymp* (painting).
C. Pissarro, *Boulevard des Italiens* (painting).
Tate Gallery, London, opened.
Bing's *Art Nouveau* Gallery opens in Paris with exhibition of Edvard Munch's paintings.
Whitechapel Art Gallery built (–99).

T **Music**

Vincent d'Indy, *Fervaal* (opera).

U **Literature**

M. Barrès, *Le Déracinéa* (1st vol. of triology, *Le Roman de l'énergie nationale* –1902).
Joseph Conrad, *The Nigger of the Narcissus*.
John Galsworthy, *From the Four Winds*.
Stefan George, *Das Jahr der Seele*.
R. Kipling, *Captains Courageous* and *Recessional*.
A. Strindberg, *Inferno*.
H. G. Wells, *The Invisible Man*.

V **The Press**

W **Drama and Entertainment**

Edmond Rostand, *Cyrano de Bergerac*.
G. B. Shaw's *Candida* produced (written 1894).
Forbes Robertson's *Hamlet* at the Lyceum.
Diamond Jubilee Celebrations throughout Britain.

X **Sport**

Y **Statistics**

L Nov: 4th, Cape railway reaches Bulawayo in Southern Rhodesia;
15th, Mathieu Dreyfus discovers the document on which his brother, Alfred Dreyfus, was convicted, to be in the writing of Major M. C. Esterházy;
28th, Count Badeni is forced to resign in Austria through German opposition to the language ordinance (of *Apr.* 1897), and the Austro-Hungarian monarchy weathers the crisis with difficulty;
—, Germany occupies Kiao-chow, North China, in retaliation for the murder of German missionaries.

M Dec: 1st, Zululand is annexed to Natal;
13th, Russia occupies Port Arthur;
16th, Peace of Constantinople between Greece and Turkey (the problem of Crete settled in *Nov.* 1898);
25th, Italy cedes Kassala to Egypt.

N British troops occupy Benin, Nigeria, in protest at human sacrifices.
Plague in Poona.
Severe famine in India.
Austro-Hungarian Socialist party splits into six nationalist groups.

z **Births and Deaths**

Apr. 3rd Johannes Brahms d. (63).
Apr. 23rd Lester Pearson b. (–).
May 27th John Cockcroft b. (–).
June 12th Anthony Eden, Viscount Avon b. (–).
July 28th Kingsley Martin b. (–).
Aug. 8th Jacob Burckhardt d. (79).
Sept. 26th Pope Paul VI (Giovanni Montini) b. (–).
Nov. 12th Aneurin Bevan b. (–1960).
Dec. 17th Alphonse Daudet d. (57).

1898 (Jan.–Sep.) Fashoda crisis—Battle of Omdurman—First German Navy Bill

A **Jan**: 11th, acquittal of Major M. C. Esterházy in trial for alleged forgery of document in Dreyfus case, provokes Zola's *J'accuse*, 13th, an open letter to the French President (for which, *Feb.* 23rd, he is imprisoned);
Anglo-Russian crisis over loan to China and
25th, Lord Salisbury suggests compromise which Russia declines to accept.

B **Feb**: 9th, Paul Kruger's re-election as President of Transvaal with massive majority;
15th, destruction of U.S.S. *Maine* in Havana;
After Greece has defaulted on obligations an international commission is appointed to control Greek finances.

C **Mar**: Finding neither U.S., 8th, nor Japan, 17th, will support her in the conflict with Russia over the loan to China, Britain decides against pressing her case to the brink of war;
27th, Russia obtains lease of Port Arthur and Britain is leased Wei-hai-wei and Kowloon;
28th, First German navy bill, introduced by Alfred von Tirpitz, begins Germany's naval expansion;
29th, Joseph Chamberlain suggests an Anglo-German alliance;
Bohemia is divided into Czech, German and mixed districts.

D **Apr**: 8th, Horatio Kitchener's victory at Atbara River;
10th, France obtains concessions in China;
19th, U.S. ultimatum to Spain to relinquish authority in Cuba;
24th, U.S. declares war on Spain.

E **May**: 1st, George Dewey destroys Spanish fleet at Manila;
3rd (–8th), bread riots in Milan are put down with heavy loss of life;
13th, Joseph Chamberlain, in Birmingham speech, criticises Russia and bids for friendship of U.S. and Germany, which creates unfavourable impression in Britain and overseas.

F **Jun**: 11th (–*Sept.* 16th), Emperor Te Tsung of China's 100 days of Reform, under guidance of K'ang Yu-wei;
14th, Anglo-French convention defines boundaries in Nigeria and Gold Coast;
28th, Luigi Pelloux forms ministry in Italy on Count Rudini's resignation.

G **Jul**: 3rd, U.S. naval victory at Santiago;
25th, U.S. invades Porto Rico, and, 26th, Spain asks for terms;
30th, Théophile Delcassé appointed French foreign secretary (–*June* 1905).

H **Aug**: 12th, transfer of islands of Hawaii to U.S.;
13th, U.S. forces capture Manila;
24th, Tsar invites powers to co-operate in reducing armaments;
30th, Anglo-German secret agreement on future of the African territories of Portugal, who is bankrupt; Britain to obtain lease of Delagoa Bay and Germany to receive parts of Mozambique and Angola;
—, Col. Henry admits the forgery of a document in the Dreyfus case.

J **Sep**: 2nd, Horatio Kitchener defeats Dervishes at Omdurman;
10th, Empress Elizabeth of Austria is murdered by an Italian anarchist at Geneva;
19th, Kitchener reaches Fashoda;
21st, Tzu-hsi, Dowager Empress of China, seizes power and revokes reforms.

O **Politics, Economics, Law and Education**

Otto von Bismarck, *Reflections and Memoirs.*

British Committee on Old-Age Pensions, chairman Lord Rothschild, is unable to accept any of the schemes proposed to it. Old-Age pensions are, however, introduced in New Zealand.

Public outcry against the meat supplied for U.S. troops fighting in the Spanish War leads to the passage of the first Food and Drugs Act.

London University bill establishes a teaching university.

P **Science, Technology, Discovery, etc.**

Pierre and Marie Curie discover radium and polonium.

W. Ramsay and M. W. Travers discover neon and metargon.

The discovery of sesquisulphide of phosphorus makes possible the safety match.

The word 'photosynthesis' is introduced.

M. J. Owen's automatic bottle-making machine.

C. von Linde's machine for the liquefaction of air.

The first flash-light photograph is taken.

Count F. von Zeppelin makes an airship.

First petrol tractor, built at Marion, Ohio.

Paris Métro system started.

Q **Scholarship**

R **Philosophy and Religion**

The U.K. Benifices Act forbids the sale of advowsons and increases the power of Anglican bishops.

S **Art, Sculpture, Fine Arts and Architecture**

Jules Dalou, *The Triumph of the Republic* (sculpture).

A. Rodin, *The Kiss* (sculpture).

T **Music**

S. Coleridge-Taylor, *Hiawatha's Wedding Feast.*

Umberto Giordano, *Fedora* (opera).

U **Literature**

T. Hardy, *Wessex Poems.*

J. K. Huysmans, *La Cathédrale.*

H. James, *The Turn of the Screw.*

H. G. Wells, *The War of the Worlds.*

O. Wilde, *Ballad of Reading Gaol.*

V **The Press**

W **Drama and Entertainment**

G. B. Shaw, *Caesar and Cleopatra.*

X **Sport**

Y **Statistics**

K Oct: William II visits Palestine and Syria (–*Nov.*).

L Nov: 4th, French evacuate Fashoda after Britain protests;
26th, Franco-Italian commercial treaty ends tariff war (since 1886);
—, following the Turkish evacuation of Crete, Prince George of Greece is appointed high commissioner in the island;
27th, Deutsche Bank secures preliminary concessions for Baghdad Railway.

M Dec: 10th, treaty of Paris between U.S. and Spain by which Spain cedes Cuba, Porto Rico and Guam and also the Philippines, as yet to be conquered, for $20 million.

N Foundation of the Boxers, an anti-foreign society in China to resist westernisation and combat Christianity.

z **Births and Deaths**

Jan. 14th C. L. Dodgson ('Lewis Carroll') d. (65).
Feb. 9th Steen Rasmussen b. (–).
Mar. 15th Henry Bessemer d. (85).
Apr. 9th Paul Robeson b. (–).
Apr. 18th Gustave Moreau d. (72).
May 19th W. E. Gladstone d. (89).
July 31st Otto von Bismarck d. (83).
Sept. 9th Stéphane Mallarmé d. (56).
Sept. 24th Howard Florey b. (–).

1899 (Jan.–Oct.) Anglo-Boer War begins—Germany secures Baghdad Railway contract

A Jan: 19th, Anglo-Egyptian convention on Sudan;
Henry Campbell-Bannerman succeeds W. V. Harcourt as leader of Liberals in Commons.

B Feb: 4th, Filipinos demand independence from U.S.;
12th, Germany buys the islands of Marianas, Caroline and Pelew in the Pacific from Spain;
15th, Tsar Nicholas II suppresses liberties in Finland;
18th, Émile Loubet is elected President of France (–1906), following Félix Faure's death;
China opposes Italy's demands for concessions at Chekiang.

C Mar: 4th, J. G. Schurman's Commission offers representative government to the Filipinos, but the revolt continues;
21st, Anglo-French convention on hinterland of Tripoli ends Fashoda crisis, but Italy protests at large concessions to France in Sahara;
24th, Petition of Johannesburg Uitlanders to Queen Victoria, reciting their grievances against the Boers;
31st (–*June* 5th), at Bloemfontein Conference Alfred Milner and Paul Kruger fail to reach agreement on Transvaal franchise.

D Apr:

E May: 18th (–*July* 21st), at first Peace Conference 26 nations meet at the Hague, at the Tsar Nicholas II's suggestion, to extend Geneva Convention to naval warfare, explosive bullets and poison gas and authorise the establishment of a permanent Court of Arbitration.

F Jun: 3rd, *cour de cassation* annuls Alfred Dreyfus's first trial and orders a retrial;
10th, U.S. Congress appoints canal commission to report on routes through Panama;
22nd, René Waldeck-Rousseau, a moderate, becomes French premier.

G Jul: 11th, Transvaal government decides immigrants in Transvaal to be enfranchised after seven years residence;
27th, Joseph Chamberlain proposes a joint British-Boer enquiry into the Transvaal franchise bills, which is unacceptable to Kruger.

H Aug: 9th, Britain purchases the possessions of the Niger Company (Protectorate proclaimed, *Jan.* 1900);
9th, Théophile Delcassé, visiting St. Petersburg, extends the Franco-Russian alliance.

J Sep: 6th, John Hay, U.S. Secretary of State, sends 'open door' note to Britain, Germany and Russia against interference in China's treaty ports;
9th, at retrial at Rennes court martial Alfred Dreyfus is condemned 'with extenuating circumstances', but, 19th, is pardoned by presidential decree, which with premier Waldeck-Rousseau's intervention in the Le Creusot strike, helps to heal divisions in France;
'Mad Mullah' raids on British and Italian Somaliland.

K Oct: 3rd, settlement of British Guiana-Venezuelan boundary dispute, largely favourable to Britain;
9th, Paul Kruger's ultimatum, which is supported, 11th, by Orange Free State, provokes, 12th, Anglo-Boer War;

O **Politics, Economics, Law and Education**

H. S. Chamberlain, *The Foundations of the XIXth Century* (published in Vienna).
London Borough Councils are established.
Board of Education takes charge of education in England and Wales.
John Dewey, *School and Society*.

P **Science, Technology, Discovery, etc.**

The magnetic recording of sound is devised.
Dortmund-Ems Canal is completed.
Aspirin is invented.
Ernst Haeckel, *The Riddle of the Universe*.

Q **Scholarship**

Lord Acton plans *The Cambridge Modern History*.
John Rylands Library, Manchester, opened.

R **Philosophy and Religion**

A. Bain, *The Realisation of the Possible*.
T. H. Green, *Prolegomena to Ethics* (posth.).
James Ward, *Naturalism and Agnosticism*.
Leo XIII's bull *Testem Benevolentiae* condemns erroneous opinions, including the 'Americanism' of Isaac Hecker.

S **Art, Sculpture, Fine Arts and Architecture**

Jules Dalou, monument to Alphard.
W. H. Thornycroft, statue of Cromwell.

T **Music**

H. Berlioz, *The Taking of Troy*, being pt. 2 of *The Trojans* (opera).
Edward Elgar, *Enigma Variations*.
J. Sibelius, Symphony no. 1 in E minor.

U **Literature**

Stefan George, *Der Teppich des Lebens*.
A. Gide, *Le Prométhée mal enchaîné*.
M. Gorki, *Foma Gordeyev*.
R. Kipling, *Stalky and Co*.
Edith Nesbit, *The Story of the Treasure Seekers*.
L. Tolstoy, *Resurrection*.

V **The Press**

W **Drama and Entertainment**

A. W. Pinero, *The Gay Lord Quex*.
National Norwegian Theatre is founded.

X **Sport**

Y **Statistics**

K Oct: 14th, by secret treaty of Windsor Portugal undertakes to prevent passage of munitions from Delagoa Bay to Transvaal;
17th, Boers defeated at Glencoe;
—, Bohemian language ordinances of *Apr.* 1897 are repealed;
23rd, Cipriano Castro assumes power in Venezuela;
30th, Piet Joubert wins battle of Nicholson's Nek, against British force under George White.

L Nov: 1st, Ladysmith, Natal, surrenders to Piet Joubert;
14th, Britain and Germany settle Togoland-Gold Coast frontier and the question of Samoa, with Britain taking Tonga and Savage Islands (confirmed *Dec.* 2nd);
19th (–25th), Kaiser William II and von Bülow visit England to discuss possible Anglo-German alliance, but Joseph Chamberlain's Leicester speech, 30th, ends rapprochement;
The Khalifa of Sudan is killed by Reginald Wingate on the White Nile.

M Dec: 10th, British defeat at Stromberg;
11th, British under Lord Methuen repulsed by Piet Cronje at Magersfontein, Orange Free State, and 15th, the 'Black week' ends with Louis Botha's repulse of Redvers Buller at Colenso, Natal;
—, Bülow in Reichstag rejects British advances for an alliance;
23rd, Germany secures Baghdad Railway contract;
24th, Netherlands adopts Proportional Representation;
Canadian and Australian Volunteers land in South Africa.

N Revisionist German Social Democrats abandon strict Marxism.
Modification of plans for federal government of Australia by conference of premiers, to meet criticism of New South Wales.

z **Births and Deaths**

Jan. 7th Francis Poulenc b. (–).
Feb. 23rd Erich Kästner b. (–).
June 3rd Johann Strauss d. (74).
July 1st Charles Laughton b. (–1965).
Aug. 16th R. W. Bunsen d. (88).
Dec. 16th Noël Coward b. (–).
— Paul Spaak b. (–).

1900 (Jan.–Aug.) Relief of Ladysmith and of Mafeking—Boxer Rising in China

A **Jan:** 1st, Frederick Lugard becomes high commissioner in Nigeria;
10th, Frederick Roberts lands in South Africa as Commander-in-Chief of British army, with Lord Kitchener as chief of staff;
Tension in Anglo-German relations through Britain's seizure of a German vessel on suspicion of carrying contraband but, 16th, Britain gives way;
Francis Joseph of Austria appoints a bureaucratic ministry under Ernst von Körber to resolve the conflict between German and Czech parties in Austria.

B **Feb:** 6th, President William McKinley appoints W. H. Taft commission to report on the Philippines;
18th, in South African War Piet Cronje surrenders to British at Paardeberg;
22nd, bitter Parliamentary conflict in Italy following the declaration by the Court of Cassation that the constitutional decrees of June 1899 are invalid;
27th, British Labour Party founded, with Ramsay MacDonald secretary;
28th, Redvers Buller relieves Ladysmith;
—, Count Muraviev, Russian foreign minister, suggests France and Germany put joint pressure on Britain to end South African War, but Germany rejects this (*Mar.* 3rd) while France takes advantage of Britain's plight to advance her interests in Morocco.

C **Mar:** 10th, Britain signs treaty with Uganda for regulating the government with the advice of a British commissioner;
13th, Frederick Roberts captures Bloemfontein;
14th, U.S. Currency Act declares paper and other money redeemable in gold;
Russian attempts to secure a naval base at Masampo in South Korea are vigorously opposed by Japan.

D **Apr:** 30th, Hawaii is organised as a territory of U.S.;
Republican bloc formed in France to defend the Republic against anti-Dreyfusard opponents.

E **May:** 1st, U.S. Congress passes the Foraker Act for establishing civil government in Puerto Rico;
17th, Relief of Mafeking;
19th, Britain annexes the Tonga Islands and
24th, annexes the Orange Free State.

F **Jun:** 5th, Pretoria taken by Redvers Buller;
12th, second German Naval Act aims at a fleet of 38 battleships in 20 years;
13th (–*Aug.* 14th), Boxer rising in China against Europeans;
18th, General Pelloux resigns following the success of the Left in Italian elections;
19th, National Republican Convention at Philadelphia re-nominates McKinley for presidency and nominates Theodore Roosevelt for vice-presidency;
20th, assassination of the German ambassador at Peking, begins the siege of the legations.

G **Jul:** 4th, armies of Roberts and Buller join forces at Vlakfontein;
14th, international expedition, including U.S. and Japan, takes Tientsin, and U.S. secretary of state, John Hay, restates policy of 'open door' in China;
29th, Humbert I of Italy assassinated by an anarchist;
French government aid wine-growers by reducing retail duties.

H **Aug:** 14th, international force relieves legations in Peking;
27th, Louis Botha is defeated at Bergendal;
31st, Frederick Roberts occupies Johannesburg.

O **Politics, Economics, Law and Education**

German Civil Law Code in force (*Jan.* 1st).
George Cadbury founds Bournville Village Trust.
Amalgamation of Castle and Union Steamship Companies.
Leslie Stephen, *The Utilitarians*.

P **Science, Technology, Discovery, etc.**

Max Planck elaborates quantum theory.
William Crookes separates uranium.
Lord Rayleigh, *Scientific Papers*.
Rediscovery by Hugo de Vries and others of Gregor Mendel's work on heredity.
The acetylene lamp is perfected.
Browning revolver invented.
R. A. Fessenden first transmits speech by wireless.
First Zeppelin trial-flight (*July* 2nd).
Elbe-Trave Canal opened.

Q **Scholarship**

Arthur Evans begins to discover Minoan culture through excavations in Crete.
Paul Claudel, *Discovery of the East*.
Victoria History of the Counties of England started.

R **Philosophy and Religion**

Henri Bergson, *On Laughter*.
Sigmund Freud, *The Interpretation of Dreams*.
Bertrand Russell, *Critical Exposition of the Philosophy of Leibniz*.
Wilhelm Wundt, *Comparative Psychology*.
C. H. Spurgeon, *Autobiography* (posth.).

S **Art, Sculpture, Fine Arts and Architecture**

Painting:

Lawrence Alma-Tadema, *Vain Courtship*.
Paul Cézanne, *Still Life With Onions*.
Claude Monet, *Water Lilies*, *Harmony in Rose*.
Auguste Renoir, *Nude in the Sun* (pastel).
J. S. Sargent, *The Sitwell Family*.
Toulouse-Lautrec, *La Modiste*.

Sculpture:

Auguste Rodin exhibition at La Place de l'Alma establishes his reputation

Architecture:

Charles Rennie Mackintosh, Glasgow School of Art.
Edwin Lutyens, Deanery Gardens, Sonning, Berks.
The Wallace Collection, Manchester Square, London, opened.

T **Music**

Gustave Charpentier, *Louise* (opera).
E. Elgar, *Dream of Gerontius* (oratorio).
G. Mahler, Fourth Symphony.
G. Puccini, *Tosca* (opera).
J. Sibelius, *Finlandia* (overture).
J. S. Bach Festival established in Bethlehem, Pennsylvania.

J Sep: 17th, proclamation of Commonwealth of Australia as a federal union of the six colonies (to come into force *Jan.* 1st 1901);
U.S. Taft Commission begins to exercise legislative power in Philippines, appropriating sums for road and harbour works.

K Oct: 6th, President Kruger, having fled to Europe, is denied an audience by Kaiser William II;
16th, in the 'Khaki' election in Britain, the Conservatives, organised by Joseph Chamberlain, remain in power, with a majority of 134 (Conservatives and Unionists 334 seats, Liberal Unionists 68; Liberals 186, Irish Nationalists 82; Labour 2). Lord Salisbury reconstructs ministry, appointing Lord Lansdowne foreign secretary;
—, Yangtze agreement between Britain and Germany to restrain foreign aggression in China and maintain open door for trade;
17th, Bernhard von Bülow succeeds Prince Hohenlohe as German chancellor;
25th, Transvaal is formally annexed by Britain at Pretoria.

L Nov: 5th, Cuban constitutional convention begins to sit at Havana;
6th, in U.S. presidential election William McKinley, Republican (292 electoral votes), defeats William Jennings Bryan, Democrat (with 155 votes), on an anti-imperialist platform;
—, Boer guerrilla raids on communications and British outposts grow in intensity in Orange River Colony and Transvaal;
9th, Russia, having completed the occupation of Manchuria with 100,000 troops, agrees with the Chinese governor to restore civil administration, but this agreement is abrogated by both central governments;
Rising of the Ashanti suppressed by British.

M Dec: 14th, secret Franco-Italian agreement to maintain French influence in Morocco and Italian interests in Tripoli.

N Beginnings of Hejaz railway to the Holy Places in Arabia, built by popular subscription as a Pan-Islamic project (–1908).
Civil War in Colombia (–1903).

U **Literature**

Colette (pseud.), first 'Claudine' novel.
J. Conrad, *Lord Jim.*
M. Gorki, *Three People.*
Charles Péguy launches *Les Cahiers de la Quinzaine* (–14).
E. Rostand, *L'Aiglon.*
G. B. Shaw publishes *Three Plays for Puritans* with prefaces.
L. Tolstoy, *The Living Corpse.*

V **The Press**

The Daily Express is founded by Arthur Pearson.

W **Drama and Entertainment**

A. Chekhov, *Uncle Vanya.*
The cake-walk dance.

X **Sport**

D. F. Davis presents international challenge cup for lawn tennis.

Y **Statistics**

Z **Births and Deaths**

Jan. 20th John Ruskin d. (81).
June 5th Stephen Crane d. (28).
June 25th Lord Louis Mountbatten b. (–).
Aug. 25th Friedrich Nietzsche d. (56).
Nov. 14th Aaron Copland b. (–).
Nov. 30th Oscar Wilde d. (44).
Dec. 22nd Alan Busch b. (–).

1901 (Jan.–Aug.) Death of Queen Victoria—Australia becomes a dominion

A **Jan:** 1st, Commonwealth of Australia comes into being with Edmund Barton, federalist and protectionist, as prime minister;
19th, William II visits England for Victoria's last days;
22nd, death of Queen Victoria; accession of Edward VII;
To combat guerrilla actions of Boers Lord Kitchener builds chain of blockhouses and starts denuding country of its farms.

B **Feb:** 8th, on receiving Russia's proposals for evacuation of Manchuria China appeals to the major powers and is supported by Britain, Japan and, with hesitancy, by Germany;
11th, death of Milan, father of Alexander I of Serbia;
23rd, Anglo-German agreement on boundary between German East Africa and Nyasaland;
27th, Russian minister of propaganda is murdered to avenge repression of student agitation;
Giuseppe Saracco overthrown for policy towards strikers in Genoa and Giuseppe Zanardelli forms ministry which is dependent on support of extreme Left;
Failures of Louis Botha's raid on Natal and Christian de Wet and James Hertzog's invasion of Cape Colony;
Botha meets Kitchener, 26th, at Middelburg, but negotiations founder on amnesty for Cape rebels.

C **Mar:** 2nd, in U.S. Orville Platt's amendment on Cuban constitution and J. C. Spooner's amendment calling for civil government in Philippines are added to Army Appropriations bill;
15th, in the Reichstag Prince von Bülow declares the Yangtze agreement of 1900 with Britain did not apply to Manchuria, and as a result the London discussions on the possibility of an Anglo-German-Japanese bloc against Russia end abruptly.

D **Apr:** 6th, on protests from Britain and Japan Russia drops draft convention with China;
18th, in the British budget proposals of Hicks Beach a higher revenue is anticipated from direct than indirect taxes for the first time.

E **May:** 29th, Lord Salisbury's confidential memorandum upholding policy of isolation marks the end of discussions for Anglo-German alliance.

F **Jun:** 12th, Cuban convention making the country virtually a protectorate of the U.S. is incorporated in the Cuban constitution as condition of the withdrawal of U.S. troops;
Moroccan mission to Paris, London and Berlin seeking an Anglo-German pact on Morocco.

G **Jul:** 1st, in France the Association Law is promulgated for compulsory regulation of all congregations and associations and the dissolution of those not authorised by the State;
4th, civil government in Philippines with W. H. Taft governor-general, who proclaims amnesty to rebels taking oath of allegiance to U.S.;
16th, Liberal ministry in Denmark;
20th, Morocco grants France control of frontier police;
22nd, Lords deliver Taff Vale judgment that a trade union can be sued in its registered name as a corporate body;
Negotiations begin in London for an Anglo-Japanese alliance;
Clerical Party in power in Holland (–1905).

H **Aug:** 17th, as expression of imperialist sentiment the Royal Titles Act adds the words 'and of the British Dominions beyond the Seas' to Edward VII's style.

O **Politics, Economics, Law and Education**
Final Pendleton Act creates U.S. Civil Service (see *Jan.* 1883).
B. S. Rowntree, *Poverty: a study of town life.*
J. P. Morgan founds United States Steel Corporation.

P **Science, Technology, Discovery, etc.**
Max Planck, *Laws of Radiation.*
W. Normann discovers process for hardening liquid fats.
Adrenalin is first manufactured.
G. Marconi transmits messages by wireless telegraphy from Cornwall to Newfoundland.
First motor-bicycle.
Trans-Siberian Railway reaches Port Arthur.

Q **Scholarship**
James Bryce, *Studies in History and Jurisprudence.*
Max Weber, *The Protestant Ethic and the Birth of Capitalism.*
British Academy founded.

R **Philosophy and Religion**
L. T. Hobhouse, *Mind in Evolution.*
S. Freud, *The Psychology of Everyday Life.*

S **Art, Sculpture, Fine Arts and Architecture**
Painting:
Paul Gauguin, *The Gold in Their Bodies.*
Edvard Munch, *Girls on the Bridge.*

T **Music**
A. Dvořák, *Russalka* (opera).
E. Elgar, Overture *Cockaigne* (op. 40).
M. Ravel, *Jeux d'Eaux*, for piano.
S. Rachmaninov, piano concerto no. 2.

U **Literature**
S. Butler, *Erewhon Revisited.*
H. Caine, *The Eternal City.*
R. Kipling, *Kim.*
Selma Lagerlöf, *Jerusalem.*
M. Maeterlinck, *Life of the Bee.*
Thomas Mann, *Buddenbrooks.*
G. W. Russell, W. B. Yeats and others, *Ideals in Ireland.*

V **The Press**
The Tatler issued.

W **Drama and Entertainment**
A. Strindberg, *Dance of Death.*

X **Sport**

J Sep: 7th, by Peace of Peking ending the Boxer Rising, China is to pay indemnity to the great powers;
14th, on death of President William McKinley, following shooting by anarchist Leon Czolgosz, Theodore Roosevelt succeeds;
25th, Ashanti Kingdom annexed to Gold Coast Colony;
Visit of Russian Emperor to France provokes anti-militarist demonstrations.

K Oct: 16th, Anglo-Japanese negotiations reopened in London by Baron Hayashi;
25th, Joseph Chamberlain's anti-German speech at Edinburgh leads (*Dec.* 27th) to breakdown in negotiations for Anglo-German alliance.

L Nov: 11th, Turkey accepts French ultimatum on violation of treaties;
18th, second Hay-Pauncefoote treaty provides for U.S. construction of Panama Canal with a neutral canal zone to be under U.S. supervision (ratified by Senate *Dec.* 16th);
25th, Prince Ito of Japan, visiting St. Petersburg, seeks Japanese concessions in Korea.

M Dec: 2nd, U.S. Supreme Court decides Puerto Ricans are not U.S. citizens;
7th, Japan drops negotiations with Russia deciding instead to conclude an alliance with Britain;
—, Anglo-Italian agreement for settling Sudan frontier;
26th, completion of Uganda railway from Mombasa to Lake Victoria.

N The Social Revolutionary Party is organised in Russia.
Italian Socialists extend their political influence through strike action.
Strikes and anarchist outrages in Belgium.
French miners, with many abstentions, vote for a general strike, but it is not carried into effect.

Y **Statistics**

Populations (in millions): China, 350; India, 294; Russia, 146; U.S., 75·9; Germany, 56·3; Japan, 45·4; Great Britain and Ireland, 41·4; France, 38·9; Italy, 32·4; Austria, 26·1.

Coal production (in mill. tons): U.S., 268; Great Britain, 219; Germany, 112; Austria, 34; Belgium, 23; Russia, 15.

Steel production (in mill. tons): U.S., 10·1; Germany, 6·2; Great Britain, 4·9; France, 1·5.

Crude petroleum production: U.S., 69·3 mill. barrels.

Z **Births and Deaths**

Jan. 15th Arnold Boecklin d. (73).
Jan. 27th Giuseppe Verdi d. (88).
Mar. 13th Benjamin Harrison d. (68).
Mar. 24th Charlotte M. Yonge d. (78).
Apr. 22nd William Stubbs d. (76).
May 23rd Edmund Rubbra b. (–).
Oct. 19th Arleigh Burke b. (–).
Oct. 23rd George von Siemens d. (62).
Nov. 3rd André Malraux b. (–).
Dec. 5th Walt Disney b. (–).
Dec. 16th Margaret Mead b. (–).
— Henri Toulouse-Lautrec d. (37).

A **Jan:** 30th, Britain ends isolation by signing treaty with Japan, providing for the independence of China and Korea. Neither State to enter separate agreements with other powers without consulting its ally.

B **Feb:** 6th, French agreement with Ethiopia to finance Jibouti-Addis Ababa railway provokes protests from Britain and Italy;
Italian government prevents general strike through calling up all railwaymen on the reserve.

C **Mar:** 20th, Franco-Russian declaration approving the principles of the Anglo-Japanese alliance, but reserving their rights to safeguard their interests.

D **Apr:** 8th, Russo-Chinese agreement for the evacuation of Manchuria;
15th, Britain adjusts the Sudanese frontier with Ethiopia;
—, murder of Sipyengin, Russian minister of interior, succeeded by Viacheslav Plehve who suppresses peasants' revolt and despoils Armenian Church.

E **May:** 12th, coal strike in U.S. (–*Oct.* 13th);
15th, national bankruptcy in Portugal;
31st, Peace of Vereeniging ends Boer War, in which British casualties numbered 5,774 killed (and 16,000 deaths from disease) against 4,000 Boers killed in action. Boers accept British sovereignty and are promised representative government and £3 million from Britain for restocking farms.

F **Jun:** 2nd, in France René Waldeck-Rousseau resigns, despite his majority in the Chamber, through lack of sympathy with extremists, and is succeeded by Émile Combes who directs a vigorous anti-clerical policy;
28th, renewal of Triple Alliance between Germany, Austria and Italy for six years;
—, Congress authorises Theodore Roosevelt to buy rights of the French Panama Company and to acquire from Colombia perpetual control of the canal zone;
30th (–*Aug.* 11th), Colonial Conference in London resolves in favour of Imperial Preference.

G **Jul:** 12th, Arthur Balfour becomes British prime minister on Lord Salisbury's retirement;
Australian Parliament passes Immigration Restriction Act and enfranchises women in federal elections, which gives women the preponderance of votes in Melbourne and Sydney constituencies.

H **Aug:**

J **Sep:** 5th, Anglo-Chinese commercial treaty;
27th, Crown Lands ordinance inaugurates white settlement of East African uplands.

K **Oct:** 13th, Theodore Roosevelt ends U.S. coal strike by threatening to work the mines with federal troops and the owners agree to the appointment of a commission to investigate miners' claims.

L **Nov:** 1st, Franco-Italian Entente, in which Italy assures France of her neutrality if France is attacked;
8th, Spain holds back from signing agreement on Morocco with France from fear of antagonising England;
13th, Persia concludes favourable tariff with Russia, discriminating against British goods.

O **Politics, Economics, Law and Education**

J. A. Hobson, *Imperialism.*
The Order of Merit established by Edward VII.
The Pilgrims, Anglo-American Association, founded.
Congress limits substitution of oleo-margarine for butter.
Reclamation Force established in U.S. for opening up the arid west, with funds for irrigation works.

P **Science, Technology, Discovery, etc.**

Oliver Heaviside states his conception of a layer in the atmosphere to aid conduction of wireless waves.
A. Cushing begins work on the pituitary body.
William Bayliss and Ernest Starling discover hormones.
C. Richet discovers cases of 'maphylaxis', or abnormal sensitiveness to anti-diptheria serum.
F. Poulsen's arc generator.
J. M. Bacon crosses Irish Channel in balloon (*Nov.*).

Q **Scholarship**

R **Philosophy and Religion**

William James, *The Varieties of Religious Experience.*
Paul Hoensbroech, *The Papacy in its Social and Cultural Influence.*

S **Art, Sculpture, Fine Arts and Architecture**

Painting:
P. Gauguin, *Horsemen on the Beach.*
C. Monet, *Waterloo Bridge.*
J. S. Sargent, *Lord Ribbesdale.*
Sculpture:
A. Rodin, *Romeo et Juliette.*
Architecture:
Cass Gilbert, New York Customs House (–07).

T **Music**

C. Debussy, *Pelléas et Mélisande* (opera).
Edward German, *Merrie England* (operetta).
F. Delius, *Appalachia.*

U **Literature**

H. Belloc, *The Path to Rome.*
J. Conrad, *Youth.*
A. Conan Doyle, *The Hound of the Baskervilles.*
A. Gide, *The Immoralist.*
R. Kipling, *Just So Stories.*
M. Gorki, *Night's Lodging.*
J. Masefield, *Salt Water Ballads.*
Émile Verhaeren, *Les Forces Tumultueuses.*

V **The Press**

The Times Literary Supplement issued.

W **Drama and Entertainment**

Gabriele D'Annunzio, *Francesca da Rimini.*
J. M. Barrie, *The Admirable Crichton.*
A. Chekhov, *Three Sisters.*

M Dec: 18th, in London the Committee of Imperial Defence holds first meeting;
—, Education Act for England and Wales provides for secondary education, places schools under Committees of local authorities and brings denominational schools into the State system;
19th, Germany, Britain and Italy blockade Venezuela in protest at Cipriano Castro's refusal to meet claims for injuries caused during revolution;
25th, German protectionist tariff;
Aswan dam opened.

N Increasing disturbance in Macedonia by Bulgarian, Serbian and Greek bands.
Beginnings of educational and economic reform in China.

X **Sport**

Y **Statistics**

Trade union membership (in mill.): U.K., 1·9; U.S., 2·0.

U.K. Textiles trade:

Imports of raw cotton	1,633 mill. lb.
Exports of cottons	5,332 mill. yds.
Exports of woollens	158 mill. yds.
Exports of linens	163 mill. yds.
Exports of silks	9·5 mill. yds.

Z **Births and Deaths**

Feb. 23rd S. R. Gardiner d. (72).
Feb. 27th John Steinbeck b. (–).
Mar. 26th Cecil Rhodes d. (41).
Mar. 29th William Walton b. (–).
Apr. 9th Lord David Cecil b. (–).
June 18th Samuel Butler d. (66).
June 19th Lord Acton d. (68).
July 5th Henry Cabot Lodge b. (–).
Sept. 29th Émile Zola d. (62).
Nov. 14th G. A. Henty d. (70).
Dec. 9th R. A. Butler b. (–).

A **Jan:** 22nd, Hay-Herrán pact for U.S. acquisition of the Panama Canal Zone, but Colombia delays ratification.

B **Feb:** Germany, Britain and Italy lift Venezuelan blockade (*Dec.* 1902) on the Hague Tribunal appointing a commission to investigate claims;
Russia and Austria call for programme of reforms for pacifying Macedonia;
Anti-trust laws in U.S. reinforced;
Joseph Chamberlain visits South Africa and, convinced of the impracticability of Alfred Milner's policy of establishing British supremacy, aims at conciliation with Boers.

C **Mar:** 15th, British conquest of Northern Nigeria completed;
18th, dissolution of French religious orders.

D **Apr:** Britain and France refuse support for construction of Baghdad Railway;
Dutch government ends railway and dock strikes by calling in troops;
Increased sickness benefits for German workers.

E **May:** 1st (–4th), Edward VII's visit to Paris begins improvement in Anglo-French relations;
15th, Joseph Chamberlain announces his conversion to Imperial Preference, which divides the Conservatives;
—, to counter Russian designs Lord Lansdowne declares that Britain would resist the establishment by any power of a fortified base on the Persian Gulf;
E. D. Morel and Roger Casement begin agitation against atrocities in Belgian Congo.

F **Jun:** 10th, murders of King Alexander I and Queen Draga of Serbia and, 15th, the Serbian Assembly elects Peter Karageorgevitch King (Peter I –1921) and restores the 1889 constitution.

G **Jul:** 6th (–9th), London visit of President Émile Loubet and Théophile Delcassé begins conversations leading to *Entente Cordiale*;
20th, following death of Leo XIII, Giuseppe Sarto is elected Pope Pius X;
21st, Irish Land Purchase Act;
25th, Arthur Henderson wins Barnard Castle, Co. Durham, by-election for Labour in three-cornered fight.

H **Aug:** 12th, Japanese note to Russia on failure to evacuate Manchuria;
29th, dismissal of Count Witte, Russian finance minister, is taken as a victory for the group favouring Russian expansion in Manchuria and Korea;
Regulation of motor-cars in Britain, with 20 m.p.h. speed limit.

J **Sep:** 16th, Francis Joseph's aim to bring Hungarian regiments into a unified army system provokes Magyar opposition;
18th, Joseph Chamberlain resigns to test feeling in country on Imperial Preference; leading free-traders also resign and Arthur Balfour reconstructs ministry with Austen Chamberlain as chancellor of exchequer.

K **Oct:** 1st (–3rd), Austro-Russian agreement at Mürzstag for reforms in Macedonia is approved by powers;
20th, settlement of Alaskan frontier by 3-power commission, in which British representative gives casting vote in favour of U.S., embitters Canada;
Anglo-Russian conversations break down through Russian unwillingness to sacrifice interests in Persia.

O **Politics, Economics, Law and Education**

Mrs. Emmeline Pankhurst founds Women's Social and Political Union (*Oct.*).
Royal Naval College, Dartmouth, established.
An infants' welfare centre opened in Ghent.
Act for controlling livestock disease in U.S.
Ebenezer Howard establishes Letchworth Garden City.

P **Science, Technology, Discovery, etc.**

Agnes Clerke, *Problems in Astrophysics.*
W. Ramsay discovers the gases krypton and xenon in the atmosphere.
J. J. Thomson, *The Conduction of Electricity Through Gases.*
Orville and Wilbur Wright make successful flight in aeroplane with a petrol engine (*Dec.* 17th).
C. T. R. Wilson's sensitive electroscope.
R. A. Zsigmondy invents the ultramicroscope.
Krupps Works, Essen, founded.
Detroit becomes the 'motor capital' of the world.
First motor taxis in London.

Q **Scholarship**

German Museum, Munich, opened.

R **Philosophy and Religion**

G. E. Moore, *Principia Ethica.*
Royal Commission on Ecclesiastical Discipline in England.
Johannes Haller, *The Papacy and Church Reform.*
Carl Munth founds Roman Catholic periodical *Hochland.*

S **Art, Sculpture, Fine Arts and Architecture**

Painting:
P. W. Steer, *Richmond Castle.*
L. Alma-Tadema, *Silver-favorites.*
National Art Collections Fund formed to prevent works of art leaving Britain.
Architecture:
J. F. Bentley, Westminster Cathedral (Campanile 273 ft.).
Giles Gilbert Scott, Liverpool Cathedral begun.
New York Chamber of Commerce and Stock Exchange built.

T **Music**

Eugène D'Albert, *Tiefland* (opera).
F. Delius, *Sea Drift.*

U **Literature**

S. Butler, *The Way of All Flesh* (posth.).
G. R. Gissing, *The Private Papers of Henry Rycroft.*
Hugo von Hofmannsthal, *Electra.*
Henry James, *The Ambassadors.*

V **The Press**

B. Croce founds *La Critica.*

W **Drama and Entertainment**

Oscar Hammerstein builds Drury Lane Theatre, New York (later the Manhattan Opera House).
Arthur Schnitzler, *Reigen.*
G. B. Shaw, *Man and Superman.*

L Nov: 3rd, fearing U.S. would choose alternative canal route if Colombia delayed further, a group of Colombians proclaims independence of Panama;

17th, by treaty of Petropolis Bolivia cedes territory to Brazil in return for rail and water outlet to the east;

Commission in Transvaal favours immigrant Chinese labour for Rand mines, which is later sanctioned by Arthur Balfour;

At London Congress the Russian Social Democratic Party splits into Menshevists, led by G. V. Plecharoff, and Bolshevists, led by N. Lenin and Lev Trotsky.

M Dec: 18th, U.S.-Panama treaty places Canal Zone in U.S. hands in perpetuity for annual rent.

N In U.S. regulation of child labour is introduced, and Elkins Act strengthens Interstate Commerce Act, 1887, by requiring railways to keep to published charges.

Foundation of Union of Liberation in Russia, supported by members of the professions, aiming at a liberal constitution.

New Zealand tariff favours British goods.

x Sport

y Statistics

Naval strength (numbers of battleships in service): Great Britain, 67; France, 39; U.S., 27; Germany, 27; Italy, 18; Russia, 18; Japan, 5.

Petroleum production (in mill. barrels): U.S., 88·7 (being 49% of world production); Russia, 80·5.

z Births and Deaths

Feb. 22nd Hugo Wolf d. (43).
May 12th Lennox Berkeley b. (–).
July 17th James Whistler d. (70).
Aug. 7th Louis Leakey b. (–).
Aug. 22nd Robert Cecil, third Marquess of Salisbury d. (73).
Oct. 22nd W. E. H. Lecky d. (87).
Oct. 28th Evelyn Waugh b. (1966).
Nov. 1st Theodor Mommsen d. (87).
Dec. 8th Herbert Spencer d. (83).
Dec. 13th John Piper b. (–).
— Paul Gauguin d. (55).
— Camille Pissarro d. (72).

1904 (Jan.–Nov.) Russo-Japanese War

A **Jan:**

B **Feb:** 4th, outbreak of Russo-Japanese War. Japan begins siege of Port Arthur and soon occupies Seoul, forcing Korea to annul her concessions to Russia.

C **Mar:** 8th, German anti-Jesuit law, 1872, revised to permit the return of individual members of the order;
11th, army bill is passed in Hungary, despite Magyar obstruction, through using guillotine;
14th, judgment in U.S. Northern Securities case declares attempted mergers of railway interests as violation of anti-Trust Act.

D **Apr:** 8th, *Entente Cordiale* settles Anglo-French differences in Morocco, Egypt and Newfoundland fishery, and Britain recognises Suez Canal Convention and surrenders claim to Madagascar;
23rd, U.S. acquires property of French Panama Canal company;
24th (–27th), visit of Émile Loubet and Théophile Delcassé to Victor Emmanuel III annoys Papacy.

E **May:** 17th, French ambassador at Vatican is recalled;
30th, Japanese occupy Dalny (Dairen), Russia.

F **Jun:**

G **Jul:** 28th, assassination of Viacheslav Plehve, Russian minister of interior;
28th, Germany signs commercial treaties with Belgium, Switzerland, Sweden and Austria-Hungary;
Rafael Reyes becomes dictator in Colombia and attempts to reorganise finances.

H **Aug:** 10th, Japanese cripple Russian fleet off Port Arthur;
11th, alteration to the drink licensing laws in Britain generates controversy but fails to deal with problem of drunkenness;
26th (–*Sept.* 3rd), Japanese defeat Russians at Liaoyang, China.

J **Sep:** 7th, on expedition to Lhasa, Francis Younghusband signs treaty with Tibet by which the Dalai Lama will not concede territory to a foreign power;
General strike in Italy, culminating in violent incidents in Milan.

K **Oct:** 3rd, Insurrection of Hereros and Hottentots in German South-West Africa (–1908);
3rd, Franco-Spanish treaty for preserving independence of Morocco, with secret clauses aiming at ultimate partition;
20th, Bolivia and Chile settle differences by treaty;
21st, Russian fleet, bound for the Far East, fires on British trawlers in Dogger Bank area of North Sea, provokes
23rd, wave of indignation in Britain, but Arthur Balfour and Lord Lansdowne remain cool and
28th, Tsar Nicholas II agrees to refer question of compensation to Hague international commission;
In Italian elections the Socialists, discredited by strike action, lose heavily.

L **Nov:** 8th, Theodore Roosevelt (Republican, with 335 electoral votes wins U.S. presidential election against Alton B. Parker (Democrat, with 133 votes);
18th, Émile Combes introduces bill for separation of Church and State in France, ending the 1801 Concordat (promulgated *Dec.* 1905);

O **Politics, Economics, Law and Education**

L. T. Hobhouse, *Democracy and Reaction.*
Workers' Educational Association founded by Albert Mansbridge.
Ten-hour day in France.
Protectionist tariff in Canada.
Paris Conference on White Slave Trade.

P **Science, Technology, Discovery, etc.**

Ernest Rutherford and F. Soddy state general theory of radioactivity.
J. P. L. T. Elster devises photo-electric cell.
An ultra-violet lamp is made.
Safety razor blades.
Work on Panama Canal begins (*May* 4th).
New York, Broadway Subway open, with electric trains from City Hall.
Rolls-Royce is founded.

Q **Scholarship**

Henry Adams, *Mont St. Michel and Chartres.*

R **Philosophy and Religion**

S **Art, Sculpture, Fine Arts and Architecture**

Painting:
Frank Brangwyn paints decorative panel in Skinners' Company Hall, London.
Max Beerbohm, 'Poets Corner' (drawings of literary men).
P. Cézanne, *Mont Sainte Victoire.*
William Nicholson's sets for first production of Barrie's *Peter Pan.*
Henri Rousseau, *The Wedding.*
Architecture:
C. R. Mackintosh, The Willow Tea Rooms, Glasgow.

T **Music**

F. Delius, *Koanga* (opera).
G. Puccini, *Madame Butterfly* (opera).

U **Literature**

G. K. Chesterton, *The Napoleon of Notting Hill.*
J. Conrad, *Nostromo.*
W. H. Hudson, *Green Mansions.*
M. R. James, *Ghost Stories of an Antiquary.*
Jack London, *Sea Wolf.*
R. Rolland, *Jean-Christophe* (–12).

V **The Press**

Alfred Harmsworth founds *The Daily Mirror.*

W **Drama and Entertainment**

J. M. Barrie, *Peter Pan.*
A. Chekhov, *The Cherry Orchard.*
T. Hardy, *The Dynasts.*
Luigi Pirandello, *Il fu Mattia Pascal.*
J. M. Synge, *Riders to the Sea.*
Abbey Theatre, Dublin founded.
First J. E. Vedrenne-Granville-Barker season at Court Theatre, London.

L Nov: 23rd, German-Russian negotiations for an alliance break down through Russia's unwillingness to sign before consulting France;
Zemstvo Congress at St. Petersburg demands a republican constitution and civil liberties.

M Dec: 10th, nationalist, anti-Austrian ministry takes office in Serbia.

N Reorganisation of French possessions as French West Africa, with capital at Dakar.
Canadian protectionist tariff.

x **Sport**

The American Walter J. Travis wins British amateur golf championship.

y **Statistics**

In U.S. two-fifths of manufacturing capital is contributed by 'trusts'.

z **Births and Deaths**

Jan. 9th George Melitonovich Balanchine b. (–).
Jan. 17th Henry Keppel d. (95).
Feb. 22nd Leslie Stephen d. (72).
Apr. 16th Samuel Smiles d. (92).
May 1st Anton Dvořák d. (62).
May 10th H. M. Stanley d. (63).
July 1st G. F. Watts d. (87).
July 2nd Anton Chekhov d. (44).
July 14th S. J. P. Kruger d. (79).
July 27th Anton Dolin b. (–).
Aug. 7th Ralph Bunche b. (–).
Aug. 26th Christopher Isherwood b. (–).
Oct. 2nd Graham Greene b. (–).
Dec. 27th Marlene Dietrich b. (–).
— Alexei Nikolaevich Kosygin b. (–).

1905 (Jan.–Oct.) Abortive revolution in Russia—Moroccan Crisis

A **Jan**: 1st, Russians surrender Port Arthur to Japanese;
22nd, 'Bloody Sunday' in St. Petersburg when workers in revolt are fired upon;
Louis Botha forms *Het Volk* organisation to agitate for responsible government in Transvaal.

B **Feb**: Insurrection in Welle District of Belgian Congo.

C **Mar**: 1st (–9th), Japanese defeat Russians at Mukden;
3rd, Tsar Nicholas II promises to undertake religious and other reforms and to call a consultative assembly;
21st, Anglo-Persian agreement to counter Russian designs in the Near East;
30th, Greeks in Crete revolt against Turkish rule;
31st, Kaiser William II's visit to Tangier sets off first Moroccan crisis.

D **Apr**: 25th, Transvaal is granted a constitution which Louis Botha regards as inadequate;
30th, Anglo-French military conversations.

E **May**: 1st (–5th), Maurice Rouvier, French premier, fails to settle Moroccan question with Germany;
8th, Union of Unions in Russia, under Paul Miliukov, combines various liberal elements demanding parliamentary institutions;
17th, Britain proposes full discussions on Morocco;
27th, Japanese annihilate Russian fleet in Tsushima Straits.

F **Jun**: 6th, Théophile Delcassé, French foreign minister since 1898, resigns under pressure from Germany;
7th, Norwegian Storting decides on separation from Sweden (ratified by plebiscite, *Aug.*).

G **Jul**: 8th, France, assured of U.S. support against unreasonable demands by Germany, agrees to a conference on Morocco;
23rd (–4th), William II and Nicholas II sign treaty of Björkö, for mutual aid in Europe (Prince von Bülow objects to the limitation to Europe and threatens to resign);
Chinese boycott U.S. goods.

H **Aug**: 12th, Anglo-Japanese alliance is renewed for ten years;
19th, Tsar Nicholas II creates an Imperial Duma, elected on limited franchise, and with only deliberative powers.

J **Sep**: 1st, Provinces of Alberta and Saskatchewan formed in Canada;
5th, by treaty of Portsmouth, mediated by Theodore Roosevelt, Russia cedes Port Arthur and Talienwan to Japan and recognises Japan's interests in Korea, but Japan fails to obtain an indemnity;
24th, Sweden acquiesces in Norway's independence;
28th, France and Germany agree to call a conference on Morocco.

K **Oct**: 20th (–30th), general strike in Russia;
26th, workers in St. Petersburg form first Soviet; mutiny on battleship *Potemkin*;
—, by Treaty of Separation between Norway and Sweden, Oscar II abdicates Norwegian crown;
30th, by 'October Manifesto' the Tsar capitulates to demands for the Duma to have legislative powers, a wider franchise for its election and civil liberties.

O **Politics, Economics, Law and Education**

N. Lenin (pseud.), *Two Tactics*.
New York state investigates insurance houses following charges of corrupt practices.
International Agricultural Institute founded in Rome.
Automobile Association, London, founded.

P **Science, Technology, Discovery, etc.**

Albert Einstein states his first theory of relativity.
Austin Motor Company founded.
First motor buses in London, where the Bakerloo and Piccadilly undergrounds are opened.
Neon signs are first displayed.

Q **Scholarship**

R **Philosophy and Religion**

Wilhelm Dilthey, *Experience and Poetry*.
G. Santayana, *Life of Reason*.
S. Freud, *Three Treatises on the Theory of Sex*.
Baptist World Alliance founded in London.

S **Art, Sculpture, Fine Arts and Architecture**

Painting:
P. Cézanne, *Les Grandes Baigneuses*.
Louis Vauxcelles coins the name 'Les Fauves' (Wild Beasts) for the group of French artists led by Henri Matisse.
Die Brücke ('The Bridge') group of artists is formed in Dresden by Ernst Kirchner to revive interest in the graphic arts (–13).
H. Matisse, *La Joie de Vivre*.
Pablo Picasso, *Boy With Pipe*.
Henri Rousseau, *The Hungry Lion*.
J. S. Sarjent, *The Marlborough Family*.

Sculpture:
Thomas Brock, memorial to Queen Victoria, outside Buckingham Palace; the posts and pedestal by Aston Webb.
W. Holman Hunt, *Pre-Raphaelitism*.

Architecture:
Flagg, Singer Building, New York (–08).
Antoni Gaudi, Casa Milà, Barcelona (–10).

T **Music**

C. Debussy, *La Mer*.
F. Delius, *A Mass of Life*.
F. Léhar, *The Merry Widow* (operetta).
R. Strauss, *Salome* (opera).
L. A. Coerne's *Zenobia*, first European production of an American opera.
A. Schweitzer, *J. S. Bach, the Musician Poet*.

U **Literature**

A. Strindberg, *Historical Miniatures*.
H. G. Wells, *Kipps*.
Edith Wharton, *House of Mirth*.
Oscar Wilde, *De Profundis*.

L Nov: 16th, Count Sergei Witte appointed premier of Russia;
18th, Prince Charles of Denmark is elected King Haakon VII of Norway;
—, Japanese exercise protectorate over Korea;
25th, Lord Rosebery attacks Henry Campbell-Bannerman's idea of Irish Home Rule, but Liberals close ranks;
28th, Sinn Fein party is founded in Dublin;
Report of Commission of Inquiry into Congo atrocities excuses Leopold II.

M Dec: 4th, Arthur Balfour resigns and, 5th, Henry Campbell-Bannerman forms Liberal ministry with Edward Grey foreign secretary, Herbert Asquith as chancellor of exchequer and R. B. Haldane as war secretary;
9th, separation of Church and State in France (as established by the 1801 Concordat); complete liberty of conscience;
12th, Tsar Nicholas II grants constitution in Montenegro;
22nd, insurrection of Moscow workers (–*Jan.* 1st 1906);
Revolution in Persia begins.

N Deterioration of Roumanian-Greek relations over Macedonian problem (–1911).
Serbia's tariff war with Austria (–1907).
Sun Yat-sen organises a union of secret societies to expel the Manchus from China.
Moslem rising in German East Africa.

v **The Press**

w **Drama and Entertainment**

Tristram Bernard, *Triplepatte.*

H. von Hofmannsthal, *Das gerettete Venedig.*

A five-cent cinema in Pittsburg shows *The Great Train Robbery.*

x **Sport**

y **Statistics**

Religious denominations (in thousands):

(a) *Britain:* Roman Catholics, 5,800; Church of England, 2,450; Presbyterian Church of Scotland, 1,170; Wesleyan Methodists, 521; Primitive Methodists, 212; Congregationalists, 498; Baptists, 426; Presbyterians, 80; Unitarians, 75; Episcopal Church of Scotland, 50; Quakers, 18; Jews, 240.

(b) *U.S.:* Roman Catholics, 12,079; Baptists, 6,166; Episcopal Methodists, 6,305; Congregational Methodists, 296; Presbyterians, 1,830; Mormons, 350; Unitarians, 90; Quakers, 90; Jews, 177.

U.K. total State expenditure: £149·5 mill.

Convictions for drunkenness in U.K.: 207,171.

z **Births and Deaths**

Jan. 2nd Michael Tippett b. (–).
Feb. 9th Adolf Menzel d. (89).
Apr. 2nd Serge Lifar b. (–).
July 1st John Hay d. (67).
Sept. 5th Arthur Koestler b. (–).
Sept. 18th Greta Garbo b. (–).
Oct. 13th Henry Irving d. (67).
Oct. 15th C. P. Snow b. (–).
Nov. 25th Patrick Devlin b. (–).
Dec. 9th Richard Jebb d. (64).
— Dag Hammarskjöld b. (–1961).

1906 (Jan.–Nov.) Liberals' landslide in Britain

A **Jan**: 1st, Helmuth von Moltke becomes chief of German general staff;
10th, Anglo-French military and naval conversations;
12th, Liberal landslide in British general election (Liberals, 377 seats, with majority of 84 over all parties; Unionists, 157; Irish Nationalists, 83; Labour, 53); Henry Campbell-Bannerman's cabinet embark on sweeping social reforms;
16th, Algeciras conference on Morocco opens (*–Apr.*);
17th, Clément Fallières elected President of France, through Georges Clemenceau's influence;
Viscount Katsura, premier of Japan, resigns.

B **Feb**: 24th, Liberal revolt in Cuba on President Tomás Palma's re-election; Theodore Roosevelt intervenes to establish a provisional government which will carry out reforms.

C **Mar**: 16th, nationalisation of Japanese railways.

D **Apr**: 5th, Count Friedrich Holstein's dismissal by William II ends fear of German war with France over Morocco;
8th, Algeciras Act signed, giving France and Spain chief control in Morocco.

E **May**: 5th, fall of Count Witte in Russia, who is succeeded by the Conservative Ivan Goremykin;
6th, Fundamental Laws promulgated in Russia;
7th, Alaska allowed to elect a delegate to U.S. Congress;
9th, Chinese decide to take over administration of Imperial Customs Service (of which Robert Hart inspector-general since 1863);
10th, first Duma meets in Russia (*–July* 21st), resulting in deadlock through the Cadets' Party's criticism of Fundamental Laws;
11th, Isvolsky becomes Russian foreign secretary;
19th, João Franco becomes premier of Spain with dictatorial powers;
30th, Giovanni Giolitti forms ministry in Italy (*–Dec.* 1909);
Turkey yields to British pressure over Egypt's frontier with Palestine.

F **Jun**: 5th, third German naval bill provides for increases in construction of battleships;
Peter Stolypin becomes premier of Russia.

G **Jul**: 4th, Britain, France and Italy guarantee the independence of Abyssinia;
12th, Alfred Dreyfus is rehabilitated;
21st, on dissolution of Duma the Cadets adjourn to Finland and issue Viborg Manifesto, calling on Russians to refuse paying taxes;
Universal suffrage bill introduced in Hungary.

H **Aug**: 15th, Edward VII's discussions with William II at Cronberg;
Anglo-Chinese convention on Tibet.

J **Sep**:

K **Oct**:

L **Nov**: 22nd, Peter Stolypin introduces agrarian reforms in Russia.

O **Politics, Economics, Law and Education**

British Patents Act secures greater protection for patentees, while Merchant Shipping Act restricts pilots' certificates to British subjects and reforms conditions in merchant navy.

School care committees established in Britain.

London *Daily News* stages Sweated Industries Exhibition to demand reforms.

Night shift work for women internationally forbidden.

Confederazione Generale de Lavoro founded in Italy.

U.S. Pure Food and Drugs Act passed, following revelations in Upton Sinclair's *Jungle* of conditions in Chicago stockyards, which prompted a federal investigation.

U.S. National Forests Commission established.

P **Science, Technology, Discovery, etc.**

J. J. Thomson undertakes work on gamma rays.

Arthur Harden and W. J. Young discover cases of catalysis among enzymes.

Automatic railway coupling first used.

Beginnings of Zuider Zee drainage scheme.

Simplon Tunnel (begun in 1898) is opened.

H.M.S. *Dreadnought* is launched.

Q **Scholarship**

Hugo Winckler leads archaeological expedition to North Cappadocia.

P. S. Allen, *Erasmi Epistolae* (–58).

W. S. Churchill, *Lord Randolph Churchill.*

R **Philosophy and Religion**

The English Hymnal (ed. Percy Dearmer and R. Vaughan Williams).

S **Art, Sculpture, Fine Arts and Architecture**

Painting:

A. Derain, *Port of London.*

G. Roualt, *At the Mirror.*

Sculpture:

Aristide Maillol, *Chained Action.*

Architecture:

Edwin Lutyens designs two churches and an institute for Hampstead Garden Suburb, founded by Henrietta Barnett.

T **Music**

Jules Massenet, *Ariane* (opera).

Ethel Smyth, *The Wreckers* (opera).

A Mozart Festival is held in Salzburg.

U **Literature**

A. Blackwood, *The Empty House.*

J. Galsworthy, *The Man of Property.*

P. Valéry, *Monsieur Teste.*

'Everyman's Library' begun.

V **The Press**

W **Drama and Entertainment**

P. Claudel, *Partage de Midi.*

A. W. Pinero, *His House in Order.*

M Dec: 6th, self-government is granted to Transvaal and Orange River Colonies;
13th, through revolt of Centre Party the Reichstag opposes expenses on colonial wars; von Bülow dissolves Reichstag and in subsequent elections the Socialists suffer losses;
Trades Disputes Act legitimises peaceful picketing in Britain.

N Crisis in French wine industry caused by declining prices.
Aga Khan founds All India Moslem League.
Utah becomes 45th state of U.S.

X Sport

Y Statistics

U.S. makes 23,000 motor vehicles (more than France) and produces 124·4 mill. barrels of petroleum.

Populations (in mill.): China, 438; Russia, 149·2; U.S., 85; Germany, 62; Great Britain, 38·9; Ireland, 4·3; France, 39·2.

Populations of cities (in mill.): London, 4·5; New York, 4; Paris, 2·7; Berlin, 2; Tokio, 1·9; St. Petersburg, 1·4; Vienna, 1·3.

Army strengths (in mill.): Russia, 13; Germany, 7·9; Austro-Hungary, 7·4; France, 4·8; Italy, 3·1; Great Britain, 0·8, with 0·4 from colonial forces.

Z Births and Deaths

Apr. 9th Hugh Gaitskell b. (–1963).
Apr. 19th Pierre Curie d. (46).
May 23rd Henrik Ibsen d. (78).
June 29th Albert Sorel d. (64).
Sept. 25th Dimitry Shostakovich b. (–).
Dec. 19th F. W. Maitland d. (56).
Dec. 30th Josephine Butler d. (78).
— Samuel Beckett b. (–).
— Paul Cézanne d. (67).

A **Jan**: 10th, universal direct suffrage in Austria.

B **Feb**: war between Honduras and Nicaragua (*–Dec.*).

C **Mar**: 5th, Second Duma meets in Russia (*–June* 16th);
Roumanian army puts down Moldavian revolt with brutality.

D **Apr**: 8th, Anglo-French convention confirms independence of Siam;
30th, Edward VII visits Rome.

E **May**: 2nd, Edward VII visits President Fallières in Paris;
14th, Imperial Conference, London;
—, Sweden adopts proportional representation for elections to both chambers and manhood suffrage for Second Chamber;
16th, Pact of Cartagena between Britain, France and Spain to counter German designs on Balearic and Canary Islands;
23rd, legislative council is erected in Mozambique.

F **Jun**: 10th, Franco-Japanese agreement to preserve 'open door' in China;
14th, female suffrage in Norway;
15th (*–Oct.* 18th), Peace Conference at the Hague, originally called at Theodore Roosevelt's suggestion in 1904, but postponed owing to war in Far East, reassembles; attempt at stopping the arms race fails, but progress is made in direction of voluntary arbitration of disputes, despite German opposition;
16th, reactionary party in Russia forces Tsar Nicholas II to dissolve the Second Duma; an electoral edict increases representation of propertied classes and reduces representation of national minorities;
26th, Commons pass Henry Campbell-Bannerman's resolution that the power of the Lords to prevent passage of bills must be restricted.

G **Jul**: 1st, revised constitution for Orange River Colony;
19th, Emperor of Korea abdicates and
25th, Japan obtains protectorate over Korea;
30th, Russo-Japanese agreement over China;
—, elections for first assembly in Philippines;
Triple alliance between Germany, Austria and Italy is renewed for six years, despite the coolness of Italy.

H **Aug**: 3rd, Kaiser William II and Tsar Nicholas II meet at Swinemünde to discuss Baghdad Railway;
4th, French fleet bombards Casablanca following anti-foreign outbreaks;
31st, Anglo-Russian Convention on Persia, Afghanistan and Tibet is signed, aligning Russia with Britain and France against the Central Powers.

J **Sep**: 5th, Edward VII meets Alexander Izvolski, Russian foreign minister, at Marienbad;
21st, risings in German South-West Africa suppressed.

K **Oct**:

L **Nov**: 14th, the Third Duma meets in Russia (–1912), elected on a restricted franchise: leads to the suppression of revolutionary outbreaks;
16th, Oklahoma is admitted as a U.S. state.

O Politics, Economics, Law and Education

First British census of production.
Medical inspection of school children in Britain.
R. Baden-Powell founds Boy Scouts.
U.S. restricts immigration.
Henry Deterding founds Royal Dutch Shell Group.

P Science, Technology, Discovery, etc.

C. Pirquet's method for diagnosing tuberculosis.
Alexis Pavlov studies conditional reflexes.
C. Ross Harrison develops tissue culture techniques.
Emil Fischer, *Researches on the Chemistry of Proteins.*
Richard Anschütz and Max Schuler perfect the gyro-compass.
A. Lumière's improved process for colour reproduction through auto-chrome plates.
Leo Bäkeland invents Bakelite.
S.S. *Lusitania* and *Mauritania* launched.

Q Scholarship

Henry Adams, *The Education of Henry Adams: a study of XXth Century Multiplicity* (privately printed).
Maurice Bloomfield, *Vedic Concordance.*
Cambridge History of English Literature (–27).

R Philosophy and Religion

H. Bergson, *L'Évolution créatrice.*
W. James, *Pragmatism.*
C. Gore, *The New Theology and the Old Religion.*
Pius X condemns modernism in encyclical *Pascendi gregis.*

S Art, Sculpture, Fine Arts and Architecture

Painting:
Exhibition of Cubist paintings, Paris.
A. Derain, *Blackfriars Bridge* and *The Bathers.*
P. Picasso, *Les Demoiselles d'Avignon.*
H. Matisse, *Luxe, Calme et Volupté.*
E. Munch, *Amor and Psyche.*
H. Rousseau, *The Snake Charmer.*
National League of Handicrafts Societies leads to extension of 'arts and crafts' movement in U.S.
Architecture:
Edward Mountford, New Central Criminal Court, London.

T Music

F. Delius, *A Village Romeo and Juliet* (opera) and *Brigg Fair* (rhapsody).
P. Dukas, *Ariadne and Bluebeard* (opera).
E. Elgar, March '*Pomp and Circumstance*' no. 4 in G (op. 39).
M. Ravel, *Spanish Rhapsody.*
R. Strauss, *Elektra* (opera).
R. Vaughan Williams, *Towards the Unknown Region.*

U Literature

J. Conrad, *Secret Agent.*
M. Gorki, *Mother.*
R. M. Rilke, *Neue Gedichte* (–08).
F. Wedekind, *Such is Life.*

1907 (Dec.)

M **Dec:** 6th, frontier between Uganda and East Africa is defined;
7th, first Nationalist Congress in Egypt under Mustapha Kemel;
8th, on Oskar II's death, Gustavus V succeeds as King of Sweden (–1950).

N Nicolai Lenin (pseud.) leaves Russia.

V The Press

W Drama and Entertainment

G. B. Shaw, *Major Barbara*.

J. M. Synge, *Playboy of the Western World*.

Julius Caesar and *The Tunnel Under the Canal* (films).

X Sport

Y Statistics

Railway mileage in operation (in thousand miles): U.S., 236·9; Russia, 44·6; Germany, 36; India, 29·8; France, 29·7; Austro-Hungary, 25·8; Great Britain and Ireland, 23·1; Canada, 22·4.

Z Births and Deaths

Feb. 2nd Dmitry Mendeléev d. (73).
Feb. 21st W. H. Auden b. (–).
May 12th J. K. Huysmans d. (59).
June 1st Frank Whittle b. (–).
Aug. 1st Eric Shipton b. (–).
Aug. 13th Basil Spence b. (–).
Aug. 15th Joseph Joachim d. (76).
Sept. 4th Edvard Grieg d. (64).
Sept. 6th Sully Prudhomme d. (67).
Sept. 12th Louis Macneice b. (–1964).
Nov. 28th Alberto Moravia b. (–).
Dec. 16th Francis Thompson d. (47).
Dec. 17th William Thomson, Lord Kelvin, d. (84).
Dec. 18th Christopher Fry b. (–).

1908 (Jan.–Nov.) Anglo-German tension—Austria annexes Bosnia and Herzegovina

A **Jan**: 4th, Mulai Hafid is proclaimed Sultan of Morocco at Fez;
27th, Count Alois Aehrenthal, Austrian foreign minister, announces the Austrian government will build railway towards Salonika.

B **Feb**: 1st, King Carlos I of Portugal and the Crown Prince are murdered in Lisbon and Manuel II becomes King (–1910).

C **Mar**:

D **Apr**: 8th, H. H. Asquith becomes British prime minister on Henry Campbell-Bannerman's resignation through ill health and David Lloyd George becomes chancellor of exchequer.

E **May**: Labour government in Australia under Andrew Fisher.

F **Jun**: 9th, Edward VII meets Nicholas II at Reval and the Tsar agrees to introduce extensive reforms in Macedonia;
14th, fourth German navy bill authorises expenditure on four further capital ships;
23rd, Shah Mohammed Ali overthrows Persian constitution of *Dec.* 1906;
—, U.S. severs diplomatic relations with Venezuela on Cipriano Castro's refusal to compensate U.S. citizens for injuries.

G **Jul**: 6th, Young Turks under Niazi Bey stage revolt at Resina in Macedonia, the government troops sent to quell them desert and, 24th, Sultan Abdul Hamid II restores the constitution of 1876;
Pan Slav Conference in Prague.

H **Aug**: 20th, Leopold II hands over Congo to Belgium (confirmed by act of Belgian Parliament, *Oct.* 18th);
23rd, Baltic Convention between Germany, Sweden, Denmark and Russia, and North Sea Convention between Britain, Germany, Denmark, France and the Netherlands to maintain the *status quo* on the shores of the two seas;
—, Abdul Aziz of Morocco is defeated at Marrakesh by Mulai Hafid, the new Sultan.

J **Sep**: 13th, German Social Democrat rally at Nuremberg;
16th, Buchlau conference between Count Aehrenthal and Alexander Izvolski, at which Austria undertakes not to oppose opening of the Straits to Russian warships and Russia agrees to Austrian annexation of Bosnia and Herzegovina;
25th, Casablanca incident, when German deserters from the French Foreign Legion are taken by force from a German consular official.

K **Oct**: 5th, Declaration of Independence of Bulgaria by Ferdinand I, who assumes the title of Tsar of Bulgaria;
6th, Austria annexes Bosnia and Herzegovina by decree;
7th, Crete proclaims union with Greece;
12th, South Africa constitutional convention meets at Durban, later removes to Capetown (–*Feb.* 1909), agreeing on a Union of South Africa;
28th, *Daily Telegraph* publishes interview with Kaiser William II in which he states the German people are hostile to Britain while he is a friend.

L **Nov**: 3rd, in U.S. presidential election William Howard Taft, Republican, with 321 electoral votes, defeats William Jennings Bryan, Democrat, with 162 votes;
9th, Alexander Izvolski, Russian foreign minister, visits London;

O **Politics, Economics, Law and Education**

F. Meinecke, *Cosmopolitanism and the National State.*
G. Sorel, *Reflections on Violence.*
Graham Wallas, *Human Nature in Politics.*
Port of London Authority established.
Berlin Copyright Convention.
Labour insurance in Russia.
Britain prohibits the manufacture and importation of phosphorus matches.

P **Science, Technology, Discovery, etc.**

Hermann Minkowski elaborates four-dimensional geometry, the mathematics of relativity.
Fritz Haber synthesises ammonia.
Two further subway lines opened in New York.

Q **Scholarship**

R **Philosophy and Religion**

Federal Council of Churches founded in U.S.

S **Art, Sculpture, Fine Arts and Architecture**

Painting:
Marc Chagall, *Nu Rouge.*
Maurice Vlaminck, *The Red Trees.*
Augustus John, *The Lord Mayor of Liverpool.*
C. Monet, *The Ducal Palace, Venice.*
Pierre Bonnard, *Nude against the Light.*
Maurice Utrillo's 'White Period' (–1914).

Sculpture:
Jacob Epstein, 'Figures', for the British Medical Association, The Strand, causes a furore of indignation.
Constantin Brancusi, *The Kiss.*

Architecture:
Peter Behrens, A.E.G. Turbine Factory, Berlin (first building of steel and glass).

T **Music**

B. Bartók, first string quartet.
E. Elgar, Symphony no. 1 in A flat (op. 55).

U **Literature**

A. Bennett, *The Old Wives' Tale.*
G. K. Chesterton, *The Man Who Was Thursday.*
Colette (pseud.), *La Retraite Sentimentale.*
W. H. Davies, *Autobiography of a Super Tramp.*
E. M. Forster, *A Room With a View.*
A. France (pseud.), *L'Île des pingouins.*
K. Grahame, *The Wind in the Willows.*

V **The Press**

Lord Northcliffe buys *The Times.*
J. L. Garvin edits *The Observer* (–42).
Ford Madox Ford founds *English Review.*

L Nov: 10th (–11th), Reichstag debate on *Daily Telegraph* interview further embitters Anglo-German relations;
14th, Liberal victory in Cuban elections leads to José Gómez's presidency (–1913).

M Dec: 2nd, revolt in Bohemia;
4th, abortive London naval conference of the powers to regulate conditions of warfare;
9th, regulation of hours of factory work for women and young persons in Germany;
17th, first meeting of Ottoman Parliament with large Young Turk majority;
28th, disastrous earthquake in South Calabria and Sicily.

N

w **Drama and Entertainment**

The Tiller Girls dance on the London Stage.

x **Sport**

Olympic Games held in London.
Jack Johnson becomes the first negro world boxing champion.

y **Statistics**

z **Births and Deaths**

Jan. 9th Simone de Beauvoir b. (–).
Jan. 25th 'Ouida' (Louise de la Ramée) d. (67).
Feb. 11th Vivian Fuchs b. (–).
Mar. 11th Edmondo de Amicis d. (61).
Apr. 22nd Henry Campbell-Bannerman d. (72).
May 28th Ian Fleming b. (–1964).
June 20th Nicolai Rimsky-Korsakov d. (63).
June 24th Stephen Grover Cleveland d. (71).
July 6th Joel Chandler Harris ('Uncle Remus') d. (60).
July 8th Nelson Rockefeller b. (–).
Aug. 25th Henri Becquerel d. (56).
Aug. 27th Donald Bradman b. (–) and Lyndon Baines Johnson b. (–).

1909 (Jan.–Nov.) Lords reject Lloyd George's budget

A **Jan**: 1st, Old-age pensions payable to all British subjects over 70;
2nd, dismissal of Yüan Shih-kai places Chinese administration in Manchu hands;
Anglo-Persian Oil Co. formed.

B **Feb**: 9th, Germany recognises France's special interests in Morocco in return for economic concessions;
13th, Kiamil Pasha, Grand Vizier of Turkey, forced to resign by the Turkish nationalists;
21st, Ferdinand I of Bulgaria visits Russia to obtain financial aid;
26th, Turkey recognises Austria's annexation of Bosnia and is paid compensation.

C **Mar**: 2nd, the powers intervene to prevent a Serbo-Austrian war;
4th, W. H. Taft inaugurated as President of U.S. (–1913);
12th, British alarm at growth of German navy leads to passage of naval bill;
25th, press censorship imposed in Egypt to control Nationalists;
31st, Serbia yields to Austria in Bosnian dispute.

D **Apr**: 13th, army counter-revolution in Constantinople against rule of Mohammedan Union;
19th, Turkey recognises Bulgarian independence;
24th, army of liberation captures Constantinople from rebels and, 27th, Young Turks depose Sultan Abdul Hamid who is succeeded by Mohammed V (–1918);
Strike of Paris postal workers (*–May*).

E **May**: 25th, Indian Councils Act gives greater powers to legislative councils, whose members are mostly directly elective, and ensures appointment of an Indian to the Viceroy's executive council.

F **Jun**:

G **Jul**: 14th, Theobald von Bethmann-Hollweg becomes German chancellor on Bernhard von Bülow's resignation;
15th, Mahommed Ali, Shah of Persia, deposed in favour of Sultan Ahmad Shah, aged 12;
24th, on Georges Clemenceau's resignation, Aristide Briand forms ministry in France;
26th, general strike in Barcelona with rioting throughout Catalonia (*–Sept.* 26th).

H **Aug**: 5th, Payne-Aldrich tariff in U.S. maintains protection, despite party pledges.

J **Sep**:

K **Oct**: 13th, Francisco Ferrer Guardia, leader of militant anti-clericals in Spain, executed;
21st, Liberal ministry in Spain;
24th, Russia and Italy sign Racconigi agreement for preserving *status quo* in Balkans;
25th, murder of Prince Ito of Japan by a Korean fanatic, leads to Japanese dictatorship in Korea.

L **Nov**: 5th, Commons pass D. Lloyd George's budget but, 30th, it is rejected by Lords.
Anglo-German conversations on control of Baghdad Railway (*–Dec.*).

O **Politics, Economics, Law and Education**

N. Lenin (pseud.), *Materialism and Empiric Criticism.*

William Beveridge, *Unemployment.*

Trade Boards Act ends 'sweating' in British industry.

Women are admitted to German universities.

Girl Guides founded in Britain.

Political action branch of Industrial Workers of the World is founded at Detroit.

House of Lords upholds Osborne Judgment (*Dec.* 2nd), making compulsory levies by trades unions for party political purposes illegal.

P **Science, Technology, Discovery, etc.**

Paul Ehrlich prepares salvarsan as cure for syphilis.

T. H. Morgan begins research in genetics.

Karl Hofmann produces synthetic rubber from butadiene.

Henry Ford's 'Model T' car.

Louis Blériot crosses the English Channel by monoplane.

R. E. Peary reaches North Pole (*Apr.* 6th).

Q **Scholarship**

R **Philosophy and Religion**

H. Bergson, *Time and Freewill, Matter and Memory.*

S. Freud lectures in U.S. on psychoanalysis.

W. James, *A Pluralistic Universe.*

S **Art, Sculpture, Fine Arts and Architecture**

Painting:

H. Matisse, *The Dance.*

P. Bonnard, *Standing Nude.*

O. Kokoschka, *Princess Montesquieu-Rohan.*

A. John, *Robin.*

W. Orpen, *Hommage à Monet.*

H. Rousseau, *Flowers in a Vase.*

E. Munch, Mural for Oslo University (–11).

Filippo Marietti first uses the term 'Futurism'.

Sculpture:

Antoine Bourdelle, *Hercules the Archer.*

H. Matisse, *The Backs* (first of four 6-ft. reliefs –1930).

Architecture:

Frank Lloyd Wright, Robie House, Chicago.

T **Music**

Sergei Diaghilev produces his Russian ballet in Paris including M. Fokine's *Les Sylphides* (to Chopin's music).

G. Mahler, Symphony no. 9.

I. J. Paderewski directs the Warsaw Conservatory.

R. Vaughan Williams, *Fantasia on a Theme by Tallis.*

U **Literature**

G. Apollinaire (pseud.), *L'Enchanteur pourrissant.*

A. Gide, *La Porte Étroite.*

H. G. Wells, *Tono-Bungay.*

V **The Press**

Daily Sketch and *Nouvelle Revue Française* issued.

M Dec: 2nd, H. H. Asquith denounces Lords for breach of constitution over finance bill and obtains dissolution of Parliament;
—, Giovanni Giolitti is overthrown in Italy and Baron Sonnino forms a government;
17th, on Leopold II's death, Albert I succeeds as King of the Belgians (–1934);
19th, Juan Gómez seizes power in Venezuela;
Civil War in Honduras (–1911).

N Compulsory military service in Australia.

W **Drama and Entertainment**

M. Maeterlinck, *The Blue Bird*.
J. M. Synge, *Deirdre of the Sorrows*.
Birmingham Repertory Company founded.
D. W. Griffiths transforms child actress Gladys Smith into Mary Pickford.
Carmen (French film).
Cinematograph Licensing Act for controlling cinemas exhibiting films in Britain.

X **Sport**

Edward VII's *Minoru* wins the Derby.

Y **Statistics**

Jewish population (in thousands): Russia, 5,215; Austro-Hungary, 2,084; U.S., 1,777; Germany, 607; Turkish Empire, 463; Britain, 240; France, 95.
Coffee production (in mill. lb.): Brazil, 1,852; Venezuela, 96; Guatemala, 82; Colombia, 79; West Indies, 70; Mexico, 68.
Tea production (in mill. lb.): India, 254; China, 208; Ceylon, 182.

Z **Births and Deaths**

Jan. 1st Barry Goldwater b. (–).
Feb. 9th Dean Rusk b. (–).
Feb. 28th Stephen Spender b. (–).
Apr. 9th Robert Helpmann b. (–).
Apr. 10th Algernon Swinburne d. (72).
May 18th George Meredith d. (81).
June 24th William Penney b. (–).
Sept. 18th Kwame Nkrumah b. (–).

1910 (Jan.–Nov.) Union of South Africa becomes a dominion—Japan annexes Korea

A **Jan:** 15th, British general election on issues of D. Lloyd George's budget, the power of the Lords and Irish Home Rule, resulting in reduced Liberal majority (Liberals, 275 seats; Labour, 40; Irish Nationalists, 82; Unionists, 273);
15th, reorganisation of French Congo as French Equatorial Africa;
Military League forces Greek assembly to refuse constitution.

B **Feb:** 10th, Swedish constitution is revised;
20th, Butros Ghali, premier of Egypt, who is a Copt, is assassinated by Nationalist fanatic.

C **Mar:** 19th, Republicans attempt to reduce power of Speaker of U.S. House of Representatives;
Luigi Luzzatti succeeds Baron Sonnino as Italian premier.

D **Apr:** 27th, Louis Botha and James Hertzog found South African party;
28th, British finance bill is finally passed;
Albanian revolt is suppressed by Turkish army.

E **May:** 6th, accession of George V on death of Edward VII (–1936);
10th, British House of Commons resolves that the Lords should have no power to veto money bills, and limited powers to postpone other bills and that the maximum lifetime of Parliament be reduced from seven to five years;
14th, Anglo-Belgian agreement assigns west shore of Lake Albert to Belgian Congo;
24th, L. Starr Jameson founds Unionist party in South Africa on imperialist platform;
26th, Pius X issues encyclical *Editio saepe*, which angers German Protestants;
27th, Prussian diet rejects reform of suffrage.

F **Jun:** 11th, Pius X, on representations by Prussia, stops circulation of encyclical of *May* 26th in Germany.

G **Jul:** 1st, Union of South Africa becomes a dominion;
4th, Russo-Japanese agreement on Manchuria and Korea.

H **Aug:** 22nd, Japan formally annexes Korea;
28th, Montenegro is proclaimed an independent kingdom under Nicholas I;
31st, Theodore Roosevelt propounds his concept of 'The New Nationalism';
Austro-Hungarian commercial treaty with Serbia.

J **Sep:** 7th, International Court of arbitration at The Hague settles Newfoundland fisheries question (referred to it in *Oct.* 1906);
15th, South African party wins first South African elections and Louis Botha becomes premier.

K **Oct:** 4th, King Manuel II of Portugal flees to England on outbreak of revolution in Lisbon and, 5th, Portugal is proclaimed a republic under Theophilo Braga;
10th, Aristide Briand calls out troops in French railway strike, a general strike is averted and, 18th, the railwaymen resume work;
18th, Eleutherios Venizelos becomes premier of Greece and begins financial reforms.

L **Nov:** 4th (–5th), Tsar Nicholas II with his new foreign minister, Sergei Sazonov, agrees with William II at Potsdam to cease opposition to the Baghdad Railway on condition that Russia is given a free hand in North Persia; (Britain is dismayed by Russia's negotiations with Germany on the railway question without consultation);
28th, H. H. Asquith again appeals to the electorate.

O **Politics, Economics, Law and Education**

First Labour Exchanges opened in Britain (*Feb.* 1st).

Development Commission instituted (*May*) to advise British Treasury on loans for developing agriculture and rural areas.

Irving Fisher, *National Vitality*.

The Industrial Syndecalist, ed. Tom Mann, runs for 10 issues.

International motor-car convention.

U.S. Postal Savings Bank established.

Season tickets are first issued on railways in Britain, which withdraw second class accommodation.

H. H. Crippen is hanged.

P **Science, Technology, Discovery, etc.**

Marie Curie, *Treatise on Radiography*.

Charles Parsons' speed-reducing gear extends use of geared turbines.

First roller bearings.

Mount Wilson 100-inch reflecting telescope completed.

Manhattan Bridge, New York, opened.

Germany's machine-tool industry overtakes Britain's.

Electrification of part of Magdeburg-Halle main-line railway.

Q **Scholarship**

Arthur Evans excavates Cnossos.

R **Philosophy and Religion**

B. Russell and A. W. Whitehead, *Principia Mathematica*.

A. Schweitzer, *The Quest of the Historical Jesus*.

E. Underhill, *Mysticism*.

S **Art, Sculpture, Fine Arts and Architecture**

Painting:

'Futurist Manifesto' signed by V. Boccioni, C. Carra, G. Balla and G. Severini.

Fernand Léger, *Nues dans le forêt*.

Amedeo Modigliani, *Cellist*.

Henri Rousseau, *Yadwiga's Dream*.

Roger Fry organises Post-Impressionist exhibition, London.

The Turner Wing at the Tate Gallery opened.

Exhibition of Islamic Art, Munich.

National Federation of Arts in U.S.

Architecture:

Max Berg, Jahrhunderthalle, Breslau (–12).

T **Music**

E. Elgar, violin concerto.

G. Puccini, *The Girl of the Golden West* (opera).

N. Rimsky-Korsakov, *The Golden Cockerel* (opera).

R. Vaughan Williams, *A Sea Symphony* (Symphony no. 1).

I. Stravinsky, *The Fire-bird* (ballet).

Thomas Beecham's first opera season at Covent Garden.

U **Literature**

A. Bennett, *Clayhanger*.

P. Claudel, *Cinq grandes odes*.

E. M. Forster, *Howard's End*.

H. Newbolt, *Songs of the Fleet*.

C. Péguy, *Le Mystère de la charité de Jeanne d'Arc*.

H. G. Wells, *The History of Mr. Polly*.

M Dec: in British general election Liberals win 272 seats; Labour, 42; Irish Nationalists, 84; Unionists, 272 (making a majority for a Parliament Bill and Home Rule 126, an increase of 4 since *Jan.*).

N Swiss railways are nationalised.
Royal Canadian Navy is formed.

V **The Press**

Lord Lothian founds *The Round Table.*

W **Drama and Entertainment**

Gerald du Maurier manages Wyndham's Theatre (–25).
A Child of the Ghetto (film).
Faust (film).
Messaline (film).
Lucretia Borgia (film).

X **Sport**

Jack Johnson's defeat of J. J. Jefferies in U.S. national boxing championship.

Y **Statistics**

Defence estimates (in £ mill.): Great Britain, 68; Germany, 64; Russia, 63; France, 52; Italy, 24; Austria-Hungary, 17.

Battleships in commission (and under construction): Great Britain, 56 (9); Germany, 33 (8); U.S., 30 (4); France, 17 (6); Japan, 14 (3); Italy, 10 (2); Russia, 7 (8).

Cotton production (in 500-lb. bales): U.S., 11·6 mill.; India, 3·8 mill.; Egypt, 1·5 mill.; China, 1·2 mill.

Wool production (in mill. lb.): Australia and New Zealand, 833; Argentina, 414; U.S., 321; Russia, 320; U.K., 141; Uruguay, 130.

Silk production (in mill. lb.): Japan, 19; China, 14; Italy, 8; Levant, 6; Austria, 0·7.

Telephones: 122,000 in use in Great Britain.

Z **Births and Deaths**

Apr. 21st. Mark Twain (Samuel Langhorne Clemens) d. (74).
June 7th Pietro Annigoni b. (–).
June 22nd John Hunt b. (–).
June 23rd Jean Anouilh b. (–).
Aug. 13th Florence Nightingale d. (90).
Aug. 27th William James d. (68).
Sept. 7th William Holman Hunt d. (83).
Oct. 17th Julia Ward Howe d. (91).
Nov. 10th Leo Tolstoy d. (82).
Dec. 4th Mary Baker Eddy d. (89).

1911 (Jan.–Jul.) Parliament Bill—Agadir Crisis—Chinese Republic proclaimed

A Jan: 7th, Carnegie Trust Co., New York, closed by state supervisor of banks;
17th, attempted assassination of Aristide Briand in French Chamber of Deputies;
20th, Ecuador refuses to submit her dispute with Peru to Hague Tribunal;
21st, National Progressive Republican League founded under Robert La Follette in U.S.;
25th, U.S. cavalry sent to preserve neutrality of Rio Grande in Mexican Civil War.

B Feb: 6th, British Labour Party elect Ramsay MacDonald chairman;
10th, Persia appoints W. Morgan Shuster to reorganise finances;
21st, U.S.-Japanese commercial treaty signed at Washington;
22nd, Canadian Parliament resolves to preserve union within British Empire, with control of own fiscal policy;
23rd, French Chamber of Deputies votes for building two battleships;
24th, Reichstag passes army bill;
27th, resignation of Aristide Briand's ministry;
28th, Andrew Fisher, Australian premier, plans to nationalise monopolies.

C Mar: 18th, Luzzatti resigns in Italy.

D Apr: 3rd, progress of Parliament bill accelerated by use of 'Kangaroo' clause;
3rd, Anglo-Japanese commercial treaty;
4th, U.S. Congress meets in extra-ordinary sessions to deal with Reciprocity agreement with Canada (ratified by Senate *July* 22nd);
11th, Jean-Jaurès announces scheme for socialist organisation of France;
13th, U.S. House of Representatives votes in favour of direct election of senators;
19th, Separation of Church and State in Portugal;
23rd (–7th), armistice in Mexican Civil War;
24th, Commons reject amendment to Parliament bill providing for referendum.

E May: 4th, D. Lloyd George introduces National Health Insurance bill;
8th, Lord Lansdowne introduces Unionist reconstruction of House of Lords bill in Lords;
15th, Commons passes Parliament Bill;
—, U.S. Supreme Court orders dissolution of Standard Oil Co.;
23rd, Russia warns Turkey to withdraw troops from Montenegro frontier;
—, H. H. Asquith opens Imperial Conference, London;
25th, Porfirio Diaz resigns presidency of Mexico;
26th, Reichstag grants Alsace-Lorraine its own legislature and large measure of autonomy.

F Jun: 8th, Birkbeck Bank, London, crashes;
11th, revised Greek constitution;
13th, reversal for Christian Socialists in Austrian election;
22nd, George V's coronation;
28th, Joseph Caillaux forms ministry in France;
—, Japanese sign commercial treaty with France.

G Jul: 1st, arrival of German gunboat *Panther* in Agadir creates international tension;
6th, Anglo-U.S. treaty for arbitration of disputes;
10th, Russia warns Germany of her support for France in Moroccan crisis;
13th, renewal of Anglo-Japanese alliance for four years;
24th, while Commons debate Lords amendments to Parliament Bill, H. H. Asquith is shouted down and Speaker adjourns the House;
26th, W. H. Taft signs Reciprocity bill with Canada.

O **Politics, Economics, Law and Education**

Copyright Act requires copies of all British publications to be given to the British Museum and five other 'copyright libraries'.

Shops Act introduces compulsory weekly half-day holidays for employees.

Coal Mines Act makes radical changes in control and management of British mines.

First British Official Secrets Act.

Investigation of alleged corruption in Ohio state reveals that a quarter of the electorate sold their votes.

A. Carnegie endows international peace foundation (*Dec.*).

Brussels Conference to control liquor supplies to backward countries.

P **Science, Technology, Discovery, etc.**

Ernest Rutherford and Frederick Soddy devise scheme for achieving the transmutation of elements.

Aeronautical map of France published.

Roald Amundsen reaches South Pole (*Dec.* 15th).

Buenos Aires to Valparaiso Railway completed.

Q **Scholarship**

British Museum's expedition to excavate Carchemish.

Cambridge Medieval History (–36).

R **Philosophy and Religion**

Hans Vaihinger, *The Philosophy of 'as If'*.

J. M. Thompson, *Miracles in the New Testament.*

World Missionary Conference, Edinburgh.

S **Art, Sculpture, Fine Arts and Architecture**

Painting:

A. Renoir, *Gabrielle with a Rose.*

Georges Braque, *Man with a Guitar.*

H. Matisse, *The Red Studio.*

Wassily Kandinsky and Franz Marc found *Blauen Reiter* ('Blue Rider') group of artists in Munich.

Da Vinci's *Mona Lisa* is stolen from the Louvre.

Sculpture:

J. Epstein, Tomb of Oscar Wilde, France.

Architecture:

Walter Gropius, Fagus Factory, Germany.

T **Music**

E. Elgar, Symphony no. 2 in E flat (op. 63).

G. Mahler, *The Song of the Earth.*

M. Ravel, *Daphnis and Chloë* (ballet).

R. Strauss, *Der Rosenkavalier* (opera).

Ermanno Wolf-Ferrari, *The Jewels of the Madona* (opera).

A. Schönberg's manual of harmony expounds the twelve-tone scale.

Irving Berlin's *Alexander's Ragtime Band.*

U **Literature**

Max Beerbohm, *Zuleika Dobson.*

Rupert Brooke, *Poems.*

T. Dreiser, *Jennie Gerhardt.*

H Aug: 1st, London dockers strike and, 7th, refuse to return until other transport workers' claims are satisfied;
10th, Lords pass Parliament bill, deciding (131–114 votes) not to insist on their amendments;
—, Commons vote to pay M.P.s £400 p.a.
14th, South Wales miners end strike after ten months;
15th, British railwaymen, under John Burns, strike (–19th);
20th, Portugal adopts a Liberal constitution;
21st, William II speaks at Hamburg on Germany's 'place in the sun' which her navy will secure for her;
31st, Franco-Russian military conversations.

J Sep: 11th, attempt to repeal Maine prohibition laws defeated;
14th, assassination of Peter Stolypin, Russian premier, and 19th, Vladimir Kokovtsoff appointed premier;
21st, in Canadian general election the Liberals, standing for Reciprocity with U.S., are defeated (the agreement is later annulled);
29th, Italy declares war on Turkey and Italian fleet bombards Tripoli coast;
—, first election in Sweden under Proportional Representation.

K Oct: 9th, H.M.S. *King George V* launched;
10th, Robert K. Borden forms Conservative ministry in Canada;
11th, revolution breaks out in Central China;
17th, Turkey promises Bulgaria to withdraw her troops and demobilise;
23rd, British cabinet changes, with Winston Churchill at Admiralty and Reginald McKenna home secretary;
26th, Chinese Republic proclaimed.

L Nov: 1st, amalgamation of London General Omnibus Co., Metropolitan and District Railway Co. and Underground Electric Railways of London;
4th, convention by which Germany allows France a free hand in Morocco in return for territory in the Congo;
5th, Italy annexes Tripoli and Cyrenaica;
6th, Francisco Madero becomes President of Mexico;
8th, A. J. Balfour resigns Unionist leadership (succeeded, 13th, by Andrew Bonar Law);
16th, Yüan Shi-kai forms cabinet in China;
—, Russia sends troops to Kazvin, Persia, on receiving no reply to ultimatum of 11th to Persia, and, 23rd, Persia concedes demands;
21st, Suffragette riots in Whitehall;
25th, Chinese revolutionaries bomb Nanking;
26th, Italy's decisive victory in Tripoli.

M Dec: 7th, Chinese edict abolishing pigtails and ordering reform of calendar;
11th, settlement of British railwaymen's dispute;
12th, George V holds Delhi Durbar;
30th, Sun Yat-sen elected president of United Provinces of China by a revolutionary assembly in Nanking.

N

U Literature (*cont.*)

H. von Hofmannsthal, *Jedermann.*
D. H. Lawrence, *The White Peacock.*
K. Mansfield (pseud.), *In a German Pension.*
J. Masefield, *The Everlasting Mercy.*
Saki (pseud.), *The Chronicles of Clovis.*
R. M. Rilke, *Duimo Elegies* (–22).
Hugh Walpole, *Mr. Perrin and Mr. Traill.*
H. G. Wells, *The New Macchiavelli.*
Edith Wharton, *Ethan Frome.*
Georgian Poetry (ed. Edward Marsh, –22).

V The Press

W Drama and Entertainment

Basil Dean opens Liverpool Repertory Theatre.
Anna Karenina (film).
The Fall of Troy (film).
Spartacus (film).
Pinocchio (film).

X Sport

Gordon-Bennett International Aviation Cup first given.

Y Statistics

Populations (in mill.): China, 325; India, 315; Russia, 167; U.S., 94; Germany, 65; Japan, 52; Great Britain, 40·8; Ireland, 4·3; France, 39·6; Italy, 34·6.
Steel production (in mill. tons): U.S., 23·6; Germany, 14·7; Great Britain, 6·4; France, 3·8; Russia, 3·8; Austria-Hungary, 2·3; Belgium, 1·9.
Rubber production (in thousand tons): Brazil and Peru, 39; West Africa, 15; Central America and Mexico, 11·7; Malaya, 9·2; East Africa, 5·3.
Petroleum production: U.S., 220·4 mill. barrels.

Z Births and Deaths

Feb. 2nd Jussi Bjoerling b. (–).
Mar. 7th Antonio Fogazzaro d. (68).
May 18th Gustav Mahler d. (50).
May 27th Hubert Humphrey b. (–).
May 29th W. S. Gilbert d. (75).
Sept. 16th Edward Whymper d. (71).

A Jan: 3rd, Ulster Unionists resolve to repudiate authority of any Irish Parliament set up under Home Rule Bill;
10th, Joseph Caillaux resigns in France and
14th, Raymond Poincaré forms cabinet;
18th, British miners ballot in favour of strike action;
Elections to German Reichstag leave the Socialists the strongest party.

B Feb: 6th, Nanking assembly endorses Yüan Shih-kai's proposals for constitutional reform;
10th, French senate ratifies Moroccan agreement;
12th, Manchu dynasty abdicates in China and a provisional republic is established;
14th, Arizona becomes a U.S. state;
15th, Labour amendment to Address, favouring a minimum wage, is rejected in Commons;
26th, British coal strike begins in Derbyshire (becoming general, *Mar.* 1st);
29th, Maurice Hankey appointed Secretary to the Committee of Imperial Defence.

C Mar: 9th, the powers ask Italy to state terms on which she would accept arbitration to end Turkish war;
14th, W. H. Taft forbids shipments of arms from U.S. to Mexico;
19th, H. H. Asquith introduces minimum wage bill to settle coal strike;
—, Tom Mann, British Syndicalist leader, arrested for inciting soldiers to mutiny;
—, U.S. excise bill, taxing net income from business sources;
28th, Commons reject women's franchise bill;
29th, government defeat in Reichstag on Post Office estimates;
—, U.S. Senate passes Reed Smoot's pension bill;
30th, Sultan of Morocco signs treaty making Morocco a French protectorate.

D Apr: 4th, Chinese Republic proclaimed in Tibet;
9th, Canadian-West Indies preferential agreement;
18th, Turkey closes Dardanelles to shipping (–*May* 1st);
19th, Dillingham Immigration bill makes literacy a condition of entrance to U.S. (later modified to meet Japanese representations);
20th, U.S. House of Representatives resolves that election expenses of presidential and vice-presidential candidates be published;
23rd, Welsh Church Disestablishment bill is introduced in Commons;
27th, Anglo-Belgian loan to China is cancelled after representations by other powers.

E May: 14th, Clayton bill, to prohibit issue of injunctions without notice, passes House of Representatives;
22nd, Count Tisza elected president of Hungarian Chamber after wild scenes;
—, Reichstag is adjourned following Socialist attacks on German emperor;
23rd, London dock strike;
28th, House of Representatives passes naval appropriations bill without provision for new battleships.

F Jun: 2nd, Clericals win Belgian elections on schools issue;
5th, U.S. marines land in Cuba;
11th, national strike of transport workers in Britain;
17th, W. H. Taft vetoes army appropriations bill;
22nd, Taft is nominated Republican presidential candidate at Chicago convention, where Theodore Roosevelt makes proposals for a new Progressive Republican Party;
25th, George Lansbury protests in Commons against forcible feeding of Suffragettes.

O **Politics, Economics, Law and Education**

Reports of Royal Commissions on Divorce and on Vivisection.

R. Casement's report on Putumayo atrocities, Peru (*July* 13th).

French *Code du Travail* promulgated.

Royal Flying Corps established.

U.S. Parcels Post inaugurated.

G.P.O. takes over British telephone systems.

P **Science, Technology, Discovery, etc.**

Albert Einstein formulates the law of photochemical equivalence.

Casimir Funck introduces word 'vitamine'.

X-ray crystallography begins.

L. O. Howard, *The House Fly, Disease Carrier*.

Drinking water is sterilised by ultra-violet rays in Manila.

Edwin Brandenberger invents Cellophane.

Henry Brearley invents stainless steel.

R. F. Scott reaches the South Pole (*Jan.* 18th).

First regular air service, between Berlin and Friedrichshaven, in rigid airships *Victoria Luise* and *Hansa*; G. H. Curtiss constructs the first sea-plane.

S.S. *Titanic* lost on maiden voyage (*Apr.* 15th), with 1,513 drowned.

Remains of Piltdown Man 'found'; later proved to be a scientific hoax.

Q **Scholarship**

E. Maude Thompson, *Introduction to Latin and Greek Palaeography*.

R **Philosophy and Religion**

E. Troeltsch, *Socialism and the Christian Church*.

B. M. Streeter, and others, *Foundations: a Statement of Christian Belief in Terms of Modern Thought*.

Church of Scotland revises Prayer Book.

S **Art, Sculpture, Fine Arts and Architecture**

Painting:

W. Orpen, *Café Royal*.

M. Chagall, *The Cattle Dealer*.

P. Picasso, *The Violin*.

F. Léger, *Woman in Blue*.

Franz Marc, *Tower of Blue Horses*.

Marcel Duchamp, *Nude Descending A Staircase*.

Albert Gleizes and Jean Metzinger publish *Du Cubisme*.

Sculpture:

A. Modigliani, *Stone Head*.

A. Bourdelle, frescoes and bas-reliefs for the Théâtre des Champs-Élysées.

George Frampton's *Peter Pan* in Kensington Gardens.

Architecture:

E. Lutyens, Viceroy's House, New Delhi.

Grand Central Railway Station, New York.

T **Music**

F. B. Busoni, *Die Brautwahl* (opera).

F. Delius, *On Hearing the First Cuckoo in Spring*.

A. Schönberg's song-cycle, *Pierrot Lunaire*.

R. Strauss, *Ariadne auf Naxos* (opera).

I. Stravinsky, *Petruschka* (ballet).

1912 (Jul.–Dec.)

G Jul: 2nd, Woodrow Wilson nominated as Democratic presidential candidate at Baltimore convention;

7th, Theobald von Bethman-Hollweg visits St. Petersburg;

9th, W. F. Massey forms ministry in New Zealand on Thomas Mackenzie's resignation;

10th, elections for French Chamber on principle of Proportional Representation;

15th, British National Health Insurance Act in force;

18th, Tewfik Pasha becomes Grand Vizier of Persia, following fall of Said Pasha's ministry;

24th, riots in London docks and at Ben Tillett's Tower Hill meeting.

H Aug: 2nd, U.S. Senate resolves to extend Monroe doctrine to foreign corporations holding territory on American continent;

5th (–16th), Raymond Poincaré visits Russia;

—, Theodore Roosevelt holds Progressive Republican Convention at Chicago;

7th, Russo-Japanese agreement determining spheres of influence in Mongolia and Manchuria;

17th, British note to restrain China from sending military expedition to Tibet;

—, Britain protests to U.S. that Panama Canal rates infringe Hay-Pauncefoote treaty of *Nov.* 1901;

19th, Britain accepts Count Berchtold's project for Balkan conversations.

J Sep: 6th, British Trades Union Congress votes against Syndicalism;

13th, revolution in Santo Domingo;

18th, Ulster Anti-Home Rule demonstrations begin at Enniskillen under Edward Carson;

23rd, Chinese government declines 6-powers loan in favour of loan by Birch, Crisp and Company of London;

29th, British and French forces pacify riots in Samos (*Sept.* 4th, Turks withdraw troops);

30th, Bulgarian and Serbian armies mobilise for war against Turkey.

K Oct: 6th, great powers back French proposals for averting Balkan war;

8th, Montenegro declares war on Turkey;

12th, Turkey declines to undertake reforms in Macedonia on which the powers insist;

14th, a fanatic wounds T. Roosevelt in Wisconsin;

16th, rebels under Porfirio Diaz occupy Vera Cruz;

17th, Turkey declares war on Bulgaria and Serbia;

18th, Italy and Turkey sign peace treaty at Lausanne by which Tripoli and Cyrenaica are granted autonomy under Italian suzerainty, and Italy restores Dodecanese Islands to Turkey.

L Nov: 3rd, Turkey asks powers to intervene to end Balkan war;

5th, Woodrow Wilson, Democrat, wins U.S. presidential election, with 435 electoral votes over W. H. Taft, Republican, with 88 votes;

Arizona, Kansas and Wisconsin adopt women's suffrage;

11th, government defeat in Commons on amendment to Home Rule bill;

—, Chile resumes diplomatic relations with Peru (after thirty months);

21st, Turkey declares terms of Balkan allies for a peace unacceptable;

26th, George Lansbury, who had resigned to test feeling of electorate on women's suffrage, is defeated in Bow by-election;

27th, run on savings banks in central and east Europe.

(*Continued opposite*)

U **Literature**

E. M. Dell, *The Way of an Eagle.*
C. J. R. Hauptmann, *Atlantis.*
P. Loti, *Le Pèlerin d'Angkor.*
Compton Mackenzie, *Carnival.*
R. Tagore, *Gitanjali.*
'New Poetry' movement in U.S.

V **The Press**

G. Dawson edits *The Times.*
The Daily Herald first issued.
H. Monro founds *Poetry Review.*

W **Drama and Entertainment**

P. Claudel, *L'Annonce faite à Marie.*
Five million Americans visit cinemas daily.
London has 400 cinemas (90 in 1909).
Quo Vadis? (film).
Sarah Bernhardt in *Queen Elizabeth* (film).
Charles Pathé produces first news film.

X **Sport**

Olympic Games held at Stockholm, in which races are timed electrically.

Y **Statistics**

Armies, including Reservists (in mill.): Russia, 5·5; Germany, 4·1; France, 3·9; Austria-Hungary, 2·3: Italy, 1·2; Japan, 1·0; British Empire, 0·9; U.S., 0·1.

U.K. Textiles trade:

Imports of raw cotton	2·1 mill. lb.
Exports of cottons	6,913 mill. yds.
Exports of woollens	180 mill. yds.
Exports of linens	213 mill. yds.
Exports of silks	11·9 mill. yds.

Trades union membership: U.K., 3,416,000.

Z **Births and Deaths**

Jan. 15th Henry Labouchere d. (80).
Feb. 10th Joseph, Lord Lister d. (85).
Mar. – Robert Falcon Scott d. (41).
Mar. 26th Tennessee Williams b. (–).
Apr. 15th W. T. Stead d. (63).
May 14th Johann A. Strindberg d. (63).
Aug. 13th Octavia Hill d. (74) and Jules Massenet d. (70).
Aug. 20th William Booth d. (83).
Sept. 1st Samuel Coleridge-Taylor d. (37).

M **Dec:** 2nd, U.S. Supreme Court orders dissolution of Union Pacific and Southern Pacific railways merger;
3rd, armistice between Turkey, Bulgaria, Serbia and Montenegro (Greece abstains);
14th, Louis Botha resigns South African premiership to form new cabinet, 20th, without James Hertzog;
19th, Prince Katsura forms cabinet in Japan;
20th, at London peace conference between Turkey and Balkan states, ambassadors of great powers accept principle of Albanian autonomy, providing Serbia has canal access to Adriatic.

N

1913 (Jan.–Jul.) Second Balkan War

A **Jan**: 2nd, Turkish garrison at Chios surrenders to Greeks;
5th, Gottlieb von Jagow becomes German foreign minister (–1916);
6th, London peace conference between Turkey and Balkan states suspended;
16th, Irish Home Rule bill passes Commons (but, 30th, is rejected by Lords);
17th, Raymond Poincaré elected President of France (–1920);
18th, Graeco-Turk naval battle off Tenedos;
21st, Aristide Briand forms cabinet in France;
23rd, Nazim Pasha is murdered in Turkish *coup* and Shevket Pasha forms ministry;
28th, Suffragettes demonstrate in London on withdrawal of franchise bill.

B **Feb**: 3rd, Bulgarians renew Turkish War (–*Apr.* 16th);
5th, Welsh Church Disestablishment bill passes Commons but, 13th, is rejected by Lords;
13th, Franco-U.S. agreement to extend 1908 arbitration convention for five years;
25th, federal income tax introduced in U.S.

C **Mar**: 4th, Woodrow Wilson inaugurated as U.S. President;
11th, Anglo-German agreement on frontier between Nigeria and Cameroons;
14th, Balkan allies accept mediation of great powers, but on unacceptable terms;
18th, King George I of Greece is murdered at Salonika;
26th, Bulgarians take Adrianople;
28th, Belgian army bill introduces universal military service;
31st, Turkey accepts recommendations of great powers for a peace.

D **Apr**: 3rd, Mrs. E. Pankhurst sentenced for inciting persons to place explosives outside D. Lloyd George's house;
8th, first Parliament of Chinese Republic opens;
16th, Turkey signs armistice with Bulgaria.

E **May**: 6th, King Nicholas of Montenegro yields Scutari to the powers until an Albanian government is created (in *Dec.*);
6th, women's franchise bill is rejected in Commons;
8th, U.S. House of Representatives passes tariff bill;
26th, Miss Emily Dawson appointed first woman magistrate in England;
30th, Canadian Senate rejects naval bill;
—, peace treaty between Turkey and Balkan states signed in London;
31st, Seventeenth Amendment to U.S. constitution, on popular election of senators.

F **Jun**: 10th, U.S. Supreme Court decides states have right to fix inter-state rail rates;
18th, Commons debate Marconi Report which acquits D. Lloyd George and other ministers of corruption in assigning imperial wireless contract to the Marconi Company;
24th (–7th), President Poincaré of France visits England;
26th, Bulgaria signs defensive treaty with Austria-Hungary;
28th, Roumania warns Bulgaria she will not remain neutral in a war;
30th, Second Balkan War opens, with Bulgaria attacking Serbian and Greek positions;
—, Reichstag passes bill to increase German army.

G **Jul**: 1st, Zanzibar is incorporated with British East Africa;
— (–9th), Hague opium conference;
7th, Commons pass Irish Home Rule bill (rejected, 15th, by Lords);
8th, Commons pass Welsh Church bill (rejected, 22nd, by Lords);
10th, Russia declares war on Bulgaria;

O **Politics, Economics, Law and Education**

Prince Bernhard von Bülow, *Imperial Germany.*

Federal Reserve Act reconstructs U.S. banking and currency system by creating federal banks.

Old-age and sickness insurance introduced in U.S., France and Holland.

Judge Archibald of U.S. federal commercial court is found guilty of corruption.

Rockefeller Foundation established.

P **Science, Technology, Discovery, etc.**

J. J. Thomson, *Rays of Positive Electricity and Their Application to Chemical Analysis.*

W. Geiger's research on radiation.

Niels Bohr's discoveries in atomic structure.

F. Soddy coins term 'isotope'.

Bela Schick discovers test for immunity from diphtheria.

Richard Willstätter discovers composition of chlorophyll.

McCollum isolates vitamin A.

Diesel-electric railway opened in Sweden.

H. Ford pioneers progressive assembly technique by means of conveyor belts.

Q **Scholarship**

G. P. Gooch, *History and Historians of the Nineteenth Century.*

R **Philosophy and Religion**

Edmund Husserl, *Pheonomenology.*

S. Freud, *Totem and Taboo.*

James Moffatt, *New Translation of the New Testament.*

S **Art, Sculpture, Fine Arts and Architecture**

Painting:

Armoury Show, New York, introduces Post-Impressionist art to U.S.

Harold Gilman, Walter Sickert and Wyndham Lewis form London Group of artists.

Walter Sickert, *Ennui.*

Stanley Spencer, *Self-Portrait.*

F. Marc, *Deer in the Forest.*

J. S. Sargent, Portrait of Henry James.

G. Apollinaire's appraisal, *The Cubist Painters.*

Sculpture:

J. Epstein, *Rock Drill.*

Eric Gill, Stations of the Cross, Westminster Cathedral.

Architecture:

Cass Gilbert, Woolworth Building, New York.

T **Music**

Alexander Scriabin, *Prometheus* (opera).

Igor Stravinsky, *The Rite of Spring* (opera).

U **Literature**

Alain-Fournier (pseud.), *Le Grand Meaulnes.*

M. Barrès, *La Colline inspirée.*

D. H. Lawrence, *Sons and Lovers.*

T. Mann, *Death in Venice.*

Ch. Péguy, *La Tapisserie de Notre-Dame.*

M. Proust, *Du côté de chez Swann* (1st part of *À la recherche du temps perdu* –27).

E. Wharton, *The Custom of the Country.*

G Jul: 12th, Turkey re-enters war, and 20th, recaptures Adrianople from Bulgaria;
23rd, 'Second Revolution' in South China (–*Sept.*);
28th, ambassadors of powers regulate establishment of Albanian principality;
31st, Balkan states sign armistice in Bucharest.

H Aug: 7th, French army bill, imposing 3 years military service;
10th, peace is signed in Bucharest.

J Sep: 3rd, Nanking falls to Yüan Shih-kai;
16th, Japan sends flotilla to Yangtze river, on China's failure to honour reparations agreement;
18th, Bulgarian-Turkish treaty settles frontier in Thrace;
24th, Ulster Unionists appoint provisional government to come into force on Home Rule bill taking effect.

K Oct: 6th, Yüan Shih-kai elected President of Chinese Republic;
17th, Serbs invade Albania;
21st, failure of royalist rising in Portugal;
28th, Britain, France and Germany withhold recognition of Victoriano Huerta's government in Mexico until U.S. defines its policy;
—, Germano-Turkish military conversations.

L Nov: 1st, naval convention of Triple Alliance;
3rd, U.S. demands withdrawal of General Huerta from Mexico;
5th, joint declaration by Russia and China recognising the autonomy of Outer Mongolia under Chinese suzerainty;
6th, Mahatma Gandhi, leader of Indian Passive Resistance movement, is arrested;
13th, Graeco-Turkish peace treaty;
17th, first vessel passes through Panama Canal;
20th, Zabern incident, in which a German officer in Alsace-Lorraine insults Alsatian recruits, embitters Franco-German relations.

M Dec: 5th, British proclamation forbids sending of arms to Ireland;
13th, Britain and France oppose Germano-Turkish military convention;
14th, Greece formally annexes Crete.

N

v The Press

S. and B. Webb found *The New Statesman* (edited by Clifford Sharp).

w Drama and Entertainment

Barry Jackson and John Drinkwater open Birmingham Repertory Theatre.
L. Pirandello, *Se non Cosi*.
The Vampire (film).
The Squaw Man (film).
The Student of Prague (film).
The foxtrot sweeps to popularity.

x Sport

y Statistics

Industrial output: increases per cent, since 1893:

	U.S.	Germany	Great Britain
Coal	210	159	75
Pig iron	337	287	50
Steel	715	522	136
Exports of raw materials	196	243	238
Exports of manufactures	563	239	121

Steel production (in mill. tons): Germany, 14; U.S., 10; Great Britain, 6; Russia, 4·2; France, 2·8.

Divorces: U.K., 801; U.S., 14,000.

z Births and Deaths

Jan. 9th Richard Nixon b. (–)
Mar. 25th Garnet Lord Wolseley d. (80).
Mar. 31st J. Pierpont Morgan d. (76).
June 2nd Alfred Austin d. (78).
Aug. 11th Angus Wilson b. (–).
Oct. 1st Rudolf Diesel d. (56).
Nov. 22nd Benjamin Britten b. (–).
— Albert Camus b. (–1960).

1914 (Jan.–Jul.) Outbreak of First World War

A **Jan**: 1st, Northern and Southern Nigeria amalgamated;
8th, Gaston Calmette, editor of *Figaro*, makes charges against Joseph Caillaux, French finance minister;
11th, Yüan Shih-kai governs without Parliament in China;
27th, President Oreste of Haiti abdicates during revolt and U.S. marines land to preserve order (General Zamon elected President, *Feb.* 8th).

B **Feb**: 4th, U.S. House of Representatives passes Burnett Immigration bill;
15th, Franco-German agreement on Baghdad Railway.

C **Mar**: 1st, unrest in Brazil, with Rio de Janiero in state of siege;
8th, Monarchist party win Spanish elections;
10th, Suffragettes damage 'Rokeby Venus' by Velasquez, in National Gallery;
14th, Turko-Serbian peace treaty;
16th, Mme Caillaux assassinates Gaston Calmette, editor of *Figaro*, for publishing love-letters;
30th, H. H. Asquith combines post of war secretary with premiership in Britain.

D **Apr**: 1st, Civil government established in Panama Canal Zone;
14th, President Wilson sends U.S. fleet to Tampico, Mexico, to enforce salute to flag and
21st, following ultimatum to Mexico, troops occupy Vera Cruz customs house.

E **May**: 6th, Lords reject women's enfranchisement bill;
10th, Liberal Unionists unite with Conservatives;
20th, Argentina, Brazil and Chile arbitrate at Niagara Falls between U.S. and Mexico;
22nd, Britain acquires control of oil properties in Persian Gulf from Anglo-Persian Oil Company;
25th, Commons pass Irish Home Rule bill;
31st, General Carranza becomes provisional president of Mexico.

F **Jun**: 11th, Niagara Falls delegates approve new Mexican government (peace with U.S. signed, 24th);
13th, René Viviani forms ministry in France;
—, Greece annexes Chios and Mytilene;
15th, Anglo-German agreement on Baghdad Railway and Mesopotamia;
28th, Archduke Francis Ferdinand of Austria and his wife assassinated at Sarajevo by a Bosnian revolutionary.

G **Jul**: 5th, General V. Huerta re-elected President of Mexico (he resigns 15th, and is succeeded by Carbajal);
10th, Ulster provisional government re-affirms Ulster's determination to resist Home Rule;
20th (–29th), President Raymond Poincaré visits Russia;
21st (–24th), British and Irish parties fail to agree at Buckingham Palace Conference;
23rd, Austro-Hungarian ultimatum to Serbia;
24th, Edward Grey proposes four-power mediation of Balkan crisis, but Serbia appeals to Russia;
26th, Austrians mobilise on Russian frontier;
—, Irish rising in Dublin;
28th, Austria-Hungary declares war on Serbia;
30th, Germany requires Russia to cease mobilisation;
—, Jean-Jaurès (aged 55) is murdered in Paris.

O **Politics, Economics, Law and Education**

Richard Huch, *The Great War in Germany*.

Edwin Cannan, *Wealth*.

Currency and Bank Notes Act, repealing Bank Charter Act, 1844, empowers Bank of England to issue £1 and 10/- notes.

French hoarding of gold, silver and copper coinage leads to Bank of France issuing 5, 10 and 20 Franc notes.

German War Raw Material Department established.

Maternity benefits for German women.

P **Science, Technology, Discovery, etc.**

A. Eddington, *Stellar Movement and the Structure of the Universe*.

J. H. Jeans, *Report on Radiation and the Quantum Theory*.

Work of National Physical Laboratory is extended to include the testing and certification of radium preparations.

James Dewar elucidates the composition of air.

Bottomley discovers fertilisation through peat.

Canadian Grand Trunk Pacific Railway completed (*Apr.* 7th).

Panama Canal officially open to traffic (*Aug.* 15th).

E. Shackleton leads Antarctic expedition (–17).

Q **Scholarship**

Edward VII Gallery of British Museum opened.

Austin Dobson, *Eighteenth-Century Studies*.

Journal of Egyptian Archaeology issued.

T. Roosevelt, *History as Literature*.

R **Philosophy and Religion**

C. D. Broad, *Perception, Physics and Psychical Research*.

Bertrand Russell, *Knowledge of the External World as a Field for Scientific Method in Philosophy*.

S **Art, Sculpture, Fine Arts and Architecture**

Painting:

A. John, *George Bernard Shaw*.

H. Matisse, *The Red Studio*.

G. Braque, *The Guitarist*.

O. Kokoschka, *The Vortex*.

Architecture:

Henry Bacon, The Lincoln Memorial, New York.

E. F. Carritt, *Theory of Beauty*.

T **Music**

Rutland Boughton, *The Immortal Hour* (opera).

F. B. Busoni, *Symphonic Nocturne*.

R. Vaughan Williams, *A London Symphony* (no. 2) and *Lark Ascending*.

U **Literature**

F. Brett Young, *Deep Sea*.

J. Conrad, *Chance*.

Henry James, *The Golden Bowl*.

James Joyce, *Dubliners*.

Miguel de Unamuno y Jugo, *Niebla*.

George Moore, *Hail and Farewell*.

H Aug: 1st, Germany declares war on Russia; France mobilises and Italy declares her neutrality;
—, German-Turkish treaty signed at Constantinople;
2nd, Germany occupies Luxembourg and sends ultimatum to Belgium to allow passage of troops;
—, Russians invade East Prussia;
3rd, Germany declares war on France and invades Belgium;
4th, Britain declares war on Germany;
—, U.S. declares her neutrality;
5th, Austria-Hungary declares war on Russia;
6th, Serbia and Montenegro declare war on Germany;
8th, British troops land in France;
—, Britain and France occupy Togoland;
10th, France declares war on Austria;
—, Germans occupy Liège;
—, *Breslau* and *Goeben* escape through Dardanelles;
12th, Britain declares war on Austria-Hungary;
14th, Russia promises autonomy to Poland in return for Polish aid;
15th, Japanese ultimatum to Germany for evacuation of Kiau-Chow;
16th, Constitutionalist army occupies Mexico City;
20th, Germans occupy Brussels;
22nd (–23rd), battles of Namur and Mons;
23rd, Russian victory at Frankenau, East Prussia;
24th, Allies retreat from Mons (–*Sept.* 7th);
26th, French cabinet reconstructed;
—, Germans cross R. Meuse and, 27th, occupy Lille;
— (–28th), Germans defeat Russians at Tannenberg;
28th, R.N. under David Beatty raids Bight of Heligoland;
—, Austria-Hungary declares war on Belgium;
30th, Germans take Amiens.

J Sep: 1st, name of St. Petersburg changed to Petrograd;
3rd, French government moved to Bordeaux;
—, Germans cross R. Marne and, 4th, occupy Rheims;
4th, Pact of London between France, Russia and Britain against a separate peace;
5th (–12th), battle of Marne, 9th (–15th), German retreat;
9th (–12th), in battle of Masurian Lakes, East Prussia, the Russians are driven back;
10th, *Emden* cruises in Bay of Bengal;
14th, Allies reoccupy Rheims;
—, Erich von Falkenhayn succeeds Helmuth von Moltke as German Commander-in-Chief;
15th (–18th), in battle of Aisne Germans withstand Allied attacks;
—, German capitulation in New Guinea;
—, bill suspends operation of Home Rule and Welsh Church bills for duration of war;
—, U.S. troops withdraw from Vera Cruz;
18th, Paul von Hindenburg appointed to command German armies in the East;
26th (–8th), battle of the R. Niemen;
27th, Russians cross Carpathians and invade Hungary;
—, Duala in Cameroons surrenders to British and French;
28th, Germans and Austrians advance towards Warsaw.

K Oct: 1st, Turkey closes Dardanelles;
9th, Antwerp surrenders to Germans;

v The Press

w Drama and Entertainment

Charlie Chaplin in *Making a Living* (film).
The Little Angel (film).
L. Baylis first produces Shakespeare at the Old Vic.

x Sport

y Statistics

Defence estimates (in £ mill.): Germany, 110·8; Russia, 88·2; Great Britain, 76·8; France, 57·4; Austria-Hungary, 36·4; Italy, 28·2.

Army strengths (at mobilisation in mill.): Germany, 4·2; France, 3·7; Russia, 1·2; Austria-Hungary, 0·8; Great Britain, 0·7; Italy, 0·7.

Navies:

	Britain	Germany	France	Russia	Italy	U.S.	Japan
Dreadnoughts	19	13	6	6	6	8	3
Pre-Dreadnoughts	39	22	20	8	8	22	13
Battle Cruisers	8	5	—	3	—	—	2
Cruisers	63	7	19	6	10	15	13
Light Cruisers	35	33	7	8	7	14	16
Destroyers	180	163	80	100	35	48	64
Submarines	44	38	75	35	20	36	14

Merchant Shipping (in mill. tons): British Empire, 21·0; Holland, 5·6; Germany, 5·5; U.S., 5·4; Norway, 2·5; France, 2·3; Italy, 1·7; Japan, 1·7; Sweden, 1·1.

Merchant shipping losses by Britain (*Aug.–Dec.*)*:* 696,542 tons.

Foreign investments (in £ mill.): Great Britain, 3,600; France, 1,740; Germany, 1,080; (U.S. has debit on account $3,000 mill.).

World aluminium production: 30,000 tons.

U.S. Motor vehicle production: 1·7 mill.

z Births and Deaths

Feb. 25th John Tenniel d. (93).
Mar. 12th George Westinghouse d. (67).
Mar. 25th Frédéric Mistral d. (84).
May 18th Pierre Balmain b. (–).
July 2nd Joseph Chamberlain d. (78).
Oct. 28th Jonas Edward Salk b. (–).
Nov. 14th Frederick, Earl Roberts, d. (82).
Dec. 1st A. T. Mahan d. (74).

K Oct: 12th, Germans occupy Ghent and Lille;
13th, Boer rebellion against British in South Africa under Christian de Wet;
14th, first Canadian troops land in England;
15th, Clayton anti-trust act in U.S.;
— (–20th), battle for Warsaw; Germans under von Mackensen are driven back by Russians;
17th (–30th), battle of Yser prevents Germans from reaching Channel ports;
26th, Russians break through in Ivangorod;
27th, Germans retreat from Poland;
29th, John A. Fisher becomes First Sea Lord;
—, Turkish warships bombard Odessa and Sebastopol;
30th (–*Nov.* 21st), first battle of Ypres; Germans fail to break through.

L Nov: 1st, Maximilius von Spee defeats R.N. under Christopher Craddock at battle of Coronel, Chile;
2nd, Russia declares war on Turkey;
3rd, large Republican gains in U.S. elections;
5th, France and Britain declare war on Turkey;
—, Britain annexes Cyprus which she has occupied since *June* 1878;
9th, *Emden* sunk off Sumatra;
18th, Germans break Russian line at Kutno;
21st, Indian troops occupy Basra;
23rd, R.N. bombard Zeebrugge.

M Dec: 2nd, Austrians take Belgrade (reoccupied by Serbians, 14th);
5th (–17th), Austrians defeat Russians at battle of Limanova, but fail to break Russian lines before Cracow;
6th, Germans take Łódź;
8th, Admiral Frederick Sturdee destroys German squadron off Falkland Islands;
10th, French government returns to Paris;
17th, British protectorate proclaimed in Egypt;
18th, Abbas II is deposed and Prince Husein Kemel becomes Khedive of Egypt.

N Mahatma Gandhi returns to India and supports the government.

1915 (Jan.–May) Italy enters the war—Dardanelles Campaign—Second battle of Ypres

A Jan: 1st, H.M.S. *Formidable* sunk in English Channel;
3rd (–4th), rebellion in Albania;
8th (–*Feb.* 5th), heavy fighting in Bassée Canal and Soissons area;
12th, House of Representatives defeats proposal for women's suffrage in U.S.;
13th, South African troops occupy Swakopmund in German South-West Africa;
18th, Japan's secret ultimatum to China regarding rights in Shantung and leases in Manchuria;
19th, German airship bombs East Anglian ports;
24th, cruiser *Blücher* sunk in battle of Dogger Bank;
28th, President Wilson vetoes U.S. Immigration bill;
30th, first German submarine attack without warning off Le Havre.

B Feb: 4th, Turks repulsed from Suez Canal;
— (–27th), Germans advance following battle in Masuria, East Prussia;
—, Foreign Office announces that any vessel carrying corn to Germany will be seized;
11th, U.S. note to Britain on use of U.S. flag on British vessels, such as *Lusitania*, and U.S. note to Germany on sinking of neutral ships;
16th (–26th), French bombard Champagne;
17th, Germans take Memel;
18th, German blockade of England comes into force with intensive submarine warfare;
19th, British and French fleets bombard Dardanelles;
27th, Russians evacuate East Prussia.

C Mar: 6th, Demetrios Gounaris forms ministry in Greece on resignation of Eleutherios Venizelos;
10th, British launch battle of Neuve Chapelle;
11th, British blockade of Germany comes into effect;
18th, cotton declared an article of contraband;
—, Anglo-French naval attack on Dardanelles fails;
22nd, Russians take Przemysl.

D Apr: 22nd (–*May* 25th), German offensive leads to second battle of Ypres;
22nd, Germans first use poison gas on Western Front;
24th, battle of St. Julien;
25th, Anglo-French forces land at Gallipoli;
26th, Britain, France and Italy sign secret convention;
—, German offensive in Courland and, 27th, in Lithuania.

E May: 1st, U.S. vessel *Gulflight* sunk by German submarines without warning;
2nd, Austro-German offensive in Galicia breaks Russian lines;
4th, Italy denounces the Triple Alliance (renewed in *Dec.* 1912);
7th, Germans sink *Lusitania* off Irish coast, with loss of 1,198 lives and U.S. is brought to verge of war with Germany;
12th, Louis Botha occupies Windhoek, capital of German South-West Africa;
13th, names of Emperors of Germany and Austria are struck off roll of Knights of the Garter;
14th, Portuguese cabinet resigns after insurrection;
15th, John Fisher, First Sea Lord, resigns, disapproving of cabinet's Dardanelles policy;
21st, Italian ambassador in Vienna is warned that Austria cannot admit nullification of Triple Alliance;
23rd, Italy declares war on Austria-Hungary;
25th, China accepts Japanese ultimatum (of *Jan.* 18th);

1915 (Jan.–May) Italy enters the war—Dardanelles Campaign—Second battle of Ypres

A **Jan**: 1st, H.M.S. *Formidable* sunk in English Channel;
3rd (–4th), rebellion in Albania;
8th (–*Feb.* 5th), heavy fighting in Bassée Canal and Soissons area;
12th, House of Representatives defeats proposal for women's suffrage in U.S.;
13th, South African troops occupy Swakopmund in German South-West Africa;
18th, Japan's secret ultimatum to China regarding rights in Shantung and leases in Manchuria;
19th, German airship bombs East Anglian ports;
24th, cruiser *Blücher* sunk in battle of Dogger Bank;
28th, President Wilson vetoes U.S. Immigration bill;
30th, first German submarine attack without warning off Le Havre.

B **Feb**: 4th, Turks repulsed from Suez Canal;
— (–27th), Germans advance following battle in Masuria, East Prussia;
—, Foreign Office announces that any vessel carrying corn to Germany will be seized;
11th, U.S. note to Britain on use of U.S. flag on British vessels, such as *Lusitania*, and U.S. note to Germany on sinking of neutral ships;
16th (–26th), French bombard Champagne;
17th, Germans take Memel;
18th, German blockade of England comes into force with intensive submarine warfare;
19th, British and French fleets bombard Dardanelles;
27th, Russians evacuate East Prussia.

C **Mar**: 6th, Demetrios Gournaris forms ministry in Greece on resignation of Eleutherios Venizelos;
10th, British launch battle of Neuve Chapelle;
11th, British blockade of Germany comes into effect;
18th, cotton declared an article of contraband;
—, Anglo-French naval attack on Dardanelles fails;
22nd, Russians take Przemysl.

D **Apr**: 22nd (–*May* 25th), German offensive leads to second battle of Ypres;
22nd, Germans first use poison gas on Western Front;
24th, battle of St. Julien;
25th, Anglo-French forces land at Gallipoli;
26th, Britain, France and Italy sign secret convention;
—, German offensive in Courland and, 27th, in Lithuania.

E **May**: 1st, U.S. vessel *Gulflight* sunk by German submarines without warning;
2nd, Austro-German offensive in Galicia breaks Russian lines;
4th, Italy denounces the Triple Alliance (renewed in *Dec.* 1912);
7th, Germans sink *Lusitania* off Irish coast, with loss of 1,198 lives and U.S. is brought to verge of war with Germany;
12th, Louis Botha occupies Windhoek, capital of German South-West Africa;
13th, names of Emperors of Germany and Austria are struck off roll of Knights of the Garter;
14th, Portuguese cabinet resigns after insurrection;
15th, John Fisher, First Sea Lord, resigns, disapproving of cabinet's Dardanelles policy;
21st, Italian ambassador in Vienna is warned that Austria cannot admit nullification of Triple Alliance;
23rd, Italy declares war on Austria-Hungary;
25th, China accepts Japanese ultimatum (of *Jan.* 18th);

O **Politics, Economics, Law and Education**

Defence of Realm Act (*Mar.* 9th) to mobilise Britain's resources.
Ministry of Munitions established.
Robert La Follette's Seamen's Act to improve conditions in U.S. merchant fleet.
Sale of absinthe is prohibited in France.
Women's Institute founded in Britain.

P **Science, Technology, Discovery, etc.**

Albert Einstein's general theory of relativity.
W. and L. Bragg devise crystal method for the diffraction of X-rays.
Kendal isolates thyroxine from thyroid gland; the dysentery bacillus is isolated.
Outbreaks of tetanus in the trenches are controlled through serum injections.
Thorburn's *British Birds* (–16).
Hugo Junkers makes first fighter aeroplane.
Royal Navy uses paravanes as protection of vessels against mines (*Oct.*).
Wegener's theory of continental drift.
Leipzig railway station, the largest in Europe, completed.

Q **Scholarship**

Aurel Stein, on his expedition to South Mongolia, discovers the remains of Marco Polo's 'city of Etzina'.

R **Philosophy and Religion**

S **Art, Sculpture, Fine Arts and Architecture**

Painting:
M. Duchamp, *The Bride Stripped Bare by Bachelors* (the first Dada-style painting).
P. Picasso, *Harlequin.*
U.S. collectors purchase many works of art at Christie's London sales to aid British Red Cross.
Hugh Lane's bequest to English and Irish National Galleries.

T **Music**

Frank Bridge, *Lament.*
M. de Falla, *The Lovespell* (opera).
Gustav Holst, *The Planets* (symphonic suite).
John Ireland, *The Forgotten Rite* (opera).
Max Reger, 'Mozart Variations'.
Clara Butt sings in aid of Red Cross.
Remains of R. de Lisle, composer of La Marseillaise, brought to the Invalides (*July* 4th).

U **Literature**

John Buchan, *The Thirty-Nine Steps.*
P. Claudel, *Corona.*
J. Conrad, *Victory.*
D. H. Lawrence, *The Rainbow.*
W. S. Maugham, *Of Human Bondage.*
F. Neumann, *Mitteleuropa.*
Ezra Pound, *Cathay* (poems).

V **The Press**

Sunday Pictorial issued.
Lord Beaverbrook buys the *Daily Express.*
The Globe is suppressed (*Nov.* 6th–20th) for spreading false rumour about Lord Kitchener's resignation.

E May: 26th, H. H. Asquith forms Coalition, with A. J. Balfour First Lord of Admiralty and R. McKenna Chancellor of Exchequer; W. S. Churchill leaves Admiralty for Chancellorship of Duchy of Lancaster;
29th, Theophilo Braga elected President of Portugal.

F Jun: 1st, first Zeppelin attack on London;
3rd, Russian southern front collapses with German recapture of Przemysl;
—, British take Amarah on R. Tigris and Mesopotamia surrenders to British;
5th, women's suffrage in Denmark;
8th, Allies take Neuville;
9th, riots in Moscow;
10th, Russian victory on R. Dniester;
15th, battle of Givenchy;
16th, D. Lloyd George appointed first minister of munitions;
21st, Christian de Wet surrenders at Bloemfontein;
23rd, Robert Lansing becomes U.S. secretary of state after W. J. Bryan's resignation, 8th;
—, German Social Democrats' manifesto asking for a peace to be negotiated;
—, Austro-German forces take Lemberg;
29th (–*July* 7th), in first battle of Isonzo Italians try to force bridgeheads held by Austrians.

G Jul: 9th, German forces in South-West Africa surrender to Louis Botha;
12th, German government takes over control of coal industry;
14th, British National Registration Act (National Register taken *Aug.* 15th);
18th (–*Aug.* 10th), second battle of Isonzo;
27th, revolution in Haiti.

H Aug: 4th, National Ministry in New Zealand;
5th, Germans enter Warsaw;
6th, fresh Allied landings at Suvla Bay, Gallipoli;
—, Bernadino Machado elected President of Portugal;
20th, Germans take Novo-Georgievsk;
—, Italy declares war on Turkey;
26th, Germans capture Brest-Litovsk.

J Sep: 6th, Russians check Germans at Tarnopol;
—, Bulgaria signs military alliances with Germany and Turkey;
8th, Nicholas Nicolaievich relieved of his command, which Tsar Nicholas II takes over in person;
9th, U.S. asks Austria to recall her ambassador (who leaves New York, *Oct.* 5th);
18th, Germany gives undertaking that her submarines will cease attacking merchant shipping until end of war;
—, Germans capture Vilna;
22nd, Joseph Joffre opens battle of Champagne but the Germans hold their own;
23rd, Greek army is mobilised;
25th (–*Oct.* 8th), in battle of Loos the British drive the Germans back towards Lens and Loos;
28th, British defeat Turks at Kut-el-Amara in Mesopotamia;
29th, U.S. loans $500 mill. to Britain and France.

K Oct: 5th, Allies land troops at Salonika;
9th, Austro-German troops occupy Belgrade;

(*Continued opposite*)

W **Drama and Entertainment**

Felix Powell and George Asaf write 'Pack Up Your Troubles in Your Old Kit Bag'.
D. W. Griffiths, *Birth of a Nation* (film).
C. B. de Mille's *Carmen* (film).
Douglas Fairbanks in *The Lamb* (film).

X **Sport**

Y **Statistics**

Merchant shipping losses by Britain (in tons): Jan.–Mar., 215,905; Apr.–June, 223,767; July–Sept., 356,659; Oct.–Dec., 307,139.

Z **Births and Deaths**

Jan. 3rd James Elroy Flecker d. (31).
Apr. 14th Alexander Scriabin d. (43).
June 10th Saul Bellow b. (–).
Aug. 26th Humphrey Searle b. (–).
Sept. 26th James Keir Hardie d. (59).
Oct. 17th Arthur Miller b. (–).
Oct. 23rd W. G. Grace d. (67).

K **Oct**: 9th, conference of Latin American states recognises Venustiano Carranza as chief of *de facto* government in Mexico (recognised by U.S. 19th);
11th, Bulgarian offensive against Serbia;
—, execution of Edith Cavell in Brussels;
12th, Allies declare they will assist Serbia under Bucharest treaty of *Aug.* 10th 1913;
—, Greece refuses Serbian appeal for aid under Serbo-Greek treaty of 1913;
13th, T. Delcassé, French foreign minister, resigns;
15th, Britain declares war on Bulgaria;
18th (–*Nov.* 3rd), third battle of Isonzo;
19th, Japan becomes signatory to treaty of London, undertaking not to make a separate peace;
20th, J. B. Hertzog's Nationalist Party's successes in South African elections leave South African Party government in a minority in the House;
28th, René Viviani resigns and
29th, Aristide Briand forms ministry in France.

L **Nov**: 5th, Chinese princes vote for establishment of a monarchy, with Yüan Shih-kai as emperor;
6th, Sophocles Skouloudis forms ministry in Greece favourable to Allies;
10th (–*Dec.* 10th), fourth battle of Isonzo;
12th, Britain annexes Gilbert and Ellice Islands;
13th, W. S. Churchill resigns from British cabinet;
21st, Italy agrees not to make a separate peace;
22nd, indecisive battle of Ctesiphon, Mesopotamia, between Turks and British.

M **Dec**: 3rd, Joseph Joffre becomes French Commander-in-Chief;
16th, Douglas Haig succeeds John French as British Commander-in-Chief in France and Flanders;
19th (–*Jan.* 8th 1916), British withdrawal from Suvla and Anzac in Gallipoli;
21st, William Robertson becomes British chief of staff;
28th, British cabinet agrees on principle of compulsory service.

N

1916 (Jan.–Jun.) Lloyd George forms coalition—Easter Rebellion in Dublin

A Jan: 19th, Russian offensive in Galicia opens;
24th, U.S. Supreme Court rules income tax law is constitutional;
27th, British Labour Party conference votes against conscription;
—, 'Spartacus' Communist group founded in Berlin;
29th, first Zeppelin raid on Paris.

B Feb: 2nd, Boris Stürmer becomes Russian premier;
9th, British military service act in force;
14th, Allies guarantee Belgium a place at the peace conference;
16th, Russians take Erzurum;
—, U.S. refuses to recognise Germany's claims to sink armed merchantmen without warning;
18th, last German garrison in Cameroons surrenders;
21st (*–Dec.* 16th), battle of Verdun;
22nd, Tsar Nicholas II opens Duma in person;
29th, first 'Black List' of firms in neutral countries, with whom trade is forbidden, is issued in Britain;
—, German order for sinking armed merchantmen at sight comes into force.

C Mar: 2nd, Russians take Bitlis (reconquered by Turks *Aug.* 7th);
9th, Germany declares war on Portugal;
15th, U.S. punitive expedition to Mexico;
—, Alfred von Tirpitz, German Minister of Marine, resigns;
—, fifth battle of Isonzo;
17th (*–Apr.* 4th) strike of Clydeside munitions workers;
20th, Allies agree on partition of Turkey;
—, Allied air attack on Zeebrugge;
22nd, Yüan Shih-kai dies;
27th, Aristide Briand opens Paris inter-allied war conference.

D Apr: 9th, German attack before Verdun;
18th, Russians take Trebizond;
21st, Roger Casement lands in Ireland (is arrested, 24th, and executed *Aug.* 3rd);
24th, Sinn Fein Easter Rebellion in Dublin (*–May* 1st);
29th, Kut-el-Amara falls to Turks.

E May: 8th, Anzacs arrive in France;
31st (*–June* 1st), in battle of Jutland, Royal Navy losses exceed those of German fleet.

F Jun: 2nd, second battle of Ypres;
4th, Alexei Brusilov begins Russian offensive;
5th (–6th), H.M.S. *Hampshire* sunk, with Lord Kitchener aboard;
6th (–24th), Allies blockade Greece;
—, Arab Revolt in Hedjaz begins;
9th, Grand Sheriff of Mecca revolts against Turkey;
10th, Republican Convention nominates Charles E. Hughes as presidential candidate;
13th, Jan Smuts captures Wilhemsthal in German East Africa;
14th, Allied economic conference in Paris;
15th, Woodrow Wilson is re-nominated Democratic presidential candidate at St. Louis convention;
17th, Italian coalition formed under Paolo Boselli;
18th, Russians take Czernowitz;
21st, battle of Carrizal between U.S. and Mexican troops;

O **Politics, Economics, Law and Education**

G. Lowes Dickinson, *The European Anarchy*.
Lionel Curtis, *The Problem of the Commonwealth*.
New Ministries Act in Britain leads to establishment of Ministry of National Service.
Cabinet Secretariat is formed (*Dec.*) in Britain.
Report of Bryce Committee on German Atrocities (*May*).
Report of Royal Commission on Irish Rebellion, under Lord Hardinge (*July* 3rd).
Report of Royal Commission on Venereal Diseases states that 10 per cent of British urban population is infected (*Mar.* 3rd).
National Savings Movement founded in Britain.
Severe rationing of food in Germany. Shortages in Paris lead to milk queues.
U.S. Shipping Board is established.
U.S. Rural Credits Law.
Products of child labour are excluded from U.S. inter-state commerce.
School of Oriental and African Studies, London University, founded.
Summer Time (daylight saving) introduced in Britain (*May* 21st).

P **Science, Technology, Discovery, etc.**

G. N. Lewis states a new valency theory, which is later stated independently by Kossel.
The Committee on the Neglect of Science, led by Ray Lankester, starts press campaign (*Feb.* 2nd) demanding greater awareness of science in Britain's schools, universities and civil service.
A Board of Scientific Societies is sponsored by the Royal Society to promote co-operation in pure and applied science and promote the application of science for the service of Britain.
The government establishes a Department of Scientific and Industrial Research (*Nov.*).
Herbert Jackson succeeds in making optical glasses of the same standard as those of the Zeiss works at Jena.
Treatment of war casualties leads to development of plastic surgery.
F. W. Mott's theory of shell-shock.
First military tanks used (*Sep.*).

Q **Scholarship**

Closure of many British museums and galleries to save manpower, but the press campaigns successfully for keeping the British Museum Reading Room and the Natural History Museum open.
Foundation of National Central Library, by Albert Mansbridge.

R **Philosophy and Religion**

Pareto, *Treatise of General Sociology*.

S **Art, Sculpture, Fine Arts and Architecture**

Painting:
Claude Monet, *Water Lilies* (murals at the Musée d'orangerie, Paris).
Georges Rouault's etchings *Guerre* and *Misère* (–27).
H. Matisse, *Bouquet*.
Dadaist anti-art cult flourishes in Zürich, headed by Tristan Tzara, Hans Arp and Giacome Ball (movement lasts –21).

Architecture:
Eugène Freyssinet, Airship Hangars at Orly, France (first giant structure in re-inforced concrete).

T **Music**

Arnold Bax, *The Garden of Fand* (orchestral work).
Leoš Janáček, *Jenufa* (opera).

F Jun: 23rd, Greece accepts Allies' demands for demobilisation;
—, Convention of Ulster Nationalists agrees to exclude Ulster under Government of Ireland act;
25th, Austrians evacuate positions in South Tirol;
26th, T. Roosevelt declines nomination as Progressive Republican presidential candidate.

G Jul: 1st, French and British troops begin Somme offensive (–*Nov.* 8th);
6th, D. Lloyd George becomes War Secretary in succession to Lord Kitchener;
9th, German commercial submarine *Deutschland* reaches U.S.;
25th, Sergei Sazonov, Russian foreign minister, resigns;
26th, U.S. protests against British 'Black List' forbidding trading with certain U.S. firms.

H Aug: 4th, Denmark sells West Indian Islands to U.S.;
—, (–6th), sixth battle of Isonzo;
19th, Royal Navy sinks German battleship *Westfalen* in North Sea;
—, Germans bombard English coast;
20th, Allied offensive in Mesopotamia begins;
27th, Roumania declares war on Austria-Hungary, and begins offensive in Transylvania;
28th, Italy declares war on Germany;
30th, Turkey declares war on Russia;
—, Paul von Hindenburg appointed German chief of general staff.

J Sep: 1st, Bulgaria declares war on Roumania;
4th, British troops take Dar-es-Salaam;
6th, Supreme War Council of Central Powers established;
14th (–18th), seventh battle of Isonzo;
15th, British first use tanks on Western Front;
18th, Greek army surrenders to Germans at Kavalla;
Alexei Brusilov's offensive checked by Germans.

K Oct: 4th, Austro-German counter-offensive in Roumania;
9th (–12th), eighth battle of Isonzo;
11th, Greece accepts Allies' ultimatum to hand over Greek fleet;
16th, Allies occupy Athens;
19th, Franco-British conference at Boulogne recognises Venizelist government of Greece at Salonika;
21st, Count Carl Stürgkh, Austrian premier, assassinated;
24th (–*Nov.* 5th), French offensive east of Verdun;
31st (–*Nov.* 4th), ninth battle of Isonzo.

L Nov: 5th, Central Powers proclaim Kingdom of Poland;
7th, Woodrow Wilson, Democrat, re-elected U.S. president with 277 electoral votes against Charles E. Hughes, Republican with 254 votes;
—, Miss Jeanette Rankin returned by Montana as first woman member of Congress;
13th, Cardinal Mercier protests against deportation of Belgians to Germany for forced labour;
21st, Emperor Francis Joseph of Austria dies, succeeded by his grand-nephew as Charles I (–1918);
—, Arthur Zimmermann becomes German foreign minister;
24th, U.S.-Mexican protocol signed at Atlantic City (but, *Dec.* 18th, President Carranza refuses to ratify);

T Music (*cont.*)

Erich Korngold, *Violanta* (opera).
E. Smyth, *The Boatswain's Mate* (opera).
Campaign against performing works by German composers makes slight headway in England.
Jazz sweeps U.S.

U Literature

J. Buchan, *Greenmantle.*
G. D'Annunzio, *La Leda Senza Gigno* (–18).
J. Joyce, *Portrait of the Artist as a Young Man.*
G. Moore, *The Brook Kerith.*
A. Quiller-Couch, *The Art of Writing.*
G. B. Shaw publishes 'Prefaces' to *Androcles and the Lion*, *Overruled* and *Pygmalion.*

V The Press

Le Populaire, French Socialist organ, issued.
Forward, British Labour newspaper, suppressed for inciting Clydeside workers to refuse making munitions.

W Drama and Entertainment

Leonid Andreyev, *He Who Gets Slapped.*
Algernon Blackwood, *Starlight Express.*
Harold Brighouse, *Hobson's Choice.*
Eugene O'Neill, *Bound East.*
The Bing Girls (revue).

X Sport

Y Statistics

Merchant shipping losses by Britain (in tons): Jan.–Mar., 325,237; Apr.–June, 270,690; July–Sept., 284,358; Oct.–Dec., 617,563.
U.S. Petroleum production: 300,767,000 tons.
Coal production: (in mill. tons): U.S., 590; Great Britain, 256·4.

Z Births and Deaths

Feb. 28th Henry James d. (72).
Mar. 11th Harold Wilson b. (–).
Apr. 22nd Yehudi Menuhin b. (–).
June 5th Horatio, Lord Kitchener, d. (66).
July 9th Edward Heath b. (–).

L Nov: 29th, Hussein is proclaimed King of the Arabs;
—, British government takes over South Wales coalfield under Defence of Realm Act because of strikes;
—, David Beatty appointed Commander-in-Chief of British fleet and John Jellicoe First Sea Lord.

M Dec: 3rd, Robert Nivelle succeeds Joseph Joffre as French Commander-in-Chief;
5th, D. Lloyd George resigns from H. H. Asquith's cabinet;
6th, Germans take Bucharest;
7th, H. H. Asquith resigns and D. Lloyd George becomes prime minister of coalition government, and (11th) forms war cabinet, including A. J. Balfour, George Curzon, Arthur Henderson and Alfred Milner;
12th, Aristide Briand forms French War Ministry;
—, U.S. Senate passes Immigration bill, with literacy test clause amended to meet Japanese criticism;
—, Germany's peace note to Allies saying the Central Powers were prepared to negotiate (reply sent 30th, via U.S. ambassador in Paris);
13th, new British offensive in Mesopotamia;
15th (–17th), French offensive between Meuse and Woëvre Plain;
19th, British government takes control of shipping and of mines;
20th, Woodrow Wilson's peace note to all belligerents;
31st, Allied ultimatum to Greece for withdrawal of forces from Thessaly.

N

1917 (Jan.–May) February and Bolshevist Revolutions in Russia—U.S. declares war on Central Powers—Germans intensify submarine warfare

A Jan: 1st, Britain, France and Italy recognise Kingdom of Hedjaz;
—, Turkey denounces treaties of Paris, 1856, and Berlin, 1878;
5th, Allies evacuate Dobrudja;
8th, Austrians take Focsani;
16th, Greece accepts Allied ultimatum of Dec. 1916;
31st, Germany's declaration to neutrals announces policy of unrestricted naval warfare.

B Feb: 2nd, bread rationing in Britain;
3rd, U.S. and Germany break off diplomatic relations;
4th (-23rd), Germans' preliminary withdrawal between Arras and Soissons;
12th, Woodrow Wilson refuses to reopen negotiations with Germany until she abandons unrestricted naval warfare;
17th, William Hughes becomes premier of Australia.

C Mar: 4th (-*Apr.* 5th), German main withdrawal on Western Front;
8th, Woodrow Wilson orders arming of U.S. merchant ships without special authority of Congress;
—, U.S. marines land at Santiago, Cuba, at request of civil government;
— (-14th) (old style, *Feb.* 23rd–*Mar.* 1st), February Revolution in Russia;
11th, British capture Baghdad;
16th, Tsar Nicholas II abdicates and Prince George Lvov, Paul Milyukov and Alexander Kerensky form ministry in Russia;
17th (-18th), British capture Bapaume and Péronne on Western Front;
19th, Alexandre Ribot forms cabinet in France;
—, Allies raise Greek blockade;
20th, Imperial war cabinet first meets in London;
26th (-*Apr.* 8th), Archibald Murray defeats Turks at Gaza;
30th, Russian provisional government guarantees independence of Poland;
31st, U.S. takes over Virgin Islands from Denmark.

D Apr: 2nd, Woodrow Wilson calls special sessions of Congress for declaration of war and
6th, U.S. declares war on Germany;
7th, Cuba declares war on Germany;
—, Kaiser William II promises universal suffrage in Prussia;
9th (-*May* 4th), in battle of Arras British third army advances 4 miles;
— (-21st), Canadians take Vimy Ridge;
11th, German Independent Labour Party founded;
14th, U.S. House of Representatives authorises 'Old Glory Loan';
16th (-20th), Germans halt French advance in second battle of Aisne;
—, food strikes in Berlin;
18th (-19th), in second battle of Gaza Turks, with German support, repulse British;
20th, U.S. and Turkey sever relations;
29th, Henri Pétain becomes chief of French staff;
30th, Frederick Maude defeats Turks at Shatt-el-Adhaim.

E May: 3rd (-5th), fresh British attack at Arras breaks Hindenburg Line;
5th, A. J. Balfour addresses U.S. House of Representatives;
— (-9th), battle of Chemin des Dames;
12th, tenth battle of Isonzo;
15th, Henri Pétain succeeds R. G. Nivelle as French Commander-in-Chief and Ferdinand Foch becomes chief of staff;
18th, U.S. selective military conscription bill;
—, Prince Lvov reforms cabinet in Russia to include Socialists;

1917 (Jan.–May) February and Bolshevist Revolutions in Russia—U.S. declares war on Central Powers—Germans intensify submarine warfare

A **Jan**: 1st, Britain, France and Italy recognise Kingdom of Hedjaz;
—, Turkey denounces treaties of Paris, 1856, and Berlin, 1878;
5th, Allies evacuate Dobrudja;
8th, Austrians take Foscani;
16th, Greece accepts Allied ultimatum of *Dec.* 1916;
31st, Germany's declaration to neutrals announces policy of unrestricted naval warfare.

B **Feb**: 2nd, bread rationing in Britain;
3rd, U.S. and Germany break off diplomatic relations;
4th (–23rd), Germans' preliminary withdrawal between Arras and Soissons;
12th, Woodrow Wilson refuses to reopen negotiations with Germany until she abandons unrestricted naval warfare;
15th, William Hughes becomes premier of Australia.

C **Mar**: 4th (–*Apr.* 5th), German main withdrawal on Western Front;
8th, Woodrow Wilson orders arming of U.S. merchant ships without special authority of Congress;
—, U.S. marines land at Santiago, Cuba, at request of civil government;
— (–14th) (old style, *Feb.* 23rd.–*Mar.* 1st), February Revolution in Russia;
11th, British capture Baghdad;
16th, Tsar Nicholas II abdicates and Prince George Lvov, Paul Milivkov and Alexander Kerensky form ministry in Russia;
17th (–18th), British capture Bapaume and Péronne on Western Front;
19th, Alexandre Ribot forms cabinet in France;
—, Allies raise Greek blockade;
20th, Imperial war cabinet first meets in London;
26th (–*Apr.* 8th), Archibald Murray defeats Turks at Gaza;
30th, Russian provisional government guarantees independence of Poland;
31st, U.S. takes over Virgin Islands from Denmark.

D **Apr**: 2nd, Woodrow Wilson calls special sessions of Congress for declaration of war and
6th, U.S. declares war on Germany;
7th, Cuba declares war on Germany;
—, Kaiser William II promises universal suffrage in Prussia;
9th (–*May* 4th), in battle of Arras British third army advances 4 miles;
— (–21st), Canadians take Vimy Ridge;
11th, German Independent Labour Party founded;
14th, U.S. House of Representatives authorises 'Old Glory Loan';
16th (–20th), Germans halt French advance in second battle of Aisne;
—, food strikes in Berlin;
18th (–19th), in second battle of Gaza Turks, with German support, repulse British;
20th, U.S. and Turkey sever relations;
29th, Henri Pétain becomes chief of French staff;
30th, Frederick Maude defeats Turks at Shatt-el-Adhaim.

E **May**: 3rd (–5th), fresh British attack at Arras breaks Hindenburg Line;
5th, A. J. Balfour addresses U.S. House of Representatives;
— (–9th), battle of Chemin des Dames;
14th, tenth battle of Isonzo;
15th, Henri Pétain succeeds R. G. Nivelle as French Commander-in-Chief and Ferdinand Foch becomes chief of staff;
18th, U.S. selective military conscription bill;
—, Prince Lvov reforms cabinet in Russia to include Socialists;

O **Politics, Economics, Law and Education**

Herman Fernau, *The Coming Democracy*.

Establishment of British Ministry of Labour and of a Civil Aerial Transport Committee.

Impact of the war makes rapid changes on the social and administrative structure of Britain.

Women in munitions factories cut their hair short as a safety precaution, and 'bobbed hair' sweeps Britain and U.S.

Reports of the Commissions on the Dardanelles (*Mar.* 8th) and on Mesopotamia Campaign (*June* 26th).

British merchant ships first sail in organised convoys (*Feb.*).

Companion of Honour and Order of British Empire founded.

P **Science, Technology, Discovery, etc.**

Institute of Technical Optics, South Kensington.

Q **Scholarship**

History (Journal of the Historical Association).

Hrozny, *The Hittite Language*.

R **Philosophy and Religion**

C. Jung, *The Unconscious*.

Maude Royden becomes assistant preacher at the City Temple, London, the first Englishwoman to have a permanent pulpit.

S **Art, Sculpture, Fine Arts and Architecture**

Painting:

P. Picasso's sets and costumes for Diaghilev's ballet *Parade* are described by G. Apollinaire as 'Surrealist'—first use of the term.

P. Bonnard, *Nude at the Fireplace*.

A. Modigliani, *Crouching Female Nude*.

J. S. Sargent, *John D. Rockefeller*.

W. Orpen, W. Rothenstein and E. Kennington are commissioned as British war artists.

Piet Mondrian launches *de Stijl* magazine in Holland.

Sculpture:

P. A. Renoir, *The Washerwoman*.

T **Music**

Arnold Bax, *Tintagel* (overture).

G. Holst, *Hymn of Jesus* (choral work).

Hans Pfitzner, *Palastrina* (opera).

Serge Prokofiev, 'Classical' Symphony.

Ottorino Respighi, *The Fountains of Rome* (rhapsody).

Albert Roussel, *Les dieux dans l'ombre des Cavernes* (orchestral work).

Igor Stravinsky's music for the ballet *The Soldier's Tale*.

E. Satie's music for the ballet *Parade*.

U **Literature**

Norman Douglas, *South Wind*.

T. S. Eliot, *Prufrock and Other Observations*.

L. Feuchtwanger, *Jew Süss* (Eng. translation 1922).

Knut Hamsun, *Growth of the Soil*.

Henry James, *The Middle Years*.

Frank Swinnerton, *Nocturne*.

Paul Valéry, *La jeune parque*.

Mary Webb, *Gone to Earth*.

Pulitzer Prizes are first awarded in U.S.

E May: 20th, mutinies in French army in Champagne;
22nd, Count Tisza, Hungarian premier, resigns;
23rd, Tuan Ch'i-jui, premier of China, dismissed.

F Jun: 2nd, Brazil revokes her neutrality and seizes German ships;
3rd, Albanian independence under Italian protection is proclaimed;
7th, battle of Messines;
10th, Sinn Fein riots in Dublin;
12th, King Constantine I of Greece abdicates in favour of second son, Alexander (–1920);
14th, U.S. mission under E. Root arrives in Petrograd;
15th, amnesty for prisoners of Irish Rebellion, 1916;
16th, first all-Russian congress of Soviets;
19th, British royal family renounces German names and titles, having adopted name of Windsor;
24th, Russian Black Sea fleet mutinies at Sebastopol;
26th, Alexander Kerensky launches Russian counter-attack;
—, first U.S. division arrives in France;
29th, Edward Allenby takes over Palestine command;
—, Greece severs relations with Central Powers.

G Jul: 1st (–9th), Russians break through at Zborov and on R. Dniester;
9th, government control of fuel and food in U.S.;
12th, Tuan Ch'i-jui resumes Chinese premiership;
13th, George Michaelis appointed German chancellor on resignation of T. von Bethmann-Hollweg;
16th (–18th), V. Lenin and other Bolsheviks fail to seize power in Petrograd;
19th, German-Austrian counter-attack in Galicia;
—, Zeppelins attack English industrial areas;
—, Reichstag passes motion for peace;
— (–*Aug.* 2nd), mutinies in German fleet;
20th, Prince Lvov resigns in Russia (succeeded 22nd, by Alexander Kerensky);
—, Corfu pact for union of Serbs, Croats and Slovenes;
25th, Irish convention meets under Horace Plunkett;
31st, Douglas Haig's offensive in third battle of Ypres (or Passchendaele) begins (–*Nov.* 10th).

H Aug: 1st, Richard von Kühlmann becomes German foreign minister;
3rd, Russians take Czernowitz;
6th, failure of German offensive at Foscani;
13th, revolt in Spain for home rule for Catalonia;
14th, China declares war on Germany and Austria;
—, Pope Benedict XV's peace note;
20th (–*Dec.* 15th), French gain positions in second battle of Verdun;
21st, Germans attack on Riga front;
25th (–8th), all-Russian conference at Moscow.

J Sep: 3rd, Germans take Riga;
8th, Lavr Kornilov, dismissed as Russian Commander-in-Chief, marches on Petrograd as leader of counter-revolutionary movement;
12th, Paul Painlevé forms cabinet in France;
15th, Russian republic proclaimed under Alexander Kerensky;
20th, British offensive near Ypres;
29th (–*Oct.* 1st), German aircraft attack London on successive nights.

V **The Press**

W **Drama and Entertainment**

G. Apollinaire, *Les Mamelles de Tirénsias.*
J. M. Barrie, *Dear Brutus.*
L. Pirandello, *Liola.*
Bubbly, with George Robey (revue).
A society is formed to produce Eugène Brieux's *Damaged Goods* in London, and the production is licensed by the Lord Chamberlain.
Mater dolorosa (film).
The Little American (film).

X **Sport**

Y **Statistics**

Merchant shipping losses by Britain (in tons): Jan.–Mar., 911,840; Apr.–June, 1,361,870; July–Sept., 952,938; Oct.–Dec., 782,889.

Z **Births and Deaths**

Jan. 29th Evelyn Baring, Earl of Cromer, d. (76).
Mar. 8th Ferdinand, Count Zeppelin, d. (79).
May 29th John Fitzgerald Kennedy b. (–1963).
July 2nd Herbert Beerbohm Tree d. (65).
Aug. 9th Ruggiero Leoncavallo d. (59).
Sept. 26th Edgar Degas d. (83).
Nov. 17th François Auguste Rodin d. (77).
Nov. 26th Leander Starr Jameson d. (64).
Dec. 17th Elizabeth Garrett Anderson d. (81).
— W. F. Cody ('Buffalo Bill') d. (71).

1917 (Oct.–Dec.)

K Oct: 15th, Germans renew offensive in East Africa at battle of Mahiwa;
22nd, Soviet congress passes resolution for armistice;
23rd, French victory on Aisne forces Germans back to Oise-Aisne canal;
24th, rout of second Italian army, in the Caporetto campaign;
28th, Vittorio Orlando becomes Italian premier.

L Nov: 1st, Count von Hertling appointed German chancellor;
2nd, A. J. Balfour's declaration on Palestine that Britain favoured the establishment of a national home for the Jewish people;
5th (–9th), Allied conference at Rapallo decides on Supreme Allied War Council (which first meets, 29th, at Versailles);
6th, Canadians and British capture Passchendaele Ridge;
7th (old style, *Oct.* 26th), Lenin leads Bolsheviks against A. Kerensky at Petrograd (October Revolution), and
8th, becomes chief of commissars of people and Lev Trotsky is appointed premier;
7th, British take Gaza;
10th (–12th), Kerensky's counter-revolution fails;
11th, Italians fall back on R. Piave;
16th, Georges Clemenceau forms cabinet in France on Paul Painlevé's fall;
17th, British take Jaffa;
20th, first notable tank battle in British advance at Cambrai;
—, Ukrainian republic proclaimed;
26th, Soviets offer armistice to Germany and Austria.

M Dec: 1st, German East Africa cleared of German troops;
5th, German and Russian delegates sign armistice at Brest-Litovsk (where peace negotiations begin 21st);
6th, Finnish republic proclaimed;
7th, U.S. declares war on Austria-Hungary;
9th, Roumania signs armistice with Central Powers at Foscani;
—, Turks surrender Jerusalem to Edmund Allenby;
10th, Italians torpedo Austrian battleship *Wien* in Trieste;
17th, Robert Borden becomes Canadian premier after Unionist election victory;
28th, Bessarabia proclaims its independence as the Moldavian republic;
—, U.S. government takes control of railways;
31st, prohibition in Canada.

N

A Jan: 8th, Woodrow Wilson propounds Fourteen Points for world peace in message to Congress;
14th, Joseph Caillaux, former premier of France, arrested for treason (sentenced to imprisonment *Apr.* 1920);
16th, strike begins in Vienna;
18th, Russian constitutional assembly opens in Petrograd but
19th, is dissolved by Bolsheviks;
20th, *Breslau* sunk in Dardanelles;
21st, Edward Carson resigns from War Cabinet;
24th, Germany and Austria decline British-U.S. peace proposals;
27th, Russia denounces Anglo-Russian treaty of 1907;
28th (–*Feb.* 3rd), strike in Berlin;
—, Bolsheviks occupy Helsinki.

B Feb: 5th, separation of Church and State in Russia;
9th, Ukraine signs peace with Central Powers;
18th, German offensive opens on Russian front;
20th (–23rd), inter-allied Labour and Socialist conference in London;
21st, Australians occupy Jericho;
25th, meat and butter rationed in London and Southern England.

C Mar: 1st, Germans occupy Kiev and, 2nd, Narva;
3rd, peace treaty of Brest-Litovsk between Russia and Central Powers, and 7th, between Germany and Finland;
12th, Turks occupy Baku (–*May* 14th);
21st, German offensive begins second battle of the Somme;
23rd, Germans shell Paris from 75 miles away;
—, Lithuania proclaims its independence;
26th, Doullens agreement for united command on Western Front, under Ferdinand Foch, signed by Georges Clemenceau and Alfred Milner.

D Apr: 1st, R.A.F. formed, replacing R.F.C.;
8th (–10th), Rome meeting of representatives of Czecho-Slovaks, Roumanians, Yugoslavs and Poles;
9th (–29th), battle of the Lys;
—, Latvia proclaims her independence;
12th, Germans take Armentières;
14th, Germans occupy Helsingfors, on Russians' withdrawal;
19th, Alfred Milner becomes British war secretary;
22nd (–23rd), Zeebrugge raid blocks entrance to Bruges Canal;
24th, British victory at Villers-Bretonneux;
29th, German major offensive on Western Front ends.

E May: 1st, Germans occupy Sebastopol;
6th, Allied break-through in Albania;
7th, Roumania signs peace treaty with Central Powers;
9th, Maurice debate in Commons on military manpower threatens D. Lloyd George's leadership;
— (–10th), British attack on Ostend;
14th, Overman bill empowers U.S. President to reorganise executive departments;
23rd, Georgia proclaims its independence;
27th (–*June* 5th), intensive German offensive on Western Front;
29th, Germans capture Soissons and Rheims.

O **Politics, Economics, Law and Education**
Oswald Spengler, *The Decline of the West* (–22).
A. F. Pollard, *The League of Nations: an Historical Argument.*
Women over 30 gain the vote in Britain.
Food shortage in Britain leads to establishment of National Food Kitchens (*Mar.*) and Rationing (*July* 14th). Prime Minister appeals to women to help with the harvest (*June* 25th).
Standard Clothing for male civilians is made by Board of Control of Textile Industries.
Ministry of Labour established in Germany (*Oct.*).
Daylight Saving introduced in U.S.

P **Science, Technology, Discovery, etc.**
Arthur Eddington, *Gravitation and the Principle of Relativity.*
Radioactive element protoactinium is discovered.
Mount Wilson telescope completed.
Three-colour traffic lights installed in New York.
Influenza epidemic (*May–June* and *September*).

Q **Scholarship**
H. R. H. Hall and Leonard Woolley begin Babylonian excavations.

R **Philosophy and Religion**
Bertrand Russell, *Mysticism and Logic.*

S **Art, Sculpture, Fine Arts and Architecture**
Painting:
Paul Klee's abstract *Gartenplan.*
John Nash, *The Cornfield.*
Paul Nash, *We are making a New World.*
Architecture:
A. Ozenfant and Le Corbusier (pseud.), *Après le Cubisme*, a manifesto on 'Purism'.
David Low's cartoons in *The Star*, newspaper.

T **Music**
B. Bartók, *Bluebeard's Castle* (opera).
E. Elgar, 'cello concerto.
G. Puccini, *Il Trittico* (operas).
S. Diaghilev's ballet company visits London.

U **Literature**
Alexander Blok, *The Twelve.*
Rupert Brooke, *Collected Poems* (posth. ed. Edward Marsh).
G. M. Hopkins, *Poems* (posth.).
Laurence Housman, *The Sheepfold.*
Lytton Strachey, *Eminent Victorians.*

V **The Press**

W **Drama and Entertainment**
James Joyce, *The Exiles.*
Luigi Pirandello, *Six Characters in Search of an Author.*
European tour of the 'Original Dixieland Jazz Band'.
The Lilac Domino (musical).

F Jun: 9th (–13th), German offensive near Compiègne;
21st, British government announces abandonment of Home Rule and conscription for Ireland.

G Jul: 6th, Montagu-Chelmsford Report on Constitution of India published;
13th, Turkish offensive in Palestine checked;
15th (–*Aug.* 4th), second battle of the Marne;
16th, execution of ex-Tsar Nicholas II and family on orders of Ural Regional Council;
18th, great Allied counter-attack opens;
22nd, Allies cross R. Marne.

H Aug: 2nd, French recapture Soissons;
—, Japanese advance into Siberia;
3rd, British force lands at Vladivostok;
8th, H. A. L. Fisher introduces Education bill for England and Wales;
15th, U.S. and Russia sever diplomatic relations;
20th, British offensive on Western Front opens;
31st, Bolshevist troops attack British embassy at Petrograd.

J Sep: 1st, British take Péronne;
4th, Hsu Shi-chang elected President of Chinese Republic;
—, Germans retreat to Siegfried Line;
10th, Mahommedan riots in Calcutta;
12th, U.S. offensive at St. Mihiel salient;
14th, Austro-Hungarian peace offer (which Allies refuse, 20th);
15th, Allied break-through in Bulgaria;
22nd, collapse of Turkish resistance in Palestine;
29th, Belgians capture Dixmude;
—, Bulgaria signs armistice with Allies;
—, Paul von Hindenburg demands immediate peace offer;
30th, George, Count Hertling, German chancellor, resigns.

K Oct: 1st, British and Arab forces occupy Damascus;
—, French take St. Quentin;
3rd, Prince Max of Baden appointed German chancellor;
— (–4th), German-Austrian note to U.S., via Switzerland, for armistice;
6th, French occupy Beirut;
9th, British take Cambrai and Le Cateau;
12th, Germany and Austria agree to Woodrow Wilson's terms, that their troops should retreat to their own territory before armistice is signed;
13th, Laon falls to French and, 17th, Lille to British troops;
17th, republic of Yugoslavia formally established;
19th, Belgians recapture Zeebrugge and Bruges;
20th, Germany suspends submarine warfare;
22nd, influenza epidemic in Britain at its height;
26th, Ludendorff dismissed;
30th, Allies sign armistice with Turkey;
—, Czechoslovakia proclaimed as an independent republic in Prague;
31st, Hungarian premier, Count Tisza, assassinated.

L Nov: 1st, Anglo-French forces occupy Constantinople;
3rd, Allies sign armistice with Austria-Hungary (to come into force 4th);

w Drama and Entertainment (*cont.*)

The Bing Boys on Broadway (revue).

Veritas Vincit (film).

Charlie Chaplin in *Shoulder Arms* and *A Dog's Life* (films).

x Sport

y Statistics

Merchant shipping losses by Britain (in tons): Jan.–Mar., 697,668; Apr.–June, 630,862; July–Sept., 512,030; Oct.–Dec., 83,952.

World total of shipping losses, 1914–1918, 15 mill. tons of which 9 mill. was British.

Naval Losses, 1914–18

	Dread-noughts	Pre-Dread-noughts	Battle Cruisers	Cruisers	Light Cruisers	De-stroyers	Sub-marines
British Empire	2	11	3	13	12	64	54
France	—	4	—	5	—	13	12
Germany	—	1	1	6	17	68	200
Austria	2	1	—	—	3	6	11
Turkey	—	1	—	—	1	3	—
Italy	1	3	—	1	2	9	7
Russia	2	2	—	2	—	18	15
Japan	1	—	1	—	2	1	—
U.S.	—	—	—	1	—	2	2

Casualties, 1914–18 (in thousands):

	Killed	*Wounded*	*Missing*
British Empire	767	2,090	132
France	1,383	2,560	—
U.S.	81	179	1
Italy	564	1,030	—
Germany	1,686	4,211	991
Russia*	1,700	2,500	

* To Peace of Brest-Litovsk.

z Births and Deaths

Mar. 6th J. E. Redmond d. (62).

Mar. 26th Claude Debussy d. (56).

Aug. 25th Leonard Bernstein b. (–).

Oct. 7th Charles Hubert Hastings Parry d. (70).

Nov. 7th Billy Graham b. (–).

Dec. 2nd Edmund Rostand d. (50).

L Nov: 3rd, German grand fleet mutinies at Kiel;
4th, Allied conference at Versailles agrees on peace terms for Germany;
5th, U.S. Congressional elections result in Republican majority of 43;
6th, Polish republic proclaimed in Cracow;
—, U.S. troops occupy Sedan;
8th, British take Maubeuge;
9th, republic proclaimed in Bavaria;
—, revolution in Berlin, Prince Max resigns, William II abdicates and a council of People's Delegates assumes power;
11th, armistice signed between Allies and Germany;
12th, Emperor Charles I abdicates in Austria (and, 13th, in Hungary);
—, Austria proclaims union with Germany;
13th, Soviet government annuls treaty of Brest-Litovsk;
14th, British Labour Party decides to secede from Coalition;
— (–21st), German fleet surrenders at sea;
—, German troops in Northern Rhodesia surrender;
—, T. Masaryk elected President of Czechoslovakia;
18th, Latvian independence;
—, Belgian troops enter Brussels and Antwerp;
22nd, D. Lloyd George and A. Bonar Law issue Coalition election manifesto;
29th, Nicholas King of Montenegro deposed and his kingdom united with Serbia under King Peter;
30th, Transylvania proclaims union with Roumania.

M Dec: 1st, Iceland becomes a sovereign state;
4th, Serbo-Croatian-Slovene Kingdom of Yugoslavia is proclaimed;
5th, Germans blockade Baltic;
6th, Allies occupy Cologne;
8th, Bolshevik rule in Estonia;
14th, in British general election Coalition have majority of 262 (Conservatives and Unionists, 395, Liberals, 163; Labour, 59, Sinn Fein, 73, others, 16);
—, Sidonio Paes, President of Portugal, assassinated;
—, Woodrow Wilson arrives in Paris for peace conference;
20th, Berlin conference of workers' and soldiers' delegates demands nationalisation of industries;
27th, Poles occupy Posen.

N

1919 (Jan.–Apr.) The Versailles Peace Conference—Mussolini founds Italian Fascist Party

A Jan: 3rd, Herbert Hoover becomes director-general of international organisation for relief in Europe.
[illegible] the Rhine.
5th, Spartacist (Communist) revolt in Berlin.
— National Socialist Party founded in Germany.
[illegible]
10th, [illegible] administration of [illegible] Railway.
[illegible]
18th(?), Rumania annexes Transylvania.
[illegible] amendment to U.S. Constitution [illegible] list of states.
[illegible] premier of Poland (to Nov. 27th).
18th, Peace Conference at Versailles opens under Georges Clemenceau's chairmanship.
21st, Sinn Fein Congress, Dublin, adopts declaration of independence.
23rd, Socialist Majority in German elections.
[illegible] Bolshevik forces.
[illegible] Peace Conference adopts principle of League of Nations.
[illegible] in Kabul.

B Feb: [illegible] president of Germany [illegible].
3rd(?), [illegible] Russian [illegible] Bolsheviks in Caucasus.
— [illegible] League of Nations meeting, Paris.
[illegible] Paris.
[illegible]
[illegible] of German Republic.
[illegible] Germany.
14th, Woodrow Wilson presents draft of League Covenant before Peace Conference (Mar. 4th [illegible]).
[illegible]
[illegible] premier, assassinated in Munich.
[illegible] Fasci del Combattimento.
[illegible] Commission under Lord Sankey (reports [illegible]).
[illegible] H. C. Lodge [illegible] campaign in U.S. against League of Nations.

C Mar: 2nd, [illegible] Grand Trunk Pacific Railway (is nationalised 1920).
10th, U.S. Supreme Court upholds conviction of Eugene V. Debs for espionage.
— [illegible] following deportation of Saad Zaghlul Pasha.
[illegible] appointed [illegible]
[illegible] navigation.
[illegible] Allenby becomes high commissioner in Egypt.
[illegible] government formed in Budapest.

D Apr: 4th, Philippines demand independence.
— Soviet Republic established in Bavaria (-May 1st).
[illegible] Valera [illegible] president of the [illegible] (imprisoned [illegible]).
[illegible] Allies evacuate Odessa.
[illegible] Red Army enters Crimea.
[illegible]
[illegible] against Prohibition.
[illegible] Montenegro [illegible] votes for union with Serbo-Croat-Slovene State (Yugoslavia).

1919 (Jan.–Apr.) The Versailles Peace Conference—Mussolini founds Italian Fascist Party

A Jan: 3rd, Herbert Hoover becomes director-general of international organisation for relief of Europe;
4th, Bolsheviks take Riga;
5th (–11th), Communist (Spartacist) revolt in Berlin;
—, National Socialist Party formed in Germany;
7th, British Labour Party decide to go into opposition;
10th, British army takes over administration of Baghdad Railway;
— (–*Feb.* 4th), Soviet Republic of Bremen;
11th, Roumania annexes Transylvania;
16th, prohibition amendment to U.S. Constitution ratified by last of states;
17th, Ignace Paderewski premier of Poland (resigns *May* 18th);
18th, Peace Conference at Versailles opens under Georges Clemenceau's chairmanship;
21st, Sinn Fein Congress, Dublin, adopts declaration of independence;
23rd, Socialist victory in German elections;
25th, Allies withdraw from Shenkunsk after Bolshevik attack;
—, Peace Conference adopts principle of League of Nations;
29th, Czechoslovakians defeat Poles in Galicia.

B Feb: 2nd, monarchy proclaimed in Portugal;
3rd (–9th), Anton Denikin's White Russian Army routs Bolsheviks in Caucasus;
—, Woodrow Wilson presides at first League of Nations meeting, Paris;
—, international Socialist conference, Berne;
—, Bolsheviks capture Kiev;
11th, Friedrich Ebert elected President of German republic;
13th, Philipp Scheidemann, Socialist, forms cabinet in Germany;
14th, Woodrow Wilson lays League of Nations Covenant before Peace Conference (adopted *Mar.* 25th);
—, Bolsheviks invade Estonia;
20th, Ameer of Afghanistan murdered;
21st, Kurt Eisner, Bavarian premier, assassinated in Munich;
23rd, Benito Mussolini founds Fasci del Combattimento;
26th, Britain sets up Coal Commission under Lord Sankey (reports *June* 23rd);
28th, H. C. Lodge begins campaign in U.S. against League of Nations.

C Mar: 9th, bankruptcy of Canadian Grand Trunk Pacific Railway (is nationalised 1920);
10th, U.S. Supreme Court upholds conviction of Eugene V. Debs for espionage;
—, Nationalist riots in Cairo, following deportation of Said Zaghlul Pasha;
16th, Karl Renner, Socialist, appointed chancellor of Austria;
21st, Danube is thrown open to navigation;
—, Edmund Allenby becomes high commissioner in Egypt;
22nd, Soviet government formed in Budapest.

D Apr: 4th, Philippines demand independence;
—, Soviet Republic established in Bavaria (–*May* 1st).
5th, Éamon de Valéra is elected president of the Sinn Fein Dáil executive (suppressed *Sept.*);
7th, Allies evacuate Odessa and
8th, Red Army enters Crimea;
10th (–14th), riots in Portugal;
11th, referendum in New Zealand declares against Prohibition;
20th, King Nicholas is dethroned in Montenegro, which votes for union with Serbo-Croat-Slovene State (Yugoslavia);

O **Politics, Economics, Law and Education**

International Labour Organisation established.

Communist Third International founded.

J. M. Keynes, *The Economic Consequences of the Peace.*

Irving Fisher, *Stabilising the Dollar in Purchasing Power.*

British Housing Act empowers local authorities to raise money by issuing bonds.

Women over 20 are enfranchised in Germany.

German Ministry of Economics is established.

P **Science, Technology, Discovery, etc.**

Observations of the total eclipse of the sun (*May* 29th) bear out Albert Einstein's theory of relativity.

Ernest Rutherford's 'transmutation', producing a simpler atom from a complex one.

F. W. Aston builds mass-spectograph and establishes the phenomena of isotopy.

Hans Vogt experiments with sound film system.

J. W. Alcock and A. W. Brown fly across the Atlantic in 16 hrs. 27 mins. (*June* 14th).

Ross Smith flies from London to Australia in 135 hours (*Dec.* 10th).

First successful helicopter flight; first motor scooter.

E. Shackleton, *South*, an account of his 1914–17 expedition.

Severe influenza epidemic (*Mar.*).

Q **Scholarship**

J. B. Huizinga, *The Waning of the Middle Ages.*

H. L. Mencken, *The American Language.*

R **Philosophy and Religion**

Henri Bergson, *L'énergie spirituelle.*

Havelock Ellis, *The Philosophy of Conflict.*

Dean W. R. Inge, *Outspoken Essays.*

Karl Barth, *The Epistle to the Romans.*

Enabling Act in Britain brings the Church Assembly into existence.

S **Art, Sculpture, Fine Arts and Architecture**

Painting:

P. Picasso, *Pierrot and Harlequin;* and sets for the *Three-Cornered Hat.*

A. Modigliani, *The Marchesa Casati.*

E. Munch, *The Murder.*

A. Munnings, *Zennor Hill.*

John Ruskin Centenary Exhibition, Royal Academy.

Sculpture:

Wax and plaster figures of dancers and horses, created by E. Degas 1890–1912, are cast in bronze.

Architecture:

The Bauhaus (School of Design, Building and Crafts) founded by W. Gropius in Weimar; transferred to Dessau, 1925.

E. Lutyens submits design for the Cenotaph, Whitehall.

T **Music**

M. de Falla, *Three-cornered Hat* (ballet).

La boutique fantasque (Diaghilev's production).

André Messager's *Monsieur Beaucaire* (operetta) with Maggie Teyte.

A. Busch founds string quartet.

D Apr: 28th, German delegates arrive at Peace Conference;
30th, Peace Conference grants German concession in Shantung to Japan, whereupon China leaves the Conference.

E May: 1st, great strike in Winnipeg (*–June* 15th);
—, Bavarian government troops capture Munich from Communists;
3rd, war between British India and Afghanistan (*–Aug.* 3rd);
6th, Peace Conference disposes of Germany's colonies, assigning German East Africa as a mandate to Britain, and German South-West Africa as a mandate to South Africa;
28th, Armenia declares its independence;
29th, Germany's counter-proposals to Peace Conference;
30th, Britain agrees on transfer of part of German South-West Africa to Belgium.

F Jun: 3rd, British reinforcements reach Archangel;
6th, Finland declares war on U.S.S.R.;
8th, Nicaragua asks U.S. for protection against Costa Rica;
9th, Red Army takes Ufa;
10th, Austria protests against terms of Peace Conference;
21st, Gustave Bauer, Socialist, forms cabinet in Germany, following P. Scheidemann's fall, 20th, for decision against signing Peace Treaty;
—, Francesco Nitti becomes premier of Italy;
—, German fleet is scuttled in Scapa Flow;
22nd, German national assembly at Weimar authorises signature of Peace Treaty (signed at Versailles, 28th);
28th, Britain and U.S. guarantee France in event of an unprovoked German attack, which U.S. later refuses to ratify.

G Jul: 12th, Britain and France authorise resumption of commercial relations with Germany;
12th, Edward Carson demands repeal of Home Rule and threatens to call out volunteers;
19th, peace celebrations in Britain;
26th, Indian government and Afghanistan peace conference at Rawalpindi (treaty signed *Aug.* 8th);
27th (–31st), race riots in Chicago;
31st, Germany adopts Weimar Constitution.

H Aug: 1st, Hungarian Socialist régime under Bela Kun overthrown;
4th, Roumanians enter Budapest;
5th, Mackenzie King elected Canadian Liberal leader;
—, Mustafa Kemal at Turkish Nationalist Congress declares himself independent of Istanbul, aiming to prevent further dismemberment of Turkey;
6th, Archduke Joseph becomes 'state governor' of Hungary (resigns 23rd, on Allies' demand);
9th, Anglo-Persian agreement at Teheran to preserve integrity of Persia;
10th, Anglo-White Russian forces defeat Soviet forces in North Dvina;
14th, revised Bavarian constitution;
15th (*–Nov.*), Prince of Wales visits Canada and U.S.;
22nd, Imperial Preference Provisions Act passed;
—, Joseph Ward resigns on break-up of Coalition in New Zealand;
23rd, U.S. Senate committee rejects Shantung clause of Versailles Treaty;
31st, press censorship abolished in Ireland.

U **Literature**

Sherwood Anderson, *Winesburg, Ohio.*
M. Beerbohm, *Seven Men.*
J. Branch Cabell, *Jurgen.*
A. Gide, *La Symphonie pastorale.*
T. Hardy, *Collected Poems.*
V. Blasco Ibáñez, *The Four Horsemen of the Apocalypse.*
W. S. Maugham, *The Moon and Sixpence.*

V **The Press**

Arthur Mee founds *Children's Newspaper.*

W **Drama and Entertainment**

G. B. Shaw, *Heartbreak House.*
Arnold Bennett and Nigel Playfair manage the Birmingham Repertory Theatre.
J'Accuse (film).
Madame Dubarry (film).
Hedda Gabler (film).
The Mystery Man (film).
Growth of broadcasting by amateurs in U.S.

X **Sport**

Suzanne Lenglen dominates Wimbledon Lawn Tennis Championships.

Y **Statistics**

Merchant fleets (in mill. tons): British Empire, 18·6; U.S., 13·1; Germany, 3·5; Japan, 2·3; France, 2·2; Norway, 1·9; Holland, 1·6; Italy, 1·4; Sweden, 1·0.

Strikes:

	No. of workers involved	No. of working-days lost
Great Britain	2,591,000	34,903,000
France	1,206,175	16,128,638
U.S.	4,160,348	—

Unemployed in Britain include 353,000 ex-servicemen.

Z **Births and Deaths**

Jan. 5th Theodore Roosevelt d. (61).
Feb. 17th Wilfrid Laurier d. (78).
Apr. 4th William Crookes d. (86).
May 18th Margot Fonteyn b. (–).
July 20th Edmund Hillary b. (–).
Aug. 8th Ernst Haeckel d. (85).
Aug. 11th Andrew Carnegie d. (84).
Aug. 27th Louis Botha d. (57).
Sept. 27th Adelina Patti d. (76).
Oct. 17th Henry Irving d. (49).
Dec. 3rd Pierre Auguste Renoir d. (78).

J Sep: 2nd, Anton Denikin's force enters Kiev;
10th, Allied peace treaty with Austria at St. Germain;
12th, Gabriele d'Annunzio leads unofficial Italian army to seize Fiume;
15th, China terminates war with Germany;
22nd, U.S. steel strike (–*Jan.* 1920);
25th, Peace Conference grants Norway sovereignty over Spitzbergen;
27th, British troops enter Archangel.

K Oct: 6th, Prohibition in Norway;
10th, Luxembourg referendum in favour of monarchy, with economic union with France;
12th, British withdraw from Murmansk;
13th, New York dock strike;
17th, Austria ratifies peace treaty;
22nd, Nicolai Yudenich, Russian counter-revolutionary, defeated by Red Army near St. Petersburg;
27th, George Curzon succeeds A. J. Balfour as British foreign secretary;
— (–8th), Woodrow Wilson vetoes Volstead Prohibition Enforcement bill, but House and Senate pass it;
28th, British War Cabinet ends;
29th, International Labour Conference at Washington.

L Nov: 7th, Allied Supreme Council demands withdrawal of Roumanian troops from Hungary;
11th, first 2-minutes' silence in Britain;
13th, U.S. Senate's resolution on article X of League of Nations Covenant amounts to virtual rejection of Peace Treaty;
15th, Red Army takes Omsk;
17th, Belgo-Dutch agreement on River Scheldt;
21st, Supreme Council gives Poland mandate over Galicia for 25 years;
27th, Peace of Neuilly between the Allies and Bulgaria;
28th, Latvia declares war on Germany;
—, Lady Astor elected first British woman M.P.

M Dec: 5th, Serbo-Croat-Slovene Kingdom agrees to peace treaties with Austria and Bulgaria;
9th, U.S. delegates leave Peace Conference;
13th, Soviets capture Kharkov from Anton Denikin;
15th, Fiume declares her independence;
16th, German troops evacuate Latvia and Lithuania;
19th, Liberals defeated in New Zealand elections;
20th, House of Representatives moves to curtail immigration;
31st, Britain, U.S., and Japan sign agreement over East Siberia.

N

A Jan: 5th, Poles and Letts capture Dvinsk from Bolsheviks;
8th, Admiral Alexander Kolchak defeated at Krasnoyarsk (he is executed by Bolsheviks *Feb.* 7th);
10th, The League of Nations comes into being;
—, Eupen and Malmédy united with Belgium;
13th, Argentina admitted to League;
16th, first meeting of Council of League in Paris;
—, Prohibition comes into force in U.S.;
—, U.S. Senate votes against joining League;
17th, Paul Deschanel becomes President of France;
23rd, Holland declines to surrender ex-Kaiser William II as demanded by Supreme Allied War Council;
28th, Turkish national pact of Ankara signed at Constantinople.

B Feb: 2nd, Estonia signs peace with U.S.S.R. and declares its independence;
8th, Bolsheviks capture Odessa;
9th, Allies cede Spitzbergen to Norway;
10th, plebiscite in Schleswig north zone favours uniting with Denmark (middle zone favours Germany, *Mar.* 14th);
13th, Switzerland is admitted to League;
15th, Allies take over Memel;
25th, Bainbridge Colby becomes U.S. secretary of state, following Robert Lansing's resignation, 13th;
26th, League takes over the Saar;
—, U.S.S.R. sends Allies new peace offer;
27th, Allies announce that Turkey will retain Constantinople, but Dardanelles to be under international control;
28th, Hungarian and, 29th, Czechoslovak constitutions are adopted.

C Mar: 1st, Nicholas Horthy elected regent of Hungary;
—, U.S. government returns railways to companies;
5th, Norway, 8th, Denmark and 10th, Netherlands are admitted to League;
10th, Ulster votes to accept Home Rule bill;
11th, Emir Feisal proclaimed King of an independent Syria;
13th (-17th), Wolfgang Kapp attempts pro-monarchist *coup d'état* in Berlin;
16th, Allies occupy Constantinople;
19th, U.S. Senate finally rejects Versailles Treaty;
28th, Bolsheviks take Novorossisk on Black Sea; collapse of Anton Denikin's White Russian army.

D Apr: 6th (-*May* 17th), French troops occupy Frankfurt, Darmstadt and Hanau until Germany evacuates Ruhr;
25th, Supreme Allied Council assigns mandates of Mesopotamia and Palestine to Britain and of Syria and the Lebanon to France;
—, Polish offensive in the Ukraine under Josef Pilsudski against U.S.S.R. (-*Oct.* 12th);
30th, conscription abolished in Britain.

E May: 5th, Woodrow Wilson rules that Communist Labor Party of America is outside scope of U.S. deportation laws;
7th, treaty of Berlin between Germany and Latvia;
8th, Poles and Ukrainians enter Kiev;
11th, Turkish national assembly meets at Ankara;
20th, President Carranza of Mexico assassinated; succeeded by Adolfo de la Huerta.

A **Jan**: 5th, Poles and Letts capture Dvinsk from Bolsheviks;
8th, Admiral Alexander Koltchak defeated at Krasnoyarsk (he is executed by Bolsheviks *Feb.* 7th);
10th, The League of Nations comes into being;
—, Eupen and Malmédy united with Belgium;
13th, Argentina admitted to League;
16th, first meeting of Council of League in Paris;
—, Prohibition comes into force in U.S.;
—, U.S. Senate votes against joining League;
17th, Paul Deschanel becomes President of France;
23rd, Holland declines to surrender ex-Kaiser William II as demanded by Supreme Allied War Council;
28th, Turkish national pact of Ankara signed at Constantinople.

B **Feb**: 2nd, Estonia signs peace with U.S.S.R. and declares its independence;
8th, Bolsheviks capture Odessa;
9th, Allies cede Spitzbergen to Norway;
10th, plebiscite in Schleswig north zone favours uniting with Denmark (middle zone favours Germany, *Mar.* 14th);
13th, Switzerland is admitted to League;
15th, Allies take over Memel;
25th, Bainbridge Colby becomes U.S. secretary of state, following Robert Lansing's resignation, 13th;
26th, League takes over the Saar;
—, U.S.S.R. sends Allies new peace offer;
27th, Allies announce that Turkey will retain Constantinople, but Dardanelles to be under international control;
28th, Hungarian and, 29th, Czechoslovak constitutions are adopted.

C **Mar**: 1st, Nicholas Horthy elected Regent of Hungary;
—, U.S. government returns railways to companies;
5th, Norway, 8th, Denmark and 10th, Netherlands are admitted to League;
10th, Ulster votes to accept Home Rule bill;
11th, Emir Feisal proclaimed King of an independent Syria;
13th (–17th), Wolfgang Kapp attempts pro-monarchist *coup d'état* in Berlin;
16th, Allies occupy Constantinople;
19th, U.S. Senate finally rejects Versailles Treaty;
28th, Bolsheviks take Novorossiisk on Black Sea; collapse of Anton Denikin's White Russian army.

D **Apr**: 6th (–*May* 17th), French troops occupy Frankfurt, Darmstadt and Hanau until Germany evacuates Ruhr;
25th, Supreme Allied Council assigns mandates of Mesopotamia and Palestine to Britain and of Syria and the Lebanon to France;
—, Polish offensive in the Ukraine under Josef Pilsudski against U.S.S.R. (–*Oct.* 12th);
30th, conscription abolished in Britain.

E **May**: 5th, Woodrow Wilson rules that Communist Labor Party of America is outside scope of U.S. deportation laws;
5th, treaty of Berlin between Germany and Latvia;
8th, Poles and Ukrainians enter Kiev;
11th, Turkish national assembly meets at Ankara;
20th, President Carranza of Mexico assassinated; succeeded by Adolfo de la Huerta;

O **Politics, Economics, Law and Education**
Prohibition in U.S. (*Jan.* 16th).
German National Economic Council established.
W. Sombart, *Der Moderne Kapitalismus.*
Oswald Spengler, *Prussianism and Socialism.*
Slump in U.S.
Welwyn Garden City is established.
Royal Institute of International Affairs, London, founded.

P **Science, Technology, Discovery, etc.**
Baade discovers the planet Hidalgo, farthest from the sun.
First chemical fumigators.
J. T. Thompson invents sub-machine gun.
The decade of 'lighter than air' airships begins.
The rise of the specialised scientific periodical.

Q **Scholarship**
Discovery of the skeletons of Peking Man ('*Sinanthropus*').
H. G. Wells, *Outline of History.*

R **Philosophy and Religion**
S. Alexander, *Space, Time and Deity.*
C. G. Jung, *Psychological Types.*
J. Maritain, *Art et scolastique.*

S **Art, Sculpture, Fine Arts and Architecture**
Painting:
Juan Gris, *Guitar, Book and Newspaper.*
S. Spencer, *Christ Bearing the Cross* and *The Last Supper.*
H. Matisse, *The Odalisque.*
A. Modigliani, *Reclining Nude.*
Spectators at Cologne Exhibition of Dadaist art allowed to smash paintings.

T **Music**
Vincent D'Indy, *The Legend of St. Christopher* (oratorio).
Erik Satie, *Socrate* (opera).
I. Stravinsky's ballets *Pulcinello* and *Le Chant du Rossignol.*
Louis Durey, Darius Milhaud, Germaine Tailleferre, Arthur Honegger, Georges Auric and Francis Poulenc form 'Les Six'.

U **Literature**
Colette, *Chéri.*
F. Wills Crofts, *The Cask; a Detective Story.*
J. Galsworthy, *In Chancery.*
Franz Kafka, *The Country Doctor.*
Sinclair Lewis, *Main Street.*
Katherine Mansfield (pseud.), *Bliss.*
Sigrid Undset, *Kristin Lavransdatter* (–22).
P. Valéry, *Le Cimetière marin.*

V **The Press**
Time and Tide issued.

W **Drama and Entertainment**
J. Galsworthy, *The Skin Game.*
E. O'Neill, *Beyond the Horizon.*

E May: 27th, Woodrow Wilson vetoes Knox peace resolution terminating state of war with Germany;
—, Leonid Krassin, Soviet trade delegate, arrives in London.

F Jun: 4th, treaty of Trianon between the Allies and Hungary;
12th, Republican Convention at Chicago nominates Warren G. Harding for presidency and Calvin Coolidge for vice-presidency;
20th, federal water power act in U.S.;
21st, Konstantin Fehrenback becomes chancellor of Germany;
—, Supreme Allied Council agrees that Germany shall make 42 annual reparations payments largely to France, Britain, Italy and Belgium;
24th, Greek offensive in Asia Minor against Turkish nationalists;
25th, The Hague selected as seat of International Court of Justice.

G Jul: 1st, Robert Borden resigns in Canada (succeeded as premier, 10th, by Arthur Meighen);
5th, Democratic convention nominates James M. Cox for presidency, F. D. Roosevelt for vice-presidency;
— (–16th), Spa Conference between Allies and Germany on reparations;
—, Schleswig is transferred to Denmark;
6th, Britain evacuates Batum;
—, U.S.S.R. offensive against Poland opens;
8th, Britain annexes East African Protectorate as Kenya Colony;
11th, plebiscite in East and West Prussia 97 per cent for Germany;
12th, U.S.S.R.-Lithuanian peace treaty;
21st, Sinn Feiners and Unionists riot in Belfast;
—, King Feisal recognises French mandate in Syria;
24th, treaty of St. Germain (signed *Sept.* 1919), comes into force;
25th, France occupies Damascus;
Greeks under King Alexander occupy Adrianople;
27th, Russians take Pinsk and cross into Poland;
28th, Teschen agreement between Czechoslovakia and Poland signed in Paris.

H Aug: 8th, U.S.S.R. again rejects proposal for armistice with Poland;
9th, British Labour organisations appoint Council of Action to arrange general strike if Britain declares war on U.S.S.R.;
10th, New States treaty between Allies, Roumania, Czechoslovakia and Poland; and frontier treaty with Roumania, Czechoslovakia and the Serbo-Croat-Slovene Kingdom (Yugoslavia);
—, Graeco-Italian treaty assigns Dodecanese Isles to Greece;
—, Constantinople government signs the Treaty of Sèvres, representing a break between the Nationalists and the Sultan;
11th, Riga treaty between U.S.S.R. and Latvia;
14th, Yugoslav-Czechoslovak alliance, which is joined, 17th, by Roumania to form 'Little Entente';
— (–16th), Poles defeat Russians at Warsaw;
18th, Milner-Zaghlul conversations provide for recognition of Egyptian independence;
19th, Poles enter Brest-Litovsk;
28th, Nineteenth Amendment gives women the vote in U.S.

J Sep: 5th, Alvaro Obregón becomes President of Mexico;
7th, Franco-Belgian military convention;
10th, Russo-British negotiations are suspended owing to Russian attempt to subsidise *Daily Herald*;

W **Drama and Entertainment** (*cont.*)

First public broadcasting station in Britain opened by G. Marconi at Writtle (*Feb.*); first broadcasting station in U.S. opened at East Pittsburgh (*Nov.* 2nd) by Westinghouse Company to give Harding-Cox election results.

Paul Whiteman's band visits Europe and the rage for jazz becomes universal.

British Board of Film Censors established.

The Cabinet of Dr. Caligari with Conrad Veidt (film).

The Mother and *Polyanna* with Mary Pickford (films).

Mary Pickford marries Douglas Fairbanks.

X **Sport**

Olympic Games held at Antwerp.

William T. Tilden, America, wins Wimbledon Lawn Tennis Championships.

Y **Statistics**

Coal production (in mill. tons): U.S., 645·5; Great Britain, 229·5; Germany, 107·5.

Petroleum production (in mill. barrels): U.S., 443; Mexico, 163; Russia, 25; Dutch East Indies, 17; Persia, 12; India, 7; Roumania, 7; Poland, 5.

Motor vehicles licensed: U.S., 8,887,000; Great Britain, 663,000.

Strikes:

	No. of workers involved	No. of working-days lost
Great Britain	1,932,000	27,011,000
U.S.	1,463,054	—
France	1,487,996	24,563,527

The Courts: In Britain 3,747 divorces are granted; 95,763 convictions for drunkenness.

Z **Births and Deaths**

Jan. 4th Benito Pérez Galdós d. (75).
Feb. 19th Robert Edwin Peary d. (64).
Mar. 24th Mrs. Humphry Ward d. (69).
May 11th William Dean Howells d. (82).
July 4th Max Klinger d. (63).
July 10th John, Lord Fisher, d. (79).
July 11th Empress Eugénie d. (94).
Sept. 1st Wilhelm Wundt d. (88).
Nov. 20th Jesse Collings d. (89).

J Sep: 23rd, Alexandre Millerand elected President of France as successor to Paul Deschanel, resigned from ill health, 16th.

K Oct: 1st, new Austrian constitution;
9th, Poland annexes Vilna;
10th, plebiscite in Carinthia favours Austria;
12th, U.S.S.R.-Polish peace treaty signed at Tartu;
20th, treaty of Ankara between France and Turkey;
—, U.S.-Chinese tariff treaty;
27th, Poland signs treaty with Danzig;
—, League of Nations headquarters are moved to Geneva.

L Nov: 2nd, Warren G. Harding, Republican, elected President of U.S. with 404 electoral votes against James M. Cox, Democrat, 137;
7th (*–Dec.* 21st), serious famine in China;
12th, by treaty of Rapallo Italy obtains Istria and cedes Dalmatia to Serbo-Croat-Slovene Kingdom (Yugoslavia) while Fiume is to be independent;
14th, Red Army takes Sebastopol;
15th, Danzig is declared a free city;
16th, end of Russian counter-revolution;
17th, Dowager Queen Olga becomes Regent of Greece;
19th, convention between Nicaragua, Honduras and Costa Rica.

M Dec: 2nd, by treaty of Alexandropol, Armenia cedes territory to Turkey;
3rd, Austria joins the League;
5th, plebiscite in Greece favours return of King Constantine (who returns 19th);
9th, Michael Hainisch elected first President of Austria;
10th, Woodrow Wilson and Léon Bourgeois awarded Nobel Peace Prize;
12th, martial law in Cork;
15th (–22nd), Brussels conference on Germany's reparations;
16th, Bulgaria, Costa Rica, Finland and Latvia, and
17th, Albania are admitted to the League;
23rd, Government of Ireland Act passed; Northern and Southern Ireland each to have own parliament;
—, Franco-British convention on boundaries of Syria and Palestine;
29th, French Socialist Conference votes for adhesion to Moscow International.

N

A Jan: 3rd, first Indian Parliament meets;
10th, Leipzig war trials before German supreme court begin;
16th, Aristide Briand forms ministry in France;
22nd, deportation of Mantes, self-styled U.S.S.R. ambassador to U.S.;
24th (–29th), Paris conference of the Allies fixes Germany's reparation payments;
25th, U.S. Senate adopts resolution on suspension of naval contracts.

B Feb: 4th, James Craig elected United Ulster leader;
8th, Jan C. Smuts gains majority of 20 in South African elections;
9th, peace treaty of Riga between U.S.S.R. and Poland;
12th, W. S. Churchill becomes colonial secretary;
18th, recall of U.S. representative from Reparation Commission;
21st, London conference of Allies on the Near East;
26th, U.S.S.R. signs treaties with Persia and, 28th, with Afghanistan;
27th, riots between Communists and Fascists in Florence.

C Mar: 1st, Turkish treaty with Afghanistan;
4th, President Warren G. Harding inaugurated;
5th, U.S. warns Costa Rica and Panama to settle frontier dispute by arbitration;
8th, French troops occupy Düsseldorf and other towns in Ruhr on grounds of Germany's failure to make preliminary reparations payment;
11th, France in treaty with Turkey renounces Cilicia;
15th, Ruanda, East Africa, ceded to Britain by Belgian convention;
16th, Anglo-U.S.S.R. trade agreement and British trade mission visits Moscow;
17th, A. Bonar Law resigns Unionist leadership in Commons;
—, Polish Constitution established;
18th, by treaty of Riga with U.S.S.R., Poland abandons claim to the Ukraine;
20th, in Upper Silesian plebiscite 63 per cent vote for incorporation with Germany;
21st, Austen Chamberlain elected Unionist leader;
23rd, Germany announces she will be unable to pay £600 mill. due as reparations on *May* 1st;
24th, British Reparation Recovery act imposes 50 per cent duties on German goods (reduced, *May* 20th, to 26 per cent);
—, Communist riots in Hamburg;
25th, U.S. refuses U.S.S.R. request to resume trading;
27th, ex-Emperor Charles's *coup* in Hungary fails;
28th, British I.L.P. refuses to affiliate with Communists;
31st, strike of British miners.

D Apr: 12th, President Harding declares U.S. could play no part in the League;
19th, Government of Ireland Act in force;
23rd, Czechoslovak-Roumanian alliance;
24th, plebiscite in Tyrol favours Germany;
—, Germany unsuccessfully asks U.S. to mediate in reparations controversy;
General Erich von Ludendorff is acquitted of breaches of laws of war by Leipzig court;
27th, Reparations Commission fixes Germany's total liability at £6,650 mill.

E May: 2nd, French troops are mobilised for occupation of Ruhr;
5th, Allied Supreme Council warns Germany that failure to pay reparations, by 12th, will lead to occupation of Ruhr;
6th, German-U.S.S.R. peace treaty signed;
8th, capital punishment is abolished in Sweden;
10th, in German cabinet crisis Julius Wirth, Catholic Centre Party, becomes chancellor;

O Politics, Economics, Law and Education

James Bryce, *Modern Democracies.*
Gilbert Murray, *The Problem of Foreign Policy.*
Bertrand Russell, *The Prospects of Industrial Civilisation.*
Stern-Rubarth, *Propaganda as a Political Weapon.*
'Chequers', presented to the nation by Lord Lee of Fareham, becomes the official country residence of the Prime Minister (*Jan.* 8th).
British Broadcasting Company founded.
British Legion founded (*May* 24th).
National Institute of Industrial Psychology, London, founded.
Belgium and Luxembourg form a customs union, though in the rest of Europe high tariffs return.
New Economic Policy in U.S.S.R. (*Mar.*) witnesses a partial return of capitalism.

P Science, Technology, Discovery, etc.

Ernest Rutherford and James Chadwick disintegrate all the elements, except carbon, oxygen, lithium and beryllium, as preliminary to splitting the atom (–24).
First medium-wave wireless broadcast, in U.S.

Q Scholarship

Institute of Historical Research, London, founded, with A. F. Pollard as director.
Lytton Strachey, *Queen Victoria.*

R Philosophy and Religion

H. Hartmann, *Philosophy of Knowledge.*
John M'Taggart, *The Nature of Existence.*
Teschner, *Telepathy and Clairvoyance.*

S Art, Sculpture, Fine Arts and Architecture

Painting:
P. Klee, *The Fish.*
Georges Braque, *Still Life with Guitar.*
Fernand Léger, *Three Women.*
E. Munch, *The Kiss.*
P. Picasso, *Three Musicians.*

Architecture:
Micheal de Klerk, Eigen Haard flats, Amsterdam.

T Music

Arthur Honegger, *King David* (opera, later revised as oratorio).
Serge Prokofiev, *Loves of Three Oranges* (opera).
Musicians' Union founded, London.

U Literature

Agatha Christie, *The Mysterious Affair at Styles.*
A. Huxley, *Crome Yellow.*
D. H. Lawrence, *Women in Love.*
John Galsworthy, *To Let.*
George Moore, *Héloïse and Abelard.*
John Dos Passos, *Three Soldiers.*
Italo Svevo, *The Confessions of Zeno.*
P. Valéry, *L'Âme de la danse.*

V The Press

E May: 11th, Germany accepts Allies' ultimatum on reparations;
14th, 29 Fascists returned in Italian elections;
19th, U.S. Emergency Quota Immigration act;
20th, Germany and China resume diplomatic relations;
28th, Walter Rathenau appointed German minister for reparations;
—, Egyptian Nationalist riots at Alexandria;
30th, plebiscite in Salzburg favours union with Germany.

F Jun: 5th, Italy, Serbia and Yugoslavia agree on control of Fiume;
7th, U.S. refuses to recognise Mexican government until international obligations are honoured;
—, first Parliament of Northern Ireland opens;
—, Roumanian-Yugoslav alliance;
19th, the powers agree to mediate between Turkey and Greece (but, 25th, Greece refuses the offer);
20th, London Imperial Conference;
22nd, Labour Conference of Great Britain rejects affiliation with Communists;
27th, Afghanistan-Persian treaty.

G Jul: 1st, Safeguarding of Industries Act in Britain to prevent dumping of foreign manufactures;
11th, British truce with Sinn Fein;
16th, Greeks defeat Turks at Kutahia;
23rd, convention for internationalisation of Danube;
25th, Belgium and Luxembourg sign 50-year economic pact;
29th, All-India Congress decides to boycott Prince of Wales's visit.

H Aug: 11th, U.S. invites powers to conference on Far East and the limitation of armaments;
12th, Allied Supreme Council refers Upper Silesia question to League;
23rd, Dáil rejects British peace offer;
24th, U.S. signs peace treaties with Austria;
—, (–*Sept.* 16th), in battle of the Sakkaria, the Turks prevent Greek forces from reaching Ankara;
25th, U.S. signs peace treaties with Germany, and 29th, with Hungary;
26th, German finance minister Mathias Erzberger assassinated;
29th (–*Dec.* 16th), state of emergency proclaimed in Germany in the face of economic crisis.

J Sep: 9th, constitution of Central American Union signed by republics of Guatemala, Honduras and San Salvador;
22nd, Estonia, Latvia and Lithuania are admitted to the League;
30th, Anglo-Russian commercial agreement;
—, French troops evacuate Ruhr.

K Oct: 6th, Franco-German agreement for supply of reparations in kind;
18th, U.S.S.R. central executive grants independence to Crimea;
19th, revolution in Lisbon;
20th, Franco-Turkish agreement signed at Ankara;
25th (–6th), Poland and Germany accept League proposal for partition of Upper Silesia;
—, ex-Emperor Charles is expelled from Hungary on failure of further attempted *coup*;
27th, Germany agrees to accept Allies' conditions on reparations.

(*Continued opposite*)

W **Drama and Entertainment**

Gabriel Marcel, *La Grâce*.
Eugene O'Neill, *The Emperor Jones*.
Jean Sarment, *Le Pêcheur d'ombres*.
Rapid development of night clubs.
Charles Chaplin in *The Kid* (film).
Hunger! Hunger! Hunger! (film).
Anne Boleyn (film).
The Adventuress from Monte Carlo (film).

X **Sport**

Australia wins the Ashes.

Y **Statistics**

Populations (in mill.): U.S.S.R., 136; U.S., 107; Japan, 78; Germany, 60; Great Britain, 42·7; France, 39·2; Italy, 38·7.
Petroleum production: U.S., 472 mill. barrels.

Strikes:

	No. of workers involved	No. of working-days lost
Great Britain	1,801,000	85,872,000
France	453,564	8,092,388
U.S.	1,099,247	—

Z **Births and Deaths**

Sept. 2nd Austin Dobson d. (81).
Sept. 27th Engelbert Humperdinck d. (67).
Dec. 16th Camille Saint-Säens d. (86).

L Nov: 1st, Otto Braun, Socialist, forms ministry in Prussia;
4th, Takashi Hara, premier of Japan, assassinated;
5th, U.S.S.R. treaty with government of Mongolia;
12th, powers recognise Albanian government;
— (–*Feb.* 6th, 1922), Washington Conference on disarmament;
Rapid fall of the German Mark.

M Dec: 6th, Britain signs peace with Ireland;
6th, Liberals defeat Conservatives in Canadian election;
7th, U.S. and Austria resume diplomatic relations;
11th, British arrest president of Indian National Congress;
13th, U.S., British Empire, France and Japan sign Washington treaty to respect each other's rights over insular possessions in the Pacific, and by this treaty the U.S. is drawn into consultation with other powers in matters of common concern;
14th, in Ödenburg plebiscite 65 per cent vote for union with Hungary, as against Czechoslovakia;
15th, Germany applies for moratorium for payments;
21st, U.S.S.R.-Turkish alliance;
—, William Hughes becomes premier of Australia in Nationalist cabinet reconstruction;
27th, Italian-U.S.S.R. commercial agreement;
29th, U.S., British Empire, France, Italy and Japan sign Washington treaty to limit naval armaments;
—, Mackenzie King, Liberal, becomes premier of Canada.

N

1922 (Jan.–Jun.) Irish Rebellion—Mussolini's march on Rome—Fall of Lloyd George

A Jan: 7th, The Dáil approves treaty with Britain and
9th, motion for re-election of Éamon de Valéra as president is defeated;
10th, Arthur Griffith elected head of provisional government of Southern Ireland;
—, strike in Rand gold mines;
13th, Cannes conference decides to postpone Germany's reparation payments;
15th, Raymond Poincaré forms ministry in France (following Aristide Briand's resignation, 12th);
—, Irish government formed under Michael Collins;
26th, legislative council of Southern Rhodesia accepts draft constitution conferring limited self-government;
31st, Walter Rathenau becomes German foreign minister.

B Feb: 1st, Washington conference approves treaties restricting submarine warfare and poison gas;
4th, Japan agrees to restore Shantung to China;
6th, Cardinal Achille Ratti elected Pope Pius XI, following Benedict XV's death, *Jan.* 22nd;
11th, nine-power treaty of Washington for securing China's independence and maintaining the 'open door';
—, U.S.-Japanese naval agreement;
—, Honduras becomes an independent republic;
15th, Permanent Court of International Justice holds first sessions at The Hague;
21st, British protectorate in Egypt ended.

C Mar: 1st, U.S.S.R.-Swedish trade agreement;
6th, U.S. prohibits export of arms to China;
10th, strikes and martial law in Johannesburg;
15th, modified reparations agreement, for Germany to pay with raw materials, signed by France and Germany (approved by Commission, 31st);
—, de Valéra organises a Republican Society, to fight Nationalists;
16th, Britain recognises Kingdom of Egypt under Fuad I, with joint Anglo-Egyptian sovereignty over Sudan;
17th, Baltic states and Poland sign agreement on neutrality;
18th, Mahatma Gandhi sentenced to six years' imprisonment for civil disobedience;
20th, President W. Harding orders return of U.S. troops from Rhineland.

D Apr: 1st, U.S. coal strike (–*Aug.* 15th);
—, South Africa denounces Mozambique Convention;
7th, Britain concedes to Standard Oil Co. rights in Palestine;
10th (–*May* 19th), economic conference of European powers at Genoa;
14th, Irish rebels seize the Four Courts, Dublin, from the Free State government;
16th, treaty of Rapallo between Germany and U.S.S.R. recognises U.S.S.R. as 'a great power' and leads to the resumption of diplomatic and trade relations.

E May: 10th, Genoa convention between U.S.S.R. and the Vatican;
15th, Germany cedes Upper Silesia to Poland;
24th, Italy signs commercial treaty with U.S.S.R.

F Jun: 5th, Medal of Congress presented to people of Verdun;
10th, bankers' committee of Reparations Commission declines to recommend international loan for Germany;
16th, polling in Southern Ireland gives majority to Pro-Treaty candidates;
20th, independent citizenship for U.S. women marrying aliens;

O Politics, Economics, Law and Education

Herbert Hoover, *American Individualism.*

C. E. Montague, *Disenchanted.*

Lady Rhondda is permitted to take a seat in House of Lords by Committee of Privileges, but this judgment is later reversed.

Report of Geddes Economy Committee leads to severe cuts in expenditure on British armed and civil services and on education.

Revival of Ku-Klux-Klan in U.S.

Fordney-McComber Act drastically raises U.S. tariff.

C. Pestalozzi, *The Argument about Co-education.*

International Union for Cultural Co-operation, Vienna.

U.S. forms 'Prohibition Navy' to prevent widespread liquor smuggling.

Marie Stopes holds series of meetings in Queen's Hall, London, advocating birth control.

P Science, Technology, Discovery, etc.

Niels Bohr's theory that electrons circulate in orbits in parallel planes around atoms.

P. S. M. Blackett's experiments in transmutation of elements.

The element hafnium discovered.

Heyrowsky's electro-chemical analysis.

Frederick Banting and Best isolate insulin and a diabetic patient in Toronto receives an insulin injection.

First ionamide dyes are prepared.

John Harwood invents self-winding wrist-watch.

The 'Austin Seven' popularises motoring.

Q Scholarship

Lord Carnarvon and Howard Carter discover the tomb of Tutankhamūn at Luxor (*Nov.*).

R Philosophy and Religion

James Dewey, *Human Nature.*

Étienne Gilson, *The Philosophy of the Middle Ages.*

E. Troeltsch, *Historismus.*

Ludwig Wittgenstein writes *Tractatus Logico-Philosophicus.*

S Art, Sculpture, Fine Arts and Architecture

Painting:

Paul Klee, *The Machine Song.*

Joan Miró, *The Farm.*

P. W. Steer, *Mrs. Raynes* and *Victor Lecour.*

Max Beerbohm, *Rossetti and his Circle* (drawings of artists).

M. Chagall, *Dead Souls* (85 etchings, published 1948).

Clive Bell publishes *Since Cézanne.*

David Low, *Lloyd George and Co.* (a book of political cartoons).

Architecture:

E. Freyssinet, Bridge of St. Pierre-du-Vauvray.

L.C.C. County Hall opened.

T Music

A. Bliss, 'Colour' Symphony.

P. Hindemith, *St. Susanna* (opera).

F. Lehár, *Frasquita* (operetta).

F **Jun**: 24th, Walter Rathenau (aged 55) is murdered by Nationalists;
26th, emergency decree in Germany to protect the economy of the republic;
28th, dispute between the Reich and Bavaria;
—, British Labour Party declines to reconsider affiliation with Communist Party;
—, siege of Four Courts, Dublin, and
30th, rebel forces surrender to Free State troops.

G **Jul**: 2nd (–5th), heavy fighting in Dublin;
8th, Chile and Peru agree to submit Tacna-Arica dispute to arbitration;
20th, League Council approves mandates for Togoland, the Cameroons and Tanganyika and
24th, for Palestine and Egypt;
29th, ultimatum of Allied Powers forbidding Greek occupation of Constantinople;
30th, Nationalists capture Tipperary.

H **Aug**: 1st, Balfour Note circulated to Allies, stating that Britain would only expect to recover from her European debtors the sum which the U.S. expected from her, thus placing the odium of war debts on U.S.;
—, Britain, France and Italy warn Greece against attempted occupation of Palestine;
4th (–8th), fighting between Fascists and Socialists in Italian cities;
22nd, Michael Collins (aged 30), chairman of Irish Provisional Government, killed by Republican ambush;
24th, Arab Congress at Nablus rejects British mandate for Palestine;
31st, Czecho-Serbo-Croat alliance signed at Marienbad;
—, Reparations Commission adopts Belgian proposal for Germany's payments by instalments on Treasury bills.

J **Sep**: 9th, William T. Cosgrave elected President of Irish Free State (following Arthur Griffith's death, *Aug.* 12th);
10th, Anglo-U.S.S.R. commercial treaty, which U.S.S.R. refuses in *Oct.* to ratify;
11th, British mandate proclaimed in Palestine while Arabs declare a day of mourning;
13th, Franco-Polish 10-year military convention;
18th, Hungary is admitted to the League;
21st, U.S. protectionist tariff;
27th, King Constantine of Greece abdicates;
30th, conscription in U.S.S.R.

K **Oct**: 4th, Austria receives international loan;
10th, Graeco-Turkish armistice;
11th, Mundania conference between Allies and Turkey ends in agreement regarding neutral zones, with Greece undertaking to evacuate Thrace;
17th, unemployed workers leave Glasgow on hunger march to London;
19th, fall of D. Lloyd George's Coalition;
23rd, A. Bonar Law forms Conservative ministry in Britain;
24th, Dáil adopts a Constitution for Irish Free State;
—, Friedrich Ebert re-elected Reich President;
27th, Italian cabinet resigns;
—, referendum in Southern Rhodesia votes against joining Union of South Africa;
28th, Benito Mussolini marches on Rome, and
30th, forms Fascist government.

L **Nov**: 1st, Kemal Pasha proclaims Turkish republic;
—, civil war renewed in China;

T **Music** (*cont.*)

M. Ravel, sonata for violin and 'cello.
O. Respighi, 'Gregorian' violin concerto.
I. Stravinsky, *Mavra* (opera).
R. Vaughan Williams, 3rd Symphony ('Pastoral')

U **Literature**

John Buchan, *Huntingtower*.
R. M. du Gard, *Les Thibault* (–40).
T. S. Eliot, *The Waste Land*.
James Joyce, *Ulysses* (published in Paris).
D. H. Lawrence, *Aaron's Rod*.
Sinclair Lewis, *Babbitt*.
Katharine Mansfield (pseud.), *The Garden Party*.
R. M. Rilke, *Sonette an Orpheus*.
Hugh Walpole, *The Cathedral*.
P.E.N., London, founded by Mrs. Dawson Scott.

V **The Press**

Criterion issued.

W **Drama and Entertainment**

B. Brecht, *Drums in the Night*.
A. A. Milne, *The Dover Road*.
B.B.C. 2LO broadcasts from Marconi House (*Nov.* 14th).
George Grossmith introduces cabaret entertainment.
The debut of the 'cocktail'.
Lilac Time (G. H. Clutsam—musical).
Films:
The Last of the Mohicans.
Glorious Adventure.
Pharaoh's Wife.
Dr. Mabuse.

Y **Statistics**

British Textile trade:

Imports of raw cotton	1,409 mill. lb.
Exports of cottons	4,313 mill. yds.
Exports of linens	77 mill. yds.
Exports of silks	5 mill. sq. yds.

T.U. membership: 5,625,000 in Great Britain.

Strikes:

	No. of workers involved	No. of working-days lost
Great Britain	552,000	19,850,000
France	307,056	3,385,902
U.S.	1,608,321	—

1922 (Nov.–Dec.)

L Nov: 2nd (–7th), Berlin conference of monetary experts on German currency;
7th, reduced Republican majority in U.S. Congressional elections;
17th, Far Eastern Republic votes for union with U.S.S.R.;
—, in British general election Conservatives win 344 seats, Labour 138 and Liberals 117;
22nd, Wilhelm Cuno becomes German chancellor;
24th, execution of Erskine Childers in Ireland;
28th, six ex-ministers of Greece executed.

M Dec: 1st, Josef Pilsudski, President of Poland, resigns;
6th, Irish Free State officially proclaimed;
7th, Northern Ireland Parliament votes for non-inclusion in Irish Free State;
15th, Franco-Canadian trade agreement;
16th, in Australian elections Nationalists win 27 seats, Labour 29 and the Country Party 14;
17th, last British troops leave Irish Free State;
26th, Reparations Commission, against British vote, declares Germany has made a voluntary default in payments.

N

z **Births and Deaths**

Jan. 5th Ernest Shackleton d. (48).
Jan. 22nd James Viscount Bryce d. (84).
Apr. 7th A. V. Dicey d. (87).
Apr. 16th Kingsley Amis b. (–).
May 15th Leslie Ward ('Spy'), d. (71).
Aug. 1st Alexander Graham Bell d. (75).
Aug. 14th Alfred Harmsworth, Lord Northcliffe, d. (57).
Aug. 18th W. H. Hudson d. (81).
Oct. 7th 'Marie Lloyd' (pseud. of Matilda Wood) d. (76).
Nov. 15th Marcel Proust d. (51).

A **Jan**: 1st, The Union of Soviet Socialist Republics established, a confederation of Russia the Ukraine, White Russia and Transcaucasia (comes into force *July* 6th);
10th, Memel, under Allied occupation, is seized by Lithuania;
11th, French and Belgian troops occupy Ruhr in consequence of Germany's failure over reparations;
19th, Germany declares policy of passive resistance, which provokes further boycott by the French, and the German economy slows to a standstill;
28th, French troops completely encircle the Ruhr;
31st, Britain accepts terms of commission for funding her war debt to U.S.

B **Feb**: 1st, Allied ultimatum to Lithuania to evacuate Memel;
2nd, Central American Republics sign treaty of amity at Washington;
—, Stanley Bruce becomes premier of Australia;
4th, Lausanne conference on the Near East breaks down through Turkey's refusal to accept proposals;
10th, Turkey's alliance with Afghanistan;
16th, conference of ambassadors assigns Memel to Lithuania, with safeguards for Poland;
24th, U.S. Labor Party convention repudiates Communism.

C **Mar**: 3rd, U.S. Senate rejects proposal to join International Court of Justice;
14th, Allies recognise Vilna and East Galicia as Polish;
21st, Secretary of State Charles Hughes declares U.S. will not recognise U.S.S.R. unless she acknowledges her foreign debts and restores alien property.

D **Apr**: 11th, Conservative government defeated (by 145 votes to 138) in Commons on motion on ex-Servicemen;
20th, Egyptian Constitution adopted;
26th, Mexico recognises oil concessions granted before 1917;
30th, Irish rebels suspend offensive operations following acceptance of terms of Éamon de Valéra's proclamation of 27th by the government.

E **May**: 8th, British note to U.S.S.R. on dissemination of anti-British propaganda;
10th, Vaslav Vorovski, U.S.S.R. delegate at Lausanne, murdered;
20th, A. Bonar Law resigns on grounds of ill health and
22nd, Stanley Baldwin forms Conservative ministry, with Neville Chamberlain as Chancellor of Exchequer;
25th, Britain, France, Italy and Belgium agree to reimburse U.S. cost of U.S. army of the Rhine;
—, independence of Transjordan under Amir Abdullah is proclaimed;
29th, Palestine Constitution suspended by British order in Council through refusal of Arabs to co-operate.

F **Jun**: 1st, New York State Prohibition Enforcement Act repealed by the governor;
9th, *coup d'état* in Bulgaria leads to fall of Alexander Stambolisky (who is assassinated, 15th);
10th, Swiss-Liechtenstein customs union;
19th, Stanley Baldwin and Andrew Mellon sign Anglo-U.S. war debt convention;
26th, German-Estonian commercial treaty.

G **Jul**: 2nd (–*Aug.* 20th), London dock strike;
10th, dissolution of non-Fascist parties in Italy;
18th, British Matrimonial Causes Act gives women equality in divorce suits;
24th, peace treaty of Lausanne between Greece, Turkey and the Allies.

O Politics, Economics, Law and Education

Alfred Marshall, *Money, Credit and Commerce.*
W. A. Appleton, *Unemployment.*
Labour and Socialist International founded (*May*).
A birth control clinic is opened in New York.

P Science, Technology, Discovery, etc.

Frederick Lindemann investigates the size of meteors and the temperature of the upper atmosphere.
L. A. Bauer analyses the earth's magnetic field.
E. N. da C. Andrade, *The Structure of the Atom.*
John B. Tytus invents continuous hot-strip rolling of steel.
Heape and Grylls make a rapid filming machine.

Q Scholarship

The Cambridge Ancient History (ed. J. B. Bury), Vol. I.
S. de Madariaga, *The Genius of Spain.*

R Philosophy and Religion

S Art, Sculpture, Fine Arts and Architecture

Painting:
M. Beckmann, *The Trapeze.*
Augustus John, *Thomas Hardy.*
P. Picasso, *Seated Woman.*
Stanley Spencer, *The Resurrection* (–1927).
M. Utrillo, *Ivry Town Hall.*

Sculpture:
Frank Dobson, *Sir Osbert Sitwell.*

Architecture:
Raymond Hood, Chicago Tribune Building.
Royal Fine Art Commission is formed in Britain to advise the government on design and siting of buildings and memorials.

T Music

B. Bartók, *Dance Suite* (opera).
M. de Falla, *Master Pédros* (opera).
G. Holst, *The Perfect Fool* (opera).
A. Honegger, *Pacific 231.*
Z. Kodály, *Háry János* Suite and *Psalmus Hungarius.*
F. Poulenc, *The House Party* (ballet).
A. Roussel, *Le Festin de l'Araignée.*
William Walton, *Façade.*
Robert Mayer founds Children's Concerts in London.

U Literature

Arnold Bennett, *Riceyman Steps.*
E. E. Cummings, *Enormous Room.*
John Drinkwater, *Collected Poems.*
Scott Fitzgerald, *Tales of the Jazz Age.*
D. H. Lawrence, *Kangaroo.*
F. Mauriac, *Génitrix.*
D. L. Sayers, *Whose Body?*

V The Press

Time Magazine and *The Adelphi* are first issued.

H Aug: 2nd, President W. G. Harding dies (aged 58), succeeded, 3rd, by Calvin Coolidge;
6th, Gustav Stresemann becomes German chancellor and foreign minister;
10th (–13th), strikes and riots in Germany;
13th, Mustapha Kemal elected President of Turkey by Angora assembly;
15th, Irish Free State troops arrest Éamon de Valéra;
27th, in Irish elections Nationalists win 63 seats, Republicans 44;
31st, Italy occupies Corfu;
— (–*Sept.* 17th), U.S. coal strike.

J Sep: 1st, earthquake in Japan;
3rd, U.S. recognises Mexican government;
—, Greece appeals to League over Corfu;
10th, Irish Free State admitted to League;
14th, Miguel Primo de Rivera assumes dictatorship in Spain;
15th, Germany's bank rate raised to 90 per cent;
26th, Germany abandons passive resistance;
27th, martial law in Germany;
28th, Abyssinia is admitted to League;
29th, Palestine mandate begins.

K Oct: 1st, failure of Black Reichswehr *coup d'état* in Germany;
—, responsible government in Southern Rhodesia;
11th, value of German Mark drops to rate of 10,000 million to £;
13th, Ankara (formerly Angora) becomes new capital of Turkey;
21st, France recognises separatist government in the Palatinate;
26th (–*Nov.* 8th), British Empire conference in London recognises the right of Dominions to make treaties with foreign powers;
29th, revised Turkish republican Constitution under Kemal Pasha.

L Nov: 8th (–9th), Adolf Hitler's *coup d'état* in Munich fails;
20th, German currency temporarily stabilised;
29th, Reparations Commission appoints two committees of experts under Charles Dawes and Reginald McKenna to investigate German economy;
30th, separatist riots in Rhineland end.

M Dec: 6th, in British general election the Conservatives, standing on platform of protective tariff to relieve unemployment, lose heavily (Conservatives, 258, Labour, 191, Liberal, 158);
8th, U.S. treaty of friendship and commerce with Germany;
17th, Greek army deposes George II;
18th, Britain, France and Spain sign convention on Tangier.

N

W Drama and Entertainment

Karel Čapek, *R.U.R.*
J. E. Flecker, *Hassan.*
Eugene O'Neill, *Anna Christie.*
Luigi Pirandello, *The Late Mattia Pascal.*
Elmer Rice, *The Adding Machine.*
G. B. Shaw, *Back to Methuselah.*
Sutton Vane, *Outward Bound.*

Films:
A Woman of Paris (directed by Charles Chaplin).
Public Opinion.
Love on the Dole.
I.N.R.I.
Skyscraper.
The Pilgrim.
Robin Hood.

X Sport

First F.A. Cup Final played at Wembley Stadium, won by Bolton Wanderers.

Y Statistics

Strikes:

	No. of workers involved	No. of working-days lost
Great Britain	405,000	10,670,000
U.S.	744,948	—
Holland	22,200	3,119,000

In Germany between 1919 and 1923 an annual average of 23,158,000 working-days lost.

Z Births and Deaths

Jan. 9th 'Katherine Mansfield' (pseud. of Kathleen Murry *née* Beauchamp) d. (35).
Feb. 1st Ernst Troeltsch d. (57).
Feb. 8th Bernard Bosanquet d. (75).
Feb. 10th Wilhelm von Röntgen d. (78).
Mar. 26th Sarah Bernhardt d. (77).
June 10th 'Pierre Loti' (pseud. of Julien Viaud) d. (73).
Sept. 23rd John Lord Morley d. (84).
Oct. 30th Andrew Bonar Law d. (65).
Dec. 4th Maurice Barrès d. (61) and Maria Callas b. (–).
Dec. 27th Gustav Eiffel d. (91).

1924 (Jan.–Jun.) First Labour Government in Britain—Dawes Report on German reparations

A **Jan**: 11th, Eleutherios Venizelos accepts premiership of Greek national assembly (–*Feb*. 4th);
21st, N. Lenin dies;
—, first Kuomin Tang (Nationalist) Congress at Canton admits Communists to the party and welcomes Russian advisers;
22nd, Stanley Baldwin resigns;
23rd, Ramsay MacDonald forms first Labour government in Britain, with Philip Snowden Chancellor of Exchequer;
24th, non-Fascist trade unions abolished in Italy;
25th, Franco-Czechoslovak alliance.

B **Feb**: 1st, Britain recognises U.S.S.R.;
2nd Caliphate abolished by Turkish national assembly;
3rd, Alexei Rykoff elected president of Council of People's Commissars in U.S.S.R.;
16th, British dock strike (–26th);
18th, Edwin Denby, U.S. navy secretary, forced to resign through connection with oil leases;
19th, Shah Ahmad of Persia deposed;
23rd, Britain reduces reparation recovery duties on German goods to 5 per cent;
28th, U.S. troops land in Honduras.

C **Mar**: 3rd, Germany signs treaty of friendship with Turkey;
9th, Italy annexes Fiume but abandons her claims to Yugoslavia's Dalmatian coast;
24th, Greece is proclaimed a republic.

D **Apr**: 1st, Adolf Hitler is sentenced to 5 years' imprisonment (but is released *Dec*. 20th);
9th, Committees under Charles Dawes and Reginald McKenna make reports on reparations issue;
11th, Socialist government in Denmark;
14th, Anglo-U.S.S.R. conference in London;
18th, League reorganises Hungary's finances;
24th, Irish boundary conference in London fails.

E **May**: 4th, in Reichstag elections Nationalists and Communists win many seats from moderates;
11th, in French elections the National bloc is defeated by a cartel of the Left;
15th, international conference on immigration held at Rome;
19th, Pan-American treaty signed to prevent conflicts between states;
26th, Calvin Coolidge signs bill limiting immigration into U.S. and entirely excluding Japanese;
—, W. Marx ministry in Germany resigns on breakdown of negotiations for coalition of Nationalists and Moderates;
31st, China recognises U.S.S.R.

F **Jun**: 10th, on murder of Giacomo Matteotti, Italian Socialist deputy, the opposition leave the Chamber;
—, Republican Convention at Cleveland nominates Calvin Coolidge for U.S. presidency and Charles Dawes for vice-presidency;
—, Alexandre Millerand, President of France, resigns;
13th, Gaston Doumergue is elected his successor and
15th, Édouard Herriot becomes premier;
24th, Democratic Convention in New York nominates J. W. Davis for presidency and William J. Bryan for vice-presidency;

O Politics, Economics, Law and Education

Ramsay MacDonald in House of Commons claims the executive is immune from judicial criticism, a reply to Mr. Justice McCardie's judgment in O'Dwyer *v.* Nairn.

Sweden returns to the gold standard.

Four universities are founded in Italy.

P Science, Technology, Discovery, etc.

Edward Appleton and M. F. Barett measure the Heaviside Layer.

Arthur Eddington discovers that the luminosity of a star is approximately a function of its mass.

The first insecticide.

'Fonofilm' system of talking pictures is developed.

World Power Conference at Wembley (*June*).

Q Scholarship

Wallis Budge edits *Baraalam and Yearsef*.

Ancient Monuments Society founded in England.

R Philosophy and Religion

S Art, Sculpture, Fine Arts and Architecture

Painting:

Gwen John, *The Convalescent*.

Juan Gris lectures at the Sorbonne on *Possibilités de la Peinture*.

Sculpture:

Charles Wheeler, *The Infant Christ* (bronze bust).

Architecture:

E. Lutyens, Britannic House, Finsbury.

T Music

Ernest Bloch, piano quintet.

George Gershwin, *Rhapsody in Blue*.

P. Hindemith's song-cycle *Das Marienleben*.

G. Puccini, *Turandot* (opera).

O. Respighi, *The Pines of Rome*.

A. Schönberg's music monodrama *Erwartung* and *Die glückliche Hand* (opera).

I. Stravinsky, wind octet.

Anton Webern, three religious songs.

S. Koussevitsky conducts Boston Symphony Orchestra.

U Literature

E. M. Forster, *A Passage to India*.

John Galsworthy, *The White Monkey*.

David Garnett, *A Man in the Zoo*.

T. Mann, *The Magic Mountain*.

St. John Perse (pseud.), *Anabase*.

Mary Webb, *Precious Bane*.

V The Press

F. M. Ford founds *Transatlantic Review*.

W Drama and Entertainment

Marc Connelly, *Green Pastures*.

Noël Coward, *The Vortex*.

F **Jun**: 25th, Britain states she will not abandon the Sudan, despite Egyptian demands for complete evacuation;
30th, J. B. Hertzog, Nationalist Party leader, forms ministry in South Africa with Labour support, following defeat of J. C. Smuts' South African Party in elections.

G **Jul**: Ramsay MacDonald refuses to sign treaty of mutual assistance prepared by League;
11th (–15th), rioting between Hindus and Moslems in Delhi;
16th, at London conference on reparations, attended by Gustave Stresemann and Édouard Herriot, the Dawes Report, which removes reparations from the sphere of political controversy, is approved.

H **Aug**: 6th, Lausanne treaty for re-establishing world peace comes into force;
16th, French delegates at London conference agree to evacuate Ruhr within a year and
18th, French troops leave Offenburg region;
29th, Reichstag approves Dawes Plan, which comes into force *Sept.* 1st.

J **Sep**: 17th, Italy abrogates treaty of Rapallo (*Nov.* 12th 1920);
20th, Britain brings Mosul controversy before the League;
29th, Germany states terms on which she will join the League, including a permanent seat on the Council;
30th, naval control of Germany abolished.

K **Oct**: 2nd, League adopts Geneva Protocol for the peaceful settlement of international disputes;
3rd, King Hussein abdicates throne of Hejaz in favour of his son Ali;
9th, Parliament is dissolved following Labour defeat on question of prosecution of *Workers' Weekly*;
—, Irish Free State bill receives royal assent (and, 17th, passes Dáil);
10th, international loan to Germany arranged in London;
25th, Foreign Office publishes the Zinoviev Letter, in which the Third International allegedly instructs Britons to provoke revolution;
—, Tsao Kun, President of China, resigns;
28th, France recognises U.S.S.R.;
29th, Conservatives win British general election with 413 seats against Labour 151, and Liberals 40.

L **Nov**: 4th, Calvin Coolidge, Republican, wins U.S. presidential election with 382 electoral votes, over J. W. Davis, Democrat, 136, and La Follette, Progressive, 13;
—, Ramsay MacDonald resigns and
6th, Stanley Baldwin forms Conservative government with Austen Chamberlain as foreign secretary and Winston Churchill as Chancellor of Exchequer;
19th, murder of Lee Stack in Cairo;
20th, revolt of Kurds in Turkey is put down with ferocity;
21st, Stanley Baldwin informs U.S.S.R. that Britain will not proceed with the treaties negotiated by the Labour government;
30th, last French and Belgian troops are withdrawn from the Ruhr;
—, Egyptian premier accepts British terms over Stack's murder.

M **Dec**: 2nd, Anglo-German commercial treaty;
7th, in German elections Nationalists and Communists lose seats to Socialists;
15th (–*Jan.* 15th 1925), cabinet crisis in Germany;
24th, Albania is proclaimed a republic.

N

W **Drama and Entertainment** (*cont.*)

H. R. Lenormand, *L'Homme et ses Fantômes.*

G. B. Shaw, *St. Joan.*

British Empire Exhibition, Wembley.

Films:

The Ten Commandments.

Reveille.

The Great Wall.

Fernand Léger's abstract *Le Ballet Mécanique.*

Wanderer of the Wasteland, a nature feature in colour.

The Admiralty film *Zeebrugge.*

X **Sport**

Olympic Games, Paris.

New Zealand 'All Blacks' Rugby Football team make undefeated tour of Britain.

Y **Statistics**

Coal production (in mill. tons): U.S., 485; Great Britain, 267·1; Germany, 124·6; France, 44·9.

Steel production (in mill. tons): U.S., 45; Germany, 9·3; Great Britain, 8·2; France, 6·9.

Strikes: 10 million days lost in U.S., and 8 million lost in Great Britain.

Z **Births and Deaths**

Jan. 21st Nikolai Lenin (pseud. of Vladimir Ilyich Ulyanov) d. (54).

Feb. 3rd Woodrow Wilson d. (67).

Apr. 21st 'Marie Corelli' (pseud. of Mary Mackay) d. (59) and Eleonora Duse d. (64).

May 29th Paul Cambon d. (78).

July 13th Alfred Marshall d. (81).

July 27th Ferruccio Busoni d. (58).

Aug. 3rd Joseph Conrad (Korzeniowski) d. (67).

Aug. 15th Robert Bolt b. (–).

Sept. 18th F. H. Bradley d. (78).

Oct. 13th Anatole France (pseud. of J. A. A. Thibaud) d. (79).

Nov. 29th Giacomo Puccini d. (66) and C. V. Stanford d. (71).

A **Jan**: 1st, Christiania, Norwegian capital, resumes name of Oslo;
5th, Mrs. Ross of Wyoming becomes first woman governor in U.S.;
6th, Allies inform Germany they will not now evacuate Cologne area on 10th;
11th, on Charles Hughes's resignation F. B. Kellogg becomes U.S. secretary of state;
15th, Hans Luther, Independent, succeeds Wilhelm Marx as German chancellor, with Gustav Stresemann as foreign minister;
16th, Lev Trotsky is dismissed from chairmanship of Russian Revolutionary Military Council;
20th, Russo-Japanese alliance;
—, Anglo-Chinese treaty of Pekin;
29th, D. Lloyd George succeeds Lord Oxford as Liberal leader.

B **Feb**: 10th, U.S.-Canadian fishing agreement;
28th, President Friedrich Ebert of Germany dies.

C **Mar**: 5th, Labour Opposition in Commons leave the House on suspension of David Kirkwood;
9th, Calvin Coolidge arbitrates in Chilean-Peruvian dispute;
12th, Britain refuses to sign Geneva protocol (of *Oct.* 1924) for the peaceful settlement of international disputes;
29th, Japanese suffrage widened.

D **Apr**: 3rd, Britain repeals Reparation Recovery Act and re-establishes sterling on a gold basis at its pre-1914 rate;
3rd, Holland and Belgium sign convention on the navigation of the Scheldt;
4th, Japan evacuates Sakhalin;
10th, Paul Painlevé becomes premier of France on Édouard Herriot's defeat;
23rd, Franco-Spanish war in Morocco against Kabyles;
25th, Paul von Hindenburg elected President of Germany.

E **May**: 1st, Cyprus is declared a British Crown Colony;
4th (–*June* 17th), Geneva Conference on arms traffic and use of poison gas in war;
12th, U.S.S.R. Constitution ratified by Soviet Congress;
30th, Joseph Coates, Reform Party, becomes premier of New Zealand, following W. F. Massey's death, 10th;
Shooting of Chinese students by municipal police in Shanghai and other incidents in Canton provokes Chinese boycott of British goods.

F **Jun**: 8th, Britain and France accept in principle Germany's proposals (of *Feb.* 9th) for a security pact to guarantee Franco-German and Belgo-German boundaries;
25th, Theodore Pangalos becomes premier of Greece in Athens *coup d'état*.

G **Jul**: 7th, South African Senate rejects colour-bar bill;
9th, revolution in Ecuador;
13th, French troops begin evacuation of Rhineland;
—, British government enquiry into coal-miners' dispute;
16th, first elected Parliament of Iraq opens in Baghdad;
18th, insurrection of the Druses in Syria (–*June* 1927);
—, Italian-Yugoslav treaty of Nettuno on Dalmatian question;
31st, Unemployment Insurance Act in Britain;
—, provisional settlement of British miners' dispute.

O **Politics, Economics, Law and Education**

Lord Beaverbrook, *Politicians and the Press.*
Adolf Hitler, *Mein Kampf*, Vol. I.
Harold Laski, *Grammar of Politics.*
Dominions Office established.
French National Economic Council appointed.
Clashes between Communists and Youthful Patriots in Paris.
Disaster to U.S. dirigible *Shenandoah* draws public attention to air defence.
State of Tennessee forbids teaching of human evolution in schools.

P **Science, Technology, Discovery, etc.**

R. A. Millikan discovers the presence of penetrating radiations in the upper atmosphere.
A. N. Whitehead, *Science and the Modern World.*
Goldberger isolates vitamins B and B_2.
Collip obtains extract of the parathyroid gland for treating tetanus.
Daventry high-power broadcasting transmitter in operation.
Clarence Birdseye extends deep-freezing process to pre-cooked foods.

Q **Scholarship**

Hilaire Belloc, *History of England.*
Viscount Grey of Fallodon, *Twenty-Five Years, 1892–1916.*

R **Philosophy and Religion**

H. Hardtman, *Psychology and the Church.*
Songs of Praise (ed. Percy Dearmer).
United Church of Canada is founded.

S **Art, Sculpture, Fine Arts and Architecture**

Painting:
Alfred Munnings, *Their Majesties returning from Ascot.*
P. Picasso, *Three Dancers.*
G. Rouault, *The Apprentice.*
Sculpture:
Constantin Brancusi, *Bird in Space.*
Jacob Epstein, *Rima* and *The Duke of Marlborough.*
Eric Gill, *Deposition.*
Alfred Gilbert, *The Shaftesbury Memorial* ('Eros').
Architecture:
W. Gropius, The Bauhaus, Dessau.

T **Music**

Ernest Bloch, *Concerto Grosso.*
F. Busoni, *Dr. Faustus* (opera).
Aaron Copland, Symphony no. I.
Franz Lehár, *Paganini* (operetta).

U **Literature**

E. E. Cummings, *XLI Poems.*
Warwick Deeping, *Sorrell and Son.*
Scott Fitzgerald, *The Great Gatsby.*
Richard Garnett, *Twilight of the Gods.*
André Gide, *Les Faux-Monnayeurs.*
Aldous Huxley, *Those Barren Leaves.*

H Aug: 7th, League advises against partition of Mosul;
15th, Norway annexes Spitzbergen;
18th, U.S. agreement with Belgium on war debts;
26th, Henri Pétain takes command of French troops in Morocco;
28th, Britain resumes diplomatic relations with Mexico, after eight years;
29th, amnesty for Kapp, pro-monarchical, conspirators in Germany of *Mar.* 1920.

J Sep: 29th, republican Constitution in Greece.

K Oct: 5th (–16th), Locarno Conference, discussing question of security pact, strikes a balance between French and German interests by drafting treaties (a) guaranteeing the Franco-German and Belgo-German frontiers, (b) between Germany and France, Belgium, Czechoslovakia and Poland respectively, and (c) a mutual guarantee between France, Czechoslovakia and Poland;
12th, U.S.S.R.-German commercial treaty;
—, risings in Syria;
18th (–20th), French fleet bombards Damascus;
19th, Italy completes occupation of Italian Somaliland under terms of 1889 Protectorate;
26th, Chinese customs conference at Peking;
29th, Conservatives win seats in Canadian elections but Mackenzie King maintains precarious Liberal government with support of Progressives;
31st, Reza Khan usurps Persian throne;
Greek army invades Bulgaria in reprisal for a soldier's murder and Bulgaria appeals to League.

L Nov: 12th, U.S. agreement with Italy on war debts;
22nd, Free State representative on Irish boundary commission resigns;
27th, Aristide Briand forms ministry in France.

M Dec: 1st, Locarno treaties signed in London;
—, British troops evacuate Cologne;
3rd, Irish boundary settled after long negotiations;
5th (–*Jan.* 20th 1926), cabinet crisis in Germany;
6th, Italy's agreement with Egypt on Cyrenaica;
15th, Greece agrees to League's penalties over her dispute with Bulgaria;
16th, League settles Mosul question in favour of Iraq;
17th, U.S.S.R. signs defensive alliance with Turkey.

N

U Literature (*cont.*)

Franz Kafka, *The Trial* (posth.).
John Dos Passos, *Manhattan Transfer*.
Gertrude Stein, *The Making of Americans* (written 1906–8).
Jules Supervielle, *Gravitations* (poems).
P. G. Wodehouse, *Carry on, Jeeves*.
Virginia Woolf, *Mrs. Dalloway*.

V The Press

The New Yorker is issued.

W Drama and Entertainment

Noël Coward, *Hay Fever*.
Ashley Dukes, *The Man With a Load of Mischief*.
Sean O'Casey, *Juno and the Paycock*.
The Charleston.

Films:
The Gold Rush.
Greed.
Miracle of the Wolves.
Owd Bob.
The Last Laugh.
The Only Way.

X Sport

Y Statistics

Railway mileage in operation: U.S., 261,871; Great Britain, 29,300; Russia, 26,255.
Wireless licences: Great Britain, 1,654,000.
Strikes: In Denmark 4 mill. working days are lost.

Z Births and Deaths

Mar. 12th Sun Yat-sen d. (58).
Mar. 20th George, Marquess of Curzon, d. (66).
Apr. 14th J. S. Sargent d. (69).
May 12th Alfred, Lord Milner, d. (71).
May 14th H. Rider Haggard d. (69).
May 22nd John French, Earl of Ypres, d. (73).
Sept. 18th Peter Sellers b. (–).
Sept. 29th Léon Bourgeois d. (74).
Nov. 20th Queen Alexandra d. (80).

General Strike in Britain—Germany joins the League

A **Jan:** 3rd (–*Aug.* 22nd), Theodore Pangalos usurps power as dictator of Greece;
4th, Moderate ministry takes office in Bulgaria, offering amnesty to all political prisoners except Communists;
8th, Ibn Saud becomes King of Hejaz on King Hussein's expulsion and changes name of Kingdom to Saudi Arabia;
14th (–30th), series of agreements between Denmark, Sweden, Norway and Finland for peaceful settlement of disputes;
20th, Hans Luther, Socialist, again becomes German chancellor;
New Code of laws in Turkey.

B **Feb:** 10th, Germany applies for admission to League of Nations;
Tension between Italy and Germany over Germanisation of South Tyrol.

C **Mar:** 11th, Éamon de Valéra resigns as head of Sinn Fein; subsequently founds Fianna Fáil;
12th, Denmark disarms;
17th, Brazil and Spain prevent Germany's admission to League;
26th, Roumanian-Polish alliance.

D **Apr:** 3rd, foundation of the *Ballilla* in Italy, a Fascist youth organisation;
7th, first of several attempts to assassinate Benito Mussolini;
22nd, Persia, Turkey and Afghanistan sign treaty for mutual security;
24th, Berlin treaty of friendship and neutrality between Germany and U.S.S.R.

E **May:** 1st (–*Nov.*), British coal strike;
2nd, U.S. troops land to preserve order in Nicaraguan revolt;
3rd (–12th), General Strike in Britain;
8th, French fleet bombards Damascus in the Revolt of Druses;
10th, Vincent Witos, leader of Peasants' Party, forms ministry in Poland;
12th, Josef Pilsudski's *coup d'état* in Poland;
17th, Wilhelm Marx, Centre, becomes German chancellor, following Hans Luther's resignation, 12th;
18th (–26th), preparatory Disarmament Conference meets, attended by U.S., but not by U.S.S.R.;
23rd, the Lebanon is proclaimed a republic by France;
26th, Riff war ends, with Abd-el-Krim's surrender to France;
31st, Gomes da Costa leads *coup d'état* in Portugal.

F **Jun:** 1st, Ignace Moscicki becomes President of Poland;
5th, Anglo-Turkish agreement on Mosul, with most of the area assigned to Iraq in accordance with League's award of *Dec.* 1925;
7th, Liberal ministry replaces Socialist government in Sweden;
10th, Spain announces her withdrawal from League, but later rescinds this;
—, Franco-Roumanian treaty;
12th, Brazil leaves the League;
26th, McNary-Haugen bill for tariff on agricultural products is defeated in U.S. Senate;
28th, W. L. Mackenzie King resigns as result of Canadian customs scandals and Arthur Meighen becomes premier of Liberal ministry.

G **Jul:** 1st, Anglo-Portuguese agreement on South-West Africa-Angola boundary;
2nd, anti-clerical legislation in Mexico;

O **Politics, Economics, Law and Education**

J. M. Keynes, *The End of Laissez-Faire.*
The Intimate Papers of Colonel House.
B. Webb, *My Apprenticeship.*
British General Electricity Board established.
Reading University founded.
Council for the Preservation of Rural England founded.
France returns to gold standard.
Kenneth Lindsay, *Social Progress and Educational Waste.*
Adoption is made legal in Britain.

P **Science, Technology, Discovery, etc.**

F. Lindemann, *The Physical Significance of the Quantum Theory.*
James Jeans formulates new stellar theory.
J. L. Baird demonstrates television in Soho (*Jan.* 26th).
Liver extract first used for treating pernicious anaemia.
Alan Cobham flies from Croydon to Cape Town and back (*Mar.*) to discover possibilities of long-distance air routes.
Flights over North Pole by Roald Amundsen and by Richard Byrd.
Scott Polar Research Institute, Cambridge, opened.

Q **Scholarship**

M. Rostovziev, *Social and Economic History of the Roman Empire.*
Speculum, a Journal of Medieval Studies issued.
G. M. Trevelyan, *History of England.*

R **Philosophy and Religion**

R. H. Tawney, *Religion and the Rise of Capitalism.*
Essays Catholic and Critical.

S **Art, Sculpture, Fine Arts and Architecture**

Painting:
M. Chagall, *Lovers' Bouquet.*
A. John, *Lady Ottoline Morrell.*
S. Spencer, Murals for Burghclere Chapel, Berkshire (–1932).
J. S. Sargent Exhibition, Royal Academy.

Sculpture:
J. Epstein, *The Visitation.*
H. Moore, *Draped reclining figure.*

Architecture:
P. Berhens, Newways, Northampton.
A. Gaudi, Church of the Sagrada Familia, Barcelona completed (begun 1883).
Le Corbusier (pseud.), *The Coming Architecture* published.

T **Music**

Alban Berg, *Wozzeck* (opera).
Arthur Honegger, *Judith* (opera).
Constant Lambert becomes first English composer to be commissioned to write music for Diaghilev's ballet with *Romeo and Juliet.*

U **Literature**

Theodore Dreiser, *An American Tragedy.*
William Faulkner, *Soldiers' Pay.*
André Gide, *Si le grain ne meurt.*

1926 (Jul.–Dec.)

G **Jul**: 9th, Gomes da Costa is overthrown in Portugal by General Antonio de Fragoso Carmona;
15th, fall of Aristide Briand's ministry through financial crisis;
23rd, Raymond Poincaré becomes premier of French National Union Ministry (–1929);
26th, Philippines legislature calls for plebiscite on independence, which is vetoed by the governor;
28th, U.S.-Panama alliance to protect the canal in wartime;
—, Belgian financial crisis: Franc is devalued and King Albert I is given dictatorial powers for six months;
30th, Albania's frontiers are fixed internationally;
31st, Afghanistan signs non-aggression pact with U.S.S.R.

H **Aug**: 10th, following devaluation of the French Franc, a sinking fund is established to redeem the national debt;
17th, Greece signs treaty of friendship with Yugoslavia;
22nd, Theodore Pangalos is overthrown and President George Kondylis is recalled to Greece.

J **Sep**: 1st, civil marriage is established in Turkey;
2nd, Italy's treaty with the Yemen begins Italian attempt to dominate east coast of Red Sea;
6th, Chiang Kai-shek reaches Hankow in his northern campaign in Chinese Civil War;
8th, Germany is admitted to the League, and in consequence
11th, Spain leaves;
16th, Italian-Roumanian treaty;
18th, Yugoslavia signs treaty of friendship with Poland;
23rd, Aristide Briand and Gustav Stresemann discuss the Rhineland and reparations at Thoiry;
25th, international convention on slavery;
—, campaign against the Mafia begins in Sicily;
—, W. L. Mackenzie King forms Liberal ministry in Canada after general election.

K **Oct**: 15th, Ignaz Seipel, Christian Socialist, forms ministry in Austria, replacing Rudolf Ramek;
19th (–*Nov.* 18th), Imperial Conference in London decides that Britain and the Dominions are autonomous communities, equal in status;
Expulsion of Lev Trotsky and Grigori Zinoviev from the Politbureau, following Josef Stalin's victory over Leftist opposition;
Union of National Peasants' Party founded in Roumania.

L **Nov**: 8th, British Parliament appoints the Simon Commission on India;
10th, Vincent Massey becomes first Canadian minister to Washington;
11th, the Hungarian Upper House, representing the landed aristocracy, is re-established;
19th, British miners call off strike (begun *May* 1st);
27th, treaty of Tirana between Italy and Albania;
Communist revolt in Java (–*July* 1927).

M **Dec**: 2nd, Liberal government in Denmark, following Socialist losses in election;
17th (–*Jan.* 28th 1927), cabinet crisis in Germany.

N British legation in Peking declares Britain's sympathy with Chinese Nationalist movement (Kuo Min Tang).

U **Literature** (*cont.*)

F. Kafka, *The Castle* (posth.).
D. H. Lawrence, *The Plumed Serpent*.
T. E. Lawrence, *Seven Pillars of Wisdom*.
W. S. Maugham, *The Casuarina Tree*.
A. A. Milne, *Winnie the Pooh*.

V **The Press**

W **Drama and Entertainment**

Paul Green, *In Abraham's Bosom*.
Margaret Kennedy and Basil Dean, *The Constant Nymph*.
Sean O'Casey, *The Plough and the Stars*.

Films:
Renoir's *Nana*.
The Last Days of Pompeii.
Ben Hur with Ramon Navarro.
John Barrymore in *Don Juan*.
Rudolph Valentino's death.

X **Sport**

J. B. Hobbs scores 16 centuries in first-class cricket.

Y **Statistics**

Populations (in mill.): U.S.S.R., 148; U.S., 115; Japan, 85; Germany, 64; Great Britain, 45; France, 41; Italy, 40.
Petroleum production: U.S. 770·8 mill. barrels.
British merchant fleet: 11·9 mill. tons (629,000 tons motor).
Strikes in Great Britain: 162,233,000 working-days lost.

Z **Births and Deaths**

Jan. 20th Charles Montagu Doughty d. (73).
Mar. 3rd Sidney Lee d. (67).
Apr. 19th Squire Bancroft d. (84).
Apr. 21st Queen Elizabeth II b. (–).
July 2nd Émile Coué d. (69).
Aug. 1st Israel Zangwill d. (62).
Dec. 5th Claude Oscar Monet d. (66).
Dec. 29th Rainer Maria Rilke d. (51).

1927 (Jan.–Aug.) German financial crisis—Washington Naval Disarmament Conference

A Jan: 1st, Chinese Kuo Min Tang (Nationalist) government established at Hankow;
29th, German cabinet crisis is resolved with Wilhelm Marx becoming chancellor;
31st, inter-Allied military control of Germany ends.

B Feb: 3rd (–13th), revolt in Portugal against the military dictatorship of General Carmona;
19th, Chinese Nationalists extract from Britain a reduction of the concessions at Hankow and Kiukiang.

C Mar: 9th, revocation of self-government in Libya;
24th, Chinese Communists seize Nanking.

D Apr: 5th, treaty of friendship between Italy and Hungary;
11th, Charles Ibáñez becomes dictator in Chile;
15th, Chiang Kai-shek organises government at Nanking;
—, U.S.S.R. and Switzerland resume diplomatic relations;
17th, bank crisis in Japan forces resignation of R. Wakatsuki's ministry;
18th, split in Kuo Min Tang between Chiang Kai-shek and the Radicals;
21st, Italian labour charter issued.

E May: 2nd (–23rd), economic conference at Geneva, attended by 52 nations, including U.S.S.R.;
4th, Henry Stimpson, U.S. secretary of state, brings together factions in Nicaragua, and U.S. is asked to supervise elections;
9th, Parliament House, Canberra, is opened;
13th, 'Black Friday' with collapse of Germany's economic system;
20th, by treaty of Jeddah Britain recognises independence of Saudi Arabia;
26th, Britain annuls trade agreement with U.S.S.R. and
27th, breaks off diplomatic relations after discovery of documents relating to Soviet intrigues against British Empire;
27th, Thomas Masaryk is re-elected President of Czechoslovakia;
Japan intervenes in Shantung, blocking advance of Chinese Nationalists on Peking.

F Jun: 2nd, revised Greek Constitution;
20th (–*Aug.* 4th), Britain, U.S. and Japan confer at Washington on naval disarmament, but fail to reach agreement;
Rupture of Yugoslav-Albanian relations following frontier incidents;
Druse revolt in Syria ends.

G Jul: 10th, assassination of Kevin O'Higgins (Nationalist minister) provokes denunciation of tactics of Irish Republicans;
15th (–16th), Socialist riots and general strike in Vienna, following acquittal of Nationalists for political murders;
27th, Belgium and Portugal make territorial adjustments in the Congo;
28th, British Trades Union Act declares certain strikes and lock-outs illegal;
Unrest in Samoa, fomented by Europeans (–*Aug.*).

H Aug: 7th, international Peace Bridge between U.S. and Canada opened;
12th, Éamon de Valéra and other Irish Republican leaders agree to take oaths and their seats in the Dáil;
22nd, Allied military control of Hungary abolished;
23rd, Nahas Pasha becomes leader of the Wafd in Egypt.

O **Politics, Economics, Law and Education**

Kemal Atatürk, *The New Turkey*.

Adolf Hitler, *Mein Kampf*, Vol. II.

T. E. Lawrence, *Revolt in the Desert*.

British Broadcasting Corporation takes over from British Broadcasting Company (*Jan.* 1st).

Industrial Health and Safety Centre, London, opened.

C. K. Ogden founds Orthological Institute.

P **Science, Technology, Discovery, etc.**

Heisenberg propounds 'the uncertainty principle' in quantum-physics.

W. Heitler and F. London make discoveries on the wave mechanics of valency.

W. Muller's work on genetics and radiation.

Siegfried Junghans's process for continuous casting of non-ferrous metal.

Albert W. Hall's improvements to fluorescent lamps.

Charles A. Lindbergh flies from New York to Paris in 37 hours (*May* 20th, 21st).

Gino Watkins leads expedition to Edge Island, Spitzbergen.

Q **Scholarship**

Leonard Woolley's discoveries at Ur.

Economic History Review issued.

R **Philosophy and Religion**

J. W. Dunne, *An Experiment with Time*.

S. Freud, *The Future of an Illusion*.

Heidegger, *Sein und Zeit*.

B. Russell, *Analysis of Matter*.

World Conference on Faith and Order, at Lausanne.

S **Art, Sculpture, Fine Arts and Architecture**

Painting:

M. Chagall, *Fables of La Fontaine* (100 etchings, published 1952).

H. Matisse, *Figures with Ornamental Background*.

Rex Whistler, frescoes for the Tate Gallery Restaurant.

Sculpture:

J. Epstein, *Madonna and Child* and *Paul Robeson*.

Hambro Thornycroft, *The Sower*, Kew Gardens, Surrey.

Eric Gill, *Mankind*; also designs the 'Sans Serif' alphabet.

T **Music**

Arthur Honegger, *Antigone* (opera with Jean Cocteau's libretto).

Ernst Křenek, *Johnny Strikes Up* (opera).

M. Ravel, violin sonata.

Dmitry Shostakovich, 1st Symphony.

I. Stravinsky, *Œdipus Rex* (opera).

Jaromir Weinberger, *Schwanda the Bagpiper* (opera).

George Antheil's 'ballet mécanique', scored for aeroplane propellers, anvils, motor horns, etc.

U **Literature**

Ernest Hemingway, *Men Without Women*.

Sinclair Lewis, *Elmer Gantry*.

Henri Michaux, *Qui je fus*.

J Sep: 2nd, in Turkish elections Mustapha Kemal is empowered to nominate all candidates, giving the People's Party a monopoly;
15th, in Irish elections Nationalists fail to win clear majority over Republicans;
16th, Paul von Hindenburg, dedicating the Tannenburg memorial, repudiates Germany's responsibility for the War (art. 231 of Versailles Treaty);
22nd, slavery abolished in Sierra Leone.

K Oct: 1st, U.S.S.R.-Persian non-aggression pact;
17th, first Labour government in Norway.

L Nov: 11th, Franco-Yugoslav treaty of friendship;
15th, Canada is elected to a seat on League Council;
22nd, Albania signs defensive alliance with Italy, in reply to the Franco-Yugoslav treaty;
—, Persia claims Bahrein Island;
30th, Maxim Litvinov, U.S.S.R. commissar for foreign affairs, proposes immediate disarmament at Geneva, but this is rejected as a 'Communist trick'.

M Dec: 13th, Lithuanian-Polish dispute is referred to League;
14th, Britain recognises Iraq's independence and promises to support her application for membership of League in 1932;
—, China and U.S.S.R. break off relations;
17th, F. B. Kellogg, U.S. secretary of state, suggests pact for renunciation of war;
18th, Chiang Kai-shek overthrows Hankow government;
27th, Josef Stalin's faction is victorious at All-Union Congress and Lev Trotsky is expelled from Communist Party as a deviationist;
Amendment to Mexican petroleum law brings improvement in relations with U.S.

N

U **Literature** (*cont.*)

Marcel Proust, *Le Temps retrouvé* (posth.).
Dorothy Richardson, *Oberland.*
Virginia Woolf, *To The Lighthouse.*
Henry Williamson, *Tarka the Otter.*

V **The Press**

W **Drama and Entertainment**

Paul Claudel, *Protée.*
Thornton Wilder, *The Bridge of San Luis Rey.*
Ben Travers, *Thark.*
The slow foxtrot.

Films:

Sound films, popularised by *The Jazz Singer*, with Al Jolson.
Underworld.
Love, with Greta Garbo.
C. B. de Mille's *King of Kings.*

X **Sport**

Helen Wills wins Ladies Lawn Tennis Championship at Wimbledon.
J. Weismüller swims 100 yards in 51 seconds.

Y **Statistics**

Z **Births and Deaths**

Feb. 18th Elbridge Thomas Gerry d. (89).
Feb. 19th Georg Brandes d. (85).
Feb. 24th Edward Marshall Hall d. (68).
May 6th Hudson Maxim d. (74).
June 1st J. B. Bury d. (76).
June 14th J. K. Jerome d. (68).
July 31st Harry Hamilton Johnston d. (69).
Aug. 4th John Dillon d. (76).

1928 (Jan.–Sep.) Kellogg-Briand Pact—Complete Women's Suffrage in Britain—Japan occupies Shantung

A **Jan**: 13th, Allied military control of Bulgaria abolished;
14th, first Conservative administration in Latvia;
29th, treaty between Germany and Lithuania provides for arbitration over Memel.

B **Feb**: 20th, Britain recognises independence of Transjordan.

C **Mar**: 16th, Nahas Pasha premier of Egypt (–*June* 25th);
25th, General Antonio Carmona elected President of Portugal;
28th, military service in France reduced to a year.

D **Apr**: 6th, Palmas Island, near Philippines, is awarded to Holland in arbitration of dispute with U.S.;
9th, Islam no longer recognised as State religion of Turkey;
13th, F. B. Kellogg submits his plan for renunciation of war to Locarno powers (Pact signed *Aug.*);
19th, Japan occupies Shantung;
21st, Aristide Briand puts forward his draft treaty for outlawing war;
22nd, National Union of the Left triumph in French elections;
27th, Oliveira Salazar becomes minister of finance in Portugal with wide powers;
29th, British ultimatum forces Egypt to provide for freedom of public meetings.

E **May**: 3rd (–11th), Sino-Japanese clashes at Tsinan;
6th, National Peasants' Party Congress in Roumania demands responsible government;
7th, women's suffrage in Britain reduced from age of 30 to 21;
12th, Italian electoral law reduces electorate from 10 million to 3 million;
20th, in German elections Socialists win at expense of Nationalists;
31st, Eleutherios Venizelos returns to Greece as premier.

F **Jun**: 9th, France convenes constituent assembly in Syria, with a Nationalist majority;
23rd, explanatory note on Kellogg-Briand pact is sent to the powers;
24th, the French Franc is again devalued;
28th, Hermann Müller, Socialist, is appointed German chancellor (following resignation of Wilhelm Marx's ministry, 13th).

G **Jul**: 17th, Obrégon, President of Mexico, assassinated; succeeded by Emilio Portes Gil;
19th, King Fuad's *coup d'état* in Egypt, where Parliament is dissolved for three years and freedom of press is suspended;
—, China annuls 'unequal treaties';
25th, Italy becomes a signatory to Tangier statute, giving Spain greater control there.

H **Aug**: 2nd, Italy signs 20-year treaty of friendship with Ethiopia;
8th, the Croats withdraw from Yugoslav Parliament to set up a separatist assembly in Zagreb;
27th, Kellogg-Briand Pact, outlawing war and providing for pacific settlement of disputes, signed in Paris by 65 states, including U.S.S.R.;
28th, all-party conference at Lucknow votes for dominion status for India, but radical members, 30th, form the Independence of India League.

J **Sep**: 1st, Albania is proclaimed a Kingdom and Zog I is elected King;
10th, Argentina nationalises oil;
11th, Portuguese treaty with South Africa regulates problems of transport and labour recruitment;
23rd, Italy signs treaty of friendship with Greece;
26th, act of League Assembly, embodying Kellogg-Briand Pact, is signed by 23 nations.

O **Politics, Economics, Law and Education**

Émile Chartier (pseud.), *Le Citoyen contre les pouvoirs.*

Benito Mussolini, *My Autobiography.*

G. B. Shaw, *The Intelligent Woman's Guide to Socialism and Capitalism.*

U.S.S.R. first Five-year Plan.

Italy returns to gold standard.

Over-production of coffee causes collapse of Brazil's economy.

P **Science, Technology, Discovery, etc.**

H. Geiger and W. Müller construct the 'Geiger counter'.

A. Fleming discovers penicillin.

The constitution of thyroxine is discovered.

T. H. Morgan, *The Theory of Sex.*

J. L. Baird gives transatlantic television transmission and demonstrates colour television in Britain.

Graf Zeppelin completes the flight Friedrichshafen to New Jersey in 4 days 15½ hours.

First east-west transatlantic flights by Köhl and by Fitzmaurice.

Q **Scholarship**

Completion of *New English Dictionary* (begun 1884).

R **Philosophy and Religion**

Revised Prayer Book of Church of England rejected by Parliament.

L. Pastor completes his *History of the Popes* (begun 1886).

Pope Pius XI's encyclical *Mortalium animus.*

Ecumenical Missionary Conference, held in Jerusalem, stresses partnership in a common undertaking.

S **Art, Sculpture, Fine Arts and Architecture**

Painting:

Max Beckmann, *Black Lilies.*

Henri Matisse, *Seated Odalisque.*

Edvard Munch, *Girl on a Sofa.*

Kenwood, Hampstead, housing Lord Iveagh's art collection, opened.

Amédée Ozenfant coins the term 'purism' in his treatise *Art.*

Architecture:

E. Scott, Shakespeare Memorial Theatre, Stratford-on-Avon.

Congrès Internationaux d'Architecture Moderne, founded in Switzerland.

T **Music**

Arnold Bax, 3rd Symphony.

George Gershwin, *An American in Paris.*

M. Ravel, *Bolero.*

A. Roussel, piano concerto.

I. Stravinsky, *Capriccio.*

Kurt Weil and Berchtold Brecht, *The Threepenny Opera.*

U **Literature**

Stephen V. Benét, *John Brown's Body.*

Aldous Huxley, *Point Counter Point.*

Christopher Isherwood, *All the Conspirators.*

D. H. Lawrence, *Lady Chatterley's Lover.*

T. F. Powys, *Mr. Weston's Good Wine.*

Upton Sinclair, *Boston.*

1928 (Oct.–Dec.)

K **Oct**: 2nd, Arvid Lindman forms Conservative ministry in Sweden;
4th (–16th), plebiscite in Germany against building new battleships fails;
6th, Chiang-Kai-shek is elected President of China.

L **Nov**: 3rd, Turkey adopts Latin alphabet;
7th, Herbert Hoover, Republican, elected U.S. President with 444 electoral votes against Albert Smith, Democrat, 87;
14th, in New Zealand elections United (Liberal) Party under Joseph Ward wins 29 seats, Reform 28 and Labour 19;
15th, Fascist Grand Council becomes part of Italian constitution, with right of nominating candidates to Chamber.

M **Dec**: 5th, Wilhelm Miklas elected President of Austria, in succession to Michael Hainisch;
6th, war between Bolivia and Paraguay;
12th, Peasants' Party wins Roumanian elections;
20th, Britain recognises Nanking government (Kuo Min Tang) of China;
22nd, Committee under Owen D. Young appointed to examine reparations question;
Arrest of a Slovak deputy in Czechoslovakia for irredentist agitation in favour of Hungary provokes ill feeling.

N Strikes in India.
Extensive railway development in East Africa.

U **Literature** (*cont.*)
Edgar Wallace, *The Squeaker*.
Virginia Woolf, *Orlando*.
W. B. Yeats, *The Tower*.

V **The Press**
Life and Letters first issued.

W **Drama and Entertainment**
Jean Giraudoux, *Siegfried*.
J. Van Druten, *Young Woodley*.

Films:
Walt Disney makes first 'Mickey Mouse' film in colour.
Charles Chaplin's *Circus*.
Eisenstein's *October*.
The Woman in the Moon.
The Patriot.

X **Sport**

Y **Statistics**

Z **Births and Deaths**
Jan. 1st Thomas Hardy d. (87).
Jan. 29th Douglas, Earl Haig, d. (66).
Feb. 15th H. H. Asquith, Earl of Oxford and Asquith, d. (75).
Apr. 10th Stanley John Weyman d. (72).
May 1st Ebenezer Howard d. (78).
July 19th John Bratby b. (–).
July 21st Ellen Terry d. (80).
Aug. 19th R. B. Haldane, Viscount Haldane, d. (72).
Sept. 3rd Roald Amundsen d. (56).
Oct. 17th Frank Dicksee d. (85).
Nov. 21st Herman Sundermann d. (71).

1929 (Jan.–Aug.) Wall Street Crash

A **Jan**: 5th, King Alexander I suppresses Yugoslav Constitution and establishes dictatorship;
—, inter-American treaty of arbitration, analogous to Kellogg-Briand Pact, signed in Washington;
21st, Croat party in Yugoslavia is dissolved;
31st, Lev Trotsky is expelled from U.S.S.R.

B **Feb**: 6th, Germany accepts Kellogg-Briand Pact;
9th, Litvinov Protocol, or Eastern Pact, between U.S.S.R., Estonia, Latvia, Poland and Roumania for renunciation of war;
11th, Lateran Treaty establishes an independent Vatican City;
27th, Turkey signs Litvinov Protocol.

C **Mar**: 6th, Bulgarian-Turkish treaty of friendship;
17th, Spanish government closes Madrid University to stifle student agitation;
24th, Fascists 'win' single-party elections in Italy;
27th, Graeco-Yugoslav pact of friendship;
28th, new Constitution in Ecuador ends military régime.

D **Apr**: 3rd, Persia signs Litvinov Protocol;
12th, Indian Trade Disputes Act and Public Safety Act to reduce radical Labour unrest;
24th, Socialist ministry formed in Denmark, following defeat of Liberals in election;
30th, Ernst Streeruwitz appointed chancellor of Austria.

E **May**: 16th, restoration of Greek Senate, abolished in 1862, in hope of stabilising republican régime;
20th, Japan evacuates Shantung;
22nd, Amir Amanullah flees from Afghanistan (Nadir Khan proclaimed King, *Oct.* 15th);
26th, Catholic Party wins Belgian elections;
30th, in British general election Labour wins 287 seats, Conservatives, 261, Liberals, 59, others, 8.

F **Jun**: 3rd, settlement of Arica-Tacna dispute, originating in 1910, by which Chile is awarded Arica, Peru gains Tacna and Bolivia acquires railway rights;
5th, Ramsay MacDonald forms Labour ministry, with Arthur Henderson Foreign Secretary, Philip Snowden Chancellor of Exchequer and J. R. Clynes Home Secretary;
7th, Young Committee recommends that Germany should pay annuities, secured on mortgage of German railways, to an international bank until 1988;
27th, Reichstag repeals Protection of Republic Act;
Kemal Atatürk suppresses Communist propaganda in Turkey.

G **Jul**: 2nd, fall of Tanarka ministry in Japan;
24th, Kellogg-Briand Pact comes into force;
25th, Pope Pius XI, no longer 'a voluntary prisoner', leaves Vatican for first time;
27th, Raymond Poincaré resigns from ill health and Aristide Briand becomes premier of France.

H **Aug**: Saudi Arabia signs treaty of friendship with Turkey (and, 24th, with Persia);
6th (–13th), at Reparations Conference at the Hague, Germany accepts Young Plan and the Allies agree to evacuate the Rhineland by June 1930;
11th, Iraq and Iran sign treaty of friendship;

O **Politics, Economics, Law and Education**

Margaret Bondfield becomes first woman privy councillor.

Collapse of U.S. Stock Exchange begins world economic crisis, bringing an era of depression and unemployment (*Oct.* 28th).

Colonial Development Fund established.

Lev Trotsky leaves U.S.S.R. for Turkey.

The term *Apartheid* is first used.

P **Science, Technology, Discovery, etc.**

Albert Einstein, *Unitary Field Theory.*

James Jeans, *The Universe Around Us.*

Adrian and Matthews, using an ultra-sensitive galvanometer, are able to follow a single impulse in a single nerve fibre.

Kodaks develop a 16 mm. colour film.

Tootal's discover a crease-resisting cotton fabric.

Graf Zeppelin airship flies round the world.

New Tilbury Dock, London, opened.

Richard Byrd flies over the South Pole.

Q **Scholarship**

14th edition of *Encyclopædia Britannica.*

Journal of Modern History issued.

R **Philosophy and Religion**

John Dewey, *The Quest for Certainty.*

Heidegger, *What is Philosophy?*

Walter Lippmann, *Preface to Morals.*

The Presbyterian Churches in Scotland unite to form The Church of Scotland.

World Conference of Lutherans at Copenhagen.

S **Art, Sculpture, Fine Arts and Architecture**

Painting:

P. Klee, *Fool in a Trance* (in one continuous line).

P. Mondrian, *Composition with Yellow and Blue.*

P. Picasso, *Woman in Armchair.*

Grant Wood, *Woman with Plants.*

Second Surrealist Manifesto. The Surrealist group is joined by Salvador Dali.

Opening of Museum of Modern Art, New York, with exhibitions of works by Cézanne, Gauguin, Seurat and Van Gogh.

Sculpture:

J. Epstein, *Night and Day*, London Transport Building, St. James's Park.

T **Music**

Paul Hindemith, *Neues von Tage* (opera).

Constant Lambert, *Rio Grande.*

William Walton, viola concerto.

A. Toscanini directs New York Philharmonic Orchestra.

Oxford History of Music begun.

U **Literature**

Robert Bridges, *The Testament of Beauty.*

Jean Cocteau, *Les Enfants terribles.*

William Faulkner, *The Sound and the Fury.*

Robert Graves, *Goodbye To All That.*

H **Aug:** Arab attacks on Jews in Palestine, following disputes over Jewish use of the Wailing Wall, Jerusalem.

J **Sep:** 5th, A. Briand proposes a European federal union;
12th, Count Grandi is appointed Italian foreign minister;
14th, U.S. joins the International Court;
16th, peace is signed between Bolivia and Paraguay;
26th, Johann Schober forms ministry in Austria supported by Christian Socialists and Nationalists.

K **Oct:** 3rd, name of Serbo-Croat-Slovene Kingdom changed to Yugoslavia;
3rd, Britain resumes relations with U.S.S.R.;
—, Julius Curtius appointed German foreign minister on Gustav Stresemann's death;
12th, Labour Party wins Australian elections and
22nd, James H. Scullin forms ministry;
31st, Egyptian constitution is restored;
Cessation of U.S. loans to Europe, following Wall Street Crash.

L **Nov:** 13th, Basle Bank for International Settlements is founded to deal with Germany's reparation payments under the Young Plan;
17th, Nikolai Bukharin and other members of the Right opposition in U.S.S.R. are expelled;
30th, second Rhineland Zone is evacuated.

M **Dec:** 6th, female suffrage in Turkey;
22nd, referendum in Germany upholds the adoption of the Young Plan;
—, U.S.S.R. signs agreement with China over Chinese Eastern railway;
Round-table conference between Viceroy and Indian party leaders on Dominion status.

N

U Literature (*cont.*)

Ernest Hemingway, *A Farewell to Arms.*
Hugo von Hofmannsthal, *Poems.*
Sinclair Lewis, *Dodsworth.*
Charles Morgan, *Portrait in a Mirror.*
J. B. Priestley, *The Good Companions.*
Erich Remarque, *All Quiet on the Western Front.*
A. de St. Exupéry, *Courrier Sud.*
Thomas Wolfe, *Look Homeward Angel.*
Virginia Woolf, *A Room of One's Own.*

V The Press

W Drama and Entertainment

P. Claudel, *Le Soulier de satin* (first performed in 1943).
Noël Coward, *Bitter Sweet.*
Jean Giraudoux, *Amphitryon 38.*
Elmer Rice, *See Naples and Die.*
G. B. Shaw, *The Apple Cart.*
R. C. Sherriff, *Journey's End.*

Films:
Bull-Dog Drummond.
Juno and the Paycock.
The Love Parade.
The Co-optimists.
Pandora's Box.
Die Generallinie.
Warner Bros. announce they will make no more 'black and white' films.

X Sport

Y Statistics

Value of world production, percentages contributed by: U.S., 34·4; U.K., 10·4; Germany, 10·3; U.S.S.R., 9·9; France, 5·0; Japan, 4·0; Italy, 2·5; Canada, 2·2; Poland, 1·7.

Z Births and Deaths

Mar. 20th Ferdinand Foch d. (78).
Mar. 23rd Roger Bannister b. (–).
May 1st Audrey Hepburn b. (–).
May 20th Archibald Primrose, Earl of Rosebery, d. (82).
July 15th Hugo von Hofmannsthal d. (55).
Aug. 5th Millicent Garrett Fawcett d. (82).
Aug. 19th Serge Diaghilev d. (57).
Sept. 3rd Gustav Stresemann d. (51).
Sept. 17th Stirling Moss b. (–).
Nov. 24th Georges Benjamin Clemenceau d. (88).
Dec. 12th John Osborne b. (–).

1930 (Jan.–Jul.) Allied occupation of Rhineland ends—Gandhi begins civil disobedience campaign

A **Jan**: 1st, Powers agree to future abolition of extra-territorial privileges in China;
—, Nahas Pasha again premier of Egypt;
23rd, Wilhelm Frick, Nazi, becomes minister in Thuringia;
28th, dictatorship of Primo de Rivera ends in Spain and General Damaso Berenguer forms ministry.

B **Feb**: 6th, Austro-Italian treaty of friendship;
18th (–*Mar.* 24th), Geneva tariff conference;
U.S. Commission in Haiti recommends reforms and the appointment of Stenio Vincent as president.

C **Mar**: 8th, U.S.-League commission reports that slavery exists in Liberia;
12th, Mahatma Gandhi opens civil disobedience campaign in India;
27th, Hermann Müller's Socialist cabinet resigns in Germany;
28th, name of Constantinople changed to Istanbul and of Angora to Ankara;
30th, Heinrich Brüning, Centre, forms a coalition of the Right in Germany, replacing the Socialists, but without a majority in Reichstag;
31st, revolt in Ethiopia, led by the empress's brother;
Publication of Reuben J. Clark's Memorandum of 1928 on Monroe doctrine.

D **Apr**: 3rd, Ras Tafari becomes Emperor Haile Selassie of Abyssinia;
22nd, Britain, U.S., France, Italy and Japan end London Conference (held since *Jan.* 21st), with signing of a treaty on naval disarmament, regulating submarine warfare and limiting aircraft carriers;
30th, Italian naval programme begun;
30th, Workman's Insurance law in France.

E **May**: 2nd, Dunning tariff in Canada imposes high duties, but gives Britain preferential treatment;
6th, Japan recognises China's tariff autonomy;
8th, breakdown of London talks on Egypt and Sudan;
17th, Young Plan for reparations in force;
19th, white women enfranchised in South Africa;
24th, Benito Mussolini champions revision of Versailles Treaty;
28th, George W. Forbes becomes premier of United Party ministry in New Zealand on Joseph Ward's retirement;
Opposition party founded in Turkey, favouring greater ties with the West.

F **Jun**: 1st, Carl Ekman forms Liberal ministry in Sweden;
8th, Crown Prince Charles is elected King of Roumania;
17th, Herbert Hoover signs Smoot-Hawley high tariff, in spite of economists' protests that it will lead to reprisals;
21st, Ismail Sidky Pasha becomes premier of Egypt;
24th, Simon Report on India published;
27th, treaty of arbitration signed by Scandinavian powers;
30th, Britain recognises independence of Iraq;
—, last Allied troops leave Rhineland.

G **Jul**: 16th, Paul von Hindenburg authorises German budget by decree on failure of Reichstag to pass it;
21st, Maxim Litvinov becomes U.S.S.R. foreign minister;
30th, National Union party (neo-Fascist), founded in Portugal;
Kurd rising on Persian-Turkish frontier.

o **Politics, Economics, Law and Education**

Albert Einstein, *About Zionism.*
Ortega y Gasset, *The Revolt of the Masses.*
C. S. Johnson, *The Negro in American Civilisation.*
J. M. Keynes, *Treatise on Money.*
Harold Laski, *Liberty and the Modern State.*
F. R. Leavis, *Mass Civilisation and Minority Culture.*
Rosenberg, *Myths of the 20th Century.*
Lev Trotsky, *Autobiography.*
Pilgrim Trust founded.
France begins construction of Maginot Line.
In U.S.S.R. 55 per cent of agricultural workers are employed on collective farms.
Smoot-Hawley Act raises U.S. tariff.
Youth Hostels Association founded in Britain.

P **Science, Technology, Discovery, etc.**

The planet Pluto discovered (*Mar.* 18th).
Debye investigates the structure of molecules with X-rays.
J. H. Northrop makes pepsin and trypsin in crystallised form.
Reppe makes artificial fabrics from acetylene base.
Perspex is invented.
Picture telegraphy service between Britain and Germany opened (*Jan.* 7th).
The photoflash bulb is invented.
Turkestan-Siberian railway completed.
Amy Johnson's solo flight, London to Australia, in 19½ days (arrives *May* 24th).
Crash of airship R.101 near Beauvais (*Oct.* 7th).
British Arctic Air Route expedition (–31).

Q **Scholarship**

L. Woolley, *Digging Up the Past.*
R. W. Chambers, *William Shakespeare.*
G. M. Trevelyan, *England Under Queen Anne* (–32).

R **Philosophy and Religion**

S. Freud, *Civilisation and its Discontents.*

S **Art, Sculpture, Fine Arts and Architecture**

Painting:
Rex Whistler, illustrations for *Gulliver's Travels.*
Grant Wood, *American Gothic.*
Van Doesburg first uses term 'Concrete Art'.
Italian Art Exhibition, Royal Academy.

Sculpture:
H. Matisse, *Tiaré.*

Architecture:
R. Hood, Daily News Building, New York.
Shreve, Lamb and Harmon, Empire State Building, New York.
E. Lutyens, Gledstone, Skipton, Yorks.

T **Music**

Arnold Schönberg, *Vom Heute auf Morgen* (opera).
I. Stravinsky, *Symphony of Psalms.*
Adrian Boult becomes musical director of B.B.C.

H Aug: 7th, Conservative ministry under R. B. Bennett replaces Liberals in Canada;
25th, Josef Pilsudski forms ministry in Poland (–*Nov.* 28th) to break down Left opposition and Radical leaders are imprisoned;
25th, Augusto Legúia resigns presidency in Peru during revolt.

J Sep: 5th, Argentina revolution, with José Uriburu as the new President;
8th (–22nd), special sessions of Canadian Parliament to enact emergency laws dealing with depression;
14th, in German elections Socialists win 143 seats and Communists 77, but National Socialists (Nazis), denouncing Versailles Treaty, gain 107 seats from Moderates;
15th, removal of press censorship in Spain brings independent demands for a republic.

K Oct: 1st, Britain restores Wei-hai-wei to China;
— (–*Nov.* 14th), Imperial Conference in London, in which Britain rejects Canadian proposal for preferential tariff to help Dominion wheat;
4th, Brazilian revolution, with Getulio Vargas as the new President;
5th (–12th), conference of Balkan powers in Athens, origin of Balkan Entente (leading to pact of *Feb.* 1934);
14th, attempted Fascist *coup d'état* in Finland;
20th, Passfield White Paper on Palestine stresses Arab land hunger and suggests halt in Jewish immigration while Arab unemployment remains, which shakes Jewish confidence in Britain;
30th, treaty of friendship between Turkey and Greece signed at Ankara.

L Nov: 11th, repressive legislation in Finland against Communism;
12th (–*Jan.* 19th 1931), Round-table conference on India in London;
14th, assassination of premier Hamaguchi of Japan;
17th (–28th), Geneva Economic Conference discusses the world depression.

M Dec: 3rd, Otto Ender, Christian Socialist, forms Austrian ministry;
9th, Preparatory Commission on Disarmament adopts draft convention for discussions at League Conference in *Feb.* 1932, but Germany and U.S.S.R. disapprove of draft;
12th, last Allied troops leave the Saar;
30th, Scandinavian states, Holland, Belgium and Luxembourg, sign Oslo agreements (–1938), against raising tariffs without prior consultation.

N

Z **Births and Deaths** (*cont.*)
Mar. 6th Alfred von Tirpitz d. (81).
Mar. 8th William Howard Taft d. (72).
Mar. 19th A. J. Balfour d. (82).
Apr. 21st Robert Bridges d. (85).
May 13th Fridtjof Nansen d. (68).
June 16th Elmer Ambrose Sperry d. (69).
July 7th Arthur Conan Doyle d. (71).
Sept. 30th F. E. Smith, Lord Birkenhead, d. (58).

T **Music** (*cont.*)
Thibaud, Cortot and Casals form a trio.
B. Gigli's début.
Camargo Ballet Society founded to encourage British ballet.

U **Literature**
W. H. Auden, *Poems.*
E. M. Delafield, *Diary of a Provincial Lady.*
T. S. Eliot, *Ash Wednesday.*
William Faulkner, *As I Lay Dying.*
Robert Frost, *Collected Poems.*
John Dos Passos, *42nd Parallel.*
J. C. Powys, *In Defence of Sensuality.*
Salvatore Quasimodo, *Acque e terre.*
Sigrid Undset, *Burning Bush.*
Hugh Walpole, *Rogue Herries.*
Evelyn Waugh, *Vile Bodies.*

V **The Press**
Daily News and *Daily Chronicle* amalgamate as *News Chronicle* (–60).
Daily Worker is first issued.
William Randolph Hearst owns 33 newspapers with total circulation of 11 mill.

W **Drama and Entertainment**
Noël Coward, *Private Lives.*
W. S. Maugham, *The Breadwinner.*
Elmer Rice, *Street Scene.*
Films:
Anthony Mann's *The Blue Angel* with Marlene Dietrich.
René Clair's *Sous les Toits de Paris.*
Alfred Hitchcock's *Murder.*
Journey's End.
Hell's Angels.
All Quiet on the Western Front.
The Big House.
Hallelujah.
Advent of the wider screen.

X **Sport**
Donald Bradman scores 334 runs for Australia in the Leeds Test Match (and in 1930/1 season makes 425 not out for New South Wales against Queensland).
Max Schmeling becomes world heavyweight boxing champion.

Y **Statistics**
Religious denominations in Great Britain (in thousands): Roman Catholics, 6,024; Church of England, 2,285; Methodists, 548; Congregationalists, 490; Baptists, 406; Presbyterians, 84; Presbyterian Church of Scotland, 1,270; Episcopal Church of Scotland, 60.
Wireless licences in U.K.: 3,092,000.
Telephone subscribers in U.K.: 1,996,000.

Z **Births and Deaths**
Jan. 13th Sebastian de Ferranti d. (66).
Mar. 2nd D. H. Lawrence d. (45).

(*Continued opposite*)

1931 (Jan.–Aug.) The Hoover Moratorium—Britain abandons gold standard

A **Jan**: 12th, Allied military control committee is dissolved;
26th, Mahatma Gandhi is released for discussions with government;
27th, Pierre Laval becomes premier of France.

B **Feb**: Oswald Mosley breaks away from British Labour Party to form New Party (which is left in the wilderness in the general election, in *Oct.*).

C **Mar**: 4th, by Delhi Pact between Viceroy (Lord Irwin) and Gandhi, civil disobedience campaign is suspended, Congress Party promises to recognise Round-table Conference and political prisoners are released;
8th, U.S.S.R.-Turkish agreement on naval reductions in Black Sea;
21st, Austro-German customs union is projected and on protests by France, Italy and Czechoslovakia is referred to the International Court in *May*, which decides against it;
26th, treaty of friendship between Iraq and Transjordan.

D **Apr**: 14th, King Alfonso flees in Spanish revolution and Alcalá Zamora becomes President of provisional government;
22nd, treaty of friendship between Egypt and Iraq, the first pact between Egypt and an Arab state.

E **May**: 5th, People's National Convention in Nanking adopts provisional constitution;
8th, Farmers' Party in power in Norway;
11th, bankruptcy of Credit-Anstalt in Austria begins financial collapse of Central Europe;
13th, Paul Doumer is elected French President (–*May* 1932).

F **Jun**: 15th, U.S.S.R.-Polish treaty of friendship and commerce;
16th, Bank of England advances money to Austria, but France withholds support;
20th, Herbert Hoover's plan for one-year moratorium for reparations and war debts;
21st, Karl Buresch, Christian Socialist, forms Austrian ministry;
24th, U.S.S.R.-Afghanistan treaty of neutrality.

G **Jul**: 1st, opening of Benguella-Katanga railway completes first trans-African railway;
—, anti-Chinese riots in Korea;
10th, Norway's annexation of East Greenland provokes Danish protest (referred to League which adjudicates against Norway in *Apr.* 1933);
13th, bankruptcy of German Danatbank leads to closure of all German banks until *Aug.* 5th;
25th, Cárlos Ibañez, President of Chile, resigns (succeeded *Oct.* 4th, by Juan Montero);
May Committee reports estimated budget deficit in Britain of £100 million and proposes drastic economies, which splits cabinet.

H **Aug**: 1st, Franco-U.S. loan to Britain;
3rd, Austria and Germany renounce customs union, Julius Curtius resigns in disgrace and Chancellor Heinrich Brüning takes over foreign affairs;
11th, London Protocol on Hoover moratorium;
19th, French loan to Hungary;
—, Layton-Wiggin report calls for six-month extension of foreign credit to Germany;
24th, Ramsay MacDonald resigns and, 25th, forms National Government to balance the budget; Labour party subsequently expels MacDonald, Philip Snowden and J. P. Thomas, who serve with him; Arthur Henderson becomes leader of rump of Labour Party.

O **Politics, Economics, Law and Education**

Norman Angell and Harold Wright, *Can Governments Cure Unemployment?*
B. Mussolini and G. Forzano, *The 100 Days*.
R. H. Tawney, *Equality*.

P **Science, Technology, Discovery, etc.**

J. Cockcroft develops high-voltage apparatus for atomic transmutations.
Ernest O. Lawrence devises the cyclotron (or 'atom-smasher').
A. Eddington, *The World of Physics*.
O. P. Karrer isolates vitamin A.
Julius A. Nieuwland invents 'Neoprene' synthetic rubber process.
I.C.I. produce petrol from coal.
Spicer-Dufay process of natural colour photography.
Zoological Gardens, Whipsnade, opened.

Q **Scholarship**

R **Philosophy and Religion**

J. Dewey, *Philosophy and Civilisation*.
Neurath, *Empirical Sociology*.
O. Spengler, *Mankind and Technology*.
Papal Encyclical *Quadragesimo Anno* on social questions.

S **Art, Sculpture, Fine Arts and Architecture**

Painting:
P. Bonnard, *The Breakfast Room*.
Otto Dix, *Girls*.
E. Hopper, *Route 6, Eastham*.
H. Matisse, *The Dance*, murals at the Barnes Foundation, Pennsylvania.
P. Nash, *Kinetics*.

Sculpture:
C. Brancusi, *Mlle Pognany*.
A. Drury, *Sir J. Reynolds* statue, Burlington House, London.
J. Epstein, *Genesis* (marble).

Architecture:
Rockefeller Center, New York (–39).

T **Music**

Francesco Malipiero, *Triumph of Love* (opera).
Hans Pfitzner, *The Heart* (cantata).
W. Walton, *Belshazzar's Feast* (choral work).
S. Rachmaninov's music is banned in U.S.S.R. as 'decadent'.

U **Literature**

L. Abercrombie, *The Sale of St. Thomas*.
G. Bernanos, *La Grande Peur des bien-pensants*.
Pearl Buck, *The Good Earth*.
Theodore Dreiser, *Dawn*.
A. de St.-Exupéry, *Vol de nuit*.
V. Sackville-West, *All Passion Spent*.
Lytton Strachey, *Portraits in Miniature*.
Tristan Tzara, *L'Homme approximatif*.

J **Sep:** 7th (*–Dec.* 1st), Gandhi attends second India Round-table Conference in London, but the Conference fails to reach agreement on the representation of religious minorities;
10th, government's economy measures provoke riots in London and Glasgow and, 15th, naval mutiny at Invergordon over pay cuts;
12th, Mexico is admitted to League;
13th, Heimwehr *coup d'état* in Austria under Fascist leader Dr. Pfrimer fails;
18th, United and Reform parties form coalition in New Zealand;
—, Japan begins siege of Mukden, using bomber seaplanes, and occupies other strategic points in Manchuria;
21st, Britain abandons gold standard, the £ falling from $4·86 to $3·49.

K **Oct:** 11th, Adolf Hitler's alliance with the commercial magnate, Hugenberg, to support the National Socialists;
16th, U.S. delegates attend League Council to discuss Japan;
20th, Protection of Republic law in Spain;
27th, in British general election National Government wins 558 seats, Opposition 56.

L **Nov:** Ramsay MacDonald forms second National Government, with Neville Chamberlain Chancellor of Exchequer and John Simon Foreign Secretary.

M **Dec:** 9th, Spanish republican Constitution with
10th, election of Alcalá Zamora President and Manuel Azaña premier;
11th, Japan abandons gold standard;
Statute of Westminster defines Dominion status.

N Joseph A. Lyons founds United Australia Party from Nationalists and Labour dissidents.
National Coffee Department is established in Brazil and begins official destruction of surplus stocks.

v The Press

Kingsley Martin edits *The New Statesman* (–60), with which the *Nation* and *Athenaeum* is amalgamated.

w Drama and Entertainment

J. Bridie, *The Anatomist.*
Noël Coward's *Cavalcade.*
E. O'Neill, *Mourning Becomes Electra.*
Dodie Smith, *Autumn Crocus.*
Lilian Baylis reopens Sadlers Wells.

Films:
Charlie Chaplin in *City Lights.*
Congress Dances.
René Clair's *The Million.*
Sagan's *Mädchen in Uniform* with Dorothea Wieck.
Lamprecht's *Emil and the Detectives.*
Frankenstein with Boris Karloff.
Trader Horn.
Gracie Fields in *Sally in Our Alley.*

x Sport

y Statistics

Populations (in mill.): China, 410; India, 338; U.S.S.R., 168; U.S., 122; Japan, 75; Germany, 64; Great Britain, 46; France, 42.
Petroleum production (in mill. barrels): U.S., 851; Venezuela, 116.

z Births and Deaths

Jan. 3rd Joseph Joffre d. (78).
Jan. 22nd Anna Pavlova d. (49).
Jan. 31st Christopher Chataway b. (–).
Feb. 23rd Nellie Melba d. (72).
Mar. 26th Timothy Healy d. (76).
Mar. 27th Arnold Bennett d. (64).
Mar. 29th Margaret McMillan d. (70).
Aug. 31st Hall Caine d. (78).
Sept. 29th William Orpen d. (52).
Oct. 18th Thomas Alva Edison d. (84).
Dec. 3rd Vincent D'Indy d. (80).

1932 (Jan.–Jun.) Geneva Disarmament Conference—F. D. Roosevelt elected U.S. President

A **Jan:** 2nd, Manchukuo republic proclaimed in Manchuria;
4th, Japanese reach Shanhaikwan on Great Wall;
—, Indian government granted emergency powers for six months, Indian National Congress is declared illegal and Mahatma Gandhi is arrested;
7th, Stimpson Doctrine, set out in note protesting against Japanese aggression in Manchuria, that U.S. will recognise no gains made by armed force;
—, Heinrich Brüning declares Germany cannot, and will not, resume reparations payments;
15th, France completes pacification of French Morocco;
22nd, U.S.S.R. second Five-year Plan begins;
25th, U.S.S.R.-Polish non-aggression pact;
28th, Japanese occupy Shanghai (*–May*).

B **Feb:** 2nd (*–July*), sixty states, including U.S. and U.S.S.R., attend Geneva Disarmament Conference, at which French proposal for international police force is opposed by Germany;
6th, Fascist *coup d'état* in Memel;
7th, by Oslo convention, Scandinavian countries, Belgium and Netherlands undertake economic co-operation;
8th, Bulgaria renounces further reparations payments;
16th, Republican majority in Irish elections;
21st, André Tardieu forms ministry in France;
27th, reorganisation of U.S. federal reserve system;
29th (*–Mar.* 3rd), Nazi revolt in Finland.

C **Mar:** 1st, Protection in Britain, with corn subsidies;
3rd, Chinese forces are driven back from Shanghai;
9th, Emperor Pu Yi, who had abdicated Chinese throne in 1912, is installed as President of Manchukuo;
—, Éamon de Valéra is elected President of Ireland;
13th, in German presidential election Paul von Hindenburg receives 18 million votes against Adolf Hitler, 11 million, and a Communist, 5 million, but below the majority required for election (new election *Apr.* 10th).

D **Apr:** 6th (–8th), London four-power conference on Danube founders since Germany and Italy decline to leave the problem to the Danubian states;
6th, British Minister of Health's circular to local authorities urging vigorous policy of slum clearance;
10th, Paul von Hindenburg (19 million votes) re-elected German President, against Hitler (13 million) and a Communist (3 million);
24th, Nazi successes in elections in Prussia, Bavaria, Württemberg and Hamburg.

E **May:** 1st, Left parties win French elections;
6th, President Paul Doumer of France murdered by Russian *émigré*;
10th, Albert Lebrun elected his successor;
16th, murder of Inukai, Japanese premier;
19th, Dáil votes for abolition of oath of loyalty to British crown, but the opposition in the Senate succeeds in preventing enactment;
20th, Engelbert Dollfuss, Austrian chancellor, forms a coalition of Christian Socialists and Agrarians;

F **Jun:** 1st, on Heinrich Brüning's resignation Franz von Papen forms a ministry in Germany with Constantin von Neurath foreign minister, from which the Nazis are excluded;

O **Politics, Economics, Law and Education**

W. Lewis, *Doom of Youth*.

John Strachey, *The Coming Struggle for Power*.

B.B.C. takes over responsibility for developing television from J. L. Baird's company.

Basic English founded as a prospective international language.

Commissioner for creating employment is appointed in Germany.

New Procedure rules in Supreme Court of Judicature in Britain to obviate attendance of witnesses through having facts proved by affidavits.

Kidnapping of C. A. Lindbergh's infant son.

P **Science, Technology, Discovery, etc.**

Chadwick's work on the 'neutron'.

Harold C. Urey and Washburn discover that electrolysed water is heavier than ordinary water.

Edwin Land discovers the synthetic light polariser.

Karl Jansky pioneers radio-astronomy.

Vitamin D discovered.

Klarges, *Graphology*.

Balloon-tyre produced for farm tractors.

Zuider Zee drainage scheme completed.

Cologne-Bonn autobahn opened.

Opening of Lambeth Bridge, London, and Sydney Harbour Bridge.

Codos flies from Paris to Hanoi in 3 days 5 hrs. 40 mins. (*Jan.*).

Q **Scholarship**

Centenary celebrations of Goethe's death include the institution of the Goethe Medal for scholarship and art.

The Folger Library, Washington, opened.

R **Philosophy and Religion**

Henri Bergson, *Les deux sources de la monde et de la religion*.

Karl Jaspers, *Philosophie*.

Karl Barth, *Christian Dogmatics*.

Reunification of the Methodist Churches in England.

S **Art, Sculpture, Fine Arts and Architecture**

Painting:

Max Beckmann, *Seven Triptychs* (–1950).

Stanley Spencer, *May Tree, Cookham*.

Sculpture:

E. Gill, *Prospero and Ariel* for Broadcasting House, London (–1937).

P. Picasso, *Head of a Woman*.

Alexander Calder exhibits 'stabiles' (sculptures moved by engines) soon followed by 'mobiles' (sculptures moved by air currents).

Architecture:

E. Lutyens Metropolitan Cathedral, Liverpool begun.

Meyer and Hand, Broadcasting House, London (–1937).

T **Music**

Arnold Bax, 'cello concerto.

George Dyson, *The Canterbury Pilgrims* (choral work).

M. Ravel, Piano Concerto in G minor.

Dmitry Shostakovich, *Lady Macbeth of Mtsensk* (opera).

Thomas Beecham founds the London Philharmonic Orchestra.

F Jun: 4th, second ministry of Édouard Herriot in France;
6th (–18th), revolt in Chile ends in appointment of Socialist government;
13th, Anglo-French pact of friendship signed at Lausanne;
16th (–*July* 9th), at Lausanne reparations conference Germany accepts proposal for a final conditional payment of 3,000 million Rm.;
—, ban in Germany on Nazi Storm Troopers (in operation since *Apr.*) is lifted;
27th, Constitution proclaimed in Siam.

G Jul: 5th, Oliveira Salazar elected premier of Portugal and establishes Fascist régime;
11th (–*Oct.* 3rd), revolution in Brazil;
15th, by Geneva protocol Austria is granted loan on condition she renounces *Anschluss* until 1952;
18th, by new language regulations in Belgium French becomes official language of Walloon provinces, Flemish the language of Flanders;
—, Turkey is admitted to the League;
20th, Franz von Papen removes Socialist premier of Prussia by show of force;
21st (–*Aug.* 20th), Imperial Economic Conference at Ottawa favours moderate imperial preference;
31st, in Reichstag elections Nazis win 230 seats, Socialists 133, Centre 97 and Communists 89, producing stalemate, since neither Nazis nor Socialists would enter a coalition;
—, war begins between Bolivia and Paraguay (the Chaco War –*June* 1935).

H Aug: 10th, revolt of Gen. José Sanjurjo in Seville is suppressed;
13th, Adolf Hitler refuses President Hindenburg's request to serve as vice-chancellor under Franz von Papen.

J Sep: 1st, in war between Peru and Colombia over Leticia harbour, Colombia appeals to the League (which in *Mar.* 1933 orders Peru to withdraw);
14th, Germany leaves disarmament conference;
—, Belgian government is granted wide powers to deal with financial crisis;
25th, Catalonia is granted autonomy, with its own flag, language and Parliament;
28th, Herbert Samuel and other Liberal free-traders resign from Cabinet over policy of imperial preference; John Simon becomes leader of Liberals supporting government.

K Oct: 2nd, Lytton Report to League on Manchuria recognises Japan's special interests and recommends an autonomous State under Chinese sovereignty, but Japanese controlled;
3rd, on end of British mandate, Iraq joins League;
4th, Julius Gömbös, anti-Semite Nationalist, forms ministry in Hungary;
31st, Eleutherios Venizelos resigns in Greece, succeeded, *Nov.* 4th, by Panyoti Tsaldaris, a moderate Royalist.

L Nov: 6th, German elections produce further deadlock, with some Communist gains from Nazis;
8th, F. D. Roosevelt wins U.S. presidential election in Democrat landslide with 472 electoral votes over Herbert Hoover, Republican, with 59;
14th, Croat party demands new Yugoslav constitution;
17th, Franz von Papen resigns, and, 24th, Adolf Hitler rejects German chancellorship;
19th (–*Dec.* 24th), third India Conference in London;
29th, Franco-U.S.S.R. non-aggression pact;
29th, Persia annuls Anglo-Persian Oil Co. agreement of 1901.

T **Music** (*cont.*)

Duke Ellington is recognised as the first composer of jazz, and the first negro musician, of distinction.

U **Literature**

W. H. Auden, *The Orators.*
L. F. Céline, *Voyage au bout de la Nuit.*
William Faulkner, *Light in August.*
Ernest Hemingway, *Death in the Afternoon.*
Aldous Huxley, *Brave New World.*
F. R. Leavis, *New Bearings in English Poetry.*
R. Lehmann, *Invitation to the Waltz.*
Rose Macaulay, *They Were Defeated.*
Henri Michaux, *Un Barbare en Asie.*
Charles Morgan, *The Fountain.*
Boris Pasternak, *Second Birth* (poems).
Jules Romains, *Les Hommes de bonne volonté* (–47).
G. B. Shaw, *The Adventures of the Black Girl in Her Search for God.*

V **The Press**

Scrutiny issued (–1953).

W **Drama and Entertainment**

B. Brecht, *The Mother.*
J. Bridie, *Tobias and the Angel.*
J. B. Priestley, *Dangerous Corner.*
Shakespeare Memorial Theatre, Stratford-on-Avon, opened.

Films:
The Blue Light
René Clair's *À Nous La Liberté.*
Gary Cooper in *A Farewell to Arms.*
Marlene Dietrich in *Shanghai Express.*
La Maternelle.
Morning Glory.
Grand Hotel.
First 'Tarzan' film.
Shirley Temple's début.
127 sound films made (8 in 1929).
The Cinema Quarterly is issued.

X **Sport**

Olympic Games held at Los Angeles.
D. R. Jardine's 'body-line' bowling in M.C.C. tour of Australia.

Y **Statistics**

Unemployment: U.S., 13·7 mill.; Germany, 5·6 mill.; Great Britain, 2·8 mill.
U.K. Textiles trade:

Raw cotton imports	1,257 mill. lb.
Exports of cottons	2,303 mill. yds.
Exports of linens	65 mill. yds.
Exports of silks	4 mill. sq. yds.

Trades union membership: Great Britain, 4,443,000.

1932 (Dec.)

M Dec: 4th, Kurt von Schleicher forms ministry in Germany, attempting to conciliate the Centre and the Left;
9th, Japanese invade Jehol;
11th, No Force Declaration of Britain, France, Germany and Italy against resorting to force for settling differences; and, with signing of Geneva Protocol on Germany's equality of rights with other nations, Germany returns to Disarmament Conference;
15th, Mexico leaves the League;
16th, National Union in Lithuania adopts Fascist programme;
18th, Édouard Herriot resigns, after defeat in Chamber of proposal to pay debt to U.S., and Paul-Boncour forms cabinet;
27th, South Africa leaves gold standard;
28th, U.S. Congressional resolution against cancellation of Germany's war debt.

N Oswald Mosley founds British Union of Fascists.
Famine in U.S.S.R.
Australian federal government is strengthened by passage of Financial Agreement Enforcement Act.

Y **Statistics** (*cont.*)

U.S.S.R. production (in mill. tons): pig iron, 6·2; steel, 5·9; coal, 64·4; oil, 21·4; fertilisers, 0·9; cement, 3·5.

Z **Births and Deaths**

Jan. 7th André Maginot d. (54).
Jan. 21st Giles Lytton Strachey d. (51).
Feb. 10th Edgar Wallace d. (57).
Mar. 7th Aristide Briand d. (69).
Mar. 14th George Eastman d. (77).
May 7th Paul Doumer d. (75).
July 6th Kenneth Grahame d. (73).
Aug. 9th Graham Wallas d. (74).
Sept. 16th Ronald Ross d. (75).

1933 (Jan.–Apr.) Hitler becomes German Chancellor—Japanese advances in China—'New Deal' in U.S.

A Jan: 2nd (–12th), rising in Barcelona of anarchists and syndicalists;
13th, U.S. Congress votes independence for Philippines after period of transition, which passes over President Hoover's veto, but is rejected, *Oct.*, by Philippine legislature;
16th, E. Venizelos again premier of Greece (–*Mar.* 10th);
24th, Éamon de Valéra's Fianna Fáil gains majority of one in Irish elections;
25th, Liberal ministry formed in Norway;
28th, Kurt von Schleicher's ministry falls in Germany, after failure to conciliate Centre and Left and
30th, Adolf Hitler is appointed Chancellor, forming a Nazi cabinet with Franz von Papen vice-chancellor, Constantin von Neurath foreign minister, Hermann Göring and Wilhelm Frick;
31st, Édouard Daladier becomes premier of France.

B Feb: 3rd, settlement of Anglo-Persian oil dispute;
6th, Twentieth Amendment to U.S. Constitution advances the President's inauguration to *Jan.* 20th, while senators and representatives are to take office on *Jan.* 3rd;
16th, fearing German threats the Little Entente (Czechoslovakia, Roumania and Yugoslavia) is reorganised, with a permanent council;
23rd (–*Mar.* 12th), Japanese occupy China north of Great Wall;
24th, League adopts Lytton Report on Manchuria, despite its rejection by Japan;
27th, Nazis engineer the Reichstag Fire, which Adolf Hitler denounces as a Communist plot, and suspends civil liberties and freedom of press.

C Mar: 4th, F. D. Roosevelt's inauguration speech on 'the policy of the good neighbor', beginnings of the New Deal;
5th, in German elections Nazis win 288 seats, Socialists, 120, Communists, 81, Centre, 74, and Nationalists, 52;
6th, Poland occupies Danzig;
— (–9th), U.S. banks closed;
7th, Engelbert Dollfuss suspends Parliamentary government in Austria;
9th, U.S. Congress grants President Roosevelt wide powers concerning currency and credit;
16th, Britain's disarmament plan for reduction in size of armies fails, as Germany insists that Storm Troopers should not be included in total;
19th, Benito Mussolini proposes pact with Britain, France and Germany (signed *July* 15th);
23rd, enabling law in Germany grants Adolf Hitler dictatorial powers until *Apr.* 1937;
26th, new Constitution in Portugal;
27th, Japan announces she will leave the League (takes effect 1935);
30th, James B. M. Hertzog forms National Coalition in South Africa and is joined by Jan C. Smuts.

D Apr: 1st, persecution of Jews begins in Germany, with national boycott of all Jewish businesses and professions;
8th, Western Australia, irritated by federal taxation, votes to secede from Commonwealth;
10th, British Labour Party moves vote of censure on government for driving thousands of unemployed to seek Poor Law assistance;
25th, Canada, and, 30th, U.S. abandon gold standard;
27th, Anglo-German trade agreement.

O **Politics, Economics, Law and Education**

Norman Angell, *The Great Illusion.*

Lev Trotsky, *History of the Russian Revolution.*

British Agricultural Marketing Scheme and U.S. Agricultural Adjustment tariff.

Oxford Union Society passes motion refusing to fight for King and Country.

German four-year plan for abolishing unemployment.

London Passenger Transport Board established.

P **Science, Technology, Discovery, etc.**

Anderson and Robert Millikin, while analysing cosmic rays, discover positive electrons ('positrons').

de Haas's work on very low temperatures.

The discovery of the Steinheim skull leads to the rejection of the theory that Neanderthal Man was in the line of descent of *Homo sapiens.*

An all-metal wireless valve is made by Marconiphone Company.

The first commercially-produced synthetic detergent is made by I.C.I.

Wiley Post flies round the world in 7 days 18 hrs. 49 mins.

Q **Scholarship**

Winston Churchill, *Marlborough: His Life and Times* (–38).

R **Philosophy and Religion**

A. N. Whitehead, *Adventures of Ideas.*

E. W. Barnes, *Scientific Theory and Religion.*

Nathan Söderblom, *The Living God* (Gifford Lectures).

Amalgamation of Protestant Churches in Germany as the German Evangelical Church (*July*).

S **Art, Sculpture, Fine Arts and Architecture**

Painting:

Herbert Read publishes *Art Now.*

Wassily Kandinsky and Paul Klee leave Germany for France and Switzerland respectively.

Sculpture:

A. Giacometti, *The Palace at 4 a.m.*

Architecture:

W. Holden, Senate House, London University.

The Warburg Institute is transferred from Hamburg to London (is incorporated in London University, 1944).

T **Music**

R. Strauss, *Arabella* (opera).

Balanchine and Kirstein found School of American Ballet.

U **Literature**

G. Duhamel, *The Pasquier Chronicle* (–45).

T. S. Eliot, *The Use of Poetry and the Use of Criticism.*

A. Malraux, *La Condition humaine.*

Thomas Mann, *The Tales of Jacob* (first volume of 'Joseph and his Brothers' –43).

J. Masefield, *The Bird of Dawning.*

G. Orwell (pseud.), *Down and Out in Paris and London.*

G. Santayana, *The Last Puritan.*

Gertrude Stein, *The Autobiography of Alice B. Toklas.*

Helen Waddell, *Peter Abelard.*

E May: 2nd, German trades unions are suppressed;
3rd, oath of allegiance to British Crown removed from Irish Constitution and Irish appeals to Privy Council made illegal;
10th, Paraguay declares war on Bolivia;
12th, U.S. agricultural adjustment act and federal emergency relief act;
—, Franco-Canadian tariff agreement;
17th, in South African elections National Coalition wins 138 seats, Opposition, 12;
—, Associations law in Spain nationalises church property and closes church schools;
18th, Tennessee Valley Authority created in U.S. to develop the valley's resources;
26th, Australia claims a third of Antarctic continent;
27th, U.S. securities act to protect investors by providing information on new security issues;
28th, Nazis win Danzig elections.

F Jun: 12th (*–July* 27th), 64 countries attend World Monetary and Economic Conference in London but fail to reach agreement on currency stabilisation, through F. D. Roosevelt's opposition (*July* 3rd), leading to rampant economic nationalism and, in Britain, to the 'buy British' campaign;
16th, U.S. National Industrial Recovery Act and Farm Credit Act;
19th, Nazi party in Austria is dissolved, but terrorist agitation continues;
20th, army *coup d'état* in Siam.

G Jul: 3rd, London convention defining the aggressor signed by U.S.S.R., the Baltic and Balkan states;
14th, political parties, other than Nazi, suppressed in Germany;
15th, Rome Pact binds Britain, France, Germany and Italy to the League Covenant, the Locarno treaties and the Kellogg-Briand Pact;
20th, concordat with Papacy defines position of Catholic Church in Germany;
23rd, National Guard ('Blue Shirts') formed in Eire to oppose É. de Valéra's Republican Army;
27th, British Commonwealth declaration on monetary and economic affairs;
—, Saudi Arabia and Transjordan sign treaty of friendship;
Assyrian Christians massacred by Iraqui (*–Aug.*).

H Aug: 5th, Polish agreement with Danzig;
25th, Canada, U.S., U.S.S.R., Australia and Argentina sign wheat agreement.

J Sep: 3rd, Irish opposition parties of National Guard and the Centre form United Ireland Party under Owen O'Duffy (but led by William Cosgrave from 22nd);
14th, Graeco-Turkish ten-year non-aggression pact.

K Oct: 11th, Latin American countries sign Rio de Janeiro non-aggression pact;
14th, Germany leaves disarmament conference and the League;
16th, Labour Party wins Norwegian elections;
23rd, Albert Sarraut forms ministry in France;
Unrest in Palestine grows.

L Nov: 12th, Nazis dominate German elections, with 92 per cent of electorate voting for Nazi candidates;
16th, British Liberal Party joins opposition;
—, President Getulio Vargas of Brazil acquires dictatorial powers;
17th, U.S. recognises U.S.S.R. and resumes trade;
19th, Right wins Spanish elections for the Cortes;
22nd, Camille Chautemps forms ministry in France.

(*Continued opposite*)

V **The Press**

Arthur Christiansen edits *The Daily Express* (–57).

W **Drama and Entertainment**

J. Bridie, *A Sleeping Clergyman.*
Gordon Daviot, *Richard of Bordeaux.*
Merton Hodge, *The Wind and the Rain.*
Eugene O'Neill, *Ah Wilderness.*
British Film Institute founded.
Odeon cinema circuit formed in Britain.

Films:
Alexander Korda's *The Private Life of Henry VIII* with Charles Laughton;
Greta Garbo in *Queen Christina.*
The Testament of Dr. Mabuse.
René Clair's *14 Juli.*
Cavalcade.
King Kong.
Poil de Carotte.

X **Sport**

National Playing Fields Association founded in London.

Y **Statistics**

Z **Births and Deaths**

Jan. 5th Calvin Coolidge d. (60).
Jan. 21st George Augustus Moore d. (80).
Jan. 31st John Galsworthy d. (66).
Apr. 22nd Frederick Henry Royce d. (60).
July 8th 'Anthony Hope' (pseud. of Anthony Hope Hawkins) d. (60).
Sept. 7th Edward Grey, Viscount Grey of Fallodon, d. (81).
Dec. 4th Stefan George d. (65).

M **Dec: 5th, Twenty-first amendment to U.S. Constitution repeals prohibition;**
9th, radical rising in Spain;
18th, Newfoundland Constitution suspended on mismanagement of economic affairs and
21st, Newfoundland loses dominion status, reverting to Crown Colony;
28th, Britain makes final payment to U.S. for war debts;
29th, Ion Duca, Liberal premier of Roumania, is murdered by Iron Guard and is succeeded by George Tartarescu;
Flight of Alexandre Stavisky, a Russian promoter, involved in fraudulent transactions in France, is exploited by Royalists and Fascists;
Jews protest at immigration restrictions in Palestine.

N

1934 (Jan.–Jun.) Dollfuss murdered—Hitler becomes Führer—Purge of Russian Communist Party begins

A Jan: 14th, Catalan elections won by Left, while in rest of Spain the Right predominates;
26th, Germany signs ten-year non-aggression pact with Poland;
30th, Édouard Daladier forms ministry in France;
—, U.S. Gold Reserve Act authorises President to revalue the dollar;
31st, Federal Farm Mortgage Corporation set up in U.S.
Turkey's five-year plan for industry begins.

B Feb: 1st (–16th), Austrian decree dissolving all political parties except Engelbert Dollfuss's Fatherland Front leads to risings; the Christian Socialists forfeit support from working classes;
5th, Corporations act in Italy;
6th (–7th), riots in Paris, and, 8th, Paul Doumergue forms National Union ministry of all parties, except Royalists, Socialists and Communists, to avert civil war;
9th, Balkan pact signed between Roumania, Greece, Yugoslavia and Turkey, as a counterpart to the Little Entente, to prevent Balkans from encroachment by the great powers, but Bulgaria is not a signatory;
12th (–13th), general strike in France;
15th, Civil Works Emergency Relief act in U.S.;
16th, Anglo-Russian trade pact;
21st (–*Mar.* 16th), French troops combat Berbers in South-West Morocco.

C Mar: 1st, Pu Yi assumes title of Emperor of Manchukuo;
8th, Labour Party for first time wins clear majority on L.C.C. over Municipal Reform and Liberal Parties;
16th (–17th), Rome protocols signed between Italy, Austria and Hungary to form Danubian bloc against Little Entente (Czechoslovakia, Roumania and Yugoslavia);
24th, Tydings-McDuffie act declares independence of the Philippines from 1945;
26th, Road Traffic Act introduces driving tests in Britain.

D Apr: 7th, Gandhi suspends civil disobedience campaign;
7th, extension of U.S.S.R.-Finnish non-aggression pact for ten years;
Socialists lead strike in Barcelona.

E May: 14th, British Unemployment bill given third reading;
15th, Karlis Ulmanis becomes dictator in Latvia;
24th, Colombia and Peru settle dispute over Leticia.

F Jun: 5th, J. C. Smuts's South African Party unites with J. B. M. Hertzog's followers in Nationalist Party to form United South African Nationalists, while other Nationalists re-form under D. F. Malan;
8th, Oswald Mosley addresses mass meeting of British Union of Fascists at Olympia;
9th, U.S.S.R. renews relations with Czechoslovakia and, 10th, with Roumania;
11th, Disarmament Conference ends in failure;
12th, political parties banned in Bulgaria;
—, Congress grants F. D. Roosevelt powers to conclude agreements for reducing tariffs;
—, Cape Parliament retains right to secede from Commonwealth in South African Status bill;
14th (–15th), Venice meeting between Hitler and Mussolini fails to bring about closer relations owing to divergent interests in the Danube Valley;
19th, U.S. Silver Purchase bill authorises President to nationalise silver;
20th, agreement on frontier between Sudan and Libya;

O **Politics, Economics, Law and Education**

Lewis Mumford, *Technics and Civilisation.*

John Wheeler-Bennett, *The Disarmament Deadlock.*

Bertrand Russell, *Freedom and Organisation.*

Peace Pledge Union founded in Britain.

British Iron and Steel Federation.

Hendon Police College founded.

Wavelengths of chief European broadcasting stations are altered, to conform with recommendations of Lucerne Committee (*Jan.* 14th).

German law for the regulation of labour.

Dr. H. Schacht's plan for the control of Germany's foreign trade (*Sept.*).

Gordonstoun School is founded.

P **Science, Technology, Discovery, etc.**

F. Joliot and I. Curie-Joliot discover induced radioactivity.

Ernest O. Lawrence's cyclotron, for producing high-velocity particles.

Enrico Fermi suggests that neutrons and protons are the same fundamental particles in two different quantum states.

Alexander Fleming and Petrie, *Recent Advances in Vaccine and Serum Therapy.*

Reichstein makes pure Vitamin C.

Phthalacyamine dyes are prepared.

Chilling process for meat cargoes discovered.

U.S.S.R. balloon *Osoaviakhim* ascends 13 miles into stratosphere (*Jan.* 30th).

Beebe descends 3,028 feet into ocean off Bermuda (*Aug.* 16th).

S.S. *Queen Mary* launched (*Sept.* 26th), and Southern Railway's first train ferry launched.

Regular air-mail service, London to Australia (*Dec.*).

Q **Scholarship**

Arnold Toynbee, *A Study of History* (–54).

Oxford History of England, ed. G. N. Clark (–65).

J. E. Neale, *Queen Elizabeth.*

Harold Nicolson, *Curzon, the Last Phase.*

R **Philosophy and Religion**

Lionel Curtis, *Civitas Dei.*

Albert Einstein, *My Philosophy.*

R. Niebuhr, *Moral Man and Immoral Society.*

William Temple, *Nature, Man and God.*

S **Art, Sculpture, Fine Arts and Architecture**

Painting:

J. Piper, *Rye Harbour.*

Stanley Spencer, *The Angel, Cookham Church.*

Architecture:

Cambridge University Library.

Wornum, Royal Institute of British Architects Building, London.

Gustav Adolf Kirche, Berlin.

T **Music**

P. Hindemith completes *Mathis der Maler* (opera), but its performance is banned in Germany.

A. Honegger's ballet, *Sémiramis.*

I. Stravinsky, *Persephone*, an opera-ballet.

John Christie founds Glyndebourne operatic festival.

1934 (Jun.–Dec.)

F Jun: 22nd, Ramsay MacDonald, ordered to rest, delegates duties to Stanley Baldwin;
23rd, Saudi Arabia and the Yemen sign peace after war of six weeks;
30th, Nazi purge in Germany with summary executions of Kurt von Schleicher, Ernst Roehm and other party leaders for alleged plot against Hitler.

G Jul: 1st, Germany suspends all cash transfers on debts abroad;
2nd, Lazaro Cárdenas elected President of Mexico;
7th, Keisuke Okada forms ministry in Japan;
12th, Belgium prohibits uniformed political parties;
14th, oil pipeline Mosul to Tripoli opened;
19th, Stanley Baldwin announces increase in size of R.A.F.;
25th, E. Dollfuss is murdered in attempted Nazi *coup* in Austria;
30th, Kurt Schuschnigg is appointed Austrian chancellor.

H Aug: 1st, Australia's prohibitive duty on imported cottons provokes boycott of Australian produce in Lancashire;
2nd, death of Paul von Hindenburg (aged 87);
19th, German plebiscite approves vesting of sole executive power in Adolf Hitler as Führer.

J Sep: 9th, Fascist and anti-Fascist demonstrations in Hyde Park, London;
12th, Baltic states sign treaty of collaboration;
17th, United Australian Party wins general election;
18th, U.S.S.R. is admitted to the League.

K Oct: 2nd, Royal Indian Navy founded;
4th, Alejandro Lerroux forms ministry of Right in Spain, provoking, 5th, strike called by the Left;
9th, King Alexander of Yugoslavia is assassinated in Marseilles;
23rd (–*Dec.* 19th), London Naval Disarmament Conference meets, but no agreement is reached;
24th, Gandhi withdraws from Indian National Congress;
—, German Labour Front founded;
30th, dissolution of Graeco-Turkish Commission of 1923.

L Nov: 3rd, Syrian Parliament is indefinitely prorogued;
7th, Joseph Lyons, United Australian Party, forms coalition ministry with Country Party in Australia;
9th, Pierre Flandin forms coalition in France;
13th, Sedition bill introduced in Britain;
20th, Depressed Areas bill introduced in Britain;
26th, abolition of titles in Turkey;
28th, Winston Churchill warns Parliament of German air menace;
30th, Egyptian Constitution of 1930 suspended;
Moroccan nationalist movement founded.

M Dec: 1st, assassination of Serge Kirov, close collaborator of Josef Stalin, leads to O.G.P.U. purge in Russian Communist Party;
5th, clashes between Italian and Ethiopian troops on Somaliland frontier;
14th, enfranchisement of women in Turkey;
16th, National Union Party provides only candidates in Portuguese elections;
19th, Japan denounces Washington treaties of 1922 and 1930;
21st, Anglo-Irish coal and cattle pact;
Daniel Salamanca, President of Bolivia, overthrown by military *coup*.

N

U **Literature**

Louis Aragon, *Hourra l'Oural* (poem).
Scott Fitzgerald, *Tender is the Night*.
Robert Graves, *I, Claudius*.
Dorothy L. Sayers, *The Nine Tailors*.
Sholokhov, *Quiet Flows the Don*.
First Soviet Writers' Conference held in Moscow under M. Gorki.

V **The Press**

Left Review (–1938).

W **Drama and Entertainment**

Jean Cocteau, *La Machine infernale*.
Sean O'Casey, *Within the Gates*.
J. B. Priestley, *Eden End*.

Films:
René Clair's *The Last Millionaire*.
Forgotten Men.
The Scarlet Pimpernel.
The Thin Man.

X **Sport**

Henry Cotton ends U.S. golfers' dominance by winning open championship at Sandwich.

Y **Statistics**

Z **Births and Deaths**

Feb. 23rd Edward Elgar d. (76).
Apr. 11th Gerald du Maurier d. (61).
May 17th Cass Gilbert d. (74).
May 25th Gustav Holst d. (59).
June 10th Frederick Delius d. (71).
July 4th Marie Curie d. (66).
Sept. 9th, Roger Fry d. (67).
Sept. 20th Sophia Loren b. (–).
Oct. 14th Arthur Schuster d. (83).
Oct. 15th Raymond Poincaré d. (74).
Nov. 23rd Arthur Wing Pinero d. (79).

1935 (Jan.–Jun.) The Saar is restored to Germany—Stresa Conference—Italy invades Abyssinia

A **Jan**: 1st, Mustapha Kemal, President of Turkey, adopts name of Kemal Atatürk when National Assembly makes family names obligatory;

4th, British cotton-spinners vote to reduce the productive capacity of the industry;

7th, Franco-Italian agreement of Marseilles, intended as preliminary to a general treaty of co-operation;

9th, Britain signs trade pact with India;

13th, Saar plebiscite favours incorporation with Germany;

15th (–17th), Grigori Zinoviev and other U.S.S.R. leaders are convicted of treason and imprisoned (Zinoviev is re-tried as a Trotskyist and sentenced to death, *Aug.* 1936);

17th, David Lloyd George's 'New Deal' speech at Bangor (*July* 22nd, the government replies to his programme);

28th, George Lansbury leads Commons storm over means test.

B **Feb**: 1st (–3rd), Anglo-German conference in London to discuss Germany's rearmament; Italy sends troops to East Africa.

C **Mar**: 1st (–11th), rising of E. Venizelos in Greece is suppressed;

7th, restoration of Saar to Germany marks beginning of Germany's expansion;

12th, 30-m.p.h. speed limit enforced in built-up areas of Britain;

16th, Germany repudiates disarmament clauses of Versailles Treaty;

20th, Labour ministry takes office in Norway;

23rd, U.S.S.R. sells her interest in Chinese Eastern Railway to Japan;

25th, Paul Van Zeeland forms ministry of National Unity in Belgium and devalues Belgian Franc.

D **Apr**: 11th (–14th), Britain, France and Italy confer at Stresa, to establish a common front against Germany;

23rd, Polish Constitution is adopted after nine years discussion.

E **May**: 2nd, Franco-U.S.S.R. treaty of mutual assistance for five years;

16th, U.S.S.R.-Czechoslovakia pact of mutual assistance;

19th, Sudete (Nazi) Party strengthens position in Czechoslovakian election;

27th, U.S. Supreme Court declares National Industrial Recovery Act to be unconstitutional;

31st, ministry of Pierre Flandin, who had demanded extensive powers, is overthrown in France.

F **Jun**: 3rd, Croats boycott Yugoslav Parliament;

4th, Pierre Laval forms ministry in France;

7th, Stanley Baldwin, Conservative, forms National Government in Britain, with Ramsay MacDonald Lord President of Council, John Simon Home Secretary and Samuel Hoare Foreign Secretary;

14th, end of Chaco War between Paraguay and Bolivia;

18th, by Anglo-German Naval Agreement Germany undertakes that her navy shall not exceed a third of tonnage of Royal Navy;

23rd, Anthony Eden offers Benito Mussolini concessions over Abyssinia, which he rejects;

27th, League of Nations Union peace ballot in Britain shows strong support for ideals of League;

—, D. Lloyd George forms Council of Action for peace and reconstruction.

O Politics, Economics, Law and Education

S. and B. Webb, *Soviet Communism: A New Civilisation.*
Victor Gollancz founds Left Book Club (first publication in *May* 1936).
Germany reintroduces compulsory military service (*Mar.* 16th).
New Deal Social Security legislation in U.S.
British Council founded.
Persia changes its name to Iran; and a University is founded at Teheran.
Bank of Canada founded (*Mar.* 11th).
L.C.C. Green Belt Scheme in operation (*Apr.* 1st).

P Science, Technology, Discovery, etc.

Robert Watson-Watt builds first practical radar equipment for detecting aircraft.
Domagk discovers protosil for treating streptococcal infections.
Polyethylene is discovered by I.C.I. chemists.
The 35 mm. 'Kodachrome' film devised.
Hydrogenerator plant, for extracting petrol from coal, opened at Billingham, Co. Durham (*June*).
Oil pipelines from Kirkuk in Iraq to Haifa and Tripolis opened (*Jan.*).
Lower Zambesi railway bridge, the longest in world, opened to traffic (*Jan.* 14th).
Malcolm Campbell at Daytona Beach, Florida, drives *Bluebird* at 276·8 m.p.h.
S.S. *Normandie* crosses Atlantic in 107 hours 33 mins.
Pan-American Airways start trans-Pacific service from California.
Princess Juliana Canal, Holland, opened.

Q Scholarship

Brockhaus Encyclopaedia completed.
R. H. Hodgkin, *History of the Anglo-Saxons.*
T. E. Lawrence, under pseudonym of T. E. Shaw, publishes translation of *The Odyssey of Homer.*

R Philosophy and Religion

J. B. S. Haldane, *Philosophy of a Biologist.*
Karl Jaspers, *Suffering and Existence.*
Margaret Mead, *Growing up in New Guinea.*
Karl Barth, *Gedo.*
F. H. Hinsley appointed Cardinal Archbishop of Westminster (*Apr.*).

S Art, Sculpture, Fine Arts and Architecture

Painting:
Salvador Dali, *Giraffe on Fire.*
Russell Flint, *Majura the Strong.*
E. Munch, *The Modern Faust.*
S. Spencer, *Workmen in the House.*
T. W. Earp, *Modern Movements in Painting.*
David Gascoigne (pseud.), *Short Survey of Surrealism.*
Exhibition of Chinese Art at Burlington House.

Sculpture:
J. Epstein, *Ecce Homo.*

Architecture:
E. Mendelssohn and Chermeyeff, The De la Warr Pavilion, Bexhill, Sussex.

T Music

Alban Berg, violin concerto.
George Gershwin, *Porgy and Bess* (folk opera).

G **Jul**: 4th, Austria, encouraged by Mussolini, abolishes anti-Hapsburg laws and restores in part imperial property;

13th, U.S.S.R.-U.S. trade pact;

25th (*–Aug.* 20th), Third International meeting declares that Communists in democratic countries should support their governments against Fascist states;

27th, French government is granted emergency financial powers;

Anti-Roman Catholic riots in Belfast.

H **Aug**: 2nd, Government of India Act reforms governmental system, separates Burma and Aden from India, grants provincial governments greater self-government and creates a central legislature at Delhi (to come into force *Apr.* 1st 1937);

14th, F. D. Roosevelt signs Social Security act;

30th, U.S. Coal Stabilization Act and Wealth Tax, which increases surtax.

J **Sep**: 10th, assembly of white settlers in Kenya denounces government policy and advocates closer union with Uganda and Tanganyika;

15th, Nuremberg laws outlaw the Jews and make Swastika the official flag of Germany.

K **Oct**: 2nd, Italy invades Abyssinia;

7th, League Council declares Italy the aggressor;

— (–17th), Kurt Schuschnigg's 'bloodless *coup d'état*' in Vienna in collaboration with Prince Starhemberg against Emil Fey, minister of interior, and his Nazi allies;

19th, League imposes sanctions against Italy;

23rd, Mackenzie King forms Liberal ministry in Canada.

L **Nov**: 3rd, Greek plebiscite favours George II;

3rd, French Socialist groups merge as Socialist and Republican Union, under Léon Blum; this soon forms close relations with Radical Socialists and Communists to found a Popular Front;

4th, German-Polish economic agreement;

5th, Milan Hodza, Agrarian party, forms ministry in Czechoslovakia;

7th, U.S.S.R.-Turkish treaties extended for ten years;

14th, in British general election Government parties win 428 seats, Opposition, 184 (Conservatives, 385, National Liberal, 32, Liberal, 17, Labour, 154, I.L.P., 4, and Communist, 1); Ramsay MacDonald is defeated by Emmanuel Shinwell at Seaham Harbour;

15th, Commonwealth of Philippines is inaugurated;

—, Canadian-U.S. reciprocal trade agreement;

20th, British miners ballot to press for wage increase;

29th, Michael Savage forms first Labour ministry in New Zealand.

T **Music** (*cont.*)

Sergei Rachmaninov, *Rhapsody on a Theme of Paganini.*
Dmitry Shostakovich, Symphony no. 1 (op. 10).
I. Stravinsky's ballet, *Game of Cards.*
William Walton, Symphony.
D. F. Tovey, *Essays in Musical Analysis* (–39).
The term 'swing' is coined.
Jazz of Negro or Jewish origin is banned from German radio (*Oct.*).

U **Literature**

W. H. Auden and C. Isherwood, *The Dog Beneath the Skin.*
Ivy Compton-Burnett, *A House and its Head.*
Cyril Connolly, *The Rock Pool.*
C. Day-Lewis, *A Time to Dance.*
Walter de la Mare, *Poems, 1919–34.*
Christopher Isherwood, *Mr. Norris Changes Trains.*
A. Malraux, *Le Temps du mépris.*
William Saroyan, *The Daring Young Man on the Flying Trapeze.*

V **The Press**

W **Drama and Entertainment**

T. S. Eliot, *Murder in the Cathedral.*
Clifford Odets, *Waiting for Lefty.*
Robert Sherwood, *The Petrified Forest.*
Emlyn Williams, *Night Must Fall.*
Ivor Novello's *Glamorous Night.*
To appease demand for American-style films, U.S.S.R. plans to found a Crimean Hollywood.

Films:
Greta Garbo in *Anna Karenina.*
D. Selznick's *David Copperfield.*
Jean Renoir's *Toni.*
Cyrano de Bergerac.
Becky Sharp.
The Lives of a Bengal Lancer.

Silver Jubilee Celebrations in Britain (*May* 6th).
Germany has regular television services.
First broadcast quiz programme, in Canada (*May* 15th).

X **Sport**

Y **Statistics**

Railway mileage in operation: U.S., 254,347; Great Britain, 62,502; U.S.S.R., 52,687; Germany, 27,218; France, 26,580.
Illiteracy: percentages of population: Egypt, 85; India, 80; Brazil, 67; Mexico, 58; Turkey, 55; Greece, 32; Spain, 31; Portugal, 30; Poland, 21; Italy, 19; U.S.S.R., 13.

M Dec: 1st, Chiang Kai-shek elected president of Chinese (Kuo Min Tang) executive;
9th, Hoare-Laval proposals on Abyssinia, which favour Italy, are wrecked by public indignation in Britain and France;
12th, Nationalists demand restitution of Egyptian Constitution of 1923;
13th, E. Beneš succeeds T. Masaryk as President of Czechoslovakia;
18th, Samuel Hoare resigns and, 23rd, Anthony Eden is appointed Foreign Secretary;
24th, U.S. Neutrality act.

N

z **Births and Deaths**

Feb. 8th Max Liebermann d. (86).
Mar. 13th George Earle Buckle d. (80).
Apr. 8th Edwin Cannan d. (74).
May 18th Paul Dukas d. (69).
May 19th T. E. Lawrence d. (46).
June 21st 'Françoise Sagan' (pseud. of Françoise Quoirez) b. (–).
July 17th G. W. Russell ('A.E.') d. (68).
Sept. 10th Huey Pierce Long d. (42).
Oct. 20th Arthur Henderson d. (72).
Oct 22nd Edward, Lord Carson, d. (61).
Nov. 20th John, Earl Jellicoe, d. (75).
Dec. 24th Alban Berg d. (50).
Dec. 25th Paul Bourget d. (83).

1936 (Jan.–Jun.) Germans troops enter Rhineland—Popular Front in France—Spanish Civil War begins—Abdication of Edward VIII

A **Jan**: 15th, Japan leaves London naval conference;
20th, accession of Edward VIII on death of George V;
22nd, Albert Sarraut forms ministry on fall of Pierre Laval through public indignation at Italian policy.

B **Feb**: 16th, in Spanish elections Popular Front wins 265 seats against 142 for the Right and 66 for the Centre parties; Manuel Azaña becomes premier and re-establishes constitution of 1931;
17th, Anglo-Irish trade pact ends tariff war;
26th, military *coup d'état* in Japan places Koki Hirota as premier.

C **Mar**: 3rd, British defence budget leaps from £122 million to £158 million, to increase Fleet Air Arm, add 250 aircraft for home defence and 4 new infantry battalions;
7th, Germany violates Treaty of Versailles by occupying demilitarised zone of Rhineland;
23rd, Italy, Austria and Hungary sign Rome pact;
25th, Britain, U.S. and France sign London naval convention;
29th, 99 per cent of electorate vote for official Nazi candidates in German elections;
31st, Lord Eustace Percy resigns from cabinet, a symptom of general dissatisfaction with Stanley Baldwin, especially for his tergiversation over the Hoare-Laval pact;
Britain's first civil defence anti-gas school opened.

D **Apr**: 1st, Austria reintroduces conscription;
7th, Cape Parliament passes Native Representation bill, permitting natives to elect three Europeans to represent them in Union Parliament, and establishing a native representative council with only advisory powers;
8th, U.S.S.R.-Mongolia treaty of mutual assistance;
10th, Cortes dismisses President Zamora of Spain;
13th, General John Metaxas becomes Greek premier;
28th, accession of King Farouk in Egypt;
Arab High Committee formed to unite Arabs against Jewish claims.

E **May**: 3rd, Popular Front wins 387 seats in French elections, other parties, 231;
5th, Italians occupy Addis Ababa, ending Abyssinian war and, 9th, Abyssinia is formally annexed by Italy;
10th, Nahas Pasha forms all-Wafdist ministry in Egypt;
—, Manuel Azaña elected President of Spain;
21st, Kurt Schuschnigg becomes leader of Austrian Fatherland Front;
22nd, J. H. Thomas, dominions secretary, resigns over budget leakage;
24th, Rexists (Fascist) win 21 seats in Belgian elections;
28th, Irish Senate is abolished.

F **Jun**: 4th, Léon Blum, Socialist, forms Popular Front ministry in France;
9th, Count Nobile Ciano appointed Italian foreign minister;
12th, 40-hour week in France;
17th, Canadian supreme court nullifies most of 'New Deal' legislation of R. B. Bennett's government in 1935;
23rd, Clement Attlee moves vote of censure on Stanley Baldwin's government for irresponsible foreign policy (defeated by 214 votes);
24th, Paul van Zeeland introduces social improvements programme in Belgium;
30th, suppression of French Fascist Party.

O **Politics, Economics, Law and Education**

A. Carr-Saunders, *World Population.*
Lancelot Hogben, *Political Arithmetic; Mathematics for the Million.*
J. M. Keynes, *General Theory of Employment, Interest and Money.*
M'Gonighe and Kirby, *Poverty and Public Health.*
J. Strachey, *The Theory and Practice of Socialism.*
Reorganisation of Bank of France.
The Ford Foundation is established.
London University moves from Kensington to Bloomsbury.

P **Science, Technology, Discovery, etc.**

Solar eclipse (*June* 19th) observed by expeditions in Kamishari, North Japan, and Omsk, Siberia.
Mrs. A. Mollison flies from England to Cape Town in 3 days 6 hrs. 25 mins. (*May* 4th–7th).
The *Wupperthal*, first diesel-electric vessel, launched.

Q **Scholarship**

A. J. Carlyle completes *History of Medieval Political Theory in the West.*
H. A. L. Fisher, *History of Europe.*
F. Meinecke, *The Origin of Historismus.*

R **Philosophy and Religion**

A. J. Ayer, *Language, Truth and Logic.*
S. Freud, *Autobiography.*
W. Sombart, *Sociology.*

S **Art, Sculpture, Fine Arts and Architecture**

Painting:
Laura Knight, *Ballet.*
P. Mondrian, *Composition in Red and Blue.*
R. Whistler, frescoes at Plas Newydd, Anglesey (–1938).
The cleaning of Velasquez's *Philip of Spain* by the National Gallery provokes controversy.

Sculpture:
Marino Marini, *The Horseman* (painted wood).

Architecture:
W. Gropius and E. M. Fry, Film Studios, Denham, Bucks.
F. L. Wright, Kaufman House, 'Falling Water', Bear Run, Pennsylvania, and office block (with umbrella columns), Racine, Wisconsin.
Crystal Palace, Sydenham, destroyed by fire.

T **Music**

C. Lambert, *Summer's Last Will and Testament.*
S. Prokofiev, *Peter and the Wolf.*

U **Literature**

W. H. Auden, *Look Stranger.*
Maurice Baring, *Have You Anything to Declare?*
Georges Bernanos, *Journal of a Country Priest.*
Aldous Huxley, *Eyeless in Gaza.*
Margaret Mitchell, *Gone With The Wind.*
H. de Montherlant, *Les Jeunes Filles* (–39).
Charles Morgan, *Sparkenbrook.*

G **Jul**: 11th, Austro-German convention acknowledges Austria's independence;
15th, League raises sanctions against Italy;
17th, munitions industry in France is nationalised;
18th, army revolt under Emilio Mola and Francisco Franco begins Spanish Civil War;
20th, by Montreux convention Turkey recovers sovereignty over Dardanelles and Bosphorus;
21st, revised means-test regulations in Britain;
24th, Junta de Defensa Nacional set up at Burgos;
Failure of Jarrow special development area scheme.

H **Aug**: 2nd, France suggests to Britain a policy of non-intervention in Spain;
4th, Franco's army captures Badajoz and advances eastwards;
11th, Chiang Kai-shek enters Canton;
24th, Germany adopts two-year compulsory military service;
26th, treaty ends British military occupation of Egypt, except Canal Zone, and forms Anglo-Egyptian alliance for 20 years.

J **Sep**: 9th, conference in London on non-intervention in Spanish Civil War;
—, France signs treaties of friendship with Syria, where mandate is to end in 1939, and, 19th, with the Lebanon;
10th, Joseph Goebbels accuses Czechoslovakia of harbouring U.S.S.R. aircraft;
27th, France, Switzerland and Holland abandon gold standard;
Japan's secret demands to China about employment of Japanese in Chinese government and presenting united front against Communists are rejected by Nanking.

K **Oct**: 1st, U.S.S.R. accedes to London naval convention of *Mar.* 25th;
—, Spanish insurgents appoint General Francisco Franco chief of state;
2nd, France devalues the Franc;
5th, Italy devalues the Lira;
6th, British Labour Party Conference rejects application of Communist Party for affiliation;
10th, Kurt Schuschnigg dissolves Heimwehr, absorbing remaining members in Fatherland Front;
12th, Oswald Mosley leads anti-Jewish march along Mile End Road, London;
14th, alarmed at German occupation of Rhineland, Belgium denounces military alliance with France and resumes liberty of action;
19th, Germany's four-year plan begins, with Hermann Goering as economic minister;
20th, Stanley Baldwin warns Edward VIII that gossip about himself and Mrs. Wallis Simpson is undermining respect for the throne;
22nd, martial law in Belgium, to combat the Rexists.

L **Nov**: 1st, following Count Ciano's visit to Berlin, Benito Mussolini proclaims Rome-Berlin axis;
3rd, in U.S. presidential election F. D. Roosevelt, Democrat, is re-elected, with 524 electoral votes over A. M. Landon, Republican, with 7, and carries every state except Maine and Vermont;
6th, siege of Madrid begins, Spanish government moves to Valencia;
9th, Vienna conference between Italy, Austria and Hungary consolidates Italian position in Danube basin;
14th, Germany denounces clauses of Versailles Treaty about internationalisation of her waterways;
16th, Stanley Baldwin warns Edward VIII that if he marries Mrs. Simpson he would offend public opinion and damage prestige of the throne;

U **Literature** (*cont.*)
Dylan Thomas, *Twenty-five Poems.*
Criticism of works of art, literature and music is forbidden in Germany.
Allen Lane founds Penguin Books, starting the paperback revolution.

V **The Press**
John and Rosamund Lehmann found *New Writing.*

W **Drama and Entertainment**
B.B.C. starts television service from Alexandra Palace (*Nov.* 2nd).
Ian Hay (pseud.), *The Housemaster.*
Terence Rattigan, *French Without Tears.*
Armand Salacrou, *Un Homme comme les autres.*
Robert Sherwood, *Idiot's Delight.*

Films:
Charlie Chaplin in *Modern Times.*
Mr. Deeds Comes to Town.
Things to Come.
As you Like It.
The Great Ziegfeld.
Shirley Temple signs five-year contract for £1,000 per week.

X **Sport**
Olympic Games in Berlin.
Max Schmeling beats Joe Louis for world heavyweight championship.

Y **Statistics**
Populations (in mill.): China, 422; India, 360; U.S.S.R., 173; U.S., 127; Japan, 89; Germany, 70; Great Britain, 47; France, 44.
Religious Denominations in U.S. (in mill.): Roman Catholics, 19·9; Baptists, 8·2; Methodists, 7; Lutherans, 4·2; Presbyterians, 2·5; Protestant Episcopal, 1·7; Mormons, 0·7.

Z **Births and Deaths**
Jan. 18th Rudyard Kipling d. (70).
Jan. 23rd Clara Butt d. (62).
Mar. 4th James ('Jim') Clark b. (–).
Mar. 11th David, Earl Beatty, d. (65).
Mar. 21st Alexander Glazounov d. (71).
Apr. 30th Alfred Edward Housman d. (77).
May 8th Oswald Spengler d. (55).
June 14th Gilbert Keith Chesterton d. (62).
June 18th Maxim Gorky d. (68).
Aug. 1st Louis Blériot d. (64).
Dec. 10th Luigi Pirandello d. (69).
— Erich Weiss ('Houdini') d. (52).

1936 (Nov.–Dec.)

L Nov: 18th, Germany and Italy recognise Franco's government in Spain;
23rd, Expropriation law in Mexico empowers government to seize private property;
24th, Germany and Japan sign Anti-Comintern Pact.

M Dec: 1st (–16th), Pan-American peace conference in Buenos Aires;
5th, new constitution in U.S.S.R., with a Supreme Council and a two-chamber Parliament;
10th, Edward VIII abdicates, becoming Duke of Windsor;
11th, accession of George VI;
12th, Chiang Kai-shek is forced to declare war on Japan;
—, abolition of office of governor-general of Ireland;
16th, protocol signed in London for non-intervention in Spain.

N Reserve Bank of New Zealand is nationalised.

1937 (Jan.–June) Japanese take Peking, Shanghai and Nanking—Rebel victories in Spain—Italy leaves the League

A Jan: 2nd, Anglo-Italian agreement on Mediterranean and for maintaining independence of Spain;
7th, Poland signs agreement with Danzig;
14th, Communists, I.L.P. and Socialist League form United Front in Britain, aiming to transform Labour movement;
15th, amnesty for Austrian Nazis;
23rd, trial of Karl Radek and other political leaders in Moscow purge;
24th, Bulgaria and Yugoslavia sign treaty of perpetual peace.

B Feb: 8th, Spanish rebels take Malaga with Italian aid;
14th, Kurt Schuschnigg claims right to decide on question of the Hapsburg restoration in Austria;
15th (-18th), conference of Balkan powers at Athens;
24th, Paraguay withdraws from the League;
27th, French defence plan creates ministry of defence, extends Maginot Line and nationalises Schneider-Creusot arms factory;
All-India Congress most successful party in Indian elections.

C Mar: 1st, Adam Koc forms Camp of National Unity in Poland; a Workers' and Peasants' Camp is formed in opposition to him;
2nd, nationalisation of oil in Mexico;
16th, Benito Mussolini visits Libya;
18th, defeat of Italian legionaries at Brihuega checks rebel threat to Madrid;
25th, Italy and Yugoslavia sign Belgrade Pact of assistance for five years.

D Apr: 1st, India's Constitution in force; All-India Party abstains from forming government, demanding complete independence;
2nd, South Africa prohibits political activity by foreigners in South-West Africa;
22nd, Kurt Schuschnigg meets Benito Mussolini in Venice;
24th, Britain and France release Belgium from obligations under Locarno treaty of 1925;
27th, Spanish rebels destroy Guernica.

E May: 1st, F. D. Roosevelt signs U.S. Neutrality act;
8th, Montreux convention abolishes Egyptian capitulations;
10th (-31st), London bus strike;
14th (-June 15th), Imperial Conference, London;
15th, Moslem rising in Albania;
26th, Egypt joins the League;
28th, on Stanley Baldwin's retirement Neville Chamberlain forms National ministry, with John Simon Chancellor of Exchequer;
31st, German fleet bombards Almeria as reprisal for Loyalists' air attack on *Deutschland*.

F June: 1st, Prince Konoye becomes Japanese premier of a national-union ministry, with Koki Hirota foreign minister;
12th, purge of U.S.S.R. generals;
14th, Dáil passes Constitution for Ireland;
18th, Spanish rebels take Bilbao;
21st, on French Senate refusing Léon Blum's demands for emergency fiscal powers he resigns and Camille Chautemps forms Radical-Socialist ministry;
23rd, Germany and Italy withdraw from non-intervention committee;
26th, Spanish rebels take Santander.
Duke of Windsor marries Mrs. Wallis Simpson in France.

1937 (Jan.–Jun.) Japanese take Peking, Shanghai and Nanking—Rebel victories in Spain—Italy leaves the League

A **Jan**: 2nd, Anglo-Italian agreement on Mediterranean and for maintaining independence of Spain;
7th, Poland signs agreement with Danzig;
14th, Communists, I.L.P. and Socialist League form United Front in Britain, aiming to transform Labour movement;
15th, amnesty for Austrian Nazis;
23rd, trial of Karl Radek and other political leaders in Moscow purge;
24th, Bulgaria and Yugoslavia sign treaty of perpetual peace.

B **Feb**: 8th, Spanish rebels take Malaga with Italian aid;
14th, Kurt Schuschnigg claims right to decide on question of the Hapsburg restoration in Austria;
15th (–18th), conference of Balkan powers in Athens;
20th, Paraguay withdraws from the League;
27th, French defence plan creates ministry of defence, extends Maginot Line and nationalises Schneider-Creusot arms factory;
All-India Congress most successful party in Indian elections.

C **Mar**: 1st, Adam Koc forms Camp of National Unity in Poland; a Workers' and Peasants' Camp is formed in opposition to him;
2nd, nationalisation of oil in Mexico;
16th, Benito Mussolini visits Libya;
18th, defeat of Italian legionaries at Brihuega checks rebel threat to Madrid;
25th, Italy and Yugoslavia sign Belgrade Pact of assistance for five years.

D **Apr**: 1st, Indian Constitution in force; All-India Party abstains from forming government, demanding complete independence;
2nd, South Africa prohibits political activity by foreigners in South-West Africa;
22nd, Kurt Schuschnigg meets Benito Mussolini in Venice;
24th, Britain and France release Belgium from obligations under Locarno treaty of 1925;
27th, Spanish rebels destroy Guernica.

E **May**: 1st, F. D. Roosevelt signs U.S. Neutrality act;
8th, Montreux convention abolishes Egyptian capitulations;
10th (–23rd), London bus strike;
14th (–*June* 15th), Imperial Conference, London;
15th, Moslem rising in Albania;
26th, Egypt joins the League;
28th, on Stanley Baldwin's retirement Neville Chamberlain forms National ministry, with John Simon Chancellor of Exchequer;
31st, German fleet bombards Almeria as reprisal for Loyalists' air attack on *Deutschland*.

F **Jun**: 1st, Prince Konoye becomes Japanese premier of a national union ministry, with Koki Hirota foreign minister;
12th, purge of U.S.S.R. generals;
14th, Dáil passes Constitution for Ireland;
18th, Spanish rebels take Bilbao;
21st, on French Senate refusing Léon Blum's demands for emergency fiscal powers he resigns and Camille Chautemps forms Radical-Socialist ministry;
23rd, Germany and Italy withdraw from non-intervention committee;
26th, Spanish rebels take Santander;
Duke of Windsor marries Mrs. Wallis Simpson in France.

O **Politics, Economics, Law and Education**

Walter Lippmann, *The Good Society.*

S. Rowntree, *The Human Needs of Labour.*

Stephen Spender and others, *The Mind in Chains; Socialism and the Cultural Revolution.*

First comprehensive wages agreement in Britain made by Lewis Ltd.

Bodkin Report on 'share pushing' in Britain.

Romansch recognised as fourth national language in Switzerland (*Dec.*).

First sit-down strikes in U.S. and Canada, in General Motors Strike.

P **Science, Technology, Discovery, etc.**

Skull of *Pithecanthropus* found in Java.

Dirac, Milne and Dingle engage in controversy about the age of the world.

Zinc protamine insulin is successfully used in cases of diabetes.

Crystalline Vitamin A and Vitamin K concentrate are obtained.

Aneurin synthesises Vitamin B.

Wallace H. Carothers makes nylon stockings.

F. Whittle's first jet engine.

U.S.S.R. establishes observation station on an ice floe near the North Pole.

Sphinx Rock meteorological station in Bernese Oberland is opened (*Oct.* 31st).

The L.M.S. Railway's 'Coronation Scot'.

Q **Scholarship**

National Maritime Museum, Greenwich, opened.

R **Philosophy and Religion**

A. Huxley, *Ends and Means.*

M. Buber, *I and Thou.*

Oxford Conference on 'Church, Community and State'.

Papal Encyclical on Atheistic Communism (*Mar.* 18th).

S **Art, Sculpture, Fine Arts and Architecture**

Painting:

Joan Miró, murals, R. Dufy's decor and P. Picasso's mural *Guernica* for Paris World Fair.

William Coldstream and Lawrence Gowing found Euston Road group of artists, advocating a return to a realistic conception of painting.

Duveen Gallery, Tate Gallery, opened.

Paul Mellon endows National Gallery of Art, Washington.

Nazi exhibition of 'Degenerate Art' in Munich.

Sculpture:

J. Epstein, *Consummatum Est.*

T **Music**

Frederick Ashton's ballet *Les Patineurs* to G. Meyerbeer's music.

Arthur Bliss, ballet *Checkmate.*

Dmitry Shostakovich, 5th Symphony.

Jaromir Weinberger, *Wallenstein* (opera).

U **Literature**

W. H. Auden and C. Isherwood, *The Ascent of F.6.*

Christopher Caudwell, *Illusion and Reality.*

Ernest Hemingway, *To Have and Have Not.*

G **Jul**: 7th, Japanese troops on manœuvres near Peking clash with Chinese; fighting spreads rapidly;

7th, Royal Commission on Palestine recommends end of mandate and establishment of Arab and Jewish states;

8th, Afghanistan, Iran, Iraq and Turkey sign non-aggression pact;

17th, naval agreements between Britain and Germany and Britain and U.S.S.R.;

22nd, Irish elections result in stalemate but Éamon de Valéra is again premier;

23rd, Matrimonial Causes bill, introduced by A. P. Herbert, facilitates divorce proceedings in England and Wales;

28th, Japanese seize Peking and, 29th, Tientsin.

H **Aug**: 6th, U.S.-U.S.S.R. trade pact;

11th, Bakr Sidqi, dictator of Iraq, assassinated;

15th, Mackenzie King appoints commission to study amendments to British North America Act.

J **Sep**: F. D. Roosevelt signs Wagner-Steagall act to provide finance for housing;

3rd, British Labour Party's declaration that war is not inevitable, reiterates Britain's role in League;

10th (–14th), at Nyon Conference, convoked by Britain, nine nations adopt system of patrol in Mediterranean to deal with piracy arising from Spanish Civil War;

25th (–28th), Benito Mussolini visits Berlin;

26th, Arabs murder British district commissioner for Galilee.

K **Oct**: 1st, Higher Arab Committee in Palestine declared illegal;

13th, Germany guarantees inviolability of Belgium;

16th, Fascist groups in Hungary form National Socialist Party;

17th, riots in Sudeten area of Czechoslovakia;

21st, Spanish rebels take Gijón, completing conquest of the North-West;

23rd, Labour defeated in Australian elections by United Australian and Country parties;

24th, Paul van Zeeland, premier of Belgium, resigns on charges of corruption over National Bank, and is succeeded by Paul Janson, Liberal;

28th, Spanish government moves to Barcelona.

L **Nov**: 3rd (–24th), Brussels conference of powers discusses Sino-Japanese War;

5th, Air Raid Precautions bill introduced in Commons;

6th, Italy joins German-Japanese Anti-Comintern Pact;

9th, Japanese take Shanghai;

15th, extraordinary session of Congress opens to promote legislative programme, but little is accomplished;

17th (–21st), Lord Halifax's visit to Adolf Hitler, to attempt peaceful settlement of Sudeten problem, marks beginning of policy of appeasement;

18th, discovery of Fascist plot in Paris;

20th, Italo-Austro-Hungarian pact is extended;

24th, Walter Funk replaces Dr. Schacht as German minister of economics;

28th, General Franco begins naval blockade of Spanish coast;

29th, Sudeten Germans leave Czech Parliament following ban on political meetings.

U **Literature** (*cont.*)

A. Malraux, *L'Espoir*.
J. P. Marquand, *The Late George Apley*.
George Orwell (pseud.), *The Road to Wigan Pier*.
J. P. Sartre, *Nausée*.
John Steinbeck, *Of Mice and Men*.

V **The Press**

Morning Post merged in *The Daily Telegraph*.

W **Drama and Entertainment**

B. Brecht, *A Penny for the Poor*.
Jean Giraudoux, *Elektra*.
L. Housman, *Victoria Regina*.
J. B. Priestley, *Time and the Conways*.
Paris World Fair.

Films:
Jean Renoir's *The Great Illusion*.
The Lost Horizon.
A Star is Born.
Camille.
The Edge of the World.

'Singing Mice' perform on U.S. radio.
George Gershwin's review *Pins and Needles*.
Billy Butlin opens Britain's first commercial holiday camp at Skegness.

X **Sport**

Y **Statistics**

Oil production (in mill. barrels): U.S., 1,277; U.S.S.R., 196; Venezuela, 182; Iran, 73; Roumania, 53; Dutch East Indies, 50; Mexico, 46.

Consumption of petroleum products (in mill. barrels) (motor fuel in brackets): U.S., 1,167 (517); U.S.S.R., 158 (24); Great Britain, 85 (43); France, 50 (25); Canada, 43 (21); Germany, 43 (20); Japan, 34 (10).

Refrigerators: U.S. has 2 mill. domestic refrigerators; Great Britain, 3,000.

1937 (Dec.)

M **Dec**: 2nd, far-reaching changes in high command of British Army imposed by Leslie Hore-Belisha;

5th (–19th), Spanish Loyalists' offensive near Teruel;

11th, Italy withdraws from the League;

12th (–13th), Japanese troops take Nanking;

14th, political parties banned in Brazil;

16th, Franco-Syrian convention;

24th, Japanese capture Hangchow;

28th, Octavian Goga, anti-Semite, forms ministry in Roumania, on fall of Nicholas Titulescu;

29th, new Irish Constitution; Irish Free State becomes Eire;

30th, Liberal Constitution Party forms ministry in Egypt;

C. R. Attlee visits Spain to encourage Republican leaders.

N

z **Births and Deaths**

Jan. 18th Frederick Pollock d. (91).
Jan. 30th Vanessa Redgrave b. (–).
Feb. 6th Elihu Root d. (91).
Mar. 16th Austen Chamberlain d. (73).
Mar. 20th John Drinkwater d. (54).
June 19th J. M. Barrie d. (77).
July 20th Guglielmo Marconi d. (63).
Aug. 11th Edith Wharton d. (75).
Sept. 14th T. G. Masaryk d. (87).
Oct. 19th Ernest, Lord Rutherford, d. (66).
Nov. 9th James Ramsay MacDonald d. (71).
Dec. 20th Erich Ludendorff d. (72).
Dec. 21st Frank Billings Kellogg d. (80).
Dec. 28th Maurice Ravel d. (62).

1938 (Jan.–Jul.) Germany annexes Austria—The 'Munich' crisis

A Jan: 4th, Britain postpones scheme for partition of Palestine and appoints commission under John Woodhead, which is boycotted by Arabs, to study boundaries (reports *Nov.* 9th);
10th, Japanese enter Tsingtao;
14th, Socialists leave French cabinet, which Camille Chautemps reorganises as a Radical Socialist ministry.

B Feb: 4th, Adolf Hitler assumes office of war minister and appoints Joachim von Ribbentrop foreign minister;
12th, Hitler forces Kurt Schuschnigg to promise release of Nazis in Austria;
15th, General Franco recaptures Teruel and drives towards the coast;
18th, French Chamber cancels Labour code;
20th, Anthony Eden resigns in protest at Neville Chamberlain's determination to seek agreement with Italy before settlement of Spanish question and is succeeded as Foreign Secretary, 25th, by Lord Halifax;
21st, Winston Churchill leads outcry against Chamberlain and, 22nd, 25 ministerialists vote against government in censure motion.

C Mar: 2nd (–15th), trial of Nikolai Bukharin and other political leaders in U.S.S.R.;
11th, German troops enter Austria, which, 13th, is declared part of the Reich;
13th, Léon Blum forms Popular Front ministry in France (–*Apr.* 10th);
19th, Lithuania capitulates to Poland's demands to reopen the frontier;
—, Mexico expropriates British and U.S. oil properties;
28th, Japanese install puppet government of Chinese Republic at Nanking.

D Apr: 10th, Édouard Daladier, Radical Socialist, forms ministry in France, supported by Léon Blum;
15th, General Franco takes Vinaroz;
16th, by Anglo-Italian pact Britain recognises Italian sovereignty over Ethiopia and Italy undertakes to withdraw troops from Spain (in force *Nov.* 16th);
23rd, Sudeten Germans demand full autonomy;
25th, British three-year agreement with Eire settles outstanding disputes;
27th, Graeco-Turkish treaty of friendship.

E May: 3rd (–9th), Adolf Hitler visits Benito Mussolini in Rome;
4th, Douglas Hyde, a Protestant, becomes first President of Eire under new Constitution;
12th, Germany recognises Manchukuo;
13th, Paul Spaak, Socialist, forms coalition in Belgium;
17th, Anglo-Turkish agreement;
18th, United Party under J. B. M. Hertzog confirmed in power in South African elections;
19th (–20th), in first Czechoslovak crisis France and Britain stand firm against Adolf Hitler's demands.

F Jun: 17th, in Eire elections Fianna Fáil win 77 seats, the Opposition, 61.

G Jul: 11th (–*Aug.* 11th), U.S.S.R. troops clash with Japanese on border of Manchukuo;
19th (–21st), George VI visits Paris;
25th, Walter Runciman visits Prague and reports in favour of Nazi claims in Czechoslovakia;
31st, Bulgaria signs non-aggression pact with Greece and other powers of Balkan Entente.

O **Politics, Economics, Law and Education**

D. Lloyd George, *The Truth About the Peace Treaties.*

National Institute of Economic and Social Research, London, founded.

Wages and Hours bill in U.S. provides for minimum wages and a maximum working week and prohibits child labour.

British Ministry of Labour Committee under Lord Amulree recommends a week's holiday with pay as a national standard.

Women's Voluntary Service founded in Britain.

P **Science, Technology, Discovery, etc.**

Ewins and Phillips synthesise sulphapyridine ('M. and B. 693').

Karrer synthesises Vitamin E.

Perlon is invented.

J. Ladisla and Georg Biro invent the ball-point pen.

Howard Hughes in monoplane *New York World Fair* flies round world in 3 days 19hrs. 17 mins. (*July* 10th–14th).

S.S. *Queen Elizabeth* launched (*Sept.* 27th).

Trolleybuses begin to replace trams in London (*Mar.* 6th).

Lancelot Hogben, *Science for the Citizen.*

Q **Scholarship**

J. B. Huizinga, *Homo Ludens.*

L. Mumford, *The Culture of Cities.*

R **Philosophy and Religion**

Voigt, *Unto Caesar.*

Edwyn Bevan, *Symbolism and Belief.*

S **Art, Sculpture, Fine Arts and Architecture**

Painting:

Raoul Dufy, *Regatta.*

Pablo Picasso, *Woman in Easy Chair.*

Georges Rouault, *Ecce Homo.*

Sculpture:

Eric Gill, 50-ft. relief for League of Nations Building, Geneva.

Architecture:

F. L. Wright, Taliesin West, Phoenix, Arizona.

T **Music**

Béla Bartók, Violin Concerto.

Aaron Copland, *Billy the Kid* (opera).

Paul Hindemith, *Nobilissima Visiona* (ballet music).

E. Moeran, Symphony in G minor.

Benny Goodman's band dominates Broadway.

U **Literature**

Cyril Connolly, *Enemies of Promise.*

C. Day-Lewis, *Overtures to Death.*

William Faulkner, *The Unvanquished.*

Graham Greene, *Brighton Rock.*

C. Isherwood, *Goodbye to Berlin.*

Paul Valéry, *Degas, Danse, Dessein.*

V **The Press**

Edward Hulton starts *Picture Post.*

H **Aug**: 12th, Germany mobilises;
21st (–23rd), Little Entente recognises right of Hungary to rearm.

J **Sep**: 7th, Sudeten Germans break off relations with Czech government after clashes between rival parties and France calls up reservists;
15th, Neville Chamberlain visits Adolf Hitler at Berchtesgaden (and, 27th, at Godesberg) and Hitler states his determination to annex Sudetenland on principle of self-determination;
18th, Anglo-French proposals for Czechs to accept Germany's terms;
22nd, Milan Hodza's cabinet resigns in Prague;
27th, Royal Navy is mobilised;
—, League pronounces Japan to be the aggressor in China;
29th, at Munich conference Neville Chamberlain, Édouard Daladier, Adolf Hitler and Benito Mussolini agree to transfer Sudetenland to Germany, while the remaining frontiers of Czechoslovakia are guaranteed; Germany becomes the dominant power in Europe and both the Little Entente and the French system of alliances in Eastern Europe are shattered.

K **Oct**: 1st, Czechs accept Polish ultimatum for cession of Teschen;
— (–10th), Germany occupies Sudetenland;
—, Alfred Duff Cooper resigns as First Lord of Admiralty;
—, League of Nations separates Covenant from Versailles Peace Treaty;
2nd, Japan withdraws from the League;
4th, end of Popular Front in France when Socialists and Communists abstain from vote of confidence;
5th, Eduard Beneš resigns in Czechoslovakia;
6th, Slovakia and, 8th, Ruthenia are granted autonomy;
21st, Japanese take Canton and, 25th, Hankow;
25th, Libya is declared to be part of Italy;
29th, Belgium withdraws from non-intervention committee.

L **Nov**: 2nd, Hungary annexes Southern Slovakia;
8th (–14th), anti-Semitic pogroms in Germany;
—, U.S. elections result in Democrats having 69 seats in Senate and 261 in House, while Republicans have 23 in Senate and 168 in House;
10th, anti-Semitic legislation in Italy;
11th, Inönü elected President of Turkey on Kemal Atatürk's death;
26th, U.S.S.R.-Polish declaration of friendship renews non-aggression pact;
30th, speeches in Italian Chamber claim Nice and Corsica for Italy;
—, Corneliu Codreanu and other members of Roumanian Iron Guard shot in government's attempts to destroy Fascism;
—, Emil Hacha elected Czech President.

M **Dec**: 1st, British national register for war service;
6th, Franco-German pact on inviolability of existing frontiers;
14th, Italian Chamber of Deputies is replaced by Chamber of Fasces and Corporations;
17th, Italy denounces 1935 agreement with France;
23rd, General Franco begins main offensive in Catalonia;
26th, Pan-American Conference makes Declaration of Peru against all foreign intervention;
28th, Iraq severs relations with France.

N

W **Drama and Entertainment**

Jean Anouilh, *Le Voyageur sans bagage.*
Philip Barry, *Here Come the Clowns.*
Jean Cocteau, *Les Parents terribles.*
Thornton Wilder, *Our Town.*
Emlyn Williams, *The Corn is Green.*

Films:
Anthony Asquith's *Pygmalion* with Leslie Howard.
Eisenstein's *Alexander Newski.*
Dance from the Volcano.
The Lady Vanishes.
Walt Disney's *Snow White and the Seven Dwarfs.*

New York World Fair.
Empire Exhibition, Glasgow.
The Lambeth Walk (dance).

X **Sport**

Len Hutton scores 364 runs against Australia at the Oval Test Match (*Aug.*).

Y **Statistics**

Coal production (in mill. tons): Great Britain, 230; Germany, including Saar, 153; U.S.S.R., 150; France, 46.
Pig-iron production (in mill. tons): U.S., 29,130; Germany, including Saar, 16,111; U.S.S.R., 14,479; Great Britain, 7,781; France, 6,679; Belgium, 3,143.
Steel production (in mill. tons): U.S., 42,906; Germany, including Saar, 20,573; U.S.S.R., 17,380; Great Britain, 11,908; France, 6,946; Belgium, 31,103.
Private cars (in mills.): U.S., 19; Great Britain, 1·7; Germany, including Austria, 1·3; Italy, 1·1; France, 0·8.
Immigration to Great Britain: 504,527.
Emigration from Great Britain: 1,609,847 British and 491,176 aliens.

Z **Births and Deaths**

Mar. 1st Gabriele D'Annunzio d. (75).
Mar. 28th Edward Mandell House d. (79).
Apr. 12th Fedor Chaliapin d. (65).
Apr. 19th Henry Newbolt d. (75).
July 4th Otto Bauer d. (57).
Aug. 7th Constantin Stanislavsky d. (75).
Sept. 13th Samuel Alexander d. (79).
Nov. 10th Kemal Atatürk d. (57).
Dec. 25th Karel Čapek d. (48).

1939 (Jan.–Jul.) Italy invades Albania—Dismemberment of Czechoslovakia —End of Spanish Civil War—German invasion of Poland begins World War II

A **Jan:** 1st (–6th), Édouard Daladier visits Algiers, Tunisia and Corsica to counter Benito Mussolini's demands for colonies in North Africa;
4th, F. D. Roosevelt asks Congress for $552 million for defence;
10th, Neville Chamberlain and Lord Halifax visit Rome for conversations with Benito Mussolini;
21st, Adolf Hitler dismisses Dr. H. Schacht, president of Reichsbank, replacing him by Walter Funk, minister of economics;
26th, Franco with Italian aid takes Barcelona.

B **Feb:** 10th, Japanese troops occupy Hainan;
27th, Britain and France recognise General Franco's government in Spain (U.S. recognition *Apr.* 1st).

C **Mar:** 10th, Joseph Tiso, premier of Slovakia, is deposed by Prague government and appeals to Hitler;
15th, German troops occupy Bohemia and Moravia, which become a protectorate ruled by Constantin von Neurath;
16th, Slovakia is placed under German 'protection', while Hungary annexes Ruthenia;
17th, Édouard Daladier is granted wide powers by French Assembly to speed rearmament;
20th, U.S. ambassador is recalled from Berlin in protest at the dismemberment of Czechoslovakia;
21st, Germany annexes Memel from Lithuania;
28th, Madrid's surrender to General Franco ends Spanish Civil War;
—, Adolf Hitler denounces Germany's non-aggression pact with Poland of *Jan.* 1934;
31st, Britain and France pledge to support Poland.

D **Apr:** 7th, Italy invades Albania;
7th, Spain joins Germany, Italy and Japan in the Anti-Comintern Pact;
11th, Hungary withdraws from League of Nations;
13th, Britain and France guarantee the independence of Roumania and Greece;
15th, F. D. Roosevelt asks Adolf Hitler and Benito Mussolini for assurances that they will not attack 31 named states;
16th, U.S.S.R. proposes a defensive alliance with Britain;
24th, Robert Menzies becomes premier of Australia, following death of J. A. Lyons (*Apr.* 7th);
27th, conscription in Britain for men aged 20–21;
—, Adolf Hitler denounces 1935 Anglo-German naval agreement.

E **May:** 4th, Vyacheslav Molotov appointed commissar of foreign affairs in place of Maxim Litvinov;
8th, Spain leaves the League;
12th, Anglo-Turkish pact of mutual assistance;
17th, Sweden, Norway and Finland reject Germany's offer of non-aggression pacts, but Denmark, Estonia and Latvia accept;
22nd, Adolf Hitler and Benito Mussolini sign ten-year political and military alliance (the 'Pact of Steel');
23rd, Parliament approves British plan for an independent Palestine by 1949, which is later denounced by Jews and by Arabs in Palestine.

F **Jun:** 8th (–11th), George VI visits U.S. at end of tour of Canada;
14th, Japanese blockade of British concession at Tientsin.

G **Jul:** 9th, Winston Churchill urges military alliance with U.S.S.R.;
26th, U.S. denounces 1911 trade pact with Japan.

O **Politics, Economics, Law and Education**

E. H. Carr, *The Twenty Years' Crisis.*

Serge Chakotin, *The Rape of The Masses.*

Clarence K. Streit, *Union Now*, advocates federal union.

M. Oakeshott, *The Social and Political Doctrines of Contemporary Europe.*

B.O.A.C. is established.

Ministry of Supply is established (*July* 11th) and Ministry of Information (*Sept.* 5th) in Britain.

Illinois Institute of Technology, Chicago, founded.

P **Science, Technology, Discovery, etc.**

Hahn and Strassman obtain isotopes of barium by bombarding uranium with neutrons.

Joliot demonstrates the possibility of splitting the atom of uranium isotope 235.

Paul Müller invents D.D.T.

Polythene is invented.

Lincoln Ellesworth surveys a large part of eastern Antarctica.

John Cobb at Bonneville Salt Flats, Utah, drives at 368·85 m.p.h. (*Aug.* 23rd).

Malcom Campbell's water speed record of 141·7 m.p.h.

Streamlined diesel train achieves 133·6 m.p.h. between Hamburg and Berlin.

Opening of Trans-Iranian Railway, Caspian Sea to Persian Gulf (*Jan.*).

Pan-American Airways begin regular commercial flights between U.S. and Europe (*May* 20th).

Q **Scholarship**

R **Philosophy and Religion**

John Dewey, *Culture and Freedom.*

Arthur Eddington, *The Philosophy of Physical Science.*

Charles Sherrington, *Man on His Nature.*

Frank Buchman re-founds 'Oxford Group' as Moral Rearmament.

S **Art, Sculpture, Fine Arts and Architecture**

Painting:

Laura Knight, *Golden Girl.*

P. Picasso, *Night Fishing at Antibes.*

S. Spencer, first of the series *Christ in the Wilderness* (–1953).

G. Sutherland, *Entrance to a Lane.*

'Granma Moses' (Anna M. Robertson) becomes famous overnight in Unknown American Painters Exhibition.

Sculpture:

J. Epstein, *Adam* (marble).

T **Music**

William Walton, Violin Concerto.

Myra Hess organises National Gallery lunch-time concerts (*Oct.*) which popularis pianoforte and chamber music in Britain.

U **Literature**

Robert Graves, *The Long Week-end.*

James Joyce, *Finnegans Wake* (written from 1922).

Richard Llewellyn, *How Green Was My Valley.*

T. Mann, *Lotte in Weimar.*

John Steinbeck, *The Grapes of Wrath.*

Jan Struther, *Mrs. Miniver.*

1939 (Aug.–Dec.)

H **Aug**: 5th, British military mission leaves for Moscow (arriving there, 11th);
18th, U.S.S.R.-German commercial agreement;
23rd, U.S.S.R.-German non-aggression pact; the 'Anti-Comintern Pact' collapses;
—, Neville Chamberlain warns Adolf Hitler that Britain will stand by Poland and pleads for settlement of Danzig question;
24th, British Parliament approves Emergency Powers bill;
25th, Anglo-Polish treaty of mutual assistance signed in London;
26th (–31st), attempts by Daladier and Chamberlain to negotiate with Hitler fail;
31st, evacuation of women and children from London begins;
—, U.S.S.R. Supreme Soviet ratifies non-aggression pact with Germany.

J **Sep**: 1st, Germany invades Poland and annexes Danzig;
2nd, British National Service bill, calling up men aged 18–41, in force;
3rd, Britain and France declare war on Germany;
—, British ministerial changes, with Winston Churchill First Lord of Admiralty;
—, Germans sink *Athenia* off Ireland;
4th, Franco-Polish agreement;
5th, J. C. Smuts premier of South Africa;
7th, Germans overrun Pomerania and Silesia and, by 10th, control western Poland;
13th, Édouard Daladier reforms ministry becoming foreign secretary himself;
17th, Germans reach Brest-Litovsk;
—, U.S.S.R. invades Poland from east;
19th, H.M.S. *Courageous* sunk;
—, R.A.F. begins 'leaflet' raids on Germany;
—, Polish government withdraws to Roumania, and Ignace Moscicki, the premier, resigns;
21st, Armand Calinescu, premier of Roumania, assassinated by the Iron Guard;
27th, emergency Budget raises standard rate of income tax in Britain to 7s. 6d. in £;
28th, Germans reach Warsaw;
—, U.S.S.R. pact with Estonia;
29th, national registration in Britain;
30th, German-U.S.S.R. treaty of amity settles partition of Poland; by 30th, British Expeditionary Force of 158,000 men sent to France.

K **Oct**: 5th, U.S.S.R. pact with Latvia;
6th, Adolf Hitler's peace-feelers are summarily rejected by Britain and France;
8th, Germany incorporates western Poland into the Reich;
10th, U.S.S.R. cedes Vilna to Lithuania;
—, deportation of Polish Jews to Lublin reserve begins;
14th, H.M.S. *Royal Oak* sunk in Scapa Flow.

L **Nov**: 3rd, F.D. Roosevelt signs bill enabling Britain and France to purchase arms in U.S. on 'cash and carry' basis, amending the Neutrality Act of *May* 1937;
7th, sovereigns of Belgium and Holland approach George VI advocating peace with Germany;
17th, Britain and France co-ordinate their economic efforts;
18th, magnetic mines, laid by U-boats, sink 60,000 tons of shipping on English east coast in a week;
30th, U.S.S.R. invades Finland, with main offensive to north of Lake Ladoga.

M **Dec**: 13th, battle of River Plate, ends 17th, with scuttling of *Graf Spee* off Montevideo;
14th, U.S.S.R. expelled from League of Nations.

N

V **The Press**

W **Drama and Entertainment**

New York Exhibition.
Swiss National Exhibition, Zürich.
T. S. Eliot, *The Family Reunion.*
George S. Kaufman, *The Man Who Came to Dinner.*
William Saroyan, *The Time of Your Life.*

Films:
Gone With the Wind.
Goodbye Mr. Chips.
The Stars Look Down.
Dawn Patrol.
Jean Renoir's *The Rules of the Game.*

Ivor Novello's *The Dancing Years* (revue).
'*Roll out the Barrel*' and '*Hang Out the Washing on the Siegfried Line*' (popular songs).
Jerome Kern '*The Last Time I Saw Paris*' (song).

X **Sport**

Y **Statistics**

Merchant fleets (in mill. tons): Great Britain, 17·8; U.S., 11·4; Japan, 5·6; Norway, 4·8; Germany, 4·4; Italy, 3·4; Netherlands, 2·9; France, 2·9.

Of 29 mill. tons of shipping passing through the Suez Canal 51 per cent was British. Of 27 mill. tons using the Panama Canal 35 per cent was U.S., 26 per cent British.

Machine tools in use: Germany, 1,177,600; U.S., 942,000; Japan, 67,260.

Aluminium: World production, 647,000 tons; Germany the chief producer, with 240,000.

Criminal offences: U.S., 1,484,811 (21,401 crimes against the person); England and Wales, 303,771 (2,899 crimes against the person).

Housing: on *May* 1st the four millionth house to be built in Britain, since *Nov.* 1918, was completed.

British war production (Sept.–Dec.): 2,924 aircraft; 314 tanks; 17 major vessels with total tonnage 22,780.

Shipping losses (Sept.–Dec., in thousand tons): Great Britain, 498; Allied, 90; Neutral, 347.

U.K. total State expenditure: £1,005 mill.

Z **Births and Deaths**

Jan. 28th William Butler Yeats d. (73).
May 22nd Ernst Toller d. (45).
June 26th Ford Madox Ford d. (66).
July 8th Havelock Ellis d. (80).
Sept. 17th Ethel M. Dell d. (58).
Sept. 23rd Siegmund Freud d. (83).
Dec. 23rd Anthony Fokker d. (49).
Dec. 31st F. R. Benson d. (81).

1940 (Jan.–Jun.) Germany invades Norway and Denmark—Churchill becomes Prime Minister—Dunkirk—Fall of France—Battle of Britain—The Blitz

A Jan: 1st, Oliver Stanley replaces Leslie Hore-Belisha as British War Secretary in government reconstruction;
8th, bacon, butter and sugar rationed in Britain;
21st, W. S. Churchill advises neutrals to side with Britain before they suffer German aggression.

B Feb: 1st, U.S.S.R. launches attacks on Karelian Isthmus and near Lake Kuhmo;
8th, British Labour Party delegation to Finland calls for substantial aid for Finns;
11th, U.S.S.R. attack on Mannerheim Line;
16th, H.M.S. *Cossack* rescues British prisoners from the *Altmark* in Norwegian waters;
21st, British women to receive old-age pension at 60.

C Mar: 3rd, U.S.S.R. troops capture Viborg;
12th, Finland signs peace treaty with U.S.S.R., ceding the Karelian Isthmus and shores of Lake Ladoga;
19th, R.A.F. raids Isle of Sylt;
20th, Paul Reynaud forms ministry in France on É. Daladier's resignation.

D Apr: 3rd, ministerial changes in Britain, with Lord Woolton as Food Minister;
4th, Treasury finances a company for trading with Balkans to intensify blockade of Germany;
9th, Germany invades Norway and Denmark;
14th, British naval forces land in Norway, but fail to take Trondheim through lack of air power.

E May: 2nd, British forces evacuate Namsos;
7th, Neville Chamberlain under fire in Commons and, 10th, resigns, when W. S. Churchill forms National government, with Clement Attlee as Lord Privy Seal, A. V. Alexander as First Lord of Admiralty and Ernest Bevin as Labour Minister;
10th, Germany invades Holland, Luxembourg and Belgium;
—, L.D.V. (later 'Home Guard') formed in Britain;
13th, W. S. Churchill's 'blood and toil' speech rallies confidence in his leadership;
14th, Dutch army surrenders, German troops turn the line of the Albert Canal and pierce French defences near Sedan;
21st, Germans capture Amiens and Arras;
22nd, British Government granted wide emergency powers;
28th, Belgium capitulates;
29th (–*June* 3rd), British forces evacuated from Dunkirk;
30th, Stafford Cripps leads trade mission to Moscow.

F Jun: 10th, Italy declares war on France and Britain;
13th, W. S. Churchill visits Paul Reynaud at Tours;
14th, Germans enter Paris;
15th, U.S. declines France's appeal for aid;
16th, France is offered union with Britain;
—, Marshal Pétain replaces Paul Reynaud as head of French administration;
17th (–23rd), Russians occupy Baltic states;
22nd, France concludes armistice with Germany;
24th, terms of French Vichy Government's armistice with Italy include the withdrawal of French colonies from the war;
27th, U.S.S.R. invades Roumania on refusal of King Carol to cede Bessarabia and Bukovina; Roumania appeals for German aid in vain.

O **Politics, Economics, Law and Education**

British Government appoints Scientific Advisory Committee under Lord Hankey to consider the advances of science in relation to national welfare.

British Colonial Development and Welfare Act for providing funds for approved development plans.

Barlow Report on the location of industry (published *Jan.*).

The George Cross is instituted (*Sept.* 23rd).

P **Science, Technology, Discovery, etc.**

Albert Einstein states in his paper to the American Scientific Congress at Washington that there is as yet no theory which can provide a logical basis for physics.

Rockefeller grant for University of California to build a giant cyclotron, under E. O. Lawrence's direction, for producing mesotrons from atomic nuclei.

Howard Florey develops penicillin as an antibiotic.

Edwin McMillan and Abelson discover neptunium (element 93).

Q **Scholarship**

R **Philosophy and Religion**

A. J. Ayer, *The Foundations of Empirical Knowledge.*

C. Jung, *The Interpretation of Personality.*

George Santayana, *The Realm of Spirit.*

S **Art, Sculpture, Fine Arts and Architecture**

Painting:

M. Beckmann, *Circus Caravan.*

W. Kandinsky, *Sky Blue.*

H. Matisse, *Rumanian blouse.*

J. Piper, *St. Mary le Port, Bristol.*

R. Whistler, *Miss Laura Ridly.*

Augustus John Exhibition, Tate Gallery.

Edward Ardizzone, Muirhead Bone, Henry Lamb, John and Paul Nash and Eric Ravillous appointed official British war artists.

T **Music**

Lennox Berkeley, Introduction and Allegro for two pianos and orchestra.

Elizabeth Lutyens, Three Pieces.

Darius Milhaud, *Médéa* (opera).

Igor Stravinsky, Symphony in C.

M. Tippett, *A Child of Our Time* (oratorio).

Agnes de Mille's ballet, *Rodeo.*

U **Literature**

Graham Greene, *The Power and the Glory.*

Ernest Hemingway, *For Whom the Bell Tolls.*

Eugene O'Neill, *Long Day's Journey into Night* (written, not produced until 1956).

Michael Sadleir, *Fanny by Gaslight.*

Upton Sinclair, *Between Two Worlds.*

Dylan Thomas, *Portrait of the Artist as a Young Dog.*

V **The Press**

W **Drama and Entertainment**

Robert Ardrey, *Thunder Rock.*

B.B.C. Radio Newsreel begun.

1940 (Jul.–Dec.)

G **Jul**: 3rd, Royal Navy sinks French fleets in Oran and North Africa;
5th, Vichy Government breaks off relations with Britain;
9th, R.A.F. begins night bombing of Germany;
—, Roumania places herself under German protection;
15th (–21st), 90 German bombers shot down over Britain;
18th, at Japan's request Britain prohibits the passage of war materials for China passing through Burma;
21st, Britain recognises Czechoslovak National Committee in London as a provisional government;
23rd, purchase tax imposed in Britain.

H **Aug**: 4th, Italians advance from Abyssinia into British Somaliland;
5th, Britain signs agreements with Polish Government in London and, 7th, with Free French under Charles de Gaulle;
8th, Indian Congress Party rejects the Viceroy's invitation to serve on War Advisory Council;
11th (–18th), Battle of Britain at its peak;
15th, 180 German planes shot down;
19th, British withdraw from British Somaliland;
23rd, all-night raid on London begins the 'Blitz'.

J **Sep**: 3rd, U.S. sells destroyers to Britain and is leased bases in Newfoundland and the Caribbean;
6th, Ion Antonescu assumes dictatorial powers in Roumania; King Carol flees;
15th, heavy raid on London with 103 German planes destroyed;
16th, Italians reach Sidi Barrani;
16th, Selective Training and Service Act in U.S.;
27th, British and Free French forces fail to occupy Dakar in Senegal;
—, Germany, Italy and Japan sign ten-year economic and military pacts;
During month Britain loses 160,000 tons of shipping.

K **Oct**: 2nd, *Empress of Britain* with child evacuees for Canada sunk;
3rd, cabinet changes following Neville Chamberlain's retirement;
4th, Adolf Hitler meets Benito Mussolini in Brenner Pass;
7th, Germans seize Roumanian oilfields;
13th (–21st), heavy raids on London;
18th, Britain reopens Burma Road;
22nd, Germany's U-boat warfare is intensified;
28th, Italy demands cession of strategic points in Greece, and Britain, answering Greece's appeal for aid, postpones offensive in Middle East.

L **Nov**: 3rd, British forces occupy Suda Bay, Crete;
4th, H.M.S. *Jervis Bay* sunk in Atlantic;
5th, F. D. Roosevelt, Democrat, is re-elected President for a third term, against Wendell L. Wilkie, Republican;
11th, British attack on Taranto cripples Italian fleet;
12th (–14th), V. Molotov in Berlin refuses to co-operate with Germany in Balkans;
20th, Anglo-U.S. agreement for partial standardisation of weapons and pooling of technical knowledge;
—, Hungary and, 23rd, Roumania, endorse German-Italian-Japanese treaty of *Sept.* 27th;
In the month's air raids, 4,558 persons killed in Britain.

(*Continued opposite*)

W Drama and Entertainment (*cont.*)

Films:

Charlie Chaplin in *The Great Dictator*.
Alfred Hitchcock's *Rebecca*.
Walt Disney's *Fantasia*.
Gaslight.
Derrière la Façade.
The Postmaster.
A Day in the New World.

German army sings 'Lili Marlene'.

X Sport

Y Statistics

Merchant shipping losses (in thousand tons): British, 2,725; Allied, 822; Neutral, 1,002.
War production in Great Britain: aircraft, 15,049; tanks, 1,397; major warships, 106 (totalling 221,935 tons).
Production in U.S.S.R. (in mill. tons): pig iron, 14·9; steel, 18·3; coal, 165·9; oil, 31·1; cement, 3·5; mineral fertilisers, 0·9.
Private cars (in mill.): U.S., 32·4; Great Britain, 2·4; France, 2·3; Canada, 1·4.
In Britain there are 3·3 mill. *telephones* and 8·9 mill. *wirelesses* in use.
Divorces: U.S., 264,000; Great Britain, 8,396.

Z Births and Deaths

Feb. 1st John Buchan, Lord Tweedsmuir, d. (63).
Mar. 16th Selma Lagerlöf d. (63).
Apr. 9th Beatrice, Mrs. Patrick Campbell, d. (75).
Apr. 18th H. A. L. Fisher d. (75).
May 7th George Lansbury d. (81).
Aug. 21st Lev Trotsky d. (61).
Aug. 30th J. J. Thomson d. (83).
Nov. 9th Neville Chamberlain d. (71).
Nov. 17th Eric Gill d. (58).
Nov. 26th Harold Harmsworth, Lord Rothermere, d. (72).

M Dec: 9th, Eighth Army under Archibald Wavell opens offensive in North Africa by attacking Sidi Barrani;
15th, Italians driven across Libyan border;
16th, Italians driven from El Wak in Italian Somaliland;
22nd, air raid on Manchester;
—, Lord Halifax is appointed British Ambassador in Washington;
23rd, Anthony Eden becomes British Foreign Secretary.

N

A Jan: 3rd, Italians surrender Bardia;
6th, F. D. Roosevelt sends Lend-Lease Bill to Congress;
10th, H.M.S. *Southampton* is sunk and H.M.S. *Illustrious* crippled by German bombers on Greek convoy;
19th, British forces take Kassala, Sudan;
26th, British forces take Biscia in Eritrea;
30th, Archibald Wavell takes Derna and advances towards Benghazi;
—, South Africans drive Italians from Kenya;
—, pro-British rising in Abyssinia.

B Feb: 6th, British occupy Benghazi;
9th, bombardment of Genoa and raids on Leghorn fail to stop German troops under General Rommel from crossing from Italy to North Africa;
19th, British troops invade Italian Somaliland from Kenya;
27th, Britain signs pact of friendship with Hungary.

C Mar: 4th, Royal Navy raids Lofoten Islands;
5th, Britain withdraws her minister from Belgrade in protest at Bulgarian collaboration with Germany;
7th, British troops invade Abyssinia;
11th, Lend-Lease Bill signed after two months' controversy in U.S.;
19th, German air raids on London resumed;
20th, Yugoslavia comes to terms with Germany;
24th, U.S.S.R. undertakes to support Turkey if she is the victim of aggression;
27th, British forces take Keren and Harar;
—, Prince Paul of Yugoslavia deposed in *coup d'état* following his pact with Adolf Hitler;
28th, three Italian cruisers sunk in battle off Cape Matapan;
31st, German counter-offensive in North Africa opens;
U-boat attacks intensified;
Pacifists in Britain, including leading Communists, organise a People's Convention to end the war.

D Apr: 5th, U.S.S.R.-Yugoslav treaty of friendship;
—, British forces take Addis Ababa and, 6th, Massawa in Eritrea;
6th, German ultimatum to Greece and Yugoslavia; Britain sends 60,000 men to Greece;
7th, Archibald Wavell evacuates Benghazi;
—, British Budget raises standard rate of income tax to 10s. in £;
11th, Blitz on Coventry;
13th, Josef Stalin signs neutrality pact with Japan;
—, Germans recapture Bardia;
18th, Yugoslav opposition collapses;
20th, Erwin Rommel attacks Tobruk;
22nd (–*May* 2nd), British evacuate Greece.

E May: 2nd, Iraq, siding with Germany, demands withdrawal of British forces;
6th, J. Stalin becomes head of Soviet government;
9th, U.S.S.R. withdraws recognition of Yugoslavia;
10th, House of Commons destroyed in London's heaviest air raid;
—, Rudolf Hess lands in Scotland;
14th, Vichy government endorses Admiral J. F. Darlan's agreement with Adolf Hitler for aiding Germany;
20th, Germans invade Crete;

o **Politics, Economics, Law and Education**

John Masefield's account of Dunkirk, *The Nine Days' Wonder*.

Edmund Wilson, *To The Finland Station.*

Double Summer Time is introduced in Britain.

Air Raid Precautions services reformed as Civil Defence (*Sept.* 4th).

Germany abandons Gothic type for Roman (*May* 31st).

B. S. Rowntree, *Poverty and Progress: A Second Social Survey of York.*

Oxford University holds degree ceremony at Harvard to honour F. D. Roosevelt (*June* 19th).

'Utility' clothing and furniture in Britain, where clothes are rationed (*June* 1st).

P **Science, Technology, Discovery, etc.**

'Manhattan Project' of atomic research begun in Chicago and Los Angeles under Pegram and H. C. Urey (*Dec.*).

Therapeutic Research Corporation of Great Britain founded to rationalise research.

The National War Formulary is compiled.

J. D. Bernal investigates the physics of air raids.

Terylene is invented by J. R. Whinfield and J. T. Dickson.

A Ferry Command aircraft crosses the Atlantic from the west in 8 hrs. 23 mins.

Q **Scholarship**

Cambridge Economic History of Europe, Volume I (–).

B. Croce, *History as the Story of Liberty.*

R **Philosophy and Religion**

Rudolf Bultmann, *New Testament and Mythology.*

Étienne Gilson, *God and Philosophy.*

Nathaniel Micklem, *The Theology of Politics.*

R. Niebuhr, *The Nature and Destiny of Man* (–43).

S **Art, Sculpture, Fine Arts and Architecture**

Painting:

F. Léger, *Divers against a Yellow Background.*

P. Nash, *Bombers over Berlin.*

Henry Moore's drawings in crayon of refugees in air-raid shelters during the London Blitz and Felix Topolski's drawings of the armed forces.

S. Spencer, *Shipbuilding in the Clyde* (–1947).

Sickert Exhibition at National Gallery.

T **Music**

Benjamin Britten, Violin Concerto.

Ernst Křenek, *Tarquin* (opera).

William Walton, *Scapino* overture.

Council for the Encouragement of Music and the Arts (C.E.M.A.) concerts begin in Britain.

U **Literature**

L. Aragon, *Le Crève-Cœur.*

I. Ehrenburg, *The Fall of Paris.*

Scott Fitzgerald, *The Last Tycoon.*

F. Werfel, *The Song of Bernadette.*

V **The Press**

R. Barrington-Ward succeeds Geoffrey Dawson as editor of *The Times.*

Daily Worker is suppressed (*Jan.* 21st).

E **May**: 20th, Abyssinian campaign ends;
22nd, Rachid Ali, ruler of Iraq, flees;
24th, H.M.S. *Hood* sunk by *Bismarck* off Greenland;
27th, *Bismarck* is sunk by Royal Navy west of Brest, but *Prinz Eugen* escapes;
29th, British evacuate Candia.

F **Jun**: 3rd, U.S.S.R. withdraws recognition of Greece;
8th, British and Free French Forces invade Syria to prevent establishment of Axis bases;
12th, first conference of Allies in London pledged to mutual assistance;
22nd, Germany invades Russia;
—, Finns invade Karelia;
27th, Hungary declares war on Russia;
28th, Germans capture Minsk.

G **Jul**: 1st, Claude Auchinleck succeeds General A. Wavell in Middle East;
6th, U.S.S.R. troops abandon occupied Poland and Baltic states, retiring to 'Stalin Line' on former frontier with Poland;
7th, U.S. troops relieve British in occupation of Iceland;
11th, cease-fire in Syria, which is administered by Allies;
12th, Anglo-Russian agreement of mutual assistance signed in Moscow;
16th, Germans pierce Stalin Line and take Smolensk;
20th, British ministerial changes, with Brendan Bracken as Minister of Information and R. A. Butler as President of Board of Education;
23rd, Britain and U.S. freeze Japanese assets to counter Japan's claims to bases in Indo-China;
25th, Germans take Tallinn;
27th, Japanese troops land in Indo-China;
—, Germans enter the Ukraine;
29th, Russian Army invading Roumania withdraws to the Dniester.

H **Aug**: 11th, W. S. Churchill and F. D. Roosevelt, meeting in the western Atlantic, sign the Atlantic Charter;
12th, Anglo-Soviet trade agreement;
18th, National Fire Service established in Britain;
25th, Britain and U.S.S.R. invade Iran following the Shah's refusal to reduce numbers of resident Germans.

J **Sep**: 3rd, Germans advance to outskirts of Leningrad and, 8th, take Schülsselburg, completing land blockade of Leningrad;
19th, Germans take Kiev;
22nd (–27th), 'Russian Tank Week' in British arms factories;
24th, Allied conference in London endorses Atlantic Charter;
29th (–*Oct.* 10th), Lord Beaverbrook and Averell Harriman visit Moscow to arrange for war supplies;
Movement in Britain for a Second Front.

K **Oct**: 1st, Germans advance from Smolensk towards Moscow;
2nd, Germans take Orel;
13th, R.A.F. bombs Nuremberg;
16th, as Germans 60 miles from Moscow the U.S.S.R. government is transferred to Kuibishev, but J. Stalin stays in Moscow;
—, Odessa falls and, 22nd, Perekop on Sea of Azov;

W Drama and Entertainment

B. Brecht, *Mother Courage and her Children.*
Joyce Cary, *Herself Surprised.*
Noël Coward, *Blithe Spirit.*
Piscator's Studio Theatre, New York, founded to present social drama.
B.B.C. Brains Trust first broadcast.
Sanger's Circus (founded 1820) closes down.

Films:
Orson Welles's *Citizen Kane.*
Leslie Howard in *The First of the Few.*
49th Parallel.
Kipps.
Marx Brothers' last film, *The Big Store.*
Nous les Gosses.
Friedmann Bach.
Das andere Ich.

X Sport

Y Statistics

Populations (in mill.): China, 450; India, 389; U.S.S.R., 182; U.S., 131; Germany, including Austria, Slovakia, West Poland, etc., 110; Japan, 105; Great Britain, 47; Brazil, 41; France, 40.
War production in Great Britain: coal, 206 mill. tons; pig iron, 7·3 mill. tons; steel, 12·7 mill. tons. 20,093 aircraft; 4,844 tanks; 170 major war vessels totalling 346,416 tons.
Merchant shipping losses (in thousand tons): Great Britain, 3,047; Allied, 1,290; Neutral, 347.
Private cars: U.S., 38.8 mill.; Great Britain, 2.2 mill.

Z Births and Deaths

Jan. 5th Henri Louis Bergson d. (81).
Jan. 8th Robert, Lord Baden-Powell, d. (83) and Amy Johnson d. (38).
Jan. 13th James Joyce d. (58).
Mar. 8th Sherwood Anderson d. (65).
Mar. 13th Tom Mann d. (84).
Mar. 28th Virginia Woolf d. (59).
May 7th James George Frazer d. (87).
May 18th Werner Sombart d. (78).
June 4th Kaiser William II d. (82).
June 15th Evelyn Underhill d. (66).
June 29th Ignaz Jan Paderewski d. (80).
July 11th Arthur Evans d. (90).
Aug. 7th Rabindranath Tagore d. (80).

K **Oct:** 22nd, Britain resumes diplomatic relations with Mexico (broken since *May* 1938);
24th, Germans take Kharkov;
25th, failure of first German offensive against Moscow.

L **Nov:** 3rd, Germans take Kursk;
12th, H.M.S. *Ark Royal* sunk near Gibraltar;
16th, second German offensive against Moscow;
18th, British begin attack in Western Desert;
25th, H.M.S. *Barham* sunk in Mediterranean;
27th, Marshal Timoshenko launches Russian counter-offensive, forcing Germans to evacuate Rostov-on-Don (taken, 23rd);
29th, Russian counter-offensive in Moscow sector.

M **Dec:** 5th, Britain declares war on Finland, Hungary and Roumania on their refusing to withdraw from the war against U.S.S.R.;
5th, Anthony Eden visits Moscow;
7th, Japanese bomb Pearl Harbor, Hawaii and British Malaya;
8th, Britain and U.S. declare war on Japan;
9th, National Service Bill in Britain lowers age of call-up to 18½ and renders single women aged 20–30 liable to military service;
—, Japanese land on Luzon; Russians recapture Tikhvin, saving Leningrad;
10th, H.M.S. *Prince of Wales* and H.M.S. *Repulse* sunk by Japanese aircraft;
11th, U.S. declares war on Germany and Italy;
17th, heavy penalties for British black-marketeers;
18th, Rommel retreats in North Africa;
19th, Penang evacuated by British;
22nd (–28th), W. S. Churchill visits Washington and Ottawa;
24th, British re-occupy Benghazi and regain control of Cyrenaica;
25th, Hong Kong surrenders to Japanese;
26th, British commandos raid Lofoten Islands and, 27th, Vaagno, near Trondheim;
30th, Russians recapture Kaluga.

N

A Jan: 2nd, Britain, U.S., U.S.S.R., China and 22 other Allies pledge themselves not to make separate peace treaties with the enemy;
9th, British recapture Bardia;
10th, Japanese invade Dutch East Indies;
11th, Japanese take Kuala Lumpur;
19th, Japanese invade Burma;
21st, Rommel launches new offensive in Western Desert;
29th, Anglo-Soviet alliance with Iran.

B Feb: 1st, British forces in Malaya withdraw to Singapore;
—, Vidkun Quisling becomes premier of Norway;
3rd, Eighth Army evacuates Derna;
11th, German battleships leave Brest for Baltic;
15th, Singapore surrenders;
19th (–22nd), W. S. Churchill reconstructs ministry, with C. R. Attlee deputy Prime Minister, Stafford Cripps Leader of House and James Grigg War Secretary;
24th, U.S. task force raids Wake Islands;
28th, Japanese land in Java.

C Mar: 10th, Rangoon falls to Japanese;
28th, British commandos raid St. Nazaire;
—, R.A.F. bombs Lübeck;
31st, Japanese successes in Burma and Andaman Islands threaten east coast of India.

D Apr: 4th, Japanese sink 3 British warships in Bay of Bengal;
6th, end of white bread in Britain;
8th (–15th), General George Marshall and Harry Hopkins in London discussing aid for Russia by launching a Second Front;
9th, Bataan surrenders to Japanese;
14th, British Budget doubles entertainment tax;
16th, Indian Congress rejects terms of self-government offered by Stafford Cripps;
23rd (–30th), German 'Baedeker' raids on Exeter, Bath, etc.;
Continuous intensive air raids on Malta while reinforcements from Italy are sent to General Rommel in North Africa.

E May: 1st, Japanese take Mandalay, while British withdraw along Chindwin Valley to India;
5th, British troops invade Madagascar;
6th, Corregidor surrenders;
8th, Germans attack Kerch Peninsula;
—, Germans attack in East Crimea;
12th, Russian gains in Kharkov region;
20th, Germans take Kerch Peninsula;
26th, V. Molotov in London signs close Anglo-Soviet treaty for prosecuting the war;
—, Rommel resumes offensive with massive tank support (–Nov. 2nd);
—, Anglo-Soviet 20-year alliance signed in London;
29th, further U.S.–U.S.S.R. lend-lease agreement;
30th, British convoy reaches Russia despite heavy air attacks;
—, mammoth R.A.F. raid on Cologne;
31st, Czech patriots assassinate Gestapo leader Heydrich.

F Jun: 2nd, British abandon Gazala-Bir Hakeim Line;
3rd, indecisive U.S.–Japanese battle of Midway Islands;

1942 (Jan.–Jun.) Fall of Singapore—Germans reach Stalingrad—Battle of El Alamein

A **Jan**: 2nd, Britain, U.S., U.S.S.R., China and 22 other Allies pledge themselves not to make separate peace treaties with the enemy;
9th, British recapture Bardia;
10th, Japanese invade Dutch East Indies;
11th, Japanese take Kuala Lumpur;
19th, Japanese invade Burma;
21st, Rommel launches new offensive in Western Desert;
29th, Anglo-Soviet alliance with Iran.

B **Feb**: 1st, British forces in Malaya withdraw to Singapore;
—, Vidkun Quisling becomes premier of Norway;
3rd, Eighth Army evacuates Derna;
11th, German battleships leave Brest for Baltic;
15th, Singapore surrenders;
19th (–22nd), W. S. Churchill reconstructs ministry, with C. R. Attlee deputy Prime Minister, Stafford Cripps Leader of House and James Grigg War Secretary;
24th, U.S. task force raids Wake Islands;
28th, Japanese land in Java.

C **Mar**: 10th, Rangoon falls to Japanese;
28th, British commandos raid St. Nazaire;
—, R.A.F. bombs Lübeck;
31st, Japanese successes in Burma and Andaman Islands threaten east coast of India.

D **Apr**: 4th, Japanese sink 3 British warships in Bay of Bengal;
6th, end of white bread in Britain;
8th (–15th), General George Marshall and Harry Hopkins in London discussing aid for Russia by launching a Second Front;
9th, Bataan surrenders to Japanese;
14th, British Budget doubles entertainment tax;
16th, Indian Congress rejects terms of self-government offered by Stafford Cripps;
23rd (–30th), German 'Baedeker' raids on Exeter, Bath, etc.;
Continuous intensive air raids on Malta while reinforcements from Italy are sent to General Rommel in North Africa.

E **May**: 1st, Japanese take Mandalay, while British withdraw along Chindwin Valley to India;
5th, British troops invade Madagascar;
6th, Corregidor surrenders;
8th, Germans attack Kerch Peninsula;
—, Germans attack in East Crimea;
13th, Russian gains in Kharkov region;
20th, Germans take Kerch Peninsula;
26th, V. Molotov in London signs closer Anglo-Soviet treaty for prosecuting the war;
—, Rommel resumes offensive with massive tank support (–*June* 2nd);
—, Anglo-Soviet 20-year alliance signed in London;
29th, further U.S.-U.S.S.R. lend-lease agreement;
30th, British convoy reaches Russia despite heavy air attacks;
—, mammoth R.A.F. raid on Cologne;
31st, Czech patriots assassinate Gestapo leader Heydrich.

F **Jun**: 2nd, British abandon Gazala-Bir Hakeim Line;
3rd, indecisive U.S.-Japanese battle in Midway Islands;

O **Politics, Economics, Law and Education**

William Beveridge, *Report on Social Security* (*Dec.* 1st).

E. H. Carr, *Conditions of Peace*.

L. B. Namier, *Conflicts; Studies in Contemporary History*.

Anglo-American Caribbean Commission is established.

Malta is awarded the George Cross in token of the heroism of the islanders under constant German air attack (*Apr.* 16th).

James Burnham, *The Managerial Revolution, or What is Happening in the World Now*.

Uthwatt Report on land development in Britain (*Sept.* 9th).

Gilbert Murray founds Oxfam.

P **Science, Technology, Discovery, etc.**

E. Fermi at Chicago splits the atom (*Dec.* 2nd).

American scientists develop ENIAC, the first electronic brain or automatic computer.

Magnetic tape is invented.

Germans launch the V-2 rocket.

The Alaska Highway is opened (*Oct.*).

Q **Scholarship**

G. M. Trevelyan, *English Social History*.

The Mildenhall hoard is discovered.

R **Philosophy and Religion**

R. G. Collingwood, *The New Leviathan*.

E. Fromm, *The Fear of Freedom*.

Reichenbach, *Philosophy Foundations of Quantum Mechanics*.

C. S. Lewis, *The Screwtape Letters*.

William Temple, appointed Archbishop of Canterbury (*Feb.* 23rd), publishes *Christianity and the Social Order*.

Kenneth Walker, *The Diagnosis of Man*.

S **Art, Sculpture, Fine Arts and Architecture**

Painting:

Pierre Bonnard, *L'Oiseau bleu*.

John Piper, *Windsor Castle*.

Graham Sutherland, *Red Landscape*.

Artists Aid Russia Exhibition at Hertford House.

T **Music**

Benjamin Britten, *Sinfonia da Requiem*.

Aaron Copland, *Lincoln Portrait*.

Roy Harris, 5th Symphony.

Carlo Menotti, *The Island God* (opera).

Edmund Rubbra, 4th Symphony.

Dmitry Shostakovich, 7th Symphony ('Leningrad').

U **Literature**

A. Camus, *L'Étranger*.

T. S. Eliot, *Little Gidding*.

John Steinbeck, *The Moon is Down*.

V **The Press**

J. L. Garvin resigns from *The Observer* (*Feb.* 28th; editor since 1928).

Stars and Stripes, daily paper for U.S. forces in Europe, published from *The Times* office (*Nov.* 2nd).

1942 (Jun.–Dec.)

F Jun: 6th, Nazis burn Lidice in Bohemia;
10th, Free French garrison at Bir Hakeim surrenders;
13th, British lose 230 tanks in desert fighting and
19th, withdraw to Sollum-Sidi Omar Line, along Egyptian frontier;
21st, Rommel takes Tobruk;
—, heavy British losses on convoy to Malta;
25th, Eighth Army retreats to Mersa Matruh;
—, R.A.F. 1,000-bomber raid on Bremen;
28th, Eighth Army retreats to El Alamein;
Germans launch counter-attack in Kharkov region.

G Jul: 1st, vote of censure debate in Commons on direction of war;
—, Coal Commission takes over colliery leases in Britain under 1938 Act;
3rd, Germans take Sebastopol;
26th, R.A.F. raids Hamburg;
27th, Second Front demonstration in Trafalgar Square;
28th, Germans take Rostov and overrun northern Caucasus;
Gregory Zhukov replaces Timoshenko as Commander of U.S.S.R. southern armies.

H Aug: 7th, Americans land in Guadalcanal;
12th (–15th), W. S. Churchill, A. Harriman and J. Stalin confer in Moscow;
15th, H.M.S. *Eagle* and H.M.S. *Manchester* lost on Malta convoy;
19th, Dieppe raid, casualties include 3,500 Canadians;
—, General Alexander replaces Auchinleck as Commander-in-Chief Middle East, while B. L. Montgomery is given command of Eighth Army;
26th, Germans reach Stalingrad;
31st, Rommel renews offensive at Alam Halfa, but is driven back to original lines.

J Sep: 12th, British convoy to Russia survives German bombing off Norway;
13th, German all-out attack on Stalingrad begins;
U.S. bombers raid France daily.

K Oct: 21st, J. C. Smuts addresses assembly of both Houses of Parliament, Westminster;
23rd, Eighth Army's attack on Rommel's line begins battle of El Alamein;
U.S. national labour service act.

L Nov: 4th, Rommel in full retreat;
8th, Allied landings in French North Africa under Dwight D. Eisenhower;
9th, Germans move into unoccupied France;
10th, Egypt is cleared of Germans;
11th, General D. Eisenhower's recognition of Admiral François Darlan as French Chief-of-State in North Africa arouses British indignation;
13th, British retake Tobruk;
—, U.S. task force at Guadalcanal beats off Japanese;
19th, Russian counter-offensive from Stalingrad surrounds besieging German Army;
22nd, British ministerial changes, with Herbert Morrison replacing Stafford Cripps in cabinet.

M Dec: 12th (–23rd), von Manstein fails to relieve Stalingrad;
16th (–20th), rout of Italians on R. Don;
19th, British and Indian troops begin advance in Burma;
21st, Eighth Army reoccupies Benghazi;
24th, Admiral F. Darlan assassinated in Algiers;
31st, Royal Navy beats off massive German air attack on convoy to Russia.

N U.S. war factories achieve maximum production.

W Drama and Entertainment

Jean Anouilh, *Antigone.*
Sean O'Casey, *Red Roses For Me.*
T. Rattigan, *Flare Path.*

Films:
Mrs. Miniver, with Greer Garson.
Coastal Command.
Holiday Inn with Bing Crosby.
How Green Was My Valley.
The Evening Visitor.
Loveletter.
Diesel.
Rembrandt.

B.B.C., Tommy Handley in *ITMA.*

X Sport

Warmerdam's record pole-jump.

Y Statistics

Steel production: World total, 175 mill. tons (U.S. leads with 70 mill.).
Great Britain's war production: 23,671 aircraft; 8,611 tanks; 173 major vessels, totalling 299,920 tons.
Merchant shipping losses (in thousand tons): Great Britain, 3,695; Allied, 4,394; Neutral, 249.

Z Births and Deaths

Jan. 22nd Walter Richard Sickert d. (81).
Mar. 12th William Bragg d. (79).
Mar. 21st Philip Wilson Steer d. (81).
July 28th William Flinders Petrie d. (89).
July 31st Francis Younghusband d. (79).
Aug. 23rd Michel Fokine d. (62).
Sept. 26th Wilson Carlile d. (92).
Oct. 14th Marie Tempest d. (78).
Nov. 21st James B. M. Hertzog d. (76).

1943 (Jan.–May) Russian victory at Stalingrad—Germans surrender in North Africa—Allies invade Italy—Mussolini falls

A **Jan**: 2nd, German withdrawal from Caucasus begins;
11th, British treaty with China renouncing extra-territorial rights;
14th (–24th), W. S. Churchill and F. D. Roosevelt confer at Casablanca on grand strategy;
15th, Japanese are driven from Guadalcanal;
18th, German air attack on London renewed;
23rd, Eighth Army enters Tripoli;
26th, Russian victory at Voronezh;
27th, civil conscription of women in Germany;
30th, Russians destroy German Army south-west of Stalingrad;
31st, Paulus surrenders at Stalingrad.

B **Feb**: 8th, Russians take Kursk;
10th, Eighth Army reaches Tunisian frontier;
14th, Russians recapture Rostov and, 16th, Kharkov;
18th, Labour M.P.'s, disobeying C. R. Attlee and H. Morrison, protest at Government's policy over Beveridge Report;
21st, George VI announces on 25th anniversary of Red Army the presentation of sword of honour to Stalingrad (handed by W. S. Churchill to J. Stalin at Teheran in *Nov.*);
—, Allied armies in North Africa come under General Dwight D. Eisenhower's supreme command;
24th, von Arnim withdraws forces through Kasserine Pass;
28th, heavy R.A.F. raid on Berlin.

C **Mar**: 1st, R.A.F. begins systematic bombing of European railway system;
7th (–11th), Eighth Army repulses heavy German counter-attacks in Tunisia;
15th, Russians forced to evacuate Kharkov;
Growing support in by-elections for candidates of Commonwealth Party, founded by Richard Acland, indicates dissatisfaction with Government's social policy, but W. S. Churchill's broadcast, 22nd, advocating four-year plan for post-war reconstruction, retrieves Government's popularity;
29th, B. L. Montgomery breaks through Mareth Line into Southern Tunisia.

D **Apr**: 6th, Rommel's retreat north from Gabes Gap enables British and U.S. armies, 8th, to link up;
8th, General S. von Arnim succeeds Rommel as Commander of Afrika Korps;
10th, Eighth Army occupies Sfax;
20th, Massacre in Warsaw ghetto;
24th, O. Wingate's commandos return to base after three months in Burmese jungle and Japanese resume offensive;
26th, U.S.S.R. breaks off diplomatic relations with London Polish Government;
Heavy air raids on Ruhr;
Bermuda Conference on refugee problem.

E **May**: 1st, compulsory arbitration in British coal industry;
—, U.S. coal-miners' strike (settled *Nov.* 3rd);
7th, Allies take Tunis and Bizerta, while Germans retire to Cap Bon Peninsula;
11th, U.S. force lands at Attu, Aleutian Islands;
12th, German Army in Tunisia surrenders;
17th, R.A.F. bombs Ruhr dams;
22nd, Third Communist International (formed 1919) dissolved;
Air offensive on Germany becomes more destructive.

O **Politics, Economics, Law and Education**

D. W. Brogan, *The American Political Scene.*
Harold Laski, *Reflections on the Revolution of Our Time.*
A. D. Lindsay, *The Modern Democratic State.*
Walter Lippmann, *U.S. Foreign Policy.*
Peter Nathan, *The Psychology of Fascism.*
U.S. Office of Economic Warfare created (*July*).
J. M. Keynes's plan for an international currency union.
First Henry Kaiser 'Liberty' ships.
United Nations Relief and Rehabilitation Administration is established.
The Nuffield Foundation formed.
Cambridge University founds a professorship of American History and Institutions.
Board of Education's *Sex Education in Schools and Youth Organisations* published to reduce venereal disease.
Forshaw and Abercrombie, *The County of London Plan.*
R. A. Brady, *Business as a System of Power.*

P **Science, Technology, Discovery, etc.**

Penicillin is successfully applied to treat chronic diseases.
Selman A. Waksman and A. Schatz discover streptomycin.
'Big inch' oil pipeline from Texas to U.S. eastern seaboard opened.
Fully-laden glider is towed across Atlantic from Montreal in 28 hrs.

Q **Scholarship**

Pilgrim Trust purchases Sir Isaac Newton's library.
J. M. Thompson, *The French Revolution.*

R **Philosophy and Religion**

J.-P. Sartre, *L'Être et le néant.*
Jacques Maritain, *Christianity and Democracy.*
C. E. Raven, *Science, Religion and the Future.*
Bertrand Griffin appointed Archbishop of Westminster as Cardinal Arthur Hinsley's successor.
Archbishop Suhard of Paris founds worker-priest movement.
Archbishop of Moscow is elected Patriarch of All Russia.

S **Art, Sculpture, Fine Arts and Architecture**

Sculpture:
H. Moore, *Madonna and Child*, Northampton.
H. G. Adam, *Reclining Figure.*

T **Music**

Arnold Bax, Violin Concerto.
Lennox Berkeley, *Divertimento.*
W. Busch, 'cello concerto.
Khachaturian, *Ode to Stalin.*
R. Vaughan Williams, Symphony no. 5 in D.
'La Pléiade' formed to finance concerts of music by French composers in Paris.

U **Literature**

Henry Green, *Caught.*
Henri Michaux, *Exorcismes.*

F Jun: 4th, French Committee of National Liberation is formed, including General Charles de Gaulle and General Henri Giraud;
11th, island of Pantelleria surrenders to Allies after bombardment;
—, agreement on post-war relief signed at end of Hot Springs Conference;
29th, U.S. forces land in New Guinea.

G Jul: 5th, German offensive on Russian front opens with battle of Kursk;
10th, Allies land in Sicily;
12th (–15th), Russian counter-offensive against Orel salient;
19th, first Allied air raid on Rome;
23rd, Palermo occupied;
26th, Benito Mussolini falls from power. Victor Emmanuel asks Marshal Badoglio to form a government;
U.S. Congress passes anti-strike act over F. D. Roosevelt's veto.

H Aug: 5th, Russians take Orel;
5th, capture of Catania gives Allies command of Sicilian Straits;
10th (–24th), W. S. Churchill, F. D. Roosevelt and Mackenzie King confer at Quebec on Far Eastern operations;
16th, U.S. troops occupy Messina;
23rd, Russians recapture Kharkov;
24th, Britain and U.S. recognise French Committee for National Liberation in Algiers;
27th, Japanese evacuate New Georgia Island.

J Sep: 3rd, Allies invade Italy;
8th, Allied landings in Salerno Bay;
—, Dwight D. Eisenhower announces Italy's unconditional surrender (made, 3rd);
10th, Eighth Army takes Taranto;
24th, Russians cross Dnieper north of Kiev;
25th, Russians take Smolensk;
30th, Fifth Army takes Naples.

K Oct: 4th, Fitzroy Maclean undertakes military mission to Marshal Tito;
6th, Kuban Peninsula in Russian hands;
12th, Portugal grants Britain facilities in the Azores;
13th, Italy declares war on Germany;
18th (–30th), Moscow Conference of Allied foreign ministers;
19th, Germans in Italy retire from Volturno river;
27th, Russians break into Nogaisk steppes.

L Nov: 1st, U.S. force lands at Bougainville in Solomons;
2nd, Moscow declaration of Allied foreign ministers on international security sets up European Advisory Commission;
4th, Eighth Army takes Isernia;
6th, Russians take Kiev;
11th, Lord Woolton appointed first British Minister of Reconstruction;
19th, release on health grounds of Oswald Mosley, imprisoned since 1940 under Defence Regulations, divides British Labour Party;
22nd, W. S. Churchill, F. D. Roosevelt and Chiang Kai-shek agree at Cairo to measures for defeating Japan;
23rd, U.S. troops occupy Makin in Gilbert Islands;
26th, Russians take Gomel;
28th (*–Dec.* 1st), W. S. Churchill, F. D. Roosevelt and J. Stalin meet at Teheran for planning overthrow of Germany.

(*Continued opposite*)

U **Literature** (*cont.*)

Ricardo Molinari, *Mundos de la Madrugada* (poems).
Romain Rolland, *Péguy*.
New Writing and Daylight, ed. J. Lehmann.

V **The Press**

Frankfurter Zeitung is suppressed by Adolf Hitler.

W **Drama and Entertainment**

J. Bridie, *Mr. Bolfry*.
Noël Coward, *This Happy Breed*.
J.-P. Sartre, *Les Mouches*.
Rogers and Hart, *Oklahoma!* (musical).
Dorothy Sayers's B.B.C. radio serial *The Man Born to be King*.

Films:
For Whom The Bell Tolls.
Orson Welles's *Jane Eyre*.
Colonel Blimp.
The Gentler Sex.
Stage-Door Canteen.
Stalingrad: One Day of War.
Summer Light.

Frank Sinatra becomes first pop idol of the teenager.

X **Sport**

Y **Statistics**

British war production: 26,263 aircraft; 8,611 tanks; 168 major vessels, totalling 292,450 tons.
Merchant shipping losses (in thousand tons): Great Britain, 1,678; Allied, 1,886; Neutral, 82.

Z **Births and Deaths**

Jan. 9th R. G. Collingwood d. (54).
Jan. 24th John Burns d. (84).
Mar. 10th Laurence Binyon d. (73).
Mar. 28th Sergei Rachmaninov d. (69).
Apr. 30th Beatrice Webb, Lady Passfield, d. (85).
June 17th Annie S. Swan (Mrs. Burnett Smith) d. (83).
July 4th Wladyslaw Sikorski d. (62).
Sept. 1st W. W. Jacobs d. (80).

M **Dec**: 12th, U.S.S.R.-Czechoslovak treaty for post-war co-operation;
26th, *Scharnhorst* sunk;
Russians succeed in recapturing two-thirds of the territory captured by Germans.

N

1944 (Jan.–Jul.) Normandy landings—Germans driven from Russia—V-bombs on England

A **Jan**: 4th, Fifth Army launches attack east of Cassino;
9th, U.S. troops take San Vittore;
—, Commonwealth Party wins Skipton by-election;
20th, R.A.F. drops 2,300 tons of bombs on Berlin (provoking, *Feb.* 9th, protests in House of Lords on bombing of German cities);
22nd, Allied landings at Nettuno and Anzio;
27th, Leningrad completely relieved.

B **Feb**: 4th, Allied troops reach Monte Cassino;
4th, Conservative majority slashed at Brighton by-election;
7th (–29th), German assaults on Anzio bridgehead;
10th, Pay-as-you-earn income tax introduced;
15th, Monte Cassino monastery bombed;
—, U.S. troops complete reconquest of Solomons;
19th (–26th), heaviest air raids on London since May 1941;
22nd, Russians take Krivoi Rog, Ukraine;
28th, British begin operations in Upper Burma;
South Wales miners' strike.

C **Mar**: 4th, Russian offensive in Ukraine begins;
6th, U.S. bombers begin daylight attacks on Berlin;
15th, Allies launch heavy attack on Monte Cassino;
19th, Russians force the Dniester;
31st, Japan transfers mineral concessions in North Sakhalin to U.S.S.R.;
Japanese troops advance on Imphal.

D **Apr**: 2nd, Russians enter Roumania;
11th, liberation of Crimea begins;
18th, Aneurin Bevan agitates for annulment of powers conferred on Minister of Labour for dealing with strikes;
22nd, Allies land at Hollandia, New Guinea.
During the month Allies drop 81,400 tons of bombs on Germany and occupied Europe.

E **May**: 1st (–16th), London conference of Dominion premiers;
—, Anglo-Spanish agreement to reduce Spain's exports of wolfram to Germany;
9th, Sebastopol liberated;
12th, Allies assault Gustav Line in Italy;
18th, Monte Cassino is taken;
21st, Allies break through the Hitler Line in Italy.

F **Jun**: 4th, Fifth Army enters Rome;
6th, 'D-Day' landings in Normandy;
10th, Russian offensive against Finland opens;
12th, Allies call on Germany's satellites to side with them;
13th, first flying-bomb dropped on London;
15th, Fifth Army takes Orvieto;
19th, U.S. troops take Saipan;
23rd (–28th), Germans encircled at Vitebsk;
27th, Allies take Cherbourg.

G **Jul**: 1st, U.S. monetary and financial conference at Bretton Woods, New Hampshire;
3rd, Russians take Minsk, capturing 100,000 Germans;
5th, British capture of Ukhrul removes threat to Imphal;

O **Politics, Economics, Law and Education**

Norman Bentwich, *Judea Lives Again.*

William Beveridge, *Full Employment in a Free Society.*

John Hilton, *Rich Man, Poor Man.*

Elspeth Huxley and Margery Perham, *Race Relations.*

Julian Huxley, *On Living in a Revolution.*

Sumner Welles, *The Time for Decision.*

R. A. Butler introduces British Education Act.

The Fleming Report recommends that British independent schools should accept selected pupils paid for by public authorities.

I.C.I. endow 80 fellowships at nine British universities.

'Black-out' restrictions are relaxed in Britain (*Sept.*).

Thomas Sharpe's plan for Greater London.

U.S.S.R. substitutes 'Hymn of the Soviet Union' for 'The Internationale'.

P **Science, Technology, Discovery, etc.**

Second uranium pile built at Clinton, Tennessee, for manufacturing plutonium for an atomic bomb.

New cyclotron of Department of Terrestrial Magnetism, Carnegie Institution, Washington, completed.

Quinine is synthesised.

Blalock successfully operates on 'blue babies'.

First non-stop flight London-Canada (*Sept.* 8th).

Q **Scholarship**

F. M. Stenton, *Anglo-Saxon England.*

B. H. Sumner, *Survey of Russian History.*

R **Philosophy and Religion**

C. Jung, *Psychology and Religion.*

L. Mumford, *The Condition of Man.*

W. Temple, *The Church Looks Forward.*

Roger Schutz founds Protestant community of Taize, near Cluny.

S **Art, Sculpture, Fine Arts and Architecture**

Painting:

G. Sutherland, *Christ on the Cross*, Northampton.

M. Beckmann, *Self-Portrait.*

T **Music**

Béla Bartók, Violin Concerto.

Paul Hindemith, *Herodias* (opera).

Ernest Moeran, *Sinfonietta.*

Dmitry Shostakovich, 8th Symphony.

Oxford University founds a faculty of music.

U **Literature**

H. E. Bates, *Fair Stood the Wind for France.*

Alex Comfort, *The Power House.*

Ivy Compton-Burnett, *Elders and Betters.*

T. S. Eliot, *Four Quartets.*

A. Huxley, *Time Must Have a Stop.*

R. Lehmann, *The Ballad and the Source.*

1944 (Jul.–Dec.)

G Jul: 9th, Caen captured;
16th, Germans withdraw from Arezzo;
18th, General Tojo resigns in Japan;
19th, Leghorn and Ancona fall to Allies;
20th, attempt to assassinate Hitler;
23rd, Russian troops cross 'Curzon Line' in Poland;
26th, U.S.S.R. recognises the Lublin Committee of Polish Liberation in Moscow as the authority for liberated Poland;
28th, Russians take Brest-Litovsk.

H Aug: 1st, Warsaw rising begins;
—, U.S. troops break through at Avranches;
13th (–20th), German Seventh Army exterminated in Falaise Gap;
15th, British land on French Riviera;
19th, Eighth Army takes Florence;
20th, Russian offensive in Bessarabia and Roumania;
25th, Charles de Gaulle enters Paris in the wake of the Allied troops and, 30th, seat of French provisional government is transferred from Algiers to Paris;
26th, Eighth Army opens attack in Adriatic sector;
30th, Russians enter Bucharest.

J Sep: 4th, Allies capture Antwerp and destroy flying-bomb sites in Pas de Calais;
—, cease-fire on Finnish front;
5th, U.S.S.R. declares war on Bulgaria;
—, Brussels is liberated;
8th, first V-2 rocket lands in Britain;
10th (–17th), W. S. Churchill and F. D. Roosevelt meet in Quebec;
11th, Americans cross German frontier near Trier;
12th, Roumanian armistice signed;
17th, British airborne forces land at Eindhoven and Arnhem, but fail to outflank the German defence of the Westwall and are withdrawn after heavy casualties;
19th, Finnish armistice signed;
28th, Canadians liberate Calais;
29th, Russians invade Yugoslavia.

K Oct: 3rd, Canadians reach R. Maas;
9th (–18th), W. S. Churchill visits Moscow;
19th, U.S. troops land in Philippines;
20th, Russians and Yugoslavs enter Belgrade;
23rd, Allies recognise General Charles de Gaulle's administration as the provisional government of France;
The Red Army advances into Hungary.

L Nov: 3rd, Flushing falls to the Allies and the port of Antwerp is reopened to shipping;
7th, F. D. Roosevelt, Democrat, wins U.S. Presidential election, for a fourth term, with 25,610,946 votes against 22,018,177 for Thomas Dewey, Republican, who fails to carry his own state of New York;
12th, *Tirpitz* sunk;
24th, Strasbourg is taken;
27th, Edward Stettinius appointed U.S. secretary of state on Cordell Hull's resignation (secretary since 1933).

(*Continued opposite*)

U **Literature** (*cont.*)

W. S. Maugham, *The Razor's Edge.*

A. Moravia, *Agustino.*

V **The Press**

W **Drama and Entertainment**

T. Rattigan, *Love in Idleness.*

J.-P. Sartre, *Huis Clos.*

Tennessee Williams, *The Glass Menagerie.*

Films:

Laurence Olivier's *Henry V.*

The Way Ahead.

Alfred Hitchcock's *Lifeboat.*

The Forgotten Village.

The White Cliffs of Dover.

Zola.

Justice is Coming.

X **Sport**

Y **Statistics**

British Commonwealth armed forces total 8·7 mill. of which Britain provides 4·5 mill.

U.S. armed forces total 7·2 mill.

Britain's electrical output totals 38·3 mill. units (increase of 12 mill. from 1939).

U.S. synthetic rubber: 763,000 tons manufactured.

Gold production (in thousand ounces): South Africa, 12,227; Canada, 2,900; U.S., 1,000; Mexico, 750.

Z **Births and Deaths**

Jan. 1st Edwin Landseer Lutyens d. (75).

Jan. 23rd Edvard Munch d. (80).

Mar. 28th Stephen Leacock d. (74).

May 9th Ethel Smyth d. (86).

May 12th Arthur Quiller-Couch ('Q') d. (80).

July 11th Lucien Pissarro d. (81).

July 18th Thomas Sturge Moore d. (74).

Aug. 19th Henry J. Wood d. (75).

Sept. 13th Heath Robinson d. (72).

Oct. 8th Wendell Wilkie d. (52).

Oct. 26th William Temple d. (63).

Nov. 7th Geoffrey Dawson d. (70).

Nov. 22nd Arthur Stanley Eddington d. (61).

Dec. 30th Romain Rolland d. (78).

M Dec: 3rd, police action against E.A.M. (Republican) demonstrations in Athens raises criticisms of British policy in Greece, and to restore confidence W. S. Churchill visits Athens (24th);

5th, Allies take Ravenna;

16th, German offensive in Ardennes ('Battle of the Bulge',—*Jan.* 5th) begins;

18th, North Burma is cleared of Japanese;

27th, Russians surround Budapest.

N

1945 (Jan.–Apr.) Germany surrenders—Roosevelt dies—Attlee forms Labour Government—The atom bomb—Japan surrenders

A Jan: 1st, 14th Army opens offensive in Burma;
3rd, Americans counter-attack Ardennes salient;
8th, Egyptian elections, boycotted by the Wafd, result in majority for Ahmed Pasha, the premier;
11th, truce in Greek civil war;
12th, Representation of the People bill introduced to settle problems of British service voters;
13th, Russian forces begin offensive in Silesia;
17th, Russians take Warsaw; 19th, Cracow, 23rd, Tilsit;
20th, provisional Hungarian government under General Miklos concludes armistice with Allies;
22nd, 14th Army take Monywa on Chindwin River;
23rd, Russians reach the Oder;
U-boats using homing torpedoes take heavy toll of British shipping in Atlantic.

B Feb: 3rd, Allies capture Colmar;
4th (–11th), W. S. Churchill, F. D. Roosevelt and J. Stalin confer at Yalta to plan for Germany's unconditional surrender, settle the Polish question and arrange for U.N. Conference at San Francisco;
5th, General Douglas MacArthur's troops enter Manila;
6th, world T.U. conference in London;
8th, Canadian offensive south-east of Nijmegen towards Rhine;
10th, Elbing captured;
13th, Budapest falls;
15th, British troops reach Rhine on ten-mile front;
16th, massive U.S. air raids on Tokyo begin;
24th, Ahmed Pasha, premier of Egypt, assassinated after announcing Egypt's declaration of war against Germany.

C Mar: 2nd, Petru Groza forms a pro-Russian government in Roumania;
7th, Cologne captured;
—, 14th Army enters Mandalay;
13th, Allies command west bank of Rhine (Nijmegen to Coblenz);
19th, U.S.S.R. denounces Turko-Soviet non-aggression pact of 1925;
23rd, General Dempsey's 2nd Army crosses Rhine;
28th, last of 1,050 V-rockets falls on Britain;
29th, Russians cross Austrian frontier;
30th, Danzig captured.

D Apr: 1st, Americans take Okinawa;
3rd, Eduard Beneš appoints a National Front government in Czechoslovakia with Zdenek Fierlinger as premier;
5th, U.S.S.R. denounces non-aggression pact with Japan of *Apr.* 1941;
—, U.S. Army takes Osnabrück;
6th, U.S. naval victory over Japanese at Kyushu;
10th, U.S. troops take Hanover, but Germans resist attack on Bremen;
11th, 8th Army reaches R. Santerno;
12th, F. D. Roosevelt dies (aged 63) and is succeeded by Harry S. Truman;
14th, Allies enter Arnhem;
17th, Paasikivi forms new coalition in Finland;
20th, Russians reach Berlin;
22nd, Bologna falls;
23rd, Allies reach River Po;
—, junction of U.S. and U.S.S.R. forces at Torgau;

O **Politics, Economics, Law and Education**

D. W. Brogan, *The Free State* (intended for re-education of Germany).
E. Cammaerts, *The Peace That Was Left.*
L. Curtis, *World War; Its Cause and Cure.*
Lord Moran, *The Anatomy of Courage.*
'Black Markets' for food, cigarettes and clothing in Europe.
France enfranchises women.
Bank of France is nationalised.
Family allowances are introduced in Britain.
Shintoism is disestablished in Japan by Allied Control Commission.

P **Science, Technology, Discovery, etc.**

The dropping of the atomic bomb (*Aug.* 6th) reveals the discovery of releasing and controlling atomic energy.
Henry Dale pleads for the abolition of secrecy in science.
Developments in 'Radar' and other wartime scientific inventions are made known.
Jánossy investigates cosmic radiation.
Synthesis of Vitamin A is prepared.

Q **Scholarship**

R **Philosophy and Religion**

R. G. Collingwood, *The Idea of Nature.*
K. Popper, *The Open Society and Its Enemies.*
M. Buber, *For the Sake of Heaven.*
Sperry, *Religion in America.*
C. J. Webb, *Religious Experience.*

S **Art, Sculpture, Fine Arts and Architecture**

Painting:
S. Spencer, series of *Resurrection* pictures (–1950).
M. Chagall, sets and costumes for *The Firebird* ballet.
E. W. Tristram, *English Medieval Wall-Painting.*

Sculpture:
A. Calder, *Red Pyramid* (mobile).
H. Moore, *Family Group.*

T **Music**

Benjamin Britten, *Peter Grimes* (opera).
Paul Honegger, *Sinfonie Liturgique.*
R. Strauss, *Metamorphosis.*
Igor Stravinsky, Symphony in three movements.
S. Prokofiev, *Sluts* (ballet).

U **Literature**

Henry Green, *Loving.*
John Hersey, *A Bell for Adano.*
P. J. Jouve, *La Vierge de Paris.*
Carlo Levi, *Christ Stopped at Eboli.*
S. Lewis, *Cass Timberlane.*
G. Orwell (pseud.), *Animal Farm.*
J.-P. Sartre, *The Age of Reason.*
E. Waugh, *Brideshead Revisited.*
K. Winsor, *Forever Amber.*

D Apr: 25th, Karl Renner becomes chancellor of provisional Austrian government;
— (–*June* 26th), U.N. Conference attended by Anthony Eden, Vyacheslav Molotov, J. C. Smuts and Edward Stettinius in San Francisco;
26th, Bremen surrenders;
—, U.S. and U.S.S.R. forces take Torgau;
27th, 5th Army takes Genoa and Verona;
28th, Allies cross Elbe;
—, Benito Mussolini killed by partisans;
29th, Venice falls;
30th, death of Adolf Hitler in Berlin.

E May: 1st, surrender of German Army on Italian front;
2nd, Berlin surrenders to Russians;
3rd, Allies enter Hamburg and, 4th, Rangoon;
7th, General Jodl makes final capitulation of Germany to General Dwight Eisenhower near Reims;
8th, 'V.E.' Day; Wilhelm von Keitel surrenders to Zhukov near Berlin;
—, Nationalist riots in Algeria;
—, Spain breaks off diplomatic relations with Germany;
9th, Russians take Prague;
10th, purge of collaborators begins in Prague;
14th, Democratic Republic of Austria established;
25th, W. S. Churchill forms Conservative 'Caretaker' ministry;
28th, French shelling of Damascus angers W. S. Churchill who requires Charles de Gaulle to order a cease-fire in Syria and the Lebanon.

F Jun: 5th, Allied Control Commission assumes control throughout Germany, which is divided into four occupation zones;
10th, José Bustamente becomes President of Peru;
11th, Liberals under Mackenzie King win Canadian elections;
15th, British Parliament prorogued;
20th, Spain is excluded from U.N.;
25th, Sean O'Kelly becomes President of Eire on Douglas Hyde's retirement;
26th, Einar Gerhardsen, Labour, forms coalition in Norway;
28th, Osobka-Morawski forms National Unity government in Poland;
29th, Czechoslovakia cedes Ruthenia to U.S.S.R.

G Jul: 1st, James F. Byrnes succeeds Edward Stettinius as U.S. secretary of state;
3rd, three-power occupation of Berlin takes effect;
5th (–12th) polling in British general election, with 1,675 candidates for 637 seats;
12th, Joseph Chifley becomes premier of Australia on John Curtin's death;
17th (–*Aug.* 2nd), Potsdam Conference, attended by J. Stalin, H. S. Truman, W. S. Churchill and C. R. Attlee, to settle the occupation of Germany;
26th, Labour landslide in British election with 412 seats, against Conservatives and supporters 213, Liberals 12;
—, Britain, U.S. and China demand Japan's unconditional surrender as the terms of peace;
27th, C. R. Attlee forms ministry with Ernest Bevin as Foreign Secretary and Hugh Dalton as Chancellor of Exchequer;
31st, Per Hansson forms Social Democrat cabinet in Sweden.

H Aug: 3rd, Germans and Hungarians in Czechoslovakia deprived of citizenship;
6th, U.S. drops atomic bomb on Hiroshima;

v **The Press**

w **Drama and Entertainment**

Ronald Duncan, *This Way to the Tomb.*

Films:

George Eisenstein's *Ivan the Terrible.*
Jean Renoir's *The Man from the South.*
Roberto Rossellini's *Rome, Open City.*
Billy Wilder's *The Lost Week-end.*
G. Gershwin, *Rhapsody in Blue.*

'Bebop' dancing in U.S.

x **Sport**

y **Statistics**

War casualties, 1939–45: Great Britain, 244,723 killed; 277,090 wounded. Rest of British Commonwealth, 109,929 killed; 197,908 wounded. U.S., 230,173 killed; 613,611 wounded. Germany, 3,000,000 military and civilian dead or missing; *c.* 1,000,000 wounded. U.S.S.R., estimated 20,000,000 military and civilian dead.

Naval losses: Royal Navy: 5 battleships, 8 aircraft carriers, 26 cruisers, 128 destroyers, 77 submarines.

U.S. Navy: 2 battleships, 5 aircraft carriers, 6 escort cruisers, 10 cruisers, 71 destroyers, 52 submarines.

Germany: 7 battleships; 2 heavy cruisers! 5 light cruisers; 25 destroyers and 974 U-boats.

Japan: 12 battleships, 15 aircraft carriers, 4 escort carriers, 16 heavy cruisers, 20 light cruisers, 126 destroyers, 125 submarines.

Merchant shipping losses (in thousand tons): Great Britain, 11,380; U.S., 3,310; Allied, 5,030; Neutral, 1,420; Germany, 8,320.

Railway mileage in operation: U.S., 240,156; U.S.S.R., 52,687; Great Britain, 50,555; France, 6,900.

Religions (in millions): *Christian*, 692 (Roman Catholics, 331; Anglican Communion and Protestant, 206; Orthodox, 144; Coptic, 10). *Non-Christian:* Confucians and Taoists, 351; Hindus, 230; Mohammedans, 209; Buddhists, 230; Animists, 136; Shintoists, 25; Jews, 16.

z **Births and Deaths**

Mar. 26th David, Earl Lloyd George, d. (81).
Apr. 11th Frederick, Lord Lugard, d. (87).
Apr. 12th Franklin Delano Roosevelt d. (63).
Apr. 28th Benito Mussolini d. (61).
Apr. 30th Adolf Hitler d. (56).
July 20th Paul Valéry d. (74).
Sept. 26th Béla Bartók d. (64).
Oct. 15th Pierre Laval d. (62).
Dec. 21st George Smith Patton d. (60).
Dec. 26th Roger, Lord Keynes, d. (73).
Dec. 28th Theodore Dreiser d. (74).

H Aug: 6th, U.S.S.R. declares war on Japan and invades Manchuria;
9th, atomic bomb dropped on Nagasaki;
13th, World Zionist Congress demands admission of 1 million Jews to Palestine;
14th, Japan's surrender ends Second World War;
—, U.S.S.R. treaty with Nationalist China for recognising the independence of Outer Mongolia;
—, General Henri Pétain sentenced to death (commuted to life imprisonment) for collaborating with Hitler;
17th, Dutch refuse to recognise Independent Indonesian Republic;
22nd, Charles de Gaulle's visit to Washington improves Franco-U.S. relations;
24th, Harry S. Truman orders cessation of lend-lease which has cost U.S. $48·5 billion.
28th, U.S. forces land in Japan, with General George Marshall supreme commander of Allied occupation.

J Sep: 2nd, Japan signs capitulation on board U.S.S. *Missouri;* Korea is placed under U.S. and U.S.S.R. occupation until a democratic government is established; Outer Mongolia is recognised as under Soviet control, while China regains sovereignty over Inner Mongolia and Manchuria, Formosa and Hainan;
2nd, independent Viet-Nam Republic formed with Ho Chi-minh President;
10th, Vidkun Quisling sentenced to death in Norway for collaboration;
11th, Allied foreign ministers in London begin drafting peace settlement for Germany;
13th, Iran requests withdrawal of British, U.S. and U.S.S.R. forces;
20th (–23rd), All-India Congress Committee under Gandhi and Pandit Nehru rejects British proposals for self-government and calls on Britain to quit India;
23rd, Egypt demands revision of Anglo-Egyptian 1936 treaty, the end of military occupation and the return of the Sudan;
27th, Congress Party and Muslim League win most seats in elections for Indian Central Legislative Assembly.

K Oct: 7th, Oliveira Salazar permits formation of opposition parties in Portugal but, 14th, reimposes press censorship;
9th, Pierre Laval sentenced to death for collaboration;
11th, breakdown of negotiations between Chiang Kai-shek and Mao Tse-tung leads to fighting between Nationalists and Communists in North China for control of Manchuria;
15th, Labour and Dominion parties in South Africa withdraw from coalition, leaving J. C. Smuts premier of a United Party government;
—, British government takes emergency powers for five years to deal with balance of payments crisis provoked by ending of lend-lease;
20th, Egypt, Iraq, Syria and Lebanon warn U.S. that the creation of a Jewish state in Palestine would lead to war; foundation of Arab League;
21st, swing to Left in elections for French Constituent Assembly, with Communists 152 seats and Socialists 151;
24th, U.N. comes into formal existence with ratification of Charter by 29 nations;
25th, Liberals in Brazil secure resignation of Getulio Vargas and the election of José Linhares as President;
30th, Danish elections leave Social Democrats the strongest single party, but Erik Eriksen forms coalition of Liberals and Conservatives.

L Nov: 3rd, Zoltan Tildy, Smallholders Party, forms coalition in Hungary;
10th, Communist-dominated government of Albania, under Enver Hoxha, recognised by Western powers;
11th, Marshal Tito's National Front wins elections to Yugoslav Constituent Assembly;

(*Continued opposite*)

L **Nov**: 13th, Charles de Gaulle elected President of French Provisional Government;
—, Achmed Soekarno becomes President of Indonesia;
18th, Communist rising in Azerbaijan province, Iran; troops sent to quell it are stopped by U.S.S.R. forces at Kazvin;
—, O. Salazar's National Union Party win Portuguese elections, boycotted by opposition;
—, Communist-dominated Fatherland Front wins Bulgarian elections;
20th, trial of Nazi war criminals before Allied tribunal opens at Nuremberg;
—, Allied Control Commission approves transfer of 6 million Germans from Austria, Hungary and Poland to West Germany pending a peace settlement;
25th, People's Party win Austrian elections;
29th, Federal People's Republic of Yugoslavia proclaimed;
30th, Alcide de Gasperi, leader of Christian Democrats, forms new coalition in Italy following Ferrucio Parri's resignation;
Strikes in U.S. (*–Mar.* 46) hamper production.

M **Dec**: 2nd, Enrico Dutra elected President of Brazil;
4th, Senate approves U.S. participation in U.N.;
6th, U.S. loan to Britain of $3·75 billion;
13th, France and Britain pledge to evacuate troops from Syria;
14th, U.S. sends George Marshall to mediate in Chinese Civil War;
18th, in Austria Leopold Figl, People's Party, forms coalition cabinet with Socialists;
27th, foreign ministers of Britain, U.S. and U.S.S.R., meeting in Moscow, call for provisional democratic government in Korea;
28th, Karl Renner elected President of Austria.

N

1946 (Jan.–May.) First meeting of U.N. General Assembly—The Nuremberg Trials

A Jan: 7th, Austrian Republic with 1937 frontiers is recognised by Western powers;
10th, truce in Chinese Civil War (–*Apr.* 14th);
—, U.N. General Assembly's first session opens in London, with Paul Spaak of Belgium president;
11th, constituent assembly in Albania proclaims a People's Republic;
20th, Charles de Gaulle resigns presidency of French provisional government through continued Communist opposition and is succeeded, 22nd, by the Socialist Félix Gouin;
31st, new Constitution in Yugoslavia, modelled on U.S.S.R.

B Feb: 1st, Trygve Lie, Norwegian Socialist, elected U.N. Secretary-General;
—, Hungarian Republic proclaimed, with Zoltan Tildy, leader of Smallholders Party, President;
13th, Trades Disputes Act, 1927, which had declared certain strikes and lockouts illegal, is repealed in Britain;
14th, Bank of England is nationalised;
17th, Christian Socialists win Belgian elections, but the position of the monarchy hampers the formation of a coalition;
24th, Juan Perón elected President of Argentina;
Strikes of steel and electrical workers in U.S. spread to other industries.

C Mar: 4th, Britain, U.S. and France appeal to the Spanish to depose General Franco;
5th, W. S. Churchill's Fulton speech appeals to the West to stand up to U.S.S.R.;
6th, France recognises Vietnam as a free State within the Indo-Chinese Federation;
10th, Britain and France begin evacuating Lebanon;
15th, U.S.S.R. adopts fourth Five-year Plan;
19th, Soviet council of ministers, with Josef Stalin chairman, replaces council of people's commissars;
22nd, Britain recognises independence of Transjordan (proclaimed *May* 25th);
26th, Allied Control Commission limits level of German production;
29th, new Constitution in Gold Coast, which becomes first British African colony with a majority of Africans in the legislature.

D Apr: 5th, U.S.S.R. agrees to withdraw troops from Iran on promise of reforms in Azerbaijan;
10th, Japanese election favours Moderate parties;
18th, League of Nations assembly dissolves itself;
19th, U.S. recognises Yugoslavia Republic;
21st, Social Democrats in East Germany merge with Communists;
29th, Anglo-U.S. committee advises against partition of Palestine.

E May: 5th, French draft constitution rejected by referendum;
9th, Victor Emmanuel III of Italy abdicates and Umberto II proclaims himself king;
17th, Mitri Antonescu, wartime premier of Roumania, sentenced to death;
—, U.S. government takes over control of railways, dislocated by strikes, and, 20th, coal mines;
20th, bill for nationalisation of coal mines in Britain passes Commons;
26th, Klement Gottwald becomes premier of Czechoslovakia following Communist victories in elections;
30th, Catholic People's Party win Dutch elections and J. Beel forms new coalition.

O **Politics, Economics, Law and Education**

F. Meinecke, *The German Catastrophe.*

Étienne Mantoux, *The Carthaginian Peace.*

Monnet plan for modernising French industry and agriculture.

In Britain the Reith committee reports on the establishment of new towns and the government sets up working parties for various industries.

U.S. Supreme Court rules (*June* 3rd) the segregation of negroes on interstate buses unconstitutional.

The Privy Council maintains the validity of a Canadian bill discontinuing appeals from Canadian courts.

Removal of social disabilities of untouchables in Bombay.

Italy enfranchises women.

P **Science, Technology, Discovery, etc.**

Edward Appleton and Donald Hay discover that sun-spots emit radio waves.

Discovery of carbon-13, an isotope for curing metabolic diseases.

Fairey Aviation Co. construct a pilotless radio-controlled rocket missile.

Electronic brain is built at Pennsylvania University.

Chester Carlson invents xerography.

The magnetic north pole observed by aircraft to be 250 miles north of charted position.

The Williamson diamond mine, Tanganyika, is found to be the world's largest.

Q **Scholarship**

R. A. Knox's translation of New Testament.

New Bodleian Library, Oxford, opened.

R **Philosophy and Religion**

Aldous Huxley, *The Perennial Philosophy.*

Bertrand Russell, *History of Western Philosophy.*

R. G. Collingwood, *The Idea of History* (posth.).

Pope Pius XII creates 32 new cardinals (*Feb.* 8th).

Committee of World Council of Churches drafts plans for a reconstructed world International Assembly.

International Christian Conference at Cambridge aims at closer relations between Protestant and Orthodox Churches.

S **Art, Sculpture, Fine Arts and Architecture**

Painting:

G. Sutherland, *Head of Thorns.*

Ben Nicholson, *Painted Relief, West Penrith.*

Sculpture:

P. Picasso founds the pottery at Vallauris.

T **Music**

The Arts Council is inaugurated in Britain.

B. Britten, *The Rape of Lucretia* (opera).

C. Menotti, *The Medium* (opera).

S. Prokofiev, *War and Peace*; *The Duenna* (operas).

D. Milhaud, 2nd Symphony.

D. Shostakovich, 9th Symphony.

Salzburg Festival reopened (*Aug.* 2nd).

F. Ashton, *Symphonic Variations* (ballet).

G. M. Balanchine, *Night Shadow* (ballet).

Jerome Robbins, *Interplay* and *Fancy Free* (ballets).

F **Jun**: Mouvement Républicain Populaire secures most votes in French elections for constituent assembly, with Communists second;
2nd, Britain and U.S. restore Azores bases to Portugal;
—, Italian referendum in favour of a republic;
3rd, South African Asiatic Land Tenure and Indian Representation bill passed;
—, Umberto II leaves Italy and Alcide de Gasperi, the premier, becomes provisional head of state;
19th, Georges Bidault elected president of French provisional government;
27th, foreign ministers of Britain, U.S., U.S.S.R. and France transfer Dodecanese Islands from Italy to Greece and areas of Northern Italy to France;
28th, Enrico de Nicola elected President of Italy;
—, widespread dismissals for incompetence in U.S.S.R. industries;
30th, referendum in Poland favours a single-house assembly and wide nationalisation.

G **Jul**: 4th, Philippine Republic inaugurated;
7th, election of Miguel Alemán, a civilian, as Mexican President leads to closer ties with U.S.;
14th, anti-Jewish pogrom in Kielce, Poland;
15th, President Truman signs bill of credit for $3.75 billion for Britain.
—, Canadian commission reports on Soviet espionage;
21st, world wheat shortage leads to bread rationing in Britain;
27th, British National Insurance Act consolidates social services;
29th (*–Oct.* 15th), Peace Conference of 21 nations that had opposed the Axis meets in Paris to draft peace treaties.

H **Aug**: 20th, Allied Control Commission dissolves Wehrmacht;
25th, 'closed shop' dispute in British transport industry begins.

J **Sep**: 1st, Greek plebiscite favours the monarchy (and, 28th, George II returns to Athens);
6th, J. F. Byrnes's speech at Stuttgart makes U.S. bid for German co-operation;
15th, People's Republic formed in Bulgaria following a referendum against the monarchy;
18th, Archbishop Stephinac of Croatia imprisoned in Yugoslavia;
30th, in verdicts of Nuremberg Tribunal, Joachim von Ribbentrop, Hermann Göring (who subsequently commits suicide) and ten other leading Nazis sentenced to death; Rudolf Hess and Walter Funk sentenced to life imprisonment; five others receive long sentences, but Dr. H. Schacht and Franz von Papen are acquitted;
London conference on Palestine meets (*–Dec.*), but is boycotted by Zionists.

K **Oct**: 5th, Tage Erlander, Social Democrat, becomes premier of Sweden on Per Hansson's death;
13th, revised French Constitution adopted with many abstentions;
—, Siam accepts U.N. verdict for returning territory to Indo-China;
23rd, U.N. General Assembly meets in New York;
30th, Britain co-ordinates armed services under a single defence committee;
Spain signs commercial agreement with Argentina following Perón's visit to Franco.

U **Literature**

Simone de Beauvoir, *Tous les hommes sont mortels.*
J. J. Gautier, *Histoire d'un fait divers.*
André Gide, *Journal, 1939–42.*
Dylan Thomas, *Deaths and Entrances.*
Robert Penn Warren, *All the King's Men.*

V **The Press**

Le Temps exonerated from the charge of collaborationist activities.
New governing body established to maintain independence of *The Observer.*

W **Drama and Entertainment**

Jean Cocteau, *L'Aigle a deux têtes.*
Eugene O'Neill, *The Iceman Cometh.*
T. Rattigan, *The Winslow Boy.*
J.-P. Sartre, *Morts sans sépulture.*

Films:
Frank Capra, *It's a Wonderful World.*
Marcel Carné, *Les Portes de la Nuit.*
J. Cocteau, *La Belle et la Bête.*
Vittorio de Sica, *Shoeshine.*
David Lean, *Great Expectations.*
Roberto Rossellini, *Paisa.*
William Wyler, *The Best Years of Our Lives.*
British TV service resumed (*June* 7th), with under 12,000 viewers.
B.B.C. Third Programme (for cultural entertainment) inaugurated (*Sept.* 29th).

X **Sport**

Joe Louis successfully defends title as world heavyweight champion for 23rd time.
Australia under Donald Bradman retain ashes in M.C.C. tour (–*Mar.* 1947).

Y **Statistics**

Populations (in mill.): China, 455; India, 311; U.S.S.R., 194; U.S., 140; Japan, 73; West Germany, 48; Italy, 47; Britain, 46; Brazil, 45; France, 40; Spain, 27; Poland, 24; Korea, 24; Mexico, 22; East Germany, 18; Egypt, 17.
European coal production (in mill. tons): Britain, 189; West Germany, 67; France, 53; Poland, 48; Belgium, 25; Holland, 9.
Petroleum production (in mill. tons): U.S., 250; Central and South America, 82; U.S.S.R., 26; Persia, 20; Saudi Arabia, 12; other Middle East states, 9; Roumania, 4.
Merchant fleets (tonnage in mill.): U.S., 57; British Empire, 20; Norway, 4; Holland, 2·1; Greece, 1·7; France, 1·3; U.S.S.R., 1·2.

L Nov: 3rd, power in Japan transferred from Emperor to elected assembly;
4th, Chinese-U.S. treaty of friendship and commerce;
—, Republicans (246 seats) win U.S. Congressional elections (with Democrats holding 188 seats);
6th, British National Health Act in force;
—, Royal Commission favours equal pay for women in Britain;
9th, President Truman removes controls, excepting those on certain food stocks and rent;
10th, elections to French national assembly give Communists 186 seats, M.R.P. 166 and Socialists 103, resulting in political deadlock;
15th, Holland recognises Indonesian Republic;
21st, Georgi Dimitrov returns from Moscow to become premier of Bulgaria;
26th, Labour retains power in New Zealand elections;
28th, nationalisation of transport bill published in London.

M Dec: 2nd, J. F. Byrnes and Ernest Bevin agree to economic fusion of British and U.S. zones of Germany;
5th, New York City is chosen as permanent headquarters of U.N.;
9th, Indian constituent assembly, boycotted by Moslem League, discusses independence;
11th, U.N. bars Spain from its activities and
14th, rejects South African proposal for incorporation of South-West Africa;
16th, Léon Blum forms Socialist government in France;
30th, U.N. atomic energy commission approves U.S. plan for control.

N Douglas MacArthur purges extreme nationalists in Japan and orders Japanese war criminals to be tried by military tribunals.
During massive strikes 116 million working-days lost in U.S., compared with 2·2 million in Britain.

z **Births and Deaths**

Jan. 29th Harry L. Hopkins d. (56).
Mar. 2nd Logan Pearsall Smith d. (80).
Apr. 21st John Maynard, Lord Keynes, d. (60).
June 3rd Michael Ivanovich Kalinin d. (71).
June 8th Gerhart Hauptmann d. (83).
June 14th John Logie Baird d. (58).
July 29th Gertrude Stein d. (72).
Aug. 13th Herbert George Wells d. (70).
Aug. 31st Harley Granville-Barker d. (69).
Sept. 16th James Jeans d. (69).
Sept. 16th Granville Bantock d. (78).
Dec. 10th Damon Runyan d. (62).

1947 (Jan.–Jun.) The Truman Doctrine—Marshall Aid—Independence of India and Pakistan— The Cominform founded

A **Jan:** 1st, British coal industry becomes nationalised;
—, Nigeria acquires modified self-government;
7th, George Marshall succeeds John F. Byrnes as U.S. secretary of state;
16th, Vincent Auriol elected President of France;
21st, J. C. Smuts refuses to place South-West Africa under U.N. trusteeship;
—, P. Ramadier forms coalition in France, on Léon Blum's resignation;
26th, Egypt breaks off diplomatic relations with Britain, for revising 1936 treaty, and for stating she will prepare the Sudan for self-government, and refers the question to the U.N.;
27th, Regional Advisory Commission for the Pacific established;
29th, U.S. abandons efforts at mediation in China.

B **Feb:** 1st, in Italy Alcide de Gasperi forms new ministry of Christian Democrats, Communists and Left Socialists;
7th, British proposal for dividing Palestine into Arab and Jewish zones with administration as a trusteeship is rejected by Arabs and Jews;
10th, by the peace treaties, signed in Paris, (i) Italy loses Adriatic Islands and part of Venezia Giulia to Yugoslavia, the Dodecanese Islands to Greece and small frontier regions to France, renounces her sovereignty over North African colonies, agrees to the establishment of Trieste as a free territory, pays reparations and reduces her forces to 300,000 men; (ii) Roumania loses Bessarabia and North Bukovina to U.S.S.R., but regains Transylvania; (iii) Bulgaria retains South Dobrudja; (iv) Hungary is reassigned 1938 frontiers; and (v) Finland cedes Petsamo to U.S.S.R.;
(*–Apr.*), fuel crisis in Britain.

C **Mar:** 3rd, N. I. Bulganin replaces Josef Stalin as U.S.S.R. defence minister;
4th, Anglo-French treaty of alliance;
10th (*–Apr.* 24th), Moscow Conference of foreign ministers fails through division between the West and U.S.S.R. over problem of Germany;
12th, Harry S. Truman in message to Congress outlines the Truman Doctrine of economic and military aid to states threatened by Communism, in announcing plan to aid Greece and Turkey;
19th, Paul Spaak forms coalition of Catholics and Socialists in Belgium;
—, Chinese Nationalists capture Communist capital of Yenan;
29th, nationalist revolt against France in Madagascar (*–July*).

D **Apr:** 2nd, U.N. Security Council appoints U.S. Trustee for Pacific islands formerly under Japanese mandate;
—, Britain refers Palestine question to U.N.;
14th, Charles de Gaulle assumes control of Rassemblement du Peuple Français (R.P.F.), to rally non-Communists in France to unity and reform;
16th, ex-President Joseph Tiso of Slovakia executed.

E **May:** 29th, Indian constituent assembly outlaws 'untouchability';
31st, Alcide de Gasperi forms government of Christian Socialists and Independents in Italy (following resignation, 13th, through friction with the Left);
—, Ferenc Nagy, premier of Hungary, falls; succeeded by Lajos Dinnyes, Smallholder;
Serious strikes in France.

F **Jun:** 2nd, German Economic Council is established;
5th, George Marshall calls for a European Recovery Programme (Marshall Aid) in Harvard speech;
17th, Burmese constituent assembly resolves for an independent republic of Burma;

O **Politics, Economics, Law and Education**

L. S. Amery, *Thoughts on the Constitution.*

G. D. H. Cole, *The Intelligent Man's Guide to the Post-War World.*

Oliver Franks, *Central Planning and Control in War and Peace.*

R. B. McCallum and Alison Readman, pioneer analysis, *The British General Election of 1945.*

Commonwealth Relations Office and Colonial Development Corporation established.

Rationing abolished in U.S.S.R. (*Dec.* 14th).

U.S. Air Force becomes independent of Army.

Old People (ed. Seebohm Rowntree).

Basic English Foundation promoted by C. K. Ogden.

P **Science, Technology, Discovery, etc.**

Britain's first atomic pile at Harwell comes into operation (*Aug.*).

British government sets up Advisory Committee on Scientific Policy.

P. M. S. Blackett's theory that all massive rotating bodies are magnetic.

The reflecting microscope is developed.

L. Essen determines the speed of radio waves in a vacuum.

First supersonic air flight.

First transatlantic automatic flight.

Capt. Odom flies round world in 73 hrs. 5 mins. (*Aug.*).

John Cobb's ground world speed record of 394·196 m.p.h. (*Sept.* 16th).

Q **Scholarship**

Discovery of main series of Dead Sea Scrolls.

H. W. Garrod, *Scholarship; Its Meaning and Value.*

F. M. Powicke, *King Henry III and the Lord Edward.*

Documents on British Diplomatic History, 1919–39, Vol. I.

H. R. Trevor-Roper, *The Last Days of Hitler.*

R **Philosophy and Religion**

E. F. Carritt, *Ethical and Political Thinking.*

A. Ruggiero, *Existentialism.*

Bishop E. W. Barnes, *The Rise of Christianity.*

C. S. Lewis, *Miracles.*

Michael Polanyi, *Science, Faith and Society.*

S **Art, Sculpture, Fine Arts and Architecture**

Painting:

W. S. Churchill, *The Loop River, Quebec.*

M. Vlaminck, *A Bunch of Flowers.*

The cleaning of Rembrandt's *Woman Bathing* and other pictures in the National Gallery provokes controversy on the principles of cleaning canvases.

Sculpture:

H. Moore, *Three Standing Figures.*

A. Gicometti, *Man Pointing.*

Architecture:

Le Corbusier (pseud.), Unité d'habitation, Marseilles.

T **Music**

Benjamin Britten, *Albert Herring* (opera).

William Walton, String Quartet in A minor.

F Jun: 23rd, U.S. Congress passes Taft-Hartley act over President Truman's veto, prohibiting use of union funds for political purposes, outlawing the 'closed shop' and strengthening the government's hands in strikes and lockouts.

G Jul: 6th, Spanish bill of succession for changing government to a monarchy on General Franco's death or resignation;
12th (–15th), 16 West European nations meet in Paris to discuss Marshall Plan for economic recovery;
20th, Dutch troops launch new offensive in Java against Indonesian forces;
28th, National Peasant Party is dissolved in Roumania.

H Aug: 1st, U.N. Security Council calls for cease-fire in Indonesia (leads to truce *Jan.* 17th 1948);
15th, Independence of India proclaimed, partitioning India; Pandit Nehru premier of India and L. Ali Khan premier of Pakistan; British authority in remaining states ends; acts of violence in Punjab between Moslems and Hindus follow;
31st, Communist successes in Hungarian elections.

J Sep: 2nd, American republics sign treaty of mutual assistance at Rio de Janeiro;
14th, Poland denounces concordat with Catholic Church;
26th, Stephen Senanayake becomes premier of Ceylon;
30th, Pakistan and the Yemen are admitted to U.N.

K Oct: 5th, Warsaw Communist conference establishes the Cominform (Communist Information Bureau) to co-ordinate activities of European Communist Parties;
19th (–26th), Charles de Gaulle's R.P.F. becomes strongest group in French municipal elections;
21st, U.N. General Assembly calls on Greece and Balkan powers to settle disputes by peaceful means;
26th, Kashmir is admitted into Indian Union, provoking crisis with Pakistan;
29th, Belgium, Netherlands and Luxembourg ratify customs union (Benelux), which becomes effective *Nov.* 1st.

L Nov: 1st, Conservative gains in British municipal elections;
13th, Social Democrats form minority cabinet in Denmark;
14th, U.N. General Assembly recognises Korea's claim to independence;
19th, P. Ramadier resigns, and 23rd, Robert Schuman forms ministry supported by Socialists and M.R.P.;
20th, Princess Elizabeth marries Philip Mountbatten, Duke of Edinburgh;
22nd, Iran assembly nullifies oil agreement with U.S.S.R.;
25th (–*Dec.* 16th), London Conference of powers on Germany fails through U.S.S.R. demands for reparations;
27th, nationalisation of Australian banks;
29th, U.N. announces plan for partition of Palestine, with Jerusalem under U.N. Trusteeship.

M Dec: 14th, Rómulo Gallegos, Democratic Action, elected President of Venezuela;
16th, U.S.S.R. currency devalued;
19th, Roumanian-Yugoslav treaty of friendship;
22nd, new Constitution in Italy centralises government and provides for popularly elected Senate;
27th, Greek government dissolves Communist Party and E.A.M.;
30th, Kashmir conflict referred to U.N.;
30th, King Michael of Roumania abdicates, under Communist pressure.

N

U **Literature**

Thomas Armstrong, *King Cotton.*
Nigel Balchin, *Lord I Was Afraid.*
Albert Camus, *The Plague.*
Kathleen Knott, *Landscapes and Departures.*
St. John Perse (pseud.), *Vents.*

V **The Press**

Size of British newspapers reduced and publication of magazines curtailed through fuel crisis (*Feb.* 17th–*Mar.* 3rd). Further reductions in size enforced on *July* 21st.

W **Drama and Entertainment**

Edinburgh Festival of the Arts is established.
Christopher Fry and Jean Anouilh, *Ring Round the Moon* (English version of the latter's *L'Invitation au Château*).
W. Douglas Home, *The Chiltern Hundreds.*
J. B. Priestley, *The Linden Tree.*
Tennessee Williams, *A Streetcar Named Desire.*

Films:
Charlie Chaplin's *Monsieur Verdoux.*
René Clair's *Le Silence est d'or.*
Henri Clouzot's *Quai des Orfèvres.*
Carol Reed's *Odd Man Out.*
Robert Hamer's *It Always Rains on Sunday.*

X **Sport**

Y **Statistics**

Religious denominations in U.S. (in mill.): Roman Catholics, 25·2; Baptists, 15; Methodists, 10·3; Lutherans, 5·2; Protestant Episcopal, 2·1; Mormons, 1.

Z **Births and Deaths**

Apr. 7th Henry Ford d. (82).
May 8th Henry Gordon Selfridge d. (90).
June 6th James Agate d. (69).
Aug. 8th Anton Denikin d. (74).
Aug. 21st Ettore Bugatti d. (65).
Sept. 20th Fionello Henry La Guardia d. (64).
Oct. 4th Max Planck d. (89).
Oct. 31st Sidney Webb, Lord Passfield, d. (88).
Dec. 14th Stanley, Earl Baldwin, d. (80).
Dec. 30th A. N. Whitehead d. (86).

1948 (Jan.–Jul.) Brussels Treaty—End of British Mandate in Palestine—Berlin blockade

A **Jan**: 1st, nationalisation of British Railways in force;
4th, Union of Burma proclaimed as an independent republic;
17th, Netherlands and Republic of Indonesia sign truce;
20th, Mahatma Gandhi is assassinated by a Hindu.

B **Feb**: 2nd, U.S. and Italy sign ten-year treaty of friendship and commerce;
4th, Ceylon becomes a self-governing dominion;
25th, Communist *coup d'état* in Czechoslovakia.

C **Mar**: 17th, Britain, France, Belgium, Netherlands and Luxembourg sign Brussels Treaty, for 50-year alliance against armed attack in Europe and providing for economic, social and military co-operation;
20th, U.S.S.R. delegates walk out of Allied Control Commission for Germany;
26th, Franco-Italian customs union concluded;
29th, Chiang Kai-shek, re-elected President of China by Nanking Assembly, is granted dictatorial powers;
31st, U.S. Congress passes Marshall Aid Act, contributing $5·3 billion for European recovery.

D **Apr**: 1st, U.S.S.R. begins to interfere with traffic between Berlin and West Germany;
6th, Central Legislature of British East Africa holds first sessions at Nairobi;
—, U.S.S.R. treaty of mutual assistance with Finland, aimed at Germany;
13th, Roumanian Constitution is remodelled on Soviet lines;
16th, Paris meeting of nations of European Recovery Programme sets up Organisation for European Economic Co-operation (O.E.E.C.);
18th, Christian Democrats win absolute majority in Italian elections.

E **May**: 7th, Hague congress of movement for European unity under W. S. Churchill;
11th, Luigi Einaudi elected President of Italy;
14th, as British mandate in Palestine ends a Jewish provisional government is formed in Israel with Chaim Weizmann President and David Ben-Gurion premier; the Arab Legion of Transjordan invades Palestine and enters Jerusalem;
15th, Egyptian troops intervene in Palestine on side of Arabs;
26th, in South African election J. C. Smuts's coalition of United and Labour parties is defeated by Nationalist Afrikander bloc, standing on *apartheid* platform;
28th, North Korea boycotts national constitutional assembly at Seoul.

F **Jun**: 1st, Britain, U.S., France and Benelux countries call for German representation in European Recovery Programme and for drafting of a federal constitution for Germany;
3rd, Daniel F. Malan forms Nationalist-Afrikander ministry in South Africa;
14th, Klement Gottwald elected President of Czechoslovak People's Republic;
18th, reform of West German currency;
19th, U.S. selective service bill for men aged 19 to 25;
28th, Yugoslavia is expelled from Cominform for hostility to U.S.S.R.

G **Jul**: 8th, William Drees, Labour, forms coalition in Holland;
15th, U.N. Security Council orders truce in Palestine;
24th, U.S.S.R. stops road and rail traffic between Berlin and the West forcing Western powers to organise airlifts (–*Sept.* 1949);
29th, Marshal Tito denies Cominform charges and is given vote of confidence by Yugoslav Communist Party, which is later purged of Cominform supporters;
30th, British Citizenship Act confers status of British subjects on all Commonwealth citizens;

O **Politics, Economics, Law and Education**

P. M. S. Blackett, *Military and Political Consequences of Atomic Energy.*

J. Jewkes, *Ordeal by Planning.*

First annual British Economic Survey.

Belgium enfranchises women; abolition of plural voting in Britain ends 'University seats'.

First World Health Assembly, Geneva (*June*).

Bread rationing in Britain ends (*July* 25th).

Institute of Advanced Legal Studies, London, founded.

British Electricity Authority takes over electrical industry.

P **Science, Technology, Discovery, etc.**

T. D. Lynsenko's denunciation of non-Michurin geneticists in U.S.S.R. leads to purges of scientific committees.

H. J. Fleure, *Some Aspects of British Civilisation.*

L. Jánossy, *Cosmic Rays and Nuclear Physics.*

Arthur Keith, *A New Theory of Human Evolution.*

Preparation of antibiotics, aureomycin and chloromycetin.

Peter Goldmark invents the long-playing record.

Transistor invented by Bell Telephone Company scientists.

Port radar installation at Liverpool Docks to supervise shipping approaches in fog, etc.

International Conference for redistribution of wavelengths (*Sept.* 15th).

Auguste Piccard constructs bathyscaphe for deep descents.

Wilfred Thesiger crosses Arabian desert and penetrates Oman Steppes.

A. C. Kinsey (and others), *Sexual Behaviour in the Human Male.*

Q **Scholarship**

British Institute of Archaeology, Ankara, opened.

J. W. Carter and Graham Pollard, *Thomas J. Wise in the Original Cloth* (investigations of Wise's literary forgeries).

W. S. Churchill, *The Gathering Storm* (first volume of *The Second World War*).

The White House Papers of Harry L. Hopkins.

L. B. Namier, *Diplomatic Prelude, 1938–9.*

R **Philosophy and Religion**

G. K. A. Bell, *Christian Unity.*

W. R. Inge, *Mysticism in Religion.*

Representatives of 147 churches from 44 countries meet in Amsterdam to inaugurate the World Council of Churches.

World Jewish Congress, Montreux.

S **Art, Sculpture, Fine Arts and Architecture**

Painting:

W. S. Churchill, who is made Honorary Academician Extraordinary, paints *The Goldfish Pool, Chartwell* and publishes *Painting as a Pastime.*

F. Léger, *Homage to David.*

Jackson Pollock, *Composition No. 1* (tachisma).

Sculpture:

Henry Moore, *Family Group* for Stevenage New Town.

Architecture:

Pier Luigi Nervi, Exhibition Hall, Turin (single-roof structure, in undulating prefabrication).

T **Music**

G **Jul**: 30th (–*Aug.* 18th), Conference of ten nations meets in Belgrade to consider the future of the R. Danube;

—, Zoltan Tildy is forced to resign in Hungary;

Amnesty is proclaimed in the Philippines, but the rebels refuse to comply.

H **Aug**: 10th, Gaston Eyskens, Christian Socialist, forms coalition in Belgium with Liberal support;

15th, Republic of Korea proclaimed in Seoul, with Syngman Rhee President;

25th, U.S.S.R. breaks off relations with U.S. for refusing to surrender a Soviet citizen against her will.

J **Sep**: 1st, Communists announce formation of a North China People's Republic;

4th, Queen Wilhelmina abdicates in Netherlands for health reasons; succeeded, 6th, by Queen Juliana;

5th, Wladyslaw Gomulka, leader of Communist Polish Workers' Party, is forced to resign for deviations;

9th, Korean People's Democratic Republic formed in North Korea, claiming authority over entire country;

10th, Henri Queuille, Radical, forms ministry in France, with Robert Schuman foreign minister;

17th, Count Folke Bernadotte, U.N. mediator in Palestine, assassinated by Jewish terrorists;

—, Hyderabad surrenders to Indian forces and agrees to join Indian Union;

18th, Indonesian Communists set up a Soviet government in Java, but are forced to withdraw;

24th, first conference in London of representatives from Britain's African colonies.

K **Oct**: 7th, Democratic-Liberal government formed in Japan by Shigeru Yoshida;

25th, U.S.S.R. vetoes proposal of non-permanent members of U.N. Security Council for ending Berlin blockade;

29th, military junta ends José Bustamente's government in Peru.

L **Nov**: 2nd, in U.S. presidential election, Harry S. Truman, Democrat, wins 303 electoral votes against Thomas E. Dewey, Republican, 189, confounding public opinion polls, and Democrats gain majority in both Houses;

7th, Charles de Gaulle's R.P.F. gains large number of seats in French elections for the Council of the Republic;

12th, Hideki Tojo and other Japanese war criminals sentenced by international military tribunal;

27th, C. R. Attlee appoints Lynskey tribunal to investigate charges of corruption against minister and officials.

M **Dec**: 1st, Arab Congress at Jericho proclaims Abdullah of Transjordan as King of Palestine;

5th, Ernst Reuter, Social Democrat, elected mayor of Berlin;

9th (–10th), U.N. General Assembly adopts convention on prevention and punishment of genocide and the declaration of human rights;

12th, conscription in Britain for men aged 18 to 26;

18th, following breakdown of negotiations the Dutch renew the offensive in Indonesia and capture the Soekarno government;

27th, refusal of Catholics in Hungary to make concessions to government leads to arrest of Cardinal Mindszenty;

(*Continued opposite*)

U **Literature**

Harold Acton, *Memoirs of An Aesthete.*
T. S. Eliot, *Notes Towards the Definition of Culture.*
Graham Greene, *The Heart of the Matter.*
A. Huxley, *Ape and Essence.*
Norman Mailer, *The Naked and the Dead.*
Howard Spring, *There is no Armour.*

V **The Press**

W **Drama and Entertainment**

Entertainment tax on British theatres is halved.
Christopher Fry, *The Lady's Not for Burning.*
Aldous Huxley, *The Gioconda Smile.*
T. Rattigan, *The Browning Version.*

Films:
Frank Capra's *The State of the Union.*
Jules Dassin's *The Naked City.*
Vittorio de Sica's *Bicycle Thieves.*
Carol Reed's *The Fallen Idol.*
Giuseppe de Santis's *Bitter Rice.*
Laurence Olivier's *Hamlet.*

B.B.C.'s 'Any Questions?'

X **Sport**

Y **Statistics**

Pig-iron production (in thousand tons): U.S., 55,085; U.S.S.R., 14,000; Great Britain, 9,425; France, 6,625; West Germany, 4,670 (with Saar, 1,125): Belgium, 3,943.
Steel production (in thousand tons): U.S., 80, 285; U.S.S.R., 16,500; Great Britain, 15,116; France, 7,255; West Germany, 5,278 (with Saar, 1,212); Belgium, 3,917.

Z **Births and Deaths**

Jan. 30th Gandhi d. (79), and Orville Wright d. (76).
Sept. 3rd Edouard Beneš d. (65).
Sept. 11th Ali Jinnah d. (71).
Oct. 18th Walther von Brauchitsch d. (67).
Nov. 14th Prince Charles b. (–).

M **Dec**: 28th, U.S., Britain, France and Benelux countries constitute themselves an International Ruhr Authority;
—, Nokrashy Pasha, premier of Egypt, assassinated.

N

1949 (Jan.–May.) North Atlantic Treaty—Apartheid—Sterling devalued —Establishment of Communist Republic of China

A **Jan**: 7th, Dean Acheson succeeds George Marshall as U.S. secretary of state;
15th, Tientsin falls to the Communists;
18th, Council for Mutual Economic Assistance formed in Moscow to further economic co-operation between U.S.S.R. and her satellites (Poland joins the Council, 25th);
20th, President Harry S. Truman, in inaugural address, states Four-Point programme, including economic aid for underdeveloped countries;
—, U.N. Security Council calls for end of hostilities in Burma;
21st, Chiang Kai-shek resigns presidency of China, following succession of reversals for Nationalist Armies.

B **Feb**: 1st, clothes rationing ends in Britain;
8th, Eire declares she is unable to participate in N.A.T.O. while Ireland remains divided.

C **Mar**: 4th, A. Vyshinsky replaces V. Molotov as U.S.S.R. foreign minister;
8th, France recognises non-Communist Viet-Nam Nationalists under Bao Dai as an independent state within the French Union;
13th, Belgium, Netherlands and Luxembourg agree to implement full economic union as soon as possible, and, 26th, France and Italy sign corresponding agreement;
31st, Newfoundland joins Dominion of Canada as tenth province.

D **Apr**: 4th, North Atlantic Treaty signed in Washington by foreign ministers of Britain, France, Belgium, Netherlands, Italy, Portugal, Denmark, Iceland, Norway, U.S. and Canada for mutual assistance against aggression in North Atlantic;
9th, U.N. International Court of Justice delivers first decision, holding Albania responsible for incidents in Corfu Channel in 1946 and awarding damages to Britain;
18th, Republic of Eire is formally proclaimed in Dublin;
19th, U.S. Foreign Assistance bill authorises $5·43 billion for European Recovery Programme.

E **May**: 5th, Statute of Council of Europe, establishing Committee of Ministers and a Consultative Assembly, signed in London by Belgium, Denmark, France, Britain, Ireland, Italy, Luxembourg, the Netherlands, Norway and Sweden (and subsequently by Greece, Iceland and Turkey); Strasbourg is chosen as seat of Council;
11th, Israel is admitted to U.N.;
—, Siam changes name to Thailand;
12th, Berlin blockade is officially lifted;
—, Far Eastern Commission terminates Japan's reparation payments to aid Japanese recovery;
14th, U.N. General Assembly invites India, Pakistan and South Africa to discuss alleged discrimination against Indian races in South Africa;
17th, Britain recognises independence of Eire, but re-affirms position of Northern Ireland within the U.K.;
23rd, German Federal Republic comes into force, with capital at Bonn;
Communist Armies in China resume offensive, to drive Nationalist Armies off the mainland.

O **Politics, Economics, Law and Education**
J. D. Bernal, *The Freedom of Necessity*.
N. Mansergh, *The Commonwealth and the Nations*.
Roy Lewis and Angus Maude, *The English Middle Classes*.
Bertrand Russell's Reith Lectures, *Authority and the Individual*.
UNESCO symposium on *Human Rights* (ed. J. Maritain).
Walter Moberly, *The Crisis in the University*.
University College of North Staffordshire founded under Lord Lindsay (becomes Keele University, 1962).

P **Science, Technology, Discovery, etc.**
Philip Hench discovers Cortisone (compound E) as cure for rheumatism.
Selman A. Waksman isolates neomycin.
First atomic bomb tests in U.S.S.R.

Q **Scholarship**
J. E. Neale, *The Elizabethan House of Commons*.
W. K. Hancock and M. M. Gowing, *British War Economy* (Official History, Civil Series).

R **Philosophy and Religion**
E. Fromm, *Man for Himself*.
A. Koestler, *Insight and Outlook*.
E. Mascall, *Existence and Analogy*.
Paul Tillich, *The Shaking of the Foundations*.
The Bible in Basic English.

S **Art, Sculpture, Fine Arts and Architecture**
Painting:
V. Passmore, *Spiral Motives*.
Graham Sutherland's portrait of W. S. Maugham.
Kenneth Clark publishes *Landscape into Art*.
Sculpture:
J. Epstein, *Lazarus*.
Architecture:
F. L. Wright, Laboratory tower for S. C. Johnson & Son, Wisconsin.

T **Music**
A. Bliss, *The Olympians* (opera).
G. Finzi, Clarinet Concerto.
A. Rawsthorne, concerto for string orchestra.
E. Rubbra's Mass *In Honorem Sancti Domini*.
Cranko-Sibelius, *Sea Change* (ballet).

U **Literature**
H. E. Bates, *The Jacaranda Tree*.
S. de Beauvoir, *The Second Sex*.
Joyce Cary, *A Fearful Joy*.
Paul Eluard, *Une Leçon de morale*.
Nancy Mitford, *Love in a Cold Climate*.
Charles Morgan, *The River Line*.
George Orwell (pseud.), *Nineteen Eighty-four*.

V **The Press**

F Jun: 2nd, Transjordan is renamed the Hashemite Kingdom of Jordan;
14th, Viet-Nam State is established at Saigon under Bao Dai, but conflict with Communists continues;
16th, Communist purge in Hungary;
27th, Liberal majority in Canadian elections;
29th, U.S. completes withdrawal of occupying forces from South Korea;
British dock strike;
South African Citizenship Act suspends automatic granting of citizenship to Commonwealth immigrants after five years, and ban on mixed marriages between Europeans and non-Europeans begins *Apartheid* programme.

G Jul: 16th, Chinese Nationalists organise Supreme Council under Chiang Kai-shek, which begins to remove forces to Formosa (completed, *Dec.* 8th);
18th, fresh agreement between Iran and Anglo-Iranian Oil Company (but is later rejected by Iran assembly);
29th, U.N. Atomic Energy Commission suspends meetings until a broader basis for agreement among powers is reached.

H Aug: 5th, U.S. aid to Nationalist China ceases;
10th, U.S. Defense Department is statutorily established;
—, Christian Socialists and Liberals form coalition ministry in Belgium;
15th, emergency legislation, authorising troops to work mines, ends Australian coal strike (begun *June* 27th).

J Sep: 2nd, U.N. Commission warns of danger of civil war in Korea;
15th, Theodor Heuss, Free Democrat, elected President and Konrad Adenauer, Christian Democrat, chancellor of West Germany;
18th, Britain devalues £ (from exchange rate of $4·03 to $2·80), and subsequently most European states devalue their currencies;
21st, Allied High Commission in Germany takes over functions of Allied Military Government;
27th, U.S.S.R. denounces treaty with Yugoslavia;
30th, Berlin Airlift ends, after 277,264 flights.

K Oct: 1st, Communist People's Republic of China proclaimed at Peiping under Mao Tse-tung, with Chou En-lai premier and foreign minister;
—, Bulgaria and, 21st, Roumania denounce treaties of friendship with Yugoslavia;
6th, President Truman signs Mutual Defense Assistance Act for military aid to N.A.T.O. countries;
7th, Democratic Republic established in East Germany with Wilhelm Pieck President and Otto Grotewohl minister-president;
9th, Socialist losses in Austrian elections;
14th, American Communist Party leaders convicted of conspiracy;
16th, defeat of rebels ends Greek Civil War (since *May* 1946);
28th, Georges Bidault forms coalition in France, following Henri Queuille's resignation over financial crisis.

L Nov: 11th (–13th), Polish United Workers' Party is purged of members with Titoist leanings;
21st, U.N. General Assembly votes for ultimate independence of Italy's former colonies;
24th, nationalisation of British iron and steel industries in force;
—, Allied High Commission makes further economic concessions to West Germany on her joining International Ruhr Authority;
26th, India adopts Constitution as a federal republic, remaining within the Commonwealth.

(*Continued opposite*)

W **Drama and Entertainment**
T. S. Eliot, *The Cocktail Party*.
Arthur Miller, *Death of a Salesman*.
Berliner Ensemble formed.

Films:
Anthony Asquith's *The Winslow Boy*.
Carol Reed's *The Third Man*, with Orson Welles.
Jean Melville's *Les Enfants terribles*.
Robert Rossen's *All The King's Men*.

X **Sport**

Y **Statistics**

Z **Births and Deaths**
Jan. 9th Thomas Handley d. (55).
Jan. 21st J. H. Thomas d. (74).
Feb. 11th Axel Munthe d. (91).
May 6th Maurice Maeterlinck d. (86).
Sept. 8th Richard Strauss d. (85).
Oct. 30th Edward R. Stettinius d. (49).

M **Dec**: 5th, U.N. General Assembly requires member states to submit information on armaments and armed forces, and
8th, calls on powers to recognise political independence of China;
14th, Israeli government moves capital from Tel Aviv to Jerusalem, disregarding U.N. resolution for internationalisation of Jerusalem;
15th, West Germany becomes full member of Marshall Plan;
16th, British Parliament bill reduces power of Lords to veto legislation;
17th, Robert Menzies, Liberal, forms new coalition in Australia;
27th, Holland transfers sovereignty to United States of Indonesia;
30th, France transfers sovereignty to Viet-Nam.

N

1950 (Jan.–May) Korean war begins—The Colombo Plan—The Schuman Plan

A **Jan**: 3rd, Wafdists return to power in Egyptian election;
5th, Alexander Diomedes, premier of Greece, resigns and his successor, Theotokis, experiences great difficulty throughout the year in forming stable government;
6th, Britain recognises Communist China;
—, Franco-German parliamentary conference in Basle;
9th, Colombo Conference of Commonwealth foreign ministers meets to prepare plans for co-operating in the economic development of Asiatic states;
12th, Nahas Pasha forms Egyptian government which includes all ministers dismissed in 1944;
—, state of emergency in Gold Coast caused by strikes;
—, capital punishment reintroduced in U.S.S.R.;
14th, Mohammed Said forms Persian government;
25th, Alger Hiss found guilty in U.S. of perjury in concealing membership of Communist Party;
27th, N.A.T.O. bilateral agreement by which U.S. provides arms to its associates signed in Washington;
—, Alcide de Gasperi forms new coalition in Italy on the withdrawal of Liberal support;
29th, first series of riots in Johannesburg provoked by racial policy;
30th, Britain, Norway, Denmark and Sweden sign agreement for economic co-operation;
31st, President Truman instructs U.S. Atomic Energy Commission to proceed with development of the hydrogen bomb.

B **Feb**: 1st, Vlko Chervenkov becomes premier of Bulgaria on Vasil Kolarov's death;
13th, Bangkok conference of heads of U.S. missions in Asiatic countries for supporting moves for independence;
14th, U.S.S.R. and Communist China sign 30-year treaty in Moscow;
20th, U.S. severs relations with Bulgaria;
23rd, British general election results in a reduced Labour majority (315 seats, Conservatives 298, Liberals 9);
28th, C. R. Attlee reconstructs his ministry.

C **Mar**: 1st, Klaus Fuchs found guilty of betraying atomic secrets to U.S.S.R. agents;
—, Chiang Kai-shek resumes presidency of Nationalist China;
3rd, France confirms autonomy of the Saar;
8th, Marshal Voroshilov states U.S.S.R. possesses the atomic bomb;
12th, Belgian referendum in favour of King Leopold III's return (government resigns, 18th, through disagreement on the question of his return);
16th, Dean Acheson's suggestions to U.S.S.R. for ending the cold war;
21st, Konrad Adenauer advocates economic union between France and Germany;
31st, House of Representatives passes foreign aid bill of $3,100 million.

D **Apr**: 1st, Britain transfers Somaliland trusteeship to Italy;
8th, Delhi pact between India and Pakistan on treatment of minorities;
11th, U.S.S.R. note to U.S. about a U.S. bomber over the Baltic;
19th, London dock strike (–*May* 1st);
27th, Communist Party is outlawed in Australia;
—, Britain recognises Israel.

E **May**: 9th, Schuman plan, for placing French and German coal industry and iron and steel production under a single authority, announced;

O **Politics, Economics, Law and Education**

A. Koestler (ed.), *The God that Failed.*

Congress for Cultural Freedom meets in West Berlin.

Legal Aid comes into force in Britain (*Oct.* 2nd).

London Stock Exchange starts compensation fund to guarantee investors against the default of member firms.

P **Science, Technology, Discovery, etc.**

U.S. Atomic Energy Commission separates plutonium from pitchblende concentrates.

Existence of 'V'-particles is confirmed in Pasadena, California, and on the Pic du Midi d'Ossau.

New calculations for the speed of light obtained through radio waves at National Physical Laboratory, Teddington, and at Stanford University.

G. T. Seaborg of California University discovers element 98 (californium).

A jet-propelled, pilotless aircraft constructed in Australia.

Danish deep-sea expedition in *Galathea* to investigate fauna.

T. Heyerdahl, *The Kon-Tiki Expedition.*

Q **Scholarship**

A. L. Rowse, *The England of Elizabeth.*

Boswell's London Journal, 1762–3 (ed. F. A. Pottle).

R **Philosophy and Religion**

Nicholas Berdyaev, *Dreams and Reality.*

N. Hardtman, *Philosophy of Nature.*

R. A. Knox, *Enthusiasm.*

A. Malraux, *Psychology of Art.*

Margaret Mead, *Social Anthropology.*

Gilbert Ryle, *The Concept of Mind.*

J.-P. Sartre, *La Mort dans l'âme.*

Holy Year of Roman Catholic Church.

Papal decree *Humani Generis* (*Aug.* 17th), against Existentialism and erroneous scientific theories.

Pope Pius XII pronounces dogma on bodily Assumption of Virgin Mary (*Nov.* 1st).

National Council of Churches of Christ is established in U.S.

S **Art, Sculpture, Fine Arts and Architecture**

Painting:

Marc Chagall, *King David.*

V. Pasmore, *Inland Sea.*

B. Berenson publishes *Aesthetics and History.*

Sculpture:

P. Picasso, *The Goat.*

A. Giacommetti, *Seven Figures and a Head.*

F. Léger, series of Flower ceramics.

Architecture:

U.N. Building, New York, completed.

Powell and Moya, Pimlico Housing Estate, Westminster.

Eugenio Montiori, Rome Railway Station.

Mario Pani and Enrique del Moral, The University City, Mexico.

T **Music**

Béla Bartók, viola concerto.

E May: 11th, foreign ministers of Britain, France and U.S. confer in London on the future of Germany;

22nd, Peking government offers Tibet regional autonomy if she joins Communist system;

30th, Albania and Yugoslavia sever relations.

F Jun: 6th, Trygve Lie, appointed to a fresh term of office as U.N. Secretary-General, announces 20-year peace plan;

15th, West Germany joins Council of Europe;

24th, Georges Bidault, French premier, resigns after a vote of confidence against his ministry;

25th, North Korean forces invade South Korea;

27th, Trygve Lie urges U.N. members to assist South Korea to repel attacks and restore peace;

28th, North Koreans capture Seoul.

G Jul: 2nd, Henri Queuille, Radical, attempts to form French government;

8th, Douglas MacArthur appointed commander of U.N. forces in Korea;

11th René Pleven forms French government in which Guy Mollet and other Socialists serve;

19th, President Truman's message to Congress urging vast military budget;

20th, U.S. Senate committee denies Senator Joseph McCarthy's charges of Communist infiltration of State Department;

22nd, King Leopold III returns to Belgium after six years' exile;

23rd, Socialist demonstrations in Brussels against Leopold.

H Aug: 1st, Leopold III abdicates in favour of Prince Baudouin;

—, U.N. Security Council, with Jacob Malik (U.S.S.R.) as chairman, discusses Korea;

11th, W. S. Churchill carries motion at Strasbourg Congress of European Movement for a European army;

15th, Paul van Zeeland forms Christian Socialist ministry in Belgium.

J Sep: 1st, North Koreans attack across Naktong River;

6th, new constitution in Syria;

7th, Hungarian decree dissolving religious orders;

12th, emergency sessions of British Parliament for defence measures for Korean War;

—, George Marshall succeeds Louis A. Johnson as U.S. Defense Secretary;

14th, U.N. forces land at Inchon, South Korea;

15th, national service in Britain is extended to two years;

19th, European Payments Union established;

20th, Control of Communists bill in U.S.;

26th, U.N. forces recapture Seoul;

—, N.A.T.O. Council decides to form an integrated European defence force;

28th, Indonesia is admitted to U.N.

K Oct: 1st, South Korean troops cross 38th parallel;

4th, Turkey agrees to co-operate with N.A.T.O. defence plans for the Mediterranean;

7th, Acheson plan for strengthening U.N.'s powers to resist aggression (adopted, 19th);

15th, East German elections result in 99 per cent support for National Front;

19th, Hugh Gaitskell succeeds Stafford Cripps as Chancellor of Exchequer;

21st, Prague conference of U.S.S.R. satellites under V. Molotov on future of Germany;

T **Music**

P. Hindemith, *Harmony of the World.*
A. Honegger, 5th Symphony.
Carlo Menotti, *The Consul* (opera).
A. Rawsthorne, Symphony no. 1.
P. Racine Fricker, Symphony op. 9.
W. Walton, violin sonata.
J. S. Bach bicentenary celebrations.
Petit-Chabrier, *Ballabile* (ballet).
N. de Valois-Gerhard, *Don Quixote* (ballet).
Robbins-Bernstein, *Age of Anxiety* (ballet).

U **Literature**

E. Hemingway, *Across the River and Into the Trees.*
Ezra Pound, *Seventy Cantos.*
Anthony Powell, *A Question of Upbringing.*
C. P. Snow, *The Masters.*

V **The Press**

W **Drama and Entertainment**

J. Anouilh, *La Répétition.*
Marcel Aymé, *Clérambard.*
Films:
René Clair's *La Beauté du diable.*
Jean Cocteau's *Orphée.*
Akira Kurosawa's *Rashomon.*
Luciano's *Sunday in August.*
Max Ophuls' *La Ronde.*
Billy Wilder's *Sunset Boulevard.*
Irving Berlin, *Call Me Madam* (musical).
Fred Hoyle's Reith Lectures, *The Nature of the Universe* (broadcasting).
'Bebop' dancing.

X **Sport**

Y **Statistics**

Populations of cities (in mill.): London, 8·3; New York, 7·8; Tokio, 5·3; Moscow, 4·1; Chicago, 3·6; Shanghai, 3·6; Calcutta, 3·5; Berlin, 3·3.

Motor cars (in mill.): U.S., 51·9; Great Britain, 4·4; West Germany, 3.

Crime: England and Wales, 461,435 crimes (of which 6,249 were crimes of violence); U.S., 1,790,030 crimes (of which 18,930 were crimes of violence).

Divorces: U.S., 385,000; Great Britain, 32,516.

Armies: U.S.S.R., 3,000,000; U.S., 591,700; France, 456,000; Italy, 250,000; Great Britain, 143,500; Egypt, 20,000.

Religious denominations in Britain (in thousands): Roman Catholics, 3,884; Church of England, 1,867; Presbyterian Church of Scotland, 1,273; Methodists, 776; Congregationalists, 387; Baptists, 338; Presbyterians, 82; Episcopal Church of Scotland, 57; Jews, 450.

K **Oct**: 21st, Chinese forces occupy Tibet;
28th, Liberal-Agrarian ministry in Denmark under Erik Eriksen;
30th, nationalist rising in Puerto Rico.

L **Nov**: 3rd, French forces withdraw from frontier of N. Indo-China;
4th, U.N. Assembly revokes 1946 resolutions on relations with Spain;
5th, Douglas MacArthur reports the massing of Chinese Communists in North Korea;
7th, in U.S. elections Republicans gain 30 seats in House of Representatives;
13th, Tibet appeals to U.N. against Chinese aggression;
27th, U.N. troops forced to withdraw in Korea;
—, Peking delegates attend U.N. as observers;
28th, Poland and East Germany proclaim the Oder–Neisse line as the frontier.

M **Dec**: 4th, C. R. Attlee visits Washington;
13th, Marshall Aid to Britain ceases;
—, S. Africa refuses to place South West Africa under U.N. trusteeship;
16th, state of emergency proclaimed in U.S. following reversals of U.N. forces in Korea;
27th, China refuses U.N. appeal for a cease-fire;
—, U.S. and Spain resume diplomatic relations;
28th, Chinese forces cross 38th parallel in Korea.

N

z **Births and Deaths**

Feb. 4th Montagu, Lord Norman, d. (78).
Mar. 6th Albert Lebrun d. (79).
Mar. 24th Harold J. Laski d. (56).
Mar. 30th Léon Blum d. (77).
July 9th Ismail Sidky Pasha d. (75).
July 22nd W. L. Mackenzie King d. (75).
Sept. 11th Jan Christian Smuts d. (80).
Nov. 2nd George Bernard Shaw d. (94).

1951 (Jan.–Jul.) Conservatives return to power in Britain—The Six sign Paris Treaty for single coal and steel authority

A **Jan**: 1st, North Korean and Chinese Communists break through U.N. lines on 38th parallel and, 4th, take Seoul;
17th, Communist China rejects U.N. Truce Committee's peace proposals for Far East;
—, Aneurin Bevan appointed British Minister of Labour;
24th, fall of Wilhelm Drees's coalition in Netherlands.

B **Feb**: 8th, President Truman orders army to control U.S. railways during strike;
13th, British Commonwealth Consultative Committee meets at Colombo to discuss development plan for S. and S.E. Asia;
14th, dissolution of David Ben-Gurion's government in Israel, following defeat in Knesset on problem of religious education;
28th, René Pleven's coalition in France falls on issue of electoral reform.

C **Mar**: 2nd, purge of Czechoslovak Communist Party;
5th, (–*June* 21st), deputy foreign ministers of Britain, France, U.S. and U.S.S.R. meet in Paris to prepare agenda for future conference, but problem of disarmament hampers progress;
7th, premier of Iran is assassinated;
9th, Herbert Morrison succeeds Ernest Bevin as British Foreign Secretary;
10th, Henri Queuille forms ministry in France, ending political deadlock;
12th, U.S. Senate Committee under Kefauver investigates crime in interstate commerce;
29th, U.S. completes draft peace treaty with Japan which she circulates to the powers;
—, Chinese government rejects Douglas MacArthur's offer of truce discussions but, 31st, India and, *Apr.* 2nd, Britain again urge truce in Korean War.

D **Apr**: 11th, President Truman relieves General MacArthur of command in Far East; succeeded by Matthew Ridgway (and, 19th, MacArthur argues against administration's policies in address to joint session of Congress);
18th, France, W. Germany, Italy, Belgium, Netherlands, and Luxembourg ('the Six'), sign Paris treaty, embodying the Schuman Plan to set up a single coal and steel authority;
22nd, Aneurin Bevan and Harold Wilson resign from Labour cabinet in protest at imposition of health service charges to meet increasing defence spending and this Bevanite revolt splits British Labour Party;
28th, Dr. Musaddiq appointed President of Iran.

E **May**: 7th (–*June* 25th), George Marshall and other witnesses testify before Foreign Relations Committee and Armed Services Committee of U.S. Senate on Douglas MacArthur's removal;
15th, North Korean forces launch offensive.

F **Jun**: 3rd, Indian Socialist Party's mammoth demonstration in Delhi in protest at the government's food and housing policies;
13th, Éamon de Valéra returns to power in Eire on defection of members of John Costello's coalition;
17th, in elections for French National Assembly Gaullists win 117 seats, Socialists, 104, Communists, 101, Independents, 99, Radicals, 95, and Popular Republicans, 86;
23rd (–29th), further attempts to negotiate armistice in Korea fail;
Guy Burgess and Donald Maclean, 'missing diplomats', flee to U.S.S.R.

G **Jul**: 3rd, India complains to U.N. Security Council against Pakistan for violating cease-fire agreement in Kashmir;

O **Politics, Economics, Law and Education**

Lord Radcliffe's Reith Lectures, *Power and the State*.

London Congress on Space Travel establishes an International Astronautical Federation (*Sept.*).

Report of Royal Commission on Betting, Lotteries and Gaming (*Apr.* 17th).

Communist-sponsored World Peace Council meets in East Berlin (*Feb.*).

P **Science, Technology, Discovery, etc.**

The 'flying spot' microscope is devised.

Krilium, a synthetic chemical, is developed from acrylonitrile for use in fertilisation.

Electric power is satisfactorily produced from atomic energy at Arcon, Idaho (*Dec.*).

Second British plutonium pile, at Sellafield, Cumberland, in operation.

Dutch-Norwegian joint atomic energy research establishment opened at Hjeller, near Oslo.

John Brown and Co. make a peat-fired gas turbine on Clydebank.

Fawley oil refinery opened (*Sept.*).

Q **Scholarship**

E. H. Carr, *A History of Soviet Russia; the Bolshevik Revolution*, Vol. I.

Stephen Runciman, *History of the Crusades* (–58).

R **Philosophy and Religion**

J.-P. Sartre, *The Psychology of Imagination*.

David Riesman, *The Lonely Crowd*.

Fraudulent Medium Act repeals provisions of Witchcraft Act, 1735, in Britain.

S **Art, Sculpture, Fine Arts and Architecture**

Painting:

S. Dali, *Christ of St. John on the Cross*.

Graham Sutherland, *Lord Beaverbrook*.

Sculpture:

Kenneth Armitage, *People in a Wind*.

Architecture:

Gerald Barry's plan for centenary of the 1851 'Great Exhibition', on the South Bank, London, with Hugh Casson director of architecture; Robert Matthew, Royal Festival Hall; Ralph Tubbs, Dome of Discovery.

Basil Spence's design for Coventry Cathedral wins award open to Commonwealth architects.

T **Music**

B. Britten, *Billy Budd* (opera).

I. Stravinsky, *The Rake's Progress* (libretto by W. H. Auden and Chester Kallman).

R. Vaughan Williams, *A Pilgrim's Progress* (opera).

Mackerras-Sullivan, *Pineapple Poll* (ballet).

Cranko-Arnell, *Harlequin in April* (ballet).

U **Literature**

Robert Frost, *Complete Poems*.

N. Monsarrat, *The Cruel Sea*.

J. D. Salinger, *The Catcher in the Rye*.

Herman Wouk, *The Caine Mutiny*.

1951 (Jul.–Dec.)

G **Jul**: 5th, International Court rules against Iran in dispute with Britain over nationalisation of Iranian oil industry and, 15th, President Truman sends Averell Harriman to Iran to urge a compromise settlement;

20th, King Abdullah of Jordan assassinated in Jerusalem.

H **Aug**: 5th, Matthew Ridgway breaks off armistice talks in Korea, charging Communists with violation of demilitarisation rules, and further negotiations fail;

—, mammoth Communist Youth Rally in Berlin;

7th, U.S. Congress rejects U.S.S.R. proposal for agreement on arms and atomic weapons, advising her first to honour existing obligations;

11th, French ministerial crisis (since elections on *June* 17th) ends with René Pleven forming a coalition of the Centre;

30th, U.S.-Philippines mutual defence pact.

J **Sep**: 8th, peace treaty with Japan signed at San Francisco by representatives of 49 powers, though U.S.S.R. and her satellites boycott final session of peace conference;

10th, foreign ministers of Britain, France and U.S. discuss plans to combat Soviet aggression and to use West German troops in N.A.T.O. army;

13th, U.N. Conciliatory Commission discusses Palestine problem with Israeli and Arab delegates, but by *Nov.* 21st the talks fail;

23rd, U.N. forces in Korea capture 'Heartbreak Ridge', north of Yanggu.

K **Oct**: 5th, House of Representatives approves $56.9 billion armed forces appropriation bill;

6th, Henry Gurney, British High Commissioner in Malaya, assassinated;

9th, David Ben-Gurion ends eight months' ministerial crisis in Israel by forming coalition;

16th, premier Ali Khan of Pakistan assassinated;

25th, in British general election Conservatives win 321 seats (net gain 23) over Labour 295 (net loss 20) and Liberal 6 (net loss 3), Irish Nationalist 2 and Irish Labour 1; and

27th, W. S. Churchill forms ministry, with Anthony Eden Foreign Secretary and R. A. Butler Chancellor of Exchequer;

25th, negotiations for armistice in Korea are renewed at Panmunjom;

27th, Egypt abrogates 1936 treaty of alliance with Britain and 1899 agreement over Sudan.

L **Nov**: 8th, Dean Acheson presents disarmament proposals to U.N. General Assembly, which U.S.S.R. counters with rival plan;

10th, France, Britain, U.S. and Turkey announce security programme for Near East;

11th, Juan Perón is re-elected President of Argentina;

14th, U.S. allegations of Communists killing Korean prisoners of war;

16th, Egypt offers to let future of Sudan be decided by plebiscite under U.N. supervision;

29th, military *coup d'état* in Syria.

M **Dec**: 6th, East and West Germany agree to send representatives to U.N. to discuss holding of free elections in Germany, but U.S.S.R. opposes the project;

13th, French National Assembly ratifies Schuman Plan (see *May* 1950) by 377 to 233 votes;

19th, Marshal Vishinsky demands U.N. to require U.S. to revoke her Mutual Security Act;

20th, Greece elected to U.N. Security Council over the U.S.S.R. candidate;

(*Continued opposite*)

V **The Press**

History Today first issued.

W **Drama and Entertainment**

J. Anouilh, *Colombe.*
Christopher Fry, *A Sleep of Prisoners.*
J.-P. Sartre, *Le Diable et le Bon Dieu.*
Peter Ustinov, *The Love of Four Colonels.*
John Whitney, *Saint's Day.*
South Pacific (musical).
The Festival of Britain.
Foundation stone of the National Theatre laid at South Bank.
British Film Censors introduce 'X certificate' classification for films totally unsuitable for anyone under 16.
Waller invents Cinerama.
Films:
Vittorio de Sica's *Miracle in Milan.*
Alfred Hitchcock's *Strangers on a Train.*
John Huston's *The African Queen.*
Max Ophuls's *Le Plaisir.*
Carol Reed's *Outcast of the Islands.*
'The Archers' (B.B.C. Light Programme).

X **Sport**

Y **Statistics**

Populations (in mill.): China, 490; India, 357; U.S.S.R., 190; U.S., 153 (of whom 136 whites, 16 negro and 0·7 other races); Japan, 85; Pakistan, 76; Great Britain, 50; West Germany, 48; Italy, 47; France, 42. S. Africa has 2·4 Europeans and 9·3 non-Europeans.

Merchant shipping (in mill. tons): U.S. 60; Gt. Britain, 12; Norway, 5·3; Greece, 3·5; Italy, 3·3; Netherlands, 2·9; France, 2·9; Japan, 2·7; U.S.S.R. 2.
80 mill. tons use Suez Canal (33·5 per cent British).
30 mill. tons use Panama Canal.

Oil production: U.S., 2,725 mill barrels; U.S.S.R., 266 mill. barrels.

Coal production (in mill. tons): U.S., 430; Great Britain, 222; U.S.S.R. 270; West Germany, 119; France, 53.

Z **Births and Deaths**

Jan. 27th Carl Mannerheim d. (83).
Feb. 19th André Gide d. (81).
Apr. 14th Ernest Bevin d. (70).
Apr. 23rd Charles Dawes d. (85).
July 13th Arnold Schönberg d. (76).
July 23rd Henri Philippe Pétain d. (95).
Aug. 21st Constant Lambert d. (45).

M **Dec:** 24th, Libya becomes an independent federation under King Idris I;
27th, failure of Korean armistice talks on exchange of prisoners and building of airfields in North Korea;
31st, Mutual Security Agency replaces Economic Co-operation Administration of Marshall Plan.

N

1952 (Jan.–Jun.) Arab League Security Pact—Mau Mau—Eisenhower elected U.S. President

A Jan: 5th, U.S. five-year loan to India;
7th, René Pleven's ministry falls through adverse Socialist vote on social security policy; and
22nd, Edgar Faure forms coalition;
14th, Tunisia unsuccessfully appeals to U.N. Security Council to state her case for autonomy;
18th, (–27th), anti-British riots in Egypt end with King Farouk's appointment of Aly Maher Pasha as premier (–*Mar.* 1st);
24th, Vincent Massey becomes first Canadian to serve as Governor-General of Canada;
25th, (–*Feb.* 4th), Franco-German crisis over administration of the Saar.

B Feb: 6th, death of George VI and accession of Queen Elizabeth II;
20th (–25th), N.A.T.O. Council, meeting in Lisbon, approves European defence project, agrees to raise 50 divisions by *Dec.* and to bring Morocco and Tunisia into the alliance;
26th, W. S. Churchill announces that Britain has produced her own atomic bomb;
29th, Edgar Faure's ministry falls, on failing to obtain National Assembly's assent to tax increases, and Antoine Pinay forms cabinet with some Gaullist support.

C Mar: 1st, in India's first national elections Pandit Nehru's Congress Party wins 364 of 489 seats in the National Assembly;
—, Aly Maher Pasha resigns in Egypt;
4th, Chinese Communists accuse U.S. forces in Korea of using germ warfare;
10th, U.S.S.R. note proposing four-power conference on unification and rearmament of Germany, to which the Western Powers reply, 23rd, that free elections would be a prerequisite, that Germany should not be empowered to rearm and that her boundaries, as settled by the Potsdam Conference, 1945, would be subject to revision;
20th, S. Africa Supreme Court invalidates race legislation of D. F. Malan;
29th, H. S. Truman announces he will not be a candidate in the presidential election;
30th, anti-French riots in Tangier.

D Apr: 8th, President Truman orders seizure of the steel industry to avert a strike;
10th, U.S.S.R. proposes that all-German elections be held under a four-power commission, instead of under U.N. supervision, and rejects the West's views on Germany's frontiers;
15th, Britain declares she will sign a mutual defence treaty with the European Defence Community;
22nd, D. F. Malan introduces bill to make S. African Parliament a high court, in order to prevent Supreme Court from invalidating race legislation;
28th, Dwight D. Eisenhower is relieved of his post as Supreme Allied Commander in Europe at his own request and succeeded by Matthew Ridgway (who is succeeded in Far East by Mark Clark).

E May: 6th, Rajendra Prasad elected President of India; and
13th, Pandit Nehru forms government;
20th, rioting of Communist prisoners of war at Koje Island prison camp, South Korea;
27th (–31st), European Defence Community treaty signed in Paris, with reciprocal N.A.T.O.-E.D.C. guarantees;
28th, Communist demonstrations in Paris.

F Jun: 1st, United National Party under Dudley Senanayake wins Ceylon elections;
18th, British scheme for Central African Federation published;

O **Politics, Economics, Law and Education**

Alan Moorehead, *The Traitors* (a discussion of the cases of the atomic scientists Fuchs, Nunn May and Pontecorvo).

Arnold Toynbee's Reith Lectures, *The World and the West*.

P **Science, Technology, Discovery, etc.**

Rapid extension of use of radio-isotopes in scientific research, medicine and industry; Britain becomes the chief exporter of isotopes.

A contraceptive tablet of phosphorated hesperidin is made.

Britain's first atomic bomb tests, in Monte Bello Islands, N.W. Australia (*Oct.* 3rd).

U.S. explodes the first hydrogen bomb, at Enimetok Atoll, Pacific (*Nov.* 6th).

President Truman lays keel of first atomic-powered submarine, *Nautilus*.

French hydro-electric power station and dam opened at Donzère-Mondragon in the Rhône Valley (*Oct.* 25th).

John Cobb is killed establishing a water speed record of 206·89 m.p.h. at Loch Ness (*Oct.* 5th).

'Smog' in London (*Dec.*).

The last London tram runs (*Jul.* 6th).

Q **Scholarship**

Kathleen Kenyon excavates the site of Jericho.

Ventris deciphers 'Linear B'.

Archaeologists use radioactive carbon tests for dating finds.

Harold Nicolson, *King George V, His Life and Reign*.

R **Philosophy and Religion**

R. Niebuhr, *Christ and Culture*.

S **Art, Sculpture, Fine Arts and Architecture**

Painting

Jackson Pollock, *Convergence*.

Augustus John publishes *Chiaroscuro*.

Sculpture:

Reg Butler, *Young Girl 52,53*.

Jacob Epstein, *Madonna and Child*, Cavendish Square, London.

M. Marini, *The Horseman*.

H. Moore, *Time-Life* Screen, London.

Architecture:

Scidmore, Owings and Merrill, Lever House, New York.

Juan O'Gorman and others, University Library, Mexico City.

Lionel Brett, Hatfield New Town.

The proposals of the Waverley Committee, restricting the export of works of art from Britain, are broadly accepted by the government.

T **Music**

Arthur Bliss, *The Enchantress*.

C. Malipiero, violin concerto.

Igor Stravinsky, *Babel* (opera).

D. Prokofiev, 7th Symphony ('Symphony of Youth').

R. Vaughan Williams, *Romance* for harmonica (for Larry Adler).

Robbins-Stravinsky, *The Cage* (ballet).

Cranko-Gardner, *Reflection* (ballet).

U **Literature**

Ray Bradbury, *The Illustrated Man*.

Ernest Hemingway, *The Old Man and the Sea*.

F **Jun**: 20th, President Truman signs foreign aid bill;
23rd, bombing of hydro-electric plants in North Korea by U.S. Air Force;
27th, London conference of U.S., France and Britain on Western foreign policy.

G **Jul**: 6th, Ruiz Cortines elected President of Mexico;
22nd, Dr. Musaddiq is re-appointed premier of Iran with emergency powers for six months;
—, Hague Court rules it has no jurisdiction in case between Iran and Anglo-Iranian Oil Co.;
23rd, General Mohammed Neguib seizes power in Egypt (forms a government *Sept.* 7th);
24th, Indian agreement with Kashmir government;
25th, European Coal and Steel Community in force;
26th, King Farouk abdicates in Egypt in favour of infant son, Fuad.

H **Aug**: 4th (–*Sept.* 25th), Honolulu Conference of three-power Pacific Council, Australia, New Zealand and U.S., as set up by Pacific Security Treaty of *Sept.* 1951;
5th, Japan resumes diplomatic relations with Nationalist China;
11th, Prince Hussain is proclaimed King of Jordan on termination of reign of King Talal, a schizophrenic;
14th, Matyas Rakosi is appointed premier of Hungary;
17th, Chinese delegates under Chou En-lai arrive in Moscow;
20th, death of Kurt Schumacher, leader of German Social Democratic Party;
23rd, Arab League Security Pact comes into force.

J **Sep**: 1st, William Drees, Labour, re-forms coalition in Netherlands after general election;
4th, General Carlos Ibáñez elected President of Chile;
5th, Britain, France and U.S. send notes to U.S.S.R. on peace treaty with Austria;
11th, federation of Eritrea with Ethiopia ratified;
18th, Finland completes reparation payments to U.S.S.R.;
21st, Conservatives and Liberals gain over Democrats and Agrarians in Swedish elections;
24th, revised Constitution in Roumania;
30th, Council of Europe adopts Eden plan, for making the Council a framework into which the Coal and Steel Community and Defence Community can be fitted.

K **Oct**: 2nd, Chinese government holds 'Asia and Pacific Peace Conference' in Peking;
3rd, U.S.S.R. demands recall of George Kennan, U.S. ambassador, for his comments about isolation of Western diplomats in Moscow;
4th, China and Mongolia sign ten-year agreement;
5th, U.S.S.R. Communist Party holds 1st Congress since 1939 and, 10th, adopts 1951–6 plan;
13th, Egyptian agreement with Sudan over waters of Nile;
17th, Council of Socialist International meets in Milan;
20th, state of emergency proclaimed in Kenya because of Mau Mau disturbances, and arrest of leaders of Kenya African Union;
22nd, Iran breaks off diplomatic relations with Britain over oil dispute;
28th, Dr. Luigi Figl forms coalition in Austria.

(*Continued opposite*)

U **Literature** (*cont.*)

F. R. Leavis, *The Common Pursuit.*
Doris Lessing, *Martha Quest.*
Dylan Thomas, *Collected Poems.*
Evelyn Waugh, *Men at Arms.*
Angus Wilson, *Hemlock and After.*

V **The Press**

William Haley becomes editor of *The Times.*
Concern in Britain over 'horror comics'.

W **Drama and Entertainment**

M. Aymé, *La Tête des Autres.*
Agatha Christie, *The Mousetrap.*
Clifford Odets, *Winter Journey.*
Films:
This is Cinerama opens on Broadway (*Sept.*).
Ingmar Bergman's *Summer With Monika.*
Charlie Chaplin's *Limelight* with Claire Bloom.
Vittorio de Sica's *Umberto D.*
Orson Welles's *Othello.*
J. Ferrer in *Moulin Rouge.*

Y **Statistics**

Z **Births and Deaths**

Mar. 4th Charles Scott Sherrington d. (94).
Apr. 21st Stafford Cripps d. (63).
Jul. 26th Eva Perón d. (30).
Nov. 9th Chaim Weizmann d. (77).
Nov. 20th Benedetto Croce d. (86).

L Nov: 4th, Republican landslide in U.S. presidential election with Dwight D. Eisenhower 442 electoral votes, in record poll, over Governor Adlai Stevenson, Democrat, 89;
16th, Field-Marshal Papagos forms ministry in Greece following success of Greek Rally in elections;
20th, Bierut elected premier of Poland;
27th, London Commonwealth Economic Conference;
Trials of Rudolf Slansky, former secretary of Czech Communist Party, and of Vladimir Clementis, former foreign minister, in Czechoslovakia for treason.
Bill to denationalise iron and steel introduced in Britain.

M Dec: 2nd, Dwight D. Eisenhower visits Korea;
3rd, U.N. General Assembly adopts Indian proposal for Korean armistice;
4th, W. S. Churchill states Britain will curtail defence expenditure;
7th, riots in French Morocco;
8th, Itzhak Ben-Zvi becomes President of Israel, following Chaim Weizmann's death, *Nov.* 9th;
10th, Egypt abolishes 1923 Constitution;
12th, Communist world conference in Vienna;
15th, China rejects Indian plan for Korean armistice;
23rd, Antoine Pinay, French premier, resigns.

N

1953 (Jan.–Jun.) Death of Stalin—Korean armistice—Egypt becomes a republic—Rise of Khruschchev

A Jan: 1st, London conference on federation of Northern and Southern Rhodesia and Nyasaland (scheme published *Feb.* 5th);
5th, W. S. Churchill visits Dwight D. Eisenhower;
6th, Asian Socialist conference at Rangoon;
8th, riots in Karachi, Pakistan;
10th, European Coal and Steel Community first meets;
12th, Yugoslav National Assembly adopts new constitution and, 14th, Marshal Josip Tito elected first President of Yugoslav Republic;
14th, Consultative Assembly of Council of Europe meets in Strasbourg to draft constitution for European Political Community (adopted *Feb.* 10th);
16th, dissolution of political parties in Egypt;
20th, Dwight D. Eisenhower is inaugurated President of U.S.;
21st, electoral reform bill passes Italian Chamber, with Communists abstaining.

B Feb: 10th, General M. Neguib is voted dictatorial powers in Egypt for three years;
12th, Anglo-Egyptian agreement on Sudan;
—, U.S.S.R. severs relations with Israel;
16th, S. African government takes emergency powers under Public Safety bill;
22nd, People's Party and Socialists win seats in Austrian elections;
24th, Rome Conference of foreign ministers of the European Defence Community countries;
28th, treaty of friendship between Greece, Turkey and Yugoslavia.

C Mar: 5th, J. Stalin dies (aged 73);
6th, G. M. Malenkov succeeds as Chairman of Council of Ministers;
16th, Marshal Tito visits London;
19th, W. German Bundestag approves Bonn agreement and Paris agreement establishing a European Defence Community;
30th, a new Danish Constitution; the Upper House is abolished and voting age reduced to 23;
31st, Dag Hammarskjöld, Sweden, elected Secretary-General of U.N. by Security Council (*Apr.* 7th elected Secretary of U.N. Assembly).

D Apr: 2nd, Julius Raab, People's Party, forms coalition in Austria;
6th, Konrad Adenauer visits New York (and, *May* 14th, London);
8th, Jomo Kenyatta and five other Kikuyu convicted of managing Mau Mau;
11th, U.N. force and Communists arrange for exchange of prisoners in Korea;
—, Vietnamese insurgents renew offensive on Laos;
13th, London conference on British West Indian federation opens;
15th, Nationalists secure clear majority in S. African elections;
18th, Mohammed Ali forms new ministry in Pakistan;
21st, Social Democrats gain clear majority in Danish elections;
30th, People's Progressive Party win first elections in British Guiana.

E May: 12th, General Gruenther (U.S.) appointed Supreme Allied Commander in Europe;
20th, France signs agreement with the Saar;
21st, Yoshida forms ministry in Japan;
25th, President Eisenhower states principles on which U.N. peace proposals for Korea were based.
Denationalisation of road transport in Britain.

F Jun: 2nd Coronation of Queen Elizabeth II;

O **Politics, Economics, Law and Education**

British Ministry of Agriculture inquiry into the disposal of Crichel Down, after prolonged agitation, eases tension between Civil Service and public.

Report of Royal Commission on Capital Punishment in Britain.

A Royal Commission is appointed to inquire into the law governing the certification and detention of mental patients.

The Beaver Committee on air pollution reports.

London Stock Exchange opens public galleries.

P **Science, Technology, Discovery, etc.**

Astronomers in Australia, S. Africa and U.S. discover a new scale of space outside the solar system.

Cosmic ray observatory is established on Mt. Wrangell, Alaska.

The Royal Observatory is moved from Greenwich to Herstmonceux, Sussex (–56).

R. Oppenheim's Reith Lectures, *Science and the Common Understanding*.

International laboratory for nuclear research opened at Meyrin, near Geneva.

U.S.S.R. explodes a hydrogen bomb (*Aug.* 29th).

W. Le Gros Clark and others prove the Piltdown Man to have been a hoax.

The 'Jindivik' pilotless 'plane.

Experimental colour TV in U.S. (*Dec.*).

Edmund Hillary and Norkey Tenzing from John Hunt's expedition climb Mt. Everest (*May* 29th).

Austro-German expedition climbs Nanga Parbat in Himalayas (*July* 4th).

Myxomatosis spreads from continental Europe to Britain, killing millions of rabbits.

Q **Scholarship**

J. Wheeler-Bennett, *Nemesis of Power; the German Army in Politics.*

Cultural Patterns and Technical Change (ed. Margaret Mead).

R **Philosophy and Religion**

Karl Jaspers, *Tragedy is not Enough.*

Rhine, *The New World of the Mind.*

Skinner, *Science and Human Behaviour.*

S **Art, Sculpture, Fine Arts and Architecture**

Painting:

B. Nicholson, *September 1953.*

Mexican Art Exhibition, Royal Academy.

Sculpture:

Henry Moore, *King and Queen*, Middleheim, Antwerp.

Barbara Hepworth, *Monolith Empyrean*, Kenwood, London.

Institute of Contemporary Art, London, holds competition for sculpture of *The Unknown Political Prisioner*, which is won by Reg Butler.

Architecture:

P. Nervi and others, UNESCO Conference Hall, Paris (–1957).

T **Music**

M. Bloch, Concerto Grosso.

B. Britten, *Gloriana* (opera).

D. Milhaud, *David* (opera).

R. Vaughan Williams, Symphony no. 7.

Thomas Beecham produces F. Delius's opera *Irmelin* (composed 1892).

Homage to the Queen (ballet; score by Malcolm Arnold).

F Jun: 3rd, London Conference of Commonwealth premiers;
7th, in Italian elections Christian Democrats and their allies win seats from Socialists and Communists;
8th, Kenya African Union is proscribed;
17th, rising against Communist government in E. Berlin;
18th, Republic proclaimed in Egypt, with General M. Neguib President;
—, South Korea releases 26,000 non-Communist North Korean prisoners;
19th, the Rosenbergs, sentenced as atomic spies in 1951, are executed in U.S.;
26th, Joseph Laniel forms ministry in France;
29th, Alcide de Gasperi resigns as premier of Italy.

G Jul: 2nd, vote of confidence in Dáil for É. de Valéra's government following setbacks in by-elections;
4th, International Confederation of Free Trade Unions meets in Stockholm;
5th, Imre Nagy forms ministry in Hungary;
10th, dismissal of L. P. Beria, U.S.S.R. minister of internal affairs (he is shot as a traitor on *Dec.* 23rd);
—, British, French and U.S. foreign ministers meet in Washington;
12th, Brigadier Chichekli becomes President of Syria;
14th, defeat of Dr. Olivier's coalition in Malta on vote of confidence;
15th, Alcide de Gasperi forms new coalition (but resigns again, 28th);
—, Kenya Supreme Court quashes Jomo Kenyatta's conviction (upheld, *Sept.* 22nd, by E. African Court of Appeal);
—, Britain proposes four-power conference on Germany;
20th, U.S.S.R. and Israel resume diplomatic relations;
27th, Korean armistice is signed at Panmunjom;
30th, Britain signs alliance with Libya.

H Aug: 6th, widespread strikes begin in France;
8th, U.S.-Korean mutual defence treaty;
10th, Liberals return to power in Canadian elections;
15th, Giuseppe Pella forms Christian Democrat ministry in Italy;
16th (–19th), attempted royalist *coup d'état* in Persia;
20th, Dr. Musaddiq, premier of Persia arrested;
—, demonstration against federation in Nyasaland by Nyasaland African Congress;
—, France deposes Sultan of Morocco;
23rd, U.S.S.R. cancels E. German reparations;
24th, Kenya government calls on Mau Mau to surrender;
30th, Hungary and Yugoslavia resume relations.

J Sep: 6th, Christian Democratic Union wins W. German elections;
12th, N. Khrushchev appointed First Secretary of Central Committee of U.S.S.R. Communist Party;
27th, Japan establishes a national defence force;
28th, Cardinal Wyszynski, primate of Poland, arrested;
30th, Social Democratic ministry formed in Denmark.

K Oct: 6th, Britain sends forces to British Guiana to prevent *coup* by the Communist People's Progressive Party;
8th, Anglo-U.S. decision to hand over administration of Zone A of Trieste to Italy;
9th, Arab Liberation movement wins Syrian elections;
12th, Labour majority in Norwegian elections;
13th, John Kotalawala forms ministry in Ceylon on D. Bandaranaike's retirement;

(*Continued opposite*)

U **Literature**

W. Faulkner, *Requiem for a Nun.*
Ian Fleming, *Casino Royale* (first 'James Bond' thriller).
Gerald Hanley, *The Year of the Lion.*
C. Day-Lewis, *An Italian Visit.*
John Wain, *Hurry on Down.*

V **The Press**

W **Drama and Entertainment**

Coronation of Queen Elizabeth II televised.
T. S. Eliot, *The Confidential Clerk.*
Graham Greene, *The Living Room.*
N. C. Hunter, *A Day by the Sea.*
Arthur Miller, *The Crucible.*
Films:
Federico Fellini's *I Vitelloni.*
William Wyler's *Roman Holiday* with Audrey Hepburn.
Fred Zinnemann's *From Here to Eternity.*
The Robe (first film in 'Cinemascope').
B'wana Devil (first 3-dimensional film).
Four Chimneys.

X **Sport**

England win the Ashes from Australia.

Y **Statistics**

Z **Births and Deaths**

Mar. 14th Klement Gottwald d. (56).
Mar. 24th Queen Mary d. (85).
June 16th Margaret Bondfield d. (80).
July 16th Hilaire Belloc d. (82).
Oct. 30th Arnold Bax d. (69).

K **Oct**: 20th, Konrad Adenauer forms new government in W. Germany;
23rd, federal Constitution of Rhodesias and Nyasaland in force;
26th, U.S. publishes report of Communist outrages in Korea;
30th, general strike in Austria, as protest against occupation.

L **Nov**: 8th, all seats in Portuguese elections won by Salazar's União Nacional;
17th, non-party government in Finland under the governor of the Bank of Finland.

M **Dec**: 4th, W. S. Churchill, President Eisenhower and Joseph Laniel meet in Bermuda;
5th, Britain and Persia resume diplomatic relations;
7th, D. Ben-Gurion resigns in Israel after prolonged tension in coalition; succeeded, 9th, by Moshe Sharett;
8th, Eisenhower proposes to U.N. General Assembly an international control of atomic energy;
18th, Godfrey Huggins, Federal Party, forms ministry in Rhodesia-Nyasaland;
20th, Fatherland Front is the sole party in Bulgarian elections;
21st, Dr. Musaddiq is sentenced to three years' confinement;
23rd, René Coty elected President of France.

N

1954 (Jan.–May) **Nasser gains power in Egypt—Fall of Dien Bien Phu—Terrorism in Algeria**

A Jan: 8th (–15th), Commonwealth finance ministers meet at Sydney, under R. G. Menzies, to consolidate economic progress of the sterling area and Commonwealth;
17th, expulsion of Milovan Djilas, who had pleaded for greater freedom of expression, from Yugoslav Communist Party;
18th, Amintore Fanfani forms ministry of Christian Democrats in Italy following Giuseppe Pella's resignation, 5th;
23rd, Report of Randall Commission on U.S. foreign economic policy;
24th, Moshe Sharett forms new coalition in Israel;
25th (*–Feb.* 18th), foreign ministers of Britain, France, U.S. and U.S.S.R. meet in Berlin to reduce world tension, but U.S.S.R. rejects proposals of the West for the reunification of Germany through free elections;
30th, A. Fanfani resigns after vote of confidence against him.

B Feb: 10th, Mario Scelba forms coalition of Christian Democrats, Social Democrats and Liberals in Italy, with Parliamentary support from Republicans;
18th, Berlin Conference of foreign ministers ends with proposal for a further conference in *Apr.* at Geneva with Chinese and Korean representatives;
25th, Colonel Nasser usurps power as premier of Egypt but, 27th, General Mohammed Neguib again in control;
—, President Chichekli of Syria flees, following army revolt (and *Mar.* 1st, Sabri el Assali forms government).

C Mar: 1st, conference of the Organization of American States, in Caracas, Venezuela;
8th, U.S.-Japanese mutual defence agreement;
9th, Centre and Right gain in Finnish election;
23rd, Israel withdraws from U.N. mixed armistice commission;
31st, U.S.S.R. offers to join N.A.T.O.

D Apr: 5th, Dwight D. Eisenhower broadcasts on the H-bomb and the Communist threat;
12th, in Belgian elections Christian Socialists lose absolute majority to Socialists and Liberals (22nd, van Acker, Socialist, forms coalition);
13th, Vladimir Petrov of the U.S.S.R. embassy in Canberra is granted asylum in Australia;
—, Dr. Jagan, former prime minister, is sentenced and British Guiana becomes a 'proclaimed area';
16th, President Eisenhower pledges support to the six E.D.C. countries;
18th, General Nasser becomes premier and military governor of Egypt;
21st, U.S. Air Force flies a French battalion to Indo-China to defend Dien Bien Phu;
—, General Zahedi becomes premier of Persia;
26th (*–July* 21st), at Geneva conference on Korea and Indo-China U.N. powers insist on free elections in Korea;
27th, G. M. Malenkov elected premier of U.S.S.R.;
28th, premiers of India, Pakistan, Burma, Indonesia and Ceylon confer at Colombo;
—, India signs commercial and cultural agreement with China;
29th, first election in Honduras.

E May: 7th, Dien Bien Phu falls to Communist Vietnamese;
13th, President Eisenhower signs St. Lawrence Seaway bill;
15th, Queen Elizabeth and Prince Philip begin Commonwealth Tour;
18th, European Convention on Human Rights in force;
29th, Thailand complains to U.N. Security Council that Communists in Indo-China threaten her security;
—, R. G. Menzies forms coalition of Liberal and Country parties in Australia;

O **Politics, Economics, Law and Education**

A. Koestler, *The Invisible Writing.*

Richard Wright, *Black Force.*

Atomic Energy Authority and Independent Television Authority are established in Britain.

Landlord and Tenant Act provides security of tenure for tenants of premises outside the scope of the Rent Act.

International Convention for preventing pollution of the sea by oil.

High Court of Chivalry sits for the first time since 1731 and rules that Manchester Palace of Varieties cannot use the arms of Manchester Corporation (*Dec.* 21st).

P **Science, Technology, Discovery, etc.**

U.S. hydrogen bomb tests at Bikini in Marshall Islands reveal the bomb's powers of destruction (*Mar.* 1st).

Composite photograph of the night sky completed by Lisk Observatory, California.

Central Observatory of U.S.S.R. Academy of Sciences, near Leningrad, opened (*May* 21st).

Bell Telephone Company develops solar battery capable of converting the sun's radiation into electricity.

An atomic-powered railway locomotive designed at Utah University.

Widespread public concern about the disposal of radioactive waste.

The connection between smoking and lung cancer is first seriously suggested.

The Eurovision network is formed.

First 'flying bedstead' aircraft, with vertical take-off.

Series of 'Comet' disasters perturb British aircraft industry.

Italian expedition under Desio climb Mt. Godwin Austen (K. 2) in the Himalayas (*July* 31st).

Q **Scholarship**

Temple of Mithras is uncovered during excavations for rebuilding in City of London.

Mortimer Wheeler, *The Indus Civilization.*

Isaac Deutscher, *The Prophet Armed* (Vol. I; a study of Trotsky –63).

R **Philosophy and Religion**

Gilbert Ryle, *Dilemmas.*

A. Schweitzer, *The Problem.*

C. E. Raven, *Natural Religion and Christian Theology.*

P. Tillich, *Love, Power and Justice.*

Billy Graham's mammoth evangelistic meetings in London, Berlin and New York.

S **Art, Sculpture, Fine Arts and Architecture**

Painting:

John Bratby, *Dustbins.*

P. Picasso, *Sylvette.*

G. Sutherland, portrait of *Churchill.*

Sculpture:

Kenneth Armitage, *Seated Group Listening to Music.*

Barbara Hepworth, *Two figures, Menhirs.*

Architecture:

E. Bedford's design for G.P.O. Tower, London, accepted (–1965).

New Barbican scheme, for development N.E. of St. Paul's Cathedral, proposed.

Historic Buildings Councils for England and Wales make public grants for repairs.

E May: 31st, state of emergency in Buganda, Uganda;
31st, Marshal Tito visits Greece.

F Jun: 2nd, John Costello (Fine Gael) forms coalition in Ireland;
12th, French government defeated in National Assembly;
15th, Convention People's Party wins Gold Coast elections and, 21st, Dr. K. Nkrumah forms government;
18th, Pierre Mendès-France becomes premier of France;
29th, following the meeting of President Eisenhower and W. S. Churchill in Washington the Potomac Charter, or six-point declaration of western policy, is issued.

G Jul: 2nd, French evacuate southern part of Red River delta, Indo-China;
17th, Theodor Heuss is elected President of W. Germany;
—, Finnish-U.S.S.R. trade pact;
20th, armistice for Indo-China signed in Geneva by which France evacuates N. Vietnam, the Communists evacuate S. Vietnam, Cambodia and Laos, and France undertakes to respect the independence of Cambodia, Laos and Vietnam;
23rd, Indo-China settlement is approved by French National Assembly.

H Aug: 9th, Greece, Yugoslavia and Turkey sign treaty of mutual assistance;
22nd, Brussels negotiations on E.D.C. treaty break down through French unwillingness to make concessions.

J Sep: 8th, S.E. Asian Defence treaty and Pacific Charter signed in Manila by Britain, France, U.S., Australia, New Zealand, Pakistan, Thailand and Philippines;
15th, All-China People's Congress in Peking;
27th, U.S. Senate Select Committee reports that Joseph McCarthy has acted improperly in making government employees hand over documents.

K Oct: 3rd, nine-power conference in London on European unity agrees that W. Germany should enter N.A.T.O.;
5th, Britain, U.S., Italy and Yugoslavia agree that the Free Territory of Trieste should be divided into Italian and Yugoslav zones;
8th, Communist forces occupy Hanoi;
11th, China appeals to U.N. against U.S. aggression over Formosa;
18th, W. S. Churchill reconstructs cabinet, with Harold Macmillan as Minister of Defence;
19th, Anglo-Egyptian agreement on evacuation of troops from Suez Canal zone;
23rd, Britain, France, U.S. and U.S.S.R. agree to end occupation of Germany, and nine-power agreement on W. European union signed;
24th, state of emergency in Pakistan; the Governor-General declares the Constituent Assembly has lost the people's confidence;
26th, France and W. Germany sign economic and cultural agreement.

L Nov: 3rd, outbreak of terrorism in Algeria leads to dissolution of Algerian Nationalist Movement for the Triumph of Democratic Liberties;
4th, High Court judgment supports legality of Uganda government in withdrawing recognition of the Kabaka;
5th, Burma signs peace treaty with Japan;
13th, success of Social Credit Party in New Zealand elections reduces National government's majority;
17th, General Nasser becomes head of state in Egypt, following fall of President Neguib, 14th;

T **Music**

P. Racine Fricker, viola concerto.
Rolf Liebermann, concerto for jazz-band and symphony orchestra.
Darius Milhaud's *La Rivière Endormie* uses 'musique concrète'.
E. Rubbra, 6th Symphony.
D. Shostakovich, 10th Symphony.
Lennox Berkeley, *Nelson* (opera).
B. Britten, *The Turn of the Screw* (opera).
A. Copland, *The Tender Land* (opera).
A. Schönberg, *Moses and Aaron* (opera).
C. Menotti, *The Saint of Bleecker Street* (opera).
W. Walton, *Troilus and Cressida* (opera).
Paris radio gives first complete performance of S. Prokofiev's *The Flaming Angel* (opera).
Richard Buckle stages Diaghilev Exhibition at Edinburgh Festival.

U **Literature**

Kingsley Amis, *Lucky Jim.*
Saul Bellow, *The Adventures of Augie March.*
John Betjeman, *A Few Late Chrysanthemums.*
William Golding, *Lord of the Flies.*
J. Masters, *Bhowani Junction.*
F. Sagan (pseud.), *Bonjour Tristesse.*
C. P. Snow, *The New Men.*
J. R. R. Tolkien, *The Lord of the Rings* (I and II).

V **The Press**

The London Magazine founded.

W **Drama and Entertainment**

Dylan Thomas's dramatic poem *Under Milk Wood* (broadcasting).
Enid Bagnold, *The Chalk Garden.*
J. van Druten, *I am a Camera* (from Christopher Isherwood).
Christopher Fry, *The Dark is Light Enough.*
Tennessee Williams, *Cat on a Hot Tin Roof.*
Sandy Wilson, *The Boy Friend* (revue).
Julian Slade, *Salad Days* (musical).
Films:
Henri Clouzot's *Les Diaboliques.*
Federico Fellini's *La Strada.*
Elia Kazan's *On the Waterfront.*
Alfred Hitchcock's *Rear Window.*
Andrzes Wajda's *A Generation.*
The Divided Heart.
The Seven Samurai.
Voyage in Italy.

X **Sport**

Roger Bannister runs a mile in 3 mins. 59·4 secs. (*May* 6th).
Miss D. Leather of Birmingham University becomes first woman to run a mile in under 5 mins. (*May* 30th).

Y **Statistics**

L Nov: 29th, Moscow Conference of representatives of Soviet satellite states opens; attended by observers from Communist China.

M Dec: 1st, U.S. signs pact of mutual security with Nationalist China;
2nd, U.S. Senate censures Joseph McCarthy;
—, J. G. Strijdom, Nationalist, forms ministry in S. Africa on D. F. Malan's retirement;
13th, Siróky forms ministry in Czechoslovakia;
14th, Enosis issue over Cyprus provokes riots in Athens;
17th, Marshal Tito visits Delhi;
20th, U.S.S.R. threatens to annul treaty of 1942 with Britain if Paris agreement of *Oct.* 23rd on Germany is ratified;
France sends 20,000 troops to Algeria.

N

z **Births and Deaths**

Jan. 11th John, Viscount Simon d. (80).
Oct. 7th Seebohm Rowntree d. (83).
Nov. 3rd Henri Matisse d. (84).

1955 (Jan.–May) Treaty for European Union ratified—West Germany enters N.A.T.O.—Emergency in Cyprus

A **Jan**: 10th, President Eisenhower asks Congress to extend Trade Agreement Act;
—, federal council of Nigeria first meets;
18th, Kenya government issue terms for surrender of Mau Mau;
21st, Einar Gerhardsen, Labour, forms ministry in Norway;
24th, President Eisenhower's message to Congress on defence of Formosa;
25th, U.S.S.R. decrees end of state of war with Germany;
—, Jacques Soustelle, Left Republican, appointed governor-general of Algeria for restoring order.

B **Feb**: 5th, Pierre Mendès-France resigns on vote of confidence;
8th, G. M. Malenkov, premier of U.S.S.R., resigns; succeeded by N. A. Bulganin;
23rd, foreign ministers of S.E.A.T.O. countries (established in *Sept.* 1954) confer at Bangkok;
—, Edgar Faure, Radical, forms ministry in France;
24th, Turkey and Iraq sign treaty of alliance, the Baghdad Pact.

C **Mar**: 2nd, defensive alliance between Egypt and Syria;
3rd, Greece, Yugoslavia and Turkey set up a representative parliamentary council;
11th, Italy, 18th, West Germany and, 27th, France ratify Paris agreement of *Oct.* 1954 for establishing European Union;
24th, new constitution in force in Tanganyika;
27th, state of emergency in Pakistan;
31st, purge of Chinese Communist Party.

D **Apr**: 1st, U.S. Senate ratifies Paris agreement;
4th, Britain signs treaty with Iraq, and Parliament decides to adhere to the Baghdad Pact (of *Feb.* 24th);
5th, W. S. Churchill resigns, succeeded, 6th, by Anthony Eden who, 7th, re-forms Conservative ministry, with Harold Macmillan Foreign Secretary and R. A. Butler Chancellor of the Exchequer;
14th, Chou En-lai visits Rangoon;
15th, U.S.S.R.-Austrian economic agreement;
17th, Vietnam appeals to U.N. over alleged breach of Geneva agreement by the Viet Minh;
20th, President Eisenhower asks Congress for $3,530 million for foreign aid appropriations;
29th, Giovanni Gronchi elected President of Italy.

E **May**: 5th, end of occupation régime in W. Germany;
6th, Britain submits dispute with Argentina and Chile over ownership of Falkland Islands to International Court; but those countries refuse to present counter-claims;
7th, U.S.S.R. annuls treaties with Britain and France in retaliation for the ratification of the Paris agreement on European Union;
9th, W. Germany is admitted a member of N.A.T.O.;
15th, Britain, France, U.S. and U.S.S.R. sign Vienna treaty restoring Austria's independence;
26th, in British general election Conservatives and supporters win 345 seats over Labour 277, Liberal 6 and Sinn Fein 2;
—, N. A. Bulganin and N. Khrushchev visit Yugoslavia (sign treaty of friendship *June* 2nd);
29th (–*June* 14th), railway strike in Britain;
30th, Sa'id al-Mufti forms ministry in Jordan, following resignation of Tawfig Anu'l-Huda.

O **Politics, Economics, Law and Education**

Walter Lippmann, *The Public Philosophy*.

Yarmolinsky Report, financed by Ford Foundation, reveals absurdities of various U.S. security precautions.

Judicial ruling that loyalty oath could not be required from tenants of New York Housing Authority.

P.E.P. Report on *World Population and Resources*.

The execution of Ruth Ellis, for murdering her lover, and new evidence in the Evans-Christie murders (1950) strengthen movement in Britain for abolishing capital punishment.

A 14-year-old negro boy is lynched in Mississippi.

First Commonwealth Law Conference, Westminster (*July*).

Cambridge Conference of Vice-Chancellors from 88 European universities discusses specialisation (*July*).

Universal Copyright Convention comes into force (*Sept.*).

Duke of Edinburgh's Award Scheme for Young People.

P **Science, Technology, Discovery, etc.**

Audouin Dolfus ascends 4½ miles above the earth to make photo-electric observations of Mars.

B. F. Burk discovers that Jupiter emits radio waves.

Radio-physicists of Massachusetts Institute of Technology develop use of Ultra High-Frequency waves.

First use of atomically-generated power in U.S., at Schenectady (*July* 18th).

Growing concern at dangers to health and heredity of nuclear radiation.

Jonas E. Salk prepares vaccine against poliomyelitis at Pittsburgh University.

Dorothy Hodgkin discovers composition of Vitamin B_{12} (a liver extract for treating pernicious anaemia).

F. Sanger establishes the structure of the molecule of insulin.

Walter Gibb, in a Canberra, flies at altitude of 65,876 feet.

U.S. and U.S.S.R. announce they will attempt launching of earth satellites in International Geophysical Year (1957–8).

Charles E. Singer, E. J. Holmyard and A. R. Hall, *A History of Technology*.

Phenomenon of 'flying saucers' attracts attention.

Q **Scholarship**

Stephen Runciman, *The Eastern Schism*.

Interrelations of Cultures: their Contribution to International Understanding (UNESCO).

R **Philosophy and Religion**

R. Bergmann, *The Metaphysics of Logical Positivism*.

H. J. Paton, *The Modern Predicament*.

S **Art, Sculpture, Fine Arts and Architecture**

Painting:

Pietro Annigoni, *H.M. The Queen*.

S. Dali, *The Lord's Supper*.

J. Bratby, *Still Life with Chip-Fryer*.

B. Buffet, *Circus*.

Oskar Kokoschka, *Thermopylae* (triptych).

F **Jun**: 6th, Western Powers propose a summit conference at Geneva to ease tension and U.S.S.R. agrees to meeting *July* 18th;
11th, President Eisenhower proposes financial and technical aid to all non-Communist countries to develop atomic energy;
15th, Britain and U.S. sign atomic energy agreement;
22nd, resignation of Scelba's coalition in Italy; Antonio Segni, Christian Democrat, forms coalition;
30th, U.S.-West Germany military aid agreement.

G **Jul**: 4th, British dock strike ends after four weeks;
—, Britain undertakes to return Simonstown naval base to S. Africa while retaining right to use it;
5th, Assembly of Western European Union holds first meeting at Strasbourg;
18th (–23rd), at Geneva summit conference of Britain, U.S., France and U.S.S.R., Anthony Eden proposes Germany should be reunified;
20th, headquarters of International Armistice Commission in Saigon sacked;
21st, Greece proposes the Cyprus question be put before U.N. General Assembly;
24th, N. A. Bulganin and N. Khrushchev visit E. Germany;
30th, conscription introduced in China;
31st, devaluation of the Pakistan rupee.

H **Aug**: 1st, Communist Youth Congress held in Warsaw;
8th, Geneva Conference on peaceful uses of atomic energy;
—, barter agreement between Egypt, U.S.S.R. and Roumania;
11th, Muslim-dominated Right wing ministry takes office in Indonesia;
13th, Irish Republican Army raids army training centre at Arborfield, Berkshire;
15th, Buganda transitional agreement signed in Kampala;
—, Indians attempt to enter Goa;
20th, riots in Morocco;
30th, London conference of foreign ministers of Britain, Greece and Turkey on Cyprus and E. Mediterranean.

J **Sep**: 6th, anti-Greek riots in Istanbul and Izmir;
16th, rising in Córdoba under General Eduardo Lonardi spreads throughout Argentina;
19th, Juan Perón resigns, going into exile; and
23rd, Lonardi assumes presidency of Argentina;
—, Bundestag votes for resumption of relations of W. Germany with U.S.S.R.
24th, President Eisenhower suffers a heart attack;
25th, John Harding appointed governor of Cyprus.

K **Oct**: 2nd, France withdraws from U.N. General Assembly meeting through hostile interference over Algeria;
12th, goodwill visits of Royal Navy to Leningrad and U.S.S.R. Navy to Portsmouth; disappearance of Commander Crabbe, frogman, at Portsmouth;
17th, following withdrawal of Sultan of Morocco to Tangier, a Council of the Throne is instituted;
—, the Kabaka returns to Buganda;
23rd, referendum in S. Vietnam advocates deposition of Emperor Bao Dai and, 26th, republic is proclaimed under Ngo Dinh Diem;
26th, R. A. Butler introduces autumn Budget, embodying credit squeeze, to deal with Britain's unfavourable balance of payments;

S **Arts, Sculpture, Fine Arts and Architecture** (*cont.*)

Sculpture:

Lynn Chadwick, *Winged figures.*

H. G. Adam, Concrete sculpture for Le Havre Museum, forecourt.

Architecture:

Le Corbusier (pseud.), La Torette, Eveaux-sur-l'Arbresle, Lyons.

Frederick Gibberd, London Airport Buildings.

Eero Saarinen, General Motors Technical Center, Michigan.

T **Music**

Rolf Liebermann, *School for Wives* (opera).

Michael Tippett, *The Midsummer Marriage* (opera).

U **Literature**

J. Cary, *Not Honour More.*

R. Church, *Over the Bridge.*

I. Ehrenburg, *The Thaw.*

The Diary of Anne Frank.

Julian Green, *The Enemy.*

Graham Greene, *The Quiet American.*

J. Lehmann, *The Whispering Gallery.*

Vladimir Nabokov, *Lolita.*

V **The Press**

W **Drama and Entertainment**

S. Beckett, *Waiting for Godot.*

Ugo Betti, *The Queen and the Rebels.*

S. Lawler, *The Summer of the Seventeenth Doll.*

A. Miller, *A View from the Bridge.*

Ronald Duncan founds English Stage Company.

Commercial television in Britain (*Sept.*).

Films:

Juan Bardem's *Death of a Cyclist.*

Ingmar Bergman's *Smiles of a Summer Night.*

René Clair's *Les Grandes Manœuvres.*

Nicholas Ray's *Rebel Without a Cause.*

Sergei Samsonov's *The Grasshopper.*

Le Mystère Picasso.

Wild Birds.

Bill Haley's *Rock Around the Clock.*

X **Sport**

Y **Statistics**

Railway mileage in operation: U.S., 234,342; Great Britain, 20,120; West Germany, 18,950; Japan, 17,200; China, 8,000.

K **Oct:** 27th (–*Nov.* 16th), four-power Geneva conference of foreign ministers on security and position of Germany;
30th, Sultan of Morocco abdicates.

L **Nov:** 1st, John Foster Dulles visits General Franco and, 6th, Marshal Tito;
2nd, D. Ben-Gurion forms ministry in Israel;
3rd, Persia joins Iraq-Turkey (Baghdad) Pact;
9th, S. Africa withdraws from U.N. General Assembly, since U.N.O. decides to continue consideration of Cruz Report of 1952 on *apartheid*;
16th, J. F. Dulles, H. Macmillan and A. Pinay issue statement on Germany in opposition to V. Molotov who had refused to discuss the question of Germany's reunification;
26th, John Harding proclaims state of emergency in Cyprus.

M **Dec:** 9th, Adnan Menderes forms ministry in Turkey;
13th, Hugh Gaitskell is elected leader of Labour Party, following C. R. Attlee's retirement;
14th, Albania, Austria, Bulgaria, Cambodia, Ceylon, Finland, Hungary, Ireland, Italy, Jordan, Laos, Libya, Nepal, Portugal, Roumania, and Spain, elected to U.N.;
20th, Anthony Eden re-forms ministry, with Harold Macmillan Chancellor of the Exchequer and Selwyn Lloyd Foreign Secretary.

N Border raids between Israel and Jordan increase in intensity.

z Births and Deaths

Mar. 11th Alexander Fleming d. (73).
Apr. 18th Albert Einstein d. (76).
July 24th Cordell Hull d. (83).
Aug. 12th Thomas Mann d. (80).
Nov. 24th Lionel Curtis d. (83).

 Suez crisis—Hungarian Revolution—S. African Treason Trial begins

A **Jan**: 1st, Sudan is proclaimed an independent democratic republic;
2nd, Communists and Poujadists (Union et Fraternité Française) gain seats in French elections;
3rd, U.S.S.R. extends technical assistance to China;
5th, Marshal Tito meets Colonel Nasser in Cairo;
8th, first U.S.S.R. ambassador to W. Germany;
18th (–*Feb.* 8th), conference on Malayan federation, recommends independence by *Aug.* 1957;
—, National People's Army formed in E. Germany;
19th, Sudan joins Arab League, as ninth member;
23rd, N. A. Bulganin proposes 20-year U.S.S.R.-U.S. pact of friendship;
24th, Jordan and Israel accept U.N. truce proposals to ease Middle East tension;
25th, Guillebaud Committee reports on British Health Service.

B **Feb**: 1st, S. Africa requests U.S.S.R. to withdraw all consulates;
—, Anthony Eden and President Eisenhower issue Declaration of Washington, reaffirming joint policy in Middle East;
—, Guy Mollet, Socialist, forms ministry in France;
3rd, U.S.S.R. provides economic aid to Bulgaria;
4th, U.S.S.R. protests to U.S. about launching of balloons with photographic equipment over Soviet territory;
11th, referendum in Malta favours integration with Britain;
12th, U.S.S.R. states that the dispatch of U.S. or British troops to the Middle East would violate U.N. Charter;
14th, at 20th Soviet Communist Party Conference, N. Khrushchev denounces policies of Stalin;
15th (–*Mar.* 23rd), lock-out in British printing industry forces many periodicals to be printed abroad;
16th, British bank rate raised to 5½ per cent, highest rate since 1932, to curb inflation;
28th, India and Indonesia sign mutual aid treaty;
29th, Pakistan becomes an Islamic Republic (*Mar.* 2nd, decides to stay in Commonwealth).

C **Mar**: 2nd, France recognises independence of Morocco (Spanish recognition, *Apr.* 7th);
—, King Hussein of Jordan dismisses General J. B. Glubb from command of Arab Legion;
5th, Britain begins jamming Athens broadcasts to Cyprus;
7th, unrest in Georgia fomented by Stalinist faction;
8th, West German Constitution amended to permit introduction of conscription;
9th, Archbishop Makarios is deported from Cyprus to the Seychelles;
12th, Greece asks Cyprus question to be put before U.N. General Assembly;
15th, G. M. Malenkov visits British electrical installations;
20th, France recognises independence of Tunisia, with Bourguiba first President;
28th, Iceland calls for revision of 1951 agreement with U.S. and withdrawal of troops.

D **Apr**: 9th, U.S.S.R.-Mongolian Republic economic pact;
10th, People's United Front, led by D. Bandaranaike, wins Ceylon elections;
17th, Cominform dissolved;
—, Harold Macmillan introduces premium savings bonds in Budget;
18th (–28th), N. A. Bulganin and N. Khrushchev visit Britain;
21st, Egypt, Saudi Arabia and Yemen sign military alliance at Jedda;
22nd, China appoints Dalai Lama chairman of committee to prepare Tibet for regional autonomy within Chinese People's Republic;

O **Politics, Economics, Law and Education**

C.N.D. members and sympathisers march from Aldermaston in protest against nuclear arms and the dangers of radiation; such dangers are discussed in a World Health Organisation report (*Aug.* 16th).

Department of Scientific and Industrial Research Act establishes a new research council with wider powers. The Department's report on *Automation* puts into perspective the impact of automatic methods on industry.

F. Pollock and A. Weber, *Revolution of the Robots.*

Britain decides to spend an extra £100 million on technological education.

Norman St. John-Stevas, *Obscenity and the Law.*

Clinton Rossiter, *Conservatism in America.*

W. H. Whyte, *The Organization Man.*

Desegregation conflict in southern states of U.S. on schooling culminates in the case of A. Lucy at Alabama University.

P **Science, Technology, Discovery, etc.**

H. P. Wilkins and P. Moore, *The Moon.*

Edward Appleton's Reith Lectures, *Science and the Nation.*

Detection of the 'neutrino' (a particle of no electric charge) at Los Alamos Laboratory, U.S.

Discovery of the anti-neutron at California University.

'Dido' reactor at Harwell opened (*Nov.* 21st).

Calder Hall, the largest nuclear power station, opened (*Oct.* 17th) and by the end of year supplies 65,000 kW.

F. W. Müller develops the ion microscope.

Tube Investments Ltd. brings into operation the first multi-purpose industrial high-energy plant in Europe.

Mullard image-dissector camera, capable of taking very rapid photographs.

Bell Telephone Company develops 'visual telephone', transmitting pictures simultaneously with sound.

Transatlantic telephone service inaugurated (*Sept.* 25th).

Peter Twiss flies at 1,132 m.p.h. in a Fairy Delta (*Mar.* 10th).

Scientists from seven countries encamp in Antarctica in preparation for International Geophysical Year.

Q **Scholarship**

Harold Acton, *The Bourbons of Naples.*

Lord Beaverbrook, *Men and Power, 1917.*

W. S. Churchill, *History of the English-Speaking Peoples* (–58).

Margery Perham, *Lugard: The Years of Adventure (1858–98).*

R **Philosophy and Religion**

A. J. Ayer, *The Revolution in Philosophy.*

R. Bultmann, *Essays Philosophical and Theological.*

Karl Mannheim, *Essays on the Sociology of Culture.*

Jean Mouroux, *The Christian Experience.*

Colin Wilson, *The Outsider.*

The German Evangelistic Churches begin revision of Lutheran text of New Testament.

The Buddhist Council, Rangoon, ends (*May*), the sixth council since 483 B.C.

S **Art, Sculpture, Fine Arts and Architecture**

Painting:

John Bratby publishes *A Painter's Credo.*

D Apr: 29th, cease-fire between Israel and Jordan, arranged by Dag Hammarskjöld, in force.

E May: 1st, Lebanon-Israel and, 2nd, Syrian-Israel cease-fires;
1st, Peronista Constitution revoked in Argentina;
9th, British Togoland plebiscite votes for integration with Gold Coast;
11th, European Coal and Steel Community adopts resolutions on a European common market and Euratom;
14th, U.S.S.R. complains U.S. 'planes have violated her air space;
22nd, Said el-Mufti forms ministry in Jordan;
—, Pandit Nehru announces plan for solving Algerian problem;
27th, India claims suzerainty over Chitral, which has been under Pakistani administration since 1947;
28th, France cedes former French settlements in India to Indian Union;
30th, life insurance nationalised in India;
31st, U.N. decides to withdraw inspection teams from Korea through frustration of their activities by North Koreans and Chinese.

F Jun: 1st, D. M. Shepilov succeeds V. Molotov as U.S.S.R. foreign minister;
2nd, Marshal Tito visits Moscow;
4th, Egypt declares she will not extend Suez Canal Company's concession after expiry in 1968;
6th, N. A. Bulganin calls on powers to match U.S.S.R.'s cuts in armed forces;
7th, in Tonbridge by-election Conservative majority drops by 8,594 votes in straight fight with Labour;
13th, last British troops leave Suez Canal base;
14th, U.S. and Britain sign agreement on atomic co-operation;
22nd, Julius Raab forms new coalition of Right in Austria;
24th, Colonel Nasser elected President of Egypt;
27th, Pakistan-U.S.S.R. trade pact;
28th, Sydney Silverman's bill for abolition of death penalty passes Commons (defeated in Lords, *July* 10th);
—, labour riots at Poznań, Poland, put down with heavy loss of life;
30th, Leeward Islands federation dissolved to enable islands to enter Caribbean federation.

G Jul: 7th, Sinhalese becomes official language in Ceylon;
9th, Duke of Edinburgh's Oxford conference on industry begins;
—, Restrictive Practices Act sets up Restrictive Practices Court in Britain;
11th, Finno-Karelian Republic abolished through incorporation in U.S.S.R. as Karelian Autonomous Republic;
17th, Kwame Nkrumah, People's Party, increases majority in Gold Coast elections;
19th (–20th), U.S. and Britain inform Egypt they cannot at present participate in financing Aswan High Dam project;
23rd, Royal Navy's first guided-missile vessel, H.M.S. *Girdle Ness*, commissioned;
26th, President Nasser seizes Suez Canal, under decree outlawing the company, provoking
26th (–31st), financial retaliations against Egypt by Britain, France and U.S.;
31st, British-West German ten-year agreement on atomic co-operation.

H Aug: 2nd, British and French nationals leave Egypt;
—, Britain rejects request of Federation of Rhodesia and Nyasaland for status as separate state within Commonwealth;

S Art, Sculpture, Fine Arts and Architecture (*cont.*)

Sculpture:

Lynn Chadwick, *Teddy Boy and Girl*.

Barbara Hepworth, *Orpheus*, Mullard House, London.

F. E. McWilliam, *Elizabeth Frink* for Harlow New Town Centre.

Architecture:

E. Saarinen's design for U.S. Embassy, London, wins open competition (–1960).

William Holford's plan for St. Paul's area published.

P. Nervi and Vitellozi, Palazzo dello Sport, Rome.

Jørn Utzon, Opera House, Sydney.

T Music

Heiss, song-cycle *Expression K* (Kafka).

Jean Martinu, *Hecube* (opera).

I. Stravinsky, *Canticum sacrum ad honorem Sancti Marci nominis.*

F. Ashton–Malcolm Arnold, *Birthday Offering* (ballet).

Humphrey Searle, *Noctambules* (ballet).

Bolshoi Ballet visits London.

U Literature

Kathleen Raine, *Collected Poems*.

Angus Wilson, *Anglo-Saxon Attitudes*.

V The Press

W Drama and Entertainment

J. Anouilh, *Poor Bitos* and *The Waltz of the Toreadors*.

J. Osborne, *Look Back in Anger*.

Angus Wilson, *The Mulberry Bush*.

English Stage Company's productions at Royal Court Theatre begin.

B. Brecht's Berliner Ensemble visits England for first London production of *The Threepenny Opera*.

Films:

Juan Bardem's *Calle Mayor*.

Ingmar Bergman's *The Seventh Seal*.

Elia Kazan's *Baby Doll* with script by Tennessee Williams.

Alain Resnais, *Nuit et Brouillard*.

A Town Like Alice.

The King and I with Yul Brunner and Deborah Kerr.

Prince Rainier of Monaco marries Grace Kelly.

'Rock and Roll' dominates dance-floors.

X Sport

Olympic Games at Melbourne.

Y Statistics

Z Births and Deaths

Feb. 10th Hugh, Viscount Trenchard d. (83).

May 20th Max Beerbohm d. (83).

June 11th Frank Brangwyn d. (89).

June 22nd Walter de la Mare d. (83)

Sept. 22nd Frederick Soddy d. (79).

H Aug: 3rd, Gold Coast League Assembly adopts Kwame Nkrumah's resolution demanding independence, which is granted by Britain, *Sept.* 18th;
4th, Indonesia repudiates debts to Netherlands;
9th, airlift of British families from Suez Canal zone;
16th, first London conference on Suez boycotted by Nasser;
21st, J. F. Dulles's plan on Suez accepted by 18 nations, but U.S.S.R., India, Indonesia and Ceylon back alternative scheme by Pandit Nehru;
22nd, John Harding, governor of Cyprus, offers surrender terms which EOKA rejects;
25th, Greece and Roumania resume diplomatic relations.

J Sep: 10th, Nasser rejects 18-nation proposals for Suez Canal;
19th, second London conference on Suez meets; and
21st, establishes Canal Users' Association (which first meets in London, *Oct.* 18th);
23rd, Britain and France refer Suez dispute to U.N. Security Council;
29th, bread subsidy ends in Britain after 15 years;
—, Joseph Grimond succeeds Clement Davies as leader of British Parliamentary Liberal Party;
30th, Admiral Karl Doenitz released from Spandau prison, Berlin.

K Oct: 2nd, Aneurin Bevan elected treasurer of British Labour Party;
8th, Israel withdraws from Israeli-Jordan mixed armistice commission;
12th, Britain informs Israel she will be obliged to assist Jordan, if attacked, under 1948 treaty;
13th, Security Council adopts Anglo-French resolution on Suez, but U.S.S.R. vetoes this;
22nd, demonstrations in Hungary call for democratic government, the return of Imre Nagy to power, the withdrawal of U.S.S.R. troops and the release of Cardinal Mindszenty;
24th, Imre Nagy is appointed minister-president of Hungary and re-elected to Politburo; state of emergency; U.S.S.R. troops intervene;
25th, unified Egyptian-Jordanian-Syrian military command;
27th, new Hungarian government under Imre Nagy, including non-Communists;
—, Franco-German agreement on Saar;
28th, release of Cardinal Wyszynski, primate of Poland;
29th, Israeli troops invade Sinai Peninsula but Britain is assured they will not attack Jordan;
—, János Kádár becomes leader of Central Committee of Hungarian Workers' Party;
30th, Anglo-French ultimatum to Egypt and Israel calls for cease-fire and withdrawal ten miles from Suez, which is accepted only by Israel;
—, Cardinal Mindszenty is released; but Soviet troops invade N.E. Hungary;
31st, Anglo-French troops bomb Egyptian airfields; public outcry in Britain over the Suez War;
—, Roy Welensky succeeds Lord Malvern as premier of Federation of Rhodesia and Nyasaland;
—, U.S. sends aid to Israel.

L Nov: 1st, Jordan disallows use of R.A.F. bases in operations against Egypt;
2nd, Gaza falls to British;
—, Hungarian government renounces Warsaw treaty and appeals to U.N. and the powers against U.S.S.R. invasion;
—, U.S.S.R. vetoes Western powers request for U.N. Security Council to consider critical state in Hungary;

(*Continued opposite*)

L **Nov**: 3rd, Britain and France accept Middle East cease-fire if U.N. force will keep the peace;
4th, U.N. General Assembly adopts Canadian resolution to send international force to Middle East, with Britain and France abstaining;
—, Soviet forces attack Budapest. Imre Nagy takes refuge in Yugoslav Embassy; defection of János Kádár who forms a 'revolutionary peasant-worker' government;
5th, British paratroops land at Port Said;
—, U.S.S.R. threatens use of rockets unless Britain and France accept cease-fire;
6th, in U.S. presidential election, Dwight D. Eisenhower, Republican, re-elected with 457 electoral votes over Adlai Stevenson, Democrat, 74 votes, but Republicans fare badly in state elections;
7th, Anglo-French cease-fire in Egypt, but Britain declares she will evacuate troops only on arrival of U.N. force;
8th, U.N. General Assembly demands withdrawal of U.S.S.R. troops from Hungary;
9th, S. Vietnam's Constituent Assembly inaugurated;
10th, Baghdad Pact boycotts Britain (–*Mar.* 1957);
12th, János Kádár refuses entry to Hungary for U.N. observers but accepts U.N. relief;
13th, Alfred Gruenther, Supreme Allied Commander Europe, warns U.S.S.R. of retaliation if she uses rockets;
15th, U.N. emergency force arrives in Egypt;
—, U.S.S.R. loan to India;
17th, Kashmir votes to be an integral part of India;
20th, Lauris Norstad succeeds Alfred Gruenther as Supreme Allied Commander Europe;
21st, U.N. General Assembly censures U.S.S.R. over Hungary;
23rd (–*Dec.* 14th), Anthony Eden leaves London for recuperation in Jamaica, with R. A. Butler deputising for him.

M **Dec**: 3rd, U.S. suspends cultural exchange programme with U.S.S.R.;
5th, mass arrests on treason charges in S. Africa of Europeans, Africans and Natives;
—, Anglo-French forces begin withdrawal from Egypt;
—, Paul Spaak appointed Secretary-General of N.A.T.O. Council;
8th, call for a general strike in Hungary leads to proclamation of martial law and mass arrests;
17th, petrol rationing in Britain;
18th, Japan is admitted to U.N.;
19th, Lord Radcliffe's proposals for Cyprus constitution published;
—, preliminary hearing against over 150 accused in Johannesburg treason trial;
22nd, last Anglo-French forces leave Port Said;
27th, U.N. fleet begins clearance of Suez Canal;
31st, President Sukarno proclaims state of siege in S. Sumatra.

N

1957 (Jan.–Mar.) Macmillan succeeds Eden—Rome Treaty for Common Market—Middle East crisis—The Rapacki plan

A **Jan**: 7th, Chou En-lai, premier of Chinese People's Republic, visits Moscow;
8th (–*Feb.* 26th), Syrian conspiracy trials, resulting in life sentences on ex-President Chichekli and others;
9th, Anthony Eden resigns;
10th, Harold Macmillan becomes Premier and, 13th, forms Conservative ministry with R. A. Butler Home Secretary, Selwyn Lloyd Foreign Secretary and Peter Thorneycroft Chancellor of the Exchequer;
20th, S. Africa denies port facilities to Indian vessels in retaliation for Indian sanctions against S. Africa.
22nd, Israeli forces complete withdrawal from Sinai Peninsula, but remain in Gaza strip;
24th, British Minister of Defence is given enlarged powers of control over defence services;
26th, Kashmir Constitution for incorporation with India in force, provoking demonstrations;
30th, U.N. General Assembly calls on S. Africa to reconsider *apartheid* policies;
31st, Trans-Iranian pipeline, Abadan–Teheran, completed.

B **Feb**: 2nd, Austria closes down offices of World Peace Council in Vienna;
9th, Japan and Poland resume diplomatic relations;
11th, Franco-U.S.S.R. trade pact;
12th, industrial rates in Britain raised to 50 per cent of net annual value (remained at 25 per cent since 1929);
14th, Labour wins Lewisham by-election from Conservatives;
—, Britain states she will reduce forces in Germany;
15th, Andrei Gromyko replaces D. T. Shepilov as U.S.S.R. foreign minister;
26th, U.N. General Assembly calls for a peaceful, democratic solution in Cyprus.

C **Mar**: 2nd (–14th), state of emergency in E. Indonesia and Thailand;
5th, U.S. Senate approves Eisenhower's doctrine for U.S. forces to protect political independence of states of Middle East;
6th, Israeli troops hand over Gaza strip to U.N. force;
—, Ghana becomes independent State within the Commonwealth and, 8th, is admitted to U.N.;
11th (–*Apr.* 11th), Singapore Constitutional Conference in London, agrees on internal self-government during 1958;
12th, Indian loan to Burma;
13th, expiration of Anglo-Jordan treaty of 1948;
14th, EOKA offers to suspend terrorist activities on release of Archbishop Makarios;
20th, Britain accepts N.A.T.O. offer to mediate in Cyprus, but rejected by Greece;
21st, Dag Hammarskjöld, U.N. Secretary-General, visits President Nasser;
— (–24th), President Eisenhower and Harold Macmillan at Bermuda Conference re-establish special relationship between Britain and U.S., which had been strained by Suez Crisis, and U.S. undertakes to make certain guided missiles available to Britain;
24th, Baghdad Pact ends boycott of Britain;
25th, Belgium, France, W. Germany, Italy, Luxembourg and Netherlands (the 'Six') sign Rome treaties for Common Market and Euratom;
27th, French company is formed to exploit mineral resources of Sahara;
28th, Britain releases Archbishop Makarios who is free to travel, except to Cyprus, and General Grivas is offered safe conduct to Greece;
29th, ships of small draught begin using Suez Canal (open to ships of maximum draught, *Apr.* 9th).

O **Politics, Economics, Law and Education**

Lord Hailey, *An African Survey* (revised).
Trevor Huddleston, *Naught for Your Comfort*.
V. P. Menon, *The Transfer of Power in India*.
W. Sargent's *The Battle for the Mind*, discusses brain-washing.
Declaration, a symposium by 'Angry Young Men'.
Desegregation crisis in Little Rock, Arkansas.
International Atomic Energy Agency is inaugurated at Vienna Conference.
Five-day week in British Civil Service.
U.S. trade recession (*Nov.*).
Richard Hoggart, *The Uses of Literacy*.

P **Science, Technology, Discovery, etc.**

International Geophysical Year begins (*July* 1st), with scientists concentrating on Antarctic exploration, oceanographic and meteorological research and the launching of satellites into space.
U.S.S.R. launches Sputnik I (*Oct.* 4th) to study the cosmosphere; weighing 180 lb., it circles the globe in 95 mins. Sputnik II is sent in orbit (*Nov.* 3rd) carrying an Eskimo dog, for studying living conditions in space.
Manchester University Jodrell Bank radio-telescope, under Bernard Lovell, tracks the Sputnik I's progress.
A new radio-telescope is built for the Mullard Observatory, Cambridge.
Artificial rain in New South Wales increases rainfall by 25 per cent and in Queensland saves crops.
Giberellin, a growth-producing hormone, is isolated.
Nobelium (element 102) is discovered at Stockholm.
H.M.C.S. *Labrador* discovers new north-west passage.
U.S.S.R. non-magnetic ship *Star* sets sail on expedition to take magnetic recordings.
U.S. expedition is flown in to South Pole.

Q **Scholarship**

Kathleen Kenyon, *Digging up Jericho*.
H. W. Parke and D. Wormell, *The Delphic Oracle*.
New Cambridge Modern History begins publication.
Arthur Bryant, *The Turn of the Tide*.
A. M. Schlesinger, *The Crisis of the Old Order, 1919–33*.

R **Philosophy and Religion**

A. J. Ayer, *The Problem of Knowledge*.
Fred Hoyle, *Man and Materialism*.
Alec Vidler, *Essays in Liberality*.
First conference of European Rabbis, under Israel Brodie.

S **Art, Sculpture, Fine Arts and Architecture**

Painting:
Francis Bacon, *Screaming Nurse*.
K. Clark's survey, *The Nude*.
Graham Sutherland, *Princess Gourielli*.

Sculpture:
H. G. Adam, *Beacon of the Dead*, monument for Auschwitz (–1958).
J. Epstein, *Christ in Majesty* for Llandaff Cathedral.
R. Whistler, *seven glasses* for U.K. Atomic Energy Authority.

D Apr: 12th, W. German nuclear physicists refuse to co-operate in production or testing of atomic weapons;
13th, demonstrations in Jordan against Eisenhower doctrine;
17th, Pandit Nehru forms new Indian Congress movement, with Krishna Menon minister of defence;
18th, representatives of Burma, Ceylon, India, Indonesia, Iraq, Japan and Syria attend first meeting in New Delhi of Asian Legal Consultative Committee;
20th, U.S. resumes aid to Israel (suspended *Oct.* 1956);
—, Japan protests to U.S.S.R. over nuclear tests;
23rd, Albert Schweitzer's letter to Norwegian Nobel Committee urging mobilisation of world opinion against nuclear tests;
24th, Ibrahim Hashem forms Right wing ministry in Jordan, following demonstrations of Committee of National Guidance;
25th, U.S. 6th Fleet sails for E. Mediterranean (provokes U.S.S.R. protest, 29th);
—, King Hussein proclaims martial law in Jordan and seals frontiers;
29th, Hussein and King Saud of Saudi Arabia state the crisis in Jordan is an internal affair.

E May: 2nd, *Die Stem Van Suid Afrika* to be S. African national anthem;
5th, Adolf Schärf elected President of Austria;
10th, U.S.S.R. appeals to U.S. and Britain to cease nuclear tests;
15th, Britain explodes first British thermonuclear bomb in megaton range in Central Pacific;
19th, Adoni Zoli forms ministry in Italy, following resignation of Segni's coalition, 6th, on withdrawal of Social Democrats' support;
21st, Guy Mollet, Socialist, resigns premiership of France;
23rd (–*June* 26th), Nigerian Constitutional Conference in London;
30th, Britain relaxes restrictions on trade with Communist China.

F Jun: 1st, ERNIE draws first premium bond prizes in Britain;
4th, increase in British tourist travel allowance to dollar area;
5th, Britain and U.S. atomic authorities agree on exchange of information;
6th, Rent Act, de-restricting many previously controlled rents, receives royal assent; Labour displays hostility in refusing to join procession to Lords;
10th, Progressive Conservatives win Canadian elections (17th, Louis St. Laurent, Liberal, resigns, and 21st, John Diefenbaker forms ministry);
12th, Maurice Bourgès-Manoury, Radical, forms ministry in France;
22nd, three British subjects sentenced to imprisonment in Cairo espionage trial.

G Jul: 4th, V. Molotov, D. J. Shepilov and G. M. Malenkov expelled from Presidium of Central Committee of Soviet Communist Party;
15th, Franco announces that the Spanish monarchy would be restored on his death or retirement;
19th (–*Aug.* 14th), the Imam of Oman revolts against the Sultan of Oman, who requests British aid;
— (–26th) bus strike in Britain;
29th, International Atomic Energy Agency comes into being;
—, Western Powers and W. Germany issue declaration on German reunification and call for free elections;
30th, Royal Commission on Local Government in Greater London Area appointed.

H Aug: 8th, President Bourguiba of Tunisia appeals to Egypt for arms;

S Art, Sculpture, Fine Arts and Architecture (*cont.*)

Architecture:

Lucio Costa prepares plans for Brasilia, new capital of Brazil.

F. Gibberd, Hinkley Point Atomic Power Station, Somerset.

Le Corbusier (pseud.), Tokio Museum (–60).

T Music

Malcolm Arnold, 3rd Symphony.

Elliott Carter, *Variations for Orchestra*.

Jean Françaix, *King Midas* (opera).

John Gardner, *The Moon and Sixpence* (opera).

P. Hindemith, *The Harmony of the World* (opera).

Francis Poulenc, *Dialogues des Carmélites*.

William Walton, 'cello concerto.

I. Stravinsky, *Agon* (ballet).

B. Britten, *Prince of the Pagodas* (ballet).

U Literature

Sibylle Beford, *A Legacy*.

John Braine, *Room at the Top*.

Jack Kerouac, *On the Road*.

C. Day-Lewis, *Pegasus*.

Iris Murdoch, *The Sandcastle*.

Roger Vailland, *The Law*.

P. White, *Voss*.

V The Press

W Drama and Entertainment

Entertainment duty abolished on living theatre in Britain and reduced on films.

S. Beckett, *Endgame*.

Robert Bolt, *The Flowering Cherry*.

John Osborne, *The Entertainer*.

My Fair Lady (musical).

Films:

Ingmar Bergman's *Wild Strawberries*.

Charlie Chaplin's *A King in New York*.

Mikhail Kalatozov, *The Cranes are Flying*.

David Lean's *The Bridge on the River Kwai*, with Alec Guinness.

Laurence Olivier's *The Prince and the Showgirl*, with Marilyn Monroe.

Otto Preminger's *Bonjour Tristesse*.

Porte des Lilas.

Quiet Flows the Don.

X Sport

Y Statistics

Production of electric power (in mill. kilowatts): U.S., 715,706; U.S.S.R. 209,480; Great Britain, 105,536; W. Germany, 91,773; Canada, 90,249; Japan, 81,303; France, 57,433.

Production of motor vehicles (in thousands): U.S., 7,200; W. Germany, 1,211; Great Britain, 1,149; France, 927; U.S.S.R., 495; Italy, 352; Japan, 45.

Rubber production (in thousand metric tons): U.S., 1,136 (synthetic); Indonesia, 696; Malaya, 648; Thailand, 135; Canada, 134 (synthetic); Cambodia and Vietnam, 101; Ceylon, 100.

H Aug: 15th, Cheddi Jagan forms government in British Guiana, following success of People's Progressive Party in elections;
30th, All-African Federal Executive Council formed in Nigeria;
31st, independence of Malayan Federation in force.

J Sep: 4th, Wolfenden Report on homosexual offences and prostitution published in Britain;
—, economic union of Egypt and Syria;
11th, U.S.S.R. complains to Turkey of concentrations of Turkish troops on Syrian borders;
14th, special session of U.N. General Assembly adopts U.N. report on Hungary;
15th, sweeping victory for Konrad Adenauer's Christian Democratic Union in W. German elections;
16th–17th, *coup d'état* in Thailand places Pote Sarasin, the new Secretary-General of S.E.A.T.O., as premier;
19th, British bank rate raised from 5 to 7 per cent;
20th, K. J. Holyoake becomes premier of New Zealand on Sidney Holland's retirement;
21st, accession of Olaf V of Norway on death of King Haakon;
23rd, Roumanian request to join Balkan Pact is refused by Greece;
26th, Dag Hammarskjöld, Sweden, re-elected Secretary-General of U.N. for further five years.

K Oct: 2nd, Rapacki Plan for a denuclearised zone in Central Europe presented to U.N. General Assembly by Polish People's Republic, supported by Czechoslovakia and E. Germany;
4th, Milovan Djilas, former Vice-President of Yugoslavia, sentenced to further term of imprisonment for spreading hostile propaganda;
7th, Labour Party returns to power in Norway;
12th, N. Khrushchev's letters to Labour and Socialist Parties in Britain and Europe urging them to prevent aggression of U.S. and Turkey in Middle East;
— (–21st), Queen Elizabeth visits Canada and U.S., and, 21st, addresses U.N. General Assembly;
16th, Syria declares state of emergency;
—, J. F. Dulles, U.S. secretary of state, warns U.S.S.R. against attack on Turkey;
19th, W. Germany severs relations with Yugoslavia, on the latter's recognition of E. Germany;
22nd, Hugh Foot appointed to succeed John Harding as governor of Cyprus;
23rd, Harold Macmillan visits Washington and, 26th, Ottawa;
26th, Marshal Zhukov, U.S.S.R. minister of defence, relieved of duties;
29th, Fulgencio Batista suspends Cuban constitution;
30th, Felix Gaillard, Radical Socialist, forms ministry in France.

L Nov: 11th, full internal self-government in Jamaica;
14th, Britain and U.S. send token consignments of arms to Tunisia provoking, 15th, French delegations to leave N.A.T.O. Conference;
—, Britain declares Bahrein an independent Arab State under British protection;
26th, International Court of Justice declares itself competent to adjudicate in India-Portuguese dispute over Portuguese enclaves in India;
27th, Pandit Nehru appeals to U.S. and U.S.S.R. to bring about effective disarmament.

(*Continued opposite*)

Z **Births and Deaths**

Jan. 16th Arturo Toscanini d. (89).
Feb. 9th Nicholas Horthy d. (88).
Mar. 11th Richard Evelyn Byrd d. (68).
Mar. 26th Édouard Herriot d. (84).
May 2nd Joseph McCarthy d. (47).
July 3rd Frederick Lindemann, Lord Cherwell d. (71).
July 11th Aga Khan d. (79)
Aug. 24th Ronald A. Knox d. (69).
Sept. 20th Jean Sibelius d. (91).
Nov. 30th Beniamino Gigli d. (67).
Dec. 18th Dorothy L. Sayers d. (64).

M **Dec**: 1st, retaliatory measures against Dutch in Indonesia following attempt on President Sukarno's life;

2nd, Bank Rate Tribunal under Lord Parker considers allegations of leakage of information;

8th, merger of four small Left wing parties in France as Union de la Gauche Socialiste;

15th, Greek resolution that Cyprus is entitled to self-determination fails to gain two-thirds majority in U.N.

19th, regular London–Moscow air service opens;

20th, European Nuclear Energy Agency inaugurated;

21st, U.S.S.R. proposals for summit conference;

30th, Maltese Legislative Assembly resolves that Malta has no obligations to Britain unless employment is found for discharged dockyard workers.

N

1958 (Jan.–Apr.) Khrushchev in power in Russia—Election of Pope John XXIII—De Gaulle elected President of France

A **Jan:** 1st, European Common Market and Euratom in force;
—, W. German forces handed over to N.A.T.O. command;
3rd (–14th), notes from British, U.S. and other powers objecting to Indonesian proclamation extending territorial waters;
—, West Indies Federation in force;
6th, Peter Thorneycroft, Enoch Powell and E. N. C. Birch resign from Harold Macmillan's government on cabinet refusing to prune estimates and
7th, D. H. Amory appointed Chancellor of the Exchequer;
8th, Marshal Bulganin again proposes summit conference;
20th, U.S.S.R. threatens Greece with economic sanctions if she agrees to installation of N.A.T.O. missile bases on her territory.

B **Feb:** 1st, Egypt and Sudan proclaim union as the United Arab Republic (and, 21st, plebiscite for President Nasser as head of state);
3rd, Benelux economic treaty signed;
5th, North Korea proposes withdrawal of all foreign troops from North and South Korea (completed *Oct.* 28th);
11th, Tunisia informs France that French warships will no longer be allowed to use Bizerta;
12th, Labour wins Rochdale by-election, with Conservatives at botton of poll;
14th, Rapacki Plan for denuclearised zone of Central Europe delivered to foreign envoys in Warsaw (rejected by U.S., *Apr.* 14th, and by Britain, *May* 18th);
—, union of Kingdoms of Iraq and Jordan in Arab Federation with King Feisal as head of state;
15th, Britain and U.S. propose summit talks be preceded by meeting of foreign ministers or of ambassadors;
17th, Edgar Whitehead forms ministry in S. Rhodesia, when Garfield Todd, former premier, was ousted from leadership of United Federal Party on account of his stand on the franchise for Africans;
—, France and Tunisia accept mediation of Britain and U.S.;
19th, Anglo-Spanish trade pact;
20th, Kwame Nkrumah sets up foundation for mutual assistance in Africa south of the Sahara;
25th, Ceylon-U.S.S.R. agreement on technical co-operation;
27th, Umma Party wins Sudanese elections.

C **Mar:** 3rd, Nuri-es-Said forms ministry in Iraq;
5th, Syria accuses King Saud of organising plot to overthrow Syrian régime and prevent union with Egypt;
14th, Marshal Bulganin, in letter to H. Macmillan about summit talks, criticises agreement for establishing U.S. missile bases in Britain;
21st, Hungarian-Chinese economic pact;
27th, Liberals win Torrington by-election from Conservatives;
—, N. Khrushchev succeeds N. A. Bulganin as chairman of U.S.S.R. Council of Ministers (Bulganin is dismissed from Communist Party Presidium, *Sept.* 6th);
31st, John Diefenbaker leads government to victory in Canadian elections.

D **Apr:** 5th, Fidel Castro begins 'total war' against President Batista's government in Cuba;
8th, President Eisenhower proposes mutual inspection as means of enforcing atomic test ban;
15th, British Budget makes 'dividend stripping' illegal;
—, confederation of independent African states meets at Accra;
16th, sweeping victory for Nationalists in S. African elections;

O **Politics, Economics, Law and Education**

J. K. Galbraith, *The Affluent Society*.

J. D. Stewart, *British Pressure Groups*.

Under First Offenders Act no adult to be imprisoned by British magistrates court if there is a more appropriate method of dealing with him.

The case of the London members of the Chemists' Federation, the first to be referred to Restrictive Practices Court, found to be against the public interest.

British Public Records Act provides for inspection of records when 50 years old.

Geneva Conference on law of the sea.

First parking meters in London.

In Morocco women are permitted to choose own husbands and polygamy is restricted.

U.S. recession continues, with peak of 5 million unemployed in March.

P **Science, Technology, Discovery, etc.**

International Geophysical Year ends (*Dec.* 31st).

Volcanic eruption on the moon observed by U.S.S.R. scientist (*Nov.* 3rd).

U.S. artificial earth satellite *Explorer I* launched at Cape Canaveral (*Jan.* 31st) to study cosmic rays, Vanguard I rocket (*Mar.* 17th) to test solar cells, and Atlas (*Dec.* 18th) to investigate radio relay.

U.S.S.R. launches Sputnik III (*May* 15th) for aerodynamic studies, and puts in orbit two dogs in a rocket to a height of 279 miles (*Aug.* 27th).

U.S. nuclear submarine *Nautilus* passes under ice cap at North Pole (*Mar.* 4th), demonstrating the practicability of shortening commercial sea routes.

U.S.S.R. launches nuclear-powered ice-breaker *Lenin*.

Discovery of submarine current in equatorial Pacific.

British Section of Commonwealth Transantarctic Expedition under Vivian Fuchs reaches South Pole (*Jan.* 20th) overland from Shackleton Base and reaches Scott Base (*Mar.* 2nd).

Stereophonic gramophone recordings.

The Rotocycle, an aerial motor-scooter, is invented.

Q **Scholarship**

Stephen Runciman, *Sicilian Vespers*.

R. H. Tawney, *Lionel Cranfield*.

J. Wheeler-Bennett, *King George VI, His Life and Reign*.

R **Philosophy and Religion**

R. S. Peters, *The Concept of Motivation*.

Ludwig Wittgenstein, *The Blue Book* and *The Brown Book* (posth.).

Conversations between Church of England and the Methodist Church, an interim report.

Church of the Brethren at 250th meeting at Des Moines, Iowa, approves ordination of women. Evangelical Church of the Palatinate decides to admit women to ordination. Legislation to admit women to Swedish Lutheran pastorate is hotly contested by the Church Assembly.

United Presbyterian Church in U.S. formed (*May*) to become the fourth largest denomination, with 3 million members.

U.S. Congregationalists and Evangelicals form United Church of Christ (*June*) with 2 million members.

Supreme Religious Centre for World Jewry is dedicated in Jerusalem (*May* 8th).

S **Art, Sculpture, Fine Arts and Architecture**

Lord Bridges' Romanes Lecture, *The State of the Arts*.

Gulbenkian Fund's Committee reviews the needs of the arts in Britain.

D **Apr:** 16th, Felix Gaillard resigns as French premier on defeat of Tunisian policy;
18th, U.S.S.R. asks U.N. Security Council to take steps to end flights of military aircraft across her Arctic frontiers;
21st, on resignation of Labour ministry in Malta the governor assumes control;
23rd, Garfield Todd leaves Edgar Whitehead's cabinet to found a new United Rhodesian Party;
26th, N. African Nationalist parties meet in Tangier.

E **May:** 2nd, state of emergency in Aden colony;
3rd, President Eisenhower proposes demilitarisation of Antarctica, subsequently accepted by the countries concerned;
5th (*–June* 21st), London bus strike;
8th, J. F. Dulles states in Berlin House of Representatives that an attack on Berlin would be regarded as an attack on the Allies;
12th, U.S. and Canada establish N. American Air Defense Command;
13th, Europeans in Algiers stage demonstrations;
14th, M. Pflimlin (M.R.P.) forms ministry in France (–28th);
15th, General Charles de Gaulle states his readiness to assume the powers of the republic; and, 19th, praises the achievements of the army of Algeria;
25th, Christian Democrats win most seats in Italian elections but have not an absolute majority;
27th, state of emergency in Ceylon;
29th, Charles de Gaulle forms government of national safety in France.

F **Jun:** 1st, Iceland extends fishery limits to 12 miles;
9th (–10th), Harold Macmillan meets President Eisenhower and J. F. Dulles in Washington;
13th, A. Gromyko, Russian foreign minister, holds discussions with ambassadors in Moscow as preliminary to summit talks;
16th, U.S.-Japanese ten-year agreement on atomic energy;
17th, announcement of execution of Imre Nagy after secret trial in Hungary;
18th, President Eisenhower admits imprudence of Sherman Adams, assistant to the President, after hearings of Senate Committee on bribery charges involving Bernard Goldfine;
19th, British plan for Cyprus involves co-operation of Greek and Turkish governments in island's administration;
20th, Indonesia bans operations of Royal Dutch Shell Oil group;
25th, Amintore Fanfani, Christian Democrat, forms Italian coalition in succession to Zoli.

G **Jul:** 1st (*–Aug.* 21st), eight-power conference of experts at Geneva on detection of nuclear explosions;
—, Sudan diverts Nile waters as first stage of Managil project;
2nd, W. German Bundestag calls on powers to solve problem of Germany's reunification;
3rd, Anglo-U.S. agreement for co-operation in development of atomic weapons;
6th, Alaska becomes 49th state of U.S. (admitted *Jan.* 1959);
14th, in Baghdad *coup d'état*, King Feisal, his heir, and premier Nuri-es-Said are murdered, and King Hussein assumes power as head of Arab Federation;
15th, at request of President Chamoun, U.S. despatches forces to Lebanon;
—, S. Africa resumes full membership of U.N.;
17th, British paratroops land in Jordan at request of King Hussein;

S **Art, Sculpture, Fine Arts and Architecture** (*cont.*)

Victorian Society founded to safeguard Victorian and Edwardian buildings threatened by demolition.

Painting:

J. Bratby, paintings for the film *The Horse's Mouth*.
Sidney Nolan, *Gallipoli* series.

Sculpture:

A. Calder, *Monumental Mobile* and *The Dog* (stabile).
H. Moore, *Reclining Figure*, UNESCO Building, Paris.

Architecture:

P. L. Nervi and G. Ponti, Pirelli Building, Milan.
O. Niemeyer, President's Palace, Brasilia.
Eero Saarinen, Yale Hockey Rink, U.S.
Mies Van der Rohe and Philip Johnson, Seagram Building, New York.
Arthur Ling, Belgrade Theatre, Coventry.

T **Music**

B. Britten, *Noye's Fludde*.
Pizzetti, *Murder in the Cathedral* (opera).
R. Vaughan Williams, Symphony no. 9 in E minor.
Humphrey Searle, *Diary of a Madman* (opera).
Van Cliburn of U.S. wins Moscow pianoforte competition.
Jeunesses Musicales meet in Brussels (*July*).
Magne, after Françoise Sagan, *Broken Date* (ballet).
L. Salzedo-Jack Carter, *Witchboy* (ballet).
F. Ashton-H.W. Henze, *Ondine* (ballet).
Macmillan-Martin, *The Burrow* (ballet).

U **Literature**

J. G. Cozzens, *By Love Possessed*.
Elaine Dundy, *The Dud Avocado*.
Lawrence Durrell, *Justine*.
Aldous Huxley, *Brave New World Revisited*.
B. Pasternak, *Dr. Zhivago*.
T. H. White, *The Sword in the Stone*.
Angus Wilson, *The Middle Age of Mrs. Eliot*.
The 'Beatnik' Movement, originating among young poets of California, spreads to Britain; devotees are unkempt, penurious and take drugs.

V **The Press**

W **Drama and Entertainment**

T. S. Eliot, *The Elder Statesman*.
Graham Greene, *The Potting Shed*.
Harold Pinter, *The Birthday Party*.
Leonard Bernstein, *West Side Story* (musical).
Brussels World Exhibition.

Films:

Marcel Carné, *Les Tricheurs*.
Jacques Tati, *Mon Oncle*.
Orson Welles, *Touch of Evil*.
Andrzej Wajda's *Ashes and Diamonds*.
The Wind Cannot Read.

1958 (Jul.–Dec.)

G **Jul**: 19th, United Arab Republic and Iraq sign treaty of mutual defence;
20th, United Arab Republic severs relations with Jordan;
22nd, Harold Macmillan rejects Khrushchev's proposal for immediate summit talks on Middle East and suggests special meeting of Security Council;
24th, first life peerages in Britain;
26th, Prince Charles is created Prince of Wales;
—, last débutantes presented at British court;
31st, N. Khrushchev visits Peking.

H **Aug**: 1st, King Hussein dissolves the Federation of Jordan with Iraq;
5th, N. Khrushchev withdraws support for Security Council meeting on Middle East and proposes meeting of U.N. General Assembly, which is accepted by Britain and U.S.;
14th, Britain, France and other N.A.T.O. countries announce relaxation for trade with Soviet bloc and Communist China; but U.S. mantains embargo with China, North Korea and North Vietnam;
23rd, Communist China begins bombarding Quemoy;
—, racial disturbances in Nottingham and, 31st, in Notting Hill.

J **Sep**: 1st, Icelandic patrols board British fishing vessels within 12-mile limit;
3rd, Hendrik Verwoerd becomes S. African premier on J. G. Strijdom's death;
5th, Lord Parker succeeds Lord Goddard as Lord Chief Justice;
7th, N. Khrushchev states that any U.S. attack on China will be regarded as an attack on U.S.S.R.;
12th, U.S. Supreme Court orders Little Rock High School, Arkansas, to admit negroes;
—, Britain states that, though not committed to defend Formosa, she supports U.S. plan;
14th, General de Gaulle meets Konrad Adenauer;
15th (–26th), Commonwealth Trade and Economic Conference, Montreal;
18th, President Eisenhower signs extension of Reciprocal Trade Agreements Act;
19th, U.N. rejects Indian proposal to consider question of China's admission to U.N.;
—, provisional government of Algeria proclaimed in Cairo;
28th, French Constitution of the Fifth Republic, submitted to referendum in France, Algeria and territories overseas (*–Oct.* 5th), gives President greater powers and strengthens position of the government in the Assembly;
30th, U.S.S.R. resumes nuclear tests (suspended since *June*).

K **Oct**: 7th, President Iskander Mirza proclaims martial law in Pakistan;
20th, successful military *coup d'état* in Siam;
23rd, U.S.S.R. loan to United Arab Republic for building Aswan Dam;
24th, Ayub Khan forms cabinet in Pakistan;
28th, Cardinal Roncalli elected Pope John XXIII on death of Pius XII.

L **Nov**: 2nd, last British troops leave Jordan;
4th, Democratic victory in U.S. mid-term Congressional elections, leaving Democrats with 62 seats in Senate (Republicans, 34) and 281 seats in House of Representatives (Republicans, 153);
10th, ten-power Geneva conference on measures against surprise attack;
12th, United Federal Party of Roy Welensky wins Rhodesian Federal elections;
—, E. Germany demands recognition by powers;
17th, Sudanese army suppresses Constitution, and Ibrahim Abboud becomes premier of Sudan;

(*Continued opposite*)

W **Drama and Entertainment** (*cont.*)

Films (*cont.*):

Vertigo.

Coronation of Pope John XXIII (on television).

X **Sport**

Water-ski-ing becomes popular.

Y **Statistics**

Electronic computers: 1,000 in use in U.S.; 160 in use in Europe.

Z **Births and Deaths**

June 17th Imre Nagy d. (62).
Aug. 26th Ralph Vaughan Williams d. (85).
Oct. 2nd Marie Stopes d. (78).
Oct. 9th Pope Pius XII d. (82).
Oct. 24th G. E. Moore d. (85).

L Nov: 23rd, Ghana and Guinea announce they will form nucleus of a union of W. African states;

30th, Neo-Gaullist Union for a New Republic (U.N.R.) gains decisive victory in French elections.

M Dec: 3rd, nationalisation of Dutch businesses in Indonesia;

8th (–13th), All-Africa People's Conference in Accra;

11th, J. M. Beel, Catholic People's Party, forms coalition in Netherlands on resignation of William Drees, Labour;

12th, General Salan is appointed inspector-general of national defence in Algeria;

15th, O.E.E.C. Council fails to reach agreement on European free trade area;

16th, N.A.T.O. Council rejects U.S.S.R. proposals on Berlin;

21st, Charles de Gaulle elected President of French Republic with 78·5 per cent of votes, the Communist candidate 13·1 and the Union des Forces démocratiques candidate 8·4;

22nd, Franco-Egyptian trade pact;

27th, Britain announces convertibility of sterling for non-resident holders;

—, France devalues the Franc and makes it convertible to non-resident holders;

30th, French W. African states decide to form a federation within the French Community;

31st, amnesty proclaimed in the Lebanon.

N

1959 (Jan.–Mar.) Castro becomes premier of Cuba—E.F.T.A. established—Conservatives increase majority in Britain

A Jan: 1st, Batista, President of Cuba, flees to Dominica and, 2nd, Manuel Urrutia becomes provisional governor, but Fidel Castro strengthens position by purges and postponement of elections;

4th, disturbances at Léopoldville, Belgian Congo, which force Belgium, 13th, to grant reforms;

6th, W. German loan to India;

8th, General de Gaulle is proclaimed President of Fifth Republic, with Michel Debré premier;

10th, U.S.S.R. proposes conference to draw up German peace treaty (West replies by suggesting four-power foreign ministers' conference, *Feb.* 16th, which meets in Geneva, *May* 11th);

17th, Federal State of Mali formed by union of Republics of Senegal and French Sudan;

19th, S. African treason trial of the accused in *Dec.* 1956 reopens;

25th, Britain signs trade pact with E. Germany;

26th, A. Fanfani, Italian premier, resigns through dissensions in Christian Democrat Party.

B Feb: 1st, Swiss referendum rejects female suffrage in federal elections;

4th, Britain and Euratom agree to co-operate in peaceful uses of atomic energy;

6th, Antonio Segni, Christian Democrat, forms Italian ministry which is supported by Liberals and Monarchists;

7th, U.S.S.R. agreement to aid Chinese industry;

9th, U.S. supply arms to Indonesia;

11th, Laos announces will recognise U.N. as sole arbiter of disputes, provoking denunciation by North Vietnam;

16th, Fidel Castro becomes premier of Cuba;

19th, agreement signed in London by premiers of Greece, Turkey and Britain for independence of Cyprus;

20th, disturbances in Nyasaland where, *Mar.* 3rd, Hastings Banda and other leaders of Nyasaland African Congress are arrested;

21st, Harold Macmillan and Selwyn Lloyd visit U.S.S.R.;

—, British one-year trade pact with Spain;

23rd (–28th), first meeting of European Court of Human Rights at Strasbourg;

26th (–*May* 20th), state of emergency in Southern Rhodesia;

28th, Anglo-Egyptian agreement on settlement of claims arising from Suez crisis.

C Mar: 1st, Archbishop Makarios returns to Cyprus from exile;

— (–9th), unsuccessful army revolt in Mosul;

9th (–23rd), Harold Macmillan and Selwyn Lloyd visit General de Gaulle, Konrad Adenauer, John Diefenbaker and President Eisenhower;

10th, U.N. Geneva Conference approves international wheat agreement;

11th, Britain signs ten-year commercial treaty with Persia;

16th, U.S.S.R. loan to Iraq;

17th, U.S.S.R. and Australia resume diplomatic relations (severed in *Apr.* 1954);

—, Colonel Grivas, EOKA leader, returns to Athens from Cyprus;

—, in Tibetan rising against Chinese garrison the Dalai Lama escapes to receive, 31st, asylum in India and, *Sept.* 9th, appeals to U.N.;

18th, Hawaii becomes 50th state of U.S.;

24th, Iraq withdraws from Baghdad Pact, thus the Anglo-Iraq agreement of 1956 lapses;

27th, U.S. aircraft first 'buzzed' in Berlin air corridor by U.S.S.R. jet fighters;

O Politics, Economics, Law and Education

World Refugee Year begins (*June* 1st)

TV coverage of British general election (*Oct.*).

Vance Packard, *The Waste-Makers.*

C. Wright Mills, *The Causes of World War III.*

Legislation in Britain to reorganise Lancashire cotton industry, to reform system for detaining mental patients and to enable a child to be legitimised by its parents' subsequent marriage. The Street Offences Act clears prostitutes from streets.

Home Secretary allows scholars to inspect the Casement Diaries.

Obscene Publications Act permits publication of V. Nabokov's *Lolita* in Britain.

The Post Office Court in U.S. decides D. H. Lawrence's *Lady Chatterley's Lover* is not objectionable.

First British drive-in bank, in Liverpool.

P Science, Technology, Discovery, etc.

Launchings of U.S.S.R. cosmic rocket Lunik I (*Jan.* 2nd) and rocket with two monkeys aboard (*May* 28th).

U.S. artificial planet Pioneer IV (*Mar.* 3rd) and British rocket Black Knight IV at Woomera (*June* 29th).

U.S.S.R. sends dogs in orbit (*July* 6th); Lunik II reaches the moon (*Sept.* 12th) and Lunik III photographs moon (*Oct.* 4th).

Alvarez discovers the neutral *xi*-particle.

Benoit's experiments with ducks are claimed to modify the laws of inheritance.

De Beers of Johannesburg manufacture a synthetic diamond (*Nov.* 17th).

Louis B. Leakey finds the skull of 'the Nutcracker Man', 600,000 years old, in Tanganyika.

Launchings in U.S. of first atomic submarine (*June* 9th) and of first atomic-powered passenger-cargo ship, *Savannah* (*July* 21st).

British hovercraft crosses the Channel in two hours (*July* 25th).

Discovery of the Arctic submarine plateau.

First section of M.1 (London–Birmingham motorway) opened (*Nov.* 1st).

Q Scholarship

Remains of Nonsuch Palace are excavated successfully during Britain's driest summer for 200 years.

Garrett Mattingly, *The Defeat of the Armada.*

I. and P. Opie, *The Lore and Language of Schoolchildren.*

R Philosophy and Religion

Pope John XXIII announces the calling of the first Vatican Council since 1870, for promoting the search for Christian unity (*Jan.* 25th).

The Vatican orders the French Worker-Priest Movement (founded 1943) to discontinue (*July* 3rd; this ban is lifted in 1965).

Karl Barth, *Dogmatics in Outline.*

Pierre Teilhard de Chardin, *The Phenomenon of Man.*

G. M. Mure, *Retreat from Truth.*

S Art, Sculpture, Fine Arts and Architecture

Painting:

John Bratby, *Coach-House Door.*

Joan Mirò's murals for UNESCO Building, Paris.

Sculpture:

Barbara Hepworth, Meridian, State House, London.

C Mar: 28th, J. E. de Quay forms Catholic People's Party ministry in Holland.
Deaths of Mau Mau prisoners at Hola Camp, Kenya.

D Apr: 4th (–*May* 30th), Ivory Coast signs series of agreements with Niger, Haute Volta and Dahomey to form Sahel-Bénin Union;
16th, Turkey's treaty of perpetual peace with Spain;
17th, Malaya and Indonesia sign treaty of friendship;
18th, Christian A. Herter succeeds J. F. Dulles as U.S. secretary of state (Dulles dies, *May* 24th);
20th, United Federal Party win Northern Rhodesian elections and African National Congress is suppressed;
26th, Cuba invades Panama;
27th, Liu Shao-chi elected Chairman of Chinese Republic in succession to Mao Tse-tung, who remains as head of Communist Party;
30th, Anglo-French trade pact.

E May: 2nd, Afro-Asian Organisation for Economic Co-operation in Cairo states exclusion of U.S.S.R.;
4th, U.S.S.R. note to Japan urges end of U.S. bases and offers to guarantee Japan permanent neutrality;
5th, Shah of Persia visits Britain; Persia replies to U.S.S.R. protest about her defence agreement with U.S. that she would agree to denuclearised zone in Middle East if the great powers agreed;
—, W. S. Tubman, True Whig, re-elected President of Liberia;
7th, Anglo-U.S. agreement enabling Britain to purchase components of atomic weapons other than warheads from U.S.;
10th, Austrian general election leads to coalition of People's Party and Socialists, *July* 16th, under Julius Raab;
11th (–*Aug.* 5th), Foreign Ministers' Conference, Geneva, to discuss Berlin and a German peace treaty;
22nd, Canadian-U.S. agreement for co-operation in use of atomic energy for mutual defence;
24th, Anglo-U.S.S.R. five-year trade pact;
25th (–*June* 4th), N. Khrushchev visits Albania;
28th, Britain announces removal of controls on imports of many consumer goods from dollar area, with increased import quotas of other goods;
30th, Iraq terminates U.S. military assistance agreements on grounds that such conflicted with Iraqi policy of neutrality.

F Jun: 3rd, Singapore becomes self-governing;
—, Iraq Petroleum Co and Lebanon settle dispute;
4th, U.S.-owned sugar mills and plantations in Cuba expropriated;
5th (–10th), Atlantic Congress, London, sponsored by N.A.T.O. Parliamentarians' Conference;
13th, Communist China's trade pact with Ceylon;
14th, U.S. agrees to provide Greece with nuclear information and supply ballistic rockets;
17th, Éamon de Valéra resigns as premier to become third President of Eire in succession to Sean O'Kelly, and, 23rd, Sean Lemass forms ministry;
20th, beginning of six-week printing strike in Britain, which affects all publications except London newspapers;
23rd, Iraq withdraws from sterling area;

S Art, Sculpture, Fine Arts and Architecture (*cont.*)

Architecture:

Basil Spence, Thorn House, London.

Frank Lloyd Wright, Guggenheim Art Museum, New York, and Beth Sholom Synagogue, Elkin Park, Pa.

British government enquiry into plans for developing Piccadilly Circus.

T Music

Pierre Boulez, *Livre du Quattuor* quartet.

Pousseur, *Rhymes from Various Sonorous Sources* (employs electronic music and two orchestras).

Francis Poulenc, *La Voix Humaine* (opera).

Purcell, Handel and Haydn anniversary concerts.

J. Cranko's *Antigone* to score by M. Theodorakis (ballet).

J. Robbins, *L'Après-midi d'un Faune* (ballet).

Peter Maxwell Davies, *St. Michael* Sonata.

U Literature

Saul Bellow, *Henderson the Rain King*.

Ivy Compton-Burnett, *A Heritage and Its History*.

William Faulkner, *The Mansion*.

Colin MacInnes, *Absolute Beginners*.

Norman Mailer, *Advertisement for Myself*.

V. S. Naipaul, *Miguel Street*.

C. P. Snow's Richmond Lecture, *The Two Cultures and the Sciences*.

Muriel Spark, *Memento Mori*.

James Thurber, *The Years with Ross*.

V The Press

Manchester Guardian renamed *The Guardian* (*Aug.* 24th).

W Drama and Entertainment

Bernard Miles opens Mermaid Theatre, the first in City of London for 300 years.

Peter Hall appointed director of Shakespeare Memorial Theatre, Stratford.

Brendan Behan, *The Hostage*.

Shelagh Delaney, *A Taste of Honey*.

Arnold Wesker, *Roots*.

Films:

Carl Bresson's *Pickpocket*.

Jean Cocteau's *Le Testament d'Orphée*.

Donskoi's *Foma Gordeyev*.

Otto Preminger's *Anatomy of Murder*.

Carol Reed's *Our Man in Havana*.

Resnais' *Hiroshima mon Amour*.

Tony Richardson's *Look Back in Anger*.

Gigi with Audrey Hepburn.

The Rickshaw Man.

S. Eisenstein publishes *Notes of a Film Director*.

Face to Face and *Monitor* series in Britain (television).

Quiz scandal in U.S., where a prize-winner admitted being supplied with answers.

S. Africa decides against introducing TV.

Regular colour TV in Cuba.

X Sport

F Jun: 25th, U.S.S.R. proposals for denuclearised zone in Balkans and Adriatic (rejected by West, *July* 11th–13th);
26th, Queen Elizabeth opens St. Lawrence Seaway.

G Jul: 1st, Heinrich Lübke elected President of W. Germany in succession to Dr. Heuss (K. Adenauer's opposition prevented Dr. Erhard standing as Christian Democrat candidate);
4th, Jamaica is granted internal self-government within West Indies Federation;
5th, Ghana boycotts S. African goods;
—, Saar is incorporated in W. German economic system;
—, President Sukarno dissolves Indonesian constituent assembly;
8th, U.S.-Liberian defence agreement;
16th, Kwame Nkrumah of Ghana and W. S. Tubman of Liberia propose holding a conference of independent African states;
17th, N. Khrushchev reaffirms guarantee of Oder-Neisse frontier and calls for European denuclearisied zone;
20th, cabinet government introduced to Trinidad and Tobago;
28th, Indian police party seized by Communist Chinese in Jammu and Kashmir area.

H Aug: 7th, Communist Chinese invade N.E. frontier of India;
—, increase in Soviet aid to Hungary;
16th, United Arab Republic restores diplomatic relations with Jordan (severed *July* 20th, 1958);
21st, Baghdad Pact changes name to Central Treaty Organisation (CENTO);
26th, President Eisenhower visits Bonn and, 27th, Britain.

J Sep: 4th, emergency in Laos, with alleged aggression of North Vietnamese;
7th, four-power statement on decision to establish new disarmament committee;
16th, President de Gaulle broadcasts on future of Algeria;
18th, N. Khrushchev addresses U.N. General Assembly on disarmament;
22nd, U.N. vote against admission of Communist China;
25th, N. Khrushchev visits Peking;
—, S. Bandaranaike, premier of Ceylon, assassinated, succeeded by W. Dahanayake.

K Oct: 8th, in British general election Conservatives under Harold Macmillan win 366 seats, Labour 258, and Liberals, 8;
20th, Inter-American Nuclear Energy Commission holds first meeting in Washington;
26th, Basic Democracies Order promulgated in Pakistan; Rawalpindi is chosen as provisional capital.

L Nov: 8th, United Arab Republic and Sudan sign agreement on sharing the Nile waters after construction of Aswan High Dam;
—, President Bourguiba's Neo-Destour Party win all seats in Tunisian assembly;
10th, U.N. General Assembly condemns *apartheid* in S. Africa and racial discrimination in any part of the world;
—, announcement of ending of emergency in Kenya after ten years;
13th, S. African Progressive Party established at Johannesburg congress;
20th (–29th), European Free Trade Association (the 'Seven'), consisting of Britain, Norway, Portugal, Switzerland, Austria, Denmark and Sweden, ratify treaty.

M Dec: 3rd, President Eisenhower's tour of European capitals (–23rd);
6th, U.N. General Assembly resolves Togoland trusteeship territory should achieve independence in *Apr.* 1960;

(*Continued opposite*)

Y **Statistics**

Cement production (in mill. metric tons): U.S., 66·8; U.S.S.R., 42·7; W. Germany, 25·1; Japan, 19; France, 14·7; Great Britain, 13·8.

Aluminium production (in mill. tons): U.S., 1·9; U.S.S.R., 0·7; Canada, 0·6; France, 0·2.

Fertilisers (in mill. tons); U.S., 45; U.S.S.R., 12; Germany, 1; Great Britain, 0·7.

Television sets: U.S., 36 mill.; Great Britain, 10 mill.; France, 1,500,000.

Z **Births and Deaths**

July 17th Alfred Munnings d. (80).
Aug. 19th Jacob Epstein d. (78).
Oct. 9th Henry Tizard d. (74).
Oct. 16th George Marshall d. (78).
Dec. 14th Stanley Spencer d. (68).

M Dec: 9th, Britain and United Arab Republic resume diplomatic relations (severed in *Nov.* 1956);
10th, U.S. begins withdrawal of troops from Iceland;
13th, U.N. decides not to intervene in question of Algeria;
19th, Western powers at Paris meeting invite N. Khrushchev to attend summit conference in *Apr.* 1960;
24th, anti-Semitic incidents in Cologne;
25th, U.S.S.R. agrees to give financial and technical aid to Syria.

N

1960 (Jan.–Apr.) Summit Meeting—Sharpeville shootings—Congo Crisis—Kennedy elected U.S. President

A Jan: 1st, independent Republic of the Cameroons proclaimed;
6th (–*Feb.* 5th), Harold Macmillan visits Ghana, Nigeria, Rhodesia and S. Africa;
9th, work on Aswan High Dam begins;
11th, U.S. protests to Cuba against expropriation of U.S. property;
12th, E.F.T.A. countries (the 'Seven') hold first ministerial meeting in Paris;
—, President Sukarno forms National Front in Indonesia;
18th, London Conference on Cyprus breaks down;
—, Kenya Constitutional Conference, London, at first boycotted by African elected members, who take their places, 25th;
19th, U.S.-Japanese treaty of mutual security;
20th, Belgian Congo conference in Brussels agrees on full independence in *June*;
24th (–*Feb.* 1st), rioting by European extremists in Algiers;
28th, Burma signs treaty of friendship with Communist China.

B Feb: 2nd, Negro sit-in campaign in U.S. lunch-counters begins;
3rd, Harold Macmillan's 'wind of change' speech in Cape Town Parliament;
5th, Anastas Mikoyan, deputy premier of U.S.S.R., opens Soviet exhibition in Havana;
8th, Queen Elizabeth announces all her descendants, except those enjoying the style of Royal Highness, to bear the name of Mountbatten-Windsor;
10th (–*Mar.* 5th), N. Khrushchev visits India, Burma and Indonesia;
14th, Ayub Khan wins presidential ballot in Pakistan;
17th, U.S.-Britain agreement to build ballistic missile early warning station at Fylingdales;
19th, Prince Andrew born (first birth to a reigning sovereign since 1857);
24th, Signor Segni resigns in Italy, and, after various other attempts, Amintore Fanfani succeeds in forming ministry, *July* 22nd;
29th, Agadir earthquake.

C Mar: 3rd, Guillebaud Committee's report on railwaymen's pay embodies principle of fair comparison with other employment;
4th, N. Khrushchev protests against likelihood of Spain granting military bases to W. Germany;
5th, Harold Macmillan elected Chancellor of Oxford University over Oliver Franks;
—, President Sukarno suspends Indonesian Parliament;
15th, ten-power disarmament committee meets in Geneva (–*June* 27th, when Communists walk out);
16th, British Labour Party executive issues declaration of objectives, which include 'clause 4' on nationalisation;
21st, D. Senanayake, United National Party, forms ministry in Ceylon following elections;
—, Pan-African demonstration against pass laws in S. Africa leads to shooting of 67 Africans at Sharpeville, and a state of emergency is proclaimed (–*Aug.* 31st); world opinion against *apartheid* is intensified;
26th, U.S. loan to United Arab Republic;
27th, President Eisenhower and Harold Macmillan issue joint statement in Washington on nuclear test negotiations;
—, General Kassem, premier of Iraq, founds Palestinian Army for the proposed independence of a Palestine Republic.

D Apr: 1st, S. African government bans African National Congress and Pan-African Congress;
4th, Sultan of Selangor becomes head of Malayan Federation;

O Politics, Economics, Law and Education

Anti-Jewish incidents in W. Germany lead to the banning of neo-Nazi political groups and a review of textbooks.

R. W. Nixon-John F. Kennedy confrontations on TV during U.S. presidential election campaign.

Brasilia becomes new capital of Brazil (*Apr.*).

240 Spanish authors plead for reform of censorship.

Churchill College, Cambridge, founded.

P Science, Technology, Discovery, etc.

Twenty satellites are in orbit.

U.S. Air Force recovers Discoverer satellite from Pacific, and U.S.S.R. recovers dogs that made 17 orbits of the earth.

U.S. launch a radio-reflector satellite (*Aug.* 12th).

R. L. Mossbauer's discoveries in gamma rays.

An optical micro-wave laser is constructed.

Surgeons at Birmingham develop a pacemaker for the heart.

Chlorophyll is synthesised simultaneously by Martin Strell of Munich and R. B. Woodward of Harvard University.

K. H. Hofman synthesises pituitary hormone.

G. N. Robinson discovers methicillin, antibiotic drug.

J. C. Kendrew elucidates three-dimensional structure of the protein myoglobin.

U.S. bathyscaphe *Trieste*, designed by Professor Piccard, dives to the bottom of Challenger Deep, 35,800 ft.

Q Scholarship

Archaeologists begin to save treasures in Aswan High Dam region of Nubia before flooding begins.

Excavations at Stonehenge by officials of Ministry of Works.

Further Biblical texts are discovered in Dead Sea region.

Gavin de Beer, *The Sciences Were Never at War*.

R Philosophy and Religion

A. J. Ayer, *Logical Positivism.*

'Kneel-in' campaign by negroes in segregated churches in U.S. Southern States.

Archbishop Fisher of Canterbury visits Jerusalem, Istanbul and Rome (*Nov.* 22nd–*Dec.* 2nd).

A church at Herne Bay, Kent, is dedicated for use jointly by Anglicans and Methodists.

Three women are admitted to pastorate of Swedish Lutheran Church.

S Art, Sculpture, Fine Arts and Architecture

Painting:

P. Picasso Exhibition, Tate Gallery.

S. Nolan 'Leda and the Swan' series (since 1945).

Arthur Boyd, *Half-Caste Bride* and William Dobell create interest in Australian artists.

J. Bratby, *Gloria with Sunflower*.

Sculpture:

Musée Léger opened at Biot with the 'Children's Garden' in the forecourt.

Architecture:

R. L. Davies, Times Building, Printing House Square (–64).

Louis I. Khan, Research Laboratory, Pennsylvania University.

O. Niemeyer, Museum and Congress Building, Brasilia, opened.

D **Apr**: 4th, British budget ends 'golden handshake' and increases profits tax to 12½ per cent;
9th, Hendrik Verwoerd wounded by David Pratt;
10th, Civil Rights bill for safeguarding negroes' voting rights passes U.S. Senate;
14th, collectivisation of E. Germany's agriculture completed;
27th, Sierra Leone constitutional conference in London proposes independence in *Apr.* 1961;
—, British Labour Opposition move vote of censure on government for lack of judgment over Blue Streak missile;
—, Syngman Rhee resigns South Korean presidency;
—, Togo becomes an independent republic;
28th (–*May* 25th), student demonstrations in Ankara and Istanbul.

E **May**: 1st, U.S. U-2 aircraft, flown by Francis Powers, shot down in Urals by U.S.S.R.;
3rd, E.F.T.A. comes into force, with 20 per cent tariff cuts between members from *July*;
—, Commonwealth Prime Ministers' Conference in London at which Eric Louw represents S. Africa;
6th, Princess Margaret marries Antony Armstrong-Jones;
7th, Leonid Brezhnev replaces Marshal Voroshilov as President of U.S.S.R.;
16th (–19th), summit meeting in Paris of N. Khrushchev, H. Macmillan, D. Eisenhower, and C. de Gaulle, which fails through U-2 affair;
17th, Kariba Dam, Rhodesia, opened;
23rd, Israel announces the arrest of Adolf Eichmann, former Gestapo chief;
27th, Adnan Menderes is overthrown in Turkey; General Cemal Gürsel assumes presidency;
—, U.S. ends aid to Cuba.

F **Jun**: 9th, Hong Kong struck by typhoon;
12th (–26th), President Eisenhower's Far East tour;
14th, President de Gaulle renews offer to Algerian provisional government to negotiate cease-fire, to which *Front de la Libération Nationale* agrees, but rejects subsequent French conditions;
15th, Japanese students riot in protest against Mutual Co-operation and Security Treaty with U.S. and Eisenhower's visit is postponed (19th, Japanese Diet ratifies treaty);
21st, Britain, France, Netherlands and U.S. provide for a Caribbean organisation for economic co-operation;
23rd, 'credit squeeze' with bank rate raised to 6 per cent in Britain;
24th, Greece, Yugoslavia and Turkey dissolve Balkan alliance of *Aug.* 1954;
25th, Mutual Co-operation Parliament meets in Indonesia;
26th, Madagascar proclaimed independent as the Malagasy Republic;
—, British Somaliland becomes independent and, 27th, joins Somalia;
30th, Bantu self-government bill in force in S. Africa;
—, independence of Congolese Republic under President Kasavubu with Patrice Lumumba premier.

G **Jul**: 1st, U.N. Food and Agriculture Organisation launches Freedom from Hunger Campaign;
—, U.S.S.R. shoots down U.S. aircraft over Barents Sea;
—, Britain and Cyprus reach agreement on British bases;
4th, Britain protests to Cuba over 'intervention' in Havana Shell Oil refinery;
5th (–6th), Congolese national army mutinies, and Europeans flee from Léopoldville area to Brazzaville;
6th, Aneurin Bevan, Deputy Leader of British Labour Party, dies (aged 62);

T **Music**

Arthur Bliss, *Tobias and the Angel.*
Pierre Boulez, *Portrait of Mallarmé.*
Hans W. Henze, *Der Prinz von Hamburg* (opera).
Ernst Křenek, *Whitsun Oratorio.*
Humphrey Seale, Symphony no. 3.

U **Literature**

John Betjeman, *Summoned by Bells.*
Lawrence Durrell, *Clea.*
Alain Robbe-Grillet, *Dans la labyrinthe.*
John Updike, *Rabbit Run.*

V **The Press**

Sunday Telegraph is issued.
The News Chronicle and *The Star* cease publication.

W **Drama and Entertainment**

Robert Bolt, *A Man For All Seasons.*
E. Ionesco, *The Rhinoceros.*
John Mortimer, *The Wrong Side of the Park.*
Harold Pinter, *The Caretaker.*
Terence Rattigan, *Ross.*
Arnold Wesker, *I'm Talking About Jerusalem.*
Fings Ain't Wot They Used T'Be (musical).
Japan begins regular colour TV.
Films:
Federico Fellini's *La Dolce Vita.*
Alfred Hitchcock's *Psycho.*
Michelangelo Antonioni's *L'Avventura.*
Otto Preminger's *Exodus.*
Karel Reisz's *Saturday Night and Sunday Morning.*
Luchino Visconti's *Rocco and his Brothers.*
Black Orpheus.
The Entertainer.
The Lady With the Little Dog.
Shadows, the cinema of improvisation.

X **Sport**

Olympic Games at Rome.
Go-Karting becomes popular.
Barbara Moore, aged 56, sets off, *Jan.* 13th, to walk from John o'Groats to Land's End; next month Billy Butlin sponsors a walk over the same course which is won by James Musgrave of Doncaster and Wendy Lewis of Liverpool.

Y **Statistics**

Total weekly hours of broadcasts to other countries: East European countries, 1,094; U.S.S.R., 1,002; China, 724; Voice of America, 602; B.B.C., 589; W. Germany, 315; France, 314.
Ownership of private cars (in mill.): U.S., 75; France, 7·3; Great Britain, 6·5; Canada, 5; W. Germany, 4·5; U.S.S.R., 3·8.
Population of cities (in mill.): Tokio, 9·6; London, 8·1; New York, 7·7; Shanghai, 6·2; Moscow, 5; Mexico City, 4·8; Buenos Aires, 4·5; Bombay, 4·1.

G **Jul**: 7th, Belgium sends troops to Congo;
8th, Lumumba appeals to U.N.
11th, Moïse Tshombe, premier of Katanga, proclaims independence of that province;
— (–12th), France agrees to independence from *Aug.* of the Republics of Dahomey, Niger, Upper Volta, Ivory Coast, Chad, Central Africa and the Congo;
14th, Léopoldville government severs relations with Belgium;
15th, U.N. emergency force arrives in Congo;
—, W. Germany agrees to compensate French victims of Nazi persecution;
18th, Hayato Ikeda, Liberal Democrat, premier of Japan;
19th, U.S.S.R. protests at U.S. proposal to equip Bundeswehr with Polaris missile;
20th, Poland asks N.A.T.O. powers to acknowledge Oder-Neisse line (*Aug.* 12th, Britain states that Germany's frontiers depended on a peace treaty);
21st, Mrs. Sirimavo Bandaranaike, Freedom Party, premier of Ceylon after elections (the first woman premier of the Commonwealth);
25th, Nyasaland Constitutional Conference in London;
27th, on Heathcoat Amory's retirement Selwyn Lloyd becomes Chancellor of the Exchequer and Lord Home Foreign Secretary.

H **Aug**: 8th, U.N. demands evacuation of Belgian troops from Congo (last leave, *Sept.* 2nd);
9th, *coup d'état* in Laos;
12th, Ceylon government takes over press;
—, Dag Hammarskjöld and U.N. troops enter Katanga;
16th, Cyprus becomes an independent republic with Archbishop Makarios President;
19th, U.S. prohibits aid funds to be used for purchasing Cuban sugar;
25th (–31st), independent African states confer at Léopoldville;
—, Russian Communist Party's manifesto condemns dogmatism of Mao Tse-tung;
29th, assassination of Hazza el-Majali, premier of Jordan;
30th, E. Germany imposes partial blockade of W. Berlin (further restrictions on entry, *Sept.* 8th).

J **Sep**: 2nd, U.S.S.R. provides aircraft for Patrice Lumumba in the Congo;
—, Cuba recognises Communist China and denounces 1952 military aid treaty with U.S.;
5th, President Kasavubu of Congo dismisses P. Lumumba and Joseph Ileo forms a ministry;
12th, George Woodcock elected T.U.C. secretary;
19th, India and Pakistan treaty on Indus waters development;
20th, Commonwealth African Assistance Plan founded;
22nd, St. Pancras rent riots by tenants hit by 1957 Rent Act;
23rd, N. Khrushchev addresses U.N. General Assembly on colonial peoples and disarmament (–*Oct.* 13th);
28th, N.A.T.O. unified system of air defence command;
29th, Harold Macmillan addresses U.N.

K **Oct**: 1st, independence of Nigerian Federation;
5th, Hugh Gaitskell battles against Labour unilateralists at Scarborough Conference;
—, S. African referendum favours republic;
11th, Lord Monckton's Report on federation of the Rhodesias and Nyasaland;
15th, trial of 800 members of Menderes' régime in Turkey.
19th, U.S. embargo on shipments to Cuba;
20th, Harold Wilson unsuccessfully opposes Hugh Gaitskell in election for leadership of Parliamentary Labour Party.

(*Continued opposite*)

Y **Statistics** (*cont.*)

TV sets (in mill.): U.S., 85; Great Britain, 10·4; W. Germany, 2; France, 1·5.

Crime in Great Britain, 398,180 indictable offences, of which 14,257 are crimes against the person. 57,363 juveniles, under 17, are indicted in U.S. total of 1,861,300 indictable offences, of which 154,930 are crimes against the person.

Britain's daily prison population totals 30,206.

Z **Births and Deaths**

Feb. 10th Aloizje Stephinac d. (62).
May 30th Boris Pasternak d. (69).
May 31st Walter Funk d. (69).
July 16th Albert Kesselring d. (74).
Aug. 19th Lewis Namier d. (72).
Sept. 7th Wilhelm Pieck d. (84).
Sept. 27th Sylvia Pankhurst d. (78).
Nov. 3rd Harold Spencer Jones d. (70).

L Nov: 1st, Harold Macmillan announces bill for facilities for U.S. Polaris submarines at Holy Loch;

8th, in U.S. presidential election, John F. Kennedy, Democrat, wins 303 votes over Richard Nixon, Republican, with 209, but Democrats lose 21 seats in House of Representatives; L. B. Johnson, Vice-President; 34,221,531 votes for Kennedy, 34,108,474 for Nixon and 502,773 for minor candidates; Kennedy subsequently nominates C. D. Dillon as secretary of treasury and R. S. McNamara defence secretary;

10th, Provisional People's Consultative Congress meets in Indonesia;

26th, National Party defeats Labour in New Zealand elections (*Dec.* 12th, K. J. Holyoake forms ministry);

28th, Mauritania becomes an independent Islamic republic.

M Dec: 2nd, Britain refuses request of Buganda for independence;

13th, Patrice Lumumba arrested and Antoine Gizenga forms ministry in Congo;

—, some 50 Labour back-benchers refuse to follow Hugh Gaitskell in defence debate;

—, revolution in Ethiopia (collapses, 19th);

14th, convention of Organisation for Economic Co-operation and Development (O.E.C.D.) signed in Paris by Canada, U.S. and 18 O.E.E.C. member countries to provide an Atlantic economic community;

—, King Baudouin of Belgium marries Doña Fabiola of Spain;

21st, King Saud takes over Saudi Arabian government on resignation of premier, Emir Faisal;

23rd, resignation of J. E. de Quay, Netherlands premier, following Protestant Parties siding with Labour on housing motion;

31st, Cuba requests U.N. Security Council to consider its complaint of U.S. aggression.

N

1961 (Jan.–Apr.) Army revolt in Algeria—S. Africa leaves the Commonwealth—The Berlin Wall—Dag Hammarskjöld dies in Congo

A **Jan**: 1st, farthings no longer legal tender in Britain;
3rd, U.S. severs relations with Cuba;
6th, Dag Hammarskjöld visits S. Africa to discuss *apartheid*;
—, (–8th), massive support in France for President de Gaulle's referendum on Algiers though 40 per cent of the electorate in Algeria abstain;
7th, Casablanca Conference of heads of state in Africa issues African Charter;
19th, Michael Ramsey appointed Archbishop of Canterbury on retirement of Archbishop Fisher;
20th, Queen Elizabeth II begins tour of India, Pakistan, Persia and Cyprus;
—, J. Kennedy inaugurated President of U.S.
26th, Britain and United Arab Republic resume full relations;
28th, Ruanda provisional government proclaims Republic, and is placed under U.N. trusteeship;
30th, civil disobedience campaign in Ceylon.

B **Feb**: 1st, Enoch Powell, British Minister of Health, increases health service charges;
4th, terrorist outbreaks in Angola;
9th, Leonid Brezhnev's 'plane intercepted by French fighter over Mediterranean;
—, President Kasavubu establishes a Central Congolese government with Joseph Ileo premier;
—, Royal Commission on British Press appointed;
10th, U.S. relinquishes rights in many defence bases in W. Indies under 1941 agreement;
11th, in Cameroons plebiscite, supervised by U.N., N. Cameroons vote for joining Nigeria, S. Cameroons for joining Cameroun;
13th, U.N. Security Council urges use of force to prevent civil war in Congo and demands enquiry into P. Lumumba's death (*Jan.* 17th);
14th, S. Africa's new decimal coinage, the Rand, in force;
16th, Cyprus votes to apply for membership of Commonwealth;
22nd, Konrad Adenauer visits London;
—, N. Khrushchev wages campaign against Dag Hammarskjöld, U.N. Secretary-General, and calls on commission of African states to supervise restoration of an independent Congo;
27th, Britain and Iceland settle fisheries dispute.

C **Mar**: 1st, John F. Kennedy establishes Peace Corps of Young Americans for overseas service;
7th, Lord Salisbury's attack on Iain Macleod, Colonial Secretary, for his liberal African policy;
8th (–17th), at meeting of Commonwealth Prime Ministers in London, H. Verwoerd announces S. Africa will leave Commonwealth on *May* 31st;
—, Congolese leaders agree on confederation under President Kasavubu;
9th, Dalai Lama appeals to U.N. to restore independence of Tibet;
21st (–*Sept.* 9th), three-power conference on discontinuance of nuclear tests;
26th, in Belgian elections Christian Socialists win most seats and form coalition with Socialists;
—, Harold Macmillan meets John F. Kennedy at Key West, Florida;
29th, in S. Africa treason trial all 28 accused are acquitted.

D **Apr**: 7th, U.N. General Assembly condemns S. African policies in South-West Africa (a U.N. Committee is later refused entry-permit to the territory);
11th, Conservative back-bench revolt by supporting amendment for bringing back the birch to R. A. Butler's Criminal Justice bill;
—, Nigeria imposes total boycott on S. African trade;

O **Politics, Economics, Law and Education**

Leon Radzinowycz, *In Search of Criminology.*

Raymond Williams, *The Long Revolution.*

Election Court rules that A. N. Wedgwood Benn is disqualified to serve as an M.P. through succession to Stansgate peerage.

Adolf Eichmann is found guilty of crimes against the Jewish people in trial in Israel (*Dec.*).

Trials in London of the spies Gordon Lonsdale and the Krogers (*Mar.*) and George Blake (*May*).

Sit-down demonstrations by C.N.D. members in Trafalgar Square, where police make 1,314 arrests (*Sept.* 17th–18th).

Freedom rides of young negroes in U.S. southern states to protest against segregation.

New Towns Commission established under Andrew Duncan.

Five Welsh counties vote for Sunday opening of public houses.

University of Sussex founded.

P **Science, Technology, Discovery, etc.**

Major Yuri Gagarin of U.S.S.R. becomes first space-man, being orbited in a 6-ton satellite (*Apr.* 12th).

Alan Shepard of U.S. makes re-entry in capsule through atmosphere (*May* 5th).

Martin Ryle concludes from radio-astronomical observations that the universe changes with time. His burial of 'the steady state' theory is challenged by Fred Hoyle.

Claus and Nagy of New York conclude from study of organisms on meteorites in museums that life in the universe must be common.

Crick and Brenner claim to determine the structure of deoxyribonucleic acid (DNA), thus breaking the genetic code.

Leucotomy operation begins controversy.

New operation for treating deafness.

The Barnet Ventilation electric lung pump.

The national electrical grids of France and Britain are connected by cable.

Britain imports methane from the Sahara to supplement coal-gas.

The Atlas computer, the world's largest, is installed at Harwell, to aid atomic research and weather forecasting.

Conference in Tanganyika (*Sept.*) for preserving African wildlife.

Q **Scholarship**

New English Bible, New Testament, appears on 350th anniversary of Authorised Version.

Lord Hankey, *The Supreme Command.*

R **Philosophy and Religion**

Stephen Neil, *Christian Faith and Other Faiths.*

R. Niebuhr, *The Self and the Dramas of History.*

Papal Encyclicals on Catholic social doctrine (*July* 14th) and for Christian reconciliation under Rome's primacy (*Aeterna Dei, Dec.*).

Preparations for Vatican Council.

Delhi meeting of World Council of Churches (*Nov.* 19th) is joined by members of Russian Orthodox Church and of Pentecostal Churches of Chile and is attended by Roman Catholic observers.

The International Missionary Council is integrated with the World Council of Churches.

Closure of Synagogues in Moscow.

D **Apr:** 11th Alphons Gorbach, People's Party, succeeds Julius Raab as Austrian chancellor;
13th, U.N. General Assembly condemns *apartheid*;
17th, Cuba invaded by rebel forces, which are defeated by Fidel Castro;
—, Selwyn Lloyd's Budget raises starting-point of surtax to £4,000;
18th, Kenya African Democratic Union agrees to form government providing a house is built for Jomo Kenyatta in Kiambu district (Kenyatta is released by governor, *Aug.* 14th);
21st, U.N. calls for elections in Ruanda and Urundi;
—, army revolt in Algeria under General Maurice Challe (collapses, 26th, rebel leaders are tried, including General Salan, *July* 11th, and sentenced *in absentia* to death);
24th, Britain and U.S.S.R. appeal for cease-fire in Laos (where the international control commission arrives, *May* 8th);
—, at Coquilhatville conference of Congolese delegates, President Tshombe of Katanga denounces President Kasavubu's agreement with U.N. and is arrested after walking out of conference;
27th, Sierre Leone becomes independent within the Commonwealth.

E **May:** 1st, Tanganyika achieves full internal self-government with Julius Nyerere as premier;
—, Kwame Nkrumah takes over control of Convention People's Party in Ghana;
9th, Ali Amini, the new premier of Persia, dissolves Parliament and bans political meetings;
11th, following sentence of 42 years on the spy George Blake, Lord Radcliffe is appointed to review security procedures;
12th, foundation of a United States of the Congo, with Léopoldville the federal capital;
24th, Cyprus becomes 16th member of Council of Europe;
25th, President Kennedy presents an extra-ordinary state of Union message to Congress for increased funds urgently needed for U.S. space, defense and air programmes;
27th, Constituent Assembly proposes new Turkish constitution;
—, Tunku Abdul Rahman, Malayan premier, proposes a Greater Malaysian Federation;
28th, last journey of 'Orient Express', Paris–Bucharest, after 78 years;
29th, Western European Union agrees that W. Germany be allowed to build destroyers equipped to fire nuclear weapons;
30th, United Arab Republic breaks off relations with S. Africa;
31st, S. Africa becomes an independent republic outside the Commonwealth, with C. R. Swart President;
—, Ghana refuses to recognise S. Africa;
—, John F. Kennedy visits France, Vienna and London.

F **Jun:** 1st (–8th), rioting during Zanzibar elections;
2nd, Latin America free trade association in force;
4th, N. Khrushchev proposes to President Kennedy a German peace conference to conclude a treaty and establish Berlin as a free city and also proposes that disarmament discussions should proceed simultaneously with test ban talks (rejected by the West, *July* 17th);
5th, U.S. Supreme Court rules that Communist Party should register as a foreign-dominated organisation (Party refuses, *Nov.* 17th);
7th, U.S.S.R.-Italian trade pact;
9th, U.N. calls on Portugal to cease repressive measures in Angola;
13th, Austria refuses application of Archduke Otto of Hapsburg to return as a private individual;

S **Art, Sculpture, Fine Arts and Architecture**

Painting:

Theft of Goya's *Duke of Wellington* from National Gallery (*Aug.* 21st).

Sculpture:

F. E. McWilliam, *Resistance.*

Architecture:

E. Maufe, Guildford Cathedral completed.

A. and P. Smithson, *The Economist* group of buildings, London (–63).

E. Saarinen, T.W.A Building, Kennedy (Idlewild) Airport, completed.

G. Maunsell and others, Hammersmith Flyover road bridge (prestressed concrete, precast sections, with electric road surface heating cables).

Hardwick's Euston portico is demolished, despite protests.

T **Music**

B. Britten, *A Midsummer Night's Dream* (opera).

Hans W. Henze, *Elegy for Young Lovers.*

S. Barbie, *Vanessa* (opera).

Zoltan Kodály, Symphony.

Luigi Nono, *Intoleranza.*

F. Ashton's new production of *Les Deux Pigeons* (Messenger—ballet).

Royal Ballet visits U.S.S.R.

U **Literature**

Richard Hughes, *The Fox in the Attic.*

John Masefield, *The Bluebells and Other Verse.*

Iris Murdoch, *A Severed Head.*

J. D. Salinger, *Franny and Zooey.*

V **The Press**

W **Drama and Entertainment**

J. Anouilh, *Becket.*

J. Osborne, *Luther.*

Harold Pinter, *The Collection.*

J. Whiting, *The Devils.*

Lionel Bart, *Oliver* (musical).

Beyond the Fringe (revue).

Films:

M. Antonioni's *La Notte.*

Anthony Mann's *El Cid.*

Alain Resnais' *L'Année dernière à Marienbad.*

Tony Richardson's *A Taste of Honey.*

François Truffaut's *Jules et Jim* with Jeanne Moreau.

Breakfast at Tiffany's with Audrey Hepburn.

Elektra.

Whistle down the Wind.

The Age of Kings (Shakespeare's historical plays—television).

'Children's Hour' ends (*Apr.*—broadcasting).

X **Sport**

Y **Statistics**

Populations (in mill.): China, 660; India, 435; U.S.S.R., 209; U.S., 179 (of which 159 white, 19 negro and 1 other races); Japan, 95; Pakistan, 94; Brazil, 66; West Germany, 54; Great Britain, 53; Italy, 50; France, 47.

F **Jun:** 19th, Britain abrogates Anglo-Kuwait agreement of 1899;
—, U.S. and U.S.S.R. representatives begin disarmament talks in Washington;
20th, Kuwait admitted to Arab League, but membership of U.N. vetoed by U.S.S.R.;
22nd, President Tshombe is freed;
25th, Abdul Karim Kassem declares Kuwait an integral part of Iraq;
30th, Britain answers Kuwait's request for troops (withdrawn, *Aug.* 13th);
—, Konrad Adenauer appeals for a German peace treaty based on right of self-determination;
Hugh Gaitskell's final victory over Labour Party unilateralists.

G **Jul:** 7th, U.S.S.R. trade fair in London;
10th (–25th), Kwame Nkrumah visits U.S.S.R.;
17th, new Constitution in force in British Guiana;
22nd, U.N. orders cease-fire after clashes between French and Tunisians in Tunisia;
23rd, referendum for new constitution in S. Rhodesia;
25th, Selwyn Lloyd's emergency Budget begins wages pause; and bank rate is raised from 5 to 7 per cent.

H **Aug:** 10th, Britain applies for membership of E.E.C.;
13th, E. Germany seals off border between E. and W. Berlin, closing the Brandenburg Gate;
15th, Hastings Banda's Malawi Congress Party victorious in Nyasaland elections;
17th (–18th), Berlin Wall constructed and the Western Powers in alarm reinforce garrison;
19th, John F. Kennedy sends Vice-President Johnson to Berlin;
21st, Cheddi Jagan's party returns to power in British Guiana elections;
25th, President de Gaulle states France will not evacuate Bizerta until international crisis is over;
27th, Ben Khedda forms provisional government in Algeria;
31st, last Spanish troops leave Morocco.

J **Sep:** 1st, U.N. breaks off relations with Katanga government; attempts of U.N. to arrest members of the government lead to heavy fighting in Elisabethville and Jadotville;
— (–6th), non-aligned powers meet in Belgrade under President Nehru and Kwame Nkrumah;
10th, Pope John XXIII appeals in TV broadcast for world peace;
14th, New Zealand introduces compulsory selective national service;
17th, Christian Democratic Union and allies lose overall majority in W. German elections;
— (–18th), Dag Hammarskjöld killed in air crash in Congo (aged 56); (U Thant acting Secretary-General from *Nov.* 3rd);
19th, Jamaican referendum to secede from W. Indies Federation;
28th, Kwame Nkrumah detains leading members of Ghana opposition;
—, army *coup* in Damascus;
29th, Syria secedes from United Arab Republic and forms Syrian Arab Republic.

K **Oct:** 5th, Shah of Persia hands over properties to Pahlevi Foundation to be used for educational and charitable purposes;
9th, Uganda Constitutional Conference ends with agreement for internal self-government in *Nov.* 1962;
10th, statement of Edward Heath, Lord Privy Seal, to E.E.C. Council of Ministers on Britain's approach to Common Market (negotiations begin, *Nov.* 8th);
—, volcanic eruption in Tristan da Cunha;
21st, President Nasser confiscates property of wealthy Egyptians;
(*Continued opposite*)

Y **Statistics** (*cont.*)

Petroleum production (in mill. barrels): U.S., 2,600 (being 60 per cent of world total); U.S.S.R., 1,075.

Cotton yarn production (percentages of world total): U.S., 28; U.S.S.R., 16; India, 12; Japan, 10; Germany, 6; Great Britain, 5.

Z **Births and Deaths**

Jan. 17th Patrice Lumumba d. (35).
Mar. 8th Thomas Beecham d. (81).
June 6th Carl Gustav Jung d. (85).
July 2nd Ernest Hemingway d. (61).
Sept. 17th A. Menderes d. (62).
Sept. 24th Sumner Welles d. (68).
Oct. 14th Paul Ramadier d. (73).
Oct. 30th Luigi Einaudi d. (87).

K **Oct**: 27th, Mauritania and Mongolia admitted to U.N.

29th, C. Karamanlis forms new ministry in Greece after victory of National Radical Union in elections.

L **Nov**: 2nd, David Ben Gurion forms new coalition in Israel after long negotiations;

8th (–*Dec.* 16th), Queen Elizabeth visits Ghana and other African territories;

16th, R. A. Butler introduces Commonwealth Immigration bill;

19th, Garfield Todd holds inaugural meeting of Rhodesian New African Party;

21st, British government fails to stop Electricity Council granting substantial wage increase, which mocks wages pause;

24th, President de Gaulle visits Harold Macmillan;

—, U.N. General Assembly resolves to treat Africa as a denuclearised zone; and

28th, calls for independence of remaining colonial peoples.

M **Dec**: 4th, Barbados Labour Party led by Grantley Adams, premier of W. Indies Federation, loses seats in Barbados elections;

4th, People's National Movement led by Eric Williams returns to power in Trinidad;

5th, U.N. force launches attack in Katanga;

6th, Order-in-Council for Southern Rhodesian Constitution; to come into effect after holding of new elections;

9th, R. G. Menzies' Liberal-Country Party returns to power in Australia following general election;

—, U.S.S.R. breaks off relations with Albania;

11th, President Nehru states the situation around Goa is critical;

15th, U.N. General Assembly rejects U.S.S.R. proposal to admit Communist China to U.N., though Britain votes in favour;

16th, U.S. loan to Ghana for Volta River project;

18th, Indian forces invade Goa (which surrenders, 19th);

—, U.N. cease-fire in Katanga; and

21st, Tshombe agrees to end secession of Katanga;

— (–22nd), Harold Macmillan meets John F. Kennedy in Bermuda;

31st, Lebanese army prevents *coup* of Syrian Popular Party in Beirut.

N

A **Jan**: 1st, Western Samoa becomes first sovereign independent Polynesian State;
3rd, President Sukarno proclaims West New Guinea an independent province;
5th (–16th), work-to-rule by Civil Service Clerical Association in protest at withdrawal of arbitration through pay pause;
6th, Princes of Laos invited to Geneva for joint negotiations;
9th, U.S.S.R.-Cuban trade pact;
14th, E.E.C. agrees on agricultural policy;
22nd, Julius Nyerere resigns in Tanganyika and Rashidj Kawawa forms ministry;
25th, African heads of state of Monrovia group (Liberia, Togo, Nigeria and Cameroun) issue Lagos Charter for pan-African co-operation;
29th, three-power conference on weapon tests at Geneva collapses.

B **Feb**: 8th, U.S. military council established in South Vietnam;
—, anti-O.A.S. riots in Paris;
10th, N. Khrushchev proposes 18-nation disarmament committee should meet at summit level;
12th, six members of C.N.D. Committee of 100 found guilty of breach of Official Secrets Act in conspiring to enter an R.A.F. base, and sentenced to imprisonment;
14th, T.U.C. agrees to join National Economic Development Council;
—, Kenya constitutional conference opens in London;
16th, anti-government riots in Georgetown, British Guiana;
23rd, U.N. Trusteeship Committee resolves to consider whether Southern Rhodesia has attained full self-government (see *Oct.* 31st).

C **Mar**: 1st, Uganda attains full internal self-government, with Benedicte Kiwanuka premier;
2nd, Britain applies to join European Coal and Steel Community;
—, in Burmese military *coup* Ne Win overthrows U Nu;
3rd, Borg Olivier, Nationalist, forms ministry in Malta;
5th, Britain applies to join Euratom;
14th, 17 foreign ministers attend Geneva disarmament conference, but France refuses to participate;
—, Eric Lubbock, Liberal, wins Orpington by-election with 7,855 majority (in 1959 election Conservative majority of 14,760);
18th, cease-fire in Algeria and establishment of *Front de la Libération Nationale* provisional government;
19th, W. Germany agrees to contribute to costs of B.A.O.R.;
23rd, Scandinavian States of Nordic Council sign Helsinki convention;
28th, Syrian army revolt fails;
31st, end of pay pause in Britain.

D **Apr**: 1st, Swiss referendum rejects manufacture or import of atomic weapons;
9th, British Budget introduces levy on speculative gains;
11th, Alexander Bustamante, Labour, forms ministry in Jamaica;
14th, M. Debré resigns in France; and
15th, Georges Pompidou forms ministry;
18th, end of West Indies Federation;
20th, O.A.S. leader Raoul Salan captured in Algiers;
22nd, renewed fighting in Laos;
25th, N. Khrushchev heads commission to draft new U.S.S.R. Constitution;
27th, United Federal Party is returned in Central African Federation elections which are boycotted by the European Opposition and all the African political parties.

O **Politics, Economics, Law and Education**

National Incomes Commission established in Britain (*Nov.* 5th)

Anthony Sampson, *The Anatomy of Britain.*

T. H. White, *The Making of the President.*

Commonwealth Immigrants Act in Britain to control immigration, especially from West Indies and Pakistan (in force *July* 1st).

British Net Book Agreement is upheld by Restrictive Practices Court.

Reorganisation of internal structure of London Stock Exchange.

Washington Supreme Court rules the reading of prayers in New York schools unconstitutional.

Annan Committee's Report on Teaching of Russian in British Schools (*June* 7th).

Rochdale Committee's Report on British Docks (*Sept.* 26th).

P **Science, Technology, Discovery, etc.**

U.S. space-men John Glenn (*Feb.*) and Malcolm Scott (*May*) are put in orbit.

Satellite Telstar, launched at Cape Canaveral (*July* 10th), circles the earth every 157·8 mins., enabling live TV pictures transmitted from Andover, Maine, to be received at Goonhilly Down, Cornwall, and in Brittany (*July* 11th).

U.S. also launch the rocket Mariner, to explore Venus, and the British satellite Aerial, to study cosmic radiation.

Further advances in molecular biology, under Max Perutz, following the discovery of DNA (in 1961).

Chudinov claims to have revived fossil algae some 250 million years old.

Twenty years after the beginning of the nuclear age U.S. has 200 atomic reactors in operation, Great Britain, 39 and U.S.S.R., 39.

Congenital malformation of babies due to side effects of thalidomide drug.

Report of Royal College of Physicians on Smoking and Health.

British weather reports give temperatures in centigrade as well as Fahrenheit (from *Jan.* 15th).

Q **Scholarship**

F. W. Deakin, *The Brutal Friendship.*

R **Philosophy and Religion**

J. L. Austin, *Sense and Sensibilia.*

Pope John XXIII insists on retention of Latin as the language of the Roman Catholic Church (*Apr.* 1st).

Vatican Council opens in Rome (*Oct.* 11th), with observer delegates from other Christian churches. Pope John orders the controversial document on Sources of Revelation to be revised.

1,100 Mormon missionaries campaign in England. Negroes are refused admission to Mormon priesthood.

8,000 English members of the Exclusive Brethren are expelled through unwillingness to accept decree forbidding contact with non-members.

S **Art, Sculpture, Fine Arts and Architecture**

Painting:

Royal Academy sells Leonardo da Vinci's cartoon of *The Virgin and Child*, which is ultimately purchased for the National Gallery.

A gallery is opened at Buckingham Palace to exhibit royal treasures.

S. Nolan, 'Kelly' series.

O. Kokoshka's autobiography, *Ringed With Vision.*

E **May**: 6th, Antonio Segni elected President of Italy on 9th ballot;
12th, S. African General Law Amendment bill imposes death penalty for sabotage;
—, British dock-workers awarded 9 per cent pay increase;
14th, Milovan Djilas, former Vice-President of Yugoslavia, given further sentence for publishing *Conversations with Stalin*;
24th, Conference of Barbados, Windward and Leeward Islands in London ends with proposals of 'Little Eight' to form new West Indies federation;
29th, state of emergency in W. Nigerian political crisis;
31st, Adolf Eichmann hanged after Israeli Court rejects appeal.

F **Jun**: 14th, European Space Research Organisation established at Paris;
14th, Conservative candidate loses deposit at W. Lothian by-election;
18th, Progressive Conservatives lose overall majority in Canadian elections, but John Diefenbaker remains as premier;
21st, U.S. concern at Chinese concentrations on mainland opposite Quemoy;
22nd, Philippines claim part of British North Borneo;
26th, Portuguese in Mozambique require Indian nationals to leave within three months of release from internment camps.

G **Jul**: 1st, Robert Soblen, sentenced to life imprisonment in U.S.A. for spying, arrives in London, following deportation from Jordan (British Home Secretary refuses to grant asylum and Soblen commits suicide, *Sept.* 11th);
—, independence of Ruanda Republic and of Kingdom of Burundi;
3rd, France proclaims independence of Algeria, following referendum of 99 per cent in favour, and the provisional government in exile returns;
4th, President Kennedy's speech envisaging partnership between U.S. and a United Europe;
12th, Conservatives at bottom of poll in Leicester North by-election;
13th, Harold Macmillan dismisses seven of his cabinet, including Lord Kilmuir, Selwyn Lloyd, David Eccles and Harold Watkinson, in an attempt to retrieve Conservative fortunes, and Reginald Maudling becomes Chancellor of the Exchequer;
20th, Laotian neutrality is guaranteed at Geneva conference;
22nd, Union movement under Oswald Mosley holds meeting in London;
31st, Britain agrees to establish a wider Malaysian Federation.

H **Aug**: 1st, attempted assassination of Kwame Nkrumah in Ghana;
6th, Jamaica becomes independent within the Commonwealth;
7th, Britain and United Arab Republic sign agreement for compensating British subjects whose property was seized after Suez;
13th, Ghana expels Archbishop of West Africa;
15th, Netherlands and Indonesia settle West New Guinea dispute;
16th, agreement signed in London for Aden to enter the Federation of S. Arabia;
—, Algeria is admitted to the Arab League;
20th, Malta requests independence within Commonwealth on breakdown of talks for financial aid;
22nd, President de Gaulle escapes assassination;
—, Arab League meets to discuss Syrian allegations of interference in internal affairs by United Arab Republic;
31st, Trinidad and Tobago become an independent nation within the Commonwealth.

J **Sep**: 1st, Singapore, and 12th, North Borneo, vote to join Malaysian Federation;
—, Persian earthquake disaster;
2nd, U.S.S.R. agrees to send arms to Cuba;

S **Art, Sculpture, Fine Arts and Architecture** (*cont.*)

Architecture:

Coventry Cathedral is consecrated (*May* 25th); architect, Basil Spence; engraved windows, John Hutton; sculpture, J. Epstein; baptistery window, J. Piper; ten nave windows, Lawrence Lee; tapestry, Graham Sutherland.

Pan-American Airways Building, New York, provides world's largest office accommodation.

T **Music**

Michael Tippett, *King Priam* (opera).
Aaron Copland-Carter, *Improvisations* (ballet).

U **Literature**

W. Faulkner, *The Reivers* (posth.).
F. R. Leavis's Richmond Lecture attacks C. P. Snow's view of the Two Cultures.
Henry Miller's *Tropic of Capricorn* is published in England.
B. Pasternak, *In the Interlude* (poems).
K. A. Porter, *Ship of Fools.*
Robert Shaw, *The Sun Doctor.*
Alexander Solzhenitsyn, *One day in the Life of Ivan Denisovich.*
Mario Tobino, *Il Clandestino.*

V **The Press**

Private Eye is issued.
The Sunday Times issues a colour supplement.

W **Drama and Entertainment**

Edward Albee, *Who's Afraid of Virginia Woolf?*
Arnold Wesker, *Chips with Everything.*
B.B.C. Television, *That Was The Week That Was.*
Pilkington Report on Broadcasting in Britain (*June* 27th) strongly supports B.B.C.
New York broadcasting station (WBA 1) performs Wagner's *Ring* in its entirety without a break.

Films:

Inmar Bergman's *Winter Night.*
Jules Dassin's *Phaedra.*
John Frankenheimer's *The Manchurian Candidate.*
David Lean's *Lawrence of Arabia.*
Orson Welles's *The Trial.*
Advice and Consent.
A Kind of Loving.
The Birds.

X **Sport**

Y **Statistics**

Of the 230 mill. population of Africa, 29 mill. are Roman Catholics, 19 mill. Protestants, and 5 mill. from Coptic and Orthodox Churches. The religions of Africa total 2,000 sects.

Z **Births and Deaths**

Jan. 16th R. H. Tawney d. (81).
Jul. 20th G. M. Trevelyan d. (86).
Nov. 7th Eleanor Roosevelt d. (78).

J **Sep**: 3rd, Katanga government accepts U Thant's plan for Congolese reunification;
7th, Laos establishes diplomatic relations with Communist China and North Vietnam;
8th, Chinese troops cross McMahon line on Indian frontier;
9th (–13th), France resumes relations with Syria, Jordan and Saudi Arabia;
19th, Commonwealth premiers endorse Britain's resumed negotiations with E.E.C. to enter Common Market;
20th, Southern Rhodesia declares Zimbabwe African People's Union an unlawful body;
25th, Fidel Castro states U.S.S.R. intends to establish a base for its fishing fleet in Cuba;
26th, Ahmed Ben Bella elected premier of Algeria;
27th, army *coup* in Yemen; Colonel Abdulla el-Sallah becomes premier;
28th, United Arab Republic amends Constitution to provide for presidential council.

K **Oct**: 1st, U.N. takes over administration of West New Guinea from British;
5th, French National Assembly censures proposed referendum to sanction future president's election by popular mandate; and Georges Pompidou resigns but de Gaulle asks him to continue in office;
9th, Uganda becomes independent within the Commonwealth;
10th, *Der Spiegel* publishes article on N.A.T.O. exercise criticising weakness of Bundeswehr (the offices of the paper are occupied by the police, 16th);
11th, Congress passes U.S. Trade Expansion Act;
—, Hugh Foot resigns as Britain's U.N. representative on colonial questions in protest against British defence of Southern Rhodesian government;
16th, cease-fire in Congo;
20th, China launches offensive on Indian border positions;
22nd, John F. Kennedy announces in broadcast the installation of U.S.S.R. missile base in Cuba;
—, William Vassall, Admiralty clerk, sentenced for spying;
24th, U.S. blockade of Cuba;
26th, Khrushchev offers to withdraw missiles if U.S. removes bases from Turkey, a condition which Kennedy rejects;
28th, French referendum favours election of president by universal suffrage;
30th, U.N. General Assembly rejects U.S.S.R. proposal to admit Communist China;
31st, Krishna Menon, Indian defence minister, resigns;
—, U.N. General Assembly requests Britain to suspend enforcement of new Constitution in Southern Rhodesia (but Constitution comes into effect, *Nov.* 1st).

L **Nov**: 2nd, President Kennedy announces U.S.S.R. has been dismantling bases in Cuba;
—, Julius Nyerere elected President of Tanganyika;
—, Greville Wynne is arrested on espionage charge in Budapest and is later extradited to U.S.S.R.;
3rd, Anastas Mikoyan visits Cuba in connection with removal of missiles;
5th, Walter Strauss, W. German defence minister, dismissed over *Der Spiegel* affair (and 19th, five Free Democrat ministers resign);
—, U.N. General Assembly demands that all nuclear tests cease by *Jan.* 1st 1963;
—, U.S. Congressional elections leave Democrats in control of both houses;
—, Saudi Arabia severs relations with United Arab Republic;
8th, Thomas Galbraith, Civil Lord of Admiralty, resigns over Vassall affair;
—, George Brown defeats Harold Wilson in election for Labour Party deputy leadership;
9th, British Guiana constitutional conference in London breaks down;
10th, President of Yemen accuses Britain of plotting to overthrow régime;

(*Continued opposite*)

z **Births and Deaths** (*cont.*)

Nov. 18th Niels Bohr d. (77).
Nov. 22nd René Coty d. (80).
Nov. 28th Queen Wilhelmina of the Netherlands d. (82).
Dec. 7th Kirsten Flagstad d. (67).

L Nov: 14th, Britain resumes negotiations with E.E.C.;
—, Harold Macmillan appoints Radcliffe tribunal to inquire into security;
20th, U.S.S.R. agrees to withdraw Ilyushin bombers from Cuba and U.S. announces end of blockade;
21st, China agrees to cease-fire on Sino-Indian border and forces subsequently withdraw;
22nd, Labour wins S. Dorset by-election through intervention of anti-common market candidate;
27th, Britain signs agreement to provide India with arms to resist Chinese aggression;
28th, President de Gaulle reprieves death sentence on Edmund Jouhaud for O.A.S. crimes;
29th, Anglo-French agreement to develop 'Concord' supersonic airliner;
30th, U Thant is elected U.N. Secretary-General.

M Dec: 4th, Western European Union Assembly in Paris calls for single N.A.T.O. nuclear force;
5th, U.S.-U.S.S.R. agreement on co-operation for peaceful uses of outer space;
—, Dean Acheson in West Point speech suggests Britain is 'just about played out'.
8th, Brunei rebellion collapses after British intervention;
9th, Tanganyika becomes a republic within the Commonwealth, with Julius Nyerere President;
11th, West German coalition of Christian Democrats, Christian Socialists and Free Democrats;
14th, Edgar Whitehead's United Federal Party defeated in Southern Rhodesia elections by Winston Field's right-wing Rhodesian Front;
—, Northern Rhodesia's first African-dominated government, under Kenneth Kaunda;
17th, committee on Lords reform recommends that an heir be able to disclaim his peerage;
18th, at Nassau meeting President Kennedy and Harold Macmillan agree that U.S. shall provide Britain with Polaris missiles instead of Skybolt;
19th, Britain acknowledges Nyasaland's right to secede from the Central African Federation;
27th, India and Pakistan reopen talks on Kashmir;
28th, U.N. troops engaged in heavy fighting in Katanga and, 29th, occupy Elisabethville.

N

A Jan: 2nd, General Lemnitzer succeeds General Norstad as Supreme Allied Commander Europe;
3rd, U.N. force captures Jadotville in Katanga;
9th, Lord Hailsham appointed minister for the North-East;
14th, President de Gaulle states objections to Britain's entry into Common Market and rejects U.S. offer of Polaris missiles;
15th, President Tshombe accepts U.N. plan for secession of Katanga;
18th, Hugh Gaitskell, Leader of British Labour Party, dies (aged 56);
22nd, President de Gaulle and Konrad Adenauer sign Franco-German treaty of co-operation;
24th, Italy accepts U.S. plan for multilateral nuclear force;
29th, Britain is refused entry into Common Market.

B Feb: 1st, Nyasaland becomes self-governing with Hastings Banda premier;
6th, U.S. places shipping restrictions on Cuba;
8th, rebels in Baghdad assassinate premier Abdel Karim Kassem and Abdul Salam Arif replaces him;
9th, U.S.S.R. releases Archbishop of Lvov after 18 years imprisonment;
14th, Harold Wilson is elected Leader of British Labour Party;
19th, U.S.S.R. agrees to withdraw troops from Cuba;
20th, U.S. recommends that surface ships should be used to carry Polaris missiles in N.A.T.O. force;
21st, Royal Society Committee reports of emigration of British scientists;
28th, L.C.C. offers 100 per cent loans for houses.

C Mar: 4th, British government proposes a unified ministry of defence;
17th, typhoid epidemic breaks out in Zermatt;
22nd, John Profumo, British Secretary of State for War, makes personal statement in Commons in face of rumours (on *June* 4th admits its untruthfulness);
25th, Terence O'Neill succeeds Lord Brookeborough as prime minister of Northern Ireland;
26th, British Consumer Council appointed under Lady Elliot;
26th, demonstration by unemployed outside Parliament.

D Apr: 1st, end of New York newspaper strike after 114 days;
3rd, Reginald Maudling abolishes Schedule A taxation and increases investment allowances in Budget;
6th, Britain and U.S. sign Polaris missile agreement;
9th, Winston Churchill becomes an honorary citizen of U.S.;
12th, first armed attack by Indonesian forces on Malaysia;
15th, disorder breaks out in last stages of C.N.D. Aldermaston March;
17th, United Arab Republic, Syria and Iraq agree to federate;
20th, first report of National Incomes Commission rejects 40-hour agreement in Scottish building industry;
22nd, Lester B. Pearson, Liberal, forms ministry in Canada, following John Diefenbaker's resignation, 17th;
22nd (–*July* 8th), general strike in British Guiana with rioting and terrorism;
25th, report of Radcliffe tribunal on Vassal spy case;
28th, Fidel Castro visits U.S.S.R.

E May: 9th, Labour gains 544 seats in England and Wales borough elections;
16th, Chief Enahoro of Nigeria is deported from Britain (*Sept.* 7th he is sentenced in Lagos; the Attorney-General, John Hobson, is later charged unsuccessfully before his Inn for his share in the deportation);

O **Politics, Economics, Law and Education**

Graham Wootton, *The Politics of Influence*.

Beeching Report on *The Reshaping of British Railways* proposes development of freight traffic and the closure of many lines.

Buchanan Report, *Traffic in Towns*.

Campaign in London against rapacious landlords of slum tenements ('Rachmanism').

Newsom Committee's Report on education recommends raising school-leaving age to 16.

Robbins Report on higher education recommends six new universities and a new ministry.

Nobel Committee inquires into moral impact of TV on the young.

Teaching machines first used in British schools.

Supreme Council of National Economy established in U.S.S.R. (*Mar.* 13th).

Campaigns against trading stamps in Britain.

P **Science, Technology, Discovery, etc.**

Discovery of anti-xi-zeno, a fundamental atomic particle of contra-terrene matter.

U.S.S.R. puts in orbit Valentina Tereshkova (*June* 16th) for three-day flight in space to study the problem of weightlessness in a woman. Another astronaut launched the same day makes 49 orbits.

U.S. astronaut Gordon Cooper, launched in an Atlas rocket, makes 22 orbits (*May* 15th).

U.S. orbit a belt of copper needles as test for secure system of global radio communications.

Space research provides much data on conditions on Mars and Venus.

Vaccine for measles is perfected.

Alan Hodgkin and John Eccles make discoveries in the transmission of nerve impulses.

Rachel Carson in her book *The Silent Spring* draws attention to the dangers of chemical pest control.

Natural gas deposits in Groningen are developed.

Friction welding is invented.

Construction of the Victoria Underground line, London, begun.

Britain endures coldest *Jan.* and *Feb.* since 1740.

Queen Elizabeth Hospital, Hong Kong, the largest in the Commonwealth, completed.

Q **Scholarship**

Alvar Ellegård, *A Statistical Method for Determining Authorship*.

A computer is used to investigate the authorship of St. Paul's Epistles.

Edward Crankshaw, *The Fall of the House of Hapsburg*.

A. Deutscher, *The Prophet Outcast; Trotsky, 1929–40*.

R **Philosophy and Religion**

John Robinson, Bishop of Woolwich, *Honest to God*, arouses widespread interest. Discussion of it includes Archbishop Ramsey's *Image Old and New*.

Alec Vidler and others, *Objections to Christian Belief*.

G. M. Carstair's Reith Lectures, *This Island Now*.

Towards a Quaker View of Sex.

Anglican-Methodist *Conversations* towards unity.

G. H. von Wright, *The Varieties of Goodness*.

John XXIII's encyclical *Pacem in Terris* (*Apr.* 11th) deals with peaceful settlement of disputes and with relations with non-Catholics and with Communists.

Vatican Council approves use of vernacular liturgies.

Mary Lusk appeals to be ordained in ministry of Church of Scotland.

E **May**: 16th, Indian-Pakistani talks on Kashmir break down;
—, Geneva Conference on General Agreement on Tariffs and Trade (G.A.T.T.) begins 'Kennedy round' negotiations for tariff cuts.

F **Jun**: 3rd, death of Pope John XXIII (aged 81); (30th, Cardinal Montini is enthroned as Pope Paul VI);
4th, John Profumo resigns from Parliament, admitting he misled the House of Commons (on *Mar.* 22nd);
11th, Constantine Karamanlis, Greek premier, resigns in protest against King Paul's state visit to Britain;
18th, new constitution for Press Council (*Dec.* 11th, Lord Devlin becomes chairman);
19th, John F. Kennedy addresses Congress on civil rights;
20th, U.S.-U.S.S.R. agreement on a 'hot line' from the White House to the Kremlin;
21st, France withdraws naval Atlantic forces from N.A.T.O.;
25th, President Tshombe is forced to resign as Katanga premier;
29th, President Kennedy visits Harold Macmillan.

G **Jul**: 9th, demonstrations occur during state visit of King and Queen of Hellenes;
10th, Edward Boyle, British Minister of Education, imposes Remuneration of Teachers Act on the Burnham Committee;
20th, end of U.S.S.R.-Chinese ideological talks in Moscow;
22nd, agreement reached for British Guiana to be granted internal self-government in 1964;
23rd, Stephen Ward found guilty at Central Criminal Court of living on immoral earnings of Christine Keeler and others;
26th, Skoplje earthquake in Yugoslavia;
30th, H. A. R. Philby, British journalist who disappeared from Beirut in *Jan.*, is granted asylum in U.S.S.R.;
31st, Peerage bill receives royal assent and A. N. Wedgwood Benn disclaims peerage.

H **Aug**: 1st, Britain agrees to grant independence to Malta in 1964;
—, minimum prison age raised to 17 by Criminal Justice Act;
5th, Britain, U.S. and U.S.S.R. sign nuclear test ban treaty (subsequently signed by 96 states, but not France, before coming into force, *Oct.* 1st);
8th, Glasgow–London mail train robbery of £2½ million near Cheddington, Bucks.;
21st, Buddhists arrested and martial law imposed in South Vietnam;
28th, 200,000 negroes take part in peaceful demonstration for civil rights in Washington;
—, Congress compels the acceptance of arbitration in U.S. rail strike;
30th, release of Kenneth Abrahams who alleges he has been abducted from Bechuanaland by South African police.

J **Sep**: 4th, riots over school desegregation in Birmingham, Alabama;
15th, negroes killed by bomb in Birmingham, Alabama;
16th, Malaya, North Borneo, Sarawak and Singapore form Federation of Malaysia which, 17th, breaks off relations with Indonesia, following Sukarno's increased hostility;
18th, U.N. Special Committee on *Apartheid* calls for prohibition of arms and petroleum traffic with South Africa;
19th, Anglo-French report favours Channel Tunnel project;
21st, V. Široký, premier of Czechoslovakia, is dismissed;
26th, Lord Denning's Report on the Profumo affair.

S **Art, Sculpture, Fine Arts and Architecture**

Painting:

Leonardo da Vinci's *Mona Lisa* exhibited in New York.

Goya Exhibition at Royal Academy.

Renewed interest in the 'Art Nouveau' period influences fabrics and design.

Sculpture:

F. E. McWilliam, 'Dame Ninette de Valois', sculpture for Covent Garden Opera House.

Architecture:

G. Bunshaft, Beinecke Library, Yale University (a windowless building).

Le Corbusier (pseud.), Carpenter Center for the Visual Arts, Harvard University.

Rohe, Museum of the 20th Century, Berlin.

James Bunning's London Coal Exchange is demolished.

Hilton Hotel, Park Lane, London.

Roebuck House, Victoria Street, a skyscraper overlooking Buckingham Palace Gardens.

T **Music**

A. Bliss, *Mary of Magdala.*

A. Brindle, *Homage to H. G. Wells.*

B. Britten, *War Requiem.*

M. Tippett, concerto for orchestra.

U **Literature**

Günter Grass, *The Tin Drum.*

Louis MacNeice, *The Burning Perch.*

Mary McCarthy, *The Group.*

Irish Murdoch, *The Unicorn.*

John Updike, *The Centaur.*

New York court allows publication of John Cleland's *Fanny Hill*, but in England magistrates courts oppose publication.

V **The Press**

Two journalists appearing before the Radcliffe tribunal are imprisoned for refusing to reveal the sources of their information for tales about the spy Vassall (*Feb.* 4th).

W **Drama and Entertainment**

John Arden, *The Workhouse Donkey.*

Rolf Hochhuth, *The Representative.*

E. Ionescu, *Exit the King.*

H. de Montherlant, *Le Chaos et la Nuit.*

Films:

Ingmar Bergman's *The Silence.*

Stanley Donen's *Charade.*

Joseph L. Mankiewicz's *Cleopatra*, costing some £12 million, with Elizabeth Taylor.

Otto Preminger's *The Cardinal.*

Carol Reed's *The Running Man.*

Tony Richardson's *Tom Jones.*

Luchino Visconti's *The Leopard.*

Billy Wilder's *Irma La Douce.*

The Beatles make the Liverpool sound international.

Capri bans transistor radios.

1963 (Oct.–Dec.)

K **Oct**: 1st, Nigeria becomes a republic within the Commonwealth, with Dr. Azikiwe President;

—, Britain agrees to join discussions about a N.A.T.O. mixed-manned nuclear fleet;

3rd, successful army *coup* in Honduras;

4th, release of Archbishop Beran of Prague after 14 years imprisonment;

—, devastating hurricane in Caribbean;

7th, U.N. Trusteeship Committee calls on Britain not to transfer armed forces of Rhodesian Federation to Southern Rhodesia;

9th, the Kabaka of Buganda becomes first President of Uganda;

11th, U.N. condemns repression in South Africa by 106 votes to 1;

15th, Ludwig Erhard becomes chancellor of West Germany on Konrad Adenauer's resignation;

18th, Harold Macmillan resigns premiership for reasons of health, and 19th, Earl of Home becomes premier (later disclaims peerage and, *Nov.* 8th, is elected M.P.);

20th, Iain Macleod and Enoch Powell refuse to serve in new Conservative ministry;

21st, government loan to Cunard Company for new liner agreed upon;

25th, Vatican Council approves principle of a fixed Easter;

26th, N. Khrushchev states U.S.S.R. would not race U.S. to the moon;

31st, Britain suspends aid to Indonesia.

L **Nov**: 1st, army *coup* in South Vietnam; President Ngo Dinh Diem assassinated;

22nd, President John F. Kennedy is assassinated by Lee H. Oswald in Dallas and L. B. Johnson is sworn in as President of U.S.;

24th, Oswald is shot by Jack Ruby;

30th, Liberal and Country Party coalition increases majority in Australian elections.

M **Dec**: 3rd, Lord Mancroft resigns from board of Norwich Union Insurance Society through Arab pressure;

4th, U.N. Security Council votes for partial embargo on arms to South Africa;

6th, Christine Keeler is sentenced for perjury in 'Lucky' Gordon case;

10th, Zanzibar becomes independent within the Commonwealth;

11th, Kwame Nkrumah dismisses Chief Justice of Ghana following acquittals in treason trials;

12th, Kenya becomes independent republic within the Commonwealth;

18th, African students riot in Red Square, Moscow, after the death of a Ghanaian;

19th, British Monopolies Commission recommends the abolition of price maintenance on car electrical equipment;

22nd, clashes in Cyprus between Greeks and Turks and, 30th, following visit by Duncan Sandys, a neutral zone is agreed upon;

—, Greek liner *Lakonia* catches fire and sinks in North Atlantic with loss of 150 lives;

25th, state of emergency in Somalia frontier region of Kenya;

31st, dissolution of Central African Federation of Rhodesia and Nyasaland.

N

X **Sport**

Y **Statistics**

Indian religious denominations (in mill.): Hindu, 366; Moslem, 47; Christian, 10; Buddhist, 3.

Z **Births and Deaths**

Jan. 29th Robert Lee Frost d. (88).
Jan. 30th Francis Poulenc d. (64).
Mar. 16th William Henry Beveridge d. (84).
Aug. 22nd William Richard Morris, Lord Nuffield d. (85).
Aug. 31st Georges Braque d. (81).
Oct. 11th Jean Cocteau d. (74).
Nov. 22nd Aldous Huxley d. (69) and John Fitzgerald Kennedy d. (46).
Dec. 30th Paul Hindemith d. (68).

1964 (Jan.–Apr.) U.S. Civil Rights Bill—Fall of Khrushchev—China explodes atom bomb—Indonesian landings in Malaya

A **Jan**: 7th, Cuba orders 400 British buses;
8th, L. B. Johnson's state of Union message proposes reduced spending on defence;
9th, anti-American riots in Panama which, 10th, breaks off diplomatic relations with U.S.;
12th, rebellion in Zanzibar, which is declared a republic, and the Sultan is banished;
15th, Cyprus constitutional conference opens in London, but fails to reach agreement
20th (–24th), mutinies of Tanganyika Rifles and of troops in Uganda and Kenya, which are quelled by British forces;
21st (–*Sept.* 17th), sixth session of 17-nation disarmament conference in Geneva;
22nd, Kenneth Kaunda, United National Independent Party, becomes first premier of Northern Rhodesia;
27th, France establishes diplomatic relations with Communist China;
28th, riots in Salisbury, Southern Rhodesia.

B **Feb**: 3rd, China challenges leadership of U.S.S.R.;
6th, Anglo-French agreement on a rail Channel Tunnel;
11th, fighting between Greeks and Turks at Limassol, Cyprus;
20th, Balzan International Foundation makes controversial award of peace prize to U.N., and Switzerland later blocks the Foundation's funds;
21st, attempted assassination of Ismet Inönü, Turkish premier;
22nd, Ghana becomes a one-party Socialist State;
23rd, Britain recognises President Abdul Amari Karume's régime in Zanzibar;
27th, Plowden Committee recommends union between Foreign Office and Commonwealth Relations Office overseas staff.

C **Mar**: 4th, government changes August Bank Holiday to last Monday in month from 1965;
6th, death of King Paul I of the Hellenes; succeeded by Constantine II;
9th, fighting in Ktima, Cyprus;
11th, South Africa withdraws from International Labour Organisation;
16th, L. B. Johnson submits £344 mill. bill to combat poverty;
19th, study on South-East of England anticipates considerable rise in population by 1981;
22nd, outbreaks of anti-Muslim violence in India;
25th, Sakari Tuomioja, Finland, appointed mediator in Cyprus dispute;
—, violence spreads in British Guiana after eight-week strike of sugar-workers (strike ends, *July* 26th);
27th, U.N. peace force under General Gyani, India, takes over in Cyprus;
30th, Easter week-end outbreaks of Mods *v.* Rockers disturbances in Clacton and other British resorts.

D **Apr**: 1st (–18th), strike of Belgian doctors;
2nd, Yemen alleges British air attack on *Mar.* 28th;
4th, Archbishop Makarios abrogates 1960 treaty between Greece, Turkey and Cyprus and heavy fighting occurs in the north-west of the island;
8th, India releases Shaikh Abdullah, former premier of Kashmir;
9th, in first elections for Greater London Council Labour win 64 seats; Conservatives, 36;
11th, Humberto Branco elected President of Brazil, following deposition of Sr. Goulart;
13th, Winston Field resigns premiership of Southern Rhodesia on policy grounds and Ian Smith forms ministry;
14th, National Development Bonds introduced in British Budget;

O **Politics, Economics, Law and Education**

Ministry of Technology formed in Britain to direct the application of science to industry (*Oct.*).

British White Paper on *Monopolies, Mergers and Restrictive Practices* (*Mar.* 5th).

In Rookes *v.* Barnard (*Jan.* 21st), the House of Lords rules that trade union officials are liable to damages claimed by a former member dismissed from employment as a result of resigning from his Union, and that the officials are not protected by the Trade Disputes Act 1906.

London Stock Exchange makes new demands on companies for information (*Aug.*).

National Commercial Bank of Scotland opens 'women only' branch in Edinburgh.

Oxford University appoints Franks Commission to examine the University's role in higher education.

Randolph Churchill, *The Fight for the Leadership of the Conservative Party.*

Warren Report on the assassination of President Kennedy (*Sept.* 17th).

F. Mauriac, *De Gaulle.*

P **Science, Technology, Discovery, etc.**

Brookhaven scientists discover the fundamental particle omega-minus through using the 'Nimrod' cyclotron.

Fred Hoyle and J. V. Narlikar of Cambridge University propound new theory of gravitation, which solves the problem of inertia.

Britain's 'Blue Streak' is launched.

Ranger VII, launched from Cape Kennedy, succeeds in obtaining close-up photographs of the moon's surface (*July* 31st).

U.S. Mariner IV and U.S.S.R. Zond II are launched with equipment for photographing Mars.

U.S. develops unmanned satellites 'Syncom' for relaying pictures of Olympic Games from Tokio, and 'Nimbus'.

Dorothy Hodgkin wins Nobel prize for work on X-ray crystallography.

The living brain of a rhesus monkey is isolated from its body by neurosurgeons at Cleveland General Hospital.

Successful experiments are made in finger-tip colour reading.

U.S. Surgeon-General's report *Smoking and Health* links lung cancer with cigarette smoking.

U.S. divers live on 'Sealab' for nine days, 192 feet down, off Bermuda coast, to study effects of depth on man's mind and body.

Britain grants licences to drill for oil and gas in the North Sea.

Emigration of British scientists, principally to U.S. (the 'Brain Drain') alarms British government.

Britain's military aircraft, TSR-2, maiden flight (*Sept.* 28th).

Opening of the Forth Bridge (*Sept.* 4th), and of the Verrazano-Narrows Bridge (the world's longest).

Q **Scholarship**

The building of Stonehenge is explained as a means of predicting the eclipse of the moon.

A. H. M. Jones, *The Later Roman Empire.*

Leslie Hotson, *Mr. W. H.*

Roy Jenkins, *Asquith.*

Alexander Werth, *Russia at War.*

R **Philosophy and Religion**

A. Koestler, *The Act of Creation.*

D **Apr**: 16th, the Committee of Public Accounts criticises Ferranti Ltd.'s profit on the Bloodhound missile as excessive (*July* 28th, a committee of investigation also criticises the Ministry of Aviation; Ferranti later offers to refund over £4 mill.);
16th, sentences totalling 307 years passed on 12 mail-train robbers;
—, Joshua Nkomo placed under restriction in Southern Rhodesia;
22nd, Greville Wynne, sentenced in Moscow, 1963, is exchanged with U.S.S.R. for Gordon Lonsdale, sentenced in London for espionage, 1961;
27th, Tanganyika and Zanzibar are united, with Julius Nyerere President (*Oct.* 29th the State is named Tanzania).

E **May**: 4th, further 'Kennedy round' G.A.T.T. talks in Geneva;
6th, South Africa passes Bantu Laws amendment bill;
14th, N. Khrushchev opens the Aswan Dam;
18th, Nationalist riots in Quebec;
19th, U.S. complains to Moscow about microphones concealed in Moscow embassy;
20th, outbreak of Aberdeen typhoid epidemic;
22nd, state of emergency in British Guiana;
24th, 300 spectators at football match in Lima die in riot;
27th, death of Pandit Nehru (aged 74); (Lala Bahadur Shastri appointed to succeed him, *June* 2nd).

F **Jun**: 9th, West Germany agrees to pay £1 mill. compensation for British victims of Nazi persecution;
11th, Greece rejects direct talks with Turkey over Cyprus;
12th, Nelson Mandela and seven others sentenced to life imprisonment for acts of sabotage in the Rivonia trial, Pretoria;
12th, U.S.S.R. and East Germany sign 20-year treaty of friendship;
13th, arrest of deputy premier of British Guiana;
19th, Congolese rebels take Albertville;
21st, breakdown of Malaysian-Indonesian talks;
30th, U.N. military operations in Congo end;
—, Spain terminates negotiations with Britain for constructing warships.

G **Jul**: 2nd, L. B. Johnson signs Civil Rights Act;
6th, Nyasaland Protectorate, renamed Malawi, becomes independent within the Commonwealth;
7th, France adopts selective military service;
8th (–15th), Commonwealth premiers meet in London;
10th, Moïse Tshombe succeeds C. Adoula as premier of the Congo;
15th, Anastas Mikoyan succeeds Leonid Brezhnev as President of U.S.S.R.;
16th, Resale Prices Act comes into force in Britain;
18th, race riots in Harlem, New York;
26th, U.S.S.R. calls for new 14-power meeting on Laos;
—, strike of British Guiana sugar-workers is called off;
27th (–30th), disturbances in Northern Rhodesia involving Lumpa Church, led by Alice Lenshina (death toll rises to 491);
—, Winston Churchill's last appearance in House of Commons;
30th, agreement for Gambia's independence in *Feb.* 1965.

H **Aug**: 2nd, a U.S. destroyer is attacked off North Vietnam; U.S. aircraft attack North Vietnam bases in reprisal;
4th, bodies of three Mississippi civil rights workers are found;
5th, Congolese rebels capture Stanleyville;
7th, People's Republic of the Congo is declared;

R **Philosophy and Religion** (*cont.*)

Howick Committee, appointed by Archbishop of Canterbury, favours retaining system of Crown appointments to bishoprics and deaneries (*Dec.* 1st).

Leslie Paul, *The Deployment and Payment of the Clergy.*

Pope Paul VI makes pilgrimage to the Holy Land (*Jan.* 4th–7th).

Roman Catholic hierarchy in England and Wales rules against use of contraceptive pill (*May* 7th); but authorises joint prayers with other churches (*Dec.* 6th).

S **Art, Sculpture, Fine Arts and Architecture**

'OP' art—geometric designs which give illusion of change of pattern.

Painting:

P. Cézanne's *Les Grandes Baigneuses* acquired by the National Gallery.

'Art of a Decade' exhibition, Tate Gallery.

Sculpture:

F. E. McWilliam, sculpture, *The Hampstead Figure*, Swiss Cottage Redevelopment Centre, London.

Architecture:

The Bull Ring, Birmingham, costing £1 mill., opened.

Basil Spence, Library and Swimming Pool at Swiss Cottage, London, opened, and his buildings for University of Sussex, near Brighton, near completion.

Ascot Racecourse new grandstand.

Shakespeare Quatercentenary Exhibition at Stratford-on-Avon and Edinburgh.

Sotheby, London, and Parke-Burnet, New York, merge.

T **Music**

Richard Rodney Bennett, *Aubade.*

Leonard Bernstein, 3rd Symphony (*Kaddish*).

B. Britten, symphony with solo 'cello.

John Cage, *Atlas Elipticales With Winter Music* (electronic version).

Gustav Mahler, 10th Symphony (posth.), completed by Deryck Cooke.

Bernard Naylor, *Stabat Mater* (oratorio).

Michael Kennedy, *The Works of Ralph Vaughan Williams.*

Wilfred Mellors, *Music in a New Found Land.*

U **Literature**

Saul Bellow, *Herzog.*

William Burroughs, *The Naked Lunch.*

William Golding, *The Spire.*

E. Hemingway, *A Moveable Feast* (posth.).

C. Isherwood, *A Single Man.*

Philip Larkin, *The Whitsun Wedding.*

J.-P. Sartre, *Les Mots.*

C. P. Snow, *Corridors of Power.*

Frank Tuohy, *The Ice Saints.*

Gore Vidal, *Julian.*

V **The Press**

T.U.C. sells shares in *Daily Herald*, which last appears *Sept.* 14th. *The Sun* takes its place, *Sept.* 15th.

W **Drama and Entertainment**

TV: B.B.C. 2 opened (*Apr.* 21st); 'The Great War' Series.

Joan Littlewood's Theatre Workshop, Stratford E., and The Windmill Theatre (non-stop vaudeville) close.

H **Aug**: 8th, Turkish planes attack Cyprus and, 9th, U.N. orders cease-fire;
11th, Alice Lenshina surrenders in Northern Rhodesia, but further incidents occur;
12th, mail-train robber Charles Wilson is rescued from Winson Green prison;
13th, General Grivas assumes command of Greek Cypriot forces;
17th, Greece withdraws units from N.A.T.O.;
24th, white mercenaries arrive in Congo to fight the rebels;
26th, Nationalist movements, People's Caretaker Council and Zimbabwe African National Union are banned in Rhodesia;
28th, an English teacher is kidnapped from Lusaka and transported to Johannesburg, where he is later released.

J **Sep**: 2nd, Indonesian army lands in Malaya and, 4th, Commonwealth troops move in;
15th, the Vatican signs an accord with Hungary;
20th, President de Gaulle begins tour of South American republics;
21st, Malta becomes an independent State within the Commonwealth;
24th, Berlin Passes agreement is signed for one year.

K **Oct**: 5th (–12th), Queen Elizabeth II visits Canada, with great security precautions in Quebec;
5th (–11th), Cairo conference of 58 non-aligned states, but Moïse Tshombe, Congo, is not permitted to attend;
7th, Hastings Banda obtains fresh powers of detention in Malawi;
14th, Martin Luther King, U.S. negro leader, is awarded Nobel peace prize;
15th, in British general election Labour win 317 seats, Conservatives, 303, with Liberals, 9; (Labour receives 44·1 per cent of votes cast, Conservatives, 43·4, and Liberals, 9·0; overall national swing to Labour 3·2 per cent);
16th, Alec Douglas-Home resigns and Harold Wilson forms Labour ministry, with Patrick Gordon Walker, defeated at Smethwick, as Foreign-Secretary, George Brown Secretary of State for Economic Affairs, James Callaghan Chancellor of the Exchequer, and Lord Gardiner Lord Chancellor;
15th, Nikita Khrushchev is replaced as First Secretary of Soviet Communist Party by Leonid Brezhnev and as prime minister by Aleksei Kosygin;
16th, China explodes an atomic bomb;
24th, Northern Rhodesia, renamed Zambia, becomes an independent republic within the Commonwealth, with Kenneth Kaunda President;
26th, British government impose 15 per cent surcharge on imports except raw materials, to close £800 mill. balance of payments gap;
27th, Harold Wilson states that a declaration of independence by Rhodesia would be an open act of defiance;
29th, further Indonesian landings on west coast of Malaya, but Commonwealth troops capture the invaders.

L **Nov**: 2nd, deposition of King Saud of Saudi Arabia, and Faisal proclaimed King;
3rd, in U.S. elections President L. B. Johnson, Democrat, with 486 electoral votes, has sweeping victory over Barry Goldwater, Republican, with 52; popular vote: Johnson, 43,126,218; Goldwater, 27,174,898; the Democrat gains in House of Representatives leave them with 295 seats against the Republicans with 140;
5th, in Rhodesian referendum 90 per cent (of a 61 per cent poll) favour independence;
—, Chou En-lai visits Moscow for summit talks of Communist states;
7th, Ian Smith rejects proposed visit of Commonwealth Secretary to Southern Rhodesia;
8th, cease-fire in force in the Yemen;
10th, Kenya becomes a single-party State;

W **Drama and Entertainment** (*cont.*)

Arthur Miller, *After the Fall.*
John Osborne, *Inadmissible Evidence.*
Peter Shaffer, *The Royal Hunt of the Sun.*
Crathorne Committee supports Sunday theatres and entertainment, but not professional sport.
Stratford-on-Avon governors support Peter Hall when attacked for producing 'Theatre of Cruelty' and *avant-garde* foreign plays at the Aldwych.
Michael Balcon's group after long struggle buys British Lion Films.
Films:
Ingmar Bergman's *The Silence.*
Peter Brooks's *Lord of the Flies.*
Stanley Kubrick's *Dr. Strangelove.*
Andrzej Munk's *The Passenger.*
Alain Resnais's *Muriel.*
François Truffaut's *Silken Skin.*
The Beatles in *A Hard Day's Night.*
Goldfinger.
The Pumpkin Eater.

X **Sport**

In Tokyo Olympic Games U.S.S.R. wins 41 gold medals; U.S., 37; Japan, 16; Germany, 13; Italy and Hungary, 10; Poland, 7; Australia and Finland, 6; Britain, Czechoslovakia and Sweden, 5.
Cassius Clay defeats Sonny Liston in World Heavy-weight Championship.
In America's Cup *Constellation* (U.S.) beats *Sovereign* (Britain).

Y **Statistics**

Merchant shipping (tonnages):
U.S., 22,430,249; U.K., 21,489,948; Liberia; 14,549,645; Norway, 14,477,112; Japan, 10,813,228; U.S.S.R., 6,957,512; Greece, 6,887,624; Italy, 5,707,817; West Germany, 5,159,186; France, 5,116,232; Netherlands, 5,110,022; Sweden, 4,308,042; Panama, 4,269, 462; British Commonwealth (excluding U.K., Canada and India), 2,783,166; Denmark, 2,431,020; Spain, 2,047,715; Canada, 1,823,387.
Oil tankers (tonnage):
Liberia, 8,619,449; U.K., 8,002,203; Norway, 7,663,906; U.S., 4,505,274; Japan, 3,145,051; Panama, 2,253,418; France, 2,208,763; Italy, 1,982,485; U.S.S.R., 1,715,956; Netherlands, 1,638,419; Greece, 1,603,082; Sweden, 1,462,796; Denmark, 883,853; West Germany, 838,740; Spain, 590,882; Argentina, 509,526.

Z **Births and Deaths**

Jan. 8th Julius Raab d. (72).
Mar. 20th Brendan Behan d. (41).
Apr. 5th Douglas MacArthur, d. (84).
June 9th Maxwell William Aitken, Lord Beaverbrook d. (85).
Aug. 12th Ian Fleming d. (56).
Sept. 18th Clive Bell d. (83) and Sean O'Casey d. (84).
Sept. 20th Herbert Hoover d. (90).
Sept. 21st Otto Grotewohl d. (70).
Oct. 15th Cole Porter d. (71).
Dec. 9th Edith Sitwell d. (77).

L Nov: 11th, food shortage in India provokes riots in Kerala;
—, James Callaghan introduces economy Budget in Britain with increased petrol tax, and announces higher old-age pensions, increase of 6d. in standard rate of income tax and capital gains and corporation taxes in 1965;
12th, Rhodesian High Court rules Joshua Nkomo's detention illegal; he and other African leaders are released, 16th, and taken to restrictive areas;
16th, British government accepts Lawrence Commission's recommendations for increasing M.P.s' salaries to £3,250;
—, Johannesburg trial begins under suppression of Communism act, of 14 whites, including Abraham Fischer, who had led defence in Rivonia trial;
17th, Britain states its intention of banning exports of arms to South Africa;
20th, pressure on the pound increases;
23rd, Britain's bank rate increased to 7 per cent;
24th, Belgian paratroopers, the Congolese army and white mercenaries capture Stanleyville from rebels and rescue hostages (and, 26th, rescue hostages from Paulis);
25th, riots in Saigon;
26th, Britain borrows $3,000 mill. from foreign bankers to save pound;
30th, Winston Churchill's 90th birthday.

M Dec: 1st, Gustavo Ordaz succeeds López Mateos as President of Mexico;
2nd, Juan Perón is detained in Brazil on way to Argentina;
4th, Federal agents in Mississippi arrest a sheriff and others in connection with the murder of civil rights workers;
6th, Harold Wilson visits L. B. Johnson in Washington;
—, Antonio Segni, President of Italy, resigns for health reasons; succeeded by Giuseppe Saragat, 28th;
—, riots in Khartoum;
8th, heavy fighting in Vietnam;
11th, Machinery of Government bill published, to permit an increased number of ministers in British House of Commons;
12th, Kenya becomes a republic within the Commonwealth with Jomo Kenyatta first President;
14th, the governor of British Guiana dismisses Cheddi Jagan, following elections, in which his People's Progressive Party lost overall majority, and appoints Forbes Burnham, People's National Congress, premier;
16th, British government, T.U.C. and employers sign a statement on productivity, prices and incomes, the first stage in incomes policy;
17th, announcement of free prescriptions in British Health Service in *Feb.* 1965;
18th, L. B. Johnson offers Panama a new canal treaty and announces that U.S. would plan a new canal;
18th, U.N. extends mandate for force in Cyprus to *Mar.* 1965;
21st, Sidney Silverman introduces bill abolishing death penalty;
—, Control of Office and Industrial Development bill published;
23rd, cyclone in Ceylon and Southern India;
30th, Cunard Q4 contract is placed with John Brown, Clydebank.

N

1965 (Jan.–Apr.) U.S. Offensive in Vietnam—India-Pakistan War—Rhodesian Unilateral Declaration of Independence

A. Jan: 1st, amalgamation of the British Foreign and Commonwealth Services as the Diplomatic Service;
2nd, President Ayub Khan gains clear victory over Miss Jinnah in Pakistan's presidential elections;
7th, Indonesia withdraws from U.N. and 8th, fresh Indonesian landings in Malaya.
14th, Prime Ministers of Northern Ireland and of Eire meet for the first time in 43 years;
—, demonstrations in London by aircraft workers against the government's policy for industry;
20th, inauguration of Lyndon Baines Johnson as 36th President of U.S.;
21st, Patrick Gordon Walker, Foreign Secretary, is defeated in Leyton by-election; he resigns, 22nd, succeeded by Michael Stewart;
30th, State Funeral of Winston Churchill;
31st, R. A. Butler retires from politics.

B. Feb: 2nd, Royal Commission on Trade Unions and Employers' Associations is appointed;
7th, U.S. aircraft bomb North Vietnam, following attacks on American areas in South Vietnam;
11th, British Medical Association advises family doctors to resign from health service (doctors vote in favour of government's proposals for new pay structure, *Aug.* 5th);
18th, Gambia becomes independent within the Commonwealth;
21st, Malcolm X, Black Muslim leader, is shot dead in Manhattan;
23rd, Roger Casement's remains are sent to the Irish Republic for reinterment;
24th, British government rejects Robbins Committee's recommendations for creating new universities;
25th, Regional Economic Planning Councils are set up in Britain.

C. Mar: 3rd, Seretse Khama becomes first premier of Bechuanaland;
7th, violence breaks out at Selma, Albama (9th, whites kill a white civil rights worker);
8th, landing of 3,500 U.S. marines in S. Vietnam;
11th, Britain's February trade figures show surplus for first time since *Aug.* 1963;
17th, Aubrey Jones is appointed first chairman of National Board for Prices and Incomes;
21st, Martin Luther King heads procession of 4,000 civil rights demonstrators from Selma to Montgomery, Alabama, to deliver petition on negro grievances;
25th, Ku Klux Klan shoot Viola Liuzzo, a white civil rights worker, in Selma;
—, Dudley Senanayake forms ministry in Ceylon following defeat of Mrs. Bandaranaike in elections;
—, West Germany extends time limit for Nazi trials from *May* 1965 to *Dec.* 1969;
28th, serious earthquake in Chile;
30th, bomb explodes in U.S. embassy, Saigon.

D. Apr: 4th, North Vietnamese Mig aircraft shoot down U.S. jets;
6th, British Budget introduces 30 per cent capital gains tax and disallows expenses incurred in business entertainment; James Callaghan, Chancellor of the Exchequer, also announces the cancellation of the TSR-2 aircraft;
7th, President Johnson proposes aid for vast development programme in South-East Asia, which Hanoi and Peking governments reject;
8th, British White Paper sets 3 to 3½ per cent as the norm for pay increases;
9th, clashes between Indian and Pakistani forces on Kutch-Sind border;
11th, tornadoes in mid-western U.S.;
17th, student demonstrations in Washington against U.S. bombing of North Vietnam;

1965 (Jan.–Apr.) U.S. Offensive in Vietnam—India–Pakistan War—Rhodesian Unilateral Declaration of Independence

A Jan: 1st, amalgamation of the British Foreign and Commonwealth Services as the Diplomatic Service;
2nd, President Ayub Khan gains clear victory over Miss Jinnah in Pakistan's presidential elections;
7th, Indonesia withdraws from U.N. and 8th, fresh Indonesian landings in Malaya;
14th, Prime Ministers of Northern Ireland and of Eire meet for the first time in 43 years;
—, demonstrations in London by aircraft workers against the government's policy for industry;
20th, inauguration of Lyndon Baines Johnson as 36th President of U.S.;
21st, Patrick Gordon Walker, Foreign Secretary, is defeated in Leyton by-election; he resigns, 22nd, succeeded by Michael Stewart;
30th, State Funeral of Winston Churchill;
31st, R. A. Butler retires from politics.

B Feb: 2nd, Royal Commission on Trade Unions and Employers' Associations is appointed;
7th, U. S. aircraft bomb North Vietnam, following attacks on American areas in South Vietnam;
11th, British Medical Association advises family doctors to resign from health service; (doctors vote in favour of government's proposals for new pay structure, *Nov.* 5th);
18th, Gambia becomes independent within the Commonwealth;
21st, Malcom X, Black Muslim leader, is shot dead in Manhattan;
23rd, Roger Casement's remains are sent to the Irish Republic for reinterment;
24th, British government rejects Robbins Committee's recommendations for creating new universities;
25th, Regional Economic Planning Councils are set up in Britain.

C Mar: 3rd, Seretse Khama becomes first premier of Bechuanaland;
7th, violence breaks out at Selma, Albama (9th, whites kill a white civil rights worker);
8th, landing of 3,500 U.S. marines in S. Vietnam;
11th, Britain's February trade figures show surplus for first time since *Aug.* 1963;
17th, Aubrey Jones is appointed first chairman of National Board for Prices and Incomes;
21st, Martin Luther King heads procession of 4,000 civil rights demonstrators from Selma to Montgomery, Alabama, to deliver petition on negro grievances;
25th, Ku Klux Klan shoot Viola Liuzzo, a white civil rights worker, in Selma;
—, Dudley Senanayake forms ministry in Ceylon following defeat of Mrs. Bandaranaike in elections;
—, West Germany extends time limit for Nazi trials from *May* 1965 to *Dec.* 1969;
28th, serious earthquake in Chile;
30th, bomb explodes in U.S. embassy, Saigon.

D Apr: 4th, North Vietnamese Mig aircraft shoot down U.S. jets;
6th, British Budget introduces 30 per cent capital gains tax and disallows expenses incurred in business entertainment; James Callaghan, Chancellor of the Exchequer, also announces the cancellation of the TSR-2 aircraft;
7th, President Johnson proposes aid for vast development programme in South-East Asia, which Hanoi and Peking governments reject;
8th, British White Paper sets 3 to 3½ per cent as the norm for pay increases;
9th, clashes between Indian and Pakistani forces on Kutch-Sind border;
11th, tornadoes in mid-western U.S.;
17th, student demonstrations in Washington against U.S. bombing of North Vietnam;

O **Politics, Economics, Law and Education**

British White Papers on *The Parliamentary Commissioner for Administration* (the 'Ombudsman', *Oct.* 12th), *A Policy for the Arts*, and *The Land Commission* (*Sept.* 22nd), which proposes 40 per cent levy on development values.

The 750th anniversary of Magna Carta and the 700th anniversary of Parliament are celebrated.

The Greater London Council (chairman, Harold Shearman) and 32 London Borough Councils come into being (*Apr.* 1st).

The Milner Holland Report on London Housing (*Mar.* 11th).

Hindi becomes official language of India (*Jan.* 26th).

Teach-Ins are held in American and British universities on Civil Rights, Vietnam and Southern Rhodesia.

George Brown introduces *The National Plan*, which aims at 25 per cent increase in Britain's output by 1970 (*Sept.* 16th).

The Queen's Awards to Industry are instituted.

The award of the M.B.E. to the Beatles in the Queen's Birthday Honours provokes controversy.

Britain agrees to adopt the metric system over ten years.

Law Commission under Mr. Justice Scarman is appointed.

Judge Elizabeth Lane is appointed first woman High Court Judge in England.

British White Paper recommends family courts (*Aug.* 24th).

Universities of Kent and Warwick are established.

University College, Cambridge, with men and women graduates, is founded.

Ministry of Education circular asks local authorities to submit plans for comprehensive schools.

P **Science, Technology, Discovery, etc.**

Soviet cosmonaut Alexei Leonov leaves spacecraft Voskhod II and floats in space for 20 minutes (*Mar.* 18th).

U.S. space-ship Gemini III is pilot-manœuvred during orbit by Virgil Grissom and John Young (*Mar.* 23rd).

Edward White walks for 20 minutes in space from U.S. Gemini IV (*June* 3rd), and Gemini V makes 120 orbits (*Aug.* 21st–29th).

Gemini VII, launched *Dec.* 4th, meets Gemini VI in orbit and returns, 18th, after record flight.

U.S. satellite Mariner IV transmits close-up photographs of Mars (*July* 15th).

First French satellite is launched (*Nov.* 26th).

Early Bird, U.S. commercial communications satellite, is first used by TV, *May* 2nd.

Soviet Antonov AN-22 makes flight with 720 passengers.

British Petroleum Company strikes oil in North Sea (*Sept.* 21st), but rig collapses, *Dec.* 27th.

Dungeness Atomic Power Station opened.

Q **Scholarship**

Yale University Press claims the 'Vinland Map' proves America was discovered by Leif Ericsson in eleventh century.

Identification of a coffin found in Stepney as containing the remains of Anne Mowbray, Duchess of York (d. 1481).

George Painter, *Marcel Proust*, Vol. II.

Arthur Schlesinger Jr., *Thousand Days.*

D Apr: 21st, 114-nation Disarmament Commission resumes talks in New York after five-year interval;
23rd, large-scale U.S. raid over North Vietnam;
27th, Britain's 15 per cent import surcharge is reduced to 10 per cent;
29th, Australia decides to send troops to Southern Vietnam.

E May: 7th, Ian Smith's Rhodesian Front has sweeping victory in Rhodesian elections;
10th, Frank Bosard and Percy Allen are sentenced in London for espionage;
11th, cyclone in East Pakistan;
12th, West Germany establishes diplomatic relations with Israel; Arab states break off relations with Bonn;
13th, Conservative gains in British borough elections;
18th (–28th), Queen Elizabeth II visits West Germany;
—, first reference on wage increase is made to Prices and Incomes Board (printing industry);
13th, Franz Jonas is elected President of Austria.

F Jun: 2nd, following a tie in Commons division on Opposition amendment to defer Corporation Tax, the Speaker gives casting vote for the government;
2nd, European hostages are reported killed by Congolese rebels;
3rd, British bank rate is cut to 6 per cent (raised to 7 per cent, *Nov.* 1964);
8th, U.S. troops are authorised to engage in offensive operations in Vietnam;
17th, at Commonwealth Prime Ministers' conference, London, a Commonwealth Secretariat is established;
19th, Ben Bella, President of Algeria, is deposed; Hovari Boumedienne heads revolutionary council;
24th, South Vietnam breaks off relations with France;
30th, India-Pakistan cease-fire signed.

G Jul: 6th, French representatives withdraw from Common Market meetings in Brussels;
8th, Harold Davies arrives in Hanoi in attempt to open peace talks;
15th, King Constantine of Greece dismisses premier Papandreou (after weeks of unrest M. Stephanopoulos becomes premier, *Sept.* 17th);
28th, Edward Heath is elected Leader of British Conservative Party, following resignation of Alec Douglas-Home, 22nd, under a new voting procedure;
30th, Medical Care for the Aged bill signed by President Johnson.

H Aug: 2nd, British White Paper on Commonwealth immigration imposes annual limit of 8,500 on work permits;
5th, Devlin Committee recommends British dockers be employed on regular weekly basis;
7th, breakdown of constitutional talks on Aden and the South Arabian federation;
9th, by mutual agreement Singapore leaves Malaysia;
11th, race riots in Los Angeles;
19th, Frankfurt court, after 20-month trial of Auschwitz prison officials, sentences six men to life imprisonment;
24th, United Arab Republic and Yemen sign cease-fire agreement.

J Sep: 1st, Pakistani troops cross Kashmir cease-fire line;
—, terrorists in Aden shoot the Speaker of the Legislative Council; (26th, Britain suspends the Constitution);
2nd, death of Harry Hylton-Foster, Speaker of the House of Commons (*Oct.* 26th, Horace King elected Speaker);

R **Philosophy and Religion**

Pope Paul VI visits New York to address U.N. General Assembly (*Oct.* 4th) and, before the Vatican Council closes, promulgates document exonerating the Jews from the death of Christ.

The Orthodox Church annuls its excommunication of the Church of Rome in 1054.

The Vatican allows the resumption of worker-priests in France (suspended 1959).

Westminster Abbey's 900th anniversary celebrations (begin *Dec.* 28th).

S **Art, Sculpture, Fine Arts and Architecture**

Painting:

M. Beckmann Exhibition, Tate Gallery.

P. Bonnard Exhibition, Royal Academy.

Goya's portrait of the Duke of Wellington (stolen in 1961) is returned to the National Gallery.

Mondrian designs dominate young dress fashions.

Dame Laura Knight, *Autobiography*.

Rembrandt's portrait of *Titus* is sold at Christie's for 760,000 guineas.

Sculpture:

A. Giacommetti Exhibition, Tate Gallery.

Michelangelo's *Pietà* on show in New York.

Architecture:

General Post Office Tower, London, opened.

New Aviary, London Zoo, designed by Lord Snowdon.

T **Music**

A. Schönberg's *Moses and Aaron* is given first complete performance, London.

L. Bernstein, *Chichester Psalms.*

W. Walton, *The Twelve.*

Malcolm Williamson, *Julius Caesar Jones* (opera with libretto by Geoffrey Dunn).

U **Literature**

Wolf Biermann, *Die Drahtharfe.*

Günter Grass, *Dog Years.*

Norman Mailer, *An American Dream.*

Robert Lowell, *Union Dead.*

V **The Press**

Circulation figures of British daily newspapers:

Daily Express, 3,981,110; *Daily Mail*, 2,424,810; *Daily Mirror*, 4,956,997; *Daily Sketch*, 826,440; *Daily Telegraph*, 1,350,529; *Daily Worker*, 60,246; *Financial Times*, 152,149; *The Guardian*, 275,900; *The Sun*, 1,361,090; *The Times*, 257,922.

W **Drama and Entertainment**

E. Bagnold, *The Chinese Prime Minister.*

J. Osborne, *A Patriot for Me.*

Frank Marcus, *The Killing of Sister George.*

Films:

Rita Tushingham in *The Knack.*

Samantha Eggar in *The Collector.*

The Beatles in *Help!*

Dr. Who and the Daleks.

Television:

The State Funeral of Sir Winston Churchill.

J Sep: 3rd, civil war breaks out in Dominica;
6th, India invades West Pakistan and bombs Lahore;
8th, Southern Rhodesia appoints an 'accredited representative' in Lisbon;
10th, British agreement with the central banks arranges for massive support for the pound;
22nd, cease-fire in war between India and Pakistan, which is subsequently violated by both sides;
24th, Mauritius constitutional conference ends with promise of independence in 1966;
29th, U.S.S.R. admits supplying arms to Hanoi.

K Oct: 1st, attempted *coup d'état* in Indonesia;
4th (–11th), Ian Smith attends talks in London on Rhodesia;
13th, President Kasavubu dismisses Moïse Tshombe, Congolese premier;
17th, demonstrations in U.S. and in London against the war in Vietnam;
19th, Un-American Activities Committee begins public hearing on Ku Klux Klan;
24th, Archbishop of Canterbury states that if the British government had to use force in Rhodesia this would have the support of Christians;
25th (–30th), Harold Wilson visits Salisbury for talks with Ian Smith and African leaders;
Kidnapping in Paris of Mehdi Ben Barka, Left Moroccan leader.

L Nov: 8th, in Canadian elections Lester Pearson again fails to obtain overall majority;
9th, Act for abolition of the death penalty in force in Britain;
11th, Ian Smith makes Rhodesian Declaration of Independence; Britain declares the régime illegal and introduces exchange and trade restrictions;
19th, British Guiana constitutional congress ends with agreement for independence in *May* 1966;
25th, General Mobutu deposes President Kasavubu of the Congo.

M Dec: 5th, General de Gaulle fails to obtain clear majority in election for the French presidency;
8th, new Rent Act in force in Britain, gives greater security to tenants;
9th, Nikolai Podgorny replaces A. Mikoyan as President of U.S.S.R.;
16th, Plowden Committee recommends British government has shareholding in aircraft firms;
17th, Britain imposes oil embargo on Rhodesia; (19th, beginning of airlift of oil to Zambia);
18th, nine African states break off diplomatic relations with Britain for not using force against Rhodesia;
19th, General de Gaulle defeats François Mitterand in election for French presidency;
22nd, British government appoints a Public Schools Commission under John Newsom;
29th, President Ho Chi Minh of North Vietnam rejects unconditional peace talks offered by U.S.;
—, independence for Bechuanaland announced for *Sept.* 1966;
31st, the executives of the Common Market Commission, The European Coal and Steel Community and Euratom merge into one executive authority.

N

W **Drama and Entertainment** (*cont.*)

Television (*cont.*)

Ban on cigarette advertising on commercial TV in Britain (from *Aug.* 1st).

'Radio Caroline' and other offshore pirate commercial radio stations are established.

X **Sport**

Ten professional British footballers are found guilty of 'fixing' matches (*Jan.* 26th).

Cassius Clay knocks out Sonny Liston in first minute of fight at Lewiston, Maine (*May* 25th).

Mme Vaucher, the first woman to climb the Matterhorn, climbs the north wall of the Matterhorn on centenary of first ascent (*July* 14th).

Karen Muir, aged 12, sets up swimming record for women's 110 yards backstroke (*Aug.* 10th).

Jim Clark wins Indianapolis 550 race and six other Grand Prix titles to become world motor racing champion.

Robert Manry reaches Falmouth after 11-week Atlantic voyage in 13½-ft. craft.

Y **Statistics**

Use of land (area in acres per head of population):

	Total area	Potentially usable	Actually used
U.S.	12·0	6·0	3·5
Canada	125·0	22·0	4·0
Great Britain	1·1	0·6	0·55
England and Wales	0·8	0·6	0·55
Japan	1·1	0·2	0·17
India	2·5	0·8	0·75

British households owning electrical goods (1955 percentages in brackets):

TV set	88 (40)
Vacuum cleaner	82 (45)
Washing-machine	56 (20)
Refrigerator	29 (10)
Telephone	22 (21)

Z **Births and Deaths**

Jan. 4th Thomas Stearns Eliot d. (76).

Jan. 24th Winston Leonard Spencer Churchill d. (90).

Feb. 15th Nat 'King' Cole d. (45).

Mar. 6th Herbert, Lord Morrison d. (77).

Mar. 17th Farouk, ex-King of Egypt d. (45)

Apr. 21st Edward Appleton d. (72).

May 21st Geoffrey de Havilland d. (82).

June 20th Bernard Baruch d. (94).

Aug. 27th Charles Édouard Jeanneret (Le Corbusier) d. (77).

Sept. 4th Albert Schweitzer d. (90).

INDEX

The scheme of this Index is described in the Introduction, pp. ix, x. Attention is drawn here to the main series of Subject Entries, in some cases running to several pages.

Abdications
Administrations, in Britain
Administrations, in US
Aid
Aircraft
Air Forces
Archaeology
Armies
Arms
Assassinations
Atomic Energy
Ballet
Broadcasting
Canals
Civil Wars
Coal
Commissions, Royal
Committees
Concertos
Conferences and Congresses
Constitutions
Coups d'état
Currency
Dances
Demonstrations
Dictionaries
Education
Elections
Electricity
Exhibitions
Exploration
Franchise, The
Films
Galleries and Museums
Journals
League of Nations
Legislation
Machines
Manifestoes
Massacres
Monarchies
Motor Car, The
Navies
Newspapers
Opera
Oratorios
Overtures, Symphonic Poems, etc.
Pacts
Parliaments and other elected assemblies
Plebiscites
Political Parties
Population
Railways
Rebellions and Revolutions
Religious Denominations
Reports
Riots and Risings
Satellites, Artificial
Steel
Strikes
Symphonies
Treaties
United Nations
Universities
Wars

INDEX

A

Aaron's Rod (D. H. Lawrence), 1922 U
Abbas I, Khedive of Egypt (1848–54), 1848 L, 1854 G
Abbas Hilmi II, Khedive of Egypt (1892–1914), 1892 A, 1893 A; deposed, 1914 M
Abbott, Sir John Joseph Caldwell, Can. Conservative politician (1821–93), premier, 1891 F, 1892 M
Abd-el-Krim, Riff leader, 1926 E
Abdication Crisis in Britain, 1936 K, M
Abdications:
  Alexander Prince of Bulgaria, 1886 J
  Amadeo I of Spain, 1873 B
  Bolivar, Simon, in Colombia, 1830 D
  Charles I, Emperor of Austria, 1918 L
  Charles IV of Spain, 1808 E
  Charles Albert of Sardinia, 1849 C
  Charles Emmanuel of Sardinia, 1798 M
  Constantine I of Greece, 1922 J
  Edward VIII of Great Britain, 1936 M
  Farouk I of Egypt, 1952 G
  Ferdinand I of Austria, 1848 M
  Gustavus IV of Sweden, 1809 C
  Hussein of Hejaz, 1924 K
  Isabella II of Spain, 1870 F
  Korean Emperor, 1907 G
  Leopold III of Belgium, 1950 H
  Louis Philippe of France, 1848 B
  Manchu dynasty in China, 1912 B
  Michael of Rumania, 1947 M
  Milan of Serbia, 1889 C
  Otto I of Greece, 1862 K
  Pedro I of Brazil, 1831 D
  Pedro II of Brazil, 1889 L
  Pedro IV of Portugal, 1828 C
  Stanislas II of Poland, 1795 6
  Victor Emmanuel of Piedmont, 1821 C
  Victor Emmanuel III of Italy, 1946 E
  Wilhelmina Queen of Netherlands, 1948 J
  William I of Netherlands, 1840 K
  William II of Germany, 1918 L
Abdul Aziz, Sultan of Morocco (1894–1908), 1908 H
Abdul Aziz, Sultan of Turkey (1861–76), 1861 F, 1866 B, E; agrees to unify Moldavia and Wallachia, 1861 M; agrees to adopt Andrássy reforms, 1876 A; deposed and murdered, 1876 E, F
Abdul Hamid I, Sultan of Turkey (1774–89), 1774 A
Abdul Hamid II, Sultan of Turkey (1876–1909), 1876 H, 1886 D, 1896 G, 1908 G, 1909 D; deposes Ismail, Khedive of Egypt, 1879 F; is forced to undertake reforms, 1895 K
Abdul Mejid I, Sultan of Turkey (1839–61), 1839 G, 1861 F
Abdullah, King of Jordan (1881–1951), proclaimed king of Palestine, 1948 M; accession as king of Jordan, 1949 E; assassinated, 1951 G
Abdullah-al-Sallal, premier of the Yemen, 1962 K
Abdul Rahman Putra, Tunku, Malay. Alliance party (b. 1903), becomes premier, 1961 E
Abecedarium, or logical machine, 1874 P
Abel, Sir Frederick, B. inventor of cordite (1827–1902), 1889 P
Abel, Niels Henrik, Nor. mathematician (1802–79), 1828 P
Abelson, F. Am. scientist, 1940 P
Abercrombie, Lascelles, B. author (1881–1938), 1931 U
Abercrombie, Sir Patrick, B. engineer and town planning consultant (1879–1957), 1943 O
Abercromby, Sir Ralph, B. general (1734–1801), 1797 B, M, 1801 C
Aberdeen, Scotland, typhoid epidemic in, 1964 E
Aberdeen, earl of. *See* Gordon, George Hamilton
Aberites (C. M. Wieland), 1774 U
Åbo (now Turku), Finland, Treaty of, Sweden with Russia, 1812 D
Aboukir, Egypt, Nelson's victory at, 1798 H; Turks defeated at, 1799 G
About Zionism (A. Einstein), 1930 O
Abrahams, Kenneth, B., alleges abduction by S. African police, 1963 H
Absinthe, sale prohibited in France, 1915 O
Absolute Beginners (C. MacInnes), 1959 U
Abstract Art, treatise on, 1912 S
Abu Hamed, Sudan, taken by Egyptians, 1897 H
Abulfeda (J. Reiske), 1789 Q
Abyssinia. *See* Ethiopia
Academies:
  British, 1901 Q
  French, replaced by Institut National, 1795 O
  Royal, London. *See under* Galleries and Museums
  Swedish, 1784
  US National Academy of Design, 1826 S
Academies of Science:
  France, Académie des Sciences Morales et Politiques, 1833 O
  Hungary, 1825 O
  Russia, observatory of, 1954 P
Accelerated motion, laws of, 1784 P
Account of Corsica . . . (J. Boswell), 1768 U
Accra, Ghana, Confederation of Independent African States at, 1958 D; All-Africa People's Conference at, 1958 M

Accumulator, electric, 1859 P
Acetate rayon ('Celanese'), invented, 1865 P
Acetic acid, synthesis of, 1845 P
Acetylene, 1836 P, 1861 P; lamp, 1900 P
Acheson, Dean, Am., lawyer and politician (b. 1893), 1893 Z, 1950 C; becomes US secretary of state, 1949 A; presents disarmament proposals to UN, 1951 L; West Point speech, 1962 M
Acheson Plan, to strengthen UN power to resist aggression, 1950 K
Achin, N. W. Sumatra, Indonesia, Dutch war against Sultan of, 1873 D
Acker, M. van, Bel. Socialist, 1954 D
Acland, Sir Richard, B. politician (b. 1906), forms Commonwealth Party, 1943 C
Acoustics, science of, founded, 1786 P; principles of, discussed, 1772 P
Acoustics (E. F. F. Chladni), 1802 P
Acque e terre (S. Quasimodo), 1930 U
Acre, Israel, bombarded by British, 1840 L
Across the River and Into the Trees (E. Hemingway), 1950 U
Acta Karolinorum (ed. von Sickel), 1867 Q
Actinometer, invented, 1825 P
Action, Council of, 1920 H
Act of Creation, The (A. Koestler), 1964 R
Acton, Harold Maris, B. author (b. 1904), 1948 U, 1956 Q
Acton, John Dalberg, lord Acton, B. historian (1834–1902), 1834 Z, 1899 Q, 1902 Z
Acton, Sir John Francis Edward, B. administrator (1736–1811), prime minister of Naples, 1799 N
Adam, Henri Georges, F. sculptor (b. 1904), 1943 S, 1955 S, 1957 S
Adam, Robert, B. architect (1728–92), 1744 S, 1769 S., 1792 Z
Adam Bede (George Eliot), 1859 U
Adams, Sir Grantley Herbert, Barbadian Labour politician, premier of West Indies Federation, 1961 M
Adams, Henry, Am. author (1838–1918), 1904 Q, 1907 Q
Adams, John, Am. statesman, 2nd president of US, Federalist (1735–1826), 1787 O, 1792 N; vice-president, 1789 D; elected president, 1796 L; inaugurated, 1797 C; defeated by Jefferson, 1800 L
Adams, John Quincy, Am. statesman, 6th president of US, Democratic Republican (1767–1848), 1767 Z; signs treaty with Spain over Florida, 1819 B; elected president, 1824 L; inaugurated, 1825 C; defeated by Jackson, 1827 L
Adams, Samuel, Am. statesman (1722–1803), 1772 L, 1776 G, 1782 L
Adams, Sherman, Am. administrator (b. 1899), assistant to president Eisenhower, 1958 F
Adams, Thomas, B. soldier (?1730–64), 1763 G
Addington, Henry, viscount Sidmouth, B. Tory politician (1757–1844), becomes premier, 1801 C; resigns, 1804 D; as home secretary suppresses seditious publications, 1817 C
Addis Ababa, Abyssinia: Treaty of, withdraws Italian protectorate, 1896 K; French influence in, 1897 C; railway to Jibouti, 1902 B; Italians occupy, 1936 E; British take, 1941 D
Adding-Machine, The (E. Rice), 1923 W
Addresses to the German Nation (J. G. Fichte), 1808 O
Address to the King (E. Burke), 1777 O
Adelaide, S. Australia, 1836 O
Adelung, Johann Christoph, G. philologist (1732–1806), 1806 Q
Aden:
ceded by Turkey, 1833 E; government of, is separated from India, 1935 H; state of emergency in, 1958 E; agreement for entering S. Arabia Federation, 1962 H; constitutional talks break down, 1965 H; terrorists shoot the Speaker, 1965 J; British suspends constitution, 1965 J
Adenauer, Konrad, G. statesman, Christian Democrat (b. 1876), 1876 Z, 1963 A; becomes chancellor of W. Germany, 1949 J; advocates Franco-German economic union, 1950 C; meets foreign leaders, 1953 D, 1958 J, 1959 C, 1961 B; reforms ministry, 1953 K; election successes, 1957 J; prevents Erhard's candidature for presidency, 1959 G; appeals for peace treaty based on self-determination, 1961 F; retires, 1963 K
Adler, Felix, Am. formerly G. religious leader (1851–1933), 1876 R
Adler, Larry, B. harmonica player, 1952 T
Administrations, in Britain:
George Grenville (Whig), 1763 D
Marquess of Rockingham (Whig), 1765 G
Earl of Chatham (Whig), 1766 G
Duke of Grafton (Whig), 1768 K
Lord North (Tory), 1770 A
Marquess of Rockingham (Whig), 1782 C
Earl of Shelburne (Whig), 1782 G
Duke of Portland ('Fox-North Coalition'), 1783 D
William Pitt (Tory), 1783 M
Henry Addington (Tory), 1801 C
William Pitt (Tory), 1804 E
Lord Grenville (Whig) ('All the Talents'), 1806 B
Duke of Portland (Tory), 1807 C
Spencer Perceval (Tory), 1809 K
Earl of Liverpool (Tory), 1812 F
George Canning (Tory), 1827 D
Viscount Goderich (Tory), 1827 H
Duke of Wellington (Tory), 1828 A
Earl Grey (Whig), 1830 L
Viscount Melbourne (Whig), 1834 G
Sir Robert Peel (Tory), 1834 L
Viscount Melbourne (Whig), 1835 D
Sir Robert Peel (Tory), 1841 H
Lord John Russell (Whig), 1846 F
Earl of Derby (Tory), 1852 B
Earl of Aberdeen (Whig Coalition), 1852 M
Viscount Palmerston (Whig-Liberal), 1855 B
Earl of Derby (Conservative), 1858 B
Viscount Palmerston (Whig-Liberal), 1859 F
Earl Russell (Whig-Liberal), 1865 K
Earl of Derby (Conservative), 1866 F
Benjamin Disraeli (Conservative), 1868 B
William Ewart Gladstone (Liberal), 1868 M
Benjamin Disraeli, later Earl of Beaconsfield (Conservative), 1874 B
William Ewart Gladstone (Liberal), 1880 D
Marquess of Salisbury (Conservative), 1885 F
William Ewart Gladstone (Liberal), 1886 B
Marquess of Salisbury (Conservative), 1886 G
William Ewart Gladstone (Liberal), 1892 H
Earl of Rosebery (Liberal), 1894 C
Marquess of Salisbury (Conservative), 1895 F
Arthur James Balfour (Conservative), 1902 G
Sir Henry Campbell-Bannerman (Liberal), 1905 M
Herbert Henry Asquith (Liberal), 1908 D
Herbert Henry Asquith (Coalition), 1915 E
David Lloyd George (Coalition), 1916 M
Andrew Bonar Law (Conservative), 1922 K
Stanley Baldwin (Conservative), 1923 E
James Ramsay MacDonald (Labour), 1924 A
Stanley Baldwin (Conservative), 1924 L
James Ramsay MacDonald (Labour), 1929 F
James Ramsay MacDonald (National Government), 1931 H

Stanley Baldwin (National Government), 1935 F
Arthur Neville Chamberlain (National Government), 1937 E
Winston Leonard Spencer Churchill (Coalition), 1940 E
Winston Leonard Spencer Churchill (Conservative 'Caretaker'), 1945 E
Clement Richard Attlee (Labour), 1945 G
Winston Leonard Spencer Churchill (Conservative), 1951 K
Sir Robert Anthony Eden (Conservative), 1955 D
Maurice Harold Macmillan (Conservative), 1957 A
Sir Alec Douglas-Home (Conservative), 1963 K
Harold Wilson (Labour), 1964 K
Administrations, in US:
George Washington (Federalist), 1789 D
John Adams (Federalist), 1797 C
Thomas Jefferson (Democratic Republican), 1801 C
James Madison (Democratic Republican), 1809 C
James Monroe (Democratic Republican), 1817 C
John Quincy Adams (Democratic Republican), 1825 C
Andrew Jackson (Democrat), 1829 C
Martin Van Buren (Democrat), 1837 C
William Henry Harrison (Whig), 1841 C
John Tyler (Whig), 1841 D
James Knox Polk (Democrat), 1845 C
Zachary Taylor (Whig), 1849 C
Millard Fillmore (Whig), 1850 G
Franklin Pierce (Democrat), 1853 C
James Buchanan (Democrat), 1857 C
Abraham Lincoln (Republican), 1861 C
Andrew Johnson (Republican), 1865 D
Ulysses Simpson Grant (Republican), 1869 C
Rutherford Richard Hayes (Republican), 1877 C
James Abram Garfield (Republican), 1881 C
Chester Alan Arthur (Republican), 1881 G
Grover Cleveland (Democrat), 1885 C
Benjamin Harrison (Republican), 1889 C
Grover Cleveland (Democrat), 1893 C
William McKinley (Republican), 1897 C
Theodore Roosevelt (Republican), 1901 J
William Howard Taft (Republican), 1909 C
Woodrow Wilson (Democrat), 1913 C
Warren Gamaliel Harding (Republican), 1921 C
Calvin Coolidge (Republican), 1923 H
Herbert C. Hoover (Republican), 1929 C
Franklin Delano Roosevelt (Democrat), 1933 C
Harry S. Truman (Democrat), 1945 D
Dwight D. Eisenhower (Republican), 1953 A
John F. Kennedy (Democrat), 1961 A
Lyndon B. Johnson (Democrat), 1963 L
Administrative Reform Association, 1855 O
Admirable Crichton, The (J. M. Barrie), 1902 U
Adoption, in Britain, legalised, 1926 D
Adolphe (B. Constant), 1807 U
Adonaïs (P. B. Shelley), 1821 U
Adoula, Mr., Congolese premier, 1964 G
Adowa, N. Ethiopia, Italian defeat at, 1896 C
Adrenalin, manufacture of, 1901 P
Adrian, Edgar Douglas, lord Adrian, B. physiologist (1889–), 1929 P
Adrianople (now Edirne), Turkey: Treaty of, between Russia and Turkey, 1829 J; Russians capture, 1878 A; Bulgarians take, 1913 C; Turks capture, 1913 G; Greeks occupy, 1920 G
Adriatic Islands, Italy cedes to Yugoslavia, 1947 B
Advancement of Science, British Association for the, 1831 P; American Association for the, 1848 P
Adventures of Augie March, The (S. Bellow), 1954 U
Adventures of Ideas (A. N. Whitehead), 1933 R
Adventures of Sherlock Holmes, The (A. C. Doyle), 1891 U
Adventures of Tom Sawyer, The (M. Twain), 1875 U
Adventures of a Black Girl in Her Search for God, The (G. B. Shaw), 1932 U
Advertisement for Myself (N. Mailer), 1959 U
Advertising, British tax on, repealed, 1853 O; of cigarettes on TV banned in Britain, 1965 W
Advice to a Young Man (W. Cobbett), 1829 U
'AE'. *See* Russell, George William
Aehrenthal, Count Alois, Aus. foreign minister, 1908 A, J
Aerated waters, 1807 P
Aeronautical map, 1911 P
Aeronautics, 1783 P, 1785 P, 1900 P. *See also* Aircraft, Aviation
Aeroplanes. *See* Aircraft
Aerostat, 1843 P
Aesthetic movement, 1882 S
Aesthetics (F. Vischer), 1846 R
Aesthetic and History (B. Berenson), 1950 S
Aesthetic Studies (G. Brandes), 1868 U
Affluent Society, The (J. K. Galbraith), 1958 O
Afghanistan:
Persia recognises independence, 1857 C
Ameer of, British subsidy to, 1879 E
murdered, 1919 B
Russian conquest in, 1884 A
frontier, Anglo-Russian compromise over, 1885 J
Africa, exploration of, 1799 P, 1850 P. *See also* Central Africa; East Africa; South-west Africa; South Africa
Africa Association, founded, 1788 F
Africa Company, British, 1820 E, 1893 G
African Assistance Plan, 1960 J
African Survey, An (Lord Hailey), 1957 O
Afrikander Bond, founded, 1879 O
Afro-Asian Organisation for Economic Co-operation, 1959 D
After the Fall (A. Miller), 1964 W
Aga Khan, 1906 N
Aga Mohammed, of Persia (d. 1797), 1794 N, 1796 N
Agadir, Morocco: Incident, 1911 G; earthquake, 1960 B
Agassiz, Jean Louis Rodolphe, Swi. naturalist and geologist (1734–1807), 1837 P, 1840 P
Age of Reason, The (T. Paine), 1794 O
Age of Reason, The (J.-P. Sartre), 1945 U
Agnosticism (T. H. Huxley), 1889 R
Agnostic's Apology (L. Stephen), 1893 R
Agrarian reforms, in Russia, 1906 L
Agricultural adjustment Tariff, US, 1933 O
Agricultural Institute, International, 1905 O
Agricultural Labourers' Union, National British, 1872 O
Agricultural Marketing Scheme, British, 1933 O
Agriculture, British Board of, 1793 P, 1889 G
Agriculture, in Britain, reforms of holdings, 1875 O
loans for, 1910 O
Agustino (A. Moravia), 1944 U
Ahmed Pasha, Egyp. premier, 1945 A, B
Ahmed Shah, of Persia (1909–24), 1909 G; deposed, 1924 B
Ahnfrau, Die (F. Grillparzer), 1817 U
Ah Wilderness (E. O'Neill), 1933 W
Aid, British:
to China, 1898 A, C, 1912 D, J
to Austria, 1932 G, K
to Indonesia, suspended, 1963 K
See also Subsidies
British Commonwealth, plan for Africa, 1960 J
plan for S.E. Asia, 1950 A

Aid—*contd.*
French, to Hungary, 1931 H
to Russia, 1888 K, 1891 G
W. German, to India, 1959 A
Indian, to Burma, 1957 C
Russian, for Bulgaria, 1956 B
for China, 1959 B
for Hungary, 1959 H
for India, 1956 L
for Iraq, 1959 C
for Syria, 1959 M
for United Arab Republic, 1958 K
technical assistance for China, 1956 A
US, to Britain, 1915 J, 1931 H, 1945 M, 1946 G
to Europe, 1929 K
to France, 1931 H
to Ghana, 1961 M
to India, 1952 A
foreign aid, under Truman Doctrine, 1947 C, 1949 A
Marshall Aid, for European Recovery, 1947 F, G, 1948 D
to Britain ends, 1950 M
aid under Foreign Assistance Bill, 1949 D, 1950 C, 1952 F, 1955 D, 1961 E
to Nationalist China ends, 1949 H
to Cuba ends, 1960 E, H
to Israel ends, 1956 K; resumed, 1957 D
to non-Communist countries for developing atomic energy, 1955 F
is offered to S.E. Asia, 1965 L
See also Lend-Lease; Loans; Marshall Plan
military, to Iraq ends, 1959 E
to NATO countries, 1949 K
to W. Germany, 1955 F
Aid, Legal, 1950 O
Aigle a deux têtes, L' (J. Cocteau), 1946 W
Aiglon, L' (Rostand), 1900 U
Aiguillon, Emmanuel Armand de Wignerod du Plessis de Richelieu, duc d', F. statesman (1720–1782), 1770 M
Aintree, Liverpool, Eng., race course, 1839 X
Air and Fire (K. W. Scheele), 1775 P
Air, composition of, 1914 P
Air, liquefaction of, 1898 P
Airborne troops, British, 1944 J
Aircraft:
Antonov AN-22, 1965 P
Blériot's, 1909 P
Concord supersonic airliner, 1962 L
flying bedstead, 1954 P
Langley's, 1896 P
petrol engine, 1903 P
pilotless, 1950 P, 1953 P
TSR-2, cancelled, 1965 D
vertical take-off, 1954 P
Wright brothers', 1903 P
Aircraft carriers, limited by London Conference, 1930 D
Aircraft detection, by Radar, 1935 P
Aircraft industry, British, Plowden Report on, 1965 M
Aircraft workers, demonstration by, 1965 A
Air defence, US, 1925 O
Air Defence Council, North American, 1958 E
Air Forces:
British. *See* Royal Air Force
German, Zeppelin raids, on England, 1915 A, F, 1917 G, J
on France, 1916 A
Churchill's warning on, 1934 L
bomber raids on Britain, 1940 G
in Battle of Britain, 1940 H, J
begin 'the Blitz' of Britain, 1940 H
bomb London, 1941 C, E, 1943 A, 1944 B
destruction of Coventry, 1941 D
attack British convoy to Greece, 1941 A
'Baedeker' raids on Britain, 1942 D
continuous bombing of Malta, 1942 D
attack British convoys to Russia, 1942 J, M
Japanese, bomb Pearl Harbor, 1941 M
sink *Prince of Wales* and *Repulse*, 1941 M
Royal, formed, 1918 D
increases in, 1934 G, 1936 C
begins bombing of Germany, 1940 G
bombs Berlin, 1943 B
bombs European railway system, 1943 C
bombs Ruhr, 1943 D, E
bombs Rome, 1943 G
bombs Cologne, 1942 E
thousand-bomber raid on Bremen, 1942 F
bombs Hamburg, 1942 G
bombs Lübeck, 1942 C
bombing of German cities, protests in Parliament at, 1944 A
bombs occupied Europe, 1944 D
production of aircraft for, 1939 Y, 1940 Y, 1941 Y, 1942 Y, 1943 Y, 1944 Y
Russian, aircraft reported to be in Czechoslovakia, 1936 J
United Nations, bombs North Korean plants, 1952 C
US (formerly US Army Air Force), daily raids on occupied France, 1942 J; daylight raids on Berlin, 1944 C, 1944 D; bombing of occupied Europe, 1944 D; becomes independent of Army, 1947 O; incidents involving aircraft of, 1950 D, 1960 E; bombing of North Vietnam, 1965 B, D
Air Mail, 1934 P
Air pollution, Beaver Committee on, 1953 O
Airports: London, 1955 S; New York, Kennedy, 1961 S
Air Raid Precautions (ARP) in Britain, legislation, 1937 L; reorganised as Civil Defence, 1941 O
Air Raids, in Britain, casualties, statistics of, 1940 L; physics of, 1941 P
Air Services, first regular (by airship), 1912 P; regular Trans-Pacific, 1935 P; regular Trans-Atlantic, 1939 P; regular London–Moscow, 1957 M
Airships: rigid, 1912 P; lighter than air, 1920 P; *R. 101* disaster, 1930 P; US *Shenandoah*, 1925 O; Count Zeppelin's, 1898 P, 1900 P; *Graf Zeppelin*, 1928 P, 1929 P
Aisne, River, France, battles of, 1914 J, 1917 D, 1917 N
Aitken, William Maxwell, Lord Beaverbrook, B. newspaper proprietor and politician (1879–1965), 1879 Z, 1915 V, 1924 O, 1941 J, 1951 S, 1956 Q, 1964 Z
Aix-la-Chapelle (now Aachen, W. Germany), Conference at, 1818 J
Akerman, John Yonge, B. antiquarian (1806–73), 1840 Q
Akkerman Convention, between Russia and Turkey, 1826 N
Alabama, State, US: becomes a US state, 1819 M; as a Confederate State, 1861 B; University, desegregation crisis in, 1956 O
Alabama, The, depredations by, 1862 G, 1872 J
Alain-Fournier, Henri Alban (originally Fournier), F. author (1886–1914), 1913 U
Alarcón, Pedro Antoine de, Sp. author (1833–91), 1859 U, 1874 U
À la recherche du temps perdu (M. Proust), 1913 U

Alaska, US state: trade monopoly in, 1799 O; purchased by US from Russia, 1867 C; law and administration of, 1884 E; frontier settled, 1903 K; elects delegates to Congress, 1906 E; becomes a US state, 1958 G
Alaska highway, 1942 P
Alastor (P. B. Shelley), 1816 U
Albania: autonomy for, accepted by peace conference, 1912 M; powers agree on establishing principality of, 1913 G; rebellion in, 1915 A; independence of, 1917 F; allied advance in, 1918 E; independence recognised, 1921 L; proclaimed a republic, 1924 M; frontier settlement, 1926 G; proclaimed a kingdom, 1928 J; Italy invades, 1939 D; republic proclaimed, 1946 A
Albee, Edward, Am. dramatist (b. 1928), 1962 W
Albert, archduke of Austria, 1866 F
Albert I, king of Belgians (1909–34), 1909 M
given dictatorial powers, 1926 R
Albert, Lake, Uganda/Congo, Anglo-Belgian pact on, 1910 E
Alberta, province, Canada, formed, 1905 J
Albert Canal, Belgium, Germans turn line of, 1940 E
Albert Edward Nyanza, Lake, Central Africa, 1887 P
Albert, Eugène Francis Charles D', B. composer (1864–1932), 1903 T
Albert Francis Charles Augustus Emmanuel, of Saxe-Coburg Gotha, Prince Consort of Great Britain (1819–61), 1819 Z, 1840 B, 1861 Z; memorial to, 1862 S
Albertville, Congo, Congolese rebels take, 1964 F
Albright, Jacob, Am. religious leader (1759–1808), founds Evangelical Association, 1807 R
Albuera, Spain, Soult defeated at, 1811 E
Alcock, Sir John William, B. aviator (1892–1919), 1919 P
Alcohol, synthesis of, 1826 P
Alcott, Louisa May, Am. authoress (1832–88), 1868 U
Aldermaston March, 1956 O
Alemán, Miguel, president of Mexico, 1946 G
Alembert, Jean Le Rond D' (1717–83), F. mathematician, 1783 Z
Aleutian Isles, N. Pacific, settled by Russians, 1785 P
Alexander of Battenberg (1879–86): elected prince of Bulgaria, 1879 D, 1883 J; appointed governor of E. Rumelia, 1886 D; abdicates, 1886 J
Alexander I of Greece (1917–20), 1917 F
Alexander I, Tsar of Russia (1778–1825), 1778 Z, 1825 M; annexes Georgia, 1801 J; meets Napoleon at Tilsit, 1807 G; designs on Finland, 1808 F; Napoleon alienates, 1811 A; issues Polish constitution, 1815 L; supports Greek rebels, 1821 C
Alexander II, Tsar of Russia (1855–81), 1855 C, 1858 O; studies emancipation of serfs, 1857 L; visits Berlin, 1875 E; assassinated, 1881 C
Alexander III, Tsar of Russia (1881–94), 1881 C, 1894 L; fails to secure *entente* with Germany, 1890 H
Alexander (Karageorgevitch), prince of Serbia, deposed, 1858 M
Alexander I, king of Serbia (1889–1903), 1893 D, 1901 B, 1903 F
Alexander I, king of Yugoslavia (1921–34), establishes dictatorship, 1929 A; assassinated, 1934 K
Alexander Cuza, prince of Rumania, 1866 B
Alexander, Albert Victor, Lord Alexander of Hillsborough, B. Co-operative Party politician (1885–1965), becomes First Lord of Admiralty, 1940 E
Alexander, Harold Rupert Leofric George, B. field-marshal (b. 1891), replaces Auchinleck as C.-in-C. Middle East, 1942 H
Alexander, Samuel, B. philosopher (1859–1938), 1859 Z, 1889 R, 1920 R, 1938 Z
Alexandra Caroline Mary Charlotte Louise Julie, princess of Denmark, Queen-consort of Edward VII of Great Britain (1844–1925), 1844 Z, 1925 Z
Alexandria, Egypt: French defeated near, 1801 C; powers sign Convention of, with Mehemet Ali, 1840 L; Cleopatra's Needle removed from, 1878 S; anti-foreign riots in, 1882 F, G; Nationalist riots in, 1921 E
Alexandrina Victoria, princess. *See* Victoria, Queen
Alexandropol, Turkey, Treaty of, between Armenia and Turkey, 1920 M
Alexinatz, Serbia, battle, 1876 J
Alfieri, Vittorio, It. dramatist (1749–1803), 1775 W, 1776 W, 1770 O, 1803 Z
Alfonso XII of Spain (1875–85), 1870 F, 1874 L, M, 1875 A
Alfonso XIII of Spain (1886–1931), flees, 1931 D
Alfred (A. von Haller), 1773 U
Alfred Ernest Albert, duke of Edinburgh (1844–1900); elected to Greek throne, 1863 B; marries Princess Marie of Russia, 1874 A
Algebra, studies in, 1770 P
Algiers, Algeria: Spanish expedition to, 1775 G; French take, 1830 G; rebels in, 1846 A
'Algiers Toast', by Cardinal Lavigerie, 1890 L
Algeciras, Conference on Morocco, 1906 A, D
Algeria: French conquest begins, 1830 G; French provisional government at, 1944 H; terrorism in, 1953 M, 1955 K, 1958 M; Nehru's plan for, 1956 E; demonstrations in, 1958 E; provisional government proclaimed, 1958 J; de Gaulle's broadcast on, 1959 J; UN declines to intervene, 1959 M; riots in, 1960 A; de Gaulle offers surrender terms to rebels, 1960 F; referendum on, 1961 A; cease-fire in, 1962 C; F.L.N. provisional government for, 1962 C; independence of, 1962 G; admitted to Arab League, 1962 H
Alice's Adventures in Wonderland (L. Carroll), 1865 U
Ali of Janina, Turkish pasha, assassinated, 1822 B
Ali Khan, premier of Pakistan, 1951 K
Alison, Archibald, B. author (1757–1839), 1790 S
Aliwal, India, battle, 1846 A
Alizarin, synthetic dye, 1869 P
Alkmaar, N. Holland, British capitulate at, 1799 K
All-Africa Federal Executive Committee, 1957 H
All-Africa People's Conference, Accra, 1958 M
All-Blacks, N. Zeal., Rugby tour, 1924 X
Allen, Percy, B. spy, 1965 E
Allen, Percy Stafford, B. classical scholar (1869–1933), 1906 Q
Allenby, Edmund, Lord Allenby, B. soldier (1861–1936), 1861 Z, 1917 F, M, 1919 C, 1936 Z
Alle Pressements alle Morte (Leobardi), 1816 U
Alliances. *See* Treaties of Alliance
Allied occupation of Germany, 1945 E; ends 1955 E; military government superseded by Allied High Commission, 1949 J
All-India Moslem League, 1906 N
Allotments, British, 1887 O
Allowances, family, 1945 O
All Passion Spent (V. Sackville-West), 1931 U
All Quiet on the Western Front (E. Remarque), 1929 U
All Sorts and Conditions of Men (W. Besant), 1882 W
All the Conspirators (C. Isherwood), 1928 U
All the King's Men (R. Penn Warren), 1946 U
Alma, USSR, battle, 1854 J
Almanack de Gotha, 1763 Q
Almanack, nautical, 1767 P

Alma-Tadema, Sir Lawrence, B. artist (1836–1912), 1900 S, 1903 S
Almayer's Folly (J. Conrad), 1895 U
Almeria, Spain, German fleet bombards, 1937 E
Almquist, Carl Jonas Love, Swe. author (1793–1846), 1832 U
Alphabet, Roman, adopted by Turkey, 1928 L
Alps, the, Europe, mountain range:
Brenner Pass through, 1772 P
Simplon Pass, carriage road through, 1800 P
Napoleon's campaigns in, 1799 H, J, 1800 E
railway through, 1853 P
Alsace-Lorraine, France: ceded to Germany, 1871 E; declared part of the Reich, 1879 H; Reichstag grants measure of autonomy to, 1911 E; returned to France, 1919 B
Altmark incident, 1940 B
Alton Locke (C. Kingsley), 1849 U
Alvensleben, Constantin von, Count, G. Diplomat, 1863 B
Alvintzi, Joseph, Aus. general (1735–1810), 1796 L
defeated at Rivoli, 1797 A
Aluminium, 1827 P; produced electrically, 1887 P; statistics of production, 1914 Y, 1939 Y, 1959 Y
Alvarez, Am. atomic physicist, 1959 P
Aly Maher Pasha, Egypt. politician, appointed premier, 1952 A; resigns, 1952 C
Amadeus I, king of Spain, formerly duke of Aosta (1845–73): elected king, 1870 L; abdicates, 1873 B
Amanullah, Emir of Afghanistan, flees, 1959 E
Amarah, on R. Tigris, British take, 1915 F
Amateur Athletic Club, 1866 X
Ambia Alagi, Abyssinia, Italians defeated at, 1895 M
Ambassadors, The (H. James), 1903 U
Amberg, Bavaria, W. Germany, 1796 H
Amelia Island, Florida, US, taken by Unionists, 1862 C
America, discovery by Leif Ericsson proved, 1965 Q
America, North-West coast, exploration of, 1790 P
America, Spanish, natural features of, studied, 1807 P
American Association for the Advancement of Science, 1848 P
American Bible Society, 1816 R
America's Cup races, 1964 X
American Colonies, under British rule:
alliance with France, 1778 B
British plans to conciliate, 1775 B, O, 1778 B, D
rejected, 1778 F
British prohibitory act against trade with, 1776 B, C
coercive legislation against, 1774 C, H
Continental Congress, first, 1774 E, J
second, 1775 E
Indians in, reserve for, 1763 K
rising of, 1763 E
trade with, 1763 K
resolution against import of British goods, 1774 M
suppression of British authority in, 1776 C
taxation by Britain, 1764 E, 1765 C, 1766 C, 1767 E, 1769 E, 1770 D
disputed, 1765 K, 1767 E, J, 1768 G, 1772 F
tracts on, 1774 O, 1775 O
vice-admiralty court on, 1764 E
American Declaration of Independence, 1776 G
American Dream, An (N. Mailer), 1965 U
American Federation of Labor, 1886 O
American Independence, the Glory and Interest of Gt. Britain (J. Cartwright), 1774 O
American Individualism (H. Hoover), 1922 O
American Language, The (H. L. Mencken), 1919 Q
American Political Scene, The (D. W. Brogan), 1943 O
American Tragedy, An (T. Dreiser), 1926 U
American Wheelmen, Society of, 1880 X
Amery, Leopold Stennett, B. Conservative politician and author (1873–1955), 1947 O
Amici, Giovanni Battista, It. astronomer and microscopist (1786–1863), 1823 P, 1846 P
Amicis, Edmondo de, It. author (1846–1908), 1884 U
Amiel, Henri Frédéric, Swi. author (1821–81), 1883 U
Amiens, France: Peace Treaty of, 1802 C, W; Germans capture, 1914 H, 1940 E
Amini, Ali, Persian premier, 1961 E
Amiot, Jean Joseph Marie, F. Jesuit missionary and orientalist (1718–93), 1789 Q
Amir Abdullah, of Transjordan, 1923 E
Amis, Kingsley, B. author (b. 1922), 1954 U
Ammonia, soda made from, 1838 P; synthesis of, 1908 P
Amnesties:
in Austria, for Nazis, 1937 A
in Bulgaria, for political prisoners, 1926 A
in France, for political offenders, 1859 D
in Germany, for Kapp conspirators, 1925 H
in Hungary, for rebels, 1856 E
in India, for political prisoners, 1931 C
in Ireland, for prisoners after rebellion, 1917 F
in the Lebanon, 1958 M
in the Philippines, for rebels, 1901 G
rejected, 1948 G
in Poland, for rebels, 1856 E
Amory, Derick Heathcote, Viscount Amory, B. Condervatice politician (b. 1899), appointed Chancellor of Exchequer, 1958 A; retires, 1960 G
Amour (P. Verlaine), 1888 U
Ampère, André Marie, F. physicist (1775–1836), 1775 Z, 1820 P, 1826 P, 1836 Z
Amphitryon 38 (J. Giraudoux), 1929 W
Amritsar, India, Treaty, 1809 D
Amsterdam, Holland: Pichegru welcomed in, 1795A; World Council of Churches founded at, 1948 R; Eigen Haard flats, 1921 S; Rijksmuseum, 1877 S
Amulree, Lord. *See* Mackenzie, William
Amundsen, Roald, Nor. explorer (1872–1928), 1872 Z, 1911 P, 1926 P, 1928 Z
Amur, River, USSR, 1852 N
Amyl, is isolated, 1849 P
Anabase (St-John Perse), 1924 U
Anaemia, pernicious, treatment for, 1926 P
Anaesthetics:
chloroform, 1847 P
cocaine, 1884 P
ether, 1842 P
Analysis, electrochemical, 1922 P
Analysis of Matter (B. Russell), 1927 R
Analysis of the Human Mind (James Mill), 1829 Q
Anarchists:
in Belgium, 1901 N
in France, 1893 C, M
in Italy, 1894 F, G, 1898 J, 1900 G
in Spain, 1933 A
in US, 1901 J
Anatomie et physiologie du système nerveux (Gall and Spurzheim), 1810 P
Anatomie générale (M. Bichat), 1801 P
Anatomist, The (J. Bridie), 1931 W
Anatomy of Britain, The (A. Sampson), 1962 O
Anatomy of Courage (Lord Moran), 1945 O
Anatomy of the Gravid Uterus (W. Hunter), 1774 P
Ancien Régime et la Révolution, L' (de Tocqueville), 1856 Q
Ancient Law (H. Maine), 1861 Q
Ancient Monuments Society, 1924 Q

Ancona, Italy: Austrians occupy, 1799 L, 1832 A; Allies take, 1944 G
Andaman Islands, Indian Ocean, Japanese successes in, 1942 C
Andernach, W. Germany, 1797 K
Andersen, Hans Christian, D. author (1805–75), 1805 Z, 1835 U, 1875 Z
Anderson, Adam, B. historian (1692–1765), 1764 Q
Anderson, Elizabeth Garrett, B. Physician (1836–1917), 1836 Z, 1866 O, 1917 Z
Anderson, James, B. economist (1739–1808), 1777 O
Anderson, Sherwood, Am. author (1876–1941), 1919 U
Andover, Maine, US, TV transmitter at, 1962 P
And Quiet Flows the Don (Sholokhov), 1934 U
Andrade, Edward Neville da Costa, B. scientist (b. 1887), 1923 P
Andrássy, Julius, count, Hung. statesman (1823–90), 1876 A, 1878 A, F
Note of religious freedom in Bosnia, etc., 1875 M
André, John, B. soldier (1751–80), 1780 J
André del Sarto (A. de Musset), 1833 U
Andrew, Prince, of Gt. Britain, 1960 B
Andreyev, Leonid N., R. dramatist (1871–1919), 1916 W
Aneurin, J. Am. scientist, 1937 P
Androcles and the Lion (G. B. Shaw), 1916 U
Angel in the House (C. Patmore), 1854 U
Angell, Sir Norman, B. economist (b. 1872), 1931 O, 1933 O
Angerstein, John Julius, B. philanthropist and art collector (1735–1823), 1824 S
Anglo-Iranian Oil Company (formerly Anglo-Persian), 1909 A, 1914 E, 1932 L; new agreement with Iran, 1949 G; Iran's dispute with, 1951 G, 1952 G, K
Anglo-Saxon Attitudes (A. Wilson), 1956 U
Anglo-Saxon England (F. M. Stenton), 1944 Q
Angola (or Portuguese West Africa), 1883 D: boundary with German South-west Africa, 1886 M, 1926 G; German designs on, 1898 H; UN calls on Portugal to cease repression in, 1961 F
Angora. *See* Ankara
'Angry Young Men', 1957 O
Animal Farm (G. Orwell), 1945 U
Animal husbandry, 1772 P
Ankara (formerly Angora), Turkey: Turkish National Pact of, 1920 A; Turkish National Assembly at, 1920 E; Treaty of, with France, 1920 K; Greek attack on, repulsed, 1921 H; becomes capital, 1923 K; name is changed from Angora, 1930 C; British Institute of Archaeology in, 1948 Q; riots in, 1960 D
Anna Christie (E. O'Neill), 1923 W
Anna Karenina (L. Tolstoy), 1873 U
Annals of the Parish (Galt), 1821 U
Annam, Viet-Nam: French trade with, 1787 N; French treaty with, 1862 F; French protectorate in, 1874 C, 1883 H, 1884 F, 1885 F, 1887 N
Annan Committee on teaching of Russian, 1962 O
Annapolis, Maryland, US, convention at, 1786 E
Annigoni, Pietro, It. artist (b. 1910), 1910 Z, 1955 S
Annobon Island, Gulf of Guinea, ceded by Portugal to Spain, 1778 N
Annonce faite à Marie, L' (P. Claudel), 1912 W
Annuals, illustrated, the first, 1823 U
Annunzio, Gabriele D', It. author (1863–1938), 1863 Z, 1884 U, 1902 W, 1916 U, 1919 J, 1938 Z
Anouilh, Jean, F. dramatist (b. 1910), 1910 Z, 1938 W, 1947 W, 1950 W, 1951 W, 1956 W, 1961 W
Anquetil Duperron, Abraham Hyacinthe, F. orientalist (1731–1805), 1771 Q, 1778 Q
Ansbach, principality, Bavaria, W. Germany, 1769 K, 1779 E; Prussia acquires, 1792 A; ceded to France, 1805 M
Anschütz, Richard, G. scientist, 1907 P
'Anstey, F.' *See* Guthrey, Thomas Anstey
Antarctica: exploration of, 1841 P. *See also* Polar Exploration; Australian claims to, 1933 E; demilitarisation of, 1958 E
Antheil, George, Am. musician (b. 1900), 1927 T
Anthems, National:
France, Marseillaise, 1792 T
Russia, substitutes 'Hymn of Soviet Union' for 'Internationale', 1944 O
Anthrax, vaccine for, 1881 P, 1883 P
Anthropogénie (E. Haeckel), 1874 P
Anthropologists, Criminal, congress of, 1887 O
Anthropology:
Nutcracker Man, 1959 P
Peking Man, 1920 Q
Piltdown Man, proved a hoax, 1953 P
Steinheim skull, 1933 P
Antibiotics:
aureomycin, 1948 P
chloromycetin, 1948 P
methicillin, 1960 P
penicillin, 1927 P, 1940 P
Anti-clericalism:
in Belgium, 1880 F
in France, 1792 L, 1877 E, 1879 F, 1880 C, 1881 R, 1902 F, 1904 L
in Mexico, 1926 G
in Prussia, 1873 E
Anti-Comintern Pact, between Germany and Japan, 1936 L; Italy joins, 1937 L; collapse of, 1939 H
Anti-Corn Law League, Manchester, 1838 J; National, 1839 C
Antietam, Maryland, US, battle, 1862 J
Anti-Gas School, in Britain, 1936 C
Anti-Goeze (Lessing), 1778 R
Antigone (J. Anouilh), 1942 W
Antigone (V. Alfieri), 1776 W
Anti-Jesuit law, in Germany, 1904 R
Anti-militarism, in France, 1901 J
Anti-neutron, discovered, 1956 P
Antiquary, The (W. Scott), 1816 U
Antiquities of Athens, The (J. Stuart and N. Revett), 1794 Q
Antiquity of Man (C. Lyell), 1863 P
Anti-Semitism:
in Britain, 1936 K
in Germany, 1878 O, 1933 D, 1935 J, 1938 L, 1959 M, 1960 O
in Hungary, 1932 K
in Italy, 1938 L
in Poland, 1939 K, 1946 G
in Rumania, 1937 M
in Russia, 1881 R
Antiseptic surgery, 1865 P
Anti-Slavery, tract on, 1786 O; movement in US, 1831 O; International Congress, Brussels, 1890 O
Anti-State Church Association, 1844 O
Anti-Trust Laws in US, 1903 B, O; railway mergers adjudged a violation of, 1904 C; other actions under, 1911 A, E, 1912 M
Antivari, Montenegro, S. Yugoslavia, 1878 C, G
Anti-xi-zeno, discovered, 1963 P
Antoine, André, F. actor-manager (1858–1920), 1887 W
Antonescu, Ion, becomes dictator in Rumania, 1950 J; sentenced to death, 1946 E
Antonioni, Michaelangelo, It. film director (b. 1912), 1960 W, 1961 W

Anton Reiser (K. Moritz), 1790 U
Antwerp, Belgium: French capture, 1832 M; surrenders to Germans, 1914 K; Belgian troops enter, 1918 L; Olympic Games, at 1920 X; Allies recapture, 1944 J; port reopened, 1944 L
Anzac, Gallipoli, British withdraw from, 1915 M
Anzac troops (Australia and New Zealand Army Corps), 1916 E
Anzio, Italy, Allied landings at, 1944 A; Germans assault allied bridgehead, 1944 B
Apartheid, in S. Africa: Nationalists win election on platform of, 1948 E; programme inaugurated, 1949 F; provokes riots in Johannesburg, 1950 A; bill to make Parliament a high court, to implement, 1952 D; UN considers Cruz Report on, 1955 L; UN calls on S. Africa to reconsider, 1957 A; UN General Assembly condemns, 1959 L, 1961 D; treason trial, 1959 A, 1956 M; Bantu self-government bill in force, 1960 F; world opinion against is intensified by Sharpeville incidents, 1960 C; D. Hammarskjöld visits S. Africa to discuss, 1961 A; UN special committee on, calls for sanctions, 1963 J; Bantu Laws Amendment bill, 1964 E
Ape and Essence (A. Huxley), 1948 U
Apollinaire, Guillaume (pseud. of Wilhelm Apollinaris de Kostrowitsky), F. formerly Pol. author (1880–1918), 1909 U, 1913 S, 1917 S, W
Apology for the Bible, An (R. Watson), 1796 R
Appeal from the New to the Old Whigs, An (E. Burke), 1791 O
Appeal to the Public on the Subject of the National Debt (R. Price), 1771 O
Appeals, from Canadian Courts to Privy Council, discontinued, 1946 O
Appearance and Reality (F. H. Bradley), 1893 R
Appeasement, policy of, origins, 1937 L
Appel à l'impartiale postérité (Mme Roland), 1793 U
Apple Cart, The (G. B. Shaw), 1929 W
Appleton, Sir Edward, B. scientist (1893–1965), 1924 P, 1946 P, 1956 P, 1965 Z
Appleton, William Archibald, B. trade union leader (1859–1940), 1923 O
Appleton, Wisconsin, US, hydro-electric plant, 1882 P
Appomattox, Virginia, US, Lee's surrender at, 1865 D
Après le Cubisme (Ozenfant and Le Corbusier), 1918 S
Après-midi d'un faune, L' (Mallarmé), 1876 U
Aqueduct, iron, at Port Cyllstan, 1805 P
Aqueduct tunnel, 1893 P
Arab Federation, formed by Iraq and Jordan, 1958 B; Hussein assumes power in, 1958 G; dissolves, 1958 H
Arabian Desert, exploration of, 1948 P
Arabian Nights, The (Burton), 1885 U
Arabic studies, 1789 Q
Arabi Pasha, Egypt. nationalist leader, 1881 J; leads anti-foreign riots, 1882 F; is banished, 1882 J
Arab League, founded, 1945 K; Security Pact, 1952 H; Algeria admitted to, 1962 H; Sudan joins, 1956 A; discusses Syrian allegations of UAR interference, 1962 H
Arabs:
- rising in German E. Africa, 1888 J
- rising of slave-holders in Congo, 1892 L
- in Palestine, attack Jews, 1929 H
  - Passfield White Paper on, 1930 K
  - Higher Committee, 1936 D, 1937 K
  - boycott Woodhead Commission, 1938 A
  - denounce plans for independent Palestine, 1939 E
  - warn US over Palestine, 1945 K

Aragon, Louis, F. poet (b. 1897), 1934 U, 1941 U
Aranda, Don Pedro Pablo Abarca y Bolea, count of, S. statesman (1719–98), 1766 F, 1775 G
Aranjuez, Madrid, Spain, Treaty of, 1801 A
Arapahoe Indians, massacre of, 1864 L
Arbitration of disputes, international, 1907 F; agreements for peaceful settlement, signed by Scandinavian states, 1926 A
Arblay, Frances D' (Fanny Burney), B. author (1752–1840), 1778 U, 1782 U, 1796 U
Arborfield, Berkshire, Eng., 1955 H
Arch, Joseph, B. trade unionist and Liberal politician (1826–1919), 1872 O
Archaeologia litteraria (J. A. Ernesti), 1768 Q
Archaeology:
- Abu Simbel treasures in Aswan High Dam region rescued, 1960 Q
- Ankara, British Institute at, 1948 Q
- Athens, British School at, 1886 Q
- Babylonian excavations, 1918 Q
- Cappadocia, Winckler's expedition to, 1906 Q
- Carchemish, excavations, 1911 Q
- Cnossos, excavations, 1910 Q
- Crete, finds in, 1900 Q
- Etzina, S. Mongolia, 1915 Q
- Halicarnassus, mausoleum of, 1857 Q
- Jericho, excavations, 1952 Q, 1857 Q
- Jerusalem, excavations, 1866 Q
- London, Temple of Mithras excavated, 1954 Q
  - remains of Anne Mowbray identified, 1965 Q
- Mildenhall hoard, 1942 Q
- Neanderthal skull found, 1856 Q
- Nineveh, discoveries at, 1845 Q
- Nippur, excavations, 1888 Q
- Nonsuch Palace, Surrey, excavated, 1959 Q
- Rome, Institute opened, 1829 Q
- Serapeum, discovered, 1850 Q
- Stonehenge, Wiltshire, excavations, 1950 Q, 1964 Q
- Troy, excavations, 1870 Q
- Tutankhamūn's tomb discovered, 1922 Q
- Ur, discoveries at, 1927 Q

Archives, British National, 1838 O, 1958 O
Archangel, Russia, British forces in, 1919 F, J
Archers, The, radio serial, 1951 W
Arc lamps, for street-lighting, 1841 P
Arcole, Veneto, Italy, 1796 L
Arcon, Idaho, US, atomic power station at, 1951 P
Arctic exploration, 1819 P, 1845 P, 1850 P; for air route, 1930 P. *See also* Polar exploration
Ardahan, N.E. Asiatic Turkey, transferred to Russia, 1878 C, G
Arden, John, B. dramatist (b. 1930), 1963 W
Ardennes, Europe, mountain range, 'Battle of the Bulge' in, 1944 M
Ardinghello (J. Heinse), 1787 U
Ardizzone, Edward, B. artist (b. 1900), 1940 S
Ardrey, Robert, Am. dramatist, 1940 W
Arezzo, Italy, Germans withdraw from, 1944 G
Argelander, Friedrich Wilhelm August, G. astronomer (1799–1875), 1862 P
Argentina: United Provinces of La Plata, independence of, 1816 G; Buenos Aires reunited with, 1860 F; frozen meat from, 1877 P
Argon, discovered, 1894 P
Argument about Co-education, The (Pestalozzi), 1922 O
Ariadne auf Naxos (H. Gerstenberg), 1767 U
Ariadne auf Naxos (R. Strauss), 1912 T
Arias, Dame Margot Fonteyn de (Margot Fonteyn), B. prima ballerina (b. 1919), 1919 Z
Arica-Tacna, S. America, dispute between Chile and Peru over, 1883 K; settled, 1929 F

Arizona, State, US: US obtains, 1848 E; Gadsden Purchase, 1854 D; as a US territory, 1863 B; conditions for statehood, 1911 H; becomes a US state, 1912 B; adopts women's suffrage, 1912 L
Arkansas, State, US: becomes a US state, 1836 F; disturbances in, 1874 E
Arkwright, Sir Richard, B. engineer (1732–92), 1769 P, 1792 Z
Armed Neutrality of the North, 1800 M, 1801 F
Armaments:
Russia proposes reduction in, 1898 H
failure to stop arms race, 1907 F
production in Britain, 1939 Y, 1940 Y, 1941 Y, 1942 Y, 1943 Y, 1944 Y
standardisation of, British-US agreement on, 1940 L
traffic in, embargoes on:
Britain to Ireland, 1913 M
UN votes for embargo to S. Africa, 1963 M
US to China, 1922 C
US to Mexico, 1912 C
traffic in, regulation of, 1889 F, 1925 E, 1949 M
traffic in, supplied by, Britain to India, 1962 L
to Tunisia, 1957 L
Russia to Cuba, 1962 J
to Egypt, 1955 H
US to Indonesia, 1959 B
See also Arms, Small
Armenia, Transcaucasia, Russia: parts of, ceded to Russia, 1827 B; massacres in, 1895 K, L, 1896 H; revolution in, 1896 H; independence declared, 1919 E
Armentières, France, Germans take, 1918 D
Armies:
comparative casualties in, World War I, 1918 Y
World War II, 1945 Y
comparative strengths of, 1875 Y, 1906 Y, 1912 Y, 1914 Y, 1950 Y
Australian, volunteers in S. Africa, 1899 M
conscription for, 1909 N
ANZACS, 1916 E
Austrian, Landwehr created, 1808 F
unified regimental system, 1903 J, 1904 C
mobilisation, 1914 G
Belgium, universal military service for, 1913 C
British, C.-in-C. of, subordinated to Secretary of State for War, 1870 F
Cardwell's reforms, 1871 H
purchase of commissions in, abolished, 1871 O
flogging in, abolished, 1881 O
expeditionary force lands in France, 1914 H
increased spending on, 1936 C
changes in higher command, 1937 M
expeditionary force lands in France, 1939 J
in Germany, reduced, 1957 B
W. Germany to contribute to cost of BAOR, 1962 C
Bulgarian, intervenes in politics, 1886 H
mobilisation of, 1912 K
Canadian, volunteers in S. Africa, 1899 M
lands in Europe, 1914 K
losses in Dieppe Raid, 1942 H
in offensive towards Rhine, 1945 B
Egyptian, intervenes in politics, 1879 B, 1881 B, 1954 C
European, Churchill proposes formation of, 1950 H
French, conscription for, 1793 H, 1798 J, 1872 G, 1913 H
equipped with Chassepot rifles, 1866 P
Lebel rifles, 1886 P
chaplains in, abolished, 1880 R
mobilises, 1914 H
mutinies, in, 1917 E
German, evacuates France, 1872 J
Bismarck advocates enlargement of, 1887 A
size of, increased, 1893 G, 1911 B, 1913 F
length of service in, reduced, 1893 G
Von Moltke as C.-in-C. of, 1906 A
mobilised for Czech crisis, 1938 H
See also Prussian Army
East German, National People's Army formed, 1956 A
West German, command of, given to NATO, 1958 A
Russian protests at proposals to equip with Polaris missiles, 1960 G
Greek, mobilised, 1915 J
intervenes in politics, 1923 M
Hungarian, rearmament of, 1938 H
Indian, sent to Malta, 1878 C
Italian, fights in Spanish Civil War, 1937 B, C
reduction in, 1947 B
Japanese, National Defence Force formed, 1953 J
NATO, plans for W. German troops to serve in, 1951 J
New Zealand, service in France, 1916 E
Palestinian, founded by Gen. Kassem, 1960 C
Prussian, reformed by Scharnhorst, 1807 N
Napoleon I limits size of, 1808 J
Landwehr and Landsturm formed, 1813 C
needle-guns for, 1858 O
Von Roon's reforms, 1859 M
See also German Army
Roumanian, brutality of, 1907 C
Russian, conscription for, 1874 A
mobilisation of, 1914 G
White Russian, collapse of, 1920 C
Serbian, mobilisation of, 1912 K
Spanish, intervention of, in politics, 1936 G
Turkish, intervention of, in politics, 1909 D
US, outcry against meat supplied to, 1898 O
troops land in France, 1917 F
first engagement with Germans, 1917 L
occupy Rhine, 1923 E
selective training and service for, 1940 J
Armies, Private:
Irish Republican Army (I.R.A.), 1933 G
National Guard, Eire, 1933 G
Nazi Storm Troopers, Germany, 1932 F, 1933 C
Armitage, Kenneth, B. sculptor (b. 1916), 1951 S, 1954 S
Armoured vehicles, 1916 P
Armour plating, of battleships, 1853 P
Arms and the Man (G. B. Shaw), 1894 W, 1898 W
Arms, Small:
Browning revolver, 1900 P
Chassepot rifle, 1866 P
Colt's armoury for, 1853 P
Gatling, machine-gun, 1862 P
Lebel rifle, 1886 P
Maxim, 1884 P
Minié rifle, 1849 P
needle-guns, 1858 O
steel gun, Krupp's, 1849 P
Thompson sub-machine gun, 1920 P
Armstrong, Louis, Am. jazz musician (b. 1900), 1900 Z
Armstrong, Thomas, B. novelist (b. 1899), 1947 U
Armstrong, Sir William George, B. engineer (1810–1900), 1845 P
Armstrong-Jones, Antony earl of Snowdon (b. 1930), 1960 E, 1965 S
Armstrong-Jones, Sir Robert, B. alienist (1857–1943), 1893 P

Arndt, Ernst Moritz, G. author (1769–1860), 1806 O, 1813 U
Arne, Thomas, B. musician (1711–78), 1778 Z
Arnell, Richard Anthony Sayer, B. musician (b. 1917), 1951 T
Arnhem, Holland, British airborne forces land, 1944 J; Allies enter, 1945 D
Arnim, Harry Karl Kurt Eduard, Count, G. diplomat (1824–81), 1874 K
Arnim, Sixt von, G. general, 1943 B, D
Arnold, Benedict, Am. soldier (1741–1804), 1775 M, 1776 K; treason of, 1780 L
Arnold, Malcolm, B. musician (b. 1921), 1953 T, 1956 T, 1957 T
Arnold, Mary Augusta. *See* Ward, Mrs. Humphrey
Arnold, Matthew, B. author (1822–88), 1822 Z, 1849 U, 1852 U, 1853 U, 1865 U, 1869 O, 1888 Z
Arnold, Thomas, B. educationalist and historian (1795–1842), 1795 Z, 1828 O, 1832 R, 1838 Q, 1842 Z
Arof, Abdul Salan, Iraqi premier, 1963 B
Around the World in Eighty Days (J. Verne), 1872 U
Arp, Jean, F. artist (1877–1966), 1916 S
Arras, France: German withdrawal from, 1917 B; battle, 1917 D, E; Germans take, 1940 E
Arrow incident, 1856 K
Art: treatises on, 1813 S, 1865 S; works of, export from Britain controlled, 1952 S; France undertakes to restore looted, 1815 L
Art Collections Fund, National, 1903 S
Art Criticism, 1775 S
Artemus Ward, His Book (C. F. Browne), 1862 U
Art et Scolastique (J. Maritain), 1920 R
Art history, treatise on, 1855 S
Articles of Religion, subscription to, 1771 R
Artificial silk, 1887 P
Artificial rain, 1957 P
Arthur, Chester Alan, Am. politician, 21st president of US (1830–86), Republican, 1881 G
Arthur Gordon Pym (E. A. Poe), 1838 U
Artists, British War, 1916 S, 1940 S
'Art Nouveau', 1893 S; influences fabrics and designs, 1963 S
Art Now (H. Read), 1933 S
Artois, Comte d'. *See* Charles X
Art of Writing, The (A. Quiller-Couch), 1916 U
Arts and crafts movement in US, 1907 S
Arts, in Britain, financial support for, 1958 S, 1965 O
Arts, US National Federation of, 1910 S
Arts Council, 1946 T
Asaf, George, B. librettist, 1915 W
Ascension Island, 1815 K
Ascent of F6 (Auden and Isherwood), 1937 U
Ascot, Berks., Eng., horseracing at, 1807 W; grandstand for, 1964 S
Ashanti, W. Africa: British protectorate in, 1896 H; war, 1824 B; kingdom is annexed to Gold Coast, 1901 J
Ashbourne, Lord. *See* Gibson, E.
Ashburton, Lord. *See* Baring, Alexander
Ashendene Press, 1894 S
Ashton, Frederick William Mallandine, B. choreographer (b. 1906), 1937 T, 1946 T, 1956 T, 1958 T, 1961 T
Ash Wednesday (T. S. Eliot), 1930 U
Asia Legal Consultative Committee, 1957 D
Asiatic Society, Royal, 1822 Q
As I Lay Dying (W. Falkner), 1930 U
Aspern, Austria, battle, 1809 E
Aspdin, Joseph, B. inventor of cement (1779–1855), 1824 P
Aspirin, 1899 P
Aspromonte, Calabria, S. Italy, Garibaldi captured at, 1862 H
Asquith, Anthony, B. film director (b. 1902), 1938 W, 1949 W
Asquith, Herbert Henry, earl of Oxford and Asquith, B. statesman (1852–1928), 1852 Z, 1880 E, 1911 G, 1925 A, 1928 Z; as home secretary, 1892 H; as chancellor of Exchequer, 1905 M; becomes premier, 1908 D; denounces House of Lords, 1909 M; appeals to electorate, 1910 A, M; opens Imperial Conference, 1911 E; introduces minimum wage bill, 1912 L; combines war secretaryship with premiership, 1914 C; forms coalition, 1915 E; resigns premiership of coalition, 1916 M
Asquith (R. Jenkins), 1964 Q
Asquith, Margot, Countess of Oxford and Asquith (*née* Tennant), B. Liberal politician, 1864 Z, 1945 Z
Assab Bay, Eritrea, 1882 M
Assassinations:
- Abbas I of Egypt, 1854 G
- Abdullah of Jordan, 1951 G
- Ahmen Pasha of Egypt, 1945 B
- Tsar Alexander III of Russia, 1881 C
- Alexander of Yugoslavia, 1934 K
- Ali Khan, 1951 K
- S. Bandaranaike, premier of Ceylon, 1959 J
- Count Bernadotte, 1948 J
- Duc de Berry, 1820 B
- Bogoliepoff, 1901 B
- A. Calinescu, of Roumania, 1931 J
- G. Calmette, 1914 C
- President Carranza, 1920 E
- Carlow I of Portugal, 1908 B
- Charles III of Parma, 1854 C
- Constantinople, Patriarch of, 1821 D
- Admiral Darlan, 1942 M
- President Diem of South Vietnam, 1963 L
- E. Dollfuss, 1934 G
- President Paul Doumer, 1932 E
- I. Duca, 1933 M
- Kurt Eisner of Bavaria, 1919 B
- Empress Elizabeth of Austria, 1898 J
- M. Erzberger, 1921 H
- King Feisal of Iraq, 1948 G
- Francis Ferdinand of Austria, 1914 F
- President Garfield of US, 1881 G
- Galilee high commissioner, 1937 J
- Gandhi, 1948 A
- George I of Greece, 1913 C
- H. Gurney, high commissioner in Malaya, 1951 K
- Gustavus III of Sweden, 1792 C
- Premier Hara of Japan, 1921 L
- Hazza-el-Majali, premier of Jordan, 1960 H
- Premier Ghali of Egypt, 1910 B
- Premier Hamaguchi of Japan, 1930 L
- Heydrich, by Czech patriots, 1942 E
- Humbert I of Italy, 1900 G
- Premier Inukai of Japan, 1932 E
- Prince Ito of Japan, 1909 K
- Jean Jaures, 1914 G
- Premier Kassim of Iraq, 1963 B
- President Kennedy of US, 1963 L
- J. B. Kléber, 1800 C
- Korea, Queen of, 1895 K
- Kotzebue, 1819 L
- Abraham Lincoln, 1865 D
- President McKinley, 1901 J
- Malcolm X, 1965 B
- Marat, 1793 G
- G. Matteotti, 1924 F

Earl of Mayo, 1872 B
Nasr-ed-Din, Shah of Persia, 1896 E
Nazim Pasha of Turkey, 1913 A
Nokrashy Pasha of Egypt, 1948 M
Premier Nuri-es-Said of Iraq, 1958 G
President Obrégon of Mexico, 1928 G
K. O'Higgins, 1927 G
President Paes of Portugal, 1918 M
Paul I, Tsar of Russia, 1801 C
Phoenix Park Murders, 1882 E
V. Plehve, 1904 G
Marshal Prim, 1870 M
Walter Rathenau, 1922 F
Rossi, Papal premier, 1848 L
President Sadi Carnot of France, 1894 F
Sipyengin, Russian minister of interior, 1902 D
Sir Lee Stack, 1924 L
A. Stambolisky, 1923 F
Stambulov, Bulgarian premier, 1895 G
P. Stolypin, Russian premier, 1911 J
Count Stürgkh, 1916 K
Count Tisza, 1918 K
V. Vorovski, 1923 E
Assassinations, attempted:
A. Briand, 1911 A
General de Gaulle, 1962 H
A. Hitler, 1944 G
Inönü, Turkish premier, 1964 B
Louis Philippe, 1835 G
B. Mussolini, 1926 D
Napoleon I, 1800 M, 1804 B
Napoleon III, 1858 A
K. Nkrumah, 1962 H
President Sukarno of Indonesia, 1957 M
H. Verwoerd, 1960 D
William I of Germany, 1878 E
Assaye, N.W. Hyderabad, India, battle, 1803 J
Assedio di Firenze, L', (Guerrazzi), 1834 U
Assembly techniquesi n factories, 1913 P
Associations, in France, regulation of, 1901 G
Assommoir, L' (É. Zola), 1877 U
Assyriology, 1864 Q
Astonishing History of Troy Town, The (A. Quiller-Couch), 1888 U
Aston, Francis William, B. physicist (1877–1945), 1919 P
Astor, Nancy Viscountess (1880–1964), B. Unionist politician, 1919 L
Astronautical Federation, International, 1951 O
Astronauts. *See under* Space flights
Astronomy, advances in, 1783 P, 1786 P, 1788 P, 1789 P, 1797 P, 1862 P, 1881 P, 1882 P, 1889 P, 1892 P, 1914 P, 1920 P, 1937 P; Jeans' stellar theory, 1926 P; new scale of space, 1953 P; composite photograph of night sky, 1954 P. *See also* Observatories
Astronomy, Radio, 1961 P
Astrophysics, treatise on, 1903 P; Eddington's discovery on luminosity of stars, 1924 P
Aswan Dam, Egypt, 1902 M; High Dam, projected, 1956 G; Russian loan for, 1958 K; work begins, 1960 A; rescue of archaeological treasures near, 1960 Q; opened, 1964 E
Asylums, Mental, in Britain, inspection, 1842 O; treatment in, 1893 P; detention of patients in, reformed, 1959 O
Atala (Chateaubriand), 1801 U
Atalanta in Calydon (A. C. Swinburne), 1865 U
Atbara, River, Sudan, Kitchener's victory at, 1898 D
Atheism, advocated, 1793 R
Athenia, sinking of, 1939 J
Athens Greece: antiquities of, 1794 Q; Elgin Marbles brought from, 1801 S; Turks enter, 1827 F; garrison revolts, 1862 K; British School of Archaeology at, 1886 Q; Allies occupy, 1916 K; Conferences of Balkan Powers in, 1930 K, 1937 B; E.A.M. demonstrations in, 1944 M; riots over Cyprus issue, 1954 M
Athletics: track events timed electrically, 1912 X; pole-jump record, 1942 X; mile record, 1954 X. *See also* Olympic Games
Atholl, John Murray, duke of (1720–74), B. owner of Isle of Man, 1765 J
Atlanta, Georgia, US: Confederate defeat at, 1864 G; Sherman occupies, 1864 J
Atlantic cable, 1865 P
Atlantic Charter, 1941 H, J
Atlantic City, Mexico, 1916 L
Atlantic Economic Community, 1960 M
Atlantic Ocean: first steamship crossing, 1818 P; regular steamship crossings, 1838 P; notable crossings, 1839 P, 1935 P; first flight across, 1919 P; notable flights across, 1928 P, 1941 P; crossing in small craft, 1965 X
Atlantis (C. J. R. Hautmann), 1912 U
Atlas computer, 1961 P
Atlas Elipticales With Winter Music (J. Cage), 1964 T
Atmolysis, gases separated by, 1863 P
Atmosphere, discovery of gases in, 1903 P; Heaviside layer in, 1902 P, 1924 P; Upper, radiation in, 1925 P; temperature of, 1923 P; A. Shepard's flight through, 1961 P
Atom, The: splitting of, 1942 P; work preliminary to, 1921 P
Atomic Bomb:
dropped on Japan, 1945 H, P
manufacture of plutonium for, 1944 P
British, first tests, 1952 B, P
thermonuclear, 1957 E
China, explodes first, 1964 K
Russia, first tests, 1949 P, 1950 C
Atomic Bomb Test Ban. *See* Nuclear Test Ban
Atomic Energy, 1945 P
Britain's agreement with Euratom on peaceful uses, of, 1959 B
with W. Germany, 1956 G
with US on co-operation and exchange of information, 1955 F, 1956 F, 1957 F
Geneva Conference on peaceful uses of, 1955 H
Netherlands agreement with Norway for joint research, 1951 P
Proposals for international control of, 1953 M
US aid to non-Communist states to develop, 1955 F
Atomic Energy Authority, British, 1954 O; International, 1957 O, G
Atomic Energy Commission, UN, 1946 M
meetings of, suspended, 1949 G
US, ordered to develop hydrogen bomb, 1950
separates plutonium, 1950 P
Atomic Energy for Defence, Canada's agreement with US, 1959 E; treatise on military consequences, 1948 O
Atomic Physics, 1934 P, 1939 P, 1940 P, 1941 P, 1948 P, 1959 P
Atomic Power Stations: electricity first produced from, 1951 P; in Britain, 1957 S, 1965 P; in US, 1955 P
Atomic-powered locomotive designed, 1954 P; passenger-cargo ship, 1959 P; submarine, 1952 P, 1959 P
Atomic Reactors: at Harwell, 1956 P; numbers in operation, 1962 P

Atomic Research:
anti-xi-zeno, fundamental particle, discovered, 1963 P
computers for, 1961 P
omega-minus, fundamental particles, discovered, 1964 P
Atomic Scientists, betrayal of secrets by, 1950 C, 1952 O, 1953 F
Atomic Theory of Chemistry, 1803 P; studies in, 1777 P
Atomic Transmutations, 1931 P
Atomic Weapons:
Britain's agreement with US for co-operation, 1958 G
for purchasing components, 1959 E
W. German physicists refuse to test, 1957 D
Swiss referendum against manufacture of, 1962 D
US Congress rejects Russian proposal for, 1951 H
See also Nuclear Test Ban
Atomic Weights: table of, 1803 P; theories about, 1815 P; settled by Karlsruhe Conference, 1860 P
Atoms:
size of, 1883 P
'Smasher' or cyclotron, 1931 P
structure of, 1913 P
transmutation of, 1919 P
Atonement, doctrine of, minister deposed for teaching against, 1831 R
Atrocities:
in Belgian Congo, 1903 E, 1905 L
in Brazil, 1912 O
by Germany, Bryce Report on, 1916 O
in Poland, at Auschwitz Prison, 1965 H
in US, murder of civil rights worker, 1965 C
At Sundown (J. G. Whittier), 1890 U
Atatürk, Kemal. *See* Kemal Atatürk
Attempt to Determine the Limits of the Frontier of the State (K. W. von Humbold), 1791 O
Attempts to Explain some of the Phenomena of Electricity (H. Cavendish), 1772 P
Attlee, Clement Richard, Earl Attlee, B. statesman and Labour Party leader (1883–), 1883 Z, 1936 F; visits Spain, 1937 M; becomes Lord Privy Seal in Churchill's Coalition, 1940 E; becomes Deputy Premier, 1942 B; at Potsdam Conference, 1945 G; forms Labour ministry, 1945 G; reconstructs ministry, 1950 B; visits Washington, 1950 M; retires from Labour Party leadership, 1955 M
Attu, Aleutian Islands, US force lands, 1943 E
Attwood, George, B. mathematician, 1784 P
Auber, Daniel Francois Esprit, F. musician (1782–1871), 1782 Z, 1830 T, 1941 T
Auckland, New Zealand, 1865 N
Auckland, Lord. *See* Eden, William
Auchinleck, Sir Claude, B. general (b. 1884), succeeds Wavell, 1941 G
replaced by Alexander, 1942 H
Auden, Wystan Hugh, B. poet (b. 1907), 1907 Z, 1930 U, 1932 U, 1935 U, 1936 U, 1937 U, 1951 T
Audubon, John James, Am. naturalist (1780–1851), 1830 P
Augier, Guillaume Victor, F. dramatist (1820–89), 1854 W
Auguste Comte and Positivism (J. S. Mill), 1865 R
Augustus III of Poland (1696–1763), elector of Saxony, 1763 K
Aureomycin, 1948 P
Auric, Georges, F. musician, 1920 T
Auriga, star in Milky Way, 1892 P
Auriol, Vincent, F. statesman (1884–1965), elected F. president, 1947 A
Aurora Leigh (R. Browning), 1857 U
Auschwitz (or Oswięcim), Poland, Prison Camp, trial of officials, 1965 H
Austen Jane, B. novelist (1775–1817), 1775 Z, 1811 U, 1813 U, 1814 U, 1816 U, 1818 U, 1817 Z
Austerlitz, Czechoslovakia, battle, 1805 M
Austin, Herbert, Lord Austin, B. motor manufacturer (1866–1941), founds motor company, 1905 P
'Austin Seven' motor car, 1922 P
Austin, John Langshaw, B. philosopher (b. 1911), 1962 R
Australia: representative government in, 1850 H; gold discovered, 1851 P; meat trade to London, 1879 P; federal confederation assembly, 1880 N; federal convention, 1897 A; federation, plans for, 1899 N; as a federal Commonwealth, 1900 J, 1901 A. *See also* Botany Bay
Australia, South, act for establishing colony, 1834 H
Australia, Western, 1870 H; votes to secede from Commonwealth, 1933 D
Austria:
union with Germany proclaimed, 1918 L
becomes part of Reich, 1938 C
Russians enter, 1945 C
Democratic Republic established, 1945 E
Allied occupation, 1945 F
protests at, 1953 K
frontiers of 1937 recognised, 1946 A
Austrian Netherlands: Barrier towns, 1782 D; independence declared, 1789 M. *See also* Belgium
Authority and the Individual (B. Russell), 1949 O
Autobahn, Cologne-Bonn, 1932 P. *See also* Motorways
Autobiography of Alice B. Toklas, The (G. Stein), 1933 U
Autobiography of a Super Tramp (W. H. Davies), 1908 U
Auto-chrome plates, 1907 P
Autocrat of the Breakfast-Table, The (O. W. Holmes), 1858 U
Automation:
aircraft, 1947 P, 1950 P
bottle-making machine, 1898 P
computers, 1942 P, 1958 Y, 1961 P
D.S.I.R. Report on, 1956 O
electronic brain, 1946 P
loom, 1895 P
railway couplings, 1906 P
railway signals, 1893 P
telephone switchboard, 1892 P
See also Machines
Automobile Association, 1905 O
Automobiles. *See* Motor Cars
Autumn Crocus (D. Smith), 1931 W
Ava, Burma, British resident at, 1826 B
Avenir des Peuples Catholiques, L' (Laveleye), 1875 R
Aventures du dernier Abencérage, Les (Chateaubriand), 1808 U
Adventures Prodigieuses de Tartarin de Tarascon (A. Daudet), 1872 U
'Average Man', concept of the, 1835 P
Aviation:
Civil Aerial Transport Committee, British, 1917 O
Flights:
Alcock and Brown, 1919 P
Croydon to Cape Town, 1926 P
glider towed from Montreal, 1943 P
Graf Zeppelin's transatlantic, 1928 P
helicopter, 1919 P
high altitude, 1955 P

Howard Hughes', 1938 P
Amy Johnson, 1930 P
Lindberg's, 1927 P
London–Canada non-stop, 1944 O
Mrs. Mollison, 1936 P
Odom's world, 1947 P
Paris–Hanoi, 1932 P
Polar, 1926 P, 1929 P
Ross Smith, to Australia, 1919 P
sea-plane, 1912 P
Transatlantic, first east-west, 1928 P
by Ferry Command, 1941 P
automatic, 1947 P
US–Europe, regular commercial, 1939 P
Wiley Post, 1933 P
Gordon-Bennett Cup, 1911 X
Space Travel, congress on, 1951 O
Avignon, France: papal estates in, seized by France, 1768 N; restored to Papacy, 1773 M; annexed by France, 1791 J
Avis au peuple français (A. Chénier), 1790 O
Avogadro, Amadeo, Conte di Quaregna, It. chemist (1776–1856), 1811 P
Avon, Viscount. *See* Eden, Anthony
Avranches, France, US break-through in, 1944 H
Axel (E. Tegner), 1822 U
Ayacucho, Peru, battle, 1824 M
Ayer, Alfred Jules, B. philosopher (1910), 1936 R, 1940 R, 1956 R, 1957 R
Aymé, Marcel, F. dramatist (b. 1902), 1950 W, 1952 W
Ayrton, William Edward, B. electrical engineer (1847–1908), 1879 P
Azaña, Manuel, Sp. politician, as premier, 1931 M, 1936 B; elected president, 1936 E
Azeglio, Massimo Taparelli d', It. political philosopher and statesman (1798–1868), 1798 Z, 1846 O, 1868 Z
Azikiwe, Dr., president of Nigeria, 1963 K
Azerbaijan, Persia, risings in, 1945 L; reforms promised, 1946 O
Azoimide, obtained from organic source, 1890 P
Azores, Atlantic, Portugal grants Britain use of bases, 1943 K; bases restored to Portugal, 1946 F

B

Babbage, Charles, B. mathematician (1792–1871), 1823 P
Babbitt (S. Lewis), 1922 U
Babist Sect, in Persia, 1843 R
Babeuf, François Noel, F. political agitator (1760–97), 1796 E
Babylonian remains, 1888 Q
Baccarat, 1891 O
Bach, Carl Philipp Emanuel, G. musician (1714–88), 1769 T, 1775 T, 1788 Z
Bach, Johann Christian, G. musician (1735–82), 1764 T, 1782 Z
Bach, Johann Sebastian, G. musician (1685–1750), choral works, revival of interest in, 1829 T
festivals of music of, 1900 T, 1950 T
Schweitzer's study of, 1905 T
Back to Methusaleh (G. B. Shaw), 1923 W
Bacon, Francis, Ir. artist (b. 1910), 1957 S
Bacon, Francis, lord Verulam, suggested as author of Shakespeare's plays, 1848 Q
Bacon, Henry, Am. sculptor, 1917 S
Bacon, John, B. sculptor (1740–99), 1796 S
Bacon, J. M., B. balloonist, 1902 P
Bacteria, Koch's techniques for fixing, 1877 P
Badajoz, Spain:
Treaty, 1801 F
British capture, 1812 D
Baden-Baden, Baden-Württemberg, W. Germany:
as a Grand Duchy, 1805 M
enters N. German Confederation, 1870 A
Trinkhalle in, 1840 S
Badeni, Casimir, Count, Aus. politician, 1895 J, 1897 L
Baden-Powell, Robert, lord Baden-Powell, B. soldier and founder of scouting movement (1857–1941), 1857 Z, 1896 K, 1907 O, 1941 Z
Badoglio, Pietro, duke of Addis Ababa, It. soldier (1870–1956), forms government on Mussolini's fall, 1943 G
'Baedeker' raids on Britain, 1942 D
Baekeland, Leo Hendrik, G. inventor (1863–1944), 1907, P
Baer, Carl von, G. physiologist (1792–1874), 1792 Z, 1827 P, 1828 P, 1874 Z
Baeviad (W. Gifford), 1794 U
Bagehot, Walter, B. economist and author (1826–77), 1826 Z, 1867 O, 1869 O, 1877 Z, 1880 O
Baghdad, Iraq:
British capture, 1917 C
coups d'état in, 1958 G, 1963 B
Pact, between Iraq and Turkey, 1955 B
Britain joins, 1955 D
Iran joins, 1955 L
boycotts Britain, 1956 L, end of boycott, 1957 C
name changed to Central Treaty Organisation, 1959 H
Railway: Germany secures contract for, 1888 K, 1899 M, 1903 D; German discussions on, 1907 H, 1909 L; Russia ceases opposition to, 1910 L; Franco-German agreement on, 1914 B; Anglo-German agreement on, 1914 F; British army administers, 1919 A
Bagnold, Enid (Lady Jones), B. dramatist, 1954 W, 1965 W
Bahaan, Burma, Japanese take, 1942 D
Bahrein Islands, Persian Gulf:
Persia claims, 1927 L
declared an independent Arab state, 1957 L
Bahr el Ghazal, River, Sudan, 1897 H
Bailey, James Anthony, Am. showman (1847–1906), 1871 W, 1889 W
Bailly, Jean Sylvain, F. revolutionary leader (1736–1793), 1789 G
Bain, Alexander, B. philosopher (1818–1903), 1855 R, 1876 R, 1899 R
Baird, John Logie, B. inventor of television (1888–1946), 1888 Z, 1926 P, 1928 P, 1932 O, 1946 Z
Baji Rao, Peshwa of Poona, 1818 F
Bakelite, 1907 P
Baku, Azerbaijan, Russians take, 1783 K; oil wells in, 1873 P; Turks occupy, 1918 C
Bakunin, Michael, R. anarchist (1814–76), 1814 Z, 1869 O, 1872 O, 1876 N, Z
Balaclava, Crimea, Russia: battle, 1854 K; telegraph to London, 1855 P
Balakirev, Mily Alexeivich, R. musician (1886–1910), 1886 Z, 1910 Z
Balanchine, George Melitonovich, Am. choreographer (b. 1904), 1904 Z, 1946 T; founds American School of Ballet, 1933 T
Balchin, Nigel Marlin, B. author (1908–), 1947 U
Balcon, Sir Michael, B. film director (b. 1896), 1964 W

Baldwin, Stanley, earl Baldwin, B. Conservative leader (1867–1947), 1867 Z, 1947 Z; becomes premier, 1923 E; resigns, 1924 A; becomes premier, 1924 L; MacDonald delegates duties to, 1934 F; forms National Government, 1935 F; dissatisfaction with, 1936 C; role in Abdication Crisis, 1936 K, L; retires, 1937 E
Balearic Islands, pact to counter German designs in, 1907 E
Balfe, Michael William, Ir. musician (1808–70), 1843 T
Balfour, Arthur James, earl of Balfour, B. statesman, Unionist and philosopher (1848–1930), 1848 Z, 1903 J, L, 1904 K, 1916 M, 1919 K, 1930 Z; forms ministry, 1902 G; resigns, 1905 M; resigns Unionist leadership, 1911 L; as First Lord of Admiralty, 1915 E; in US, 1917 E; Declaration on Palestine, 1917 L; Balfour Note, 1922 H; as philosopher, 1879 R, 1895 R
Balkans: Russia's agreement with Italy on preserving *status quo* in, 1909 K; Count Berchtold's conversations on, 1912 H; War of Turkey against Bulgaria, Serbia, Montenegro and Greece, 1912 K, L, M, 1913 C, E; Montenegro renews, 1913 B; Pact, 1934 P; Britain forms company to trade in, 1940 D; Rumania refused accession to Pact, 1957 J
Balla, Giacomo, It. artist (1874–), 1910 S, 1916 S
Ballad and the Source, The (R. Lehmann), 1944 U
Ballad of Reading Gaol, The (O. Wilde), 1898 U
Ballads and Other Poems (H. W. Longfellow), 1842 U
Ballads and Sonnets (D. G. Rossetti), 1881 U
Ball-bearings, 'cup and cone', invented, 1869 P
Ballet:
American School of, 1933 T
Ballet mécanique, 1927 T
Royal, visits Russia, 1961 T
Russian, under Diaghilev, visits Paris, 1909 T
Age of Anxiety, 1950 T
Agon (Stravinsky), 1957 T
Antigone (Cranko), 1959 T
Après-midi d'un faune, L' (Robbins), 1959 T
Ballabile (Petit-Chabrier), 1950 T
Birthday Offering (Ashton-Arnold), 1956 T
Boutique Fantasque, La (Diaghilev), 1919 T
Broken Date (Magne), 1958 T
Burrow, The (Macmillan-Martin), 1958 T
Cage, The (Robbins-Stravinsky), 1952 T
Casse-Noisette (Tschaikovsky), 1891 T
Chant de Rossignol, Le (Stravinsky), 1920 T
Checkmate (Bliss), 1937 T
Daphnis and Chloë (Ravel), 1911 T
Deux Pigeons, Les (Ashton-Messenger), 1961 T
Don Quixote, 1950 T
Façade (Walton), 1923 T
Fancy Free (Robbins), 1946 T
Festin de l'Araigné, Le (Roussel), 1923 T
Game of Cards (Stravinsky), 1935 T
Harlequin in April, 1951 T
Homage to the Queen (M. Arnold), 1953 T
House Party, The (Poulenc), 1923 P
Improvisations (Copland-Carter), 1962 T
Interplay (J. Robbins), 1946 T
Night Shadow (Balanchine), 1946 T
Nobilissima Visiona (Hindemith), 1938 T
Noctambules (Searle), 1956 T
Ondine (Ashton-Henze), 1958 T
Parade (Diaghilev–Satie), 1917 S, T
Patineurs, Les (Ashton), 1937 T
Petruschka (Stravinsky), 1912 T
Pineapple Poll, 1951 T
Prince of the Pagodas (Britten), 1957 T
Pulcinello (Stravinsky), 1920 T
Reflection (Cranko-Gardner), 1952 T
Rite of Spring, The (Stravinsky), 1913 T
Rodeo (de Mille), 1940 T
Sea Change (Cranko-Sibelius), 1949 T
Sémiramis (Honegger), 1934 T
Sluts (Prokofiev), 1945 T
Soldier's Tale, The (Stravinsky-Diaghilev), 1917 T
Swan-Lake (Tschaikovsky), 1878 T
Sylphides, Les (Fokine-Chopin), 1909 T
Symphonis Variations (Ashton), 1946 T
Three-cornered Hat (de Falla), 1919 S, T
Witchboy (J. Carter), 1958 T
Ballilla, Italian Fascist youth organisation, 1926 D
Balloons: ascents by, 1783 P, 1785 P, 1863 P, 1902 P, 1934 P; photography from, Russian protests to US about, 1956 B
Ballou, Hosea, Am. Universalist minister (1771–1852), 1805 R
Ball-point pen, 1938 P
Balmaceda, José, Chilean president, 1891 J
Balmain, Pierre, F. couturier (b. 1914), 1914 Z
Balta Liman, treaty between Russia and Turkey, 1849 E
Baltic Convention, 1908 H
Baltic Sea, Britain bars French fleet from, 1772 G
Baltic States Russian occupation of, 1940 F
Baltimore, Maryland, US: Congress at, 1776 K; Roman Catholic Bishop, 1790 R; Swedenborgian Church in, 1792 R; steam engine from, 1829 P; Roman Catholic Council at, 1852 R; Democrat Convention at, 1912 G
Baluchistan, N. W. Pakistan, is united with India, 1887 K
Balzac, Honoré de, F. author (1799–1850), 1799 Z, 1829 U, 1831 U, 1832 U, 1834 U, 1841 U, 1845 U, 1846 U, 1850 Z
Balzan International Foundation, 1964 B
Bampton Lectures, Oxford, 1780 R
Bancroft, George, Am. historian (1800–91), 1834 Q
Bancroft, Sir Squire, B. actor-manager (1841–1926), 1841 Z, 1866 W, 1926 Z
Banda, Hastings, premier of Malawi (b. 1905), arrested as leader of African Congress Party in Nyasaland, 1959 B; becomes premier of Nyasaland, 1963 A; acquires powers of detention, 1964 K
Bandaranaike, Dudley, Ceyl. politician, 1953 K, 1956 D
Bandaranaike, Mrs. Sirimavo, Ceyl. politician, Freedom Party, becomes premier, 1960 F; is defeated, 1965 C
Bandaranaike, Solomon, Ceyl. politician (1899–1959), 1959 J
Bandinel, James, B. divine (1734–96), 1780 R
Bangkok, Thailand, 1782 N; Conference of heads of US Asiatic missions at, 1950 B; SEATO Conference at, 1955 B
Bangor, N. Wales, 1935 A
Bankrupt, The (Ostrovsky), 1847 W
Bankruptcy. *See* Crises, Financial
Banks, Sir Joseph, B. scientist (1743–1820), 1788 F, 1799 P
Banks and Banking:
in Australia, nationalisation of, 1947 L
in Austria, failure of Credit-Anstalt, 1931 D
in Belgium, scandal over National Bank, 1937 K
in Britain:
Baring Bros., failure of, 1890 O
Birkbeck Bank fails, 1911 F
England, Bank of, buildings for, 1795 S, 1803 S
suspends cash payments, 1797 B
resumes cash payments, 1817 K, 1821 E

Bank Charter Act for, 1833 H, 1844 G
repealed, 1914 O
issues Treasury notes, 1914 O
advances money to Austria, 1931 F
is nationalised, 1946 B
agrees with central banks for support for, £, 1965 J
provincial banks, run on, 1796 M
bank holidays, 1871 W, 1964 C
bank rate, notable changes in, 1957 J, 1960 F, 1961 G, 1964 L, 1965 F
bank rate tribunal, 1957 M
'women only' branch, in Edinburgh, 1964 O
drive-in, in Liverpool, 1959 O
in Canada, bank of Canada, 1935 O
Newfoundland Bank fails, 1894 L
in France, Bank of France, 1801 O
issues Franc notes, 1914 O
reorganised, 1936 O
is nationalised, 1945 O
in Germany, Agricultural Co-operative land, 1849 O
Deutsche, 1898 L
Reichsbank, 1875 O, 1876 O
Schacht is dismissed from, 1939 A
Danatbank, fails, 1931 G
bank rate raised to 90 per cent, 1923 J
in Italy, Milan People's Bank, 1866 O
in Japan, 1882 O, 1927 D
in New Zealand, Reserve Bank nationalised, 1936 N
in Switzerland, Basel Bank, for Germany's reparations payments, 1929 L
in Turkey, Ottoman Bank, Constantinople, attacked, 1896 H
in US, Bank of North America, 1791 O
uniform banking system provided, 1863 B, 1864 F
Federal Bank created, 1913 O
Postal Savings Bank, 1910 O
closure of banks in crisis, 1933 C
Bannister, Roger Gilbert, B. athlete (b. 1929), 1929 Z, 1954 X
Banting, Frederick, Can. biochemist (1891–), 1922 P
Bantry Bay, Cork, Eire, Hoche's expedition to, 1796 M
Bantu self-government bill, S. Africa, 1960 F
Banville, Théodore de, F. author (1823–91), 1842 U
Bao Dai, ex-emperor of Viet-Nam (b. 1911), 1949 C; establishes Viet-Nam state, 1949 F; deposed, 1955 K
Bapaume, N.E. France, British capture, 1917 C
Bar, in Podolia, formerly Poland, now Russia, Confederation, 1768 H
Baraalam and Yearsef (ed. Budge), 1924 Q
Barbare en Asie, Un (H. Michaux), 1932 U
Barber, Samuel, Am. musician (b. 1910), 1961 T
Barber of Seville (P. Beaumarchais), 1775 W
Barbier, Henri Auguste, F. poet and dramatist (1805–82), 1831 U
Barbizon School of French Artists, 1831 S
Barometer, 1771 P
Barcelona, Spain: French capture, 1808 B; risings in, 1842 K; Alfonso XII at, 1875 A; general strike in, 1909 G; rising by Monarchists, 1933 A; strike by Socialists, 1934 D; government moves to, 1937 K; places: Casa Mila, 1905 S; Church of the Sagrada Familia, 1926 S
Barchester Towers (A. Trollope), 1857 U
Barden, Juan Antonio, F. film director (b. 1910), 1955 W, 1956 W
Bardia, Cyrenaica, Libya: Italians surrender, 1941 A; Germans recapture, 1941 D; British take, 1942 A
Bardo, Tunisia, Treaty of, 1881 E
Barham, Richard Harris, B. author (1788–1845), 1840 U
Baring, Alexander, lord Ashburton, B. diplomat (1774–1848), 1842 H
Baring, Evelyn, Lord Cromer, B. statesman and diplomat (1841–1917), as British agent in Egypt, 1883 J, 1893 A
Baring, Maurice, B. author (1874–1945), 1936 U
Barlow, Sir Montague, B. economist, 1940 O
Barnard Castle, Durham, by-election, 1903 G
Barnardo, Thomas John, B. philanthropist (1845–1905), 1865 O
Barnes, E. W., B. churchman and scientist, Bishop of Birmingham (1874–1953), 1933 R, 1947 R
Barnes, Thomas, B. journalist (1784–1841), 1817 V
Barnett, Dame Henrietta Octavia Weston, B. social reformer (1851–1936), 1906 S
Barnum, Phineas Taylor, Am. showman (1810–91), 1850 W, 1871 W, 1889 W
Barotseland, N. Rhodesia, 1891 F
Barrack Room Ballads (R. Kipling), 1892 U
Barras, Paul François Nicolas, Comte de, F. revolutionary (1755–1829), 1797 J
Barrès, Maurice, F. author (1862–1923), 1862 Z, 1888 U, 1891 U, 1897 U, 1913 U, 1923 Z
Barrie, Sir James Matthew, B. dramatist (1860–1937), 1860 Z, 1889 U, 1891 U, 1902 W, 1917 W, 1937 Z
Peter Pan, 1904 S, W
Barrier Towns, Austrian Netherlands, 1782 D
Barrington, Samuel, B. admiral (1729–1800), 1778 L
Barrington-Ward, Robert McGowan, B. journalist (1891–1948), 1941 V
Barrow, Sir John, B. Arctic explorer (1764–1848), 1919 P
Barry, Sir Charles, B. architect (1795–1860), 1840 S, 1858 S
Barry, Sir Gerald Reid, B. journalist (b. 1899), as director-general of Festival of Britain, 1951 S
Barry, Philip, Am. dramatist (1896–1949), 1938 W
Barrymore, John, Am. film actor (1882–1942), 1926 W
Bar-sur-Aube, France, French defeat at, 1814 B
Bartenstein, Russo-Prussian Convention of, 1807 D
Britain joins, 1807 F
Barton, Sir Edmund, Australian Federalist, premier, 1901 A
Baryta, discovered, 1774 P
Bart, Lionel, B. musician (b. 1930), 1961 W
Barth, Heinrich, G. explorer (1821–65), 1850 P, 1852 P
Barth, Karl, Swi. theologian (1886–1965), 1886 Z, 1919 R, 1932 R, 1935 R, 1959 R
Barthélemy, Jean-Jacques, F. educationalist (1716–1795), 1787 Q
Bartók, Béla, Hung. musician (1881–1945), 1881 Z, 1908 T, 1918 T, 1923 T, 1938 T, 1944 T, 1945 Z, 1950 T
Baruch, Bernard, Am. financier (1870–1965), 1870 Z, 1965 Z
Baseball:
first played, 1839 X
rules codified, 1845 X
first US professional club, 1868 X
US National League founded, 1876 X
American Association, 1882 X
Base constitutionelle de la république de genre humain (Cloots), 1793 O
Basic English, 1932 O
Foundation, 1947 O

Basle, Switzerland: bishopric annexed by France, 1793 C; Peace of, between France and Prussia, 1795 D; Austro-French secret agreement on, 1797 K; Zionist Conference at, 1897 R; Franco-German Parliamentary Conference at, 1950 A
Basra, S.E. India, occupied by Indians, 1914 L
Bass, George, B. naval surgeon (d. 1812), 1798 P
Bassée Canal, Belgium, 1915 A
Bassein, Bombay, India, treaty, 1802 M
Bastien-Lepage, Jules, F. artist (1848–84), 1879 S
Basutoland, S. Africa: comes under British protection, 1843 M; annexed by Britain, 1868 C; is united with Cape Colony, 1871 H
Basutos, tribe, S. Africa, 1877 D
Batavian Republic (Holland), 1795 E, 1797 K, 1801 B
Directory established in, 1798 A
Bateau Ivre, Le (A. Rimbaud), 1895 U
Bates, Herbert Ernest, B. author (b. 1905), 1944 U, 1949 U
Batetelas, in Upper Congo, rising of, 1897 J
Bath, Somerset, Eng., bombed, 1942 D
Baths and wash-houses, public, 1844 O
Bathyscape, 1948 P, 1960 P
Batistá, Fulgencio, president of Cuba, 1957 K, 1958 D
flees, 1959 A
Battery:
carbon-zinc, 1841 P
solar, 1954 P
Battle for the Mind, The (W. Sargent), 1957 O
Batum, S.W. Georgia, Russia: transferred to Russia, 1878 C, G; British evacuate, 1920 G
Baudelaire, Charles Pierre, F. author (1821–67), 1821 Z, 1857 U, 1863 S, 1866 U, 1867 Z
Baudouin, King of the Belgians, succeeds Leopold III, 1950 H; marries, 1960 M
Baudrillant, Henri Joseph Léon, F. economist (1821–1892), 1865 O
Bauer, Gustav, G. Socialist leader, 1919 F
Bauer, L. A., G. physicist, 1923 P
Bauer, Otto, Aus. Socialist leader (1881–1938), 1938 Z
Bauer, Ferdinand Christian, G. theologian (1792–1860), 1846 Q
Bautzen, E. Germany, battle, 1813 E
Bavaria: Austrian claims to, 1777 M, 1778 A, 1797 K; passes to Elector Palatine, 1777 M; War of Succession, 1778 G, 1779 E; Joseph II attempts to exchange Austrian Netherlands for, 1785 A, G, 1790 M; becomes a kingdom, 1805 M; alliance with N. German Confederation, 1870 L; republic proclaimed, 1918 L
Bayer, Adolf von, G. chemist (1835–1917), 1880 P
Bayliss, Lilian, B. theatrical manager (1874–1937), 1914 W, 1931 W
Bayliss, Sir William Maddock, B. physiologist (1866–1924), 1902 P
Bayonne, France, siege of, 1813 L
Bayreuth, Bavaria, W. Germany: principality, 1769 K, 1779 E; Prussia acquires, 1792 A; Festpielhaus in, 1876 T
Bax, Sir Arnold Edward Trevor, B. musician (1883–1953), 1916 T, 1917 T, 1928 T, 1932 T, 1943 T
Beaconsfield, Earl of. *See* Disraeli, Benjamin
Beale, Dorothea, B. educationalist (1831–1906), 1831 Z, 1906 Z
Beardsley, Aubrey, B. artist (1872–98), 1893 S, 1894 S
Bearings, roller, 1910 P
Beatrice Cenci (F. D. Guerazzi), 1854 U
Beattie, James, B. poet and philosopher (1735–1803), 1770 R
Beatles, The, B. group of musicians, 1963 W, 1964 W, 1965 O, W
Beatnik Cult, The, 1958 U
Beatty, David, Earl Beatty, B. naval officer (1871–1936), 1871 Z, 1914 H, 1916 L, 1936 Z
Beaver Committee on air pollution in Britain, 1953 O
Beauharnais, Eugène de, F. soldier (1781–1824), stepson of Napoleon I, 1813 K
Beauharnais, Josephine de (*née* Marie Rose Josephine Tascher de la Pagerie; married Napoleon I). *See* Josephine
Beaumarchais, Pierre Augustin Caron de, F. dramatist (1732–99), 1775 W, 1784 W, 1787 W, 1799 Z
Beauty contest, first, 1888 W
Beaverbrook, Lord. *See* Aitken, William Maxwell
Beauvoir, Simone de, F. author (b. 1908), 1908 Z, 1946 U, 1949 U
Bebel, Ferdinand August, G. Socialist (b. 1840), 1867 H
Bebop dancing, 1945 W, 1950 W
Beccaria-Bonesana, Cesare, Marchese de, It. publicist (1735–94), 1764 O
Bechuanaland, S. Africa: exploration of, 1802 P; British protectorate in, 1885 C; under a British governor, 1890 N; annexed to Cape Colony, 1895 L; to be independent, 1965 M
Becket (J. Anouilh), 1961 W
Beckett, Samuel, Ir. dramatist (b. 1906), 1906 Z, 1955 W, 1957 W
Beckford, Peter, B. sportsman (1740–1811), 1781 X
Beckford, William, B. author (1759–1844), 1786 U
Beckmann, Max, G. artist (1884–1950), 1923 S, 1928 S, 1932 S, 1940 S, 1944 S, 1965 S
Becque, Henri François, F. dramatist (1837–99), 1882 W, 1885 W, 1887 W
Becquerel, Henri, F. chemist (1852–1908), 1852 Z, 1908 Z
Bedchamber Question, 1839 E
Bedford, Eric, B. architect, 1954 S
Bedford, Sibylle, Am. author (b. 1911), 1957 U
Bedford, Dukes of. *See under* Russell
Bednore (now Nagar), in Mysore, India, 1783 D
Beebe, William, Am. marine biologist (b. 1877), 1934 P
Beecham, Sir Thomas, B. musician (1879–1961), 1910 T, 1932 T, 1953 T, 1961 Z
Beecher, Henry Ward, Am. preacher (1813–76), 1847 R
Beecher Stowe, Harriet, Am. author (1811–96), 1852 U
Beeching, Richard, Lord Beeching, B. administrator (b. 1913), 1963 O
Beel, J. M., Du. politician, leader of Catholic People's Party, 1958 M
Beer, Sir Gavin de, B. scientist and administrator (b. 1899), 1960 Q
Beer, Jacob. *See* Meyerbeer, Giacomo
Beerbohm, Sir Max, B. author and artist (1872–1956), 1872 Z, 1904 S, 1911 U, 1919 U, 1922 S, 1956 Z
Beethoven, Ludwig van, G. musician (1771–1827), 1771 Z, 1783 T, 1827 Z
Fidelio, 1805 T, 1814 T
Liederkreis, 1816 T
Mass in D, 1822 T
overtures, 1807 T, 1810 T
piano concertos, 1800 T, 1801 T, 1805 T, 1809 T
piano sonatas, 1799 T, 1802 T, 1807 T, 1811 T
string quartets, 1801 T, 1806 T
symphonies, 1800 T, 1802 T, 1806 T, 1808 T, 1812 T
Choral, 1824 T, 1825 T
violin concerto, 1806 T, 1844 T
Wagner's essay on, 1870 T

Before Dawn (G. Hauptmann), 1889 U
Behan, Brendan, Ir. dramatist (1923–64), 1959 W, 1964 Z
Behrens, Peter, G. architect (1868–1940), 1908 S, 1926 S
Beirut, The Lebanon: British bombard, 1840 J; French occupy, 1918 K
Bel Ami (G. de Maupassant), 1885 U
Belfast, Northern Ireland, riots in 1920 G, 1935 G
Belfry of Bruges, The (H. W. Longfellow), 1846 U
Belgium: declared independent of Austria, 1789 M; Britain withholds recognition, 1790 A; revolution in, suppressed, 1790 M; French liberate, 1793 C; incorporated with France, 1795 K; ceded to France, 1797 K; independence, 1830 L; Holland forced to recognise, 1832 M; recognised by Treaty of London, 1839 D; neutrality, guaranteed by Prussia, 1870 H; Germany invades, 1914 H, 1940 E; capitulates to Germany, 1940 E; Allies liberate, 1944 L. *See also* Austrian Netherlands
Belgrade, Yugoslavia: Joseph II fails to capture, 1788 K; Austrians take, 1789 K; Russians capture, 1811 B; bombarded by Turkey, 1862 F; Austrians capture, 1914 M; occupation by Austrians and Germans, 1915 K; Pact of Assistance, 1937 C; British minister withdrawn from, 1941 C; liberated, 1944 K; Conference on R. Danube, 1948 G; meeting of non-aligned powers at, 1961 J; university, 1964 O
Bélisaire (J. F. Marmontel), 1767 R
Bell, Andrew, B. educationalist (1750–1832), 1797 O
Bell, Sir Charles, B. neurologist (1774–1842), 1807 P, 1811 P, 1830 P
Bell, Clive, B. art critic (1881–1964), 1881 Z, 1922 S, 1964 Z
Bell, George Kennedy Allen, B. churchman, bishop of Chichester (1883–1958), 1948 R
Bell, Gertrude Margaret Lowthian, B. traveller and archaeologist (1868–1926), 1868 Z, 1926 Z
Bell, Graham Alexander, Am. inventor and physicist (1847–1922), 1847 Z, 1876 P, 1922 Z
Bell, Henry, B. marine engineer (1767–1830), 1783 P, 1812 P
Bell, John, Am. politician, Constitutional Unionist (1797–1869), 1860 L
Bellamy, Edward, Am. author (1850–98), 1888 U
Bell for Adano, A (J. Hersey), 1945 U
Bellini, Vincenzo, It. musician (1810–35), 1801 Z, 1827 T, 1831 T, 1835 Z
Belloc, Hilaire, B. author (1870–1953), 1895 U, 1902 U, 1925 Q
Bell Telephone Company, 1848 P, 1954 P, 1956 P
Bellow, Saul, Am. author (b. 1915), 1954 U, 1959 U, 1964 U
Bemis Heights, New York, US, battles, 1777 J, K
Benares, India, Rajah of, deposed, 1781 F
Ben Barka, Mehdi, Moroccan Left leader, kidnapped, 1965 K
Ben Bella, Ahmed, premier of Algeria, 1962 J; deposed, 1965 F
Benedict XV, Pope (1914–22), Giacomo della Chiesa, It., 1917 H, 1922 B
Benefit of Clergy, in Britain, abolished, 1827 F
Benefit Societies, 1769 O
Benelux countries, full economic union of Belgium, Netherlands and Luxembourg, 1949 C
Beneš, Eduard, Czech statesman (1884–1948), 1935 M, 1938 K, 1945 D
Benét, Stephen Vincent, Am. poet (1898–1943), 1928 U
Bengal, India: Clive's reforms, 1765 E; British settlement of, 1793 N
Bengal Asiatic Society, 1784 Q
Bengal Atlas (J. Rennell), 1779 P
Benghazi, Cyrenaica, Libya: British occupy, 1941 A, B; evacuate, 1941 D; recapture, 1941 M; occupation by 8th Army, 1942 M
Benin, Nigeria, British occupation, 1897 N
Ben-Gurion, David, Israeli statesman (1886–), 1886 Z; becomes premier, 1948 E; resigns, 1951 B; forms coalition, 1951 K; resigns, 1953 M; forms ministries, 1955 L, 1961 L
Benn, Anthony Neil Wedgwood (formerly Viscount Stansgate), B. Socialist politician (b. 1925), election court rules disqualification through succession to peerage, 1961 O; disclaims peerage, 1963 G
Bennett, Arnold, B. novelist (1867–1931), 1867 Z, 1908 U, 1910 U, 1919 W, 1923 U, 1931 Z
Bennett, Joan, Am. film actress (b. 1910), 1910 Z
Bennett, Richard, Viscount Bennett, Canad. Conservative politician (1870–1947), 1930 H, 1936 F
Bennett, Richard Rodney, B. musician (b. 1936), 1964 T
Bennigsen, Rudolf von, G. Liberal leader (1824–1902), 1859 G, 1866 L
Bennington, Vermont, US, battle, 1777 H
Benoit, biologist, 1959 P
Benson, Sir Francis ('Frank') Robert, B. actor-manager (1858–1939), 1858 Z, 1939 Z
Bentham, Jeremy, B. writer on jurisprudence (1748–1832), 1776 O, 1787 O, 1789 O, 1791 O, 1802 O, 1824 V, 1832 Z, 1834 O
Bentham, Sir Samuel, B. engineer (1787–1831), 1793 P
Bentinck, Lord George Cavendish, B. Tory politician (1802–48), 1849 B
Bentinck, William Henry Cavendish, Duke of Portland, B. Tory leader, becomes nominal premier, 1783 D; becomes premier, 1807 C, D; resigns, 1809 J
Bentinck, Lord William Cavendish, B. Indian administrator (1774–1834), as governor-general, 1829 O, 1832 H
Bentley, John Francis, B. architect (1839–1902), 1903 S
Bentwich, Norman, B. lawyer and Jewish leader (1883–1965), 1944 O
Benz, Karl, G. motor manufacturer (1844–1929), 1885 P, 1893 P
Benzene, is isolated, 1824 P; structure of, 1865 P
Ben-Zvi, Itzhak, president of Israel, 1952 M
Beowulf, editions of, 1815 Q, 1833 Q
Beran, Archbishop of Prague, release of, 1963 K
Béranger, Pierre Jean de, F. poet (1780–1857), 1815 U
Berbers, in Morocco, French action against, 1934 B
Berbice, B. Guiana, taken by British, 1796 N; retained by Britain, 1814 H
Berchtesgaden, Bavaria, W. Germany, Chamberlain visits, 1938 J
Berchtold, Count, Aus. foreign minister, 1912 H
Berdyaev, Nicolas, B. philosopher, 1950 R
Berenguer, Damaso, Sp. general and politician, 1930 A
Berenson, Bernhard, Am. art critic (1865–1959), 1950 S
Beresina, River, Russia, French disaster at, 1812 L
Berg, Alban, Aus. musician (1885–1935), 1885 Z, 1926 T, 1935 T, Z
Berg, Max, G. architect, 1910 S
Bergendal, S. Africa, Botha's defeat at, 1900 H
Bergen-op-Zoom, Holland, 1799 J

Bergman, Ingmar, Swe. film director (b. 1918), 1952 W, 1955 W, 1956 W, 1957 W, 1962 W, 1963 W, 1964 W
Bergman, Torbern Olof, Swe. chemist (1735–84), 1774 P
Bergmann, R., G. philosopher, 1955 R
Bergson, Henri, F. philosopher (1859–1941), 1859 Z, 1889 R, 1896 R, 1900 R, 1907 R, 1909 R, 1919 R, 1932 R
Beria, Leonid, R. minister of internal affairs, 1953 G
Bericht über die Wissenschaftslehre (J. G. Fichte), 1806 Q
Bering Sea, N. Pacific, seal fishery, 1892 B
Bering Strait, survey of coasts, 1778 P
Berkeley, Sir George, B. colonial administrator (1819–1905), 1872 K
Berkeley, Lennox, B. musician (b. 1903), 1903 Z, 1940 T, 1943 T, 1954 T
Berlin, Germany:
- Napoleon occupies, 1806 K
- Napoleon's decrees, 1806 L
  - revoked, 1810 L
- Napoleon threatens to invade, 1811 K
- Conference between Prussia, Russia and Austria on integrity of Ottoman Empire, 1833 K
- revolution in, 1848 E
- Treaty, between Prussia and Denmark, 1850 G
- meeting of Three Emperors at, 1872 J
- Memorandum on armistice in Bulgaria, 1876 E
- Congress on Eastern Question, 1878 F, G
- Treaty on Eastern Question, 1878 G
  - adjustment to, 1880 L, 1881 G
- Conference on Africa, 1884 L
- Congress for protection of workers, 1890 C
- Copyright Convention, 1908 O
- air service to, 1912 P
- political parties in, 1916 A
- strikes in, 1918 A
- revolution in, 1918 L
- Spartacist revolt in, 1919 A
- Treaty, between Germany and Latvia, 1920 E
- Kapp's attempted coup in, 1920 C
- Conference on German currency, 1922 L
- Treaty between Germany and Russia, 1926 D
- Olympic Games in, 1936 X
- Mussolini visits, 1937 J
- bombing of, 1943 B, 1955 A, C
  - protests in Parliament against, 1944 A
- Russians reach, 1945 D
- surrenders to Allies, 1945 E
- Allied occupation of, 1945 G
- interference to communications, 1948 D
- Russian blockade and Anglo-US airlift, 1948 G, K, 1949 E, J
- E. Reuter as mayor, 1948 M
- Cultural Freedom Congress, 1950 O
- Communist Youth Rally, 1951 H
- World Peace Council, 1951 O
- anti-Communist rising, 1953 F
- foreign ministers meet in, 1954 A
- Dulles's speech in, 1958 E
- NATO Council rejects Russian proposals on, 1958 M
- US aircraft buzzed in air corridor, 1959 C
- blockade by E. Germany, 1960 H
- Wall constructed, 1961 H
  - passes agreement for crossing, 1964 J
- musical events in, 1829 T, 1882 T
- places in:
  - A.E.G. Turbine factory, 1908 S
  - Atlas Museum, 1824 S
  - Brandenburg Gate, 1791 S, closure of, 1961 H
  - Charlottenburg Technical High School, 1884 O
  - Frederick the Great monument, 1851 S
  - Gustav Adolf Kirche, 1934 S
  - Museum of Twentieth Century, 1963 S
  - National Theatre in, 1796 W
  - Schauspielhaus, 1819 S
  - University, 1810 O, 1818 Q
- population, 1801 Y, 1941 Y, 1881 Y, 1906 Y, 1950 Y

Berlin, Irving, Am. musician (b. 1888), 1888 Z, 1911 T, 1950 W
Berliner, Emil, G. inventor (1851–1929), 1887 P
Berliner Ensemble, 1949 W
Berlioz, Hector, F. musician (1803–69), 1803 Z, 1834 T, 1837 T, 1838 T, 1846 T, 1844 T, 1854 T, 1855 T, 1863 T, 1869 Z, 1899 T
Bermuda (or Somers Islands):
- Conference on Refugees, 1943 D
- Churchill and Eisenhower meet in, 1953 M

Bernadotte, Folke, Count, Swe. statesman (d. 1948), as UN mediator in Palestine, 1948 J
Bernadotte, Jean, F. general, as heir to Charles XIII of Sweden, 1810 H, 1818 B. *See also* Charles XIV
Bernal, John Desmond, B. physicist (1901–64), 1941 P, 1949 O
Bernanos, Georges, F. author (1888–1948), 1931 U, 1936 U
Bernard, Claude, F. physiologist (1813–78), 1813 Z, 1850 P, 1854 P, 1878 Z
Bernard, Tristram, F. dramatist (1866–1947), 1905 W
Berne, Switzerland: French occupy, 1798 C; Union général des postes at, 1874 O; International Socialist Conference at, 1919 B
Bernhardt, Sarah, F. actress (1845–1923), 1845 Z, 1862 W, 1881 W, 1923 Z; as film actress, 1912 W; portrait, 1879 S
Bernstein, Leonard, Am. musician (b. 1918), 1918 Z, 1950 T, 1958 W, 1964 T, 1965 T
Bernstorff, Andreas Peter, Count, Da. statesman (1735–97), 1784 E
Bernstorff, Johann Hartwig Ernst, Count von (1712–72), 1770 J
Berry, Charles Ferdinand, Duc de, heir to French throne, 1820 B, J
Berry, Duchesse de, F. Legitimist, 1832 L
Berthollet, Claude Louis, F. chemist (1748–1822), 1785 P, 1803 P
Bertillon, Louis Adolphe, F. statistician (1821–83), 1883 P, 1890 O
Bertrand, Joseph Louis François, F. mathematician (1822–85), 1864 P
Berzelius, Jöns Jacob, Swe. chemist (1779–1848), 1814 P
Besançon, Doubs, France, Parlement of, 1783 G
Besant, Sir Walter, B. author (1836–1901), 1882 W
Bessarabia, Russia: Russia restores conquests in, to Turkey, 1792 A; Russia obtains, 1812 E; Austria demands Russian cession of, 1855 M; ceded by Russia, 1856 C; disturbances in, 1878 G; proclaims independence, 1917 M; Russia demands cession of, 1940 F; Russian offensive in, 1944 H; Rumania cedes to Russia, 1947 B
Bessel, Friedrich Wilhelm, G. astronomer (1784–1846), 1818 P
Bessemer, Sir Henry, B. engineer (1813–98), 1813 Z, 1856 P, 1859 P, 1878 P, 1898 Z
Bessenyei, György, Hun. dramatist (1747–1811), 1772 W
Bethlehem, Pa., US, Bach Festival in, 1900 T
Bethmann-Hollweg, Theobald von, G. statesman (1856–1921), as Chancellor, 1909 G, 1912 G; resigns, 1917 G
Betjeman, John, B. poet (b. 1906), 1954 U, 1960 U

Betti, Ugo, It. dramatist, 1955 W
Betting, lotteries and gaming, Royal Commission on, 1951 O
Between Two Worlds (U. Sinclair), 1940 U
Bevan, Aneurin, B. Socialist (1897–1960), 1897 Z, 1944 D; becomes Minister of Labour, 1951 A; resigns from Cabinet, 1951 D; elected Treasurer of Labour Party, 1956 J; death, 1960 G
Bevan, Edwyn, B. churchman, 1938 R
Beveridge, William Henry, lord Beveridge, B. economist (1879–1963), 1879 Z, 1909 O, 1944 O, 1963 Z
  Plan for Social Security, 1942 O
    policy over, 1943 B
Bevin, Ernest, B. trade union leader and statesman (1881–1951), 1881 Z, 1946 M, 1951 Z; becomes Minister of Labour, 1940 E; becomes Foreign Secretary, 1945 G; resigns, 1951 C
Bewick, Thomas, B. wood-engraver (1753–1823), 1797 P, 1800 U
Bexhill, Sussex, England, 1935 S
Beyle, Marie Henri, F. author under pseudonym 'Stendhal' (1783–1842), 1783 Z, 1822 U, 1823 U, 1830 U, 1839 U, 1842 Z
Beyond Good and Evil (F. Nietzsche), 1886 U
Beyond Human Endurance (B. Björnson), 1883 U
Beyond the Horizon (O'Neill), 1920 W
Bhowani Junction (J. Masters), 1954 U
Biarritz, France, Napoleon III meets Bismarck at, 1865 K
Biberach, Bad-Württ., W. Germany, Austrian defeat at, 1800 E
Bible, The:
  New Testament, editions:
    Basic English, 1949 R
    Greek (ed. Westcott and Hort), 1881 Q
    Knox translation, 1946 Q
    Lutheran revision, 1956 R
    Moffatt's translation, 1913 R
    New English Bible, 1961 Q
    Revised Version, 1870 R, 1881 R
    studies and commentaries, 1775 Q, 1846 Q, 1919 R, 1941 R
  Old Testament, studies, 1776 Q, 1779 R, 1783 R, 1862 R
    Codex Sinaiticus, 1844 Q, 1859 Q
    Dead Sea Scrolls, 1947 Q, 1960 Q
Bible in Spain, The (G. Borrow), 1843 U
Bibliographical Society, 1842 Q
Bibliotheca Historica Medii Aevi (ed. G. Potthast), 1862 Q
Bichat, Marie François Xavier, F. anatomist and physiologist (1771–1802), 1771 Z, 1801 P, 1802 Z
Bicycle: 'bone-shaker', 1865 P; P. Michaux's, 1867 P; American, 1878 P; 'Rover' safety, 1885 P; pennyfarthing, world tour on, 1886 W
Bicycle, Motor, 1901 P
Bidassoa, Spain, River, 1813 K
Bidault, Georges, F. politician (1899–), elected president of provisional government, 1946 F; forms coalition, 1949 K; resigns premiership, 1950 F
Biddle, James, Am. naval officer (1783–1848), 1846 N
Bielefeld, N. Rhine, W. Germany, epileptic hospital, 1868 O
Biermann, Wolf, G. poet (b. 1936), 1965 U
Bierstadt, Albert, Am. formerly G. artist (1830–1902), 1878 S
Bierut, M., Pol. Communist, forms ministry, 1952 L
Bigelow, E. B., Am. inventor (1814–79), 1845 P
Biglow Papers, The (J. R. Lowell), 1848 U
Bikini, Marshall Islands, Pacific, US hydrogen bomb tests, in, 1954 P
Bilbao, Spain, rebels take, 1937 F
Bilderdijck, Willem, Du. poet (1756–1831), 1786 U
Billingham, Co. Durham, England, 1935 P
Billroth, Albert Christian Theodor, Aus. surgeon (1829–94), 1872 P
Bing Girls, The, a revue, 1916 W
Biochemistry, science of, founded, 1838 P
Biology, term first used, 1802 P; first International Congress on, 1821 P
Biot, France, 1960 S
Birch, Evelyn Nigel Chetwode, B. Conservative politician (b. 1906), resigns, 1958 A
Bird of Dawning, The (J. Masefield), 1933 U
Birdseye, Clarence, Am. pioneer of frozen food, 1925 P
Birds of America (J. J. Audubon), 1830 P
Birkbeck, George, B. founder of mechanics' institutes (1776–1841), 1823 O
Birkbeck Bank, London, fails, 1911 F
Birkenhead, Earl of. *See* Smith, Frederick Edwin
Bir Hakeim, Cyrenaica, Libya, French surrender at, 1942 F
Birmingham, England: Boulton's works at, 1775 P, 1802 W; co-operative workshop at, 1777 O; riots, 1791 G; Chartist rising, 1839 G; Repertory Company, 1909 W, 1913 W, 1919 W; surgery at, 1960 P
Birmingham, Alabama, US, school desegregation riots in, 1963 J
Biro, Georg, Hun. inventor, 1938 P
Birth Control: F. Place advocates, 1822 O; M. Stopes's campaign, 1922 O; New York clinic, 1923 O; through phosphorated hesperidin in tablets ('the pill'), 1952 P; Roman Catholic ruling against use of, 1964 R
Birthday Party, The (H. Pinter), 1958 W
Births, Registration of, in Britain, 1836 H
Biscia, Eritrea, British take, 1941 A
Biscuit manufacture, by steam process, 1841 P
Bismarck, Otto Eduard Leopold von, Prince, G. statesman (1815–98), 1815 Z, 1864 K, 1898 Z; becomes minister president of Prussia, 1862 J; 'Blood and Iron' speech, 1862 J; rules without budget, 1862 K; meets Napoleon III, 1865 K; indemnified for unconstitutional rule, 1866 J; begins *Kulturkampf*, 1871 G; remodels Prussian local government, 1872 M; plot against, 1874 K; preserves *entente* with Russia, 1875 B; declines to mediate in Russo-Turkish War, 1877 M; proposes legislation against Radicals, 1878 E; at Congress of Berlin, 1878 F; introduces sickness insurance, 1883 E; organises Berlin Conference on Africa, 1884 L; advocates larger army, 1887 A; publishes Germano-Austrian alliance, 1888 B; dismissed, 1890 C; memoirs, 1898 O
Bismarck Archipelago, N.E. New Guinea, annexed by Germany, 1885 E
Bitlis, Turkey, Russians take, 1916 C
Bitter Sweet (N. Coward), 1929 W
Bizerta, Tunisia: seized by French, 1881 D; accepts French protectorate, 1881 E; Allies take, 1943 E; banned to French warships, 1958 B; de Gaulle states French will not evacuate until end of crisis, 1961 H
Bizet, Georges, F. musician (1838–75), 1838 Z, 1867 T, 1872 T, 1875 Z
Bjoerling, Jussi, Swe. singer (b. 1911), 1911 Z
Björkö, Treaty, between Germany and Russia, 1905 G
Björnson, Björnstjerne, Nor. author (1832–1910), 1857 U, 1883 U, 1889 U
Black, Joseph, B. engineer (1728–99), 1764 P, 1769 P

Blackburne, Francis, B. divine (1705–87), 1766 R
Blackett, Sir Patrick Maynard Stuart, B. physicist (b. 1897), 1922 P, 1947 P, 1948 O
Black Force (R. Wright), 1954 O
Blackley, William Lewery, B. churchman and advocate of old-age pensions (1830–1902), 1879 O
Black List, British, for war-time trade, 1916 B, G
Black Market, 1941 M, 1945 O
Blackmore, Richard Doddridge, B. novelist (1825–1900), 1869 T
Black-out, in Britain, relaxed, 1944 O
Black Reichwehr *coup d'état* fails, 1923 K
Black Sea: Russian Fleet for, 1776 N; Royal Navy sent into, 1854 A; neutrality of, 1855 M, 1856 C; repudiated, 1871 C
Blackstone, Sir William, B. judge (1723–80), 1765 O, 1780 Z
Blackwood, Algernon, B. author (1869–1951), 1906 U, 1916 W
Blackwood, Frederick Temple Hamilton-Temple, Marquess of Dufferin and Alva, B. statesman (1826–1902), report on Egypt, 1883 E
Blaine, James Gillespie, Am. Republican politician (1830–93), loses presidential election, 1884 L
Blair, Eric, B. author under pseudonym of 'George Orwell' (1903–50), 1937 U, 1945 U, 1949 W
Blair, Hugh, B. Presbyterian divine (1718–1800), 1777 R
Blake, George, B. spy, 1961 E, O
Blake, William, B. poet and artist (1757–1827), as poet, 1783 U, 1789 U, 1794 U, 1804 U; as artist, 1820 S
Blanc, Louis, F. politician and economist (1811–82), 1811 Z, 1839 O, 1841 O, 1847 O, 1848 B, 1882 Z
Blanchard, Jean Pierre, F. balloonist (1753–1809), 1785 P
Blanco, Antonio Guzmán, president of Venezuela, 1889 K
Bland, R. P., Am. Congressman, 1878 B
Blankenburg, W. Germany, kindergarten at, 1837 O
Blanketeers, March of, 1817 C
Blasco, Ibáñez, Sp. author, 1919 U
Blauer Reiter ('Blue Rider'), group of artists, 1911 S
Blavatsky, Helena Petrovina, R. theosophist (1831–1891), 1875 R
Bleach, Chlorine used as a, 1785 P
Bleaching powder, process for making, 1870 P
Blennerhasset's Island, US, 1806 N
Blériot, Louis, F. aviator (1872–1936), 1872 Z, 1909 P, 1936 Z
Blind, schools for, 1791 O
Bliss, Sir Arthur, B. musician (1891–), 1891 Z, 1922 T, 1937 T, 1949 T, 1952 T, 1960 T, 1963 T
Bliss (K. Mansfield), 1920 U
Blithe Spirit (N. Coward), 1941 W
Bloch, Ernest, Am. musician (b. 1880), 1880 Z, 1924 T, 1925 T, 1953 T
Blockade, defined, 1856 D
Blockades:
by Britain, of France and her Allies, 1806 D, 1807 A, L, 1809 D
of Germany, 1915 B, C, 1940 D
of Greece, 1916 F
of US, 1811 L, 1812 F
Bloemfontein, S. Africa: Convention, 1854 B; Roberts captures, 1900 C
Blok, Alexander, R. poet (1880–1921), 1918 U
Blondin, pseudonym of Jean François Gravelet, F. tight-rope walker and acrobat (1824–97), 1859 W
Blood, treatise on the, 1794 P
Blood pressure, recorded by kymograph, 1865 P
Blood River, Natal, Zulus defeated at, 1838 M
Bloom, Claire, B. actress (b. 1931), 1952 W
Bloomer, Amelia Jenks, Am. reformer of women's clothes (1818–94), 1849 O
Bloomfield, Maurice, B. orientalist, 1907 Q
Bloomfield, Robert, B. rustic poet (1766–1823), 1800 U
Blount, James H., Am. diplomat, 1893 B
Blücher, Gebhard Leberecht von, Prussian general (1742–1819), 1813 H, 1814 B; crosses Rhine, 1813 M; at Waterloo, 1815 F
'Blue babies', operations, 1944 O
Bluebells and other verse, The (J. Masefield), 1961 U
Bluebird, driven by M. Campbell, 1935 P
Blue Bird, The (M. Maeterlinck), 1909 W
'Blue Shirts', in Ireland, 1933 G
Blue Streak, missile, 1964 P
Blum, Léon, F. Socialist (1872–1950), 1872 Z, 1935 L, 1950 Z; forms Popular Front ministry, 1936 F; resigns, 1937 F; forms Popular Front ministry, 1938 C; supports Daladier, 1938 D; becomes premier, 1946 M; resigns, 1947 A
Boat Race, Oxford and Cambridge, 1829 W
'Bobbed hair', 1917 O
Bobbin net machine, 1809 P
Boccherini, Luigi, It. musician (1743–1805), 1787 T
Boccioni, Umberto, It. sculptor (1882–1916), 1910 S
Böckh, Philipp August, G. classical scholar (1785–1867), 1817 Q, 1824 Q
Bocklin, Arnold, Swi. artist (1827–1901), 1827 Z, 1864 S, 1872 S, 1901 Z
Bode, Johann Elert, G. astronomer (1747–1826), 1774 P
Bodkin Report on share-pushing, 1937 O
Boehm, Sir Joseph Edgar, B. formerly Aust. sculptor (1834–90), 1869 S
Boers, in Natal, defeat Zulus, 1838 M
J. Chamberlain aims at conciliation, 1903 B
Bogardus, James, Am. civil engineer (1800–74), 1851 P
Bohemia: ruled by Maria Theresa, 1765 H; Peasants' Revolt in, 1775 B; serfdom abolished, 1780 K; Germans occupy, 1939 C
Bohr, Niels, Da. physicist (1885–1962), 1913 P, 1922 P
Boïeldieu, François Adrien, F. musician (1775–1834), 1799 T
Boiler plating, by ductile steel, 1856 P
Bokhara, Russia, 1873 H
Boldrewood, Rolf. *See* Browne, T. A.
Bolívar, Simon, leader of S. American independence (1783–1830), 1783 Z, 1810 D, 1811 G, 1813 G, 1819 O, 1830 Z; invades Venezuela, 1816 B; organises independent Venezuela, 1817 K; declares Venezuela independent, 1818 L; in Colombia, 1820 L; defeats Spanish, 1821 F, 1824 H; as emperor of Peru, 1823 J; attempts to unite S. American republics, 1826 F; alleged tyranny of, 1827 A; abdicates in Colombia, 1830 D
Bolivia (or Upper Peru): becomes independent of Peru, 1825 H; federation with, Peru, 1836 K; dissolved, 1839 A; boundary with Chile settled, 1874 H
Bologna, Italy, in Napoleonic campaigns, 1797 B, G, 1801 G
Bolometer, invented, 1881 P
Bolshoi Ballet, visits London, 1956 T
Bolt, Robert Oxton, B. dramatist (b. 1924), 1924 Z, 1957 W, 1960 W
Bomb, Atomic: plutonium for, 1944 P; dropped on Japan, 1945 H, P; Britain produces own, 1952 P; Russia's, 1949 P, 1950 C. *See also* Atomic Research; Nuclear Warfare; Test Ban

Bomb, Flying, 1944 F. *See also* Rockets
  sites for launching, destroyed, 1944 J
Bomb, Hydrogen, 1950 A, 1952 L, 1954 D, 1953 P, 1954 P
Bombay, India: untouchables in, 1946 O; population, 1960 Y
Bon, Cape, Tunisia, Germans retire to, 1943 E
Bonald, Louis Gabriel Ambroise, Vicomte de, F. philosopher and politician (1754–1840), 1796 O
Bonanza Creek, Yukon, Canada, gold discovered at, 1897 P
Bonaparte Family, banished from France, 1886 F
Bonaparte, Charles Louis Napoleon. *See* Napoleon III
Bonaparte, Jerome, appointed King of Westphalia, 1807 H
Bonaparte, Joseph, King of Naples, 1806 C
Bonaparte, Louis, King of Holland, 1806 F
Bonaparte, Napoleon. *See* Napoleon I
Bonaparte et les Bourbons (Chateaubriand), 1814 O
Bond, George Phillips, Am. astronomer (1825–65), 1851 P
'Bond, James', 1953 S
Bondfield, Margaret Grace, B. Labour politician (1873–1953), 1873 Z, 1929 O, 1953 Z
Bone, Sir Muirhead, B. artist (1876–1953), 1940 S
Bonjour Tristesse (F. Sagan), 1954 U
Bonn, W. Germany: university, 1818 O; becomes capital of Federal Republic, 1949 E; Eisenhower visits, 1959 H
Bonn Catalogue of Stars, 1862 P
Bonnard, Pierre, F. artist (1867–1947), 1908 S, 1909 S, 1942 S, 1965 S
Bonnet, Charles, Swi. naturalist and philosopher (1720–93), 1764 R, 1769 R
Bonneville Salt Flats, Utah, US, 1939 P
Bonpland, Aimé Jacques Alexandre, F. traveller and botanist (1783–1858), 1807 P
Book of Mormon (J. Smith), 1830 R
Book of Nonsense (E. Lear), 1846 U
Book of the Thorn and the Rose (C. Almquist), 1832 U
Boole, George, B. mathematician and philosopher (1815–64), 1847 P, 1854 R
Boomplatz, S. Africa, Boer defeat at, 1848 H
Booth, Abraham, B. Baptist minister (1734–1806), 1768 R
Booth, Charles, B. sociologist (1840–1916), 1891 O
Booth, William, B. Evangelical leader (1829–1912), 1829 Z, 1865 R, 1878 R, 1890 O, 1912 Z
Bopp, Franz, G. philologist (1791–1867), 1816 Q, 1833 Q
Bordeaux, France: Wellington takes, 1814 C; National Assembly meets at, 1871 B; Government moved to, 1914 J
Borden, Sir Robert, Can. Unionist politician (1854 1937), as premier, 1911 K, 1917 M; resigns, 1920 G
Boring mill, 1774 P
Boris III, King of Bulgaria (1918–43), as Crown Prince, 1896 B
Boris Godunov (Pushkin), 1825 U
Borneo, North: British protectorate over, 1888 E; Philippines claim to, 1962 F; votes to join Malaysian Federation, 1962 J
Borodin, Alexander, R. musician (1834–87), 1834 Z, 1877 T, 1887 T, Z, 1890 T
Borodino, Russia, 1812 J
Borrow, George, B. author (1803–81), 1803 Z, 1843 U, 1851 U, 1857 U, 1881 Z
Bosanquet, Bernard, B. philosopher (1848–1923), 1888 R, 1923 Z
Boselli, Paolo, It. politician, forms coalition, 1916 F
Bosnia, Yugoslavia: Russian intrigues in, 1767 N; rebellion in, 1875 G, M; reforms in, 1878 C
Bosnia and Herzegovina, Yugoslavia: Russia agrees to Austrian annexation, 1908 J; Austria annexes, 1908 K; Turkey recognises, 1909 B
Bosphorus, The: closed to warships, 1841 G; Turkey recovers sovereignty over, 1936 G
Bossard, Frank, B. spy, 1965 E
Boston, Mass., US: riot, 1768 J; massacre, 1770 C; assembly threatens secession from Britain, 1772 B; 'Tea Party', 1773 M; Continental Army at, 1775 E; British evacuate, 1776 C; street-lighting in, 1822 P; Slavery Abolition Society, 1832 O; Lowell Institute, 1839 Q; Church of Christ Scientist, 1879 R; Symphony Orchestra, 1924 T
Boston (U. Sinclair), 1928 U
Bostonians, The (H. James), 1886 U
Boswell, James, B. author (1740–95), 1786 U, 1791 U, 1795 Z; meets Johnson, 1763 U
Boswell's London Journal (ed. Pottle), 1950 Q
Botany Bay, Australia: discovered, 1770 P; penal settlement in, 1788 A
Botha, Louis, S. Afr. soldier and statesman (1862–1919), 1862 Z, 1899 M, 1900 H, 1915 G, 1919 Z; raid on Natal fails, 1901 B; meets Kitchener, 1901 B; forms *Het Volk*, 1905 A; on Transvaal constitution, 1905 D; founds S. African Party, 1910 D; becomes premier, 1910 J; ministerial changes, 1912 M; occupies Windhoek, 1915 E
Botta, Carlo Giuseppe Guglielmo, It. historian (1766–1837), 1824 Q
Böttinger, Karl August, G. archaeologist (1760–1835), 1811 Q
Bottle-making machine, 1898 P
Boubouroche (G. Courteline), 1893 W
Boucher, François, F. artist (1703–70), 1765 S, 1770 Z
Boucicault, Dion, Ir. actor and dramatist (1822–90), 1860 W
Bougainville, Louis Antoine de, F. navigator (1729–1811), 1764 N, 1766 N, P
Bougainville, Solomon Isles, US task force at, 1943 L
Boughton, Rutland, B. musician (1878–), 1878 Z, 1914 T
Boulanger, George Ernest Jean Marie, F. general (1837–91), 1887 K, 1888 C, D, 1889 A; becomes War minister, 1886 A; excluded from Rouvier's ministry, 1887 E; flight, 1889 D; suicide, 1891 J
Boule de Suif (G. de Maupassant), 1880 U
Boulez, Pierre, F. musician (b. 1925), 1959 T, 1960 T
Boulogne, France: Louis Napoleon's attempted rising, 1840 H; Conference at, 1916 K
Boult, Sir Adrian Cedric, B. musician (b. 1889), 1930 T
Boulton, Matthew, B. engineer (1728–1809), 1775 P, 1785 P, 1807 P
Boumedienne, Houari, Algerian general, 1965 F
Bound East (O'Neill), 1916 W
Bourbons of Naples, The (H. Acton), 1956 Q
Bourdelle, Antoine, F. sculptor (1861–1929), 1909 S, 1912 S
Bourgeois, Léon Victor Auguste, F. Radical politician and author (1851–1925), 1851 Z, 1895 L, 1920 M, 1925 Z
Bourgès-Manoury, F. Radical politician, forms ministry, 1957 F
Bourget, Paul Charles Joseph, F. author (1852–1935), 1883 U, 1885 U
Bourguiba, President of Tunisia and leader of Neo-Destour Party, 1956 C, 1957 H, 1959 L
Bourke, Richard Southwell, Earl of Mayo, B. administrator (1822–72), viceroy of India, 1872 B
Bournville Village Trust, 1900 O

Bouvard et Pécuchet (G. Flaibert), 1881 U
Bowell, Sir Mackenzie, Can. statesman, 1894 M
Bowles, William Lisle, B. poet and antiquary (1762–1850), 1789 U
Bowring, Sir John, B. author and traveller (1792–1872), 1821 U, 1854 O
Boxer, Rising, 1898 N, 1900 F, 1901 J
Boxing:
with bare fists, 1860 X
Queensberry codifies rules, 1866 X
US national championship, 1910 X
world championships, 1908 X, 1930 X, 1936 X, 1965 X
Boycott, Charles Cunningham, Ir. land-agent (1832–1897), 1880 N
Boycotts:
of British goods, by China, 1935 E
of S. African goods, by Ghana, 1959 G
by India, 1957 A
by Nigeria, 1961 D
Boyd, Arthur, Austral. artist (b. 1920), 1960 S
Boyle, Sir Edward Charles Gurney, B. Conservative politician (b. 1923), 1963 G
Boys' Brigade, The, founded, 1883 O
Boy Scouts, 1907 O
Brabant, Belgium, constitution of, revoked, 1789 K
Bracebridge Hall, or the Humourist (W. Irving), 1822 U
Bracken, Brendan, Viscount Bracken, B. journalist and Conservative politician (1901–58), 1941 G
Bradbury, Ray, Am. author (b. 1920), 1952 U
Bradford, Yorks, England, Independent Labour Party founded at, 1893 A
Bradlaugh, Charles, B. politician and free-thinker (1833–91), 1860 V; refuses to take Parliamentary oath, 1880 E
Bradley, Francis Herbert, B. philosopher (1846–1924), 1846 Z, 1876 R, 1883 R, 1893 R, 1924 Z
Bradley, James, B. divine and astronomer (1693–1762), 1818 P
Bradman, Sir Donald, Austral. cricketer (b. 1908), 1908 Z, 1930 X, 1946 X
Bradshaw, George, B. originator of railway guides (1801–53), 1841 V
Braga, Theophilo, President of Portugal, 1910 K, 1915 E
Braganza, house of, flee from Portugal, 1807 L; return to Portugal, 1815 F
Bragg, Sir Lawrence, B. scientist (b. 1890), 1915 P
Bragg, Sir William, B. scientist (1862–1942), 1862 Z, 1915 P, 1942 Z
Brahms, Johannes, G. musician (1833–97), 1833 Z, 1853 T, 1868 T, 1869 T, 1897 Z
double concerto, 1887 T
overtures, 1881 T
piano concertos, 1861 T, 1882 T
requiem, 1873 T
songs, 1896 T
symphonies, 1876 T, 1877 T, 1883 T, 1885 T
violin concerto, 1879 T
Braid, James, B. surgeon (?1795–1860), 1842 P
Braille, Louis, F. inventor of Braille system (1809–1852), 1934 P
Brailoff, Russia, battle, 1809 J
Brain, electric responses of, 1875 P
Brain drain, 1963 B, 1964 P
Brain, electronic, 1942 P, 1946 P
Brain, John Gerard, B. author (b. 1922), 1957 U
Brains Trust, BBC, 1941 W
Brainwashing, 1957 O
Brake, Westinghouse railway, 1868 P
Branco, Humberto, President of Brazil, 1964 D
Brancusi, Constantin, It. sculptor (1876–1957), 1908 S, 1925 S, 1931 S
Bramah, Joseph, B. locksmith (1748–1914), 1778 P, 1784 P, 1795 P
Brand, Henry Bouverie William, Viscount Hampden, B. politician and Speaker of the House of Commons (1814–92), 1881 A
Brand (H. Ibsen), 1866 W
Brandenberger, Edwin, Swi. inventor, 1912 P
Brandes, Georg, Dan. author (1842–1927), 1842 Z, 1868 U, 1872 Q, 1927 Z
Brandis, Christian August, G. philosopher and philologist (1790–1867), 1835 Q
Brandywine, Pa., US, battle, 1777 J
Brangwyn, Sir Frank, B. artist (1867–1956), 1904 S
Braque, Georges, F. artist and sculptor (b. 1882), 1882 Z, 1911 T, 1914 S
Braschi, Giovanni Angelo, Pope Pius VI (1775–99), 1782 C
Brasilia, Brazil, becomes capital, 1960 O
buildings, 1957 S, 1958 S, 1960 S
Bratby, John Randall, B. artist (b. 1928), 1928 Z, 1954 S, 1955 S, 1956 S, 1958 S, 1959 S, 1960 S
Braun, Otto, G. politician, premier of Prussia, 1921 L
Braut von Messina, Die (F. Schiller), 1803 U
Brave New World (A. Huxley), 1932 U
Brave New World Revisited (A. Huxley), 1958 U
Brazzaville, Congo, 1960 G
Bratton, G., Am. engineer, 1873 P
Brazil: becomes an empire, 1816 A; independence, 1822 K, 1823 F; recognised by Portugal, 1825 H; Dom Pedro's tyranny in, 1823 L; becomes a republic, 1889 L; coffee production in, 1909 Y
Brazza, Pierre Paul François de, Count, F. explorer of Africa (1852–1905), 1880 F, 1886 D
Bread:
rationed in Britain, 1917 B, 1946 G, 1948 O
subsidy in Britain ends, 1956 J
white, baking of, ends in Britain, 1942 D
Breadwinner, The (W. S. Maugham), 1930 W
Brearley, Henry, B. metallurgist, 1912 P
Brecht, Bertolt, G. dramatist (1898–1956), 1922 W, 1928 T, 1932 W, 1937 W, 1941 W; Berliner Ensemble of, 1956 W
Breckinridge, John Cabell, Am. S. Democrat politician (1821–75), opposes Lincoln, 1860 L
Bremen, W. Germany: annexed by Napoleon, 1810 M; Soviet republic formed, 1919 A; surrenders to Allies, 1945 D
Brenner Pass, through Alps, 1772 P
Brenner, Sydney, S. Afr. chemist (b. 1927), 1961 P
Breslau (now Wroclaw), Poland: gymnasium, 1765 O; Institute of Physiology, 1839 O; Jewish Seminary, 1854 R; Jahrhunderthalle, 1910 S
Bresslau, H., G. student of diplomatic, 1889 Q
Bresson, Carl, film director, 1959 W
Brest, France, first submarine at, 1801 P
Brest-Litovsk, Russia: Germans take, 1915 H; Russia's armistice with Germany at, 1917 M; Peace Treaty, between Russia and Central Powers, 1918 O; annulled, 1918 L; Poles enter, 1920 H; Germans reach, 1939 J; Russians capture, 1944 G
Brett, John Watkins, B. telegraphic engineer (1805–1862), 1850 P
Brett, Lionel, B. architect (b. 1913), 1952 S
Bretton Woods, New Hampshire, US, UN Monetary Conference at, 1944 G
Brewster, Sir David, B. scientist (1781–1868), 1813 P, 1816 P
Brezhnev, Leonid, R. leader (b. 1906), becomes USSR president, 1960 E; 'Plane intercepted,

1961 B; Mikoyan succeeds, 1964 G; becomes first secretary of Soviet Communist Party, 1964 K
Briand, Aristide, F. statesmen (1862–1932), 1862 Z, 1925 L, 1932 Z; becomes premier, 1909 G; averts strike, 1910 K; attempted assassination, 1911 A; resigns, 1911 B; forms cabinet, 1913 A; at Allied Conference, 1916 C; forms War Ministry, 1916 M; as premier, 1921 A; resigns, 1922 A; meets Stresemann, 1926 J; proposals for outlawing war, 1928 D; again premier, 1929 G; proposes European federal union, 1929 J. *See also* Kellogg-Briand Pact
Bride of Abydos (Byron), 1813 U
Brideshead Revisited (E. Waugh), 1945 U
Bridge, Frank, B. musician (1879–1941), 1915 T
Bridge of San Luis Rey, The (T. Wilder), 1927 W
Bridges, Edward, Lord Bridges, B. civil servant (b. 1892), 1958 S
Bridges, Robert, B. poet (1844–1930), 1844 Z, 1929 U, 1930 Z
Bridges:
- cast-iron, 1773 P, 1850 P
- tubular, 1849 P
- Forth, 1890 P, 1964 P
- Lambeth, 1932 P
- Lower Zambesi, 1935 P
- Manhattan, 1910 P
- Menai, 1819 P, 1849 P
- Niagara Falls Suspension, 1852 P
- New York-Brooklyn, 1872 P
- Peace, 1927 H
- Saltash, 1853 P
- Sydney Harbour, 1932 P
- Verrazano Narrows, 1964 P

Bridie, James (pseud. of Osborne Henry Mavor), B. dramatist (1888–1951), 1931 W, 1932 W, 1933 W, 1943 W
Bridport, Lord. *See* Hood, Alexander
Brienne, Étienne Charles de Loménie de, Cardinal Archbishop of Toulouse, F. ecclesiastic and statesman (1727–94), 1787 D, 1787 G, 1788 H
Brieux, Eugène, F. dramatist (1868–1932), 1917 W
Brighouse, Harold, B. author (1882–1958), 1916 W
Bright, John, B. Liberal politician (1811–89), 1811 Z, 1882 G, 1886 F, 1889 Z
Brighton, Sussex, England: Pavilion, 1815 S; by-election, 1944 B
Brighton Rock (G. Greene), 1938 U
Brihuega, Spain, 1937 C
Brindle, Arthur, Am. musician (b. 1920), 1963 T
Brindley, James, B. engineer (1712–72), 1772 Z
Brisbane, Queensland, Australia, 1859 N
Brissot, Jacques Pierre, F. revolutionary (1754–93), 1791 K, 1793 F
Bristol, England: roads in, 1815 P; riots in, 1831 K
Bristow, George Frederick, Am. musician (1825–98), 1855 T
British and Foreign Bible Society, 1804 R
British Army of Rhine (BAOR), W. Germany agrees to assist costs of, 1962 C
British Association for the Advancement of Science, 1831 P, 1861 P, 1870 P
British Birds (T. Bewick), 1797 P
British Birds (Thorburn), 1915 P
British Broadcasting Company, 1921 O
British Broadcasting Corporation:
- takes over from British Broadcasting Company, 1917 O
  - Boult becomes musical director, 1930 T
  - develops TV, 1932 O
  - TV service begun, 1936 W; resumed, 1946 W
    - BBC Two, 1964 W
- Programmes, Sound:
  - *Any Questions?* 1948 W
  - *The Archers*, serial, 1951 W
  - *Brains Trust*, 1941 W
  - *ITMA*, 1942 W
  - *Children's Hour*, ends, 1961 W
  - *The Man Born to be King*, 1943 W
  - *Radio Newsreel*, 1940 W
  - *Under Milk Wood*, 1954 W
  - Reith Lectures, notable, 1949 O, 1950 W, 1951 O, 1952 O, 1953 P, 1956 P, 1963 R
  - Third Programme, 1946 W
- Programmes, TV:
  - *The Age of Kings*, 1961 W
  - *BBC Three*, 1965 W
  - Coronation of Elizabeth II, 1953 W
  - *Monitor*, 1959 W
  - *Great War* series, 1964 W
  - *That Was The Week That Was*, 1962 W

British Columbia: becomes British colony, 1858 H; joins Dominion of Canada, 1871 G
British Council, 1935 O
British Economic Survey, 1948 O
British Fossils (R. Owen), 1846 P
British General Election of 1945, The (McCallum and Readman), 1947 O
British Guiana: British capture, 1796 N, 1803 J; Britain retains, 1814 H; boundary with Venezuela, 1895 G, L, M, 1899 K; forces sent to restore order, 1953 J; becomes a proclaimed area, 1954 D; state of emergency in, 1964 E; deputy premier arrested, 1964 F; to be independent in 1966, 1965 M
British Institution for the Development of the Fine Arts, 1805 S
British Legion, 1921 O
British Lion Films, 1964 W
British Medical Association, advises doctors to resign from health service, 1965 B
British Museum. *See under* London
British Overseas Airways Corporation, 1939 O
British Petroleum Company, strikes oil in North Sea, 1965 R
British Pressure Groups (J. D. Stewart), 1958 O
British War Economy (Hancock and Gowing), 1949 Q
British West Indian Federation, London Conference on, 1953 L
Britten, Edward Benjamin, B. musician (b. 1913), 1913 Z, 1941 T, 1942 T, 1945 T, 1946 T, 1947 T, 1951 T, 1953 T, 1957 T, 1958 T, 1961 T
Broad, Charlie Dunbar (b. 1887), B. philosopher, 1914 R
Broadcasting:
- wavelengths, settled, 1934 O; redistributed, 1948 P
- comparative survey of foreign broadcasts, 1960 Y
- in Britain:
  - first station, 1920 W
  - from Marconi House, 1922 W
  - Daventry transmitter, 1925 P
  - BBC chartered, 1927 O
  - Pilkington Report, 1962 W
  - pirate radio stations, 1965 W
  - *See also* British Broadcasting Corporation
- in France, operatic first performance, 1954 T
- in Greece, Britain jams Athens broadcasts to Cyprus, 1956 C
- in US:
  - by amateurs, 1919 W
  - of election results, 1920 W
  - East Pittsburgh station, 1920 W
  - medium wave, 1921 P

Brock, Sir Isaac, B. soldier (1769–1812), 1812 K
Brock, Sir Thomas, B. sculptor (1847–1922), 1905 S

Brockden Brown, Charles, Am. author (1771–1810), 1798 U
Brockhaus, Friedrich Arnold, G. publisher (1772–1823), 1796 Q
Brockway, Zebulon Reed, Am. penologist (1827–1920), 1876 O
Brodie, Israel, B. Rabbi (b. 1895), 1957 R
Brogan, Sir Denis William, B. political scientist (b. 1900), 1943 O, 1945 O
Broken Pitcher, The (H. Kleist), 1811 U
Bromberg Canal, Germany, 1772 P
Brontë, Charlotte (afterwards Nicholls), B. novelist (1816–55), 1816 Z, 1847 U, 1855 Z
Brontë, Emily, B. novelist (1818–48), 1847 U
Brook, Peter Stephen Paul, B. producer (b. 1925), 1964 W
Brooke, Basil, lord Brookeborough, N. Ir. premier (b. 1888), 1963 C
Brooke, Henry, Ir. author (?1703–83), 1765 U
Brooke, Rupert, B. poet (1887–1915), 1911 U, 1918 U
Brookeborough, Lord. *See* Brooke, Basil
Brook Kerith, The (G. Moore), 1916 U
Brooklyn, New York, US, Plymouth Congregational Church, 1847 R
Brougham, Henry, Lord Brougham, B. Whig politician (1779–1868), 1779 Z, 1827 O, 1868 Z
Brown, Sir Arthur Whitten, B. aviator, 1919 P
Brown, Ford Madox, B. artist (1821–93), 1852 S
Brown, George Alfred, B. Labour politician (b. 1914), elected deputy leader of Party, 1962 L; minister of Economic Affairs, 1964 K, 1965 O
Brown, John, Am. abolitionist (1800–59), 1800 Z, 1859 Z; at Pottawatomie Creek, 1856 E; raid on Harper's Ferry, 1859 K
Brown, John, and Company, Clydebank shipbuilders, 1951 P, 1964 M
Brown, Joseph Rogers, Am. inventor (1810–76), 1862 P
Brown, Thomas, B. philosopher (1778–1820), 1804 R, 1820 R
Brown University, Providence, Rhode Island, US, 1764 O
Browne, C. F., Am. author under pseudonym 'Artemus Ward' (1834–67), 1862 U
Browne, Thomas Alexander, Austral. author under pseudonym 'Rolf Boldrewood' (1826–1915), 1888 U
Browning, Elizabeth Barrett, B. poet (1806–61), 1806 Z, 1826 U, 1850 U, 1857 U, 1861 Z
Browning, John Moses, Am. inventor (1855–1926), 1900 P
Browning, Robert, B. poet (1812–89), 1833 U, 1835 U, 1868 U
Browning Version, The (T. Rattigan), 1948 W
Bruce, James, B. explorer (1730–94), 1772 P, 1790 P
Bruce, Michael, B. poet (d. 1767), 1767 U
Bruce, Stanley, Lord Bruce, Austral. statesman (b. 1883), 1923 B
Brucke, Die ('The Bridge'), group of artists, 1905 S
Bruckner, Anton, Aus. musician (1824–96), 1824 Z, 1864 T, 1871 T, 1879 T, 1884 T, 1892 T, 1896 Z
Brudenell, James, Earl of Cardigan, B. soldier (1797–1868), 1797 Z
Bruges, Belgium, Canal, blockaded, 1918 D
Belgians recapture, 1918 K
Brugsch, Heinrich Karl, G. Egyptologist (1827–94), 1883 Q
Brunei, Borneo, British protectorate over, 1888 E
Brunel, Isambard Kingdom, B. engineer (1806–59), 1806 Z, 1843 P, 1852 S, 1853 P, 1859 Z
Brüning, Heinrich, G. Centre Party politician (b. 1885), forms ministry, 1930 C, 1931 H; resolves to end reparations payments, 1932 A; resigns, 1932 F
Brunner, Yul, Am. film actor, 1956 W
Bruno (F. Schelling), 1802 R
Brunswick, Karl Wilhelm Ferdinand, Duke of, Aus. general (1735–1806), issues manifesto, 1792 G
Brusilov, Alexei, R. general, 1916 F, J
Brussels, Belgium: riots, 1787 A; revolution in, suppressed, 1790 M; French capture, 1792 L; Liberal meeting in, 1846 F; Palais de Justice in, 1866 S; population, 1881 Y; Conference on Slave Trade, 1889 F, 1890 O; Conference on liquor traffic, 1911 O; Germans occupy, 1914 H; Edith Cavell executed in, 1915 K; Belgian troops enter, 1918 L; Conference on Sino-Japanese War, 1937 L; Germans invade, 1940 E; liberated, 1944 J; Treaty, 1948 C; Socialist demonstrations in, 1950 G; Common Market meeting at, 1950 G
Brutal Friendship, The (F. W. Deakin), 1962 Q
Bryan, William Jennings, Am. Democrat politician (1860–1925), 1915 F; defeated in presidential elections, 1896 L, 1900 L, 1908 L; nominated for vice-presidency, 1924 F
Bryant, Sir Arthur, B. historian (b. 1899), 1957 Q
Bryant, William Cullen, Am. author (1794–1878), 1817 U
Bryce, James, Lord Bryce, B. jurist, historian and politician (1838–1922), 1838 Z, 1864 Q, 1888 O, 1901 Q, 1916 O, 1921 O, 1922 Z
Buber, Martin, Israeli philosopher (1878–1965), 1878 Z, 1937 R, 1945 R
Buchan, John, Lord Tweedsmuir, B. author and diplomat (1875–1940), 1875 Z, 1915 U, 1916 U, 1922 U, 1940 Z
Buchanan, James, Am. Democrat (1791–1868), president of US (1857–61), elected, 1856 L; inaugurated, 1857 C
Buchanan Report on Traffic in Towns, 1963 O
Bucharest, Rumania: occupied by Russians, 1769 L; Austrians capture, 1789 K; Treaty, between Turkey and Russia, 1812 E; legislative assembly at, 1861 M; University, 1864 O; Peace Treaty, 1886 C; armistice at, 1913 G; peace signed at, 1913 H; Germans take, 1916 M; Russians enter, 1944 H
Buch der Lieder (H. Heine), 1827 U
Buchlau Conference, 1908 J
Buchman, Frank, Am. founder of Moral Re-armament (1878–1961), 1939 R
Büchner, Georg, G. author (1813–37), 1835 U
Buck, Pearl S., Am. author, 1931 U
Buckingham Palace Conference, 1914 G
Buckle, George Earle, B. journalist (1854–1935), 1854 Z, 1935 Z
Buckle, Henry Thomas, B. historian (1821–62), 1821 Z, 1857 Q, 1862 Z
Buckle, Richard, B. author (b. 1916), 1954 T
Buda, Hungary, united with Pesth, 1873 L
Budapest, Hungary: Hungarian Academy of Sciences, 1825 O; becomes capital, 1873 L; Convention on Eastern Question, 1877 A; opera in, 1888 T; Soviet government formed in, 1919 C; Roumanians enter, 1919 H; Russians surround, 1944 M; Russians take, 1945 B; Russian attack on, 1956 L
Buddenbrooks (T. Mann), 1901 U
Buddhist Council, Rangoon, 1956 R
Budge, Wallis, B. archaeologist (1857–1934), 1924 Q
Budgets, notable:
in Britain, Peel's free trade, 1842 D
Gladstone's, 1853 D
Hicks-Beach's, 1901 D

Lloyd George's, 1909 L
deficit, 1931 G, H
increased defence spending, 1936 C
leakage, 1936 E
emergency, 1939 J
standard rate of income tax raised to ten shillings, 1941 D
entertainment tax doubled, 1942 D
defence spending curtailed, 1952 M
emergency, 1955 K
increased profits tax, 1960 D
starting-point of surtax raised, 1961 D
emergency, 1961 G, 1964 L
corporation tax, 1965 D
in Germany, Reichstag fails to pass, 1930 G
in US, defence spending, 1939 A, 1950 G, 1951 K
Johnson proposes reduction in, 1964 A
See also Taxation
Buenos Aires, Argentina: surrenders to British, 1806 F; British attack, 1807 N; independence, 1811 H; recognised, 1824 M; separated from Argentina, 1854 D; enters Argentine Confederation, 1859 K; reunited with Argentina, 1860 F; railway to, 1911 P; Pan American Conference at, 1936 M; population, 1960 Y
Buffalo, N.Y., US, British burn, 1813 M
1936 M; population, 1960 Y
Buffalo Bill (W. F. Cody), Am., 1917 Z
Buffet, Bernard, F. artist (b. 1928), 1955 S
Buffon, Georges Louis Leclerk, Comte de, F. naturalist (1707–88), 1778 P, 1786 P, 1788 Z
Bug, River, Russia and Poland, 1795 K
Buganda, Uganda: state of emergency, 1954 E; agreement for, signed, 1955 H; request for independence refused, 1960 M
Bugatti, Ettore, It. racing-car designer, 1947 Z
Bukovina, Austria, formerly in Moldavian principality: occupied by Austria, 1774 J; ceded to Austria, 1775 E
Building Techniques:
cast-iron frame building, 1851 P
reinforced concrete, 1910 S, 1916 S
steel-frame, 1890 P
steel and glass, 1908 S
undulating prefabrication, 1948 S
Building Societies, in Britain, 1874 O
Bukharin, Nikolai, R. politician, expelled, 1929 L; tried, 1938 C
Bukovina, now in Russia: Russia demands cession of, 1940 F; Rumania cedes to Russia, 1947 B
Bulawayo, Rhodesia:
British occupy, 1893 L
Cape railway to, 1897 L
Bulganin, Nikolai, R. leader (b. 1895), 1895 Z, 1947 L; becomes premier, 1955 B; visits Yugoslavia, 1955 E; visits E. Germany, 1955 G; proposes pact with US, 1956 A; visits Britain, 1956 D; calls for reduction in armed forces, 1956 F; proposes Summit Conference, 1958 A; criticises Anglo-US agreement on bases, 1958 C
Bulgaria: risings in, 1876 A, 1877 A; massacres by Turks, 1876 C; autonomy agreed, 1878 G; boundaries reduced, 1878 E–G; independence declared, 1908 K; recognised by Turkey, 1909 D; Russia declares war on, 1944 J; Republic proclaimed, 1946 J
Bulgarian Horrors, The (W. E. Gladstone), 1876 J
Bull Run, Virginia, US, battles of, 1861 G, 1862 H
Buller, Sir Redvers, B. soldier (1839–1908), 1899 M, 1900 F, G; relieves Ladysmith, 1900 B
Bulls, papal. *See* Papal Bulls
Bülow, Bernhard von, Prince, G. statesman (1849–1929), 1849 Z, 1901 C, 1905 G, 1913 O, 1929 Z; as Foreign Secretary, 1897 K; rejects British advances for alliance, 1899 M; becomes Chancellor, 1900 K
Bülow, Friedrich Wilhelm, baron von, Pruss. general, 1813 H, J
Bulwer, William Henry Lytton Earle, lord Bulwer, B. diplomat (1801–72), 1850 D
Bulwer-Lytton, Edward George, lord Lytton, B. novelist (1803–73), 1803 Z, 1834 U, 1835 U, 1843 U, 1873 Z
Bultmann, Rudolf, G. theologian, 1941 R, 1956 R
Bunbury, Sir Thomas Charles, B. racehorse owner (1740–1821), 1779 X
Bunche, Ralph J., Am. diplomat, 1904 Z
Bunker Hill, Mass., US, battle, 1775 F
Bunning, James Bunstone, B. architect (1802–63), 1846 S, 1963 S
Bunsen, Christian Charles Josias, baron von, G. diplomat (1791–60), 1856 O
Bunsen, Robert Wilhelm von, G. chemist (1811–99), 1811 Z, 1841 P, 1850 P, 1859 P, 1861 P, 1899 Z
Bunshaft, Gordon, Am. architect (b. 1907), 1963 S
Burckhardt, Jacob, Swi. art historian (1818–97), 1818 Z, 1855 S, 1860 S, 1897 Z
Burdett, Sir Francis, B. Whig politician (1770–1844), 1818 F
Buren, Martin van, Am. Democrat (1782–1862), president of US (1837–41), inaugurated, 1837 C
Buresch, Karl, Aus. Christian Socialist, forms ministry, 1932 F
Bürger, Gottfried August, G. poet (1748–94), 1773 U, 1786 U
Burgess, Guy, B. diplomat, flees to Russia, 1951 F
Burgess, Thomas, François, Boer politician (1834–81), president of Transvaal, 1872 G
Burghclere Chapel, Berkshire, England, 1926 S
Burgos, Spain, British withdraw from, 1812 J
Burgoyne, John, B. soldier and dramatist (1722–92), 1777 J, 1786 W; surrenders at Saratoga, 1777 K
Burk, B. F., Am. scientist, 1955 P
Burke, Arleigh Albert, Am. admiral, 1901 Z
Burke, Edmund, B. statesman (1729–97), 1764 U, 1782 G, 1790 C, 1797 Z; proposes economic reform, 1780 E; in Rockingham's coalition, 1782 C; impeaches W. Hastings, 1787 E; condemns French Revolution, 1790 B; writings, 1769 O, 1770 O, 1774 O, 1775 O, 1777 O, 1790 O, 1791 O, 1796 O
Burke, Thomas Henry, B. administrator (1829–82), 1882 E
Burma: war with Siam, 1767 H; acknowledges suzerainty of China, 1769 N; British Wars with, 1852 D, M, 1853 F, 1885 K; Britain annexes, 1886 A; British occupation recognised by China, 1886 G; government of, separated from India, 1935 H; Japanese invade, 1942 A; North region is cleared of Japanese, 1944 M; independent Republic proclaimed, 1948 A
Burma Road, S.E. Asia, 1940 G, K
Burne-Jones, Sir Edward Coley, B. artist (1833–98), 1833 Z, 1884 S, 1896 S, 1898 Z
Burney, Charles, B. musicologist (1726–1814), 1773 T, 1776 T
Burney, Fanny. *See* Arblay, Frances D'
Burnham, Forbes, Guianian, People's National Congress, forms ministry, 1964 M
Burnham, James, Am. author, 1942 O
Burning Bush (S. Undset), 1930 U
Burning Peach, The (L. MacNeice), 1963 U
Burns, John, B. trade union leader (1858–1943), 1858 Z, 1911 H, 1943 Z

Burns, Robert, Scottish poet (1759–96), 1786 U, 1790 U, 1796 Z
Burnside, Ambrose Everitt, Am. Unionist general (1824–81), 1862 M
Burroughs, William, Am. author, 1964 U
Burslem, Staffs., England, 1769 P
Burton, Sir Richard Francis, B. explorer and scholar (1821–90), 1854 P, 1856 P, 1885 U
Burundi, Kingdom, independence proclaimed, 1962 G
Bury, John Bagnell, B. classical scholar and historian (1861–1927), 1861 Z, 1923 Q, 1927 Z
Busa, Nigeria, British protectorate over, 1895 A
Busch, Alan, B. musician, 1900 Z, 1943 T
Busch, Wilhelm, G. caricaturist (1832–1908), 1859 S
'Bus. *See* Omnibus
Bushnell, David, Am. inventor of torpedo (1750–1824), 1777 P
Business as a System of Power (R. A. Brady), 1943 O
Busoni, Ferruccio Benvenuto, It. musician (1866–1924), 1912 T, 1925 T
Buss, Frances Mary, B. educationalist (1827–94), 1850 O
Bustamante, Alexander, Jamaic. Labour leader, 1962 D
Bustamente, José, Peruv. president, 1945 F, 1948 K
Butadiene, synthetic rubber from, 1909 P
Bute, John Stuart, Earl of, B. Tory (1713–92), becomes prime minister, 1763 D
Butler, Josephine Elizabeth (*née* Grey), B. social reformer (1828–1906), 1828 Z, 1906 Z
Butler, Richard Austen, Lord Butler, B. Conservative politician (b. 1902), 1902 Z, 1941 G; introduces Education Act, 1944 O; becomes Chancellor of Exchequer, 1951 K; introduces credit squeeze, 1955 K; deputises for Eden, 1956 L; becomes Home Secretary, 1957 A; introduces Criminal Justice bill, 1961 D; introduces Commonwealth Immigration bill, 1961 L; retires from politics, 1965 A
Butler, Reg, B. sculptor (b. 1913), 1952 S, 1953 S
Butler, Samuel, B. author (1835–1902), 1835 Z, 1872 U, 1901 U, 1902 Z, 1903 U
Butler, William, B. soldier (d. 1781), 1778 L
Butlin, Sir William Edmund ('Billy'), B. founder of holiday camps (b. 1899), 1937 W
Butt, Clara, B. singer (1873–1936), 1873 Z, 1915 T, 1936 Z
Butter, substitute for, statutory limit to, 1902 O
Buxar, Bengal, India, battle, 1764 K
By Love Possessed (J. G. Cozzens), 1958 U
Byrd, Richard, Am. admiral and explorer (1888–1957), 1926 P, 1929 P
Byrnes, James F., Am. statesman (b. 1879), becomes US secretary of state, 1945 G; bids for German co-operation with US, 1946 J; retires, 1947 A
Byron, John, B. navigator (1723–86), 1766 N, P
Byron, George Gordon, Lord Byron, B. poet (1788–1824), 1788 Z, 1807 U, 1809 U, 1813 U, 1814 U, 1816 U, 1817 U, 1818 U, 1819 U, 1824 D

C

Cabanis, Pierre, F. physiologist (1757–1808), 1789 O
Cabaret entertainment, 1922 W
Cabell, James Branch, Am. author (1879–1958), 1919 U
Cabet, Etienne, F. author and politician (1788–1856), 1842 O
Cabinet Secretariat, British, formed, 1916 O
Cabinet, War, end of British, 1919 K
Cable-making machine, 1792 P
Cable, submarine, 1850 P
Cable, transatlantic, 1857 P, 1865 P
Cabral, Costa, fount of Thomar, Port. dictator (1796–1854), 1846 E
Cadbury, George, B. chocolate manufacturer and social reformer (1839–1922), 1900 O
Cadiz, Spain, French troops enter, 1823 H
Cadmium, a metallic element, 1818 P
Caecilian Society for Performance of Sacred Music, 1785 T
Caen, France, Allies take, 1944 G
Caesar and Cleopatra (G. B. Shaw), 1898 W
Caesium, an element, is isolated, 1861 P
Cage, John, Am. musician, 1964 T
Cahiers de la Quinzaine, Les (C. Péguy), 1900 U
Caillaux, Joseph, F. Republican (1863–1940), forms ministry, 1911 F; resigns, 1912 A; becomes finance minister, 1914 A; wife of, kills G. Calmette, 1914 C; arrested for treason, 1918 A
Caillebotte, Gustave, F. art collector, 1894 S
Caine, Sir Thomas Henry Hall, B. novelist (1853–1931), 1853 Z, 1894 U, 1901 U, 1931 Z
Caine Mutiny, The (H. Wouk), 1951 U
Ca Ira! (F. Freiligrath), 1846 U
Caird, John, B. theologian and philosopher (1820–1898), 1880 R
Cairo, Egypt, 1811 C; J. B. Kléber in, 1800 C; falls to British, 1801 F; British occupation, 1882 J; Nationalist riots in, 1919 C; Stack's murder in, 1924 L; Conference of Allies on war in Far East, 1943 L; Afro-Asian Organisation meets in, 1959 D; Conference of non-aligned states at, 1964 K
Calais, France: submarine cable from, 1850 P; is liberated, 1944 J
Calcium carbonate, decomposition of, 1862 P
Calculating machine, 1823 P
Calculus, 1852 P, 1864 P
Calcutta, India: E. India Company in, 1764 N, 1775 N; Anglican bishop appointed, 1814 R; riots, 1918 J; population, 1950 Y
Calder, Alexander, Am. sculptor (b. 1898), 1932 S, 1945 S, 1958 S
Calder Hall, Cumb., England, nuclear power station, 1956 P
Caleb Williams (W. Godwin), 1794 U
Calendars:
  Chinese, reformed, 1911 M
  French Revolutionary, 1792 J
  Vatican Council approve principle of fixed Easter, 1963 K
Caledonian Canal, Scotland, 1803 P
Calhoun, John Caldwell, Am. statesman (1782–1850), 1844 D
Calico, printing by copper cylinder, 1783 P
California, State, US: gold rush, 1847 P; US obtains, 1848 E; admitted to Union, 1850 G; *Wellingtonia gigantea* in, 1853 P; earthquake, 1892 O; University, cyclotron at, 1940 P
Californium, element, 1950 P
Calinescu, Armand, Rum. premier, assassinated, 1939 J
Callaghan, James, B. Labour politician (b. 1912), chancellor of Exechequer, 1964 K, L
Callas, Maria (G. B. Meneghini), Am. prima donna (b. 1923), 1923 Z
Calmette, Gaston, F. journalist (1858–1914), 1914 A, C

Calonne, Charles Alexandre de, F. statesman (1734–1802), 1783 L, 1785 N; financial reforms rejected, 1787 B; is banished, 1787 D
Calverley, Charles Stuart, B. poet and parodist (1831–84), 1872 U
Camargo Ballet Society, 1930 T
Cambacérès, Jean Jacques Régis de, duke of Parma, F. politician (1753–1824), 1796 O
Cambodia: as French Protectorate, 1863 H; as French Colony, 1887 N; independence, 1954 G
Cambon, Paul, F. statesman (1843–1924), 1843 Z, 1924 Z
Cambrai, France: British advance on, 1917 L; British take, 1918 K
Cambridge, England, University:
  Evangelical movement, 1783 R
  religious tests abolished, 1871 O
  residence for women, 1871 O
  professorship of experimental physics, 1871 P
  Institutions:
    Churchill College, 1960 O
    Fitzwilliam Museum, 1837 S
    Girton College, 1869 O
    Library, 1934 S
    Mullard Observatory, 1957 P
    Richmond Lectures, 1959 U, 1962 U
    Scott Polar Research Institute, 1926 P
    University Extension Lectures, 1870 O
Cambridge, Mass., US: moon photographed from, 1851 P; Harvard University, Carpenter Center, 1963 S
Cambridge, duke of. *See* George William Frederick
Cambridge Ancient History, The (ed. Bury), 1923 Q
Cambridge Economic History of Europe, 1941 Q
Cambridge History of English Literature, The, 1907 Q
Cambridge Medieval History, The, 1911 Q
Cambridge Modern History, The, 1899 Q
Cambridge Modern History, The New, 1957 Q
Cambridge Philological Society, 1868 Q
Camden, S. Carolina, US, 1780 H
Camden Society, 1838 Q
Camera:
  image-dissector, 1956 P
  photo'-flash bulb, 1930 P
  See also Photography
Cameroons, The, S.W. Africa: German occupation, 1884 D; Anglo-German convention, 1892 K; frontier with Nigeria, 1893 C, 1913 C; frontier with French Congo, 1894 C; Germans surrender, 1916 B; League mandate for, 1922 G; becomes independent republic, 1960 A; North, plebiscite for joining Nigeria, 1961 B; South, plebiscite for joining Cameroun, 1961 B
Camilla (F. Burney), 1796 U
Campaign for Nuclear Disarmament (C.N.D.):
  Aldermaston March, 1956 O, 1963 O
  sit-down demonstrations, 1961 O
  trial of Committee of 100 members, 1962 B
Campbell, Alexander, Scot, minister, founder of 'Campbellites' (1788–1866), 1831 R
Campbell, Colin, lord Clyde, B. soldier (1792–1863), 1792 Z, 1863 Z; relieves Lucknow, 1857 L
Campbell, John, Scot, author (1708–75), 1763 R, 1774 O
Campbell, Sir Malcolm, B. racing-champion (1885–1945), 1935 P, 1939 P
Campbell, Mrs. Patrick (Beatrice, *née* Tanner), B. actress (1865–1940), 1865 Z, 1940 Z
Campbell, Thomas, B. poet (1777–1844), 1799 U, 1809 U
Campbell-Bannerman, Sir Henry, B. Liberal statesman (1836–1908), 1836 Z, 1905 L, 1906 A; as War Secretary, 1895 F; leader of Liberal Party, 1899 A; becomes premier, 1905 M; moves to restrict Lords' powers, 1907 F; retires, 1908 D
Campe, Joachin Heinrich, G. educationalist (1746–1818), 1785 O
Camperdown, N. Holland, battle, 1797 K
Camperdown, lord. *See* Duncan, Adam
Campo Formio, N. Italy, Peace between France and Austria, 1797 K
Camponanes, Pedro Rodriguez It. author (1723–1802), 1775 O
Camps, holiday, 1937 W
Camus, Albert, F. author (1913–1960), 1913 Z, 1942 U, 1947 U
Canada:
  ceded to Britain, 1763 B
  Quebec Act for, 1774 D
  American troops driven from, 1776 C
  Upper and Lower, established, 1791 E
  emigration to, 1816 O
  frontier with US, defined, 1818 K, 1842 H, 1846 F
  railways in, 1836 P, 1886 P
  Council for, 1839 H
  Union of Upper and Lower, 1840 G
  discovery of northern coasts, 1850 P
  Dominion established, 1867 C
  Purchase of Hudson's Bay Co. territories, 1869 L
  British Columbia joins Dominion,1871 G
  Confederation, 1872 G
  resolution on preserving union with Britain, 1911 B
Canadian Question, The (G. Smith), 1891 O
Canals:
  Bromberg, 1772 P
  Bruges, blocked, 1918 D
  Caledonian, 1803 P
  Corinth, 1893 P
  Dortmund–Ems, 1899 P
  Eider to Baltic, 1784 P
  Elbe–Trave, 1900 P
  Ellesmere, 1805 P
  Firth–Clyde, 1790 P
  Göta, 1832 P
  Kiel, 1895 P
  Manchester Ship, 1893 P
  Oxford-Birmingham, 1790 P
  Panama, opened, 1914 P. For negotiations, building, traffic, etc., *see under* Panama
  Regent's, London, 1820 P
  Suez, opened, 1869 L
    Britain purchases shares in, 1875 L. For negotiations, building, traffic, etc., *see under* Suez
Canary Islands, Pact to counter German designs in, 1907 E
Canberra, Australia, 1954 D
  Parliament House, 1927 E
Candia. *See* Crete
Candida (G. B. Shaw), 1897 W
Candid Examination of Theism, A (G. Romanes), 1878 Q
Candolle, Augustin de, F. botanist (1778–1841), 1813 P
Can Government Cure Unemployment? (Angell and Wright), 1931 O
Cannan, Edwin, B. economist (1861–1935), 1914 O
Canned Foods, 1874 P, 1880 P, 1892 P
Cannes, France, Conference on Reparations, 1922 A
Canning, George, B. statesman, Tory (1770–1827), 1770 Z, 1807 C; duel with Castlereagh, 1809 J; returns to Cabinet, 1816 F; resigns, 1820 M; becomes foreign secretary, 1822 J; role in inde-

Canning, George B.—*contd.* pendence of S. American states, 1924 M; sends troops to Portugal, 1826 M; becomes premier, 1827 D; death, 1827 G
Canning, Stratford de, Lord Stratford de Canning, B. diplomat (1786–1880), 1854 A
Canonisations, 1887 R
Canova, Antonio, It. sculptor (1757–1822), 1779 S, 1782 S, 1793 S, 1802 S, 1808 S, 1815 S, 1822 Z
Canton, China: opened to British commerce, 1842 H; falls to British and French, 1851 M; R.N. bombards, 1856 L; anti-British incidents, 1925 E; Chiang Kai-shek enters, 1936 H; Japanese take, 1938 K
Canzoni e Versi (Leopardi), 1824 U
Cape Breton Island, Canada, ceded to Britain, 1763 B
Čapek, Karel, Czech. author (1890–1938), 1890 Z, 1923 W, 1938 Z
Cape of Good Hope (Cape Colony), S. Africa: British seizure prevented, 1781 D; British occupation, 1795 J, 1806 A; becomes British Colony, 1814 H; astronomical observations from, 1834 P; landing of convicts forbidden, 1849 L; Basutoland added to, 1871 H; responsible government in, 1872 K
Capetown, S. Africa, 1908 K; Macmillan's speech in Parliament, 1960 B
Capital (Marx, English edition), 1886 O
Capitalism, study of, 1901 Q
Capital Punishment:
in Britain, royal commission, 1953 O
movement for abolition, 1955 O
Silverman's bill, 1956 P, 1964 M
abolition, 1965
in Russia, reintroduced, 1950 A
in Sweden, abolished, 1921 E
Capitals:
Australia (Canberra), 1927 E
Brazil (Brasilia), 1957 A, 1960 O
Canada (Ottawa), 1858 O
Congo (Léopoldville), 1961 E
French W. Africa (Dakar), 1904 N
W. Germany (Bonn), 1949 E
Hungary (Budapesth), 1873 L
Italy (Florence), 1864 J; (Rome), 1870 K
New Zealand (Wellington), 1865 N
Norway (Oslo), 1925 A
Pakistan (Rawalpindi), 1959 K
Queensland (Brisbane), 1859 N
Transvaal (Pretoria), 1860 D
Viet-Nam (Saigon), 1949 F
Turkey (Ankara), 1923 K
U.S.A. (New York), 1788 J; (Washington), 1800 F, 1801 C
Capo d'Istria, Count, elected president of Greece, 1827 D; assassinated, 1831 K
Caporetto Campaign, Italy, Italians routed, 1917 K
Cappellari, Bartolommeo Alberto. *See* Gregory XVI, Pope
Cappadocia, North, archaeological expedition to, 1906 Q
Capra, Frank, Am. film director, 1946 W, 1948 W
Caprera, Isle, off Sardinia, 1867 L
Caprices de Marianne, Les (A. de Musset), 1833 U
Caprivi, Georg Leo von, G. chancellor and general (1831–99), 1890 C, 1894 K
Captains Courageous (R. Kipling), 1897 U
Carabobo, Venezuela, 1821 F
Caracas, Venezuela, Conference of Organisation of American States, 1954 C
Carbajal, president, of Mexico, 1914 G
Carbonari, Italian secret society, 1820 G, 1821 C
Carbon dioxide, 1774 P
Carbonic acid, 1774 P
Carbon-13, isotope, 1946 P
Carbon-zinc battery, 1841 P
Carchemis, Turkey, archaeological expedition to, 1911 Q
Cárdenas, Lazaro, president of Mexico, 1934 G
Cardigan, earl of. *See* Brundenell, J
Cardwell, Edward, lord Cardwell, B. Liberal politician (1813–86), 1813 Z, 1871 H, 1886 Z
Caretaker, The (H. Pinter), 1960 W
Carey, Henry Charles, Am. economist (1793–1879), 1858 O
Carey, Joseph Maull, Am. Republican politician (1845–1924), 1894 H
Cariatides, Les (T. de Banville), 1842 U
Caribbean Commission, 1942 O
Caribbean Organisation for Economic Co-operation, 1960 F
Caribbean Sea, British bases leased to US, 1940 J
Carinthia, plebiscite in, 1920 H
Carl August, elector of Saxe-Weimar (1758–1828), 1816 E
Carlile, Wilson, B. evangelical leader (1847–1942), 1847 Z, 1882 R, 1942 Z
Carlist War, in Spain, 1834 G
Carlos I, King of Portugal, 1907 B
Carlos, Don, proclaimed King of Spain, 1872 D, 1876 B
Carlsbad Decrees, 1819 J
Carlson, Chester, Am. inventor of xerography, 1946 P
Carlyle, Alexander James, B. historian of philosophy (1861–1943), 1936 Q
Carlyle, Thomas, B. essayist and historian (1795–1881), 1795 Z, 1828 U, 1833 U, 1837 Q, 1841 U 1843 U, 1845 U, 1858 Q, 1881 Z
Carme sui sepolcri (U. Foscolo), 1807 U
Carmen (P. Mérimée), 1847 W
Carmona, Antonio de Fragosa, Sp. general and dictator, 1926 G, 1927 B, 1928 C
Carnarvon, earl of. *See* Herbert
Carnatic, The, region of Madras, S. India, 1799 N; Hyder Ali conquers, 1780 J
Carné, Marcel, F. film director, 1946 W, 1958 W
Carnegie, Andrew, B. steel manufacturer and philanthropist (1835–1919), 1835 Z, 1880 P, 1886 O, 1911 O, 1919 Z
Carnegie Trust Co., 1911 A
Carnival (C. Mackenzie), 1912 U
Carnot, Lazare Nicolas Marguerite, F. soldier (1753–1823), 1797 J, 1803 P, 1810 O
Carnot, Nicolas Léonard Sadi, F. physician (1796–1832), 1824 P
Carol I, King of Rumania (1866–1914), formerly Charles of Hohenzollern, 1866 B
Carol II, King of Rumania, 1940 F; flees, 1940 J
Carolina, South, state, US: tariff problems in, 1833 A, C; leaves Union, 1860 M
Caroline Princess of Wales (1768–1821), 1820 M, 1821 A, G, H; demands recognition as Queen, 1820 F; bill to dissolve marriage with George IV, 1820 G, L; enquiry into conduct of, 1820 L
Caroline Matilda, Queen of Denmark (1751–75), sister of George III, 1770 J
Caroline Islands, Pacific: Germany's dispute with Spain, 1885 M; Germany purchases, 1899 B
Carothers, Wallace, H., Am. inventor of nylon stockings, 1937 P
Carpenter, Malcolm Scott, Am. cosmonaut, 1962 P
Carpenter, Mary, B. philanthropist (1807–77), 1851 O
Carpet-sweeper, 1865 P
Carpets, manufacture by Brussels loom, 1845 P

Carr, Benjamin, Am. musician (1769–1831), 1796 T
Carr, Edward Hallett, B. historian (b. 1892), 1939 O, 1942 O, 1951 Q
Carrà, Carlo, It. artist (b. 1881), 1910 S
Car-racing, 1965 X
Carranza, Venustiano, president of Mexico, 1914 E, 1915 K, 1916 L, 1920 E
Carré, E. C., F. inventor of freezing-machine, 1850 P
Carriage-lathe, 1797 P
Carritt, Edgar Frederick, B. philosopher (1876–1961), 1914 S, 1947 R
Carrizal, Mexico, battle, 1916 F
Carroll, John, Am. Roman Catholic bishop (1735–1815), 1790 R
Carroll, Lewis. *See* Dodgson, Charles
Carr-Saunders, Sir Alexander, B. economist (b. 1886), 1936 O
Carry on, Jeeves (P. G. Wodehouse), 1925 U
Carson, Edward, lord Carson, B. Unionist politician (1854–1935), 1854 Z, 1912 J, 1935 Z; resigns from Cabinet, 1918 A; demands repeal of Home Rule, 1919 G
Carson, Rachel, Am. author (b. 1907), 1963 P
Carstairs, George, B. philosopher (b. 1916), 1963 R
Carstens, Armus Jacob, G. artist (1754–98), 1795 S
Cartagena Pact, between Britain, France and Spain against Germany, 1907 E
Carte, Richard D'Oyly, B. promoter of opera (1844–1901), 1881 W
Carter, Elliot, Am. musician (b. 1908), 1957 T
Carter, Howard, B. artist and archaeologist (1874–1939), 1922 Q
Carter, Jack, Am. musician, 1958 T
Carter, John Waynglebe, B. bibliographer (b. 1905), 1948 Q
Carthaginian Peace, The (E. Mantoux), 1946 O
Cartography, 1779 P
Cartoons:
political, 1784 S, 1918 S, 1922 S
satirical, 1779 S
strip, 1859 S
Cartridge-cases, brass, 1882 P
Cartwright, Edmund, B. dissenting minister and cotton-spinning pioneer (1743–1823), 1786 P
Cartwright, George, B. explorer, 1798 P
Cartwright, John, B. political reformer (1740–1824), 1774 O, 1776 O
Cask, The (F. Wills Crofts), 1920 T
Casson, Sir Hugh, B. architect (b. 1910), 1951 S
Cass Timberlane (S. Lewis), 1945 U
Castelar y Ripoli, Emilio, Sp. statesman (1832–99), 1873 J, 1874 A
Castelfidardo, Italy, Cavour's victory at, 1860 J
Castiglione delle Stiviere, Lombardy, Italy, 1796 H
Cast-iron bridge, 1773 P
Castle, The (Kafka), 1926 U
Castle of Otranto, The (H. Walpole), 1765 U
Castle Rackrent (M. Edgeworth), 1800 U
Castlereagh, viscount. *See* Stewart, Robert
Castner, H. Y., Am. chemist (1858–99), 1894 P
Castro, Cipriano, Venezuelan leader, 1899 K, 1902 M, 1908 F
Castro, Fidel, Cuban politician (b. 1921), 1958 D, 1959 A, 1961 D; becomes premier, 1959 B; states Russia will establish base in Cuba, 1962 J; visits Russia, 1963 D
Casuarina Tree, The (W. S. Maugham), 1926 U
Catalina (H. Ibsen), 1850 W
Catalogue of Nebulae (W. Herschel), 1786 P
Catalogue of the Languages of the Nations (Hervás y Panduro), 1800 Q
Catalonia, Spain: home rule movement, 1917 H; autonomy granted, 1932 J
Catalysis among enzymes, 1906 P
Catania, Sicily, Allies capture, 1943 H
Catcher in the Rye, The (J. D. Salinger), 1951 U
Cateau, Le, France, 1918 K
Catéchism des Industriels (St. Simon), 1823 O
Cathar, India, annexed by E. India Company, 1832 H
Cathay (E. Pound), 1915 U
Cathédrale, La (J. K. Huysmans), 1898 U
Cathedral, The (H. Walpole), 1922 U
Catherine II ('The Great') empress of Russia (1762–96), 1764 N, 1766 R, 1780 F, 1781 B, 1787 A, Q, 1796 L
Catherine Furze (M. Rutherford), 1893 U
Cathode rays, experiments with, 1897 P
Catholic Association, in Ireland, 1823 E
Catholic Emancipation, in Britain: Pitt advocates, 1800 J; Pitt resigns on issue of, 1801 C; Grenville refuses to grant, 1807 C; bills for, defeated, 1813 E, 1821 D, 1825 E; Wellington supports, 1829 C; achieved, 1829 D
Catholic Parties. *See under* Political Parties
Cat on a Hot Tin Roof (T. Williams), 1954 W
Caton, H., F. electrical engineer, 1875 P
Cato Street conspiracy, 1820 B
Caucasus, Russian acquisitions south of, 1829 J
Caudwell, Christopher, Am. author, 1937 U
Caught (H. Green), 1943 U
Causes of World War III (C. Wright Mills), 1959 O
Cavaignac, Louis, F. general (1802–57), 1848 F
Cavalcade (N. Coward), 1931 W
Cavalotti, Felice, It. Radical, 1896 C
Cave, Sir Stephen, B. politician (1820–80), 1875 M, 1876 C
Cavell, Edith, B. nurse (1865–1915); executed, 1915 K
Cavendish, lord Frederick Charles, B. administrator (1836–82), chief secretary for Ireland, murdered, 1882 E
Cavendish, Henry, B. natural philosopher (1731–1810), 1766 P, 1784 P, 1785 P, 1789 P, 1798 P, 1810 Z
Cavendish, Spencer, Compton, marquess of Hartington, duke of Cambridge, B. Liberal (1833–1908); elected leader, 1875 B; notes against Liberal government, 1886 F
Cavendish, William, duke of Devonshire (1808–91), 1870 O, 1891 M
Cavour, Camillo, Count, It. statesman (1810–61), 1810 Z, 1859 O, 1861 Z; as minister of Piedmont, 1850 K, 1852 L; meets Napoleon III, 1858 G; rejects Austrian ultimatum for Sardinia to disarm, 1859 D; recalled to Sardinia, 1860 A; defeats papal troops, 1860 J
Cawnpore, India: British massacred, 1857 F, G; British recapture, 1857 M
Cayenne, F. Guiana, 1809 N
Cayley, Arthur, B. mathematician (1821–95), 1845 P
Cecil, lord David Gascoyne, B. author (b. 1902), 1902 Z
Cecil, Robert, Arthur Talbot Gascoyne, 3rd marquess of Salisbury, B. Conservative statesman (1830–1903), 1830 Z, 1885 L, 1895 L; becomes foreign secretary, 1878 D; attends Berlin Conference, 1878 F; becomes Conservative leader, 1881 D; becomes prime minister and foreign minister, 1885 F; resigns, 1886 A; forms ministry, 1886 G; resigns, 1892 G, H; forms ministry, 1895 F; proposes partition of Turkey, 1895 H; reforms ministry, 1900 K; upholds British isolation, 1901 E; retires, 1902 G

Cecil, Robert Arthur James Gascoyne, 5th marquess of Salisbury, B. Conservative politician (b. 1893), attacks British policy on Africa, 1961 C
Cecilia (F. Burvey), 1782 U
Cecil, or the Adventures of a Coxcomb (C. Gore), 1841 U
Celanese, invented, 1865 P
Celibates, The (G. Moore), 1895 U
Céline, L. F., F. author, 1932 U
Cellophane, invented, 1912 P
Cell, photo-electric, 1904 P
Cell theories, 1839 P, 1863 P
Cellular, theory of plants, 1838 P
Celluloid, invented, 1869 P; roll-films, 1889 P
Cement, Portland, 1824 P
Cement production, statistics of, 1932 Y, 1940 Y, 1959 Y
Censorship:
of art and criticism, in Germany, 1936 U
of films, in Britain, 1920 W, 1951 W
of music, in Germany, 1934 T, 1935 T
in Russia, 1931 T
of plays, in France, 1775 W, 1800 W
of press. *See* Press, censorship of
Census of population, first accurate, 1801 Y
Census of production, British, first, 1907 O
Centaur, The (J. Updike), 1963 U
Central African Federation (of Northern and Southern Rhodesia and Nysaland): scheme for, 1952 F; Britain rejects request for status as separate state within Commonwealth, 1956 H; elections for, boycotted by European opposition and all African parties, 1962 D; Nyasaland's right to secede acknowledged, 1962 M; UN asks Britain to transfer forces of, to Southern Rhodesia, 1963 K; Dissolved, 1963 M. *See also* Malawi: Rhodesia; Zambia
Central African Republic, French, becomes independent, 1960 G
Central America, Confederation of United Provinces of, 1823 G
Central American Union (of Guatemala, Honduras and San Salvador), constitution, 1921 J
Central Planning and Control in War and Peace (O. Franks), 1947 O
Central Treaty Organisation (CENTO), name changed from Baghdad Pact, 1959 H
Centre Parties. *See under* Political Parties
Ceres, first asteroid, discovered, 1801 P
Cetywayo, Zululand, captured, 1879 H
Ceylon: Dutch surrender to Britain, 1795 B; Britain retains, 1801 K, 1815 C; tea production in, 1909 Y; becomes self-governing dominion, 1948 B; state of emergency in, 1958 E
Cézanne, Paul, F. artist (1839–1906), 1839 Z, 1867 S, 1872 S, 1873 S, 1874 S, 1877 S, 1883 S, 1884 S, 1890 S, 1900 S, 1904 S, 1905 S, 1906 Z, 1964 S
Chabrier, Alexis Emmanuel, F. musician (1841–94) 1883 T, 1950 T
Chad, Lake, Cen. Africa: explored, 1823 P, 1852 P; land east of, leased to Germany, 1893 L
Chad Republic, becomes independent, 1960 G
Chadwick, Sir Edwin, B. sanitary reformer (1800–95), 1800 Z, 1842 O, 1890 Z
Chadwick, Lynn Russell, B. sculptor (b. 1914), 1955 S, 1956 S
Chadwick, Sir James, B. physicist (b. 1891), 1921 P, 1932 P
Chagall, Marc, R. artist (b. 1887), 1908 S, 1912 S, 1922 S, 1926 S, 1927 S, 1945 S, 1950 S
Chakotin, Serge, R. political economist, 1939 O
Chaliapin, Feodor Ivanovich, R. bass singer, 1873 Z, 1938 Z
Chalk Garden, The (E. Bagnold), 1954 W
Challe, Maurice, F. soldier, leads Algerian revolt, 1961 D
Chalmers, Thomas, Scot. church leader (1780–1847), 1843 R
Chamberlain, Austen, B. Conservative and Unionist leader (1863–1937), 1863 Z, 1937 Z; becomes chancellor of Exchequer, 1903 J; elected Unionist leader, 1921 C; becomes foreign secretary, 1924 L
Chamberlain, Houston Stewart, B. political author (1855–1927), 1899 O
Chamberlain, Joseph, B. Liberal Unionist leader (1836–1914), 1836 Z, 1896 L, 1897 G, 1914 Z; becomes president of Board of Trade, 1880 D; votes against Liberal government, 1886 F; becomes Liberal Unionist leader, 1891 M; as Colonial Secretary, 1895 F, 1897 F; bids for *entente* with Germany, 1898 C, E; stand on issue of Transvaal franchise, 1899 G; Leicester speech, 1899 L; organises Conservative electoral victory, 1900 K; anti-German speech, 1901 K; visits S. Africa, 1903 B; is converted to Imperial Preference, 1903 E; resigns to test feeling on Imperial Preference, 1903 J
Chamberlain, Neville, B. Conservative politician (1869–1940), 1869 Z, 1940 Z; as Chancellor of Exchequer, 1923 E, 1931 L; forms National ministry, 1937 E; censured for appeasement of Italy, 1938 B; visits Hitler, 1938 J; at Munich Conference, 1938 J; meets Mussolini, 1939 A; fails in negotiations over Poland, 1939 H; resigns from premiership, 1940 E; retires, 1940 K
Chamber Music, notable, by:
Bartók, 1908 T
Beethoven, 1806 T
Bloch, 1924 T
Boccherini, 1787 T
Boulez, 1959 T
Franck, 1880 T
Haydn, 1771 T, 1781 T, 1797 T
Mozart, 1785 T
Schubert, 1819 T, 1825 T
Stravinsky, 1924 T
Walton, 1947 T
Trio to perform, formed by Thibaud, Cortot and Casals, 1930 T
Chamber of Commerce, London, 1882 O
Chambers, John Graham, B. athlete and journalist (1843–83), 1866 X
Chambers, Robert, B. publisher and author (1802–1871), 1844 P
Chambers, Raymond William, B. author (1874–1942), 1930 Q
Chambers, Sir William, B. architect (1726–96), 1776 S
Chambord, Henri Charles Ferdinand, comte de, F. pretender as 'King Henri V' (1820–83), 1820 J, 1873 H, 1883 H; Antwerp Declaration, 1872 A; Frohsdorf Letter, 1873 K; refuses to accept tricolour, 1873 K
Chambre Chronophotographique, 1888 P
Chamiso, Adalbert von, G. poet (1781–1838), 1813 U
Chamoun, President of Lebanon, 1958 G
Champagne, France, 1917 E: French bombardment, 1915 B; Joffre's offensive, 1915 J
Champlain, Lake, N. America, 1776 K, 1814 J
Chance (J. Conrad), 1914 U
Chancellorsville, Va., US, Confederate victory at, 1863 E
Chandernagore, Bengal, India, French settlement, 1778 N

Chandler, Richard, B. antiquary and traveller (1738–1810), 1775 P
Channel Tunnel: first mooted, 1882 O; report on, 1963 J; rail, Anglo-French agreement on, 1964 B
Chansons (Béranger), 1815 U
Chantrey, Sir Francis Legatt, B. sculptor (1782–1841), 1782 Z, 1817 S
bequest, 1841 A
Chaos et la Nuit, 1963 W
Chaplin, Charles, Am. film actor and director (b. 1889), 1889 Z, 1914 W, 1918 W, 1921 W, 1923 W, 1928 W, 1931 W, 1936 W, 1940 W, 1947 W, 1952 W, 1957 W
Chappe, Claude, F. engineer (1763–1805), 1793 P
Charcot, Jean Martin, F. physician (1825–93), 1825 Z, 1873 P, 1893 Z
Chadin, Jean Baptiste Siméon, F. artist (1699–1779), 1775 S
Chardonnet, Hilaire, Comte de, F. inventor (1839–1924), 1887 P
Charge of the Light Brigade, 1854 K
Charity bazaars, 1833 O
Charleroi, S.W. Belgium, 1794 F
Charles, archduke of Austria (1771–1847), general, 1796 H, 1799 F, J, 1800 D
Charles I, emperor of Austria (1916–18), 1916 L; abdicates, 1918 L; *coup d'état* fails, 1921 C, K
Charles, Prince of Wales (b. 1948), 1948 Z
created Prince of Wales, 1958 G
Charles, Prince of Denmark, elected King Haakon of Norway, 1905 L
Charles X, King of France (1757–1836), 1826 N; as Comte d'Artois, 1791 G; accession, 1824 J; dissolves National Guard, 1827 D; appoints Polignac premier, 1829 H; dissolves chambers, 1830 E; ordinances of, 1830 G; abdicates, 1830 H
Charles, Prince of Hohenzollern, becomes Carol I of Rumania, 1866 B
Charles III, duke of Parma, 1854 C
Charles, Crown Prince of Roumania, elected King, 1930 F
Charles III, King of Spain (1759–88), 1767 C
Charles IV, King of Spain (1788–1808), 1800 K; abdicates, 1808 E
Charles XIII, King of Sweden (1809–18), 1809 C, 1818 B; adopts Bernadotte as heir, 1810 H; becomes King of Sweden and Norway, 1814 L
Charles XIV, King of Sweden (1818–44), 1818 B, 1844 C. *See also* Bernadotte, Jean
Charles XV, King of Sweden (1859–72), 1859 G
Charles Albert, Prince of Carignan, 1821 C, D
Charles Albert, King of Sardinia (1831–49), 1847 K; grants constitution, 1848 B; abdicates, 1849 C
Charles Edward Louis Philip Casimir, the 'Young Pretender' to British throne (1720–88), 1788 A
Charles Emmanuel II, King of Sardinia (1796–1802), 1798 M
Charles Felix, King of Sardinia (1821–31), 1821 C
Charles Theodore, elector Palatine, King of Bavaria (1777–99), 1777 M, 1778 M, 1785 A
Charles O' Malley (C. Lever), 1841 U
Charles IX (J. Chénier), 1789 W
Charleston, S. Carolina, US, 1781 K; surrenders to British, 1780 E; siege of, 1865 B
Charlottesville, Va., US, university, 1817 S
Charpentier, Gustave, F. musician (1860–1956), 1900 T
Chartier, Émile, F. author (pseud.), 1928 O
Chartism: beginnings, 1836 F; points, 1838 O; London Convention, 1839 B; Parliament rejects petition, 1839 G, 1842 D; riots, 1839 G, L, 1842 H
Chartreuse de Parme, La (Stendhal), 1839 U
Chassepot, A. A., F. gunsmith (1833–1905), 1866 P
Chataway, Christopher John, B. athlete, 1931 Z
Chateaubriand, François René, vicomte de, F. author (1768–1848), 1768 Z, 1797 O, 1801 U, 1802 U, 1805 U, 1809 U, 1814 O, 1848 T, Z
Chatham, Earl of. *See* Pitt, William
Châtillon, France, peace negotiations, 1814 B
Chattanooga, Tenn., US: Confederate defeat at, 1863 L; Sherman's march from, 1864 E
Chatterton, Thomas, B. poet (1752–70), 1765 U, 1770 Z
Chaumette, Pierre Gaspard, F. revolutionary (1763–1794), 1793 R
Chaumont, France, treaty between Allies, 1814 C
Chautemps, Camille, F. Radical Socialist, 1933 L, 1937 F, 1938 A
Chebichev, Pafnutiy Lvovich, R. mathematician (1821–94), 1850 P
Cheddington, Bucks, England, mail train robbery near, 1963 H
Chef-d'œuvre inconnu, Le (H. de Balzac), 1831 U
Chekhov, Anton, R. dramatist (1860–1904), 1860 Z, 1896 W, 1900 W, 1902 W, 1904 W, Z
Chekiang, E. China, Italy demands concessions in, 1899 B
Chemical analysis, 1913 P
Chemical terms, treatise on, 1787 P
Chemin des Dames, France, battle, 1917 E
Chemists' Federation, British, 1958 O
Chemistry, College of London, 1845 O
Chemistry of Diet, The (J. Liebig), 1840 P
Chemistry of the Sun, The (J. N. Lockyer), 1887 P
Chemistry, Organic, Wöhler founds study of, 1828 P
Chemistry, treatise on, 1789 P
Chénier, André Marie de, F. author (1762–94), 1790 O, 1794 U
Chénier, Marie Joseph Blaise de, F. dramatist (1764–1811), 1789 W, 1791 W
Chequers, Bucks, England, becomes official residence of prime minister, 1921 O
Cherasco, Piedmont, N. Italy, peace signed at, 1796 E
Cherbourg, France, Allies take, 1944 F
Chéri (Colette), 1920 U
Chermayeff, L., Am. architect (b. 1900), 1935 S
Cherokee alphabet, 1824 Q; Indians, 1830 E
Cherry Orchard, The (Chekhov), 1904 W
Cherry Valley, N. York, US, massacre, 1778 L
Cherubini, Maria Luigi Carlo, It. musician (1760–1842), 1791 T, 1797 T, 1800 T
Chervenkov, Vulko, Bulg. premier, 1950 B
Cherwell, lord. *See* Lindemann, F.
Chesapeake and *Shannon*, naval action, 1813 F
Chesapeake Bay, Maryland, US, French occupy, 1781 H
Chester, Ches., England, Fenian outrages in, 1867 B
Chesterfield, earl of. *See* Stanhope
Chesterton, Gilbert Keith, B. author (1874–1936), 1904 U, 1908 U
Chevalier, Maurice, F. actor and singer, 1888 Z
Chevalier, Sulpice Guillaume, F. caricaturist under pseudonym of Gavarni (1801–66), 1857 S
Cheyenne Indians, massacred, 1864 C
Chiang Kai-shek, Chin. Nationalist leader (b. 1887), 1887 Z; northern campaign, 1926 J; opposes Radicals in Kuo Min Tang, 1927 D; overthrows Hankow government, 1927 M; elected president of China, 1928 K; elected Kuo Min Tang president, 1935 M; enters Canton, 1936 H; declares war on Japan, 1936 M; meets Churchill, 1943 L; negotiations with Mao Tse-tung founder, 1945 K; Nanking Assembly grants dictatorial powers,

Chiang Kai-shek—*contd.*
1948 C; resigns presidency of China, 1949 A; removes forces to Formosa, 1949 G; resumes presidency of Nationalist China, 1950 C
Chiaramonti, Luigi Barnaba, It., Pope Pius VII (1800–23), 1800 C, 1814 R
Chiaroscuro (A. John), 1952 S
Chiavenna, Switzerland, France annexes, 1797 K
Chicago, Ill., US: Sankey and Moody mission, 1870 R; labour riots, 1886 E; world exhibition, 1893 W; stockyards, exposure of conditions in, 1906 O; Republican convention at, 1912 F; Progressive Republican convention at, 1912 H; race riots, 1919 G; university, atomic research, 1941 P, 1942 P
buildings in, 1890 P
Chicago Tribune building, 1923 S
Illinois Institute of Technology, 1939 O
Robie House, 1909 S
Skyscraper, the first, 1883 P
population, 1950 Y
Chichekli, President of Syria, 1953 G, 1954 B, 1957 A
Chief Truths of Revelation (A. von. Haller), 1772 R
Chiesa, Giacomo della, It. Pope Benedict XV (1854–1922), 1917 H
Chifley, Joseph, Austral. premier, 1945 G
Childe Harold's Pilgrimage (Byron), 1812 U
Childers, Robert Erskine, Ir. author and Republican politician (1870–1922), 1922 L
Children of the Ghetto, The (I. Zangwill), 1897 U
Chile: revolts against Joseph Bonaparte, 1810 J; independence proclaimed, 1818 B; nitrates trade, 1830 P; state religion, 1833 E; territorial settlements with Bolivia, 1866 H, 1874 H; relations with Peru, 1912 L; dispute with Argentine, 1925 C
Chillianwalla, Punjab, battle, 1849 A
Chilton Hundreds, The (W. Douglas-Home), 1947 W
Chimney-sweeps act, in Britain, 1834 O
China: Inland mission, 1865 R; open ports, 1895 D; loans to, 1895 A, C; French concessions in, 1898 D; 'open-door', note, 1899 J; policy, 1800 G, 1900 K; customs service, 1906 E; tea production, 1909 Y; Republic proclaimed, 1911 K; Kuo Min Tang (Nanking) government, recognised by Britain, 1928 M; extra-territorial rights, Britain renounces, 1943 A; North China People's Republic, 1948 J; People's Republic proclaimed, 1949 K; UN calls for recognition of, 1949 M; Britain recognises, 1950 A. *See also under* Civil wars
Chindwin Valley, Burma, operations in, 1942 E
Chinese Prime Minister, The (E. Bagnold), 1965 W
Chios, Island: Turks capture, 1822 D; massacre, 1822 D, F; garrison surrenders to Greece, 1912 A; Greece annexes, 1914 F
Chippendale, Thomas, B. furniture-maker (d. 1779), 1779 Z
Chippewa, Wis., US, battle, 1814 G
Chips with Everything (A. Wesker), 1962 W
Chitral, Pakistan, India claims suzerainty over, 1956 E
Chivalry, High Court of, 1954 O
Chivington, Colonel, Am. soldier, 1864 L
Chladni, E. F. F., It. physicist (1756–1827), 1786 P, 1802 R
Chlorine: discovered, 1774 P; used as bleach, 1785 P; is liquefied, 1823 P
Chloroform, 1847 P
Chloromycetin, 1948 P
Chlorophyll: pronounced necessary for photosynthesis, 1837 P; composition discovered, 1913 P; synthesis of, 1960 P
Choderlos de Laclos, Pierre Ambroise François (1741–1803), F. author, 1772 U
Choiseul, Étienne François, duc de, F. statesman (1719–85), 1770 H, M
Cholera epidemic, 1830 O
Cholet, N.W. France, Vendéan defeat at, 1793 H
Chopin, Frédéric, Pol. musician (1810–49), 1810 Z, 1832 T, 1833 T, 1839 T, 1840 T, 1845 T, 1909 T
Choral Works:
Appalachia (Delius), 1902 T
Belshazzar's Feast (Walton), 1931 T
Canterbury Pilgrims, The (Dyson), 1932 T
Heart, The (Pfitzner), 1931 T
Hiawatha's Wedding Feast (Coleridge-Taylor), 1898 T
Hymn of Jesus (Holst), 1917 T
Lark Ascending (Vaughan Williams), 1914 T
Mass of Life, A (Delius), 1905 T
Rio Grande (Lambert), 1929 T
Sea Drift (Delius), 1903 T
Seasons, The (Haydn), 1801 T
Song of the Earth (Mahler), 1911 T
Summer's Last Will and Testament (Lambert), 1936 T
Symphony of Psalms (Stravinsky), 1930 Y
Towards the Unknown Region (Vaughan Williams), 1907 T
Twelve, The (Walton), 1965 T
See also under Mass, settings of; Operas; Oratorios
Chouans, Les (Balzac), 1829 U
Chou En-lai, Chinese leader (b. 1898): as premier and foreign minister, 1949 K; visits Moscow, 1952 H, 1957 A, 1964 L; visits Rangoon, 1955 D
Christiania, Norway. *See* Oslo
Christian VIII, of Denmark (1839–48), 1839 M, 1846 G, 1848 A
Christian IX, of Denmark (1863–1906), 1863 L
Christian Frederick of Denmark, elected King of Norway, 1814 D
Christ and Culture (R. Niebuhr), 1952 R
Christian Democrats. *See under* Political parties
Christian Dogmatics (K. Barth), 1932 R
Christian Experience (J. Monroux), 1956 R
Christian Faith and other Faiths (S. Neil), 1961 R
Christian Scientists. *See under* Religious Denominations
Christiansen, Arthur, B. journalist (1904–63), 1933 V
Christianity and Democracy (J. Maritain), 1943 R
Christianity and the Social Order (W. Temple), 1942 R
Christian Mysticism (J. Görres), 1836 R
Christian Socialism, 1849 R
Christian Socialists. *See under* Political parties
Christian Unity (G. K. A. Bell), 1948 R
Christian Year, The (J. Keble), 1827 R
Christie, Agatha, B. author, 1921 U, 1952 W
Christie, John, founder of Glyndebourne Festival (1882–1962), 1934 T
Christie, Manson and Co., London, art sales at, 1915 S
Christmas Carol, A (C. Dickens), 1843 U
Christ Stopped at Eboli (Levi), 1945 U
Chromosomes, term coined, 1888 P
observed, 1876 P
Chrome Yellow (A. Huxley), 1921 U
Chronicles of Clovis, The (Saki), 1911 U
Chrysler's Farm, Montreal, Canada, US defeat at, 1813 L
Chudinov, Dr. K., R. scientist, 1962 P
Church, Richard William, B. churchman (1815–90), 1891 R
Church, Richard, B. author (b. 1893), 1955 U
Church and the Churches, The (Döllinger), 1861 R
Church Army, founded, 1882 R

Churchill, Randolph Henry Spencer, lord Randolph Churchill, B. Conservative statesman (1849–94), 1887 A; a member of the 'Fourth Party', 1880 E; Dartford speech, 1886 K; resigns chancellorship of Exchequer, 1886 M; life, by W. S. Churchill, 1906 Q
Churchill, Randolph Frederick Edward Spencer, B. journalist (b. 1911), 1964 O
Churchill, Sir Winston Leonard Spencer, B. statesman, orator and historian (1874–1965), 1874 Z
First Lord of Admiralty, 1911 K
becomes Chancellor of Duchy of Lancaster, 1915 E
resigns from Cabinet, 1915 L
appointed Colonial Secretary, 1921 B
becomes chancellor of Exchequer, 1924 L
warns of German air manace, 1934 L
opposes Chamberlain over Italy, 1938 B
urges military alliance with Russia, 1939 G
appointed First Lord of Admiralty, 1939 J
advises neutrals to side with Britain, 1940 A
forms National Ministry, 1940 E
'blood and toil' speech, 1940 E
visits Reynaud, 1940 F
offers France union with Britain, 1940 F
meets Roosevelt in W. Atlantic, 1941 H
visits Washington and Ottawa, 1941 M
reconstructs ministry, 1942 B
confers in Moscow, 1942 H
at Casablanca Conference, 1943 A
presents Stalingrad sword, 1943 B
speech on post-war reconstruction, 1943 C
at Quebec conference, 1943 H
at Cairo conference, 1943 L
meets Roosevelt and Stalin at Teheran, 1943 L
in Quebec, 1944 J
visits Moscow, 1944 K
visits Athens, 1944 M
at Yalta Conference, 1945 B
forms Conservative 'Caretaker' ministry, 1945 E
requires de Gaulle to order cease-fire in Syria, 1945 E
at Potsdam Conference, 1945 G
resigns, 1945 G
Fulton speech, 1946 C
at Hague Congress for European Unity, 1948 E
favours a European army, 1950 H
forms Conservative ministry, 1951 K
announces Britain has own atom bomb, 1952 B
visits Eisenhower, 1953 A, 1954 F
at Bermuda Conference, 1953 M
reforms ministry, 1954 K
resigns, 1955 D
becomes honorary US citizen, 1963 D
last appears in Commons, 1964 G
90th birthday, 1964 L
death, 1965 Z
state funeral, 1965 A, W
as artist, 1947 S, 1948 S
as author:
life of father, 1906 Q
Marlborough, 1933 Q
Second World War, 1948 Q
History of English-speaking Peoples, 1956 Q
portrait, 1954 T
Churchill College, Cambridge, 1960 O
Church Looks Forward, The (W. Temple), 1944 R
Church of England. *See under* Religious Denominations
Ciano, Count Nobile, It. foreign minister, 1936 F, L
Cicero, manuscripts of, discovered, 1819 Q
Cigarette advertising, on TV, banned, 1965 W. *See also under* Diseases, lung cancer
Cigarettes, black market in, 1945 O
Cimarosa, Domenico, It. musician (1749–1801), 1792 T
Cimetière marin, Le (P. Valéry), 1920 U
Cincinnati, Ohio, US: Democrat convention at, 1872 E; Red Stockings baseball club, 1868 X
Cinema, The: forerunners of, 1888 P, 1894 W; cinematograph invented, 1895 P; sound films, 1927 W; wide screen, 1930 W; 'Cinerama', 1951 W; 'Cinemascope', 1953 W
in Britain, licensing, 1909 W
picture theatres in London, 1912 W
Odeon circuit, 1933 W
in US, five-cent, 1905 W
attendances, 1912 W
See also Films
Cinq grandes odes (P. Claudel), 1910 U
Cinq-mars (A. de Vigny), 1826 U
Cinque Maggio, Il (A. Manzoni), 1821 U
Cintra, Convention of, 1808 H
Circumnavigation, voyage of, 1766 P
Circus, the, 1941 W
Cisalpine Republic (Italy), 1797 G, K, 1799 D, 1801 B, 1802 A
Cispadane Republic (Italy), 1796 K; merged with Cisalpine Republic, 1797 G
Cité Antique, La (Fustel de Coulanges), 1864 Q
Citoyen contre les pouvoirs, Le (E. Chartier), 1828 O
City of Dreadful Night, The (F. Thompson), 1880 U
Civil Aerial Transport Committee, British, 1917 O
Civil and Penal Legislation (J. Bentham), 1802 C
Civil Defence, in Britain, 1936 C, 1941 O
Civil Disobedience:
in Ceylon, 1961 A
in India, 1922 C, 1930 C, 1931 C, 1934 D
Civilization and its Discontents (S. Freud), 1930 R
Civil List, British, scrutiny of, 1780 D
Civil Rights, in US: 14th Amendment to secure, 1866 F, 1867 C, 1870 C; Kennedy's speech on, 1963 F; Negroes' peaceful demonstrations, 1963 H; Act signed, 1964 G; Workers, murder of, 1964 H, M, 1965 C; Workers' procession to Montgomery, 1965 C
Civil Service, in Britain, Commission founded, 1854 O
posts open to competition, 1870 F, O
effect of Crichel Down inquiry on, 1953 O
five-day week in, 1957 O
clerical officers work to rule, 1962 A
in US, reform of, 1883 A
Pendleton Act for, 1901 D
Civil Wars:
in Afghanistan, 1863 F
in Chile, 1891 A
in China, 1922 L, 1926 J, 1927 C, D, M, 1945 K, 1946 A
Japanese intervention, 1927 E, 1928 E
Britain recognises Nanking government, 1928 M
Marshall attempts mediation, 1945 M
US abandons mediation, 1947 A
Tientsin falls to Communists, 1949 A
Nationalist reversals, 1949 A
Communists resume offensive, 1949 E
Nationalists remove to Formosa, 1949 G
in Colombia, 1900 N
in Dominica, 1965 J
in Greece, 1944 M, 1945 A, 1946 E, 1949 K
in Honduras, 1909 M
in Indonesia, 1947 G, M
in Korea, 1949 J
in Mexico, 1911 A, D, 1912 C, K, 1914 D
in Portugal, 1847 G

Civil Wars—*contd.*
in Samoa, 1880 L
in Spain (Carlist), 1834 G, 1840 F, 1872 D, E, 1875 A, 1876 B
(Franco's), opens, 1936 G
siege of Madrid, 1936 L
non-intervention in, 1936 H, J, M, 1938 K
Italian troops in, 1937 B, C, 1938 D, 1938 A
destruction of Guernica, 1937 D
German fleet bombards Almeria, 1937 E
Bilbao falls, 1937 E
piracy resulting from, 1937 J
rebels take Gijón, 1937 K
government moves to Barcelona, 1937 K
Franco's naval blockade, 1937 L
Attlee visits, 1937 M
withdrawal of Italian troops, 1938 D
Franco's Caledonian offensive, 1938 M
Franco takes Barcelona, 1939 A
Madrid surrenders, 1939 C
in Switzerland, 1847 K
in US: War for Bleeding Kansas, 1854 E, 1856 E
War of 1861–5, opens, 1861 D
battle of Bull Run, 1861 G
Trent affair, 1861 L
Grant takes Fort Henry, 1862 B
Alabama case, 1862 G
Jackson's victory over Unionists at Bull Run, 1862 H
Lee's victory at Fredericksburg, 1862 M
Confederate victory at Chancellorsville, 1863 E
Lee defeats Confederates at Gettysburg, 1863 G
Sherman marches Unionist Army through Georgia, 1864 E, G
Savannah surrenders to Unionists, 1864 M
Richmond surrenders to Grant, 1865 D
ends, 1865 E
Civitas Dei (L. Curtis), 1934 R
Cività Vecchia, Italy, French troops at, 1867 K
Clacton, Essex, England, Mod *v.* Rockers at, 1964 C
Claim of Our Age to Legislation, The (F. Savigny), 1814 O
Clair, René, F. film director (b. 1898), 1930 W, 1931 W, 1932 W, 1933 W, 1934 W, 1947 W, 1950 W, 1955 W
Clairvoyance, studies in, 1921 R
Clandestino II (M. Tobino), 1962 U
Clare, John, B. poet (1793–1864), 1793 Z, 1827 U, 1864 Z
Clare, county, Ireland, election, 1828 F
Clarendon, Lord. *See* Villiers, G. W. F.
Clarendon Press, Oxford, 1781 Q
Clark, Sir George Norman, B. historian (b. 1890), 1934 Q
Clark, George Rogers, Am. soldier (1752–1818), 1779 B
Clark, Sir Kenneth, B. art critic (b. 1903), 1949 S, 1957 S
Clark, Sir Wilfred le Gros, B. anatomist (b. 1895), 1953 P
Clark, James ('Jim'), B. racing driver, 1936 Z, 1965 X
Clark, Mark Wayne, Am. general (b. 1896), 1952 D
Clark, Reuben J., Am. politician, writes memo on Monroe Doctrine, 1930 C
Clarke, Sir Andrew, B. Colonial official (1824–1902), 1873 N
Clarkson, Thomas, B. anti-slavery agitator (1760–1846), 1786 O
Classical scholarship, 1796 Q, 1802 Q, 1850 Q, 1869 Q
Claudel, Paul, F. author (1868–1955), 1900 Q, 1906 W, 1910 U, 1912 W, 1915 U, 1927 W, 1929 W
Claudius, Matthias, G. author (1740–1815), 1771 U
Claus, Am. scientist, 1961 P
Clausius, Rudolf, Julius Emmanuel, G. physicist (1822–88), 1850 P
Clavigo (Goethe), 1774 U
Clay, Cassius, Am. boxer, 1964 X, 1965 X
Clay, Henry, Am. Whig politician (1777–1852), 1833 C, 1844 L; defeated by Jackson for presidency, 1832 C; compromise resolution on slavery, 1850 A
Claybury, Essex, England, asylum at, 1893 P
Clayhanger (A. Bennett), 1910 U
Clayton-Bulmer treaty, 1850 D
Clea (L. Durrell), 1960 U
Cleland, John, B. novelist (1709–89), 1963 U
Clemenceau, Georges, F. statesman (1841–1929), 1841 Z, 1906 A, 1909 G, 1918 C, 1929 Z; becomes premier, 1917 L; as Chairman of Peace Conference, 1919 A
Clemens, Samuel Langhorne, Am. writer under pseudonym of 'Mark Twain' (1835–1910), 1835 Z, 1869 U, 1875 U, 1884 U, 1910 Z
Clement XIII, Pope (1758–69), It. Cardinal (Carlo della Torre Rezzonico), 1763 R, 1764 R, 1766 R, 1769 B
Clement XIV, Pope (1769–74), It. Cardinal (Lorenzo Ganganelli), 1768 N, 1769 E, 1773 G
Clementi, Muzio, It. musician (1752–1832), 1817 T
Clementis, Vladimir, Czech. foreign minister, executed, 1952 C
Cleopatra (V. Alfieri), 1775 W
Cleopatra's Needle, 1878 S
Clérambaud (M. Aymé), 1950 W
Clerical Parties. *See under* Political Parties
Clerk, Sir Dugold, B. engineer (1831–79), 1879 P
Clerke, Agnes May, B. historian of anatomy (1842–1907), 1903 P
Clerk-Maxwell, James, B. physicist (1831–79), 1831 Z, 1873 P, 1879 P, Z
Cleveland, Grover Stephen, Am. Statesman (1837–1903) Democrat, president of US (1885–8, 1893–6), 1837 Z, 1895 M, 1908 Z; wins presidential election, 1884 L; inaugurated, 1885 C; defeated, 1888 C; elected, for further term, 1892 L; withdraws treaty annexing Hawaii, 1893 B; repeals Sherman silver act, 1893 L; repeals McKinley tariff, 1894 E; opposes Wilson-Gormann tariff, 1894 H
Cleveland, Ohio, US: Republican convention at, 1924 F; hospital, surgery at, 1964 P
Cleves, ceded to France, 1805 M
Cliburn, Van, Am. pianist, 1958 T
Clifford, John, B. Baptist (1836–1923), 1891 R
Clifford, Thomas, B. inventor, 1790 P
Clifford, William Kingston, B. mathematician (1845–79), 1873 P
Clinton, Sir Henry, B. general (?1738–95), 1778 F, 1780 E, J
Clinton, De Witt, Am. Republician (1769–1828), 1812 L
Clinton, Tenn., US, uranium pile at, 1944 P
Clive, Robert, lord Clive, B. governor of Bengal (1725–73), 1765 E, 1767 A, 1772 C, 1773 Z
Clodin, Claude Michel, F. sculptor (1745–1814), 1806 S
Cloister and the Hearth, The (C. Reade), 1861 U
Cloots, Jean Baptiste du Val de Grace, baron ('Anacharsis'), F. politician (1755–94), 1792 O, 1793 O
'Closed shop' dispute, in Britain, 1946 H; in US, outlawed, 1947 F
Clothes-rationing in Britain, 1941 O
ends, 1949 B
Clothing, standard, in Britain, 1918 O, 1941 O

Clough, Anne Jemima, B. educationalist (1820–92), 1871 O
Clouzot, Henri, F. film director, 1947 W, 1954 W
Clubs: Left Book, 1935 O
night, 1921 W
political, in France, 1790 N
for women, 1892 O
Clutsam, G. H., composer of light opera, 1922 W
Clyde, lord. *See* Campbell, Colin
Clyde, River, Scotland, 1812 P
Clydeside, Scotland, munition workers in, 1916 V
Clymer, George, B. inventor (1754–1834), 1813 P
Clynes, John Robert, B. Labour politician (1869–1949), as home secretary, 1929 F
Cnossos, Crete, excavations at, 1910 Q
Coal:
extraction of petrol from, 1931 P, 1935 P
gas. *See* Gas, coal
mines, in Australia, strike, 1949 H
in Britain, statutory control, 1911 O
Sankey commission, 1919 B, 1919 O
strikes, 1922 D, 1944 B
enquiry into, 1925 G
Commission takes over colliery leases, 1942 G
compulsory arbitration, 1943 E
nationalisation, 1946 E, 1947 A
in France and Germany, Schuman plan for, 1950 E
in Germany, government control, 1915 G
in US, stabilisation act for, 1935 H
strike, 1943 E
production, statistics of, in Austria, 1870 Y, 1871 Y, 1890 Y, 1901 Y
in Belgium, 1901 Y, 1946 Y
in Britain, 1821 Y, 1831 Y, 1841 Y, 1851 Y, 1861 Y, 1870 Y, 1871 Y, 1880 Y, 1890 Y, 1895 Y, 1901 Y, 1913 Y, 1916 Y, 1920 Y, 1924 Y, 1928 Y, 1941 Y, 1946 Y, 1951 Y
in France, 1831 Y, 1841 Y, 1851 Y, 1861 Y, 1870 Y, 1871 Y, 1880 Y, 1890 Y, 1895 Y, 1924 Y, 1938 Y, 1946 Y, 1951 Y,
in Germany, 1851 Y, 1870 Y, 1871 Y, 1880 Y, 1890 Y, 1895 Y, 1901 Y, 1913 Y, 1920 Y, 1924 Y, 1938 Y, 1946 Y, 1951 Y
in Holland, 1946 Y
in Poland, 1946 Y
in Russia, 1861 Y, 1880 Y, 1890 Y, 1901 Y, 1932 Y, 1938 Y, 1940 Y, 1951 Y
in US, 1821 Y, 1851 Y, 1870 Y, 1871 Y, 1880 Y, 1890 Y, 1895 Y, 1901 Y, 1913 Y, 1916 Y, 1920 Y, 1924 Y, 1946 Y, 1951 Y
used in steel production, 1861 P
traffic, Anglo-Irish pact for, 1934 M
Coal Questions, The (W. S. Jevons), 1865 O
Coalbrookdale, Salop, England, bridge, 1773 P
Coates, Joseph, N.Z. politician, Reform Party, 1925 E
Cobb, John, B. racing-driver (d. 1952), 1939 P, 1947 P, 1952 P
Cobbett, William, B. essayist and politician (1766–1835), 1792 O, 1802 V, 1816 V, 1829 U, 1830 U, 1835 Z
Cobden, Richard, B. Liberal and free-trader (1804–1865), 1804 Z, 1835 O, 1865 Z; founds Anti-Corn Law League, 1838 J; signs commercial treaty with France, 1860 A
Cobden Club, London, founded, 1866 O
Cobham, Sir Alan, B. aviator (b. 1894), 1894 Z, 1926 P
Coblenz, W. Germany, French *émigrés* at, 1791 G
Coburg, Francis Josiah, duke of, general (d. 1806), 1789 G, J, K, 1794 F
Cocaine, used as anaesthetic, 1884 P
Cochin-China: Franco-Spanish blockade, 1858 M; France annexes, 1862 F; France organises, 1887 N
Cockcroft, Sir John, B. atomic physicist (b. 1897), 1897 Z, 1931 P
Cocktail, the, 1922 W
Cocktail Party, The (T. S. Eliot), 1949 W
Cocteau, Jean, F. author and film producer (1889–1963), 1889 Z, 1927 T, 1929 U, 1934 W, 1938 W, 1946 W, 1950 W, 1959 W
Code du Travail, 1912 O
Codes of Law:
in Austria, civil, 1811 O
in Britain, criminal, reformed by Peel, 1827 F
in French, treatise on, 1796 O
Napoleonic, 1807 O
in Germany, civil, 1900 O
criminal, 1872 O
in Japan, penal, 1880 G
in Turkey, 1926 A
Codex Sinaiticus, 1844 Q, 1859 Q
Codreanu, Corneliu, Rum. politician, 1938 L
Codos, Paul, Am. aviator, 1932 P
Cody, William Frederick ('Buffalo Bill'), Am. (d. 1917), 1917 Z
Coeducation, study of, 1922 O
Coelebs in Search of a Wife (H. More), 1809 U
Coerne, Louis Adolphe, Am. musician (1870–1922), 1905 T
Coffee:
in Brazil, over-production, 1928 O, 1931 N
world production, 1909 Y
Cohn, Gustav, G. economist (1840–1918), 1885 O
Coinage:
in Britain, treatises on, 1805 O, 1854 O, 1930 O
florins introduced, 1854 O
farthings no longer legal tender, 1961 A
in Germany, 1873 O
in S. Africa, the Rand introduced, 1961 B
in Switzerland, 1850 O
in US, the dollar introduced, 1792 O
policy of free silver, 1896 L
See also Currency
Coke, Thomas, William, earl of Leicester, B. agriculturist (1752–1842), 1772 P
Colby, Bainbridge, Am. secretary of state, 1920 B
Coldstream, Sir William Menzies, B. artist (b. 1908), 1937 S
Cole, George Douglas Howard, B. economist (1889–1959), 1947 O
Cole, Nat 'King', Am. jazz singer (1920–65), 1965 Z
Cole, Thomas, Am. artist (1801–48), 1825 S
Colebrooke, Henry Thomas, B. orientalist (1765–1837), 1805 Q, 1822 Q
Colenso, John William, B. churchman, bishop of Natal (1814–83), 1862 R, 1863 R
Colenso, Natal, S. Africa, Bullers repulsed at, 1899 M
Coleridge, Samuel Taylor, B. poet and philosopher (1772–1834), 1772 Z, 1794 W, 1798 U, 1816 U, 1817 U, 1828 R, 1834 Z
Coleridge-Taylor, Samuel, B. musician (1875–1912), 1875 Z, 1898 T, 1912 Z
Colette, Sidonie Gabrielle, F. author (1873–1954), 1900 U, 1908 U, 1920 U
Collection, The (H. Pinter), 1961 W
Collective farms:
in E. Germany, 1960 D
in Russia, 1939 O
Colleen Bawn, The (D. Boucicault), 1860 W
Colley, Sir George Pomeroy, B. soldier (1835–81), 1881 A, B
Colline inspirée, La (M. Barrès), 1913 U

Collings, Jesse, B. Liberal (1831–1920), 1831 Z, 1886 A, 1920 Z
Collingwood, Robin George, B. philosopher and historian (1889–1943), 1889 Z, 1942 R, 1943 Z, 1945 R, 1946 R
Collins, Lottie, B. music-hall artiste, 1892 W
Collins, Michael, Ir. revolutionary leader (1890–1922), 1890 Z, 1922 H
forms government, 1922 A
Collins, William Wilkie, B. novelist (1824–89), 1860 U, 1868 U
Collip, James Bertram, B. pathologist (b. 1892), 1925 P
Colman, George, the younger, B. dramatist (1762–1836), 1797 W
Colmar, E. France, 1945 B
Cologne, W. Germany: archbishop, 1837 R; Roman Catholic working-men's club, 1847 R; Cathedral, 1880 S; Allies occupy, 1918 M, 1925 A; art in, 1920 S; British evacuate, 1925 M; bombing, 1942 E; Allies take, 1945 C; anti-Semitism in, 1959 M
Colomba (P. Mérimée), 1840 U
Colombe (J. Anouilh), 1951 W
Colombia: Republic formed from Venezuela and New Grenada, 1819 M; truce with Spain, 1820 L; Panama joins, 1821 L; Britain recognises independence, 1824 M; Venezuela secedes from, 1830 J; dissolution of Union, 1831 L; grants Panama Canal concession, 1878 E; delays ratification of Hay-Herrán Pact, 1903 E, L; coffee production in, 1909 Y
Colombo, Ceylon: Conference of Commonwealth foreign ministers, 1950 A; Plan, 1951 B; Conference of Asian premiers, 1954 D
Colonial Conference, British, first, 1887 D. *See also under* Conferences
Colonial Development Corporation, 1947 O
Colonial Development Fund, 1929 O
Colonial Secretaryship, British, 1768 A; revived, 1854 F
Colonial Society, German, 1882 O
Colorado State, US: US obtains, 1848 E; becomes a US state, 1876 H; grants for irrigation in, 1894 H
Colour Bar. *See* Apartheid; Civil Rights
Colour film, 16 mm., 1929 P
Colour films, 1929 W
Colour photography, Spier-Dufay process, 1931 P
Colour reproduction, process for, 1907 P
Colour sensitising, 1873 P
Colour TV, 1953 P
Colours, theory of, 1810 P
Colt, Samuel, Am. gunsmith (1814–62), 1835 P, 1853 P
Columbia, S. Carolina, US, Unionists take, 1865 B
Columbus, Ohio, US, state capital, 1839 S
Combes, Émile, F. anti-clerical, 1902 F, 1904 L
Combination of Gases, The (J. L. Gay-Lussac), 1808 P
Comédie humaine, La (Balzac), 1829 U
'Comet' aircraft, 1954 P
Comets:
calculation of orbits, 1797 P
Encke's, 1818 P
photography of, 1881 P
Comfort, Alex, B. philosopher and poet (b. 1920), 1944 U
Comics, horror, 1952 V
Comic Tales (C. M. Wieland), 1765 U
Cominform (Communist Information Bureau): established, 1947 K; Yugoslavia expelled from, 1948 F; dissolved, 1956 D
Coming Architecture, The (Le Corbusier), 1926 S
Coming Democracy, The (Fernau), 1917 D
Coming Struggle for Power (J. Strachey), 1932 O
Comité d'Études du Haut-Congo, 1878 L
Commandos and Task Forces:
British, raid Norway, 1941 M
raid St. Nazaire, 1942 C
raid Dieppe. 1942 H
Wingate's, in Burma, 1943 D
raid Wake Islands, 1942 B
raid Aleutian Islands, 1943 E
raid New Guinea, 1943 F
raid Solomon Islands, 1943 F
in Philippines, 1944 K
Commentaries on the Laws of England (W. Blackstone), 1765 O
Commissions, British Royal:
betting, lotteries and gaming, 1951 O
capital punishment, 1953 O
Dilke on housing, 1884 O
divorce, 1912 O
ecclesiastical discipline, 1903 R
equal pay for women, 1946 L
fine arts, 1923 S
Greater London, 1957 G
land, 1965 O
law, 1965 O
Lawrence, on M.P's. salaries, 1964 L
mental patients, 1953 O
mines, 1842 O
monopolies, 1963 M
National Incomes, 1962 O
Newson, public schools, 1965 W
new towns, 1961 O
Palestine, 1937 G, 1938 A
press, the, 1961 B
science, 1870 O
Simon, on India, 1926 L
Trades Unions and Employers' Associations, 1965 B
vivisection, 1912 O
Woodhead, on Palestine, 1938 A
Commissions, US:
for Haiti, 1930 B
Taft, on Philippines, 1900 B
Commissions, Anglo-US, for Caribbean, 1942 O
US-League, on slavery in Liberia, 1930 C
Committees, British:
Amultree, on holidays with pay, 1938 O
Beaver, on air pollution, 1953 O
Burnham, on teachers' pay, 1963 G
Craythorne, on Sunday entertainment, 1964 W
Devlin, on docks, 1965 H
Fraser, on TV and the young, 1963 O
Guillebaud, on health service, 1956 A
Guillebaud, on railwaymen's pay, 1960 C
Hankey, scientific advisory, 1940 O
Howick, on ecclesiastical appointments, 1964 R
May, on budget deficit, 1931 G
neglect of science, 1916 P
Newsom, on education, 1963 O
Plowden, on diplomatic service, 1964 B
Plowden, on aircraft industry, 1965 M
Reith, on new towns, 1946 O
Royal Society, on emigration of scientists, 1963 B
Uthwatt, on land development, 1942 O
Waverley, on export of works of art, 1952 S
Committees, international:
Lucerne, on wavelengths, 1934 O
Young, on reparations, 1928 M, 1929 F
See also under United Nations
Committees, US, Un-American Committee, hearing on Ku-Klux-Klan, 1965 K

Common, Andrew Ainslie, B. astronomer (1841–1903), 1881 P
Common Market or European Economic Community (EEC), ('The Six'): resolution on, adopted by European Coal and Steel Community, 1956 E; Rome Treaty for, 1957 C; in force, 1958 A; Britain applies for membership, 1961 H; Heath's statement to, 1961 K; agreement on agriculture, 1962 A; Commonwealth premiers endorse Britain's attempt to enter, 1962 J; Britain resumes negotiations, 1962 L; de Gaulle's objection to British entry, 1963 A; France leaves council meeting, 1965 G; merger of executive authority of, with Euratom and ECSC, 1965 M
Common Pursuit, The (F. R. Leavis), 1952 U
Common Sense (T. Paine), 1776 O
Commons Preservation Society, 1865 O
Commonwealth and other Nations, The (N. Mansergh), 1949 O
Commonwealth, British:
- S. Africa retains right to secede, 1934 F
- citizens of, become British subjects, 1948 G
- foreign ministers of, confer in Colombo, 1950 A
- London economic conference, 1952 L
- premiers of, confer in London, 1953 F, 1960 E, 1961, C 1962 J, 1964 G, 1965 F
- finance ministers of, meet at Sydney, 1954 A
- trade and economic conference, Montreal, 1958 J
- S. Africa leaves, 1961 E
- Cyprus votes to apply for membership, 1961 B
- premiers of, endorse Britain's attempt to enter Common Market, 1962 J
- secretariat established, 1965 F
- limit imposed to immigrants to Britain from, 1965 H
- African states leave, 1965 M

Commonwealth Party. *See under* Political Parties
Commonwealth Relations Office: established, 1942 O; overseas staff amalgamated with foreign service, 1964 B, 1965 A
Communards, French, 1871 G
Communism:
- International, 1876 O, 1919 O, 1943 E
- Russo-Chinese ideological talks, 1963 G, 1964 B
- *See also under* Communist; Deviations; International; Political Parties

Communist International, 1876 O; Third, 1919 O, 1943 E
Communist League, founded in Paris, 1836 O
Communist Manifesto, 1848 O
Communists. *See under* Political Parties
Comparative Grammar (F. Bopp), 1833 Q
Comparative Psychology, 1859 R, 1900 R
Comparative Zoology, 1796 P
Compass, gyro, 1907 P
- mariners, reform of, 1879 P

Compensation:
- Austria, to Turkey, for annexing Bosnia, 1909 B
- in Britain, workmen's, 1897 O
- in France, for nobility, 1825 D
- W. Germany, to Britain, for victims of Nazi persecution, 1964 F

Compiègne, France, German offensive near, 1918 F
Complaintes (J. Laforgue), 1885 U
Complete Duty of Man (H. Venn), 1763 R
Compound E. (Cortisone), discovered, 1949 P
Comprehensive schools, in Britain, 1965 O
Compte Rendu (J. Necker), 1781 O
Compton-Burnett, Ivy, B. author, 1935 U, 1944 U, 1959 U
Comte, Auguste, F. philosopher (1798–1857), 1798 Z, 1830 R, 1865 R, 1957 Z
Computers:
- Atlas, 1961 P
- statistics of machines in use, 1958 Y
- used for investigating authorship, 1963 Q
- *See also under* Automation

Concept of Mind (G. Ryle), 1950 R
Concept of Motivation (R. S. Peters), 1958 R
Concertina, invented, 1829 T
Concertos:
- clarinet, Finzi, 1949 T
- jazz band, 1954 T
- pianoforte, Beethoven, 1800 T, 1801 T, 1805 Y, 1809 T
  - Brahms, 1861 T, 1882 T
  - Grieg, 1868 T
  - Rachmaninov, 1901 T, 1935 T
  - Ravel, 1932 T
  - Roussel, 1928 T
  - Schumann, 1841 T
  - Tchaikovsky, 1875 T
- viola, Bartók, 1950 T
  - Walton, 1922 T
- violin, Bartók, 1938 T
  - Bax, 1943 T
  - Beethoven, 1806 T
  - Berg, 1935 T
  - Brahms, 1879 T
  - Britten, 1941 T
  - Elgar, 1910 T
  - Fricker, 1954 T
  - Malipiero, 1952 T
  - Mendelssohn, 1844 T
  - Respighi, 1922 T
  - Walton, 1932 T
- violin and 'cello, Brahms, 1887 T
- violoncello, Bax, 1932 T
  - Busch, 1943 T
  - Elgar, 1918 T
  - Walton, 1957 T

Concord, Mass., US, battle, 1775 D
'Concord' airliner project, 1962 L
Concordats of Papacy:
- with Austria, 1855 H
- with Belgium, 1828 G
- with France, 1801 G; ended, 1905 M
- with Germany, 1933 G
- with Hungary, 1964 H
- with Netherlands, 1827 F
- with Poland, denounced, 1947 J

Concrete, reinforced, 1849 P, 1877 P
'Concrete Art', 1930 S
Condenser, invented, 1765 P, 1769 P
Condition humaine, La (A. Malraux), 1933 U
Condition of Man (L. Mumford), 1944 R
Condition of the Working Classes in England (F. Engels), 1845 O
Conditions for Peace (E. H. Carr), 1942 O
Condorcet, Marie Jean Antoine Nicholas Caritat, marquis de, F. mathematician, philosopher and revolutionary (1743–94), 1793 O, 1794 Z
Conduction of Electricity through Gases, The (J. J. Thomson), 1903 P
Confederate States, US, formed, 1861 B
Confederation of the Rhine, 1806 K; dissolved, 1813 K
Confederation of Independent African States, 1958 D
Confederazione Generale de Lavoro, 1906 O
Conferences, and Congresses:
- African Wild Life, 1961 P
- Aix-le-Chapelle, 1818 J
- Algeciras, on Morocco, 1905 G, J, 1906 A
- All-African People's, Accra, 1958 M
- Allied, War of 1914–18, 1916 C

Conferences, and Congresses—*contd.*
Allied, War of 1939–45 for allied leaders:
Cairo, 1943 L
Casablanca, 1943 A
London, 1941 F, J
Moscow, 1942 H, 1943 K
Potsdam, 1945 G
Quebec, 1943 H
Teheran, 1943 L
Yalta, 1945 B
Architecture, Modern, 1928 S
Athens, of Balkan powers, 1930 K, 1937 B
Atlantic, of NATO Parliamentarians, 1959 F
Bangkok, of heads of US Asiatic missions, 1950 B
of SEATO, 1955 B
Basle, Franco-German Parliamentary, 1950 A
Belgrade, on R. Danube, 1948 G
Berlin, on Eastern Question, 1878 F, G
on protection of workers, 1890 C
on workers and soldiers, 1918 M
on Germany's currency, 1922 L
on cultural freedom, 1950 O
of foreign ministers, 1954 A, B
Bermuda, on refugees, 1943 D
between Eisenhower and Macmillan, 1957 C
Berne, of International Socialists, 1919 B
Bloemfontein, on Transvaal franchise, 1899 C
Bretton Woods, UN monetary and financial, 1944 G
British Colonial London, 1887 D, 1902 F
in Ottawa, 1894 F
British Commonwealth, of Dominion premiers, 1944 E
Economic, London, 1952 L
Law, London, 1955 O
Premiers, London, 1953 F, 1960 E, 1961 C, 1964 G, 1965 F
British Guiana, constitutional, 1962 L, 1965 L
British Imperial, London, 1907 E, 1911 E, 1921 F, 1923 K, 1926 K, 1930 K, 1937 E
Brussels, on Abolition of Slave Trade, 1889 F
on Germany's reparations, 1920 M
on Sino-Japanese War, 1937 K
on Belgian Congo, 1960 A
Buchlau, 1908 J
Buckingham Palace, on Irish Home Rule, 1914 G
Buenos Aires, Pan American, 1936 M
Cairo, of non-aligned states, 1964 K
Cambridge, of International Christians, 1946 R
of European vice-chancellors of universities, 1955 O
Cannes, on reparations, 1922 A
Caracas, of Organisation of American States, 1954 C
Casablanca, of Allied leaders, 1943 A
of heads of African states, 1961 A
Chinese Customs Service, 1925 K
Colombo, of Commonwealth foreign ministers, 1950 A
of Asian premiers, 1954 D
Copenhagen, of Lutherans, 1929 R
Coquilhatville, on Congo, 1961 D
Cracow, Pan-Slav, 1892 O
Dublin, of Sinn Fein, 1919 A
Erfurt, held by Napoleon, 1808 K
European Rabbis, 1957 R
Geneva, on arms traffic, 1925 E
on disarmament, 1926 E
economic, 1927 E, 1930 L
on tariffs, 1930 B
disarmament, 1932 B
Germany leaves, 1932 J
returns, 1932 M
No Force Declaration by, 1932 M
Germany leaves, 1933 K
ends, 1934 F
monetary, 1933 F
on world health, 1948 O
on Korea and Indo-China, 1954 D
Summit, 1955 F, G
on atomic energy, 1955 H
on detection of nuclear explosions, 1958 G
on surprise attack, 1958 L
on law of the sea, 1958 O
on Germany, 1959 E
disarmament, 1962 C, 1964 A
France, boycotts, 1962 C
on Laos, 1962 G
GATT, 1963 E
Genoa, on economic affairs, 1922 D
Hague, The, Peace, 1899 E
for European Unity, 1948 E
Honolulu, of Pacific Council, 1952 H
Hot Springs, on post-war relief, 1943 F
Jerusalem, on missions, 1928 R
Laibach, 1820 L, 1821 A, B
Latin American states, on Mexico, 1915 K
Lausanne, on Near East, 1923 B
on Faith and Order, 1927 R
Léopoldville, of independent African states, 1960 H
'Little Eight', for new West Indies federation, 1962 E
Locarno, 1925 K
London, on Greek independence, 1930 B
on Belgium, 1830 M, 1831 A, C, F, K
on Danish question, 1864 D
on neutrality of Luxembourg, 1867 E
on Black Sea clauses of 1856 Treaty, 1871 C
of Russian Social Democratic Party, 1903 L
naval, 1908 M
on Turkey and Balkans, 1912 M, 1913 A
of Allied Labour and Socialist Parties, 1918 B
on Near East, 1921 B
Anglo-Russian, 1924 D
on reparations, 1924 G
Round Table on India, 1929 M, 1930 L, 1931 C, 1931 J, 1932 L
naval disarmament, 1930 D, 1934 K
Japan leaves, 1936 A
monetary, 1933 F
on rearmament, 1935 B
on non-intervention in Spain, 1936 J
world trades unions, 1945 B
on Palestine, 1946 J
on Germany, 1947 L, 1950 E
on British Africa, 1948 J
to combat Russian aggression, 1951 J
on space travel, 1951 O
on Western foreign policy, 1952 F
on Rhodesias and Nyasaland, 1953 A
on British W. Indian federation, 1953 D
on European unity, 1954 K
of foreign ministers of Britain, Greece and Turkey, 1955 H
on Singapore constitution, 1957 C
on Nigerian constitution, 1957 E
on Kenya constitution, 1960 A, 1962 B
on Cyprus, 1960 A, 1964 A
on Sierra Leone constitution, 1960 D
on Nyasaland constitution, 1960 G
on Uganda constitution, 1961 K
on Mauritius constitution, 1965 J
Lucknow, all party, on India's status, 1928 H
Milan, of Socialist International, 1952 K

Montreal, on Commonwealth trade, 1958 J
Moscow, All-Union Soviet, 1927 M
of Soviet writers, 1934 U
of foreign ministers, 1947 C
of Russian Communist Party, 1952 K
on Soviet satellites, 1954 L
Münchengratz, 1833 J
Mundania, between Allies and Turkey, 1922 K
Munich, on Czechoslovakia, 1938 J
Nablus, of Arabs on Palestine, 1922 H
New Grenada, 1816 B
Nyon, on Mediterranean, 1937 J
Oxford, on Church, Community and State, 1937 R
Duke of Edinburgh's, on Industry, 1956 G
Panama, Pan American, under Bolivar, 1826 F
Paris, Peace, 1856 B, 1946 G
Summit, preliminary negotiations for, 1958 A, B, F, 1959 M
achieved, 1960 E
Peking, Asia and Pacific, 1952 K
All-China People's, 1954 J
Peru, Pan-American, makes Declaration of Peru, 1938 M
Prague, between France, Germany and Austria, 1813 G
Pan-Slav, 1848 F, 1908 G
of Soviet satellites, 1950 K
Rangoon, of Asian Socialists, 1953 A
Rastadt, 1797 M, 1799 D
Reichenbach, 1790 F
Rome, on immigration, 1924 E
of EDC foreign ministers, 1953 B
San Francisco, 1945 B, D
Peace between Allies and Japan, 1951 J
Spa, on reparations, 1920 G
Stockholm, of free trade unions, 1953 G
Stresa, between Britain, France and Italy, 1935 D
Tangier, N. African Nationalists, 1958 D
Troppau, 1820 K, L, M
Tucuman, 1816 G
Verona, 1822 K, L, M
Versailles, Peace, 1918 L, 1919 A
Belgium guaranteed place at, 1916 B
adopts principle of League of Nations, 1919 A
League Covenant laid before, 1919 B
Vienna, 1814 L, 1815 F, 1820 E
on Danube basin, 1936 L
World Communist, 1952 M
Warsaw, Communist, 1947 K
Communist Youth, 1955 H
Washington, on Samoa, 1887 F
Pan-American, 1889 K
International Labour, 1919 K
on disarmament, 1921 L
scientific, 1940 P
Wavelengths, redistribution of, 1948 P
Wembley, Power, 1924 P
Zemstvo, 1904 L
Zionist, 1945 H
Confessional (F. Blackburne), 1766 R
Confessions (Rousseau), 1781 U
Confessions of an Opium Eater (T. de Quincey), 1821 U
Confessions of Zeno (I. Svevo), 1921 U
Confidential Clerk, The (T. S. Eliot), 1953 W
Conflicts (L. B. Namier), 1942 O
Congo, Belgian: Colonisation, 1878 L; rivalry with Portuguese, 1884 B; colony established, 1885 B; Belgian advances in, 1893 F; atrocities in, 1903 E, 1905 L; revolt in, 1905 B; Leopold II hands over to Belgium, 1908 H; frontier settled, 1927 G; Brussels conference promises independence, 1960 A; independence as Congolese Republic, 1960 F. *See also* Congolese Republic
Congo, French: de Brazza in, 1886 D, 1888 M; boundary with Cameroons settled, 1894 C; reorganised, 1910 A
Congo, International Association of, recognised, 1884 M
Congolese Republic:
independence, 1960 F
army mutinies, 1960 G
Belgium sends troops to, 1960 G
Lumumba appeals to UN, 1960 G
Léopoldville government severs relations with Belgium, 1960 G
UN demands evacuation of Belgian troops, 1960 G
UN troops enter Katanga, 1960 H
Russia provides aircraft for Lumumba, 1960 J
Kasavubu dismisses Lumumba, 1960 J
Lumumba arrested, 1960 M
Kasavubu establishes central government, 1961 B
Lumumba's death, 1961 B
UN urges use of force, 1961 B
Khruschev calls for supervised restoration of independent Congo, 1961 B
Congolese leaders agree on Confederation under Kasavubu, 1961 C
Coquilhatville conference, 1961 D
Tshombe arrested, 1961 D
United States of Congo formed, 1961 E
Tshombe freed, 1961 F
UN breaks with Katanga government, 1961 J
Hammarskjöld killed in air crash, 1961 J
UN force attacks Katanga, 1961 M
cease-fire in Katanga, 1961 M
Tshombe ends secession of Katanga, 1961 M
UN plan for reunification of Congo, 1962 J
cease-fire, 1962 K
UN troops occupy Elisabethville, 1962 M
capture Jadotville, 1963 A
Tshombe accepts plan for Katanga secession, 1963 A
Tshombe is forced to resign, 1963 F
rebels take Albertville, 1964 F
UN operations end, 1964 F
rebels take Stanleyville, 1964 H
People's Republic proclaimed, 1964 H
white mercenaries in, 1964 H
Stanleyville recaptured from rebels, 1964 L
Kasavubu dismisses Tshombe, 1965 K
Mobutu deposes Kasavubu, 1965 L
Congo, River, Stanley traces source of, 1875 P; explorations of Stanley and de Brazza, 1880 F; Portuguese designs near, 1884 B; free trade on, 1884 L; Anglo-Portuguese agreement on, 1890 L
Congo, Upper, Arab rising in, 1892 L, 1897 J
Congregationalists. *See under* Religious Denominations
Congresses. *See* Conferences
Coningsby (B. Disraeli), 1844 U
Connaissance de Dieu (A. Gratry), 1855 R
Connolly, Cyril Vernon, B. author and journalist (b. 1903), 1935 U, 1938 U
Connelly, Marc, Am. dramatist (b. 1890), 1924 W
Conquest of Peru, The (W. H. Prescott), 1846 Q
Conrad, Joseph (Tedor Josef Konrad Korzeniowski), B. formerly Pol. novelist (1857–1924), 1857 Z, 1895 U, 1897 U, 1900 U, 1904 U, 1907 U, 1914 U, 1915 U, 1924 Z
Conscience, Hendrik, Belg. poet (1812–83), 1837 U
Conscription (military service):
in Austria, 1936 D

Conscription—*contd.*
in Britain, cabinet favours, 1915 M
Labour Party opposes, 1916 A
Act in force, 1916 B
ministry of, 1916 O
ends, 1920 D
for men of 20, 1929 D
for men between 19 and 41, 1939 J
for men, lowered to 18½, 1941 M
for women, 1941 M
for men between 18 and 26, 1948 M
extended for two years, 1950 J
in China, 1955 G
in France, 1872 G
reduced, 1928 C
selective, adopted, 1964 G
in Germany, reintroduced, 1935 O, 1936 H
West German constitution amended to permit, 1956 C
in Japan, 1872 N
in New Zealand, selective, 1961 J
in Russia, 1874 A, 1922 J
in US, selective, 1917 E
under National Labor Service Act, 1942 K
Selective Service bill, 1948 F
See also Armies
Conservation of energy, theory of, 1837 P, 1842 P
Conservative Parties. *See under* Political Parties
Conservatism in America (C. Rossiter), 1956 O
Considérant, Victor Prosper, F. Socialist (1809–93), 1836 O
Considérations sur la France (J. de Maistre), 1796 O
Considérations sur la Revolution française (A. de Staël), 1818 O
Considérations sur le Gouvernement (P. Malouet), 1789 O
Conspiracy of Pontiac, The (F. Parkman), 1851 Q
Constable, John, B. artist (1776–1837), 1776 Z, 1809 S, 1817 S, 1820 S, 1821 S, 1827 S, 1828 S, 1837 Z
Constant de Rebecque, Henri Benjamin, F. author and politician (1767–1830), 1767 Z, 1807 U, 1813 O, Z
Constantine I, King of Greece (1913–17, 1920–22), 1917 F; plebiscite favours return, 1920 M; abdicates, 1922 J
Constantine II, King of Greece (1964–); accession, 1964 C; dismisses Papandreou, 1965 G
Constantine, prince, grandson of Catherine II of Russia, 1781 B
Constantinople, Turkey: protection of Christians in 1724 G; treaty, 1784 A; conference, 1876 M, 1877 A; Britain resolves to declare war, if Russia occupies, 1877 G; Armenians in, massacred, 1895 K, L; Russians propose to seize, 1895 K, 1896 L; Armenian revolution in, 1896 H; Peace, between Greece and Turkey, 1897 M; army revolt, 1909 D; Allies occupy, 1918 L, 1920 C; Turkey to retain, 1920 B; Allies forbid Greek occupation, 1922 G; name changed to Istanbul, 1930 C. *See also* Istanbul
Constant Nymph, The (M. Kennedy), 1926 W
Constitutional History of England (H. Hallam), 1827 Q
Constitutional History of England (W. Stubbs), 1874 Q
Constitutional View of the War Between the States (A. H. Stephens), 1868 O
Constitution of Church and State (S. T. Coleridge), 1828 Q
Constitutions:
Aden, suspended, 1965 J
Aden and S. Arabia Federation, talks break down, 1965 H
Argentina, 1853 E, 1956 E
Australia, representative government in, 1850 H, 1855 G
responsible government in W. Australia, 1870 H, 1890 K
federal, opposed, 1891 C
discussed, 1897 A, 1899 N
achieved, 1900 J
Austria, 1848 D, E, 1849 C
abolished, 1851 M
amended by October Diploma to provide for federation, 1860 K
is centralised by February Patent, 1861 B
opposition to, 1861 H
annulled, 1865 J
revised, 1867 M, 1920 K
Austrian Netherlands, revoked, 1789 K
Baden, 1818 H
Bavaria, 1818 E, 1919 H
Belgium, 1831 B
Brazil, promised, 1821 B
plans for, 1823 L
in force, 1826 C, 1891 B
British Guiana, in force, 1961 G
conference breaks down, 1962 L
agreement for internal self-government, 1963 G
conference, 1965 L
Brunswick, 1830 J
Bulgaria, 1879 B, 1881 G, 1883 J
Canada, legislative assemblies for Upper and Lower, 1791 E
Cape Colony, 1853 G
responsible government in, 1872 K
Central American Union, 1921 J
Chile, 1833 E
China, provisional, adopted, 1931 E
Croatia, internal self-government, 1873 L
Cuba, convention for framing, 1900 L
Platt amendment on, 1901 C
in force, 1901 F
suspended, 1957 K
Cyprus, proposals for, 1956 M
conference, 1964 A
Czechoslavakia, 1920 B
autonomy for Slovakia and Ruthenia, 1938 K
Denmark, 1842 F, 1863 L
ultimatum for repeal, 1864 A
revised, 1866 G
for single chamber, 1953 C
Ecuador, 1830 J, 1929 C
Egypt, responsible government in, 1878 M
by Organic law, 1883 E
suspended, 1923 D
restored, 1929 K
suspended, 1934 L
Nationalists demand revision, 1935 M
abolished, 1952 M
Eire, 1922 K
oath of allegiance to British Crown removed from, 1933 E
passes Dáil, 1937 F
Finland, 1861 D
suppressed, 1899 B
France, Estates General summoned, 1788 H
Third Estate undertakes to frame, 1789 F
Louis XVI accepts, 1790 G
constitutional monarchy, 1791 J
revised, 1793 F
for Directory, 1795 H
of Year VIII (Consulate), 1799 M

Fifth, 1802 H
First Empire, 1804 E
Louis XVIII's Charter, 1814 F
Napoleon's 'champ de Mai', 1815 F
Constitutional Charter, 1830 H
Republican, 1848 L
revised, 1851 M
Louis Napoleon given monarchical powers, 1852 A
Second Empire, 1852 M
Senate becomes an Upper House, 1870 C
Walloon amendment, 1875 A
Republican, 1875 A, B, G
National Assembly summons new Senate and Chamber, 1876 C
Chamber is moved from Versailles to Paris, 1879 L
exclusion from presidency of members of former dynasties, 1884 H
life senatorships abolished, 1884 H
Boulanger campaigns for revision, 1888 D
draft, rejected by referendum, 1946 E
revised, adopted, 1946 K
Fifth Republic, 1958 J
Germany, 1849 C
Empire, 1871 D
Weimar Republic, 1919 G
W. Germany's amended to permit conscription, 1956 C
Greece, adopted, 1822 A
revised, 1844 C
democratic, 1864 L
revised, 1910 A, 1911 F
Republican, 1924 C
further revisions, 1925 J, 1927 F, 1929 E
Gold Coast, 1946 L
Hanover, 1819 M, 1831 C, 1833 J
suppressed, 1837 G
new, imposed, 1840 H, 1855 E
Hesse-Cassel, 1830 J, 1831 A
Holland, 1848 C
Hungarian, 1867 B, 1920 B
Iceland, self-government for, 1874 G
India, Montagu-Chelmsford Report on, 1918 G, 1937 D
as federal republic, 1949 L
Italy, conflict over, 1900 B
Fascist grand council becomes part of, 1928 L
revised, 1938 M
Republican, 1946 F, 1947 M
Jamaica, suspended, 1839 D
self-government for, 1957 L, 1959 G
Japan, 1889 B, 1946 L
Kashmir, for incorporation in India, 1957 A
Kenya, conference, 1960 A, 1962 B
Libya, self-government revoked, 1927 C
Mauritius, conference, 1965 J
Mexico, congress for framing, 1822 E
Montenegro, 1905 M
Mozambique, legislative council in, 1907 E
Naples, promised, 1820 G, 1848 B
Natal, 1837 F, 1893 E
Newfoundland, suspended, 1933 M
New Granada, 1832 B
New Zealand, representative government in, 1852 F, 1856 N
centralised, 1875 K, 1876 N
Nigeria, modified self-government for, 1947 A
Conference, 1957 E
Norway, 1814 D, L, 1884 N
Nyasaland, Conference, 1960 G
Orange River Colony, self-government for, 1906 M, 1907 G
Palestine, suspended, 1923 E
Persia, overthrown, 1908 F
Peru, 1836 K
Philippines, offered by US, 1899 C
Piedmont, 1848 C
Poland, guaranteed by Russia and Prussia, 1764 D
Diet, 1788 K
a free, 1791 B, E
abrogated, 1792 E
revised, 1815 L
abolished, 1832 B
revised, 1921 C, 1935 D
Portugal, 1821 A, 1822 J
annulled, 1823 F
revised, 1826 D
Liberal, supported by Quadruple Alliance, 1834 D
revised, 1911 H, 1933 E
Prussia, promised, 1815 E
granted, 1848 C, M
Liberal, 1850 A
S. Rhodesia, 1922 A, 1923 K
referendum for, 1961 G
new, in force, 1962 K
Rome, 1848 C
revoked, 1850 D
Rumania, responsible government demanded, 1928 E
remodelled, 1948 D
revised, 1952 J
Russia, support for a liberal, 1903 N
Zemstvo Congress demands Republican, 1904 L
Parliamentary institutions demanded, 1905 E
ratified by Soviet Congress, 1925 E
revised, 1936 M
commission to draft new, 1962 D
Sardinia, 1848 C
Saxe-Weimar, 1816 E
Saxony, 1830 J, 1831 J
Serbia, 1835 N
restored, 1894 E, 1903 F
Siam, 1932 F
Sierra Leone, conference, 1960 D
Singapore, conference, 1957 E
becomes self-governing, 1959 F
S. Africa, convention for drafting, 1908 K
Spain, 1812 C
annulled, 1814 E
restored, 1820 A, C
powers demand abolition, 1823 A
Quadruple Alliance support for a liberal, 1834 D
liberal granted, 1837 F, 1845 E
re-established, 1856 J
annulled, 1856 K
revised, 1869 F
republican, 1873 B
Cortes provide for two-chamber legislature, 1876 A
republican, 1831 M
restored, 1936 B
Sudan, suppressed, 1958 L
Sweden, guaranteed by Russia and Prussia, 1764 D
revised, 1865 M, 1910 B
Switzerland, 1813 M, 1848 J, 1874 E
Syria, 1950 J
Tanganyika, 1955 L
internal self-government for, 1961 E
Tasmania, self-government for, 1856 N
Transvaal, agitation for self-government, 1905 A
granted, 1905 D, 1906 M

Constitutions—*contd.*
Transylvania, abrogated, 1784 G
Trinidad, cabinet government introduced, 1959 G
Turkey, partial autonomy for Serbs, 1817 L
revised, 1876 M
restored, 1908 G
republican, 1923 K
new, proposed, 1961 E
Tuscany, 1848 B
abolished, 1852 E
Uganda, conference, 1961 K
United Arab Republic, 1962 J
United States of America, first, 1777 L
framed, 1787 E, J
in force, 1788 F
first ten amendments to, 1789 C
ratified, 1791 M
11th amendment, 1794 M
12th amendment, on presidential ballots, 1804 J
13th amendment, 1865 M
14th amendment, 1866 F
states to draw up constitutions, 1867 C
15th amendment, not to revoke suffrage, 1870 C
presidential succession, 1886 E
Negro Rights and Force bill, 1892 L
17th amendment, on popular election of senators, 1913 E
18th amendment, on prohibition, 1919 A
19th amendment, on women's franchise, 1920 H
20th amendment, advancing president's inauguration, 1933 B
21st amendment, repeals prohibition, 1933 M
Venezuela, 1811 G, 1821 F
Venice, 1797 E
Württemberg, 1819 J
Yugoslavia, suppressed, 1929 A
revision demanded, 1932 L
new, 1946 A
Consumers' Council, in Britain, 1963 C
Contemplation de la nature (C. Bonnet), 1764 R
Contemplations, Les (V. Hugo), 1856 U
Contes d'Éspagne et d'Italie (A. de Musset), 1829 U
Contes Drôlatiques (H. de Balzac), 1832 U
Continental Drift, theory of, 1915 P
'Continental System', Napoleon's: in operation, 1806 L; Prussia joins, 1807 G; Portugal refuses to enter, 1807 L; Austria joins, 1808 B; Sweden joins, 1810 A; Napoleon's annexations in Germany, to strengthen, 1810 M; pressure on Sweden to continue in, 1812 A; Prussia to adhere to, 1812 B
Contraband of War, defined, 1856 D
Contraband, British Black List, 1916 B, G
Contraceptive Pills: devised, 1952 P; Roman Catholics oppose use of, 1964 R. *See also under* Birth Control
Control of Inflation, The (J. E. Meade), 1958 O
Controls:
Allied, of Bulgaria, abolished, 1928 A
Committee dissolved, 1931 A
Allied Control Commission for Germany, 1945 F
limits German protection, 1946 C
dissolves Wehrmacht, 1946 H
Russian delegates leave, 1948 C
British, of mines and shipping, 1916 M
of textile industries, 1918 O
of trade with China, removed, 1957 E
of trade with dollar area, removed, 1959 E
of office and industrial development, 1964 M
NATO countries, trade with Soviet block, relaxed, 1958 H
US, of food and fuel, 1917 G
of railways, 1917 M
ends, 1920 C
removed, 1946 L
See also under Currency; Rationing
Conventions (Diplomatic):
Akkerman, Russia with Turkey, 1826 K
Anglo-Russian, to prevent Baltic trade with France, 1793 C
Annapolis, under Madison and Hamilton, 1786 E
Bartenstein, between Russia and Prussia, 1807 D; Britain joins, 1807 F
Brussels, to control liquor traffic, 1911 O
Cintra, French army in Portugal with Britain, 1808 H
Graeco-Turkish, 1881 G
Hague, The, to fix limits of territorial waters, 1882 F
Irish, 1917 G
London, on Transvaal, 1884 B
Marsa, between France and Tunis, 1883 F
Moss, between Sweden and Norway, 1814 H
Motor car, 1910 O
Philadelphia, 1787 E
Pretoria, between Britain and Transvaal, 1893 L
Slavery, 1826 J
Tauroggen, between Russia and Prussia, 1812 M
Uddevalla, between Denmark and Sweden, 1788 L
See also Treaties
Conventions, of US Political Parties (notable):
Democratic, first, 1832 L, 1912 G, 1916 F, 1920 G, 1924 F
Progressive Republican, 1912 H
Republican, 1912 F, 1916 F, 1920 F, 1924 F
Conversations (Anglican-Methodist), 1963 R
Conversations with Stalin (M. Djilas), 1962 E
Conversions, religious, notable:
Boris of Bulgaria, 1896 B
Newman, 1845 R
Conveyor-belts, 1913 P
Convicts, transportation of:
from Britain, to Botany Bay, 1823 G
to Cape Colony, forbidden, 1849 L
to Tasmania, 1849 L
suspended, 1853 N
from France, 1851 O
Convoy system, 1917 O
Convoys, notable:
British, to Malta, 1942 F, H
to Russia, 1942 E, J, M
Conway, Henry Seymour, B. soldier and politician (1721–95), 1766 G
Conway, William Martin, lord Conway, B. explorer and art critic (1856–1937), 1896 P
Cook, James, B. navigator (1728–79), 1768 P, 1770 P, 1775 P, 1776 P, 1777 P, 1778 P, 1779 Z
Cook, Thomas, B. travel agent (1808–92), 1841 W
Cooke, Deryck, B. musician, completes Mahler symphony, 1964 T
Coolidge, Calvin, Am. Republican (1872–1933), 30th president of US (1923–9), 1872 Z, 1924 E, F, 1925 C; nominated vice-president, 1920 F; succeeds Harding as president, 1923 H; wins presidential election, 1924 L
Coomassie, Ghana, British capture, 1896 A
Cooper, Anthony Ashley, 7th earl of Shaftesbury, B. social reformer (1801–85), 1842 O
Cooper, Duff, lord Norwich, B. Conservative politician and diplomat (1890–1954), resigns ftom cabinet, 1938 K
Cooper, Gary, Am. film actor, 1932 W
Cooper, Gladys, B. actress (b. 1889), 1889 Z
Cooper, Gordon, Am. astronaut, 1963 P

Cooper, James Fenimore, Am. novelist (1789–1851), 1789 Z, 1821 U, 1823 U, 1826 U, 1840 U, 1851 Z
Co-operative Movement:
Birmingham tailors, 1777 O
Rochdale pioneers, 1844 O
Cooperstown, New York, US, baseball first played at, 1839 X
Coote, Sir Eyre, B. soldier (1726–83), 1781 G
Copeland, Ralph, B. astronomer (1837–1905), 1882 P
Copenhagen, Denmark: Veterinary and Agricultural College, 1773 P; battle, 1801 D; Royal Navy bombards, 1807 J; Town Hall, 1893 S
Copland, Aaron, Am. musician (b. 1900), 1900 Z, 1925 T, 1938 T, 1942 T, 1954 T, 1962 T
Copley, John Singleton, B. artist (1737–1815), 1778 S, 1780 S
Copper deposits, in Katanga, 1891 D
Coptic Church. *See under* Religious Denominations
Copyright:
Berlin convention, 1908 O
British Act, 1911 O
revised international convention (U.C.C.), 1955 O
Coräes, Adamantios, Greek patriot (1748–1833), 1803 O
Corbeaux, Les (Becque), 1882 W
Corbett, Matthew Ridley, B. artist (1850–1902), 1894 S
'Corbusier, Le'. *See* Jeanneret, C. E.
Corday d'Armont, Charlotte, F. revolutionary (1768–93), 1793 G
Cordeliers Club, Paris, 1790 N
Cordite, invented, 1889 P
'Corelli, Marie'. *See* Mackay, Mary
Corfu, Greece: Pact, for union of Serbs, Croats and Slovenes, 1917 G; Italy occupies, 1923 H; Greece appeals to League, 1923 H; Albania held responsible for incidents in, 1949 D
Corinne (A. de Staël), 1807 U
Corinth Canal, Greece, 1893 P
Cork, Eire, martial law in, 1920 M
Corn, treatise on, 1815 O
Corn is Green, The (E. Williams), 1938 W
Corn Law Rhymes (E. Elliott), 1831 O
Corn Laws, British: tracts on, 1777 O, 1831 O; revised, 1815 C; agitation for repeal, 1819 H; by Anti-Corn-Law league, 1838 C, J; amended, 1822 G, 1828 G, 1842 D; repealed, 1846 E
Corn Trade, in France, 1763 E, 1774 J, 1776 J
Cornelius, Peter von, G. artist (1783–1867), 1825 S, 1858 T
Cornwallis, Charles, marquess of Cornwallis, B. soldier and Governor-General of India (1738–1805), 1780 H, 1781 A, C, J; capitulates at Yorktown, 1781 K; as Governor-General of India, 1786 B; defeats Tippoo at Seringapatam, 1791 E; reforms, 1793 N
Corona (P. Claudel), 1915 U
Coronel, S. America, naval battle, 1914 L
Corot, Jean Baptiste Camille, F. artist (1796–1875), 1796 Z, 1850 S, 1851 S, 1859 S, 1870 S, 1873 S, 1875 Z
Corpus Inscriptionis Graecum (ed. Böckh), 1824 Q
Corpus Juris Civilis, 1872 Q
Corregidor, Philippines, surrenders, 1942 E
Corridors of Power (C. P. Snow), 1964 U
Corruption, political:
in Britain, sale of Parliamentary seats forbidden, 1809 F
Lynskey tribunal to investigate, 1948 L
in Sicily, 1848 A
in US, by Tweed Ring in New York, 1871 G
in Ohio, 1911 O
judicial, 1913 O
Sherman Adams affair, 1958 F
See also Secret Societies
Corsair, The (Byron), 1814 U
Corsica, Island: France purchases, 1768 G; Paoli expelled, 1769 H; British occupy, 1793 G; British abandon, 1796 N; Italy claims, 1938 L; Daladier visits, 1939 A
Cort, Henry, B. iron-master (1740–1800), 1784 P
Corti, Ludovico, Count, It. diplomat (1823–88), 1878 F
Cortines, Ruiz, president of Mexico, 1952 G
Cortisone (Compound E), 1949 P
Corunna, Spain, 1809 A
Corvée, The, in France, 1776 A
Cosgrave, William Thomas, Sinn Fein leader, president of Eire (b. 1880), 1922 J, 1933 J
Cosmic radiation, 1945 P
Cosmic rays:
analysis of, 1933 P
observatory for, 1953 P
studied by artificial satellite, 1958 P
Cosmic Rays and Nuclear Physics (L. Janossy), 1948 P
Cosmopolitanism and the National State (F. Meinecke), 1908 O
Cosmos (A. von Humboldt), 1845 P
Cossacks, revolt of, 1773 K, 1774 J
Costa, Gomes da, Port. politician, 1926 E, G
Costa, Lucio, Brazil, architect, 1957 S
Costa Rica:
enters Central American Federation, 1823 G
frontier dispute with Panama, 1921 C
Costello, John Aloysius, Ir. Fine Gael politician (b. 1891), premier, 1891 Z, 1951 F, 1954 F
Costa, Charles de, Belg. author (1829–79), 1867 U
Cotman, John Sell, B. artist (1782–1842), 1803 S
Cotta, Johann Friedrich, G. publisher (1764–1832), 1798 V
Cotton, Thomas Henry, B. golfer (b. 1907), 1934 X
Cotton gin, invented, 1793 P
Cotton industry:
in Britain, trade in, 1772 Y, 1782 Y, 1792 Y, 1802 Y, 1812 Y, 1822 Y, 1832 Y, 1842 Y, 1852 Y, 1862 Y, 1872 Y, 1882 Y, 1892 Y, 1902 Y, 1912 Y, 1922 Y, 1932 Y
statistics of weavers, 1806 Y
spinners reduce productivity, 1935 A
reorganisation of Lancashire industry, 1959 O
in US, grants of exports, 1793 P, 1910 Y, 1940 Y, 1961 Y
Cotton, raw production, 1910 Y, 1961 Y
Cotton, sea-island, 1786 P
Cotton, spinning by steam, 1785 P
Cotton, tariffs, 1882 O, 1934 H
Coty, René, F. last president of 4th Republic (1882–1962), 1962 Z; elected president, 1953 M
Coubertin, Pierre de, F. re-founder of Olympic Games (1863–1937), 1863 Z
Coué, Émile, F. psychologist (1857–1926), 1857 Z, 1926 Z
Coulomb, Charles Augustin, F. natural philosopher (1736–1806), 1777 P, 1779 P, 1785 P
Council for the Encouragement of Music and the Arts (CEMA), 1941 T
Council of Europe:
Assembly drafts constitution of European Political Community, 1953 A
Cyprus joins, 1961 E
Count of Monte Cristo, The (A. Dumas), 1844 U
Country Doctor, The (F. Kafka), 1920 U
Country Party. *See under* Political Parties

Coups d'état:
in Austria, Schuschnigg's 'bloodless', 1935 K
in Bolivia, 1934 M
in Bulgaria, 1923 F
in Burma, 1962 C
in Czechoslovakia, Communist, 1948 B
in Egypt, by King Fuad, 1928 G
by Neguib, 1952 G
by Nasser, 1954 B
in Finland, Fascist, 1930 K
in France, by Louis Napoleon, 1851 M
in Greece, 1925 F
in Honduras, 1963 K
in Iraq, 1958 G
in Japan, 1936 B
in Lithuania, Fascist, 1932 B
in Persia, 1908 F, 1909 G
in Poland, by Pilsudski, 1926 E
in Portugal, 1828 F, 1926 E
in Siam, military, 1933 F, 1958 K
in Syria, 1951 L, 1961 J
in Thailand, 1957 J
in Turkey, 1909 D, 1913 A, 1960 E
in Venezuela, 1909 M
in Viet-Nam, 1960 H, 1963 L
in Yemen, 1962 J
Coups d'état, attempted:
in Austria, by ex-Emperor Charles, 1921 C
by Pfrimer, 1931 J
Nazi, 1934 G
in France, by Louis Napoleon, 1840 H
by Boulanger, 1887 K
Fascist, 1937 L
in Germany, by Kapp, 1920 C
Black Reichwehr, 1923 K
Hitler's in Munich, 1923 L
in Indonesia, 1965 K
in Persia, royalist, 1953 H
in Syria, alleged, 1958 C, 1961 M
Coupling, railway, automatic, 1906 P
Courbet, Gustave, F. artist (1819–77), 1819 Z, 1894 S, 1850 S, 1855 S, 1867 S, 1877 Z
Courland, now Russia, German offensive in, 1915 D
Cournot, Antoine Augustine, F. economist and mathematician (1801–77), 1888 O
Courrier Sud (St.-Exupéry), 1929 U
Course of Positive Philosophy (A. Comte), 1830 R
Courteline, Georges, F. dramatist (1858–1929), 1893 W
Courtois, B., F. chemist, 1811 P
Courts:
in Britain, Court of Appeal, 1873 C
Court of Chivalry, 1954 O
Divorce, 1857 O
Judicial Committee of Privy Council, 1876 L
Canadian appeals to, discontinued, 1946 O
Irish appeals to, made illegal, 1933 E
House of Lords, jurisdiction of, 1876 L
Supreme Court of Judicature, 1873 C
procedure revised, 1932 O
in Germany, industrial, 1890 G
in Holland, feudal, suppressed, 1784 G
in Japan, reformed, 1875 D
International Court of arbitration, 1899 E. *See also* International Court
See also Codes of Law; Judgments; Legislation
Cousine Bette, La (H. de Balzac), 1846 U
Cousins, Frank, B. trades unionist and Labour politician, 1904 Z
Couture, Thomas, F. artist (1815–79), 1847 S
Coventry, England:
bombing, 1941 D
cathedral, 1951 S, 1962 S
Belgrade Theatre, 1958 S
Coward, Noël, B. dramatist and composer (b. 1899), 1899 Z, 1924 W, 1925 W, 1929 W, 1931 W, 1941 W, 1943 W
Cowpens, S. Carolina, US, battle, 1781 A
Cowper, Francis Thomas de Grey, earl Cowper, B. administrator (1834–1905), lord lieutenant of Ireland, 1882 E
Cowper, William, B. poet (1731–1800), 1779 R, 1782 U, 1800 Z
Cox, David, B. landscape artist (1783–1859), 1813 S
Cox, James Middleton, Am. Democrat (b. 1870), fights presidential election, 1920 G, L
Cozens, Alexander, B. landscape artist (d. 1786), treatise by, 1785 S
Cozzens, James Gould, Am. author (b. 1903), 1958 U
Crabbe, George, B. poet (1754–1832), 1781 U, 1783 T, 1817 U, 1832 Z
Crabbe, Commander, B. naval officer, disappearance of, 1955 K
Cracow, Poland: Austrians take, 1795 K; becomes independent republic, 1815 P; rising, 1846 B; occupied by Austrians and Russians, 1846 C; annexed by Austrians, 1846 L; Pan-Slav Conference, 1892 O; Russians hold line at, 1914 M; Russians take, 1945 A
Cradock, Sir Christopher George, B. admiral (1862–1914), 1914 L
Craig, Sir James Henry, B. general (1748–1812), 1795 J
Craig, James, Viscount Craigavon, United Ulster leader (1870–1940), 1921 B
Craik, Mrs. *See* Mulock, Dinah
Crane, Stephen, Am. author (1871–1900), 1871 Z, 1900 Z
Cranford (E. Gaskell), 1853 U
Cranko, John, B. choreographer (b. 1927), 1949 T, 1951 T, 1952 T, 1959 T
Crankshaw, Edward, B. journalist and historian (b. 1909), 1963 Q
Craythorne Committee on Sunday entertainment, 1964 W
Cream separator, invented, 1877 P
Crease-resisting fabric, 1929 P
Crêche, the first, 1769 O
Creighton, Mandell, B. churchman and historian (1843–1901), 1886 Q
Creole, Der (Zshokke), 1830 U
Creole incident, 1841 L
Crete (Candia), Island, Levant: Egyptians capture, 1824 D; Mehemet Ali surrenders, 1840 G, L; Turkish ultimatum to Greeks in, 1866 M; revolts against Turks, 1866 J, 1896 B, G, H, 1897 B; Greeks leave, 1869 B; proclaims union with Greece, 1897 B, M, 1908 K; Turks evacuate, 1898 L; Greek revolt, 1905 C; Greece annexes, 1913 M; Britain occupies, 1940 L; Germany invades, 1941 E; excavations in, 1900 Q
Creuzer, Georg Friedrich, G. philosopher (1771–1858), 1810 Q
Crève-cœur, Le (L. Aragon), 1941 U
Crichel Down Inquiry, 1953 O
Crick, Francis Henry Compton, B. chemist (b. 1916), 1961 P
Cricket:
MCC move to Lord's Cricket Ground, 1787 X
codifies Laws, 1788 X
English county championships, 1890 X
record scores:
Grace's triple centuries, 1876 X

Hobbs's record number of centuries, 1926 X
Hutton's test innings, 1938 X
English XI's tours of Australia:
first, 1862 X
first official tour, 1880 X
England *v.* Australia test matches, 1921 X, 1930 X, 1938 X, 1946 X, 1953 X
Crime, statistics of convictions for:
in Britain, 1873 Y, 1939 Y, 1950 Y, 1960 Y
in US, 1939 Y, 1950 Y, 1960 Y
Crimea, Russia: Russia conquers from Turkey, 1771 F; Turkey cedes, 1774 G; Turkey agrees to annexations, 1784 A; Allied landings, 1854 J. *See also under* War, Crimean. Red Army enters, 1919 D; independence, 1921 K; plans for film studios in, 1935 W; German attack in, 1942 E; Russians begin liberation, 1944 D
Crime and Punishment (F. Dostoievsky), 1866 U
Crime de Sylvestre Bonnard, Le (A. France), 1881 U
Criminal, The (C. Lombroso), 1876 O
Criminals: identification of, 1890 O; First Offenders Act, 1958 O. *See also* Convicts
Criminology, science of, founded, 1876 O
Crippen, Hawley Harvey, Am. murderer (1861–1910), 1910 O
Cripps, Sir Stafford, B. Labour politician (1889–1952), 1889 Z, 1950 K; leads mission to USSR, 1940 E; becomes Leader of House, 1942 B; offers India self-government, 1942 D; replaced in war cabinet by Morrison, 1942 L
Crisis, agricultural, 1946 G
Crisis, economic:
in Australia, 1873 O
in Austria, 1811 B, 1873 E, 1931 E
in Belgium, 1926 G, 1932 J, 1935 C
in Brazil, 1928 O
in Britain, 1846 O, 1866 O, 1890 O, 1929 O, 1931 G, H, J,
through ending of Lend-Lease, 1945 K
over balance of payments, 1949 J, 1955 K, 1956 B
Butler's credit squeeze, 1955 K, 1961 G, 1964 K, 1964 L
pressure on pound, 1964 L; is eased, 1965 C
in Canada, 1849 K
in Europe, 1873 O, 1929 O, 1949 J
in France, 1788 H, 1926 G, H, 1935 G, 1936 K, 1949 K
in Germany, 1921 H, L, 1922 F, 1923 A, J, K, 1927 C, 1931 G, H
in Italy, 1936 K
in Japan, 1927 D
in Portugal, 1902 E
in US, 1784 N, 1873 J, O, 1920 O, 1929 O, 1933 C, 1957 O, 1958 O
World, 1929 U
Crisis, fuel, British, 1947 B, V
Crisis in the University, The (W. Moberley), 1949 O
Crisis of the Old Order (A. M. Schlesinger), 1957 Q
Crispi, Francesco, It. statesman (1819–1901), 1887 G, 1891 A, 1893 M, 1896 C
Cristina, Queen Regent of Spain, 1840 K
Critic, The (R. B. Sheridan), 1779 W
Critical Exposition of the Philosophy of Liebnitz (B. Russell), 1900 R
Criticism of Political Economy (K. Marx), 1859 O
Critique of Judgment (Kant), 1790 R
Critique of Practical Reason (Kant), 1788 R
Critique of Pure Reason (Kant), 1781 R
attacks on, answered, 1783 R
Critique of Revelation (J. G. Fichte), 1792 R
Croats, boycott Yugoslav Parliament, 1928 H, 1935 F. *See also under* Political Parties
Croce, Benedetto, It. philosopher (1866–1952), 1866 Z, 1903 V, 1941 Q, 1952 Z
Crofts, Freeman Wills, B. Author of detective stories, 1920 U
Crome, John Bernay, B. artist (1794–1842), 1803 S
Cromer, Lord. *See* Baring, Evelyn
Crompton, Samuel, B. inventor (1753–1827), 1779 P
Cromwell's Letters and Speeches (T. Carlyle), 1845 Q
Cronberg, Germany, 1906 H
Cronje, Piet Arnoldus, Boer general (1840–1911), 1899 M, 1900 B
Crookes, Sir William, B. scientist (1832–1919), 1832 Z, 1861 P, 1900 P, 1919 Z
Crosby, Harry L. ('Bing'), Am. film actor, 1942 W
Crosby, Brass, B. politician (1729–93), 1771 C
Cross, Charles Frederick, B. chemist (1885–1935), 1892 P
Cross, Richard Asheton, lord Cross, B. Conservative politician (1823–1914), 1874 B, 1885 F
Crotchet Castle (T. L. Peacock), 1831 U
Crown Point, New York, US, 1775 E
Croydon, Surrey, England, tram-road at, 1801 P
Crucible, The (A. Miller), 1953 W
Cruelle Énigme (P. Bourget), 1885 U
Cruel Sea, The (N. Monsarrat), 1951 U
Cruz Report on apartheid, 1955 L
Crystallography, studies in, 1784 P, 1813 P, 1838 P; X-ray, 1912 P
Ctesiphon, Mesopotamia, battle, 1915 L
Cuba: US acquisition urged, 1854 K; risings, 1895 N; US war with, 1898 D, E, G, M; ceded by Spain, 1898 M; becomes virtually a protectorate of US, 1901 F; revolt, 1906 B; US marines land, 1912 F, 1917 C; expropriation of sugar mills, 1959 F; US protests at, 1960 A; recognises Communist China, 1960 J; Kennedy's broadcast on Russian bases, 1962 K; Russia's offer to withdraw missiles, 1962 K; US blockade, 1962 K, L; Kennedy announces Russia begins dismantling bases, 1962 L; Russia withdraws bombers, 1962 L; US places shipping restrictions on, 1963 B; Russia agrees to withdraw troops, 1963
Cubism, 1907 S, 1912 S, 1914 S
Cubist Painters, The (Apollinaire), 1913 S
Cubitt, Joseph, B. civil engineer (1811–72), 1851 S
Cuddalore, off Madras, India, naval battle, 1782 G
Cugnot, Nicolas Joseph, F. engineer (1725–1804), 1762 P
Ciudad Rodrigo, Spain, battles, 1810 G, 1812 A
Cullen, William, B. physician (1710–90), 1774 P
Cultural Co-operation, International Union for, 1922 O
Culture and Anarchy (M. Arnold), 1869 O
Culture and Freedom (Dewey), 1939 R
Culture of Cities (L. Mumford), 1938 Q
Cummings, Edward Estlin, Am. poet (1874–1962), 1923 U, 1925 U
Cunard Company, 1963 K, 1964 M
Cuneiform inscriptions, 1837 Q
Cuno, Wilhelm, G. chancellor, 1922 L
Curie, Marie (*née* Sklodowska), F. scientist (1867–1934), 1867 Z, 1898 P, 1910 P, 1934 Z
Curie, Pierre, F. scientist (1860–1906), 1860 Z, 1898 P, 1906 Z
Curie-Joliot, F. scientist, 1934 P
Currency:
International Union proposed, 1943 O
in Belgium, Franc devalued, 1926 G, 1935 C

Currency—*contd.*
in Britain, bullion committee's report, 1810 J
Bank of England resumes cash payments, 1817 K, 1820 E
Bank Charter Act, limits fiduciary issue, 1844 G
Treasury notes issued, 1914 O
return to gold standard, 1925 D
treatise on, 1930 O
pound devalued, 1931 J, 1949 J
dollar travel allowances increased, 1957 F
convertibility of sterling for non-resident holders, 1958 M
foreign support for pound, 1965 J
Commonwealth Declaration on monetary affairs, 1933 G
in Europe, devaluation in, 1949 J
in France, Assignats issued, 1788 M
Franc notes issued, 1914 O
Franc made convertible, 1958 M
in Germany, experts confer on, 1922 L
rapid decline in Mark, 1923 K
temporary stability, 1923 L
suspension of cash transfers, 1934 G
reformed, 1948 F
in Iraq, withdrawal from sterling area, 1959 F
in Italy, Lira devalued, 1936 K
in Pakistan, devalued, 1955 G
in Russia, devalued, 1947 M
in US, specie payments resumed, 1879 A
paper money redeemable in gold, 1900 C
federal reserves reorganised, 1932 B
president authorised to revalue, 1934 A
See also Coinage; Gold Standard
Curtatone, Italy, Austrian victory, 1848 E
Curtin, John, Austral. Labour leader (1885–1945), 1945 G
Curtis, Lionel George, B. statesman (1872–1955), 1872 Z, 1916 O, 1934 R, 1945 O, 1955 Z
Curtiss, Glenn Hammond, Am. aviator (1878–1930), 1912 P
Curtius, Julius, G. diplomat, 1929 K, 1931 H
Curtius, T., G. chemist, 1890 P
Cushing, Harvey Williams, Am. neurological surgeon (1869–1939), 1902 P
Curzon, George Nathaniel, lord Curzon of Kedleston, B. diplomat (1859–1925), 1916 M, 1919 K
'Curzon Line', Poland, Russians cross, 1944 G
Curzon, the Last Phase (H. Nicolson), 1934 Q
Custom of the Country (E. Wharton), 1913 U
Customs Unions:
Austro-German, projected, 1931 C
Austro-Hungarian, 1850 O
Benelux, 1947 K
Ceylon and South India, 1964 M
European Economic Community, 1957 C, 1958 A. *See also* Common Market
Franco-Italian, 1948 C
German, 1888 K
E. Pakistan, 1965 E
Prussia, with Hesse-Darmstadt, 1827 N. *See also* Zollverein
US, 1789 G
Custozza, Italy, battles, 1848 G, 1866 F
Cuvier, Georges Léopold Chrétien, F. naturalist (1769–1832), 1769 Z, 1796 P, 1812 P, 1832 Z
Cuyper, P. J. H., Du. architect, 1877 S
Cyanide, used for extracting gold and silver, 1887 P
Cyclades Isles, 1827 K
Cycling Clubs, in England, 1878 X; in US, 1880 X
Cyclotron, the (or 'atom smasher'), 1931 P, 1934 P; giant, at California University, 1940 P; for Carnegie Institution, Washington, 1944 O; 'Nimrod', 1964 P
Cylinders, for steam engines, 1774 P
Cyprus:
British occupation, 1878 F, G
Britain annexes, 1914 L
declared a British colony, 1925 D
'Enosis' issue over, 1954 M, 1955 G, H
state of emergency, 1955 L
Athens broadcasts to, jammed, 1956 C
Makarios deported, 1956 C
Greece demands reference of problems to UN, 1956 C
EOKA rejects Harding's surrender terms, 1956 H
UN calls for peaceful solution, 1957 B
EOKA offers to suspend terrorism, 1957 C
UN offers to mediate, 1957 C
Greek resolution fails in UN, 1957 M
British plan for Graeco-Turkish joint administration, 1958 F
agreement for independence signed, 1959 B
London Conference breaks down, 1960 A
agreement on bases, 1960 G
becomes independent Republic, 1960 H
fighting between Greeks and Turks, 1964 B, C, D
UN mediator appointed, 1964 C
UN peace force takes over, 1964 C
Greece rejects direct talks with Turkey, 1964 F
Turkish 'planes bomb, 1964 H
UN orders cease-fire, 1964 H
Gen. Grivas assmues command of Greek Cypriot forces, 1964 H
UN extends mandate for force, 1964 M
Cyrano de Bergerac (E. Rostand), 1897 W
Cyrenaica: annexed by Italy, 1911 L; becomes autonomous under Italian suzerainty, 1912 K; Italian-Egyptian agreement on, 1925 M
Czech language: studies in, 1818 Q; ordinances, 1897 D, L, 1899 K
Czechoslovakia: US recognises, 1918 J; independent republic proclaimed, 1918 K; irredentist agitation in, 1928 M; first crisis, 1938 E; second crisis, 1938 J; Hitler annexes, 1939 C
Czechoslovak National Committee in London, 1940 G
Czech Question, The (T. G. Masaryk), 1895 O
Czernowitz (now Chernovtsky), Russia, Russians take, 1916 F, 1917 H
Czolgosz, Léon, Am. anarchist, 1901 J

D

Dadaist Movement, 1915 S, 1916 S, 1920 S
Daguerre, Louis Jacques Mandé, F. pioneer of photography (1789–1851), 1789 Z, 1839 P, 1851 Z
Dahl, Vladimir Ivanovich, R. lexicographer (1802–1872), 1861 Q
Dahn, Julius Sophus Felix, G. author (1834–1900), 1876 U
Dahomey, West Africa: King of, 1892 N; French protectorate over, 1893 L; proclaimed a French colony, 1894 F; becomes an independent Republic, 1960 G
Daimler, Gottlieb, G. inventor of petrol engine (1834–1900), 1882 P, 1885 P
Dairen. *See* Dalny
Daisy Miller (H. James), 1878 U
Dakar, in Senegal, W. Africa, 1904 N, 1940 J
Dakota, North, State, US, becomes state, 1889 B
Dakota, South, State, US, becomes state, 1889 B

Daladier, Edouard, F. Radical Socialist politician (b. 1884), forms ministries, 1933 A, 1934 A, 1938 D; at Munich Conference, 1938 J; visits Algiers, 1939 A; empowered to rearm, 1939 C; attempts to negotiate with Hitler, 1939 N; reforms ministry, 1939 J; resigns, 1940 C
Dalai Lama of Tibet: appointed to prepare Tibet for regional autonomy, 1956 D; escapes, 1959 C; appeals to UN, 1961 C
Dale, Sir Henry Hallett, B. scientist (b. 1875), 1945 P
Dalhousie, Earl of. *See* Ramsay, James
Dali, Salvador Felipe Jacinte, Sp. artist (b. 1904), 1929 S, 1934 S, 1951 S, 1955 S
Dallas, Tex., US, Kennedy assassinated at, 1963 L
Dalmatia: Austria obtains, 1797 K; ceded to Yugoslavia, 1920 L; Italy abandons claims in, 1924 C
Dalny (Dairen), Russia, Japanese occupy, 1904 E
Dalou, Jules, F. sculptor (1838–1902), 1898 S, 1899 S
Dalton, Hugh, B. Labour politician (1888–1962), as chancellor of Exchequer, 1945 G
Dalton, John, B. chemist and natural philosopher (1766–1844), 1766 Z, 1803 P, 1808 P, 1844 Z
Dalrymple, Sir Henry, B. soldier, 1808 H
Damaged Goods (E. Brieux), 1917 W
Damaraland, exploration of, 1850 P
Damascus, Syria: Allies occupy, 1918 K; French occupy, 1920 G; French bombard, 1925 K, 1926 E, 1945 E; army *coup* in, 1961 J
Dame aux Camélias, La (A. Dumas), 1848 U
Damian, F., Aus. instrument maker, 1829 T
Dams:
  Aswan, 1902 M
  Aswan High, finance for, 1956 G, 1958 K; work begins, 1960 A; rescue of antiquities in area, 1960 Q; opened, 1964 E
  Kariba, Rhodesia, 1960 E
  Zola, France, 1843 P
Dana, James Dwight, Am. geologist (1813–95), 1837 P
Dance of Death (A. Strindberg), 1901 U
Dances:
  Bebop, 1945 W, 1950 W
  Cake-walk, 1900 W
  Charleston, 1925 W
  Foxtrot, 1913 W
  Lambeth Walk, 1938 W
  Lancers, 1836 X
  Polka, 1835 W
  Quadrille, 1815 W
  Rock and Roll, 1956 W
  Slow Foxtrot, 1927 W
  Waltz, 1812 W
Dangerous Corner (J. P. Priestley), 1932 W
Danish language, 1775 O
Dannecker, Johann Heinrich von, G. sculptor (1758–1841), 1794 S
Dans le labyrinthe (Robbe-Grillet), 1960 U
Danton, George Jacques, F. revolutionary (1759–94), 1790 N, 1792 L; leads Committee of Public Safety, 1793 D; executed, 1794 D
Danton's Death (G. Buchner), 1835 U
Danube, River: Napoleon crosses, 1809 E; Vienna Note demands free passage, 1854 H; freedom of navigation, 1856 C; crossed by Russians, 1877 F; open to navigation, 1919 C; convention for internationalisation, 1921 G; London Conference on, 1932 D; Italian designs on, 1936 L; Belgrade Conference on, 1948 G
Danubian *Bloc*, 1934 C; Italian and German rival interests in, 1934 F
Danubian Principalities. *See under* Moldavia and Wallachia
Danzig, Poland: as a free city, 1772 H; ceded to Prussia, 1790 C, 1793 E; Polish treaty with, 1920 K; declared a free city, 1920 L; Poland occupies, 1933 C; elections won by Nazis, 1933 E; Polish agreement with, 1933 H, 1937 A; Germany annexes, 1939 J; Russians take, 1945 C
Darby, John Nelson, B. founder of Plymouth Brethren (1800–82), 1827 R
Dardanelles, The: Royal Navy in, 1807 B; Treaty of, 1809 A; Turkey closes, to all except Russian warships, 1833 G; closed to warships in peace-time, 1841 G; British and French fleets off, 1853 F; Austria agrees to opening to Russian warships, 1908 J; Turkey closes, 1912 D, 1914 K; British and French bombard, 1915 B; Campaign, Allied attack fails, 1915 C; Fisher resigns over disagreement in Cabinet about, 1915 E; Report of Commission on, 1917 O; international control of, 1920 B; Turkey renounces sovereignty over, 1936 G
Dar-es-Salaam, Tanganyika, British take, 1916 J
Dargomijsky, Alexander Sergeivich, R. musician (1813–69), 1856 T
Daring Young Man on the Flying Trapeze, The (W. Saroyan), 1935 U
Dark is Light Enough, The (C. Fry), 1954 W
Darlan, Jean François, F. admiral (d. 1942), agreement with Hitler, 1941 E; recognised by Eisenhower, 1942 L; assassinated, 1942 M
Darlington, Dur., England, railway opened, 1825 P
Darmesteter, James, F. antiquarian (1849–94), 1892 Q
Darmstadt, W. Germany, French occupy, 1920 C
Dartmouth, Devon, England, Royal Naval College, 1903 O
Dartmouth, Earl of. *See* Legge, W.
Darwin, Charles, B. scientist (1809–82), 1809 Z, 1831 O, 1839 P, 1858 P, 1859 P, 1868 P, 1871 P, 1882 Z
Darwin, Erasmus, B. scientist (1731–1802), 1794 P, 1802 Z
Darwin and After Darwinism (G. J. Romanes), 1892 R
Dashwood, Edmée Elizabeth M., B. author under pseudoym of 'E. M. Delafield' (1890–1943), 1930 U
Dassin, Jules, F. film director, 1948 W, 1962 W
Daudet, Alphonse, F. author (1840–97), 1866 U, 1872 S, U, 1885 U
Daughters of the American Revolution, 1890 O
Daumier, Honoré, F. artist (1808–79), 1808 Z, 1830 S, 1841 S, 1879 Z
Daventry, Northants, England, transmitter, 1925 P
David, Jacques Louis, F. artist (1749–1825), 1783 S, 1785 S, 1788 S, 1793 S, 1799 S, 1800 S, 1801 S, 1807 S, 1825 Z
David Copperfield (C. Dickens), 1849 U
Davies, Sir Clement, B. Liberal politician (1895–1962), 1956 J
Davies, Harold, Am. diplomat (b. 1914), 1965 G
Davies, Peter Maxwell, B. musician, 1959 T
Davies, R. L., B. architect, 1960 S
Davies, William Henry, B. poet (1871–1940), 1908 U
Daviot, Gordon, B. dramatist, 1933 W
Davis, D. F., B. tennis enthusiast, 1900 X
Davis, Jefferson, Am. Confederate (1808–89), Resolutions for federal slave trade, 1860 B; selected president of Confederate States, 1861 B
Davis, John W., Am. Democrat (1873–1955), in presidential election, 1924 F, L
Davy, Sir Humphry, B. natural philosopher (1778–1829), 1778 Z, 1800 P, 1806 P, 1812 P, 1815 P, 1829 Z

Dawes, Charles Gates, Am. Republican (1865–1951), investigates German economy, 1923 L; Report on Reparations, 1924 D, G, H; nominated for vice-presidency, 1924 F

Dawes, Henry Laurence, Am. lawyer and Republican (1816–1903), 1887 B

Dawn (T. Dreiser), 1931 U

Dawson, Emily, N. magistrate, 1913 E

Dawson, Geoffrey, B. journalist (1874–1944), 1874 Z, 1912 V, 1941 V, 1944 Z

Day by the Sea, A (N. C. Hunter), 1953 W

Day-Lewis, Cecil, B. poet (b. 1904), 1935 U, 1938 U, 1953 U, 1957 U

Daylight Saving:
in Britain, introduced, 1916 O
Double Summer Time, 1941 U
in US, 1918 O

Daytona Beach, Florida, US, *Bluebird's* record at, 1935 P

Daza, Hilarión, Bolivian politician, 1876 N

DDT, invented, 1939 P

Dead Sea Scrolls, 1947 S, 1960 Q

Dead Souls (N. Gogol), 1835 U

Deafness, treatment for, 1961 P

Deak Party, in Hungary, 1875 C

Deakin, Frederick William Dampier, B. historian (b. 1913), 1962 Q

Dean, Basil, B. theatre manager, 1911 W, 1926 W

Deane, Silas, Am. diplomat (1737–89), 1776 G

Dear Brutus (J. M. Barrie), 1917 W

Dearmer, Percy, B. hymnologist (1867–1936), 1906 R, 1925 R

Death in the Afternoon (E. Hemingway), 1932 U

Death in Venice (T. Mann), 1913 U

Death of a Salesman (A. Miller), 1949 W

Death Penalty:
in Britain, reduced for offences, 1823 G, O
abolition, bills introduced, 1956 F, 1964 M
in force, 1965 L
in S. Africa, imposed for sabotage, 1962 E

Deaths and Entrances (D. Thomas), 1946 U

Deaths, registrations of, in Britain, 1836 H

Débâcle, La (É. Zola), 1892 U

De Beers Mining Corporation, 1880, 1959 P

Debré, Michel, F. Radical, 1959 A, 1962 D

Debs, Eugene, Am. trade union leader (1855–1926), 1919 C

Debt, National, British, sinking fund for, 1786 C

Debts, Indonesian to Netherlands, repudiated, 1956 H

Debussy, Claude, F. musician (1862–1918), 1862 Z, 1892 W, 1894 T, 1902 T, 1905 T, 1918 Z

Debutantes, presentation of, discontinued, 1958 G

'Decadence', of Russian composers, alleged, 1931 T

Decazes, Élie, Duc de, F. foreign minister (1780–1860), 1818 M; 1820 B

Decazes, Louis Charles Élie, F. statesman (1819–86), 1875 D

Decimal System, The (J. Bowring), 1854 O

Declaration of Independence, American, 1776 G

Declaration of Rights of Man, in France, 1789 H

Declaration of Frankfurt, for Allied invasion of France, 1813 M

Declaration of Paris, defines blockade and contraband of war, 1856 D

Declaration of Commonwealth on Monetary Affairs, 1933 G

Declaration of Third International against Fascism, 1935 G

Declaration, 1957 O

Declaratory Act, 1766 C

Decline and Fall of the Roman Empire (E. Gibbon), 1776 Q

Decline of the West, The (O. Spengler), 1918 O

Decoration, interior, 1893 S

Decrees:
Berlin, revoked, 1810 L
Carlsbad, by the Frankfurt Diet, 1819 J
Fontainbleau, for confiscating British goods, 1810 K
Milan, 1807 M; revoked, 1810 L
Rambouillet, for sale of US ships seized by France, 1810 C

Deep-freezing of food, 1925 P

Deephaven (S. O. Jewett), 1877 U

Deeping, Warwick, B. author (d. 1950), 1925 U

Deep Sea (F. Brett Young), 1914 U

Deep-sea exploration, 1960 P, 1964 P

Deere, John, Am. inventor (1804–86), 1846 P

Defeat of the Armada, The (G. Mattingley), 1959 Q

Defence Estimates, comparative, 1870 Y, 1910 Y, 1914 Y

Defence, British spending on, 1951 D

Defence, British Minister of, given enlarged powers, 1957 A

Defence, British Ministry, unified, 1963 B

Defence Committee, British, 1946 K

Defence Ministry, in France, 1937 B

Defence of Guenevere, The (W. Morris), 1958 U

Defence of Philosophic Doubt (A. J. Balfour), 1879 R

Defence of the Constitution of Government of the US (J. Adams), 1787 O

Defence of Usury (J. Bentham), 1787 O

Defense Department, US, establishment, 1949 H

Degas, Danse, Dessein (P. Valéry), 1938 U

Degas, Edgar, F. artist (1834–1917), 1834 Z, 1866 S, 1868 S, 1872 S, 1874 S, 1885 S, 1917 Z, 1919 S

Degli ultimi casa de Romagna (M. D' Azeglio), 1846 O

Deirdre of the Sorrows (J. M. Synge), 1907 U

Delacroix, Eugène, F. artist (1798–1863), 1798 Z, 1822 S, 1824 S, 1829 S, 1831 S, 1846 S, 1849 S, 1857 S, 1863 Z

Delafield, E. M. *See* Dashwood, E. E. M.

Delagoa Bay, S.E. Africa: Captured by Portuguese, 1781 N; Portuguese claim is upheld, 1875 N; railway concession in, 1883 M; railway to Transvaal, 1895 G; British designs on, 1898 H; munitions to Transvaal, prevented, 1899 K

De la défense de places fortes (L. Carnot), 1810 O

De la Démocratie en Amerique (A. de Tocqueville), 1835 O

De l'Allemagne (Mme de Staël), 1810 U

De la littérature allemande (Frederick the Great), 1780 U

De l'amour (Stendhal), 1822 U

Delane, John Thadeus, B. journalist (1817–79), 1817 Z, 1841 V, 1879 Z

Delany, Shelagh, B. dramatist (b. 1938), 1959 W

Delavigne, Jean François, F. author (1793–1843), 1818 U

Delaware, State, US, 1777 L, 1778 G
River, steamboat on, 1787 P

Delcassé, Théophile, F. statesman (1852–1923), 1852 Z, 1898 G, 1899 H, 1903 G, 1905 F, 1915 K, 1923 Z

De l'esprit de conquête et de l'usurpation dans les rapports avec la civilisation Européenne (B. Constant), 1813 O

Delhi, India: British capture, 1857 J; Durbar, 1911 M; Hindu and Moslem riots in, 1924 G; Pact, between Viceroy and Gandhi, 1931 C; Central legislature at, 1935 H; Pact, on minorities, 1950 D; World Council of Churches meets, etc., 1961 R

Delibes, Léo, F. musician (1836–91), 1836 Z, 1870 T, 1876 T, 1891 Z
Delisle, Léopold Victor, F. historian (1826–94), 1852 Q
Delititiae Sapientiae (E. Swedenborg), 1768 R
Delius, Frederick, B. musician (1863–1934), 1863 Z, 1902 T, 1903 T, 1904 T, 1905 T, 1907 T, 1912 T, 1934 Z, 1953 T
Dell, Ethel M. (Savage), B. novelist (1881–1939), 1881 Z, 1912 U, 1939 Z
Delphic Oracle, The (Parke and Warmell), 1957 Q
Delphine (A. de Staël), 1802 U
Deluc, Jean André, Swi. geologist and meteorologist (1727–1817), 1771 P, 1778 P
Demerara, British Guiana:
  British capture, 1796 N
  British retain, 1814 H
Democratic Vistas (W. Whitman), 1871 U
Democracy and Re-action (L. T. Hobhouse), 1904 O
Democratic Parties. *See under* Political Parties
Demonstrations:
  in Algiers, by Europeans, 1948 E
  in Belgium, against Leopold III, 1950 G
  in Britain, by Blanketeers, 1817 C
    by Chartists, 1848 D
    by Socialists in Trafalgar Square ('Bloody Sunday'), 1887 L
    by ex-servicemen, 1923 D
    by Fascists and anti-Fascists, 1934 J
    for Second Front, 1942 G
    CND Aldermaston March, 1956 O, 1963 D
    CND sit-down, 1961 O
    by unemployed, 1963 C
    during visit of King and Queen of Hellenes, 1963 G
    of aircraft-workers, 1965 A
    against war in Viet-Nam, 1965 K
  in France, by Communists, 1952 E
  in Germany, by Communist Youth, 1951 H
  in India, by Socialists, 1951 F
  in Kashmir, against incorporation with India, 1957 A
  in Jordan, against Eisenhower doctrine, 1957 D
  in Nyasaland, against federation, 1953 H
  in Poland, against Russian rule, 1861 B
  in Russia, by students, 1901 B
  in S. Africa, against pass-laws, 1960 C
  in Spain, by students, 1929 C
  in Turkey, by students, 1960 D
  in US, by civil rights workers, 1963 H, 1965 C
    against war in Viet-Nam, 1965 D, K
  See also Political Parties; Riots; Strikes
Demos (G. R. Gissing), 1886 U
Dempsey, Sir Miles, B. general (b. 1896), 1945 C
De mundi sensibilis et intelligibilis forma et principiis (I. Kant), 1770 R
Denby, Edwin, Am. politician, 1924 B
Denikin, Anton, R. general (d. 1947), 1919 B, J, M, 1920 C
Denison, George Anthony, B. churchman (1805–96), 1856 R
Denmark: Struensee's rule in, 1770 J, M, 1772 A; cedes Oldenburg to Russia, 1773 K; invades Sweden, 1788 J; Germany invades, 1940 D
Dennewitz, W. Germany, battle of, 1813 J
Denning, Alfred, lord Denning, B. lawyer (b. 1899), 1963 J
Deontology; or the Science of Morality (J. Bentham), 1834 O
Deoxyribonucleic acid (DNA), structure of, determined, 1961 P, 1962 P
Department of Scientific and Industrial Research (DSIR), 1956 O
Deployment of Payment of the Clergy (L. Paul), 1964 R
Depositions of Monarchs:
  Alexander Cuza, of Rumania, 1866 B
  Isabella II, of Spain, 1868 J
  See also Abdications; Monarchies
Depressed areas, in Britain, 1934 L, 1936 G
Depretis, Agostino, It. politician (1813–87), 1876 C, 1887 G
De Profundis (O. Wilde), 1905 U
Deptford, Kent, England, power station, 1890 P
  phosphate factory, 1843 P
Déracinés, Les (M. Barrès), 1897 U
Derain, André, F. artist (1880–1954), 1906 S, 1907 S
Derby, Earls of. *See under* Stanley
Derna, Tripoli: Wavell takes, 1941 A; British evacuate, 1942 B
Dervishes, in Sudan, 1885 G, 1894 G
Descent of Man, The (C. Darwin), 1871 P
Deschanel, Paul, F. statesman, president of France 1920 A, H
Deserted Village, The (O. Goldsmith), 1770 U
Design, US National Academy, 1826 S
Desio, M., It. mountaineer, 1954 P
Desmarest, Nicolas (1725–1815), F. geologist, 1774 P
Des Moines, Iowa, US, 1958 R
Desmoulins, Lucie Simplice Camille Benoist, F. revolutionary (1760–94), 1794 D
Dessau, E. Germany, 1919 S, 1925 S
De Statu Ecclesiae (J. Febronius), 1763 R
De Stijl, 1917 S
Destinée sociale (V. Considérant), 1836 O
Destinées, Les (A. de Vigny), 1864 U
Detective Stories, 1920 U, 1921 U
Deterding, Henry, 1907 O
Detergent, Synthetic, 1933 P
Detroit, Michigan, US: Indian rising, 1763 E; surrenders to British, 1812 H; US recapture, 1813 H; motor industry at, 1903 P
Deutscher, Isaac, B. historian (b. 1407), 1954 Q, 1963 Q
Deutschland ein Wintermarchen (H. Heine), 1844 U
Deux Sources de la monde et de la religion, Les (H. Bergson), 1932 R
Development Commission, British, 1910 O
Development Hypothesis, The (H. Spencer), 1852 P
Development of the Frog (R. Remak), 1850 P
Deviations, by Communists: Trotsky's, 1927 M; in Yugoslavia, 1948 J; in Poland, 1948 J; in China, 1955 C
Devils, The (J. Whiting), 1961 W
Devil's Island, French Guiana, 1894 M
Devlin, Patrick, Lord Devlin, B. lawyer (b. 1905), 1905 Z, Chairman of Press Council, 1963 F; presides over Committee on Docks, 1965 H
Devonshire, Dukes of. *See under* Cavendish
Dewar, Sir James, B. chemist (1842–1923), 1894 P, 1914 P
Dewey, George, Am. colonial, 1898 E
Dewey, John, Am. philosopher (1859–1952), 1899 O, 1922 R, 1929 R, 1931 R, 1939 R
Dewey, Thomas E., Am. Republican (b. 1902), 1944 L, 1948 L
Diabetes, treatment of, 1937 P
Diable et le Bon Dieu, Le (J.-P. Sartre), 1951 W
Diaghilev, Serge, R. choreographer (1872–1929), 1872 Z, 1909 T, 1917 S, 1918 T, 1919 T, 1926 T, 1929 Z
Diagnosis of Man, The (K. Walker), 1942 R
Dialogues des Carmélites (F. Poulenc), 1957 T

Dialogues of Natural Religion (D. Hume), 1779 R
Dialogues sur le Commerce des Blés (F. Galiani), 1770 O
Diamonds: discovered in Orange Free State, 1870 N; Kimberley diamond fields annexed by Britain, 1871 K; Rhodes amalgamates Rand companies, 1888 O; Williamson mine, Tanganyika, 1946 P; synthetic diamonds, 1959 P
Diamond Necklace Affair, 1785 F
Diana of the Crossways (G. Meredith), 1885 U
Diary of Anne Frank, The 1955 U
Diary of a Provincial Lady (E. M. Delafield), 1930 U
Diary of a Witness of the War in Africa (P. Alarcón), 1859 U
Diastase, enzyme, separated from barley, 1832 P
Diaz, Porfirio, president of Mexico (1830–1911), 1877 D, 1884 M, 1911 E, 1912 K
Dicey, Albert Venn, B. jurist (1835–1922), 1835 Z, 1860 O, 1922 Z
Dick, Sir William Reid, B. sculptor, 1879 Z
Dickens, Charles, B. novelist (1812–70), 1812 Z, 1836 U, 1837 U, 1838 U, 1840 U, 1843 U, 1849 U, 1859 U, 1861 U, 1864 U, 1870 U, Z
  edits *Daily News*, 1846 V
Dickinson, Goldsworthy Lowes (1862–1932), 1916 O
Dickson, J. T., Am. inventor of Terylene, 1941 P
Dicksee, Sir Francis Bernard (Frank), B. artist (1853–1928), 1853 Z, 1928 Z
Dictionaries:
  Classical (Lemprière), 1788 Q
  Etymological English (Skeat), 1879 Q
  French (Littré), 1863 Q
  German (Grimm), 1854 Q
  Grand Dictionnaire Universel du XIXe Siècle (Larousse), 1866 Q
  Greek-English Lexicon (Liddell and Scott), 1843 Q
  Hebrew and Chaldaic, 1812 Q
  Musique (Rousseau), 1767 T
  New English Dictionary (later known as *The Oxford Dictionary* (ed. Murray)), 1884 Q, 1928 Q
  Philosophist (Voltaire), 1764 R
  Russian (Dahl's), 1861 Q
  Russian ('Imperial'), 1787 Q
  Sanskrit, 1819 Q, 1856 Q
  Tartare-Mantchou-français (Amiot), 1789 Q
  Totius Latinitatis Lexicon (Forcellini), 1769 Q
  Totius Latinitatis Lexicon (Facciolati), 1771 Q
  Webster's, 1828 Q
Dictionary of German Biography, 1875 Q
Dictionary of National Biography, 1885 Q
Diderot, Denis, F. philosopher (1713–84), 1766 R, 1775 R, 1784 Z
Diefenbaker, John George, Canad. Progressive Conservative (b. 1895), 1895 Z, 1962 F; forms ministry, 1957 F; Macmillan visits, 1959 C; resigns, 1963 D
Diem, Ngo Dinh, President of South Viet-Nam, 1963 L
Dien Bien Phu, North Viet-Nam: US flies French battalion to defend, 1954 D; falls, 1954 E
Dieppe, France, raid on, 1942 H
Diesel, Rudolf, G. engineer (1857–1913), 1857 Z, 1892 P, 1913 Z
Diesel-electric railway, 1913 P
Diesel-electric vessel, 1936 P
Diet, treatise on, 1840 P
Diets. *See* Parliaments, etc.
Dietrich, Marlene, Am. formerly G. film actress (b. 1904), 1904 Z, 1930 W, 1932 W
Dieu et l'État (M. Bakunin), 1882 O
Diez, Friedrich Christian, G. philologist (1794–1876), 1836 Q
Diffusion of Useful Knowledge, Society for, 1827 O
Digestion, human, study of, 1822 P
Digging Up Jericho (K. Kenyon), 1957 Q
Digging Up the Past (L. Woolley), 1930 Q
Dilemmas (G. Ryle), 1954 R
Dilettanti Society of London, 1764 Q
Dilke, Sir Charles Wentworth, B. Radical Liberal politician (1843–1911), 1872 C, 1884 O, 1886 U
Dillon, Clarence Douglas, Am. Rep. politician (b. 1909), 1960 L
Dillon, John, Ir. Nationalist leader (1851–1927), 1851 Z, 1886 L, 1927 Z
Dilthey, Wilhelm, G. philosopher, 1905 R
Dimitrov, Georgi, president of Bulgaria, 1946 L
Dimyes, Lajos, Hung., Smallholder Party leader, 1947 E
Dingle, Herbert, B. scientist (b. 1890), 1937 P
Dingley, Nelson, Am. politician (1832–99), 1897 G
Diomedes, Alexander, Gr. premier, 1950 A
Diphtheria, immunity test, 1913 P
Diplomatic, Science of, 1889 Q
Diplomatic Prelude, 1938–9 (L. B. Namier), 1948 Q
Diplomatic Service, British, 1965 A
Dirac, Paul Adrien Maurice, B. scientist (b. 1902), 1937 P
Disarmament:
  Washington Conferences on, 1921 H, L, M, 1922 F
  by Denmark, 1926 C
  Preparatory Conference on, 1926 E
  Litvinov proposes immediate, 1927 L
  Preparatory Commission on, 1930 D, M
  British Plan for, fails, 1933 C
  Germany leaves Conference on, 1933 K
  Naval Conference on, 1934 K
  Acheson's proposals to UN, 1951 L
  Russia calls on West to reduce forces, 1956 F
  Nehru appeals to Russia and US, 1957 L
  Committee meets at Geneva, 1959 J, 1960 C
  Washington discussions on, 1961 F
  Russia proposes meeting at Summit level, 1962 B
  Seventeen nations meet at Geneva, 1962 C, 1964 A
    France boycotts, 1962 C
    talks resumed, 1965 D
Disarmament Deadlock, The (J. Wheeler-Bennett), 1934 O
Disasters:
  Airship R.101, 1930 P
  Comet aircraft, 1954 P
  S.S. *Lakonia*, 1963 M
  at Lima football stadium, 1964 E
  S.S. *Titanic* sunk, 1912 P
  See also Earthquakes; Famines; Fires
Discourse Before the Congress Angostura (S. Bolivar), 1819 O
Discourse on Popular Education (P. Campanares), 1775 O
Discovery, voyages of, 1768 P, 1775 P, 1776 P, 1777 P, 1778 P, 1831 P. *See also under* Exploration
Discovery of the East (P. Claudel), 1900 Q
Disease, germ theory of, 1861 P
Diseases:
  chronic, treated by penicillin, 1943 P
  lung cancer, 1954 P
  metabolic, cures for, 1946 P
  pernicious anaemia, treatment for, 1955 P
  streptococcus infections, treatment for, 1935 P
  tetanus, controlled by serum, 1915 P
  venereal, 1916 O, 1943 O
    cure for, 1909 P
  See also Epidemics
Disease, Livestock, 1857 O, 1903 O
Disenchanted (C. E. Montague), 1927 O

Disestablishment, of Irish Church, 1869 G
of Welsh Church, proposed, 1891 K
effected, 1919 R
Dish-washer, mechanical, 1865 P
Disintegration of elements, 1921 P
Disney, Walt, Am. film director (b. 1901), 1901 Z, 1928 W, 1938 W, 1950 W
Displaced persons, aid to, 1945 O
Disquisitiones arithmeticae (K. F. Gauss), 1801 P
Disquisitions relating to Matter and Spirit (J. Priestley), 1777 R
Disraeli, Benjamin, Earl of Beaconsfield, B. Conservative statesman and author (1804–81), 1804 Z, 1873 C, 1874 R, 1875 J, 1879 L, 1881 Z
becomes leader of Conservatives, 1849 B
becomes Chancellor of Exchequer, 1852 A, M
Reform Bill introduced by, defeated, 1859 C
leads Commons, 1866 G
becomes prime minister, 1868 B, 1874 B
resigns, 1868 M, 1880 D
stand on Eastern Question, 1875 M, 1877 G
created Earl of Beaconsfield, 1876 H
at Berlin Conference, 1878 F
goes to country on Irish Home Rule issue, 1880 C
death, 1881 D
as a novelist, 1826 U, 1844 U, 1845 U, 1870 U, 1880 U
Dissertation on Animal and Vegetable Science (Spallanzani), 1780 P
Dissertation on Miracles (J. Campbell), 1763 R
Dittersdorf, Karl Ditters von, Aus. musician (1739–1799), 1780 T, 1786 T
Dividend-stripping, 1958 D
Divorce:
in Austria, established, 1783 O
in Britain, 1857 O
royal commission on, 1912 O
women granted equality in litigation, 1923 G
Herbert's Act, 1937 G
in France, instituted, 1792 R
re-established, 1884 G
statistics of, in Britain and US, 1913 Y, 1920 Y, 1940 Y, 1950 Y
Divorces, notable:
Napoleon, from Josephine, 1809 M
Dilke, 1886 O
Parnell, 1890 O
Dixieland Jazz Band, 1918 W
Dixmude, Belgium, 1918 J
Djilas, Milovan, Yugoslav politician: expelled from Communist Party, 1954 A; sentence on, increased, 1957 K, 1962 E
Dnieper River, Russia: ceded by Turkey, 1774 G; Russians cross, 1943 J
Dniester River, Russia: Russian boundary reaches, 1792 A; victory over Germans at, 1915 F; Russian withdrawal to, 1941 G; Russians force crossing, 1944 C
Dobell, William, Austral. artist, 1960 S
Dobrovsky, Joseph, Hung. philologist (1753–1829), 1783 U, 1818 Q
Dobrudja, Russia: Turkey cedes, 1878 G; Allies evacuate, 1917 A; Bulgaria acquires Southern area, 1947 B
Dobson, Austin, B. author (1840–1921), 1840 Z, 1914 Q, 1921 Z
Dobson, Frank, B. sculptor (b. 1888), 1888 Z, 1923 S
Docks: Liverpool, radar installation at, 1948 P; Rochdale Committee on, 1962 D; workers' pay increased, 1962 E; Devlin Committee on, 1965 H. *See also* Strikes
Doctor Jekyll and Mr. Hyde (R. L. Stevenson), 1886 U
Doctor Zhivago (B. Pasternak), 1858 U
Doctors:
in Belgium, strike, 1964 D
in Britain, advised by B.M.A. to leave Health Service, 1965 B
Doctrina numerum vetrum (J. Eckhel), 1792 Q
Doctrines, Theological:
authority of Pentateuch denied, 1862 R
Eternal punishment, denied, 1863 R
Immaculate Conception, 1854 R
Real Presence, 1856 R
Documents of British Diplomatic History 1919–39, 1942 Q
Dodecanese Islands, Aegean: restored to Turkey, 1912 K; assigned to Greece, 1920 H; Italy transfers to Greece, 1946 F, 1947 B
Dodgson, Charles Lutwidge, B. author under pseudonym of 'Lewis Carroll' (1832–98), 1832 Z, 1865 U, 1871 U, 1898 Z
Dodsworth (S. Lewis), 1929 U
Doenitz, Karl, G. admiral (b. 1892), released from prison, 1956 T
Doesburg, Von, 1930 S
Dog Beneath the Skin, The (Auden and Isherwood), 1935 U
Dogger Bank, North Sea: incident, 1904 K; battle, 1915 A
Dogmatics in Outline (K. Barth), 1959 R
Dog Years (G. Grass), 1965 U
Dohnányi, Ernst von, Hung. musician, 1877 Z
Dolfus, Audouin, F. astronomer, 1955 P
Dolin, Anton (Patrick Healey-Kay), B. dancer and choreographer (b. 1904), 1904 Z
Dollfuss, Engelbert, Aus. Christian Socialist (1892–1934), 1934 B; becomes Chancellor, 1932 E; suspends Parliamentary government, 1933 C; murdered, 1934 G
Dollinger, Johann Joseph Ignaz von, G. theologian (1799–1890), 1799 Z, 1856 R, 1861 R, 1869 R, 1871 R, 1890 Z
Doll's House, The (H. Ibsen), 1879 W
Dolomite, for lining furnaces, 1878 P
Domagk, Gerhard, G. pathologist (b. 1895), 1935 P
Dominica Island, W. Indies: ceded to Britain, 1763 B; seized by France, 1778 J
Dominican Order, 1938 R
Dominion Office, 1925 O
Dominion Party. *See under* Political Parties
Dominion Status, 1931 M
Don, River, Russia, Italians routed on, 1942 M
Doña Luz (J. Valera), 1879 U
Doña Perfecta (Perez-Galdos), 1876 U
Don Carlos (Schiller), 1787 W
Doncaster, Yorks, England: St. Leger horse race, 1776 X; cotton factory, 1786 P
Donen, Stanley, Am. film director, 1963 W
Dongola, Sudan, Kitchener takes, 1896 J
Donizetti, Gaetano, It. musician (1798–1848), 1798 Z, 1832 T, 1835 T, 1840 T, 1843 T, 1848 Z, 1859 W
Don Juan (Byron), 1818 U
Don Juan Tenorio (J. Zorilla Y Moral), 1844 U
Donkin, Bryan, B. engineer, 1768 Z
Données Immédiates et la conscience (H. Bergson), 1889 R
Don Pacifico affair, 1850 A, D
Donsokoi, Mark, R. film director, 1959 W
Donzère-Mondragon, France, power station at, 1952 P
Doom of Youth (W. Lewis), 1932 O

Doornkop, S. Africa, 1896 A
Dorpat (now Tartu), Estonia, university, 1802 O
Dorset South, English constituency, by-election, 1962 L
Dortmund-Ems Canal, Germany, 1899 P
Dos Passos, John, Am. novelist (b. 1896), 1896 Z, 1921 U, 1925 U, 1930 U
Dost Mohammed of Afghanistan, 1863 F
Dostoievsky, Feodor, R. novelist (1821–81), 1821 Z, 1846 U, 1866 U, 1868 U, 1870 U, 1880 U, 1881 Z
Double Summer Time, 1941 O
Doughty, Charles Montagu, B. explorer (1843–1926), 1843 Z, 1888 P, 1926 Z
Douglas, John Sholto, eighth marquess of Queensbery, B. sportsman (1844–1900), 1866 X, 1895 U
Douglas, Norman, B. author (1868–1952), 1917 U
Douglas, Stephen, Am. Northern Democrat (1813–1861), senatorial campaign with Lincoln, 1858 H; as presidential candidate, 1860 L
Doullens Agreement, 1918 C
Doumer, Paul, F. statesman (1857–1932), 1857 Z; elected president, 1931 E; assassinated, 1932 E
Doumergue, Gaston, president of France (1863–1937), 1924 F
Doumergue, Paul, F. politician, forms National Union ministry, 1934 B
Dover, Kent, England, submarine cable from, 1850 P
Dover Road, The (A. A. Milne), 1922 W
Down and Out in Paris and London (G. Orwell), 1933 U
Doyle, Sir Arthur Conan, B. novelist (1859–1930), 1859 Z, 1891 U, 1902 U, 1930 Z
Draga, Queen of Serbia, 1903 F
Dragashen, Turkey, 1821 F
Drahtharfe, Die (W. Biermann), 1965 U
Drake, Edwin, L., Am. oil driller (1819–80), 1859 P
Drama, French classical, revival of, 1838 W
Dramatic criticism, 1767 W
Draper, Henry, Am. chemist (1837–82), 1881 P
Dreadnought, H.M.S., 1906 B
Dream of Gerontius, The (J. H. Newman), 1866 U
Dreams and Reality (N. Berdyaev), 1950 R
Drees, Willem, Du, Labour leader, 1948 G, 1951 A, 1952 J, 1958 M
Dreiser, Theodore, Am. author (1871–1945), 1871 Z, 1911 U, 1926 U, 1931 U, 1945 Z
Dresden, E. Germany: occupied by Russians and Prussians, 1813 C; battle, 1813 H; revolts in, suppressed, 1849 E; Conference on German Unification, 1850 M, 1851 E; artists in, 1905 S
Dress, women's, reform of, 1849 O
Dreyfus, Alfred, F. soldier (1859–1935), 1896 C, 1897 L, 1898 A; arrested, 1894 K; convicted, 1894 M; retired, 1899 F; pardoned, 1899 J; rehabilitated, 1906 G
Dreyse, J. N. von, G. gunsmith (1787–1867), 1836 P
Drinkwater, John, B. poet (1882–1937), 1882 Z, 1913 W, 1923 U, 1937 Z
Driving Tests, in Britain, 1934 C
Droysen, Johann Gustav, G. historian (1808–84), 1855 Q
Drugs:
analgesic, 1887 P
antibiotic, 1946 P, 1960 P; side effects of, 1962 P
dangerous, 1839 G, H, L, 1958 F; taken by Beatniks, 1958 U
synthetic, 1886 P
Drugs, legislation for controlling:
British, 1860 O, 1875 O
US, 1898 O, 1906 O
Drummond, Thomas, B. engineer (1767–1840), 1796 P
Drums in the Night (B. Brecht), 1922 W
Drum Taps (W. Whitman), 1866 U
Drunkenness, statistics of convictions for, 1905 Y, 1920 Y
Drury, A., B. sculptor, 1931 S
Druses, in Syria, revolt of, 1925 G, K
Druten, J. Van, B. dramatist, 1928 W, 1954 W
Duala, Cameroons, 1914 J
Dubarry, Marie Jeanne Bécu, comtesse (1746–93), F. adventuress, 1769 D, 1770 M
Dublin, Eire: Royal Irish Academy in, 1782 O; Bottle Riots in, 1822 M; University College, 1854 O; Phoenix Park murders, 1882 E; Abbey Theatre, 1904 W; Sinn Fein riots in, 1917 F; Sinn Fein Congress, 1919 A; Four Courts, seizure of, by rebels, 1922 D, F
Dubliners (J. Joyce), 1914 U
Duca, Ion, Rum. Liberal, 1933 M
Duchamp, Marcel, F. artist (1887–), 1912 S, 1915 S
Ducis, Jean François, F. dramatist (1733–1816), 1769 W
Du côté de chez Swann (M. Proust), 1913 U
Du Cubisme (Gleizes and Metzinger), 1912 S
Dud Avocado, The (E. Dundy), 1958 U
Dudevin, Amandine. *See* Sand, George
Dudley, Staffs., England, riots in, 1874 B
Dufaure, Jules Armand Stanislas, F. Left-Centre politician (1728–1881), 1877 M
Dufferin, Lord. *See* Blackwood, Frederick
Dufrénoy, Ours Pierre Armand Petit, F. geologist (1792–1857), 1841 P
Dufy, Raoul, F. artist (1877–1953), 1937 S, 1938 S
Duhamel, Georges, F. author (b. 1884), 1884 Z, 1933 U
Duimo Elegies (R. M. Rilke), 1911 U
Dukas, Paul, F. musician (1865–1935), 1965 Z, 1907 T, 1935 Z
Dukes, Ashley, B. dramatist (b. 1885), 1925 W
Dulcigno, S. Yugoslavia, 1880 L
Dulles, John Foster, Am. secretary of state (1888–1959), 1955 L; visits Franco and Tito, 1955 L; Suez plan, 1956 H; Berlin speech, 1958 E; meets Macmillan, 1958 F; retires, 1959 D
Dulwich, Surrey, England, art gallery, 1814 S
Dumas, Alexander, pseudonym of Alexandre Davy de la Pailleterie, F. author (1802–70), 1802 Z, 1848 U
Dumas, Jean Baptiste André, F. chemist (1800–84), 1824 P, 1834 P
Dumouriez, Charles François, F. general (1739–1823), 1792 C, L; defeated at Neerwinden, 1793 C; deserts to Allies, 1793 D
Dumping of manufactures, 1921 G
Dunant, Henri, Swi. founder of Red Cross (1828–1910), 1864 O
Duncan, Adam, Lord Camperdown, B. admiral (1731–1804), 1797 E, K
Duncan, Sir Andrew, B. administrator (b. 1905), 1961 O
Duncan, Ronald, B. dramatist (b. 1886), 1945 W, 1955 W
Dundas, Henry, Lord Melville, B. Tory politician (1742–1811), 1782 E
Dundy, Elaine, Am. author (b. 1929), 1958 U
Dungeness, Kent, England, atomic power station at, 1965 P
Dunkirk, France, British evacuation from, 1940 E account of, 1941 O
Dunlap, William, Am. artist (1766–1839), 1834 S
Dunlop, John Boyd, B. veterinary surgeon and inventor (1840–1921), 1888 P
Dunn, Geoffrey, B. actor, 1965 T

Dunne, John William, B. philosopher (d. 1949), 1927 R
Dunning, John, Lord Ashburton, B. Whig politician (1731–83), 1780 D
Dunning Tariff in US, 1930 E
Du Pape (de Maistre), 1817 R
Düppel, Schleswig, W. Germany, 1864 D
Dupuis, Charles François, F. author and politician (1742–1809), 1795 Q
Durban, S. Africa, 1908 K
Durey, Louis, F. musician (b. 1888), 1920 K
Durham, Lord. *See* Lampton, J. G.
Durham Report on Canada, 1839 B
Durham, N. Carolina, US, Johnston's surrender at, 1865 D
Durrell, Lawrence George, B. author (b. 1912), 1958 U, 1960 U
Duruy, Jean Victor, F. statesman (1811–94), 1865 O
Duse, Eleonora, It. actress (1861–1924), 1861 Z, 1872 W, 1891 W, 1924 Z
Düsseldorf, W. Germany: French occupy, 1921 C; Art gallery, 1926 S
Du système industriel (St. Simon), 1821 O
Dutra, Enrico, president of Brazil, 1945 M
Dutrochet, René Joachim Henri, F. physiologist (1776–1847), 1837 P
Dvina, River, Russia, 1772 H, 1795 K, 1920 A
Dvořák, Anton, Bohemian musician (1841–1904), 1841 Z, 1828 T, 1880 T, 1901 T, 1904 Z
  Stabat Mater, 1883 T
  Symphonies, 1882 T, 1893 T
  in US, 1892 T
Dyce, William, B. artist (1806–64), 1828 S
Dyer, H. G., B. chemist, 1838 P
Dyes:
  Aniline, 1856 P
  Ionamide, 1922 P
  Phthalacyamine, 1934 P
  Synthetic, 1869 P
Dynamite, invented, 1866 P
Dynamo, with ring armature, 1870 P
Dynamic Sociology (L. Ward), 1883 O
Dynasts, The (T. Hardy), 1904 W
Dysentery bacillus, isolated, 1915 P
Dyson, Sir George, B. musician (b. 1883), 1932 T

E

Earl, Ralph, Am. artist (1751–1801), 1775 S
Early Bird, communications satellite, 1965 P
Earth, The:
  current, discovered, 1862 P
  density of, determined, 1798 P
  dynamic theory of, 1788 P
  magnetic field of, analysed, 1923 P
Earthly Paradise (W. Morris), 1868 U
Earthquakes:
  Agadir, 1960 B
  California, 1892 O
  Chile, 1965 C
  Persia, 1962 J
  Sicily and S. Calabria, 1908 M
  Skopje, Yugoslavia, 1963 G
East Africa, British: Anglo-German agreement on, 1886 L; Anglo-Italian agreement on, 1894 E; British protectorate in, 1895 G; settlement of uplands, 1902 J; frontier with Uganda, 1907 M; becomes Kenya, 1920 G; Central Legislature, 1948 D. *See also* Kenya
East Africa, German: Arab rising in, 1888 J; cleared of German troops, 1917 M; assigned as mandated territory to Britain, 1919 E. *See also* Tanganyika
East Africa Company, British: formed, 1887 E; occupies Uganda, 1890 M, 1893 C; treaty with Leopold II, 1890 E; dissolved, 1895 G
East Africa Company, German, 1885 B; cedes rights to Germany, 1890 K
Eastern Questions, The: Napoleon's problem, 1808 K; Vienna note on, 1853 G; Congress of Berlin on, 1878 G. *See also* Russophobia
Eastern Schism, The (S. Runciman), 1955 Q
East Galicia, 1772 H
East India Company, British: administration of India, 1767 A, 1772 C, D; regulating Act for, 1773 E; Fox's Bill to reform, 1783 M; Pitt's Act, 1784 H; acquires Poona, 1802 M; monopoly in Indian trade abolished, 1813 O; Bentinck's reforms, 1829 O; powers transferred to Crown, 1858 H; end of rule in Straits Settlements, 1867 D
East Lynne (Mrs. Henry Wood), 1861 U
Eastman, George, Am. photographer (1854–1932), 1854 Z, 1885 P, 1888 P, 1889 P, 1932 Z
Eau de Javel (chlorine), 1785 P
Ebert, Friedrich, G. statesman (1871–1925), 1871 Z, 1925 B; as president of G. republic, 1919 B, 1922 K
Ecce Homo (J. R. Seeley), 1866 R
Eccles, David McAdam, lord Eccles, B. Conservative politician (b. 1904), dismissed from cabinet, 1962 G
Eccles, Sir John Carew, Austral. neurologist (b. 1903), 1963 P
Ecclesiastical Commissioners, 1836 R
Ecclesiastical Courts, proceedings in, notable, 1856 R, 1857 R, 1863 R, 1890 R
Ecclesiastics, imprisonment of notable, 1937 R
  Card. Mindszenty, 1948 M
  Abp. Stephinac, 1946 J
  Card. Wyszynski, 1953 J
  releases from, 1963 B, K
Eckhel, Joseph Hilarius, Aus. numismatist (1737–98), 1792 Q
Eclipses, solar, 1936 P
Economic Affairs, British Ministry of, 1964 K
Economic Consequences of the Peace (J. M. Keynes), 1919 O
Economic Council, French National, 1925 O
Economic Council, German, 1947 F
Economic Reform, in Britain, 1780 E
Economics, Ministry of, German, 1919 O
Economic Studies (W. Bagehot), 1880 O
Economic Survey, British, 1948 O
Economic Warfare, US Office of, 1943 O
Ecuador: Republic established, 1830 J; leaves Union of Colombia, 1831 L; becomes a theocracy, 1873 K; dispute with Peru, 1911 A
Eddington, Sir Arthur Stanley, B. scientist (1882–1944), 1882 Z, 1914 P, 1918 P, 1924 P, 1931 P, 1939 R, 1944 Z
Eddy, Mary Baker, Am. founder of Christian Science (1821–1910), 1821 Z, 1875 R, 1879 R, 1910 Z
Eden, Anthony, Viscount Avon, B. Conservative statesman (b. 1897), 1897 Z; offers Mussolini concessions over Abyssinia, 1935 F; becomes foreign secretary, 1935 M; resigns, 1938 B; re-appointed foreign secretary, 1940 M; in Moscow, 1941 M; at UN Conference, 1945 D; foreign secretary, 1951 K; plan for Europe, 1952 H; becomes premier, 1955 D; proposes reunification of Germany, 1955 G; reforms ministry, 1955 M; with Eisenhower issues Washington Declaration, 1956 B; recuperates, 1956 L; resigns, 1957 A

Eden, William, baron Auckland, B. diplomat (1744–1814), 1786 J
Eden End (J. B. Priestley), 1934 W
Edge Island, Spitzbergen, expedition to, 1927 P
Edgeworth, Maria, B. novelist (1767–1849), 1800 U
Edinburgh, Scotland:
  Bank with 'women only' branch, 1964 O
  Festival, 1947 W
  Scott Museum, 1840 S
  University, 1855 O
Edinburgh, Dukes of. *See* Alfred Ernest Albert; Philip
Edinburgh Letter (Lord J. Russell), 1845 L
Edison, Thomas Alva, Am. inventor (1847–1931), 1847 Z, 1872 P, 1876 P, 1880 P, 1882 P, 1894 W, 1931 Z
Edo Bay, Japan, 1846 N
Education:
    theories, co-education, 1922 O; Pestalozzi, 1781 O
    treatises, 1775 O, 1803 O, 1806 O, 1861 O
    for blind, 1784 O, 1791 O
  in Austria, 1770 O, 1868 O
    clerical control of, 1855 H
  in Belgium, political crises over control of, 1880 F, 1895 H, 1912 F
    primary, 1879 G
    secondary, 1850 O
  in Britain, adult, 1834 O, 1854 O, 1904 O
    schools, monitorial system for, 1797 O
      religious foundations, 1808 O, 1811 O
      State grant for, 1833 O
      reforms urged, 1867 O
      board schools established, 1870 O
      elementary, 1890 O
      Board of Education, 1899 O
      denominational schools brought within State system, 1902 M
      school care committees, 1906 O
      medical inspectors in, 1907 O
      Fisher's Act, 1918 H
      cuts in expenditure for, 1922 O
      Butler's Act, 1944 O
      Newsom Committee Report, 1963 O
      proposal to raise leaving age to sixteen, 1963 O
    schools, secondary, girls', 1880 O
      in Wales, 1889 O
      in Britain, 1902 M
    schools, comprehensive, circular about, 1965 O
      teaching of Russian in, 1962 O
    schools, independent, Fleming Report on, 1944 O
      Commission on, 1965 M
    higher education, Robbins Report on, 1963 O
    technological, increased spending on, 1956 O
    teachers' training colleges, first, 1846 O
    women's higher, 1849 O, 1869 O, 1871 O
  in China, reformed, 1902 N
  in Denmark, Veterinary and Agricultural College, 1773 P
    reforms in, 1784 E
  in France, compulsory, 1793 O, 1882 O
    École Normale, 1794 O
    École Polytechnique, 1795 O
    Écoles Centrales, 1795 O
    clerical control of, 1822 F, 1833 F
    primary, 1882 C
    secondary, 1865 O
  in Germany, technical, 1884 O
    university, 1909 O
  in Ireland, Maynooth College, 1845 F
  in Israel, religious, 1951 B
  in Italy, 1877 O
  in Prussia, elementary, 1763 O, 1765 O
    secondary, 1859 O
    religious, 1788 R, 1892 C
  in Spain, 1766 F
    clerical control, 1851 C
    Church schools closed, 1933 E
  in US, degrees awarded to women, 1841 O
    scientific and technological, 1862 O
    graduate schools, 1876 O
    Teaching of evolution forbidden in Tennessee, 1925 O
    desegregation crisis, 1957 O, 1958 J
    reading of prayers in New York unconstitutional, 1962 O
  See also Universities
Education, Moral, Intellectual, Physical (H. Spencer), 1861 O
Education of Henry Adams (H. Adams), 1907 Q
Éducation sentimentale, L' (G. Flaubert), 1869 U
Edward VII, King of Gt. Britain and Ireland (1901–1910), 1841 L, 1874 J, 1907 J, 1910 E; as Prince of Wales, visits India, 1875 H; witness in Tranby Croft case, 1891 O; accession, 1901 A; style, 1901 H; visits Paris, 1903 E, 1907 E; discussions with William II, 1906 H; visits Rome, 1907 D; meets Nicholas II, 1908 F; as race-horse owner, 1896 X, 1909 X
Edward VIII, King of Gt. Britain (b. 1894); as Prince of Wales, visits Canada and US, 1919 H; visits India, 1921 G; accession, 1936 A; relations with Mrs. Wallis Warfield Simpson, 1936 K, L; abdicated, 1936 M; becomes Duke of Windsor, 1936 M; marries Mrs. Simpson, 1937 F
Eggar, Samantha, B. film actress, 1965 W
Egoist, The (G. Meredith), 1879 U
Egmont (Goethe), 1788 W
Egypt: French interest in, 1795 Q; French expeditions to, 1798 E, G, H, 1799 G, H; Turks recover possession of, 1801 K; British and French armies leave, 1801 K; Turkey recognises independence, 1833 E; becomes possession of Mehemet Ali, 1840 G, L, 1841 B; finances, 1875 M, 1876 C, 1884 F; Anglo-French control of, 1876 L, 1878 M, 1879 J, 1882 L; Gambetta Note on, 1882 A; Nationalist Movement in, 1881 B, J; British occupation, 1882 J, 1883 A; Anglo-French differences in, settled, 1904 D; Milner-Zaghlul conversations on, 1920 H; British Protectorate in, ends, 1922 B; Republic proclaimed, 1953 F; forms, with Syria, United Arab Republic, 1958 B. *See also* Suez Canal; Suez Crisis; United Arab Republic
Egyptology, 1883 Q
Ehrenberg, Christian Gottfried, G. bacteriologist (1795–1876), 1854 P
Ehrenburg, Ilya, R. author (b. 1891), 1891 Z, 1941 U, 1955 U
Ehrlich, Paul, G. chemist (1854–1915), 1909 P
Eichhorn, Johann Gottfried, G. theologian (1752–1827), 1783 R
Eichhorn, Karl Friedrich, G. jurist (1781–1854), 1808 Q
Eichmann, Adolf, G. Gestapo chief, arrested, 1960 E; trial, 1961 O; hanged, 1962 E
Eider River, W. Germany, linked by canal to Baltic, 1784 P
Eiffel, Gustav, F. engineer (1834–1923), 1834 Z, 1923 Z
Eighteenth-Century Studies (A. Dobson), 1914 Q
Einaudi, Luigi (1874–1961), president of Italian Republic (1948–55), 1948 E

Eindhoven, Holland, British airborne forces at, 1944 J
Einstein, Albert, Am. scientist and philosopher (1879–1955), 1879 Z, 1912 P, 1929 P, 1934 R, 1940 P, 1955 Z; theories of relativity, 1905 P, 1915 P, 1919 P; on Zionism, 1930 O
Einthoven, Willem, Du. physiologist (1860–1927), 1860 Z, 1927 Z
Eire: Irish Free State proclaimed, 1922 M; name changed from Irish Free State, 1937 M; Republic formally proclaimed, 1949 D; Britain recognises, 1949 E; Prime Minister meets Northern Ireland premier, 1965 A. *See also* Ireland; Irish Home Rule; Rebellions
Eirenicon (E. B. Pusey), 1865 R
Eisenach, E. Germany, Protestant Conference at, 1852 R
Eisenhower, Dwight David, Am. soldier and statesman, 34th president of US (1953–61), Republican (b. 1890), 1890 Z, 1954 E, 1955 A, 1958 E, J
  commands Allied landings in N. Africa, 1942 L
  as supreme commander in N. Africa, 1943 B
  on Italy's unconditional surrender, 1943 J
  Jodl's capitulation to, 1945 E
  retires from post of Supreme Allied Commander, 1952 D
  elected president, 1952 L, inaugurated, 1953 A
  visits Korea, 1952 M
  meets Churchill, 1953 A, 1953 M, 1954 F
    on principles of UN peace proposals for Korea, 1953 E
    proposes control of atomic energy, 1953 M
    broadcasts on Communist threat, 1954 D
    message to Congress on Formosa, 1955 A
    asks for foreign aid, 1955 D, F
    heart attack, 1955 J
    re-affirms joint policy in Middle East, 1956 B
    re-elected, 1956 L
    at Bermuda Conference, 1957 C
    proposes mutual inspection for atom tests, 1958 D
    meets Macmillan, 1958 F, 1959 H, L
    admits S. Adams's imprudence, 1958 F
    visits Germany and Britain, 1959 H
    tours Europe, 1959 M
    issues joint declaration on nuclear test negotiations, 1960 C
    at Summit meeting, 1960 E
    tours Far East, 1960 F
Eisenhower Doctrine, for US forces to protect independence of Middle East States, 1957 C, D
Eisenstein, Sergei, R. film director, 1928 W, 1938 W, 1945 W, 1959 W
Eisner, Kurt, Bavarian premier, 1919 B
Either-or (S. Kierkegaard), 1843 R
Ekman, Carl, Swe. Liberal politician, 1930 F
El Alamein, Egypt, battle, 1942 K
Elba, Isle of: Britain captures, 1796 G; Napoleon I banished to, 1814 D
Elbe, River, W. Germany, closed by Danes, 1801 C, D; Canal to Trave, 1900 P; Allies cross, 1945 D
Elbing, W. Germany, Allies take, 1945 B
Elder Statesman, The (T. S. Eliot), 1958 W
Elders and Betters (I. Compton-Burnett), 1944 U
Election Court, in Britain, 1961 O
Elections:
  in Australia, 1922 M, 1929 K, 1934 J, 1937 K, 1961 M, 1963 L
  in Austria, 1911 F, 1945 L, 1949 K, 1953 B, 1959 E
    presidential, 1920 M
  in Barbados, 1961 M
  in Belgium, 1880 F, 1912 F, 1929 E, 1936 E, 1946 B, 1954 D, 1961 C
  in Britain:
    By-elections, notable:
      Clare (O'Connell), 1828 F
      Barnard Castle (won by Labour), 1903 G
      Bow (Lansbury), 1912 L
      Skipton (Commonwealth Party), 1944 A
      Brighton, 1944 B
      Tonbridge, 1956 F
      Lewisham, 1957 B
      Rochdale, 1958 B
      Torrington (Liberal), 1958 C
      Orpington (Liberal), 1962 C
      W. Lothian, 1962 F
      Leicester, N., 1962 G
      S. Dorset (Labour), 1962 L
      Leyton (foreign secretary loses), 1965 A
    General, 1784 C, 1790 L, 1806 K, M, 1807 D, F, 1818 F, 1820 B, 1831 D, 1868 M, 1874 B, 1880 C, D, 1885 L, 1886 G, 1892 G, ('Khaki') 1900 K, Liberal landslide—1906 A, 1910 M, 1918 M, 1922 L, 1923 M, 1924 K, 1929 E, 1931 K, 1935 L, Labour landslide—1945 G, 1950 B, 1951 K, 1955 E, 1959 K, 1964 K
    Act to prevent fraudulent votes in 1763 G
    spending of parties and candidates in, limited, 1883 H
    arrangements for National Service voters, 1945 A
    pioneer study of, 1947 O
    TV coverage of, 1959 O
  local government, 1963 E, 1964 D, 1965 E
  in British Guiana, 1953 D, 1957 H, 1961 H, 1964 M
  in Bulgaria, 1945 L
  in Canada, 1878 K, 1911 J, 1917 M, 1921 M, 1926 J, 1945 F, 1949 F, 1953 H, 1957 F, 1962 F, 1965 L
  in Central African Federation, 1962 D
  in Ceylon, 1952 F, 1956 D, 1960 C, 1965 C
  in Cuba, 1908 L
  in Czechoslovakia, 1935 E, 1946 E
  in Danzig, 1933 E
  in Denmark, 1926 M, 1945 K, 1953 D
  in Egypt, 1945 A, 1950 A
  in Eire, 1922 F, 1923 H, 1927 J, 1932 B, 1933 A, 1938 F
    presidential, 1932 C
  in Finland, 1954 C
  in France:
    General, 1816 J, 1817 J, 1818 M, 1827 L, 1830 G, 1848 E (on universal suffrage), 1879 A, 1889 D
    multiple candidates forbidden in, 1889 G
    proportional representation in, 1912 G, 1924 E, 1932 E, 1936 E, 1945 K, 1946 F, 1946 L, 1948 L, 1951 F, 1956 A, 1958 L
    presidential, 1848 M, 1879 A, 1885 M, 1887 M, 1899 B, 1906 A, 1913 A, 1920 J, 1931 E, 1932 E, 1946 F, 1947 A
    referendum for election by universal suffrage, 1962 K, 1965 K
    municipal, 1947 K
  in Germany:
    For Reichstag, 1874 A, 1878 G, 1906 M, 1912 A, 1919 A, 1924 E, 1924 M, 1928 E, 1930 J, 1932 G, 1932 L, 1933 C, L, 1936 C, 1953 J, 1957 J, 1961 J
    presidential, 1925 D, 1932 C, D, 1959 G
    holding of free, discussed, 1951 M, 1952 D, 1954 A, 1957 G
    provincial, 1932 D
  in East Germany, 1950 K
  in Gold Coast, 1954 F, 1956 G

Elections—*contd.*
in Greece, 1952 L
in Holland, 1946 E, 1952 J
in Honduras, 1954 D
in Hungary, 1947 H
in India, 1937 B, 1945 J, 1952 C
in Italy:
General, 1904 K, 1921 E
single-party, 1929 C, 1948 D, 1953 F, 1958 E
presidential, 1946 F, 1948 E, 1962 E
in Japan, 1890 G, 1946 D
in New Zealand, 1890 D, 1919 M, 1928 L, 1946 L, 1954 L
in Nicaragua, 1927 E
in Norway, 1933 K, 1953 K
in Pakistan, presidential, 1965 A
in Philippines, 1907 G
in Portugal, 1934 M, 1945 L, 1953 L
in Northern Rhodesia, 1959 D
in Southern Rhodesia, 1962 M, 1965 E
in South Africa, 1910 J, 1924 F, 1933 E, 1938 E, 1948 E, 1953 D, 1958 D
in Spain, 1914 C, 1933 L, 1934 A, 1936 B
in Sudan, 1958 B
in Sweden, 1907 E, 1911 J, 1952 J
in Syria, 1953 K
in Turkey (single party), 1927 J
in US:
Congressional, 1914 L, 1918 L, 1922 L, 1938 L, 1946 L, 1950 L, 1958 L, 1962 L
presidential, 1796 L, 1800 L, 1804 J, 1812 L, 1824 L, 1827 L, 1832 L, 1844 L, 1852 L, 1856 L, 1860 L, 1872 L 1876 L, 1877 A, 1884 L, 1896 L, 1900 L, 1908 L, 1912 L, 1920 L, 1920 W, 1924 L, 1928 L, 1932 L, 1936 L, 1944 L, 1948 L, 1952 L, 1956 L, 1960 L, 1964 L
force bill to control, facts, 1890 F
expenses of, to be published, 1912 D
TV coverage of, 1960 O
senatorial, by direct system, 1911 D
State, disputed, 1874 E
in Yugoslavia, 1945 L
in Zanzibar, 1961 F
voting in, by ballot, in Britain, 1872 G
in Canada, 1874 N
in US, 1804 J
Elective Affinities, The (Goethe), 1809 U
Electra (H. von Hofmannsthal), 1903 U
Electricity Authority, British, 1948 O
Electrical Consumer Goods, in Britain, 1965 Y
Electrical Engineers, British Institution of, 1889 P
Electrical Exhibition, Munich, 1883 P
Electrical Grids, linking of British and French, 1961 P
Electrical Industry, British, power station for, 1890 P; taken over by Electricity Authority, 1948 O; output, 1944 Y, 1957 Y
Electrical precipitation, 1884 P
Electrical Researches of the Hon. Henry Cavendish, 1879 P
Electrical Self-induction, 1834 P
Electrical Standards, 1861 P
Electrical Waves, detection of, 1896 P
Electricity:
accumulator for, 1859 P
A.C. motor for, 1888 P
carbon filament lamps, 1878 P
carbon-zinc battery, 1841 P
conduction of, through gases, 1903 P
Galvani's observations, 1789 P
generating station, 1882 P
hydro-electric power stations, 1882 P, 1952 P
produced from atomic energy, 1951 P
produced from steam turbine, 1884 P
transformer for, 1831 P
Voltaic pile, 1798 P
Volta's cell, 1800 P
Electricity, Treatises on, 1789 P, 1814 P, 1820 P, 1826 P, 1839 P, 1843 P, 1873 P, 1879 P
Electricity, Uses of:
for lighthouses, 1858 P
for lighting, 1872 P, 1878 P, 1880 P, 1881 P
for lung pump, 1961 P
for motive power, 1879 P
to coat metals with nickel, 1843 P
to heat steel furnace, 1879 P
to power railways, 1879 P, 1895 P, 1904 P, 1910 P
to power submarine, 1896 P
to power washing-machine, 1869 P
to prepare potassium and sodium, 1806 P
Electricity Board, British, 1926 O
Electro-chemical analysis, 1822 P
Electrodynamics (A. Ampère), 1826 P
Electrolytic process for making soda, 1894 P
Electro-magnetism, discoveries relating to, 1819 P, 1821 P
Electro-magnetic Waves, 1887 P
Electronic brain, 1942 P, 1946 P
Electronic music, 1959 T, 1964 T
Electronic Power Production, comparative, 1959 Y
Electrons: term first used, 1891 P; Bohr's theory, 1922 P; positive ('positrons'), 1933 P
Electroscope, 1903 P
Elegy on the Death of Pushkin (M. Y. Lermontov), 1837 U
Elegy Written in Spring (M. Bruce), 1767 U
Elektra (J. Giraudoux), 1937 W
Elements:
Disintegration of, 1921 P
Law for classification of, 1869 P
Transmutation of, 1911 P, 1922 P
Elements, Named:
Californium (98), 1950 P
Germanium, 1886 P
Hafnium, 1922 P
Nobelium, 1957 P
Scandium, 1879 P
Éléments de Geométrie (A. Legendre), 1794 P
Elements of Chemical Philosophy (H. Davy), 1812 P
Elements of Political Economy (James Mill), 1821 P
Elements of the Philosophy of the Human Mind (D. Stewart), 1792 R
Elements of Psycho-Physics (G. T. Fechner), 1860 P
Elements of Systematic Morality (W. Whewell), 1846 R
Elenchus Zoophytorum (P. S. Pallas), 1767 P
Elevators, 1780 P, 1875 P
Elgar, Sir Edward, B. musician (1857–1934), 1857 Z, 1899 T, 1901 T, 1907 T, 1934 Z; *Dream of Gerontius*, 1900 T; symphonies, 1908 T, 1911 T; violin concerto, 1910 T; cello concerto, 1918 T
Elgin Marbles, 1801 S, 1816 S
Elgin Treaty, 1854 F
Elias (W. Bilderdijck), 1786 U
Elias, Ney, G. explorer, 1885 P
Élie de Baumont, Jean Baptiste Armand, F. geologist (1798–1858), 1841 P
Eliot, George. *See* Evans, Mary Ann
Eliot, Thomas Stearns, B. author (1888–1965), 1917 U, 1922 U, 1930 U, 1933 U, 1935 W, 1939 W, 1942 U, 1944 U, 1948 U, 1949 W, 1953 W, 1958 W, 1965 Z
Elisabethville, Congo, UN troops occupy, 1962 M

Elixiere des Teufels, Die (E. Hoffmann), 1815 U
Elizabeth II, Queen of Gt. Britain, since 1952; birth, 1926 Z; as Princess, marriage, 1947 L; accession, 1952 B; coronation, 1953 F, W; Commonwealth Tour, 1954 E; visits Canada and US, 1957 K, 1964 K; addresses UN, 1957 K; opens St. Lawrence Seaway, 1959 F; descendants not being Royal Highnesses, to bear name Mountbatten-Windsor, 1960 B; tours India, Pakistan and Cyprus, 1961 A; visits African territories, 1961 L; visits W. Germany, 1965 E; Awards to industry, 1965 O
Elizabeth, Empress of Austria, 1898 J
Elizabethan House of Commons, The (J. E. Neale), 1949 Q
Elizabeth City, N. Carolina, US, taken by Unionists, 1826 B
Elkin Park, Pa., US, Synagogue in, 1859 S
Elle et Lui (G. Sand), 1859 U
Ellegård, Alvan, 1963 Q
Ellesworth, Lincoln, Am. explorer, 1939 P
Ellington, Duke, Am. jazz musician (b. 1899), 1932 T
Elliott, Ebenezer, B. author (1781–1849), 1831 O
Elliptic functions, study of, 1928 P
Ellis, Henry Havelock, B. psychologist (1859–1939), 1897 R, 1919 R
Ellis, Ruth, B. murderess, 1955 O
Elmer Gantry (S. Lewis), 1927 U
Elmira, N.Y., US, reformatory at, 1876 O
El Obeid, Sudan, British defeat at, 1883 L
El Salvador, forms union with Nicaragua and Honduras, 1895 F
Elsie Venner (or *The Professor*) (O. W. Holmes), 1861 U
Elster, J.P.L.T., G. electrician, 1904 P
Éluard, Paul, F. author (1895–1952), 1949 U
El Wak, It. Somaliland, 1940 M
El Zanjón, Cuba, Convention of, 1878 B
Emancipation:
  of serfs, in Russia, 1861 C
  of slaves in US, Lincoln's declaration, 1862 J
  of women, Mill's treatise on, 1869 O. *See also under* Franchise
Émaux et Camées (T. Gautier), 1852 U
Embargoes:
  by American Colonies, against British goods, 1774 M
  by Britain, on oil for Rhodesia, 1965 M
  by Russia, on British ships, 1800 L
  by US, on British goods, 1812 D
  by US, on shipments to Cuba, 1960 K
Embryology, Comparative, science of, established, 1828 P
Emerson, Ralph Waldo, Am. author (1803–82), 1803 Z, 1836 R, 1840 R, 1850 U, 1882 Z
Emigration:
  British, to US, 1830 Y, 1840 Y, 1850 Y, 1860 Y, 1870 Y, 1880 Y, 1890 Y, 1938 Y
  of British scientists, 1963 B, 1964 P
  Irish to US, 1830 Y, 1840 Y, 1850 Y, 1860 Y, 1870 Y, 1880 Y, 1890 Y
Émigrés, French, 1789 K
Émile (Rousseau), attacks on, 1763 O
Emilia Galotti (Lessing), 1772 W
Eminent Victorians (L. Strachey), 1918 U
Emir Faisal, of Saudi Arabia, 1960 M
Emma (J. Austen), 1816 U
Emmet, Robert, Ir. politician (1778–1803), leader of United Irishmen, 1803 G
Empedocles on Etna (M. Arnold), 1852 U
Emperor Jones, The (E. O'Neill), 1921 W
Empirical Sociology (Neurath), 1931 R
Empty House, The (A. Blackwood), 1906 U
Ems, W. Germany:
  Punctation of, 1786 R
  refuted by Pius VI, 1789 R
  Telegram, 1870 G
Enchanteur pourrissant, L' (G. Apollinaire), 1909 U
Encke, Johann Franz, G. astronomer (1791–1865), 1818 P
Encyclicals, Papal:
  Aeterna Dei, 1961 R
  on Atheistic Communism, 1937 R
  Editio Saepe, 1910 E, F
  Humani generis, 1950 R
  Mortalium animus, 1928 R
  Pacem in Terris, 1963 R
  Pascendi gregis, 1907 R
  Quadragesimo Anno, 1931 R
  Rerum novarum, 1891 R
Encyclopaedias:
  Brockhaus, 1796 Q, 1935 Q
  Encyclopædia Britannica, 1771 Q, 1929 Q
  Penal Jurisprudence, 1800 O
  Protestant Theology, 1853 R
Ender, Otto, Aus. Christian Socialist, 1930 M
Endgame (S. Beckett), 1957 W
End of Laissez-Faire, The (J. M. Keynes), 1926 O
Ends and Means (A. Huxley), 1937 R
Endymion (J. Keats), 1818 U
Enemies of Promise (C. Connolly), 1938 U
Enemy of the People, An (H. Ibsen), 1882 U
Enemy, The (J. Green), 1955 U
Énergie spirituelle, L' (H. Bergson), 1919 R
Energy, conservation of, laws of, 1837 P, 1842 P, 1851 P
Enfants terribles, Les (J. Cocteau), 1929 U
Enfranchisement. *See under* Franchise
Engels, Friedrich, G. Socialist (1820–95), 1820 Z, 1845 O, 1848 O, 1895 Z
Enghien, Louis Antoine Henri de Bourbon Condé, Duc d', F. (1722–1804), 1804 C
Engines:
  internal combustion, 1885 P
  jet, 1937 P
  oil, 1873 P
  petrol, 1882 P, 1892 P
    for aeroplane, 1903 P
  railway, atomic-powered, 1954 P
    steam, 1814 P, 1825 P, 1829 P
  single-cylinder, 1885 P
  steam, 1765 P, 1774 P, 1775 P, 1800 P, 1811 P, 1813 P
    for railway. *See above under* railway
    for ships, 1803 P, 1807 P, 1812 P, 1815 P, 1818 P, 1820 P
England, Ireland and America (R. Cobden), 1835 O
England of Elizabeth, The (A. L. Rowse), 1950 Q
England under Queen Anne (G. M. Trevelyan), 1930 Q
English Bards and Scots Reviewers (Byron), 1809 U
English Channel: Blériot flies across, 1909 P; hovercraft crosses, 1959 P
English Constitution, The (W. Bagehot), 1867 O
English Middle Classes, The (Lewis and Maude), 1949 O
English Social History (G. M. Trevelyan), 1942 Q
English Stage Company, 1955 W
English Water Colour Society, 1804 S
Enahoro, Chief, of Nigeria, 1963 E
Eniwetok Atoll, Pacific, hydrogen bomb tests at, 1952 P
Enniskillen, Northern Ireland, 1912 J
Enormous Room (E. E. Cummings), 1923 U
En Route (J. K. Huysmans), 1895 U

Ensor, James, Belg. artist (1860–1949), 1884 S, 1888 S
Entente Cordiale, between Britain and France, 1903 G, 1904 D
Entente, Little, between Czechoslovakia, Roumania and Yugoslavia, 1923 H, 1933 B; Balkan counterpart of, 1934 B; Rome Protocols counter, 1934 C
Entertainer, The (J. Osborne), 1957 W
Enthusiasm (R. A. Knox), 1950 R
Entomology, studies in, 1775 P
Environs of London, The (D. Lysons), 1792 Q
Enzymes, the first, 1832 P; catalysis among, 1906 P
EOKA, in Cyprus, 1956 H
Eothen (A. W. Kinglake), 1844 U
Épaves, Les (C. Baudelaire), 1866 U
Epidemics:
  Cholera, in Europe, 1830 O
  Influenza, 1918 K, 1919 P
  Typhoid, 1963 C, 1964 C
Epigonen (K. Immermann), 1836 U
Epirus, Greece, granted to Greece by Turkey, 1881 G
Episcopal Church. *See under* Religious Denominations
Episodios Nactionales (B. Pérez-Galdós), 1879 U
Epistola ad Episcopos Catholicos pro causa Italica (Passaglia), 1859 O
Époques de la nature (G. Buffon), 1778 P
Epsom, Surrey, England, The Derby first run at, 1779 X
Epstein, Sir Jacob, B. sculptor (1880–1959), 1880 Z, 1908 S, 1911 S, 1913 S, 1925 S, 1926 S, 1927 S, 1928 S, 1929 S, 1931 S, 1935 S, 1937 S, 1939 S, 1949 S, 1952 S, 1957 S, 1959 S, 1962 S
Equality (R. H. Tawney), 1901 O
Equal pay for women, in Britain, proposed, 1946 L
Erard, Sébastien, F. inventor of pianoforte (1752–1831), 1780 P, 1823 T
Erasmus, letters of, edited, 1906 Q
Erbförster, Die (O. Ludwig), 1850 W
Erewhon, or Over the Range (S. Butler), 1872 U
Erewhon Revisited (S. Butler), 1901 U
Erfurt, E. Germany: is incorporated in France, 1807 H; Congress, between Napoleon and his vassals, 1808 K; Parliament, 1850 C, D; Social Democrat Congress at, 1890 K
Erhard, Ludwig, G. Christian Democrat (b. 1879): Adenauer prevents candidature for presidential election, 1959 G; becomes Chancellor, 1963 K
Erie, Lake, N. America, US actions on, 1813 J
Eriksen, Eric, Da. politician, forms ministry, 1945 K, 1950 K
Eritrea: as Italian Colony, 1890 E; Mahdist attack on, 1893 M; is federated with Ethiopia, 1952 J
Erivan, in Armenia, Russia: ceded to Russia, 1827 B; Persian defeat at, 1827 K
Erlander, Tage, Swe. Social Democrat, 1946 K
Ermland, Poland, 1772 H
Ernest Augustus, Duke of Cumberland (1771–1851), as King of Hanover, 1837 F, G, M, 1840 H, 1851 L
Ernesti, Johann August, G. theologian and philologist (1707–81), 1764 Q, 1768 Q
'ERNIE', used for premium bonds draws, 1957 F
Ernst und Falk (Lessing), 1777 R
Eros, sculpture by Gilbert, 1925 S
Erskine, John, B. lawyer (1695–1768), 1773 O
Erskine, Thomas, B. lawyer and theologian (1788–1870), 1820 R
Erzberger, Matthias, G. finance minister, 1921 H
Erzerum, Turkey, Russians take, 1916 B
Eschenburg, Johann Joachim, G. critic (1743–1820), 1775 W
Espartero, Baldomero, Sp. soldier and politician (1792–1879), 1840 F, 1840 K, 1841 E; risings against, 1842 K, M; defeated, 1843 G; recalled, 1847 J; becomes premier, 1854 H; replaced by O'Donnell, 1856 J
Espionage:
  in Britain:
    Fuchs, 1950 C
    Lonsdale, 1961 O
    Blake, 1961 E, O
    Vassall, 1962 K
    Radcliffe Tribunal Report on, 1963 D
    Bossard and Allen, 1965 E
  in Canada, 1946 G
  in Egypt, 1957 F
  in Russia, Wynne, 1962 L; concealed microphones, 1964 E
  in US, the Rosenbergs, 1953 F
Espoir, L' (Malraux), 1937 U
Essai de Cristallographie (J. de l'Isle), 1772 P
Essai de monde et de critique (E. Renan), 1859 R
Essai de Statique Chimique (C. Berthollet), 1803 P
Essai d'une théorie sur la structure des cristaux (R. Haüy), 1784 P
Essai historique, politique et moral sur les Révolutions (Chateaubriand), 1797 O
Essai sur la langue et la littérature chinoises (J. P. A. Rémusat), 1811 Q
Essai sur la Peinture (D. Diderot), 1766 S
Essai sur le Despotisme (Mirabeau), 1772 O
Essai sur l'Indifférence (H. F. R. de Lamennais), 1817 R
Essais de Psychologie contemporaine (P. Bourget), 1883 U
Essay on Beethoven (R. Wagner), 1870 T
Essay on Church Reforms (T. Arnold), 1832 R
Essay on Finance (R. Giffen), 1879 O
Essay on Goethe (T. Carlyle), 1828 Q
Essay on Mind, with other poems (E. B. Browning), 1826 U
Essay on Slavery (Clarkson), 1786 O
Essay on the Development of Christian Doctrine (J. H. Newman), 1845 R
Essay on the First Principles of Government (J. Priestley), 1768 O
Essay on the History of Civil Society (A. Ferguson), 1766 O
Essay on the Nature and Immutability of Truth (J. Beattie), 1770 R
Essay on the Nature and Principles of Taste (A. Alison), 1790 S
Essay on the Principle of Population (T. R. Malthus), 1790 O
Essay on the Vedas (H. T. Colebrooke), 1805 Q
Essays and Reviews (F. Temple and M. Pattison), 1860 R
Essays Catholic and Critical, 1926 R
Essays in Criticism (M. Arnold), 1865 U
Essays in Liberality (A. Vidler), 1957 R
Essays in Musical Analysis (D. F. Tovey), 1935 T
Essays of Elia (C. Lamb), 1820 U
Essays on the Active Powers of the Human Mind (T. Reid), 1788 R
Essays on the Sociology of Culture (K. Mannheim), 1956 R
Essays Philosophical and Theological (R. Bultmann), 1956 R
Essen, W. Germany, Krupps works at, 1810 P, 1903 P
Essen, P., Am. scientist, 1947 P
Essence of Christianity (L. Feuerbach), 1841 R

Essequibo, B. Guiana: British capture, 1796 N; Britain retains, 1814 H
Estaing, Charles Hector, Comte d', F. admiral (1729–94), 1778 G
Esterhazy, Marie Charles, F. soldier, 1897 L
Esther Waters (G. Moore), 1894 U
Estonia: Bolshevik rule in, 1918 M; Bolsheviks invade, 1919 B; declares independence, 1920 B
Eternal City, The (H. Caine), 1901 U
Ethan Frome (E. Wharton), 1911 U
Ether, used as anaesthetic, 1842 P, 1846 P
Ether Alcohol, constitution of, 1832 P
Ethical and Political Thinking (E. F. Carritt), 1947 R
Ethical Culture, Society for, 1876 R
Ethical Studies (F. H. Bradley), 1876 R
Ethics, Treatises on, 1785 R, 1874 R, 1876 R, 1879 R, 1882 R, 1903 R, 1947 R, 1957 R
Ethiopia (Abyssinia): exploration of, 1772 P; British expedition to, 1868 A; frontiers defined, 1891 C, 1902 D; Italian claims to, 1889 E, 1891 B; Italian troops in, 1895 C; Italy withdraws protectorate, 1896 K; independence is guaranteed, 1906 B; Italy invades, 1935 K; Italy annexes, 1936 E; Allies liberate, 1941 C, E
Ethnological Society founded, 1843 O
Ethnographie moderne des races sauvages (L. A. Bertillon), 1883 P
Euler, Leonhard, Swi. mathematician (1707–83), 1770 P, 1772 P, 1783 Z
Eupen, Belgium, 1920 A
Euratom: resolution on, adopted by ECSC, 1956 E; Rome Treaty for, 1957 C; in force, 1958 E; Britain agrees to co-operate with, 1959 B; Britain applies to join, 1962 C; merger of executive authority, 1965 M
Euripides, works of, edited, 1802 Q
European Advisory Commission, Allied, 1943 L
European Anarchy, The (G. Lowes Dickinson), 1916 O
European Coal and Steel Community (ECSC): in force, 1952 G, 1953 A; resolution of, on Common Market, 1956 E; Britain applies to join, 1962 C; merger of executive authority, 1965 M
European Convention on Human Rights, 1954 E
European Defence Community (EDC): NATO approves, 1952 B; Britain proposes defence treaty with, 1952 D; Paris Treaty signed, 1952 E
European Economic Community (EEC) or 'Common Market': Foreign ministers of 'The Six', at Rome Conference, 1953 B; W. German Bundestag approves, 1953 C; Eisenhower pledges support to, 1954 D; Brussels negotiations founder, 1954 H; Britain applies for membership, 1961 H; E. Heath's statement to, 1961 K; Agreement on agriculture, 1962 A; Commonwealth premiers endorse Britain's attempted entry, 1962 J; Britain resumes negotiations with, 1962 L; Britain is refused entry, 1963 A
European Economic Co-operation, Organisation for (OEEC), 1948 D
European Free Trade Association (EFTA): 'The Seven' sign a treaty, 1959 L; first meeting, 1960 A; in force, 1960 E
European Nuclear Energy Agency, 1957 M
European Payments Union, 1950 J
European Political Systems (P. Feuerbach), 1800 O
European Recovery Programme, under Marshall Aid: formed, 1947 F; Paris discussions on, 1947 G, 1948 D; Marshall Aid, US Acts, 1948 F, 1949 D; German representation in, demanded, 1948 F; achieved, 1949 M
European Union: Hague Conference on, 1948 E; Strasbourg Conference on, 1950 H; Nine-power agreement on, 1954 D; Paris Treaty for, ratified, 1955 C, D; provokes Russia to annul treaties, 1955 E; Assembly meets at Strasbourg, 1955 G; Paris Assembly calls for single NATO nuclear force, 1962 M
Europe, Council of: Statute of, 1949 E; W. Germany joins, 1950 F; adopts Eden Plan, 1952 J
Eurovision network, 1954 P
Euston Road School of Artists, 1937 S
Eutaw, N. Carolina, US, 1781 J
Evangelical Alliance, American, 1866 R
Evangelicals. *See under* Religious Denominations
Evans, Sir Arthur, B. archaeologist (1851–1941), 1851 Z, 1900 Q, 1910 Q, 1941 Z
Evans, Mary Ann, B. novelist under pseudonym 'George Eliot' (1819–80), 1819 Z, 1857 U, 1859 U, 1860 U, 1861 U, 1871 U, 1880 Z
Evans, Oliver, Am. wheelwright (1755–1819), 1780 P
Evaporated milk, 1847 P
Evatt, Herbert Vere, Austral. Labour Party leader (b. 1894), 1894 Z
Evelina (F. Burney), 1778 U
Eve of St. Agnes, The (J. Keats), 1820 U
Everest, Mount, climbed, 1953 P
Everlasting Mercy, The (J. Masefield), 1911 U
Everyman's Library, 1906 U
Evidence from Scripture of the Second Coming of Christ (W. Miller), 1842 R
Evidences of Christianity (W. Paley), 1794 R
Evolution, term coined, 1852 P
teaching of, forbidden, 1925 O
theories of, 1948 P
Evolution of Ethics (T. H. Huxley), 1893 P
Évolution créatrice, L' (H. Bergson), 1907 R
Ewald, Johannes, Da. poet and dramatist (1743–81), 1770 W
Ewart, William, B. Whig politician (1798–1869), 1850 O
Ewins, Arthur James, B. biochemist (1882–1957), 1938 P
Examination of the British Doctrine which subjects to capture a Neutral Trade (J. Madison), 1806 O
Exclusive Brethren. *See under* Religious Denominations
Exclusive Commercial State (J. G. Fichte), 1800 O
Excommunications, notable, 1871 R, 1885 O
Excursion, The (W. Wordsworth), 1814 U
Exeter, Devon, England, bombed, 1942 D
Exhibitions and World Fairs:
The Great Exhibition, Hyde Park, 1851 W
Paris, 1855 S
International, London, 1862 W
Paris, 1867 W
Chicago, 1893 W
British Empire, Wembley, 1924 W
Paris, 1937 W
Empire, Glasgow, 1938 W
New York, 1939 W
Swiss National, Zürich, 1939 W
Festival of Britain, 1951 S, W
Brussels, 1958 W
Exhibitions, Art:
in Britain:
Act to facilitate, 1866 S
Post-Impressionist, London, 1910 S
Ruskin, 1919 S
Sargent, 1926 S
Italian Art, 1930 S
Chinese Art, 1935 S
Augustus John, 1940 S
Sickert, 1941 S
Aid Russia, 1942 S

Exhibitions, Art—*contd.*
in Britain—*contd.*
Mexican Art, 1953 S
Picasso, 1960 S
Goya, 1963 S
'Art of a Decade', 1964 S
Beckmann, 1965 S
Bonnard, 1965 S
Giacometti, 1965 S
in France, Impressionist, 1874 S, 1877 S, 1886 S
van Gogh, 1891 S
Rodin, 1900 S
Cubist, paintings, 1907 S
in Germany, Islamic Art, Munich, 1910 S
Nazi Exhibition of 'Degenerate Art' 1937 S
in US, Armoury of Post-Impressionists, 1913 S
Unknown American Painters, 1939 S
of *Mona Lisa*, 1963 S
Exhibitions, Miscellaneous:
Electrical, Munich, 1883 P
Aeronautic, Vienna, 1888 P
Sweated Industries, London, 1906 O
Diaghilev, Edinburgh, 1954 S
Shakespeare Quatercentenary, 1964 S, W
Exiles, The (J. Joyce), 1918 W
Existence and Analogy (E. Mascall), 1949 R
Existentialism, Papal decree against, 1950 R
Existentialism (Ruggiero), 1947 R
Exit the King (E. Ionescu), 1963 W
Exorcismes (H. Michaud), 1943 U
Expansion of England, The (J. R. Seeley), 1883 Q
Expectancy of life, observations on, 1769 O
Expedition of Humphry Clinker, The (T. Smollett), 1771 U
Experience and Pottery (W. Dilthey), 1905 R
Experimental Inquiry into the Nature and Properties of Heat (J. Leslie), 1804 P
Experiments and Instruments depending on the relations of Air to Heat and Moisture (J. Leslie), 1813 O
Experiment with Time (J. W. Dunne), 1927 R
Exploration:
Africa, 1772 P, 1795 P, 1799 P, 1850 P, 1852 P, 1854 P, 1855 P, 1856 P, 1871 P, 1875 P
N. America, 1790 P
S. America, 1799 P
Pacific, 1766 P, 1768 P, 1770 P, 1775 P, 1776 P, 1778 P
N.W. Passage, 1850 P
N. Pole, 1871 P, 1888 P, 1893 P, 1900 P, 1906 P, 1909 P, 1926 P
S. Pole, 1903 P, 1908 P, 1910 P, 1912 P, 1934 P, 1935 P
Spitzbergen, 1927 P
under water, 1934 P
Exposition des Droits de l'Homme (Sièyes), 1789 O
Exposition du système du monde (P. Laplace), 1796 P
Extraterritorial privileges in China, agreement to abolish, 1930 A
Eyeless in Gaza (A. Huxley), 1936 U
Eylau, Russia, formerly E. Prussia, battle, 1807 B
Eyskens, Gaston, Belg. Christian Socialist, 1948 H

F

Faber, Frederick Williams, B. ecclesiastic (1814–63), 1849 R
Fabian Essays (G. B. Shaw), 1889 O
Fabian Society, 1884 O
Fabiola, Doña y Aragon, Sp. Princess, marries King Baudouin I of Belgium, 1960 M
Fables (J. Kriloff), 1809 U
Fabricius, Johann Christian, Da. entomologist (1745–1808), 1775 P
Facciolati, Jacopo, It. philologist (1682–1769), 1771 Q
Factories:
in Britain, cotton spinning, 1785 P, 1786 P
legislation for, 1825 F, 1833 H, 1844 F, 1847 F, O, 1867 O, 1906 O
munitions, 1917 O
Owen's model, 1800 O
women in, 1906 O, 1917 O
in Germany, employment of women, 1908 M
inspection of, 1891 F
Faugét, Émile, F. author (1847–1915), 1892 O
Fairbanks, Douglas Elton (Sr.), Am. film actor (d. 1939), 1915 W, 1920 W
Fairey Aviation Company, 1946 P
Fair Stood the Wind for France (H. E. Bates), 1944 U
Fairs, World. *See under* Exhibitions
Fairy Tales (H. Andersen), 1835 U
Fairy Tales (J. and W. Grimm), 1812 U
Faisal, King of Saudi Arabia (1907–58), 1964 L; heads Arab Federation, 1958 B; murdered, 1958 G
Faisal, King of Syria, 1920 C, G
Falaise Gap, France, defeat of Germans in, 1944 H
Falconet, Étienne Maurice, F. sculptor (1716–91), 1763 S, 1766 S
Falk, Paul Ludwig Adalbert, G. politician (1827–1900), 1873 E
Falkenhagen, Erich von, G. general, 1914 J
Falkland Isles, S. America: discovered by France, 1764 N; claimed by Britain, 1766 N; Anglo-Spanish dispute over, 1770 H; Spain sells to Britain, 1771 A; Britain proclaims sovereignty over, 1833 A; battle, 1914 M; Britain's dispute with Argentina and Chile, 1955 E
Falla, Manuel de, Sp. musician (b. 1876), 1915 T, 1919 T, 1923 T
Fallières, Clément Armand, F. Republican (1841–1931), 1883 A; elected President, 1906 A
Fall of Paris, The (I. Ehrenburg), 1941 U
Fall of Robespierre, The (Coleridge, Southey and Lovell), 1794 W
Fall of the House of Habsburg (E. Crankshaw), 1963 Q
Falmer, near Brighton, Sussex, England, Sussex University, 1964 S
Family allowances, 1945 O
Family Reunion (T. S. Eliot), 1939 W
Famines:
in China, 1920 L
in India, 1769 N, 1873 N, 1877 N, 1897 N, 1964 L
in Ireland, 1846 N
in Italy, 1898 E
in Japan, 1783 N
in Russia, 1892 N, 1932 N
world wheat shortage, 1946 G
Fanfani, Amintore, It. Christian Democrat (b. 1908), 1954 A; forms coalitions, 1958 F, 1960 B; resigns, 1959 A
Fanny by Gaslight (M. Sadleir), 1940 U
Fanny Hill (Cleland), 1963 U
Fantasias. *See under* Rhapsodies
Fantin-Latour, Henri, F. artist (1836–1904), 1870 S
Faraday, Michael, B. natural philosopher (1791–1867), 1791 Z, 1821 P, 1823 P, 1825 P, 1831 P, 1834 P, 1839 P, 1843 P, 1867 Z
Far Eastern Commission, terminates Japan's reparations payments, 1949 E
Far Eastern Republic, Siberia, votes for union with USSR, 1922 L
Farewell to Arms, A (E. Hemingway), 1929 U

Far From the Madding Crowd (T. Hardy), 1874 U
Farmer's Boy, The (R. Bloomfield), 1800 U
Farm mortgage corporation, US, 1934 A
Farms, collective, 1930 O
Farms credit act, US, 1933 F
Farnborough, Surrey, England, prize fight at, 1860 X
Farouk I, King of Egypt (1920–65), 1952 G, 1965 Z
accession, 1936 D
abdicates, 1952 G
Fascism, studies in, 1943 O
Fascists. *See under* Political Parties
Fashoda, Sudan, 1896 F; French occupy, 1897 G; Kitchener reaches, 1898 J; French evacuate, 1898 L; crisis ends, 1899 C
Fatherland Front. *See under* Political Parties
Fathers and Sons (I. Turgeniev), 1862 U
Fats, liquid, process for hardening, 1901 P
Faulkner, William, Am. author (1897–1961), 1926 U, 1929 U, 1930 U, 1932 U, 1938 U, 1953 U, 1959 U, 1962 U
Faure, Edgar, F. Radical politician, 1952 A, B, 1955 B
Faure, Félix, F. Moderate Republican politician (1841–99), elected president, 1895 A, 1899 B
Faust (Goethe), 1808 W, 1831 W
Faust (N. Lenau), 1836 U
Fauves, Les, group of French artists, 1905 S
Faux-Monnayeurs, Les (A. Gide), 1925 U
Fawcett, Millicent Garrett, B. suffragette (1847–1929), 1847 Z, 1929 Z
Fawley, Hants, England, oil refinery at, 1951 P
Fayette, N.Y., US Mormon Church at, 1830 D
Fearful Joy, A (J. Cary), 1949 U
Fear of Freedom, The (E. Fromm), 1942 R
Feast of Reason, 1793 R
Feast of Supreme Being, 1794 R
Febronius, Justinus. *See* Hontheim
Fechner, Gustav Theodor, G. physicist (1801–87), 1860 P
Federal Union, advocated, 1929 J, 1939 O
Federation of Employers, British National, 1873 O
Federation of Labor, American, 1881 O
Fehrenbach, Konstantin, G. Chancellor, 1920 F
Feldhoven Caves, near Hochdel, W. Germany, 1856 Q
Fellini, Federico, It. film director (b. 1920), 1953 W, 1954 W, 1960 W
Fenian outrages, 1857 K, 1866 B, 1867 B, J, M, 1883 C
in Quebec, 1870 E
Féodora (V. Sardou), 1882 U
Ferdinand and Isabella (W. H. Prescott), 1837 Q
Ferdinand I of Austria (1835–48), 1835 C; flees, 1848 E; returns to Vienna, 1848 H
Ferdinand I of Bulgaria (1887–1918), 1887 G, 1896 G, 1908 K, 1909 B
Ferdinand I of Naples (1759–1825), 1798 L, 1815 F, 1820 G, 1825 A
Ferdinand II of Naples (1830–59), 1830 L, 1859 E; grants constitution, 1848 B
Ferdinand of Saxe-Coburg, elected prince of Bulgaria, 1887 G
Ferdinand VII of Spain (1814–33), 1814 E, 1822 L, 1833 J; as Crown Prince, renounces throne, 1808 E; Venezuela's allegiance to, 1810 D, 1811 G; Napoleon to restore, 1813 M; restored to throne, 1815 F; fails to keep to constitution, 1820 A, C, L; refuses to leave Madrid, 1823 F; restored by French, 1823 K; abrogates Salic Law, 1830 C
Ferguson, Adam, B. philosopher (1725–1816), 1766 O
Fermentation, lactic, 1857 P
Fermi, Enrico, Am. atomic physicist (1901–54), 1934 P; splits the atom, 1942 P
Fernando Po, Island, in Gulf of Guinea, ceded by Portugal to Spain, 1778 N
Fernau, Hermann, 1917 O
Ferranti Ltd., profit on Bloodhound missile, 1964 D
Ferrara, N. Italy, formerly a Papal State, 1797 G, 1801 G; ceded to France, 1797 B; Austrians occupy, 1847 G
Ferrari, Giuseppe, It. philosopher (1812–76), 1847 R
Ferrer, Guardia Francisco, Sp. anti-clerical, 1909 K
Ferrer, José, Am. film actor (b. 1912), 1952 W
Ferry Jules, François Camille, F. Republican statesman (1832–93), 1883 B, 1885 C; Tunisian policy, 1881 L, 1884 L; Egyptian policy, 1884 F
Ferstel, H. von, Aust. architect (1828–83), 1856 S
Fertilisation, study of, 1763 P, 1779 P
through krilium, 1951 P
through peat, 1914 P
Fertilisers, production of, statistics of, 1932 Y, 1940 Y, 1959 Y
Festivals:
of Britain, 1951 S, W
Champ de Mars, 1790 G
Edinburgh, 1947 W, 1954 T
Glyndebourne, 1934 T
Hambach, 1832 E
Reason, 1793 R
Salzburg, 1946 T, 1955 S
Wartburg, 1817 K
Fessenden, Reginald Aubrey, Am. scientist, 1900 P
Fêtes galantes (P. Verlaine), 1869 U
Feuchtwanger, Lion, G. author (1884–1958), 1917 V
Feuerbach, Ludwig Andreas, G. theologian (1804–72), 1841 R
Feuerbach, Paul Johann Anslem, G. jurist (1775–1833), 1800 O
Feuillet, Octave, F. author (1821–90), 1858 U
Few Late Chrysanthemums, A (J. Betjeman), 1954 U
Fey, Emil, Aus. minister of interior, 1935 K
Fianna Fail. *See under* Political Parties
Fichte, Immanuel Hermann von, G. philosopher (1797–1879), 1837 R
Fichte, Johann Gottlieb, G. philosopher and statesman (1762–1814), 1792 R, 1794 R, 1796 O, 1798 R, 1800 O, 1806 R, 1808 O, 1812 R, 1814 Z, 1818 R; as rector of Berlin University, 1810 O; Herder's attack on, 1799 R
Fick, Am. speculator, leader of the 'Erie Ring', 1872 A
Fiction:
English Romantic School, 1765 U
Gothic novel, 1794 U
historical novel, 1765 U
Field, John, B. musician (1782–1837), 1814 T
Field, Winston Joseph, Rhodesian Front politician (b. 1904), 1962 M, 1964 D
Fields, Gracie, B. actress (b. 1899), 1931 W
Fielinger, Zdenek, Czech. National Front leader, 1945 D
Fieschi, Giuseppe, Corsican Radical (1790–1836), 1835 G
Fight for the Leadership of the Tory Party (R. Churchill), 1964 O
Figli, Leopold, Aust. People's Party leader, 1945 M, 1952 K
Fiji Islands, Britain annexes, 1874 K
Filangieri, Gaetano, It. lawyer (1752–88), 1780 O
Filles du feu, Les (G. de Nerval), 1854 U
Fillmore, Millard, Am. Whig (1800–74), 13th president of US (1850–3), 1850 G, 1856 L
Film Censors, British Board of, 1920 W
introduces 'X' certificate, 1951 W

Filming machine, rapid, 1923 P
Film Institute, British, 1933 W
Film, roll, 1889 P
Films, sound, 1919 P, 1927 W, 1932 W
colour, 1924 W, 1928 W, 1929 P, W
Films:
Accuse, J', 1919 W
Adventuress from Monte Carlo, The, 1921 W
Advice and Consent, 1962 W
African Queen, The, 1951 W
Alexander Newski, 1938 W
All Quiet on the Western Front, 1930 W
All the King's Men, 1949 W
Anatomy of Murder, 1959 W
Andere Ich, Das, 1941 W
Anna Karenina, 1911 W, 1935 W
Anne Boleyn, 1921 W
Année Dernière à Marienbad, L', 1961 W
À Nous la Liberté, 1932 W
Ashes and Diamonds, 1958 W
As You Like It, 1936 W
Avventura, L', 1960 W
Baby Doll, 1956 W
Ballet Mécanique, Le, 1924 W
Beauté du Diable, La, 1950 W
Becky Sharp, 1935 W
Belle et la Bête, La, 1946 W
Ben Hur, 1926 W
Best Years of Our Lives, The, 1946 W
Bicycle Thieves, 1948 W
Big House, The, 1930 W
Big Store, The, 1941 W
Birds, The, 1962 W
Birth of a Nation, 1915 W
Black Orpheus, 1960 W
Blue Angel, The, 1930 W
Blue Light, The, 1932 W
Bonjour Tristesse, 1957 W
Breakfast at Tiffany's, 1961 W
Bridge on the River Kwai, The, 1957 W
Bull-Dog Drummond, 1929 W
B'wana Devil, 1953 W
Cabinet of Dr. Caligari, The, 1920 W
Calle Major, 1946 W
Camille, 1937 W
Cardinal, The, 1963 W
Carmen, 1909 W, 1915 W
Cavalcade, 1933 W
Charade, 1963 W
Child of the Ghetto, A, 1910 W
Cid, El, 1961 W
Circus, 1928 W
Citizen Kane, 1941 W
City Lights, 1931 W
Cleopatra, 1963 W
Coastal Command, 1942 W
Collector, The, 1965 W
Colonel Blimp, 1943 W
Congress Dances, The, 1931 W
Co-optimists, The, 1929 W
Cranes Are Flying, The, 1957 W
Cyrano de Bergerac, 1935 W
Dance from the Volcano, 1938 W
David Copperfield, 1935 W
Dawn Patrol, The, 1939 W
Day in the New World, A, 1940 W
Death of a Cyclist, 1955 W
Derrière la Façade, 1940 W
Diaboliques, Les, 1954 W
Diesel, 1942 W
Divided Heart, The, 1954 W
Dr. Mabuse, 1922 W
Dr. Strangelove, 1964 W
Dr. Who and the Daleks, 1965 W
Dog's Life, A, 1918 W
Dolce Vita, La, 1960 W
Don Juan, 1926 W
Edge of the World, The, 1937 W
Elektra, 1961 W
Emil and the Detectives, 1931 W
Enfants terribles, Les, 1949 W
Entertainer, The, 1960 W
Evening Visitor, The, 1942 W
Exodus, 1960 W
Fallen Idol, The, 1948 W
Fall of Troy, The, 1911 W
Fantasia, 1940 W
Farewell to Arms, A, 1932 W
Faust, 1910 W
First of the Few, The, 1941 W
Foma Gordeyev, 1959 W
Forgotten Men, 1934 W
Forgotten Village, The, 1944 W
Forty-Ninth Parallel, 1941 W
For Whom the Bell Tolls, 1943 W
Four Chimneys, 1953 W
Frankenstein, 1931 W
Friedmann Bach, 1941 W
From Here to Eternity, 1953 W
Gaslight, 1940 W
Generallinie, Die, 1929 W
Generation, A, 1954 W
Gentler Sex, The, 1943 W
Gigi, 1959 W
Glorious Adventure, 1922 W
Goldfinger, 1964 W
Gold Rush, The, 1925 W
Gone With the Wind, 1939 W
Goodbye Mr. Chipps, 1939 W
Grandes Manœuvres, Les, 1955 W
Grand Hotel, 1932 W
Grasshopper, The, 1955 W
Great Dictator, The, 1940 W
Great Expectations, 1946 W
Great Illusion, The, 1937 W
Great Train Robbery, The, 1905 W
Great Well, The, 1924 W
Great Ziegfeld, The, 1936 W
Greed, 1925 W
Hallelujah, 1930 W
Hamlet, 1948 W
Hard Day's Night, A, 1964 W
Hedda Gabler, 1919 W
Hell's Angels, 1930 W
Help! 1965 W
Henry V, 1944 W
Hiroshima Mon Amour, 1959 W
Holiday Inn, 1942 W
How Green Was My Valley, 1942 W
Hunger! Hunger! Hunger! 1921 W
I.N.R.I., 1923 W
Irma La Douce, 1963 W
It Always Rains on Sunday, 1947 W
It's A Wonderful World, 1946 W
Ivan the Terrible, 1945 W
I Vitelloni, 1953 W
Jane Eyre, 1943 W
Journey's End, 1930 W
Jules et Jim, 1961 W
Julius Caesar, 1907 W
Juno and the Paycock, 1929 W
Justice is Coming, 1944 W
Kid, The, 1921 W
Kind of Loving, A, 1962 W

King and I, The, 1956 W
King in New York, A, 1957 W
King Kong, 1933 W
King of Kings, 1927 W
Kipps, 1941 W
Knack, The, 1965 W
Lady Vanishes, The, 1938 W
Lady With the Little Dog, The, 1960 W
Lamb, The, 1915 W
Last Days of Pompeii, The, 1926 W
Last Millionaire, The, 1934 W
Last of the Mohicans, The, 1922 W
Lawrence of Arabia, 1962 W
Leopard, The, 1963 W
Lifeboat, 1944 W
Limelight, 1952 W
Little American, The, 1917 W
Little Angel, The, 1914 W
Lives of Bengal Lancer, 1935 W
Look Back in Anger, 1959 W
Lord of the Flies, 1964 W
Lost Horizon, The, 1937 W
Lost Week-end, The, 1945 W
Love, 1927 W
Loveletter, 1942 W
Love on the Dole, 1923 W
Love Parade, The, 1929 W
Lucrezia Borgia, 1910 W
Madame Dubarry, 1919 W
Mädchen in Uniform, 1931 W
Making a Living, 1914 W
Manchurian Candidate, The, 1962 W
Man from the South, The, 1945 W
Mater dolorosa, 1917 W
Maternelle, La, 1932 W
Messalina, 1910 W
Million, The, 1931 W
Miracle in Milan, 1951 W
Miracle of the Wolves, 1925 W
Mr. Deeds Comes to Town, 1936 W
Mrs. Miniver, 1942 W
Modern Times, 1936 W
Mon Oncle, 1958 W
Monsieur Verdoux, 1947 W
Morning Glory, 1932 W
Mother, The, 1920 W
Moulin Rouge, 1952 W
Murder, 1930 W
Muriel, 1964 W
Mystère Picasso, Le, 1955 W
Mystery Man, The, 1919 W
Naked City, The, 1948 W
Nana, 1926 W
Notte, La, 1961 W
Nous les Gosses, 1941 W
Nuit et Brouillard, 1956 W
October, 1928 W
Odd Man Out, 1947 W
One Day of War, 1943 W
Only Way, The, 1925 W
On the Waterfront, 1954 W
Orphée, 1950 W
Othello, 1952 W
Our Man in Havana, 1959 W
Outcast of the Islands, 1951 W
Owd Bob, 1925 W
Paisa, 1946 W
Pandora's Box, 1929 W
Passenger, The, 1964 W
Patriot, The, 1928 W
Payday, 1922 W
Phaedra, 1962 W
Pharaoh's Wife, 1922 W
Pickpocket, 1959 W
Pilgrim, The, 1923 W
Pinocchio, 1911 W
Plaisir, 1951 W
Poil de Carotte, 1933 W
Polyanna, 1920 W
Porte des Lilas, 1957 W
Portes de la Nuit, Les, 1946 W
Postmaster, The, 1940 W
Prince and the Showgirl, The, 1957 W
Private Life of Henry VIII, 1933 W
Psycho, 1960 W
Public Opinion, 1923 W
Pumpkin Eater, The, 1964 W
Pygmalion, 1938 W
Quai des Orfèvres, 1947 W
Quatorze Juli, 1933 W
Queen Christina, 1933 W
Queen Elizabeth, 1912 W
Quiet Flows the Don, 1957 W
Quo Vadis? 1912 W
Rashomon, 1950 W
Rear Window, 1954 W
Rebecca, 1940 W
Rebel Without a Cause, 1955 W
Rembrandt, 1942 W
Reveille, 1924 W
Rhapsody in Blue, 1945 W
Rickshaw Man, The, 1959 W
Robe, The, 1953 W
Robin Hood, 1923 W
Rocco and his Brothers, 1960 W
Rock Around the Clock, 1955 W
Roman Holiday, 1953 W
Rome, Open City, 1945 W
Ronde, La, 1950 W
Rules of the Game, The, 1939 W
Running Man, The, 1963 W
Sally in Our Alley, 1931 W
Saturday Night and Sunday Morning, 1960 W
Scarlet Pimpernel, The, 1934 W
Seven Samurai, The, 1954 W
Seventh Seal, The, 1956 W
Shadows, 1960 W
Shanghai Express, 1932 W
Shoeshine, 1946 W
Shoulder Arms, 1918 W
Silence, The, 1964 W
Silence est d'or, Le, 1947 W
Silken Skin, 1964 W
Skyscraper, 1923 W
Smiles of a Summer Night, 1955 W
Snow White and the Seven Dwarfs, 1938 W
Sous les Toits de Paris, 1930 W
Spartacus, 1911 W
Squaw Man, The, 1913 W
Stage-Door Canteen, 1943 W
Stalingrad, 1943 W
Star is Born, A, 1937 W
Stars Look Down, The, 1939 W
State of the Union, The, 1948 W
Strada, La, 1954 W
Strangers on a Train, 1951 W
Student of Prague, The, 1913 W
Summer Light, 1943 W
Summer with Monika, 1952 W
Sunday in August, 1950 W
Sunset Boulevard, 1950 W
Taste of Honey, A, 1961 W
Ten Commandments, The, 1924 W
Testament d'Orphée, Le, 1959 W

Films—*contd.*
Testament of Dr. Mabuse, The, 1933 W
Thin Man, The, 1934 W
Things to Come, 1936 W
Third Man, The, 1949 W
This is Cinerama, 1952 W
Tom Jones, 1963 W
Toni, 1935 W
Touch of Evil, 1958 W
Town Like Alice, A, 1956 W
Trader Horn, 1931 W
Trial, The, 1962 W
Tricheurs, Les, 1958 W
Tunnel Under the Canal, The, 1907 W
Umberto D, 1952 W
Underworld, 1927 W
Vampire, The, 1913 W
Veritas Vincit, 1918 W
Vertigo, 1958 W
Voyage in Italy, 1954 W
Wanderer of the Wasteland, 1924 W
Way Ahead, The, 1944 W
Whistle Down The Wind, 1961 W
White Cliffs of Dover, The, 1944 W
Wild Birds, 1955 W
Wild Strawberries, 1957 W
Wind Cannot Read, The, 1958 W
Winslow Boy, The, 1949 W
Winter Light, 1962 W
Woman in the Moon, The, 1928 W
Woman of Paris, A, 1923 W
Zeebrugge, 1924 W
Zola, 1944 W
Finch-Hatton, George Williams, Earl of Winchilsea (1791–1858), 1829 C
Fine Arts, 1805 S, 1961 S, 1882 O, 1900 S
Fingerprints, 1885 P, 1890 O
Finland: invaded by Sweden, 1788 F; Russian territory in, 1790 H; Russian aggression in, 1807 G, 1812 D; liberties suppressed, 1899 B; Republic proclaimed, 1917 M; signs peace with Central Powers, 1918 C; Russia invades, 1939 C; Russian offensive against, 1944 F, J
Finnegans Wake (J. Joyce), 1939 U
Finno-Karelian Republic, incorporated in USSR, 1956 G
Finzi, Gerald, B. musician (b. 1901), 1949 T
Fire, studies in, 1824 P
Fires, notable:
Crystal Palace, 1936 S
Houses of Parliament, 1834 K
Reichstag, 1933 B
First Lines of the Practice of Physic (W. Cullen), 1774 P
First Principles (H. Spencer), 1862 O
Fischer, Abram, S. Afr. lawyer, 1964 L
Fischer, Emil, G. chemist (1852–1919), 1852 Z, 1887 P, 1907 P, 1919 Z
Fischer, Kuno, G. philosopher (1824–1907), 1852 R
Fisher, Andrew, Aus. Labour politician, 1908 E, 1911 B
Fisher, Geoffrey Francis, B. churchman (b. 1887), Archbishop of Canterbury, 1960 R, 1961 A
Fisher, Herbert Albert Laurens, B. historian and Liberal statesman (1865–1940), 1865 Z, 1918 H, 1936 Q, 1940 Z
Fisher, Irving, Am. economist (1867–1948), 1910 O, 1919 O
Fisher, John, lord Fisher, B. admiral (1841–1920), 1841 Z, 1920 Z; as First Lord of Admiralty, 1914 K; resigns over Dardanelles policy, 1915 E
Fisheries:
Bering Sea Seal, 1892 B
Icelandic, 1958 F, J, 1961 B
Newfoundland, 1763 B
US—Canadian agreement on, 1925 B
Fitch, John, Am. inventor (1743–98), 1787 P
Fitzgerald, Edward, B. poet and translator (1809–83), 1809 W, 1859 U, 1883 Z
Fitzgerald, F. Scott, Am. author (1896–1940), 1923 U, 1925 U, 1934 U, 1941 U
Fiume, Italy: d'Annunzio attempts seizure, 1919 J; independence, 1919 M, 1920 L; agreement on, 1921 F; Italy annexes, 1924 C
Five Checks to Antinomianism (J. W. Fletcher), 1771 R
Five Great Monarchies of the Ancient Eastern World (H. Rawlinson), 1862 Q
Fizeau, Armand Hippolyte Louis, F. physicist (1819–96), 1849 P
Flagg, Ernest, Am. architect (1857–1939), 1905 S
Flamandes, Les (E. Verhaeren), 1883 U
Flandin, Pierre, F. Radical politician, 1934 L, 1935 E
Flare Path (T. Rattigan), 1942 W
Flash-light photography, 1898 P
Flaubert, Gustave, F. author (1821–80), 1821 Z, 1856 U, 1862 U, 1869 U, 1874 U, 1880 Z, 1881 U
Flax, machine for spinning, 1812 P
Flaxman, John, B. designer and sculptor (1755–1826), 1775 S, 1824 S
Flecker, James Elroy, B. poet (1884–1915), 1884 Z, 1915 W, 1923 W
Fleet Air Arm, British, increase in, 1936 C
Flegeljahre (Jean Paul), 1804 U
Fleming, Sir Alexander, B. scientist (1881–1955), 1881 Z, 1928 P, 1934 P, 1955 Z
Fleming, Ian Lancaster, B. author (1908–64), 1908 Z, 1953 U, 1964 Z
Fleming Report on independent schools, 1944 O
Flemish language, 1870 O; admitted in courts of Flanders, 1873 N; becomes official language of Flanders, 1932 G
Fletcher, John William, B. divine (1729–85), 1771 R
Fleure, Herbert John, B. zoologist (b. 1877), 1948 P
Fleurs du Mal, Les (Baudelaire), 1857 U
Fleurus, S.W. Belgium, battle, 1794 F
Flights. *See* Aeronautics; Aeroplanes; Space
Flinders, Matthew, B. naval officer (1774–1814), 1774 Z
Flogging, in British forces, abolished, 1881 O
Flood, Henry, Ir. statesman (1732–91), 1779 M
Floquet, Charles Thomas, F. Republican (1828–96), 1888 Q
Florence, Italy: peace of, 1801 C; becomes Italian capital, 1864 J; riots in, 1921 B; Eighth Army takes, 1944 H
Florey, Sir Howard, B. pathologist (1898–), 1898 Z, 1940 P
Florida, State, US: as a British colony, 1763 B, K; Spanish claims to, 1779 F; Spanish conquest of, 1782 F; restored to Spain, 1783 J; US boundary with, 1795 K; US obtains from Spain, 1819 B; becomes a US State, 1845 C; as a Confederate State, 1861 B
Florin, the, introduced, 1854 O
Flotow, Friedrich von, G. musician (1812–83), 1847 T
Flowering Cherry, The (R. Bolt), 1957 W
Fluorescent lamps, 1927 P
Fluorine, preparation of, 1886 P
Flushing, Holland, liberated, 1944 L
Flying-bombs, 1944 F; launching sites for, 1944 J
'Flying-saucers', 1955 P

'Flying-spot' microscope, 1951 P
Fly Leaves (C. S. Calverley), 1872 U
Foch, Ferdinand, F. soldier (1851–1929), 1851 Z, 1929 Z; as French Chief of Staff, 1917 E; as united commander on Western Front, 1918 C
Focshani, Rumania, Turkish defeat at, 1789 G
Fogazzaro, Antonio, It. author (1842–1911), 1842 Z, 1874 O, 1911 Z
Fokine, Michael, R. dancer and choreographer (1880–1942), 1909 T
Fokker, Anthony, G. aircraft designer (1890–1939), 1890 Z, 1939 Z
Folklore, German, 1778 U, 1810 R
Follette, Robert La, Am. Republican politician (1855–1925), 1911 A, 1915 O; as Progressive presidential candidate, 1924 L
Foma Gordeyev (M. Gorki), 1899 U
Fommenah, Ghana, treaty of, 1874 B
Fonseca, Manoel Deodoro da, Brazil, general, 1891 L
Fontainebleau, France:
  Treaty, abrogates Barrier Treaty, 1715, 1784 K
  Treaty, between France and Spain against Portugal, 1807 K
  decree, for confiscating British goods, 1810 K
Fontane, Theodor, G. author (1818–98), 1878 U
Fonteyn, Margot. *See* Arias, Margot Fonteyn de
Food:
  canned, 1874 P, 1880 P, 1892 P
  frozen, 1925 P
  legislation relating to, British, 1860 O, 1875 O
    American, 1898 O, 1906 O, 1917 G
  shortages and rationing, in Britain, 1918 O
    in France, 1916 O
    in Germany, 1916 O, 1917 D
Food Kitchens, 1918 O
Fool of Quality, The (H. Brooke), 1765 U
Foot, Hugh, lord Caradon, B. administrator and diplomat (b. 1907), as governor of Cyprus, 1957 K; resigns as Britain's representative to U.N., 1962 K
Football, Association, in Britain, 1863 X
  F.A. Cup, 1871 X
    at Wembley, 1923 X
  first international match, 1872 W
  League, 1888 X
  Players convicted of fixing matches, 1965 X
Foraker, Joseph Benson, Am. Republican (1846–1917), 1900 E
Forbes, George W., New Zealand United Party leader, 1930 E
Forbes-Robertson, Sir Johnston, B. actor (1853–1937), 1897 W
Forced labour, of Belgians deported to Germany, 1916 L
Forcellini, Egidio, It. classical scholar (1688–1768), 1769 Q, 1771 Q
Ford, Ford Madox (F. M. Hueffer), B. author and editor (1873–1939), 1873 Z, 1908 V, 1924 V, 1939 Z
Ford, Henry, Am. motor-car manufacturer (1863–1947), 1863 Z, 1909 P, 1913 P, 1947 Z
Ford Foundation, 1936 O
Foreign investments, statistics of comparative, 1914 Y
Foreign Service, British, amalgamation of overseas staffs of Foreign Office and Commonwealth Relations Office, 1964 B, 1965 A
Forests, US National Commission, 1906 O
Forever Amber (K. Winsor), 1945 U
Forgery, notable, 1789 R
Formosa (or Taiwan), S.E. China: rebellion in, 1787 N; ceded to Japan, 1895 D; China renounces sovereignty over, 1945 J; Chiang Kai-shek removes to, 1949 G, 1954 K; Britain supports US plan for, 1958 J
Formulary, National War, 1941 P
Fors Claviger (J. Ruskin), 1871 O
Forster, Edward Morgan, B. author (1879–), 1879 Z, 1908 U, 1910 U, 1924 U
Forster, William Edward, B. Liberal statesman (1818–86), 1818 Z, 1870 O, 1886 Z
Fort Clark, N. Carolina, US, captured by Unionists, 1861 H
Fort Donelson, Tenn., US, taken by Grant, 1862 B
Forth Bridge, Scotland, 1890 P, 1964 P
Fort Henry, Tenn., US, taken by Grant, 1862 B
For the Sake of Heaven (M. Buber), 1945 R
Fort Hudson, Missouri, US, surrenders to Unionists, 1863 G
Fortification, study of, 1810 O
Fort Lee, New Jersey, US, 1776 L
Fort St. George, Canada, 1813 E
Fort Sumpter, in Charleston Harbour, S. Carolina, US, 1861 D
Fort Ticonderoga, New York, US, 1775 E
Forty-hour week, in France, 1936 F
Forty-ninth parallel, as Canadian–US frontier, 1818 K
Forty-Second Parallel (J. Dos Passos), 1930 U
For Whom the Bell Tolls (E. Hemingway), 1940 U
Forzano, Giovacchino, It. politician, 1931 O
Foscani, Italy: taken by Austrians, 1917 A; German offensive, 1917 H, M
Foscolo, Ugo, Niccolo Ugo, It. author (1778–1827), 1778 Z, 1797 W, 1798 U, 1807 U, 1827 Z
Fossils, study of, 1837 P, 1846 P, 1962 P
Fouché, Joseph, duc de Otranto, F. politician (1763–1820), 1800 W
Foundations: a Statement of Christian Belief... (ed. Streeter), 1912 R
Foundations of Belief, The (A. J. Balfour), 1895 R
Foundations of Empirical Knowledge (A. J. Ayer), 1940 R
Foundations of Political Economy (Cohn), 1885 O
Foundations of Psychology (Waitz), 1846 R
Foundations of the XIXth Century (H. S. Chamberlain), 1899 O
Foundations:
  Balzan International, 1964 B
  Carnegie Peace, 1911 O
  Ford, projects sponsored by, 1955 O
  Nuffield, 1943 O
  Pahlavi, 1961 K
Fountain, The (C. Morgan), 1932 U
Fouqué, Friedrich Heinrich, Freiherr de la Motte, G. author (1777–1843), 1811 U
Four-dimensional geometry, 1908 P
Four Horsemen of the Apocalypse, The (Ibáñez), 1919 U
Four-minute mile, 1954 X
Fournier, Henri. *See* Alain-Fournier
Fournier de Pescay, François, F. medical practitioner and scientific author (1771–1833), 1822 P
Four Quartets (T. S. Eliot), 1944 U
Fourteen sonnets written chiefly on picturesque spots (W. Bowles), 1789 U
Fox, Charles James, B. Whig politician (1749–1806), 1782 C, E, G, 1790 C, 1806 J; coalition with North, 1783 D, M; supports Parliamentary Reform, 1783 E; India Bill, 1783 M; welcomes French Revolution, 1790 B; leads Whig rump, 1794 G; excluded from Pitt's cabinet, 1804 E; becomes foreign secretary, 1806 B
Fox, Henry, baron Holland, B. Whig politician (1705–74), 1763 D
Fox in the Attic, The (R. Hughes), 1961 U
Fragment on Government, A (J. Bentham), 1776 O

Fragonard, Jean Honoré, F. artist (1733–1806), 1766 S, 1776 S, 1806 Z
Frampton, Sir George, B. architect and sculptor (1860–1928), 1912 S
Françaix, Jean, F. musician (b. 1912), 1957 T
France:
botanical survey, 1813 P
frontier with Spain, 1856 M
geological map, 1841 P
France and England in the New World (F. Parkman), 1865 Q
France, Anatole. *See* Thibaut, J. A. A.
Francesca da Rimini (G. D'Annunzio), 1902 W
Francesca da Rimini (S. Pellico), 1855 W
Franchise, The:
in Australia, for women, 1902 G
in Austria, reformed, 1873 D
problem of women's, 1893 K
universal, 1907 A
in Belgium, universal male, demanded, 1885 N; achieved, 1893 O
women's, 1948 O
in Britain, attempts to widen, 1810 E, 1811 O, 1818 F, 1831 C, J
removal of Roman Catholic disabilities, 1829 D
widened by First Reform Bill, 1832 F
antiquated forms, eliminated, 1832 F
Chartists demand manhood, 1838 O
assimilation of county and borough, motion for, 1851 B
extended, 1867 D, 1884 M
plural voting abolished, 1891 K
for women, bills rejected, 1912 C, 1913 E, 1914 E
by-election on issue of, 1912 L
Suffragette demonstrations, 1913 A, D, 1914 C
at age of thirty, 1918 O
at age of twenty-one, 1928 E
abolition of university seats, 1948 O
in Denmark, women's 1915 F
age limit reduced, 1953 C
in France, limited, 1817 B
electoral colleges regulated, 1820 F
plural voting introduced, 1820 F
extension, demanded, 1847 G
universal, 1848 E, L; abolished, 1850 E
women's, 1945 O
in Germany:
universal, promised in Prussia, 1917 D
women's 1919 O
in Holland, reformed, 1887 F
widened, 1896 F
proportional representation adopted, 1899 M
in Hungary, universal, 1906 G
in Italy, extended, 1881 N
reformed, 1882 A
reduced, 1928 E
women's, 1946 O
in Japan, extended, 1925 C
in New Zealand, manhood, 1889 N
women's, 1893 O
in Norway, 1907 F
in Russia, for propertied classes, 1907 F
in S. Africa, controversy in Transvaal, 1899 C, G
for white women, 1930 E
in Spain, universal, 1890 C
in Sweden, proportional representation, 1911 J
in Switzerland, women ineligible to vote in federal elections, 1959 B
in Turkey, women's 1934 M
in US:
rights of Negro voters, attempts to protect, 1890 F
safeguarded by Civil Rights Bill, 1960 D
women's adopted in Arizona, Kansas and Wisconsin, 1912 L
proposal for, defeated, 1915 A
achieved, by 19th Amendment, 1920 H
Francis I, Holy Roman Emperor (1745–65), 1765 H
Francis II, Holy Roman Emperor (1792–1806), emperor of Austria (1804–35), 1792 C, 1804 H, 1809 B, 1835 C; resigns as Holy Roman Emperor, 1806 H
Francis I, of Naples, King of the Two Sicilies (1825–1830), 1825 A, 1830 L
Francis II, King of the Two Sicilies (1859), 1859 E; flees, 1860 J; surrenders to Garibaldi, 1861 B
Francis Ferdinand, archduke of Austria, assassinated, 1914 F
Francis Joseph I, emperor of Austria (1848–1916), 1848 M, 1900 A, 1916 L; concordat with Pius IX, 1855 R; crowned King of Hungary, 1867 F; army reforms, 1903 J
Franck, César, Belg. musician (1822–95), 1822 Z, 1858 T, 1872 T, 1880 T, 1884 T, 1885 T, 1889 T, 1895 Z
Franco, Francisco, Sp. general and dictator (b. 1892), 1955 L; leads army revolt, 1936 G, H; rebels elect chief of state, 1936 K; recognised by Germany and Italy, 1936 L; begins naval blockade, 1937 L; retakes Teruel, 1938 B; offensive in Catalonia, 1938 M; recognised by powers, 1939 B; Western powers appeal for overthrow of, 1946 L; proposes monarchy on death or resignation, 1947 G, 1957 G
Franco, Jono, Sp. politician, becomes premier, 1906 E
François Charles Joseph, King of Rome, 1811 C
Frankenau, formerly E. Prussia, Germany, 1914 M
Frankenheimer, John, Am. film director, 1962 W
Frankenstein (Mary Shelley), 1818 U
Frankfurt, Declaration of, 1813 M
Frankfurt-am-Main, W. Germany; Diet at, 1816 L; Professors discuss Germany's reunification at, 1846 E; Vorparlement meets at, 1848 C; German National Assembly meets at, 1848 E; Princes meet to reform Confederation, 1863 H; annexed by Prussia, 1866 H, J; Franco-German Peace Treaty, 1871 E; French occupation, 1920 D
Frankland, Sir Edward, B. chemist (1825–99), 1849 P
Franklin, Benjamin, Am. diplomat and inventor (1706–90), 1776 G, 1782 E, L, 1790 Z
Franklin, Sir John, B. Arctic explorer (1786–1847), 1786 Z, 1845 P, 1847 Z; search for, 1850 P
Franks, Oliver Sherwell, lord Franks, B. economist and administrator (b. 1905), 1947 O, 1960 C
Franny and Zooey (J. D. Salinger), 1961 U
Franz Josef Land, discovered, 1873 P
Fraudulent mediums, legislation against, 1951 R
Frau Sorge (H. Sudermann), 1887 U
Frazer, Sir James George, B. anthropologist (1854–1941), 1854 Z, 1890 Q, 1941 Z
Frederick II ('The Great'), King of Prussia (1740–1786), 1763 B, O, 1767 D, 1769 H, K, 1770 J, R, 1786 H; as author, 1768 L, 1780 U; role in first Partition of Poland, 1772 H; forms League of German Princes, 1785 G; monument, 1851 S
Frederick the Great (T. Carlyle), 1858 Q
Frederick III, emperor of Germany (1888), as Crown Prince, 1870 H; as emperor, 1888 C, F
Frederick VI, of Denmark (1808–39), 1839 M
Frederick VII, of Denmark (1848–63), 1848 A, 1863 L
Frederick Augustus, duke of York and of Albany, B. soldier (1763–1827), 1793 J, 1799 J, K
Frederick Christian, renounces Norwegian throne, 1814 H

Frederick William II, of Prussia (1786–97), 1786 H, 1790 F, 1791 G, 1795 D, 1797 L
Frederick William III, of Prussia (1797–1840), 1797 L, 1812 M, 1840 F; open letter to, 1797 O; dismisses Stein, 1807 A; meets Napoleon, 1807 G; declares war on France, 1813 C; promises constitution, 1815 E
Frederick William IV, of Prussia (1840–61), 1840 F, 1850 R, 1861 A; summons Diet, 1847 B; grants constitution, 1848 C; refusal to be elected 'emperor', 1849 C, D; summons Erfurt Parliament, 1850 C; insanity, 1857 K, 1858 K
Fredericksburg, Va., US, Lee's victory at, 1862 M
Frederikshavn, Treaty of, 1809 J, 1810 A
Freedom and Organisation (B. Russell), 1934 O
Freedom from Hunger Campaign, 1960 G
Freedom of Necessity, The (J. D. Bernal), 1949 O
Freedom of Worship. *See* Religious Toleration
Freedom Parties. *See under* Political Parties
Free French Government, 1940 H
Committee of National Liberation, 1943 F
Freeman, Edward Augustus, B. historian (1823–92), 1823 Z, 1867 Q, 1892 Z
Free State, The (D. W. Brogan), 1945 O
Free Trade:
Austro-German customs union projected, 1931 C
in Britain:
with Ireland, 1780 M
relaxation of navigation laws, 1821 E, 1822 F, 1823 E, G, D, 1825 G, 1894 F, K
Cobden's pamphlet, 1835 O. *See also* Anti-Corn Law League
The Times declares for, 1839 A
budgets, 1842 D, 1845 D
Russell's conversion to, 1845 L
repeal of Corn Laws, 1846 E
Gladstone's budget, 1853 O, 1861 D
treaty with France, 1860 A
in Prussia:
Gentz's plea, 1797 O
internal, 1805 O, 1818 E
'Zollverein', 1819 K, 1826 M, 1818 A, 1829 E, 1833 C, 1835 E
See also Common Market; EFTA; Tariff Questions
Free Trade Association, Latin American, 1961 F
Freiligrath, Ferdinand, G. poet (1810–76), 1846 U
Fréjus, S.E. France, 1799 K
Frémont, John Charles, Am. Republican (1813–90), 1856 L
French, John, earl of Ypres, B. soldier (1852–1925), 1915 M
French Committee of National Liberation, 1943 F
French Equatorial Africa, 1910 A
French Guiana, 1800 M, 1801 J
French Revolution. *See* Revolution, French
French Revolution, The (T. Carlyle), 1837 Q
French Revolution, The (J. M. Thompson), 1943 Q
French Without Tears (T. Rattigan), 1936 W
Frere, Sir Henry Bartle Edward, B. colonial administrator (1815–84), 1877 C, 1878 M
Fresnel, Augustin Jean, F. physicist (1788–1827), 1815 P, 1822 P
Freud, Sigmund, Aus. psychologist (1856–1939), 1856 Z, 1895 R, 1900 R, 1901 R, 1905 R, 1909 R, 1913 R, 1927 R, 1930 R; autobiography, 1936 R
Freycinet, Charles Louis de Saulces de, F. Moderate Republican politician (1828–1912), 1882 A, 1886 A, M
Freyssinet, Eugène, F. architect, 1916 S, 1922 S
Freytag, Gustave, G. dramatist (1816–95), 1853 W
Frick, Wilhem, G. Nazi, 1930 A, 1933 A
Fricker, Peter Racine, B. musician (b. 1920), 1950 T, 1954 T
Friction: experiments, 1778 P, 1798 P; laws of, 1779 P
Friedland, W. Germany, battle, 1807 F
Friedrich, Johann, G. theologian (1836–1912), 1869 R
Friedrich, Kaspar David, G. artist (1774–1840), 1808 S, 1809 S, 1835 S
Friendly Societies, in Britain, 1876 O
Fries, Jakob Friedrich, G. philosopher (1773–1843), 1808 R
Friesland, East, W. Germany, ceded to Hanover, 1815 F
Frith, William Powell, B. artist (1819–1909), 1858 S
Frithjofs Saga (E. Tegner), 1825 U
Frobel, Friedrich Wilhelm August, G. philosopher and educationalist (1782–1852), 1816 O, 1837 O
Frogs, treatise on, 1850 P
Fröhliche Wissenschaft, Die (F. Nietzsche), 1882 U
From Another Shore (A. Hertzen), 1850 U
Fromm, Erich, B. sociologist, 1942 R, 1949 R
From the Four Winds (J. Galsworthy), 1897 U
Frost, Robert, Am. poet (b. 1874), 1930 U, 1951 U
Froude, James Anthony, B. historian (1818–94), 1818 Z, 1848 R, 1856 Q, 1894 Z
Frou-frou (W. Halévy), 1869 W
Fructose, synthesis of, 1887 P
Fruits, canned, 1892 P
Fry, Christopher, B. dramatist (b. 1907), 1947 W, 1948 W, 1951 W, 1954 W
Fry, Elizabeth, B. prison-reformer (1780–1845), 1813 O
Fry, E. M., B. architect, 1936 S
Fry, Roger Eliot, B. artist and critic (1866–1934), 1866 Z, 1910 S, 1934 Z
Fry, William Henry, Am. musician (1815–64), 1863 T
Fuad I, King of Egypt, 1922 C, 1928 G
Fuad II, King of Egypt, 1952 G
Fuchs, Klaus, Am. atomic spy, 1950 C, 1952 O
Fuchs, Sir Vivian Ernest, B. explorer (b. 1908), 1908 Z, 1958 P
Full Employment in a Free Society (W. Beveridge), 1944 O
Fuller, Sarah Margaret, Am. journalist and social reformer (1810–50), 1840 R
Fulton, Robert, Am. civil engineer (1765–1815), 1765 Z, 1801 P, 1803 P, 1807 P
Fulton, Missouri, US, Churchill's speech at, 1946 C
Fumigators, chemical, 1920 P
Funck, Casimir, Pol. chemist (1884–1941), 1912 P
Fundamenta Astronomiae (F. W. Bessel), 1818 P
Fundamentalism, defined, 1895 R
Fundamental particles, 1964 P
Funk, Walter, H. economics minister (1891–1960), 1937 L, 1939 A, 1946 J
Furnaces, blast, 1829 P; gas-fired, 1861 P
Furniture, 'Utility', 1941 O
Fuseli, Henry, B. painter (1741–1825), 1782 S
Fustel de Coulanges, Numa Denis, F. archaeologist, (1830–89), 1864 Q
Future of An Illusion (Freud), 1927 R
Futurism, term coined, 1909 S
Futurist Manifesto, 1910 S
Fylingdales, Yorks, England, early warning station, 1960 B

G

Gabes Gap, Tunisia, Rommel retreats through, 1943 D

Gabon, now independent state of French Community, as French Equatorial Africa, 1888 M
Gabriel, Ange Jacques, F. architect (1698–1782), 1765 S
Gadsden Purchase, of US Far West territories, 1854 D
Gaeta, Cen. Italy, 1848 L, 1849 B; Francis II surrenders to Garibaldi, 1861 B
Gagarin, Yuri, R. cosmonaut (b. 1934), 1961 P
Gage, Thomas, B. soldier (1721–87), 1775 D
Gageure imprévue, La (M. J. Sedaine), 1768 W
Gaillard, Félix, F. Radical Socialist (b. 1919), 1957 K, 1958 D
Gainsborough, Thomas, B. artist (1727–88), 1770 S, 1777 S, 1788 Z
Gaisford, Thomas, B. classical scholar (1779–1855), 1793 Q
Gaitskell, Hugh Todd Naylor, B. Labour Party leader (1906–63), 1906 Z, 1960 M, 1963 A; becomes Chancellor of Exchequer, 1950 K; elected Party leader, 1955 M; conflict with Labour unilateralists, 1960 K, 1961 F; defeats Wilson in election for leadership, 1960 K
Gaius, Institutes of, discovered, 1816 Q
Galathea, deep-sea expedition by the, 1950 P
Galbraith, John Kenneth, Am. economist (b. 1908), 1958 O
Galbraith, Thomas Galloway, B. Conservative politician (b. 1917), 1962 L
Galiani, Ferdinando, It. economist (1728–87), 1770 O
Galicia, Poland, 1809 K; Polish designs on, 1790 C; taken by Austria, 1795 K; Russian offensive in, 1916 A; Germano-Austrian counter-attack, 1917 G; Poles defeated in, 1919 A; mandate over, assigned to Poland, 1919 L; recognised as Polish, 1923 C
Galilee, N. Israel, British district commissioner for, 1937 J
Gall, Franz Joseph, G. anatomist and physiologist (1758–1828), 1810 P
Galle, Johann Gottfried, G. astronomer (1812–90), 1846 P
Gallegos, Rómulo, Venezuelan leader of Democratic Action Party, 1947 M
Galleries and Museums:
  in Britain:
    closure of, 1916 Q
    Bethnal Green Museum, 1874 Q
    British Museum, public admission to, 1879 W
      Edward VII Gallery opened, 1914 Q
      Reading Room, 1916 Q
      See also under London
    Buckingham Palace Gallery, 1962 S
    Dulwich Art Gallery, 1814 S
    Fitzwilliam Museum, Cambridge, 1837 S
    National Gallery, 1824 S, 1832 S
      damage by Suffragettes, 1914 C
      cleaning of pictures in, 1936 S, 1947 S
      theft and return of Goya's 'Wellington', 1961 S, 1965 S
      acquires Cézanne's 'Les Grandes Baigneuses', 1964 S
      See also under Exhibitions, Art
    National Maritime Museum, Greenwich, 1937 Q
    National Portrait Gallery, 1857 S
    Natural History Museum, S. Kensington, 1881 P, 1916 Q
    Royal Academy, founded, 1768 S
      Chantrey bequest to, 1841 S
      sells Leonardo da Vinci cartoon, 1962 S
      See also under Exhibitions, Art
    Science Museum, S. Kensington, 1857 O
    Tate Gallery, 1897 S
      Turner Wing of, 1910 S
      Duveen Gallery at, 1937 S
      See also under Exhibitions, Art
    Wallace Collection, 1900 S
    Whitechapel Art Gallery, 1897 S
  in France:
    'Art Nouveau', 1897 S
    Louvre, The, 1793 S
      theft of *Mona Lisa* from, 1911 S
    Musée d'Orangerie, 1916 S
  in Germany:
    Atlas Museum, Berlin, 1824 S
    German Museum, Munich, 1903 O
    Museum of Twentieth Century, Berlin, 1963 S
  in Holland, Rijksmuseum, Amsterdam, 1877 S
  in Ireland, Lane bequest to, 1915 S
  in Italy, Brera Gallery, Milan, 1806 S
    Rome Museum, 1769 Q
  in Japan, Tokio Museum, 1957 S
  in US:
    Guggenheim Art Museum, 1953 S, 1959 S
    Museum of Modern Art, New York, 1929 S
    National Gallery of Art, Washington, 1937 S
    Philadelphia Museum, 1769 Q
    See also under Exhibitions, Art
Gallican Articles of Religion of 1682, observation enforced, 1766 R; adopted in Italy, 1786 R
Gallipoli, Turkey: Anglo-French landings, 1915 D, H; British withdrawal from Suvla and Anzac, 1915 M
Gallium, element, discovered, 1871 P
Galois, Evaniste, F. mathematician (1811–32), 1846 P
Galsworthy, John, B. novelist and dramatist (1867–1933), 1867 Z, 1933 Z; as novelist, 1879 U, 1906 U, 1920 U, 1921 U, 1924 U; as dramatist, 1920 W
Galt, John, B. novelist (1779–1839), 1821 U
Galton, Sir Francis, B. forensic scientist, 1850 P, 1869 P, 1885 P
Galvani, Luigi, It. physiologist (1737–98), 1771 P, 1789 P, 1798 Z
Galvanometer, invented, 1826 P; mirror, 1858 P
Gambetta, Léon, F. Moderate Republican statesman (1838–82), 1838 Z, 1870 J, 1882 Z; forms ministry, 1881 L; Note on Egypt, 1882 A; loses power, 1882 A
Gambia: taken over by Britain, 1821 E; becomes Crown Colony, separate from Sierra Leone, 1843 D; independence agreed, 1964 G; becomes independent, 1965 B
Gamma rays, 1906 P, 1913 P, 1960 P
Gandamak, Afghanistan, treaty of, 1879 E
Gandhi, Mohandas Karamchand, Ind. statesman and social reformer (1869–1948), 1869 Z; arrested, 1913 L; returns to India, 1914 N; imprisoned, 1922 C; opens civil disobedience campaign, 1930 C; released for discussions, 1931 A; signs Delhi Pact, 1931 C; at Round Table Conference, 1931 J; re-arrested, 1932 A; suspends civil disobedience campaign, 1934 D; withdraws from Indian National Congress, 1934 K; rejects proposals for self-government, 1945 J; assassinated, 1948 A
Ganganelli, Lorenzo, It. (1705–74), elected Pope Clement XIV, 1769 E
Garbo, Greta (*née* Gustafsson), Swe. film actress (b. 1905), 1905 Z, 1927 W, 1933 W, 1935 W
Garciá-Gutiérrez, Antonio, Sp. author (1812–84), 1836 U
Gard, R. M. du, F. author, 1922 U
Garden Party, The (K. Mansfield), 1922 U

Gardiner, Gerald, lord Gardiner, B. lawyer and Labour Party politician (b. 1900), becomes Lord Chancellor, 1964 K
Gardiner, Samuel Rawson, B. historian (1829–1902), 1829 Z, 1863 Q, 1902 Z
Gardner, John, Am. musician, 1957 T
Garfield, James Abraham, Am. Republican (1831–1881), inaugurated 20th president of US, 1881 C; assassinated, 1881 G
Garibaldi, Giuseppe, It. statesman and soldier (1807–82), 1807 Z, 1882 Z; defends Rome, 1849 G; forms Italian National Association, 1857 H; proclaims Victor Emmanuel King of Italy, 1860 K; takes surrender of Francis II of Naples, 1861 B; is captured, 1862 H; March on Rome, 1867 K, L
Garnett, David, B. author (b. 1892), 1924 U, 1925 U
Garnier, Jean Louis Charles, F. architect (1825–98), 1861 S
Garrick, David, B. actor (1718–79), 1779 Z
Garrison, William Lloyd, Am. anti-slavery leader and journalist (1805–79), 1831 O
Garrod, Heathcote William, B. author and critic (b. 1878), 1947 Q
Garson, Greer, Am. film actress (b. 1908), 1942 W
Garvin, James Louis, B. journalist (1867–1947), 1868 Z, 1808 V, 1942 V, 1947 Z
Gasperi, Alcide de, It. statesman (1881–1954), Christian Democrat; forms coalitions, 1945 L, 1947 B, E, 1950 A, 1953 G; becomes provisional head of state, 1946 F
Gas, Coal, system of heating and lighting by, 1798 P; used for street-lighting, 1802 W, 1809 P, 1812 P, 1822 P
Gascoigne, David. *See under* Sanderson, Cobden
Gases, chemistry of, 1766 P
diffusion of, laws on, 1829 P
kinetic theory of, 1850 P
partial pressure, law of, 1803 P
separation of, 1863 P
Gases:
krypton, 1903 P
natural, 1963 P, 1964 P
xenon, 1903 P
Gaskell, Elizabeth Cleghorn (*née* Stevenson), B. novelist (1810–65), 1810 Z, 1848 U, 1853 U, 1865 Z
Gas-mantle, 1886 P
Gas, Poison: Hague Convention on, 1899 E; first used, 1915 D; banned by Washington Conference, 1922 B; Geneva Conference on, 1925 E; anti-gas school, British, 1936 C
Gastein, Austria, Convention of, 1865 H
Gas turbine, peat-fired, 1951 P
Gates, Horatio, Am. general (1728–1806), 1777 K, 1780 K
Gathering Storm, The (W. S. Churchill), 1948 Q
Gatling, Richard Jordan, Am. gunsmith (1818–1903), 1862 P
Gaudi, Antoni, It. architect (1852–1926), 1905 S, 1926 S
Gauguin, Paul, F. artist (1848–1903), 1848 Z 1876 S, 1884 S, 1891 S, 1897 S, 1901 S, 1902 S, 1903 Z
Gaulle, Charles André Joseph Marie de, F. statesman and soldier (b. 1890), 1890 Z, 1962 L, 1963 A
becomes leader of Free French, 1940 H
enters Paris, 1944 H
heads French Provisional Government, 1944 K
orders cease-fire in Syria and Lebanon, 1945 E
visits Washington, 1945 H
elected president of Provisional Government, 1945 L
resigns, 1946 A
controls Rassemblement du Peuple Français, 1947 D, 1948 L
is prepared to take office, 1958 E
forms government, 1958 E
meets Adenauer, 1958 J
elected president, 1958 M
proclaimed president of Fifth Republic, 1959 A
meets Macmillan, 1959 C, 1961 L
broadcasts on Algeria, 1959 J
at Summit meeting, 1960 E
offers terms to Algerian rebels, 1960 F
on Tunisian crisis, 1961 H
attempted assassination, 1962 H
asks Pompidou to remain in office, 1962 K
objects to Britain entering Common Market, 1963 A
rejects offer of Polaris missile, 1963 A
tours S. America, 1964 J
fails to obtain clear majority for presidency, 1965 M
defeats Mitterand in presidential election, 1965 M
Gaulle, De (F. Mauriac), 1964 O
Gauss, Karl Friedrich, G. mathematician and astronomer (1777–1855), 1772 Z, 1801 P, 1809 P, 1833 P, 1855 Z
Gautier, Théophile, F. author (1811–72), 1811 Z, 1925 U, 1852 U, 1872 Z
Gavarni. *See* Chevalier, Sulpice
Gay Lord Quex, The (A. W. Pinero), 1899 U
Gay-Lussac, Joseph Louis, F. Chemist (1778–1850), 1778 Z, 1807 P, 1808 P, 1850 Z
Gaza, in Egyptian-controlled Sinai: Turks defeated at, 1917 C; battle, 1917 D; British take, 1917 L, 1956 L
Gazala–Bir Hakeim Line, Western Desert, 1942 F
Gear, speed-reducing, for turbines, 1910 P
Gebir (W. S. Landor), 1798 U
Geddes Committee, 1922 O
Gedo (K. Barth), 1935 R
Geiger, H., Am. physicist, 1913 P, 1928 P
Geiger Counter, 1928 P
Gendre de M. Poirier, Le (Angier and Sandeau), 1854 W
Genera Crustaceorum et Insectorum (P. A. Latreille), 1806 P
General Agreement on Tariffs and Trade (GATT), Geneva, Conferences on, 1963 E, 1964 E
General History of the Science and Practice of Music (J. Hawkins), 1776 T
General Motors, sit-down strike, 1937 O
General Theory of Employment (J. M. Keynes), 1936 O
General Warrants, 1763 D
General Plantarum (A. de Jussieu), 1789 P
General Post Office, takes over British telephone system, 1912 O
Generating Stations. *See under* Electricity
Genetic Code, breaking of, 1961 P
Genetics, research in, 1909 P, 1927 P
Geneva, Switzerland:
Lemanic Republic in, 1798 A
Protestant revivalists in, 1810 R
Convention, on Red Cross, 1864 D
Court of Arbitration, 1872 J
League of Nations moves to, 1920 K
building for, 1938 S
Protocol, adopted by League of Nations, 1924 K
Britain refuses to sign, 1926 C
Conference on Arms Traffic, 1925 E
Conferences on Economic Affairs, 1927 E, 1930 L
Disarmament Conference, 1927 L
Protocol, on Germany's equality of rights, 1932 M
World Health Assembly, 1948 U

Geneva—*contd.*
Conference on Korea and Indo-China, 1954 D
Summit Conference proposed, 1955 F, G
Conference of foreign ministers on Germany, 1955 K, 1959 E
Conference on atomic energy, 1955 H
Conference on detection of nuclear explosions, 1958 G
Conference on surprise attack, 1958 L
Conference on law of the sea, 1958 O
Wheat agreement, 1959 C
Disarmament Committee, 1960 C
Conference on atomic weapon tests, 1962 A
negotiations on Laos, 1962 A, G
Disarmament Conference, 1962 C, 1964 A
France boycotts, 1962 C
Génie du Christianisme, Le (Chateaubriand), 1802 U
Genius of Spain (de Madariaga), 1923 Q
Genoa, Italy: sells Corsica to France, 1768 G; Ligurian Republic in, 1797 F; capitulates to French, 1800 F; under French domination, 1805 F; Conference on Economic Affairs, 1922 D; Convention, between Russia and Vatican, 1922 E; British bombard, 1941 B; Allies capture, 1945 D
Genocide, convention on prevention of, 1948 M
Gentz, Friedrich von, G. publicist (1764–1832), 1797 O
Geographical Society, The Royal, London, 1830 P
Geography in its Relation to Nature and History (K. Ritter), 1817 P
Geology, studies in, 1775 P, 1815 P, 1816 P, 1830 P, 1839 P
Geometry, four-dimensional, 1908 P
line, invented, 1865 P
synthetic, founded, 1832 P
treatises on, 1794 P, 1854 P
Geophysical Year, International, 1957 P, 1958 P
George III, King of Great Britain and Ireland (1738–1820), 1766 G, 1769 A, 1782 C, 1795 L; Dunning's motion on power of, 1780 D; derangement of, 1788 L; recovery of, 1789 B; insanity, 1811 B; death, 1820 A; library, 1923 Q
George IV, King of Great Britain and Ireland (1820–30), 1823 Q, 1830 F; as Prince of Wales, 1789 B; as Prince Regent, 1811 B, 1812 B, 1815 K, 1819 M; attack on, 1817 A; accession, 1820 A; relations with Caroline, Princess of Wales, 1820 F, G, 1821 G
George V, King of Great Britain, etc. (1910–36), accession, 1910 E; coronation, 1911 F; holds Delhi Durbar, 1911 M; Buckingham Palace Conference, 1914 G; adopts name of Windsor, 1917 F; Silver Jubilee celebrations, 1935 W; death, 1936 A
George VI, King of Great Britain, etc. (1932–52), accession, 1936 M; visits Paris, 1938 G; visits Canada and US, 1939 F; peace feelers to, 1939 L; presents sword to Stalingrad, 1943 B; death, 1952 B
George V, King of Hanover (1851–66), 1851 L, 1855 E
George XIII, Prince of Georgia, 1780 J
George I, King of Greece (1863–1913), 1863 C; murdered, 1913 C
George II, King of Greece (1890–1947), 1935 L; as Crown Prince, 1898 L; deposed, 1923 M; returns to Athens, 1946 J
George, Henry, Am. political economist (1839–97), 1879 O
George, Stefan, G. author (1868–1933), 1868 Z, 1890 V, 1897 U, 1899 U, 1933 Z
George William Frederick, Duke of Cambridge (1819–1904), B. soldier, 1895 F
Georgetown, B. Guiana, riots in, 1962 B
Georgia, Russia: Russian intervention in, 1783 K, 1787 H; Russian annexation, 1801 J; independence proclaimed, 1918 E
Georgia, State, US: dispute with Cherokee Indians, 1830 E; as a Confederate State, 1861 B; Sherman's march through, 1864 E, J
Georgian Poetry (ed. E. Marsh), 1911 U
Gérard, François, F. artist (1770–1837), 1789 S
Gerettete Venedig, Das (H. von Hofmannsthal), 1905 W
Gerhardsen, Einar, Norw. Labour leader, as premier, 1945 F. 1955 A
Gerhardt, Charles Frédéric, F. chemist (1816–56), 1852 P
Géricault, Théodore, F. artist (1790–1824), 1790 Z, 1819 S, 1824 Z
Germain, George Sackville, Viscount, B. soldier and politician (1716–85), 1775 L
German (formerly Jones), Sir Edward, B. musician (1862–1936), 1902 T
German Catastrophe, The (F. Meinecke), 1946 O
German Confederation: established under Austria, 1815 F; Diet of, 1816 L; issues Carlsbad Decrees, 1819 J; to interfere in states unable to maintain public order, 1820 E; reserves rights in Schleswig-Holstein, 1846 F; suspended, 1848 E; replaced by the Reich, 1848 F; Prussia attempts revival through Erfurt Parliament, 1850 C, D; Austria revives Frankfurt Bundestag, 1850 E; Prussia reorganises, 1851 E, 1866 H; Princes meet to reform, 1863 H; declared at an end, 1866 F
Germanium, element, discovered, 1886 P
German Legal Antiquities (J. G. Grimm), 1828 Q
German literature, introduced to England by Carlyle, 1828 W
German Mythology (J. G. Grimm), 1835 Q
German Empire established, 1871 A, D
Germantown, Pennsylvania, US, battle, 1777 K
Germany, Unification of: national revival against Napoleon, 1806 O; Prussian despatch on, 1849 A; by Parliamentary means fails, 1849 F; Dresden Conference fails, 1850 M; work of German National Association for, 1859 J; under Prussia's lead, 1865 K, 1866 H, 1871 A, D
Germany:
Allied military control ends, 1927 A
Allied occupation, 1945 F, 1954 K, 1955 E
economic fusion of British and US zones, 1946 M
problem of, differences between Russia and West on, 1952 C
Britain proposes four-power conference on, 1952 G, 1955 K
Russia rejects proposals for reunification through free elections, 1954 A
Russia refuses to discuss reunification, 1955 L
West German Bundestag asks for solution to problem, 1958 G
East Germany demands recognition, 1958 L
Russian proposals on Berlin rejected, 1958 M
Foreign ministers' conference on Berlin and peace treaty, 1959 E
Adenauer appeals for peace treaty based on self-determination, 1961 F
Khrushchev proposes a peace conference and Berlin as a free city, 1961 F
Berlin Wall, 1961 H
See also Berlin; Germany, East; Germany, West
Germany, East: Democratic Republic established, 1949 K; frontier with Poland settled, 1950 L; demands recognition, 1958 L

Germany, West: federal constitution demanded, 1948 F; Federal Republic in force, 1949 E
Germany and the Revolution (J. Görres), 1820 O
Germinal (É. Zola), 1885 U
Germ theory of disease, 1861 P
Germ warfare, China accuses US troops in Korea of using, 1952 C
Gerry, Elbridge Thomas, Am. lawyer and philanthropist (1837–1927), 1837 Z, 1874 O, 1927 Z
Gershwin, George, Am. musician (1898–1937), 1924 T, 1928 T, 1935 T, 1937 W
Gerstenberg, Heinrich Wilhelm von, G. poet and critic (1737–1823), 1766 U, 1767 U
Gertrude of Wyoming (T. Campbell), 1809 U
Geschichte der Poesie der Griechen und Römer (K. Schlegel), 1798 Q
Gesenius, Heinrich Friedrich, G. orientalist (1786–1842), 1812 Q
Gesner, Abraham, Canad. geologist (1797–1864), 1854 P
Gettysburg, Pennsylvania, US, Lee's defeat at, 1863 G
Ghali, Butros, Egyptian premier, assassinated, 1910 B
Ghana: becomes independent, 1957 C; becomes a one-party state, 1964 B. *See also* Gold Coast
Ghent, Belgium: Treaty, between Britain and US, 1814 M; Peace, 1815 A; University, 1816 O; infants' welfare centre, 1903 O; Germans occupy, 1914 K
Ghosts (H. Ibsen), 1881 W
Ghost Stories of An Antiquary (M. R. James), 1904 U
Giaour, The (Byron), 1813 U
Giacometti, Alberto, Swi. sculptor (1901–66), 1933 S, 1947 S, 1950 S, 1965 S
Gibb, Walter, B. aviator (b. 1919), 1955 P
Gibberd, Frederick, B. architect (b. 1908), 1955 S, 1957 S
Gibbon, Edward, B. historian (1737–94), 1764 U, 1776 O, 1794 Z
Giberellin, hormone, 1957 P
Gibraltar: siege of, 1779 F; relief of, 1780 A, 1782 K
Gibson, Edward, Lord Ashbourne, Ir. attorney-general (1837–1913), 1885 H
Gide, André, F. author (1869–1951), 1899 U, 1902 U, 1909 U, 1919 U, 1925 U; *Journal*, 1889 U, 1946 U
Giffen, Sir Robert, B. administrator and economist (1837–1910), 1879 O
Gifford, William, B. author (1756–1826), 1794 U
Gigli, Benjamino, It. singer (1890–1957), 1930 T
Gijón, Spain, falls to rebels, 1937 K
Gilbert, Sir Alfred, B. sculptor (1854–1934), 1925 S
Gilbert, Cass, Am. architect (1859–1934), 1859 Z, 1902 S, 1913 S, 1934 Z
Gilbert, Sir Joseph Henry, B. Congregationalist minister and agriculturalist (1779–1852), 1843 P
Gilbert, Sir William Schwenck, B. dramatist (1836–1911), 1836 Z, 1875 T, 1896 T, 1911 Z
Gilbert and Ellice Islands, S. Pacific, Britain annexes, 1915 L
Gilchrist, Percy, B. metallurgist (1851–1935), 1878 P
Gill, Arthur Eric Rowton, B. stone-carver, engraver and typographer (1882–1940), 1882 Z, 1913 S, 1925 S, 1927 S, 1928 S, 1932 S, 1938 S, 1940 Z
Gillray, James, B. caricaturist (1757–1815), 1779 S
Gilman, Harold, B. artist (1876–1919), 1913 S
Gilson, Étienne, F. historian and philosopher (b. 1884), 1922 R, 1941 R
Gin, cotton, invented, 1793 P
Gioberti, Vincenzo, It. political author (1801–52), 1851 P
Giocanda Smile, The (A. Huxley), 1948 W
Giolitti, Giovanni, It. statesman (1842–1928), 1909 M, 1911 C; becomes premier, 1892 E; falls, 1893 M; forms second ministry, 1906 E
Giordano, Umberto, It. musician (1867–1934), 1898 T
Girard, Philippe Henri de, F. engineer (1775–1845), 1812 P
Giraudoux, Jean, F. dramatist (1882–1944), 1928 W, 1929 W, 1937 W
Girl Guides, 1909 O
Girodet de Roussy, Anne Louis, F. artist (1767–1824), 1793 S
Girondins in France: in power, 1792 L; overthrown, 1793 F; execution of prominent, 1793 K; survivors admitted to Convention, 1794 M
Girtin, Thomas, B. artist (1775–1802), 1797 S, 1800 S, 1802 S
Gissing, George Robert, B. author (1857–1903), 1886 U, 1891 U, 1903 U
Gitanjali (R. Tagore), 1912 U
Givenchy, France, battle, 1915 F
Gizenga, Antoine, Congolese politician, 1960 M
Glaciers, treatise on, 1840 P
Gladstone, William Ewart, B. statesman and Liberal (1809–98), 1809 Z, 1898 Z
becomes chancellor of Exchequer, 1852 M
Free Trade budget, 1853 D
leads House of Commons, 1865 K
forms first ministry, 1868 M
resigns after government defeat, but returns to office, 1872 C
both premier and chancellor of Exchequer, 1873 H, 1880 D
hopes to abolish income tax, 1874 B
resigns, 1874 B
attacks papal infallibility, 1874 R
resigns Liberal Party leadership, 1875 A
publishes *The Bulgarian Horrors*, 1876 J
conducts Midlothian campaign, 1879 L
forms second ministry, 1880 D
introduces Irish land act, 1881 H
Third Reform Bill, 1884 M
resigns, 1885 F
forms third ministry, 1886 B
introduces Irish Home Rule bill, 1886 D
defeated over, 1886 F
forms fourth ministry, 1892 H
delivers Romanes Lecture, 1892 Q
resigns, 1894 C
speeches on Armenian massacres, 1896 J
Glasgow, Scotland: School of Art, 1900 S; riots in, 1931 J; Empire Exhibition, 1938 W
Glass Menagerie, The (T. Williams), 1944 W
Glass, optical, 1916 P
Glatz (now Klodzkow), Poland, restored by Austria, 1763 B
Glazounov, Alexander, R. musician (1865–1936), 1865 Z, 1936 Z
Gleizes, Albert, F. artist (1881–1953), 1912 S
Glencoe, S. Africa, Boer defeat at, 1899 K
Glenn, John, Am. cosmonaut (b. 1921), 1962 P
Gloucester, England, Sunday School at, 1780 R
Gloucestershire County Cricket Club, 1870 X
Glubb, Sir John Bagot, B. soldier (b. 1897), 1956 C
Gluck, Christoph Willibald von, G. musician (1714–1787), 1767 T, 1774 T, 1775 S, 1777 T, 1779 T, 1787 Z
Glyndebourne, Sussex, England, operatic festival at, 1934 T
Gneisenau, August Wilhelm Anton, Count Neithandt von, Pruss. soldier (1760–1831), 1812 A

Gnesen, Poland, ceded to Prussia, 1793 E
Goa, Indians invade, 1955 H, 1961 M
Goblet, René, F. Moderate Republican (1828–1905), 1886 M, 1887 E
God and Philosophy (E. Gilson), 1941 R
Goddard, Rayner, lord Goddard, B. judge (b. 1877), 1958 J
Goderich, Viscount. *See* Robinson, F. J.
Godesberg, W. Germany, Chamberlain visits, 1938 J
Godoy, Alvarez de Faria Manuel de, Duke of El Alcudia, Sp. dictator (1767–1851), 1792 N, 1798 C, 1800 E
God that Failed, The (ed. A. Koestler), 1950 Q
Godwin Austen, Mount (K2), in Himalayas, 1954 P
Godwin, William, B. political author (1756–1836), 1793 O, 1794 U
Goebbels, Joseph, G. Nazi leader, 1936 J
Goethe, Johann Wolfgang, G. poet, dramatist and philosopher (1750–1832), 1774 U, 1775 U, 1794 U, 1809 U, 1811 U, 1819 U, 1821 U; *Faust*, 1808 W, 1832 W; other plays, 1773 W, 1787 W, 1788 W, 1791 W, 1792 W; scientific works, 1790 P, 1791 P, 1810 P; *Wilhelm Meister*, 1795 U; centenary medal, 1932 Q
Goetz von Berlichingen (Goethe), 1773 W
Goeze, Johann Melchior, G. pastor (1717–86), 1778 R
Goga, Octavian, Rum. anti-Semite, 1937 M
Gogh, Vincent van, Du. artist (1853–90), 1853 Z, 1884 T, 1888 T, 1889 T, 1890 Z, 1891 T
Gogol, Nicolai, R. author (1809–52), 1809 Z, 1833 U, 1835 U, 1842 U, 1952 Z
Goito, Italy, battles, 1848 D, E
Go-Karting, 1960 X
Gold, discoveries of:
  in Australia, 1851 F, P
  in Canada, 1897 P
  in S. Africa, 1885 P
  in US, 1847 P, 1866 P
Gold, extraction by cyanide, 1887 P
  production, statistics of, 1944 Y
Goldberger, W., G. biochemist, 1925 P
Gold Coast: taken over by British government, 1821 E; Britain purchases forts from Denmark, 1850 G; Britain purchases Dutch trading-posts, 1872 B; frontiers with Togoland settled, 1886 G, 1899 L; frontiers defined, 1898 F; independence granted, 1956 H. *See also* Ghana
Golden Bough, The (J. G. Frazer), 1890 Q
Golden Bowl, The (H. James), 1914 U
Golden Legend (H. W. Longfellow), 1851 U
Goldfine, Bernard, Am. businessman, 1958 F
Golding, William, B. author (b. 1911), 1954 U, 1964 U
Goldmark, Karl, Hung. musician (1882–1911), 1875 T
Goldmark, Peter, Am. technologist, 1948 P
Goldsmith, Oliver, B. author (1728–74), 1766 U, 1767 U, 1767 W, 1770 U, 1773 W, 1774 Q, Z
Gold Standard:
  Britain returns to, 1925 D
    abandons, 1931 J
  Canada abandons, 1933 D
  France returns to, 1926 O
    abandons, 1936 J
  Germany adopts, 1871 O
  Holland abandons, 1936 J
  Italy returns to, 1928 O
  Japan adopts, 1897 C
    abandons, 1931 M
  S. Africa abandons, 1932 W
  Sweden returns to, 1924 O
  Switzerland abandons, 1936 J
  US adopts, 1873 O
    abandons, 1933 D
Goldstücker, Theodor, G. scholar (1821–72), 1856 Q
Goldwater, Barry, Am. Republican Senator (b. 1909), 1909 Z; defeated by Johnson, 1964 L
Goldwyn, Samuel, Am. film producer (b. 1882), 1882 Z
Golf: British championships, 1860 X, 1886 X, 1904 X, 1934 X; Royal and Ancient Golf Club, St. Andrews, 1834 X
Gollancz, Victor, B. publisher (b. 1893), 1935 O
Goluchowski, Agenor, Aus. statesman (1849–1921), 1895 E
Gömbös, Julius, Hung. politician, anti-Semite Nationalist, 1932 K
Gomel, Russia, Russians take, 1943 L
Gómez, José, Cuban president (1908–13), 1908 L, 1909 M
Gomulka, Wladyslaw, Pol. Communist, expelled for deviations, 1948 J
Goncharov, Ivan Alexandrovich, R. author (1812–1891), 1859 U, 1870 U
Goncourt, Edmond de, F. author (1822–96), 1822 Z, 1896 Z
Goncourt, Jules de, F. author (1830–70), 1864 U
Gone to Earth (M. Webb), 1917 U
Gone With The Wind (M. Mitchell), 1936 U
Gooch, George Peabody, B. historian (b. 1873), 1913 Q
Goodbye to All That (R. Graves), 1929 U
Goodbye to Berlin (C. Isherwood), 1938 U
Good Companions, The (J. B. Priestley), 1929 U
Good Earth, The (P. Buck), 1931 U
Goodman, Benny, Am. band leader, 1938 T
Good Natur'd Man, The (O. Goldsmith), 1767 W
Good Society, The (W. Lippmann), 1937 O
Goodwood, Sussex, England, horse-racing at, 1802 X
Goodyear, Charles, Am. inventor (1800–60), 1839 P
Goonhilly Down, Cornwall, England, 1962 P
Göransson, G. F., Swe. steelmaker (1819–1900), 1858 P
Gorbach, Alphons, Aus. People's Party leader, 1961 D
Gorchakov, Prince Alexander Mikhailovich, R. diplomat (1798–1883), 1875 E
Gordon, Adam Lindsay, Austral. poet (1833–70), 1867 U
Gordon, Aloysius ('Lucky'), 1963 M
Gordon, Charles George, B. soldier (1833–85), 1884 B, 1885 A
Gordon, George Hamilton, Earl of Aberdeen, B. Whig statesman (1784–1860), 1784 Z, 1846 K, 1860 Z; forms coalition, 1852 M; resigns, 1855 B
Gordon, Lord George, B. agitator (1751–93), 1780 F
Gordonstoun School, Morayshire, Scotland, 1934 O
Gordon Walker, Patrick Chrestian, B. Labour politician (b. 1907); appointed Foreign Secretary, 1964 K; resigns on by-election defeat, 1965 A
Gore, Mrs. Catherine Grace Frances, B. author (1799–1861), 1831 W, 1841 W
Gore, Charles, B. churchman (1853–1932), 1890 R, 1892 R, 1907 R
Gore, Spencer, B. lawn-tennis player, 1877 X
Goree, Island, West Indies: restored to France, 1763 B; France recovers, 1783 J; attack on, 1799 E
Goremykin, Ivan, R. Conservative, 1906 E
Gorham, George Cornelius, B. divine (1787–1857), 1850 R

Göring, Hermann, G. Nazi politician (1893–1946), 1893 Z, 1933 A; becomes economics minister, 1936 K; sentenced by Nuremberg tribunal, 1946 J
Gorki, Maxim, R. novelist (1868–1936), 1868 Z, 1899 U, 1900 U, 1902 U, 1907 U, 1934 U, 1936 Z
Gorman, Arthue Pue, Am. Democrat (1839–1906), 1894 H
Görres, Johann Joseph von, G. author (1776–1848), 1820 O, 1821 U, 1836 R
Gorst, Sir John Eldon, B. lawyer and Conservative politician (1835–1916), 1880 E
Goschen, George Joachim, Viscount Goschen, B. Liberal politician (1831–1907), 1876 L; as chancellor of Exchequer, 1887 A, 1888 D
Gota Canal, Sweden, 1832 P
Gotha, Sweden, 1874 E
Gothic novel, the, 1794 U
Gothic style of architecture, 1845 S
Gothic type, abandoned by Germany, 1941 O
Gottenberg, Sweden, system of liquor control, 1866 O
Göttingen, West Germany: *Hainbuch* in, 1772 U; telegraph at, 1833 P; brothers Grimm dismissed from University, 1837 M
Gottwald, Klement, Czech. Communist (1896–1953), 1896 Z, 1953 Z; becomes premier, 1946 E; becomes president of Republic, 1948 F
Gouda, Holland, 1787 F
Gough, Hugh, lord Gough, B. soldier (1779–1869), 1846 B
Gouin, Félix, F. Socialist, 1946 A
Goulart, João Belchior, Brazilian politician (b. 1918), deposed from presidency, 1964 D
Gould, Sir Francis Carruthers, B. caricaturist (1844–1925), 1844 Z, 1925 Z
Gounod, Charles François, F. musician (1818–93), 1818 Z, 1859 T, 1882 T, 1893 Z
Gournaris, Demetrios, Gr. politician, 1915 C
Government Inspector, The (N. Gogol), 1833 U
Gowing, Lawrence Burnett, B. artist (b. 1918), 1937 S
Gowing, Margaret M., B. historian, 1949 Q
Goya, Francisco y Lucientes, Sp. artist (1747–1828), 1795 S, 1796 S, 1799 S, 1800 S, 1805 S, 1808 S, 1810 S, 1814 S, 1815 S, 1816 S, 1819 S, 1828 S, 1850 S
portrait of Wellington, 1812 S, 1961 S, 1965 S
Grace, William Gilbert, B. cricketer (1848–1915), 1848 Z, 1865 X, 1870 X, 1876 X, 1915 Z
Grâce, La (G. Marcel), 1921 W
Grafton, Augustus Henry Fitzroy, Duke of, B. Whig statesman (1735–1811), 1766 G, 1769 A, 1770 A, 1775 L, 1776 C
Graham, Thomas, B. chemist (1805–69), 1829 P, 1863 P
Graham, William Franklin ('Billy'), Am. evangelist, 1918 Z, 1954 R
Grahame, Kenneth, B. author (1859–1932), 1859 Z, 1908 U, 1932 Z
Gramido, Convention, 1847 G
Grammar of Assent (J. H. Newman), 1870 R
Grammar of Politics (H. Laski), 1925 O
Grammar of the Romance Languages (F. C. Dietz), 1836 Q
Gramme, Z. T., F. electrician (1826–1901), 1870 P
Gramophone, 1887 P; stereoscopic recordings for, 1958 P
Granadian Confederation, 1858 D
Grande Peur des bien pensants, La (Bernanos), 1931 U
Grandi, Count, It. politician (b. 1895), 1929 J
'Grandma Moses', Am. artist, 1939 S
Grand Trunk Pacific Railway, 1919 C
Grant, Ulysses Simpson, Am. Unionist general and Republican leader, president of US (1822–85), 1822 Z, 1862 B, 1864 E, 1872 A, 1876 M, 1885 Z; elected president, 1868 L, 1869 C; re-elected, 1872 L
Granville, lord. *See* Leveson-Gower, G. G.
Granville-Barker, Harley Granville, B. actor, producer and dramatist (1877–1946), 1877 Z, 1904 W, 1946 Z
Grapes of Wrath, The (J. Steinbeck), 1939 U
Graphology (Klarges), 1932 P
Grass, Günter, G. author, 1963 U, 1965 U
Grasse, François Joseph Paul, Comte de, F. naval officer (1722–88), 1781 D, H, 1782 D
Gratry, Auguste Joseph Alphonse, F. author and theologian (1805–72), 1855 R
Grattan, Henry, Ir. statesman (1746–1820), 1779 M, 1780 D; makes Irish Declaration of Rights, 1782 D
Gravelet, Jean François. *See* Blondin
Gravellotte, France, battle, 1870 H
Graves, Robert Ranke, B. author (b. 1895), 1929 U, 1934 U, 1939 U
Gravitation and the Principle of Relativity (A. Eddington), 1918 P
Gravitation, theory of, 1964 P
Gravitations (Supervielle), 1925 U
Gray, Thomas, B. poet (1716–1771), 1768 U, 1771 Z
Greater London Council, 1964 D, 1965 O
Great Expectations (C. Dickens), 1861 U
Great Gatsby, The (S. Fitzgerald), 1925 U
Great Illusion, The (N. Angell), 1933 O
Great Lakes, N. America, agreement to limit naval forces on, 1817 D
Great Salt Lake, Utah, Mormons' trail to, 1846 F
Great War in Germany, The (R. Huch), 1914 O
Greece (W. M. Leake), 1812 O
Greece:
antiquities in, 1764 Q
restoration of empire, planned by Russia, 1781 B
independence, cause of, 1803 D
War of Independence from Turkey, 1821 C, D, F, K, 1822 F, G, 1824 D, G, K, 1827 D, F
proposals for British protection, 1825 F
Sultan rejects mediation, 1827 M
powers allow France to intervene in Morea, 1828 G
constitution adopted, 1822 A
independence proclaimed, 1822 A
guaranteed by powers, 1829 C, J, 1830 B
blockaded, for aiding Rumelian rebels, 1886 E
finances to be controlled by international commission, 1898 B
blockade of, 1916 F
Italy's demands to, 1940 K
German ultimatum to, 1941 D
British expedition to, 1941 D
Russia withdraws recognition of, 1941 F
Greek, Classical, studies in, 1781 Q, 1802 Q
Greeley, Horace, Am. journalist and Democratic politician (1811–72), as presidential candidate, 1872 E, L
Green, Henry, B. author (b. 1905), 1943 U, 1945 U
Green, John Richard, B. historian (1837–83), 1874 Q
Green, Julian, F. author (b. 1900), 1955 U
Green, Paul, Am. dramatist (b. 1894), 1926 W
Green, Thomas Hill, B. philosopher (1836–82), 1836 Z, 1882 Z, 1899 R
Green Belt, 1935 O
Greene, Graham, B. author (b. 1904), 1904 Z, 1928 U, 1940 U, 1948 U, 1953 W, 1955 U, 1958 W
Greene, Nathaniel, Am. soldier (1742–86), 1777 J, 1781 C, J

Greenland: discovery of interior, 1870 P; crossed by Nansen, 1888 P; Norway annexes East Greenland, 1931 G
Green Mansions (W. H. Hudson), 1904 U
Greenmantle (J. Buchan), 1916 U
Green Pastures (M. Connelly), 1924 W
Greenwich, Kent, England, National Maritime Museum at, 1937 Q
Greenwich Mean Time, adopted by France, 1911 C
Gregory XVI, Pope (Bartolommeo Alberto Cappellari), It. (1765–1846), 1831 B, 1832 R
Grein, J. T., B. theatrical producer, 1891 W
Grenada, Isle, W. Indies, 1763 B, K; captured by France, 1779 G; captured by Britain, 1796 N
Grenville, George, B. Whig statesman (1712–70), 1763 D, 1765 C, G
Grenville, Thomas, B. diplomat (1755–1846), 1782 E
Grenville, lord. *See* Wyndham, William
Grétry, André, Belg. musician (1741–1813), 1784 T
Greuze, Jean Baptiste, F. artist (1725–1805), 1765 S, 1777 S, 1805 Z
Grévy, Jules, F. Republican politician (1813–91), elected president, 1879 A; re-elected, 1885 M; resigns after scandals, 1887 K, M
Grey, Charles, Earl Grey, B. Whig statesman (1764–1845), 1794 G, 1832 E; becomes premier, 1830 L; dissolves Parliament, 1831 D; resigns, 1834 G
Grey, Edward, Viscount Grey of Fallodon, B. Liberal statesman (1862–1933), 1862 Z, 1895 C, 1933 Z; as foreign secretary, 1905 M, 1914 G; memoirs, 1925 Q
Griechen und Römer, Die (Schlegel), 1797 Q
Grieg, Edvard, Nor. musician (1843–1907), 1843 Z, 1868 T, 1907 Z
Griesbach, Johann Jakob, G. New Testament scholar (1745–1812), 1775 Q
Griffin, Bernard, Cardinal Archbishop of Westminster (1899–1956), 1943 R
Griffith, Arthur Ir. politician (1872–1922), 1922 J; as head of S. Ireland provisional government, 1922 A
Griffith, David Wark, Am. film director (1875–1948), 1909 W, 1915 W
Grigg, Sir James, B. administrator and politician (1890–1964), becomes war secretary, 1942 B
Grillparzer, Franz, Aus. author (1791–1872), 1791 Z, 1817 U, 1818 U, 1834 U, 1872 Z
Grimm, Jakob, G. author and philologist (1785–1863), 1785 Z, 1812 U, 1819 Q, 1828 Q, 1835 Q, 1837 M, 1848 Q, 1854 Q, 1863 Z
Grimm, Wilhelm, G. author and philologist (1786–1859), 1786 Z, 1812 U, 1837 M, 1859 Z
Grimond, Joseph, B. Liberal leader (b. 1913), 1956 J
Griqualand West, Cape Province, S. Africa, annexed by Cape Colony, 1872 K
Gris, Juan, Sp. artist (1887–1927), 1920 S, 1924 S
Grissom, Virgil, Am. cosmonaut, 1965 P
Grivas, George, Cypriot-born Greek general (b. 1898), as EOKA leader, 1957 L; returns to Athens, 1959 C; assumes command of Greek Cypriot forces, 1964 H
Gromyko, Andrei, R. diplomat (b. 1909), appointed foreign minister, 1957 B; holds discussions preliminary to Summit talks, 1958 F
Gronchi, Giovanni, It. Christian Democrat (b. 1887), elected president of Italy, 1955 D
Groningen, Holland, natural gas deposits in, 1963 P
Gropius, Walter, Am., formerly G., architect (b. 1883), 1883 Z, 1911 S, 1919 S, 1925 S, 1936 S
Grossbeeren, Germany, battle, 1813 H
Grosskhophta, Der (Goethe), 1792 W
Grossmith, George, Junior (1874–1935), B. comedian and promoter of entertainment, 1922 W
Grote, George, B. historian and Radical politician (1794–1871), 1794 Z, 1821 O, 1846 Q, 1871 Z
Grotefend, Georg Friedrich, G. epigraphist (1775–1853), 1837 Q
Grotewohl, Otto, E. Germ. Communist leader (d. 1964), 1964 Z
becomes minister president, 1949 K
Group, The (M. McCarthy), 1963 U
Grove, Sir George, B. musicologist (1820–1900), 1878 T, 1883 T
Growing Up in New Guinea (M. Mead), 1935 R
Growth of the Soil (K. Hamsun), 1917 U
Groza, Petru, Rum. Communist, 1945 C
Gruenther, Aldred, Am. general (b. 1899), as Supreme Allied Commander Europe, 1953 E, 1956 L
Grüne, Heinrich, Der (G. Keller), 1851 U
Grylls, inventor of rapid filming-machine, 1923 P
Guadalcanal, Pacific: US task forces at, 1942 H, L; Japanese driven from, 1943 A
Guadaloupe, W. Indies, 1794 N; restored to France, 1763 B; British take, 1810 N
Gualdeloupe Hidalgo, Treaty, between US and Mexico, 1848 B
Guam, S. Pacific, ceded by Spain to US, 1898 M
Guarantees:
by Britain and France, for independence of Rumania and Greece, 1939 D
by Germany, for Belgium's inviolability, 1937 K
Guardi, Francesco, Venetian painter (1712–93), 1763 S, 1782 S
Guardian Angel (O. W. Holmes), 1867 U
Guatemala: independence declared, 1821 J; enters Central American Federation, 1823 G; movement for a federal Central America in, 1887 N; coffee production in, 1909 Y
Guerazzi, Francisco Domenico, It. publicist (1804–1873), 1834 U, 1854 U
Guernica, Spain, destroyed by rebels, 1937 D
Guernica (P. Picasso), 1937 P
Guerrero, Vincente, Mexic. leader, 1821 B
Guess, George. *See* Sequoyah
Guiana, British. *See* British Guiana
Guides, railway, 1841 V
Guildford Cathedral, Surrey, 1961 S
Guilds, Religious, abolished in Tuscany, 1786 R
Guilford, Conn., US, battle, 1781 C
Guillebaud, Claude William, B. economist (b. 1890), as chairman of committee on Health Service, 1956 A; on railwaymen's pay, 1960 C
'Guillotine', use of, in Parliamentary procedure, 1904 C
Guinea, French, W. Africa, 1882 F, 1893 C
Guinea, Spanish, protectorate in, 1885 A
Guinness, Sir Alec, B. actor (b. 1914), 1957 W
Guinness, Edward, lord Iveagh, B. brewer and philanthropist (1847–1927), 1928 S
Guizot, François, F. politician and historian (1787–1874), 1787 Z, 1829 Q, 1846 K; becomes premier, 1847 J
Gujerat, India, Sikhs defeated at, 1849 B
Gulbenkian, Nubar Sarkis, Iran. financier and philanthropist (b. 1896), establishes Fund, 1958 S
Guldberg, Ove Höegh, Da. statesman (d. 1788), 1772 A
Gun-cotton, 1846 P
Gunpowder, experiments with, 1778 P
Gura, Ethiopia, 1876 C
Gurkhas, in Nepal, Indian warriors: conquer Nepal, 1768 N; British war with, 1814 K

Gurney, Sir Henry, B. high commissioner in Malaya (d. 1951), 1951 K
Gürsel, Cemal, Turk. soldier, 1960 E
Gustafsson, Greta. *See* Garbo, Greta
Gustav Line, in Italy, 1944 E
Gustavus III, King of Sweden (1746–92), 1772 G, H, 1784 O, 1789 B, 1791 M, 1792 C
Gustavus IV, King of Sweden (1792–1809), 1809 C
Gustavus V, King of Sweden (1907–50), 1907 M
Gustavus Adolphus Society, 1832 R
Guy Mannering (W. Scott), 1815 U
Guys, Constantin, F. draughtsman (1802–92), 1863 S
Gwalior, Cen. India, 1802 K, 1803 H
Gyani, General, Ind., commands UN peace force in Cyprus, 1964 C
Gymnasium, the first, 1765 O
Gyro-compass, 1907 P

H

Haakon VII, King of Norway (1905–57), 1905 L, 1957 J
Haas, Paul, B. chemist (1877–1960), 1933 P
Habeas Corpus Act, British, suspended, 1777 M, 1817 C
suspension repealed, 1818 A
Haber, Fritz, G. chemist (1868–1934), 1908 P
Hacha, Emil, Czech. president, 1938 L
Haeckel, Ernst Heinrich, G. biologist (1834–1919), 1868 P, 1874 P, 1899 P
Hafnium, element, discovered, 1922 P
Hagen, Friedrich Heinrich von der, G. philologist (1780–1856), 1810 U
Haggard, Sir Henry Rider, B. novelist (1856–1925), 1856 Z, 1886 U, 1925 Z
Hague, The, Holland:
Treaty, for Britain to subsidise Allies, 1794 D
Communist Conference at, 1872 O
Convention, on territorial waters, 1882 F
international commission at, 1904 K
Peace Conference at, 1907 F
International Court of Arbitration, settlements by, 1903 B, 1910 J, 1911 A
International Court of Justice, Permanent, at, 1920 F, 1922 B
Iran *v.* Iranian Oil Company dispute outside jurisdiction, 1952 G
Congress on European Unity, at, 1948 E
Hahn, Otto, G. atomic physicist (b. 1874), 1939 P
Hahnemann, Samuel, G. doctor (1755–1843), 1810 P
Haifa, Israel, pipelines to, 1935 P
Haig, Douglas, Earl Haig, B. soldier (1861–1928), 1861 Z, 1915 M, 1917 G, 1928 Z
Hail and Farewell (G. Moore), 1914 U
Haile Selassie (Ras Tafari), Emperor of Abyssinia, 1930 D
Hailey, William Malcolm, Lord Hailey, B. administrator (b. 1872), 1957 O
Hainan Tao, Island, Kwangtung, China: Japanese occupy, 1939 B; China regains sovereignty over, 1945 J
Hainault, Belgium, constitution revoked, 1789 K
Hainsich, Michael, Aus. statesman, Socialist (1858–1941), president of Austria, 1920 M, 1928 M
Haiti: US marines land, 1914 A; US commission in, 1930 B
Haldane, John Burdon Sanderson, B. biochemist (1892–1964), 1935 R
Haldane, Richard Burdon, Viscount Haldane, B. Liberal statesman and lawyer (1856–1928), 1905 M
Halévy, Ludovic, F. dramatist (1834–1908), 1869 W
Haley, William ('Bill'), Am. singer, 1955 W
Haley, Sir William John, B. journalist (b. 1901), 1952 V
Half-tone blocks, 1880 V
Halicarnassus, mausoleum of, discovered, 1857 Q
Halifax, Lord. *See* Wood
Hall, Albert W., Am. scientist, 1927 P
Hall, Alfred Rupert, B. historian of technology (b. 1920), 1955 P
Hall, Asaph, Am. astronomer (1829–1907), 1877 P
Hall, Harry Reginald Holland, B. archaeologist (1873–1930), 1918 Q
Hall, Marshall, B. physiologist (1790–1857), 1832 P
Hall, Peter, B. theatre director (b. 1930), 1959 W, 1964 W
Hall, Robert, B. Baptist minister (1764–1831), 1791 R
Hallam, Henry, B. historian (1777–1859), 1777 Z, 1818 Q, 1827 Q, 1859 Z
Haller, Albrecht von, G. theologian (1708–77), 1772 R
Haller, Johannes, G. Catholic priest and historian, 1903 R
Ham, France, Louis Napoleon imprisoned in, 1840 H
Hamaguchi, Japanese premier, Minseito Party, assassinated, 1930 L
Hambach, W. Germany, Festival, 1832 E
Hamburg, W. Germany: Danes enter, 1801 C; annexed by Napoleon, 1810 M; Russians occupy, 1813 C; Communist riots in, 1921 C; R.A.F. bombs, 1942 G; Allies enter, 1945 E
Hamburgische Dramaturgie (Lessing), 1767 W
Hamer, Robert, Am. film director, 1947 W
Hamilton, Alexander, Am. statesman (?1757–1804), president of US, Federalist, 1786 E, 1789 D, 1790 B, 1792 N
Hammarskjöld, Dag (Hjalmar Agne Carl), Swe. statesman (1905–61), becomes UN Secretary-General, 1953 C; arranges Israel-Jordan cease-fire, 1956 D; visits Nasser, 1957 C; re-elected UN Secretary-General, 1957 J; enters Katanga, 1960 H; visits S. Africa, 1961 A; Khrushchev's campaign against, 1961 B; killed in air crash, 1961 J
Hammerstein, Oscar I, Am. composer and theatre manager (1847–1919), 1903 W
Hammerstein, Oscar II, Am. librettist (b. 1895), 1895 Z
Hampden Clubs, 1811 O
Hampden, Viscount. *See* Brand, H. B. W.
Hampstead Garden Suburb, London, England, 1906 S
Hampton Roads, Virginia, US, naval action in, 1862 C
Hamsun, Knut. *See* Pederson, Knut
Hanau, W. Germany, French occupation, 1920 D
Hancock, John, Am. statesman (1737–93), 1775 G
Hancock, Sir Keith, Austral. economic historian (b. 1898), 1949 Q
Handbook of Climatology (J. Hann), 1897 P
Handbook to the History of Graeco-Roman Philosophy (C. Brandis), 1835 Q
Handbuch der Urkundenlehre für Deutschland und Italien (H. Bresslau), 1889 Q
Handel, George Frederick, G. musician (1685–1759), *Messiah* by, notable performances of, 1770 T, 1772 T; anniversary concert, 1959 T
Handicrafts Societies, National League of US, 1907 S

Handley, Thomas ('Tommy'), B. comedian (1894–1949), 1942 W
Hangchow, China, Japanese take, 1937 M
Hankey, Maurice, Lord Hankey, B. cabinet secretary (1877–1964), 1940 O, 1961 Q; becomes secretary of Committee of Imperial Defence, 1912 B
Hankow, China: Kuo Min Tang government at, 1927 A; reduction of British concessions at, 1927 B; Japanese take, 1938 K
Hanley, Staffs., England, riots at, 1874 B
Hanley, Gerald Anthony, B. author (b. 1916), 1953 U
Hann, Julius, Aus. meteorologist (1839–1921), 1897 P
Hanoi, North Vietnam: French reverses at, 1885 C; Communist occupy, 1954 K
Hanover, W. Germany: Prussians overrun, 1801 D, 1805 M; French occupation of, 1803 F, 1806 D, K; Northern, annexed by Napoleon, 1810 M; proclaimed a Kingdom, 1814 K; Salic law in, 1837 F; invaded by Prussia, 1866 F; incorporated in Prussia, 1866 H, J; royal territory outside, confiscated by Prussia, 1868 C; US troops take, 1945 D
Hansen, T., Aus. architect (1813–91), 1861 S
'Hansom' cabs, 1834 P
Hansson, Per A., Swe. Social Democrat (d. 1946), 1945 G, 1946 K
Hara, Takashi, Jap. premier, 1921 L
Harar, Ethiopia: assigned to Italy, 1894 E; British take, 1941 C
Harcourt, Sir William George Granville Venables Vernon, B. Liberal politician (1827–1904), 1886 B, 1892 H, 1899 A; becomes home secretary, 1880 D; becomes Liberal leader, 1896 K
Harden, Sir Arthur, B. chemist (1865–1940), 1906 P
Hardenberg, Friedrich von, G. author under pseudonym of 'Novalis' (1772–1801), 1772 Z, 1799 U, 1800 U, 1801 Z
Hardenberg, Karl August von, Prince, Pruss. statesman (1750–1822), 1810 F, 1811 J
Hardie, James Keir, B. Socialist leader (1856–1915), 1856 Z, 1893 A, 1915 Z
Harding, John, Lord Harding of Petherton, B. soldier and administrator (b. 1896), as governor of Cyprus, 1955 J, L, 1956 H, 1957 K
Harding, Warren Gamaliel, Am. statesman, Republican (1865–1923), president of US (1921–3), 1922 C, 1923 H; nominated, 1920 F; elected president, 1920 L; inaugurated, 1921 D; declares US could play no part in League of Nations, 1921 D
Hardinge, Charles, lord Hardinge, B. administrator (1858–1944), 1916 O
Hardtmann, Eduard von, G. philosopher (1842–1906), 1869 R
Hardy, Thomas, B. author (1840–1928), 1840 Z, 1928 Z
novels, 1872 U, 1874 U, 1878 U, 1887 U, 1891 U, 1896 U
plays, 1904 W
poems, 1898 U, 1919 U
Hargreaves, James, B. inventor (d. 1778), 1764 P, 1778 Z
Harlow New Town, Essex, England, 1956 S
Harmonica, music for, 1952 T
Harmony of the World (P. Hindemith), 1950 T
Harmsworth, Alfred, Viscount Northcliffe, B. journalist and newspaper proprietor (1865–1922), 1865 Z, 1896 V, 1904 V, 1922 Z; buys *The Times*, 1908 V
Harmsworth, Harold, Lord Rothermere, B. newspaper proprietor (1868–1940), 1868 Z, 1940 Z
Harnack, Adolf, G. theologian (1851–1912), 1886 R
Harper's Ferry, W. Virginia, US, John Brown's raid on, 1859 K
Harriman, Averell, Am. secretary of state, diplomat and Governor of New York (b. 1891), 1891 Z, 1941 J; confers in Moscow, 1942 H; negotiates in Iran, 1951 G
Harris, Joel Chandler, Am. author under pseudonym of 'Uncle Remus' (1848–1908), 1848 Z, 1908 Z
Harris, Roy, Am. musician (b. 1898), 1942 T
Harrison, Benjamin, Am. Republican (1833–1901), 23rd president of US (1889–93), 1833 Z, 1888 L, 1889 C; defeated in election, 1892 L
Harrison, C. Ross, B. pathologist, 1907 P
Harrison, William Henry, Am. Whig (1773–1841), president of US, 1841 D
Hart, J. C., Am. author, investigates Shakespeare-Bacon controversy, 1848 Q
Hart, Moss, Am. dramatist (b. 1904), 1943 W
Hart, Robert, Am. inspector-general of Chinese Customs service (1863–1906), 1906 E
Harte, Bret, Am. author and editor (1836–1902), 1868 V, 1869 U
Hartford, Conn., US, Colt's armoury at, 1853 P
Hartington, Marquess of. *See* Cavendish, S. C.
Hartmann, H., G. philosopher, 1921 R, 1925 R, 1950 R
Harwell, Berks, England, British nuclear research station at, 1947 P, 1956 P, 1961 P
Harwood, John, B. horologist, 1922 P
Hashem, Ibrahim, Jordan Right-wing politician, 1957 D
Hassan (J. E. Flecker), 1923 W
Hastings, Warren, B. governor-general of India (1732–1818), 1772 D, 1773 J, 1774 O, 1775 N, 1778 N, 1781 F; plundering by, 1781 F; recalled, 1782 E; returns to England, 1785 F; is impeached, 1787 E; trial, 1788 B; acquittal, 1795 D
Hatfield New Town, Herts, England, 1952 S
Hatteras, N. Carolina, US, Fort, captured by Unionists, 1861 H
Hauptmann, Gerhart, G. author (1862–1946), 1862 Z, 1889 U, 1912 U, 1946 Z
Haussmann, Georges Eugène, baron, F. town-planner (1809–91), 1853 S
Haüy, René Just, F. mineralogist (1743–1822), 1784 P
Haüy, Valentin, F. founder of blind school (1745–1822), 1784 O
Havana, Cuba, West Indies, 1898 B, 1900 L; Spain exchanges Florida for, 1763 B; Russian exhibition in, 1960 B
Have You Anything to Declare? (M. Baring), 1936 U
Havelock, Sir Henry Marshman, B. soldier (1830–97), 1857 J
Havilland, Sir Geoffrey de, B. aircraft designer, 1965 Z
Hawaii: independence recognised, 1842 M, 1843 L; republic proclaimed, 1893 A; problem of US annexation, 1893 B; transferred to US, 1898 H; organised as US territory, 1900 D; becomes a US state, 1959 C
Hawke, Edward, lord Hawke, B. admiral (1705–81), 1781 Z
Hawkins, Anthony Hope, B. novelist under pseudonym of 'Anthony Hope' (1863–1933), 1863 Z, 1894 U, 1933 Z
Hawkins, Sir John, B. musicologist (1719–89), 1776 T
Hawthorne, Nathaniel, Am. author (1804–64), 1804 Z, 1850 U, 1851 U, 1853 U, 1864 Z

Haxthausen, August Franz Ludwig Maria von, G. political economist (1792–1866), 1843 O
'Hay, Ian', B. author and dramatist, pseudonym of 'John Hay Beth' (1876–1952), 1936 W
Hay, John, Am. secretary of state (1838–1905), Note on 'Open-door' in China, 1899 J, 1900 G; treaty with Britain (Pauncefoote) on Panama, 1901 L; pact with Colombia (Herrán) on Panama Canal, 1903 A
Haydn, Joseph, Aus. musician (1732–1809), 1785 T, 1809 Z
Creation, The, 1798 T
Masses, 1766 T, 1796 T
Seasons, The, 1801 T
String quartets, 1771 T, 1781 T, 1797 T
Symphonies, 1764 T, 1772 T, 1777 T, 1780 T, 1784 T, 1788 T, 1791 T, 1794 T, 1795 T
anniversary concert, 1959 T
Haydon, Benjamin Robert, B. artist (1786–1846), 1786 Z, 1816 S, 1846 Z
Hayes, Rutherford Birchard, Am. Republican (1822–1893), 19th president of US (1877–81), 1876 L, 1877 A, C
Hay Fever (N. Coward), 1925 W
Hazlitt, William, B. essayist (1778–1830), 1778 Z, 1818 U, 1821 U, 1825 U, 1830 Z
Hazza-el-Majali, Jordan premier, assassinated, 1960 H
Headlong Hall (T. L. Peacock), 1816 U
Healey-Kay, Patrick. *See* Dolin, Anton.
Health, in Britain, report on, 1844 O
Health Service:
British, 1911 E, 1912 E, 1946 L
charges imposed, 1951 D
Guillebaud Committee on, 1956 A
charges increased, 1961 B
charges abolished, 1964 M
B.M.A. advises general practitioners to resign from, 1965 B
US, medical care for the aged, 1965 G
Health, World Assembly, 1948 O
Healy, Timothy, Ir. politician, 1855 Z, 1931 Z
Heape, A., Am. inventor of filming-machine, 1923 P
Hearst, William Randolph, Am. newspaper proprietor (1863–1951), 1930 V
Heart of Midlothian (W. Scott), 1818 U
Heart of the Matter, The (G. Greene), 1948 U
Heat:
experiments concerning, 1778 P, 1840 P
generated by friction, 1798 P
radiant, discoveries in, 1831 P
treatises on, 1804 P, 1822 P, 1835 P, 1843 P
Heating, by gas, devised, 1798 P
Heat Rays, variability of, 1850 P
Heath, Edward Richard George, B. Conservative leader (b. 1916), 1916 Z; statement on Britain's approach to the Common Market, 1961 K; elected Conservative leader, 1965 G
Heathcoat, John, B. manufacturer (1783–1861), 1809 P
Heaviside, Oliver, B. mathematical physicist (1850–1925), 1902 P
Heaviside Layer, measured, 1924 P
Hébert, Jacques René, F. revolutionary (1757–94), 1793 R; partisans of, 1794 C
Hebrew, study of, 1812 Q
Hecker, Isaac Thomas, Am. Catholic priest (1819–1888), 1858 R; opinions condemned by Pope Leo XIII, 1899 R
Hecuba (Euripides), 1802 Q
Hedda Gabler (H. Ibsen), 1890 W
Heenan, John C., Am. pugilist, 1860 X
Heeren, Arnold Hermann Ludwig, G. historian (1760–1842), 1800 O
Hegel, Georg Wilhelm Friedrich, G. philosopher (1770–1831), 1770 Z, 1801 R, 1807 R, 1812 R, 1817 R, 1821 R, 1831 Z; succeeds Fichte, 1818 R
Heidegger, Martin, G. philosopher (b. 1889), 1927 R, 1929 R
Heilmann, Josué, F. inventor (1796–1848), 1845 P
Heine, Heinrich, G. poet (1797–1856), 1797 Z, 1821 U, 1826 U, 1827 U, 1844 U, 1851 U, 1856 Z
Heinrich von Ofterdingen (Novalis), 1799 U
Heinse, Johann Jacob Wilhelm, G. author (1749–1803), 1787 U
Heir at Law, The (G. Colman), 1797 W
Heiress, The (J. Burgoyne), 1786 W
Heir of Redclyffe (C. M. Yonge), 1853 U
Heisenberg, Werner, G. physicist (b. 1901), 1927 P
Heitler, Walter Heinrich, G. physicist (b. 1904), 1927 P
Hejaz (later Saudi Arabia): railway, 1900 N; Arab revolt in, 1916 F; Kingdom recognised, 1917 A; name changed to Saudi Arabia, 1926 A
Helicopter, 1917 P
Heligoland, Island, W. Germany: retained by Britain, 1814 A, 1815 F; exchanged with Germany for Zanzibar, 1890 G
Heligoland Bight, N. Sea, battle, 1914 H
Heliopolis, Turkey, Kléber's victory at, 1800 C
Helium, discovered, 1896 P
Helmholtz, Hermann, G. instrument-maker (1821–1894), 1847 P, 1850 P, 1851 P, 1856 P, 1858 P, 1862 P
Héloïse and Abelard (G. Moore), 1921 U
Helpmann, Robert Murray, Austral. actor and choreographer (b. 1909), 1909 Z
Helsinki (or Helsingfors), Finland: Bolsheviks occupy, 1918 A; Germans occupy, 1918 D
Helvetian Republic, under Napoleon (Switzerland), 1798 C, H, 1801 B
Hemingway, Ernest Miller, Am. author (1900–61), 1927 U, 1929 U, 1932 U, 1937 U, 1940 U, 1950 U, 1952 U
Hemlock and After (A. Wilson), 1952 U
Hemming, J., B. chemist, 1838 P
Hench, Philip Showalter, Am. physician (b. 1896), 1949 P
Henderson, Arthur, B. Labour politician (1863–1935), 1903 G, 1916 M; becomes foreign minister, 1929 F; leads rump of Labour Party, 1931 H
Henderson the Rain King (S. Bellow), 1959 U
Hendon, Middlesex, England, Police College, 1934 O
Henle, Friedrich, Gustav Jakob, G. pathologist and anatomist (1809–85), 1809 Z, 1846 P, 1885 Z
Henley, Oxfordshire, England, Regatta, 1839 X
Henry, Prince of Prussia, 1771 A
Henry VIII (J. Chénier), 1791 W
Henry, Patrick, Am. statesman (1736–99), 1763 M, 1765 E
Henty, George Alfred, B. author (1832–1902), 1832 Z, 1902 Z
Henze, Hans Werner, G. musician (b. 1926), 1956 T, 1958 T, 1960 T, 1961 T
Hepburn, Audrey, Belg. film actress (b. 1929), 1929 Z, 1953 W, 1959 W, 1961 W
Hepplewhite, George, B. cabinet-maker, 1786 Z
Hepworth, Barbara, B. sculptor (b. 1903), 1953 S, 1954 S, 1955 S, 1959 S
Heraclius II, of Georgia, recognises Russian sovereignty, 1783 K
Herat, Afghanistan, 1856 L
Herbart, Johann Friedrich, G. philosopher (1776–1841), 1806 O, 1813 R, 1824 R

Herbert, Sir Alan Patrick, B. author and lawyer (b. 1890), 1890 Z, 1937 G
Herbert, George Edward Stanhope Molyneux, lord Carnarvon, B. archaeologist (1860–1923), 1922 Q
Herbert, Henry Howard Molyneux, lord Carnarvon, B. Conservative politician (1831–90), as colonial secretary, 1875 H
Herder, Johann Gottfried von, G. author (1744–1803), 1769 U, 1772 Q, 1773 U, 1775 U, 1778 U, 1782 U, 1784 R, 1799 R, 1803 Z
Here Come the Clowns (P. Barry), 1938 W
Heredia, José Maria de, F. poet (1842–1905), 1893 U
Hereditary Genius, its Laws and Consequences (F. Galton), 1869 P
Heredity, laws of: established, 1866 P; rediscovered 1900 P; modified by Benoit, 1959 P
Hereros, in East Africa, rising of, 1904 K
Heresy: in Italy, Church's jurisdiction in, abolished, 1850 R
in Prussia, penalties for, 1788 R
Heritage and Its History (I. Compton-Burnett), 1959 U
Hermann, K. S. L., G. chemical manufacturer, 1818 P
Hermes, Georg, G. Catholic theologian (1775–1831), 1819 R
Hermetic-sealing, 1765 P
Hernani (V. Hugo), 1830 U
Herne Bay, Kent, England, church for Anglican-Methodist joint use, 1960 R
Hero of Our Time (M. Y. Lermontov), 1839 U
Hérold, Louis Joseph Ferdinand, F. musician (1791–1833), 1831 T
Herriot, Édouard, F. statesman, Radical Socialist (1872–1957), 1872 Z, 1957 Z; as premier, 1924 F, G; ministry falls, 1925 D; forms new ministry, 1932 F; resigns, 1932 M
Herschel, Sir John Frederick William, B. astronomer (1792–1871), 1792 Z, 1825 P, 1834 P, 1871 Z
Herschel, Sir William, B. astronomer (1738–1822), 1781 P, 1783 P, 1786 P, 1789 P, 1800 P, 1802 P, 1822 Z
Herself Surprised (J. Cary), 1941 U
Hersey, John, Am. author (b. 1914), 1945 U
Herstmonceux, Sussex, England, Royal Observatory moved to, 1953 P
Herter, Christian Archibald, Am. diplomat (b. 1895), 1895 Z; succeeds Dulles as secretary of state, 1959 D
Herling, Georg, Count von, G. Centre Party (1843–1919), becomes Chancellor, 1917 L
Hertz, Henrik, Da. author (1797–1870), 1845 W
Hertz, Rudolf, G. physicist (1857–94), 1887 P
Hertzberg, Ewald Friedrich, Count von, Pruss. minister (1725–95), 1791 G
Hertzen, Alexander, R. author (1812–70), 1850 U
Hertzog, James Barry Munnik, S. Afr. statesman, Nationalist and soldier (1866–1942), 1866 Z, 1942 Z; as Boer general, 1901 B; founds S. African party, 1910 D; is left out of Botha's cabinet, 1912 M; leads Nationalist Party to success, 1915 K; forms ministry, 1924 F; forms coalition, 1933 E; forms United S. African Nationalists, 1934 F; resigns premiership, 1938 E
Hervás y Panduro, Sp. philologist (1735–1809), 1800 Q
Herzegovina, Yugoslavia: rebellion, 1875 G, M; reforms, 1878 L. *See also* Bosnia
Herzl, Theodor, Hung. founder of political Zionism (1860–1904), 1897 R
Herzog, Johann Jakob, G. Protestant theologian (1805–82), 1853 R
Herzog (S. Bellow), 1964 U
Hesperidin, phosphorated, as contraceptive tablet, 1952 P
Hesperus (Jean Paul), 1795 U
Hess, Dame Myra, B. pianist (d. 1965), 1939 T
Hess, Rudolph, G. Nazi (b. 1894), lands in Scotland, 1941 E; sentenced by Nuremberg tribunal, 1946 J
Hesse, Grand Duchy, W. Germany: Prussia invades, 1866 F; Prussia incorporates, 1866 H, J
Hessian mercenaries, Britain recruits, 1776 H, M
Het Volk organisation in Transvaal, 1905 A
Heuss, Theodor, G. Free Democrat (b. 1884), 1954 G; becomes W. German president, 1949 J; retires, 1959 G
He Who Gets Slapped (L. Andreyev), 1916 W
Hey, Donald Holroyde, B. physicist (b. 1904), 1946 P
Heydrich, Reinhard, G. Gestapo leader, 1942 E
Heyerdahl, Thor. Nor. author and ethnologist (b. 1914), 1950 P
Heyne, Christian Gottlob, G. classical scholar (1729–1812), 1767 Q
Heyrowsky, J., Am. scientist, 1922 P
Heyse, Paul Johann Ludwig, G. author (1830–1915), 1873 U
Hibbert Lectures on Comparative Religion, 1878 Q
Hicks, William, B. general in Egyptian army (1830–1883), 1883 L
Hicks-Beach, Michael Edward, Earl of St. Aldwyn, B. Conservative politician (1837–1916), 1885 F; budget of, 1901 D
Hidalgo, planet, 1920 P
High Commission in Germany, Allied: takes over from Allied Military Government, 1949 J; makes concessions to Germany on joining Ruhr Authority, 1949 L
High Price of Bullion (D. Ricardo), 1809 O
Hildesheim, W. Germany, ceded to Hanover, 1815 F
Hill, John, B. quack physician (?1716–75), 1770 P
Hill, Octavia, B. philanthropist (1838–1912), 1838 Z, 1864 O, 1912 Z
Hill, Sir Rowland, B. inventor of penny-postage (1795–1879), 1795 Z, 1840 O, 1879 Z
Hill, Ureli Corelli, Am. musician (1802–75), 1842 T
Hillary, Sir Edmund, N.Z. mountaineer (b. 1919), 1919 Z, 1953 P
Hiller, Johann Adam, G. musician (1728–1804), 1781 T
Hilton, John, B. socialist and economist (1883–1943), 1940 O
Hindemith, Paul, Swi. musician (b. 1895), 1922 T, 1924 T, 1929 T, 1938 T, 1944 T, 1950 T, 1957 T
Hindenburg, Paul von, G. soldier and statesman (1847–1934), 1847 Z, 1914 J, 1934 H; as chief of general staff, 1916 M; demands peace offer, 1918 J; elected president of Germany, 1925 D; repudiates Germany's war guilt, 1927 J; authorises budget by decree, 1930 G; re-elected president, 1932 C, D
Hindenburg Line, British break through, 1917 E
Hindi, becomes official language of India, 1965 O
Hindus. *See under* Religious Denominations
Hinsley, Arthur, B. Cardinal Archbishop of Westminster (1865–1943), 1935 R, 1943 R
Hiroshima, Japan, atomic bomb on, 1945 H
Hirota, Koki, Japanese premier, 1936 A, 1937 F
His House in Order (A. W. Pinero), 1906 W
Hiss, Alger, Am. Communist, 1950 A
Histoire contemporaine, L' (A. France), 1896 U
Histoire de dix ans (L. Blanc), 1841 O
Histoire de France (J. Michelet), 1833 Q
Histoire de la Civilisation en France (F. Guizot), 1829 Q

Histoire de la Conquête d'Angleterre par les Normands (Thierry), 1825 Q
Histoire de la Révolution française (J. Michelet), 1847 Q
Histoiré de la Révolution française (L. Thiers), 1823 Q
Histoire de Port-Royal (Sainte-Beuve), 1840 U
Histoire des Origines du christianisme (E. Renan), 1863 R
Histoire d'un fait divers (J. T. Gautier), 1946 U
Histoire naturelle des animaux (Lamarck), 1815 P
Histoire naturelle des oiseaux (G. Buffon), 1786 P
Historic Buildings Council, grants by, 1954 S
Historical Association, The, 1917 Q
Historical Miniatures (A. Strindberg), 1905 U
Historical Research, Institute of, London, 1921 Q
Historismus (E. Troeltsch), 1922 R
History and Historians of the Nineteenth Century (G. P. Gooch), 1913 Q
History as Literature (T. Roosevelt), 1914 Q
History as the Story of Liberty (B. Croce), 1941 Q
History of America (W. Robertson), 1771 Q
History of Ancient Art (J. J. Winckelmann), 1764 Q
History of Caliph Vathek, The (W. Beckford), 1786 U
History of Charles V (W. Robertson), 1769 Q
History of Civilization (H. T. Buckle), 1857 Q
History of Creation, The (E. Haeckel), 1868 P
History of Dogma (Harnack), 1886 R
History of England (H. Belloc), 1925 Q
History of England (Lord Macaulay), 1848 Q
History of England (G. M. Trevelyan), 1926 Q
History of England from the Death of Wolsey to the Defeat of the Armada (J. A. Froude), 1856 Q
History of England from the Earliest Period (S. Turner), 1799 Q
History of England in the Eighteenth Century (W. E. H. Lecky), 1878 Q
History of England Principally in the Seventeenth Century (L. von Ranke), 1859 Q
History of England, 1603–56 (S. R. Gardiner), 1863 Q
History of English Law (Pollock and Maitland), 1894 Q
History of English Poetry (T. Warton), 1774 U
History of Europe (H. A. L. Fisher), 1936 Q
History of European Morals, A (W. E. H. Lecky), 1869 Q
History of France, Principally in the Sixteenth and Seventeenth Centuries (L. von Ranke), 1852 Q
History of German Law (K. F. Eichhorn), 1808 Q
History of Germany in the Nineteenth Century (Treitschke), 1879 Q
History of Great Britain (D. Hume), 1763 Q
History of Greece (G. Grote), 1846 Q
History of Greece (W. Mitford), 1784 Q
History of Greece (C. Thirlwall), 1835 Q
History of Henry Esmond, The (W. M. Thackeray), 1852 U
History of Herodotus, The (ed. H. Rawlinson), 1858 Q
History of Italian Literature (G. Tiraboschi), 1782 Q
History of Italy (C. Botta), 1824 Q
History of Latin Christianity (H. Milman), 1855 Q
History of Materialism (F. Lange), 1866 R
History of Medieval Political Theory in the West (A. J. Carlyle), 1936 Q
History of Mr. Polly, The (H. G. Wells), 1910 U
History of Modern Philosophy (K. Fischer), 1852 R
History of Music (C. Burney), 1776 T
History of Protestant Dogma (G. J. Planck), 1781 R
History of Prussian Policy (J. Droysen), 1855 Q
History of Roman Law in the Middle Ages (F. Savigny), 1815 Q
History of Rome (T. Arnold), 1838 Q
History of Rome (T. Mommsen), 1853 Q
History of Soviet Russia (E. H. Carr), 1951 Q
History of Technology, A (Singer, Holymard and Hall), 1955 P
History of the Anglo-Saxons (R. H. Hodgkin), 1935 Q
History of the Apostolic Church (P. Schaff), 1851 R
History of the Consulate and Empire (L. Thiers), 1845 Q
History of the Corruptions of Christianity, A (J. Priestley), 1782 R
History of the Crimean War (A. W. Kinglake), 1863 Q
History of the Crusades (S. Runciman), 1951 Q
History of the Czech Language (J. Dobrovsky), 1818 Q
History of the Earth and Animated Nature (O. Goldsmith), 1774 Q
History of the English-Speaking Peoples (W. S. Churchill), 1956 Q
History of the French Revolution (L. Blanc), 1847 O
History of the French Revolution (H. von Sybel), 1853 Q
History of the German Languages (J. Grimm), 1848 Q
History of the Index of Forbidden Books (Reusch), 1883 R
History of the Inquisition in Spain (J. Llorente), 1817 R
History of the Italian Republics (J. Sismondi), 1807 Q
History of the Jews (H. H. Milman), 1829 Q
History of the Norman Conquest (E. A. Freeman), 1867 Q
History of the Oxford Movement (R. W. Church), 1891 R
History of the Peninsular War (W. Napier), 1828 Q
History of the Popes (Pastor), 1928 R
History of the Popes (L. von Ranke), 1834 Q
History of the Reformation in Germany (L. von Ranke), 1839 Q
History of the Revolt of the Netherlands under the Spanish Régime (F. Schiller), 1788 Q
History of the Rise and Influence of Rationalism in Europe, A (W. E. H. Lecky), 1865 Q
History of the Roman and Teutonic People (L. von Ranke), 1824 Q
History of the Russian Empire (N. Karamzin), 1816 Q
History of the Russian Revolution (L. Trotsky), 1933 O
History of the United Netherlands (J. R. Motley), 1860 Q
History of the United States (G. Bancroft), 1834 Q
History of Thomas Friis, The (S. C. F. Schandorph), 1881 U
History of Trade Unionism (S. and B. Webb), 1894 O
History of Western Philosophy (B. Russell), 1946 R
Hitchcock, Alfred Joseph, Am. film producer-director (b. 1899), 1930 W, 1940 W, 1944 W, 1951 W, 1954 W, 1960 W
Hitchens, Ivon, B. artist (b. 1893), 1893 Z
Hitler, Adolf, G. dictator (1889–1945), 1889 Z, 1931 K, 1943 V, 1945 D
  Munich *coup* fails, 1923 L
  imprisoned, 1924 D
  Mein Kampf, 1925 O, 1927 O
  opposes Hindenburg, 1932 C
  refuses to serve under von Papen, 1932 H
  rejects Chancellorship, 1932 L
  appointed Chancellor, 1933 A
  denounces Reichstag Fire as Communist plot, 1933 B
  is granted dictatorial powers, 1933 E
  meets Mussolini, 1934 F, 1938 E, 1940 K
  alleged plot against, 1934 F
  is vested with sole power as Führer, 1934 H

Hitler—*contd*.
Halifax visits, 1937 L
becomes war minister, 1938 B
annexes Austria, 1938 C
attitude to Sudeten question, 1938 E, J
Chamberlain's visits to, 1938 J
dismisses Schacht, 1939 A
dismembers Czechoslovakia, 1939 C
denounces non-aggression pact with Poland, 1939 C
denounces Anglo-German naval agreement, 1939 D
pact with Mussolini, 1939 E
invades Poland, 1939 J
attempted assassination of, 1944 G
study of last days of, 1947 Q
Hitler Line, in Italy, 1944 E
Hittite Language, The (Hrozny), 1917 Q
Hjeller, near Oslo, Norway, atomic research station, 1951 P
Hoare, Samuel John Gurney, Viscount Templewood, B. Conservative politician (1880–1959): becomes foreign secretary, 1935 F; resigns, following outcry at proposals on Abyssinia, 1935 M
Hoare–Laval Pact, with Mussolini on Abyssinia, proposed, 1935 M
Hoban, James, Am., formerly Ir., architect (1762–1831), 1792 S
Hobart, Tasmania, 1804 K
Federal convention at, 1897 A
Hobbs, Sir John Berry, B. cricketer (1882–1964), 1882 Z, 1926 X
Hobhouse, Leonard Trelawny, B. philosopher and journalist (1864–1929), 1901 R, 1904 R
Hobson, John Atkinson, B. economist and publicist (1858–1940), 1902 P
Hobson, Sir John Gardiner Sumner, B. lawyer and Conservative politician (b. 1912), attorney-general, 1963 E
Hobson's Choice (Brighouse), 1916 W
Hoche, Lazare, F. general (1768–97), 1794 G, 1796 M
Ho Chi-Minh, president of North Vietnam, 1945 J, 1965 M
Hochhuth, Rolf, G. dramatist, 1963 W
Höchstedt, Germany, battle, 1800 F
Hodge, Merton (Horace Emerton), B. dramatist (1904–58), 1933 W
Hodgkin, Alan Lloyd, B. neurologist (b. 1914), 1963 P
Hodgkin, Dorothy Crowfoot, B. scientist (b. 1910), 1955 P, 1964 P
Hodgkin, Robert H., B. historian (d. 1943), 1935 Q
Hodza, Milan, Czechoslovak politician, Agrarian party, 1935 L, 1938 J
Hoelderlin, Friedrich, G. author and translator (1770–1843), 1804 Q
Hoensbroech, Paul, G. churchman, 1902 R
Hoffmann, August Heinrich, G. author (1798–1874), 1841 T, 1847 U
Hoffmann, Ernst Theodor Wilhelm, G. author (1776–1822), 1776 Z, 1815 U, 1822 Z
Hofmann, Karl, G. chemist, 1909 P
Hofmann, K. H., G. chemist, 1960 P
Hofmannsthal, Hugo von, Aus. poet (1884–1929), 1884 Z, 1903 U, 1905 W, 1911 U, 1929 U, Z
Hogben, Lancelot, B. social biologist (b. 1895), 1936 O, 1938 P
Hogarth, William, B. artist (1697–1764), 1764 Z
Hogg, Quintin McGarel, formerly Viscount Hailsham, Conservative politician (b. 1907), appointed minister for North-East, 1963 A
Hoggart, Richard, B. author and critic (b. 1918), 1957 O
Hohenlinden, Bavaria, W. Germany, battle, 1800 M
Hohenlohe-Schillingsfürst, Chlodwig Karl Victor, Prince of, G. statesman (1819–1901); Chancellor, 1894 K; retires, 1900 K
Hola Camp, Kenya, deaths of Mau Mau prisoners in, 1959 C
Holbach, Paul Henri Thiry, Baron d', F. philosopher and natural historian (1723–89), 1770 R
Holden, William, B. architect, 1933 S
Hölderlin, Johann Christian Friedrich, G. author (1770–1843), 1797 U
Holford, Sir William Graham, B. town-planner (b. 1907), 1956 S
Holiday camps, 1937 W
Holidays, Bank, in England and Wales, 1871 W, 1964 C
Holidays with pay, 1938 O
Holkar, Maharaja of Indore, 1802 K, 1804 D
Holkham, Norfolk, England, 1772 P
Holland (the Netherlands): sides with American Colonists, 1778 J; Britain declares war on, 1780 L; Germany invades, 1940 E. *See also under* Netherlands, The United
Holland, Edward Milner, B. lawyer (b. 1902), reports on London housing, 1965 O
Holland, Sir Sidney George, N.Z. National Party leader (b. 1893), 1957 J
Hollandia, New Guinea, 1944 D
Holman Hunt, William, B. artist (1827–1910), 1827 Z, 1848 S, 1860 S, 1905 S, 1910 Z
Holmes, Oliver Wendell, Am. author (1809–94), 1809 Z, 1858 U, 1861 U, 1867 U, 1894 Z
Holmyard, E. J., Am. historian of technology, 1955 P
Holst, Gustav, B. musician (1874–1934), 1874 Z, 1915 T, 1917 T, 1923 T, 1934 Z
Holstein, Duchy, W. Germany: Russia cedes claim to, 1776 D; Saxon and Hanoverian troops enter, 1863 M; ceded to Austria and Prussia, 1864 K; acquired by Austria, 1865 H; Prussia annexes, 1866 F. *See also* Schleswig-Holstein Question
Holy Alliance, 1815 J, K, 1833 K; United Netherlands joins, 1816 F; Sweden joins, 1817 E
Holy Loch, Firth of Clyde, nr. Dunoon, Scotland, facilities for US Polaris submarines at, 1960 L
Holyoake, Keith Jacks, N.Z. National Party leader (b. 1904), 1957 J, 1960 L
Holy Roman Empire: dismembered by Peace of Lunéville, 1801 B; reconstruction of, 1803 B; end of, 1806 H
Holy Roman Empire, The (J. Bryce), 1864 Q
Homage to H. G. Wells (Brindle), 1963 T
Home, Sir Alec (Alexander Frederick) Douglas- (formerly 14th Earl of Home), B. Conservative leader (b. 1903); appointed foreign secretary, 1960 G; becomes premier, 1963 K; renounces peerage, 1963 K; resigns, 1964 K; resigns Conservative Party leadership, 1965 G
Home, William Douglas-, B. dramatist (b. 1912), 1947 W
Home Guard, in Britain, 1940 E
Homeopathy, science of, founded, 1810 P
Homer, Winslow, Am. artist (1836–1910), 1865 S, 1877 S
Homeric studies, 1781 Q, 1795 Q
Home Rule, for Ireland. *See* Ireland, Home Rule for
Homme approximatif, L' (T. Tzana), 1931 U
Homme comme les autres, Un (A. Salaam), 1936 W
Homme et ses fantômes, L' (Lenormand), 1924 W
Homme qui rit, L' (V. Hugo), 1869 U
Hommes de bonne volonté, Les (J. Romains), 1932 U

Homo Ludens (Huizinga), 1938 Q
Homosexual offences, Wolfenden Report on, 1957 J
Hondschoote, Belgium, 1793 J
Honduras: Britain takes, 1798 N; enters Central American Federation, 1823 G; union with Nicaragua and El Salvador, 1895 E; war with Nicaragua, 1907 B; civil war, 1909 M; becomes independent Republic, 1922 B; US troops in, 1924 B
Honegger, Arthur, Swi., later Am., musician (b. 1892), 1920 T, 1921 T, 1923 T, 1926 T, 1927 T, 1934 T, 1945 T, 1950 T
Honest to God (J. Robinson), 1963 R
Hong Kong: British take, 1839 H; British sovereignty over, 1841 A; surrenders to Japan, 1941 M; typhoon strikes, 1960 F; hospital in, 1963 P
Honolulu, Hawaii, meeting of Pacific Council, 1952 H
Honours and Awards:
in Britain:
Victoria Cross, 1856 A
Order of Merit, 1902 O
Garter Roll, Emperors of Germany and Austria removed from, 1915 E
Companion of Honour, 1917 O
Order of British Empire, 1917 O
George Cross, 1940 O, 1942 O
life peerages, 1958 G
Queen's Awards to Industry, 1965 O
in France, Legion of Honour, 1802 E
in Germany, Goethe medal, 1932 Q
in US, Congressional Medal, awarded to Verdun, 1922 F
See also Nobel Prizes
Hontheim, Johann Nikolaus von (Justinus Febronius), G. Bishop of Treves (1701–90), 1763 R
Hood, Alexander, lord Bridport, B. admiral (1727–1814), occupies Toulon, 1793 H
Hood, John Bell, Am. Confederate general (1831–79), 1864 G
Hood, Raymond, Am. architect (1881–1934), 1923 S, 1930 S
Hooker, Sir William Jackson, B. director of Kew Gardens (1785–1865), 1835 P, 1841 P
Hoover, Herbert, Am. statesman, Republican (1874–1964), president of US (1929–33), 1874 Z, 1922 O, 1930 F, 1964 Z; as director of relief for Europe, 1919 A; election, 1928 L; proposes moratorium for war debts, 1931 F, H; Roosevelt defeats, 1932 L; vetoes Philippines independence, 1933 A
'Hope, Anthony.' *See* Hawkins, Anthony Hope
Hopkins, Gerard Manley, B. poet (1844–89), 1918 U
Hopkins, Harry L., Am. Democrat statesman (1890–1946), 1890 Z, 1942 D, 1946 Z, 1948 Q
Hopper, Edward, Am. artist (b. 1882), 1931 S
Hoppner, John, B. artist (1758–1810), 1786 S
Horace (Corneille), produced, 1838 W
Hore-Belisha, Leslie, lord Hore-Belisha, Conservative politician (1894–1957); war secretary, 1937 M, 1940 A
Horen (ed. F. Schiller), 1794 U
Hormones, discovered, 1902 P
Giberellin, 1957 P
pituitary, is synthesised, 1960 P
Hornby, Charles Harry St. John, B. printer and connoisseur (1867–1946), 1894 S
Horror comics, 1952 V
Horse-racing:
in Britain, Ascot, grandstand rebuilt, 1964 S
Cesarewitch, The (Newmarket), 1839 X
Derby, The (Epsom), 1779 X
won by Edward VII, 1896 X, 1909 X
Goodwood, 1802 X
Grand National, The (Aintree), 1839 X
Newmarket, 1809 X
St. Leger, The (Doncaster), 1776 X
in France, Grand Prix de Paris (Longchamp), 1863 X
Prix du Jockey Club, 1836 X
in US, 1818 X, 1894 X
Hort, Fenton John Anthony, B. churchman and New Testament scholar (1828–92), 1881 Q
Horthy de Nagybanya, Nicholas, Hung. admiral and regent (1868–1957), 1920 C, 1957 Z
Hospitals:
in Britain, Elizabeth Garrett Anderson, 1866 O
in France, 1789 O
in Germany, epileptic, 1868 O
in Hong Kong, 1963 P
Hostage, The (B. Behan), 1959 W
'Hot line', White House–Kremlin, 1963 F
Hotson, Leslie, Am. Shakespearean scholar (b. 1897), 1964 Q
Hot Springs Conference, 1943 F
Hot-strip rolling of steel, 1923 P
Hottentots, E. Africa, rising of, 1904 K
'Houdini.' *See* Weiss, E.
Houdon, Jean Antoine, F. sculptor (1741–1828), 1764 S, 1771 S, 1775 S, 1779 S, 1781 S, 1783 S; visits US, 1785 S
Hound of the Baskervilles, The (A. C. Doyle), 1902 U
Hourra l'Oural (L. Aragon), 1934 U
Hours of Idleness (Byron), 1807 U
House and its Head, A (I. Compton-Burnett), 1935 U
House, Edward Mandell, Am. statesman (1858–1938), 1858 Z, 1926 O, 1938 Z
House Fly, Disease Carrier, The (L. O. Howard), 1912 P
Housemaster, The (I. Hay), 1936 W
House of Mirth, The (E. Wharton), 1905 U
House of Seven Gables (N. Hawthorne), 1851 U
House of the Dead, The (F. Dostoievsky), 1870 U
Housing:
in Britain, artisans, 1867 O, 1884 O, 1890 O
building under act of 1919, 1919 O, 1939 Y
slum clearance, 1932 D, 1950 S
landlord and tenant act, 1954 O
rent act, de-restricts previously controlled rents, 1957 F
rent riots, 1960 J
L.C.C. offers 100 per cent. loans for house purchase, 1963 B
'Rachmanism', 1963 O
rent act, 1965 M
Milner Holland report on rented accommodation in London, 1965 O
See also Building Societies; New Towns
in India, protests at, 1951 F
in US, finance for, under Wagner-Steagall Act, 1937 J
Housman, Albert Edward, B. poet and classica scholar (1859–1936), 1859 Z, 1896 U, 1936 Z
Housman, Laurence, B. author (1865–1959), 1918 U, 1937 W
Howard, Henry Charles, earl of Surrey, later duke of Norfolk, B. Conservative politician (1791–1856), 1829 O
Howard, John, B. philanthropist (?1726–90), 1770 O
Howard, Leslie, B. film actor (1893–1943), 1938 W, 1941 W
Howard, L. O., B. physician, 1912 P
Howard's End (E. M. Forster), 1910 U
Howe, Elias, Am. inventor (1819–67), 1846 P

Howe, Julia Ward, Am. author (1819–1910), 1819 Z, 1910 Z
Howe, Richard, Earl Howe, B. admiral (1726–99), 1782 K, 1794 F
Howe, Sir William, B. soldier (1729–1814), 1776 C, J, 1777 J
Howells, William Dean, Am. author (1837–1920), 1837 Z, 1882 U, 1920 Z
How Gertrude Teaches her Children (J. H. Pestalozzi), 1801 O
How Green Was My Valley (R. Llewellyn), 1939 U
Howick Committee on ecclesiastical appointments, 1964 R
Hoxha, Enver, Albanian Communist leader, 1945 L
Hoyle, Fred, B. astronomer (b. 1915), 1950 W, 1957 R, 1961 P, 1964 P
Hrozny, Bedrich, Hung. archaeologist (b. 1879), 1917 Q
Hsu Shi-chang, president of China, 1918 J
Huber, Johann Nepomuk, G. philosopher and leader of Old Catholics (1830–79), 1869 R
Hubertusburg, Treaty of, 1763 B
Hübsch, Heinrich, G. architect (1795–1863), 1840 S
Huch, Richard, G. author, 1914 O
Huckleberry Finn (M. Twain), 1884 U
Huddleston, Trevor, B. churchman (b. 1913), 1957 O
Hudson, William Henry, B. author (1841–1922), 1904 U
Hudson River, New York, US, 1807 P
Hudson's Bay Company, territories of, purchased by Canada, 1869 L
Hué, Annam, 1884 F
Hueffer, Ford. *See* Ford, Ford Madox
Huerta, Adolfo de la, Mex. president, 1920 E
Huerta, Victoriano, Mex. general, 1913 K, L, 1914 G
Hufeland, Gottlieb, G. economist (1760–1817), 1807 O
Huggins, Godfrey, lord Malvern, premier of Central African Federation (b. 1883), 1953 M; retires, 1956 K
Hughes, Charles E., Am. Republican (1862–1948), nominated Republican candidate, 1916 F; as secretary of state, 1923 C, 1925 A
Hughes, David Edward, B. electrician (1831–1900), 1878 P
Hughes, Howard, Am. aviator, 1938 P
Hughes, Richard, B. author (b. 1900), 1961 U
Hughes, Thomas B. author (1822–96), 1857 U
Hughes, William, Austral. politician, Labour, later Nationalist, as premier, 1917 B, 1921 M
Hugo, Victor, F. poet and dramatist (1802–85), 1802 Z, 1819 U, 1829 U, 1830 U, 1831 U, 1832 W, 1838 U, 1856 U, 1859 U, 1862 U, 1866 U, 1869 U, 1874 U, 1885 Z
Huis Clos (J.-P. Sartre), 1944 W
Huizinga, J. B., Du. historian, 1919 Q, 1938 Q
Hull, Cordell, Am. statesman (1871–1955), secretary of state (1933–44), 1944 L
Human Nature (J. Dewey), 1922 R
Human Nature in Politics (G. Wallas), 1908 U
Human Needs of Labour, The (S. Rowntree), 1937 O
Human Rights:
UN declaration on, 1948 M
European convention on, 1954 E
European court of, 1959 B
Human Rights (ed. J. Maritain), 1949 O
Human Sacrifices:
in Ashanti, 1874 B
in Benin, 1879 N
Humbert I, King of Italy (1878–1900), 1878 A; assassinated, 1900 G
Humboldt, Alexander von, G. astronomer and explorer (1769–1859), 1769 Z, 1799 P, 1807 P, 1808 R, 1845 P
Humboldt, Karl Wilhelm von, G. philologist and author (1767–1835), 1791 O; becomes Prussian education minister, 1810 O
Hume, David, Scot. philosopher and historian (1711–76), 1763 Q, 1776 Z, 1779 R
Hume, Joseph, B. Radical (1777–1855), 1824 O
Humperdinck, Engelbert, G. musician (1854–1921), 1854 Z, 1893 T, 1921 Z
Humphrey, Hubert, Am. Democrat, vice-president (b. 1911), 1911 Z
Hundred Days, The (Mussolini and Forzano), 1931 O
Hundred Days, Napoleon's, 1815 C
Hundred Days of Reform, by Te Tsung, 1898 F
Hung Siu-tsuen, Chin. rebel, 1850 K
Hungarian literature, 1783 U
Hungary: under Maria Theresa, 1765 H; serfdom abolished, 1780 K; Red Army advances in, 1944 K; republic proclaimed, 1946 B; crisis of 1956. *See under* Revolutions, Hungarian
Hunger (K. Hamsun), 1890 U
Hunger Marches, in Britain, 1922 K, L
Hungerpastor, Der (W. Raabe), 1864 U
Hunt, Sir Henry Cecil John, B. mountaineer (b. 1910), 1910 Z, 1953 P
Hunt, Leigh, B. author (1785–1859), 1785 Z, 1808 V, 1816 U, 1859 Z
Hunt, William Holman. *See under* Holman Hunt
Hunter, John, B. surgeon and anatomist (1728–93), 1794 P
Hunter, Norman Charles, B. dramatist (b. 1908), 1953 W
Hunter, William, B. anatomist (1718–83), 1774 P
Huntingdon, Selina Hastings, Countess of (1707–91), 1771 R, 1779 R
Huntingtower (J. Buchan), 1922 U
Hurricanes, 1963 K
Hurry on Down (J. Wain), 1953 U
Huskisson, William, B. Tory statesman (1770–1830), 1770 Z, 1830 J; as president of Board of Trade, 1823 A, O; resigns from Wellington's ministry, 1828 E
Hussein, Kemel, Khedive of Egypt, 1914 M
Hussein, King of Hejaz (1916–24), abdicates, 1924 K; expelled, 1926 A
Hussein, King of Jordan (b. 1935), 1952 H; dismisses General Glubb, 1956 C; proclaims martial law, 1957 D; as head of Arab Federation, 1958 G; dissolves Arab Federation, 1958 H; asks for British support, 1958 G
Husserl, Edmund, G. philosopher, 1913 R
Huston, John, Am. film director (b. 1906), 1951 W
Hutchinson, Horatio Gordon ('Horace'), B. golfer (1859–1932), 1886 X
Hutchinson, Thomas, B. governor of Massachusetts Colony (1711–80), 1774 B
Hutton, James, B. geologist (1726–97), 1788 P
Hutton, John, B. artist (b. 1927), 1962 S
Hutton, Sir Leonard, B. cricketer (b. 1916), 1938 X
Huvé, Jean Jacques, F. architect, 1845 S
Huxley, Aldous Leonard, B. author (1894–1963), 1894 Z, 1921 U, 1925 U, 1928 U, 1932 U, 1936 U, 1937 R, 1944 U, 1946 R, 1948 U, W, 1958 U
Huxley, Elspeth, B. traveller and author (b. 1907), 1944 O
Huxley, Sir Julian, B. scientist (b. 1887), 1887 Z, 1944 O
Huxley, Thomas Henry, B. scientist (1825–95), 1825 Z, 1858 P, 1870 P, 1889 R, 1893 P

Huysmans, Joris Karl, F. novelist (1848–1907), 1848 Z, 1891 U, 1895 U, 1898 U, 1907 Z
Hyacinthe, Père. *See* Loyson, Hyacinthe
Hyatt, J. W., Am. inventor of celluloid (1837–1920), 1869 P
Hyde, Douglas, president of Eire (d. 1949), 1938 E, 1945 F
Hyderabad, India: Nizam of, 1766 L, 1790 G, 1792 B, 1798 J, 1799 E; joins Indian Union, 1948 J
Hyder Ali, Ind. ruler (*c.* 1722–82), 1763 N, 1769 F, 1782 M; usurps throne of Mysore, 1764 N; conquers the Carnatic, 1780 J; defeated by Coote, 1781 G
Hydraulic press, invented, 1795 P
Hydro-electric plant, 1882 P, 1886 P, 1935 P, 1952 P
Hydrogen, density of, 1766 P
  sulphuretted, 1777 P
Hydrogen Bomb:
  Russia explodes, 1953 P
  US development of, 1950 A, 1952 P, 1954 P
Hydrography, studies in, 1855 P, 1872 P
Hydrophobia, cured, 1885 P
Hyer, Tom, Am. boxer, 1841 X
Hylton-Foster, Sir Harry, B. Conservative politician and Speaker of House of Commons (1905–1965), 1965 J
Hymnals:
  English Hymnal, The, 1906 R
  Olney Hymns (Cowper and Newton), 1779 R
  Songs of Praise, 1925 R
Hymn of Jesus (A. Holst), 1917 T
Hyndman, Henry Mayers, B. Socialist (1842–1921), 1886 B
Hypatia (C. Kingsley), 1853 U
Hyperion (J. Hölderlin), 1797 U
Hyperion (J. Keats), 1819 U
Hypnotism, 1842 P

I

I am a Camera (J. van Druten and C. Isherwood), 1954 W
Iambes, Les (H. Barbier), 1831 U
I and Thou (M. Buber), 1837 R
Ibáñez, Cárlos, Chil. dictator, 1927 D, 1931 G, 1952 J
Ibn Saud, King of Saudi Arabia (*c.* 1880–1953), 1926 A
Ibrahim, son of Mohammed Ali of Egypt, 1826 D, 1832 E; routs Turks, 1839 F; evacuates Syria, 1840 L; viceroy of Egypt, 1848 L
Ibrahim Abboud, Sudan. politician, 1958 L
Ibsen, Henrik, Nor. dramatist (1828–1906), 1828 Z, 1850 W, 1864 U, 1866 W, 1867 U, 1877 W, 1879 W, 1881 W, 1882 W, 1884 W, 1890 W, 1896 W, 1906 Z; plays of, introduced to London, 1891 W
Ice-breaker, nuclear-powered, 1958 P
Iceland: self-government granted, 1874 G; becomes a sovereign state, 1918 M; Allied occupation, 1941 G; demands withdrawal of US troops, 1956 C; US troops withdraw, 1959 M
Icelandic, study of, 1810 Q, 1811 Q
Iceman Cometh, The (O'Neill), 1946 W
Ice Saints, The (F. Tuohy), 1964 U
I, Claudius (R. Graves), 1934 U
Idaho, State, US: organised as US territory, 1863 C; becomes a US state, 1890 G; grants for irrigation in, 1894 H
Idea of History, The (R. G. Collingwood), 1946 R
Idea of Nature, The (R. G. Collingwood), 1945 R
Ideals in Ireland (G. W. Russell and others), 1901 U
Ideas towards a Philosophy of History (J. G. von Herder), 1784 R
Iddesleigh, Earl. *See* Northcote, Stafford
Idiot, The (F. Dostoievsky), 1868 U
Idiots' Delight (R. Sherwood), 1936 W
Idlewild, N. York, US, Kennedy Airport, 1961 S
Idris I, King of Libya, 1951 M
Idstedt, Austria, 1850 G
Idylls of the King (Tennyson), 1859 U
If Christ Came to Chicago (W. T. Stead), 1893 R
Iffland, August, G. theatrical director (1759–1814), 1796 W
Ignatiev, Nikolai Pavlovich, R. diplomat (1832–1908), 1878 C
Ikeda, Hayato, Jap. Liberal Democrat, 1960 G
Île de Bourbon, Indian Ocean, British take, 1810 G
Île des pingouins, L' (A. France), 1908 U
Ileo, Joseph, Congol. politician, 1960 J
Il fu Mattia Pascal (L. Pirandello), 1904 W
Ili Valley, N.W. China, Russia acquires posts in, 1879 J
Illinois, state, US: becomes a US state, 1818 M; population, 1818 M; prohibition enforced in, 1851 O
Illiteracy, statistics of comparative, 1935 Y
Illuminations, Les (A. Rimbaud), 1886 U
Illusion and Reality (Caudwell), 1937 U
Illustrated Man, The (R. Bradbury), 1952 U
Illustrations, half-tone block for, 1880 V
Illustrations . . . of the Principles of Population (F. Place), 1822 P
Illyria: Austria cedes to France, 1809 K; France promises restoration, 1812 C
Image-dissector camera, 1956 P
Image Old and New (M. Ramsay), 1963 R
Imaginary Conversations (W. S. Landor), 1824 U
Immermann, Karl Lebrecht, G. poet (1796–1840), 1836 U, 1838 U
Immigration:
  Rome Conference on, 1924 E
  to Australia, restricted, 1855 N, 1902 G
  to Britain, statistics, 1938 Y
    controlled by Commonwealth Immigration Act, 1961 L, 1962 O
    limit on Commonwealth immigrants imposed, 1965 H
  to Canada, by British schoolchildren, 1940 K
  to New Zealand, of Japanese, restricted, 1881 F
  to Palestine, of Jews, 1930 K
    Jewish protests at restrictions, 1933 M
  to Transvaal, 1896 L
    of Chinese, 1903 L
  to US from Britain and Ireland, statistics, 1840 Y, 1850 Y, 1860 Y, 1870 Y, 1880 Y, 1890 Y
    of Chinese, banned, 1882 E
    restrictions on, 1907 O
    of Japanese, 1912 D
    literacy made a condition of, 1912 D
    bill for controlling, 1914 B
      vetoes, 1915 A
    bill for controlling, 1916 M
      curtailed, 1919 M
    emergency quota act, 1921 E
    limits on, 1924 E
    of Japanese, excluded, 1924 E
Immoralist, The (A. Gide), 1902 U
Imperial Chemical Industries (I.C.I.), 1931 P, 1935 P; endows fellowships, 1944 O
Imperial Conferences, London, 1907 E, 1911 E, 1926 K

Imperial Council (Reichrat), Austria, 1860 C
Imperial Defence, Committee of, British, 1902 M, 1912 B
Imperial Federation League, in Canada, 1884 D
Imperial Germany (von Bülow), 1913 O
Imperialism (J. A. Hobson), 1902 P
Imperial Preference, 1903 J, 1932 G
Imperial War Cabinet, British, first meets, 1917 C
Imphal, India, Japanese advance on, 1944 C
Impressionism, 1874 S, 1901 S
Impressionist Exhibitions, 1877 S, 1886 S
Improvements in Education as it respects the Industrious Classes (J. Lancaster), 1803 O
I'm Talking About Jerusalem (A. Wesker), 1960 W
Inadmissible Evidence (J. Osborne), 1964 W
In a German Pension (K. Mansfield), 1911 U
In Chancery (J. Galsworthy), 1920 U
Inchbald, Elizabeth, B. dramatist and actress (1753–1821), 1791 W
Inchon, Korea, 1950 J
Incomes, pioneer study of, 1855 O
Incomes and wages, in Britain:
  railwaymen's pay, 1960 C
  wages pause, 1961 G, 1962 A; ends, 1962 C
  dockers, increased, 1962 E
  National Incomes Commission, 1963 D
  teachers' salaries, 1963 G
  Statement of Intent on productivity, prices and incomes, 1964 M
  doctors, new pay structure proposed for, 1965 B
  Prices and Incomes Board, 1965 C
  the norm for pay increases, 1965 D
  printers, wage claim, 1965 E
  See also Prices; Strikes
In Darkest England and the Way Out (W. Booth), 1890 O
In Defence of Sensuality (J. C. Powys), 1930 U
Indemnities:
  Burma, to Britain, 1826 B
  China, to Russia, 1881 B
    to powers, 1901 J
  France, to Allies, 1818 J, K
    to Germany, 1871 E
  Japan, to powers, 1864 J
  Turkey, to Russia, 1878 C
  US, to Mexico, 1848 E
Independent Labour Party. *See under* Political Parties
Independent Television Authority, 1954 O
Independent Theatre Society, London, 1891 W
Index, papal, 1814 R, 1883 R
India, British administration of. *See under* East India Company, British
  French settlements in, 1763 B, 1793 N
  Native states. *See* Delhi; Kanara; Mysore; Murshidabad; Oudh
  Mutiny, 1857 E, F, G, J, L, M
  Queen Victoria proclaimed Empress, 1877 A
  Indian National Congress, first, 1886 N
  tea production in, 1909 Y
  Simon Commission on, 1926 L
  All-party conference votes for dominion status, 1928 H
  Labour unrest in, 1929 D
  Round Table Conference on, 1929 M
  All-India Congress demands British withdrawal, 1945 J
  Independence, discussions on, 1946 M; achieved, 1947 M
  Hyderabad joins Indian Union, 1948 J
  Chinese invade, 1959 H, 1962 J, K, L
Indiana, state, US, becomes a US state, 1816 M
Indiana (G. Sand), 1832 U
Indianapolis, US, car-racing at, 1965 X
Indians, in US: settlement of, 1830 E; Dawes Act for, 1887 B. *See also under* Massacres
India-rubber cloth, 1791 P
Indigo, synthetic, 1880 P
Indo-China, Japanese land in, 1941 G
Indonesian Republic:
  Dutch refuse to recognise, 1945 H
    recognise, 1946 L
    transfer sovereignty to, 1949 M
  Britain suspends aid to, 1963 K
  talks with Malaysia fail, 1964 F
Indore, Cen. India, 1802 K, 1818 A
Induction, magnetic-electric, laws of, 1851 P
Indus Civilization, The (M. Wheeler), 1954 Q
Indus, Waters, treaty for development, 1960 J
Industrial Democracy (S. and B. Webb), 1897 O
Industrial Health and Safety Centre, London, 1927 O
Industrial Output, comparative tables of increases in, 1913 Y
Industrial Psychology, National Institute of, London, 1921 O
Industrial Workers of the World, Political Branch of, 1909 O
Indy, Vincent D', F. musician (1851–1931), 1851 Z, 1897 T, 1920 T, 1931 Z
Infanticide, in India, abolished, 1870 O
Infants' Welfare Centre, 1903 O. *See also* Crêche
Inferno (A. Strindberg), 1897 U
Influence of a Low Price of Corn on the Profits of Stock, The (D. Ricardo), 1815 O
Influence of Sea Power on History (A. T. Mahan), 1890 Q
Influenza epidemics, 1918 K, 1919 P
Information, Ministry of, British, 1939 O
Infra-red solar rays, 1800 P
Inge, William Ralph, B. churchman and author (1864–1954), 1919 R, 1948 R
In God's Way (B. Björnson), 1889 U
Ingoldsby Legends, The (R. H. Barham), 1840 U
Ingres, Jean Auguste Dominique, F. artist (1780–1867), 1780 Z, 1808 S, 1823 S, 1824 S, 1842 S, 1856 S, 1859 S, 1867 Z
Injections, of insulin, 1922 P, 1937 P
Inkerman, Russia, battle, 1854 C
In Memoriam (Tennyson), 1850 U
Innocents Abroad, The (M. Twain), 1869 U
Inn Quarter, Austria: acquired from Bavaria, 1779 E; ceded to Bavaria, 1809 K
Inni Sacri (A. Manzoni), 1813 U
Innsbruck, Austria, 1848 E
Inoculations against anthrax, 1883 P
Inönü, Ismet, Turk. politician, 1938 L, 1964 B
In Quest of the Historical Jesus (A. Schweitzer), 1910 R
Inquiry Concerning Political Justice, The (W. Godwin), 1793 O
Inquiry into the Nature and Causes of the Wealth of Nations (A. Smith), 1776 U
Inquiry into the Nature and Progress of Rent, An (T. R. Malthus), 1815 U
Inquiry into the Human Mind (T. Reid), 1764 R
Inquiry into the Relation of Cause and Effect (T. Brown), 1804 R
Inquisition, The:
  in Italy, abolished in Tuscany, 1765 H
    Napoleon abolishes in Italian States, 1808 R
    revived, 1814 R
  in Portugal, abolished, 1821 A
  in Spain, seizes Goya's *Capriccios*, 1796 S
    Napoleon abolishes, 1808 R

revived, 1814 R
abolished, 1820 C
account of, 1817 R
Insects, classification of, 1775 P
Insecticides, 1924 P
Inscriptiones Aegypticae (H. Brugsch), 1883 Q
Inscriptions, cuneiform, 1846 Q
In Search of Criminology (L. Radzinowycz), 1961 O
Insight and Outlook (A. Koestler), 1949 R
Inspections, medical, of schoolchildren, 1907 O
Institute of Advanced Legal Studies, London, 1948 O
Institute of Economic and Social Research, National, London, 1938 O
Institute of Historical Research, London, 1921 O
Institute of International Affairs, London, 1920 O
Institute of Mechanics, Liverpool, 1834 O
Institute of Technical Optics, S. Kensington, 1917 P
Institute of Technology, Chicago, 1939 O
Institute of Technology, Massachusetts, develops use of ultra-high-frequency waves, 1955 P
Institutes of the Law of Scotland (J. Erskine), 1773 O
Institutiones theologicae dogmaticae (J. Wegscheider), 1815 R
Instrumentation, treatise on, 1844 T
Insulin, is isolated, 1922 P
structure of, 1955 P
zinc protamine, for treating diabetes, 1937 P
Insurance Societies, British, 1769 O, 1963 M
in India, nationalised, 1956 E
in US, alleged corruption, 1905 O
Insurance:
old age, in Britain, 1909 A, 1913 O, 1940 B, 1964 L
in France, 1850 O
in Germany, 1883 E, 1889 E
sickness, in Britain, 1913 O
in France, 1930 D
in New Zealand, 1898 O
unemployment, in Britain, 1925 G
in Denmark, 1891 M
Intelligent Man's Guide to the Post-War World, The (G. D. H. Cole), 1947 O
Intelligent Woman's Guide to Socialism and Capitalism (G. B. Shaw), 1928 O
Internal Evidence for the Truth of Revealed Religion (T. Erskine), 1820 R
International, Labour and Socialist, 1923 O
International, Communist, 1876 O; Bakunin expelled from, 1872 O; Third, 1919 O; French Socialists adhere to, 1920 M; Zinoviev Letter, 1924 K; declaration in support of governments against Fascism, 1935 G; dissolved, 1943 E
International Justice, Permanent Court of, The Hague, 1922 B; US Senate rejects proposal to join, 1923 C; US joins, 1929 J; decides against Austro-German customs union, 1931 C; ruling in Anglo-Iranian dispute, 1951 G; Britain submits Falkland Isles dispute to, 1955 E; to hear India's dispute with Portugal, 1957 L
International Labour Organisation, 1919 O
S. Africa leaves, 1964 C
International Working-Men's Association, 1876 O
Interpretation of Dreams, The (S. Freud), 1900 R
Interpretation of Personality, The (Jung), 1940 R
Inter-relations of Cultures (UNESCO), 1955 Q
In the Interlude (B. Pasternak), 1962 U
Intimate Papers of Colonel House, The, 1926 O
Introduction aux Travaux Scientifiques du XIXe Siècle (St. Simon), 1807 O
Introduction to Algebra (L. Euler), 1770 P
Introduction to Greek and Latin Palaeography (E. M. Thompson), 1912 Q
Introduction to Philosophy (J. F. Herbart), 1813 R
Introduction to the Law of Nature and Notions (Mackintosh), 1799 O
Introduction to the Principles of Morals and Legislation (J. Bentham), 1789 O
In't Wonderjaar (H. Conscience), 1837 U
Inukai, Japanese premier, 1932 E
Invergordon, Scotland, mutiny at, 1931 J
Invisible Man (H. G. Wells), 1897 U
Invisible Writing, The (A. Koestler), 1954 O
Invitation au Château, L' (Anouilh), 1947 W
Invitation to the Waltz (R. Lehmann), 1932 U
Inwood, William, B. architect (1771–1843), 1819 S
Iodine, discovered, 1811 P
Ionamide dyes, 1922 P
Ionesco, Eugène, F. dramatist (b. 1912), 1960 W, 1963 W
Ionian Islands: France occupies, 1797 F; conquered by Turks and Russians, 1788 C; independence recognised, 1801 K; British protectorate over, 1815 L; cede Parga, 1819 D; conference on, 1863 L; ceded by Britain to Greece, 1864 C
Ion microscope, 1956 P
Iowa, US, becomes a US state, 1846 M
Iphigenie auf Tauris (Goethe), 1787 W
I Promessi Sposi (A. Manzoni), 1825 U
Ipsara, Island, Aegean, Turks capture, 1824 G
Iran (formerly Persia): name changed from Persia, 1935 O; Allies invade, 1941 H
Iraq: independence recognised, 1927 M, 1930 F; massacre of Assyrian Christians, 1933 G; severs relations with France, 1938 M; demands withdrawal of British, 1941 E; forms, with Jordan, the Arab Federation, 1958 B; Arab Federation dissolved, 1958 H; petroleum company's dispute with Lebanon, 1959 F; federates with United Arab Republic, 1963 D
Ireland, John, B. musician (1879–1962), 1915 T
Ireland:
Whiteboys Revolt in, 1763 G
Protestant Volunteers in, 1779 C
free trade with Britain, 1779 M, 1780 M
Home Rule for, demanded, 1780 D, 1782 D
granted, 1782 E
Gratton's Parliament, 1782 E
French attempt invasion, 1798 H, K
Union with England, 1800 C, 1801 A
Famine, 1845 N
Coercion bill for, rejected, 1846 F
Disestablishment of Church, 1869 G
land legislation for, 1870 H
Land League, 1880 L
Land Act, 1881 H, J
disturbances in, 1881 A, C, 1882 E, G
eviction of tenants, 1882 N
agrarian outrages, 1882 N
loans to tenants, 1885 H
Crimes Act, 1887 A
Rebellion, 1916 O
emigration to US, 1830 Y, 1840 Y, 1850 Y, 1860 Y, 1870 Y, 1880 Y, 1890 Y, 1900 Y
See also Eire; Irish Free State; Irish Home Rule
Ireland, Northern: first Parliament of, 1821 F; boundary settled, 1825 L, M; votes for non-inclusion in Irish Free State, 1922 M; Britain re-affirms position of, 1949 E; premier meets prime minister of Eire, 1965 A
Irène (Voltaire), 1778 U
Irish Free State: officially proclaimed, 1922 M; becomes Eire, 1937 M. *See also* Eire

Irish Home Rule:
Disraeli goes to country on issue of, 1880 C
Gladstone's bill, 1886 D
defeated, 1886 F
issue of, 1891 K
Lords reject bill, 1893 J
issue splits British Liberal Party, 1894 C
Campbell-Bannerman on, 1905 L
as election issue, 1910 A
Ulster Unionists resolve to repudiate, 1912 A, J
Liberals defeated over, 1912 L
Lords reject bill for, 1913 A, G
Ulster Unionists appoint provisional government, 1913 J
bill passes Commons, 1914 E
suspended for duration of war, 1914 J
Ulster determines to resist, 1914 G
Buckingham Palace Conference on, 1914 G
Rebellion, 1916 O
Iris Convention meets, 1917 G
Sinn Fein Congress adopts declaration of independence, 1919 A
Britain abandons, 1918 F
Carson demands repeal of, 1919 G
Ulster votes to accept bill, 1920 C
Belfast riots, 1920 G
under Government of Ireland Act, 1920 M, 1921 D
British truce with Sinn Fein, 1921 G
Dáil rejects British peace offer, 1921 H
Anglo-Irish Peace treaty, 1921 M
Dáil approves, 1922 A
Irish Free State, 1922 M
Irish Republican Army (IRA), 1933 G, 1955 H
Irish Republican Brotherhood, 1857 K. *See also under* Fenians
Iron and Steel:
British Federation, 1934 O
nationalisation, in force in Britain, 1949 L
denationalised, 1952 L
in France and Germany, Schuman Plan for, 1950 E
production of, in Austria, 1870 Y
in Belgium, 1938 Y, 1948 Y
in Britain, 1806 Y, 1818 Y, 1825 Y, 1835 Y, 1841 Y, 1851 Y, 1860 Y, 1861 Y, 1870 Y, 1871 Y, 1875 Y, 1880 Y, 1895 Y, 1913 Y, 1938 Y, 1941 Y, 1948 Y
in France, 1841 Y, 1851 Y, 1860 Y, 1861 Y, 1870 Y, 1871 Y, 1875 Y, 1880 Y, 1895 Y, 1938 Y, 1948 Y
in Germany, 1861 Y, 1870 Y, 1871 Y, 1875 Y, 1880 Y, 1913 Y, 1938 Y, 1948 Y
in Russia, 1851 Y, 1880 Y, 1932 Y, 1938 Y, 1940 Y, 1948 Y
in US 1860 Y, 1861 Y, 1870 Y, 1880 Y, 1913 Y, 1938 Y, 1948 Y
Iron, cast, building-frame of, 1851 P
Iron, wrought, Cort's process for, 1784 P
Iron Guard. *See under* Political Parties
Iron steamship, 1820 P
Irredentist Movement in Italy, 1878 N
Irrigation works, 1894 H, 1902 O
Irving, Sir Henry, B. actor (1838–1917), 1838 Z, 1856 W, 1866 W, 1878 W, 1917 Z
Irving, Washington, Am. author (1783–1859), 1783 Z, 1809 U, 1820 U, 1822 U, 1832 U, 1859 Z
Irwin, Lord. *See* Wood, Edward
Isabella II, Queen of Spain (1833–68), 1833 J, 1843 L, 1868 J, 1870 F, 1874 L
Isandhlwana, Zululand, S. Africa, massacre at, 1879 A
Isernia, Italy, Eighth Army takes, 1943 L
Isherwood, Christopher William Bradshaw, B. author (b. 1904), 1904 Z, 1928 U, 1935 U, 1937 U, 1938 U, 1954 U, 1964 U
Isidore decretals admitted as forgery, 1789 R
Islam, Holy Places, 1900 N
Ismail, Khedive of Egypt (1830–95), 1863 A, 1866 E, 1879 F
Ismail, Russia, captured from Turkey, 1790 M
Ismail, Sidky Pasha, becomes Egyptian premier, 1930 F
Isomorphism, theory of, 1819 P
Isolation, British policy of, ends, 1902 A
Isonzo, Italy, battles of, 1915 F, G, K, L, 1916 C, H, J, K, 1917 E
Isotope, term coined, 1913 P
235, possibility of splitting, 1939 P
radio-, 1952 P
Isotopy, phenomena of, established, 1919 P
Israel: provisional government formed, 1948 E; recognised by Britain, 1950 D; W. Germany establishes relations with, 1965 E. *See also under* Jerusalem; Middle East Crisis; Suez Crisis
Istanbul, Turkey: name changed from Constantinople, 1930 C; riots in, 1955 H, 1960 D
Istria, Italy: Austria obtains, 1797 K; Italy obtains, 1920 L
Italian National Association, 1857 H
Italian, The (A. Radcliffe), 1795 U
Italian Visit, An (C. Day-Lewis), 1953 U
Italian War and the Mission of Prussia (F. Lassalle), 1859 O
Italy:
Republic established, 1802 A
unification of, Garibaldi's plans for, 1857 H, 1860 E, H, J
Napoleon III's designs, 1858 G
plebiscites for, 1860 C, K, L
British support for, 1860 H
Kingdom of Italy proclaimed, 1860 K, 1861 B
France and Prussia agree upon, 1865 K
achievements towards, 1866 K, 1870 K
Allies invade, 1943 J
cedes territory to France, 1946 F
It is Never Too Late to Mend (C. Reade), 1856 U
Ito, Prince of Japan (1841–1909), 1892 F, 1901 L, 1909 K
ITMA, 1942 W
Iturbide, Augustus, president of Mexico, 1822 E, 1823 C
Ituzaingo, Brazil, battle, 1827 B
Ivangorod, Russia, Russians break through at, 1914 K
Ivanhoe (W. Scott), 1820 U
Iveagh, Lord. *See* Guinness, Edward
Ivory Coast (French West Africa): French Protectorate over, 1889 A; French colony established, 1893 C
Ivory Coast Republic, independence for, 1960 G
Izmir, Turkey, riots in, 1955 J
Izvolski, Alexander, R. foreign minister (1856–1919), 1906 E, 1908 J; meets Edward VII, 1907 J; visits London, 1908 L

J

Jacaranda Tree, The (H. E. Bates), 1949 U
J'accuse (É. Zola), 1898 A
Jackson, Andrew, Am. statesman, Democrat (1767–1845), 1845 Z; 7th president of US (1828–37), 1767 Z, 1827 L, 1829 C, 1832 L, 1833 A, C, H

Jackson, Sir Barry, B. theatrical manager (1879–1961), 1913 W
Jackson, Sir Herbert, B. scientist (1863–1936), 1916 P
Jackson, Thomas Jonathan ('Stonewall'), Am. Confederate general (1824–63), 1862 H, 1863 E
Jacksonville, Flor., US, 1862 C
Jacobins Club, 1790 N. *See also* Political Parties
Jacobsen, Jens Peter, Da. author (1847–85), 1880 U
Jadis et naguère (P. Verlaine), 1884 U
Jadotville, Katanga, Congo, UN force captures, 1963 A
Jaeger, Werner, G. philosopher, 1888 Z
Jaffa (Yafo), Israel, British take, 1917 L
Jagan, Cheddi, B. Guian. People's Party leader (b. 1918), sentenced, 1954 D; forms ministry, 1957 H, 1961 H; dismissed, 1964 M
Jagow, Gottlieb von, G. foreign minister (1863–1917), 1913 A
Jahr der Seele, Das (S. George), 1897 U
Jamaica, becomes independent, 1962 H
James, Henry, Am. author (1843–1916), 1843 Z, 1876 U, 1877 U, 1878 U, 1881 U, 1886 U, 1895 U, 1898 U, 1903 U, 1913 S, 1914 U, 1916 Z, 1917 U
James, Montague Rhodes, B. scholar (1862–1936), 1904 U
James, William, Am. philosopher (1842–1910), 1842 Z, 1890 R, 1902 R, 1907 R, 1909 R, 1910 Z
Jameson, Sir Leander Starr, S. African statesman (1849–1912), 1849 Z, 1891 F, 1893 L, 1894 A, 1896 A, 1912 Z; raid into Transvaal, 1895 M; founds Unionist Party, 1910 E
Jameson Raid, Report on, 1897 G
Jammu, India, disturbances in, 1959 G
Janáček, Leoš, Czech. musician (1854–1928), 1916 T
Jane Eyre (C. Brontë), 1847 U
Janissaries, Turkish, dissolved, 1826 F
Janossy, Lajos, Hung. scientist (b. 1912), 1948 P
Jansky, Karl, radio-astronomer, 1932 P
Janson, Paul, Belg. Liberal, 1937 K
Japan: extra-territorial concessions in, 1886 E; art of, introduced to West, 1867 S; US forces land in, 1945 H
Jardin de Bérénice (M. Barres), 1891 U
Jarrow, Durham, England, development scheme, 1936 G
Jaspers, Karl, Swi. philosopher (b. 1883), 1883 Z, 1932 R, 1935 R, 1953 R
Jassy, Moldavia, Russia, peace treaty of, 1792 A
Jauraie, La, Vendée, France, treaty, 1795 B
Jaurès, Auguste Marie Joseph Jean–, F. Socialist leader (1859–1914), 1859 Z, 1911 D, 1914 G
Java: restored to Netherlands, 1816 M; Japanese land in, 1942 B; war in, 1947 G; Communists in, 1948 J
Jay, John, Am. diplomat (1745–1829), 1794 L
Jazz: sweeps US, 1916 T; Original Dixieland Band, 1918 W; becomes universal, 1920 W
Jean Calas (J. Chénier), 1791 W
Jean-Christophe (R. Rolland), 1904 U
Jeanneret, Charles Édouard ('Le Corbusier'), F. architect (1887–1965), 1887 Z, 1918 S, 1926 S, 1929 S, 1952 S, 1955 S, 1957 S, 1963 S, 1965 S
Jeans, Sir James, B. astronomer (1877–1946), 1877 Z, 1914 P, 1926 P, 1929 P, 1946 Z
Jebb, John, B. theologian (1736–86), 1771 R
Jebb, Sir Richard Claverhouse, B. classical scholar (1841–1905), 1841 Z, 1905 Z
Jedermann (H. von Hofmannsthal), 1911 U
Jefferson, Thomas, Am. statesman (1743–1826), 3rd president of US, Republican (1801–9), 1776 G; 1778 N, 1784 D, 1792 N, 1798 N, 1801 C, 1807 F, 1817 S, 1826 Z; as secretary of state, 1789 D; defeated by John Adams, 1796 L; elected president, 1800 L; second term, 1805 C
Jeffries, John, Am. physician and scientist (1744–1818), 1785 P
Jeffries, J. J., Am. boxer, 1910 X
Jehovah's Witnesses. *See under* Religious Denominations
Jellicoe, John Rushworth, Earl Jellicoe, B. admiral (1859–1935), 1916 L
Jemappes, Hainault, Belgium, Austrian defeat at, 1792 L
Jena, Germany, Zeiss optical factory at, 1846 P
Jenkins, Roy Harris, B. Labour politician and author (b. 1920), 1964 Q
Jenkinson, Robert Banks, Earl of Liverpool, B. Tory politician (1770–1828), 1805 O; premier, 1812 E, 1827 A
Jenner, Edward, B. physician (1749–1823), 1796 P
Jennie Gerhardt (T. Dreiser), 1911 U
Jenyns, Soame, B. philosopher (1704–87), 1776 R
Jericho, Jordan: Australians occupy, 1918 B; Arab Congress of, 1948 M; excavations at, 1952 Q
Jerome, Jerome Klapka, B. author (1859–1927), 1859 Z, 1889 U, 1927 U
Jerusalem, Israel/Jordan: Russian Orthodox Church establishes monastery, 1860 R; excavations at, 1866 Q; surrenders to Allenby, 1917 M; missionary conference at, 1928 R; Arab-Jew conflict over Wailing Wall, 1929 H; UN trusteeship for, 1947 L; Arabs enter, 1948 E; Israel attempts to found capital, 1949 M; Religious Centre for World Jewry, 1958 R
Jerusalem (W. Blake), 1804 U
Jerusalem (S. Lagerlöf), 1901 U
Jerusalem (M. Mendelssohn), 1783 R
Jervis, John, lord St. Vincent, B. admiral (1735–1823), 1797 B
Jesuits (Society of Jesus):
 dissolution demanded, 1769 A
 dissolved, 1773 G
 revived, 1814 R
 in France, suppressed, 1764 L, 1879 F, 1880 C, R
  allowed to return, 1826 N
  attacked, 1828 F
 in Germany, laws against, 1872 F, 1904 R
 in Parma, expelled, 1768 N
 in Poland, expelled, 1774 N
 in Spain and Sicilies, expelled, 1767 C
Jet engine, 1937 P
Jeu de paume (A. Chénier), 1790 O
Jeune captive (A. Chénier), 1794 O
Jeune parque, La (P. Valéry), 1917 U
Jeunes filles, Les (H. de Montherlant), 1936 U
Jeunesses musicales, 1958 T
Jevons, William Stanley, B. economist (1835–82), 1865 O, 1871 O, 1874 P, 1882 O
Jewett, Sarah Orme, Am. author (1849–1909), 1877 U
Jewkes, John, B. economist (b. 1902), 1948 O
Jews, The:
 disabilities of, tract on, 1781 R
 in Britain, removal of disabilities, 1858 G, O
 in France, admitted to civil liberties, 1790 R
  consistorial organisation of, 1806 R
 in Germany, Prussian, emancipated, 1812 R
  seminary in Breslau, 1854 R
  influence of, 1878 O
  persecution of, 1933 D, 1935 J
  Eichmann's trial for crimes against, 1961 O
 in Palestine, Balfour Declaration on national home for, 1917 L

Jews, The—*contd.*
in Palestine—*contd.*
protests at immigration restrictions, 1933 M
admission to Palestine demanded, 1945 H
See also Israel; Jerusalem
in Poland, deported to Lublin, 1939 K
pogrom, 1946 G
in Russia, persecuted, 1881 R
closure of synagogues, 1961 R
statistics of, 1909 Y
World Conference, Montreux, 1948 R
Conference of Rabbis, 1957 R
Religious Centre for World Jewry, Jerusalem, 1958 R
See also Anti-Semitism; Israel
Jew Suss (Feuchtwanger), 1917 U
Jibouti railway to Addis Ababa, 1902 B
'Jindivik' pilotless plane, 1953 P
Jingoism, in Britain, 1878 A
Jinnah, Miss, Pakist., 1865 A
Joachim, Joseph, G. violinist (1831–1907), 1831 Z, 1844 T, 1879 T, 1907 Z
Jocelyn (A. de Lamartine), 1836 U
Jodl, General, G., capitulates to Eisenhower, 1945 E
Jodrell Bank, England, radio-telescope, 1957 P
Joffre, Joseph, F. general and statesman (1852–1931), 1852 Z, 1916 M, 1931 Z; takes offensive, 1915 J; as commander-in-chief, 1915 M
Johannes IV, King of Ethiopia (1872–89), 1888 M, 1889 L
Johannesburg, S. Africa, 1892 J, 1896 A; Uitlanders petition, 1899 C; Roberts occupies, 1900 H; strikes in, 1922 C; race riots in, 1950 A; Progressive Party established at, 1959 L; trial in, 1964 L
John VI, King of Portugal (1816–26), 1792 N, 1816 A, C, 1820 B, M, 1821 D, J, 1823 F, 1824 D, 1826 C
John XXIII, Pope (Cardinal Angelo Roncalli), 1963 F; elected Pope, 1958 K, W; decides to call Vatican Council, 1959 R; appeals for world peace, 1961 J; insists on retention of Latin, 1962 R; encyclical, *Pacem in Terris*, 1963 R
John, Augustus, B. artist (1879–1961), 1908 S, 1909 S, 1911 S, 1914 S, 1923 S, 1926 S, 1940 S
John, Gwen, B. artist, 1924 S
John Brown's Body (S. V. Benét), 1928 U
John Gabriel Borkman (Ibsen), 1896 W
John Gilpin (W. Cowper), 1785 U
John Halifax Gentleman (D. Muloch), 1857 U
John Inglesant (J. H. Shorthouse), 1880 U
Johnson, Amy (later Mollison), B. airwoman (1903–1941), 1903 Z, 1930 O, P, 1936 P, 1941 Z
Johnson, Andrew, Am. statesman, Republican (1808–75), 17th president of US (1865–70), 1864 L, 1865 D
acquitted after impeachment, 1868 E
Johnson, C. S., Am. author, 1930 O
Johnson, Jack, Am. boxer, 1908 X, 1910 X
Johnson, Louis Arthur (b. 1891), Am. defence secretary, 1950 J
Johnson, Lyndon Baines, Am. statesman, Democrat (b. 1908), 36th president of US, since 1963, 1908 Z, 1965 A
appointed vice-president, 1960 L
visits Berlin, 1961 H
succeeds as president, 1963 L
proposes reduced defence budget, 1964 A
submits poverty bill, 1964 C
signs Civil Rights Act, 1964 G
defeats Goldwater, 1964 L
meets H. Wilson, 1964 M
offers Panama a new Canal treaty, 1964 M
proposes aid for S.E. Asia, 1965 D
signs Medical Care for Aged bill, 1965 G
Johnson, Philip, Am. architect (b. 1906), 1958 S
Johnson, Samuel, B. author, lexicographer and wit (1709–84), 1763 U, 1764 U, 1775 U, 1779 U, 1784 Z, 1785 R, 1796 S
Johnston, Sir Harry Hamilton, B. explorer and administrator (1858–1927), 1858 Z, 1927 Z
Johnston, Joseph Eggleston, Am. Confederate general (1807–91), 1865 D
Jókai, Maurus, Hung. novelist (1825–1904), 1846 U
Joliot, F. Curie, F. physicist, 1934 P, 1939 P
Jolson, Al, Am. singer, 1927 W
Jonas, Franz, president of Austria, 1965 E
Jones, Aubrey, B. Conservative politician (b. 1911), as Chairman of Prices and Incomes Board, 1965 C
Jones, Arnold Hugh Martin, B. ancient historian (b. 1904), 1964 Q
Jones, Edith. *See* Wharton, Edith
Jones, Edward. *See* German, Sir Edward
Jones, Sir Harold Spencer, B. astronomer (b. 1890), 1890 Z
Jones, Henry Arthur, B. dramatist (1851–1929), 1882 U
Jones, John Paul, Am. naval officer (1747–92), 1779 J
Jones, Sir William, B. orientalist (1764–94), 1784 Q, 1789 Q
Jordan, Hashemite Kingdom of: name changed from Transjordan, 1949 F; forms, with Iraq, Arab Federation, 1958 B; Arab Federation ended, 1958 H
Jorrocks's Jaunts and Jollities (R. S. Surtees), 1838 U
Joseph and His Brothers (T. Mann), 1933 U
Joseph Delorme (Sainte-Beuve), 1829 U
Joseph II, Emperor of Austria (1765–90), 1768 M, 1769 H, K, 1770 J, 1780 F, L, 1783 F, 1784 K, 1787 A, 1788 B, K, 1790 B; as Archduke of Austria, 1763 B; elected emperor, 1765 H; claims Lower Bavaria, 1777 M, 1778 A; reforms, 1781 K, L, 1782 C; abrogates Barrier Treaty, 1782 D; attempts to exchange Bavaria for Netherlands, 1785 A, G, 1786 K
Joseph, Archduke of Austria (1872–1931), as 'state governor' of Hungary, 1919 H
Joseph I, King of Portugal (1750–77), insanity of, 1774 N
Joseph (Bonaparte), King of Naples, 1806 C, 1810 D, J; becomes King of Spain, 1808 F; flees from Madrid, 1808 H; flees from Spain, 1813 F
Josephine (Marie Rose Josephine Tascher de la Pagenie) (1763–1814), F. empress, as Josephine Beauharnais, marries Napoleon Bonaparte, 1796 C; Napoleon divorces, 1809 M
Joubert, Barthélemy Catherine, F. general (1769–99), 1798 L, M
Joubert, M., F. financier, 1876 L
Joubert, Piet Jacobus, Boer general (1834–1900), 1899 K, L
Jouffroy d'Abbans, Claude François Dorothée, Marquis de, F. pioneer of steam navigation (1751–1832), 1783 P
Jouhaud, Edouard, Alger, OAS leader, sentence reprieved, 1962 L
Joule, James Prescott, B. physicist (1818–89), 1818 Z, 1840 P, 1843 P, 1889 Z
Jourdan, Jean Baptiste, F. general (1762–1833), 1794 F, 1795 F, 1796 F, H, 1799 C
Journal Intime (H. F. Amiel), 1883 U
Journalist, The (G. Freytag), 1853 W
Journalists, Society of Women, 1884 V
Journal of a Country Priest (G. Bernanos), 1936 U

Journal of Transactions . . . on the Coast of Labrador (G. Cartwright), 1792 P
Journals:
Action française, 1899 V
Adelphi, The, 1923 V
Aeronaute, L', 1963 P
Allgemeine Zeitung, 1798 V
American Historical Review, 1895 Q
Athenaeum, 1931 V
Atlantic Monthly, 1857 V
Blackwood's Magazine, 1817 V, 1857 V
Blätter fur die Kunst, 1890 V
Botanical Magazine, 1777 P
Caricature, La, 1830 S
Catholic, The, 1856 R
Children's Newspaper, The, 1919 V
Cinema Quarterly, The, 1932 W
Civilta Cattolica, La, 1850 R
Constitutionnel, Le, 1849 V
Cornhill Magazine, The, 1860 V
Criterion, 1922 V
Critica, La, 1903 V
Critical Journal of Philosophy, 1801 R
Deutsche Museum, Das, 1810 V
Dial, The, 1840 R
Economic History Review, 1927 Q
Economist, The, 1843 V
Edinburgh Press, The, 1802 V, 1825 Q
Egyptian Archaeology, 1914 Q
English Historical Review, 1886 Q
English Review, The, 1908 V
Field, The, 1853 V
Fortnightly Review, The, 1865 V
Forward, is suppressed, 1916 V
Fraser's Magazine, 1838 U
Harper's Weekly, 1856 V
History, 1917 Q
History Today, 1951 V
Hochland, 1903 V
Illustrated London News, The, 1842 V
Industrial Syndecalist, The, 1910 O
John Bull, 1820 V
Knickerbocker Magazine, 1833 V
Lancet, The, 1823 P
Left Review, 1934 V
Liberator, The, 1831 O
Life and Letters, 1928 V
London Magazine, The, 1954 W
Mind, 1876 R
Musical Times, The, 1844 T
National Reformer, The, 1860 V
Nation and Athenaeum, 1931 V
New Statesman, The, 1913 V, 1931 V
New Writing and Daylight, 1943 U
New Yorker, The, 1925 U
Nineteenth Century, The, 1877 U
Nouvelle Revue Française, 1909 V
Overland Monthly, The, 1868 V
Pall Mall Gazette, 1865 V
Penny Magazine, 1832 V
Poetry Review, 1912 V
Political Register, 1816 V
Populaire, Le, 1916 V
Private Eye, 1962 V
Punch, 1841 V, 1896 V
Quarterly Review, 1809 V
Review of Reviews, 1890 V
Revue des deux Mondes, 1829 V
Round Table, The, 1910 V
Saturday Review, The, 1855 V
Scrutiny, 1932 U
Sketch, The, 1893 V
Spectator, The, 1828 V
Speculum, 1926 Q
Spiegel, Der, 1962 K, L
Stijl, De, 1917 S
Strand Magazine, 1891 U
Studio, The, 1893 S
Symboliste, Le, 1886 V
Tablet, The, 1840 V
Tatler, The, 1901 V
Time and Tide, 1920 V
Time Magazine, 1923 V
Times Literary Supplement, 1902 V
Transatlantic Review, 1924 V
Truth, 1877 R
Westminster Review, 1824 V
Zeitschrift für Philosophie, 1837 R
See also under Newspapers
Journals, scientific, development of, 1920 P
Journey from St. Petersburg to Moscow (A. Radistscheff), 1790 O
Journey to the Western Islands of Scotland, A (S. Johnson), 1775 U
Journey's End (R. C. Sherriff), 1929 W
Jouve, P. J., F. poet, 1945 U
Jowett, Benjamin, B. soldier and educationalist (1817–93), 1870 O
Joyce, James, Ir. author (1882–1941), 1882 Z, 1914 U, 1916 U, 1918 W, 1922 U, 1939 U, 1941 Z
Judea Lives Again (N. Bentwich), 1944 O
Jude the Obscure (T. Hardy), 1896 U
Judgments, Notable:
in Britain, Taff Vale, 1901 G
in US, in Dred Scott case, 1856 C
Puerto Ricans not US citizens, 1901 M
in Northern Securities case, 1904 C
Income Tax ruled unconstitutional, 1916 A
Debs's conviction for espionage upheld, 1919 L
National Industrial Recovery Act declared unconstitutional, 1935 E
Segregation of Negroes on buses declared unconstitutional, 1946 O
on loyalty oaths of New York tenants, 1955 O
for desegregation in Little Rock Schools, 1958 J
that Communist Party should register as foreign-dominated body, 1961 F
reading of prayers in schools rules unconstitutional, 1962 O
Judiciary, British:
Court of Chivalry revived, 1954 O
Family Courts proposed, 1965 O
Judicial Committee of Privy Council, 1856 R
Canadian appeals to, discontinued, 1946 O
Supreme Court of Judicature, 1873 C
Russian, reformed, 1864 M
Judson, Egbert Putnam, Am. inventor (1812–93), 1893 P
Julian (G. Vidal), 1964 U
Juliana, Queen of Netherlands, 1948 J
Jung, Carl Gustav, Swi. psychologist (1876–1961), 1917 R, 1920 R, 1940 R, 1944 R
Jungfrau, Switzerland, mountain, 1811 P
Junghans, Siegfried, G. metallurgist, 1927 P
Junin, Prince, 1824 H
Jungle (U. Sinclair), 1906 O
Jungle Box, The (R. Kipling), 1894 U
Junius', Letters of, 1768 V, 1769 A, 1770 F
Juno and the Paycock (O'Casey), 1925 W
Junot, Androche, F. general (1771–1813), 1808 M
Junta de Defensa Nacional, in Spain, 1936 G
Jupiter, planet, emission of radio waves from, 1955 P,
Jurandes, privileged corporations in France, abolished, 1776 B

Jurgen (J. B. Cabell), 1919 U
Jussieu, Antoine Laurent de, F. botanist (1748–1836), 1789 P
Justice, La (Sully-Prudhomme), 1878 U
Justine (L. Durrell), 1858 U
Just So Stories (R. Kipling), 1902 U
Jutland, battle of, 1916 E
Juveniles, employment of, 1819 O
  in Britain, legislation to control, 1825 F, 1833 M, 1842 M, 1844 F, 1847 F
  in Germany, regulated, 1908 M
  in US, regulated, 1903 N
    products of labour by, excluded from inter-state commerce, 1916 O
    forbidden, 1938 P
Juvenile offenders, 1854 O, 1964 C, E
  courts for, 1965 O
  reformatories for, 1851 O, 1876 O

K

Kabaka, The, of Buganda, recognition of, withdrawn 1954 L; returns to Uganda, 1955 K; becomes president of Uganda, 1963 K
Kabale und Liebe (Schiller), 1784 W
Kabul, Afghanistan:
  British capitulate at, 1842 A
  British legation at, massacred, 1879 J
Kádár, János, Hung. Communist, becomes leader of Central Committee of Workers' Party, 1956 K; defection of, 1956 L; refuses entry of UN observers, 1956 L
Kaffaria, Colony, S. Africa, united with Cape Colony, 1865 C
Kafka, Franz, Aus. author (1883–1924), 1920 U, 1925 U, 1926 U, 1956 T
Kahn, Gustave, F. poet (1859–1941), 1886 V
Kahn, Louis, I., Am. architect (b. 1917), 1960 S
Kaiser, Henry, Am. industrialist (b. 1882), 1943 O
Kajar dynasty, Persia, 1794 N
Kaleidoscope, invented, 1816 P
Kalinin, Mikhail Ivanovich, R. statesman (1875–1946), 1875 Z, 1946 Z
Kalisch, Cen. Poland: Prussia acquires, 1793 E; treaty, between Prussia and Russia, 1813 B
Kallman, Chester, Am. librettist, 1951 T
Kalstozov, Mikhail, R. film director, 1957 W
Kaluga, Russia, Russians recapture, 1941 W
Kamishari, N. Japan, solar eclipse observed at, 1936 P
Kamitz, Wenzel Anton, Prince von, Aus. chancellor (1711–94), 1768 M
Kampala, Uganda, 1955 H
Kampf, Ein (J. Dahn), 1876 U
Kanara, State, Bombay, India, 1763 N
Kandinsky, Wassily, R., later Am., artist (1866–1944), 1911 S, 1912 S, 1933 S, 1940 S
Kandy, King, of Ceylon, 1815 A
Kandyan Provinces, Ceylon, 1815 C
Kangaroo (D. H. Lawrence), 1923 U
K'ang Yu-wei, Chin. reformer, 1898 F
Kansas, state, US: settlement of, 1854 E; Civil war on slavery issue, 1856 E; becomes a US state, 1861 A; adopts women's suffrage, 1912 L
Kant, Immanuel, G. philosopher (1724–1804), 1770 R, 1781 R, 1783 R, 1784 R, 1785 R, 1788 R, 1790 R, 1793 R, 1795 R, 1797 R, 1798 R, 1799 R, 1804 Z
Kapital, Das (K. Marx), Vol. I, 1867 O; Vol. II, 1885 O; Vol. III, 1895 O; English edition of Vol. I, 1886 O
Kapp, Wolfgang, G. politician, leader of attempted *coup*, 1920 C
  followers of, pardoned, 1925 H
Karamzin, Nikolai Mikhailovich, R. historian (1765–1826), 1793 U, 1816 Q
Karachi, Pakistan, riots in, 1953 A
Karamanlis, Constantine, Greek politician, 1961 K, 1963 F
Karelia, Finland: Russians attack, 1940 B; ceded to Russia, 1940 C; Finns invade, 1941 F
Kariba Dam, Rhodesia, 1960 E
Karloff, Boris (W. H. Pratt), Am. film actor (b. 1887), 1931 W
Karlsruhe, W. Germany, chemical conference at, 1860 P
Karrer, O. Paul, Swi. biochemist (b. 1889), 1931 P, 1938 P
Kars, Russia: Russian take, 1855 L; Turkey transfers to Russia, 1877 L, 1878 C, G
Karume, Abdul Aman, president of Zanzibar, 1964 B
Kasavubu, Joseph, Congolese leader (b. 1910), 1961 C; as president of Congolese Republic, 1960 F; dismisses Lumumba, 1960 J; dismisses Tshombe, 1965 K; is deposed, 1965 L
Kashmir, India: admitted into Indian Union, 1947 K; problem of, referred to UN, 1947 M; fighting in, 1951 G; India's agreement with, 1952 G; votes for integration with India, 1956 L; is incorporated in India, 1957 A; disturbances, 1959 G; talks between India and Pakistan on, 1962 M; failure of, 1963 E
Kassala, Sudan: Dervishes take, 1885 G; Italians take, 1894 G; ceded to Egypt, 1897 M; British take, 1941 A
Kassem, Abdul Kerim, general, premier of Iraq, founds Palestinian Army, 1960 C; declares Kuwait part of Iraq, 1961 F; is assassinated, 1963 B
Kasserine Pass, Tunisia, 1943 B
Kästner, Erich, G. author, 1899 Z
Katanga, Congo: settled by Company, 1891 D; UN troops enter, 1960 H; UN breaks off relations, 1961 J; cease fire in, 1961 M; Tshombe ends secession of, 1961 M; UN plans for, 1962 J, 1963 A
Kätchen von Heilbronn, Das, 1808 W
Katsura, Japanese Prince, 1906 A, 1912 M
Katzbach, Germany, battle, 1813 H
Kaufman, George S., Am. dramatist (b. 1889), 1889 Z, 1939 W
Kaunda, Kenneth, Zambian, leader of National Independent Party (b. 1924); premier of Northern Rhodesia, 1962 M, 1964 A; president of Zambia, 1964 K
Kavalla, Greece, Greeks surrender at, 1916 J
Kawawa, Rashidj, Tanzanian politician, forms ministry, 1962 A
Kay, John, B. inventor (1704–64), 1764 Z
Kay-Shuttleworth, Sir T. P. *See under* Shuttleworth
Kazan, Elia, Am. film director, 1954 W, 1956 W
Kazviv, Persia, 1911 L
Kean, Edmund, B. actor (1787–1833), 1787 Z, 1814 W, 1820 W, 1833 W, Z
Keats, John, B. poet (1795–1821), 1795 Z, 1818 U, 1819 U, 1820 U, 1821 Z
Keble, John, B. divine and poet (1792–1866), 1792 Z, 1827 R, 1833 R, 1866 Z
Kedah, N.W. Malaya: Rajah of, 1786 H; becomes Siamese territory, 1826 F
Keele, Staffordshire, England, University college at, 1949 O

Keeler, Christine, B. model, 1963 G, M
Kefauver Committee on Crime in US inter-state commerce, 1951 C
Keilhau, formerly in Thuringia, now in Rudolstadt, E. Germany, Froebel's community at, 1816 O
Keitel, Wilhelm von, G. general, 1945 E
Keith, Sir Arthur, B. anthropologist (1866–1955), 1948 P
Kekulé, Friedrich August, G. chemist (1829–96), 1829 Z, 1865 P, 1896 Z
Keller, Gottfried, G. author (1819–90), 1819 Z, 1846 U, 1851 U, 1890 Z
Kellogg, Frank Billings, Am. statesman (1856–1937), 1856 Z, 1937 Z; becomes secretary of state, 1925 A; proposes pact for renunciation of war, 1927 M, 1928 D
Kellogg-Briand pact, 1928 D, F, H; embodied in Act of League Assembly, 1928 J; Germany accepts, 1929 B; in force, 1929 G; Rome Pact endorses, 1933 G
Kellogg, William Pitt, Am. politician, Republican governor of Louisiana (1830–1918), 1874 F
Kelly, Grace, Princess of Monaco (b. 1933), 1956 W
Kelly, William, B. steel engineer (1811–88), 1851 P
Kelmscott Press, 1890 S
Kelvin, lord. *See* Thomson, William
Kemble, John Mitchell, B. historian (1807–57), 1833 Q, 1849 Q
Kemel Atatürk, Turk. statesman (1881–1938), 1881 Z, 1907 M, 1919 H, 1922 L, 1923 K, 1927 J, 1938 L, 1938 Z; elected president of Turkey, 1923 H; suppresses Communist propaganda, 1929 F; takes name Atatürk, 1935 A; as author, 1927 O
Kemp, George Meikle, Scot. architect (1795–1844), 1840 S
Kenilworth (W. Scott), 1821 U
Kendall, James, B. chemist (b. 1889), 1915 P
Kendrew, John Cowdery, B. biophysicist (b. 1917), 1960 P
Kennan, George, Am. diplomat (b. 1904), Russia demands recall of, 1952 K
Kennedy, John Fitzgerald, Am. statesman, Democrat (1917–63), 35th president of US (1961–3), 1917 Z, wins presidential election, 1960 L
inaugurated, 1961 A
meets Macmillan, 1961 C, M, 1962 M, 1963 F
establishes Peace Corps, 1961 C
extra-ordinary State of Union message, 1961 E
visits Europe, 1961 E
sends L. B. Johnson to Berlin, 1961 H
envisages partnership with a United Europe, 1962 G
broadcast on installation of Russian missile base in Cuba, 1962 K
'Kennedy Round' tariff negotiations, 1963 E, 1964 E
speech on Civil Rights, 1963 F
is assassinated, 1963 L
Warren Report on assassination, 1964 O
Kennedy, Margaret, B. author, 1926 W
Kennedy, Michael, B. musicologist, 1964 T
Kennicott, Benjamin, B. Biblical scholar (1718–83), 1776 Q
Kennington, Eric Henri, B. artist (d. 1960), 1917 S
Kentucky, State, US: becomes a US state, 1792 F; legislature, 1798 N
Kenwood House, Middlesex, 1764 S, 1928 S, 1953 S
Kenya (formerly East African Protectorate), 1920 G; white settlers advocate closer ties with Uganda and Tanganyika, 1935 J; Italians driven from, 1941 A; emergency, 1953 D, 1959 L; becomes an independent Republic, 1963 M, 1964 M
Kenyatta, Jomo, Kenya, Nationalist leader (b. 1893), convicted of managing Mau Mau, 1953 D, G; released, 1961 D; becomes president of Kenya, 1964 M
Kenyon, Kathleen Mary, B. archaeologist (b. 1906), 1957 Q
Keppel, Henry, B. naval officer (1809–1904), 1809 Z, 1904 Z
Kenala, India, riots in, 1964 L
Kerch Peninsula, Russia, Germans attack, 1942 E
Keren, Ethiopia, British take, 1941 C
Kerensky, Alexander, R. politician (1881–1926), 1917 C, F; becomes premier, 1917 G; proclaims Republic, 1917 J; falls, 1917 L
Kermadec Isles, Pacific, annexed by New Zealand, 1887 A
Kern, Jerome, 1939 W
Kerosene, first manufactured, 1854 P
Kerouac, Jack, Am. author (b. 1922), 1957 U
Kerr, Deborah, B. film actress (b. 1923), 1956 W
Kerr, Robert Schomberg, Marquess of Lothian, B. administrator and journalist (1874–1930), 1910 V
Kerry, Munster, Ireland, Fenian outrages in, 1867 B
Kesselring, Albert, G. soldier (1886–1960), 1960 Z
Ketteler, Wilhelm Emmanuel, G. bishop of Mainz (1811–77), 1856 R
Kew Gardens, Surrey, England, 1835 P, 1840 P
Keyes, Roger, lord Keyes, B. naval officer (1872–1945), 1872 Z, 1945 Z
Keynes, John Maynard, B. economist (1883–1946), 1883 Z, 1919 O, 1926 O, 1930 O, 1936 O, 1943 O, 1946 Z
Key West, Florida, US, 1961 C
Khachaturian, Aram (b. 1908), R. musician, 1943 T
Khan, Ayub, Pakist. leader, 1965 A; forms ministry, 1958 K; elected president, 1960 B
Khana, Seretse, Bechuanaland politician (b. 1921), 1965 C
Kharkov, Russia: Bolsheviks capture, 1919 M; Germans take, 1941 K; fighting near, 1942 E; Russians recapture, 1943 B, H; Russians evacuate, 1943 C
Khartoum, Sudan: Gordon at, 1884 B; Mahdi takes, 1885 A; riots in, 1964 M
Khedda, Ben, Alger. leader, 1961 H
Khiva, Russia, Russians assume control of, 1873 H
Khorasan, in Khuzistan, Persia, 1796 N
Khrushchev, Nikita, R. statesman (b. 1894), 1894 Z, 1958 H, 1962 D, 1963 K
appointed first secretary of Central Committee, 1953 J
visits Yugoslavia, 1955 E
visits E. Germany, 1955 G
denounces Stalin's policies, 1956 B
visits Britain, 1956 D
appeals to Labour and Socialist parties to prevent US aggression in Middle East, 1957 K
proposals for immediate summit meeting rejected, 1958 G
visits Peking, 1958 G
warns US against attacking China, 1958 J
visits Albania, 1959 E
reaffirms Oder–Neisse Line as German frontier, 1959 G
calls for denuclearised zone in Europe, 1959 G
addresses UN, 1959 J, 1960 J
visits Peking, 1959 J
invited to Summit Conference, 1959 M
visits India, Burma and Indonesia, 1960 B
protests against possibility of Spain providing bases for W. Germany, 1960 C
attends Summit Conference, 1960 E

Khrushchev—*contd.*
wages campaign against Hammarskjöld, 1961 B
proposes a German peace conference, 1961 F
proposes disarmament and test-ban talks proceed simultaneously, 1961 F
proposes disarmament committee meet at summit level, 1962 B
in Cuban crisis, 1962 K
opens Aswan Dam, 1964 E
is replaced by Brezhnev and Kosygin, 1964 K
Kiamil Pasha, grand vizier of Turkey, 1909 B
Kiao-chow, Shantung, N. China: Germany occupies, 1897 L; Japan demands German withdrawal, 1914 H
Kidd, Benjamin, B. sociologist (1858–1916), 1894 O
Kidnappings:
of Lindbergh's son, 1932 O
of English teacher from Lusaka, 1964 H
Kiel, W. Germany: acquired by Prussia, 1865 H; Canal, 1895 P; Treaty, between Denmark and Sweden, 1914 A, D; German naval mutiny at, 1918 L
Kielce, Poland, pogrom in, 1946 G
Kierkegaard, Søren, Dan. theologian (1813–55), 1813 Z, 1843 R, 1855 Z
Kiev, Russia: Germans occupy, 1918 C; Bolsheviks take, 1919 B; Denikin's force enters, 1919 J; Poles enter, 1920 E; Germans take, 1941 J; Russians recapture, 1943 L
Kikuyu, tribe in Kenya, 1953 D
Killing of Sister George, The (F. Marcus), 1965 W
Kilmainham Treaty, between Parnell and British government, 1882 E
Kilmuir, Lord. *See* Maxwell Fyfe, D.
Kiln, tunnel, 1839 P
Kim (R. Kipling), 1901 U
Kimberley, Earl of. *See* Wodehouse, John
Kimberley, Griqualand West, S. Africa: Britain annexes diamond fields, 1871 K; amalgamation of mining companies, 1888 O; railway reaches, 1885 L
Kinder der Welt (P. Heyse), 1873 U
Kindergarten, the first, 1837 O
Kinetic theory of gases, 1850 P
Kinetoscope, the, 1894 W
King, Edward, B. churchman, Bishop of Lincoln (1829–1910), 1890 R
King, Horace, B. Labour politician (b. 1901), elected Speaker, 1965 J
King, Martin Luther, Am. Negro leader (b. 1929), 1964 K, 1965 C
King, William Mackenzie, Can. statesman, Liberal (1874–1950), 1874 Z, 1919 H, 1937 H; becomes premier, 1921 M; maintains ministry with Labour support, 1925 K; resigns, 1926 F; forms ministry, 1926 J, 1935 K, 1945 F; confers with Churchill and Roosevelt, 1943 H
'King and Country' debate, in Oxford Union, 1933 O
King Cotton (T. Armstrong), 1947 U
King George V, His Life and Reign (H. Nicolson), 1952 Q
King George VI, His Life and Reign (J. Wheeler-Bennett), 1958 Q
King Henry III and the Lord Edward (F. M. Powicke), 1947 Q
Kinglake, Alexander William, B. traveller and author (1809–91), 1844 U, 1863 Q
King René's Daughter (H. Hertz), 1845 U
Kingsley, Charles, B. author, churchman and social reformer (1819–75), 1819 Z, 1849 U, 1853 U, 1854 U, 1863 U, 1875 Z; founds Christian Socialism, 1849 R
King's Mountain, N. Carolina, US, battle, 1780 K
King Solomon's Mines (R. Haggard), 1886 U
Kinsey, A. C., Am. psychologist (b. 1907), 1948 P
Kipling, Rudyard, B. author (1865–1936), 1865 Z, 1888 U, 1892 U, 1894 U, 1897 U, 1899 U, 1901 U, 1902 U, 1936 Z
Kipps (H. G. Wells), 1905 U
Kirchhoff, Johann Wilhelm Adolf, G. classical scholar (1826–1908), 1859 P
Kirchner, Ernst, G. artist, 1905 S
Kirk, Sir John, B. naturalist and administrator (1832–1922), 1873 F
Kirkuk, Iraq, pipelines from, 1935 P
Kirkwood, David, B. Labour politician, 1925 C
Kirov, Serge, R. politician, 1943 M
Kirstein, Lincoln Edward, Am. choreographer (b. 1907), 1933 T
Kiss, The (Rodin), 1898 S
Kitchener, Horatio, Lord Kitchener, B. soldier (1850–1916), 1850 Z, 1915 V, 1916 F, G; in Sudan, 1896 J, 1898 D; in S. Africa, 1900 A, 1901 A
Kinkiang, China, British concessions at, reduced, 1927 B
Kiwanuka, Benedicte, premier of Uganda, 1962 C
Klanges, J., Am. graphologist, 1932 P
Kléber, Jean Baptiste, F. general (1753–1800), 1800 C
Klebs, Edwin, G. pathologist (1834–1913), 1834 Z
Klee, Paul, Swi. artist (1879–1940), 1918 S, 1921 S, 1922 S, 1929 S, 1933 S
Kleist, Heinrich von, G. author (1777–1811), 1808 W, 1811 U
Klenze, Les, G. architect (1784–1864), 1816 S, 1830 S, 1846 T
Klenk, Micheal de, Du. architect, 1921 S
Klinger, Friedrich Maximilian von, G. dramatist (1752–1831), 1776 W
Klinger, Max, G. artist (1857–1920), 1857 Z, 1897S, 1920 Z
Klondyke, Yukon, Canada, gold rush, 1897 P
Klopstock, Friedrich Gottlieb, G. poet (1724–1803), 1771 U, 1773 U
'Kneel-in' campaigns in American churches, 1960 R
Knickerbocker's History of New York (W. Irving), 1809 U
Knight, Dame Laura, B. artist, 1936 S, 1939 S, 1965 S
Knott, Kathleen, B. poet, 1947 U
Knowledge of the External World (B. Russell), 1914 R
Knowles, Sir James Thomas, B. journalist and architect (1831–1908), 1869 R, 1877 V
Knox, Ronald Arbuthnot, B. Roman Catholic dignitary and Biblical scholar (1888–1957), 1888 Z, 1946 Q, 1950 R, 1957 Z
Knox peace resolution, 1920 E
Koc, Adam, Pol. politician, 1937 C
Koch, Robert, G. physician (1843–1910), 1877 P, 1883 P
Kodak box camera, 1888 P
Kodak company, 1929 P
Kodachrome film, 1935 P
Kodály, Zoltan, Hung. musician (b. 1882), 1923 T, 1961 T
Koestler, Arthur, Hung. author (b. 1905), 1905 Z, 1949 R, 1950 O, 1954 O, 1964 R
Koffee, King, of Ashanti, 1824 B
Koje Island, Korea, riots in prison camp, 1952 E
Kokoschka, Oskar, Aus. artist (b. 1886), 1886 Z, 1909 S, 1914 S, 1926 S, 1955 S, 1962 S
Kokovtsoff, Vladimir, R., becomes premier, 1911 J
Kolarov, Vassil, Bulg. politician, 1950 B

Kolbe, Adolphe Wilhelm Hermann, G. chemist (1818–84), 1845 P
Köller, Franz, Aus. inventor of tungsten-steel, 1855 P
Kölliker, Rudolph von, G. scientist (1817–1905), 1840 P
Kolozsvár, Hungary, diet at, 1865 M
Kölreuter, Joseph Gottlieb, G. botanist (1733–1806), 1763 P
Koltchak, Alexander, R. admiral, 1920 A
Kondylis, George, president of Greece, 1926 H
Konieh, Turkey, battle, 1832 M
Königgratz, formerly Sadowa, Austria, battle, 1866 G
Konoye, Jap. Prince, becomes premier, 1937 F
Kon-Tiki Expedition, The (T. Heyerdahl), 1950 P
Kopper, Karl, G. philosopher, 1945 R
Körber, Ernst von, Aust. politician (1860–1919), 1900 A
Korda, Sir Alexander, B. film producer (1893–1956), 1893 Z, 1933 W
Korea:
 declared independent, 1876 B, 1895 L
 US trading rights in, 1882 E
 declares war on China, 1894 G
 Queen assassinated, 1895 K
 Russian position in, recognised, 1896 E
 intervention of Russia and Japan in, 1897 K
 Japan seeks concessions in, 1901 L
 independence guaranteed, 1902 A
 Russian concessions annulled, 1904 B
 Japanese interests in, recognised by Russia, 1905 J
 Japanese protectorate over, 1905 L, 1907 G
 Japanese dictatorship in, 1909 K
 Russo-Japanese agreement on, 1910 G
 Japan annexes, 1910 H
 is placed under US and USSR occupation, 1945 J
 the Allies demand democratic government in, 1945 M
 Republic proclaimed, 1948 H
 Democratic Republic formed, 1948 J
 US withdraws occupying force, 1949 F
 See also under Wars, Korean
Korngold, Erich Wolfgang, Aus. musician (1897–1957), 1916 T
Kornilov, Lavr, R. general, 1917 J
Korsákov, Alexander Mikhailovich, R. general, 1799 J
Korzeniowski, Josef Konrad. *See* Conrad, Joseph
Kościuszko, Tadeusz Andrzej, Pol. Nationalist (1746–1817), 1794 C
Kössel, H., G. chemist, 1916 P
Kossuth, Louis, Hung. patriot (1802–94), 1848 J
Kostrowitsky, Wilhelm. *See* Apollinaire, Guillaume
Kosygin, Alexei Nikolaevich, R. statesman (b. 1904), 1904 Z
 becomes premier, 1964 K
Kotalawala, Sir John, Ceyl. premier, 1953 K
Kötzebue, August, G. dramatist (1761–1819), 1797 W, 1819 C, H
Koussevitsky, Sergei, Am. musician (1874–1951), 1924 T
Kowloon, China, leased to Britain, 1898 C
Krafft-Ebing, Richard, baron, G. psychologist (1840–1902), 1886 P
Krasnoyarsk, Russia, 1920 A
Krassin, Leonid, R. trade delegate, 1920 E
Krause, Karl Christian Friedrich, G. philosopher (1781–1832), 1804 R
Kray de Krajof, Paul, Baron Kray, Aus. general (1735–1804), 1779 D, 1800 D
Křenek Ernst, Hung. musician (b. 1893), 1927 T, 1941 T, 1960 T
Kreutzer Sonata, The (L. Tolstoy), 1890 U
Kriloff, Ivan, R. author (1768–1844), 1809 U
Krilium, synthetic chemical, 1951 P
Krishna Menon, Vengali Krishnan, Ind. statesman (b. 1897), 1897 Z, 1957 D, O
Kristin Lavransdatter (S. Undset), 1920 U
Kritische Walder (Herder), 1769 U
Krivoy Rog, Ukraine, Russia, Russians recapture, 1944 B
Kroger, Helen and Peter, B. spies, 1961 O
Kronstadt, Russia, French navy visits, 1891 G
Kropotkin, Peter Alexeivich, R. revolutionary (1842–1921), 1884 O
Kruger, Stephanus Johannes Paulus, S. African statesman (1825–1904), 1825 Z, 1880 M, 1899 C, G, 1904 Z; president of Transvaal, 1883 C, 1893 D, 1898 B; William II's telegram to, 1896 A; ultimatum to Britain, 1899 K; flight, 1900 K
Krumir Tribe, N. Africa, raids by, 1881 C
Krupp, Alfred, G. metallurgist (1812–87), 1812 Z, 1849 P, 1887 Z
Krypton, gas, 1903 P
Ktima, Cyprus, 1964 C
Kuala Lumpur, Malaya, Japanese take, 1942 A
Kuban, Russia: Russia annexation, 1783 G; agreed by Turkey, 1784 A; Russia's recapture, 1943 K
Kubicks, Stanley, Am. film director, 1964 W
Kubla Khan (S. T. Coleridge), 1797 U, 1816 U
Kühlmann, Richard von, G. foreign minister, 1917 H
Kuhmo Lake, Finland, Russian attack near, 1940 B
Kuibishev, Russia, government moved to, 1941 K
Ku-Klux-Klan, in US, 1922 O, 1965 C, K
Kulturkampf, in Germany, 1871 G
Kumasi, Ghana, 1874 B
Kun, Bela, Hung. Socialist, 1919 H
Künstler, Die (F. Schiller), 1789 U
Kunstmythologie (K. A. Böttiger), 1811 Q
Kuo Min Tang. *See under* Political Parties
Kurak, Russia, Russians take, 1943 B
Kurdla, India, 1795 C
Kurds, tribe, rising by, 1930 G
Kurosawa, Akira, Jap. film director, 1950 W
Kursk, Russia: Germans take, 1941 L; German offensive at, 1943 G
Kutahia, Turkey, battle, 1921 G
Kutchuk-Kainardji, Bulgaria, peace signed at, 1774 G
Kut-el-Amara, Mesopotamia, 1915 J, 1916 D
Kutno, Russia, Germans break through at, 1914 L
Kuwait: admitted to Arab League, 1961 F; Kassem declares is part of Iraq, 1961 F; British troops sent to, 1961 F
Kwang-su, Emperor of China (1875–1908), 1875 A
Kyber Pass, E. Afghanistan, British occupy, 1879 E
Kymograph, for measuring blood pressure, 1865 P
Kynoch, George, B. gunsmith (1834–91), 1882 P
Kynshu, Japan, US naval mutiny at, 1945 D

L

Là-bas (J. Huysmans), 1891 U
Labiche, Eugène Maria, F. dramatist (1815–88), 1860 W
Labouchere, Henry du Pré, B. Liberal politician (1831–1912), 1831 Z, 1912 Z
Labour, treatise on, 1848 O

Labour codes:
in France, 1912 O
in Italy, 1927 D
Labour Day, May Day celebrations, 1890 O
Labour Department, German, founded, 1892 C
Labour Exchanges in Britain, 1910 O
Labour, Ministry, British, 1917 O
minister's powers for dealing with strikes, agitation against, 1944 D
Labour, Ministry, in Germany, 1918 O
Labour Parties. *See under* Political Parties
Lachmann, Karl Konrad Friedrich Wilhelm, G. classical scholar (1793–1851), 1850 Q
Lacordaire, Jean Baptiste Henri, F. ecclesiastic (1802–61), 1838 R
Ladisla, J., Hung., inventor, 1938 P
Ladoga, Lake, Finland, shores of, ceded to Russia, 1940 C
Lady Chatterley's Lover (D. H. Lawrence), 1928 U; publication of, 1959 O
Lady of Shalott, The (Tennyson), 1832 U
Lady of the Lake, The (W. Scott), 1810 U
Ladysmith, Natal, S. Africa: surrenders to Joubert, 1899 L; relieved, 1900 B
Lady's Not for Burning (C. Fry), 1948 W
Lady Windermere's Fan (O. Wilde), 1892 W
Lafayette, Marie Joseph Paul Yves du Motier, Marquis de, F. soldier (1757–1834), 1791 G; in America, 1777 D, 1781 J; commands National Guard, 1789 G; portrait, 1825 S
La Fontaine et ses Fables (H. Taine), 1853 Q
Laforgue, Jules, F. poet (1860–87), 1885 U
Lagerlöf, Selmar, Swe. author (1858–1940), 1858 Z, 1901 U, 1940 Z
Lagos, Nigeria, as a British Colony, 1886 A
Lagos Charter for Pan-African Co-operation, 1962 A
Lagrange, Joseph Louis, Comte de, F. mathematician (1737–1813), 1788 P, 1797 P, 1813 Z
Laguardia, Fionello Henry, Am. mayor of New York (1882–1947), 1882 Z, 1947 Z
Lahore, Pakistan, Treaty, between Britain and Sikhs, 1846 C
Laibach, now Yugoslavia, Conference, 1820 M, 1821 A, B
Laienbrever (L. Schefer), 1834 U
Laing's Neck, Transvaal, S. Africa, British defeat at, 1881 A
Lakanal, Joseph, F. politician (1762–1845), 1795 O
Lake, Gerard, lord Lake, B. soldier (1744–1803), 1797 C, 1798 F
Lallement, Pierre, F. inventor of 'bone-shaker' bicycle, 1865 P
Lamarck, Jean Baptiste Antoine de Monnel, Chevalier de, F. naturalist (1744–1829), 1803 P, 1809 P, 1815 P
Lamarque, General, F., 1832 F
Lamartine, Alphonse de, F. author (1790–1869), 1790 Z, 1820 U, 1823 U, 1836 U, 1869 Z; heads provisional government, 1848 B
Lamb, Charles, B. essayist (1775–1834), 1775 Z, 1807 U, 1820 U, 1834 Z
Lamb, Henry, B. artist (1883–1960), 1940 S
Lamb, Mary, B. author (1764–1847), 1807 U
Lamb, William, Viscount Melbourne, B. Whig statesman (1779–1848), 1779 Z, 1839 E; forms ministry, 1834 G; resigns, 1834 L; forms ministry, 1835 D; resigns, 1841 H
Lambert, Constant, B. musician (1905–1951), 1905 Z, 1926 T, 1929 T, 1936 T, 1951 Z
Lambeth Walk, The, 1938 W
Lambton, John George, Earl of Durham, B. colonial governor (1792–1840), 1838 E, K; report on Canada, 1839 B
Lamennais, Hughes, Félicité Robert de, F. author (1782–1854), 1782 Z, 1817 R, 1830 O, 1834 R, 1854 Z
Lamp, acetylene, 1900 P
carbon filament, 1878 P
fluorescent, 1927 P
miner's safety (Davy), 1815 P
ultra violet, 1904 P
Lanark, New, Scotland, 1800 O
Lancaster, Joseph, B. educationalist (1778–1838), 1778 Z, 1803 O, 1808 O, 1838 Z
Land, Edwin, B. scientist, 1932 P
Land, use of, comparative statistics of, 1965 Y
Land:
in Britain, nationalisation advocated, 1775 O
Uthwatt Report on, 1942 O
Land Commission, 1965 O
in Ireland, Land League, 1878 K
land purchase, 1903 G
in S. Africa, land tenure legislation, 1946 F
in US, squatters' rights, 1841 N
minimum prices fixed, 1820 D
Lander, John, B. explorer of Africa (1807–39), 1830 P
Lander, Richard Lemon, B. explorer of Africa (1804–34), 1830 P
Landon, A. M., Am. Republican, 1936 L
Landor, Walter Savage, B. author (1775–1864), 1775 Z, 1798 U, 1824 U, 1864 Z
Landscape into Art (K. Clark), 1949 S
Landscapes and Departures (K. Knott), 1947 U
Landseer, Sir Edwin Henry, B. artist (1802–73), 1818 S
Lane, Sir Allen, B. publisher (b. 1902), 1936 U
Lane, Elizabeth, B. judge (b. 1905), 1965 O
Lane, Sir Hugh, bequest by, 1915 S
Lange, Friedrich Albert, G. philosopher (1828–75), 1866 R
Langensalza, W. Germany, 1866 F
Langhans, Karl Gotthard, G. architect (1732–1808), 1791 S
Langley, Samuel Pierpont, Am. physicist and astronomer (1834–1906), 1881 P, 1896 P
Language and Wisdom of the Indians (F. Schlegel), 1808 Q
Language, Truth and Logic (A. J. Ayer), 1936 R
Languages:
Czech, in Bohemia, ordinances for, 1897 D, L; repealed, 1899 K
Basic English, 1932 O, 1947 O, 1949 R
Dutch, in S. Africa, 1879 O
Esperanto, 1887 O
Flemish, in Flanders provinces of Belgium, 1873 N, 1878 O, 1932 G
German, enforced in Bohemia, 1783 F
Hindi, official language of India, 1965 O
Latin, Pope John XXIII insists on retention of, 1962 R
Romanset, in Switzerland, 1937 O
Sinhalese, in Ceylon, 1956 G
Laniel, Joseph, French politician, 1953 F, M
Lankester, Edwin, B. scientist (1814–74), 1884 P
Lankester, Sir Edwin Ray, B. scientist (1847–1929), 1916 P
Lansbury, George, B. Labour politician (1859–1940), 1859 Z, 1912 L, 1935 A; resigns to fight by-election on issue of women's vote, 1912 L
Lansdowne, Marquess of. *See* Petty-Fitzmaurice

Lansing, Robert, Am. Secretary of State (1864–1928), 1915 F, 1920 B
Laocoön (Lessing), 1766 Q
Laon, France: battle, 1814 C; French take, 1918 K
Laos, Viet Nam, 1953 D; French protectorate over, 1893 N; France pledges to respect inpependence, 1954 G; recognises UN as arbiter, 1959 B; emergency in, 1959 G; *coup* in, 1960 H; disturbances in, 1961 D; Princes, invited to Geneva talks, 1962 A; fighting resumed, 1962 D; Geneva Conference guarantees neutrality of, 1962 G; establishes relations with Communist China and Vietnam, 1962 J; Russia calls for conference on, 1964 G
Laplace, Pierre Simon, Marquis de, F. mathematician and astronomer (1749–1827), 1788 P, 1796 P, 1812 P, 1827 Z
Larkin, Philip, B. poet (b. 1922), 1964 U
Larousse, Pierre, F. lexicographer, 1866 Q
Laski, Harold Joseph, B. political scientist (1893–1950), 1893 Z, 1925 O, 1930 O, 1943 O, 1950 Z
Lassalle, Ferdinand, G. Socialist (1825–64), 1825 Z, 1859 O, 1861 O, 1862 O, 1864 Z
Last Chronicle of Barset, The (A. Trollope), 1867 U
Last Days of Hitler, The (H. R. Trevor-Roper), 1947 Q
Last Days of Pompeii, The (Lytton), 1834 U
Last of the Barons, The (Lytton), 1843 U
Last of the Mohicans, The (J. F. Cooper), 1826 U
Last Puritan, The (G. Santayana), 1933 U
Last Tycoon, The (S. Fitzgerald), 1941 U
Late George Apley, The (J. P. Marquand), 1937 U
Late Mattia Pascal, The (Pirandello), 1923 W
Lateran Treaty, for independence of Vatican City, 1929 B
Later Roman Empire, The (A. H. M. Jones), 1964 Q
Latham, Peter, B. sportsman, 1895 X
Lathanum discovered, 1839 P
Lathe, carriage, 1797 P
  screw-cutting, 1800 P
Latreille, Pierre André, F. naturalist (1762–1833), 1806 P
Latvia, independence of, 1918 D, L
Lauder, Sir Harry, B. comedian, 1870 Z, 1950 Z
Lauenberg, W. Germany: duchy, annexed by Napoleon, 1810 M; part of, returned to Denmark, 1815 F; ceded by Denmark to Austria and Prussia, 1864 K; purchased by Prussia, 1865 H
Laughton, Charles, B. actor (1899–1965), 1899 Z, 1933 W, 1965 Z
Laurent, Auguste, F. chemist (1807–53), 1846 P
Laurier, Sir Wilfred, Can. statesman (1841–1919), 1896 G
Lausanne, Switzerland: Treaty, between Italy and Turkey, 1912 K; Conference, 1923 B, E; Treaty, between Greece, Turkey and Allies, 1923 G; Treaty, for establishing World Peace, 1924 H; Conference on Faith and Order, 1927 R; Anglo-French Treaty of friendship, 1932 F; Reparations Conference at, 1932 F
Laval, Carl Gustaf Patrik de, Swe. engineer (1845–1913), 1877 P, 1887 P
Laval, Pierre, F. politician (1883–1945), 1883 Z, 1945 Z; as premier, 1931 A, 1935 F; proposals with Hoare, on Italy, 1935 M; falls, 1936 A
Lavater, Johann Kaspar, Swi. author (1741–1801), 1767 U
Laveleye, Émile Louis Victor de, Belg. author (1822–92), 1875 R
Lavengro (G. Borrow), 1851 U
Lavigerie, Charles Martial Allemand, F. Cardinal (1825–92), 1890 L
Lavoisier, Antoine Laurent, F. chemist (1743–94), 1774 P, 1780 P, 1787 P, 1789 P, 1794 Z
Law, Andrew Bonar, B. Conservative politician (1858–1923), 1858 Z, 1918 L, 1923 Z; becomes Unionist leader, 1911 L; resigns leadership, 1921 C; becomes premier, 1922 K; resigns, 1923 E
Law, International, Geneva Conference on law of the sea, 1958 O
Law:
  in Britain, commission, 1965 O
  in Russia, land, 1843 O
    codified, 1830 O
  See also Codes of law; Legislation
Law, studies in, 1789 O, 1798 O, 1814 O, 1815 Q
Law of Conservation of Energy (J. Mayer), 1842 P
Law of the Constitution (A. V. Dicey), 1886 O
Law, The (R. Vailland), 1957 U
Lawes, Sir John Bennett, B. agriculturalist (1814–1900), 1843 P
Lawler, L. Austral. dramatist, 1955 W
Lawn-tennis:
  invented, 1874 X
  Wimbledon championships, 1877 X, 1895 X, 1919 X, 1920 X, 1927 X
  Lawn Tennis Association founded, 1888 X
  Davis Cup, 1900 X
  US championships, 1881 X
Lawrence, David Herbert, B. author (1885–1930), 1885 Z, 1911 U, 1913 U, 1915 U, 1921 U, 1922 U, 1923 U, 1926 U, 1928 U, 1930 Z, 1959 O
Lawrence, Ernest O., Am. nuclear physicist (1901–1958), 1931 P, 1934 P, 1940 P
Lawrence, Richard Smith, Am. inventor (1817–92), 1855 P
Lawrence, Sir Thomas, B. artist (1769–1830), 1769 Z, 1811 S, 1830 Z
Lawrence, Thomas Edward ('Lawrence of Arabia', *alias* 'T. E. Shaw'), B. soldier and author (1888–1935), 1888 Z, 1926 U, 1927 O, 1935 Q
Lawrence Commission on MPs. salaries, 1964 L
Laws of Radiation (Max Planck), 1901 P
Laws of Thought on which are founded the Mathematical Theories of Logic and Probabilities, The (G. Boole), 1854 R
Layard, Sir Austen Henry, B. archaeologist (1817–1894), 1845 Q
Lay of the Last Minstrel, The (W. Scott), 1805 U
Lay patronage, issue of, in Scotland, 1843 R
Lays of Ancient Rome (T. B. Macaulay), 1842 U
Layton-Wiggin Report on credit for Germany, 1931 H
Lazarus, Moritz, G. philosopher (1824–1903), 1859 R
Leacock, Stephen, B. humorist, 1869 Z, 1944 Z
Leaflet Raids on Germany, 1939 J
League of Nations:
  Peace Conference adopts principle of, 1919 A
  Wilson presides at first meeting, 1919 B
  Covenant of, laid before Peace Conference, 1919 B
    campaign in US against, 1919 B, L, 1920 A, C
    comes into force, 1920 A
    is endorsed by Rome Pact, 1933 G
    is separated from Versailles Treaty, 1938 K
  Council first meets, 1920 A
  admissions to. *See below* under League Membership
  takes over Saar, 1920 B
  moves to Geneva, 1920 K
  Harding declared US could play no part in, 1921 D
  approves mandated territories, 1922 G
  Greece appeals to, over Corfu, 1923 J
  re-organises Hungarian finances, 1924 D

League of Nations—*centd.*
Germany's terms for joining, 1924 J
adopts Geneva protocol, 1924 K
advises against partition of Mosul, 1925 H, M
Bulgaria appeals to, over Greece, 1925 K, M
Council, Canada acquires seat on, 1927 L
decides Lithuanian-Polish dispute, 1927 M
Act of, embodies Kellogg-Briand Pact, 1928 J
rules against Norway's annexation of Greenland, 1931 G
Council, US delegates attend, 1931 K
orders Peru to withdraw from Columbia, 1932 J
Lytton Report on Manchuria, to, 1932 K
adopted, 1933 B
holds Peace Ballot, 1935 F
imposes sanctions against Italy, 1935 K, 1936 G
Britain's role in, Labour Party view of, 1937 J
pronounces Japan the aggressor, 1938 J
separates Covenant from Versailles Treaty, 1938 K
Assembly dissolved, 1946 D
League of Nations, membership of:
Abyssinia joins, 1923 J
Albania joins, 1920 M
Argentine joins, 1920 A
Austria joins, 1920 M
Bulgaria joins, 1920 M
Costa Rica joins, 1920 M
Denmark joins, 1920 C
Egypt joins, 1937 E
Estonia joins, 1921 J
Finland joins, 1920 M
Germany, gives terms for membership, 1924 J
applies for membership, 1926 B
membership prevented by Brazil and Spain, 1926 C
joins, 1926 J
leaves, 1933 K
Holland, joins, 1920 C
Hungary joins, 1922 J
leaves, 1939 D
Iraq joins, 1932 K
Irish Free State joins, 1923 J
Italy leaves, 1937 M
Japan announces she will leave, 1933 E
leaves, 1938 K
Latvia joins, 1921 J
Lithuania joins, 1921 J
Mexico joins, 1932 M
Norway joins, 1920 C
Paraguay leaves, 1937 B
Russia joins, 1934 J
is expelled from, 1939 M
Spain threatens withdrawal from, 1926 F, J
leaves, 1939 E
Switzerland joins, 1920 B
Turkey joins, 1932 G
US Senate rejects membership, 1920 A, C
League of Nations, The (A. F. Pollard), 1918 O
Leake, William Martin, B. classical scholar and numismatist (1777–1860), 1812 O
Leakey, Louis Seymour Bazett, B. archaeologist (b. 1903), 1903 Z, 1959 P
Lean, David, B. film producer (b. 1908), 1946 W, 1957 W, 1962 W
Lear, Edward, B. artist and humorist (1812–88), 1846 U
Leather, D., B. athlete, 1954 X
'Leatherstocking' novels of J. F. Cooper, 1823 U
Leaves of Grass (W. Whitman), 1855 U
Leavis, Frank Raymond, B. author and critic (b. 1895), 1930 O, 1932 U, 1952 U, 1962 U
Lebanon, The: mandated to France, 1920 D; Republic proclaimed, 1926 E; cease-fire in, 1945 E; British and French evacuate, 1946 C; amnesty in, 1958 M
Lebas, Louis Hippolyte, F. architect (1782–1860), 1823 S
Leben des Quintus Fixlein (Jean Paul), 1796 U
Leblanc, Nicholas, F. chemist (1742–1806), 1787 P
Lebon, Philippe, F. chemist (1769–1804), 1798 P
Lebrun, Albert, F. statesman (1871–1950), 1871 Z, 1932 E, 1950 Z
Lecky, William Edward Hartpole, B. historian (1838–1903), 1838 Z, 1865 Q, 1869 Q, 1878 Q, 1903 Z
Lecocq, Alexandre Charles, F. composer (1832–1918), 1872 T
Leçon de morale, Une (P. Éluard), 1949 U
Leconte de Lisle, Charles Marie, F. author (1818–1894), 1884 U
Lectures on Dramatic Art and Literature (A. Schlegel), 1809 U
Lectures on the Decorative Arts (O. Wilde), 1882 S
Lectures on the Eastern Church (A. P. Stanley), 1861 Q
Lectures on the English Poets (W. Hazlitt), 1818 U
Lectures on the Feudal and English Laws (F. S. Sullivan), 1772 O
Lectures on the Philosophy of the Human Mind (T. Brown), 1820 R
Leda Senza Cigno, La (D'Annunzio), 1916 U
Lee, Ann., B. revivalist (1736–84), 1774 R
Lee, Arthur Hamilton, lord Lee of Fareham (1868–1947), 1921 O
Lee, Lawrence, B. artist, 1962 S
Lee, Richard Henry, Am. statesman (1732–94), 1776 E, F
Lee, Robert Edward, Am. Confederate general (1807–70), 1862 M, 1864 E; defeated at Gettysberg, 1863 G; capitulates at Appomattox, 1865 D
Lee, Sir Sidney, B. author and editor, 1859 Z, 1926 Z
Leech, John, B. caricaturist (1817–64), 1817 Z, 1841 V, 1864 Z
Leeds, Yorkshire, England: coal carriage at, 1811 P; Yorkshire college founded, 1874 O
Leeward Islands, Federation of, 1956 F
Left Book Club, 1935 O
Legacy, A (S. Bedford), 1957 U
Legal aid, in Britain, 1950 O
Legal Studies, Institute of Advanced, London, 1948 O
Légende des Siècles, La (V. Hugo), 1859 U
Légende d'Uylenspiegel (C. de Coster), 1867 U
Legendre, Adrien Marie, F. mathematician (1752–1833), 1794 P
Legends or Flowers (M. Tompa), 1854 U
Léger, Fernand, F. artist (1881–1955), 1912 S, 1921 S, 1924 W, 1941 S, 1948 S, 1950 S
Legge, William, Earl of Dartmouth, B. politician (1731–1801), 1775 L
Leghorn, Italy: British raid, 1941 B; Allies take, 1944 G
Legion of Honour, 1802 E
Legislation:
in Australia, Financial Agreement Enforcement, 1932 N
Immigration restriction, 1902 G
for troops to work mines during strike, 1949 H
in Austria, anti-Hapsburg laws abolished, 1935 G
in Britain, Agricultural Holdings, 1875 O
Air Raid Precautions, 1937 L

Legislation

Aliens, 1792 M
Allotments, 1887 O
Apothecaries, 1815 O
Appellate Jurisdiction, 1876 L
Apprentices (1563), repealed, 1814 O
Artisans' Dwellings, 1867 O, 1890 O
Ashbourne, for loans to Irish tenants, 1885 H
Asylums, inspection of, 1842 O
Australia Government, 1850 H
Ballot, 1872 G
Bank Charter, 1844 G
Bankruptcy, 1883 G
Benefices, 1898 R
British Citizenship, 1948 G
British North America, 1867 C
British Possessions, 1846 H
Building Societies, 1874 O
Burials, 1880 R
Canada Constitution, 1791 E, 1840 G
Cash payments, 1819 G
Chimney Sweeps, 1834 O
Cinematograph Licensing, 1909 W
Coal Mines, 1911 O
Colonial Welfare and Development, 1940 O
Combinations, 1800 O
  repealed, 1824 O, 1825 G
Commonwealth Immigration, 1961 L, 1962 O
Control of Office and Industrial Development, 1964 M
Conventicle, repealed, 1812 R
Copyhold, 1887 O
Copyright, 1911 O
Corn Laws, 1815 C
  amended, 1822 G, 1828 G
  repealed, 1846 E
Corrupt Practices in elections, 1883 H
Criminal Justice, 1961 D, 1963 H
Curwen's, to prevent sale of Parliamentary seats, 1809 F
Death penalty, Abolition of, 1956 F, 1965 L
Defence of Realm, 1915 O
Department of Scientific and Industrial Research, 1956 O
Depressed Areas, 1934 L
Ecclesiastical Titles, 1851 H
  repealed, 1871 R
Education (Forster's), 1870 H, O
Education, 1902 M
Education (Fisher's), 1918 H
Education (Butler's), 1944 O
Education for Wales, 1889 O
Emergency Powers, 1939 H
Employers' Liability, 1880 O
Enabling, for Church Assembly, 1919 R
Factory, 1833 H, 1844 F, 1847 F
Factory Inspection, 1867 H
First Offenders, 1958 O
Food and Drugs, 1860 O, 1875 O
Fraudulent Mediums, 1951 R
Government of India, 1935 H
Government of Ireland, 1920 M, 1921 D
Habeas Corpus, suspended, 1793 C, 1801 D, 1817 C, 1818 A
  in Ireland, 1866 B, 1881 C
Health and Morals of Apprentices, 1802 O
Horne Tooke, 1801 F
Housing, 1919 O
Hovering, against smuggling, 1784 G
Imperial Preference Provisions, 1919 H
Indian Councils, 1909 E
Industrial and Provident Societies, 1876 O
Irish Coercion, 1881 A
Irish Crimes, 1887 A
Irish Free State, 1924 K
Irish Land, 1870 H, 1881 H
Irish Land Purchase, 1903 G
Irish University, 1873 C
Jewish Disabilities, removal of, 1858 G
Judicature, 1873 O
Juvenile Offenders, 1854 O
Labourers' Dwellings, 1874 O
Landlord and Tenant, 1954 O
Legitimisation, 1959 O
Libel, 1792 O
Local Government, 1888 H
Machinery of Government, 1964 M
Married Women's Property, 1870 H, 1882 O
Matrimonial Causes, 1857 O, 1923 G, 1937 G
Mental Health, 1959 O
Merchant Shipping, 1906 O
Military Service, 1916 B
Mines (Ashley's), 1842 H
Mines Inspection, 1850 O
Municipal Corporations, 1835 J
National Health Insurance, 1912 C
National Health Service, 1946 G
National Insurance, 1946 G
Nationalisation of Coal Mines, 1946 E
Nationalisation of Iron and Steel, 1949 L
  repealed, 1952 L
Nationalisation of Transport, 1946 L, 1951 O, 1953 E
National Registration, 1915 G
National Service, 1939 J
Naval Construction, 1909 C
Naval Defence, 1889 E
Navigation, modified, 1822 F, 1823 G, 1825 G
  repealed, 1849 F
New Ministries, 1916 O
Obscene Publications, 1959 O
Official Secrets, 1911 O
Parliament, 1911 O, 1949 M
Patent, 1906 O
Peerage Renunciation, 1963 G
Plimsoll's Merchant Shipping, 1875 O
Poor Law Amendment, 1834 O
Prevention of Crimes, Ireland, 1882 G
Protection of Prince Regent, 1817 C
Public Exhibitions, 1866 S
Public Health, 1848 O, 1875 H, 1891 O
Public Libraries, 1850 O
Public Records, 1838 O, 1958 O
Public Worship, 1855 R, 1874 R
Reform, of Parliament, 1832 F, 1867 H, 1884 M
Regency, 1811 B
Regulation of Children and Women's Work, 1867 H
Relief of Distress for Ireland, 1880 H
Remuneration of Teachers, 1863 G
Rent, 1957 F, 1965 M
Reparations Recovery, 1921 C
  repealed, 1925 D
Representation of the People, 1945 A
Resale Prices, 1964 G
Restrictive Practices, 1956 G
Road Traffic, 1934 C
Roman Catholic Relief, 1829 D
Safeguarding of Industries, 1921 G
Sedition, 1934 L
Seditious Meetings, 1795 L, 1817 C
Shops, 1911 O
'Six Acts', 1817 M
Street Offences, 1959 O
Ten Hours, 1847 O

Legislation—*contd.*
in Britain—*contd.*
Test and Corporations, repealed, 1828 E
Theatres, 1843 W
Tithe Commutation, 1836 H
Trade Disputes, 1906 M
Trade Disputes, 1927, repealed, 1946 B
Trade Unions, 1871 F, 1927 G
Traitorous Correspondence, 1793 C
Unemployment, 1934 E
Unemployment Insurance, 1925 G
University Test, abolition, 1871 F
Warehousing of Goods, 1823 E
Welsh Church Disestablishment, 1912 D
Westminster, Statute of, on Dominion Status, 1931 M
Witchcraft, repealed, 1951 R
Workmen's Compensation, 1897 O
in Canada, Elgin's Reciprocity, 1854 F
Emergency, in depression, 1930 J
in Egypt, Organic Law, 1883 E
in Finland, against Communism, 1930 L
in France, amnesty for Communards, 1880 G
anti-Jesuit, 1879 F
Army, 1913 H
Association Law, 1880 C, 1901 G
Excluding Bourbons, and Bonapartists, 1832 D
Fixing Prices and Wages, 1793 L
Forbidding Multiple Candidates, 1889 G
Indemnity, to compensate nobles, 1825 D
Labour Code, cancelled, 1938 B
Press Laws, 1824 J, 1827 D, 1828 D
'September' Laws, 1835 J
in German Confederation, for interfering in states unable to maintain order, 1820 E
in Germany, anti-Jesuit, 1904 C, R
anti-Socialist, 1878 K, 1890 K
Army, 1886 M, 1893 G, 1911 B, 1913 H
Enabling Law, grants dictatorial powers, 1933 E
Labour regulations, 1916 O, 1934 O
'May Laws', against Ultramontane clergy, 1874 E, 1878 B
Navy, 1898 C, 1900 F, 1906 F, 1908 F
'Nuremberg Laws', 1935 J
Old-age insurance, 1889 E
Protectionist, 1879 G
Protection of Republic, repealed, 1929 F. *See also* Prussia
In India, Public Safety, 1929 D
Trade Disputes, 1929 D
Untouchability outlawed, 1947 E
in Ireland, Abolition of Oath of Loyalty, 1932 E, 1933 E
Maynooth College, 1795 R
in Italy, against Anarchists and Socialists, 1894 G
Corporations, 1934 B
Electoral Reform, 1953 A
Law of Guarantees, 1871 E
in Mexico, anti-clerical, 1926 G
expropriations, 1936 L
petroleum, 1927 M
in New Zealand, Immigration, 1881 F
in Pakistan, Basic Democracies Order, 1959 K
in Prussia, 'May Laws' to control clergy, 1873 E
County Organisation, 1872 M. *See also* Germany
in Russia, Fundamental, 1906 E
in S.Africa, Aliens Immigration, in Transvaal, 1896 L
Asiatic Land Tenure, 1946 F
Bantu self-government, 1960 F
Bantu Amendment, 1964 E
Citizenship, 1949 F
General Law Amendment, 1962 E
Glen Grey, in Cape Colony, 1894 M
High Court of Parliament, 1952 D
Indian Representation, 1946 F
Native Representation, 1936 D
Public Safety, 1953 B
status, 1934 F
suppression of Communism, 1964 L
in Spain, Associations, 1933 E
Protection of Republic, 1931 K
Salic, abrogated, 1830 C
Succession, 1947 G
in Sweden, Unity and Security, 1789 B
in Switzerland, Mediation, 1803 B
revoked, 1813 M
in Turkey, Reform Edict, 1856 B
in US, Acts of Congress, resolutions to nullify in particular states, 1798 N, 1799 N
Passed over president's veto, 1867 C, 1894 H, 1919 K, 1933 A, 1943 G, 1947 F
Agricultural Adjustments, 1933 E
Aliens, 1798 N
Anti-Strike, 1943 G
Anti-Trust, 1903 B, O
Basic Reconstruction, 1867 C
Bland-Allison, for silver standard, 1878 B
Burnett, Immigration, 1914 B
Carey, to encourage irrigation, 1894 H
Civil Rights, 1866 F, 1960 D, 1964 G
Civil Works Emergency Relief, 1934 B
Clay Tariff, 1833 C
Clayton, prohibiting injunction without notice, 1912
Coal Stabilization, 1935 H
Combat Poverty, 1964 C
Control of Communists, 1950 J
Control of Livestock Disease, 1903 O
Currency, 1900 C
Dawes, for dividing lands amongst Indians, 1887 B
Desert Land, 1877 C
Dillingham, Immigration, 1912 D
Elkins, Inter-state Commerce, 1903 N
Embargo, 1807 M, 1809 C
Emergency Quota Immigration, 1921 E
Emergency Relief, 1933 E
Excise, 1912 C
Farm Credit, 1933 F
Federal Reserve, 1913 O
Food and Drugs, 1898 O, 1906 O
Foraker, 1900 E
Force, for collecting revenue, 1833 C
Force, to control elections, 1890 F
Fordney-McComben, Tariff, 1922 O
Foreign Aid, 1952 F
Foreign Assistance, 1949 D
Fugitive Slaves, 1793 N, 1850 G
Funding, 1790 B
Gold Reserve, 1934 A
Inter-state Commerce, 1887 B
Kansas-Nebraska, 1854 E, G
La Follette, Seamen's, 1915 O
Land, 1784 D, 1820 D
Lend-Lease, 1941 A, C
Limiting Butter Substitution, 1902 O
Marshall Aid, 1948 C
Medical Care for the Aged, 1965 G
Mutual Defense Assistance, 1949 K
Mutual Security, Russia demands revocation, 1951 M
National Banking, 1863 B, 1864 F
National Industrial Recovery, 1933 F
declared unconstitutional, 1935 E

National Labor Service, 1942 K
Neutrality, 1935 M, 1937 E
amended, 1939 L
Non-Intercourse, 1809 C, 1811 B
Organic, for administration of Alaska, 1884 E
Overman, for re-organising departments, 1918 E
Pendleton, for reforming Civil Service, 1883 A, 1901 O
Pre-emption Distribution, 1841 N
Presidential Succession, 1886 E
Reciprocal Trade Agreements, 1958 J
Rural Credit, 1916 O
St. Lawrence Seaway, 1954 E
Securities, 1933 E
Seditions, 1798 N
Selective Training and Service, 1940 J, 1948 F
Sherman, anti-Trust, 1890 G
Sherman, for compulsory silver-purchase, 1893 L
Silver Purchase, 1934 F
Smoot, Pensions, 1912 L
Social Security, 1935 H, O
Tariff, 1832 G
Taft-Hartley, for Union Funds, 1947 F
Tenure of Office, 1867 C, 1868 B
Trade Agreement, 1955 A
Trade Expansion, 1962 K
Tydings-McDuffie, for Philippine independence, 1934 C
Volstead, Prohibition, 1919 K
Wages and Hours, 1938 O
Wagner-Steagall, to finance housing, 1937 J
Water-power, 1920 F
Wealth Tax, 1935 N
Législation orientale (A. H. Anquetil Duperron), 1778 Q
Legitimation of child born before parents' marriage, 1959 O
Legúia, Augusto, Peruv. president, 1930 H
Léhar, Franz, Aus. musician (1870–1947), 1905 T, 1922 T, 1925 T
Lehmann, John, B. author (b. 1907), 1936 V, 1943 U, 1955 U
Lehmann, Rosamund, B. author, 1932 U, 1936 V, 1944 U
Lehrs, Karl, G. classical scholar (1802–78), 1869 Q
Leicester, North, Eng. constituency, by-election, 1962 G
Leighton, Frederick, lord Stretton, B. artist (1830–1896), 1890 S, 1896 S
Leipzig, E. Germany, 1822 P: Gewandhaus concerts, 1781 T; 'Battle of The Nations', 1813 K, anniversary of, 1817 K; Conservatoire, 1843 T; railway station, 1915 P; war trials at, 1921 A, D
Lélia (G. Sand), 1833 U
Lemanic Republic (Switzerland), 1798 A
Le Mans, France, 1793 M
Lemass, Séan, Ir. politician (b. 1899), 1959 F
Lemberg, Poland: Austrian occupation, 1769 B; Austro-German force takes, 1915 E
Lemnitzer, Lynam L., Am. soldier (b. 1899), Supreme Allied Commander, Europe, 1963 A
Lemon, Mark, B. journalist (1809–70), edits *Punch*, 1841 V
Lemprière, John, B. classical scholar (1765–1824), 1788 Q
Lend-lease, by US, 1941 A, C; revised agreement with Russia, 1942 E; ends, 1945 H, K; total cost of 1945 H
Lenglen, Suzanne, F. tennis champion, 1919 X
Lenin, Nicolai (Vladimir Ilich, originally Oulianov) R. statesman (1870–1924), 1870 Z, 1903 H, 1924 A
leaves Russia, 1907 N
seizes power, 1917 G
becomes chief of commissars, 1917 L
writings, 1905 O, 1909 O
Leningrad (formerly St. Petersburg), Russia:
Germans advance to outskirts, 1941 J
Russians relieve, 1941 M, 1944 A
Lennox, Charles, Duke of Richmond, B. sportsman (1735–1806), 1780 F, 1802 X
Lenormand, H. R., F. dramatist, 1924 W
Lens, Russia, Germans retire towards, 1915 J
Lenshina, Alice, Rhodes. religious fanatic, 1964 G, H
Lenz, Jacob Michael Reinhold, G. author (1751–92), 1776 W
Leo XII, Pope, Cardinal Annibal della Genga (1823–9), concordat with United Netherlands, 1827 F
Leo XIII, Pope, Cardinal Giocchino Pecci (1878–1903), 1878 B, 1891 R, 1899 R, 1903 G
Leoben, Styria, Austria, Peace, between France and Austria, 1797 D
Leonard and Gertrude (J. H. Pestalozzi), 1781 O
Leoncavallo, Ruggiero, It. musician (1858–1917), 1858 Z, 1892 T, 1917 Z
Leonore (G. A. Bürger), 1773 U
Leonov, Alexei, R. cosmonaut, 1965 P
Leopardi, Giacomo, Count, It. author (1798–1837), 1798 Z, 1816 U, 1824 U, 1827 U, 1837 Z
Leopold II, Holy Roman Emperor (1790–2), 1790 B, 1792 C; as grand duke of Tuscany, 1765 H, 1786 R; calls for support for Louis XVI, 1791 G
Leopold I, of Belgium (Prince Leopold of Saxe-Coburg), 1831 F, 1865 M
Leopold II, of Belgium (1865–1909), 1865 M, 1895 J, 1909 M; sends expedition to Congo, 1880 F; establishes Belgian Congo, 1885 B, 1891 D; plans for East Africa, 1890 E; claims land on Upper Nile, 1894 E, H; excused of Congolese atrocities, 1905 L; hands over Congo to Belgium, 1908 H
Leopold III, of Belgium (b. 1901), referendum favours return, 1950 C; returns, 1950 G; abdicates, 1950 H
Leopold, Prince of Hohenzollern, 1870 G
Leopold, Prince of Saxe-Coburg, 1831 F
Leopold II, Duke of Tuscany (1824–59), purchases Lucca, 1846 M; recalled, 1849 D; abolishes constitution, 1852 E
Léopoldville, Congo: disturbances in, 1959 A, 1960 G; conference of Independent African States in, 1960 H; becomes federal capital, 1961 E
Le Play, Pierre Guillaume Frédéric, F. engineer and economist (1800–82), 1855 O, 1864 O
Lermontov, Mikhail Yurevich, R. poet and novelist (1814–41), 1837 U, 1839 U
Lerroux, Alejandro, Sp. Right-wing leader, 1934 K
Leslie, Sir John, B. mathematician and natural philosopher (1766–1832), 1804 P, 1813 P
Lespinasse, Jean de, F. author (1732–76), 1764 U
Lesseps, Ferdinand de, F. diplomat and maker of Suez Canal (1805–94): organises Canal Company, 1879 H; trial for corruption, 1892 L, 1893 C
Lessing, Doris, B. author (b. 1919), 1952 U
Lessing, Gotthold Ephraim, G. author (1729–81), 1766 Q, 1767 W, 1769 U, 1772 W, 1777 R, 1778 R, 1779 W, 1781 Z
Leticia, Peru, dispute between Peru and Columbia over, 1832 J, 1934 E
Letters covering the Aesthetic Education of Mankind (Schiller), 1795 U

Letters of Jacopo Ortis (U. Foscolo), 1798 U
Letters of Janus (Döllinger, Huber and Friedrich), 1869 R
Letters on a Regicide Peace (E. Burke), 1796 O
Letters on the Curiosities of Literature (H. Grenstenberg), 1766 U
Letter to a Member of the National Assembly (E. Burke), 1791 O
Letter to a Noble Lord, A (E. Burke), 1796 O
Letters to His Son (Lord Chesterfield), 1774 U
Letter to the Sheriffs of Bristol, A (E. Burke), 1777 O
Letters to Travis (R. Porson), 1788 R
Lettres à une princesse d'Allemagne (L. Euler), 1732 P
Lettres de la Montagne (J. J. Rousseau), 1763 O
Lettres de mon moulin (A. Daudet), 1866 W
Lettres physiques et morales sur les montagnes (J. A. Deluc), 1778
Leucotomy, 1961 P
Levana (Jean Paul), 1807 U
Lever, Charles James, Ir. author (1806–72), 1846 U
Leverrier, Urbain Jean Joseph, F. astronomer (1811–1877), 1846 P
Leveson-Gower, Granville George, Earl of Granville, B. Whig-Liberal statesman (1815–91), as foreign secretary, 1851 M, 1880 D, 1883 A
Levi, Carlo, It. author and artist, 1945 U
Lewis, Clive Staples, B. author (1893–63), 1942 R, 1947 R
Lewis, G. N., B. chemist, 1916 P
Lewis, Ltd., of Gt. Britain, 1937 O
Lewis, Matthew Gregory, B. author (1775–1818), 1795 U
Lewis, Roy, B. author (b. 1913), 1949 O
Lewis, Sinclair, Am. author (1885–1951), 1920 U, 1922 U, 1927 U, 1929 U, 1945 U
Lewis, Wyndham, B. artist (1884–1957), 1913 S
Lewisham, Kent, England, by-election, 1957 B
Lewiston, Maine, US, 1965 X
Lexington, Mass., US, battle, 1775 D
Leyton, Essex, England, by-election, 1965 A
Liaisions dangereuses, Les (Choderlos de Laclos), 1772 U
Liao Tung, N.E. China, 1895 D, E
Liaoyang, China, Russian defeat at, 1904 H
Liaquat Ali Khan, Pakis. premier, 1947 H
Libel Act, British, 1792 O
  Seditious, penalties increased, 1819 M
Libel Actions, notable: Wilkes (seditious), 1763 D; publishers of 'Junius' (seditious), 1770 F; Ruskin *v.* Whistler, 1878 S; G. Cumming *v.* Lycett Green (Tranby Croft), 1891 O
Liberals. *See under* Political Parties
Liberation, Union of, in Russia, founded, 1903 N
Liberia: founded, 1822 N; proclaimed an independent republic, 1847 H; independence recognised, 1862 F; boundary with Sierra Leone, 1885 L
Liberté du travail, La (M. Baudrillant), 1865 O
Liberty and the Modern State (H. Laski), 1930 O
'Liberty' ship, 1943 O
Libraries:
  in Britain, Cambridge University, 1934 S
    circulating, 1842 O
    copyright, 1911 O
    John Rylands, Manchester, 1899 Q
    I. Newton's purchased, 1943 Q
    public, Ewart's Act for, 1850 P
    See also British Museum
  in France, Bibliothèque Impériale, Paris, 1852 Q
  in Germany, Berlin public, 1850 O
  in Spain, National, Lisbon, 1796 Q
Library, The (G. Crabbe), 1781 U
Libya: self-government, revoked, 1927 C; frontier with Sudan, 1934 F; declared part of Italy, 1938 K; becomes an independent federation, 1951 M
Lichfield House Compact, 1835 C
Lichtenberg, George Christoph, G. physicist (1742–1799), 1777 P
Liddell, Henry George, B. churchman and Greek scholar (1811–98), 1843 Q
Lidice, Bohemia, Nazis burn, 1942 F
Lie, Trygve Haivdan, Nor. statesman (b. 1896), 1896 Z; elected UN Secretary-General, 1946 B; second term, 1950 F; urges UN members to assist S. Korea, 1950 F
Lieber, Francis, Am., formerly G., publicist (1800–1872), 1838 O
Liebermann, Max, G. artist (1849–1935), 1849 Z, 1881 S, 1935 Z
Liebermann, Rolf, G. musician, 1954 T, 1955 T
Liebig, Justus von, baron, G. chemist (1803–73), 1803 Z, 1832 P, 1838 P, 1840 P, 1873 Z
Liège, Belgium, Germans occupy, 1914 H
Lifar, Serge, R. dancer and choreographer (b. 1905), 1905 Z
Life and Labour of the People of London (C. Booth), 1891 O
Life-insurance, in India, nationalised, 1956 E
Life of Jesus (D. F. Strauss), 1835 R
Life of Johnson (J. Boswell), 1791 U
Life of Nelson (R. Southey), 1813 U
Life of Reason (G. Santayana), 1905 R
Life of Savonarola (P. Villari), 1859 Q
Life of the Bee, The (M. Maeterlinck), 1901 U
Life peerages, 1958 G
Lifts. *See* elevators
Light, defraction of, 1815 P
  experiments concerning, 1800 P
  polarisation of, discovered, 1809 P
  speed of, re-calculated, 1950 P
  velocity of, measured, 1849 P
Lighthouses:
  lenses for, 1822 P
  New Eddystone, 1878 P
  S. Foreland, lit by electricity, 1858 P
Light in August (W. Faulkner), 1932 U
Lighting:
  electric, 1878 P, 1880 P
  gas, 1798 P, 1802 W, 1809 P, 1812 P
  'limelight', 1796 P
Lightning conductors, 1769 P
Light of Nature Pursued, The (A. Tucker), 1765 R
Ligurian Republic (Genoa), N.W. Italy, 1797 F, 1801 B; is united with France, 1805 F
Lilac Domino, The, 1918 W
Liliencron, Detley von, G. author (1844–1909), 1888 U
Lille, France: German occupation, 1914 H, K; British capture, 1918 K
Lima, Peru, riots at football match, 1964 E
Limanova, Italy, Austrian victory at, 1914 M
Limassol, Cyprus, 1964 B
Lime, 1862 P
Lime, chloride of, 1798 P
'Limelight' invented, 1796 P
Lincoln, Abraham, Am. statesman, Republican (1809–65), 16th president of US (1861–5), 1809 Z; senatorial campaign with Douglas, 1858 H; elected president, 1860 L; inaugurated, 1861 C; calls for militia, 1861 D; declares all slaves to be free, 1862 J, 1863 O; re-elected, 1864 L; assassinated, 1865 D
Lind, Jenny (*alias* Johanna Maria), B., formerly Swe. singer (1820–87), 1838 W, 1850 W

Lindbergh, Charles A., Am. aviator, 1927 P; son of, kidnapped, 1932 O
Linde, C. von, G. inventor, 1898 P
Lindemann, Frederick Alexander, Lord Cherwell, B. scientist (1886–1957), 1923 P, 1926 P, 1957 Z
Linden Tree, The (J. B. Priestley), 1947 W
Lindman, Arvid, Swe. pol., Conservative, 1928 K
Lindsay, Alexander Dunlop, Lord Lindsay of Birker, B. author and administrator (1879–1952), 1943 O, 1949 O
Lindsay, Kenneth, B. educationalist and sociologist (b. 1897), 1926 Q
Linear B, interpretation of, 1952 Q
Linear transformations, theory of, 1845 P
Linens: British exports, 1772 Y, 1782 Y, 1792 Y, 1802 Y, 1812 Y, 1822 Y, 1832 Y, 1842 Y, 1852 Y, 1862 Y, 1872 Y, 1882 Y, 1892 Y, 1902 Y, 1912 Y, 1922 Y, 1932 Y
Ling, Arthur George, B. architect (b. 1913), 1958 S
Linhares, José, Braz. president, 1945 K
Linotype, 1886 V
Linnean Society, founded, 1788 P
Linnaeus (Carl von Linné), Swe. botanist (1707–78), 1778 Z
Liola (L. Pirandello), 1917 W
Lionel Cranfield (R. H. Tawney), 1958 Q
Lippmann, Walter, Am. journalist (b. 1889), 1929 R, 1937 O, 1943 O, 1955 O
Liquefaction of air, 1898 P
Liquor traffic:
Brussels Conference on suppressing traffic to undeveloped peoples, 1889 F
Conventions to control traffic, 1890 G, 1911 O
in Britain, licensing, local veto on, proposed, 1891 K
hours, 1904 H
Welsh counties vote on Sunday opening, 1961 O
in France, sale of absinthe prohibited, 1915 O
in Sweden, state control, 1866 O
in US, Prohibition, in Maine, 1851 N
Anti-Saloon League, 1893 N
Volstead Act for, 1919 K, 1920 A
See also Prohibition
Lisbon, Portugal:
Royal Academy of Sciences, 1779 P
National Library, 1796 Q
John VI agrees to remove government to, 1821 D
revolts in, 1824 D, 1921 K
British troops in, to support Q. Maria, 1827 A
occupied by Dom Pedro's followers, 1833 G
NATO Council meets in, 1952 B
Lisk, Calif., US, observatory, 1954 P
Lissa, Italy, naval battle off, 1866 G
List, Friedrich, G. economist (1789–1846), 1789 Z, 1841 O, 1846 Z
Lister, Joseph, Lord Lister, B. surgeon (1827–1912), 1827 Z, 1865 P, 1912 Z
Liston, Sonny, Am. boxer, 1964 X, 1965 X
Liszt, Franz, Hun. musician (1811–86), 1811 Z, 1822 T, 1845 T, 1846 T, 1849 T, 1850 T, 1854 T, 1857 T
Lithography, invented, 1798 P
Lithuania: Russia acquires, 1793 E; German offensive in, 1915 F; independence in, 1918 L; re-opens frontier with Poland, 1938 C
Little Entente (of Czechoslovakia, Rumania and Yugoslavia). *See under* Entente
Little Gidding (T. S. Eliot), 1932 U
Little Minister, The (J. M. Barrie), 1891 U
Little Rock, Arkansas, US, desegregation crisis in, 1957 O, 1958 J
Little Women (L. A. Alcott), 1808 U
Littlewood, Joan, B. producer, 1964 W
Littré, Paul Emile, F. lexicographer (1801–81), 1863 Q
Litvinov, Maxim, R. politician (1876–1951), 1929 B, 1939 E
proposes disarmament, 1927 L
becomes foreign secretary, 1930 G
Litvinov Protocol, 1929 B, D
Liu, Shao-chi, Chin. politician, elected chariman of Republic, 1959 D
Liuzzo, Viola, Am. Civil Rights worker, 1965 C
Liver extract, 1926 P
Liver, glycogenic function of, 1850 P
Liverpool, Lord. *See* Jenkinson, Robert Banks
Liverpool, Lancs., England: blind school, 1791 O; railway to Manchester, 1830 P; Mechanics' Institute, 1834 O; baths and wash-houses in, 1844 O; automatic signals at, 1893 P; cathedrals, 1903 S, 1932 S; Repertory Theatre, 1911 W; Radar installations in Docks, 1948 P; drive in bank, 1959 O
Lives of the Poets (S. Johnson), 1779 U
Living Corpse, The (L. Tolstoy), 1900 U
Living God, The (N. Söderblom), 1933 R
Living Room, The (G. Greene), 1953 W
Livingstone, David, B. explorer and missionary (1813–73), 1813 Z, 1841 P, R, 1852 P, 1855 P, 1871 P, 1873 Z
meets Stanley, 1871 L
Landaff, Wales, cathedral, 1957 S
Llanthony Abbey, Wales, 1862 R
'Llewellyn, Richard.' *See* Lloyd, R. D. V. L.
Llorente, Juan Antonio, Sp. Secretary of Inquisition (1756–1823), 1817 R
'Lloyd, Marie.' *See* Wood, Matilda
Lloyd, Richard Dafydd Vivian Llewellyn, B. author under pseudonym of 'Richard Llewellyn', 1939 U
Lloyd, Selwyn, B. Conservative politician (b. 1904), 1957 A; becomes foreign secretary, 1955 M; overseas tours, 1959 B, C; appointed chancellor of exchequer, 1960 G; begins wages pause, 1961 G; Macmillan dismisses, 1962 G
Lloyd-George, David, Earl Lloyd-George, B. statesman, Liberal (1863–1945), 1863 Z, 1938 O, 1945 Z
appointed chancellor of exchequer, 1908 D
budget of, rejected by Lords, 1909 L; election on issue of, 1910 A; passed, 1910 D
introduces health service bill, 1911 E
home attacked by suffragettes, 1913 D
acquitted of corruption over Marconi affair, 1913 E
as minister of munitions, 1915 F
as war secretary, 1916 G
resigns from Asquith's cabinet, 1916 M
forms war cabinet, 1916 M
leadership threatened, 1918 E
issues Coalition manifesto, 1918 L
Coalition falls, 1922 K
becomes leader of Liberal party, 1925 A
'New Deal' speech, 1935 A
forms Council of Action, 1935 F
Lloyd-George and Co. (D. Low), 1922 S
Lloyd's Register of Shipping, 1834 V
Loana, Italy, Austrian defeat at, 1795 L
Loans. *See* Aid
Lobengula, King of Matabele, 1888 B, K
Local Defence Volunteers (LDV), British, later Home Guard, 1940 E
Local Government:
in Britain, chartered boroughs reformed, 1835 J
boards created, 1871 H
county councils established, 1888 H
London County Council, 1889 O

Local Government,—*contd.*
in Britain—*contd.*
Labour Party majority on, 1934 C
offers 100 per cent. housing loans, 1963 B
parish councils, 1894 O
London Borough Councils, 1899 O, 1965 O
Royal Commission on Greater London, 1957 G
Greater London Council established, 1965 O
in France, administrative departments, 1789 L
re-organised, 1790 B
in Ireland, 1840 H
in New Zealand, reformed through centralisation, 1875 K
in Prussia, municipal councils, 1808 L
provincial councils of state, 1817 C
provincial diets, 1823 N
remodelled, 1872 M
in Russia, reform of, 1820 F
provincial courts (Zemstvos) established, 1864 A
Local history, study of, 1900 Q
Locarno Conference, 1925 K
Locarno treaties, 1925 M; Rome pact endorses, 1933 G; Belgium released from obligations under, 1937 D
Lock, Bramah's patent, 1784 P
Lock-outs, in British printing industry, 1956 B
Lockyer, Sir Joseph Norman, B. astronomer (1836–1912), 1887 P
Lodge, Henry Cabot, Am. diplomat (b. 1902), 1902 Z, 1919 B
Lodge, Sir Oliver, B. physicist (1851–1940), 1884 P
Lodomerica, Poland, 1772 H
Lodz, Poland, Germans take, 1914 M
Lofoten Islands, Royal Navy raids, 1941 C, M
Logic, studies in, 1843 R, 1854 R, 1883 R
Logic (J. S. Mill), 1843 R
Logical positivism, 1922 R, 1955 R, 1960 R
Logic on the Morphology of Thought (B. Bosanquet), 1888 R
Lolita (V. Nabokov), 1955 U, 1959 O
Lombardy, Italy: ceded to France, 1797 K; Republic established, 1796 E; restored to Austria, 1815 F; Sardinia surrenders, 1848 H; ceded by Austria to France, 1859 G
Lombroso, Cesare, It. crimonologist (1836–1909), 1876 O
Lonardi, Edouardo, Argentine general, president, 1955 J
London, England:
events:
riots in, 1764 A
street lighting in, 1812 P
Spa Fields riots, 1816 M
monopoly of theatre managements ended, 1843 W
medical school for women, 1875 P
political meetings in Trafalgar Square, 1886 B
on 'Bloody Sunday', 1887 L
London County Council, 1889 O
Borough Councils, 1899 O
Port of London Authority, 1908 O
Suffragette riots, 1911 L
Tower Hill riot, 1912 G
air attack on, 1917 J
television demonstrated in Soho, 1926 P
riots, 1931 J
London Passenger Transport Board, 1933 O
Fascist meetings, 1934 F, J
green-belt scheme, 1935 O
'bus strike, 1937 E
evacuation from, 1939 H
Blitz, 1940 H, J, 1941 C, E, 1943 A, 1944 B, F
Second Front demonstration, 1942 G
flying bombs on, 1944 F
UN General Assembly meets, 1946 A
racial disturbances at Notting Hill, 1958 H
rent riots at St. Pancreas, 1960 J
CND sit-down demonstrations, 1961 O
places, buildings and institutions, in or near:
Adelphi, The, 1769 S
Airport, 1955 S
Albert Hall, Royal, opened, 1872 W
Albert Memorial, 1862 S
Aldwych Theatre, 1964 W
Almack's gaming house, 1763 W
Argyll Rooms, 1813 T
Bank of England, 1795 S, 1803 S
Bedford College for Women, 1849 O
Bethnal Green Museum, 1874 Q
Bloomsbury, University moves to, 1936 O
Britannic House, Finsbury, 1924 S
British Museum, buildings, 1816 S, 1823 S, 1845 S, 1914 Q
as copyright library, 1911 O
public admission to, 1879 W
royal library, 1823 Q
Broadcasting House, 1932 S
Brooks' Club, 1763 W
Buckingham Palace, Nash's building, 1825 S
Victoria Memorial at, 1905 S
Cenotaph, Whitehall, 1919 S
Central Criminal Court, 1907 S
Chamber of Commerce, 1882 O
City Temple, 1917 R
Cleopatra's Needle, 1878 S
Clerkenwell, 1867 M
Coal Exchange, 1846 S, 1963 S
Cobden Club, 1866 O
College of Chemistry, 1845 O
County Hall, 1922 S
Covent Garden Opera House, 1858 S, 1910 T
sculpture in, 1963 S
Crystal Palace, 1850 S
concerts at, 1855 T
Drury Lane Theatre, 1775 W
Economist buildings, 1961 S
Elizabeth Garrett Anderson Dispensary, 1866 O
Euston portico, demolished, 1961 S
Exeter Hall, 1853 R
Festival Hall, 1951 S
G.P.O. Building, St. Martin le Grand, 1823 S
G.P.O. Tower, 1954 S, 1965 S
Hammersmith Flyover, 1961 S
Hilton Hotel, 1963 S
Houses of Parliament, destroyed by fire, 1834 K
rebuilt by Barry, 1840 S
destruction by bombs, 1941 E
Hyde Park, Great Exhibition in, 1851 W
Imperial Institute, 1893 O
Industrial Health and Safety Centre, 1927 O
Institute of Contemporary Art, 1953 S
Institute of Technical Optics, 1917 P
Kensington Gardens, 'Peter Pan' in, 1912 S
King's College, 1830 O
King's Cross Station, 1851 S
Lambeth Bridge, 1932 P
Literary Club, 1764 U
London Library, 1841 Q
London School of Economics, 1895 O
London Transport Building, St. James's Park, 1929 S
Lord's Cricket Ground, 1787 X
Lyceum Theatre, Irving's Company at, 1878 W
Mermaid Theatre, 1959 W

National Gallery, 1824 s, 1832 s, 1838 s
concerts in, 1939 T
National Portrait Gallery, 1857 s, 1896 s
National History Museum, 1881 P
Newgate Prison, 1813 O
Olympia, Barnum and Bailey's Show at, 1889 W
Oratory, The, 1849 R
Paddington Station, 1852 s
Pall Mall, lit by gas, 1809 P
Philosophical Society, 1869 R
Piccadilly Circus, 'Eros'(Shaftesbury Memorial) in, 1925 s
enquiry for development, 1959 s
Pimlico housing estate, 1950 s
Pioneer Club, 1892 O
Public Record Office, 1838 O
Queen's Hall, Promenade Concerts in, 1895 T
Regent's Canal, 1820 P
Regent Street, Nash's improvements to, 1811 s
Polytechnic, 1882 O
Royal Academy, 1768 s
Royal Academy of Music, 1822 T, 1861 T
Royal College of Music, 1883 T
Royal College of Surgeons, 1800 P
Royal Court Theatre, 1904 W
English Stage Company at, 1956 W
Royal Courts of Justice, 1868 s
R.I.B.A. Building, 1933 s
Royal Institute of International Affairs, 1920 O
Royal Geographical Society, 1830 P
Sadlers Wells Theatre, 1931 W
St. Marylebone, reform of tenements in, 1864 O
St. Pancras Church, 1819 s
St. Paul's Cathedral, notable monuments in, 1796 s, 1858 s
interior decorations for, 1891 s
New Barbican Scheme, 1954 s, 1956 s
Savoy Theatre, 1881 W
Science Museum, 1857 O
Senate House, Bloomsbury, 1933 s
Skinners' Company Hall, 1904 s
Skyscrapers in, 1963 s
Somerset House, 1776 s
Spa Fields Chapel, 1779 R
Swiss Cottage Library and Swimming Pool, 1964 s
Stock Exchange, compensation fund, 1950 O
public galleries, 1953 O
re-organised, 1962 O
Stratford East, Theatre Workshop, 1964 W
Tate Gallery, 1897 s
Temple of Mithras, 1954 Q
Thorn House, 1959 s
Times, The, Building, 1960 s
University, 1836 O, 1860 O, 1898 O
moves to Bloomsbury, 1936 O
University College, 1826 O
Underground railway development, 1905 P, 1963 P
Wallace Collection, 1900 s
Waterloo Bridge, 1811 s
Westminster Abbey, anniversary celebrations, 1965 R
Westminster Cathedral, 1895 R, 1903 s, 1913 s
Whitechapel Art Gallery, 1897 s
Windmill Theatre, closes, 1964 W
Wyndhams Theatre, 1910 W
Zoological Society, Royal, 1826 P
Zoo, London, Aviary at, 1965 s
musical events in: 1785 T, 1813 T, 1825 T, 1844 T, 1855 T, 1876 T, 1895 T, 1916 T, 1918 T, 1923 T, 1940 T
population: 1801 Y, 1841 Y, 1881 Y, 1906 Y 1950 Y, 1960 Y
London, Treaties, Protocols, etc:
protocol on French intervention in Greece, 1828 G
protocol recognises Greek independence, 1827 G, 1828 L, 1829 C
Treaty, recognises Belgian independence, 1839 D
Treaty of Quadruple Alliance with Mehemet Ali, 1840 G, L
Treaty on Schleswig-Holstein, 1850 H
Treaty guarantees Denmark's integrity, 1852 E
protocol demands Turkish reforms, 1877 C, D
Naval convention, 1936 C
London, F., B. scientist, 1927 P
London, Jack, Am. author (1876–1916), 1904 U
Lonely Crowd, The (D. Riesman), 1951 R
Long, Crawford, Am. surgeon (1815–78), 1842 P
Long, Huey Pierce, Am. politician (1893–1935), 1893 Z, 1935 Z
Longchamps, France, horse-racing at, 1863 X
Long Day's Journey into Night (O'Neill), 1940 U
Longfellow, Henry Wadsworth, Am. poet (1807–82), 1807 Z, 1839 U, 1842 U, 1846 U, 1851 U, 1855 U, 1880 U, 1882 Z
Long-playing records, invented, 1948 P
Long Revolution, The (R. Williams), 1961 O
Long Week End, The (R. Graves), 1939 U
Longwy, France, Prussians capture, 1792 J
Lonsdale, Gordon, B. spy, 1961 O, 1964 D
Look Back in Anger (J. Osborne), 1956 W
Look Homeward Angel (T. Wolfe), 1929 U
Looking Backwards, 2000–1887 (E. Bellamy), 1888 U
Look Stranger (W. H. Auden), 1936 U
Loom: automatic, 1895 P; Brussels power, 1845 P
Loos, France, battle, 1915 J
Lord I was Afraid (N. Balchin), 1947 U
Lord Jim (J. Conrad), 1900 U
Lord of the Flies, The (W. Golding), 1954 U
Lord of the Rings, The (J. Tolkein), 1954 U
Lords, House of, Committee recommends an heir be able to disclaim peerage, 1962 M
Lore and Language of Schoolchildren, The (I. and P. Opie), 1959 Q
Loren, Sophia, It. film actress, 1934 Z
Loris-Melikov, Michael, Count, R. minister of Interior (1825–88), 1880 E
Lorna Doone (R. D. Blackmore), 1869 U
Lorraine, Duchy, France, 1766 B
Los Alamos, New Mex., US, laboratory at, 1956 P
Los Angeles, Calif., US: Olympic Games at, 1932 X; atomic research in, 1941 P; race riots in, 1965 H
Lothair (B. Disraeli), 1870 U
Lothian, Lord. *See* Kerr
Lothian, West, Scotland, by-election, 1862 F
'Loti, Pierre.' *See* Viaud, Julien
Lotte in Weimar (T. Mann), 1939 U
Lottery, national, in US, 1776 O
Lotus-Eaters, The (Lord Tennyson), 1832 U
Lotze, Rudolf Hermann, G. philosopher (1817–81), 1841 R, 1856 R
Loubet, Émile, F. statesman (1838–1929), 1838 Z, 1929 Z; elected president, 1899 B; visits London, 1903 G; visits Italy, 1904 D
Louis XV, King of France (1715–74), 1769 D, 1774 E
Louis XVI, King of France (1774–93), 1774 E, H, 1781 E
as Dauphin, 1765 M
marriage, 1770 E
mediates in Scheldt crisis, 1784 K
banishes Parlement of Paris, 1787 H
summons Estates General, 1787 L, 1789 H
summons notables, 1788 L

Louis XVI—*contd.*
dismisses Necker, 1789 G
moved from Versailles to Paris, 1789 K
accepts constitution, 1790 G
vetoes decree of Legislative Assembly, 1791 L
a prisoner, 1791 D
attempted flight, 1791 F
trial, 1792 M
execution, 1793 A
Louis XVIII, King of France (1814–24), 1816 J, 1824 J; enters Paris, 1814 E; issues Constitutional Charter, 1814 F; flees, 1815 C; returns to Paris, 1815 G
Louis (Bonaparte), King of Holland, 1806 F; abdicates, 1810 G
Louis Napoleon. *See* Napoleon III
Louis Philip Joseph, Duke d'Orléans ('Philippe Egalité', 1747–93), 1793 L
Louis Philippe Albert d'Orléans, Comte de Paris, 1848 B, 1850 G
Louis Philippe, King of the French (1830–48), 1773 Z, 1830 G, 1831 B, 1835 G; elected King, 1830 H; abdicates, 1848 B; death, 1850 G
Louis Philippe, Comte de Paris (1838–94), 1872 L, 1873 H
Louis I, King of Portugal (1861–89), 1861 L
Louis, Joe, Am. boxer, 1936 X, 1946 X
Louisiana, state, US: acquired by Spain from France, 1763 B; Spain sells to France, 1800 K, 1801 A; US purchases from France, 1803 D; Burr's expedition to, 1806 N; slavery to be abolished, except in Missouri, 1820 C; as a Confederate state, 1861 B; rival governors in, 1874 F
Lourdes, France, pilgrimages to, 1858 R
Louvain, Belgium: riots, 1787 A; seminary, 1786 K
Louw, Eric, S. African Nationalist (b. 1890), 1960 E
Love in a Cold Climate (N. Mitford), 1949 U
Love in Idleness (T. Rattigan), 1944 W
Lovell, Sir Bernard, B. astronomer (b. 1913), 1957 P
Love of Four Colonels, The (P. Ustinov), 1951 W
Love, Power and Justice (P. Tillich), 1954 R
Loving (H. Green), 1945 U
Low, Sir David, N. Zeal. cartoonist (1891–1965), 1891 Z, 1918 S, 1922 S
Lowe, Robert, Viscount Sherbrooke, B. Liberal (1811–92), 1868 M
Lowell, James Russell, Am. author and diplomat (1819–91), 1843 U, 1848 U, 1857 V
Lowell, John, Jnr., Am. businessman and philanthropist (1799–1836), 1839 Q
Lowell, Robert, Am. poet (b. 1917), 1965 U
Lowell, Robert, B. poet (1770–96), 1794 W
Lowth, Robert, B. divine (1710–87), 1779 R
Loyson, Hyacinthe, F. priest ('Père Hyacinthe'), 1872 R
Lubbock, Eric Reginald, B. Liberal (b. 1928), 1962 C
Lübeck, E. Germany: Napoleon annexes, 1801 C, 1810 M; bombed, 1942 C
Lübke, Heinrich, W. German president (b. 1894), 1959 G
Lublin, Poland, Jews deported to, 1939 K
Lublin Committee of Polish Liberation in Moscow, 1944 G
Lucca, Duchy, Italy, sold to Leopold of Tuscany, 1846 M
Lucerne Committee on broadcasting, 1934 O
Luciano, S., It. film director, 1950 W
Lucinde (Schlegel), 1799 U
Lucknow, India, relief of, 1857 J, L
Lucky Jim (K. Amis), 1954 U
Luddites, in Britain, 1812 C
Ludendorff, Erich, G. soldier (1865–1937), 1865 Z, 1918 K; acquitted of breaches of rules of war, 1921 D
Ludwig, Karl Friedrich Wilhelm, G. physiologist (1816–95), 1865 P
Ludwig, Otto, G. dramatist (1813–65), 1850 W
Lugard, Frederick, Lord Lugard, B. administrator in Africa (1858–1945), 1858 Z, 1890 M, 1900 A, 1945 Z
Lugard; The Years of Adventure (M. Perham), 1956 Q
Luisa Fernanda, Sp. Princess (1832–95), marries Duc de Montpensier, 1846 K
Luise (J. H. Voss), 1795 U
Lumière, Auguste, F. inventor (1862–1954), 1895 P, 1907 P
Lumière, Louis, F. inventor (1864–1948), 1895 P
Lumpa Church, N. Rhodesia, 1964 G
Lumumba, Patrice, Congol. leader (1926–61): becomes premier, 1960 F; dismissed, 1960 J; arrested, 1960 M
Lunatics, treatment of, reformed, 1792 O. *See also* Asylums
Lunéville, France, Treaty, 1801 B
Lung cancer, connexion with smoking, 1954 P, 1962 P
Lung pump, electric, 1961 P
Lusaka, S. Africa, 1964 M
Lusitania, S.S., sinking of, 1915 E
Lusk, Mary, Scottish lay preacher, 1963 R
Luther (J. Osborne), 1961 W
Luther, Hans, G. Independent Socialist (1879–1934): as Chancellor, 1925 A, 1926 A; resigns, 1926 E
Lutyens, Sir Edwin, B. architect (1869–1944) 1869 Z, 1900 S, 1906 S, 1919 S, 1924 S, 1930 S, 1932 S, 1944 Z
Lutyens, Elizabeth, B. musician (b. 1906), 1940 T
Lützen, Germany, battle, 1813 E
Luxemburg: capitulates to French, 1795 F; becomes independent Grand Duchy, 1839 D; neutrality guaranteed, 1867 E; is separated from Netherlands, 1890 L; Germans occupy, 1914 H; Germany invades, 1940 E
Lux Mundi (ed. C. Gore), 1890 R
Luxor, Egypt, Tutankhamun's tomb at, 1922 Q
Luzon, Philippines, Japanese landings, 1941 M
Luzzatti, Luigi, It. premier (1841–1928), 1911 C, D
Lvov, Archbishop of, released, 1963 B
Lvov, Prince George of, R. premier, 1917 C, E, G
Lyell, Sir Charles, B. geologist (1767–1849), 1830 P, 1863 P
Lyne, Joseph Leycester ('Father Ignatius'), F. priest (1837–1908), 1862 R
Lynskey Tribunal, 1948 L
Lyons, France, riots of silk-weavers in, 1831 L, 1834 D
Lyons, Joseph A., Austral. politician (1879–1939), 1939 D
founds United Australian Party, 1931 N
forms Coalition, 1934 L
Lyrical Ballads (Wordsworth and Coleridge), 1798 U, 1800 U
Lys, The, south of Ypres, France, German attack at, 1918 D
Lysenko, Trofin Denisovich, R. geneticist (b. 1898), 1948 P
Lysons, David, B. antiquarian and topographer (1762–1834), 1792 Q
Lytton, Lord. *See* Bulwer-Lytton
Lytton Report on Manchuria, 1932 K, 1933 B

M

Maas, River, Holland, Canadian troops reach, 1944 K
Macadam, John Loudon, B. road-builder (1756–1836), 1815 P
Macao, S.E. China, Portugal acquires, 1887 M
MacArthur, Douglas, Am. soldier (1880–1964), 1880 Z, 1964 Z; enters Manila, 1945 B; orders trials of Japanese war criminals, 1946 N; commands UN force in Korea, 1950 G, L; China rejects offer of truce by, 1951 C; removed from Korean command, 1951 D; investigations on removal, 1951 E
Macaulay, Thomas Babbington, Lord Macaulay, B. historian and Liberal politician (1800–59), 1800 Z, 1825 Q, 1842 Q, 1848 Q, 1859 Z
Macaulay, Rose, B. author (d. 1958), 1932 U
McCallum, Ronald Buchanan, B. author and psephologist (b. 1893), 1947 O
McCarthy, Joseph, Am. Republican (1909–1957), 1909 Z; Senatorial Committee denies charges by, 1950 G; Senatorial Committee reports improper action by, 1954 J, M
McCarthy, Justin, Ir. politician and author (1830–1912), succeeds Parnell as Nationalist leader, 1890 M
McCarthy, Mary, Am. author (b. 1912), 1963 U
McCollum, B. biochemist, 1913 P
McCormick, Cyrus, Am. engineer (1809–84), 1834 P
MacDonald, James Ramsay, B. Labour leader (1866–1937), 1866 Z, 1937 Z
  appointed Labour Party Secretary, 1900 B
  elected Labour Party Chairman, 1911 B
  becomes premier, 1924 A
  refuses to sign treaty of Mutual Assistance, 1924 G
  on the immunity of the executive, 1924 O
  resigns, 1924 L
  becomes premier, 1929 F
  forms first National government, 1931 H
  is expelled from Labour Party, 1931 H
  forms second National government, 1931 L
  is ordered to rest, 1934 F
  serves under Baldwin, 1935 F
  defeated in election, 1935 L
MacDonald, Sir John Alexander, Can. Conservative leader (1815–91), 1878 K, 1891 F
Macedonia, now in Yugoslavia:
  reforms in, 1878 G
  movement for independence, 1893 N
  raids into, 1895 F
  activities of External Revolutionary Organisation, 1895 F
  disturbances in, 1902 N
  reforms for pacification demanded, 1903 B
    Austro-Russian agreement on, 1903 K
  agitation in, 1905 N
  Nicholas II, agrees to reforms, 1908 F
  Young Turks revolt, 1908 G
  Turkey declines to undertake reforms, 1912 K
Machado, Bernadino, president of Portugal, 1915 H
McEnery, Samuel Douglas, Am. Democrat (1837–1910), 1874 F
Machine infernale, La (J. Cocteau), 1934 W
Machinery, exports from Britain legalised, 1843 P
Machines:
  automatic computer, 1942 P
  bottle-making, 1898 P
  cable-making, 1792 P
  combing, 1845 P
  for liquefaction of air, 1898 P
  for manufacture of coated photographic paper, 1885 P
  for proving laws of accelerated motion, 1784 P
  logical, 1874 P
  nail-making, 1786 P, 1790 P, 1806 P
  rapid filming, 1923 P
  sewing, 1846 P, 1851 P
  sounding, 1872 P
  teaching, 1963 O
  threshing, 1784 P
  type-setting, 1897 P
  universal milling, 1862 P
  wood-working, 1793 P
  See also under automation
Machine-tool industry:
  British, 1800 P, 1910 P, 1939 Y
  German, 1910 P, 1939 Y
  US, 1853 P, 1910 P, 1939 Y
Machine-tools:
  for small arms manufacture, 1853 P
  plane, 1776 P
  turret-lathe, 1855 P
Macintosh, Charles, B. chemist and inventor (1766–1843), 1766 Z, 1823 P
MacKay, Mary, B. novelist under pseudonym of 'Marie Corelli' (1855–1924), 1855 Z, 1924 Z
McKenna, Reginald, B. Liberal (1863–1943), as Home Secretary, 1911 K; as Chancellor of Exchequer, 1915 E; investigates German economy, 1923 L; reports on reparations, 1924 D
Mackenzie, Sir Compton, B. author (b. 1883), 1883 Z, 1912 U
Mackenzie, Thomas, N. Zeal. politician, 1912 G
Mackenzie, William Lyon, Canad. rebel, 1837 M, 1838 A
Mackenzie, William Warrender, Lord Amulree, B. administrator (1860–1942), 1938 O
McKinley, William, Am. Republican (1843–1901), 25th president of US (1897–1901), 1900 B, F, 1901 J; wins presidential elections, 1896 L, 1900 L; inaugurated, 1897 C
  tariff, 1890 K, 1892 L
    repealed, 1894 E
Mackinnon, Sir William Henry, B. general (1857–1929), 1890 E
Mackintosh, Charles Rennie, B. architect (1868–1928), 1900 S, 1904 S
Mackintosh, Sir James, B. philosopher (1765–1832), 1791 O, 1799 O
Mack von Leiberich, Karl, Baron, Aus. general (1752–1828), defeated at Ulm, 1805 K
MacInnes, Colin, B. author (b. 1929), 1959 U
Maclean, Donald, B. diplomat, flees to Russia, 1951 F
Maclean, Sir Fitzroy, B. soldier, and Conservative politician (b. 1911), 1943 K
Macleod, Ian Norman, B. Conservative politician (b. 1913), as Colonial Secretary, Lord Salisbury attacks policy of, 1961 C; refuses to serve under Douglas-Home, 1963 K
Maclure, William, B. merchant and geologist (1763–1840), 1809 P
Macmahon, Marie Edmé Patrice Maurice de, Duke of Magenta, F. Marshal (1809–93), 1875 N, 1877 E; defeated, 1870 H; elected president, 1873 E, L; resigns, 1879 A
McMahon Line, Indian frontier, Chinese troops cross, 1962 J
McMillan, Edwin, Am. scientist, 1940 P
McMillan, Margaret, B. educationalist, 1860 Z 1931 Z

Macmillan, Maurice Harold, B. statesman, Conservative (b. 1894), 1894 Z, 1955 L, 1958 F
minister of defence, 1954 K
foreign secretary, 1955 D
chancellor of Exchequer, 1955 M
introduces premium savings bonds, 1956 D
forms ministry, 1957 A
at Bermuda Conference with Eisenhower, 1957 C
visits US and Canada, 1957 K
resignations from ministry, 1958 A
tours Commonwealth, 1958 A, 1959 C
meets Eisenhower, 1958 F
rejects Russian proposal for immediate Summit talks, 1958 G
visits Russia, 1959 B
leads Conservatives to victory in election, 1959 K
visits Africa, 1960 A
'Wind of change' speech, 1960 B
elected Chancellor of Oxford University, 1960 C
issues joint declaration on nuclear tests, 1960 C
at Summit meeting, 1960 E
addresses UN, 1960 J
announces facilities for US Polaris submarines, 1960 L
meets de Gaulle, 1961 L
meets Kennedy, 1961 C, M, 1962 M, 1963 F
dismisses seven cabinet ministers, 1962 G
appoints Radcliffe tribunal, 1962 L
resigns premiership, 1963 K
McNamara, Robert Strange, Am. defense secretary (b. 1916), 1960 L
McNaught, William, B. engineer (1813–81), 1945 P
MacNeice, Louis, B. author (1907–65), 1907 Z, 1963 U
Macready, William Charles, B. actor (1793–1873), 1851 W
M'Taggart, John, B. philosopher (1866–1925), 1921 R
McWilliam, Frederick Edward, B. sculptor (b. 1909), 1956 S, 1961 S, 1963 S, 1964 S
Madagascar: Anglo-French expedition to, 1845 F; French commercial treaty with, 1868 H; liberation of slaves in, 1877 K; French war with, 1883 F; French control of, 1885 M; French conquest of, 1894 L; France annexes, 1896 H; Britain surrenders claims, 1904 D; British invade, 1942 E; Nationalist revolt in, 1947 C; becomes independent as Malagasy Republic, 1960 F
Madame Bovary (G. Flaubert), 1856 U
Madariaga, Salvador de, Sp. author (b. 1886), 1886 Z, 1923 Q
Mademoiselle de Maupin (F. Gautier), 1835 U
Madero, Francisco, President of Mexico, 1911 L
Madison, James, Am. statesman (1751–1836), 4th president of US (1809–17), 1785 R, 1787 O, 1786 E, 1798 N, 1799 N, 1800 L, 1806 O; inaugurated, 1809 C; orders war preparations against Britain, 1811 L; presidential election, 1812 L
'Mad Mullah', in Somaliland, 1899 J
Madoc (R. Southey), 1805 U
Madras, India, East India Company at, 1769 F
Madrid, Spain: treaty, 1801 J; Murat occupies, 1808 C; capitulates to Napoleon, 1808 M; Nationalist rising against French, 1808 E; rebels in, 1808 H; Wellington enters, 1812 H; Prado Museum, 1818 S; Monarchists in, 1873 D; University, closed by government, 1929 C; siege, 1936 L; surrenders to Franco, 1939 C
Maestricht, Belgium, Joseph II renounces claim to, 1785 L
Maeterlinck, Maurice, Belg. author (1862–1949), 1862 Z, 1889 U, 1892 W, 1901 U, 1909 U, 1949 Z
Mafeking, Cape Province, S. Africa, relieved, 1900 E
Mafia, in Sicily, 1926 J
Magdala, Ethiopia, 1868 D
Magic Mountain, The (T. Mann), 1924 U
Magenta, Italy, battle, 1859 F
Magersfontein, Orange Free State, S. Africa, 1899 M
Maginot, André, F. military expert, 1877 Z, 1932 Z
Maginot Line, France, 1930 O; extended, 1937 B
Magna Carta, 750th anniversary celebrations, 1965 O
Magnano, Italy, battle, 1799 D
Magnetic detection of electrical waves, 1896 P
Magnetic mines, 1939 L
Magnetic North Pole, 1946 P
Magnetic recordings, 1899 P; expedition to take, 1957 P
Magnetic tape, 1942 P
Magnetic waves, 1825 P
Magnetism, studies in, 1807 P, 1851 P, 1923 P
Magyars, oppose Francis Joseph, 1903 J, 1904 C
Mahan, Alfred Thayer, Am. admiral and naval historian (1840–1914), 1840 Z, 1890 Q, 1914 Z
Mahdi, The, Egyptian revolutionary. *See* Mahommed Ahmed ibn Seyyid Abdullah
Mahdists, attack Eritrea, 1893 M
Mahiwa, E. Africa, German attack on, 1917 K
Mahler, Gustave, Aus. musician (1860–1911), 1860 Z, 1888 T, 1895 T, 1900 T, 1909 T, 1911 T, Z, 1964 T
Mahmud II, Sultan of Turkey (1808–39), 1808 G, 1839 F; dissolves Janissaries, 1826 F; rejects Allies' rights to mediate in Greek war, 1827 M
Mahommed Ahmed ibn Seyyid Abdullah, Dongolese leader of Egyptian revolutionaries ('The Mahdi'), (d. 1885), 1883 L, 1884 B, K, 1885 F
Mahommed Ali, Shah of Persia, deposed, 1909 G
Mohamed V, Sultan of Turkey (1909–18), 1909 D
Mahrattas, Indian tribe of W. and Central India, 1770 N, 1773 J, 1795 C; British alliance with, 1790 E; British war against, 1802 K, 1803 H
Mai, Angelo, It. cardinal and philologist (1782–1854), 1819 Q
Maid of Orleans, The (F. Schiller), 1801 U
Mailer, Norman, Am. author (b. 1923), 1948 U, 1959 U, 1965 U
Maillol, Aristide, F. sculptor (1861–1944), 1906 S
Mail-train robbery, 1963 H, 1964 D
Maine, state, US: enters Union, 1820 C; prohibition in, 1851 N, O; repeal of, defeated, 1911 J; remains Republican, 1936 L
Maine, Sir Henry James Sumner, B. jurist (1822–1888), 1861 Q, 1885 O
Main Streams of XIXth Century Literature (G. Brandes), 1872 Q
Main Street (S. Lewis), 1920 U
Maisky, Ivan, R. diplomat, 1884 Z
Maison Tellier, Le (G. de Maupassant), 1881 U
Maistre, Joseph de, F. author (1755–1821), 1796 O, 1809 O, 1817 R
Maistre, Xavier de, F. author (1763–1852), 1763 Z, 1794 U
Maitland, Frederic William, B. historian (1850–1906), 1850 Z, 1887 Q, 1894 Q, 1906 Z
Major Barbara (G. B. Shaw), 1907 W
Majuba Hill, Natal, S. Africa, B. defeat at, 1881 B
Makarios III, Archbishop of Cyprus (b. 1913), deported to Seychelles, 1956 C; released, 1957 C; returns to Cyprus, 1959 C; becomes president of Cyprus Republic, 1960 H; abrogates 1960 Treaty, 1964 D
Makin, Gilbert Isles, Pacific, US occupy, 1943 L
Making of Americans, The (G. Stein), 1925 U
Making of the President, The (T. H. White), 1962 O
Malaga, Spain, falls to rebels, 1937 B

Malagasy Republic (formerly Madagascar), independence, 1960 F
Malan, Douglas Francois, S. Afr. Nationalist (1877–1955), 1934 F; forms ministry, 1948 F; race legislation invalidated by Supreme Court, 1952 C, D; retires, 1954 M
Malaria: parasite observed, 1880 P; bacillus discovered, 1897 P
Malawi, Republic (formerly Nyasaland), becomes an independent republic, 1964 G
Malay States, 1873 N
Malaya: Japanese attack on, 1941 M; independent federation proposed, 1956 A, 1957 H
Malaysian Federation: proposed, 1961 E, 1962 G; Singapore and N. Borneo vote to join, 1962 J; formed, 1963 J
Malcolm X, Am. Black Muslim leader, 1965 B
Malenkov, George Maximilianovich, R. leader (b. 1901), chairman of Council of Ministers, 1953 C; premier, 1954 D; resigns, 1955 B; visits Britain, 1956 C; expelled from Soviet Central Committee, 1957 G
Malesherbes, Chrétien Guillaume de Lamoignon de F. statesman (1721–94), 1775 G, 1776 E
Malet conspiracy against Napoleon, 1812 K
Mali, Federated state of, 1959 A
Malik, Jacob, R. politician, 1950 H
Malipiero, Francesco, It. musician, 1931 T, 1952 T
Mallarmé, Stéphane, F. author (1842–98), 1842 Z, 1876 U, 1898 Z
Malmédy is united with Belgium, 1920 A
Malmö, Sweden, truce between Denmark and Prussia, 1848 H
Malone, Edmund, B. literary critic (1714–1812), 1778 Q
Malouet, Pierre Victor, F. publicist and politician (1740–1814), 1789 O
Malraux, André, F. author (b. 1901), 1901 Z, 1933 W, 1935 U, 1937 U, 1950 R
Malta: captured by France, 1798 F; Britain takes, 1800 J, L; restored to Knights of St. John, 1801 K; restored to Britain, 1815 F; Indian troops sent to, 1878 C; air attack on, 1942 D; convoys to, 1942 F, H; awarded George Cross, 1942 O; legislative assembly demands employment for dockyard workers, 1957 M; governor assumes control, 1958 D; requests independence within Commonwealth, 1962 H; Britain agrees to grant independence, 1963 H; becomes independent, 1964 J
Malthus, Thomas Robert, B. political economist (1766–1834), 1766 Z, 1798 O, 1815 O, 1820 P, 1834 Z
Malvern, Lord. *See* Huggins, Godfrey
Malus, Étienne Louis, F. physicist (1775–1812), 1809 P
Mälzel, Johann Nepomuk, G. inventor of metronome (1772–1838), 1814 T
Mamelles de Tirésias, Les (G. Apollinaire), 1917 W
Mamelukes, massacre of, 1811 C
Man, Isle of, fiscal rights in, 1765 J
Managerial Revolution, The (J. Burnham), 1942 O
Managil Project, Sudan, 1958 G
Man and Materialism (F. Hoyle), 1957 R
Man and Superman (G. B. Shaw), 1903 W
Man Born to be King (D. L. Sayers), 1943 W
Manchester, England, 1774 R, 1817 C; Peterloo Massacre in, 1819 H; Anti-Corn Law League founded in, 1838 J, O; Owens College, 1851 O, 1880 O; Church Congress at, 1863 R; Fenianism in, 1867 J; University, 1880 O; Ship Canal, 1893 P; John Rylands Library, 1899 Q; Corporation's suit with Palace of Varieties, 1954 O; Jodrell Bank radio telescope, 1957 P
Manchukuo: Republic proclaimed, 1932 A; Pi Yi becomes president, 1932 L; emperor of, 1934 C; Germany recognises, 1938 E; Japanese-Russian clash on borders, 1938 G
Manchuria: Russo-Chinese convention on, 1896 J; Russia's right to operate railway in Northern, 1896 F; Russian occupation, 1900 L; Russian evacuation, 1901 B, 1902 D, 1903 H; Russo-Japanese agreement on, 1910 G, 1912 H; Japanese leases in, 1915 A; Japanese occupation of, 1931 J; republic proclaimed, 1932 A; Lytton Report on, 1932 K, 1933 B; China regains sovereignty over, 1945 J; fighting for control of, 1945 K
Manchus, in China, expulsion of, demanded, 1905 N
Mancroft, Stormont Mancroft Samuel, Lord Mancroft, B. financier (b. 1901), 1963 M
Mandalay, Upper Burma: British occupy, 1885 L; Japanese take, 1942 E; 14th Army enters, 1945 C
'M. and B.' (sulphapyradine), 1938 P
Mandated Territories:
  by Supreme Allied Council, 1919 L, 1920 D
  British in Iraq, ends, 1932 K
    in Palestine ends, 1948 E
  See also under League of Nations
Mandela, Nelson, S. African politician, sentenced, 1964 F
Manet, Édouard, F. artist (1832–83), 1832 Z, 1858 S, 1859 S, 1860 S, 1862 S, 1863 S, 1865 S, 1867 S, 1868 S, 1873 S, 1877 S, 1882 S, 1883 Z
Man for All Seasons, A (R. Bolt), 1960 W
Man for Himself (Fromm), 1949 R
Manfred (Byron), 1817 U
'Manhattan Project', for splitting atom, 1941 P
Manhattan Transfer (J. Dos Passos), 1925 U
Manifestoes:
  African Charter, issued by Casablanca Conference, 1961 A
  Atlantic Charter, 1941 H, J
  Brunswick's, Duke of, 1792 G
  Communist, 1848 O
  Fundamental Rights, German, 1848 M
    abolished, 1851 N
  Futurist, 1910 S
  Human Rights, UN declaration on, 1948 M
  Lagos Charter, for Pan-African Co-operation, 1962 A
  Lassalles Working-Class Programme, 1862 O
  Nationalisation, British Labour Party retains 'clause 4', 1960 C
  October Manifesto, by Canadians for union with US, 1849 K
  October, in Russia, 1905 K
  Ostend, advises US acquisition of Cuba, 1854 K
  Peace, by German Social Democrats, 1915 F
  Pillnitz, Declaration, 1791 H
  Polish National Committee, 1863 A
  Potomac Charter, 1954 F
  Rights of Man, French Declaration of, 1789 H
  Russian Communist Party condemns Mao Tse-tung's dogmatism, 1960 H
  Scharnhorst's, for reforming Prussian army, 1807 N
  Spanish Liberal, 1854 G
  Surrealist, 1929 S
  Tamworth, by Peel, 1834 M
  Viborg, issued by Russian Cadets, 1906 G
  Washington Declaration, on Anglo-US policy in Middle East, 1956 B
  Western Powers, for German re-unification and free elections, 1957 G

Manila, Philippines: Spain regains, 1763 B; Spanish fleet destroyed at, 1898 E; US captures, 1898 H; sterilisation of water in, 1912 P; US troops enter, 1945 B
Manin, Daniele, It. revolutionary (1804–57), 1848 C
Man in the Zoo, A (D. Garnett), 1924 U
Manitoba, Province, Canada, 1870 E
Mankiewicz, Joseph L., Am. film director (b. 1909), 1963 W
Mankind and Technology (O. Spengler), 1931 R
Mann, Anthony, B. film director, 1930 W, 1961 W
Mann, Horace, Am. educationalist (1796–1859), 1837 O
Mann, Thomas, G. author (1875–1955), 1901 U, 1913 U, 1924 U, 1933 U, 1939 U
Mann, Tom, B. syndicalist and trades union leader (1856–1941), 1910 O, 1912 C
Mannerheim, Carl, Baron, Fin. soldier (1868–1951), 1868 Z
Mannerheim Line, Finland, Russian attack on, 1940 B
Mannheim, W. Germany, 1795 J, 1819 C
Mannheim, Karl, G. philosopher, 1956 R
Manning, Henry Edward, B. cardinal (1808–92), 1850 R, 1869 R
Man of Property, The (J. Galsworthy), 1906 U
Man on His Nature (C. Sherrington), 1939 R
Manry, Robert, Am. sailor, 1965 X
Mansbridge, Albert, B. founder of WEA (1876–1952), 1904 O
Mansergh, Philip Nicholas, B. author (b. 1910), 1949 O
'Mansfield, Katherine.' *See* Murray, Kathleen
Mansfield, Earl of. *See* Murray
Mansfield Park (J. Austen), 1814 U
Mansion, The (W. Faulkner), 1959 U
Man's Place in Nature (T. H. Huxley), 1863 P
Manstein, Field Marshal, G., fails to relieve Stalingrad, 1942 M
Mantes, Russian agent in US, 1921 A
Manteuffel, Otto von, Prussian premier, 1850 L
Mantoux, Étienne, F. historian, 1946 O
Mantua, Italy: attempted relief, 1796 H; surrenders to French, 1797 B
Manual of Rational Pathology (F. G. J. Henle), 1846 P
Manuel II of Portugal (1908–10), 1908 B, 1910 K
Manufactured goods, comparative statistics of increases in production, 1913 Y
Manuscripts, discoveries, 1842 R, 1948 Q
Man versus the State, The (H. Spencer), 1884 O
Man Who Came to Dinner, The (G. S. Kaufman), 1939 W
Man Who was Thursday, The (G. K. Chesterton), 1908 U
Man With A Load of Mischief, The (A. Dukes), 1925 W
Manxman, The (Hall Caine), 1894 U
Manzoni, Alessandro, It. author (1785–1873), 1785 Z, 1813 U, 1821 U, 1825 U, 1873 Z
Maoris, in New Zealand: chiefs surrender to Britain, 1840 B; revolts, 1843 F, 1845 C, 1863 E; British wars with, 1860 C, 1861 C, 1865 J, 1868 F
Mao-Tse-tung, President of China (b. 1893), 1949 K; negotiations with Chiang Kai-shek break down, 1945 K; resigns as chairman of Republic, 1959 D; dogmatism of, condemned by Russian Communist Party, 1960 H
Maps and Atlases: Bengal Atlas, 1779 P; aeronautical map of France, 1911 P; geological, 1841 P; the Vinland, 1965 Q
Marakeesh, Morocco, 1908
Marat, Jean Paul, F. revolutionary (1743–93), 1793 G
Marc, Franz, G. artist (1880–1916), 1911 S, 1912 S, 1913 S
Marc au diable, La (G. Sand), 1846 U
Marcel, Gabriel, F. dramatist (b. 1889), 1921 W
Marcel Proust (G. Painter), 1865 Q
Marchand, Major, F. soldier, 1896 F, 1897 G
Marconi, Guglielmo, It. inventor of wireless telegraphy (1874–1937), 1874 Z, 1895 P, 1901 P, 1920 W, 1937 Z
Marconi Scandal, 1913 F
Marconiphone Company, 1933 P
Marcus, Frank, B. dramatist, 1965 W
Mare, Walter de la, B. poet (1873–1956), 1873 Z, 1935 U, 1956 Z
Marengo, Italy, Napoleon's victory at, 1800 F
Mareth Line, N. Africa, Montgomery breaks through, 1943 C
Marey, Etienne Jules, P. physiologist and inventor (1830–1904), 1888 P
Margaret, Princess, Countess of Snowdon (b. 1930), 1960 E
Margarine, invented, 1869 P; substitution for butter, limited in US, 1912 O
Maria I, Queen of Portugal (1777–1816), 1777 B, 1816 C; as Regent, 1774 N
Maria II, Queen of Portugal (1826–53), 1831 D, 1853 L; accession as an infant, 1826 E; British support for, 1826 M, 1827 A; returns to Lisbon, 1833 G; restoration, 1834 E, J
Maria Christina, Queen Regent of Spain, 1854 H
Maria Theresa, Archduchess of Austria, Queen of Hungary and Bohemia, wife of the Holy Roman Emperor Francis I (1717–80), 1765 H, 1780 L
Mariage de Figaro (P. Beaumarchais), 1784 W
Marianne Island, Pacific, bought by Germany, 1899 B
Marie Alexandrovna, R. Princess, married Alfred, Duke of Edinburgh, 1874 A
Marie Antoinette, daughter of Empress Maria Theresa of Austria (1755–1793): marries Louis XVI, 1770 E; discredited by Diamond Necklace affair, 1785 H; executed, 1793 K
Marie-Louise, of Austria, married Napoleon I, 1810 B
Mariette, Auguste Ferdinand Francois, F. Egyptologist (1821–81), 1850 Q
Marienbad, now Czechoslovakia, 1907 J, 1922 H
Marine Biological Association, 1884 P
Marinetti, F. T., F. poet (1876–1944), 1909 S
Marini, Marino, It. sculptor (b. 1901), 1936 S, 1952 S
Marion, Ohio, US, 1898 P
Maritain, Jacques, F. theologian (b. 1882), 1920 R, 1943 R, 1949 U
Marius the Epicurean (W. Pater), 1885 U
Marlborough, His Life and Times (W. S. Churchill), 1933 Q
Marmion (W. Scott), 1808 U
Marmont, Auguste Frédéric Louis, Duke of Ragusa, F. general (1774–1852), 1812 G
Marmontel, Jean François, F. author (1723–99), 1767 R, 1770 U
Marne, River, France, battles, 1914 J, 1918 G
Marquand, John Phillips, B. author (1893–1960), 1937 U
Marquis, Frederick James, lord Woolton, B. Conservative (1893–1964), 1941 D, 1943 L
Marriage:
in Austria, civil, 1783 O, 1894 R
Roman Catholic control of, 1855 H

in Britain, of Nonconformists, 1833 R
registration, 1836 H
civil, in England and Wales, 1857 O
in France, civil, 1792 R
in Germany, mixed, in Prussia, 1837 R
civil, 1874 O
in Italy, minimum age of brides raised, 1892 O
in Morocco, women permitted to choose husbands, 1958 O
in S. Africa, mixed, forbidden, 1949 F
in Turkey, civil, 1926 J
in US, polygamy among Mormons, 1843 R
See also under Divorce
Marriage, notable:
King Baudouin, 1960 M
Princess Elizabeth, 1947 L
Luisa Fernanda with Duc de Montpensier, 1846 K
Marie Antoinette, 1770 E
Princess Margaret, 1960 E
Napoleon's, 1796 C, 1810 B
Prince Rainer to Grace Kelly, 1956 W
Duke of Windsor, 1937 F
Married Women's property act, in Britain, 1870 H, 1882 O
Marryat, Frederick, B, novelist (1792–1848), 1836 U
Mars, planet: satellites of discovered, 1877 P; photo-electric observations, 1955 P; conditions in, 1963 P; photographs of, 1964 P, 1965 P
Marsa, Tunisia, convention, 1883 F
Marseilles, France, Franco-Italian agreement, 1935 A
Marsh, Sir Edward, B. civil servant and promoter of literature (1872–1953), 1911 U, 1918 U
Marshall, Alfred, B. economist (1842–1924), 1842 Z, 1890 O, 1923 O, 1924 Z
Marshall, George Catlett, Am. general and statesman (1880–1959), 1880 Z, 1942 D, 1951 E; commands Allied occupation of Japan, 1945 H; attempts mediation in China, 1945 M; becomes Secretary of State, 1947 A; calls for European Recovery Programme (Marshall Aid), 1947 F; retires, 1949 A; becomes defense secretary, 1950 J
Marshall Plan, 1947 F, 1948 C; Germany becomes a full member of, 1949 M; aid to Britain ceases, 1950 M; replaced by Mutual Security Agency, 1951 M
Marshall, John, Am. jurist (1755–1835), 1819 O
Mars-la-Tour, France, Prussian victory at, 1870 H
Martens, Georg Friedrich von, G. jurist and diplomat (1756–1821), 1791 Q
Martha Quest (D. Lessing), 1952 U
Martial Law: in Belgium, 1936 K; in Germany, 1923 J
Martignac, Jean Baptiste Sylvere Gay, Vicomte de, F. Doctrinaire Royalist (1778–1832), becomes premier, 1828 A; attacks Jesuits, 1828 F; is dismissed, 1829 H
Martin, John, B. artist (1789–1854), 1822 S
Martin, Kingsley, B. journalist (b. 1897), 1897 Z, 1931 V
Martin, Pierre Émile, F. engineer (1824–1915), 1861 P
Martineau, James, B. Unitarian divine (1805–1900), 1888 R
Martinu, Botuslav, Czech. musician (1890–1959), 1956 T
Martinique, West Indies: restored to France, 1763 B; Britain captures, 1794 N, 1809 N
Marx Brothers, Am. film actors, 1941 W
Marx, Heinrich Karl, G. Socialist (1818–83), 1818 Z, 1847 O, 1848 O, 1867 O, 1883 Z, 1885 O, 1886 O, 1895 O
Marx, Wilhelm, G. Centre Party Chancellor (1863–1936), 1924 E, 1925 A, 1926 E, 1927 A, 1928 F
Mary, Queen Consort of King George V of Gt. Britain (Princess Mary of Teck), 1867 Z, 1953 Z
Mary Barton (E. Gaskell), 1848 U
Marylebone Cricket Club (M.C.C.), 1787 X, 1788 X, 1814 X
Mary Stuart (F. Schiller), 1800 W
Marzeppa (Byron), 1819 U
Masampo, Korea, 1900 C
Masaryk, Thomas Garrigue, Czech. statesman (1850–1937), 1850 Z, 1895 O, 1935 M, 1937 Z; elected president of Czechoslovakia, 1918 L; re-elected, 1927 E
Mascall, Eric Lionel, B. churchman (b. 1905), 1949 R
Masefield, John, B. poet (b. 1878), 1878 Z, 1902 U, 1911 U, 1933 U, 1941 O, 1961 U
Mashonaland, Rhodesia, 1890 J
Maskelyne, Nevil, B. astronomer (1732–1811), 1767 P
Masks and Faces (C. Reade), 1852 W
Mass, Roman Catholic, in vernacular, 1786 R, 1964 R
musical settings of, notable, 1766 T, 1796 T, 1783 T, 1949 T
Massacres:
of Armenians by Turks, 1895 K, L, 1896 H
Gladstone on, 1896 J
of Assyrian Christians, 1933 G
of British by Afghans, 1841 L, 1879 J
by Indians, at Cawnpore, 1857 F, G
by Zulus, at Isandhlwana, 1879 A
of Bulgarians, by Turks, 1876 C
of Christians, by Druses in Syria, 1860 J
of French, during 'June Days', 1848 F
of Greeks, at Chios, by Turks, 1822 D
of Irish family at Maamtrasna, 1882 H
of Turks, by Greeks, 1821 K
of Poles, by Russians, at Warsaw, 1861 B
of Indians in US, at Wyoming, 1778 G
at Cherry Valley, 1778 L
of Anapahoe Indians, 1864 L
of Cheyenne Indians, 1864 L
of US pro-slavers at Pottawatomie Creek, 1856 E
Massachusetts, state, US: Colonial assembly dissolved, 1768 G; committees of correspondence in, 1772 L; coercive acts against, 1774 C; educational reforms in, 1837 O
Massachusetts Institute of Technology, 1865 O; develops ultra-high-frequency waves, 1955 P
Massachusetts Spy, The, 1770 V
Massawa, Eritrea: Italians occupy, 1885 B; British take, 1941 D
Mass Civilization and Minority Culture (F. R. Leavis), 1930 O
Masséna, André, F. general, Duke of Rivoli (1756–1817), 1799 F, J
Massenet, Jules, F. musician (1842–1912), 1842 Z, 1884 T, 1894 T, 1906 T, 1912 Z
Massey, Vincent, Canad. statesman (b. 1887), 1887 Z; becomes Canadian minister to Washington, 1926 L; becomes Governor General of Canada, 1952 A
Massey, William Ferguson, N. Zeal. politician (1856–1925), 1856 Z, 1925 E; becomes premier, 1912 G
Mass-spectrograph, 1919 P
Mastai-Ferretti, Giovanni Maria, It. cardinal, Pope Pius IX (1846–78), 1792 Z, 1878 Z; elected Pope, 1846 F. *See under* Pius IX
Masters, John, B. author (b. 1914), 1954 U
Masters, The (C. P. Snow), 1950 U
Masuria, Poland (formerly East Prussia), battles, 1914 J, 1915 B

Matabeleland, Rhodesia: under British protection, 1888 B; mineral rights in, 1888 K; risings in, 1893 G; revolt in, crushed, 1893 L; British occupation, 1894 A
Matapan, Cape, Italy, naval battle off, 1941 C
Matches:
friction, invented, 1827 P
phosphorus, prohibited in Britain, 1908 O
safety, 1898 P
Mateos, López, Mex. president, 1964 M
Materialism and Empiric Criticism (Lenin), 1909 O
Maternity benefits, in Germany, 1914 O
Mathematical Logic (G. Boole), 1847 P
Mathematics of Commerce (A. Cournot), 1838 O
Mathematics:
algebraic equations, 1846 P
bi-quaternions, 1873 P
calculus of forms, 1852 P
linear transformations, theory of, 1845 P
numbers, theory of, 1854 P
of relativity, 1908 P
primary numbers, treatise on, 1850 P
See also Geometry
Matière et Mémoire (H. Bergson), 1896 R
Matisse, Henri, F. artist and sculptor (1869–1954), 1869 Z, 1905 S, 1907 S, 1909 S, 1911 S, 1914 S, 1916 S, 1920 S, 1927 S, 1928 S, 1930 S, 1931 S, 1940 S, 1954 S
Matteotti, Giacomo, It. Socialist, 1924 F
Matterhorn, The, Switzerland, ascents, 1865 X, 1965 X
Matthew, Robert, B. architect, 1951 S
Matthews, Sir Bryan, B. scientist (b. 1906), 1929 P
Mattingly, Garrett, Am. historian (d. 1963), 1959 Q
Mattini, Il (G. Parini), 1763 U
Mauberge, France, British take, 1918 L
Maud and Other Poems (Tennyson), 1855 U
Maude, Angus, B. Conservative politician (b. 1912), 1949 O
Maude, Frederick Stanley, B. soldier (1864–1917), 1917 D
Maudling, Reginald, B. Conservative politician (b. 1917), Chancellor of Exchequer, 1962 G, 1963 D
Maudslay, Henry, B. engineer (1771–1831), 1797 P, 1800 P
Maufe, Sir Edward, B. architect (b. 1883), 1961 S
Maugham, William Somerset, B. author (1874–1965), 1874 Z, 1915 U, 1919 U, 1926 U, 1930 W, 1944 U, 1965 Z; portrait, 1949 S
Mau Mau terrorists in Kenya, 1952 K, 1953 D, H; Kenya government's terms for surrender, 1955 A; prisoners' deaths at Hola Camp, 1959 C
Maunsell, G., B. architect, 1961 S
Maupassant, Guy de, F. author (1850–93), 1850 Z, 1880 U, 1881 U, 1883 U, 1885 U, 1888 U, 1893 Z
Maupeon, René Nicolas Charles Augustin, F. statesman (1714–92), 1770 M, 1771 A
Maurepas, Jean Frédéric Phéypeaux, Comte de, F. statesman (1701–81), 1774 E
Mauriac, François, F. author (b. 1885), 1964 O
Maurice, Frederick Denison, B. churchman (1805–1872), 1849 R, 1853 R, 1854 O
Maurice, Sir Frederick (1871–1951), B. soldier and administrator, 1918 E
Maurier, Sir Gerald Hubert Edward Busson de, B. actor-manager (1873–1934), 1873 Z, 1910 W, 1934 Z
Mauritania, becomes an independent Islamic republic, 1960 L
Mauritius, Indian Ocean: British take, 1810 G; constitutional conference promises independence, 1965 J
Maury, Jean Giffrein, F. churchman (1746–87), Cardinal Archbishop of Paris, 1800 C
Maury, Matthew Fontaine, Am. hydrographer (1806–73), 1855 P
Mavor, Osborne Henry. *See* Bridie, James
Max, Prince of Baden, 1918 K, L
Maxim, Sir Hiram, Am. gunsmith (1840–1916), 1884 P
Maxim, Hudson, Am. inventor, 1853 Z, 1927 Z
Maximilian, Archduke of Austria (1832–67), becomes Emperor of Mexico, 1864 D; loses French support, 1867 C; is executed, 1867 F
Maximilian III, King of Bavaria (1745–77), 1777 M
Max-Müller, Friedrich, B. orientalist and philologist (1823–1900), 1875 Q, 1878 R
Maxwell-Fyfe, David, Lord Kilmuir, Conservative politician, Lord Chancellor (b. 1900), 1962 G
May, Princess of Teck. *See* Mary, Queen
May, Nunn, B. atomic spy, 1952 O
May, Philip William ('Phil'), B. cartoonist (1864–1903), 1896 V
May Committee on Britain's budget deficit, 1931 G
May Day Labour celebrations, 1890 O
Mayence, France, 1792 K, 1793 G, 1797 M
Mayer, Julius, G. physicist (1814–87), 1842 P
Mayer, Sir Robert, B. promoter of children's concerts (b. 1879), 1923 T
Mayerling, near Vienna, Austria, 1889 A
Maynooth College, Ireland: founded, 1795 R; British grant to, 1845 F
Mayo, county, Eire, boycotting in, 1880 N
Mayo, Earl of. *See* Bourke, R. S.
Mazzini, Giuseppe, It. statesman (1805–72), 1805 Z, 1832 O, 1834 B, 1872 Z; proclaims Roman Republic, 1849 B
Meade, Margaret, B. anthropologist (b. 1901), 1901 Z, 1935 R, 1950 R, 1953 Q
Meade, George Gordon, Am. Unionist general (1815–72), 1863 G
Meade, James Edward, B. economist (b. 1907), 1935 A
Means-test, in Britain, 1935 A, 1936 G
Measles, vaccine for, 1963 P
Meat:
chilling process for, 1934 P
frozen, 1877 P, 1879 P
Mécanique analytique (Lagrange), 1788 P
Mechanics, studies in, 1788 P
Medical practitioners, unqualified, prohibited from practising, 1815 O. *See also* Health Service
Medieval history, study of, 1866 Q
Médiations poétiques (A. de Lamartine), 1870 U
Mediterranean, Anglo-French agreement on, 1937 A
Mee, Arthur, B. journalist (1875–1943), 1919 V
Meerut, India, mutiny of, 1857 E
Meetings: British act to prevent seditious, 1817 C; in Egypt, British ultimatum for free, 1928 D; political in Persia, banned, 1961 E
Mège-Mouries, H., F. chemist (1817–80), 1869 P
Mehemet Ali, Egypt. ruler (d. 1849), 1811 C; quits Greece, 1828 H; Turkey recognises independence in Egypt, 1833 E; powers reserve right to treat with, 1839 G; terms of Quadruple Alliance to, 1840 G, L; is forced to submit, 1840 J, K; death, 1849 H
Meighen, Arthur, Can. politician (1874–1960), 1920 G, 1926 F
Meiji, dynasty in Japan, 1868 A
Meikle, Andrew, B. millwright and inventor (1719–1811), 1748 P
Meinecke, Frederick, G. historian (1862–1959), 1908 O, 1936 Q

Mein Kampf (A. Hitler), 1925 O, 1927 O
Melba, Nellie, Austral. operatic singer (1861–1931), 1861 Z, 1931 Z
Melbourne, Australia, Olympic Games at, 1956 X
Melbourne, Viscount. *See* Lamb, William
Meline, Félix Jules, F. Conservative Republican (1838–1912), 1891 N, 1896 D
Mellon, Andrew William, Am. politician (1855–1937), 1923 F
Mellon, Paul, Am. executive art collector and benefactor (b. 1907), 1937 S
Mellini, Macedonio, It. physicist (1798–1854), 1831 P, 1850 P
Mellors, Wilfrid, B. musicologist, 1964 T
Melville, Herman, Am. author (1819–91), 1819 Z, 1846 U, 1851 U, 1891 Z
Melville, Jean, Am. film director, 1949 W
Memel, Lithuania: Germans capture, 1915 B; under Allied Control, 1920 B; seized from Allies by Lithuania, 1923 A, B; German-Lithuanian arbitration treaty, 1928 A; Germany annexes, 1939 C
Memento Mori (M. Spark), 1959 U
Mémoires d'Outre-tombe (Chateaubriand), 1848 U
Memoirs of an Aesthete (H. Acton), 1948 U
Menai Straits, England: suspension bridge, 1819 P; tubular railway bridge, 1849 P
Men and Power (Lord Beaverbrook), 1956 Q
Men at Arms (E. Waugh), 1952 U
Mencken, H. L., Am. critic (1880–1956), 1919 Q
Mendel, Gregor, R. biologist (1822–82): establishes laws of heredity, 1866 P; work of, rediscovered, 1900 P
Mendeléev, Dimitry Ivanovich, R. chemist (1834–1907), 1834 Z, 1869 P, 1907 Z
Mendelssohn, Moses, G. philosopher (1729–86), 1767 R, 1781 R, 1783 R, 1785 U
Mendelssohn, E., Am. architect, 1935 S
Mendelssohn-Bartholdy, Felix, G. musician (1809–1847), 1809 Z, 1826 T, 1829 T, 1833 T, 1842 T, 1846 T, 1844 T, 1847 Z
establishes Leipzig Conservatoire, 1843 T
as conductor, 1839 T
Menderes, Adnam, Turk. politician (1899–1961), 1955 M, 1960 E
Mendes-France, Pierre, F. Radical-Socialist (b. 1907), as premier, 1954 F; resigns, 1955 B
Meneghini, G. B. *See* Callas, Maria
Menelek, King of Ethiopia (1889–1911), 1889 L, 1891 B, 1897 E; as Menelek of Shoa revolts against Johannes IV, 1888 M; denounces Italian claims, 1891 B
Menon, Krishna. *See* Krishna Menon
Menotti, Gian Carlo, It. musician (b. 1911), 1942 T, 1950 T, 1954 T
Menschenhass und Reue (A. Kötzebue), 1797 W
Mensheviks. *See under* Political Parties
Menshikov, Prince Alexander, R. emissary to Turkey (1787–1869), 1853 D, E
Mental Evolution in Man (G. T. Romanes), 1888 R
Mental Health, treatment of, 1792 O, 1893 P, 1953 O, 1959 O. *See also* Asylums
Mental Patients, Royal Commission on, 1953 O
system of detention reformed, 1959 O
Mentana, Italy, Garibaldi's defeat at, 1867 L
Mentone, France, purchased from Monaco, 1862 B
Menuhin, Yehudi, Am. violinist (b. 1916), 1916 Z
Men without Women (E. Hemingway), 1927 U
Menzel, Adolph Friedrich Erdmann von, G. artist (1815–1905), 1815 Z, 1875 S, 1905 Z
Menzies, Sir Robert Gordon, Austral. Liberal statesman (b. 1894), 1894 Z, 1954 A; becomes premier, 1939 D; forms new coalition, 1949 M, 1954 E, 1961 M
Mercure, Paris journal, 1770 V
Merchant Shipping:
in Britain, contract for Cunard Q4 liner, 1964 M
control of, 1875 O
construction in wartime, 1940 Y, 1941 Y, 1942 Y, 1943 Y
convoy system for, 1917 O
'Liberty' ships, 1943 O
reforms in, 1906 O
registered tonnage, 1786 Y, 1806 Y, 1826 Y, 1836 Y, 1846 Y, 1856 Y, 1866 Y, 1876 Y, 1886 Y, 1896 Y, 1914 Y, 1919 Y, 1926 Y, 1939 Y, 1946 Y, 1951 Y, 1964 Y
wartime losses, 1914 Y, 1915 Y, 1916 Y, 1917 Y, 1918 Y, 1939 L, Y, 1940 J, Y, 1941 Y, 1942 Y, 1943 Y, 1944 Y, 1945 A, Y
in US, conditions in, improved, 1915 A
Wilson arms, without Congressional authority, 1917 C
world tonnages, 1914 Y, 1919 Y, 1939 Y, 1946 Y, 1951 Y, 1964 Y
losses in war, 1918 Y, 1945 Y
Mercier, Cardinal, Belg., 1916 L
Mercury, planet, rotation of, 1889 P
Meredith, George, B. author (1828–1909), 1828 Z, 1859 U, 1862 U, 1879 U, 1885 U, 1902 Z
Mérimée, Prosper, F. author (1803–70), 1803 Z, 1830 U, 1840 U, 1847 W, 1870 Z
Merrill, John Ogden, Am. architect (b. 1896), 1952 S
Mersah Matruh, Libya, British retreat to, 1942 F
Mery, Russia, Afghanistan cedes, 1884 A
Méryon, Charles, F. artist (1821–68), 1852 S
Mesmer, Franz Anton, Aus. physician (1733–1815), 1778 O, 1815 Z
Mesopotamia, Syria: Anglo-German agreement on, 1914 F; surrenders to Britain, 1915 F; Allied offensive, 1916 H; British offensive, 1916 M; Report of Commission on, 1917 O; mandate of, to Britain, 1920 D
Messager, André, F. musician, 1919 T
Messeniennes, Les (J. Delavigne), 1818 U
Messiah (G. F. Klopstock), 1773 U
Messina, Sicily, US troops occupy, 1943 H
Messines, France, battle, 1917 F
Metakritik (J. G. Herda), 1799 R
Metamorphose der Pflanzen (Goethe), 1790 O
Metamorphosis (R. Strauss), 1945 T
Metaphysical Foundations of the Theory of Right (Kant), 1797 R
Metaphysics (R. Lotze), 1841 R
Metaphysics of Logical Positivism (Bergmann), 1955 R
Metargon, discovered, 1898 P
Metaxas, John, Greek general and politician, becomes premier, 1936 D
Meteorites, study of, 1961 P
Meteors, size of, investigated, 1923 P
Meteorological Society, Royal, 1850 P
Meteorological Stations, 1937 P
Meteorology, studies in, 1897 P
Methene, British imports from Sahara, 1961 P
Methicllin, anti-biotic drug, 1960 P
Méthode de nomenclature chimique (A. Lavoisier), 1787 P
Methodists. *See under* Religious Denominations
Methods of Ethics (H. Sidgwick), 1874 R
Methuen, Paul, lord Methuen, B. soldier (1845–1932), 1899 M
Metric system, Britain's proposed change to, 1965 O

Metropolitan Police Force, London, founded, 1829 O
Metternich, Clemens, Prince, Aus. statesman (1773–1859), 1773 Z; as chief minister, 1809 H; agrees to peace conference, 1813 F; mediates Prussian armistice with France, 1813 F; presides over German confederation, 1816 L, 1819 J, L; presides at Vienna Conference, 1820 E; Six articles for re-actionary government, 1832 F
Metz, Moselle, N.E. France, France surrenders, 1870 K
Metzinger, Jean, F. artist (1883–1956), 1912 S
Meuse, River, France: Germans cross, 1914 H; French offensive near, 1916 M
Mexico:
revolt against Spain, 1810 J
declares independence, 1813 L
fresh proposals for independence, 1821 B
Emperor of, elected, 1822 E
becomes a republic, 1823 C
Britain recognises independence, 1824 M
Texas becomes independent of, 1836 C, D
US war with, 1846 D, E
Convention, following suspension of foreign debts, 1861 K
withdrawal of French troops in, 1865 K
coffee production in, 1909 Y
US punitive expedition to, 1916 C, F
Britain resumes diplomatic relations, 1941 K
Mexico, New, US: US negotiations for purchase, 1846 D; US obtains, 1846 H, 1848 E; admitted to statehood on conditions, 1911 H
Mexico City, Mexico: US captures, 1847 J; occupied by Constitutionalist Party, 1914 H; University, 1952 S; population, 1960 Y
Meyer, John Rudolf, Swi. mountaineer, 1811 P
Meyer, Konrad Ferdinand, Swi. poet (1825–98), 1887 U
Meyer, Nathan, Lord Rothschild, B. financier (1840–1915), 1898 O
Meyerbeer, Giacomo (Jakob Liebmann Beer), G. musician (1791–1864), 1791 Z, 1820 T, 1836 T, 1849 T, 1851 T, 1864 Z, 1937 T
Meyrin, near Geneva, Switzerland, international nuclear research laboratory near, 1953 P
Miall, Edward, B. Liberal politician (1809–81), 1844 O
Michael, King of Roumania, abdicates, 1947 M
Michael II, King of Serbia (1839–42), 1839 F
Michael III, Prince of Serbia (1860–68), 1868 F
Michaelis, George, G. Chancellor (1857–1943), 1917 G
Michaux, Henri, F. author (b. 1899), 1927 U, 1932 U, 1943 U
Michaux, Pierre, F. manufacturer of bicycles (d. 1883), 1867 P
Michelet, Jules, F. historian (1798–1874), 1798 Z, 1933 Q, 1847 Q, 1874 Z
Michigan, state, US, becomes a US state, 1837 A
Micklem, Nathaniel, B. theologian (b. 1888), 1941 R
Microgeology (C. Ehrenberg), 1854 P
Microphone, invented, 1878 P
Microscopes:
study of, 1770 P
'flying spot', 1951 P
ion, 1956 P
reflecting, 1947 P
ultramicroscope, 1903 P
Microscopic Investigations in the Structure . . . of Plants and Animals (T. Schwann), 1839 P
Microscopic study, 1770 P
Micro-wave laser, 1960 P
Middle Age of Mrs. Eliot, The (A. Wilson), 1958 U
Middleburg, S. Africa, 1901 B
Middle-classes, British, survey of, 1949 O
Middle East Crisis:
proposals for de-nuclearised zone, 1959 E
US 6th Fleet sails for Mediterranean, 1957 D
concentration of Turkish troops on Syrian borders, 1957 J
Syria declares state of emergency, 1957 K
Dulles warns Russia against attacking Turkey, 1957 K
Khrushchev appeals to Labour and Socialist Parties to prevent US aggression, 1957 K
Lebanon, amnesty in, 1958 M
Baghdad *coup*, 1958 G
Lebanon requests US troops, 1958 G
British paratroops land in Jordan, 1958 G
leave Jordan, 1958 L
See also Egypt; Israel; Jordan; Lebanon; Palestine; Suez
Middlemarch (G. Eliot), 1871 U
Middle Years, The (H. James), 1895 U, 1917 U
Midhat Pasha, Turk. politician (1822–84), 1876 E, 1877 B
Midlothian campaign, Gladstone's, 1879 L
Midway Islands, Pacific, battle in, 1942 F
Mignet, François, F. historian (1796–1884), 1796 Z, 1884 Z
Miguel, Dom Maria Evariste, Portug. pretender (1802–56), 1824 D, 1826 E, 1828 F, 1832 G; Spanish support for, 1826 M; as lieutenant in Portugal, 1827 G; as Regent, 1828 B; followers of, defeated, 1833 G; surrenders and abdicates, 1834 D; supporters of, rise, 1846 E
Miguel Street (V. S. Naipaul), 1959 U
Miklas, Wilhelm, Aus. president, 1928 M
Miklas, General, Hung. politician, 1945 A
Mikoyan, Anastas, R. politician (b. 1895), opens Havana exhibition, 1960 B; visits Cuba, 1962 L; becomes president of USSR, 1964 G; is replaced, 1965 M
Mikrokosmos (R. Lotze), 1856 R
Milan, Italy:
Napoleon enters, 1796 E
Murat occupies, 1800 F
Napoleon is crowned in, 1805 E
Brera Gallery in, 1806 S
Napoleon issues decrees against British trade, 1807 M
revoked, 1810 L
Peace, between Sardinia and Austria, 1849 H
liberated by French troops, 1859 F
People's Bank, 1866 O
Socialist International meets, 1952 K
Pirelli Building, 1958 S
Milan III, Prince of Serbia, 1839 F
Milan IV, Prince, later King, of Serbia (1868–89), 1868 F, 1882 C, 1889 C, 1901 B
Mildenhall, Suffolk, England, Anglo-Saxon treasure hoard at, 1942 Q
Mile, The, Bannister's record, 1954 X
Miles, Bernard, B. actor and producer (b. 1907), 1959 W
Milhaud, Darius, F. musician (b. 1892), 1920 T, 1930 T, 1940 T, 1946 T, 1953 T, 1954 T
Military and Political Consequences of Atomic Energy (P. Blackett), 1948 O
Military Conventions:
Anglo-French, 1905 D, 1906 A
Franco-Belgian, 1920 J
Franco-Polish, 1922 J
Franco-Prussian discussions for, 1911 H

Germano-Turkish, 1913 K
opposed by Britain and France, 1913 M
Militia:
in Britain, 1786 F. *See also* Local Defence Volunteers
in France, National Guard, 1789 G
Milinkov, Paul, R. Liberal, 1905 E, 1917 C
Milk:
evaporated, 1847 P
powdered, 1855 P
Milky Way, The, 1892 P
Mill, James, B. utilitarian philosopher (1773–1836), 1821 O 1829 Q
Mill, John Stuart, B. philosopher (1806–73), 1806 Z, 1843 R, 1844 R, 1848 O, 1859 O, 1860 O, 1862 R, 1865 R, 1867 R, 1869 R, 1873 U, Z
Millais, Sir John Everett, B. artist (1829–96), 1829 Z, 1848 S, 1850 S, 1896 Z
Mille, Agnes de, Am. choreographer, 1940 T
Mille, Cecil Blount de, Am. film director (b. 1881), 1881 Z, 1915 W, 1927 W
Miller, Arthur, Am. dramatist (b. 1915), 1915 Z, 1949 W, 1953 W, 1955 W, 1964 W
Miller, Henry, Am. author (b. 1891), 1962 U
Miller, Hugh, B. author and geologist (1802–56), 1838 P, 1846 U
Miller, Joachim, Am. author (?1841–1913), 1871 U
Miller, William, Am. leader of Second Adventists (1782–1849), 1831 R, 1842 R
Millerand, Alexandre, F. politician, President of France, 1920 H, 1924 F
Millesino, N. Italy, Austrian defeat at, 1796 D
Millet, Jean François, F. artist (1814–75), 1831 S, 1846 S, 1848 S, 1857 S, 1859 S
Mill, boring, 1774 P
Millikan, Robert Andrews, Am. physicist (1868–1953), 1925 P, 1933 P
Milling-machine, universal, 1862 P
Mill on the Floss, The (G. Eliot), 1860 U
Mills, C. Wright, Am. author, 1959 O
Milman, Henry Hart, B. churchman and author (1791–1868), 1829 Q, 1855 Q
Milne, Alan Alexander, B. journalist and author (1882–1956), 1922 W, 1926 U
Milne, Edward Arthur, B. mathematician (1896–1950), 1937 P
Milner, Alfred, Lord Milner, B. administrator (1854–1925), 1899 C, 1916 M, 1918 C; as high commissioner for S. Africa, 1897 H; policy criticised, 1903 B; as war secretary, 1918 D; conversations with Zaghlul on Egypt, 1920 H
Milner, John, B. Roman Catholic priest, Bishop of Castabala (1752–1826), 1810 R
Milosh (Obrenovich), of Serbia, 1835 N; Sultan limits authority of, 1838 M; abdicates, 1839 F; restored, 1858 M
Milton (W. Blake), 1804 U
Mimas, a satellite, discovered, 1789 P
Mind in Chains, The, 1937 O
Mind in Evolution (L. T. Hobhouse), 1901 R
Mindszenty, Cardinal, Hungarian: arrested, 1948 M; released, 1956 K
Mines, Coal:
in Britain, royal commission on, 1842 H
inspection, 1850 O
government control of, 1916 M
strikes, 1921 L, 1926 E, L
government enquiry, 1925 G
ballot, to press for wage increase, 1935 L
nationalisation of, 1946 E, 1947 A
in France, general strike, 1901 N
Mines, Diamond, in Tanganyika, 1946 P
in Transvaal, Chinese labour for, 1903 L
Mines, explosive, 1915 P
magnetic, 1939 L
Mines, School of, London, 1850 O
Minghetti, Marco, It. premier (1818–86), 1873 J, 1874 E, 1876 C
Minié, C. E., F. gunsmith, 1849 P
Minkowski, Herman, G. mathematician (1864–1909), 1908 P
Minna of Barnhelm (Lessing), 1767 W
Minnelieder, 1803 Q
Minnesota, state, US: becomes a US state, 1858 E; Sioux rising in, 1862 H
Minoan culture, discovery of, 1900 Q
Minorca, Island, Spain: ceded to Britain, 1763 B; Spanish capture, 1782 B; Spain retains, 1783 J; Britain captures, 1798 L
Minsk, Russia: Germans take, 1941 F; Russians recapture, 1944 G
Mirabeau, Gabriel Honoré de Riquetti, Comte de, F. statesman (1749–91), 1772 O; as Louis XVI's agent, 1790 E; elected President of Assembly, 1791 A; death, 1791 D, Z
Miracles (C. S. Lewis), 1947 R
Miracles in the New Testament (J. M. Thompson), 1911 R
Miranda, Francisco de, Sp. politician, 1811 G, 1812 G
Miranda (Fogazzaro), 1874 U
Mir Kasim, Nabwab of Murshidabad, 1763 G
Mirò, Joan, Sp. artist (b. 1893), 1922 S, 1937 S, 1959 S
Mirza, Iskander, President of Pakistan, 1958 K
Misérables, Les (V. Hugo), 1862 U
Mrs. Dalloway (V. Woolf), 1925 U
Mrs. Minniver (Jan Struther), 1939 U
Missiles:
Bloodhound, 1964 D
Blue Streak, 1960 D
launched, 1964 P
guided, vessels for, 1956 G
US to make available to Britain, 1957 C
pilotless, radio-controlled, 1946 P
Polaris, bases in England, Bulganin's note on, 1958 C
for Bundeswehr, Russia protests at, 1960 G
agreement from US to provide to Britain, in place of Skybolt, 1962 M
de Gaulle rejects offer of, 1963 A
US recommends surface ships of NATO fleet should carry, 1963 B
Anglo-US agreement on, 1963 D
Russian, in Cuba, 1962 M, L
V2 rockets, 1942 P, 1944 J, 1945 C
See also Rockets
Missionary Societies:
American Bible Society, 1816 R
American Sunday School Union, 1824 R
Baptist, British, 1792 R
British and Foreign Bible Society, 1804 R
China Inland Mission, 1865 R
Church Army, 1882 R
Church Missionary Society, 1799 R
International Missionary Council, 1961 R
Jerusalem conference on, 1928 R
Methodist, British, 1813 R
Missions to Africa, 1841 R
Presbyterian, Britain, 1846 R
Religious Tract Society, 1799 R
World Conference, 1911 R
World Student Christian Federation, 1895 R
Miss Julie (Strindberg), 1888 W

Mississippi River, US, navigation rights, 1795 K
Mississippi state, US, 1955 O; is admitted to Union, 1817 M; as a Confederate state, 1861 B; arrest of sheriff in connexion with murder of Civil Rights workers, 1964 M
Missolonghi, Greece: Byron's death, 1824 D; falls to Ibrahim, 1826 D
Missouri Compromise, 1820 C; repealed, 1854 E
Missouri state, US, enters Union as a slave state, 1821 H
Mr. Bolfrey (J. Bridie), 1943 W
Mr. Midshipman Easy (F. Marryat), 1836 U
Mr. Norris Changes Trains (C. Isherwood), 1935 U
Mr. Perrin and Mr. Trail (H. Walpole), 1911 U
Mr. Weston's Good Wine (T. F. Powys), 1928 U
Mr. W. H. (L. Hotson), 1964 Q
Mistral, Frédéric, F. poet (1830–1914), 1830 Z, 1854 U, 1914 Z
Mitchell, Margaret, Am. author, 1936 U
Mitford, Mary Russell, B. author (1787–1855), 1787 Z, 1824 U, 1855 Z
Mitford, Nancy, B. author (b. 1904), 1949 W
Mitford, William, B. historian of Greece (1744–1827), 1784 Q
Mithridates (J. C. Adelung), 1806 Q
Mitscherlich, Eilhardt, G. chemist (1794–1863), 1819 P
Mitteleuropa (F. Neumann), 1915 U
Mitterand, François, F. Socialist, 1965 M
Mitylene, Greece: Greek victory at, 1824 K; Greece annexes, 1914 F
Moberly, Sir Walter, B. administrator (b. 1881), 1949 O
Mobiles, invented, 1932 S
Mobulu, Congol. general, deposes Kasavubu, 1965 L
Moby Dick (H. Melville), 1851 U
Modena, Italy, 1797 G
Modern Democracies (J. Bryce), 1921 O
Modern Democratic State (A. D. Lindsay), 1943 O
Moderne Kapitalismus, Der (W. Sombart), 1920 O
Modern Instance, A (W. D. Howells), 1882 U
Modernism, condemned, 1907 R
Modern Love (G. Meredith), 1862 U
Modern Predicament, The (H. J. Paton), 1955 R
Modigliani, Amedeo, It. artist and sculptor (1884–1920), 1910 S, 1912 S, 1917 S, 1919 S, 1920 S
Mods *v.* Rockers, 1964 C, E
Moeran, Ernest John, B. musician (1894–1950), 1938 T, 1944 T
Moffatt, James, B. translator of Bible (1870–1944), 1913 R
Mohammed Ali, Pakis. premier, 1953 D
Mohammed, Ali, Shah of Persia, 1908 F
Mohammed Ali, Khedive of Syria, 1832 D, F
Mohammed ben Abdullah, 'Mad Mullah', Somali chief, 1899 J
Mohammed Said, Khedive of Egypt (1822–63) 1854 G, 1863 A
Mohammed Said, Pers., forms government, 1950 A
Mohl, Hugo von, G. botanist (1805–72), 1846 P
Mohr, Karl Friedrich, G. pharmacist (1806–79), 1837 P
Moines de l'Occident (C. de Montalembert), 1860 Q
Moissan, Henri, F. chemist (1852–1907), 1886 P
Mola, Emilio, Sp. general, 1936 G
Moldavia, 1812 E; Russians occupy, 1769 J; Russia restores conquests to Turkey, 1792 A; is united with Wallachia, to form Roumania, 1861 M; republic (Bessarabia), 1917 M. *See also* Bessarabia; Roumania; Wallachia
Moldavia *and* Wallachia, Danubian Principalities, 1858 H, L; become independent from Turkey, 1829 J; Russians quash revolts, 1848 G; Russo-Turkish joint occupation, 1849 E; Russia invades, 1853 G; Austrians occupy, during war, 1854 F, H, M; Vienna Four Points guarantee integrity of, 1854 H; Austria defends in return for guarantee of Italian possessions, 1854 M; guaranteed by powers, 1856 C; powers decide on union between Wallachia and Moldavia, 1858 H
Molecular biology, advances in, 1961 P
Molecules, structure of, 1930 P
Molinari, Ricardo, Argentin. poet (b. 1913), 1943 U
Mollet, Guy, F. Socialist, serves under Pleven, 1950 G; forms ministry, 1956 B; resigns, 1957 E
Mollison, Amy. *See* Johnson, Amy
Molotov, Vaycheslav, R. diplomat and politician (b. 1890), 1890 Z, 1942 E, 1956 F; as foreign minister, 1939 E; in Berlin, 1940 L; at UN Conference, 1945 D; replaced as foreign minister, 1949 C; presides at Prague Conference, 1950 K; refuses to discuss Germany's unification, 1955 L; is expelled from Soviet Central Committee, 1957 G
Molteno, Sir John Charles, S. Afr. politician (1814–1886), 1872 K
Moltke, Helmuth von, Count, G. soldier (1800–91), 1800 Z, 1891 Z
Moltke, Helmuth von, G. general (1848–1916), 1906 A, 1914 J
Mombassa, Kenya, railway to, 1901 M
Mommsen, Theodor, G. historian (1817–1903), 1817 Z, 1853 Q, 1863 Q, 1871 Q, 1872 Q, 1903 Z
Monaco, Principality:
sells Mentone and Roquebrune to France, 1862 B
Mona Lisa, theft, 1911 S
Monarchies:
in Albania, 1828 J
in Austria-Hungary, dual, 1867 B, F
question of Hapsburg restoration, 1937 B
in Belgium, 1830 L, 1831 B, F
problems of, 1946 B
in Britain, change in royal style, 1901 H
renunciation of German titles, 1917 F
in Bulgaria, 1879 D, 1886 L, 1887 G, 1946 J
in China, 1912 B
in France, July, 1830 H
falls, 1848 B
Second Empire, 1852 A, M
hope of restoration ended, 1877 K
in Greece, 1832 H, 1935 L
candidates for, 1863 B, C
plebiscite favours, 1946 J
in Hanover, 1814 K, 1837 F
in Hawaii, 1893 B
in Hungary, 1784 G
in Italy, under Napoleon, 1805 E, 1808 F
under Victor Emmanuel, 1860 K
ends, 1946 F
in Japan, Meiji dynasty restored, 1868 A
in Luxemburg, 1919 K
in Mexico, 1864 D
in Montenegro, 1901 H
in Naples, 1808 F
in Norway, 1814 D, L, 1905 K, L
in Poland, 1791 E
in Portugal (Braganza), 1807 L, 1815 F, 1822 J, 1826 D, E, 1834 E, 1910 K, 1919 B
in Roumania, 1866 B, 1930 F
in Saxony, 1806 M
in Serbia, 1882 C
in Spain, 1802 E, F, 1812 C, 1873 B, D, 1874 L, M
Hohenzollern candidate for, 1870 G

Duke of Aosta elected to, 1870 L
bill for succession, 1947 G
Franco's announcement on, 1957 G
in Sweden, 1818 B
in Syria, 1920 C
in Turkey, 1924 B
in Tuscany, proposed, 1800 K
in Westphalia, 1807 H
See also Abdications
Monasteries:
Austrian Empire, dissolved, 1781 R
in Britain, founded, 1862 R
in France, regulated, 1778 R
in Italy, dissolved, 1873 G
in Portugal, suppressed, 1834 R
Monboddo, James Burnett, Lord, B. judge (1714–1799), 1773 Q
Monckton, Walter, Lord Monckton, B. lawyer (d. 1964), report on Rhodesia and Nyasaland, 1960 K
Monde ou l'on s'ennuie, Le (E. Pailleron), 1881 W
Mondovi, Piedmont, N. Italy, Napoleon's victory at, 1796 D
Mondrian, Piet, Du. artist (1872–1944), 1917 S, 1929 S, 1936 S; designs, 1965 S
Monet, Claude Oscar, F. artist (1840–1926), 1840 Z, 1866 S, 1869 S, 1875 S, 1881 S, 1892 S, 1900 S, 1902 S, 1908 S, 1916 S, 1926 Z
'Impression Sunrise', 1874 S
Money, Credit and Commerce (A. Marshall), 1923 O
Mongolia: Russo-Japanese agreement on, 1912 H; declaration on Outer, 1913 L; Stein's expedition to South, 1915 Q; Russian treaty with, 1921 L; independence of Outer, 1945 H; Outer becomes under Soviet control, 1945 J; China regains Inner, 1945 J
Monier, Joseph, F. gardener and inventor of reinforced concrete (1823–1906), 1849 P, 1877 P
Monk, The (M. G. Lewis), 1795 U
Monmouth, New Jersey, US, battle, 1778 F
Monnet Plan for French industry, 1946 O
Monod, Frédéric, F. Protestant leader (1810–49), 1848 R
Monopolies:
East India Company's in Indian trade, abolished, 1813 O
Commission recommends abolition of price maintenance in Britain, 1963 M
Monopolies, Mergers and Restrictive Practices (White Paper), 1964 O
Monotype typesetting machine, 1897 P
Monroe, James, Am. statesman (1758–1831), 5th President of US (1817–25), 1758 Z; inaugurated, 1817 C; second term, 1821 C
Monroe Doctrine, 1823 M; Canning counters, 1824 M; Britain declares is not binding, 1854 E; US resolves to extend, 1912 H; Clark memorandum on, 1930 C
Monroe, Marilyn, Am. film actress (d. 1961), 1957 W
Monrovia Group, of heads of African state (Liberia, Togo, Nigeria and Cameroon), 1962 A
Mons, France: battle, 1914 H; Allies retreat from, 1914 H
Monsaratt, Nicolas, B. author (b. 1913), 1951 U
Monsieur Teste (P. Valéry), 1906 U
Montagn, John, earl of Sandwich, B. naval officer (1718–92), 1776 T
Montagu-Chelmsford Report on India, 1918 G
Montague, Charles Edward, B. author (1867–1928), 1922 O
Montalembert, Charles de, F. author (1810–70), 1810 Z, 1860 Q, 1870 Z
Montana, state, US: becomes US territory, 1864 E; created a state, 1889 B; returns first woman member of Congress, 1916 L
Mont Blanc, France, climbed, 1787 P
Mont Cenis tunnel, Switzerland, 1871 P
Monte Bello Islands, N.W. Australia, British atom bomb tests at, 1952 P
Monte Cassino, Italy: monastery bombed, 1944 B; assault on, 1944 C; falls, 1944 E
Montenegro, now S. Yugoslavia: Russian intrigues in, 1767 N; frontiers fixed, 1858 L; declares war on Turkey, 1876 G; enlargement and independence of, 1878 C, G; occupies Dulcigno, 1880 L; proclaimed an independent kingdom, 1910 H; Turkey is warned to withdraw troops from frontier, 1911 E; Turkish troops withdrawn, 1911 K; is united with Serbia, 1918 L; votes for union with Yugoslavia, 1919 D. *See also* Yugoslavia
Montero, Juan, Chil. president, 1931 G
Monte Video, Uruguay: Portuguese attack on, 1775 C; *Graf Spee* scuttled off, 1939 M
Montgolfier, Jacques Etienne, F. balloonist (1745–1799), 1783 P
Montgolfier, Michel, F. balloonist (1740–1810), 1783 P
Montgomery, Bernard Law, Viscount Montgomery, B. soldier (b. 1887), 1887 Z; commands 8th Army, 1942 H; breaks through Mareth Line, 1943 C
Montgomery, Albama, US: Congresses at, to form Confederate states, 1861 B; Civil Rights procession to, 1965 C
Montherlant, Henri de, F. author (b. 1896), 1936 U, 1963 W
Month in the Country, A (I. Turgeniev), 1872 U
Montini, Giovanni, It. Cardinal (b. 1879), Pope Paul VI (since 1963), 1892 Z, 1963 F
Montiori, Eugenio, It. architect, 1950 S
Montluccon, France, peace with Vendéans at, 1800 A
Montmorin de St. Hérem, Armand Marc, Comte de, F. diplomat (1745–92), 1787 K; becomes foreign minister, 1787 B
Montpensier, Antoine Marie Philipe Louis, Duc de (1824–90), 1846 K
Mont St. Michel and Chartres (H. Adams), 1904 Q
Montreal, Canada: rebellion in, 1849 D; Commonwealth trade conference at, 1958 J
Montreux, Switzerland: Convention, 1937 E; World Jewish Congress at, 1948 R
Monumenta Germaniae Historica (ed. Pertz), 1826 Q
Monumenti antichi inediti (J. J. Winckelmann), 1767 Q
Monywa, on Chindwin River, Burma, 14th Army takes, 1945 A
Moody, Dwight Lyman, Am. evangelist (1837–99), 1870 R, 1873 R
Moon, The:
Lunik II reaches, 1959 P
photographs, 1851 P
by Lunik III, 1959 P
by satellite, 1964 P
space research for flights to, 1963 K
volcanic eruption of, 1958 P
Moon, The (Wilkins and Moore), 1956 P
Moon and Sixpence, The (W. S. Maugham), 1919 U
Moon is Down, The (J. Steinbeck), 1942 U
Moonstone, The (W. Collins), 1868 U
Moore, George Augustus, B. novelist (1852–1933), 1852 Z, 1885 U, 1894 U, 1895 U, 1914 U, 1916 U, 1921 U, 1933 Z
Moore, George Edward, B. philosopher (1873–1958), 1903 B

Moore, Henry, B. sculptor (b. 1898), 1926 S, 1940 S, 1941 S, 1943 S, 1945 S, 1947 S, 1948 S, 1953 S, 1957 S, 1958 S
Moore, Sir John, B. soldier (1761–1809), 1809 A
Moore, P., B. astronomer, 1956 P
Moore, Thomas, B. poet (1779–1852), 1779 Z, 1807 T, 1852 Z
Moorehead, Alan, B. historian (b. 1910), 1952 O
Moral Man and Immoral Society (K. Niebuhr), 1934 K
Moral Order and Progress (S. Alexander), 1889 R
Moral Philosophy, 1846 R
Moral Rearmament, 1939 R
Moran, Lord. *See* Wilson, Charles McMoran
Moravia, Alberto, It. novelist (b. 1907), 1907 Z, 1944 U
Moravia, Germans occupy, 1939 C
Moravian Brethren, reform of, 1764 R
More, Hannah, B. author (1745–1833), 1788 O, 1809 U
Morea, The, Greece, 1781 B; guaranteed by the powers, 1828 L
Moréas, Jean, F. poet (1856–1910), 1884 U, 1886 V
Moreau, Gustave, F. painter (1826–98), 1866 S
Moreau, Jean, F. general (1763–1813), 1796 F, 1800 E, F
Moreau, Jean, F. actress (b. 1930), 1961 W
Morel, Edmund, D., B. Labour politician (1873–1924), 1903 E
Morgan, Charles, B. author (1894–1958), 1929 U, 1932 U, 1936 U, 1949 W
Morgan, Daniel, Am. soldier (1736–1802), 1781 A
Morgan, John Pierpont, Am. banker and connoisseur (1837–1913), 1837 Z, 1901 O, 1913 Z
Morgan, Thomas H., B. geneticist, 1909 B, 1928 P
Morgenthau, Henry, Am. statesman, 1856 Z, 1946 Z
Morghen, Raffaello Sanzio, It. engraver (1758–1833), 1792 S
Mörike, Eduard Friedrich, G. poet (1804–75), 1838 U
Morillo, Pablo, defeats Bolivar, 1816 B
Moritz, Karl Philipp, G. author (1757–93), 1790 U
Morland, George, B. artist (1763–1804), 1791 S
Morley, John, Lord Morley, B. Liberal, 1838 Z, 1923 Z
Mormons. *See* Religious denominations
Morocco:
  French war in, 1844 H, J
  Spanish wars in, 1859 K, 1860 D
  France advances interests in, 1900 B, M
  Anglo-German pact on, is sought, 1901 F
  France is granted control of frontier, 1901 G
  Franco-Spanish agreements on, 1902 L, 1904 K
  Anglo-French differences settled, 1904 D
  Crisis, first, 1905 C, E
    conference on, 1905 G, J
  Crisis, second, 1906 D
  Algericas Conference, 1906 A, D
  Franco-Spanish control in, 1906 D
  Civil War, 1908 H
  Germany recognises France's interests in, 1909 B
  Agadir Crisis, 1911 F, G
  Franco-German convention, 1911 L
  French agreement on, 1912 B
  becomes a French protectorate, 1912 C
  pacification of, 1932 A
  Berber revolt in S.W., 1934 B
  France deposes Sultan, 1953 H
  Sultan abdicates, 1955 K
  independence recognised, 1956 C
  Spanish troops leave, 1961 H
Morrill, Justin Smith, Am. financier (1810–98), tariff of, 1861 C
Morris, William, B. poet, artist and Socialist (1834–96), 1834 Z, 1861 S, 1896 Z; as artist, 1890 S, 1896 S; as author, 1858 U, 1868 U, 1876 U
Morrison, Herbert, Lord Morrison, B. Labour leader (1888–1965), 1965 Z; replaces Cripps in war cabinet, 1942 L; becomes foreign secretary, 1951 C
Morse, Samuel Finley Breese, Am. artist and inventor (1791–1872), 1791 Z, 1825 S, 1832 P, 1844 P, 1872 Z
Mort, T. S., Austral. pioneer of refrigeration (1816–1878), 1861 P
Mort dans l'âme, La (Sartre), 1950 R
Morte d'Arthur and other Idylls (Lord Tennyson), 1842 U
Morts sans sépultre (Sartre), 1946 W
Mortimer, John, B. dramatist (b. 1923), 1960 W
Morton, William Thomas, Am. dentist (1819–68), 1846 P
Mosaics, glass, 1891 S
Mosander, Karl Gustav, Swe. scientist (1797–1858), 1839 D
Moscicki, Ignace, Pol. premier, 1926 F, 1939 J
Moscow, Russia:
  Napoleon's occupation, 1812 J
  Napoleon's retreat from, 1812 K
  Kremlin built, 1838 S
  revolt of workers, 1905 M
  riots in, 1915 F
  British trade missions visit, 1921 C, 1940 E
  Soviet Writers' Conference, 1934 U
  purges in, 1937 A
  failure of first German offensive towards, 1941 K
  Stalin remains in, 1941 K
  Second German offensive against, 1941 L
  war leaders confer in, 1942 H
  conference of Allied foreign ministers, 1943 K, 1945 M, 1947 C
  Churchill visits, 1944 K
  Council for Mutual Economic Assistance in, 1949 A
  isolation of Western diplomats, 1952 K
  conference of Soviet satellites in, 1954 L
  concealed microphones in US embassy, 1964 E
  population, 1950 Y, 1960 Y
Moser, Justus, G. publicist (1720–94), 1775 O
Moslem League. *See under* Political Parties
Moslems. *See under* Religious denominations
Mosley, Sir Oswald, B. Fascist (b. 1896), 1896 Z; founds New Party, 1931 B; founds British Union of Fascists, 1932 N; holds Fascist meetings, 1934 F, 1962 G; anti-Jewish activities, 1936 K; is released from detention, 1943 L
Moss, Convention of, between Sweden and Norway, 1814 H
Mossbauer, R. L., Am. scientist, 1960 P
Mosul: controversy before League, 1924 J; question of Partition, 1925 H, M; Anglo-Turkish agreement on, 1926 F; pipe-line to Tripoli, 1934 G; revolt, 1959 C
Mother (M. Gorki), 1907 U
Mother, The (B. Brecht), 1932 W
Mother Courage (B. Brecht), 1941 W
Motion, accelerated, laws of, 1784 P; theory of, 1858 P
Motion of the Solar System in Space (W. Herschel), 1783 P
Motley, John Lothrop, Am. historian (1814–77), 1814 Z, 1856 Q, 1860 Q, 1877 Z
Motor bicycle, 1901 P
Motor 'buses, in London, 1905 P
Motor car:
  Benz's four-wheel, 1893 P

single-cylinder engine for, 1885 P
first Paris–Rouen trial run, 1894 X
'Austin 7', 1922 P
'Ford model T', 1909 P
companies:
Austin, 1905 P, 1922 P
Ford, 1909 P
Rolls-Royce, 1904 P
convention for, 1910 O
regulations, in Britain:
speed limit, 1903 H, 1935 C
driving tests, 1934 C
parking meters, 1958 O
production, statistics of, 1906 Y, 1914 Y, 1957 Y
vehicles licensed, statistics of, 1920 Y, 1938 Y, 1940 Y, 1941 Y, 1950 Y, 1960 Y
Motor, electric, A.C., 1888 P
Motor scooter, 1919 P
Motorways, M.1, 1959 P
Mots, Les (J. P. Sartre), 1964 U
Mott, Sir Frederick Walter, B. neurologist (1853–1926), 1916 P
Mouches, Les (J. P. Sartre), 1943 W
Mountaineering:
ascent of Mt. Blanc, 1787 P
ascent of Mt. Everest, 1953 P
ascent of Mt. Godwin Austen, 1954 P
ascent of Jungfrau, 1811 P
ascent of Nanga Parbat, 1953 P
ascent of Matterhorn, 1865 X, 1965 X
Mount Athos, Greece, 1842 R
Mountbatten, Louis, Lord, Earl Mountbatten of Burma (b. 1900), 1900 Z
Mountbatten-Windsor, surname to be borne by Elizabeth II's descendants, not being Royal Highnesses, 1960 B
Mountford, Edward, B. architect (1855–1908), 1907 S
Mount Wilson, US telescope, 1910 P, 1918 P
Mourning Becomes Electra (E. O'Neill), 1931 W
Mouroux, Jean, F. philosopher, 1956 R
Mousetrap, The (A. Christie), 1952 W
Moussoursky, Modeste Petrovich, R. musician (1839–81), 1839 Z, 1874 T, 1881 Z
Mouth-organ, invented, 1829 T
Moveable Feast, A (E. Hemingway), 1964 U
Mouvement Républican Populaire. *See under* Political Parties
Mowbray, Anne, Duchess of York (d. 1481), coffin of, 1965 Q
Mozambique, 1895 N, 1907 E; German designs on, 1898 H; Indian nationals required to leave, 1962 F
Mozart, Wolfgang Amadeus, G. musician (1756–91), 1791 Z
chamber music, 1795 T
Eine kleine Nachtmusik, 1787 T
mass, 1783 T
operas: *Cosi fan Tutti*, 1790 F
Don Giovanni, 1787 T
Figaro, 1786 T
Magic Flute, 1791 T
other operas, 1768 T, 1781 T, 1789 T
requiem, 1791 T
symphonies: 'Jupiter', 1788 T
'Prague', 1787 T
other symphonies, 1781 T, 1788 T
Salzburg festival, 1906 T
Mudie, Charles Edward, B. founder of circulating library (1818–90), 1842 O
Mugwumps, The, or Reformist Republicans in US, 1884 L
Muhlenberg, William Augustus, Am. episcopalian (1796–1877), 1853 O
Muir, Karen, S. Afr. swimmer, 1965 X
Mukden, Manchuria: Russian defeat at, 1905 C; Japanese siege, 1931 J
Mulai Hafid, Sultan of Morocco, 1908 A, H
Mulberry Bush, The (A. Wilson), 1956 W
Müller, F. W., Swi. scientist, 1956 P
Müller, Hermann, G. Socialist (b. 1890), becomes Chancellor, 1928 F; resigns, 1930 C
Müller, Paul, Swi. chemist, inventor of DDT, 1939 P
Müller, Wilhelm, G. scientist, 1927 P, 1928 P
Mulock, Dinah Maria (afterwards Mrs. Craik), B. author (1826–87), 1857 U
Mumford, Lewis, Am. author (b. 1895), 1895 Z, 1934 O, 1938 Q, 1944 R
Mummer's Wife (G. Moore), 1885 U
Munch, Edvard, Nor. artist (1863–1944), 1863 Z, 1897 S, 1901 S, 1907 S, 1909 S, 1919 S, 1921 S, 1928 S, 1935 S, 1944 Z
Münchengrätz Conference, between Russia, Prussia and Austria, 1833 J
Münchhausen (K. Immermann), 1838 U
Mundania Conference, between Allies and Turkey, 1922 K
Mundos de la Madrugada (R. Molinari), 1943 U
Mundoseer, India, treaty, 1818 A
Munich, Bavaria, W. Germany:
Glyptothek, 1816 S
Ludwigskirche, 1825 S
University, 1826 O
Propylaea, 1846 S
School of theologians, led by Döllinger, 1856 R
Archbishop of, 1871 R
electrical exhibition, 1883 P
German museum, 1903 O
'Blue Rider' school of artists, 1911 S
government troops regain from Communists, 1919 E
exhibition of 'Degenerate Art', 1937 S
conference on Czechoslovakia, 1938 J
Munitions, Ministry, British, 1915 F, O
Munitions:
workers, 1916 V; women workers, 1917 O
in Britain, production, 1941 Y, 1942 Y, 1943 Y, 1944 Y
special weeks, 1941 J
in France, nationalised, 1937 B
in US, factories achieve maximum production, 1942 N
See also under Armaments
Munk, Andrzej, R. film director, 1964 W
Munnings, Sir Alfred, B. artist (1878–1959), 1919 S, 1925 S
Munro, Sir Hector, B. soldier (1726–1805), 1764 K, 1778 N
Munro, Hector Hugh, B. author under pseudonym of 'Saki' (1870–1916), 1911 U, 1912 U
Munth, Carl, G. Roman Catholic propagandist, 1903 V
Munthe, Axel, Swe. physician and author, 1857 Z, 1949 Z
Murad V, Sultan of Turkey, 1876 E, H
Murat, Joachim, King of Naples, F. general (1767–1815), 1800 F, 1806 L, 1812 M, 1915 D, E; becomes King of Naples, 1808 F; deserts Napoleon, 1814 A; is shot, 1815 K
Muraviev, Michael, Count, R. diplomat, 1900 B
Murchison, Sir Roderick Impey, B. geologist (1792–1871), 1839 P
Murder in the Cathedral (T. S. Eliot), 1935 W

Murdoch, Jean Iris, B. author (b. 1919), 1957 U, 1961 U, 1963 U
Murdock, William, B. engineer, inventor of coal gas lighting (1754–1839), 1802 W
Mure, Geoffrey Reginald Gilbert, B. philosopher (b. 1893), 1951 R
Murger, Henri, F. author (1822–61), 1822 Z, 1848 U, 1861 Z
Murmansk, Russia, British withdraw from, 1919 K
Murray, Archibald, B. soldier, 1917 C
Murray, George Gilbert Aimé, B. author (1866–1957), 1921 O, 1942 O
Murray, Sir James Augustus Henry, B. lexicographer (1837–1915), 1884 O
Murray, William, Earl of Mansfield, B. judge (1705–1793), 1769 A, 1772 O
Murray, Kathleen, N. Zeal. author under pseudonym of 'Katherine Mansfield' (1888–1923), 1888 Z, 1911 U, 1920 U, 1922 U, 1923 Z
Murshidabad, India, Nabwab of, 1763 G
Mürzstag Agreement, between Austria and Russia on Macedonian reforms, 1903 K
Musaddiq, Dr. Z., Iran, politician: becomes premier, 1951 D; granted special powers, 1952 G; arrested, 1953 H; sentenced, 1953 M
Musäus, John Karl August, G. author (1735–87), 1786 U
Museums. *See* Galleries and Museums
Music, metaphysics of, 1870 T
Music, Royal College of, London, 1883 T
Musicals:
- *Call Me Madam*, 1950 W
- *Fings Ain't What they Used T'Be*, 1960 W
- *Lilac Time*, 1922 W
- *My Fair Lady*, 1957 W
- *Oklahoma*, 1943 W
- *Oliver*, 1961 W
- *South Pacific*, 1951 W
- *West Side Story*, 1958 W
- *See also* Reviews

Musicians Union, London, 1921 T
Music in a New Found Land (W. Mellors), 1964 T
'Musique concrete', 1954 T
Muskets, 1800 P
Musset, Alfred de, F. author (1810–57), 1810 Z, 1829 U, 1833 U, 1857 U
Mussolini, Benito, It. dictator (1883–1945), 1883 Z, 1935 G
- founds Fasci del Combattimento, 1919 B
- march on Rome, 1922 K
- attempts on life, 1926 D
- autobiography, 1928 O
- champions revision of Versailles treaty, 1930 E
- *The 100 Days*, 1931 O
- proposes four-power pact, 1933 C
- meets Hitler, 1934 F, 1937 J, 1938 E, 1940 K
- rejects concessions over Abyssinia, 1935 F
- proclaims Rome-Berlin axis, 1936 L
- in Libya, 1937 C
- meets Schuschnigg, 1937 D
- in Berlin, 1937 J
- at Munich Conference, 1938 J
- demands colonies in N. Africa, 1939 A
- talks with Chamberlain and Halifax, 1939 A
- pact with Hitler, 1939 E
- falls, 1943 G
- is killed by partisans, 1945 D

Mustapha IV, Sultan of Turkey (1807–8), 1807 E, 1808 G
Mutual Economic Assistance, Council for, 1949 A
Mutual Security Agency, in US, 1951 M
Mutinies, notable:
- Royal Navy, at Spithead, 1797 D
  - at Nore, 1797 E, F
  - at Invergordon, 1931 J
- of Congolese National Army, 1960 G
- of French Army, 1917 E
- of German Fleet, 1917 G, 1918 L
- of Russian Fleet, 1917 F
- of troops in Tanganyika, Uganda and Kenya, 1964 A

My Apprenticeship (B. Webb), 1926 O
My Imprisonment (S. Pellico), 1832 O
My Life, Poetry and Truth (Goethe), 1811 U
Myoglobin, discoveries in, 1960 P
My Philosophy (A. Einstein), 1934 R
Mysore, India, 1763 N, 1769 F, 1782 M; Hyder Ali usurps throne, 1764 N; signs peace with Britain, 1784 C; to Britain, 1792 B; shared between Britain and Hyderabad, 1799 E; annexed by East India Company, 1831 N
Mystère de la charité de Jeanne d'Arc (Péguy), 1910 U
Mysteries of Udolpho, The (A. Radcliffe), 1794 U
Mysterious Affairs at Styles, The (A. Christie), 1921 U
Mystery of Edwin Drood (C. Dickens), 1870 U
Mysticism (E. Underhill), 1910 R
Mysticism of Logic (B. Russell), 1918 R
Mysticism in Religion (W. R. Inge), 1948 R
Mythology, German, 1835 Q
Myths of the 20th Century (Rosenberg), 1930 U
Myxomatosis, 1953 P

N

Nablus Congress on Palestine, 1922 H
Nabokov, Vladimir, Am., formerly R., author (b. 1899), 1955 U, 1959 O
Nachtigal, Gustav, G. explorer of Central Africa (1834–85), 1869 P
Nadar, A., F. photographer and balloonist, 1863 P
Nadir Khan, King of Afghanistan, 1929 E
Nagar, formerly Bednore, Mysore, India, 1783 D
Nagasaki, Japan, atomic bomb on, 1945 H
Nagib, Mohammed, Egypt. general (b. 1900), 1954 B; seizes power, 1952 G; is voted dictatorial powers, 1953 B; becomes president of Egypt, 1953 F; falls, 1954 L
Nagpur, India, 1817 L; Britain annexes, 1853 M
Nagy, Ferenc, Hung. politician, 1947 E
Nagy, Imre, Hung. leader (1896–1958), 1953 G; recall demanded, 1956 K; forms ministry, 1956 K; takes refuge, 1956 L
Nagy, P., Am. scientist, 1961 P
Nahas Pashas, Egypt. Wafd leader, 1927 H, 1936 E; as premier, 1928 C, 1930 A, 1950 A
Nail-making machine, 1786 P, 1790 P
Naipaul, Vidiadhar Surprajprasad, W. Ind. author (b. 1932), 1959 U
Nairobi, Kenya, East African legislature at, 1948 D
Naked and the Dead, The (N. Mailer), 1948 U
Naked Lunch, The (Burroughs), 1964 U
Naktong, River, Korea, 1953 J
Names, family, obligatory in Turkey, 1935 A
Namier, Sir Lewis Bernstein, B. historian (1888–1960), 1888 Z, 1942 O, 1948 Q, 1960 Z
Namsos, Norway, British evacuate, 1940 E
Namur, Belgium, 1785 A
- battle, 1914 H

Nana (E. Zola), 1880 U
Nancy, France, mutiny in, 1790 H

Nanga Parbat, Himalayas, ascent of, 1953 P
Nanking, China: treaty, ends Opium War, 1842 H; confirmed, 1843 K; falls to rebels, 1850 K; bombed by revolutionaries, 1911 L; falls to Yüan Shih-Kai, 1913 J; National Convention in, 1931 E; Communists seize, 1927 C; Chiang Kai-shek at, 1927 D; Japanese take, 1937 M; puppet government at, 1938 C; National Assembly, 1948 C
Nansen, Fridtjof, Norw. explorer (1861–1930), 1861 Z, 1888 P, 1893 P, 1930 Z
Napier, Sir Charles, B. soldier (1782–1853), conquers Sund, 1843 A
Napier, Robert Cornelis, Lord Napier, B. soldier (1810–90), 1868 A, D
Napier, Sir William Francis Patrick, B. soldier and military historian (1785–1860), 1828 Q
Naples, Italy, 1768 N, 1815 K; British influence in, 1779 N; French overrun, 1798 M; Suvorov recaptures, 1799 F; French evacuate, 1801 K; French re-enter, 1806 B; San Carlos Opera House, 1810 S; Garibaldi enters, 1860 J; plebiscite supports union with Sardinia, 1860 K; Allies capture, 1943 J
Napoleon I (Napoleon Bonaparte), F. emperor (1769–1821), 1769 Z, 1800 K, 1806 R, 1808 R
takes Toulon, 1793 M
'whiff of grapeshot', 1795 K
marries Josephine de Beauharnais, 1796 C
takes command in Italy, 1796 D
wins battle of Lodi, 1796 E
defeats Wurmser, 1796 H
wins battle of Rivoli, 1797 A
advances to Vienna, 1797 B
founds Ligurian Republic, 1797 F
given command of French forces invading England, 1797 K
occupies Alexandria, 1798 G
in Syria, 1799 A, C, E
defeats Turks, 1799 G
lands at Fréjus, 1799 K
overthrows Directory, 1799 L
becomes First Consul, 1799 M, 1800 B
crosses Great St. Bernard Pass, 1800 E
defeats Austrians at Marengo, 1800 F
becomes president of Italian Republic, 1802 A
creates Legion of Honour, 1802 E
becomes First Consul for life, 1802 H
conspiracies against, 1804 B, 1812 K
proclaimed Emperor, 1804 E, M
crowned King of Italy, 1805 E
occupies Berlin, 1806 K
meets Alexander I at Tilsit, 1807 G
imprisons Pope Pius VII, 1809 G
divorces Josephine, 1809 M
marries Marie-Louise, 1810 B
annexes Holland, 1810 G
disputes with Pius VII, 1811 F
invades Russia, 1812 F
occupies Moscow, 1812 J
retreats from Moscow, 1812 K
returns to Paris, 1812 M
victory at Lützen, 1813 E
victory at Dresden, 1813 H
banished to Elba, 1814 D
lands in France ('Hundred Days'), 1815 C
issues Constitutions of Le Champ de Mai, 1815 F
defeated at Waterloo, 1815 F
abdicates, 1815 F
banished to St. Helena, 1815 H
art treasures looted by, 1815 S
death, 1821 Z
remains brought to Paris, 1840 M
Napoleon III (Charles Louis Napoleon Bonaparte), F. emperor (1808–73), 1808 Z, 1860 L, 1863 S
is exiled, 1836 K
attempts rising at Boulogne, 1840 H
escapes to London, 1846 E
elected president of France, 1848 M
coup d'etat, 1851 M
is granted monarchical powers, 1852 A
proclaimed Emperor, 1852 M
marries Eugénie de Montijo, 1853 A
birth of heir, 1856 C
meets Cavour, 1858 G
meets Bismarck, 1865 K
promises French neutrality in Austro-Prussian War, 1866 F
announces cession of Venezia to Italy, 1866 G
withdraws support from Maxmilian of Mexico, 1867 C
attempts to buy Duchy of Luxemburg, 1867 E
adopts Parliamentary system, 1869 G
capitulates at Sedan, 1870 J
death, 1873 A
Napoleon of Notting Hill, The (G. K. Chesterton), 1904 U
Narlikar, Jayant Vishnu, B. scientist, 1964 P
Narva, Russia, Germans occupy, 1918 C
Narvarez, Ramon Maria, Sp. soldier and politician (1800–68), defeats Espartero, 1843 G; becomes premier, 1864 J; is dismissed, 1865 F
Nash, John, B. architect (1752–1835), 1811 S, 1815 S, 1825 S
Nash, John Northcote, B. artist (b. 1893), 1918 S, 1940 S
Nash, Paul, B. artist (1889–1946), 1889 Z, 1918 S, 1940 S, 1941 S, 1946 S
Nasir Ud-Din, Shah of Persia (1848–96), 1848 K, 1896 E
Nasmyth, James, B. engineer (1808–90), 1839 P
Nassau, Bahamas, Kennedy meets Macmillan at, 1962 M
Nassau, Duchy, annexed by Prussia, 1866 H, J
Nasser, Gamal Addal, Colonel, Egypt. leader (b. 1918), usurps power, 1954 B; becomes premier, 1954 D; becomes head of state, 1954 L; meets Tito, 1956 A; elected president of Egypt, 1956 F; seizes Suez Canal, 1956 G; boycotts London Conference on Suez, 1956 H; rejects Dulles's proposals, 1956 J; Hammarskjold visits, 1957 C; becomes president of United Arab Republic, 1958 B; confiscates property, 1961 K
Natal, S. Africa: Dutch settlers found Republic, 1837 F; British war with Boers in, 1842 N; is proclaimed a British colony, 1843 E; combined with Cape Colony, 1844 E; segregation in, 1846 N; becomes a Crown Colony, 1856 G; self-government for, 1893 E
Natalia (N. Karamzin), 1793 U
Nathan, Peter, B. author, 1943 O
Nathan the Wise (Lessing), 1779 W
National anthems:
French (Le Marseillaise), 1792 T
Russian, 1944
S. African, 1957 U
National Apostasy (J. Keble), 1833 R
National Art Collections Fund, British, 1903 S
National Council of Churches of Christ, US, 1950 R
National Debt, British, interest on, reduced, 1888 D
National Development Bonds, 1964 D
National Economic Council, German, 1920 O
National Economic Development Council, T.U.C. joins, 1962 B
National Forests Commission, US, 1906 O

National Guard, French, 1789 J
dissolved, 1827 D
National Incomes Commission, British, 1962 O
first report, 1963 D
National Insurance in Britain, 1946 L
Nationalisation:
in Argentina, of oil, 1928 J
in Australia, of banks, 1947 L
of monopolies, proposed, 1911 B
in Britain, of Bank of England, 1946 G
of coal mines, 1946 E, 1947 A
of iron and steel, 1949 L
repealed, 1952 L
of land, advocated, 1775 O
of railways, 1946 L, 1948 A
of road transport, repealed, 1953 E
Labour Party retains 'clause 4', 1960 C
in Canada, of Grand Trunk Pacific Railway, 1919 C
in France, of Bank of France, 1945 O
of Church property, 1789 L
of munitions industry, 1936 G, 1937 B
in Germany, of industries, demanded, 1918 M
in India, of life insurance, 1956 E
in Indonesia, of Dutch businesses, 1958 M
in Iran, of oil industry, 1951 G
in Japan, of railways, 1906 C
in Mexico, of oil and minerals, 1926 E
in New Zealand, of Reserve Bank, 1936 N
in Poland, 1946 F
in Russia, of industries, dismissals for incompetence, 1946 F
in Spain, of Church property, 1933 E
in Switzerland, of railways, 1910 N
in US, of silver, president empowered to order, 1934 F
Nationalist Parties. *See under* Political Parties
National Life and Character; a Forecast (C. H. Pearson), 1893 O
National Parties. *See under* Political Parties
National Plan, The (British White Paper), 1965 O
National Registration, in Britain, 1915 G, 1938 M
National Savings Movement, 1916 O
National Socialists. *See under* Political Parties
National Society, The, for educating the poor, 1811 O
National System of Political Economy (F. List), 1841 O
National Theatre, British, 1951 W
National Trust, The, founded, 1895 O
National Vitality (I. Fisher), 1910 O
Natural History of Selbourne (G. White), 1789 P
Naturalism and Agnosticism (J. Ward), 1899 R
Natural Religions and Christian Theology (C. Raven), 1954 R
Natural Theology (W. Paley), 1802 R
Nature (R. W. Emerson), 1836 R
Nature and Destiny of Man, The (R. Niebuhr), 1941 R
Nature, Man and God (W. Temple), 1934 R
Nature of Existence, The (McTaggart), 1921 R
Nature of the Corn Laws (J. Anderson), 1777 O
Nature of the Universe, The (F. Hoyle), 1950 W
Naught for Your Comfort (T. Huddleston), 1957 O
Nausée (Sartre), 1937 U
Nautical Almanac, 1767 P
Nauvoo City, Illinois, US, 1846 F
Navarro, Raymon, Am. film actor, 1926 W
Navarre, France, Spain invades, 1793 C
Navarino Bay, Greece, battle, 1827 K
Navies:
Agreements: International, London Naval Convention, 1936 C
Russia accedes to, 1936 K
Britain with Germany, 1935 F, 1937 G
Hitler denounces, 1939 D
Britain with Russia, 1937 G
Russia with Turkey, on Black Sea, 1931 C
US with Japan, 1922 B
Conferences: London Naval, 1908 M
Washington, restricts submarine warfare, 1922 B
London Naval Disarmament, 1930 D, 1934 K
Japan leaves, 1936 A
Naval Strengths, comparative, 1838 Y, 1903 Y, 1914 Y, 1918 Y, 1945 Y
Navies:
Austrian, *Wien* sunk, 1917 M
Brazilian, 1891 L
Royal:
actions, at Trafalgar, 1805 K
at Naravino Bay, 1827 K
off Dardanelles, 1853 F, 1895 K
sent into Black Sea, 1854 A
sent to Constantinople, 1878 A, B
bombards Alexandria, 1882 G
Cossack rescues prisoners from *Altmark*, 1940 B
sinks French Fleet in Oran, 1940 G
raids Lofoten Islands, 1941 C
sinks *Bismarck*, 1941 E
convoys to Malta, 1942 F, H
to Russia, 1942 J, M
construction, etc., increase in, 1791 C
extensive building programme, 1889 E
Dartmouth R.N. College, 1903 E
battleships, 1903 Y
Spencer programme, 1894 N
Dreadnought launched, 1906 P
bill for increasing, 1909 C
battleships, 1910 Y
George V launched, 1911 K
losses of capital ships, notable, *Formidable*, 1915 A
Hampshire, 1916 F
total in World War I, 1918 Y
Courageous, 1939 J
Royal Oak, 1939 K
Jervis Bay, 1940 L
Illustrious, 1941 A
Southampton, 1941 A
Hood, 1941 E
Ark Royal, 1941 L
Barnham, 1941 L
Prince of Wales, 1941 M
Repulse, 1941 M
losses in Bay of Bengal, 1942 D
Eagle, 1942 H
Manchester, 1942 H
total, in World War II, 1945 Y
mutinies, 1797 D, E, F, 1931 J
miscellaneous, flogging abolished, 1881 O
paravanes used, 1915 P
acquires US destroyers, 1940 J
first guided-missile vessel, 1956 G
Canadian, Royal, formed, 1910 N
Canada rejects Navy bill, 1913 E
H.M.C.S. *Labrador*, 1957 P
Danish, surrenders to Britain, 1807 J
Egyptian, destroyed at Navarino Bay, 1827 K
French, visits Kronstadt, 1891 G
construction of battleships, 1903 Y, 1910 Y, 1911 B
losses, 1918 Y
in Oran, sunk, 1940 G
German, of 1848, auctioned, 1853 N
expansion under Tirpitz, 1898 C, 1900 F

battleship construction, 1903 Y, 1910 Y
increased under Navy bills, 1906 F, 1908 F
alarm at growth of, 1909 C
in World War I:
actions, etc.: *Breslau* and *Goeben* escape through Dardanelles, 1914 H
Emden sunk, 1914 L
Blücher sunk, 1915 A
Westfalen sunk, 1916 H
Breslau sunk, 1918 A
submarines, attack without warning, 1915 A, E, 1916 B
attacks intensified, 1915 B
not to attack merchantmen, 1915 J
unrestricted attacks, 1917 A
attacks suspended, 1918 K
Kiel mutinies, 1918 L
plebiscite against building battleships fails, 1928 K
not to exceed a third of tonnage of Royal Navy, 1935 F
bombards Almeira, 1937 E
in World War II:
Graf Spee scuttled, 1939 M
Bismarck sunk, 1941 E
Prinz Eugen escapes, 1941 E
Scharnhorst sunk, 1943 M
Tirpitz sunk, 1944 L
U-boats:
lay magnetic mines, 1939 L
attacks intensified, 1940 K, 1941 C
use homing torpedoes, 1945 A
losses, 1945 Y
W. German, agreement for building destroyers for firing nuclear weapons, 1961 E
Greek, is handed over to Allies, 1916 K
Indian, 1934 K
Italian, construction of battleships, 1910 Y, 1930 D
losses at Taranto, 1940 L
losses off Cape Matapan, 1941 C
Japanese: is attacked, 1864 J
battleships in, 1903 Y, 1910 Y
losses, 1945 Y
Merchant. *See* Merchant Navy.
NATO: US recommends surface ships in, to carry Polaris missiles, 1963 B
France withdraws Atlantic force from, 1963 F
mixed-manned nuclear fleet, discussed, 1963 K
Russian: in Bosphorus, 1833 B
visits Toulon, 1893 K
battleships in, 1903 Y, 1910 Y
crippled by Japanese, 1904 H
fires on British trawlers, 1904 K
mutinies, 1917 F, G
visits Portsmouth, 1955 K
Spanish, Britain fails to win contract for building warships for, 1964 F
Swedish, destroyed by Russians, 1788 G
Turkish, destruction at Navarino, 1827 K
destruction at Sinope, 1853 L
US, created, 1798 G
Chesapeake, incident, 1807 F, M
first steam warship, 1815 P
battleships in, 1903 Y, 1910 Y
naval appropriations bill, 1912 E
contracts suspended, 1921 A
defeats Japanese at Kynshu, 1945 A
losses, 1945 Y
Nautilus atom-powered submarine, 1957 P
sails for E. Mediterranean, 1957 D
Navigators Island, Pacific, 1766 P
Naylor, Bernard, B. musician, 1964 T
Nazarener group of German artists, 1810 S, 1828 S
Nazim Pasha, Turk. leader, murdered, 1913 A
Nazis. *See under* Political Parties
Neale, Sir John Ernest, B. historian (b. 1890), 1949 Q
Neanderthal skull, discovered, 1856 Q
Nebraska, state, US: settlement of, 1854 E; becomes a US state, 1867 C
Nebular hypothesis, enunciated by Laplace, 1796 P
Necker, Jacques, Swi. financier (1732–1804), 1776 K, 1780 N, 1781 E, O, 1790 J, 1804 Z; is recalled as F. finance minister, 1788 H; Louis XVI dismisses, 1789 G
Necker, Suzanne, Swi. literary hostess (d. 1794), 1764 U
Neerwinden, Belgium, battle, 1793 C
Negapatam, Madras, India: British capture, 1781 L; is ceded to Britain, 1784 C
Neglect of Science Committee, 1916 P
Negroes, in US, emancipated, 1863 O. *See also under* Civil Rights
Negro in American Civilization, The (C. S. Johnson), 1930 O
Nehru, Shri Jawahalal, Indian statesman, leader of Indian Congress (1889–1964), 1945 J
becomes premier, 1947 H, 1952 E
leads Congress Party to victory in election, 1952 C
plan for solving Algerian problem, 1956 E
plan for solving Suez Crisis, 1956 H
forms new ministry, 1957 D
appeals for disarmament, 1957 L
at Belgrade meeting of non-aligned powers, 1961 J
stand on Goa, 1916 M
death, 1964 E
Neill, Stephen Charles, B. churchman (b. 1900), 1961 R
Neisse, E. Germany, 1769 H
Nelson, Horatio, Lord Nelson, B. admiral (1758–1805), at Cape Vincent, 1797 B; at Nile, 1798 H; at Copenhagen, 1801 D; at Trafalgar, 1805 K
Nelson, James Beaumont, B. engineer (1792–1865), 1829 P
Nemesis of Faith (J. A. Froude), 1848 R
Nemesis of Power (J. Wheeler-Bennett), 1953 Q
Nemours, Louis Charles Philippe Raphaël, Duc de (1814–96), 1831 B
Neo-classicism, 1775 S
Neomycin, 1949 P
Neon, discovered, 1898 P
signs, 1905 P
'Neoprene' synthetic rubber process, 1931 P
Nepal: Gurkhas conquer, 1768 N; British war with, 1814 K
Neptune, planet, 1846 P
Neptumium, element, 1940 P
Nerval, Gérard de, F. author (1808–55), 1854 U, 1855 U
Nerve-centres, reflex action of, discovered, 1832 P
Nerves, treatise on, 1873 P
Nervi, Pier Luigi, It. architect and structural engineer (b. 1891), 1948 S, 1953 S, 1956 S, 1958 S
Nervous impulses:
of single nerve fibres, 1929 P
speed of, established, 1850 P
transmission of, work in, 1963 P
Nervous System of the Human Body, The (C. Bell), 1830 P
Nervous System, studies in, 1830 P
Nesbit, Edith (Mrs. E. Bland), B. author of children's books (1858–1924), 1899 U
Nesselrode, Karl Robert von, R. diplomat (1814–96), 1844 F
Net Book Agreement in Britain upheld, 1962 O

Netherlands, Kingdom of. *See* Holland
Netherlands, Austrian, France conquers, 1792 L
Netherlands, The United, 1815 F, 1816 F; concordat with Pope Leo XII, 1827 F; is divided into Holland and Belgium, 1831 A, F, K
Nettuno Treaty, on Dalmatia, 1925 G
Netto, Italy, Allied landings at, 1944 A
Neuchâtel, France, 1805 M
Neue Armadis, Der (C. M. Wieland), 1771 U
Neue Gedichte (R. M. Rilke), 1907 U
Neufchâtel, Switzerland: rising against Republic, 1856 J; Prussia renounces sovereignty, 1857 E
Neumann, Franz Ernest, G. physicist and mathematician (1798–1895), 1851 P
Neumann, Franz, G. author, 1915 U
Neun Bücher preussischer Geschichte (L. von Ranke), 1847 Q
Neurath, Constantin von, G. diplomat (1873–1956), as foreign minister, 1932 F, 1933 A; rules Bohemia and Moravia, 1939 C
Neurath, K., G. sociologist, 1931 R
Neurology, studies in, 1830 P, 1854 P
Neustadt, W. Germany, 1770 J
Neutral Nations, rights of, 1802 O, 1806 O
'Neutrino', the, detected, 1956 P
Neutrons, research into, 1832 P
Neuilly Peace treaty, between Allies and Bulgaria, 1919 L
Neuve Chapelle, France, battle, 1915 C
Neuville, France, Allies take, 1915 F
Nevada, state, US, US obtains, 1848 E
Nevinson, Henry Wood, B. essayist and journalist, 1856 Z, 1941 Z
Newark, Canada, 1913 M
New Bearings in English Poetry (F. R. Leavis), 1932 U
New Berne, N. Carolina, US, Unionist take, 1862 C
Newbolt, Sir Henry John, B. poet (1862–1938), 1910 U
New Brunswick, enters Dominion of Canada, 1867 C
New Caledonia: France annexes, 1853 J; nickel ore deposits in, 1876 P
New Cambridge Modern History, 1957 Q
Newcastle-upon-Tyne, Northumb. England, railway bridge, 1850 P
'Newcastle Programme' of British Liberal Party, 1891 K
New Critique of Reason (J. F. Fries), 1808 R
New Deal:
- in Britain, Lloyd George's proposed programme for, 1935 A
- in Canada, legislation for, nullified, 1936 F
- in USA, Roosevelt introduces, 1933 C
  - social security legislation, 1935 O

New Delhi, India, Asian Legal Consultative Committee at, 1957 D
New Economic Policy (NEP), in Russia, 1921 O
New English Art Club, 1886 S
New Foundations of Political Economy (G. Hafeland), 1807 O
Newfoundland: French fishing rights off, 1763 B; Anglo-French fishery dispute settled, 1904 D, 1910 J; loses Dominion status for mismanagement, 1933 M; bases in, leased to US, 1940 J; joins Dominion of Canada, 1949 C
New Georgia Island, Japanese evacuate, 1943 G
New Grenada: revolt against Spanish, 1810 E; Congress, 1816 B; with Venezuela, forms Colombia, 1819 M; leaves Union of Colombia, 1831 L; becomes independent, 1831 L
New Grub Street (G. Gissing), 1891 U
New Guinea, 1883 N; Northern, annexed by Germany, 1885 E, N; Southern, British protectorate in, 1885 N; Germans capitulate, 1914 J; US landings in, 1943 F; West, proclaimed as an Indonesian province, 1962 A, H; UN takes over administration, 1962 K
New Hampshire, state, US, 1788 F
New Hebrides, 1887 L
Ne Win (Maung Shu Maung), Burmese general (b. 1911), 1962 C
New Jersey, state, US, 1776 L
New Leviathan, The (R. G. Collingwood), 1942 R
New Macchiavelli, The (H. G. Wells), 1911 U
Newman, John Henry, B. cardinal (1801–90), 1801 Z, 1845 R, 1870 R, 1890 Z; *Apologia*, 1864 R; *Tract 90*, 1841 R
Newman, Robert, B. concert promoter (d. 1926), 1895 T
Newmarket, Cambs., England, horse-races at, 1809 X, 1839 X
New Men, The (C. P. Snow), 1954 U
New Mexico, US, Gadsden Purchase, 1854 D
New Orleans, La., US: US purchases from France, 1803 D; British defeat at, 1815 A; siege of, 1862 D
Newport, Mons., Wales, Chartist rising at, 1839 L
Newport, Rhode Island, US, 1778 H, 1780 G
Newsom, Sir John, B. publisher and educationalist (b. 1910), 1963 O, 1965 M
New South Wales, Australia: opposes federation, 1891 C; role in federation, 1899 N; artificial rain in, 1957 P
Newsfilms, 1912 W
Newspapers:
- in Britain:
  - illustrated, 1890 V
  - national daily, circulation figures for, 1965 V
  - provincial, affected by strike, 1959 F
  - Sunday, the first, 1780 V
  - taxes on, 1798 V, 1819 M; abolished, 1855 V
- in US, New York strike, 1963 D
- *See also* Journals; Press, freedom of
- *Berliner Tageblatt*, 1882 V
- *Berlin Post*, war-scare by, 1875 C
- *Birmingham Post*, 1857 V
- *Boston Centinel*, 1784 V
- *Catholic Times, The*, 1860 V
- *Collier's Weekly*, 1888 V
- *Daily Chronicle*, merges with *Daily News*, 1930 V
- *Daily Express, The*, 1900 V, 1965 V; Beaverbrook buys, 1915 V; Christiensen becomes editor, 1933 V
- *Daily Graphic, The*, 1890 V
- *Daily Herald, The*, 1912 V; Russia attempts to subsidise, 1920 H; last appears, 1964 V
- *Daily Mail, The*, 1896 V, 1965 V
- *Daily Mirror, The*, 1904 V, 1965 V
- *Daily News, The*, 1846 V, 1906 O, 1930 V
- *Daily Sketch, The*, 1909 V, 1965 V
- *Daily Telegraph, The*, 1855 V, 1965 V; interviews Kaiser, 1908 K, L; merger with *Morning Post*, 1937 V
- *Daily Worker, The*, 1930 V, 1965 V; suspended, 1941 V
- *Evening News, The*, 1881 V
- *Evening Standard, The*, 1827 V
- *Figaro, Le*, 1854 V; charges against Caillaux, 1914 A; editor murdered, 1914 C
- *Financial Times, The*, 1888 V, 1965 V
- *Frankfurter Zeitung*, 1856 V; suppressed, 1943 V
- *Globe, The*, 1803 V, 1824 V; suppressed, 1915 V
- *Guardian, The* (formerly *Manchester Guardian*), 1959 V, 1965 V
- *Manchester Guardian, The*, 1821 V; Scott as editor, 1872 V; renamed, 1959 V

Matin, Le, 1884 V
Mattino, Il, 1891 V
Morning Chronicle, The, 1769 V
Morning Post, The, 1772 V; merged in *Daily Telegraph*, 1937 V
Neue Freie Presse, 1864 V
News Chronicle, The, 1930 V
ceases publication, 1960 V
News of the World, The, 1843 V
New York Daily Graphic, 1880 V
New York Evening Post, 1801 V
New York Herald, 1835 V
New York Times, 1851 V
New York Tribune, 1841 V; uses linotype, 1886 V; editor stands for presidency, 1872 E, L
Northern Star, 1838 V
Observer, The, 1791 V; Garvin as editor, 1908 V, 1942 V; under independent governing body, 1946 V
Petit Journal, Le, 1863 V
Presse, Le, 1836 V
St. James's Chronicle, 1763 V
Scotsman, The, 1817 V
Siecle, Le, 1836 V
Star, The, 1888 V, 1918 S; ceases publication, 1960 V
Stars and Stripes, 1942 V
Sun, The, 1964 V, 1965 V
Sunday Pictorial, The (late *Sunday Mirror*), 1915 V
Sunday Telegraph, The, 1960 V
Sunday Times, The, 1822 V; issues colour supplement, 1962 V
Temps, Le, exonerated from charges of collaboration, 1946 V
Times, The, 1788 V
sends out first war correspondent, 1808 V
is printed by steam, 1814 V
Barnes appointed editor, 1817 V
declares for free trade, 1939 A
Delane appointed editor, 1841 V
on 'Parnellism and Crime', 1887 A
action regarding Parnell's letters, 1888 G
bought by Northcliffe, 1908 V
Dawson appointed editor, 1912 V
Barrington Ward appointed editor, 1941 V
Haley appointed editor, 1952 V
Times of India, The, 1838 V
Tribuna, La, 1883 V
Weekly Political Register, 1802 V
Workers' Weekly, prosecution of, 1924 K
New System of Chemical Philosophy (J. Dalton), 1808 P
New Testament and Mythology (R. Bultmann), 1941 R
New Theology and the Old Religion, The (C. Gore), 1907 R
New Theory of Human Evolution, A (A. Keith), 1948 P
New Theory of the Earth (J. Hutton), 1788 P
Newton, Sir Charles Thomas, B. archaeologist (1816–94), 1857 Q
Newton, Sir Isaac, B. scientist (1642–1727), library of, 1943 Q
Newton, John, B. divine (1725–1807), 1779 R
New towns, in Britain, 1946 O; Hatfield, 1952 S; Commission, 1961 O
New Turkey, The (Kemel Attaturk), 1927 O
New View of Society, A (R. Owen), 1813 O
New World of the Mind, The (Rhine), 1953 R
New Writing, 1936 V
New York, N.Y., US:
Stamp Act Congress, 1765 K
assembly suspended, 1767 F
falls to Howe, 1776 J
becomes federal capital, 1788 J
trades unions in, 1833 N
corruption in, 1871 G
Tammany Hall in, 1888 L
Austrian ambassador recalled from, 1915 J
Wall Street Crash, 1929 K, O
World Fair, 1938 W
Exhibition, 1939 W
UN headquarters in, 1946 M
Harlem race riots, 1964 G
places, buildings and institutions in or near:
Brooklyn, Barnum and Bailey's Circus, 1871 W
Carnegie Music Hall, 1891 T
Chamber of Commerce, 1903 S
Customs House, 1902 S
Daily News Building, 1930 S
Drury Lane Theatre (later Manhattan Opera House), 1903 W
Empire State Building, 1930 S
Grand Central Station, 1912 S
Guggenheim Art Museum, 1959 S
Hudson Terminal Building, 1909 T
Idlewilde Air Terminal, 1958 S
Jockey Club, 1894 X
Kinetoscope Parlour, 1894 W
Lever House, 1952 S
Lincoln Memorial, 1914 S
Manhattan bridge, 1910 P
Manhattan Opera House, 1903 P
Metropolitan Opera, 1883 T
Museum of Modern Art, 1929 S
National Conservatory, 1892 T
New Crotoun tunnel, 1893 P
Pan American Airlines Building, 1962 S
Pearl Street generating station, 1882 P
Philharmonic Society, 1842 T
Piscator's Studio Theatre, 1941 W
Rockefeller Center, 1931 S
Seagram Building, 1958 S
Singer Building, 1905 S
Stock Exchange, 1903 S, 1929 K, O
Subway, 1904 P, 1908 P
UN Building, 1950 S
Woolworth Building, 1913 S
art in, 1825 S, 1913 S
drama in, 1820 W
music in, 1770 T, 1796 T, 1842 T, 1859 T
university extension lectures, 1850 O
population, 1801 Y, 1841 Y, 1881 Y, 1906 Y, 1950 Y, 1960 Y
New York State, US, investigations of insurance houses in, 1905 O
New Zealand: coast of, charted, 1768 P; proclaimed a British Colony, 1841 E; Maoris sign treaty of Waitangi, 1840 B; Maori revolt, 1843 F. *See also under* Wars, Maori; female franchise in, 1893 O
Ney, Michel, F. marshal (1769–1815), 1813 J; takes Cuidad Rodrigo, 1810 G; is shot, 1815 M
Nezib, Syria, Turks routed at, 1839 F
Ngami, Lake, Bechuanaland, Central Africa, 1802 P, 1841 P
Ngo Dinh Diem, S. Vietnam, 1955 K
Niagara, N. America:
British capture Fort, 1813 M
Bible Conference at, 1895 R
Falls, suspension bridge, 1852 P
Blondin crosses, 1859 W
hydro-electric installations, 1886 P, 1896 P
Conference between US and Mexico, 1914 E, F
Niazi Bay, Young Turk leader, 1908 G

Nicaragua: enters American Federation, 1823 G; union with Honduras and El Salvador, 1895 F; war with Honduras, 1907 B; asks for protection against Costa Rica, 1919 F; US supervises elections in, 1927 E
Nice, France: France annexes, 1792 L; is ceded to France, 1796 E, 1860 C; Italy claims, 1938 L
Nicholas I, of Montenegro (1860–1918), 1910 H, 1913 E, 1918 L, 1919 D
Nicholas I, Tsar of Russia (1825–1855), 1796 Z, 1825 M, 1830 L, 1843 O, 1855 C; relations with Poland, 1831 A, 1832 B; suggests partition of Turkey, 1844 F; visits London, 1844 F; orders occupation of Danubian Principalities, 1853 E
Nicholas II, Tsar of Russia (1894–1917), 1894 L, 1899 B, E, 1904 K, 1905 M, 1916 B
visits London, 1896 K
promises reforms, 1905 C
signs treaty of mutual aid with Germany, 1905 G
suppresses Duma, 1905 H
capitulates to Duma's demand for legislative powers, 1905 K
dissolves Duma, 1907 F
meets William II, 1907 H
meets Edward VII, 1908 F
agrees to Macedonian reforms, 1908 F
ceases to oppose Baghdad Railway, 1910 L
takes over Russian command, 1915 J
abdicates, 1917 C
executed, 1918 G
Nicholas Nickleby (C. Dickens), 1838 U
Nicholson, Ben, B. artist (b. 1894), 1894 Z, 1946 S, 1953 S
Nicholson, Sir William Newzam Prior, B. artist (1872–1949), 1904 S
Nicholson's Well, Natal, S. Africa, battle, 1899 K
Nickel, metals coated with, 1843 P; deposits in New Caledonia, 1876 P
Nicola, Enrico, President of Italy, 1946 F
Nicolai, Carl Otto Ehrenfried, G. musician (1810–1849), 1848 T
Nicolai, Christoph Friedrich, G. author (1733–1811), 1765 R
Nicolaievich, Nicholas, R. grand duke, 1915 J
Nicholson, Sir Harold, B. author (b. 1886), 1934 Q, 1952 Q
Niebla (Unamuno y Jugo), 1914 U
Niebuhr, Berthold, G. historian (1777–1831), 1777 Z, 1811 Q, 1814 O, 1816 Q, 1821 R, 1831 Z
Niebuhr, Reinhold, Am. philosopher (b. 1892), 1934 R, 1941 R, 1961 R
Niels Lyhne (Jacobsen), 1880 U
Niemen, River, Russia, 1795 K; Napoleon crosses, 1812 F; battle, 1914 J
Niemeyer, Oscar, Brazil. architect (b. 1907), 1958 S, 1960 O
Niemöller, Martin, G. Protestant, 1892 Z
Niepce, Joseph, F. physicist (1765–1833), 1765 Z, 1827 P, 1833 Z
Nietsche, Friedrich Wilhelm, G. philosopher (1844–1900), 1844 Z, 1882 U, 1883 U, 1886 U, 1900 Z
Nieuwland, Julius A., G. chemist, 1931 P
Niger Company, British, 1895 A; sells possessions to Britain, 1899 H; Niger Republic, independence of, 1960 G
Niger, River, Africa: M. Park explores, 1795 P; expeditions to, 1805 P, 1830 P; British protectorate over, 1885 F
Niger, Upper, French conquest, 1883 N
Nigeria: Presbyterian missions in, 1846 R; Anglo-French agreement on, 1890 H; boundaries defined, 1893 L, 1898 F, 1913 C; protectorate, 1899 H; North, British conquest of, 1903 C; amalgamation of North and South, 1914 A; becomes a republic within the Commonwealth, 1963 K
Nigerian Federation, independence of, 1960 K
Nigger of the Narcissus, The (J. Conrad), 1897 U
Night clubs, 1921 W
Nightingale, Florence, B. pioneer of nursing (1820–1910), 1820 Z, 1910 Z
Nightmare Abbey (T. L. Peacock), 1818 U
Night Must Fall (E. Williams), 1935 W
Nihilists. *See under* Political Parties
Nikki, near Dahomey, W. Africa, 1895 A
Nikolaier, Arthur, G. physician (1862–1934), 1884 P
Nikolsburg, Austria, peace treaty, 1866 G, H
Nile, River:
expeditions to discover source of, 1772 P, 1790 P, 1856 P
battle, 1798 H
Upper, territory near, 1890 E
left bank of, assigned to Leopold II, 1894 E, H
Franco-Belgian co-operation on, 1895 J
White, British action on, 1899 L
waters of, Egyptian-Sudan agreements on, 1952 K, 1959 L
diversion of, 1958 G
Nine Days' Wonder, The (J. Masefield), 1934 U
Nine Tailors, The (D. L. Sayers), 1934 U
Nineteen Eighty Four (G. Orwell), 1949 W
Ninety-three (V. Hugo), 1874 O
Nineveh, ancient Assyrian capital, excavations of, 1845 Q
Nippur, Iraq, excavations of Babylonian remains at, 1888 Q
Nitrates, shipped from S. America, 1830 P
Nitric acid, composition of, discovered, 1785 P
Nitrogen, discovery of, 1772 P
Nitroglycerine, 1846 P
Nitrous oxide, Davy's researches concerning, 1800 P
Nitti, Francesco, It. premier, 1919 F
Nivelle, Robert George, F. soldier (1856–1924), 1916 M, 1917 E
Nixon, Richard Milhons, Am. Republican (b. 1913), 1913 Z
defeated in presidential election, 1960 L
Nkrumah, Kwame, Ghanian leader, People's Party (b. 1909), 1909 Z
forms ministry, 1954 F
increases majority, 1956 G
demands independence for Gold Coast, 1956 H
founds mutual assistance in Africa, 1958 B
proposes conference of independent African states, 1959 G
takes over Convention People's Party, 1961 E
visits Russia, 1961 G
at Belgrade meeting of non-aligned powers, 1961 J
detains opposition leaders, 1961 J
attempted assassination, 1962 H
dismisses chief justice of Ghana, 1963 M
See also under Ghana; Gold Coast
Nkomo, Joshua, Rhodes. Nationalist leader Zimbabwe People's Union Party (b. 1917), placed under restriction, 1964 D; detention of, declared illegal, 1964 L
Nobel, Alfred, Swe. inventor (1833–96), 1833 Z, 1866 P, 1896 Z; establishes prizes, 1896 O
Nobel Prizes, notable awards, 1920 M, 1964 P, K
Nobelium, element 102, 1957 P
Noble, Fraser, B. administrator (b. 1918), reports on influence of TV on the young, 1963 O
Nobili, Leopoldo, It. physicist (1784–1835), 1826 P
Nocturne (F. Swinnerton), 1917 U
No Force Declaration, 1932 M

Nogaisk Steppes, Russia, Russians penetrate, 1943 K
Nokrashy, Pasha, of Egypt, 1948 M
Nolan, Sidney Robert, Austral. artist (b. 1917), 1958 S, 1960 S, 1962 S
Non-aggression Pact, Russia with Persia, 1927 K
  Russia with Germany, 1939 H
Non-intervention in Spanish Civil War, Germany and Japan withdraw from Committee, 1937 F
Nono, Luigi, It. musician, 1961 T
Nonsuch Palace, Surrey, England, site of, excavated, 1959 Q
Nootka Sound, British Columbia, Canada, Anglo-Spanish crisis concerning, 1789 F, 1790 E, K
Nordan, Max Simon, G. philosopher and Zionist (1849–1911), 1897 R
Nordenskjöld, Niels Adolfe Erik, Swe. explorer (1832–1901), 1870 P
Nore, The, England, naval mutiny at, 1797 E, F
Norman, Montagu, Lord Norman, B. economist and financier (1871–1950), 1871 Z, 1950 Z
Normandie, S.S., 1935 P
Normann, Wilhelm, G. chemist, 1901 P
Norse, Old, study of, 1811 Q
Norstad, Lauris, Am. soldier (b. 1907), as supreme Allied Commander in Europe, 1956 L, 1963 A
North, Frederick, Lord North, Earl of Guildford, B. Tory (1732–92), 1767 J, 1778 B, 1782 C; appointed prime minister, 1770 A; resigns, 1782 C; declines to form ministry, 1783 B; opposes Parliamentary Reform, 1783 E; forms Coalition with Fox, 1783 D, M
North American Air Defense Council, 1958 E
Northampton, Northants, England, Bradlaugh as M.P. for, 1880 E
Northanger Abbey (J. Austen), 1818 U
North Atlantic Treaty, signed, 1949 D
North Atlantic Treaty Organization (NATO):
  Eire refuses to participate in, 1949 B
  US military aid for, 1949 K
  bilateral agreement, 1950 A
  Council decides to form European defence force, 1950 J
  Turkey agrees to co-operate with, 1950 K
  plans to use W. German troops, 1951 J
  approval of European defence project, 1952 B
  Morocco and Tunis to enter, 1952 B
  Russia offers to join, 1954 C
  conference on European unity agrees W. Germany should enter, 1954 K
  W. Germany enters, 1955 E
  offers to mediate in Cyprus, 1957 C
  France leaves conference, 1957 L
  W. German forces handed over to, 1958 A
  missile bases in Greece, Russian threats over, 1958 A
  Council rejects Russian proposal on Berlin, 1958 M
  Parliamentarian's Conference of, sponsors Atlantic Congress, 1959 F
  Poland asks for acknowledgement of Oder–Neisse frontier, 1960 G
  unified air defence council, 1960 J
  exercises, *Der Spiegel's* articles on, 1962 K, L
  W. European Union calls for a single nuclear force, 1962 M
  US recommends surface ships of, to carry Polaris missiles, 1963 B
  France withdraws force from fleet, 1963 F
  mixed-manned nuclear fleet, discussed, 1963 K
  Greece withdraws from, 1964 H
North Briton, The, 1763 D, 1764 B
'North, Christopher.' *See* Wilson, John
Northcliffe, Lord. *See* Harmsworth, Alfred
Northcote, Stafford Henry, Earl of Iddesleigh, B. Conservative (1818–87), 1854 O, 1874 B, 1881 D
Northern Circars, Madras, India, ceded to Britain, 1766 L
Northern Securities case, US, 1904 C
North German Confederation: formed, 1867 D; Baden seeks to enter, 1870 A; alliances with Bavaria and Württemburg, 1870 L
North Pole. *See* Polar Expeditions.
Northrop, John Howard, Am. inventor (b. 1891), 1895 P, 1930 P
North Sea Convention, 1908 H
North-West Passage: expeditions to discover, 1818 P, 1845 P, 1850 P; new passage discovered, 1957 P
North-West Territory, US, 1787 G
Norway: Swedish annexation suggested, 1812 D; ceded by Denmark to Sweden, 1814 A; statholdership abolished, 1873 N; is separated from Sweden, 1905 F, J, K; Germany invades, 1940 D
Norwegian National Theatre, 1899 W
Norwich School of Artists, 1803 S
Nostromo (J. Conrad), 1904 U
Notes of a Film Director (S. Eisenstein), 1959 W
Notes Towards the Definition of Culture (T. S. Eliot), 1948 O
Not Honour More (J. Cary), 1955 U
Notion of a Universal History in a Cosmopolitan Sense (Kant), 1784 R
Nottingham, Notts., England, racial disturbances in, 1958 H
Notre-Dame de Paris (V. Hugo), 1831 U
Nouveau Christianisme (St. Simon), 1825 R
Nouveaux Principes d'Économie Politique (J. Sismondi), 1819 O
Nouvelles génevoises (R. Töpffer), 1839 U
Nouvelles Méditations Poétiques (A. de Lamartine), 1823 U
'Novalis.' *See* Hardenberg, Friedrich von
Novara, Piedmont, Italy, battles, 1821 D, 1849 C
Nova Scotia: ceded to Britain, 1763 B; enters Dominion of Canada, 1867 C
Novel, The:
  gothic, 1794 U
  historical, 1809 U
  romantic, 1765 U
Novello, Ivor, B. actor and composer (1893–1951), 1935 W, 1939 W
Novi, Italy, 1799 H
Novo-Georgievsk, Russia, Germans take, 1915 H
Novoroissik, on Black Sea, Russia, 1920 C
Nu, U., Burmese leader (b. 1907), overthrown, 1962 L
Nubar Pasha, Egyptian Nationalist, 1878 H, 1879 B
Nuclear Energy: European Agency, 1957 M; Inter-American Commission, 1959 K
Nuclear ice-breaker, 1958 P
Nuclear Power Stations, 1956 P
Nuclear Radiation, fears of danger to health from, 1955 P
Nuclear Research: Meyrin International Laboratory, 1953 P; US provides Greece with information, 1959 F
Nuclear Submarines, 1958 P, 1963 P
Nuclear Tests:
  Japan protests to Russia, 1957 D
  Schweitzer urges condemnation of, 1957 D
  British test bombs of megaton range, 1957 E
  Russia appeals to West to cease, 1957 E
  Geneva conference on detection of, 1958 G
  Russia resumes tests, 1958 J
  Anglo-US declaration on negotiations, 1960 C
  Three-power conference on, 1961 C
    fails, 1962 A

Nuclear Tests—*contd.*
Russia proposes ban talks should proceed simultaneously with disarmament talks, 1961 F
UN Assembly demands end of tests, 1962 L
Test Ban Treaty signed, 1963 H
Nuclear Warfare:
Conference on surprise attack, 1958 L
W. German fleet for firing missiles approved by W. European Union, 1961 E
US plan for multi-lateral force, 1963 A
NATO mixed-manned fleet, discussed, 1963 K
Denuclearised Zones:
Rapacki Plan for, 1957 K; rejected by US and Britain, 1958 B
negotiations for zone in Middle East, 1959 E
Russia proposes zone in Balkans, 1959 F
Russia calls for zone in Europe, 1959 G
UN resolves to treat Africa as zone, 1961 L
Nude, The (K. Clark), 1957 S
Nuffield Foundation, 1943 O
Numbers, Theory of, 1854 P
Numismatics, studies in, 1792 Q, 1840 Q
Nuncomar, Indian official (d. 1775), 1775 N
Nuremberg, W. Germany: Social Democrat rally, 1908 J; Laws, against Jews, 1935 J; Tribunal, of war criminals, 1946 J
Nuri-es-Said, Iraq. politician, 1958 C, G
'Nutcracker Man', 1959 P
Nyasaland: proclaimed a British protectorate, 1891 F; frontier settled, 1901 B; right to cede from Central African Federation, acknowledged, 1962 M; becomes self-governing, 1963 A; becomes independent republic as Malawi, 1964 G. *See also* Central African Federation; Malawi
Nyerere, Julius, Tanzanian leader (b. 1922): becomes premier of Tanganyika, 1961 E; resigns, 1962 A; elected President of Tanganyika, 1962 L; elected President of Tanzania, 1964 D
Nylon stockings, invented, 1937 P

O

Oakeshott, Michael, B. philosopher (b. 1903), 1939 O
Oberland (D. Richardson), 1927 U
Oberlin, Jean Frédéric, G. pastor and philanthropist (1740–1826), 1769 O
Oberon (C. M. Wieland), 1780 U
Objections to Christian Belief (ed. A. Vidler), 1963 R
Oblamov (I. Goncharov), 1859 U
Obregón, Alvaro, president of Mexico, 1920 J, 1928 G
O'Brien, James, B. Chartist leader (1805–64), 1848 G
O'Brien, William Smith, Ir. Nationalist leader (1803–64), 1886 L
Obscenity and the Law (N. St. John-Stevas), 1956 O
Observations on a late Publication on the Present State of the Nation (E. Burke), 1769 O
Observations on Civil Liberty and the Justice and Policy of the War with America (R. Price), 1776 O
Observations on Magnetism (J. Gay-Lussac), 1807 P
Observations on the Geology of the U.S. (W. Maclure), 1809 P
Observations sur les hôpitaux (P. Cabanis), 1789 O
Observatories:
in Britain, Mullard, Cambridge, 1957 P
Royal, Herstmonceux, 1953 P
in Russia, Central, of the USSR Academy of Sciences, 1954 P
in US Lisk, California, 1954 P
Mt. Wrangell, Alaska, 1953 P
Ocana, Spain, Spanish defeat at, 1809 L
O'Casey, Sean, Ir. dramatist (1884–1964), 1884 Z, 1925 W, 1926 W, 1934 W, 1942 W, 1964 Z
Oceanography:
surveys, 1872 P, 1934 P, 1950 P, 1959
through bathyscaphe, 1948 P, 1964 P
Ochakóv, on Black Sea, Russia: Russians capture, 1788 M, 1791 C; Turkey cedes, 1792 A
O'Connell, Daniel, Ir. Nationalist leader (1775–1847), 1775 Z, 1835 C; establishes Catholic Association, 1823 E; wins Clare election, 1828 F
O'Connor, Feargus, Ir. Chartist leader (1794–1855), 1838 O, V
Ödenburg, plebiscite for union with Hungary, 1921 M
Odeon cinema circuit in Britain, 1933 W
Ode on the Intimations of Immortality (W. Wordsworth), 1807 U
Oder, River, Cen. Europe, 1772 P, 1945 A
Oder–Neisse line, 1950 L; Poland asks for acknowledgment of, 1960 G
Odes (F. Klopstock), 1771 U
Odes (V. Hugo), 1819 U
Ode to a Nightingale (J. Keats), 1820 U
Ode to the West Wind (P. B. Shelley), 1820 U
Odessa, Russia: port founded, 1791 N; Turks bombard, 1914 K; Allies evacuate, 1919 D; Bolsheviks, capture, 1920 B; Germans take, 1941 K
Odets, Clifford, Am. dramatist (b. 1906), 1935 W, 1952 W
Odom, Capt., Am. aviator, 1947 P
O'Donnell, Leopold, duke of Tetuan, Sp. general and Liberal politician (1809–67), 1854 G, 1856 J, K, 1865 F, 1867 L
O'Duffy, Eoin, Ir. politician (1892–1944), 1933 J
Odyssey of Homer, The (T. E. Lawrence's translation), 1935 Q
Oecumenical movement, 1928 R, 1959 R, 1961 R
Oersted, Hans Christian, Da. physicist (1777–1851), 1819 P
Oesophagus, resection of, 1872 P
Offenbach, Jacques, F. musician (1819–80), 1819 Z, 1858 T, 1880 Z, 1881 T
Offenburg, W. Germany, French troops leave, 1924 H
Of Human Bondage (W. S. Maugham), 1915 U
Of Mice and Men (J. Steinbeck), 1937 U
Ogden, Charles Kay, B. originator of Basic English (1889–1957), 1927 O, 1947 O
O'Gorman, Juan, Mexic. architect (b. 1905), 1952 S
O'Higgins, Kevin Christopher, Ir. Nationalist (1892–1927), 1927 G
Ohio: becomes a US state, 1803 C; steam engine to, 1829 P; abandons liquor licensing, 1851 O; corruption in, 1911 O
Ohm, Gearg Simon, G. physicist (1787–1854), 1787 Z, 1827 P, 1843 P, 1854 Z
Oil:
in Argentine, nationalised, 1928 J
in Britain, refinery at Fawley, 1951 P
licences to drill in N. Sea, 1964 P
company strikes oil in N. Sea, 1965 P
embargo placed on oil for Rhodesia, 1965 M
airlift to Zambia in operation, 1965 M
in Iran, nationalised, 1951 G
agreement with Russia is nullified, 1947 L
in Mexico, concessions in, 1923 D
expropriations of British and US properties, 1938 C
in Roumania, seized by Germans, 1940 K
Oil Companies:
Anglo-Persian agreement annulled by Persia, 1932 L

dispute settled, 1933 B. See also Anglo-Fronien Oil Co
Iraq Petroleum, dispute with the Lebanon settled, 1959 F
Royal Dutch Shell Oil, banned by Indonesia, 1958 F
Shell Oil refinery, Havana, dispute with Cuba, 1960 G
Standard Oil Co., 1922 D
US leases for, scandal over, 1924 B
Oil-engine, 1873 P
Oil pipe-lines:
Abadan–Teheran, completed, 1957 A
Kirkuk, Iraq, to Haifu and Tripolis, 1935 P
Mosul–Tripoli, 1934 G
from Texas ('big inch'), 1943 P
Oil pollution of sea, 1954 O
Oil production. *See under* Petrol
Oil tanker fleets, comparative tonnages, 1964 Y
Oil wells, in Pennsylvania, 1859 P
in Baku, 1873 P
Oise–Aisne Canal, France, Germans forced back to, 1917 K
Okada, Keisuke, Jap. premier, 1934 G
O'Kelly, Sean, president of Eire, 1945 F, 1959 F
Oken, Lorenz, G. scientist (1779–1851), 1822 P
Okinawa, Rynkyn Islands, Pacific, US take, 1945 D
Oklahoma, state, US: opened to settlement, 1889 D; admitted as a US state, 1907 L
Olaf V, King of Norway, 1957 J
Olbers, Henrich Wilhelm Matthias, G. astronomer (1758–1840), 1797 P, 1801 L
Old-age pensions, in Britain, advocated, 1879 O
Rothschild's Committee on, 1898 O
introduced, 1909 A
women to receive at 60, 1940 B
increased, 1964 L
in France, 1850 O
in Germany, 1889 E
in New Zealand, 1898 O
Old Curiosity Shop, The (C. Dickens), 1840 U
Oldenburg, W. Germany, grand duchy: ceded by Denmark to Russia, 1773 K; Napoleon annexes, 1811 A
Old Faith and the New, The (D. F. Strauss), 1872 R
Old Man and the Sea, The (E. Hemingway), 1952 U
Old Mortality (W. Scott), 1816 U
Old People (S. Rowntree), 1947 O
Old Red Sandstone (H. Miller), 1841 U
Old Wives' Tale, The (A. Bennett), 1908 U
Oleo-margarine, substitution for butter limited, 1902 P
Olga, dowager Queen of Greece, 1920 L
Oliver Twist (C. Dickens), 1837 U
Olivenza, Spain, ceded to Spain, 1801 F
Olivier, Borg, Maltese Nationalist Party, 1953 G, 1962 C
Olivier, Sir Laurence, B. actor (b. 1907), 1944 W, 1948 W, 1957 W
Ollivier, Oliver Émile, F. statesman (1825–1912), 1870 A
Olmütz, Czechslovakia, Punctation of, 1850 L
Olney Hymns (Cowper and Newton), 1779 R
Olympia, Greece, 'Hermes' of Praziteles found at, 1875 S
Olympic Games: Athens, 1896 X; London, 1908 X; Stockholm, 1912 X; Antwerp, 1920 X; Paris, 1924 X; Los Angeles, 1932 X; Berlin, 1936 X; Melbourne, 1956 X; Rome, 1960 X; Tokio, 1964 P, X
Omaha, Nebraska, US, Populist Convention at, 1892 G
Oman, revolt of the Imam, 1957 G
Oman, Steppes, Arabia, 1948 P
Ombudsman, The (or Parliamentary Commissioner) in Britain, 1965 O
Omdurmann, Khartum, Sudan, 1884 K; Kitchener's victory at, 1898 J
Ommanney, Erasmus, B. admiral (1810–75), 1850 P
Omnibus:
horse-drawn, 1892 P
motor, 1905 P
ordered by Cuba, 1964 A
Omsk, Siberia, Russia: Red Army takes, 1919 L; solar eclipse observed at, 1936 P
On American Taxation (E. Burke), 1774 O
On Crimes and Punishments (C. Beccaria), 1764 O
On Discovery in Medicine (J. G. Zimmermann), 1764 P
One Day in the Life of Ivan Denisovich (A. Solzhenitsyn), 1962 U
O'Neill, Eugene Gladstone, Am. dramatist (1888–1953), 1916 W, 1920 W, 1921 W, 1923 W, 1931 W, 1933 W, 1940 W, 1946 W
O'Neill, Terence, N. Ir. premier, 1963 C
On Heroes and Hero-Worship (T. Carlyle), 1841 U
On Labour (W. T. Thornton), 1869 O
On Laughter (H. Bergson), 1900 R
On Liberty (J. S. Mill), 1859 O
On Literature (A. de Staël), 1800 U
On Living in a Revolution (J. Huxley), 1944 O
On Primary Numbers (P. L. Chebichev), 1850 P
Ontario, Canada, enters Dominion of Canada, 1867 C
On the Archetypes and Homologies of the Vertebrate Skeleton (Owen), 1848 P
On the Civil Amelioration of the . . . Jews (M. Mendelssohn), 1781 R
On the Conservation of Energy (H. Helmholtz 1847 P
On the Eve (I. Turgeniev), 1860 U
On the Hypotheses forming the Foundation of Geometry (G. Riemann), 1854 P
On the Notion of the Theory of Science (J. G. Fichte), 1794 R
On the Origins of Speech (Herder), 1772 P
On the Road (J. Kerouac), 1957 U
OP Art, 1964 S
'Open-door' policy in China, 1907 F, 1922 B
Open Society and Its Enemies, The (K. Popper), 1945 R
Opera:
Abu Hassan (Weber), 1811 T
Aida (Verdi), 1871 T
Albert Herring (B. Britten), 1947 T
Alcestre (Gluck), 1767 T
Antigone (Honegger), 1927 T
Antigone (Piccini), 1771 T
Arabella (R. Strauss), 1933 T
Archers of Switzerland, The (B. Carr), 1796 T
Ariadne and Bluebeard (P. Dukas), 1907 T
Ariane (Massenet), 1906 T
Armide (Gluck), 1777 T
Babel (Stravinsky), 1952 T
Barber of Baghdad (Cornelius), 1858 T
Barber of Seville (G. Paisiells), 1780 T
Barber of Seville (Rossini), 1816 T
Bartered Bride, The (Smetana), 1866 T
Bastien and Bastienne (Mozart), 1768 T
Benvenuto Cellini (Berlioz), 1837 T
Billy Bud (Britten), 1951 T
Billy the Kid (A. Copland), 1938 T
Bluebeard's Castle (Bartok), 1918 T
Boatswain's Mate, The (E. Smyth), 1916 T
Bohème, La (Puccini), 1896 T

Opera—*contd.*
Bohemian Girl, The (Balfe), 1843 T
Boris Godunof (Moussourgski), 1874 T
Bride of Lammermoor (Donizetti), 1859 W
Caliph of Baghdad (Boieldieu), 1799 T
Cavalleria Rusticana (P. Mascagni), 1890 T
Cenerentola, La (Rossini), 1810 T
Christopher Columbus (D. Milhand), 1930 T
Comte Dry, Le (Rossini), 1828 T
Consul, The (C. Menotti), 1950 T
Coppelia (Delibes), 1870 T
Corregedior, The (H. Wolf), 1896 T
Cosi fan tutte (Mozart), 1789 T, 1790 T
Crown Diamonds (Auber), 1841 T
Danaides, Les (A. Salieri), 1784 T
David (D. Milhand), 1953 T
Diary of a Madman (H. Searle), 1958 T
Dr. Faustus (Busoni), 1925 T
Doctor and Apotheker (Dittersdorf), 1786 T
Don Carlos (Verdi), 1867 T
Don Giovanni (Mozart), 1787 T
Don Pasquale (Donizetti), 1843 T
Duenna, The (Prokofiev), 1946 T
Elisir d'Amore, L' (Donizetti), 1832 T
Enchantress, The (Bliss), 1952 T
Ernani (Verdi), 1844 T
Erwartung (Schönberg), 1924 T
Eugene Onegin (Tchaikovsky), 1879 T
Fair Maid of Perth, The (Bizet), 1867 T
Falstaff (Verdi), 1893 T
Faust (Gounod), 1859 T
Fedora (U. Giordano), 1898 T
Ferdinand Cortez (Spontini), 1809 T
Fervaal (D'Indy), 1897 T
Fidelio (Beethoven), 1805 T, 1814 T
Fille du Régiment, La (Donizetti), 1840 T
Flaming Angel, The (Prokofiev), 1954 T
Fledermaus, Die (J. Strauss), 1874 T
Flying Dutchman, The (Wagner), 1843 T
Forgotten Rite, The (J. Ireland), 1915 T
Forza del Destino (Verdi), 1862 T
Fra Diavolo (Auber), 1830 S
Frieschütz, Der (Weber), 1838 W
Gazza Ladra, La (Rossini), 1817 T
Girl of the Golden West, The (Puccini), 1910 T
Gloriana (Britten), 1953 T
Glückliche Hand, Die (Schönberg), 1924 T
Golden Cockerel, The (Rimsky-Korsakov), 1910 T
Gondoliers, The (Sullivan), 1889 T
Götterdämmerung (R. Wagner), 1874 T
Grand Duke, The (Sullivan), 1896 T
Hansel and Gretel (Humperdinck), 1893 T
Harmony of the World, The (Hindemith), 1957 T
Hecube (Martinu), 1956 T
H.M.S. Pinafore (Sullivan), 1878 T
Herodias (P. Hindemith), 1944 T
Hugenots, The (Meyerbeer), 1836 T
Idomeneo (Mozart), 1781 T
Immortal Hour, The (R. Boughton), 1914 T
Intoleranza (L. Nono), 1961 T
Iolanthe (Sullivan), 1882 T
I Pagliacci (Leoncavallo), 1892 T
Iphigenia in Aulis (Gluck), 1774 T
Iphigenia in Tauris (Gluck), 1779 T
Irmelin (Delius), 1953 T
Island of God, The (C. Menotti), 1942 T
Italian in Algiers, The (Rossini), 1813 T
Ivan the Terrible (Rimsky-Korsakov), 1873 T
Jenufa (Janáček), 1916 T
Jewels of the Madonna, The (Wolf-Ferrari), 1911 T
Johnny Strikes Up (E. Krenek), 1927 T
Joseph (Méhul), 1807 T
Judith (Honegger), 1926 T
Julius Caesar Jones (Williamson), 1965 T
King David (Honegger), 1921 T
King Midas (Françaix), 1957 T
King Priam (M. Tippett), 1962 T
Koanga (Delius), 1904 T
Lady Macbeth of Mtensk (Shostakiovich), 1932 T
Life for the Czar, A (Glinka), 1836 T
Lodoiska (Cherubini), 1791 T
Lohengrin (Wagner), 1850 T
Louise (G. Charpentier), 1900 T
Loves of Three Oranges, The (De Falla), 1921 T
Lovespell, The (De Falla), 1915 T
Lucy of Lammermoor (Donizetti), 1835 T
Macbeth (Verdi), 1847 T
Madam Angot's Daughter (Lecocq), 1872 T
Madame Butterfly (Puccini), 1904 T
Magic Flute (Mozart), 1791 T, 1955 T
Manon (Massenet), 1884 T
Manon Lescaut (Puccini), 1893 T
Margherita d'Anjon, 1820 T
Marriage of Figaro, The (Mozart), 1786 T
Martha (Flotow), 1847 T
Masaniello (Auber), 1828 T
Master Pédros (De Falla), 1923 T
Mastersingers, The (Wagner), 1868 T
Mathis der Maler (Hindemith), 1934 T
Mavra (Stravinsky), 1922 T
Medea (Cherubini), 1797 T
Médéa (D. Milhand), 1940 T
Medium, The (Menotti), 1946 T
Merrie England (E. German), 1902 T
Merry Widow, The (Léhar), 1905 T
Merry Wives of Windsor, The (Nicolai), 1848 T
Midsummer Marriage, The (M. Tippett), 1955 T
Midsummer Night's Dream, A (Britten), 1961 T
Mignon (Thomas), 1866 T
Moon and Sixpence, The (J. Gardner), 1957 T
Moses and Aaron (Schönberg), 1954 T, 1965 T
Murder in the Cathedral (Pizzetti), 1958 T
Nelson (L. Berkeley), 1954 T
Neues vom Tage (Hindemith), 1929 T
Norma (Bellini), 1831 T
Notre Dame de Paris (Fry), 1863 T
Oedipus Rex (Stravinsky), 1927 T
Olympians, The (Bliss), 1949 T
Orpheus in the Underworld (Offenbach), 1858 T
Othello (Verdi), 1887 T
Palestrina (Pfitzner), 1917 T
Parsifal (Wagner), 1882 T
Pearl Fishers, The (Bizet), 1863 T
Pelléas et Mélisande (Debussy), 1902 T
Perfect Fool, The (Holst), 1923 T
Peter Grimes (Britten), 1945 T
Pietra del Paragone, La, 1812 T
Pilgrim's Progress, A (Vaughan Williams), 1951 T
Pirata, Il (Bellini), 1827 T
Pirates of Penzance, The (Sullivan), 1880 T
Porgy and Bess (G. Gershwin), 1935 T
Prince Igor (Borodin), 1887 T, 1890 T
Prinz von Hamburg, Der (H. W. Henze), 1960 T
Queen of Sheba (Goldmark), 1875 T
Queen of Spades (Tchaikovsky), 1890 T
Rake's Progress, The (Stravinsky), 1951 T
Rape of Lucretia, The (Britten), 1946 T
Rhinegold, The (Wagner), 1869 T
Richard Coeur de Lion (Grétry), 1784 T
Rienzi (Wagner), 1842 T
Rigoletto (Verdi), 1851 T
Ring, The, Wagner's text of, 1853 T
first complete performance, 1876 T
broadcast without a break, 1962 W

Rip Van Winkle (Bristow), 1855 T
Rosenkavalier, Der (R. Strauss), 1911 T
Ruddigore (Sullivan), 1887 T
Russalka (Dargomijsky), 1856 T
Russalka (Dvořák), 1901 T
Russlan and Ludmilla (Glinka), 1842 T
Saint of Bleecker Street, The (Menotti), 1954 T
St. Susanna (Hindemith), 1922 T
Salome (R. Strauss), 1905 T
Savonarola (C. V. Stanford), 1884 T
School for Wives (Liebermann), 1955 T
Schwanda the Bagpiper (Weinberger), 1927 T
Secret Marriage, The (D. Cimarosa), 1792 T
Seraglio, Il (Mozart), 1782 T
Sicilian Vespers (Berlioz), 1855 T
Siegfried (Wagner), 1876 T
Snow Maiden, The (Rimsky-Korsakov), 1882 T
Socratie (E. Satie), 1920 T
Sonnambula, La (Bellini), 1831 T
Sylvia (Delibes), 1876 T
Tales of Hoffmann, The (Offenbach), 1881 T
Tancredi (Rossini), 1813 T
Tannhauser (Wagner), 1845 T
Tarquin (Kreňek), 1941 T
Tender Land, The (A. Copland), 1954 T
Thais (Massenet), 1894 T
Threepenny Opera, The (Weil and Brecht), 1928 T
London production of, 1956 W
Tiefland (D'Albert), 1903 T
Tobias and the Angel (Britten), 1960 T
Tosca (Puccini), 1900 T
Traviata, La (Verdi), 1853 T
Trial by Jury (Sullivan), 1875 T
Tristan and Isolde (Wagner), 1859 T, 1865 R
Trittico, Il (Puccini), 1918 T
Triumph of Love (Malipiero), 1931 T
Troilus and Cressida (Walton), 1954 T
Trojans, The, Part I (Berlioz), 1863 T
Part II (The Taking of Troy), 1899 T
Trovatore, Il (Verdi), 1853 T
Turandot (Puccini), 1924 T
Turn of the Screw, The (Britten), 1954 T
Vanessa (S. Barber), 1961 T
Vestal Virgin, The (Spontini), 1807 T
Village Romeo and Juliet, A (Delius), 1907 T
Violanta (Korngold), 1916 T
Voie Humaine, La (Poulenc), 1959 T
Vom Heute auf Morgen (Schönberg), 1930 T
Walkürie, Die (Wagner), 1870 T
Wallenstein (Weinberger), 1937 T
War and Peace (Prokofiev), 1946 T
Water-Carrier, The (Cherubini), 1800 T
William Tell (Rossini), 1829 T
Wozzeck (Berg), 1926 T
Wreckers, The (E. Smyth), 1906 T
Zampa (Hérold), 1831 T
Zenobia (L. Coerne), 1905 T
Opera ballet: *Persephone* (Stravinsky), 1934 T
Operetta:
Frasquita (Léhar), 1922 T
Monsieur Beaucaire (Messager), 1919 T
Paganini (Léhar), 1925 T
See also under Musicals
Operette morali (Leopardi), 1827 U
Ophthalmoscope, 1851 P
Ophuls, Max, F. film director, 1950 W, 1951 W
Opie, Iona, B. author (b. 1923), 1959 Q
Opie, John, B. artist (1761–1807), 1781 S, 1783 S
Opie, Peter, B. author (b. 1918), 1959 Q
Opinions of Nature (A. von Humboldt), 1808 R
Opium: British war with China over, 1839 G, H, L; trade to China, legalised, 1858 F
Oporto, Portugal: battle, 1809 E; revolution in, 1820 H
Oppenheim, Robert, Am. physicist (b. 1918), 1953 P
Optical glass, 1846 P, 1916 P
Optical instruments, 1846 P
Optical studies, 1791 P, 1856 P
Optics, principles of, discussed, 1772 P
Opuscules physiques et Chimiques (A. Lavoisier), 1774 P
Oran, Algeria, French fleet sunk, 1940 G
Orange Free State, S. Africa: established, 1854 B; diamonds discovered in, 1870 N; supports Kruger, 1899 K; British annexes, 1900 E
Orange River Colony, S. Africa, 1848 H
Orangemen, riot in Dublin, 1822 M
Oratorios:
Amadis de Gaule (J. C. Bach), 1779 T
Beatitudes, Les (C. Franck), 1872 T
Canticum sacrum and honorem Sancti Marci nominis, 1956 T
Chichester Psalms (L. Bernstein), 1965 T
Childhood of Christ, The (Berlioz), 1854 T
Child of Our Time, A (M. Tippett), 1940 T
Creation, The (Haydn), 1798 T
Damnation of Faust (Berlioz), 1846 T
Djinns, Les (C. Franck), 1884 T
Dream of Gerontius (Elgar), 1900 T
Elijah (Mendelssohn), 1846 T
German Requiem, A (Brahms), 1868 T
Israelities in the Wilderness, The (C. P. E. Bach), 1775 T
Job (K. von Dittersdorf), 1780 T
Job (C. H. H. Parry), 1892 T
Legend of St. Christopher, The (D'Indy), 1920 T
Mary of Magdala (Bliss), 1963 T
Messiah, The (Handel), notable performances of, 1770 T, 1772 T
Moses in Egypt (Rossini), 1818 T
Noye's Fludde (Britten), 1958 T
Passion Cantata (C. P. E. Bach), 1769 T
Prophet, The (Meyerbeer), 1849 T
Psalmus Hungarius (Kodály), 1923 T
Psalm 150 (Bruckner), 1892 T
Redemption, The (F. Gounod), 1882 T
Requiem (Verdi), 1874 T
St. Matthew Passion (Bach), revival of, 1829 T
Sampson and Delilah (C. Saint-Saëns), 1877 T
Stabat Mater (Dvořák), 1883 T
Stabat Mater (B. Naylor), 1964 T
Stabat Mater (Rossini), 1841 T
Te Deum (Bruckner), 1884 T
Twelve, The (Walton), 1965 T
Whitsun Oratorio (E. Kreňek), 1960 T
Orators, The (W. H. Auden), 1932 U
Oratory of St. Francis de Sales, 1841 R
Orchestras, notable:
Berlin Philharmonic, 1882 T
Boston Symphony, 1924 T
London Philharmonic, 1932 T
New York Philharmonic, 1929 T
Ordaz, Gustav, Mex. president, 1964 M
Ordeal by Planning (J. Jewkes), 1948 O
Ordeal of Richard Feverel, The (G. Meredith), 1859 U
Ordnance Survey, British, established, 1791 P
Örebro, Sweden, Treaty of, alliance between Sweden and Russia, 1812 G
Oregon, state, US: Canadian-US joint occupation, 1818 K; becomes a US state, 1859 B; laws of, applied to Alaska, 1884 E
Orel, Russia, Russian offensive at, 1943 G, H
Oreste, president of Haiti, 1914 A
Orfila, Mathieu, Joseph Bonaventure, F. chemist (1787–1853), 1814 P

Organic Compounds, theory of, 1852 P
Organisation du travail, L' (L. Blanc), 1839 O
Organisation Man, The (W. H. Whyte), 1956 O
Organisation of American States, Conference of, 1954 C
Organisation of European Economic Cooperation (OEEC): formed, 1948 D; Convention for Economic Cooperation signed, 1960 M
Organon of Therapeutics (S. Hahnemann), 1810 P
Orientales, Les (V. Hugo), 1829 U
Oriental studies, 1778 Q, 1784 Q, 1789 Q, 1875 Q
Oriental and African Studies, School of, London, 1916 O
Orient Express, 1883 P, 1961 E
Origin and Progress of Language (Lord Monboddo), 1773 Q
Origine de tons les cultes (C. F. Dupois), 1795 Q
Origines de la France contemporaine (H. Taine), 1873 O
Origin of Historismus, The (F. Meinecke), 1936 Q
Origin of Species by Natural Selection, The (C. Darwin), 1859 P
Origin of the Ovum (K. Baer), 1827 P
Origins of Commerce, The (Anderson), 1764 Q
Orlando (V. Woolf), 1928 U
Orlando, Vittorio, It. premier (1860–1936), 1917 K
Orléans family, banished from France, 1852 A, 1886 F
Orly, France, airship hangars at, 1916 S
Ornithology, studies in, 1786 P, 1830 P
Orpen, Sir William, B. artist (1878–1931), 1878 Z, 1900 S, 1909 S, 1917 S, 1931 Z
Orphanage, Dr. Barnardo's homes, 1866 O
Orpington, Kent, England, by-election, 1962 C
Orsini, Felice, It. anarchist (1819–58), 1858 A, B
Orsova, S.W. Rumania, ceded to Austria, 1791 H
Ortega y Gasset, José, Sp. philosopher and historian, 1930 O
Orthological Institute, 1927 O
Orton, Arthur, B. impostor (1837–83), 1874 O
Orvieto, Italy, Fifth Army takes, 1944 F
Orwell, George. *See* Blair, Eric
Osborne, John James, B. dramatist (b. 1929), 1929 Z, 1956 W, 1957 W, 1961 W, 1964 W, 1965 W
Osborne, Judgment, 1909 O
Oslo, Norway (formerly Christiana): university, 1811 O; name changed from Christiana, 1925 A; agreement on tariffs, 1930 M; Convention on Scandinavian economic cooperation, 1932 B
Oscar I, King of Sweden (1844–59), 1844 C, 1859 G
Oscar II, King of Sweden (1872–1907), 1907 M; abdicates Norwegian Crown, 1905 K
O'Shea, William Henry, Ir. politician (1840–1905), 1890 O
Osnabrück, Germany, US army takes, 1945 D
Osobka-Morawski, Polish Communist, forms ministry, 1945 F
Ostend, Belgium: manifesto, advising US acquisition of Cuba, 1854 K; British take, 1918 E
Ostrolenke, Poland, Polish rebels defeated at, 1831 E
Ostrovsky, Alexander Nicolaievich, R. author (1823–86), 1847 W, 1860 W, 1872 W
Oswald, Lee, H., Am. assassin, 1963 L
Otis, E. G. Am. civil engineer (1811–61), 1857 P
Ottawa, Canada: becomes capital, 1858 O; Parliament House at, 1859 S; Colonial Conference in, 1894 F; Imperial Economic Conference in, 1932 G; Churchill visits, 1941 M
Otto, of Bavaria, Prince, elected King of Greece, 1832 H
Otto, Archduke of Habsburg, refused to return to Austria, 1961 F
Otto I, King of Greece (1832–62), 1832 H, 1843 J, 1862 K
Oudh, India:
  Nabwab of, defeated, 1764 K
    alliance with E. India Company, 1773 J
    treasures of, plundered, 1781 N
  Britain annexes, 1856 B
Oudney, Walter, B. naval surgeon and explorer (1790–1824), 1823 P
'Ouida'. *See* Ramée, Marie Louise de la
Oulianov. *See* Lenin
Our Mutual Friend (C. Dickens), 1864 U
Our Town (T. Wilder), 1938 W
Our Village (M. Mitford), 1824 U
Outcasts of Poker Flat, The (B. Harte), 1869 U
Outline of History (H. G. Wells), 1920 Q
Outlines and Experiments respecting Sound and Light (T. Young), 1800 P
Outpourings of a Monk (W. Wackenroder), 1797 U
Outrages:
  in Belgium, by anarchists, 1901 N
  in Britain, attack on Prince Regent, 1817 A
    Peterloo massacre, 1819 H
    Cato Street Conspiracy, 1820 B
    sinking of *Lusitania*, 1915 E
    sinking of *Athenia*, 1939 J
    sinking of *Empress of Britain*, 1940 K
    See also under Fenianism; Suffragettes
  in Czechoslovakia, Nazi burning of Lidice, 1942 F
  in France, by anarchists, 1858 A, 1893 L, M
  in India, between Moslems and Hindus, 1947 H
    anti-Moslem violence, 1964 C
  in Korea, by Communists, alleged, 1953 K
  in S. Africa, Sharpeville shootings, 1960 C
  in US, against Negroes in Alabama, 1963 J
    murders of Civil Rights Workers, 1964 H, M
  See also Assassinations; Kidnappings
Outram, Sir James, B. soldier (1805–64), 1857 J
Outsider, The (C. Wilson), 1956 R
Outspoken Essays (W. R. Inge), 1919 R
Outward Bound (S. Vane), 1923 W
Ouvriers européens, Les (P. Le Play), 1855 O
Overbeck, Johann Friedrich, G. artist (1789–1869), 1810 S, 1824 S
Overend and Gurney, London firm of bill discounters, failure of, 1866 O
Overruled (G. B. Shaw), *Preface to*, 1916 U
Over the Bridge (R. Church), 1955 U
Overtures, Symphonic Poems, etc.:
  Academic Festival (Brahms), 1881 T
  Après-midi d'un Faune, L' (Debussy), 1894 T
  Cockaigne (Elgar), 1901 T
  Coriolanus (Beethoven), 1807 T
  Dance Suite (Bartok), 1923 T
  Death and Transfiguration (R. Strauss), 1889 T
  Dieux dans l'ombre des Cavernes, Les (A. Roussel), 1917 T
  Don Juan (R. Strauss), 1888 T
  1812 (Tchaikovsky), 1880 T
  Elegy for Young Lovers (Henze), 1961 T
  Enigma Variations (Elgar), 1899 T
  Faust Overture (Wagner), 1840 T
  Finlandia (Sibelius), 1900 T
  Firebird Suite (Stravinsky), 1910 T
  Fountains of Rome, The (Respighi), 1917 T
  Francesca da Rimini (Tchaikovsky), 1876 T
  Harold in Italy (Berlioz), 1834 T
  Háry János Suite (Kodály), 1923 T
  Italian Capriccio (Tchaikovsky), 1880 T
  Italian Serenade (H. Wolf), 1894 T
  Karelia Suite (Sibelius), 1893 T
  Leonora No. 3 (Beethoven), 1807 T

Lincoln Portrait (A. Copland), 1942 T
Mazeppa (Liszt), 1854 T
Mer, La (Debussy), 1905 T
My Fatherland (Smetana), 1874 T
On Hearing the First Cuckoo of Spring (Delius), 1912 T
Pacific 231 (Honegger), 1923 T
Perfect Fool, The (Holst), 1923 T
Pictures from an Exhibition (Moussourgski), 1874 T
Planets, The, Suite (Holst), 1915 T
Romeo and Juliet (Berlioz), 1838 T
Romeo and Juliet (Tchaikovsky), 1864 T
Rouet D'Omphale, Le (Saint-Saëns), 1871 T
Scapino (Walton), 1941 T
Scheherezade (Rimsky-Korsakov), 1888 T
Symphonic Nocturne (Busoni), 1914 T
Symphonic Variations (Franck), 1885 T
Thus Spake Zarathustra (R. Strauss), 1896 T
Till Eulenspiegel's Merry Pranks (R. Strauss), 1895 T
Tintagel (Bax), 1917 T
Tragic (Brahms), 1881 T
Variations on a Theme of Haydn (St. Anthony Chorale) (Brahms), 1873 T
Variations for Orchestra (E. Carter), 1957 T
Overtures to Death (C. Day-Lewis), 1938 U
Owen, Robert, B. Socialist and philanthopist (1771–1858), 1771 Z, 1800 O, 1813 O, 1834 A, C, 1858 Z
Owen, Sir Richard, B. naturalist (1804–92), 1846 P, 1848 P
Owens, M. J., Am. inventor, 1898 P
Owings, Nathaniel Alexander, Am. architect (b. 1903), 1952 S
Oxford Committee for Famine Relief (OXFAM), 1942 O
Oxford Conference on Church, Community and State, 1937 R
Oxford Group, 1939 R
Oxford History of England (ed. G. Clark), 1934 Q
Oxford History of Music, 1929 T
Oxford Movement, The, 1833 R, 1841 R, 1845 R
Oxford Union Society, 1823 W, 1933 O
Oxford University:
appoints Franks Commission, 1964 O
Balliol College, under Jowett, 1870 O
Bampton Lectures, 1780 R
Conference on Industry, Duke of Edinburgh's, 1956 G
Keble College, founded, 1870 O
Macmillan elected Chancellor, 1960 C
music faculty founded, 1944 T
Natural science honours school, 1850 O
Pitt Rivers Museum, 1874 Q
Professorship of modern history at, 1866 Q
religious tests abolished, 1871 F, O
Roosevelt honoured by, at Harvard, 1941 O
Oxford and Asquith, earl and countess of. *See* Asquith
Oxford and Cambridge boat race, 1829 W
Oxygen, is liquefied, 1894 P
Ozenfant, Amédée, F. artist (b. 1886), 1918 S, 1928 S

P

Paardeberg, S. Africa, Cronje surrenders at, 1900 B
Pace-maker, the, for cardiac therapy, 1960 P
Packard, Vance Oakley, Am. author (b. 1914,) 1959 O
Pacific, Advisory Commission for, 1947 A
Pacific Charter, 1954 J
Pacific Council, under Security Treaty of 1951, 1952 H
Pacific Islands, US trusteeship for, 1947 D
Pacific Ocean, submarine current in, 1958 P
Pacts:
Anti-Comintern (Germany with Japan), 1936 L
Italy joins, 1937 L
Spain joins, 1939 D
collapse of, 1939 H
Baghdad (Turkey and Iraq), 1955 B
Britain accedes to, 1955 D
Iran joins, 1955 L
end of boycott to Britain, 1957 C
changes name to Central Treaty Organisation (CENTO), 1959 H
Balkan (Rumania, Greece, Yugoslavia and Turkey), 1934 B
Balkan, Greece prevents Rumania from joining, 1957 J
Belgrade (armistice between Italy and Yugoslavia), 1937 C
Delhi (between British Viceroy and Gandhi), 1931 C
Delhi (between India and Pakistan, in minorities), 1950 D
Eastern (or Litvinov Protocol, between Estonia, Latvia, Poland, Rumania and Russia), 1929 B
Iran joins, 1929 D
Turkey joins, 1929 B
Four-Power (Britain, France, Germany and Italy), 1932 C, G
Kellogg-Briand, for international peace, 1928 F, H
Germany accepts, 1929 B
in force, 1929 G
Rome Pact endorses, 1933 G
Rome, four-power, 1933 G
Rome (between Italy, Austria and Hungary), 1936 C
Rome-Berlin Axis, 1936 L
'Pact of Steel' (between Hitler and Mussolini), 1939 E
Afghanistan with Iran, Iraq and Turkey (non-aggression), 1937 G
Britain with Hungary (amity), 1941 B
Britain with Italy (over Ethiopia), 1938 D
Britain with Spain (over Spanish exports of wolfram to Germany), 1944 E
Britain with Turkey (mutual assistance), 1939 E
France with Germany (on inviolability of frontiers), 1938 M
France with Russia (non-aggression), 1932 L
Germany with Italy and Japan (economic and military), 1940 J
endorsed by Hungary and Rumania, 1940 L
Germany with Poland (non-aggression), 1934 A
Hitler denounces, 1939 C
Germany with Scandinavian and Baltic states, offered (non-aggression), 1939 E
Greece with Bulgaria (non-aggression), 1938 G
Greece with Turkey (non-aggression), 1933 J
Italy with Austria and Hungary, 1937 L
Latin American states (non-aggression), 1933 K
Russia with Estonia, 1939 J
Russia with Finland (non-aggression), 1934 D
Russia with Germany (non-aggression), 1939 H
Russia with Japan (neutrality), 1941 D
denounced by Russia, 1945 D
Russia with Latvia, 1939 K
Russia with Poland (non-aggression), 1932 A, 1938 L
Turkey with Russia (1925), denounced, 1945 C

Pacts—*contd.*
US with Nationalist China (mutual security), 1954 M
US with Japan (defence), 1954 C
US with Philippines (defence), 1951 H
Yugoslavia with Germany, 1941 C
See also under Treaties
Pacts, Trade. *See* Treaties, Commercial
Paderewski, Ignaz Jan, Pol. statesmen and pianist (1860–1941), 1860 Z, 1887 T, 1909 T, 1941 Z
becomes premier of Poland, 1919 A
Paes, Sidonio, president of Portugal, 1918 M
Pagannini, Niccolo, It. violinist (1784–1840), 1784 Z, 1793 T, 1805 T, 1940 Z
Pailleron, Édouard Jules Henri, F. author (1834–90), 1881 W
Pailleterie, Alexandre Davy de la. *See* Dumas, Alexander
Paine, Thomas, B. radical and political pamphleteer (1737–1809), 1776 O, 1791 O, 1792 O, M, 1794 O, 1809 Z
Painlevé, Paul, F. premier, 1917 J, L, 1925 D
Painter, George, B. author (b. 1915), 1965 Q
Painter's Credo, A (J. Bratby), 1956 S
Painting as a Pastime (W. S. Churchill), 1948 S
Paisiello, Giovanni, It. musician (1741–1816), 1780 T
Pajou, Augustin, F. sculptor (1730–1809), 1768 S, 1791 S
Pakistan: independence proclaimed, 1947 H; becomes an Islamic republic, 1956 B
Palacky, Francis, Czech. historian and politician (1798–1876), 1848 F
Palaeography, study of, 1852 Q, 1912 Q
Palatinate, Elector of, 1777 M
Palermo, Sicily: revolt in, 1848 A; Neapolitans enter, 1849 E; Garibaldi takes, 1860 E; Allies occupy, 1943 G
Palestine:
frontier with Egypt, 1906 E
Balfour declaration on, 1917 L
Turkish collapse in, 1918 J
mandate of, to Britain, 1920 D
boundary with Syria settled, 1920 M
League mandate for, 1922 G, H
Arab Congress rejects, 1922 H
Greece is warned against attempt to occupy, 1922 H
British mandate begins, 1923 J
Separatism in, 1923 K, L
unrest in, 1933 K
Jewish immigration to, restricted, 1933 M
Arab High Committee formed, 1936 D
end of mandate recommended, 1937 G
murder of district commissioner, 1937 J
Britain proposes partition, 1938 A
plan for independence, 1939 E
admission of Jews to, demanded, 1945 H
Arab states' warning to US, 1945 K
advice against partition, 1946 D
British proposal for partition under trusteeship is rejected, 1947 B
Britain refers problem to UN, 1947 D
UN plan for future of, 1947 L
Arabs invade, 1948 E
UN Conciliatory Commission discusses, 1951 J
Israel-Jordan raids, 1955 N
UN truce is accepted, 1956 A
Hammarskjöld arranges cease-fire, 1956 D, E
Israel withdraws from mixed armistice commission, 1956 K
Britain states she must assist Jordan if attacked, 1956 K
Israeli troops invade Sinai, 1956 K
withdrawal, 1957 A
Israel hands over Gaza strip to UN, 1957 C
See also Israel; Jerusalem; Jordan
Palestinian Army, formed by Kassem, 1960 C
Paley, William, B. theologian (1743–1805), 1785 R, 1794 R, 1802 R
Pa-li-Chan, China, Chinese defeat at, 1860 J
Palingénésie philosophie (C. Bonnet), 1769 R
Palladium, discovered in platinum, 1804 P
Pallas, Peter Simon, G. naturalist (1741–1811), 1767 P, 1768 P
Palmas Island, near Philippines, Pacific, awarded to Holland, 1928 D
Palmerston, Viscount. *See* Temple, Henry
Palo Alto, New Mexico, US, battle, 1846 E
Pamirs, mountain range, Central Asia, 1885 P
Pampeluna, Spain, surrenders to British, 1813 K
Pan African Congress. *See under* Political Parties
Panama: declares independence and joins Colombian Republic, 1821 L; is given federal status, 1855 A; becomes independent, 1903 L; Canal Zone placed in US hands, 1903 M; frontier dispute with Costa Rica, 1921 C; is invaded from Cuba, 1959 D
Panama Canal:
concession for building, 1878 E
Lesseps organises French Company for building, 1879 H
Scandal in France concerning, 1892 L, 1893 C
reports on routes, 1899 F, 1903 L
treaty for US construction of, 1901 L
US purchases French company's rights, 1902 F, 1904 D
Hay-Herrán Pact for US acquisition, 1903 A
Canal Zone placed in US hands, 1903 M
construction begins, 1904 P
rates for, alleged to infringe 1901 Treaty, 1912 H
first vessel passes, 1913 L
civil government in Canal Zone, 1914 D
is officially open to traffic, 1914 P
alliance for defence of, 1926 G
US plans for a new canal, 1964 M
statistics of ships using, 1939 Y, 1951 Y
Pan American Airways, 1939 P
Pan American Conferences, 1889 K, 1938 M
Pan American Congress, under Bolivar, 1826 F
Pangalos, Theodore, Greek dictator, 1925 F, 1926 A
is overthrown, 1926 H
Pan German League, 1891 O
Pankhurst, Emeline, B. suffragette (1858–1928), 1903 P, 1913 D
Pankhurst, Estelle Sylvia, B. suffragette (1882–1960), 1882 Z, 1960 Z
Pangkor, Isle, Malaysia, Britain acquires, 1826 F
Pani, Mario, It. architect, 1950 S
Pan-Islam movement, 1900 N
Panmunjohn, Korea, 1951 K, 1953 G
Panopticon, Bentham's, 1791 O
Pan-Slav Conferences, 1848 F, 1892 O, 1908 G, 1918 D
Pan Slav Pact, of Corfu, for union of Serbs, Croats and Slovenes, 1917 G
Pantelleria, Island, Mediterranean, surrenders to Allies, 1943 F
Paoli, Pasquale, Corsican general and patriot (1725–1807), 1769 H
Papacy, The:
concordat with Austria, 1855 H
revoked, 1870 G
concordat with France, 1801 R
ended, 1905 M
concordat with Prussia, 1821 R

concordat with Spain, 1851 C
Decree of Papal Infallability, 1870 R
law of guarantees for, 1871 E
undertakes arbitration, 1885 M
See also under Vatican, The
Papacy and Church Reform, The (J. Haller), 1903 R
Papacy in its Social and Cultural Influence, The (P. Hoensbroech), 1902 R
Papagos, Greek field-marshal, forms ministry, 1952 L
Papal Infallability, discussed, 1864 R, 1869 R; declared, 1870 R; Gladstone attacks, 1874 R
Papal Bulls, notable:
condemning nationalism, 1835 R
Dominus ac Redemptor, 1773 G
Quod Nunquam, 1874 E
Testem Benevolentiae, 1899 R
See also under Encyclicals
Papal States, 1763 R, 1766 R, 1781 L
Avignon is regained, 1773 M
annexed by France, 1809 E
Austria evacuates, 1838 K
French expedition to, 1849 D, G
Papandreon, Greek premier, 1965 G
Papen, Franz von, G. Socialist (b. 1880), forms ministry, 1932 F; removes Prussian premier, 1932 G; Hitler refuses to serve under, 1932 H; resigns, 1932 L; becomes Vice-Chancellor, 1933 A; is acquitted by Nuremberg Tribunal, 1946 J
Paperbacks, 1936 U
Paper, duties on, British, repealed, 1861 O
Paper money:
in Britain, issue restricted, 1844 O
Treasury Notes are issued, 1914 O
in France, Assignats are issued, 1789 O
Franc Notes are issued, 1914 O
Papineau, Louis Joseph, Can. rebel, 1837 L
Papplewick, Notts., England, cotton spinning factory at, 1785 P
Paracelsus (R. Browning), 1835 U
Paraguay, independence of, 1811 H
Parathyroid gland, extract of, 1925 P
Paravanes, 1915 P
Parents terribles, Les (J. Cocteau), 1938 W
Pareto, G., It. Sociologist, 1916 R
Parga, Greece, Italy obtains, 1819 D
Parini, Giuseppi, It. poet (1729–99), 1763 U
Paris, France:
events:
Parlement, meets, 1785 N
demands summoning of Estates General, 1787 H
is banished to Troyes, 1787 H
is banished, 1788 A
Bastille is sacked, 1789 G
Champs de Mars festival, 1790 G
political clubs, 1790 N, 1794 L
Louis XVI attempts to go to St. Cloud, 1791 D
Massacre of Champs de Mars, 1791 G
Massacre of Swiss Guard at Les Tuileries, 1792 H
Revolutionary Commune, 1792 H, 1794 G
execution of Louis XVI, 1793 A
Napoleon installed in Tuileries, 1800 B
Allies enter, 1814 C
July Revolution, 1830 G
Napoleon I's remains removed to Les Invalides, 1840 M
street-lighting in, 1841 P
reform banquets are prohibited, 1848 B
Revolution in, 1848 B, E, F, M, L
reconstruction of, 1853 S
World Fair at, 1855 S, W
siege, 1870 J
capitulates to Prussians, 1871 A
Commune is established, 1871 C
defeated, 1871 E
anarchist outrages, 1893 C
Edward VII visits, 1903 E
postal strike, 1909 D
French government returns to, 1914 M
Zeppelin raids on, 1916 A
is shelled by Germans, 1918 C
riots in, 1934 B
World Fair, 1937 S, W
George VI visits, 1938 G
Germans enter, 1940 F
is liberated, 1944 H
French Provisional government is transferred from Algiers, 1944 H
Communist demonstrations, 1952 E
EFTA meeting, 1960 A
anti-OAS riots, 1962 B
buildings, institutions and places in or near:
Arc de Triomphe, 1806 S, 1836 S
Bibliothèque Impériale, 1852 Q
Bing's 'Art Nouveau' Gallery, 1897 S
blind school in, 1784 O
Bois de Boulogne, 1853 S
Champs de Mars, art exhibition in, 1890 S
Comedie Française, 1862 W, 1881 W
Conservatoire de Musique, 1795 T
École des Chartes, 1821 Q
École Polytechnique, 1795 O
Eiffel Tower, 1889 S, W
Hôtel de Ville, 1889 P
Invalides, 1915 T
Institut National, 1795 O
Louvre, The, 1793 S, 1911 S
Salon d'Apollou in, 1849 S
Luxembourg, 1846 S, 1894 S
Madeline, The, 1763 S, 1845 S
Metro, The, 1898 P
Montmartre music halls, 1891 S
Musée d'Orangerie, 1916 S
Notre Dame, 1845 S
Notre Dame de Lorette, 1823 S
Opera House, 1861 S
Pantheon, 1764 S
Pasteur Institute, 1880 O
Place de la Concorde, 1765 S
St. Eustache Church, 1793 R
St. Sulpice, 1857 S
Salon, 1775 S, 1831 S, 1867 S, 1876 S, 1877 S
secession of artists from, 1890 S
Salon des Indépendants, 1891 S, 1901 S
Salon des Refuses, 1863 S
Théâtre des Champs-Elysees, 1912 S
Théâtre Français, 1838 W
Théâtre Libre, 1887 W
Unesco building, 1953 S, 1959 S
art in: Impressionist exhibitions, 1874 S, 1877 S, 1886 S
Gris's lectures on painting, 1924 S
ballet in: 1909 T
literary salons in, 1764 U
music in, 1943 T
public restaurants, 1770 O
the theatre in, 1775 W, 1875 W, 1881 W
population, 1801 Y, 1841 Y, 1881 Y, 1906 Y
Treaties and Peace Negotiations at, 1763 B, 1782 E, 1814 E, 1815 L, 1856 C, D, 1857 C, 1951 D, 1955 C, D, E
Paris, Comte de. *See* Louis Philippe
Parisienne, La (H. F. Becque), 1885 W

Park, Mungo, B. explorer of Africa (1771–1806), 1795 P, 1805 P
Park, W., of Musselburgh, B. golf champion, 1860 X
Parke, Herbert William, B. ancient historian (b. 1894), 1957 Q
Parke-Bernet, of New York, fine art auctioneers, 1964 S
Parker, Alton Brooks, Am. Democrat (1852–1926), 1904 L
Parker, Hubert Lister, Lord Parker of Waddington, B. judge (b. 1900), 1957 M, 1958 J
Parkes, Sir Henry, Austral. statesman (1815–96), 1880 N, 1891 C
Parking meters, in London, 1958 O
Parkman, Francis, Am. historian (1820–93), 1820 Z, 1851 Q, 1865 Q, 1893 Z
Parliaments and other elected assemblies:
in Albania, Constituent Assembly, 1946 A
in Alsace-Lorraine, separate legislature granted, 1911 E
in Australia, federal, 1927 E
in Austria, States General promised, 1848 C
Reichstag meets, 1848 G
suspended, 1933 C
in Bohemia, committee of Diet suppressed, 1783 F
in Brazil, legislative assembly, 1824 C
in Britain, 700th anniversary celebrations, 1965 O
debates, printing of, 1771 C
emergency sessions, 1950 J
House of Commons, electors' rights, 1782 E
members, Anglican clergy not eligible, 1801 F
Dissenters in, 1844 O
Jewish, first, 1858 O
property qualifications abolished, 1858 O
Roman Catholic, first, 1829 O
salaries for, 1911 H, 1964 L
university, abolished, 1948 O
women, first, 1919 L
ministers in, increase in, 1964 M
privilege, 1763 E, L, 1771 C
procedure, Kangaroo clause, 1911 D
obstruction to, by Irish members, 1881 A
tie in division, 1965 F
House of Lords, powers of, attempt to restrict, 1907 F, 1910 E
Parliament Bill, 1911 D, E, G, H
to veto legislation reduced, 1949 M
committee recommends an heir be able to disclaim peerage, 1962 M
in British East Africa, Central legislature, 1948 D
in Burma, constituent assembly, 1947 F
in Canada, special sessions of, 1930 J
in Cape Colony, 1853 G
in China, Nanking Revolutionary Assembly, 1912 B
Republican assembly, 1913 D
People's National Convention, 1931 E
Nanking Nationalist Assembly, 1948 L
in Czechoslovakia, Sudetens leave, 1937 L
in Egypt, legislative council, 1883 E
in Eire, Dail, rejects British peace offer, 1921 H, 1922 J
votes for abolition of loyalty oath, 1932 E
Senate abolished, 1936 E
passes constitution, 1937 F
in France: States-General, demand for summoning, 1783 G
meets, 1789 E
third estate declares it is a National Assembly, 1789 F
Journal des Débats of, 1789 O
proceedings of, 1790 E
National Assembly dissolves itself, 1791 J
Legislative Assembly, 1791 J, K
is suspended, 1792 H
National Convention, 1792 J
Senate is enlarged, 1802 H
Tribunate is suppressed by Napoleon, 1807 J
Senate, 1814 D
National Assembly, 1848 E
is dissolved, 1849 A
power of legislative is increased, 1860 L
financial powers extended, 1861 L
National Assembly, at Bordeaux, 1871 B
principle of elections to Chamber, 1912 G
Constituent Assembly, 1946 F
in Germany: Diet of Confederation, 1803 B, 1816 L, 1819 L, 1820 E
revolutionaries fail to take over, 1833 D
National Assembly, 1848 E, 1849 C, D
moves to Stuttgart and is dissolved, 1849 F
Erfurt, summoned by Frederick William IV, 1850 C, D
Frankfurt Bundestag, revived, 1850 E
Prussia recognises, 1850 L
votes for federal action against Denmark, 1863 K
North German Reichstag, 1867 H
Imperial Reichstag, rejects legislation against Radicals, 1878 E
conflict in, over army bill, 1886 M
Bismarck's speech on Russian designs, 1888 B
Weimar Republic National Assembly, 1919 F
Reichstag Fire, 1933 B
West German Bundestag, votes to resume relations with Russia, 1955 J
in Gold Coast, Africans secure majority on legislature, 1946 C
in Greece, National Assembly, 1832 H, 1843 J, 1924 A
Senate is restored, 1929 E
sets up representative Parliamentary Council with Yugoslavia and Turkey, 1955 C
in Holland, States-General, 1783 K
in Holstein, Estates resolve on independence, 1844 L
in Hungary, Diet re-opened, 18-5 J
dissolved, 1861 H
at Kolozsvár, decrees for incorporation of Transylvania, 1865 M, 1867 B
Chamber, wild scenes in, 1912 E
Upper House re-established, 1926 L
in India, legislative council given greater powers, 1909 E
first Parliament, 1921 A
central legislature at Delhi, 1935 M
Constituent Assembly, 1946 M, 1947 E
dissolved, 1959 G
in Indonesia, suspended, 1960 C
Mutual Co-operation Parliament, 1960 F
in Iraq, first Parliament, 1925 G
in Ireland, Gratton's, 1782 E
passes Act of Union, 1800 C
See also Eire
in Northern Ireland, first, 1921 F
in Israel, Knesset, 1951 B
in Italy, first, 1860 D
proclaims Victor Emmanuel King, 1861 B
Chamber of Deputies is replaced by Fasces and Corporations, 1938 M
Senate to be popularly elected, 1947 M
is reformed, 1953 A

in Japan, first Diet, promise of calling, 1881 N
meets, 1890 L
power of emperor transferred to Assembly, 1946 L
in Korea, N. Koreans boycott constitutional assembly, 1948 E
in Mexico, Constitutional Congress, 1822 E
in Naples, suspended, 1849 C
in Nigeria, federal council, 1955 A
in Norway, national assembly, 1814 D
Storting meets, 1905 F
in Pakistan, Constituent Assembly, loss of confidence in, 1954 K
in Philippines, assembly, 1907 G
legislative reject independence, 1933 A
in Poland, Diet, 1812 F, 1831 A
referendum favours single-house assembly, 1946 F
in Portugal, Cortes established, 1821 A, 1826 D
in Prussia, Diet is summoned by Frederick William IV, 1847 B
national assembly, 1848 E
Upper House reconstituted, 1854 K
Diet rejects military budget, 1862 K
indemnifies Bismarck for unconstitutional rule, 1866 J
special creations of peers to pass legislation, 1872 M
in Russia, Decembrists demand summoning of assembly, 1825 M
assembly of notables is called, 1881 C
representative assembly is demanded, 1905 E
Duma, first, 1905 H, 1906 E
is dissolved, 1906 G
second, 1907 C
is dissolved, 1907 F
third, 1907 L
meeting of, 1916 B
Soviet two-chamber, 1936 M
in South Africa, Cape Assembly meets, 1853 G
reports on Jameson Raid, 1896 A
constitutional convention, 1908 K
native representation in Cape Parliament, 1936 D
in Spain, Cortes meets, 1812 C
to meet annually, 1856 J
in Syria, constituent assembly, 1928 F
is prolonged indefinitely, 1934 L
in Tangier, Council of the Throne, 1955 K
in Transjordan, Arab Congress, 1948 M
in Turkey, first, 1908 M
national assembly at Ankara, 1920 D
abolishes Caliphate, 1924 B
constituent assembly, 1961 E
in US, New York Assembly, 1787 D
first Congress meets, 1789 C
extraordinary sessions of Congress, 1911 D, 1917 D, 1937 L
presidential messages to Congress, notable, 1918 A
House of Representatives elects J. Q. Adams president, 1824 C
Speaker of, attempts to reduce power of, 1910 C
Senate, stops Force Bill, 1890 F
popular elections for, 1913 E
in S. Vietnam, Constituent Assembly for, 1956 L
in West European Union, Strasbourg assembly first meets, 1955 G
in Yugoslavia, Croats withdraw from, 1928 H, 1935 F
constituent assembly, 1945 L

Parliamentary Reform in Britain:
advocated, 1774 O, 1776 O, 1816 M, 1821 D
Yorkshire petition for, 1780 B
manhood suffrage proposed, 1780 F
Pitt's scheme for, 1783 E; defeated, 1785 D
issue of, splits Whig Party, 1794 G
sale of Parliamentary seats is forbidden, 1809 F
bills for, defeated, 1810 E, 1818 E, F, 1821 E, 1831 C, J
agitation for, 1819 H
Russell's campaign for, 1819 M
election of issue of, 1831 D
riots favour, 1831 K
new bill in Commons, 1831 M
1st Reform Bill passes Commons, 1832 C; Lords, 1832 F
in Scotland, 1832 G
in Ireland, 1832 H
Chartist demands for, 1838 O
bill introduced by Disraeli, defeated, 1859 C
2nd Reform Bill, 1867 H
Trevelyan's bill to extend franchise, 1874 E
3rd Reform Bill, 1884 M
re-distribution of seats, 1885 F
power of Lords, 1910 E
Quinquennial Parliaments proposed, 1910 E
Parliament Bill, progress accelerated by 'Kangaroo' clause, 1911 D
Lansdowne's reconstruction bill, 1911 E
Parliament Bill, passes Commons, 1911 E
Lords amendments to, 1911 G
passes Lords, 1911 H
in Ireland, 1790 K
Parma, Duchy, Italy, 1767 C; confiscated by Clement XIII, 1768 N; forms, with Tuscany, Kingdom of Etruria, 1801 B; Napoleon annexes, 1802 K; ceded by Austria, 1859 G
Parma, Duke of. *See* Cambacérès, Jean
Parnassus School of Poets, 1853 U
Parnell, Charles Stewart, Ir. Nationalist politician (1846–91), 1887 A; as president of Irish Land League, 1878 K; followers of, acquitted, 1880 L; imprisoned for inciting Irish, 1881 K; is party to Kilmainham 'treaty', 1882 E; calls on Irish in Britain to vote Conservative, 1885 L; dispute with *The Times*, 1888 G; resigns leadership of Irish Nationalists, 1890 M; divorce action, 1890 O
Paroles d'un Croyant (H. F. R. Lamennais), 1834 R
Paroles d'un Révolté (P. A. Kropotkin), 1884 O
Parri, Ferrucio, It. politician, resigns, 1945 L
Parry, Sir Charles Hubert Hastings, B. musician (1848–1918), 1848 Z, 1892 T, 1918 Z
Parsons, Sir Charles, B. marine engineer (1854–1931), 1884 P, 1910 P
Partage de Midi (P. Claudel), 1906 W
Parthenopaen Republic, in Piedmont, 1798 A
Pasadena, Calif., US, atomic research at, 1950 P
Pasmore, Victor, B. artist (b. 1908), 1949 S, 1950 S
Pasquier Chronicle, The (G. Duhamel), 1933 U
Passage to India (E. M. Forster), 1924 U
Passaglia, Carlo, It. churchman (1812–87), 1859 O
Passchendaele, W. Flanders, Belgium: battle (or 3rd Battle of Ypres), 1917 G; British and Canadians capture Ridge, 1917 L
Passfield, Lord and Lady. *See* Webb
Passfield White Paper on Arabs and Palestine, 1930 K
Past and Present (T. Carlyle), 1843 U
Pasternak, Boris, R. author (1890–1960), 1890 Z, 1932 U, 1958 U, 1962 U
Pasteur, Louis, F. biologist and chemist (1822–95), 1857 P, 1861 P, 1864 P, 1880 P, 1881 P, 1885 P
Pastor, L., G. ecclesiastical historian, 1928 R

Pastrengo, Italy, Austrians defeated at, 1848 D
Patent law:
in Britain, 1906 O
in Germany, 1877 O
in US, 1790 P
Pater, Walter Horatio, B. author (1839–94), 1839 Z, 1873 Q, 1885 U, 1894 Z
Pathé, Charles, F. photographer (1873–1957), 1912 W
Pathfinder, The (J. F. Cooper), 1840 U
Path to Rome, The (H. Belloc), 1902 U
Patmore, Coventry Kersey Dighton, B. poet (1823–1896), 1854 U
Paton, Herbert James, B. philosopher (b. 1887), 1955 R
Patriot for Me, A (J. Osborne), 1965 W
Patriotic Phantasies (J. Moser), 1775 O
Patriots. *See under* Political Parties
Patti, Adelina, It. operatic singer (1843–1919), 1843 Z, 1859 W, 1919 Z
Pattison, Mark, B. churchman and author (1813–84), 1860 R, 1867 O
Patton, George Smith, Am. soldier, 1885 Z, 1945 Z
Paul I, King of Greece, 1964 C
visits Britain, 1963 F, G
Paul I, Tsar of Russia (1796–1801), 1796 L, 1797 N, 1801 C
Paul VI, Pope, It. (Cardinal Giovanni Montini, b. 1897), 1897 Z; elected Pope, 1963 F; makes pilgrimage to Holy Land, 1964 R; addresses UN, 1965 R; closes Vatican Council, 1965 R
Paul, Prince, of Yugoslavia, is deposed, 1941 C
Paul, Jean. *See* Richter, Jean Paul
Paul-Boncour, Joseph, F. politician (1873–1943), 1932 M
Paul et Virginie (St. Pierre), 1789 U
Pauline (R. Browning), 1833 U
Paul Report on Development of Clergy, 1964 R
Pavlov, Alexis Petrovich, R. pathologist, 1907 P
Pavlova, Anna, R. prima ballerina, 1931 Z
Paxton, Joseph, B. architect (1803–65), 1803 Z, 1850 S, 1865 Z
Pay-as-you-earn Income Tax in Britain, 1944 B
Payer, Julius, Aus. explorer, 1873 P
Payne-Aldrich tariff in US, 1909 H
Paysans, Les (H. de Balzac), 1845 U
Peace Ballot, 1935 F
Peace Conference, Versailles: opens, 1919 A; German delegates at, 1919 D; US delegates leave, 1919 M. *See also under* Conferences, Versailles
Peace Corps of Young Americans, for overseas service, 1961 C
Peace Foundation, Carnegie, 1911 O
Peace Pledge Union, 1934 O
Peace That Was Left (E. Cammaerts), 1945 O
Peace Treaties. *See* Treaties of Peace
Peacock, Thomas Love, B. novelist (1785–1866), 1785 Z, 1816 U, 1818 U, 1831 U, 1866 Z
Pearl Harbor, Philippines, Japanese bomb, 1941 M
Pearson, Sir Arthur, B. newspaper owner (1866–1921), 1900 V
Pearson, Charles Henry, B. Colonial administrator and historian (1830–94), 1893 O
Pearson, Lester Bowles, Canad. Liberal leader (b. 1897), 1897 Z, 1963 D, 1965 L
Peary, Robert Edwin, Am. explorer (1856–1920), 1856 Z, 1909 P, 1920 Z
Peasants:
in Prussia, proprietorship, 1811 J
in Russia, services of, 1797 N
Peasants Parties. *See under* Political Parties
Peat:
fertilisation through, 1914 P
for firing gas turbine, 1951 P
Peau de Chagrin (H. de Balzac), 1831 U
Pecci, Joachim, It. Cardinal, Pope Leo XIII (1810–1903), 1891 R; elected Pope, 1878 B
Péché de M. Antoine, Le (G. Sand), 1847 U
Pêcheur d'ombres, Le (J. Sarment), 1921 W
Pêcheurs d'Island (P. Loti), 1886 U
Pederson, Knut, Norw. author under pseudonym of 'Knut Hanson' (1859–1936), 1893 U, 1917 U
Pedro, Dom, Emperor of Brazil, 1822 K, 1823 L, 1825 M, 1832 G, 1833 G; abdicates, 1831 D; becomes Peter IV of Portugal, 1826 C. *See* Peter IV
Pedro II, King of Brazil, 1889 L
Peel, Sir Robert, B. Conservative statesman (1788–1850), 1788 Z, 1819 G, 1829 O, 1850 Z; as Home Secretary, reforms, 1822 A, 1823 G, 1827 F; founds London Metropolitan Police, 1829 F; becomes premier, 1834 L; issues Tamworth Manifesto, 1834 M; resigns, 1835 D; fails to form ministry, 1839 E; forms ministry, 1841 H; free trade budgets, 1842 D, 1845 D; resigns on issue of free trade, but returns to office, 1845 M; repeals Corn Laws, 1846 E; resigns, 1846 F
Peel, Samuel, B. inventor, 1791 P
Peerages, in Britain: life, introduced, 1958 G; Stansgate peerage, election court ruling, 1961 O; Lords Committee recommends an heir be able to disclaim, 1962 M; renunciations, 1963 G, K
Peer Gynt (H. Ibsen), 1867 W
Pegasus (C. Day-Lewis), 1957 U
Pegram, G. B., Am. scientist, 1941 P
Pegu, Lower Burma, Britain annexes, 1852 M
Péguy, Charles, F. author and critic (1873–1914), 1900 U, 1910 U, 1913 U
Péguy (R. Rolland), 1943 U
Peiping, China, 1949 K
Peixoto, Floriano, Brazil. dictator, 1891 L
Peking, China: Chinese rebels attack, 1850 K; treaty, ratifying earlier treaties between Britain, China and France, 1860 K; siege of legations in, 1900 F; relieved, 1900 H; treaty, ends Boxer rising, 1901 J; treaty, between Britain and China, 1925 A; British legation in, 1926 N; Japanese siege, 1937 G; All-China People's Congress at, 1954 J
Peking Man ('Sinanthropus'), 1920 Q
Pélerin d'Angkor, Le (P. Loti), 1912 U
Pelew, Island, in Pacific, Germany purchases, 1899 B
Pella, Giuseppe, It. Christian Democrat (b. 1902), 1953 H, 1954 A
Pelléas et Melisande (M. Maeterlinck), 1892 W
Pellico, Silvio, It. author (1788–1854), 1832 O, 1855 W
Pelloux, Luigi, It. general and Moderate Left politician (1839–1924), 1898 F, 1900 F
Pemba, Island, off Zanzibar, Britain acquires, 1890 G, H
P.E.N. (Poets, Essayists, Novelists), London, 1922 U
Pen:
ball-point, 1938 P
steel, 1780 P
Penal Reform, tracts advocating, 1764 O. *See also under* Capital Punishment, Abolition of
Penal settlements, in Botany Bay, 1788 A
Penang, Malaya: ceded to Britain, 1786 H; British evacuate, 1941 M
Pendennis (W. M. Thackeray), 1850 U
Pendleton, George Hart, Am. lawyer (1825–89): reforms US Civil Service, 1883 A; reforms completed, 1901 O

Penguin Books, 1936 U
Penicillin: discovered, 1928 P; developed, 1940 P; used for treating chronic diseases, 1943 P
Peninsular War. *See under* Wars
Penjdeh, Afghanistan, Russians occupy, 1885 C
Penney, Sir William George, B. atomic scientist (b. 1909), 1909 Z
Pennsylvania, state, US: as British Colony, 1776 L
University, sends archaeological expedition, 1888 Q
builds electronic brain, 1946 P
research laboratory, 1960 S
Penny for the Poor, A (B. Brecht), 1937 W
Penobscot, Maine, US, 1779 H
Pensacola, Florida, US, Spanish capture, 1781 G
Pensions, old-age:
in Britain, advocated, 1879 O
Rothschild committee on, 1898 O
introduced, 1909 A
women, to receive at 60, 1940 B
increased, 1964 L
in France, 1850 D
in Germany, 1889 E
in New Zealand, 1898 O
People's Parties. *See under* Political Parties
Pepita Jimenez (J. Valera), 1848 U
Pepsin, 1930 P
Perak, Malay, independence of, 1826 F
Perception, Physics and Psychical Research (C. D. Broad), 1914 R
Perceval, Spencer, B. Tory premier (1762–1812), 1809 K; assassinated, 1812 E
Percy, Lord Eustace, B. Conservative politician, minister without portfolio (1887–1958), resigns, 1936 C
Percy, Thomas, B. antiquarian and poet, Bishop of Dromore (1729–1811), 1765 U, 1811 Z
Père Duchesne (ed. J. Hébert), 1793 R
Père Goriot, Le (H. de Balzac), 1834 U
Perekop, on Sea of Azov, Russia, Germans take, 1941 K
Perennial Philosophy, The (A. Huxley), 1946 R
Pérez Galdós, Benito, Sp. poet (1845–1920), 1845 Z, 1876 U, 1879 U, 1920 Z
Perham, Dame Margery, B. historian of Africa (b. 1895), 1944 O, 1956 Q
Perkin, Sir William Henry, B. chemist (1838–1907), 1856 P
Perlon, invented, 1938 P
Perón, Eva, Argent., 1922 Z, 1952 Z
Perón, Juan d', President of Argentina (b. 1895), 1946 B, K; re-elected President, 1951 L; resigns, 1955 J; detained in Brazil, 1964 M
Péronne, France, British capture, 1917 C, 1918 J
Perry, Matthew Calbraith, Am. naval officer (1794–1858), 1854 C
Perryville, Kentucky, US, battle, 1862 K
Perse, St. John, F. poet (Alexis St. Léger), 1924 U, 1947 U
Pershing, John Joseph, Am. soldier (1860–1948), 1917 L
Persia (late Iran): Babist sect in, 1843 R; Russian advance into, 1849 N; Russian interests in, 1903 K, 1910 L; Anglo-Russian convention on, 1907 H; concessions to Russia, 1911 L; changes name to Iran, 1935 O. *See also under* Iran
Persia, Shah of: visits Britain, 1959 E; hands over properties for educational and charitable purposes, 1961 K
Persian Gulf, bases on, 1903 E
Perspex, invented, 1930 P
Persuasion (J. Austen), 1818 U
Perthes, Friedrich Christoph, G. philosopher (1772–1843), 1810 V
Pertz, Georg Heinrich, G. historian (1795–1876), 1826 Q
Peru: revolt in Upper, 1809 G; independence, 1821 G; nitrates' trade, 1830 P; federation with Bolivia, 1836 K, dissolved, 1839 A; independence recognised, 1865 A; declares war on Spain, 1866 A; Declaration of, 1938 M
Perutz, Max Ferdinand, B. biologist, 1962 P
Peshawar, India: Sikhs capture, 1834 E; Treaty, between Britain and Afghanistan, 1855 C
Peshaw of Poona, 1802 K; surrenders independence to Britain, 1802 M
Pestalozzi, C., Swi. educationalist, 1922 O
Pestalozzi, Johann Heinrich, Swi. educationalist (1746–1827), 1781 O, 1801 O
Pest control, chemical, dangers of, 1963 P
Pesth, Hungary, is united with Buda, 1873 L
Pétain, Henri Philippe, F. marshal (1856–1951), 1925 H; as chief of staff, 1917 D; as commander-in-chief, 1917 E; replaces Reynaud as head of administration, 1940 F; sentenced for collaboration, 1945 H
Peter IV of Portugal (Dom Pedro, 1826–8), 1826 C, D, 1834 J; abdicates, 1828 C. *See also under* Pedro, Dom
Peter V of Portugal (1853–61), 1853 L, 1861 L
Peter I of Serbia (1903–21), 1903 F, 1918 L
Peter Abelard (H. Waddell), 1933 U
Peter and the Wolf (Prokofiev), 1936 T
'Peterloo Massacre', Manchester, 1819 H
Peter Pan (J. M. Barrie), 1904 S, W
Peter Plymley's Letters (S. Smith), 1808 R
'Peter Porcupine' pamphlets (W. Cobbett), 1792 O
Peter Schlemihl (A. Chamisso), 1813 U
Petrie, Sir William Flinders, B. archaeologist (1853–1942), 1853 Z, 1942 Z
Petrified Forest, The (R. Sherwood), 1935 W
Petrograd, Russia: name changed from St. Petersburg, 1914 J; Bolsheviks seize power, 1917 G; Kornilov's march on, 1917 J; October Revolution in, 1917 L; Bolsheviks attack British Embassy, 1918 H. *See also* St. Petersburg
Petrol: is produced from coal, 1931 P, 1935 P; is rationed in Britain, 1956 M; Mexican laws concerning, 1927 M
Petroleum, consumption, comparative statistics of, 1937 Y
Petroleum production:
in America, Central and South, 1946 Y
in Dutch East Indies, 1937 Y
in Iran, 1937 Y
in Mexico, 1920 Y, 1937 Y
in Panama, 1946 Y
in Rumania, 1860 Y, 1937 Y, 1946 Y
in Russia, 1903 Y, 1920 Y, 1932 Y, 1937 Y, 1940 Y, 1946 Y, 1951 Y
in Saudi Arabia, 1946 Y
in US, 1860 Y, 1863 Y, 1873 Y, 1883 Y, 1893 Y, 1901 Y, 1903 Y, 1906 Y, 1911 Y, 1916 Y, 1920 Y, 1921 Y, 1926 Y, 1937 Y, 1946 Y, 1951 Y, 1961 Y
in Venezuela, 1937 Y
Petrol engine, Daimler's, 1882 P
developed, 1892 P
for aeroplane, 1903 P
for tractor, 1898 P
Petropolis, Treaty between Bolivia and Brazil, 1903 L
Petrov, Vladimir, R. diplomat, 1954 D
Petsumo, Russia, Finland cedes to Russia, 1947 B

Petty, William, Earl of Shelburne, Marquess of Lansdowne, B. Tory statesman (1737–1805), 1763 J, 1766 G, 1768 K, 1782 C, 1783 B; becomes premier, 1782 G
Petty-Fitzmaurice, Henry Charles Keith, Marquess of Lansdowne, B. conservative (1845–1927), 1903 E, 1904 K; becomes foreign secretary, 1900 K; introduces reconstruction of House of Lords bill, 1911 E
Pflimlin, Pierre, F. leader of M.R.P. (b. 1907), 1958 E
Pfrimer, Dr. Aus. Fascist, 1931 J
Pfitzner, Hans Erich, G. musician (1869–1942), 1917 T, 1931 T
Phaedon (M. Mendelssohn), 1767 R
Pharmaceutical Society, British, founded, 1841 P
Phenomena of Man, The (P. de Chardin), 1959 R
Phenacetin, 1887 P
Phenomenology (E. Husserl), 1913 R
Phenomenology of Spirit (G. W. F. Hegel), 1807 R
Philadelphia, Pennsylvania, US:
  museum, 1773 Q
  Continental Congresses at, 1774 J, M, 1775 E, G
  British occupy, 1777 J
  British evacuate, 1778 F
  mint, 1792 O
  American Association for the Advancement of Science founded at, 1848 P
  International Working Men's Association at, 1876 O
Philby, H. A. R., B. journalist, defects to Russia, 1963 G
Philharmonic Society, London, 1813 T
Philip, Prince, Duke of Edinburgh (b. 1921), marries Princess Elizabeth, 1947 L; Oxford Conference, 1954 E
Philippe Egalité, Duke of Orléans (d. 1793), 1793 L
Philip II (W. H. Prescott), 1855 Q
Philippines, Islands:
  recovered by Spain, 1763 B
  Spain cedes to US, 1898 M
  demand independence, 1899 B
  Taft Commission for, 1900 B
  appropriations for public works in, 1900 J
  Spooner's amendment for civil government in, 1901 C
  Civil government in, 1901 G
  independence demanded, 1919 D
    US votes for, 1933 A
    Tydings-McDuffie Act for, 1934 C
  as Commonwealth, 1935 L
  US landings in, 1944 K
  republic inaugurated, 1946 G
Phillips, H., B. scientist, discovers 'M. and B.', 1938 P
Phillpotts, Henry, B. churchman (1778–1869), 1852 R
Philology, comparative, 1772 Q. *See also under* Dictionaries
Philosophe sans le savoir (M. J. Sedaine), 1765 W
Philosophes Francais du XIX siècle, Les (H. Taine), 1856 R
Philosophie (K. Jaspers), 1932 R
Philosophie de la misère (P. J. Proudhon), 1846 O
Philosophical Foundations of Quantum Mechanics (Reichenbach), 1942 R
Philosophical Introduction to Christian Theology (A. Schopenhauer), 1919 R
Philosophical Society, London, founded, 1869 R
Philosophical Systems (K. C. F. Krause), 1804 R
Philosophy and Civilization (Dewey), 1931 R
Philosophy of A Biologist (J. Haldane), 1935 R
Philosophy of 'As If', The (Vaihingen), 1911 R
Philosophy of Conflict (H. Ellis), 1919 R
Philosophy of History (G. Ferrari), 1847 R
Philosophy of Inductive Sciences (W. Whewell), 1840 P
Philosophy of Knowledge (H. Hardtmann), 1921 R
Philosophy of Law (F. J. Stahl), 1830 P
Philosophy of Nature (N. Hardtmann), 1950 R
Philosophy of Nature (Schelling), 1797 R
Philosophy of Physical Science, The (A. Eddington), 1939 R
Philosophy of Religion (J. Caird), 1880 R
Philosophy of Right (G. W. Hegel), 1821 R
Philosophy of the Active and Moral Powers of Man (D. Stewart), 1818 Q
Philosophy of the Middle Ages, The (E. Gilson), 1922 R
Philosophy of the Unconscious, The (E. Hardtmann), 1869 R
Philosophy, studies in, 1764 R, 1783 R, 1798 R, 1799 R, 1854 R, 1856 R, 1866 R, 1900 R, 1929 R
  political, survey of, 1939 O
  scholastic, 1922 R
Phoenix, Arizona, US, 1938 S
Phonograph, The, invented, 1876 P. *See also under* Gramophone
Phosphates, factory for, 1843 P
Phosphorus, sesquisulphide of, discovered, 1898 P
Phosphorus matches, sale of, prohibited in Britain, 1908 O
Photochemical equivalence, law of, 1912 P
Photo-electric cell, 1904 P
Photographie judiciare (L. A. Bertillon), 1890 O
Photography:
  the first photograph, 1802 P
  box camera, 1888 P
  coated photographic paper, 1885 P
  colour, 1873 P
    Spier-Dufuy process for, 1931 P
  daguerreotype, perfected, 1839 P
  flash bulb for, 1930 P
  Fox Talbot's negative, 1839 P
  half-tone block used for daily newspaper, 1880 V
  produced on metal plate, 1827 P
  roll film, 1889 P
  very rapid, by image-dissector camera, 1956 P
  See also Camera; Cinematography
Photographs:
  of comets, 1881 P
  of Mars, by satellite, 1964 P, 1965 P
  of the moon, 1840 P, 1951 P, 1964 P
  of the night sky, composite, 1954 P
Photosynthesis of plants, 1857 P, 1898 P
Phtalacyamine dyes, 1934 P
Physical Geography of the Sea (M. Maury), 1855 P
Physical Laboratory, National, Teddington, 1914 P
Physical Significance of the Quantum Theory (Lindemann), 1926 P
Physics and Politics (W. Bagehot), 1869 O
Physics, Atomic, 1931 P, 1932 P, 1941 P, 1942 P, 1943 P, 1944 P, 1945 P
Physiological Optics (H. Helmholtz), 1856 P
Physiological Psychology (W. Wundt), 1874 R
Physiology, Institute of, Breslau, 1839 O
Piacenza, N. Italy, Duchy, Napoleon annexes, 1802 K
Pianoforte, the first, 1780 P
Piave, River, N.E. Italy, Italians retreat to, 1917 L
Piazzi, Giuseppe, It. astronomer (1746–1826), 1801 P
Picasso, Pablo Ruiz y, Sp. artist (b. 1881), 1881 Z, 1905 S, 1907 S, 1912 S, 1915 S, 1919 S, 1921 S, 1923 S, 1925 S, 1929 S, 1932 S, 1938 S, 1939 S, 1954 S, 1960 S
  ballet sets by, 1917 S

'bone' period, 1928 S
mural, 1937 P
as sculptor, 1950 S
founds Vallauris pottery, 1946 S
Piccard, Auguste, Belg. marine biologist (b. 1884), 1948 P, 1960 P
Piccinni, Nicola, It. musician (1728–1800), 1771 T
controversy with Gluck, 1779 T
Pic du Midi, France, atomic research at, 1950 P
Pichegru, Charles, F. general (1761–1804), 1794 E, M, 1795 J
captures Dutch fleet, 1795 A
Pickford, Mary (née Smith), Am. film actress (b. 1893), 1893 Z, 1909 W, 1920 W
Pickwick Papers (C. Dickens), 1836 U
Picture of Dorian Grey, The (O. Wilde), 1891 U
Pictures, cleaning of, 1936 S, 1947 S
Pictures of Travel (H. Heine), 1826 U
Picture-telegraphy, 1930 P
Pieck, Wilhelm, president of East German Republic (1875–1960), 1949 K
Piedmont, Italy: Joubert occupies, 1798 L; Parthenopaer Republic established in, 1799 A; Napoleon annexes, 1802 J; Austrian intervention in, 1821 D
Pierce, Franklin, Am. Democrat (1804–69), 14th president of US (1853–7), 1852 L, 1853 C
Pierre et Jean (G. de Maupassant), 1888 U
Pigtails, abolished in China, 1911 M
Pilgrims, The, founded, 1902 O
Pilgrim Trust, The, founded, 1930 O; benefaction through, 1943 Q
Pilkington Report on Broadcasting in Britain, 1962 W
Pillars of Society, The (H. Ibsen), 1877 W
Pillnitz, near Dresden, E. Germany, Declaration of, 1791 H
Pilotless aircraft, 1950 P, 1953 P
missiles, 1946 P. *See also* Rockets
Pilsudski, Jozef Clemens, Pol. statesman (1867–1935), 1920 D, 1922 M, 1926 E, 1930 H
Piltdown Man, 1912 P; proved to be a hoax, 1953 P
Pinay, Antoine, F. politician, 1952 B, M, 1955 L
Pinckney, Charles Cotesworth, Am. lawyer and Federalist (1746–1825), 1800 L
Pinckney, Thomas, Am. diplomat (1750–1828), 1795 K
Pinel, Philippe, F. alienist (1745–1826), 1791 P
Pinero, Sir Arthur Wing, B. dramatist (1855–1934), 1855 Z, 1888 W, 1893 W, 1899 W, 1906 W, 1934 Z
Pinsk, in Pripet Marshes, Russia, Russians take, 1920 G
Pinter, Harold, B. dramatist (b. 1930), 1958 W, 1960 W, 1961 W
Pioneers, The (J. F. Cooper), 1823 U
Piper, John, B. artist (b. 1903), 1903 Z, 1934 S, 1940 S, 1942 S, 1962 S
Piracy:
Algerian, 1775 G
arising from Spanish Civil War, 1937 J
Piraeus, Greece: Royal Navy blockades, 1850 A; French and British occupation, 1854 E; blockade of, 1897 B, C
Pirandello, Luigi, It. dramatist (1867–1936), 1867 Z, 1904 W, 1913 W, 1917 W, 1918 W, 1923 W, 1936 Z
Pirot, Serbia, 1885 L
Pirquet, Charles, F. physician, 1907 P
Pissarro, Camille, F. artist (1831–1903), 1831 Z, 1872 S, 1874 S, 1897 S, 1903 Z
Pissarro, Lucien, F. artist (1863–1944), 1863 Z, 1944 Z
Pithecanthropus, skull of, 1937 P
Pitman, Sir Isaac, B. inventor of shorthand (1813–97), 1837 P
Pitt, William, Earl of Chatham, B. statesman (1708–1778), 1766 G, 1769 B, 1778 Z, 1780 S; illness, 1767 C; proposes conciliation with America, 1775 B, 1778 D
Pitt, William (The Younger), B. Tory statesman (1759–1806), 1790 L, 1792 M
as Chancellor of Exchequer, 1782 G
declines to form ministry, 1783 B
proposes Parliamentary Reform, 1783 E
becomes premier, 1783 M
opposition to dwindles, 1784 C
gains support through elections, 1784 C
reduces excise duties, 1784 F
India bill, 1784 H
motion for Parliamentary Reform defeated, 1785 D
establishes Sinking Fund, 1786 C
excise scheme, 1786 F
policy over Belgian independence, 1790 A
seeks to maintain neutrality, 1791 H
subsidises Allies, 1793 C
begins peace negotiations, 1796 C
increases newspaper tax, 1798 V
advocates Catholic Emancipation, 1800 J
resigns from premiership, 1801 C
forms second ministry, 1804 E
death, 1806 A
Pitt-Rivers, Augustus Henry Lane Fox, B. anthropologist and archaeologist (1827–1900), 1874 Q
Pittsburgh, East, Pennsylvania, US, broadcasting station at, 1920 W
Pittsburgh, West, Pennsylvania, US, 1881 O; early cinema in, 1905 W; university, 1955 P
Pituitary body, study of, 1902 P
hormone, is synthesised, 1960 P
Pius VI, Pope (Cardinal Giovanni Angelo Braschi), It. (1717–99), elected Pope 1775, 1782 C; admits forged decretals, 1789 R; refutes Ems articles, 1789 R; cedes Romagna and Bologna to France, 1797 B; leaves Romes, 1798 B
Pius VII, Pope (Cardinal Luigi Barnaba Chiaramonti), It. (1740–1823), 1808 B, 1811 F, 1815 S; elected Pope, 1800 C; concordat with Napoleon, 1801 G; crowns Napoleon, 1804 M; Napoleon imprisons, 1809 G; restores Inquisition and Index, 1814 R; restored to Papal Estates, 1815 F
Pius IX, Pope (Cardinal Giovanni Maria Mastai-Ferretti), It. (1792–1878), 1792 Z, 1847 G, 1854 R, 1867 R, 1881 R; elected Pope, 1846 F; disassociates himself from Italian Nationalism, 1848 D; flees to Gaeta, 1848 L; is restored by French, 1849 G, 1850 D; revokes Constitution, 1850 D; concordat with Francis Joseph of Austria, 1855 R; issues Syllabus of Errors, 1864 R; temporal power is attacked, 1859 O; calls Vatican Council, 1870 R; annuls German May Laws, 1874 E
Pius X, Pope (Cardinal Giuseppe Sarto), It. (1835–1914), elected Pope, 1903 G; condemns Modernism, 1907 R; encyclical *Editio Saepe*, 1910 E, F
Pius XI, Pope (Cardinal Achille Ratti), It. (1857–1939), 1922 B, 1928 R; leaves Vatican, 1929 G
Pius, XII, Pope (Cardinal Eugene Pacelli), It. (1876–1958), 1876 Z; elected 1939, 1946 R; pronounces on bodily assumption, 1950 R; death, 1958 K
Pizzetti, Ildebrando, It. musician (b. 1880), 1958 T
Place, Francis, B. Radical reformer and pioneer of birth control (1771–1854), 1822 P, 1824 O
Plague, The (A. Camus), 1947 U
Plain Tales from the Hills (R. Kipling), 1888 U
Planck, Gottlieb Jakob, G. Protestant divine (1751–1833), 1781 R

Planck, Max Karl Ernst Ludwig, G. physicist (1858–1947), 1858 Z, 1900 P, 1901 P, 1947 Z
Plane, machine, 1776 P
Planetary system, laws of, 1788 P
Planets, The:
  Hidalgo, 1920 P
  Jupiter, emission of radio waves from, 1955 P
  Mars, satellites of, discovered, 1877 P
    photo-electric observations, 1955 P
    data on, from space research, 1963 P
    photographs of, 1964 P, 1965 P
  Mercury, rotation of, 1889 P
  Neptune, 1846 P
  Pallas, 1801 P
  Pluto, 1930 P
  Uranus, discovered, 1781 P
  Venus, observations of transit of, 1768 P, 1882 P
    is explored by satellites, 1962 P, 1963 P
Plans:
  Acheson, to increase powers of UN to resist aggression, 1950 K
  Colombo, to aid S.E. Asia, 1950 A, 1951 B
  Eden, for Council of Europe, 1952 H
  Germany's 4-year, 1946 K
  Marshall, for European recovery, 1947 A, F, 1948 C, 1949 M, 1950 M, 1951 M
  Rapacki, for denuclearised military zone, 1957 K, 1958 B
  Russia's first 5-year, 1928 P
    subsequent 5-year, 1932 A, 1946 C, 1952 K
  Schuman, for iron and steel community, 1950 E
  Turkey's 5-year, 1928 P
Planté, R. L. Gaston, F. electrical engineer (1834–1889), 1859 P
Plants, cellular theory of, 1838 P
  classification of, 1789 P
  fertility of, 1793 P
  growth of, chemicals needed for, 1843 P
Plata, La, United Provinces of (Argentina), independence, 1816 G. *See also* Argentina
Plate River, S. America, vice-royalty, 1776 N
  naval battle, 1939 M
Platinum, found in Urals, 1820 P
  palladium discovered in, 1804 P
Platt, Orville Hitchcock, Am. Republican (1827–1905), 1901 C
Playboy of the Western World (J. M. Synge), 1907 W
Playfair, Sir Nigel Ross, B. producer (1874–1934), 1919 W
Playing Fields Association, National, 1933 X
Pleasures of Hope, The (T. Campbell), 1799 U
Pleasures of Memory, The (S. Rogers), 1792 U
Plebiscites:
  in British Togoland, for integration with Gold Coast, 1956 E
  in Cameroons, 1961 B
  in Carinthia, 1920 H
  in France, for Louis Napoleon's constitution, 1851 M
    for revival of French Empire, 1852 L
  in Germany, against battleships, 1928 K
    vesting Hitler with power as *Führer*, 1934 H
  in Greece, for King Constantine's return, 1920 M
    for George II, 1935 L
    favouring monarchy, 1946 J
  in Naples, favouring union with Sardinia, 1860 K
  in Norway, for separation from Sweden, 1905 F
  in Odenburg, for union with Hungary, 1921 M
  in Philippines, demanded, 1926 G
  in Prussia, 1920 G
  in Saar, for incorporation in Germany, 1935 A
  in Salzburg, for union with Germany, 1921 E
  in North Schleswig, annulled, 1878 K
  in Schleswig, 1920 B
  in Upper Silesia, for incorporation in Germany, 1921 C
  in Sudan, 1951 L
  in Taca and Arica, S. America, 1883 K
  in Tuscany, etc., favouring union with Sardinia, 1860 C
  in Tyrol, favouring Germany, 1921 D
  in Umbria, for union with Sardinia, 1860 L
  in United Arab Republic, for Nasser to be head of state, 1958 B
  in Venezia, 1866 K
  See also Referenda
Plecharoff, G. V., R. politician, 1903 H
Plehve, Viacheslav, R. minister of interior, 1902 D, 1904 G
Pleiade, La, formed to finance performance of French music, 1943 T
Pleven, René, F. statesman (b. 1901), 1950 G, 1951 B, H, 1952 A
Plevna, Bulgaria, 1877 M
Plimsoll, Samuel, B. politician and social reformer (1824–98), 1875 O
Plombières, France, Napoleon III meets Cavour at, 1858 G
Plough and the Stars, The (O'Casey), 1926 W
Plowden Committee on Public Expenditure, 1964 B
Plowden Committee on British Aircraft Industry, 1965 M
Plückner, Julius, G. mathematician (1801–68), 1865 P
Plumed Serpent, The (D. H. Lawrence), 1926 U
Plunckett, Sir Horace Curzon, Ir. statesman (1854–1932), 1917 G
Pluralistic Universe, A (W. James), 1909 R
Pluto, planet, 1930 P
Plutonium:
  manufacture, 1944 P
  separation from pitchblende concentrates, 1950 P
  Sellafield Pile, 1951 P
Plymouth Brethren. *See under* Religious Denominations
Pneumatic tyre, 1888 P
Po, River, Italy, Allies reach, 1945 D
Pobédonostev, Constantine Petrovich, R. jurist (1827–1907), 1881 R
Podgorny, Nikolai V., R. president of USSR (b. 1907), 1965 M
Poe, Edgar Allan, Am. author (1809–49), 1809 Z, 1827 U, 1838 U, 1850 U, 1849 Z
Poelaert, Joseph, Belg. architect (1816–79), 1866 S
Poèmes Antiques (de Lisle), 1853 U
Poèmes saturniens (P. Verlaine), 1866 U
Poems and Ballads (A. C. Swinburne), 1866 U
Poems by Two Brothers (A. and C. Tennyson), 1827 U
Poems Chiefly in the Scottish Dialect (R. Burns), 1786 U
Poems Chiefly Lyrical (Lord Tennyson), 1830 U
Poems of the English Roadside (G. Meredith), 1862 U
Poetical Studies (W. Blake), 1783 U
Poincaré, Raymond, F. statesman (1860–1934), 1860 Z; forms ministry, 1912 A; visits Russia, 1912 H, 1914 G; elected President of France, 1913 A; visits Britain, 1913 F; as premier, 1922 A; of National Union ministry, 1926 G; resigns, 1919 G
Point Counter Point (A. Huxley), 1928 U
Poison Gas: first used, 1915 D; banned by Washington Conference, 1922 B; Geneva Conference on, 1925 E

Poischwitz, Germany, armistice between Prussia and France at, 1813 F
Poisson, Siméon Denis, F. mathematician (1781–1840), 1811 P, 1835 P
Poland:
constitution in, 1764 D
Russian intrigues, in, 1766 N, 1767 D, L
Civil War in, 1768 H
Partition of, proposed, 1768 M, 1769 B, H, 1771 H
first, 1772 H
Russians invade, 1792 E
Second Partition, 1793 A, E
Third Partition, 1795 A, K, 1797 A
becomes independent, 1812 F
Russian designs on, 1814 L
East Poland is ceded to Russia, 1815 F, L
West Poland is ceded to Prussia, 1815 F
independence proclaimed, 1831 A
Russian, is divided into provinces, 1863 C
Russian provinces autonomy to, 1914 H
Kingdom is proclaimed by Central Powers, 1916 L
Russia guarantees independence, 1917 C
Republic proclaimed, 1918 L
Germany invades, 1939 J
Russia invades, 1939 J
Polish government in London, 1940 H
Russia severs relations with, 1943 D
Lublin Committee for Polish Liberation, in Moscow, 1944 G
frontier with East Germany agreed, 1950 L
Polanyi, Michael, B. formerly Czech., chemist and philosopher (b. 1891), 1947 R
Polar Discovery:
Scott Polar Research Institute, Cambridge, 1926 P
North Pole, Nansen's expedition, 1893 P
Peary reaches, 1909 P
flights over, 1926 P
observation station near, 1937 P
magnetic N. Pole, position of, 1946 P
Nautilus passes under ice cap, 1958 P
Arctic submarine plateau discovered, 1959 P
South Pole, Amundsen at, 1911 P
Scott at, 1912 P
Shackleton's expedition, 1914 P
flights over, 1929 P
survey of East Antarctica, 1939 P
Commonwealth Transantarctic expedition, 1957 P, 1958 P
Polaris submarines, facilities for, at Holy Loch, 1960 L. *See also under* Missiles
Polariser, synthetic light, 1932 P
Police forces:
international, proposed, 1932 B
Metropolitan, Peel founds, 1829 O
Hendon Police College, 1934 O
Policy for the Arts, A, 1965 O
Polignac, Prince Jules de, F. Ultra Royalist (1780–1847), 1829 H
Poliomyelitis, Salk vaccine against, 1955 P
Political Arithmetic (A. Young), 1774 O
Political Arithmetic; Mathematics for the Million (L. Hogben), 1936 O
Political Economy, treatises on, 1844 O, 1848 O, 1885 O
Political Ethics (F. Lieber), 1838 O
Political Parties:
in Algeria, Front de la libération nationale, 1960 F, 1962 C
Nationalist movement for the Triumph of Democratic Liberties, dissolved, 1953 L
in Australia, Communist, outlawed, 1950 D
Country, forms coalition with United Australia, 1934 L
election success, 1937 K
Labour, in power, 1908 E, 1929 K
losses to United Australia, 1931 N
election defeat, 1937 K
Liberal-Country, in power, 1961 M
Nationalist, 1922 M, 1931 M
United Australia founded, 1931 N
in power, 1934 J
election success, 1937 K
in Austria, Agrarian, joins coalition with Christian Socialist, 1932 E
Christian Socialist, reversal for, 1911 F
in power, 1926 K, 1930 M, 1931 F
supports Schober, 1929 J
forfeits support of working classes, 1934 B
Fatherland Front, becomes sole party, 1934 B
under Schuschnigg's leadership, 1936 E, K
National Socialist (Nazi), 1931 J
is dissolved, 1933 F
attempted *coup*, 1934 G
Schuschnigg's *coup* against, 1935 K
amnesty for, 1937 A
release of members, forced, 1938 B
People's, 1945 L, M
in power, 1953 B, D
forms coalition with Socialists, 1959 E
Socialist, split in, 1897 N
election losses, 1949 K
election success, 1953 B
forms coalition with People's, 1959 E
in Barbados, Labour, election losses, 1961 M
in Bavaria, Communist, *coup* by, 1919 D
expelled from Munich, 1919 E
in Belgium, Catholic, in power, 1929 E
Christian Democrat, in power, 1950 H
Christian Socialist, in power, 1946 B, 1952 A
forms coalition with Liberals, 1949 H
loses majority, 1954 D
forms coalition with Socialists, 1961 C
Clerical, unites with Liberals, 1928 G
in power, 1880 F, 1912 F
Democrat (or Vonckists), lose power, 1790 C
Labour, 1885 N
Liberals, 1846 F
unite with Clericals, 1828 G
defeated, 1880 F
in power, 1937 K
forms coalition with Christian Socialists, 1942 H
Rexist (Fascist), 1936 E, K
Socialist, demonstrate against Leopold III, 1950 G
Vonckist. *See* Democrat
uniformed parties, prohibited, 1934 G
in Brazil, Liberal, 1945 K
political parties banned, 1937 M
in Britain, British Union of Fascists, founded, 1932 N
mass meetings and demonstrations, 1934 F, J, 1962 G
Commonwealth, 1943 C
by-election success, 1944 A
Communist, application for affiliation with Labour Party rejected, 1936 K
supports Pacifist People's Convention, 1941 C
Conservative (and Unionist), based on Tamworth manifesto, 1834 M
in power, 1841 H
split by repeal of Corn Laws, 1846 E
Disraeli elected leader, 1849 B
in power, 1852 B, 1858 B, 1866 F, 1874 B

Political Parties—*contd.*
in Britain, Conservative (and Unionist)—*contd.*
defeated, 1880 D
leadership, under Northcote, 1881 D
in power, 1885 F
electoral success, 1886 G
defeated, 1892 G
in power, 1895 F
divided on issue of Imperial Preference, 1903 E
out of office, 1905 M
defeated in election, 1906 A
Bonar Law succeeds to leadership, 1911 L
A. Chamberlain elected leader, 1921 C
in power, 1922 L
defeated in election, 1923 M
in power, 1924 L
defeated in election, 1929 E
in power, 1945 E
defeated in election, 1945 G
successes in local elections, 1947 L
in power, 1951 K
losses in by-elections, 1958 B, C, 1962 C, F, G
Macmillan becomes leader, 1957 A
wins general election, 1959 K
back-bench revolt, 1961 D
Home elected leader, 1963 J
account of struggle for leadership, 1964 O
defeated in election, 1964 K
by-election success, 1965 A
local election successes, 1965 E
Heath elected leader, 1965 G
'Fourth, The', a Conservative splinter-group, 1880 E
Independent Labour (I.L.P.), founded 1892 G, 1893 A
refuses affiliation with Communists, 1921 C
forms United Front, 1937 A
'King's Friends', 1770 A
Labour, founded, 1900 B
wins by-election, 1903 G
elects MacDonald Chairman, 1911 B
against conscription, 1916 A
newspaper suppressed, 1916 V
secedes form Coalition, 1918 L, 1919 A
appoints Council of Action, 1920 H
refuses affiliation with Communists, 1921 F, 1922 F, 1936 K
in power, 1924 A
defeated, 1924 L
leaves Commons on Kirkwood's suspension, 1925 C
in power, 1929 E
expels MacDonald and those serving with him, 1931 H
rump of, led by Henderson, 1931 H
wins majority on L.C.C., 1934 C
declares that war is not inevitable, 1937 J
sends delegations to Finland, 1940 B
divided by Mosley's release, 1943 L
in power, 1945 G
majority reduced, 1950 B
split by Bevanite revolt, 1951 D
defeated in election, 1951 K
Gaitskell elected leader, 1955 M
by-election successes, 1957 B, 1958 B
hostility to Rent Act, 1957 F
retains 'clause 4' on nationalisation, 1960 C
censures government over 'Blue Streak' missile, 1960 D
unilateralist conflict in, 1960 K
back-benches refuse to follow Gaitskell on defence, 1960 M
Gaitskell's victory over unilateralists, 1961 F
by-election successes, 1962 L
Wilson elected leader on Gaitskell's death, 1963 B
wins first G.L.C. election, 1964 D
wins general election, 1964 K
Liberal, in power, 1830 L. *See also* Whig
out of office, 1841 H
in power, 1846 F
out of office, 1852 B
in power, 1852 M, 1855 B
defeated, 1858 B
in power, 1859 F
defeated, 1866 F
in power, 1868 M
back bench revolt, 1873 C
electoral defeat, 1874 B
Hartington elected leader, 1875 B
wins election, 1880 D
out of office, 1885 F
returns to power, 1886 B
back bench revolt over Home Rule, 1886 F
falls from power, 1886 G
adopts Newcastle Programme, 1891 K
wins election, 1892 G
defeated, being split by Home Rule, 1894 C
Rosebery resigns leadership, 1896 K
Campbell Bannerman as leader, 1899 A
closes ranks over Irish Home Rule, 1905 L
in power, 1905 M
electoral landslide, 1906 A
majority is reduced, 1910 A
Lloyd George becomes leader, 1925 A
joins opposition to National government, 1933 L
downfall, 1945 G
Grimond elected leader, 1956 J
wins Torrington by-election, 1958 C
by-election successes, 1962 C
holds balance between major parties, 1964 K
Liberal Unionist, under J. Chamberlain, 1891 M
Rosebery becomes premier, 1894 C
unites with Conservatives, 1914 E
Municipal Reform, 1934 C
National Liberal, 1932 J
New Party, Mosley's, 1931 B
Social Democratic Federation, 1886 B
Socialist, mass meeting, 1887 L. *See* Labour Party
Socialist League, forms United Front, 1937 A
Syndicalist, 1912 C
Tory, in power, 1807 C
out of office, 1830 L
attempts to form government, 1834 L, M
Peel refounds, on Tamworth Manifesto, 1834 M
Peelites coalesce with Whigs, 1852 M. *See* Conservative Party
Unionist. *See under* Conservative
United Front, 1937 A
Whig, led by Bedford, 1763 J
led by Rockingham, 1776 K
split on issue of Reform, 1794 G
fall from power, 1807 C
in power, 1830 L
defeated, 1841 H
coalesce with Peelites, 1852 M
in British Guiana, People's National Congress, 1964 M
People's Progressive, 1953 D, 1957 H
in Bulgaria, are banned, 1934 F
Communist, excluded from amnesty, 1926 A

Fatherland Front (Communist), 1945 L
is unopposed, 1953 M
in Canada, Conservative, in power, 1878 K, 1911 K, 1925 K, 1930 H
Liberal, adopts reciprocity, 1890 K
in power, 1896 G
defeated, 1911 J
elect Mackenzie King as leader, 1919 H
in power, 1921 M
defeated, 1925 K
in power, 1925 K
defeated, 1930 H
in power, 1945 F, 1949 F, 1953 H
defeated, 1957 F
Progressive Conservative, in power, 1957 F
loses overall majority, 1962 F
Unionist, 1917 M
in Ceylon, Freedom Party, in power, 1960 G
People's United Front, 1956 C
United National, in power, 1952 E
in Chile, Socialist, in power, 1932 F
in China, Communist, 1936 J
is purged, 1955 C
Kuo Min Tang (Nationalist), 1924 A
British sympathy with, 1926 N
split in, 1927 D
See also under Civil Wars, in China
in Cuba, Liberal, 1908 L
in Czechoslovakia, Agrarian, 1935 L
Communist, in power, 1946 E
stages *coup*, 1948 B
is purged, 1951 C
National Front, 1945 D
Sudete (Nazi), 1935 E
in Danzig, Nazi, 1933 E
in Denmark, Liberal, in power, 1901 G, 1926 M
Social Democrats, electoral success, 1945 K
in power, 1947 L, 1953 D, J
Socialist, in power, 1924 D, 1929 D
in Egypt, dissolution of all, 1953 A
Liberal Constitution, in power, 1937 M
Nationalist, 1882 A, B, 1907 M, 1909 C, 1910 B, 1919 C, 1921 E
demands constitutional reform, 1935 L
Wafd, boycotts elections, 1945 A
in power, 1936 E, 1950 A
leadership of, 1927 H
in Eire, Fianna Fail, founded, 1926 C, 1938 F
gains majority, 1933 A
Irish Republican Army (IRA), 1933 G
National Guard (Blue Shirts), 1933 G
forms United Ireland Party, 1933 J
Nationalist, 1923 H
Republican, 1922 C
tactics of, denounced, 1927 G
agrees to take seats in Dail, 1927 H
in power, 1932 B
Sinn Fein, adopts declaration of independence, 1919 A
elects de Valera president of Dail executive, 1919 D
de Valera resigns from leadership, 1926 C
United Ireland, founded, 1933 J
See also under Ireland
in Finland, Fascist, 1930 K, 1932 B
in France, Communist League, 1836 O, 1848 E
Communist Party, 1925 O, 1946 F
electoral successes, 1946 L, 1956 A
stages demonstrations, 1952 E
Dantonist, 1794 G
Democratic Republications, 1800 M
Fascist, suppressed, 1936 F
plot by, 1937 L
Girondist, 1791 K, 1792 C, 1794 M
fall of, 1792 L, 1793 F
Hébertistes, 1794 C
Jacobins, in power, 1792 L
Liberal, electoral success, 1830 G
Monarchist, 1877 E
'Mountain, The' (Moderates), 1794 G
Mouvement Républican Populaire (MRP), success in elections to Constituent Assembly, 1946 F
National Union of Left, electoral success, 1928 D
Popular Front, 1935 L
dominates elections, 1936 E
forms ministry, 1936 F
ends, 1938 K
Progressive, 1896 D
Radical, 1895 L
in power, 1948 J
Radical Socialist, 1938 A
Rassemblement du peuple Françaisè (RPF), 1947 D
success in local elections, 1947 K
success in elections, 1948 L
Republican, 1832 F, 1876 C, 1879 A
electoral success, 1889 D
Republican *bloc*, 1900 D
Socialist, 1916 V
votes to adhere to Moscow International, 1920 M
leave Chautemps's Cabinet, 1938 A
in power, 1946 M, 1956 B
adverse vote of, on social security policy, 1952 A
Socialist and Republican Union, 1935 L
Third Party, 1863 L, 1869 G
Ultra Conservative, in power, 1821 M
defeated, 1827 L
Ultra Royalist, 1817 J
Union de la Gauche Socialiste, formed, 1957 M
Union et Fraternité Française (Poujadist), electoral successes, 1956 A
Union for a New Republic (UNR), electoral successes, 1958 L
Youthful Patriot, 1925 O
in Germany, Catholic (Centre), 1870 M, 1874 A, 1921 E
revolts, 1906 M
Christian Democratic, 1949 J, 1957 J
loses overall majority, 1961 J
Communist, 1916 A, 1930 J
('Spartacist'), 1919 A
electoral successes, 1924 E
lose seats to Socialists, 1924 M
Conservative, 1876 O, 1878 G
Democrats (South German), 1832 E
Free Democrat, 1949 J
Independent Labour Party, 1917 D
Labour Front, 1934 K
Liberal (Prussia), 1856 O
Liberal (North German), split in, 1866 L
Liberal, split by protection, 1879 G
attempts to control army appropriations, 1886 M
National Liberal (North German), 1866 L
National Socialist (Nazi), formed, 1919 A
electoral successes, 1924 E, 1932 D
through denouncing Versailles Treaty, 1930 J
excluded from Von Papen's ministry, 1932 F
Storm Troopers of, 1932 F, 1933 C

Political Parties—*contd.*
in Germany, National Soc.—*contd.*
refuses to enter coalition with Socialists, 1932 G
in power, 1933 A
engineers Reichstag Fire, 1933 B
becomes sole party, 1933 G, L
is purged, 1934 F
dominates elections, 1936 C
leading Nazis sentenced by Nuremberg Tribunal, 1946 J
neo-Nazi groups banned, 1960 O
time limit for trials of members, extended, 1965 C
Revisionist Social Democrats, 1899 N
Social Democrat, adopts Marxist Programme, 1890 K
holds rally, 1908 J
demands peace negotiations, 1915 F
Socialist, 1867 H
is driven underground, 1878 K
electoral losses, 1906 M
becomes strongest party, 1912 A
attacks Kaiser, 1912 E
in power, 1919 A
wins elections, 1924 M, 1930 J
loses power, 1930 C
will not enter coalition with Nazis, 1932 G
Socialist Workingmen's, 1874 E
in East Germany, Communist, merges with Social Democrats, 1946 D
National Front (Communist), 1950 K
Social Democrat, merges with Communists, 1946 D
in Ghana (or Gold Coast), Convention People's, 1954 F, 1956 G
Nkrumah takes over, 1961 E
becomes one party state, 1964 B
in Greece, Communist, dissolved by government, 1947 M
E.A.M. (Republican), 1944 M
dissolved by government, 1947 M
Greek Rally, 1952 L
Military League, 1910 A
National Radical Union, 1961 K
in Holland, Calvinist, 1889 M
Catholic, 1889 M
Catholic People's Party, 1946 E
in power, 1959 C
Clerical, in power, 1901 G
Labour, is supported by Protestant Parties, 1960 M
Liberal, fall of, 1889 M, 1896 F
Patriot, 1786 N
in Hungary, Communist, electoral successes, 1947 H
is purged, 1949 F
Deak, 1875 C
Liberal, in power, 1847 C
Nationalist, anti-Semite, 1932 K
National Socialist (Fascist), 1937 K
Smallholders, 1945 L, 1946 B
in power, 1947 E
Workers, 1956 K
in India, National (or All-India) Congress, 1886 N
boycotts Prince of Wales's visit, 1921 G
President of, arrested, 1921 M
recognises Round Table Conference, 1931 C
declared illegal, 1932 A
electoral success, 1937 B
demands independence, 1937 D
refuses to serve on War Council, 1940 H
rejects terms for self-government, 1942 D, 1945 J
electoral success, 1945 J, 1952 C
Independence of India League, 1928 H
Moslem League, 1906 N
electoral success, 1945 J
boycotts constituent assembly, 1946 M
Socialist, protests at food and housing policies, 1951 F
in Indonesia, National Front, 1960 A
in Ireland, Nationalist, under O'Connell, make compact with Whigs, 1835 C
in House of Commons, 1880 D, 1881 A, 1886 G, 1887 L, 1892 G, 1895 G, 1900 K
McCarthy succeeds Parnell as leader, 1890 M
Sein Fein, 1905 L
United Irishmen, 1790 K
Ulster Unionists, 1912 A, 1913 J
agree to exclude Ulster from Government of Ireland Act, 1916 F
leadership of, 1921 B
See also under Eire
in Italy, Christian Democrats, in power, 1948 D
electoral success, 1953 F, 1958 E
dissensions among, 1959 A
form coalition with Independents, 1947 E
Fascist, founded, 1919 B
electoral success, 1921 E
forms government, 1922 K
founds *Ballilla* Youth organisation, 1926 D
grand Council of, becomes embedded in Constitution, 1928 L
Liberal, withdraws support from Government, 1950 A
supports Segni's ministry, 1959 B
Monarchist, supports Segni's ministry, 1959 B
Radical, 1896 C
Socialist, uses strike action, 1901 N
is discredited by strikes, 1904 K
in Jamaica, Labour, in power, 1962 D
in Japan, parties are founded, 1881 N
Democratic-Liberal, in power, 1948 K, 1960 G
National Union, 1937 F
in Kenya, Kenya-African Union, members are arrested, 1952 K
party is proscribed, 1953 F
forms government, 1961 D
becomes a single-party state, 1964 L
in Latvia, Conservative, in power, 1928 A
in Liberia, True Whig, 1959 E
in Lithuania, National Union (Fascist), 1932 M
in Malawi, Nyasaland African Congress, 1953 H, 1959 B
in Malta, Labour, ministry resigns, 1958 D
in Morocco, Nationalist, 1934 L
in New Zealand, Conservative, defeated, 1890 D
Labour, in power, 1890 D, 1935 L, 1946 L
Liberal, 1890 D
defeated, 1919 M
National, in power, 1960 L
Reform, 1925 E
forms coalition with United Party, 1931 J
Social Credit, electoral success, 1954 L
United (Liberal), in power, 1928 L
in Norway, Labour, in power, 1927 K, 1933 K, 1935 C, 1955 A, 1957 K
electoral success, 1953 K
Liberal, in power, 1933 A
in Palestine, Higher Arab Committee, declared illegal, 1937 K
in Poland, Communist Workers', 1948 J
National Unity Camp, 1937 C, 1945 F
Peasants', in power, 1926 E
United Workers', is purged of Titoists, 1949 L

Workers' and Peasants' Camp, 1937 C
in Portugal, National Union (neo Fascist), 1930 G
becomes the sole party, 1934 M, 1945 L, 1953 L
Republican, 1882 O
Opposition parties are formed, 1945 K
in Rhodesia, African Nationalist Congress, is suppressed, 1959 D
People's Caretaker Council, is banned, 1964 H
Rhodesian Front, electoral success, 1962 M, 1965 E
Rhodesia New Africa, formed, 1961 L
United Federal Party, 1953 M, 1958 B
electoral success, 1959 D, 1962 D
electoral defeat, 1962 M
United Nationalist Independent, 1964 A
United Rhodesia, formed, 1958 D
Zimbabwe African People's Union declared unlawful, 1962 J, 1964 H
in Rumania, Iron Guard (Fascist), 1933 M, 1938 L, 1939 J
National Peasants', 1926 K, 1928 E
in power, 1928 M
is dissolved, 1947 G
in Russia, Cadets, 1906 E, G
Communist (formerly Bolshevist), 1903 L
seizes power, 1917 G
Trotsky expelled from, 1927 M
purges of, 1933 N, 1937 A
O.G.P.U. purge of, 1934 M
holds Congress, 1952 K
condemns Mao Tse-tung's dogmatism, 1960 M
Menshevist, 1903 L
Nihilist, 1880 E
Populist, 1876 N
Social Democratic, splits, 1903 L
Social Revolutionary, 1901 N
in Serbia, Nationalist, 1904 M
Nationalist Radical, 1883 L
in South Africa, African National Congress is banned, 1960 D
Dominion, withdraws from coalition, 1945 K
Labour, withdraws from coalition, 1945 K
Nationalist, electoral successes, 1915 K
in power, 1924 F
is reformed under Malan, 1934 F
secure clear majority, 1953 D
sweeping electoral victory, 1958 D
Nationalist-Afrikander *bloc*, in power, 1948 E
Pan African Congress, demonstrates against pass laws, 1960 C
is banned, 1960 D
Progressive, 1959 L
South Africa Party, 1910 D, 1915 K
Unionist, 1910 E, J
United S. African, Nationalist, 1934 F, 1938 E
in power, 1945 K
in Spain, Liberal, in power, 1909 K
Monarchist, in power, 1914 C
Popular Front, electoral success, 1936 B
Socialist, 1934 D
in Sudan, Umma, in power, 1958 B
in Sweden, Conservative, 1928 K
Liberal, in power, 1926 F, 1930 F
Social Democrat, in power, 1945 G
in Switzerland, Liberal, 1847 K
in Syria, Arab Liberation, in power, 1953 K
Nationalist, 1928 F
Syrian Popular, 1961 M
In Trinidad, People's National Movement, in power, 1961 M
in Tunisia, Neo-Destour, 1959 L
in Turkey, Communist, propaganda by, suppressed, 1929 F
Liberal, 1877 B
Mohammedan Union, revolt against, 1902 D
Nationalist, 1909 B, 1919 H
breaks with Sultan's government, 1920 H
People's, has monopoly, 1927 J
Young Turk, 1896 N, 1908 G
dominates first Ottoman Parliament, 1908 M
Opposition parties are founded, 1930 E
in US, parties are formed, 1792 N
Communist, is outside scope of deportation laws, 1920 E
leaders of, are convicted of conspiracy, 1949 K
McCarthy's charges of infiltration by, denied, 1950 G
Control of Communists bill, 1950 J
supreme court rules must register as a foreign-dominated body, 1961 F
Constitutional Union, 1860 L
Democrat, landslides, 1932 L, 1964 L
in power, 1948 L
electoral successes, 1958 L
in control of Senate and House of Representatives, 1962 L
Federal, 1792 N
fall of, 1800 L
Labor, repudiates Communism, 1923
Liberal Democrat, 1872 E
Mugwumps (Reformist Republican), 1884 L
National Progressive Republican League, 1911 A
National Prohibition, 1869 J
National Republican, is absorbed by Whigs, 1833 N
Northern Democrat, 1860 L
Populist, 1892 B, G, L, 1896 L
Progressive, 1924 L
Progressive Republican, 1912 F, H
Republican, is established, 1854 G
electoral successes, 1914 L, 1946 L, 1950 L
electoral landslide, 1952 L
Southern Democrat, 1860 L
Tammany Hall (Democrat Organisation in New York), 1888 L
Whig, 1833 N
Working Men's, 1827 N
See also under Conventions
in Venezuela, Democratic Action, 1947 M
in Yugoslavia, Communist, is purged of Cominform supporters, 1948 G
Croat, is dissolved, 1929 A
is reformed, 1932 L
National Front, 1945 L
See also under Administrations; Elections; Parliaments
Political Survey of Great Britain, A (J. Campbell), 1774 O
Politicians and the Press (Lord Beaverbrook), 1925 O
Politics of Influence (G. Wooton), 1963 O
Politiques et Moralistes francaises du XIX siècle (E. Faguet), 1892 O
Polk, James Knox, Am. Democrat (1795–1849), 11th president of US (1845–9), 1844 L, 1845 C; sends troops to Mexico, 1846 D
Pollard, Albert Frederick, B. historian (1869–1948), 1918 O, 1921 Q
Pollard, Graham, B. bibliographer (b. 1903), 1948 Q
Pollock, Sir Frederick, B. jurist (1845–1937), 1845 Z, 1894 Q, 1937 Z
Pollock, F., Am. sociologist, 1956 O

Pollock, Jackson, Am. artist (b. 1920), 1948 S, 1952 S
Polonium, discovered, 1898 P
Polyethylene, 1935 P
Polygamy:
in Africa, condoned, 1863 R
in Morocco, restricted, 1958 O
in US, authorised among Mormons, 1843 R
Polythene, invented, 1939 P
Pombal, Sebastiano Jose de Carvalho E. Mello, Marquess, Port. statesman (1699–1782), 1774 N, 1777 B
Pomerania, Swedish, Sweden recovers, 1810 A; France re-occupies, 1812 A
Pomerania, Western (or Hither), France annexes, 1807 J; Prussia obtains, 1814 A, 1815 F
Pompadour, Jeanne Antoinette Poisson Le Normant D'Étioles, Marquis de, F. mistress of Louis XV (1721–65), 1765 S
Pomp and Circumstance, March, No. 4 (Elgar), 1907 T
Pompidou, Georges Jean Raymond, F. politician (b. 1911), 1962 D, K
Poncelet, Jean Victor, F. mathematician (1788–1867), 1822 P
Pondicherry, India, French settlement, 1778 N
Pondoland, S. Africa, Britain annexes, 1894 J
Pontecorvo affair, 1952 O
Ponti, Gio, It. architect (b. 1891), 1958 S
Pontiac, Indian chief of Ottawa tribe (1720–69), 1763 E
Pontoise, France, artists at, 1872 S
Poona, Central India, 1802 K, M, 1817 L; comes under British control, 1818 F; plague in, 1897 N
Poor Bitos (J. Anouilh), 1956 W
Poor Folk (F. Dostoievsky), 1846 U
Poor Lisa (N. Karamzin), 1793 U
Poor Relief:
in Britain, Speenhamland system, 1795 O
out-door relief prohibited by Poor Law Amendment Act, 1834 O
in Ireland, 1838 G
in Italy, by religious bodies, 1841 R
in US, bill to combat poverty, 1964 C
Pope, Albert Augustus, Am. engineer (1843–1909), 1878 P
'Pop Stars', 1943 W, 1963 W
Popular Front. *See under* Political Parties
Popular Government (H. Maine), 1885 O
Population:
observations on, 1769 O
treatises on, 1798 P, 1936 O
first census, 1801 Y
world, report on, 1955 O
movements in Britain, 1964 C
Population Statistics, of Countries:
Austria, 1821 Y, 1851 Y, 1891 Y, 1901 Y
Brazil, 1941 Y, 1946 Y, 1961 Y
Britain, 1801 Y, 1811 Y, 1821 Y, 1831 Y, 1841 Y, 1851 Y, 1861 Y, 1871 Y, 1881 Y, 1891 Y, 1901 Y, 1911 Y, 1921 Y, 1926 Y, 1931 Y, 1936 Y, 1941 Y, 1946 Y, 1951 Y, 1961 Y
China, 1911 Y, 1931 Y, 1936 Y, 1941 Y, 1946 Y, 1951 Y, 1961 Y
Egypt, 1946 Y
France, 1801 Y, 1811 Y, 1821 Y, 1831 Y, 1841 Y, 1851 Y, 1861 Y, 1871 Y, 1881 Y, 1891 Y, 1901 Y, 1906 Y, 1911 Y, 1921 Y, 1926 Y, 1931 Y, 1936 Y, 1941 Y, 1946 Y, 1951 Y, 1961 Y
Germany, 1801 Y, 1811 Y, 1821 Y, 1831 Y, 1841 Y, 1851 Y, 1861 Y, 1871 Y, 1881 Y, 1891 Y, 1901 Y, 1906 Y, 1911 Y, 1921 Y, 1926 Y, 1931 Y, 1936 Y, 1941 Y, 1946 Y, 1951 Y, 1961 Y
India, 1901 Y, 1911 Y, 1931 Y, 1946 Y, 1951 Y, 1961 Y
Ireland, 1801 Y, 1821 Y, 1831 Y, 1841 Y, 1851 Y, 1861 Y, 1871 Y, 1881 Y, 1891 Y, 1901 Y, 1906 Y, 1911 Y, 1921 Y, 1926 Y, 1931 Y
Italy, 1801 Y, 1821 Y, 1851 Y, 1861 Y, 1871 Y, 1881 Y, 1891 Y, 1901 Y, 1911 Y, 1921 Y, 1926 Y, 1946 Y, 1951 Y, 1961 Y
Japan, 1871 Y, 1891 Y, 1901 Y, 1911 Y, 1921 Y, 1926 Y, 1931 Y, 1936 Y, 1941 Y, 1946 Y, 1951 Y
Korea, 1946 Y
Mexico, 1946 Y
Pakistan, 1961 Y
Poland, 1946 Y
Russia, 1861 Y, 1901 Y, 1906 Y, 1911 Y, 1921 Y, 1926 Y, 1931 Y, 1936 Y, 1941 Y, 1946 Y, 1951 Y, 1961 Y
South Africa, 1951 Y
Spain, 1946 Y
US, 1801 Y, 1831 Y, 1851 Y, 1861 Y, 1871 Y, 1881 Y, 1891 Y, 1901 Y, 1906 Y, 1911 Y, 1921 Y, 1926 Y, 1931 Y, 1936 Y, 1941 Y, 1946 Y, 1951 Y, 1961 Y
Populations of Chief Cities. *See Index under entries for places concerned*
Populists. *See under* Political Parties
Porson, Richard B., Greek scholar (1759–1808), 1788 R, 1793 Q, 1802 Q
Portal, Sir Gerald Herbert, B. diplomat (1858–94), 1893 C
Port Arthur, China: Japanese victory at, 1894 L; agreements over, 1895 D, E; Russians occupy, 1897 M; Russians lease, 1898 C; railway to, 1901 P; Japanese siege, 1904 B; Russian fleet defeated off, 1904 H; surrenders to Japanese, 1905 A; ceded to Japan, 1905 J
Porte Étroite, La (Gide), 1909 U
Port Egmont, Falkland Isles, 1766 N
Porter, Cole, Am. composer of popular songs, 1893 Z, 1964 Z
Porter, Katherine A., Am. novelist, 1962 U
Portes Gil, Emilio, Mex. leader, 1928 G
Port Hamilton, Korea, British occupy, 1885 D
Portland, Duke of. *See* Bentinck, W. H. C.
Porto Novo, Coromandel Coast, Madras, India, 1781 G
Portrait in a Mirror (C. Morgan), 1929 U
Portrait of a Lady (H. James), 1881 U
Portrait of Mallarmé (P. Boulez), 1960 T
Portrait of the Artist as a Young Dog (D. Thomas), 1940 U
Portrait of the Artist as a Young Man (J. Joyce), 1916 U
Portraits in Miniature (Lytton Strachey), 1931 U
Port Said, Egypt, British troops land, 1956 L
Portsmouth, Hampshire, England, Treaty of, between Russia and Japan, 1905 J
Portugal: attacks Monte Video, 1775 C; re-organises S. American colonies, 1776 N; joins League of Armed Neutrality, 1782 G; suppression of monasteries in, 1834 R; separation of Church and State, 1911 D
Posen, Poland: Prussia acquires, 1793 E; Treaty of, Saxony with France, 1806 M; Archbishop of, 1837 R; expropriation of Polish landowners, 1886 D; Polish occupation, 1918 M
Positivism, 1830 R, 1855 R, 1865 R
'Positrons' (positive electrons), 1933 P
Postal Services:
in Britain, penny post, 1840 O
parcel post, 1880 O
airmail to Australia, 1934 P

in Germany, letter post, 1800 O
in US, parcel post, 1912 O
postal savings banks, 1910 O
Posters, notable, 1891 S
Post-Impressionism, 1913 S
Potassium: electrical preparation of, 1806 P; deposits, exploited, 1860 P
Potemkin, Grigory Aleksandrovich, R. statesman (1739–91), favourite of Catherine II, 1776 N, 1788 M
Potemkin, Russian battleship, mutiny aboard, 1905 K
Potomak Charter, 1954 F
Potsdam, E. Germany, Conference of Allied leaders at, 1945 G
Potter, Thomas Bayley, B. politician (1817–98), 1866 O
Potthast, August, G. historian (1824–98), 1862 Q
Potting Shed, The (G. Greene), 1958 W
Pottle, Frederick Albert, Am. scholar (b. 1897), 1950 Q
Poujade, M., F. politician, founder of Union et Fraternité Française, 1956 A
Poulenc, François, F. musician (b. 1899), 1899 Z, 1920 T, 1923 T, 1957 T, 1959 T
Poulson, Frederick, Am. electrician, 1902 P
Pound, Ezra, Am. poet (b. 1885), 1885 Z, 1915 U, 1950 W
Pound, Roscoe, Am. lawyer (1870–1965), 1870 Z, 1965 Z
Pousseur, Henri, F. musician, 1959 T
Poverty and Progress (B. S. Rowntree), 1941 O
Poverty and Public Health (M'Gonighe and Kirby), 1936 O
Poverty: a Study of Town Life (B. S. Rowntree), 1901 O
Poverty of Philosophy, The (P. J. Proudhon), 1847 O
Powder, bleaching, 1870 P
Powdered milk, 1855 P
Powell, Anthony Dymoke, B. author (b. 1905), 1950 U
Powell, Enoch, B. Conservative politician (b. 1912), resigns from Cabinet, 1958 A; becomes Minister of Health, 1961 B; refuses to serve under Home, 1963 K
Powell, Felix, B. musician, 1915 W
Power, electric, produced from atomic energy, 1951 P
plants. *See under* electricity
Power and the Glory, The (G. Greene), 1940 U
Power and the State (Lord Radcliffe), 1951 O
Power House, The (A. Comfort), 1944 U
Power of Darkness, The (L. Tolstoy), 1885 U
Powers, Francis, Am. pilot, 1960 E
Powicke, Sir Frederick Maurice, B. medieval historian (b. 1879), 1947 Q
Powys, John Cowper, B. author (b. 1872), 1930 U
Powys, Theodore Francis, B. author (d. 1953), 1928 U
Poznam, Poland, riots in, 1956 F
Practical View of the Religious System (W. Wilberforce), 1797 R
Pragmatism (W. Jones), 1907 R
Prague, Czechoslovakia: Congress, 1813 G; Czech revolt in, 1848 F; music school in, 1848 T; Peace of, 1866 H; University, 1882 O; Pan Slav Conference in, 1908 G; Russians take, 1945 E; purge of collaborators in, 1945 E; Conference of Soviet Satellites in, 1950 K
Prasad, Rajendra, Indian president, 1952 E
Pratt, Charles, Earl of Camden, B. judge (1714–94), 1763 E
Pratt, David, S. African, wounds Verwoerd, 1960 D
Pratt, Orsen, Am. Mormon leader (1811–81), 1833 R
Praxiteles, *The Hermes* of, found at Olympia, 1875 S
Prayer Books:
Church of England, revised, 1928 R
Church of Scotland, revised, 1912 R
vernacular liturgies approved by Vatican Council, 1963 R
Precious Bane (M. Webb), 1924 U
Precipice, The (I. Gontscharov), 1870 U
Precipitation, electrical, 1884 P
Preface to Morals (W. Lippmann), 1929 R
Preliminary Sketch of Bi-quarternions (W. K. Clifford), 1873 P
Prelude The (W. Wordsworth), 1805 U
Preminger, Otto, Am. film director (b. 1906), 1957 W, 1959 W, 1960 W, 1963 W
Premium Savings Bonds, 1956 D, 1957 F
Prempeh, King of Ashanti, 1896 A
Pre-Raphaelite Brotherhood, 1848 S
Pre-Raphaelitism (W. Holman Hunt), 1905 S
Presbyterians. *See under* Religious Denominations
Prescott, William Hickling, Am. historian (1796–1859), 1796 Z, 1837 Q, 1846 Q, 1855 Q, 1859 Z
Presentations of débutantes at Court, ends in Britain, 1958 G
Present Condition of Civilisation in Greece (A. Coraës), 1803 O
Present State of Music in Germany, the Netherlands and the United Provinces (C. Burney), 1773 T
Preservation of Rural England, Council for, 1926 O
Preserving, process of, 1765 P
Press, The:
in Britain, cheap, 1816 V, 1846 V
press campaigns, to reform sweated industries, 1906 O
on neglect of science, 1916 P
Royal Commission on, 1961 B
Press Council, 1963 F
journalists imprisoned for refusing to reveal sources of information, 1963 V
in France, cheap, 1836 V
in US, cheap, 1835 V
See also under Journals; Newspapers
Press, The, Censorship of:
advocated by Pope Gregory XVI, 1837 R
in Austria, abolished, 1781 K
clerical control in force, 1855 H
in Belgium, abolished, 1831 B
in Britain, seditious publications suppressed, 1817 C
Daily Worker suspended, 1941 V
relaxations through Obscene Publications Act, 1959 O
in Ceylon, imposed, 1960 H
in Denmark, abolished, 1770 M, 1784 E
in Egypt, imposed, 1909 C, 1928 G
in France, relaxed, 1796 C, 1819 E, 1830 H, 1868 E, 1881 O
re-imposed, 1800 V, 1820 C, 1822 C, 1824 J, 1827 D, F, 1828 D, 1830 G, 1835 J, 1850 J, 1852 B
in Germany, imposed, 1819 J, 1851 E, 1933 B, 1943 V
Gentz's plan for freedom, 1797 O
in Ireland, abolished, 1919 H
in Portugal, imposed, 1945 K
in Transvaal, restrictions imposed, 1896 L
in Turkey, abolished, 1876 M
Pressburg, Germany, Peace between Austria and France, 1805 M

Presses, Private:
  Ashendene, 1894 S
  Kelmscott, 1896 S
Pressure-cooking, for canned foods, 1874 P
Pretender, Young. *See* Charles Edward Louis Philip Casimir
Pretenders, The (H. Ibsen), 1864 W
Pretoria, Transvaal, S. Africa: becomes capital of Transvaal, 1860 D; Treaty, between Britain and Boers, 1881 D; Convention, over Swaziland annexation, 1893 L; is fortified, 1896 A; Buller takes, 1900 F; Britain annexes Transvaal at, 1900 K; Rivonia trial in, 1964 F.
Pretorius, Marthinius, President of Transvaal (1819–1901), 1856 M
Prevention of Cruelty to Children, Society for, 1864 O
Prevost, Constant, F. geologist (1787–1856), 1824 P
Price, Richard, B. Nonconformist minister and author (1723–91), 1769 O, 1771 O, 1776 O
Prices, Wages and Incomes:
  in Britain, minimum wage, 1912 B, C
    comprehensive wages agreement, 1937 O
    electrical workers wage increase, 1961 L
    National Incomes Commission, 1962 O
    resale price maintenance on electrical equipment, etc., abolition recommended, 1963 M
    resale prices act, in force, 1964 G
    Prices and Incomes Board, National, 1965 C
      printers' wage claim referred to, 1965 E
  in France, prices are fixed, 1793 J
  in Germany, courts for adjusting wages, 1890 B
  in US, minimum wage, 1938 O
Pride and Prejudice (J. Austen), 1813 U
Priestley, John Boynton, B. author (b. 1894), 1894 Z; *The Good Companions*, 1929 W; plays, 1932 W, 1934 W, 1937 W, 1947 W
Priestley, Joseph, B. Nonconformist minister and chemist (1733–1804), 1767 P, 1768 O, 1772 P, 1777 R, 1782 R, 1804 Z; discovers oxygen, 1774 P; rioters attack, 1791 G
Prim, Juan, Marquis de los Castillejas, Sp. general and statesman (1814–70), 1868 J
Primrose, Archibald Philip, Lord Rosebery, B. Liberal statesman and historian (1847–1929), 1847 Z, 1889 O, 1905 L, 1929 Z; as foreign secretary, 1886 B, 1892 H; becomes premier, 1894 C; seeks *entente* with Germany, 1894 F; resigns, 1895 F; resigns Liberal leadership, 1896 K
Primrose League, founded, 1882 O
Prince Edward Island, joins Dominion of Canada, 1873 G
Princess Casamassima, The (H. James), 1886 U
Princeton, New Jersey, US, battle, 1777 A
Principe des moeurs chez toutes les nations ou catechisme universel (St. Lambert), 1798 R
Principe Générateur des Constitutions Politiques (de Maistre), 1809 O
Principes fondamenteux de l'equilibre et du mouvement (L. Carnot), 1803 P
Principia Ethica (G. E. Moore), 1903 R
Principia Mathematica (Russell and Whitehead), 1910 R
Principles of Economics (A. Marshall), 1890 O
Principles of Ethics (H. Spencer), 1879 R
Principles of Geology (C. Lyell), 1830 P
Principles of Logic, The (F. H. Bradley), 1883 R
Principles of Moral and Political Philosophy (W. Paley), 1785 R
Principles of Political Economy (T. R. Malthus), 1820 O
Principles of Political Economy (J. S. Mill), 1848 O
Principles of Political Economy and Taxation (D. Ricardo), 1817 O
Principles of Psychology (W. James), 1890 R
Principles of Psychology (H. Spencer), 1855 R
Principles of Social Service (H. Carey), 1858 D
Pringsheim, Nathaniel, G. botanist (1823–1904), 1856 P
Printing:
  printing press, improved, 1813 P
    hydraulic, 1795 P
    Staples' iron, 1800 P
    steam, 1814 V
  linotype, 1886 V
  monotype type-setting machine, 1897 P
  type-casting machine, 1838 P
  See also Presses, Private
Printing of calicoes, machine for, 1783 P
Printing industry, in Britain, lock-out in, 1956 B
Prisoner of Zenda, The (A. Hope), 1894 U
Prison Reform, advocated, 1777 O, 1813 O
  in Britain, 1823 G, 1958 O, 1963 H
  in Turkey, 1856 B
Prisons: panopticon designed, 1791 O
  statistics of criminals in, 1960 Y
  escapes, notable, 1964 H
  See also Convicts; Transportation
Privateering, abolished, 1856 D
Private Lives (N. Coward), 1930 W
Private Papers of Henry Rycroft (G. R. Gissing), 1903 U
Privy Council. *See under* Judicature, in Britain
Probabilities, studies in the theory of, 1854 R
Probate of wills, civil, in Britain, 1857 O
Problem of Foreign Policy (G. Murray), 1921 O
Problem of Knowledge, The (A. J. Ayer), 1957 R
Problem of the Commonwealth, The (L. Curtis), 1916 O
Problems in Astrophysics (A. M. Clerke), 1903 P
Problem, The (A. Schweitzer), 1954 T
Production:
  census of, in Britain, 1907 O
  values of world, comparative percentages, 1888 Y, 1929 Y
  war, in Britain, 1939 Y, 1940 Y, 1941 Y, 1942 Y, 1943 Y, 1944 Y
Production of Heat by Voltaic Electricity (J. P. Joule), 1843 P
Professor, The (or *Elsie Venner;* O. W. Holmes), 1861 U
Profumo, John Dennis, B. Conservative politician (b. 1915), Secretary of State for war, misleads Commons, 1963 C; resigns, 1963 F
Progress and Poverty (H. George), 1879 O
Progress of Metaphysical, Ethical and Political Philosophy (D. Stewart), 1815 R
Progressives. *See under* Political Parties
Prohibition:
  in Canada, 1917 M
  in New Zealand, referendum against, 1919 D
  in Norway, 1919 K
  in US, in Illinois, 1851 O
    in Maine, 1851 O, 1911 J
    National Prohibition Party formed, 1869 J
    Anti-Saloon League founded, 1893 N
    Volstead Act, 1919 A
      passes over president's veto, 1919 K
      in force, 1920 A, O
    liquor running, 1922 O
    'Prohibition Navy', 1922 O
    repealed in New York state, 1923 G
    repealed, 1933 M

Projet de Code Civil (J. Cambacérès), 1796 O
Prokofiev, Serge, R. musician (b. 1891), 1917 T, 1921 T, 1936 T, 1945 T, 1946 T, 1952 T, 1954 T
Prolegomena to any Possible Metaphysic (I. Kant), 1783 R
Prolegomena to Ethics (T. H. Green), 1899 R
Prolegomena to Homer (F. Wolf), 1795 Q
Promethée mal enchainé, Le (A. Gide), 1899 U
Prometheus (A. Scriabin), 1913 T
Prometheus Unbound (P. B. Shelley), 1820 U
Propaganda as a Political Weapon (Stern-Rubarth), 1921 O
Prophet Armed, The (I. Deutscher), 1954 Q
Prophet Outcast, The (I. Deutscher), 1963 Q
Proportional Representation: adopted in Netherlands, 1899 M; adopted in Sweden, 1907 E
Prospects of Industrial Civilization (B. Russell), 1921 O
Prostitution in Britain, 1904 O; Wolfenden Report on, 1957 J; Street Offences Act, 1959 O
Protactinium, radio-active element, 1918 P
Protection. *See under* Tariff Questions
Protection of Ancient Buildings, Society for, 1877 S
Protée (P. Claudel), 1927 W
Proteins, chemistry of, 1907 P
Protestant Ethic and the Birth of Capitalism, The (W. Weber), 1901 Q
Protestants. *See under* Religious Denominations
Protocols:
  London, on French intervention in Greece, 1828 G
    recognises Greek independence, 1828 L, 1929 C
    on Belgium, 1831 A
  St. Petersburg, between Britain and Russia, over Greece, 1826 D
  non-intervention in Spanish Civil War, 1936 M
Protoplasm, term first used, 1840 P; Mohl's discovery, 1846 P
Proudhon, Pierre Joseph, F. political philosopher (1809–65), 1809 Z, 1840 P, 1846 O, 1847 O, 1865 Z
Proust, Louis Joseph, F. chemist (1754–1826), 1815 P
Proust, Marcel, F. novelist (1871–1922), 1871 Z, 1913 U, 1922 Z, 1927 U
Provencal culture, revived by Mistral, 1854 U
Providence, Rhode Island, US, Brown University, 1764 O
Prufrock and other Observations (T. S. Eliot), 1917 U
Prussia: education in, 1763 O; acquires rights in Ansbach and Bayreuth, 1769 K, 1779 E; gains through first partition of Poland, 1772 H; joins League of Armed Neutrality, 1781 E; gymnasia reformed, 1810 O; historiographer of, 1841 Q. *See also* Germany
Prussia, East, Germany: Russians evacuate, 1914 H, 1915 B; plebiscite in, 1920 G
Prussia, West, Germany: Polish landowners expropriated, 1886 D; plebiscite in, 1920 G
Prussianism and Socialism (O. Spengler), 1920 U
Prussia's Right to Saxony (B. Niebuhr), 1814 O
Pruth, River, Russia, 1853 G
Przemysl, Russia: Russians take, 1915 C; Germans recapture, 1915 F
Psephology, 1947 O, 1948 L, 1962 O
Psychical Research, Society for, 1882 P
Psychical research, studies in, 1914 R
Psycho-analysis, science of, founded, 1895 R
  Freud's lectures on, 1909 R
Psychological Types (C. Jung), 1920 R
Psychology, Industrial, Institute of, 1921 O
Psychology and Religion (C. Jung), 1944 R
Psychology and the Church (Hardtmann), 1925 R
Psychology of Art (A. Malraux), 1950 R
Psychology of Everyday Life (S. Freud), 1901 R
Psychology of Fascism, The (P. Nathan), 1943 O
Psychology of Imagination, The (J. P. Sartre), 1951 R
Psychology, Comparative, 1859 R
Psychology, studies in, 1824 R, 1846 R, 1855 R, 1890 R, 1900 R, 1913 R
Psychology of Sex, 1886 P, 1897 R
Psychopathia Sexualis (Krafft-Ebing), 1886 P
Public Economy of Athens, The (P. Böckh), 1817 Q
Public Health, legislation for, 1891 O
Public Lectures, free, 1839 Q
Public Meetings, Right of holding:
  in Britain, curtailed, 1795 L, 1819 M
  in France, 1868 F
  in Germany, restricted, 1878 K
  in Transvaal, restricted, 1896 L
Public Opinion Polls, confounded by Truman's presidential election, 1948 L
Public Philosophy, The (W. Lippmann), 1955 O
Puccini, Giacomo, It. musician (1858–1924), 1858 Z, 1893 T, 1896 T, 1900 T, 1904 T, 1910 T, 1918 T, 1924 T, Z
Puddling process, Cort's, 1784 P
Puerto Rico: US invades, 1898 G; Spain cedes to US, 1898 M; Foraker Act for, 1900 E; decision on US citizenship, 1901 M; Nationalist Rising in, 1950 K
Pugachoff, Emel'yon Ivanovich, R. pretender (?1741–75), 1773 K, 1774 J
Pugilism. *See* Boxing
Puissance motrice de Feu (N. Carnot), 1824 P
Pulitzer Prizes, 1917 U
Pullman dining-car, first, 1879 P
Pump, lung, 1961 P
Pump, steam, 1841 P
Purcell, Henry, B. musician (1658–1695), anniversary concert, 1959 T
Purcell Society, founded, 1876 T
Purges:
  in China, 1955 C
  in Czechoslovakia, 1951 C
  in Germany, 1934 F
  in Hungary, 1949 F
  in Russia, 1933 N, 1934 M, 1937 A, F
    of Scientific Committees, 1948 F
'Purism', in art, 1918 S, 1928 S
Purkinje, Johannes Evangelista, G. biologist (1781–1869), 1840 P
Pusey, Edward Bouverie, B. churchman (1800–82), 1836 R, 1865 R
Pushkin, Alexander, R. author (1799–1837), 1799 Z, 1820 U, 1822 U, 1825 U, 1828 U, 1832 U, 1837 Z
Putumayo, Peru, atrocities in rubber industry in, Casement's Report on, 1912 G
Puvis de Chavannes, Pierre, F. artist (1824–98), 1878 S, 1889 S, 1890 S
Pu Yi, Emperor of China (to 1912), installed as Emperor of Manchukuo, 1932 C, 1934 C
Pygmalion, Preface to (G. B. Shaw), 1916 U
Pyramids, The, Egypt, battle of, 1798 G

Q

'Q'. *See* Quiller-Couch
Quakers. *See under* Religious Denominations
Quantum theory, 1900 P
  report on, 1914 P
  studies in, 1926 P, 1942 P
  uncertainty principle, 1927 P
Quasimodo, Salvatore, It. poet, 1930 U

Quay, J. E. de, Du. Catholic People's Party leader, 1959 C, 1960 M
Quebec, Canada: assigned to Britain, 1763 K; attack on, 1775 M; enters Dominion of Canada, 1867 C; Fenianism in, 1870 E; Conference of Allied leaders at, 1943 H; Churchill meets Roosevelt in, 1944 J; Nationalist riots in, 1964 E; Queen Elizabeth's visit, 1964 K
Queen and the Rebels, The (U. Betti), 1955 W
Queen Elizabeth, S.S., launched, 1938 P
Queen Mab (P. B. Shelley), 1813 U
Queen Mary, S.S., launched, 1934 P
Queensbury, Marquess of. *See* Douglas, John Sholto
Queensland, Australia: is separated from N.S. Wales, 1859 A; requests to annex New Guinea, 1883 N; boycotts Hobart Convention, 1897 A; artificial rain in, 1957 P
Queenston Heights, US, battle, 1812 K
Queen Victoria (G. Lytton Sprachey), 1921 Q
Quemoy: Chinese bombard, 1958 H; US concern over, 1962 F
Qu'est-ce-que la Propriete? (P. J. Proudhon), 1840 O
Qu'est-ce-que le Tiers Etat? (Sieyes), 1789 O
Quest for Certainty, The (Dewey), 1929 R
Question of Upbringing, A (A. Powell), 1950 U
Quetelet, Lambert Adolphe Jacques, F. philosopher (1796–1874), 1835 P
Queiulle, Henri, F. Radical, 1950 G; forms ministry, 1948 J; resigns, 1949 K; forms ministry, 1951 C
Quiberon, France, British aid to insurgents in, 1795 F
Quiberon Bay, France, Emigres defeated at, 1794 G
Quiet American, The (G. Greene), 1955 U
Qui je fus (H. Michaux), 1927 U
Quiller-Couch, Sir Arthur, B. novelist and critic under pseudonym of 'Q' (1863–1944), 1863 Z, 1888 U, 1916 U, 1944 U
Quincey, Thomas de, B. author (1785–1859), 1785 Z, 1821 U, 1859 Z
Quinine, is synthesised, 1944 O
Quintana, Marcel, Sp. poet (1772–1857), 1772 Z
Quisling, Vidkun, Norw. puppet premier, 1942 B
sentenced for collaboration, 1945 J
Quiz programmes, 1935 W
Quoinez, François, F. author under pseudonym of 'Françoise Sagan' (b. 1935), 1935 Z, 1950 U, 1958 T
Quo Vadis? (H. Sienkiewicz), 1895 U

R

Raab, Julius, Aus. People's Party leader (1892–1964), 1964 Z; forms coalitions, 1953 D, 1956 F, 1959 E; retires, 1961 D
Raabe, Wilhelm, G. author (1831–1910), 1864 C
Rabbit Run (J. Updike), 1960 U
Rabbits, in Britain, killed by myxomatosis, 1953 P
Racconigi agreement, Russia with Italy, on Balkans, 1909 K
Race Relations (E. Huxley and M. Perham), 1944 O
Rachel, Elisa, F. actress (1820–58), 1838 W
Rachid Ali, of Iraq, flees, 1941 E
Rachmaninoff, Sergei, R. musician (1873–1943), 1873 Z, 1901 T, 1935 S, 1943 Z; music is banned in Russia, 1931 T
'Rachmanism', exploitation of tenants of rented dwellings, campaign against, 1963 O
Racial Problems:
UN condemns discrimination, 1959 L
in Britain, disturbances, 1958 H
in South Africa, bill for segregation rejected, 1925 G
discrimination over franchise, 1930 E
alleged discrimination against Indians, 1949 E
riots in Johannesburg, 1950 A
Malan's apartheid legislation invalidated by courts, 1952 C
in force, 1952 D
Sharpeville shooting, 1960 C
See also under Apartheid; Treason trials
in US, riots in Chicago, 1919 G
Negro lynching, 1955 O
Harlem riots, 1964 G
Los Angeles riots, 1965 H
segregation on 'buses ruled unconstitutional, 1946 O
desegregation in schools, 1956 O
crisis in Arkansas, 1957 O
Little Rock High School required to admit Negroes, 1958 J
crisis in Birmingham, 1963 J
discrimination against Negroes, in Mormon priesthood, 1962 R
lunch-counter sit-in, 1960 B
'kneel-in' campaign in churches, 1960 R
freedom rides, 1961 O
Negro voting rights safeguarded to Civil Rights Bill, 1960 D
Kennedy's speech of Civil Rights, 1963 F
Negro peaceful demonstrations, 1963 H
Negro petition on grievances, delivered at Montgomery, 1965 C
See also under Civil Rights Campaign
Racine, Wiscon., US, 1936 S
Racine et Shakespeare (Stendhal), 1823 U
Racing, horse. *See* horse-racing
Racquets, championship, 1895 X
Rackham, Arthur, B. illustrator, 1867 Z, 1939 Z
Radar, equipment devised, 1935 P; developments are publicised, 1945 P; port installation, 1948 P
Radcliffe, Cyril John, lord Radcliffe, B. judge (b. 1899), 1951 O; proposals for Cyprus Constitution, 1961 E; reviews security procedures, 1961 E; heads tribunal on security, 1962 L, 1963 D, V
Radcliffe, Mrs. Anne, B. author (1764–1823), 1794 U, 1795 U
Radek, Karl, R. politician, 1937 A
Radetsky, Joseph, Count of Radetz, Aus. soldier (1766–1858), 1832 A, 1848 C, D, G
Radiant heat, discoveries in, 1831 P
Radiation:
Geiger counter for measure of, 1927 P
'Positrons' discovered, 1933 P
Report on, 1914 P
researches in, 1913 P, 1927 P
Radiation, Cosmic, studies in, 1925 P, 1953 P, 1962 P
Radiation, Nuclear, disposal of radio-active waste, 1954 P, 1955 P, 1956 O
Radio-activity: theory of, 1904 P, 1918 P; induced, 1934 P; carbon tests, for dating archaeological finds, 1952 Q
Radio Caroline, pirate radio station, 1965 W
Radio communication, global, test for, 1963 P
Radiography, Treatise on, 1910 P
Radio-isotopes, extended use of, 1952 P
Radio-reflector satellite, 1958 P, 1960 P
Radio-telescopes:
Jodrell Bank, 1957 P
Mullard Observatory, Cambridge, 1957 P
Radio, Transistor, is banned in Capri, 1963 W
is invented, 1948 P

Radio Waves:
emitted from Jupiter, 1955 P
speed of, 1947 P
speed of light through, 1950 P
sunspots emitted from, 1946 P
Radistcheff, Alexander, R. author (1749–1802), 1790 O
Radium: discovered, 1898 P; testing of preparations of, 1914 P
Radstadt Conference, 1797 M, 1799 D
Radzinowycz, Leon, B., formerly Pol., legal historian and criminologist (b. 1906), 1961 O
Raeburn, Sir Henry, B. portrait painter (1756–1823), 1803 S, 1809 S
Raffles, Sir Thomas Stamford, B. colonial governor (1781–1826), 1819 B, 1826 P
Ragged School Union, 1844 O
Raikes, Robert, B. promoter of Sunday Schools (1735–1811), 1780 R
Railways:
corridor-train, 1890 P
couplings, automatic, 1906 P
diesel electric system, 1913 P
electric, 1879 P, 1895 P
Pullman dining car, 1879 P
signals, automatic, 1893 P
train ferry, 1934 P
truck, refrigerated, 1888 P
tunnel, first, 1826 P
Railways:
in Africa, first trans-African, 1931 G
in Australia, Sydney–Melbourne, 1883 P
in Austria, Budweis–Lintz, 1832 P
mileage in operation, 1907 Y
in Britain, Beeching Report, 1963 O
City and S. London, 1890 P
Great Western, 1842 P
Liverpool–Manchester, 1826 P, 1829 P, 1830 J, P
London, the first train into, 1836 P
London Metropolitan, 1864 P
Underground, 1890 P, 1898 P, 1905 P, 1963 P
amalgamated with Metropolitan, 1911 L
London Midland and Scottish, *Coronation Scot*, 1937 P
mileage in operation, 1840 Y, 1850 Y, 1860 Y, 1870 Y, 1880 Y, 1890 Y, 1935 Y, 1945 Y, 1955 Y
nationalisation, in force, 1948 A
season tickets, 1910 O
standard gauge on, 1942 P
Stockton and Darlington, 1825 P
in Canada, the first, 1836 P
Canadian Grand Trunk, 1914 P, 1919 L
Canadian Pacific Railway, 1881 M, 1886 P
mileage in operation, 1907 Y
in China, 1888 P
Chinese Eastern, agreement on, 1929 M
Russia sells interest in, 1935 C
mileage in operation, 1955 Y
North Manchurian, 1896 F
in East Africa, 1928 N
in Ethiopia, finance for, 1902 B
in France, Paris Metro, 1898 P
mileage in operation, 1880 Y, 1890 Y, 1935 Y, 1945 Y
in Germany, electric, 1910 R
Leipzig station, 1915 P
mileage in operation, 1907 Y, 1935 Y, 1955 Y
in Greece, railway to Salonika, proposed, 1908 A
in India, mileage in operation, 1907 Y
in Iran, Trans-Iranian, 1939 P
in Iraq, Baghdad Railway, German interests in, 1888 K, 1898 L, 1899 M, 1903 D
discussions on, 1907 H, 1909 L, 1910 L
international agreements on, 1914 B, F
British army administers, 1919 A
in Italy, Rome Station, 1950 S
in Japan, nationalisation of, 1906 C
mileage in operation, 1955 Y
in Russia, Trans-Siberian, 1891 G, 1891 P, 1901 P
Turkestan–Siberian, 1930 P
mileage in operation, 1860 Y, 1880 Y, 1890 Y, 1907 Y, 1925 Y, 1935 Y, 1945 Y
In Saudi Arabia, Hejaz Railway, 1900 N
in South Africa, Cape Railway, 1885 L, 1892 J
to Rhodesia, 1897 L
from Delagoa Bay to Transvaal, 1883 M, 1895 G
in South America, 1894 P, 1911 P
in Sweden, 1913 P
in Switzerland, Trans-Alpine, 1853 P
nationalisation of, 1910 N
in Turkey, Orient Express, 1883 P, 1961 E
in Uganda, 1901 M
in US, first steam locomotive, 1829 P
mileage in operation, 1840 Y, 1850 Y, 1860 Y, 1870 Y, 1880 Y, 1890 Y, 1907 Y, 1925 Y, 1935 Y, 1945 Y, 1955 Y
New York Subway, 1904 P, 1908 P
regulation of, by Elkins Act, 1903 N
by Interstate Commerce Act, 1887 B
mergers of, judged to violate anti-Trust laws, 1904 C, 1912 M
rates for, 1913 F
strike, military control during, 1951 B
war-time control of, 1917 M, 1920 C
Rain, artificial, 1957 P
Rainbow, The (D. H. Lawrence), 1915 U
Raine, Kathleen (Mrs. Madge), B. poet (b. 1908), 1956 U
Rainier, Prince of Monaco (b. 1923), 1956 W
Rajput States, India, under British protection, 1818 A
Rakósi, Matyas, Hungarian Communist, 1952 H
Rama I, King of Siam (1782–1809), 1782 N
Ramadier, Paul, F. Socialist (1888–1961), 1947 A, L
Rambouillet Decrees, for sale of US ships seized by French, 1810 C
Rameau, Jean Philippe, F. musician (1683–1764), 1764 Z
Ramée, Marie Louise de la, B. novelist under pseudonym of 'Ouida' (1839–1908), 1839 Z, 1867 U, 1908 Z
Ramek, Rudolf, Aus. politician, 1926 K
Ramsay, Allan, B. artist (1713–84), 1767 S
Ramsay, James, earl of Dalhousie, B. administrator (1812–60), as governor-general of India, 1848 A
Ramsay, Sir William, B. scientist (1852–1916), 1896 P, 1898 P, 1903 P
Ramsden, Jesse, B. engineer (1735–1800), 1770 P, 1800 Z
Ramsey, Arthur Michael, B. churchman (b. 1904), 1963 R; appointed Archbishop of Canterbury, 1961 A; speaks on use of force in Rhodesia, 1965 K
Rand, S. Africa: gold mines in, Chinese labour for, 1903 L; strike in, 1922 A
Randall Commission, on US foreign economic policy, 1954 A
Rangoon, Burma: British capture, 1824 E; falls to Japanese, 1942 C; Allies enter, 1945 E; Asian Socialist Conference at, 1953 A; Buddhist Council meets at, 1956 R

Ranke, Leopold von, G. historian (1795–1886), 1795 Z, 1824 Q, 1834 Q, 1839 Q, 1841 Q, 1847 Q, 1852 Q, 1859 Q, 1886 Z
Rankin, Jeanette, Am. Irish woman member of Congress, 1916 L
Rapacki Plan, for denuclearised zone in Europe, 1957 K
  rejected by Britain and US, 1958 B
Rapallo, Italy: Allied Conference at, 1917 L; Treaty, Italy with Yugoslavia, 1920 L; Italy abrogates, 1924 J; Treaty, German with Russia, 1922 D
Rape of the Masses, The (S. Chakotin), 1939 O
Rask, Rasmus Christian, Dan. philologist (1787–1832), 1811 Q
Rasmussen, Steen, Dan. architect, 1898 Z
Ras Tafari. *See* Haile Selassie
Rates, in Britain:
  church abolished, 1868 R
  industrial, raised, 1957 B
Rathenau, Walter, G. industrialist and economist (1867–1922), 1867 Z; becomes minister for Reparation, 1921 E; as Chancellor, 1921 E, 1922 A; is murdered, 1922 F
Rationing:
  in Britain, bread, 1917 B, 1946 G, 1948 O
    clothes, 1941 O, 1949 B
    food, 1918 B, 1940 A
    petrol, 1956 M
    penalties for black-marketeers, 1941 M
  in Germany, food, 1916 O
  in Russia, abolished, 1947 O
Ratisbon, Germany, Diet, reconstructs German states, 1803 B
Ratti, Achille, It. cardinal (1857–1939), elected Pope Pius XI, 1922 B
Rattigan, Terence Mervyn, B. dramatist (b. 1911), 1936 W, 1942 W, 1944 W, 1946 W, 1948 W, 1960 W
Räuber, Die (Schiller), 1781 W
Rauch, Christian Daniel, G. sculptor (1727–1857), 1851 S
Ravel, Maurice, F. musician (1875–1937), 1875 Z, 1901 T, 1907 T, 1911 T, 1922 T, 1927 T, 1928 T, 1932 T, 1937 Z
Raven, Charles Earle, B. theologian (1885–1963), 1943 R, 1954 R
Ravenna, Italy, falls to Allies, 1944 M
Ravilious, Eric, B. artist (d. 1942), 1940 S
Rawalpindi, Pakistan: Sikhs surrender at, 1849 C; and Afghanistan Peace Conference, 1919 G; designated provisional capital, 1959 K
Rawlinson, Sir Henry Creswiek, B. orientalist and soldier (1810–95), 1846 Q, 1858 Q, 1862 Q
Rawsthorne, Alan, B. musician (b. 1905), 1949 T, 1950 T
Ray, Nicholas, B. film director, 1955 W
Rayleigh, Lord. *See* Strutt, J. W.
Rayon, manufacture of, 1892 P
Rays, cosmic, observatory for, 1953 P
Rays of Positive Electricity and Their Application to Chemical Analysis (J. J. Thomson), 1913 P
Razor blades, safety, 1904 P
Razor's Edge, The (W. S. Maugham), 1944 U
Reaction Committee, appointed by German Diet, 1851 N
Reactors, atomic, statistics of, 1962 P
Re-armament:
  in France, 1939 C
  in Germany, 1935 B
  See also under Conferences
Read, Sir Herbert, B. artist and critic (b. 1893), 1933 S
Reade, Charles, B. author (1814–84), 1852 U, 1856 U, 1861 U
Reading, Berks, University, 1926 O
Reading, colour, finger-tip, 1964 P
Readman, Alison, B. psephologist, 1947 O
Realization of the Possible (A. Bain), 1899 R
Realm of Spirit (G. Santayana), 1940 R
Reaping-machine, 1834 P
Rebellions and Revolutions:
  nations undergoing, to be expelled from Concert of Europe, 1820 L
  in Albania, suppressed, 1910 D, 1915 A
  in Algeria, 1961 D, 1965 F
  in American Colonies. *See* Wars, War of American Independence
  of Arabs, in Turkey, 1916 F, L, 1917 A
  in Argentina, against Joseph Bonaparte, 1810 E, 1930 J
  in Austria, 1848 C, E, K
  in Austrian Empire, of Peasants in Bohemia, 1775 B
    in Transylvania, 1784 G
    by Czechs, 1848 F
    in Bohemia, 1908 M
  in Austrian Netherlands, 1789 K, 1790 M
  in Belgium, 1830 H, L, M, 1831 H
  in Brazil, 1930 K, 1932 G
  in Brunei, 1962 M
  in Brunswick, 1830 J
  in Canada, under Papineau, 1837 L, M
    under Mackenzie, 1837 M, 1838 A
    Lord Durham's leniency towards rebels criticised, 1838 K
    Red River Rebellion, 1869 K, 1870 E
  in Chile, 1810 J, 1932 F
  in China, by White Lotus Society in Shantung, 1774 N
    Taiping, 1850 K, 1855 K, 1911 K, L, M, 1912 B, 1913 J
  in Congo, 1905 B, 1965 F
  in Crete, 1866 J, 1896 B, G, H, 1905 C
  in Cuba, 1906 B
    by Castro, 1958 D
  in Dutch East Indies, 1894 N
  in Eastern Rumelia, 1886 D, E
  in Ecuador, 1925 G
  in Ethiopia, 1930 C
  in Finland, by Nazis, 1932 B
  in France:
    Revolution of 1789:
      Third Estate declares itself to be National Assembly, 1789 F
        takes Tennis Court Oath, 1789 F
      sack of Bastille, 1789 G
      abolition of feudal system, 1789 H
      March of women to Versailles, 1789 H
      Declaration of Rights of Man, adopted, 1789 H
      nationalisation of church property, 1789 L
      civil constitution of clergy, 1790 L, R
      English views of, 1790 B, 1791 G
      Paris Commune, 1792 H, 1794 G
      sack of Tuileries, 1792 H
      Republic proclaimed, 1792 J
      Revolutionary Calendar, 1792 J
      Convention offers assistance to all peoples for overthrowing governments, 1792 L
      decree for revolutionary institutes to be adopted in lands occupied by French armies, 1792 M
      abolition of Christianity, 1793 K
      execution of Louis XVI, 1793 A

Committee of Public Safety, 1793 D, G
Reign of terror, 1793 F
Marie Antoinette executed, 1793 K
Rising of royalists in La Vendee, 1793 C, K, M, 1796 C
Feast of Reason, 1793 R
mass executions, 1794 F
Terror ends, 1794 G
White Terror, 1795 E
'Day of the Sections', 1795 K
Directory established, 1795 L
rising of Royalists in Brittany, 1795 F, 1796 C
Royalist re-action prevented, 1797 J
Consulate established, 1799 M
See also under Wars
July Revolution, 1830 G
influence of, 1831 B
by Republicans, 1832 F
1848 Revolution:
Lamartine's provisional government, 1848 B
Communists rise, 1848 E
'June Days', 1848 F
Republican constitution, 1848 L
Paris, rising, 1870 J
in Geneva, 1792 M
in Germany, crushed, 1833 D, 1848 C
in Berlin, 1918 L
Spartacist, 1919 A
in Haiti, 1915 G
in Hesse, 1830 J
in Hesse-Cassel, 1850 J, L
in Hungary, 1848 J, K
Revolution of 1956:
demonstrations call for democratic government, 1956 K
Nagy forms ministry, 1956 K
Russian troops intervene, 1956 K
Hungarian government renounces Warsaw treaty and appeals to UN, 1956 L
Kádár's deflection, 1956 L
Soviet attack on Budapest, 1956 L
Nagy seeks refuge, 1956 L
mass arrests, 1956 M
UN report on, 1957 J
in Iraq, 1963 B
in Ireland, Whiteboys Rebellion, 1763 G
Ulster Rebellion, 1797 C
1798 A, F
Emmet's rebellion, 1803 G
Sinn Fein Easter Rebellion, 1916 D, O
amnesty for rebels, 1917 F
Sinn Fein, 1922 D, F, G
amnesty for rebels, 1923 D
in Japan, Satsuma Rebellion, 1877 J
in Java, Communist Revolt, 1926 L
in Macedonia, Young Turk revolt, 1908 G
in Madagascar, against French, 1947 C
in Matabeleland, 1893 L
in Mexico, against Spain, 1810 J
in Milan, 1848 C
in Modena, 1831 B, 1859 D
in Moldavia, against Turks, 1821 C, 1907 C
in Mosul, 1959 L
in Naples, 1820 G, 1821 B, C, 1848 E
in New Grenada, 1810 E
in Nicaragua, 1926 E
in Papal States, 1831 B, 1832 A
in Parma, 1831 B, 1848 C, 1859 D
in Persia, 1905 M
by Kurds, 1930 G
in Peru, 1809 G, 1930 H
in Philippines, against Spain, 1872 N, 1948 G
in Poland, against Russia, 1830 L, 1831 A
suppressed, 1831 E, J, 1848 E, 1863 A, B
in Portugal, 1820 H, 1910 K, 1921 K
against Carmona, 1927 B
in Rhodesia, 1965 L
in Russia, Cossack Rebellion, 1773 K, 1774 J
Peasants' Revolt, 1902 D
Revolution of 1905:
Bloody Sunday, 1905 A
Tsar promises to call assembly, 1905 C, 1905 H, K
General Strike, 1905 K
Potemkin mutiny, 1905 K
first Soviet formed, 1905 K
October manifesto, 1905 K
Moscow workers revolt, 1905 M
revolutionary outbreak suppressed, 1907 L
Revolution of 1917, February:
separation of Church and State, 1917 B
beginnings, 1917 C
all-Russia congress of Soviets, 1917 F
Lenin and Bolsheviks seize power, 1917 G
all-Russia conference, 1917 H
Kornilov's counter-revolution, 1917 J
Republic proclaimed, 1917 J
Soviet Congress resolves on armistice, 1917 K
Revolution of 1917, October:
outbreak, 1917 L
armistice with Germany, 1917 M
Bolsheviks dissolve constituent assembly, 1918 A
in San Domingo, 1791 H, 1865 E, 1912 J
in Saxony, 1830 J
in Serbia, revolt of Nationalist Radicals, 1883 L
in Sicily, 1848 A, D
in South Africa, Boer revolt, 1914 K
in Spain, 1820 A, L
crushed by French troops, 1823 K, 1840 K
O'Donnell's revolt, 1854 G, 1868 J
for Catalonian home rule, 1917 H, 1931 D
Sanjurjo's revolt in Seville, 1932 H
in Syria, Revolt of Druses, 1925 G, K, 1927 F
army revolt, 1954 B, 1962 C
in Transvaal, of Boers against British, 1881 A, B, D
in Transylvania, 1784 G
in Turkish Empire, by sheriff of Mecca, 1916 F
in Tuscany, 1859 D
in Venezuela, 1902 M
in Venice, 1848 C
in US, Pontiac's Rebellion, 1763 E
Shay's Rebellion, in Massachusetts, 1786 J
Whiskey Insurrection in Pennsylvania, 1794 M
Dore Rebellion, in Rhode Island, 1841 K
in Wallachia, against Turks, 1821 C
in Zanzibar, 1964 A, B
See also Civil Wars; *Coup d'états;* Riots and Risings; Wars
Recent Advances in Vaccine and Serum Therapy (Fleming and Petrie), 1934 P
Recessional (R. Kipling), 1897 W
Recherche de l'Absolu, La (H. de Balzac), 1834 U
Recherches Chimiques sur la Végétation (N. de Saussure), 1797 P
Recherches sur les ossements fossiles de quadrupèdes (G. Cuvier), 1812 P
Recherches Théoriques et expérimentals sur la force de torsion . . . (C. A. Coulomb), 1785 P
Reciprocity. *See* Tariff Questions
Recits des temps mérovingiens (A. Thierry), 1850 Q
Reclamation force, US, 1902 P
Reconstruction, Ministry, in Britain, 1943 L

Recording, magnetic, 1899 P
Records, gramophone, long-playing, 1948 P
Records, Public, in Britain, 1838 O, 1958 O
access to, 1958 O
Recueil des traités (G. Martens), 1791 Q
Red Cross League, 1864 O
Red Cross, British, funds for, 1915 S, T
Reden über die Religion (F. Schleiermacher), 1799 R
Red Flag, The, 1899 T
Redgauntlet (W. Scott), 1824 O
Redgrave, Vanessa, B. actress, 1939 Z
Red River Rebellion, in Canada, 1869 K, 1870 E
Red Room, The (A. Strindberg), 1879 W
Red Roses for Me (O'Carey), 1942 W
Red Sea, Italian domination of east coast of, 1926 J
Reed, Sir Carol, B. film director (b. 1906), 1947 W, 1948 W, 1949 W, 1951 W, 1959 W, 1963 W
Reed, Ezekiel, Am. inventor, 1786 P
Referenda:
in Belgium, for return of Leopold III, 1950 C
in Britain, for Parliament Bill, proposal for, rejected, 1911 D
in Bulgaria, against monarchy, 1946 J
in France, rejects draft constitution, 1946 E
approves Constitution of Fifth Republic, 1958 J
on Algiers, 1961 A, 1962 G
favours president's election by universal suffrage, 1962 K
in Germany, on Young Plan for reparations, 1929 M
in Italy, favours republic, 1946 F
in Jamaica, to secede from West Indies Federation, 1961 J
in Luxembourg, on monarchy, 1919 K
in Malta, favours union with Britain, 1956 B
in New Zealand against Prohibition, 1919 D
in Poland, for single-house assembly, 1946 F
for wide nationalisation, 1946 F
in S. Rhodesia, for new constitution, 1961 G
favours independence, 1964 L
in S. Africa, for a Republic, 1960 K
in Switzerland, against female suffrage, 1959 B
against import or manufacture of atomic weapons, 1962 D
in S. Vietnam, for a republic, 1955 K
See also under Plebiscites
Reflecting microscope, 1947 P
Reflections and Memoirs (Otto von Bismarck), 1898 O
Reflections on the Revolution in France (E. Burke), 1790 O
Reflections on the Revolution of our Time (H. Laski), 1943 O
Reflections on Violence (G. Sorel), 1908 O
Reflex-action, of nerve-centres, discovered, 1832 P
Reflexes, conditioned, 1907 P
Réflexions sur la formation et le distribution des richesses (A. Turgot), 1765 O
Reform:
in Britain, of Church, essay on, 1832 R
of Parliament. *See* Parliamentary Reform
in Russia, shelved, 1880 E
Reformatories, proposed for juvenile offenders, 1851 O
founded, 1876 O
Reformatory Schools for . . . Juvenile Offenders (M. Carpenter), 1851 O
Réforme Sociale, La (Le Play), 1864 O
Reform Parties. *See under* Political Parties
Refrigeration: early development, 1850 P; cold store, 1861 P; railway truck, 1888 P; Chilling process for meat, 1934 P
Refrigerators, domestic, statistics, 1937 Y, 1965 Y
Refugees: Bermuda Conference on, 1943 D; UNRRA established, 1943 O; World Refugee Year, 1959 O
Regencies, in Britain:
bills for, 1765 G, 1811 B, 1812 B
in force, 1788 M, 1789 B, 1811 B
Prince Regent. *See under* George IV
Regensberg, Bavaria, W. Germany, the Walhalla near, 1830 S
Reger, Max, G. musician (1873–1916), 1915 T
Regional economic planning councils, British, 1965 B
Registrations of births, deaths and marriages, in Britain, 1836 H
Registration, national, British, 1939 J
Reichenbach, E. Germany: Conference and treaty, 1790 F; Treaty, Austria with Russia and Prussia, 1813 F
Reichstein, Tadeus, Swi. chemist (b. 1897), 1934 P
Reichstag Fire, 1933 B
Reid, Thomas, B. philosopher (1710–96), 1764 R, 1788 R
Reigen (A. Schnitzler), 1903 W
Reign of Grace (A. Booth), 1768 Q
Reinecke Fuchs (Goethe), 1794 U
Reis, Philipp, G. scientist, 1861 P
Reiske, Johann Jacob, G. Arabic scholar (1716–74), 1789 Q
Reisz, Karel, B. film director, 1960 W
Reivers, The (W. Faulkner), 1962 U
Réjane, Gabrielle (Charlotte Réju), F. actress (1857–1923), 1875 W
Relativity:
Einstein's first theory of, 1905 P
general theory of, 1915 P
mathematics of, 1908 P
studies in, 1918 P, 1919 P
Relief for Europe, 1919 A
Religion and the Rise of Capitalism (R. H. Tawney), 1926 R
Religion in America (Sperry), 1945 R
Religion within the Boundaries of Reason (I. Kant), 1793 R
Religious Denominations:
African sects, statistics of, 1962 Y
Anglican Communion, first colonial bishop appointed, 1814 R
Pan Anglican synod, first, 1867 R
See also Church of England
Baptist World Alliance, 1905 R
Baptists, British, form Baptist Union, 1812 R
union of, 1891 R
statistics, 1905 Y, 1930 Y, 1950 Y
US, statistics, 1840 Y, 1905 Y, 1936 Y, 1947 Y
Black Muslims, US, 1965 B
Buddhists, Indian, 1963 Y
in S. Vietnam, arrested, 1963 H
Chile, state religion in, 1833 E
Christadelphians, 1844 R
Christian Scientists, 1879 R, 1936 Y, 1947 Y
Church of England, advowsons, sale of prohibited, 1898 R
Anglican orders, validity of, 1891 R
Anglo-Catholic party in, 1846 R, 1860 R, 1891 R
appointments, Howick Committee on, 1964 R
bishops, powers of, increased, 1898 R
Suffragan, revival of, 1869 R
Christian Socialist party in, 1849 R
Church Assembly, 1919 R
Congress, 1863 R
Convocation, revived, 1852 R, 1860 R
appoints Committee to prepare Revised Version of Bible, 1870 R

ecclesiastical discipline, commission on, 1903 R
English Church Union, 1860 R
Evangelical Party in, 1783 R, 1846 R
Methodists, relations with, 1958 R, 1960 R, 1963 R
Oxford Movement in, 1833 R, 1846 R, 1860 R, 1891 R
Paul Report, on deployment of clergy, 1964 R
Prayer Book of 1928, rejected by Parliament, 1928 R
ritualistic practices in, 1857 R, 1874 R
proceedings against, 1890 R
Roman Catholic Church, relations with, 1894 R
statistics, 1905 Y, 1930 Y, 1945 Y, 1950 Y
See also Anglican Communion
Church of Ireland, revenues of, 1835 D
is disestablished, 1869 R
Church of Jesus Christ of Latter-Day Saints (Mormons), founded, 1825 R
in England, 1962 R
in US, 1830 D, R, 1833 R, 1843 R
leave for Salt Lake City, 1846 F, 1847 R
Negroes refused admission to priesthood in, 1962 R
Church of Scotland, Free, 1843 R
Church of Scotland, Presbyterian, General Assembly deposes Campbell, 1831 R
Prayer Book revised, 1912 R
re-grouping of, 1847 R, 1929 R, 1930 T
appeal of woman for ordination in, 1963 R
statistics, 1905 Y, 1945 Y, 1950 Y
Church of the Brethren, US, 1958 R
Church of Wales, disestablishment, proposed, 1891 K
legislation for, opposed, 1912 D, 1913 B, G
bill suspended for duration of war, 1914 J
Congregationalists, in Britain, 1905 Y, 1930 Y, 1945 Y, 1950 Y
in US, 1905 Y, 1936 Y, 1945 Y, 1947 Y, 1958 R
Coptic, in Africa, 1962 Y
in Egypt, 1910 B
Église Libre, French, 1848 R
Episcopal Church of Scotland, ministers ordained in, permitted to hold English benefices, 1864 R
re-grouping, 1930 T
statistics, 1905 Y, 1930 Y, 1945 Y, 1950 Y
Episcopal Church in US, 1801 R, 1853 R
statistics, 1905 Y, 1936 Y, 1945 Y, 1947 Y
Evangelicals, in Germany, revived, 1809 R, 1850 R
Union, formed by Lutheran and Reformed, 1817 R
angered by papal encyclical, 1910 E, F
in Palatinate, 1958 R
statistics, 1945 Y
in US, Evangelical Association (or 'New Methodists'), 1807 R
Evangelical Alliance, 1866 R, 1958 R
defines Fundamentalism, 1895 R
Billy Graham's revivals, 1954 R
statistics, 1905 Y, 1936 Y, 1945 Y, 1947 Y
Exclusive Brethren, British, expulsions from, 1962 R
French National Church, 1848 R, 1872 R
separation of Church and State, 1905 R
Hindus, Indian, 1924 G, 1945 Y, 1947 H, 1963 Y
Illuminati, Bavarian, 1776 R
Islam, 1945 Y
no longer state religion in Turkey, 1928 D
Jehovah's Witnesses, founded, 1871 R
Jews, statistics of, 1905 Y, 1909 Y, 1936 Y, 1947 Y, 1950 Y
See also main index under Jews
Lumpar Church, N. Rhodesia, 1964 G
Lutherans, World Conference, 1929 Y
German. *See under* Evangelicals
Swedish, 1958 R
admits women to pastorate, 1960 R
US. *See under* Evangelicals
statistics, 1905 Y, 1936 Y, 1945 Y
Mennonites, in Canada, 1786 R
Methodists, British, Wesleyan, deed of declaration for, 1784 R
New Connexion leaves, 1797 R
founds missionary Society, 1813 R
re-union of, 1932 R
conversations with Church of England, 1958 R, 1963 R
statistics, 1837 Y, 1905 Y, 1930 Y, 1950 Y
US, Wesleyan, presbyters ordained, 1784 R
statistics, 1837 Y, 1840 Y, 1905 Y, 1936 Y, 1947 Y
Mormons. *See* Church of Latter Day Saints
Moslems, 1886 M
in Albania, rising by, 1937 E
in India, 1924 G, 1947 H
violence against, 1964 C
in Indonesia, 1955 H
statistics, 1945 Y, 1963 Y
Old Catholics, 1871 R, 1874 R
Orthodox Church, annuls excommunication of Church of Rome, 1965 R
in Africa, statistics, 1962 Y
in Armenia, despoiled, 1902 D
in Russia, claims protectorate over Ottoman Christians, 1853 E, 1860 R
separation of Church and State, 1917 B
election of Patriarch of All-Russia, 1943 J
attends World Council of Churches meeting, 1961 R
in Turkish Empire, civil power of heads of, abolished, 1856 B
statistics, 1945 Y
Pentecostal Churches, in Chile, attends World Council of Churches meeting, 1961 R
Plymouth Brethren, 1827 R
Presbyterian, in Britain, 1846 R
invited Congregations of, 1876 R
statistics, 1905 Y, 1930 Y, 1950 Y
in Scotland, United Church, 1847 R
separate churches unite, 1929 R
See also Church of Scotland
statistics, 1905 Y, 1950 Y
in US, revision of Catechism, 1788 R, 1810 Q, 1837 R
United Church formed, 1958 R
statistics, 1840 Q, 1905 Y, 1947 Y
Protestants, French (Huguenot), General Assembly of, revived, 1872 R
German, Eisenarch, Conference of, 1852 R. *See also under* Evangelicals; Lutherans
Welsh, leave Anglican Church, 1811 R
Quakers. *See* Society of Friends
Relief Church of Scotland, 1847 R
Roman Catholic, Vatican Councils, 1870 R, 1962 R
sends observers to World Council of Churches meeting, 1961 R
statistics, 1945 Y
See also main index under Encyclical, papal; Papacy; Papal Bulls; Vatican
in Africa, statistics, 1962 Y
in Belgium, 1895 H

Religious Denominations—*contd.*
Roman Catholic—*contd.*
in Britain, penal laws against, eased, 1778 E, 1780 F
Catholic emancipation for, advocated, 1800 R
achieved, 1828 R
first M.P., 1829 O
appointment of bishops, 1810 R
hierarchy established, 1850 R
ecclesiastical titles act, 1851 R
repealed, 1871 R
converts to, 1845 R, 1850 R
joint prayers authorised, 1964 R
martyrs canonised, 1887 R
ruling on contraceptive pill, 1964 R
statistics, 1780 Y, 1869 Y, 1905 Y, 1930 Y, 1950 Y
in France, civil constitution of clergy, 1790 R
non-juring priests threatened with death penalty, 1793 R
concordat with Papacy, 1801 G
repealed, 1905 R
no longer state religion, 1830 H, R
worker-priest movement, 1943 R, 1965 R
statistics, 1945 Y
in Germany, aims at a national church, 1786 R
Ems articles rejected by Pius VI, 1789 R
Kulturkampf against, 1871 G
Ultramontane clergy, 1856 R, 1874 E
concordat with Papacy, 1933 G
statistics, 1945 Y
in Holland, hierarchy established, 1853 R
in Hungary, refuse concessions to government, 1948 M
in Italy, vernacular liturgy, 1786 R
in Poland, concordat is denounced, 1947 J
in Scotland, hierarchy is restored, 1878 R
statistics, 1905 Y, 1950 Y
in Spain, to be sole faith, 1851 C
property is nationalised, 1933 E
in Sweden, combated by Gustavus Adolphus Society, 1832 R
in Switzerland, protected by *Sonderbund*, 1845 M
in US, first bishopric:
plenary council, 1852 R
Sulpician seminary, 1791 R
statistics, 1840 Y, 1905 Y, 1936 Y, 1947 Y
Salvation Army, in Britain, founded, 1865 R 1878 R
Second Adventists, in US, 1831 R, 1842 R
Shakers, the, in US, 1774 R
Societé des Amis, Geneva, 1810 R
Society of Friends (Quakers), statistics, 1905 Y, 1936 Y, 1945 Y, 1947 Y, 1950 Y
Stundists, in Russia, 1858 R
Swedenborgians, in US, 1792 R
Unitarians, statistics, 1905 Y, 1936 Y, 1945 Y, 1947 Y, 1950 Y
United Brethren in Christ, US, 1800 R
United Church of Canada, 1925 R
United Church of Christ (Congregationalist and Evangelical), in US, 1958 R
United Free Church of Scotland, 1843 R
United Presbyterian Church, US, formed, 1958 R
United Secession Church of Scotland, 1847 R
US Federal Council of Churches, 1908 R
See also under Oecumenical Movement
Religious Orders and Committees:
Dominicans, 1838 R
Jesuits. *See main index under* Jesuits, The
in Austria, made independent of Rome, 1781 L
in Belgium, Louvain Seminary, 1786 K
in Britain, revived, 1862 R
Community of the Resurrection (Anglican), 1892 R
in France, orders, dissolved, 1792 R
prohibited from teaching, 1828 F
abolished, 1875 E, 1903 C
Communities, decree for non-authorised, 1800 C
Protestant Community of Taizé, 1944 R
in Hungary, dissolved, 1950 J
in Sardinia, contemplative orders dissolved, 1855 R
in US, Paulist Fathers, 1858 R
Sisters of Charity of St. Joseph, 1809 R
Religious Houses. *See* Monasteries
Religious Toleration:
is condemned by Gregory XVI, 1832 R
in Austria, 1781 K, 1782 C, 1894 R
in Belgium, 1831 B
in Bosnia and Herzegovina, demanded, 1875 M
in Britain, relief for Protestant Dissenting minister, 1778 E
Saville's Act modifies penal laws for Roman Catholics, 1778 E, 1780 F
registration of Dissenters' Chapels, 1779 R
position of Protestant Dissenters eased, 1812 R
Test and Corporation Acts, repealed, 1828 E
Catholic Emancipation, 1828 R
religious tests, for office, abolished, 1867 R
in universities, abolished, 1871 O
in Denmark, 1770 M
in France, opposed, 1767 R
for Protestants, 1787 R, 1795 B
toleration advocated, 1830 O
achieved, 1905 M
in Germany, advocated, 1777 R, 1783 R
emancipation of Jews, 1812 R
in Russia, 1766 R
in Turkey, 1856 B, 1876 M
in US, in Virginia, 1785 R
principles of, advocated by Presbyterians, 1788 R
Religious Experience (C. J. Webb), 1945 R
Reliques of Ancient English Poetry (T. Percy), 1765 U
Remak, Robert, G. biologist and naturalist (1815–1892), 1850 P
Remarque, Erich, G. author, 1929 U
Rembrandt, picture by, cleaning of, 1947 S
Remington, Philo, Am. manufacturer (1816–89), 1873 P
'Remus, Uncle.' *See* Harris, Joel Chandler
Rémuset, Jean Pierre Abel, F. orientalist (1788–1832), 1811 Q
Renan, Ernest, F. philosopher (1823–92), 1823 Z, 1857 R, 1859 R, 1863 R, 1883 R, 1892 Z
René (Chateaubriand), 1805 U
Renée Mauperin (J. Goncourt), 1864 U
Rennell, James, B. geographer (1742–1830), 1779 P
Renner, Karl, Aus. Socialist, 1919 C, 1945 D
elected president of Austria, 1945 M
Rennie, John, B. civil engineer (1761–1821), 1811 S
Renoir, Jean, F. film director (b. 1890), 1926 W, 1935 W, 1937 W, 1939 W, 1945 W
Renoir, Pierre Auguste, F. artist (1841–1919), 1841 Z, 1868 S, 1874 S, 1876 S, 1879 S, 1883 S, 1911 S, 1917 S, 1919 Z
Rent, treatise on, 1815 O
Reparations:
Bulgarian, to Allies, further payments renounced, 1932 B
China, to Japan, not honoured, 1913 J
Finland, to Russia, 1952 J
Germany, to Allies, Supreme Allied Council agrees on payments, 1920 F
Spa Conference on, 1920 G

Brussels Conference on, 1920 M
Allies fix payments, 1921 A
US representative is recalled from commission, 1921 B
Germany announces default, 1921 C
British Reparation Recovery Act, 1921 C
repealed, 1925 D
Germany's failure to pay leads to occupation of Ruhr, 1921 C, E
US declines to mediate in controversy, 1921 D
Commission fixes liability, 1921 D
Germany accepts Allies' ultimatum, 1921 E
to supply France with reparations in kind, 1921 K
Germany applies for moratorium, 1921 M
payments postponed by decision at Cannes Conference, 1922 A
to pay with raw materials, 1922 C
Bankers' Committee declines to recommend loan, 1922 F
Balfour Note on, 1922 H
Commission permits payments by instalments on Treasury bills, 1922 H
Commission declares Germany defaulted voluntarily, 1922 M
Commission appoints Dawes and McKenna Committees, 1923 L
Ruhr is occupied, 1923 A
Britain reduces reparations import duty, 1924 B
Reports of Dawes and McKenna Committees, 1924 D
approved, 1924 G
London Conference, 1924 G
Stresemann's discussions with Briand, 1926 J
Young Committee, 1928 M, 1929 F
Hague Conference, 1929 H
Young Plan, 1929 H
upheld by referendum, 1929 M
in force, 1930 E
to be made through Basle Bank, 1929 L
Hoover proposes moratorium, 1931 F
London protocol on, 1931 H
Brunning declares Germany will pay no more, 1932 A
Layton-Wiggin Report, for extending credit, 1931 H
Lausanne Conference, requires final payment, 1932 F
demanded by Russia, 1947 L
Russia cancels East German, 1953 H
Italy, Allies impose, 1947 B
Japan, terminated, 1949 E
See also War debts
Répétition, La (J. Anouilh), 1950 W
Reports, notable:
Annan Committee, on teaching of Russian, 1962 O
Barlow, on location of industry, 1940 O
Beeching, on reshaping British railways, 1963 O
Beveridge, on social security, 1942 O, 1943 B
Bodkin, on share-pushing, 1937 O
Bryce Committee, on German Atrocities, 1916 O
Buchanan, on traffic in towns, 1963 O
Capital Punishment, royal commission, 1953 O
Chadwick, on sanitary reform, 1842 O
Cruz, on apartheid, 1955 L
Dardanelles Commission, 1917 O
Denning, on the Profumo Affair, 1963 O
Durham, on Canada, 1839 B
Fleming, on independent schools, 1944 O
Geddes Economy Committee, 1922 O
Health of Towns, 1844 O
Irish Rebellion, Commission, 1916 O
Lytton, on Manchuria, 1932 K, 1933 B
Mesopotamia Campaign, 1917 O
Milner Holland, on London housing, 1965 O
Monckton, on Rhodesia and Nyasaland, 1960 K
Montagu-Chelmsford, on India, 1918 G
Newsom, on education, 1963 O
Northcote-Trevelyan, on Civil Service, 1854 O
Pilkington, on broadcasting, 1962 W
Radcliffe Tribunal, on security procedure, 1963 D
Randall Commission, on US foreign economic policy, 1954 A
Robbins Committee, on higher education, 1963 O
rejected by government, 1965 B
Rochdale Committee, on British docks, 1962 O
Sankey Coal Commission, 1919 B, O
Simon, on India, 1930 F
Smoking and Health, by Royal College of Physicians, 1962 P
Venereal Disease, Royal Commission on, 1916 O
Warren, on Kennedy's assassination, 1964 O
Wolfenden, on homosexual offences and prostitution, 1957 J
Yarmolinsky, on US security precautions, 1955 O
See also under Committees and Commissions; Plans
Report on Radiation and the Quantum Theory (Jeans), 1914 P
Reppe, J., inventor of artificial fabrics, 1930 P
Representative, The (R. W. Emerson), 1850 U
Representative, The (R. Hochhuth), 1963 W
Republicans. *See under* Political Parties
République universalle, La (J. B. Cloots), 1792 O
Requiem for a Nun (W. Faulkner), 1953 U
Resaca de la Palma, New Mexico, battle, 1846 E
Resale price maintenance, in Britain, 1964 G
Researches, Chemical and Philosophical, Chiefly Concerning Nitrous Oxide (H. Davy), 1800 P
Reasearches in Electricity (M. Faraday), 1839 P
Researches on the Chemistry of Proteins (E. Fisher), 1907 P
Resection of oesophagus, 1872 P
Reshaping of British Railways, The (Dr. R. Beeching), 1963 O
Resina, Macedonia, 1908 G
Resnais, Alain, F. film director, 1956 W, 1959 W, 1961 W, 1964 W
Respighi, Ottorino, It. musican (1879–1936), 1917 T, 1922 T, 1924 T
Respiration, study of, 1780 P
Ressel, Joseph, Aus. engineer (1793–1857), 1827 P
Restaurants, public, first, 1770 U
Restrictive Practices in Britain:
Court, is established, 1956 G
first case before, 1958 O
upholds net book agreement, 1962 O
White Paper, 1964 O
Resurrection (L. Tolstoy), 1899 U
Rethel, Alfred, G. wood-engraver (1816–59), 1849 S
Retraite Sentimentale, La (Colette), 1908 U
Retreat from Truth (G. R. Mure), 1959 R
Return of the Native, The (T. Hardy), 1878 U
Réunion, Isle, Indian Ocean, becomes a French Colony, 1764 N
Reusch, Franz Heinrich, G. theologian (Old Catholic) (1823–1900), 1883 R
Reuter, Ernst, G. Social Democrat, Chief Burgomeister of Berlin (1889–1953), 1948 M
Reval, Estonia, 1908 F
Rêve et la Vie, La (G. de Nerval), 1855 U
Revett, Nicholas, B. architect and draughtsman (1720–1804), 1794 Q
Reviews (publications). *See* Journals

Reviews (Theatrical):
Beyond the Fringe, 1961 W
Bing Boys of Broadway, The, 1918 W
Boy Friend, The, 1945 W
Bubbly, 1917 W
Dancing Years, The, 1939 W
Glamorous Nights, 1935 W
Pins and Needles, 1937 W
Salad Days, 1954 W
Revolt in the Desert (T. E. Lawrence), 1927 O
Revolt of Islam (P. B. Shelley), 1817 U
Revolt of the Masses (Ortega y Gasset), 1930 O
Revolution in Philosophy, The (A. J. Ayer), 1956 R
Revolution in Tanner's Lane, The (M. Rutherford), 1888 U
Revolution of the Robots (F. Pollock and A. Weber), 1956 O
Revolutions. *See* Rebellions and Revolutions
Revolution Society, The (London), 1789 L
Revolver, Colt's, 1835 P. *See also under* Arms
Reyes, Rafael, Colombian dictator, 1904 G
Reynaud, Paul, F. politician (b. 1878), 1940 C, F
Reynolds, Sir Joshua, B. artist (1723–92), 1764 U, 1768 S, 1773 S, 1775 S, 1780 S, 1784 S, 1786 S, 1787 S, 1892 Z
statue of, 1931 S
Reza Khan, usurps Persian Throne, 1925 K
Rhapsodies:
Bolero (Ravel), 1928 T
Brigg Fair (Delius), 1907 T
Capriccio (Stravinsky), 1928 T
España (Chabrier), 1883 T
Fantasia on a theme by Tallis (R. Vaughan Williams), 1909 T
On a theme of Paganini (S. Rachmaninoff), 1935 T
Rhapsody in Blue (G. Gershwim), 1924 T
Spanish Rhapsody (M. Ravel), 1907 T
Rhee, Syngman, Korean president (b. 1875), 1948 H, 1960 D
Rheims, France: Germans occupy, 1914 J; Allies recapture, 1914 J; Germans take, 1918 E
Rheumatism, cure for, 1949 R
Rhine, Joseph Banks, Am. philosopher (b. 1895), 1935 R
Rhine, Confederation of, 1815 F
Rhine, River, Europe:
French army reaches, 1794 K
France cedes conquests on right bank, 1795 D
Austrian conquests on right bank, 1795 J
Moreau's campaign, 1796 F
Prussia yields land on left bank to France, 1796 H
cession of left bank to France agreed upon, 1797 K
free navigation, 1797 K
France annexes left bank, 1798 C
France is assigned left bank, 1801 B
British troops reach, 1945 B
Dempsey crosses, 1945 C
Rhineland, The: ceded to Prussia, 1815 F; US troops evacuate, 1922 C; costs of US army in, 1923 E; French troops evacuate, 1925 G; Franco-German discussions on, 1926 J; Allied evacuation of, 1929 H, L, 1930 F; Germany occupies demilitarized zone, 1936 C
Rhinoceros, The (E. Ionescu), 1960 W
Rhinoscope, invented, 1860 P
Rhode Island, state, US: as British Colony, 1772 F; Howe captures, 1776 J; Dorr Rebellion, 1841 K
Rhodes, Cecil John, B. imperialist and benefactor (1853–1902), 1853 Z, 1888 K, O, 1902 Z; heads S. Africa Company, 1889 K; becomes premier of Cape Province, 1890 G; resigns premiership, 1896 A; connexion with Jameson Raid, 1897 G
Rhodesia (formerly S. Rhodesia):
is organised by British S. Africa Company, 1895 E
votes against joining Union of S. Africa, 1922 K
constitution for, 1923 K
Federation of N. and S. Rhodesia and Nyasaland in force, 1953 K. *See also* Central African Federation
state of emergency, 1959 B
UN Trusteeship Committee resolves to consider whether full self-government is attained, 1962 B
asks Britain not to transfer Federation forces to, 1963 K
Nationalist movement in, is banned, 1964 H
Wilson warns that a UDI would be an act of defiance, 1964 K
Nkomo placed in a restriction area, 1964 L
referendum favours independence, 1964 L
Smith rejects visit by Commonwealth Secretary, 1964 L
appoints 'accredited' representative to Lisbon, 1965 J
Wilson's talks with Smith, 1965 K
Archbishop Ramsey's remarks on the use of force, 1965 K
Smith makes UDI, 1965 L
Britain declares Smith regime illegal, 1965 L
Britain imposes trade and exchange restrictions, 1965 L
nine African states sever relations with Britain for not using force against rebels, 1965 M
Britain imposes oil embargo, 1965 M
Rhodesia, Northern:
German troops surrender, 1918 L
Federation with S. Rhodesia and Nyasaland in force, 1953 K. *See also* Central African Federation
become independent republic, 1964 K
is renamed Zambia, 1964 K
See also under Zambia
Rhodesian Front. *See under* Political Parties
Rhondda, Margaret, Lady (1883–1958), B. Liberal, attempts to take seat as peer, 1922 O
Rhymes from Various Sonorous Sources (Pousseur), 1959 T
Ribbentrop, Joachim von, G. diplomat, National Socialist (1893–1946), 1893 Z
as foreign minister, 1938 B
sentenced by Nuremberg Tribunal, 1946 J
Ribot, Alexandre Félix Joseph, F. politician (1842–1927), 1895 A, L, 1917 C
Ricardo, David, B. economist (1772–1823), 1772 Z, 1809 O, 1817 O
Ricci, Lorenzo, It. bishop of Pistoria and Prata, 1786 R
Rice, Elmer, Am. dramatist (b. 1892), 1923 W, 1929 W, 1930 W
Riceyman Steps (A. Bennett), 1923 U
Richard of Bordeaux (G. Daviot), 1933 W
Richardson, Dorothy (Mrs. Alan Odle), B. author (d. 1957), 1927 U
Richardson, Tony, B. stage and film director (b. 1928), 1959 W
Richelieu, Armand Emmanuel Sophie Septemanie du Plessis, Duc de, F. royalist politician (1766–1822), 1818 M, 1820 B, C, 1821 M
Richet, Charles, F. physician, 1902 P
Rich Man, Poor Man (J. Hilton), 1944 O
Richmond, duke of. *See* Lennox
Richmond, Sir William Blake, B. artist (1842–1921), 1891 S

Richmond, Virginia, US surrenders to Grant, 1865 D
Richter, Hans, G. musician (1843–1912), 1876 T
Richter, Jean Paul Friedrich, G. author under pseudonym 'Jean Paul' (1763–1825), 1763 Z, 1793 U, 1795 U, 1796 U, 1800 U, 1804 U, 1807 U, 1825 Z
Riddle of the Universe, The (E. Haeckel), 1899 P
Riders to the Sea (J. M. Synge), 1904 W
Ridgway, Matthew Bunker, Am. general (b. 1895), succeeds MacArthur in Korea, 1951 D; breaks off Korea armistice talks, 1951 H; becomes supreme Allied Commander in Europe, 1952 D
Ried, Austria, Treaty, Bavaria with Austria, 1813 K
Riel, Louis, Can. insurgent (1844–85), 1869 K
Riemann, Georg Friedrich Bernhard, G. mathematician (1826–66), 1854 P
Rienzi (Lytton), 1835 O
Riesman, David, Am. sociologist, 1951 R
Rieti, Naples, Italy, Austrians crush rebels at, 1821 C
Riga, Latvia: Germans attack, 1917 H, J; Bolsheviks take, 1919 A; Treaty, between Russia and Poland, 1921 B, C
Right of Search, British, countered by Armed Neutrality, 1780 C, L
Rights of Man, The (T. Paine), 1791 O, 1792 M, O
Rights of Neutral Nations in Time of War, The (D. Webster), 1802 O
Rilke, Rainer Maria, G. poet (1875–1926), 1875 Z, 1907 U, 1911 U, 1922 U, 1926 Z
Rimbaud, Arthur, F. author (1854–91), 1854 Z, 1873 U, 1886 U, 1891 Z, 1895 U
Rime of the Ancient Mariner (S. T. Coleridge), 1798 U
Rimnik, near Martinesti, Wallachia, Turkish defeat at, 1789 J
Rimsky-Korsakov, Nicholas, R. musician (1844–1908), 1844 Z, 1865 T, 1873 T, 1882 T, 1888 T, 1908 Z, 1910 T
Ring and the Book, The (R. Browning), 1868 U
Ringed with Vision (O. Kokoshka), 1962 S
Ring Round the Moon (C. Fry—J. Anouilh), 1947 W
Rinnovamente Civile d'Italia, Il (V. Gioberti), 1851 O
Rio de Janeiro, Brazil: as capital of Portuguese colonies in S. America, 1776 N; non-aggression pact, 1933 K; treaty of Mutual Assistance, by American Republics, 1947 J
Rio de la Plata (Argentina), revolts against Joseph Bonaparte, 1810 E
Rio Grande, US troops sent to, 1911 A
Riots and Risings:
  in Aegean Isles, against Turks, in Samos, 1912 J
  in Albania, by Moslems, 1937 E
  in Algiers, 1846 A
    against French, 1881 G
    by Nationalists, 1945 E, 1954 L, M, 1955 A
    by Europeans, 1960 A
  in Argentina, at Córdoba, 1955 H
  in Armenia, by Nationalist Revolutionaries, 1890 M
  in Ashanti, suppressed, 1900 L
  in Austria, by Socialists, 1927 G
  in Austrian Netherlands, 1787 A
  in Bosnia and Herzegovina, against Turks, 1875 G, M
  in Brazil, 1914 C
  in Britain, pro-Wilkes riots, 1764 A, 1768 E
    Gordon Riots, 1780 F
    against sympathisers with French Revolution, 1791 G
    Spa Fields Riots, 1816 M
    in Derbyshire, 1817 F
    in Bristol, 1831 K
    by Chartists, 1839 G, L, 1842 H
    election riots, 1874 B
    in Wales, 1911 C
    by Suffragettes, 1911 L
    at London Docks, 1912 G
    provoked by government economies, 1931 J
  in British Guiana, 1962 B, 1963 D, 1964 C
  in Bulgaria, 1876 A, E
  in Canada, in Montreal, against British, 1849 D
    in Quebec, by Nationalists, 1964 E
  in China, Boxer Rising, 1900 F, 1901 J
  in Congo, by Arab Slave-holders, 1892 L
    of Bartebelas, 1897 J
    anti-Belgian, 1959 A
  in Crete, of Christians, against Turks, 1894 N, 1896 G, 1897 B
  in Cuba, 1875 J, 1895 N
  in Cyprus, between Greeks and Turks, 1963 M
  in Czechslovakia, 1937 K
  in Eastern Rumelia, 1885 J
  in Egypt, Nationalist Risings, 1881 J, 1882 F, 1919 C, 1921 E
    anti-British, 1952 A, 1964 M
  in Ethiopia, pro-British, 1941 A
  in France, bread riots in Paris, 1795 D
    by Lyons silk-weavers, 1831 L, 1834 D
    by Republicans, in Paris, 1834 D
    by Communists, in Paris, 1849 F
    anti-government, in Paris, 1934 B
    anti-OAS, in Paris, 1962 B
  in Formosa, 1787 N
  in Germany, by students, 1817 K
    in Hamburg, by Communists, 1921 C
    in Rhineland, by Separatists, 1923 L
    anti-Communist, in East Berlin, 1953 F
  in German East Africa, by Arabs, 1888 J
    by Moslems, 1905 N
  in German South West Africa, 1904 K, 1907 J
  in Greece, in Thessaly, 1878 A
    pro-Venizelos rising, suppressed, 1935 C
    in Athens, about Cyprus issue, 1954 M
  in Holland, 1787 F, J
  in India, by Mohammedans, in Calcutta, 1918 J
    in Delhi, 1924 G
    anti-Muslim riots, 1964 C
    food riots, 1964 L
  in Iran, by Communists, in Aberdaijan, 1945 L
  in Ireland, at Dublin, 1822 M
    in Tipperary, 1848 G
    Sinn Fein, in Dublin, 1914 G, 1917 F
      and Unionist Riots in Belfast, 1920 G
    anti-Roman Catholic, in Belfast, 1935 G
  in Italy, riots in Sicily, 1894 N
    between Communists and Fascists, in Florence, 1921 B
    between Fascists and Socialists, 1922 H
  in Jamaica, riots, 1839 E
  in Japan, by students, against treaty with US, 1960 F
  in Korea, anti-Chinese, 1931 G
    of Communist prisoners at Koje Camp, 1952 E
  in Matabeleland, against British Africa Company, 1893 G, 1896 K
  in Mozambique, 1895 N
  in Morocco, 1955 H
  in New Zealand, Maori Risings, 1845 C, 1863 E
  in Nyasaland, 1959 B
  in Pakistan, riots in Karachi, 1953 A
  in Panama, 1964 A
  in Peru, at Lima, 1964 E
  in Philippines, 1896 H
    against US, 1899 B, C

Riots and Risings—*contd.*
in Poland, 1794 C, L
in Cracow, 1846 B, C, L
Warsaw Rising, 1944 H
Labour riots at Poznan, 1956 F
in Portugal, Miguelist Rising, 1846 E
Royalist rising, 1913 K, 1915 E, 1919 D
in Puerto Rico, Nationalist rising, 1950 K
in Rhodesia, rising by Matabeles, 1893 G, 1896 C, K
in N. Rhodesia, 1964 G
in S. Rhodesia, 1964 A
in Rumania, by Serbs in Belgrade, 1862 F
agrarian rising, 1888 D
in Russia, Decembrist rising, 1825 M
riots in Moscow, 1915 F
risings in Georgia, by Stalinists, 1956 L
African students riot in Moscow, 1963 M
in South Africa, race riots, 1950 A
in Spain, risings against Espartero, 1842 K
Carlist risings, 1873 D, J
in Catalonia, 1909 G
by anarchists and Syndicalists, in Barcelona, 1933 A
by Radicals, 1933 M
in Syria, 1925 K
in Switzerland, of Prussian royalist, against Neufchatel republic, 1856 J
in Tangier, anti-French, 1952 C
in Tibet, against China, 1959 L
in Turkey, by Janissaries, 1826 F
Army, 1909 D
anti-Greek, in Istanbul, 1955 J
by students, 1960 D
in US, by Sioux, in Minnesota, 1862 H
by Knights of Labor, in Chicago, 1886 E
race riots, in Chicago, 1919 G
over desegregation in schools, 1963 J
race riots, in Harlem, 1964 G
in Los Angeles, 1965 H
in Viet Nam, riots in Saigon, 1964 L
in Zanzibar, 1961 F
See also under Coup d'états; Rebellions and Revolutions
Rip Van Winkle (W. Irving), 1809 U
Rise and Progress of the Arts of Design in the U.S. (W. Dunlap), 1834 S
Rise of Christianity, The (E. W. Barnes), 1947 R
Rise of the Dutch Republic, The (J. R. Motley), 1856 Q
Risings. *See* Riots and Risings
Ristich, Jovan, Serb. regent (1831–99), 1876 F, 1889 C
Ristori, Adelaide, It. actress (1822–1906), 1855 W
Ritter, Karl, G. geographer, 1817 P
Rivals, The (R. B. Sheridan), 1775 W
Rivera, Miguel de Primo, Sp. dictator, 1923 J, 1930 A
River Line, The (C. Morgan), 1949 W
Riviera, French, British land in, 1944 H
Rivière Endormie, La (D. Milhaud), 1954 T
Rivoli, Italy, Austrian defeat at, 1797 A
Rivonia trial, S. Africa, 1964 F, L
Road carriage, steam, 1769 P
Roads:
Autobahn, in Germany, 1932 P
construction of, 1764 P, 1815 P
Hammersmith, flyover, 1961 S
M.1 motorway, 1959 P
road surface-heating cables, 1961 S
speed limit, in Britain, 1935 C
Telford's, in Scottish Highlands, 1802 P
Road to Wigan Pier, The (G. Orwell), 1937 U
Road Traffic, Buchanan Report on, 1963 P
Roanoke Island, N. Carolina, US, Unionists take, 1862 B
Robbe-Grillet, Alain, F. author (b. 1922), 1960 U
Robbery Under Arms (R. Boldrewood), 1888 U
Robbins, Jerome, Am. choreographer (b. 1918), 1946 T, 1950 T, 1959 T
Robbins, Lionel, lord Robbins, B. economist (b. 1898), 1963 O
Robert, N. L., F. inventor, 1798 P
Roberts, Frederick, lord Roberts, B. soldier (1832–1914), as C-in-C in S. Africa, 1900 A, C, G,
Robertson, Anna M. ('Grandma Moses'), Am. artist, 1939 S
Robertson, William, B. historian (1721–93), 1769 Q, 1771 Q, 1793 Z
Robertson, Sir William, B. soldier (1860–1933), 1915 M
Robeson, Paul, Am. singer and actor, 1898 Z
Robespierre, Maxmilien François Marie Isadore de, F. revolutionary (1758–94), 1790 N, 1793 G, 1794 G, R
Robey, Sir George, B. comedian (1869–1954), 1917 W
Robinson, Frederick John, viscount Goderich, earl of Ripon, B. Tory (1782–1859), 1827 H, 1828 A
Robinson, G. N., B. chemist, 1960 P
Robinson, Heath, B. humorist (1872–1944), 1872 Z, 1944 Z
Robinson, Henry Crabb, B. journalist (1775–1867), 1808 V
Robinson, John, B. bishop of Woolwich (b. 1919), 1963 R
Robinson, Mary ('Perdita'), B. actress (1758–1800), 1780 S
Rob Roy (W. Scott), 1818 U
Rochambeau, Jean Baptiste Donation de Vimeur, F. soldier (1725–1807), 1780 G
Rochdale pioneers of co-operation, 1844 O
Rochdale, Lancs, England, by-election, 1958 B
Rochdale Committee on British Docks, 1962 O
Rochebouet, Gaetan de Grimaudet de, F. politician, 1877 L
Rochefort, Henri, Marquis de Rochefort Lucay, F. Communard (1830–1912), 1871 G
Rock and Roll dancing, 1956 W
Rockefeller, John Davison, Am. industrialist and philanthropist (1839–1937), 1839 Z, 1870 P, 1937 Z
Rockefeller, Nelson, Am. politician (b. 1908), 1908 Z
Rockefeller Foundation, 1913 O, 1940 P
'Rockers', hooliganism by, 1964 C, E
Rockets:
artillery, 1805 P
ballistic, 1959 F
German V2, 1942 P, 1944 J, 1945 C
pilotless, 1946 P
space, 1958 P, 1959 P, 1963 P
See also under Atomic weapons; Aviation
Rockingham, marquess of. *See* Watson-Wentworth
Rock Pool, The (C. Connolly), 1935 U
Roderick Hudson (H. James), 1876 U
Rodgers, Richard, Am. musician (b. 1902), 1943 W
Rodin, Auguste, F. sculptor (1840–1917), 1840 Z, 1864 S, 1877 S, 1879 S, 1884 S, 1898 S, 1900 S, 1902 S
Rodney, George Brydges, B. admiral (1719–92), 1780 A, D, 1782 D
Roebuck, John, B. chemist and inventor (1718–94), 1794 Z
Roehan, Ernst, G. Politician, executed, 1934 F

Rogers, Samuel, B. poet (1763–1855), 1792 U
Rogue Herries (H. Walpole), 1930 U
Rohan, Louis René Edouard de, F. Cardinal Archbishop of Strasbourg (1734–1803), 1785 H
Rohe, Ludwig, Mies von de, Am. architect (b. 1886), 1958 S, 1963 S
Rohilkland (now Bareilly), India, 1774 D
Rohillas, tribe of Afghan marauders, 1774 D
Roi s'amuse, Le (V. Hugo), 1832 W
Rokeby Venus (of Velasquez), damaged by Suffragettes, 1914 C
Roland de la Platière, Jean Marie, F. Girondin leader (1734–93), 1792 L
Roland, Manon Jean, F. author (1754–93), 1793 U
Rolf Krage (J. Ewald), 1770 W
Rolland, Romain, F. author (1866–1944), 1866 Z, 1904 U, 1943 U, 1944 Z
Roller-bearings, 1910 P
Roll-film, celluloid, 1889 P
Rolling-mill, steam, 1790 P
Rolls-Royce motor company, 1904 P
'Rolls, Series', of Chronicles and Memorials of the Middle Ages, 1857 Q
Romains, Jules, F. author (b. 1885), 1932 U
Romagna, Italy, 1797 B, G, 1801 G
Roman alphabet, Turkey adopts, 1928 L
Roman Catholicism. *See* Religious Denominations
Romances sans Paroles (P. Verlaine), 1874 U
Roman Constitutional Law (T. Mommsen), 1871 Q
Roman de l'énergie nationale, Le (M. Barrès), 1897 U
Roman d'un jeune homme pauvre (O. Feuillet), 1858 U
Romanes, George John, Can. scientist (1848–94), 1878 R, 1888 R, 1892 R
Romanes Lectures, at Oxford, notable, 1892 Q, 1958 S
Roman History (B. Niebuhr), 1811 Q
Roman Law, in Canada, 1774 D
Roman Republic established, 1798 B, 1849 B
Roman Russe, Le (E. Vogué), 1886 U
Romanset language, 1937 O
Romantic Movement in England, 1765 U, 1800 U
Romany Rye, The (G. Borrow), 1857 U
Romanzero (H. Heine), 1851 U
Rome, Italy:
  French take, 1798 B
  Republic established, 1798 B
  Ferdinand IV enters, 1798 L
  French recapture, 1798 M
  French occupation, 1808 B
  restoration of art treasures to, 1815 S
  Republic proclaimed, 1849 E
  French troops restore Pius IX, 1849 G
  Pius IX revokes constitution, 1850 D
  French garrison in, 1850 D
  Italy renounces claim to, 1864 J
  Garibaldi's march on, 1867 K
  Italian troops enter, 1870 H
  becomes capital of Italy, 1870 K
  Conference of criminal anthropologists at, 1887 O
  Mussolini's march on, 1922 K
  Conference on Immigration, 1924 E
  Protocol, Italy with Austria and Hungary, 1934 C
  Pact, between Italy, Austria and Hungary, 1936 C
  Air raids on, 1943 G
  Fifth Army enters, 1944 F
  Conference of EDC foreign ministers, 1953 B
  Treaties, for Common Market and Euratom, 1957 C
  Olympic Games at, 1960 X
Rome—buildings and institutions in:
  Archaeological Institute, 1829 Q
  Braccio Nuovia, Vatican Museum, 1817 S
  Catacombs, The, 1864 Q
  International Agricultural Institute, 1905 O
  Palazzo delo Sport, 1956 S
  Pio-Clemantiano Museum, 1769 Q
  Railway Station, 1950 S
  Vatican Library, discovery in, 1819 Q
Romé de L'Isle, Jean Baptiste Louis, F. mineralogist (1736–90), 1772 P
Rommel, Erwin, G. general, 1941 B, D; retreats in, N. Africa, 1941 M; new offensives, 1942 A, E; takes Tobruk, 1942 F; retreats after El Alamein, 1942 L; replaced by von Arnim, 1943 D
Romney, George, B. artist (1734–1802), 1775 S
Roncalli, Angelo, It. Cardinal (1881–1963), elected Pope John XXII, 1958 K. *See also under* John XXIII
Röntgen, Wilhelm, G. physicist (1845–1923), 1895 P
Room at the Top (J. Braine), 1957 U
Room of One's Own (V. Woolf), 1929 U
Room With a View, A (E. M. Forster), 1908 U
Roon, Albert von, Prussian minister of war, 1859 M
Roosevelt, Anna Eleanor, Am., wife of F. D. Roosevelt, chairman of UNESCO Commission on human rights (1884–1962), 1962 Z
Roosevelt, Franklin Delano, Am. statesmen, Democrat (1882–1945), 32nd president of US (1933–45), 1882 Z, 1934 F, 1941 O
  nominated vice-president, 1920 G
  elected president, 1932 L
  inauguration, 1933 C
  New Deal, 1933 C, 1937 J
  Congress grants wide powers to, 1933 C
  opposes currency stabilization, 1933 F
  signs Social Security Act, 1935 H
  re-elected, 1936 L
  signs Neutrality Act, 1937 E
  defence budget, 1939 A
  asks Hitler and Mussolini for assurances against aggression, 1932 D
  'Cash and Carry' bill, 1939 L
  re-elected, 1940 L
  sends Lend-Lease bill to Congress, 1941 A
  meets Churchill in W. Atlantic, 1941 H
  vetoes anti-strike act, 1943 G
  at Quebec Conference, 1943 H
  at Cairo Conference, 1943 L
  at Teheran Conference, 1943 L
  at Yalta Conference, 1945 B
  death, 1945 D
Roosevelt, Theodore, Am. statesman, Republican (1859–1919), 26th president of US (1901–9), 1859 Z, 1900 F, 1902 F, 1907 F, 1919 Z
  succeds as president on McKinley's death 1901 J
  ends coal strike, 1902 K
  re-elected, 1904 L
  mediates between Russia and Japan, 1905 J
  intervenes in Cuba, 1906 B
  on 'the New Nationalism', 1910 H
  proposes new Progressive Republican Party, 1912 F, H
  declines nomination, 1916 F
  as author, 1914 Q
Root, Elihu, Am. lawyer and statesman (1845–1937), 1845 Z, 1917 F, 1937 Z
Roots (A. Wesker), 1959 W
Roquebrune, France, purchased from Monaco, 1862 B
Rosas, Juan de, Argent. dictator, 1835 N, 1852 B
Rose and the Ring, The (W. M. Thackeray), 1855 U
Rosebery, lord. *See* Primrose, Archibald
Rosenbergs, Am. atomic spies, 1953 F

Rosenberg, Arthur, G. author, 1930 O
Rosmersholm (H. Ibsen), 1886 W
Ross, Sir James Clark, B. admiral and explorer (1800–62), 1841 P
Ross, Sir John, B. Arctic navigator (1777–1856), 1818 P
Ross, Mrs. of Wyoming, Am. first woman governor of a state, 1925 A
Ross, Sir Ronald, B. discoverer of the mosquito cycle in malaria (1857–1932), 1857 Z, 1879 P, 1932 Z
Ross (T. Rattigan), 1960 W
Rosselini, Roberto, It. film director (b. 1906), 1945 W, 1946 W
Rossen, Robert, Am. film director, 1949 W
Rossetti, Dante Gabriel, B. artist and poet (1828–82), 1828 Z, 1882 Z
 as artist, 1848 S, 1863 S
 as poet, 1870 U, 1881 U
Rossi, Michele de, It. archaeologist, 1864 Q
Rossini, Gioacchino, It. musician (1792–1868), 1792 Z, 1810 T, 1812 R, 1813 T, 1816 T, 1817 T, 1818 T, 1828 T, 1829 T, 1841 T, 1868 Z
Rossiter, Clinton, Am. political scientist, 1956 O
Rostand, Edmond, F. author (1868–1918), 1868 Z, 1879 U, 1900 U, 1918 Z
Rostov on Don, Russia: Germans evacuate, 1941 L; Germans take, 1942 G; Russians recapture, 1943 B
Rostovziev, M., R. later Am. historian (1870–1952), 1926 Q
Rothamsted, Herts., England, experimental plant station at, 1843 P
Rothenstein, Sir William, B. artist (1872–1945), 1917 S, 1924 S
Rothermere, lord. *See* Harmsworth, Harold
Rothière, La, France, battle, 1814 B
Rothschild, lord. *See* Meyer, Nathan
Rôtisserie de la Reine Pédauque (A. France), 1893 U
Rotocycle, invented, 1958 P
Rouault, Georges, F. artist (1871–1958), 1906 S, 1916 S, 1925 S, 1938 S
Rouge et le Noir, Le (Stendhal), 1830 U
Rouget de Lisel, Claude Joseph, F. author (1760–1836), 1792 T, 1915 T
Rougon-Macquart, Les, series of novels (E. Zola), 1871 U
Roumania:
 created by unification of Moldavia and Wallachia, 1861 M
 monarchy in, 1866 B
 Russians invade, 1877 D
 declares war on Turkey, 1877 E
 to be independent, 1878 C, G
 union with Transylvania proclaimed, 1918 L
 Russia invades, 1940 F
 asks for German protection, 1940 G
 Russians enter, 1944 D, H
 armistice with Russia, 1944 J
Rousseau, Henri, F. artist (1844–1910), 1904 S, 1905 S, 1907 S, 1909 S, 1910 S
Rousseau, Jean Jacques, F. philosopher (1712–78), 1763 O, 1767 T, 1781 U, 1778 Z
Rousseau, Pierre Etienne Théodore, F. artist (1812–1867), 1831 S
Roussel, Albert, F. musician (1869–1937), 1917 T, 1923 T, 1928 T
Roussillon, S. France, Spain invades, 1793 C
Rouvier, Maurice, F. Republican (1842–1930), 1887 E, 1905 E
Rowing:
 Henley Royal Regatta, 1839 X
 Oxford and Cambridge Boat Race, 1829 X
Rowlandson, Thomas, B. artist and caricaturist (1756–1827), 1784 S
Rowntree, Joseph, B. manufacturer and philanthropist, 1836 Z, 1925 Z
Rowntree, Seebolm B., B. chocolate manufacturer and sociologist (1871–1954), 1901 O, 1937 O, 1941 O, 1947 O
Rowse, Alfred Leslie, B. historian (b. 1903), 1950 Q
Royal Academy, London, founded, 1768 S
Royal Academy of Music, London, founded, 1861 T
Royal Dutch Shell Oil Group, formed, 1907 O
 operations in Indonesia, banned, 1958 F
Royal Flying Corps, formed, 1912 O; replaced by Royal Air Force, 1918 D
Royal Historical Society, founded, 1868 Q
Royal Hunt of the Sun, The (P. Shaffer), 1964 W
Royal Institute, The, founded, 1799 P
Royalists. *See under* Political Parties
Royal Literary Fund, founded, 1790 U
Royal Marriage Act, in Britain, 1772 C
Royal Niger Company, British, 1886 G
Royal Society, sponsors board of scientific studies, 1916 P
 committee on emigration of scientists, 1963 B
Royce, Sir Frederick Henry, B. automobile engineer (1863–1933), 1863 Z, 1933 Z
Royden, Agnes Maude (Mrs. G. W. H. Shaw), B. Congregational minister (1876–1956), 1917 R
Ruanda, East Africa: is ceded to Britain, 1921 C; republic proclaimed, 1961 A; UN calls for elections, 1961 D; independence, 1962 G
Rubaiyát of Omar Khayyam (E. Fitzgerald), 1859 U
Rubber production, comparative statistics, 1911 Y, 1957 Y
Rubber, synthetic, 1902 Y, 1931 P
 production, comparative statistics, 1944 Y, 1957 Y
Rubber tyre, 1888 P
Rubber, vulcanised, 1839 P
Rubbra, Edmond, B. musician (b. 1901), 1942 T, 1949 T, 1954 T
Rubidium, an element, is isolated, 1861 P
Ruby, Jack, Am. strip-tease parlour proprietor, shoots Kennedy's assassin, 1963 L
Ruckert, Friedrich, G. poet (1788–1866), 1814 U
Rudin (I. Turgeniev), 1855 U
Rudini, Antonio Starabba, marquis di, It. statesman (1839–1908), 1896 C, 1891 A, 1892 E, 1898 F
Rudolf, Crown Prince, Archduke of Austria (1857–1889), 1889 A
Ruff's Guide to the Turf, 1842 X
Rugby, Warwickshire, England, School, under Arnold, 1828 O
Rugby Football, 1924 X
Rügen, E. Germany: French occupation, 1812 A; Prussians enter, 1814 A; ceded to Prussia, 1815 F
Ruggiero, Guido de, It. philosopher, 1947 R
Ruhr, W. Germany: German evacuation, demanded, 1920 D; French occupation, 1921 C, E, J; Franco-Belgian occupation, 1923 A; evacuation, 1924 L, H; bombing, 1943 D, E; International Authority constituted, 1948 M, Germany joins, 1949 L
Raines, on méditations sur les révolutions des empires, Les (C. Volney), 1791 Q
Rumelia, Eastern, 1878 G; disturbances in, 1885 J, L, 1886 D, E
Rumford, Count. *See* Thompson, Benjamin
Runciman, Sir Stephen, B. historian (b. 1903), 1951 Q, 1955 Q, 1958 Q
Runciman, Walter, viscount Runciman, B. Liberal National (1870–1949), visits Prague, 1938 G
Runge, Philipp Otto, G. artist (1777–1810), 1805 S

Runyon, Alfred Damon, Am. author and journalist, 1884 Z, 1946 Z
R.U.R. (Čapek), 1923 W
Rural credits, US, 1916 O
Rural Rides (W. Cobbett), 1830 U
Rush-Bagot agreement, 1817 D
Rusk, Dean, Am. diplomat (b. 1909), 1909 Z
Ruskin, John, B. author, artist and social reformer (1819–1900), 1819 Z, 1900 Z; as author, 1865 U, 1871 O; as artist, 1843 S, 1849 S, 1851 S, 1919 S; Whistler's libel action against, 1878 S
Ruslan and Ludmila (A. Pushkin), 1820 U
Russell, Bertrand, earl Russell, B. philosopher (b. 1872), 1872 Z, 1900 R, 1910 R, 1914 R, 1918 R, 1921 O, 1927 R, 1934 O, 1946 R, 1949 O
Russell, Francis, fifth duke of Bedford, B. Whig (1765–1805), 1796 O
Russell, George William, B. poet under pseudonym 'AE' (1867–1935), 1867 Z, 1901 U, 1935 Z
Russell, John, duke of Bedford, B. Whig politician (1710–71), 1763 R
Russell, lord John, B. Whig-Liberal statesman (1792–1878), 1792 Z, 1845 M, 1864 D, 1878 Z
campaigns for Parliamentary Reform, 1819 M, 1821 E, 1831 C
William IV refuses his appointment as leader of Commons, 1834 L
is converted to free trade, 1845 L
becomes prime minister, 1846 F
resigns, but returns to premiership, 1851 B
resigns, 1852 B
forms second ministry, 1865 K
resigns, 1866 F
Russia (Union of Soviet Socialist Republics):
intrigues in Poland, 1767 D, L, 1768 H
share in first partition of Poland, 1772 H
acquires Oldenburg, 1773 K
acquires the Crimea and mouth of R. Dnieper, 1774 G
Russia plans to restore Greek empire, 1781 B
share in second partition of Poland, 1793 A, E
share in third partition of Poland, 1795 H, K
frontier treaty with US, over Alaska, 1824 D
USSR recognised as 'a great power', 1922 D
Union is formally established, 1923 A
Britain recognises USSR, 1924 B
US recognises USSR, 1933 L
Germany invades, 1941 F
Russia (R. Cobden), 1835 O
Russia America Company, 1799 O
Russia at War (A. Werth), 1964 Q
Russian literature, introduced to England, 1821 U
Russophobia:
in Britain, 1835 O, 1838 K, 1878 A, C, F, 1904 K, 1923 E. *See also* Wars, Crimean War
in Germany, 1770 J, 1771 G, 1772 H, 1882 B, 1888 B
in Roumania, 1883 K
Ruthenia: annexed by Hungary, 1939 C; ceded to Russia, 1945 F
Rutherford, Ernest, lord Rutherford, B. scientist (1871–1937), 1871 Z, 1896 P, 1904 P, 1911 P, 1919 P, 1921 P, 1937 Z
Rutherford, John, B. physician (1695–1779), 1772 P
'Rutherford, Mark.' *See* White, W. H.
Ruy Blas (V. Hugo), 1838 U
Rykoff, Alexei, R. politician, 1924 B
Ryle, Gilbert, B. philosopher (b. 1900), 1950 R, 1954 R
Ryle, Martin, B. radio astronomer (b. 1918), 1961 P

S

Saar, The, W. Germany:
League of Nations takes over, 1920 B
last Allied troops leave, 1930 M
plebiscite for incorporation in Germany, 1935 A
restored to Germany, 1935 C
autonomy of, 1950 C
crisis over administration of, 1952 A
Franco-German agreement on, 1956 K
incorporated in W. German economic system, 1959 G
Saarinen, Eero, Am. architect (1910–61), 1955 S, 1956 S, 1958 S, 1961 S
Sabbatarianism in England, 1835 R
Sabri el Assali, Syrian leader, 1954 B
Saburov, Pierre Alexandrovich, R. diplomat, 1879 K
Sachs, Julius Wilhelm, G. botanist (1832–97), 1862 P
Sackville-West, Victoria Mary, B. author (1892–1964), 1931 U
Sacred Heart, celebration of, sanctioned, 1766 R
Sacrilege, made a capital offence in France, 1825 O
Sadi-Carnot, Marie François, F. statesman (1837–1894), elected president of France, 1887 M; assassinated, 1894 F
Sadleir, Michael, B. author and publisher (1888–1957), 1940 U
Sadowa, now Königgratz, Austria, battle, 1866 G
Sadras, Madras, India, battle, 1782 B
Safety legislation in factories, earliest, 1802 O
Safety-match, invented, 1898 P
Sagerre (P. Verlaine), 1881 U
Saghalein, Russia, Japanese evacuate, 1925 D
Sagan, Françoise. *See* Quoirez, Francoise
Sahara, N. Africa: exploration, 1869 P; concessions to France in, 1899 C; French company to exploit resources, 1957 C; methane from, 1961 P; Sahel-Bénin Union formed, 1959 D
Sa'id el-Mufti, Jordan. leader, 1955 E, 1956 E
Said Pasha, premier of Persia, 1912 G
Said Zaghlul Pasha, Egypt-Nationalist, deposed, 1919 C
Saigon, Viet Nam: treaty between France and Annam, 1862 F; becomes capital, 1949 F; headquarters of Armistice Commission wrecked, 1955 G; riots in, 1964 L; bomb explodes in US embassy in, 1965 C
St. Aldwyn, earl. *See* Hicks-Beach, M. E.
St. Andrews, Fife, Scotland, Royal and Ancient Golf Club, 1834 X
St. Bernard Pass, Great, Switzerland, Napoleon's army crosses, 1800 E
St. Christopher (or St. Kitts), Island, W. Indies, 1782 B
St. Claire Deville, Étienne Henri, F. chemist (1818–1881), 1855 P
Sainte-Beuve, Charles Augustin, F. author (1804–1869), 1804 Z, 1829 U, 1840 U, 1849 U, 1869 Z
St. Exupéry, Antoine de, F. author (1900–44), 1929 U, 1931 U
St. Eustacius, Island, W. Indies, 1781 L
St. Germain, France, Treaty of, Allies with Austria, 1919 J, 1920 G
Austria ratifies, 1919 K
St. Gotthard tunnel, through Alps, 1882 P
St. Helena, Napoleon banished to, 1815 H
St. Joan (G. B. Shaw), 1924 W
St. John-Stevas, Norman, B. Conservative and author (b. 1927), 1956 O
St. Juan, N.W. America, adjudication over, 1872 K
St. Julien, France, battle, 1915 D

St. Just, Antoine Louis Léon de Richebourg de, F. revolutionary (1767–94), 1793 G, 1794 G
St. Kitts. *See* St. Christopher
St. Lambert, Jean François de, F. poet (1716–1803), 1768 U, 1798 R
St. Laurent, Louis Stephen, Can. Liberal (b. 1882), 1957 F
St. Lawrence River, Canada, improvements to, 1847 P
St. Lawrence Seaway, N. America, 1954 E, 1959 F
St. Leger, Anthony, B. soldier and sportsman, 1776 X
St. Louis, Missouri, US: Populist Party founded at, 1892 B; Democratic convention at, 1916 F
St. Lucia, W. Indies: restored to France, 1763 B; Britain captures, 1778 L; France recovers, 1783 J; changes hands in Napoleonic wars, 1794 N, 1795 F, 1796 N, 1803 F
St. Lucia Bay, S. Africa, annexed by Britain to Natal, 1884 L
St. Martin, Louis Claude de, F. philosopher (1743–1803), 1775 R
St. Mihiel, France, US offensive at, 1918 J
St. Nazaire, France, Britain raids, 1942 C
St. Petersburg (later Leningrad), Russia:
monument to Peter the Great, 1766 S
Alliance, Allies against France, 1794 J
Treaty, 1801 F
Bourse, 1804 S
Alliance between Britain and Russia to liberate N. Germany, 1805 D
Austria joins, 1805 H
Theological Seminary founded, 1809 R
St. Isaac's Cathedral, 1817 S
Protocol, between Britain and Russia over Greek independence, 1826 D
docks in, electrically lit, 1872 P
Treaty, China with Russia, 1881 B
revolution in, 1905 A
first Soviet formed in, 1905 K
population, 1881 Y, 1906 Y
name changed to Petrograd, 1914 J
See also Leningrad
St. Pierre, Jacques Henri Bernardin de, F. author (1737–1814), 1784 R, 1789 U
St. Privat, Corrèze, France, French defeat at, 1870 H
St. Quentin, Aisne, France: French defeat at, 1871 A; French take, 1918 K
St. Saëns, Charles Camille, F. musician (1835–1921), 1835 Z, 1871 T, 1877 T, 1921 Z
Saint's Day (J. Whitney), 1951 W
Saint Simon, Claude Henri de Rouvray, comte de, F. Socialist (1760–1825), 1807 O, 1821 O, 1823 O, 1825 R
Saints, The Battle of the, off Dominica, W. Indies, 1782 D
St. Vincent, Cape, Portugal, naval battles, 1780 A, 1797 B
St. Vincent, Island, in Windward Islands: ceded to Britain, 1763 B; French capture, 1779 F
Saipan, Island, Marianas, Pacific, US take, 1944 F
Saison en Enfer, Une (A. Rimbaud), 1873 U
Saisons, Les (J. de St. Lambert), 1768 U
Sakhalin, North, Japan, mineral concessions in, 1944 C
Sakkaria, Turkey, battle, 1921 H
Sakuntalà (trans. W. Jones), 1789 Q
Salacrou, Armand, F. dramatist (b. 1895), 1936 W
Salamanca, Spain, Wellington's victory, 1812 G
Salamanca, Danielo, president of Bolivia, 1934 M
Salammbó (G. Flaubert), 1862 U
Salan, Raoul, F. Algerian rebel, leader of O.A.S., 1958 M, 1961 D, 1962 D
Salazar, Oliviera, Port. dictator (b. 1889), 1889 Z, 1928 D, 1945 K, L, 1953 L; elected premier, 1932 G
Salbai, Madras, India, Treaty of, 1782 E
Sale of St. Thomas (L. Abercrombie), 1931 U
Salerno, Italy, Allied landings at, 1943 J
Salic Law: in Hanover, 1837 F; in Spain, abrogated, 1830 C
Salieri, Antonio, It. musician (1750–1825), 1784 T
Salinger, Jerome David, Am. author (b. 1919), 1951 U, 1961 U
Salisbury, Rhodesia: founded, 1890 J; riots in, 1964 A
Salk, Jonas Edward, Am. scientist (b. 1914), 1914 Z, 1955 P
Salonika, Macedonia, Greece: railway to, proposed, 1908 A; Allied landings, 1915 K; Venizelos government at, 1916 K
Saltash, Cornwall, bridge, 1853 P
Salt Lake City, Utah, US, 1847 R
Salt Water Ballads (J. Masefield), 1902 U
Salvarsan, prepared, 1909 P
Salvation Army, 1865 R, 1878 R
Salzburg, Austria: archbishopric of, Austrian designs on, 1797 K; Austria cedes to Bavaria, 1809 K; plebiscite favours union with Germany, 1921 E; Mozart Festival, 1906 T, 1946 T
Salzedo, Leonard Lopes, Am. choreographer (b. 1921), 1958 T
Samarkand, Uzbek, Russia, occupied by Russians, 1868 E
Samoa (formerly Navigator's Isles), S.W. Pacific: US treaty with, 1878 A; commercial treaty with Germany, 1879 A; King of, recognised by powers, 1880 C; Washington Conference on, 1887 F; unrest in 1927 G; Anglo-German settlement on, 1899 L; West Samoa becomes independent, 1962 A
Sampson, Anthony, B. journalist (b. 1926), 1962 O
Samsonov, Sergei, R. film director, 1955 W
Samuel, Herbert, viscount Samuel, B. Liberal statesman (1870–1963), 1870 Z, 1932 J, 1963 Z
Sanctions:
by League of Nations against Italy, 1935 K
raised, 1936 G
Russia threatens Greece with, 1958 A
UN calls for, against S. Africa, 1963 J
against Rhodesia, 1965 L
Sand, George, pseudonym of Amandine Dudevin (née Dupin), F. author (1804–76), 1804 Z, 1832 U, 1833 U, 1846 U, 1847 U, 1859 U
Sandcastle, The (I. Murdoch), 1957 U
Sand Creek, Colorado, US, massacre at, 1864 L
Sandeau, Léonard Sylvain Julien (*alias* Jules), F. novelist and dramatist (1811–83), 1854 W
Sanderson, Cobden, B. art critic (under pseudonym of 'David Gascoigne'), 1935 S
San Domingo, East Hispanola, W. Indies: part ceded to France, 1795; independent republic established, 1821 M; annexed by Spain, 1861 C; revolt in, 1865 E
Sand River Convention, establishing Transvaal, 1852 A; violated, 1877 D
Sandwich, earl of. *See* Montagu, John
Sandwich, Kent, golf course, championship at, 1934 X
Sandwich Islands, S. Seas, 1775 P
Sandys, Duncan, B. Conservative politician (b. 1908), visits Cyprus, 1963 M
San Francisco, US, UN Conference at, 1945 D
Sanger, Frederick, B. scientist (b. 1913), 1955 P
Sanger's Circus, 1941 W
San Ildefonso, Old Castille, Spain:
Treaty, Spain with France, 1796 H
Treaty, Spain with US, 1800 K

Sanitation, in Britain:
Chadwick's report, 1842 O
legislation, 1848 O
London's main drainage completed, 1875 P
See also Health, Public
San Jacinto, Mexico, battle, 1836 D
Sanjurjo, José, Sp. general, 1932 H
Sankey, Ira David, Am. evangelist (1840–1908), 1870 R, 1873 R
Sankey, John, lord Sankey, Labour politician and lawyer (1866–1948), reports on coal industry, 1919 B
San Salvador: asks for incorporation in US 1822 M; enters Central American Federation, 1823 G
San Sebastian, Spain, capitulates to Wellington, 1813 J
Sanskrit, study of, 1784 Q, 1819 Q
Sans-serif alphabet, Gill's, 1927 S
Santa Fé, New Mexico, US captures, 1846 H
Santander, Spain, falls to rebels, 1937 F
Santayona, George, Sp. author (1863–1952), 1905 R, 1933 U, 1940 R
Santerno River, Italy, 8th Army reaches, 1945 D
Santiago, Chile: US Navy at, 1898 G; US marines land, 1917 C
Santis, Giuseppe de, It. film director, 1948 W
San Vittore, Italy, US troops take, 1944 A
Saône River, France, 1783 P
Sap, circulation of, in plants, 1846 P
Sappho (F. Grillparzer), 1818 U
Saracco, Giuseppe, It. politician, 1901 B
Saragat, Giuseppe, It. president, 1964 M
Sarajevo, Yugoslavia, assassination at, 1914 F
Sarassin, Pote, Thai, Secretary-general of SEATO, and premier of Thailand, 1957 J
Sarawak, N.W. Borneo, British protectorate over, 1888 C
Sardou, Victorien, F. dramatist (1831–1908), 1882 U, 1887 W, 1891 W
Sargent, John Singer, Am. artist (1856–1925), 1856 Z, 1882 S, 1886 S, 1900 S, 1902 S, 1905 S, 1913 S, 1917 S, 1925 Z, 1926 S
Sargent, W., Am. author, 1957 O
Sarment, Jean, F. dramatist (b. 1897), 1921 W
Sarotoga, New York, British capitulate at, 1777 K
Saroggon, William, Am. author (b. 1908), 1935 U, 1939 U
Sarraut, Albert, F. politician, 1933 K, 1936 A
Sarto, Giuseppe, It. cardinal (1835–1914), elected Pope Pius X, 1903 G
Sartor Resartus (T. Carlyle), 1833 U
Sartre, Jean Paul, F. author (b. 1905), 1937 U, 1943 R, W, 1944 W, 1945 U, 1946 W, 1950 R, 1951 R, W, 1964 U
Saskatchewan, Canada, becomes a province, 1905 J
Satellites, cosmic, 1789 P
Satellites, artificial:
Aerial, to study cosmic radiation, 1962 P
Atlas, to investigate radio relay, 1958 P
ball of copper needles in orbit, 1963 P
Discoverer, recovered, 1960 P
Early Bird, for tele-communications, 1965 P
Explorer I, to study cosmic rays, 1958 P
French launch first, 1965 P
Gagarin's flight, 1961 P
launching of first, anticipated, 1955 P
Mariner IV, for photographing Mars, 1964 P, 1965 P
Nimbus, for meteorological survey, 1964 P
Pioneer IV, 1959 P
radio-reflector, 1960 P
Ranger VII, for photographing moon's surface, 1964 P
Sputnik I and II launched, 1957 P
Sputnik III launched, 1958 P
Syncom, for relaying TV pictures, 1964 P
Telstar, for tele-communications, 1962 P
Vanguard I, to test solar cells, 1958 P
Zone Z, for photographing Mars, 1964 P
See also under Aviation; Rockets
Satie, Erik, F. musician (1866–1925), 1916 T, 1920 T
Saud, King of Saudi Arabia (b. 1905), 1957 D; attempted *coup* in Syria, 1958 C; takes over government, 1960 M; is disposed, 1964 L
Saudi Arabia (formerly Hejaz): name changed from Hejaz, 1926 A; independence recognised, 1927 E
Saussure, Horace Bénédict de, Swi. physicist (1740–99), 1787 P, 1797 P
Savage, Ethel. *See* Dell, Ethel M
Savage, Michael Joseph, N. Zeal. Labour leader (1872–1940), 1935 L
Savage Islands, Pacific, Britain acquires, 1899 L
Savannah, Georgia, US: British capture, 1778 H; British evacuate, 1781 K; Sherman occupies, 1864 M
Savigny, Friedrich Karl von, G. jurist (1779–1861), 1779 Z, 1814 O, 1815 O
Savile, Sir George, B. politician (1726–84), 1778 E
Savings, National, 1916 O
Savonarole (N. Lenau), 1837 U
Savoy: serfdom abolished, 1770 O; France annexes, 1792 L; is ceded to France, 1796 E, 1860 C
Saw circular, invented, 1780 P
Sax, Antoine (*alias* Adolphe), Joseph, Belg. maker of musical instruments (1814–94), 1840 T
Saxe-Weimar, Germany, constitution in, 1816 E
Saxophone, invented, 1840 T
Saxony, W. Germany: evacuated by Prussians, 1763 B; elector of, becomes King of Poland, 1791 E; becomes a Kingdom, 1806 M; King of, rules Duchy of Warsaw, 1807 G; flees, 1813 L; Prussia invades, 1866 F; cedes territory to Prussia, 1866 H
Say, Jean Baptiste, F. economist (1767–1832), 1803 O
Sayers, Dorothy Leigh (Mrs. A. Fleming), B. author (1893–1957), 1893 Z, 1923 U, 1934 U, 1943 W, 1957 Z
Sayers, Tom, B. boxer (1826–65), 1860 X
Sazonov, Sergei, R. diplomat (1866–1937), 1913 L, 1916 G
Scale, twelve-tone, 1911 T
Scandals:
in Belgium, financial corruption, 1937 K
in Britain, Lynskey tribunal investigates charges of corruption, 1948 L
Profumo affair, 1963 C, F, G, J
footballers fix match results, 1965 X
in France, trafficking in Legion of Honour medals, 1887 M
Panama, 1892 L
Dreyfus, 1894 K, 1899 J
in Italy, bank, 1893 M
in US, oil companies' leases, 1924 B
TV Quiz, 1959 W
Sherman Adams affair, 1958 F
Scandium, the element, 1879 P
Scarborough, Yorks, England, Labour Party Conference at, 1960 K
Scarlet Letter, The (N. Hawthorne), 1850 U
Scarman, Sir Leslie George, B. judge (b. 1911), 1965 O

Scelba, Mario, It. People's Party leader (b. 1910), 1954 B, 1955 F
Scènes de la Vie Bohème (H. Murger), 1848 U
Scenes from Clerical Life (G. Eliot), 1857 U
Schacht, Hjalmar, G. economist (b. 1877), 1877 Z; plans to control Germany's foreign trade, 1934 O; Funk replaces him, as economics minister, 1937 L; dismissed from Reichsbank, 1939 A; Nuremberg tribunal acquits, 1946 J
Schadow, Friedrich Wilhelm, G. artist (1789–1862), 1876 S, 1842 S
Schaff, Philip, Am., formerly Swi., theologian (1819–93), 1851 R
Schandorph, Sophus Christian Frederick, Dan. author (1836–1901), 1881 U
Schärf, Adolf, Aust., elected president, 1957 E
Scharnhorst, Gerhard Johann David von, Pruss. general (1755–1813), 1807 N, 1812 B
Schatz, A., Am., scientist, 1943 P
Scheele, Karl Wilhelm, Swe. chemist (1742–86), 1774 P, 1775 P, 1777 P, 1781 P, 1786 Z
Schefer, Leopold, G. poet and novelist (1784–1862), 1834 U
Scheidermann, Philipp, G. Socialist (1865–1942), 1919 B, F
Scheldt, River, Europe: navigation of, 1783 K, 1784 K, 1785 L; is opened to commerce, 1792 L; British expedition to, 1809 D, G; agreement to open to commerce, 1839 D; Belgo-Dutch agreements on, 1919 L, 1925 D
Schelling, Friedrich Wilhelm Joseph, G. philosopher (1775–1854), 1775 Z, 1797 R, 1800 R, 1801 R, 1802 P, 1854 Z, 1856 R
Schenectady, US, atomic power station at, 1955 P
Schérer, Barthélemy Louis Joseph, F. general (1747–1804), 1795 L, 1799 D
Schiaparelli, Giovanni Virginio, It. astronomer (1835–1910), 1889 P
Schick, Bela, Hun. scientist (b. 1877), 1913 P
Schiller, Friedrich, G. author (1759–1805), as dramatist, 1781 W, 1784 W, 1787 W, 1799 W, 1800 W, 1801 W, 1804 W
other works, 1788 Q, 1789 U, 1794 U, 1795 U, 1803 U
bust of, 1794 S
death, 1805 Z
Schinkel, Karl Friedrich, G. architect and artist (1781–1841), 1819 S, 1824 S, 1851 S
Schizophrenia, 1852 H
Schlegel, August, G. author (1767–1845), 1767 Z, 1809 U
Schlegel, Karl Wilhelm Friedrich von, G. critic and scholar (1772–1829), 1797 Q, 1798 Q, 1799 U, 1808 Q
Schleicher, Kurt von, G. politician (d. 1934), 1932 M, 1933 A, 1934 F
Schleiden, Matthias Jacob, G. biologist (1804–81), 1838 P, 1846 P
Schleiermacher, Friedrich Ernst Daniel, G. theologian (1768–1834), 1799 R, 1823 R
Schlesinger, Arthur Meier, Jr., Am. historian (b. 1917), 1957 Q, 1965 Q
Schleswig-Holstein Question: Holstein Estates resolve on independence, 1844 L; German Confederation reserves rights in Duchies, 1846 G, J; Frederick VII announces Denmark will incorporate Holstein, 1848 C; Prussia invades Denmark, 1848 E; Frederick VII decides to incorporate Schleswig Duchy in Denmark, 1848 L; settled by Treaty of Berlin, 1850 G; position guaranteed by Treaty of London, 1850 H; Schleswig is incorporated in Denmark, 1863 C, L; ultimatum to Denmark, 1864 A; Austrian and Prussian troops enter, 1864 B; War, 1864 D, F; Denmark cedes to Austria and Prussia, 1864 K; convention of Gastein re-arranges conquests, 1865 H; Prussia acquires, 1865 H; Duchies are incorporated in Prussia, 1866 M; plebiscite in, 1920 B; is transferred to Denmark, 1920 G
Schliemann, Heinrich, G. archaeologist (1822–90), 1870 O
Schmeling, Max, G. boxer, 1930 X, 1936 X
Schnaebelé, F. frontier official, incident concerning, 1887 D
Schnitzler, Arthur, Aus. dramatist (1862–1931), 1903 W
Schober, Johann, Aus. Moderate (1874–1946), 1929 J
Scholar Gipsy, The (M. Arnold), 1853 U
Scholarship; Its Meaning and Value (H. W. Garrod), 1947 Q
Scholes, Christopher Latham, Am. printer and inventor (1819–90), 1873 P
Schönbein, Christian Friedrich, G. chemist (1799–1868), 1799 Z, 1846 P, 1848 Z
Schönberg, Arnold, Am., formerly G., musician 1874 Z, 1912 T, 1924 T, 1930 T, 1954 T, 1965 T
expounds 12-tone scale, 1911 T
Schönbrunn, W. Germany, Treaties, between France and Prussia, 1805 M, 1809 K
School and Society (J. Dewey), 1899 O
School for Coquettes (C. Gore), 1831 W
School for Scandal, The (R. B. Sheridan), 1778 W
Schools. *See under* Education
Schopenhauer, Arthur, G. philosopher (1788–1860) 1788 Z, 1819 R, 1860 Z, 1870 T
Schubart, Christian Friedrich Daniel, G. poet (1739–91), 1785 U
Schubert, Franz, G. musician (1797–1828), 1797 Z, 1814 T, 1816 T, 1818 T, 1820 T, 1823 T, 1825 T, 1827 T, 1828 Z
Erl King, 1816 T
'Great C. Major' Symphony, 1828 T, 1839 T
Trout Quintet, 1819 T
'Unfinished' Symphony, 1822 T
Schuler, Marx, G. scientist, 1907 P
Schultze, Marx Johann Sigismund, G. microscopic anatomist (1825–74), 1863 P
Schumacher, Kurt, G. Social Democrat, 1952 H
Schuman, Robert, F. statesman (1886–1963), 1947 L, 1948 J
Plan, 1950 E
embodied in Paris Treaty, 1951 D
ratified by France, 1951 M
Schumann, Robert, G. musician (1810–56), 1810 Z, 1834 T, 1838 T, 1840 T, 1849 T, 1850 T, 1853 T
Schurman, Jacob Gould, Am. administrator and educationalist (1854–1942), leads Philipines Commission 1899 C
Schuschnigg, Kurt von, Aus. politician (b. 1897), 1937 B; appointed Chancellor, 1934 G; *coup* in Vienna, 1935 K; becomes leader of Fatherland Front, 1936 E; dissolves Heimwehr, 1936 K; meets Mussolini, 1937 D; promises release of Nazi prisoners, 1938 B
Schuster, Sir Arthur, B. physicist (1851–1934), 1851 Z, 1934 Z
Schutz, Roger, F. Protestant, 1944 R
Schutzenberger, Paul, F. chemist (1829–97), 1865 P
Schwann, Theodor, G. botanist (1810–82), 1810 Z, 1839 P, 1882 Z
Schwanzenberg, Prince Karl, Philipp zu, Aus. general (1771–1820), 1813 M, 1814 B

Schwarzenberg, Prince Friedrich zu (1800–70), 1850 L
Schweitzer, Albert, F. missionary-surgeon, theologian and musician (1875–1965), 1875 Z, 1905 T, 1910 R, 1954 R, 1957 D, 1965 Z
Schwind, Moritz, G. artist (1804–71), 1854 S
Science:
American Association for the Advancement of, 1848 P
British Association for the Advancement of, 1831 P
British Committee on the Neglect of, 1916 P
degrees at London University, 1860 O
Science and Health (M. B. Eddy), 1875 R
Science and Human Behaviour (Skinner), 1953 R
Science and the Common Understanding (R. Oppenheim), 1953 P
Science and the Modern World (A. N. Whitehead), 1925 P
Science and the Nation, 1956 P
Science, Faith and Society (M. Polanyi), 1947 R
Science for the Citizen (L. Hogben), 1938 P
Science of Antiquity (F. Wolf), 1807 Q
Science of Ethics (L. Stephen), 1882 R
Science of Legislation (G. Filangieri), 1780 O
Science of Rights (J. G. Fichte), 1796 O
Science, Religion and the Future (C. E. Raven), 1943 R
Sciences Were Never at War, The (G. de Beer), 1960 Q
Scientific Advisory Committee, British, 1940 O
Scientific and Industrial Research, Department of, in Britain (DISR), 1916 P
Scientific Papers (Lord Rayleigh), 1900 P
Scientific Policy, British Advisory Committee on, 1947 P
Scientific Studies, British Board of, 1916 P
Scientific Theory and Religion (E. W. Barnes), 1933 R
Scooter, motor, 1919 P
Scotland:
Highlands of, roads in, 1802 P
Secretary of State, for, first appointed, 1885 H
legislation for, 1894 N
Scott, Charles, Prestwich, B. journalist (1846–1932), 1872 V
Scott, Mrs. Dawson, B. founder of P.E.N., 1922 U
Scott, E., B. architect, 1928 S
Scott, Sir Francis Clayton, B. soldier (1834–1902), 1896 A
Scott, Sir George Albert, B. architect (1811–78), 1862 S
Scott, Sir Giles Gilbert, B. architect (b. 1880), 1903 S
Scott, Robert, B. churchman and Greek scholar (1811–87), 1843 Q
Scott, Robert Falcon, B. Polar explorer (1868–1912), 1868 Z, 1912 Z
reaches S. Pole, 1912 P
Scott, Sir Walter, B. novelist and poet (1771–1832), 1771 Z, 1805 U, 1808 U, 1809 V, 1810 U, 1814 U, 1815 U, 1816 U, 1818 U, 1820 U, 1821 U, 1824 U, 1826 U
Museum for, in Edinburgh, 1840 S
Scott, Winfield, Am. Whig (1786–1866), 1852 L
Scott Polar Research Institute, Cambridge, 1926 P
Scouting Movement, 1907 O
Scramble for Africa:
Britain warns Germany against infringement of rights, 1883 D
Belgium drive in Congo region, 1884 B, 1885 B
Berlin Conference, 1884 L
See also under Congo; Nigeria; Rhodesia; Somaliland; South West Africa
Screw, ship's, invented, 1827 P
Screwtape Letters (C. S. Lewis), 1942 R
Scriabin, Alexander, R. musician (1872–1915), 1872 Z, 1913 T, 1915 Z
Scriptores rerum Bohemicarum (J. Dobrovsky), 1783 U
Scullin, James Henry, Austral. Labour leader (1876–1953), 1929 K
Scurvy, is conquered, 1775 P
Seaborg, Glenn Theodore, Am. chemist (b. 1912), 1950 P
Seagull, The (A. Chekhov), 1896 W
Seaham, Harbour, Co. Durham, England, election in, 1935 L
Sea-island cotton, 1786 P
'Sealab', 1964 P
Seaplanes, 1912 P
Searle, Humphrey, B. musician (b. 1915), 1915 Z, 1956 T, 1960 T
Search, right of, at sea, 1850 M
Sears, R. D., Am. lawn-tennis player, 1881 X
Sea Spray and Smoke Drift (A. L. Gordon), 1867 U
Season Tickets on railways, 1910 O
Sea Wolf (J. London), 1904 U
Sebastopol, Russia: harbour begun, 1776 N; siege of, 1854 K; storm at, 1854 L; allies enter, 1855 J; Turks bombard, 1914 K; Germans occupy, 1918 E; Red Army takes, 1920 L; Germans enter, 1942 G
Second Birth (B. Pasternak), 1932 U
Second Adventists. *See under* Religious Denominations
Second Front, movement for, 1941 J; Anglo-US talks on, 1942 D; British demonstrations favouring, 1942 G
Second Mrs. Tanqueray, The (A. W. Pinero), 1893 U
Second Sex, The (S. de Beauvoir), 1949 U
Secret Agent (J. Conrad), 1907 U
Secret ballot, in Britain, 1872 G
Secret Societies:
in China, Boxers, 1898 N
White Lotus, in Shantung, 1774 N
union of, organised, 1905 N
in Ireland, Irish Republican Brotherhood, 1857 K
The Invincibles, 1882 H
in Italy, the Carbonari, 1820 G, 1821 C
Mafia, in Sicily, 1926 J
in Macedonia, revolutionary organisations, 1893 N, 1895 F
in Russia, Land and Liberty, 1876 O
Will of the People, 1879 O
in US, Ku-Klux Klan, 1922 O
shoot Civil Rights worker, 1965 C
before Un-American Committee, 1965 K
See also under Armies, private
Secrets Act, Official, British, 1911 O
Security Pacts:
Arab League, 1952 H
France, with Czechoslovakia and Poland, 1925 K
Germany's proposals for, 1925 F, K
See also under Pacts
Security procedures, Radcliffe review of, 1961 E
Sedaine, Michel Jean, F. dramatist (1719–97), 1765 W, 1768 W
Sedan, Ardennes, N.E. France: French defeat at 1870 J; US troops occupy, 1918 L; Germans break through near, 1940 E
Seditious meetings. *See under* Public Assembly
Seditious publications. *See under* Censorship
Seebeck, Thomas Johann, G. scientist (1770–1839), 1821 P
Seeley, Sir John Robert, B. historian (1834–95), 1883 Q

See Naples and Die (E. Rice), 1929 W
Segantini, Giovanni, It. artist (1858–99), 1891 S
Segni, Antonio, It. Christian Democrat (b. 1891), forms ministry, 1955 F; resigns, 1957 E; forms ministry, 1959 B; resigns, 1960 B; elected president of Italy, 1962 E; resigns presidency, 1964 M
Segregation. *See* Apartheid; Racial Problems
Sein und Zeit (Heidegger), 1927 R
Seipel, Ignaz, Aus. Christian Socialist, 1926 K
Selangor, Malay: independence, 1826 F; Sultan of, heads Malaysian Federation, 1960 D
Self and the Dramas of History, The (R. Niebuhr), 1961 R
Selfridge, Harry Gordon, B. formerly Am. businessman, 1858 Z, 1947 Z
Self-winding watch, 1922 P
Selim III, Sultan of Turkey (1789–1807), 1789 D, 1807 E
Sella, Quintius, It. politician and financier (1827–84), 1874 E
Sellafield, Cumb., England, atomic power station at, 1951 P
Sellassie, Haile, emperor of Ethiopia (b. 1892), 1892 Z
Selma, Alabama, US: violence in, 1965 C; Civil Rights procession from, 1965 C
Selznick, David Oliver, Am. film director (b. 1902), 1935 W
Semaphore (or optical telegraph), 1793 P
Sembilan, Islands, Malaysia, B. acquires, 1826 F
Seminaries:
in France, closed, 1791 R
in Ireland, Maynooth established, 1795 R
in Russia, established at St. Petersburg, 1809 R
See also under Monasteries; Religious Communities
Semler, Johann Salomo, G. Biblical critic (1725–91), 1771 R
Senanyake, Dudley Stetton Ceyl. United National Party leader (b. 1911), 1952 F, 1960 C, 1965 C
Senanyake, Stephen, Ceyl. United Party leader (d. 1957), 1947 J
Senefelde, Alois, G. inventor (1771–1834), 1798 R
Senegal, West Africa: ceded to Britain, 1763 B; captured by France, 1779 A; France recovers, 1783 J; forms, with Sudan, Mali Republic, 1959 A
Senior, Nassau William, B. economist (1790–1864), 1790 Z, 1864 Z
Se non cosi (L. Pirandello), 1913 W
Sensations of Tones (H. Helmholtz), 1862 P
Sense and Sensibilia (J. L. Austin), 1962 R
Sense and Sensibility (J. Austen), 1811 U
Sense and the Intellect (A. Bain), 1855 R
Sentences, criminal: first offenders act, 1958 O; 42 years imprisonment, 1961 E. *See also under* Death penalty; Penal Reform
Sentimental Journey, A (L. Sterne), 1768 U
Seoul, Korea: incidents against Japanese in, 1882 G; palace, seized by Japanese, 1894 G; Japanese occupy, 1904 B; Constituent Assembly, boycotted by N. Korea, 1948 E; N. Koreans capture, 1950 F; UN force recaptures, 1950 J
Separator, cream, invented, 1877 P
Sequoyah (*alias* George Guess), Am. Indian (1770–1843), invents Cherokee alphabet, 1824 Q
Serbia: Russian ultimatum to Turkey about, 1826 D; Russian influence in, 1826 K; independence, 1829 J; declares war on Turkey, 1876 G, 1877 M; independence guaranteed, 1878 C, G; monarchy in, 1903 F; to have canal access to Adriatic, 1912 M
Serbo-Croat-Slovene Kingdom. *See* Yugoslavia
Serbs:
gain partial autonomy, 1817 L
rising of, in Belgrade, 1862 F
Serfdom:
emancipation of, plea for, 1790 O
in Austria, abolished, 1781 L, 1848 J
in Bohemia, abolished, 1780 K
revolts against, 1775 B
in Denmark, abolished, 1784 E
in Hungary, abolished, 1780 K
in Prussia, emancipated, 1807 K
in Russia, problem studied, 1857 L
emancipation of, 1858 O, 1861 C
in Savoy, abolished, 1771 O
See also Slaves
Seringapatam, Mysore, S. India, battles, 1791 E, 1799 E
Serrano y Dominguez, Francisco, duke de la Torre, Sp. statesman (1810–85), 1874 A
Serres Chaudes (M. Maeterlinck), 1889 U
Serum:
anti-diphtheria, 1902 P
for tetanus, 1915 P
Salk, for poliomyelitis, 1955 P
See also Vaccines
Servitude et grandeur militaires (A. de Vigny), 1835 U
Sesame and Lilies (J. Ruskin), 1865 U
Seton, Elizabeth Ann Bayley, Am. founder of the Sisters of Charity of St. Joseph (1774–1821), 1809 R
Seurat, Georges, F. artist (1859–91), 1884 S, 1886 S
Seven Men (M. Beerbohm), 1919 U
'Seven, The' (EFTA), 1959 L. *See also* European Free Trade Association
Severini, Gino, It. artist (b. 1883), 1910 S
Severn, River, England, tunnel, 1886 P
Severed Head, A (I. Murdoch), 1961 U
Seville, Spain, revolt in, 1932 H
Sèvres, France, treaty of, 1920 H
Sewing-machine, 1846 P, 1851 P
Sex Education in Schools, 1943 O
Sex, Treatise on, 1905 R
Sexual Behaviour in the Human Male (Kinsey), 1948 P
Seychelles Islands: Britain captures, 1794 N; Makarios deported to, 1956 C
Seymour, Horatio, Am. Democrat (1810–86), 1868 L
Sfax, Tunisia, British occupy, 1943 O
Shackleton, Sir Ernest Henry, B. explorer (1874–1922), 1874 Z, 1914 P, 1919 P, 1922 Z
Shaffer, Peter Levin, B. dramatist (b. 1926), 1964 W
Shahn, Benn, Lithuanian artist (b. 1898), 1945 S
Shaikh Abdullah, Kashmir premier, 1964 D
Shakers, The, Sect, 1774 R
Shakespeare, William, B. dramatist (1563–1616):
Plays, production of, notable, 1769 W, 1814 W, 1820 W, 1833 W, 1897 W, 1914 W
filmed, 1944 W, 1948 W, 1952 W
televised, 1961 W
quatercentenary exhibition, 1964 S, W
studies, 1778 Q
translations, 1775 W
Shakespeare-Bacon controversy, 1848 Q
Shaking of the Foundations, The (P. Tillich), 1949 R
Shanghai, China: is opened to British commerce, 1842 H; falls to rebels, 1850 K; anti-British incidents in, 1925 E; Japanese occupy, 1932 A; Chinese driven from, 1932 C; Japanese take, 1937 L; population, 1950 Y, 1960 Y
Shanhaikwan, China, Japanese troops reach, 1932 A

Shantung, China: rebellion in, 1774 N; Japanese ultimatum on rights in, 1915 A; German concession in, granted to Japan, 1919 D; US Senate rejects clause of Versailles treaty about, 1919 H; restored to China, 1922 B; Japanese intervention in, 1927 E, 1928 D; evacuate, 1929 E
Share-pushing, 1937 O
Sharett, Moshé, Israel leader (b. 1894), 1953 M, 1954 A
Sharpe, Thomas, B. town-planner (b. 1901), 1944 O
Sharpeville, S. Africa, shooting of demonstrators at, 1960 C
Shastri, Lal Bahandra, Indian leader (d. 1966), succeeds Nehru, 1964 E
Shatt-el-Adhaim, Mesopotamia, Turks defeated at, 1917 D
Shaw, George Bernard, B. author (1856–1950), 1856 Z, 1900 U, 1932 U, 1950 Z
  as dramatist, 1892 W, 1894 W, 1897 W, 1898 W, 1903 W, 1907 W, 1919 W, 1923 W, 1924 W, 1929 W
  political works, 1898 O, 1928 O
  Prefaces to published plays, 1916 U
  portrait, 1914 S
Shaw, Robert, B. author (b. 1927), 1962 U
Shawe, T. E. *See* Lawrence, T. E.
Shays, Daniel, Am. insurgent (1747–1825), 1786 J
Shearman, Sir Harold, B. Labour politician (b. 1895), first chairman of Greater London Council, 1965 O
Sheepfold, The (L. Housman), 1918 U
Shelburne, earl of. *See* Petty, William
Shelley, Mary Wollstonecroft, B. author (1797–1851), 1797 Z, 1818 U
Shelley, Percy Bysshe, B. poet (1792–1822), 1792 Z, 1813 U, 1816 U, 1817 U, 1820 U, 1821 U, 1822 Z
Shell Oil Company, dispute with Cuba over Havana refinery, 1960 G
Shell-shock, 1916 P
Shenkunsk, Russia, Allies withdraw from, 1919 A
Shenstone, William, B. poet (1714–63), 1765 U
Shepard, Alan, Am. astronaut, 1961 P
Shepherd's Calendar, The (J. Clare), 1827 U
Shepilov, Dmitri Trofimovitch, R. leader (b. 1904): becomes foreign minister, 1956 F; is superseded, 1957 B; is expelled from Soviet Central Committee, 1957 G
Shepstone, Sir Theophilis, S. African statesman (1817–93), 1877 D
Sheridan, Richard Brinsley, B. dramatist (1751–1816), 1775 W, 1778 W, 1779 W, 1816 Z
Sheriff, Robert Cedric, B. author (b. 1896), 1929 W
Sherman, John, Am. financier and statesman (1823–1900), introduces Anti-Trust law, 1890 G
Sherman, William Tecumseh, Am. Unionist general (1820–91), 1864 G, M, 1865 D; march through Georgia, 1864 E
Sherrington, Sir Charles Scott, B. physiologist (1857–1952), 1857 Z, 1939 R, 1952 Z
Sherwood, Robert Emmet, Am. dramatist (1896–1955), 1935 W, 1936 W
She Stoops to Conquer (O. Goldsmith), 1773 W
Shevket Pasha, Turk, leader, forms ministry, 1913 A
Shiloh, Tenn., US, Confederate success at, 1862 D
Shimonoseki, Japan, Treaty, 1895 D; fleet attacked in, 1864 J
Shintoism, disestablished in Japan, 1945 O
Shinwell, Emmanuel, B. Labour politician, defeats MacDonald in Seaham Harbour election, 1935 L
Shipka Pass, Central Bulgaria, Turks capitulate at, 1878 A
Ship of Fools (K. A. Porter), 1962 U
Ships:
  atomic powered, 1959 P
  guided-missiles, 1956 G
  iron, 1820 P
  iron-clad, 1861 P
  non-magnetic, 1957 P
  screw for, invented, 1827 P
  steam, 1783 P, 1803 P, 1807 P, 1812 P
Shipping:
  embargoes on, 1800 M, 1801 A, C, 1803 E
  in Britain, modification of navigation laws, 1822 F, 1825 G
    Lloyd's Register, 1834 V
    government control, 1916 M
    loan to Cunard Company, 1963 K
  in US, note to Britain on use of US flag, 1915 B
    note to Germany on sinking of neutral ships, 1915 B
    Shipping Board, 1916 O
  for tonnages. *See under* Merchant shipping
Shipton, Eric Earle, B. mountaineer, 1907 Z
Shotokhov, Mikhal, R. author, 1934 U
Shops, early-closing of British, 1911 O
Shorthand, invented, 1837 P
Short History of the English People (J. R. Green), 1874 Q
Shorthouse, Joseph Henry, B. author (1834–1903), 1880 U
Short Survey of Surrealism (D. Gascoigne), 1935 S
Shostakovich, Dmitry, R. musician (b. 1906), 1906 Z, 1927 T, 1932 T, 1937 T, 1942 T, 1944 T, 1946 T, 1954 T
Shrapnel, Henry, B. soldier and inventor (1761–1842), 1803 P
Shreveport, Louisiana, US, Confederates surrender at, 1865 E
Shropshire Lad, A (A. E. Housman), 1896 U
Shumla, Bulgaria, battle, 1774 G
Shuttleworth, Sir Thomas Phillips Kay, B. educationalist (1804–77), 1840 O
Shuvalov, Peter Andreivich, R. diplomat (1827–89), 1878 E, F
Siam: Burmese invade, 1767 H; France maintains as buffer state, 1893 G; Anglo-French agreements on, 1893 M, 1896 A; independence confirmed, 1907 D; changes name to Thailand, 1949 E. *See also under* Thailand
Sibelius, Jean Julius Christian, Fin. musician (1865–1957), 1865 Z, 1893 T, 1899 T, 1900 T, 1957 Z
Siberia: Japanese advance into 1918 H; East, British, US, and Japanese agreement on, 1919 M
Siberian Highway, 1781 P
Sica, Vittorio de, It. film director (b. 1901), 1901 Z, 1946 W, 1948 W, 1951 W, 1952 W
Sicilian Vespers (S. Runciman), 1958 Q
Sicily, Italy: Kingdom of Two Sicilies (Sicily and Naples), 1767 C; declared independent of Naples, 1848 D; forced to submit to Naples, 1849 E; plebiscite supports union with Sardinia, 1860 K; Allies land in, 1943 G
Sickel, Theodor von, G. historian, 1867 Q
Sickert, Walter Richard, B. artist (1860–1942), 1860 Z, 1886 S, 1913 S, 1941 S, 1942 Z
Siddons, Sarah (née Kemble), B. actress (1755–1831), 1775 W, 1784 S, 1812 W, 1831 Z
Sidgwick, Henry, B. philosopher (1838–1900), 1874 R, 1882 P
Sidi Barrani, Cyrenaica, N. Africa, 1940 J, M
Sidi Omar, Cyrenaica, N. Africa, British withdrawal to, 1942 F
Sidmouth, Viscount. *See* Addington

Sidqi, Bakr, Iraq. premier, 1937 H
Siege of Corinth (Byron), 1816 U
Siegfried (J. Giraudoux), 1928 W
Siegfried Line, Germany, Germans retreat to, 1918 J
Siemens, Ernst Werner von, G. electrician (1816–92), 1816 Z, 1879 P, 1892 Z
Siemens, Sir William, B. metallurgist and electrician (1823–83), 1856 P, 1861 P
Siemkiewicz, Henryk, Pol. author (1849–1916), 1895 U
Sierra Leone, W. Africa: is settled as asylum for slaves, 1788 H; Sierra Leone Company is formed, 1792 N; becomes Crown Colony, 1808 A; taken over by Britain, 1821 E; boundaries defined, 1882 F, 1885 L; becomes independent, 1961 D
Sieyès, Emmanuel Joseph, F. abbé and politician (1758–1836), 1789 O, 1836 Z
Signals, railway, automatic, 1893 P
Signs of the Times (C. von Bunsen), 1856 O
Sigurid the Volsung (W. Morris), 1876 U
Sigwart, Christoph, G. philosopher (1830–94), 1873 R
Sikhs: British treaty with, 1809 D; British wars against, 1834 E, 1845 M, 1846 A, B, C, 1848 C, 1849 A, B, C
Silas Marner (G. Eliot), 1861 U
Si le grain ne meut (Gide), 1926 U
Silent Spring, The (R. Carson), 1963 P
Silesia, Germany: Austria renounces claim to, 1768 K; ceded to Prussia, 1866 H
Upper, plebiscite for incorporation in Germany, 1921 C; future of, referred to League, 1921 H, K; partition of, 1921 K; cession to Poland, 1922 E
Silestria, Rumania, battle, 1809 J
Silk, artificial, 1887 P
Silk manufactures, British exports, 1772 Y, 1782 Y, 1792 Y, 1802 Y, 1822 Y, 1842 Y, 1852 Y, 1862 Y, 1872 Y, 1882 Y, 1892 Y, 1902 Y, 1912 Y, 1922 Y, 1932 Y
production, comparative statistics, 1910 Y
Silver:
compulsory purchase repealed, 1893 L
extraction by cyanide, 1887 P
Roosevelt empowered to nationalise, 1934 F
standard in US, 1878 B
Silver King, The (H. A. Jones), 1882 W
Silverman, Sidney, B. Labour politician (b. 1895), advocates abolition of death penalty, 1956 F
introduces new death penalty abolition bill, 1964 M
Simeon, Charles, B. evangelical churchman (1759–1836), 1783 R
Simon, John, viscount Simon, B. National Liberal politician (1873–1954), 1873 Z, 1935 F, 1954 Z; leads commission on India, 1926 L; becomes foreign secretary, 1931 L; elected National Liberal Leader, 1932 J; as chancellor of Exchequer, 1937 E
Simon, Jules, F. philosopher and statesman (1814–1896), 1877 E
Simonstown, S. Africa, naval base, returned by Britain to S. Africa, 1955 G
Simple Story, A (E. Inchbald), 1791 W
Simplon Pass, Alps: carriage-road, 1800 P; tunnel, 1906 P
Simpson, Sir James Young, B. physician (1811–70), 1811 Z, 1847 P, 1870 Z
Simpson, Mrs. Wallis Warfield (later duchess of Windsor), Am., 1936 K, L
marries duke of Windsor, 1937 F
'Sinanthropus' (Peking Man), 1920 Q
Sinatra, Francis Albert (Frank), Am. singer and film actor (b. 1917), 1943 W
Since Cezanne (C. Bell), 1922 S
Sinclair, Sir John, B. administrator and economist (1754–1835), 1791 O
Sinclair, Upton, Am. author (b. 1878), 1878 Z, 1906 O, 1928 U, 1940 U
Sind, India, Napier conquers, 1843 A, H
Sindhia, of Gwalior, Ind. ruler, 1802 K, 1803 H, J, M
Sindhia, India, peace signed with East India Company, 1805 L
Sinecures, proposals for abolition in Britain, 1780 E
Sinfonie Liturgique (P. Honegger), 1945 T
Singapore: East India Company's settlement at, 1819 B; falls to Japanese, 1942 B; votes to join Malaysian Federation, 1962 J
Singer, Charles, E., B. historian of technology (1876–1960), 1955 P
Singer, Isaac Merritt, Am. inventor (1811–75) 1851 P
'Singing-mice', 1937 W
Single Man, A (C. Isherwood), 1964 U
Sinhalese, becomes official language of Ceylon, 1956 G
Sinn Fein. *See under* Political Parties
Sinope, Turkey, battle of, 1853 L, P
Sioux rising in Minnesota, 1862 H
Siphon recorder, 1867 P
Sipyengin, R. minister of interior, 1902 D
Siroký, Vilian, Czech. Communist (b. 1902), 1954 M, 1963 J
Sisley, Alfred, F. artist (1840–99), 1874 S
Sismondi, Jean Charles Leonard de, Swi. historian (1773–1842), 1773 Z, 1807 Q, 1819 O, 1842 Z
Sistova, Bulgaria, peace of, 1791 H
Sitwell, Dame Edith, B. author, 1887 Z, 1964 Z
Six Characters in Search of an Author (L. Pirandello), 1918 W
Six, Les, French school of musicians, 1920 T
'Six, The' (France, W. Germany, Italy, Belgium, Netherlands and Luxembourg forming the Common Market), sign Paris Treaty, 1951 D. *See also* Common Market; European Economic Community
Skeat, Walter William, B. philologist (1835–1912), 1879 Q
Skegness, Lincs., England, holiday camp at, 1937 W
Sketch Book of Geoffrey Crayon, Gent, The (W. Irving), 1820 U
Sketches by Boz (C. Dickens), 1836 U
Skiing, water, 1958 X
Skinner, Burrhus, Am. psychologist (b. 1904), 1953 R
Skipton, Yorks., England, by-election, 1944 A
Sklodowska, Marie. *See* Curie, Marie
Skobelev, Mikhail Dimitriévich, R. general and diplomat (1843–82), 1882 B
Skopje, Yugoslavia, earthquake at, 1963 G
Skouloudis, Sophocles, Greek premier, 1915 L
Skutari, Turkey, 1913 E
Skyscrapers, 1857 P, 1883 P, 1930 S, 1964 S
Slade, Julian, B. composer and dramatist (b. 1930), 1954 W
Slansky, Rudolf, Czech. Communist (d. 1952), 1952 L
Slav influence in Austria-Hungary, 1879 H
Slavery:
tract advocating abolition, 1786 O
Anti-Slavery Congress, 1890 O
International Convention for abolition, 1926 J
in Africa, abolished, 1884 L

in Brazil, abolished, 1888 E
in Britain, Lord Mansfield's decision in Somerset's case, 1772 O
in British Empire, abolished, 1834 O
Creole incident with US, 1841 L
decision over restoration of fugitive slaves, 1875 J
Jamaican riots following emancipation, 1839 E
in French Colonies, abolished, 1794 N
in Liberia, colony established for freed US slaves, 1822 N
reported to persist, 1930 C
in Madagascar, liberation of, 1877 K
in Russia, pleas for emancipation, 1790 O
in Sierra Leone, asylum for slaves, 1788 H
in US, Jefferson champions rights of slaves, 1778 N
in part of Louisiana purchase, abolished, 1820 C
fugitive slaves, legislation about, 1793 N, 1850 G
Abolition Society founded, 1832 O
Wilmot Proviso on, 1846 H
Clay's compromise resolution on, 1850 A
pro-slavers massacred, 1856 E
Lincoln's declaration against slavery, 1862 J
Lincoln declares emancipation of negro slaves, 1863 O
slavery abolished by 13th Amendment, 1865 M
in Zanzibar, abolished, 1897 D
Slave Trade:
Brussels Conference on abolition, 1889 F
Africa—US, prohibited, 1808 A
African, abolished, 1884 L
Brussels convention to eradicate, 1890 G
in Britain, Parliamentary motion for abolition, 1788 E
in Denmark, abolished, 1792 N, O
in Spain, ended, 1817 J
in US, forbidden in District of Columbia, 1850 J
Dredd Scott case, 1856 C
J. Davis's resolutions, 1860 B
in Zanzibar, abolished, 1873 F
Sleeping Clergyman (J. Briche), 1933 W
Sleep of Prisoners, A (C. Fry), 1951 W
Slivnitza, Bulgaria, Serbs defeated at, 1885 L
Slogans, 'Buy British' campaign, 1933 F
Slovakia: Southern, Hungary annexes, 1938 L; is placed under German 'protection', 1939 C. *See also* Czechoslovakia
Slum clearance, in Britain, 1864 O, 1867 O, 1932 D
See also under Housing
Smallholders. *See under* Political Parties
Small House at Allington, The (A. Trollope), 1864 U
Smallpox, vaccination against, 1796 P
Smeaton, John, B. engineer (1724–92), 1792 Z
Smeatonian Club, 1771 P
Smetana, Friedrich, Bohemian musician (1824–84), 1824 Z, 1848 T, 1866 T, 1874 T, 1884 Z
Smethwick, Warwicks., England, election, 1964 K
Smiles, Samuel, B. author (1812–1904), 1812 Z, 1904 Z
Smirke, Sir Robert, B. architect (1780–1867), 1780 Z, 1823 S, 1845 S, 1867 Z
Smith, Adam, B. political economist (1723–90), 1776 O, 1790 Z
Smith, Albert Emanuel, Am. Democrat (1873–1947), 1928 L
Smith, Mrs. Burnett, B. novelist under pseudonym of 'Annie S. Swan' (1872–1943), 1872 Z, 1943 Z
Smith, Dodie (Mrs. Alec Beesley; pseudonym of C. L. Anthony), B. dramatist, 1931 W
Smith, Frederick Edwin, B. lawyer (1872–1930), 1872 Z, 1930 Z
Smith, Gladys. *See* Pickford, Mary
Smith, Goldwin, B. controversionalist (1823–1910), 1823 Z, 1891 O, 1910 Z
Smith, Sir Harry George Wakelyn, B. soldier (1787–1860), 1846 A, 1848 B
Smith, Henry John Stephen, B. mathematician (1826–83), 1854 P
Smith, Ian, Rhodes. politician, leader of Rhodesian front (b. 1919): forms ministry, 1964 D; rejects visit by Commonwealth Secretary, 1964 L; talks with Wilson, 1965 K; proclaims U.D.I., 1965 L
Smith, Joseph, Am. Mormon leader (1805–44), 1825 R, 1830 R, 1843 R
Smith, Lloyd Logan Pearsall, B., formerly Am., author (1865–1946), 1865 Z, 1946 Z
Smith, Sydney, B. ecclesiastic (1771–1845), 1771 Z, 1808 R
Smith, Sir Ross Macpherson, B. aviator (1892–1922), 1919 P
Smith, William, B. geologist (1769–1839), 1815 P, 1816 P
Smith, William Henry, B. Conservative politician and newsagent (1825–91), 1887 A
Smith, Sir William Sidney, B. naval officer (1764–1840), 1799 C
Smithson, Alison, and Peter Denham (b. 1923), B. architects, 1961 S
'Smog', in London, 1952 P
Smoke (I. Turgeniev), 1867 U
Smoking of Cigarettes: connexion with lung cancer, 1954 P; report of Royal College of Physicians on, 1962 P
Smolensk, Russia: Russian defeat at, 1812 H; Germans capture, 1941 G; Germans advance from, 1941 K; Russians recapture, 1943 J
Smollett, Tobias, B. author (1721–71), 1771 U, Z
Smoot, Reed, Am., Senator for Utah (1862–1947), 1912 C
Smoot-Hawley tariff, 1930 F
Smuggling in Britain, checked, 1784 G. *See also under* Free Trade
Smuts, Jan Christian, S. Afr. statesman (1870–1950), 1870 Z, 1916 F, 1950 Z; electoral defeat, 1924 F; joins Hertzog's cabinet, 1933 E; unites with Hertzog's followers to form United South African Nationalists, 1934 F; becomes premier, 1939 J; addresses British Parliament, 1942 K; at UN Conference, 1945 D; heads United Party ministry, 1945 K; refuses to place South-West Africa under UN trusteeship, 1947 A; coalition led by, defeated by Nationalist-Afrikander *bloc*, 1948 E
Smyth, Ethel Mary, B. musician (1858–1944), 1906 T, 1916 T
Snow, Charles Percy, lord Snow, B. novelist and scientist (b. 1905), 1905 Z, 1950 U, 1954 U, 1962 U, 1964 U; delivers Richmond Lecture, 1959 U
Snowden, Sir Philip, B. Labour politician (1864–1937), as chancellor of Exchequer, 1924 A, 1929 F; is expelled from Labour Party, 1931 H
Snowden, lord. *See* Armstrong-Jones, Anthony
Snow Maiden, The (A. Ostrovsky), 1872 W
Soane, Sir John, B. architect (1753–1837), 1795 S, 1803 S
Soblen, Robert, American spy (d. 1962), asylum for, refused in Britain, 1962 G
Sobrahan, India, battle, 1846 B
Sobrero, Ascacio, It. chemist (1811–70), 1846 P
Social and Economic History of the Roman Empire (Rostovziev), 1926 Q
Social and Political Doctrines of Contemporary Europe, The (M. Oakeshott), 1939 O
Social Anthropology (M. Mead), 1950 R
Social Democrats. *See under* Political Parties

Socialism:
condemned by Pius IX, 1849 R
state, advocated, 1862 O
Jaurès advocates, 1911 D
studies in, 1936 O, 1937 O
Socialism and the Christian Church (E. Troeltsch), 1912 R
Socialist Parties. *See under* Political Parties
Socialist Party, in Britain. *See under* Political Parties, Labour Party
Social Progress and Educational Waste (K. Lindsay), 1926 O
Social Question, The (A. Wagner), 1871 O
Social Revolution (B. Kidd), 1894 O
Social Security:
in Belgium, 1936 F
in Britain, Beveridge Plan, 1942 O. *See also under* legislation
in Canada, 1936 F
in France, 1952 A
in Germany, 1903 D
in US, 1935 H. *See also under* New Deal
Social Statics (H. Spencer), 1850 O
Society Islands, Pacific, explored, 1768 P
Society of Jesus. *See* Jesuits
Sociology (W. Sombart), 1936 R
Sociology, studies in, 1846 O, 1850 O, 1853 R, 1858 O, 1873 O, 1916 R
Soda manufacturing processes for, 1787 P, 1838 P, 1861 P, 1894 P
Soddy, Frederick, B. scientist (1877–1956), 1877 Z, 1904 P, 1911 P, 1913 P, 1956 Z
Söderblom, Nathan, Swe. theologian (1866–1947), 1933 R
Sodium, electrical preparation of, 1806 P
Sofia, Bulgaria: military *coup* in, 1886 H; Macedonian revolutionaries in, 1895 F
Sohab and Rustrum (M. Arnold), 1853 U
Soissons, France: battles near, 1915 A; German withdrawal from, 1917 B; Germans take, 1918 E; French recapture, 1918 H
Solar battery, 1954 P
Solar cells tested by satellite, 1958 P
Soldaten Die (J. Lenz), 1776 W
Soldiers' Pay (W. Faulkner), 1926 U
Solferino, Italy, Austrian defeat at, 1859 F
Soloman, H., Am. manufacturer of canned foods, 1874 P
Solomon Islands, Pacific, US recovers, 1944 B
Solvay, Ernest, Belg. chemist (1838–1922), 1861 P
Solzhenitsyn, Alexander, R. author, 1962 U
Somalia, 1960 F
Somaliland, British: exploration, 1854 P; protectorate established, 1884 N; Mad Mullah raids on, 1899 J; Italian advance into, 1940 H; becomes independent, 1960 F; joins Somalia, 1960 F
Somaliland, French, boundary defined, 1897 C
Somaliland, Italian: Mad Mullah raids on, 1899 J; occupation completed, 1925 K; becomes protectorate, 1925 K; clashes on Abyssinian frontier with, 1934 M; British troops invade, 1941 B; trusteeship is transferred to Italy, 1950 D
Sombart, Werner, G. economist (1863–1934), 1863 Z, 1920 O, 1936 R
Some Aspects of British Civilization (H. L. Fleure), 1948 P
Somerville, William, B. physician and explorer of Africa (1771–1860), 1802 P
Somme, River, France, battles, 1916 G, 1918 C
Sömmering, Samuel Thomas, G. anatomist and inventor, 1809 P
Sonatas, notable:
by Beethoven, *Appassionate*, 1807 T
Les Adieux, 1811 T
Moonlight, 1802 T
Pathétique, 1799 T
Kreutzer, 1803 T
St. Michael for wind instruments (P. M. Davies), 1959 T
by Ravel, 1922 T, 1927 T
by Walton, 1950 T
Sonderbund, The, in Switzerland, 1845 M; War of, 1847 K
Sonette am Orpheus (R. M. Rilke), 1922 U
Song-cycles:
Heiss, *Expression K*, 1956 T
Hindemith, *Das Marienleben*, 1924 T
Schönberg, *Pierrot Lunaire*, 1912 T
Song of Bernadette, The (F. Werfel), 1941 U
Song of Hiawatha, The (H. W. Longfellow), 1855 U
Songs of Experience (W. Blake), 1794 U
Songs of Innocence (W. Blake), 1789 U
Songs of Praise (hymnal), 1925 R
Songs of the Fleet (H. Newbolt), 1910 U
Songs, Popular:
Alexander's Ragtime Band (I. Berlin), 1911 T
Hang Out the Washing on the Siegfried Line, 1939 W
Last Time I Saw Paris, The (J. Kern), 1939 W
Lili Marlene, 1940 W
Pack Up Your Troubles, 1915 W
Roll Out the Barrel, 1939 W
Tar-ra-ra-boom-de-ay, 1892 W
Sonnets from the Portuguese (E. B. Browning), 1850 U
Sonnino, Sidney, baron (1847–1922), It. statesman, 1902 M
Son of a Servant, The (A. Strindberg), 1886 U
Sons and Lovers (D. H. Lawrence), 1913 U
Sophocles, tragedies of, translated into German, 1804 Q
Sorel, Albert, F. historian (1842–1906), 1842 Z, 1885 Q, 1906 Z, 1908 O
Sorrell and Son (W. Deeping), 1925 U
Sorrows of Werther (Goethe), 1774 U
Soubirous, Bernadette, of Lourdes, 1858 R
Soulie de satin (P. Claudel), 1929 W
Soult, Nicholas Jean, F. soldier (1769–1851), 1769 Z, 1809 E, 1811 E, L, 1851 Z
Sounds and the Fury, The (W. Faulkner), 1929 U
Sound, experiments concerning, 1800 P; treatise on, 1877 P
Sound films, 1919 P, 1927 W
Sounding-machine, Kelvin, 1872 P
Sous l'Oeil des Barberes (M. Barrès), 1808 U
Soustelle, Jacques, F. Left Republican, governor-general of Algeria, 1955 A
South (E. Shackleton), 1919 P
South Africa:
Smith annexes country between Orange and Vaal rivers, 1848 B
problems of federation in, 1875 H, 1877 C, 1880 F
War. *See under* Wars, Britain with Boers
becomes a dominion, 1910 G
Portuguese labour in, regulated, 1928 J
becomes an independent republic outside the Commonwealth, 1961 E
See also under Cape of Good Hope; Transvaal
South African Company British: is chartered, 1889 K; founds Salisbury, 1890 J; organises Rhodesia, 1895 E
South African Republic, of Transvaal, established, 1852 A
See under Transvaal.

South Carolina, State, US: rejects tariff act, 1832 G; as Confederate state, 1861 B
Southcott, Joanna, B. fanatic (1750–1814), 1814 Z
South East Asia Treaty organisation (SEATO): Conference at Bangkok, 1955 B; Sarassin appointed Secretary-General, 1957 J
South-East England, study on development of, 1964 C
Southey, Robert, B. author (1774–1843), 1774 Z, 1794 W, 1801 U, 1805 U, 1813 Q, 1814 U
South Foreland lighthouse, Kent, England, 1858 P
South Pole. *See under* Polar Exploration
South Seas, discoveries in, 1775 P
Southwest Africa: German colonies in, 1883 D; German occupation, 1884 D; boundary with Angola, 1886 M; risings in, 1904 K; German forces surrender to British, 1915 G; assigned as mandated territory to S. Africa and Belgium, 1919 E; political activities by foreigners in, prohibited, 1937 D; UN rejects S. African proposal for incorporation, 1946 M; Smuts refuses to place under UN trusteeship, 1947 A, 1950 M
South Wind (N. Douglas), 1917 U
Souvenirs d'enfance et de jeunesse (Renan), 1883 U
Soviet Communism: A New Civilization, S. and B. Webb, 1935 O
Spa, Belgium: beauty contest at, 1888 V; Conference on Reparations at, 1920 G
Spaak, Paul, Belg. statesman Socialist (b. 1899), 1899 Z; forms coalition, 1938 E; president of U.N. General Assembly, 1946 A; Secretary-general of NATO, 1956 M
Space craft, pilot-manoeuvred, 1965 P
Space flights:
dogs sent in orbit in, 1958 P, 1959 P
monkeys sent in orbit in, 1959 P
G. Cooper, 1963 P
Y. Gagarin, 1961 P
J. Glenn, 1962 P
A. Leonov, 1965 P
M. Scott Carpenter, 1962 P
A. Shepard, 1961 P
V. Tereshkova, 1963 P
Space, Outer, US-Russian agreement on peaceful use of, 1962 M
Space Research: Programmes for launching satellites, 1955 P; Sputniks I and II, launched, 1957 P; Lunik I, launched, 1959 P; Lunik II, reaches moon, 1959 P; Lunik III, photographs moon, 1959 P; Gemini III–VI launched, 1965 P
Space Research Organisation, European, 1962 F
Space, scale of, 1953 P
Space Travel, London Congress on, 1951 O
Space, walks in, 1965 P
Space, Time and Deity (S. Alexander), 1920 R
Spain: Social classes in, 1773 N; troops finally leave South America, 1824 M; frontier with France, defined, 1856 M
Spallanzani, Lazaro, It. scientist (1729–99), 1765 P, 1779 P, 1780 P
Spangenberg, August Gottlieb, G. theologian (1704–92), bishop of Moravian Brethren, 1764 R
Spark, Muriel, B. author, 1959 U
Sparkenbrook (C. Morgan), 1936 U
'Spartacus' Communist group in Berlin, 1916 A, 1919 A
Species, origin of, propounded by Darwin, 1859 P
Species, variation of, 1858 P
Specimens of the Russian Poets (J. Bowring), 1821 U
Spectrum analysis, 1859 P, 1861 P
Speech, transmission of first, 1861 P; by telephone, 1876 P; by wireless, 1900 P
Speeches, notable:
Acheson, at West Point, 1962 M
Balfour, in Washington, 1917 E
Bismarck's 'Blood and Iron', 1862 J
Burke, on Conciliation with America, 1775 O
on French Revolution, 1790 B
J. Chamberlain, at Leicester, 1899 L
Lord R. Churchill, at Dartford, 1886 K
W. S. Churchill, 'Blood and Toil', 1940 E
at Fulton, 1946 C
Dulles, in Berlin, 1958 E
Eisenhower, on Communist threat, 1954 D
Kennedy, on Cuba, 1962 K
Lavigerie's 'Algiers Toast', 1890 L
Lloyd George's 'New Deal' at Bangor, 1935 A
H. Macmillan's 'Wind of Change', in Capetown, 1960 B
G. Marshall, at Harvard, 1947 F
Palmerston's, 'Civis Romanus Sum', 1850 F
F. D. Roosevelt, on 'Policy of the Good Neighbour', 1933 C
Speed limit, in Britain, for motor vehicles, 1903 H, 1935 C
Speed records:
ground, by Campbell, 1935 P
by Cobb, 1939 P, 1947 P
locomotive, 1939 P
water, by Campbell, 1939 P
by Cobb, 1952 P
Speed-reducing gear, for turbines, 1910 P
Speenhamland, Berks., England, system of poor relief, 1950
Speke, John Hanning, B. explorer (1827–64), 1854 P, 1856 P
Spence, Sir Basil, B. architect (b. 1907), 1907 Z, 1951 S, 1959 S, 1962 S, 1964 S
Spence, Thomas, B. bookseller and author (1750–1814), 1775 O
Spencer, Herbert, B. philosopher (1820–1903), 1850 O, 1852 P, 1855 R, 1861 O, 1862 O, 1873 O, 1879 R, 1884 O
Spencer, John Poyntz, earl Spencer, B. Liberal politician (1835–1910), as first lord of Admiralty, 1894 N
Spencer, Sir Stanley, B. artist (1891–1959), 1891 Z, 1913 S, 1920 S, 1922 S, 1923 S, 1926 S, 1934 S, 1935 S, 1939 S, 1941 S, 1945 S, 1959 Z
Spender, Stephen, B. poet and critic (b. 1909), 1909 Z, 1937 O
Spengler, Oswald, G. philosopher (1880–1936), 1880 Z, 1918 O, 1920 O, 1931 R, 1936 Z
Speranski, Mikhail Mikhailovich, Count, R. statesman (1772–1839), 1830 U
Sperry, Elmer Ambrose, Am. inventor (1861–1930), 1861 Z, 1930 Z
Sperry, William Learoyd, Am. author (1882–1954), 1945 R
Spezia, N. W. Italy, 1888 B
Sphinx Rock, Bernese Oberland, meteorological station, 1937 P
Sphymograph, 1878 P
Spicer-Dufuy process for colour photography, 1931 P
Spicheren, Alsace-Lorraine, France, German victory at, 1870 H
Spinning jenny, 1864 P
Spinning machine, for cotton, 1762 P; for flax, 1812 P
Spinning mule, Crompton's, 1779 P
Spire, The (W. Golding), 1964 U
Spirit of Hebrew Poetry, The (Herder), 1782 U

Spirit of the Age (E. Arndt), 1806 O
Spirit of the Age; or Contemporary Portraits (W. Hazlitt), 1825 U
Spiritualism, in US, 1848 R
Spithead, Hampshire, England, naval mutiny at, 1797 D
Spitzbergen, Norway: assigned to Norway, 1919 J; ceded to Norway, 1920 B; Norway annexes, 1925 H; expedition to, 1927 P
Splitting the atom, 1942 P
Spontaneous generation, 1765 P, 1870 P
Spontini, Gasparo Luigi Pacificio, It. musician (1774–1851), 1809 T
Spooner, John Coit, Am. Republican (1843–1919), 1901 C
Sportsman's Sketches, A (I. Turgeniev), 1852 U
Sportsylvania Courthouse, Virginia, US battle, 1864 E
Sprengel, Kurt, G. botanist (1766–1833), 1793 P
Spring, Howard, B. author (1889–1966), 1948 U
Spring's Awakening (F. Wedekind), 1891 U
Spurgeon, Charles Haddon, B. nonconformist preacher (1834–92), 1852 R, 1900 R
Spurzheim, Johann, G. phrenologist (1776–1832), 1810 P
'Spy', cartoonist. *See* Ward, Leslie
Spy, The (J. F. Cooper), 1821 U
Squeaker, The (E. Wallace), 1928 U
Stabiles, 1932 S
Stabilising the Dollar in Purchasing Power (I. Fisher), 1919 O
Stack, Sir Lee, B. governor of Sudan (1868–1924), 1924 L
Staël, Anne Louis Germaine Necker, baronne de Staël-Holstein, F. author (1766–1817), 1766 Z, 1800 U, 1802 U, 1807 U, 1810 U, 1817 Z, 1818 U
Stahl, Friedrich Julius, G. ecclesiastical lawyer (1802–61), 1830 O
Stainless steel, invented, 1912 P
Stalin, Joseph, R. statesman (1879–1953), 1879 Z, 1926 K, 1934 M, 1947 C, 1953 C
  victorious at All-Union Congress, 1927 M
  makes neutrality pact with Japan, 1941 D
  becomes head of USSR government, 1941 E
  meets Churchill, in Moscow, 1942 H
    and Roosevelt at Teheran, 1943 L
  Ode to, 1943 T
  at Yalta Conference, 1945 B
  at Potsdam Conference, 1945 G
  as chairman of Council of Ministers, 1946 C
  policies of, denounced by Khrushchev, 1956 B
Stalingrad, Russia: Germans reach, 1942 H; sword presented to, 1943 B
'Stalin Line', Russia, Russian troops retire to, 1941 G
Stalky and Co. (R. Kipling), 1899 U
Stambolisky, Alexander, Bulgarian politician, 1923 F
Stambulov, Stephen, Bulgarian Nationalist (d. 1895), 1886 J, 1895 G
Stamford University, US, 1950 P
Stamp Act, Britain, imposes on American Colonies, 1765 C
  repealed, 1766 B
Stamp Act Congress, in America, 1765 K
Stamp duties, in Britain, reduced, 1836 H
Stamps, postage. *See under* Postal services
Stamps, trading, campaign against, 1963 O
Standard Oil Company: Rockefeller founds, 1870 P; dissolution ordered, 1911 E; rights in Palestine, 1922 D
Standards, electrical, 1861 P
Stanford, Sir Charles Villiers, B. musician (1852–1924), 1852 Z, 1884 T, 1924 Z
Stanhope, Charles, third earl Stanhope, B. Whig politician and scientist (1753–1816), 1774 O, 1800 P
Stanhope, Philip Dormer Stanhope, earl of Chesterfield (1694–73), 1773 Z, 1774 U
Stanislaus Lesczcynski, King of Poland (1733–6), ruler of Lorraine (1730–66), 1766 B
Stanislaus II (Pontiatowski), King of Poland (1764–1795), 1768 H, 1791 E; elected King, 1764 J; abdicates, 1795 L
Stanislavsky, Constantin, R. choreographer (1863–1938), 1863 Z, 1938 Z
Stanley, Arthur Penrhyn, B. churchman and scholar (1815–81), 1861 Q
Stanley, Edward, 14th earl of Derby, B. Conservative statesman (1799–1869), 1799 Z, 1851 B, 1859 C, 1869 Z
  becomes premier, 1852 B, 1858 B, 1866 G
  resigns, 1852 M, 1859 F, 1868 B
Stanley, Edward Henry, 15th earl of Derby, B. Conservative (1826–93), 1878 D; as foreign secretary, 1874 B; protests against Jingoism, 1878 A
Stanley, Sir Henry Morton, B. explorer of Africa (1840–1904), 1840 Z, 1875 P, 1880 F, 1887 P; meets Livingstone, 1871 P
Stanley, James, B. machinist (1831–81), 1885 P
Stanley, Oliver Frederick George, B. Conservative politician (1896–1950), War Secretary, 1940 A
Stanleyville, Congo: rebels capture, 1964 H; is recaptured, 1964 L
Stansgate, peerage, election court ruling on, 1961 O
Stansgate, viscount. *See* Benn, A. N. W.
Starch, discovery concerning, 1862 P
Starhemberg, Prince, Aus., 1935 K
Starlight Express (A. Blackwood), 1916 W
Starling, Ernest Henry, B. physiologist (1866–1927), 1902 P
Stars:
  codification of, 1818 P, 1862 P
  luminosity of, 1924 P
  measurements of, 1837 P
  revolutions of, 1802 P
  See also Astronomy
State in Relation to Labour, The (W. S. Jevons), 1882 O
State of the Arts, The (Lord Bridges), 1958 S
State of the Prisons of England, The (J. Howard), 1777 O
Statement of the Question of Parliamentary Reform (G. Grote), 1821 O
Statistical Account of Scotland, The (J. Sinclair), 1791 O
Statistical Method for Determining Authorship (A. Ellegärd), 1963 Q
Statute of Liberty, 1886 S
Stavinsky, Alexandre, R. promoter, 1933 M
Stead, William Thomas, B. journalist (1849–1912), 1890 V, 1893 R
'Steady-State' theory, 1961 P
Steam engine:
  early constructions, 1765 P, 1774 P
  invention perfected, 1775 P
  compound, 1845 P
  for cotton spinning, 1785 P
  Puffing Billy, 1812 P
  Rocket, The, 1829 P
  rotary motion, 1785 P
  Stephenson's first effective, 1814 P
  Trevithick's, 1800 P

in US, first engine, 1829 P
Westinghouse brakes for, 1868 P
Steam-hammer, Nasmyth's, 1839 P
Steam, measurement of heat of, 1764 P
Steam-pump, 1841 P
Steam road-carriage, 1769 P
Steam-roller, 1859 P
Steam rolling-mill, 1790 P
Steamships: paddle-wheel, 1783 P, Fitch's, 1787 P; early vessels, 1803 P, 1807 P, 1812 P; iron, 1820 P; screw for, 1839 P. *See also under* Merchant Shipping
Steamships, notable:
Great Eastern, 1859 P
Lusitania, 1907 P, 1915 E
Mauritania, 1907 P
Normandie, 1935 P
Queen Mary, 1934 P
Savannah, 1818 P
Titanic, 1912 P
Steamship Companies, 'Castle' and 'Union' lines amalgamate, 1900 O
Cunard, loan to, 1964 M
Steel:
'basic' process for, 1878 P
Bessemer's process, 1856 P
Carnegie's large furnace, 1880 P
cheap, 1856 P, 1857 P, 1861 P
continuous hot-strip rolling, 1923 P
ductile, 1856 P
electric arc to heat, 1879 P
furnace lined with dolomite, 1877 P
open-hearth process, 1861 P
stainless, invented, 1912 P
steel-making converter, 1851 P
tungsten, 1855 P
Cf. Iron
Steel Corporation, US, Morgan founds, 1901 O
Steel-framed buildings, 1890 P
Steel pens, 1780 P
Steel Production:
in Austria, 1890 Y, 1911 Y
in Britain, 1820 Y, 1875 Y, 1885 Y, 1890 Y, 1896 Y, 1901 Y, 1911 Y, 1913 Y, 1924 Y, 1938 Y, 1941 Y, 1948 Y
in France, 1875 Y, 1885 Y, 1890 Y, 1896 Y, 1901 Y, 1911 Y, 1913 Y, 1924 Y, 1938 Y, 1948 Y
in Germany, 1875 Y, 1885 Y, 1890 Y, 1896 Y, 1901 Y, 1911 Y, 1913 Y, 1924 Y, 1938 Y, 1948 Y
in Russia, 1890 Y, 1911 Y, 1913 Y, 1932 Y, 1938 Y, 1940 Y, 1948 Y
in US, 1890 Y, 1896 Y, 1901 Y, 1911 Y, 1924 Y, 1938 Y, 1942 Y, 1948 Y
Steer, Philip Paul Wilson, B. artist (1860–1942), 1860 Z, 1886 S, 1903 S, 1922 S, 1942 Z
Stein, Sir Aurel, B. archaeologist (1862–1943), 1915 Q
Stein, Gertrude, Am. author (1874–1946), 1874 Z, 1925 U, 1933 U, 1946 Z
Stein, Heinrich Friedrich Karl, baron von und zum, G. statesman (1757–1831), 1804 K, 1807 A, G, 1808 M, 1810 F, 1826 Q
Steinbeck, John, Am. author (b. 1902), 1902 Z, 1939 U, 1942 U
Steiner, Jakob, Swe. mathematician (1796–1863), 1832 P
Steinheim skull, 1933 P
Steintal, Alsace, France, Crêche at, 1769 O
Steinthal, Heymann, G. philosopher (1823–99), 1859 R
Steinway, William, Am. formerly G. piano manufacturer (1835–96), 1853 T
Stellaland Republic, in Bechuanaland, S. Africa, 1873 J, 1885 C
Stellar Movement and the Structure of the Universe (Eddington), 1914 P
Stendhal. *See* Beyle, Marie Henri
Stenton, Sir Frank Merry, B. historian (b. 1880), 1944 Q
Stephanopoulos, Stephanhos, Greek leader of Social Populist Party (b. 1893), 1965 G
Stephen, Sir Leslie, B. author and philosopher (1832–1904), 1832 Z, 1882 R, 1885 Q, 1893 R, 1900 O, 1904 Z
Stephens, Alexander Hamilton, Am. Confederate, 1868 O
Stephens, Uriah, Smith, Am. garment cutter, founder of Knights of Labor (1821–82), 1869 O
Stephens, W., Am. cyclist, 1886 W
Stephenson, George, B. engineer (1781–1848), 1781 Z, 1814 P, 1848 Z, 1850 P
Rocket, 1829 P
Stephinac, Aloizje, Yugoslav Cardinal (1898–1960), Archbishop of Zagreb and primate of Yugoslavia, imprisoned, 1946 J
Stereophonic gramophone recordings, 1958 P
Sterilisation of water, by ultra-violet rays, 1912 P
Sterne, Lawrence, B. author (1713–68), 1767 U, 1768 O, Z
Stern-Rubath, G. political scientist, 1921 O
Stettinius, Edward, Am. Secretary of State (1900–1949), appointed secretary of state, 1944 L; at UN Conference, 1945 D; retires, 1945 G
Stevenage New Town, Herts., England, 1948 S
Stevens, Alfred, B. artist (1818–75), 1858 S
Stevenson, Adlai, Am. Democrat (b. 1900), defeated in presidential elections, 1952 L, 1956 L
Stevenson, Elizabeth. *See* Gaskell, Elizabeth
Stevenson, Sir John Andrew, Ir. musician (1760–1833), 1807 T
Stevenson, Robert Louis, B. author (1850–94), 1850 Z, 1879 U, 1881 U, 1883 U, 1886 U, 1894 Z, 1896 U
Steward, J. D., B. author, 1958 O
Stewart, Dugald, B. philosopher (1753–1828), 1782 R, 1792 R, 1815 R, 1828 R
Stewart, Michael, B. Labour politician (b. 1906), becomes foreign secretary, 1965 A
Stewart, Robert, viscount Castlereagh, marquess of Londonderry, B. statesman, Tory (1769–1822), 1769 Z, 1807 C; fights duel with Canning, 1809 J; becomes foreign secretary, 1812 C; suicide, 1822 H
Stijl, The, 1917 S
Stimpson, Henry Lewis, Am. secretary of state, Republican (1867–1950), 1927 E
Stimpson Doctrine, 1932 A
Stock Exchange, London: compensation fund, 1950 O; public galleries opened, 1953 O; re-organisation of, 1962 O; requires companies to supply information, 1964 O
Stock Exchange, New York: built, 1903 S; crash, 1929 O
Stockholm, Sweden: national theatre, 1773 W; treaty, Britain with Sweden, 1813 C; music in, 1838 W; Town Hall, 1909 O; Olympic Games in, 1912 X; Confederation of Free Trade Union meets at, 1953 G
Stockton-on-Tees, Durham, England, railway opened, 1825 P
Stockach, Baden, W. Germany, 1799 C
Stolypin, Peter, R. premier (*d.* 1911), 1906 F; agrarian reforms of, 1906 L; assassinated, 1911 J

Stonehenge, Wiltshire, England, excavations at, 1957 Q, 1964 Q
Stoney, Johnstone, B. physicist (1826–1911), 1891 P
Stonyhurst College, England, 1794 O
Stopes, Marie Carmichael, B. pioneer of birth control (1890–1958), 1890 Z, 1922 O, 1958 Z
Storm-Troopers, Nazi, 1932 F, 1933 C
Story of Agathon, The (C. M. Wieland), 1766 U
Story of Rimini, The (L. Hunt), 1816 U
Story of the Treasure Seekers, The (E. Nesbitt), 1899 U
Stowe, Harriet Beecher, Am. author (1811–96), 1811 Z, 1896 Z
Strachey, Giles Lytton, B. author (1880–1932), 1880 Z, 1918 U, 1921 Q, 1931 U, 1932 Z
Strachey, John, B. Labour politician and author (1902–63), 1932 O, 1936 O
Straits Settlements: becomes Crown Colony, 1867 D; under Clarke's governorship, 1873 N; treaty of federation of, 1896 G
Stranger, The (A. Kötzebue), 1797 W
Strasbourg, Bas-Rhin, France: Napoleon III's revolt at, fails, 1836 K; surrenders to Prussians, 1870 K; University, 1872 O; Allies recapture, 1944 L; becomes seat of Council of Europe, 1949 E; Congress of European Unity at, 1950 H; Assembly of W. European Union meets at, 1955 G; European Court of Human Rights meets at, 1959 B
Strassfurt, near Magdeburg, E. Germany, 1860 P
Strassman, W., atomic physicist, 1939 P
Strata Identified by Organised Fossils, 1816 P
Stratford upon Avon, Warwickshire, England, Shakespeare Memorial Theatre at, 1928 S, 1932 W, 1959 W
Strauss, David Friedrich, G. theologian (1808–74), 1835 R, 1872 R
Strauss, Franz Josef, West Germ. Christian Democrat (b. 1915), dismissed from Ministry of Defence over *Der Spiegel* affair, 1962 L
Strauss, Johann, the younger, Aus. musician (1825–1899), 1867 T, 1874 T
Strauss, Richard, G. musician (1864–1949), 1888 T, 1889 T, 1895 T, 1896 T, 1905 T, 1907 T, 1911 T, 1912 T, 1933 T, 1945 T
Straussfedern (J. Musäus), 1786 U
Stravinsky, Igor, R. musician (b. 1882), 1882 Z, 1910 T, 1912 T, 1913 T, 1920 T, 1922 T, 1924 T, 1927 T, 1928 T, 1930 T, 1934 T, 1935 T, 1940 T, 1945 T, 1951 T, 1952 T, 1956 T, 1957 T
Strayed Reveller, The (M. Arnold), 1849 U
Streeruwitz, Ernst, Aus. Chancellor, 1929 D
Street, George Edmund, B. architect (1824–88), 1868 S
Streetcar Named Desire, A (T. Williams), 1947 W
Streeter, Burnett Hillman, B. theologian (1874–1937), 1912 R
Street-lighting:
by gas, in London, 1822 P
by electricity, in Paris, 1841 P
in London, 1878 P
in New York, 1880 P
Street Scene (E. Rice), 1930 W
Strehlenau, Nikolas Franz Niembsch von, Aus. poet under pseudonym 'Nikolas Lenau' (1802–50), 1836 U, 1837 U, 1842 U
Streit, Clarence, K., Am. journalist, advocate of federal union (b. 1896), 1939 O
Strell, Martin, G. chemist (b. 1916), 1960 P
Streptococcal injections, treatment for, 1935 P
Streptococcus, discovery of, 1880 P
Streptomycine, 1943 P, 1946 P
Stresa, Italy Conference, between Britain, France and Italy, 1935 D
Stresemann, Gustave, G. statesman (1878–1929), 1878 Z, 1925 A, 1929 K; becomes Chancellor, 1923 H; as foreign minister, 1925 A; meets Briand, 1926 J
Strife of the Faculties (I. Kant), 1798 R
Strijdom, Johannes Gerhardus, S. African Nationalist (1893–1958), 1954 M, 1958 J
Strikes:
in Australia, coal miners, 1949 H
in Austria, in Vienna, 1918 A
general, 1927 G, 1953 K
in Belgium, general, 1893 D, 1901 N
doctors, 1964 D
in Britain, tailors, 1777 O
strikes effectively prohibited, 1825 G
general, plan for, fails, 1834 A
agricultural workers, 1874 B
London dockers, 1889 H, T
peaceful picketing permitted, 1906 M
South Wales miners, 1911 C, H
London dockers, 1911 H, 1912 E, G
railwaymen, 1911 H, M
coal miners, 1912 A, B, C
transport workers, 1912 F
munition workers, 1916 C
South Wales miners, 1916 L
statistics of working days lost, 1919 Y, 1920 Y, 1921 Y, 1922 Y, 1923 Y, 1924 Y
general strike to be called if Britain declares war on USSR, 1920 H
coal miners, 1921 C, 1922 D
London dockers, 1923 G
dockers, 1924 B
coal miners, 1926 E, L
general strike, 1926 E
statistics of working days lost, 1926 Y
illegality of certain strikes under Trade Unions Act, 1927 G
London busmen, 1937 E
South Wales coal miners, 1944 B
power of Minister of Labour in, agitation against, 1944 D
repeal of Trades Disputes Act, 1946 B
statistics of working days lost, 1946 N
dockers, 1949 F, 1950 D
railwaymen, 1955 E
dockers, 1955 G
'busmen, 1957 G, 1958 E
printers, 1959 F
in British Guiana, general strike, 1963 D, 1964 G
sugar workers, 1964 C, G
in Canada, in Winnipeg, 1919 E
sit-down, in motor industry, 1937 C, O
in Denmark, statistics, 1925 Y
in France, principle of general strike, 1895 A
at Le Creusot, 1899 J
coal miners, 1901 N
postal workers, 1909 D
general strike averted, 1910 K
railwaymen, 1910 K
statistics of working days lost, 1919 Y, 1920 Y, 1921 Y, 1922 Y
strike action, 1947 E, 1953 H
in Germany, food strike in Berlin, 1917 D
in Berlin, 1918 A
general, 1923 A, Y
in Gold Coast, 1950 A
in Holland, dockers, 1903 D
railwaymen, 1903 D
statistics, 1923 Y

in India, 1928 N
in Italy, in Genoa, 1901 B
in chief cities, 1901 N
general, prevented, 1902 B
general, 1904 J
in Russia, general, 1905 K
in South Africa, 1922 C
in Spain, general, in Barcelona, 1909 G
by Socialists in Barcelona, 1934 D
frequent, 1934 K
in US, iron and steel workers, 1892 F
coal miners, 1902 E, K
steel workers, 1919 J
New York dockers, 1919 K
statistics of working days lost, 1919 Y, 1920 Y, 1921 Y, 1922 Y, 1923 Y, 1924 Y
coal miners, 1923 H
sit-down, in motor industry, 1937 O
coal miners, 1943 D
widespread, 1945 L
steel and electrical workers, 1946 B
federal government takes over mines and railways, 1946 E
statistics of working days lost, 1946 N
position under Taft-Hartley Act, 1947 F
military control during railway strike, 1951 B
steel workers, averted, 1952 D
New York newspaper men, 1963 D
in Uruguay, call for general strike, 1956 M
See also under Trade Unions
Strindberg, August, Swe. author (1849–1912), 1849 Z, 1879 W, 1886 U, 1888 W, 1897 U, 1901 U, 1905 U, 1912 Z
Stromberg, S. Africa, British defeat at, 1899 M
Stromeyer, F., Swe. chemist, 1818 P
Structure of the Atom, The (E. Andrade), 1923 P
Struensee, Johann Frederick, Dan. politician (1731–1772), 1770 J, M, 1772 A
Struther, Jan, pseudonym of Mrs. A. K. Placzek (née Joyce Anstruther), Am. author (1901–53), 1939 U
Strutt, John William, lord Rayleigh, B. scientist (1842–1919), 1877 P, 1894 P, 1900 P
Struve, Friedrich Georg Wilhelm, G. astronomer (1793–1864), 1837 P
Struwwelpeter (A. H. Hoffmann), 1847 U
Stuart, James, B. artist and architect (1713–88), 1794 Q
Stubbs, George, B. artist (1724–1806), 1766 S
Stubbs, William, B. medieval historian and bishop of Oxford (1825–1901), 1825 Z, 1866 Q, 1874 Q, 1901 Z
Studien über Hysterie (S. Freud), 1895 R
Studies in History and Jurisprudence (J. Bryce), 1901 Q
Studies in the Free Investigation of the Canon (J. Semler), 1771 R
Studies in the History of the Renaissance (W. Pater), 1873 Q
Studies in the Psychology of Sex (H. Ellis), 1897 R
Studies of Glaciers (Agassiz), 1840 P
Study of History, A (A. Toynbee), 1934 Q
Study of Religion, A (J. Martineau), 1888 R
Study of Sociology (H. Spencer), 1873 P
Sturdee, Sir Frederick Charles Doveton, B. admiral (1859–1925), 1914 M
Stürgkh, Carl, Count, Aus. premier, 1916 K
Sturmer, Boris, R. premier, 1916 B
Sturm und Drang in literature, 1766 U
Sturm und Drang (F. M. von Klinger), 1776 W
Subjection of Women, The (J. S. Mill), 1869 O
Submarine cables, 1850 P, 1866 P
Submarines:
atomic powered, 1952 P, 1959 P
commercial, 1916 G
electric, 1896 P
the first, 1801 P
nuclear, *Nautilus*, passes under Polar ice-cap, 1958 P
Polaris, facilities for, at Holy Loch, 1960 L
Submarine Warfare:
by Germany; in World War I, sinkings without warning, 1915 A, E
intensified, 1915 B
undertaking not to attack merchant shipping, 1915 J
sinkings of merchant shipping without warning, 1916 B
unrestricted warfare, 1917 A
suspended, 1918 K
losses, 1918 Y
in World War II, lay magnetic mines, 1939 L
warfare intensified, 1940 K, 1941 C
use homing torpedoes, 1945 A
losses, 1945 Y
restricted by Washington Conference, 1922 B
regulated by London Conference, 1930 D
Subsidies, paid by Britain to Allies, 1809 D, 1813 C, F. *See also under* Loans
Subsidies, bread, in Britain, 1956 J
Substitution, chemical law of, 1834 P
Such is Life (F. Wedekind), 1907 W
Sudan:
exploration of, 1869 P
British occupation, 1882 J
British evacuation, 1883 L, 1885 A
under Dervish control, 1885 G
British campaigns in, 1896 G, J, 1897 G, H, 1898 D, J, L, 1899 L
Anglo-Egyptian convention on, 1899 A
frontier settlements, 1901 M, 1902 D, 1934 F
Anglo-Egyptian joint sovereignty over, 1922 C
Britain refuses Egyptian demands to evacuate, 1924 F
Anglo-Egyptian talks on, 1930 E
military operations in, end, 1945 J
preparation for self-government, 1947 A
Egypt abrogates 1899 convention, 1951 K
Anglo-Egyptian agreement on, 1953 B
proclaimed an independent republic, 1956 A
forms, with Egypt, United Arab Republic, 1958 B
Sudermann, Hermann, G. author (1857–1938), 1857 Z, 1887 U, 1938 U
Sudetenland, Czechoslovakia: riots in, 1937 K; S. Germans leave Czech Parliament, 1937 L; Halifax discusses problem with Hitler, 1937 L; Germans in demand autonomy, 1938 D; France and Britain oppose Germany, 1938 E; Runciman's role in talks, 1938 G; is transferred to Germany, 1938 J
Sue, Eugène, F. novelist (1804–57), 1844 U
Suez Canal, Egypt:
opened, 1869 L
statistics of shipping using, 1870 Y, 1880 Y, 1939 Y, 1951 Y
Britain purchases shares in, 1875 L
Russia is warned against attempting blockade of, 1877 E
Constantinople Convention declares open to all nations, 1888 K
Convention on, 1904 D
Turks are repulsed from, 1915 B
Britain occupies Canal Zone, 1936 H

Suez Canal—*contd.*
Anglo-Egyptian agreement on evacuation of Canal Zone, 1954 K
Egypt not to extend Canal Company's concession, 1956 F
last British troops leave Canal Zone, 1956 F
Nasser seizes, 1956 G
Canal-Users Association established, 1956 H
air lift of British families from Canal Zone, 1956 H
London Conferences on, 1956 H, J
Dulles Plan for, rejected by Nasser, 1956 J
Nehru's plan for, 1956 H
Britain and France refer dispute to UN, 1956 J
Anglo-French ultimatum to Egypt and Israel, 1956 K
Israel invades Sinai, 1956 K
Israel accepts demands for cease-fire, 1956 K
Anglo-French bombing of Egypt, 1956 K
Britain and France accept cease-fire if UN force will keep peace, 1956 L
UN sends force, 1956 L
British paratroops land at Port Said, 1956 L
Anglo-French cease-fire, 1956 L
Anglo-French withdrawal, 1956 M
UN fleet clears Canal, 1956 M
is re-opened to shipping, 1957 C
Anglo-Egyptian settlement of claims, 1959 B
compensation for British subjects, 1962 H
Suffering and Existence (K. Jaspers), 1935 R
Suffrage, The. *See under* Franchise, The
Suffragettes, in Britain, 1903 O; riots by, 1911 L; forcible feeding, of, 1912 F; demonstrations by, 1913 A; outrages by, 1913 D, 1914 C
Suffren St. Tropez, Pierre André de, F. admiral (1729–88), 1781 D
Suffolk Convention, Massachusetts, US, 1774 H
Suhard, Archbishop of Paris, 1943 R
Sukarno, Archmed, Indonesian president (b. 1901), 1945 L, 1948 M, 1956 M; attempted assassination, 1957 M; dissolves Constituent assembly, 1959 G; forms National Front, 1960 A; suspends Parliament, 1960 C; proclaims West New Guinea an Indonesian province, 1962 A; increases hostility to Malaysia, 1963 J
Sullivan, Sir Arthur Seymour, B. musician (1842–1900), 1842 Z, 1875 T, 1878 T, 1880 T, 1882 T, 1887 T, 1889 T, 1900 Z; ends partnership with Gilbert, 1896 T; music arranged as ballet, 1951 T
Sullivan, Francis Stoughton, B. jurist (1719–76), 1772 Q
Sully-Prudhomme, René François Armand, F. poet (1839–1907), 1878 U
Sulphapyridine ('M and B'), 1938 P
Summer of the Seventeenth Doll, The (Lawler), 1955 W
Summertime, 1916 O
Summit meeting: proposed, 1958 A; preliminary talks, 1958 B, F; Khrushchev's proposals for immediate meeting rejected, 1958 G; Western powers invite Russia to, 1959 M; meeting in Paris achieved, 1960 E
Summoned by Bells (J. Betjeman), 1960 U
Sumner, Benedict Humphrey, B. historian (1893–1951), 1944 Q
Sumter, Thomas, Am. soldier (1736–1832), 1780 H
Sun, The:
eclipses of, 1919 P, 1936 P
rays of, measurement of heat of, 1825 P
infra-fed, 1800 P
spots, 1946 P
Sunday rest:
in Austria, 1850 O
in Britain, revival of Sabbatarianism, 1835 R
Sunday Schools:
in Britain, 1780 R
London Society for establishing, 1785 R
in US, 1824 R
Sun Doctor, The (R. Shaw), 1962 U
Sun Yat-Sen, Chi. statesman (1867–1925), 1867 Z, 1905 N, 1911 M, 1925 Z
Supervielle, Jules, F. author (1884–1961), 1925 U
Supply, British Ministry of, 1939 O
Supreme Allied War Council, 1917 L, 1921 E
Supreme Command, The (Lord Hankey), 1961 Q
Supreme Council of National Economy, Russian, 1963 O
Supreme War Council of Central Powers, 1916 J
Surgeons, Royal College of, London, 1800 P
Sur l'homme et le développment de ses faculties (L. A. J. Quetelet), 1835 P
Surrealism, 1917 S, 1929 S, 1935 S
Surrey, earl of. *See* Howard, Henry
Survey of Russian History (B. H. Sumner), 1944 Q
Surtees, Robert Smith, B. sporting novelist (1803–1864), 1838 U
Sutherland, Graham Vivian, B. artist (b. 1903), 1939 S, 1942 S, 1944 S, 1946 S, 1949 S, 1951 S, 1954 S, 1957 S, 1962 S
Sutlej River, W. Pakistan, British gains beyond, 1846 C
Suvla, Gallipoli, Turkey: Allied landings, 1915 H; withdrawal, 1915 M
Suvorov, Alexander Vasilievich, Count Suvarov Rimniksy, R. soldier (1729–1800), 1789 G, 1790 M, 1799 D, F, H, J
Svevo, Italo, It. author, 1921 U
Swakopmund, S.W. Africa, occupied, 1915 A
Swan, Annie, S. *See* Smith, Mrs. Burnett
Swan, Sir John William, B. physicist and electrician (1828–1914), 1878 P, 1880 P
Swart, Charles Robberts, S. Afri. Nationalist (b. 1901), president of Republic, 1961 E
Swastika, becomes German flag, 1935 J
Swaziland, S. Africa, annexed by Transvaal, 1893 L
Sweated industries, campaign to reform British, 1906 O
legislation to end, 1909 O
Sweden: Constitution in, 1764 D, 1769 K, M; monarchy in, 1772 G, H; union with Norway, 1813 C; acquiesces in Norway's independence, 1905 J
Swedenborg, Emanuel, Swe. theologian (1688–1772), 1768 R, 1772 Z
Swedenborgians. *See under* Religious Denominations
Sweet Lavender (A. W. Pinero), 1888 W
Swimming records, 1927 X, 1965 X
Swinburne, Algernon Charles, B. poet (1837–1909), 1837 Z, 1865 U, 1866 U, 1878 U, 1909 Z
Swinemunde, Poland, emperors meet at, 1907 H
'Swing', term coined, 1935 T
Swinnerton, Frank Arthur, B. author (b. 1884), 1917 U
Swiss Songs (J. K. Lavater), 1767 U
Switchboard, telephone, automatic, 1892 P
Switzerland: Cantons regain independence, 1803 B; single coinage in, 1850 P
Sword in the Stone, The (T. H. White), 1958 U
Sybil, or the Two Nations (B. Disraeli), 1845 U
Sybilline Leaves (S. T. Coleridge), 1817 U
Sybel, Heinrich von, G. historian (1817–95), 1853 Q
Sydney, N.S. Wales, Australia: cold store, at 1861 P; railway to Melbourne, 1883 P; convention for

federation at, 1891 C; harbour, bridge, 1932 P; Commonwealth finance ministers meet at, 1954 A;
Opera House, 1956 S
Syllabus of Errors, issued by Pius IX, 1864 R; Döllinger opposes, 1869 R
Sylt, Isle of, W. Germany, 1940 C
Sylvester, James Joseph, B. mathematician (1814–1897), 1852 P
Sylvain (J. F. Marmontel), 1770 U
Symbolism and Belief (E. Bevan), 1938 R
Symbolism of the Ancients (G. F. Creuzer), 1810 Q
Symbolist Movement, 1855 U, 1886 V
Symphonic Poems and Suites. *See* Overtures, etc.
Symphonie Pastorale, La (A. Gide), 1919 U
Symphonies, named:
Choral (Beethoven), 1824 T, 1825 T
Classical (Prokofiev), 1917 T
Clock (Haydn), 1794 T
Colour (Bliss), 1922 T
Drum Roll (Haydn), 1795 T
Eroica (Beethoven), 1804 T
Fantastique (Berlioz), 1830 T
Farewell (Haydn), 1772 T
Faust (Liszt), 1857 T
From the New World (Dvořák), 1893 T
Great C Major (Schubert), 1839 T
Haffner (Mozart), 1782 T
Italian (Mendelssohn), 1833 T
Jupiter (Mozart), 1788 T
Kaddish (Bernstein), 1964 T
Leningrad (Shostokovich), 1942 T
London (Haydn), 1795 T
London (Vaughan Williams), 1914 T
Oxford (Haydn), 1788 T
Paris (Haydn), 1784 T
Pastoral (Beethoven), 1808 T
Pastoral (Vaughan Williams), 1922 T
Pathétique (Tschaikovisky), 1893 T
Philosopher, The (Haydn), 1764 T
Prague (Mozart), 1787 T
Rhenish (Schumann), 1850 T
Roxolane, La (Haydn), 1777 T
Scottish (Mendelssohn), 1842 T
Sea (Vaughan Williams), 1910 T
Surprise (Haydn), 1791 T
Toy (Haydn), 1780 T
Unfinished (Schubert), 1822 T
Youth (Prokofiev), 1952 T
Symphonies, other notable:
Arnold, 1957 T
Bax, 1928 T
van Beethoven, 1800 T, 1802 T, 1804 T, 1806 T, 1808 T, 1812 T, 1824 T, 1825 T
Borodin, 1877 T
Brahms, 1876 T, 1877 T, 1883 T, 1885 T
Britten, 1964 T
Bruckner, 1884 T
Copland, 1925 T
Dvořák, 1889 T
Elgar, 1908 T, 1911 T
Franck, 1889 T
Fricker, 1950 T
Harris, 1942 T
Honegger, 1950 T
Kodály, 1961 T
Mahler, 1895 T, 1900 T, 1909 T, 1964 T
Milhaud, 1946 T
Moeran, 1938 T
Rawsthorne, 1950 T
Rubbra, 1942 T, 1954 T
Searle, 1960 T
Shostokovich, 1927 T, 1937 T, 1944 T, 1946 T, 1954 T
Sibelius, 1899 T
Stravinsky, 1940 T, 1945 T
Tschaikovsky, 1877 T, 1889 T
Vaughan Williams, 1943 T, 1953 T, 1958 T
Walton, 1935 T
Syndicalism, British T.U.C. votes against, 1912 J
Syndicalists. *See* Political Parties
Synge, John Millington, Ir. dramatist (1871–1909), 1904 W, 1907 W, 1909 W
Synnöve Solbakken (B. Björnson), 1857 U
Synthetic diamonds, 1959 P
Synthetic fibres:
artificial silk, 1887 P
nylon, 1937 P
rayon, 1892 P
terylene, 1941 P
Synthetic rubber, 1909 P, 1944 Y
Syria: ceded by Turkey to Egypt, 1833 E; Turks invade, 1839 D; Ibrahim evacuates, 1840 L; is assigned to Mehemet Ali, 1840 G, L; massacres in, 1860 J; independence, 1920 C; mandated to France, by League, 1920 D, G, 1922 G; boundary with Palestine settled, 1920 M; Allied invasion of, 1941 F; cease fire in, 1941 G, 1945 E; France and Britain pledge to evacuate, 1945 M; Arab Republic formed, 1961 J; alleges UAR interference, 1962 H; federated with UAR, 1963 D
Syrtes, Les (J. Moréas), 1884 U
System der Sittenlehre (J. G. Fichte), 1798 R
Système de la Nature (P. Holbach), 1770 R
Système des animaux sans vertebres (Lamarck), 1809 P
Systemma Entomologiae (J. C. Fabricius), 1775 P
System of Assigned Rights (F. Lassalle), 1861 O
System of Comparative Surgery (C. Bell), 1807 P
System of Conjugation (F. Bopp), 1816 Q
System of Minerology (J. Dana), 1837 P
System of Transcendental Idealism (F. W. Schelling), 1800 R

T

Taaffe, Eduard Franz Joseph von, Count, Aus. statesman (1833–95), 1879 H, 1893 K
Tableau du Progrès de l'Esprit humain (Condorcet), 1793 O
Table Talk (W. Cowper), 1782 U
Table Talk (W. Hazlitt), 1821 U
Tablets, contraceptive, 1952 P
Tacna-Arica dispute, S. America, 1883 K, 1922 G
Taff Vale judgment, 1901 G
Taft, William Howard, Am. Republican statesman (1857–1930), 27th president of US (1909–13), 1857 Z, 1911 G, H, 1912 C, F, 1930 Z; heads commission on Philippines, 1900 B, J; governor of Philippines, 1901 G; elected president, 1908 L; inaugurated, 1909 C; vetoes army bill, 1912 F; loses presidential election to Wilson, 1912 L
Tagore, Rabindranath, Ind. poet (1861–1941), 1861 Z, 1912 U, 1941 Z
Tahiti, Society Islands, Pacific: France annexes, 1880 F; Gauguin settles in, 1891 S
Tailleferre, Germaine, F. musician (b. 1892), 1920 T
Taine, Hippolyte, F. author (1828–93), 1828 Z, 1853 Q, 1856 R, 1865 R, 1873 O, 1893 Z
Tait, Archibald Campbell, B. churchman (1811–82), 1867 R
Taiping Rebellion in China, 1851 N, 1855 C
Taiwan, China. *See* Formosa

Taizé, near Cluny, France, Protestant community at, 1944 R
Take Your Choice (J. Cartwright), 1776 O
Talal, King, of Jordan, reign of, is terminated, 1952 H
Talbot, William Henry Fox, B. pioneer of photography (1800–77), 1800 Z, 1839 P, 1877 Z
Tale of Two Cities, A (C. Dickens), 1859 U
Tales from Shakespeare (C. and M. Lamb), 1807 U
Tales of Jacob (T. Mann), 1933 U
Tales of Peter Lebrecht (L. Tieck), 1797 U
Tales of the Grotesque and Arabesque (E. A. Poe), 1840 U
Tales of the Hall (G. Crabbe), 1817 U
Tales of the Jazz Age (S. Fitzgerald), 1923 U
Talienwan, China, is ceded to Japan, 1905 J
Talleyrand-Périgord, Charles Maurice de, F. diplomat (1754–1838), 1797 G, 1799 G, L, 1814 D, 1838 Z
Tallinn, Russia, Germans take, 1941 G
Tamerlane (E. A. Poe), 1827 U
Tampico, Mexico, US troops sent to, 1914 D
Tamworth Manifesto, Peel issues, 1834 M
Tam O'Shanter (R. Burns), 1790 U
Tanganyika: Germany annexes, 1885 B; League mandate for, 1922 G; internal self-government for, 1961 E; becomes republic within Commonwealth, 1962 M; is united with Zanzibar, 1964 D; changes name to Tanzania, 1964 D. *See also under* Tanzania
Tanganyika, Lake, Africa: exploration of, 1856 P; British Africa Company acquires land near, 1890 E
Tangier, Morocco: William II visits, 1905 C; convention on, 1923 B; Spanish control in, 1928 G; Sultan of Morocco visits, 1955 K; North African Nationalists meet at, 1958 D
Tanglewood Tales (N. Hawthorne), 1853 U
Tankara ministry in Japan, falls, 1929 G
Tanks, military: first used in warfare, 1916 J, P; used in British advance on Cambrai, 1917 L; notable battles in Western Desert, 1942 E, F; British production of, 1939 Y, 1940 Y, 1941 J, Y, 1942 Y, 1943 Y
Tannenburg, Poland: Russians defeated at, 1914 E; memorial, 1927 J
Tanner, Beatrice. *See* Campbell, Mrs. Patrick
Tanzania, formed by union of Tanganyika and Zanzibar, 1964 D
Tape, magnetic, 1942 P
Tapestries, Morris's, 1861 S
Tapisserie de Notre-Dame, La (C. Péguy), 1913 U
Taranto, Italy, British attack on, 1940 L; falls to Eighth Army, 1943 J
Tarare (P. Beaumarchais), 1787 W
Tardieu, André, F. premier, 1932 B
Tariff Questions:
  Pan-American plans for reciprocity, 1889 K
  Geneva Conference on, 1930 B
  Oslo agreement on, 1930 M
  General Agreement on Trade and Tariffs (GATT), negotiations on ('Kennedy Round'), 1963 E, 1964 E
  in Australia, duty on Lancashire cottons, 1934 H
  in Belgium and Luxembourg, customs union, 1912 O
  in Belgium, Holland, Luxembourg, customs union ('Benelux'), formed, 1947 K
  in Britain: free trade, beginnings of, 1821 E; completed, 1849 F, H
    imperial preference, issue of, 1897 G, 1902 F, 1903 E
      Chamberlain resigns to test feeling on, 1903 J
      Act passed, 1919 H
      Britain rejects, with Canada, 1930 K
      favoured by Ottawa Conference, 1932 G
      Samuel resigns on issue of, 1932 J
    protection is introduced, 1932 C
    duties on German Reparation goods, 1921 C; reduced, 1924 B
    tariff war with Ireland ended, 1936 B
    Anglo-Irish pact on coal and cattle, 1934 M
    import surcharge imposed, 1964 L; reduced, 1965 D
  in Canada, right to fix tariffs, 1846 H
    protection, 1878 H
    reciprocity with US urged, 1890 K
    protectionist in force, 1904 O
    preferential agreement with W. Indies, 1912 D
    customs scandals, 1926 F
    Dunning tariff, 1930 E
    gives Britain preference, 1930 E
    Britain rejects preference, 1930 K
    reciprocal trade agreement with US, 1935 L
    See also under US
  in Central and S. America, Latin American Free Trade Association, 1961 F
  in China, boycott of US goods, 1905 G
    Japan recognises right of China to fix, 1930 E
  in Egypt, economic union with Syria, 1957 J
  in Europe, high tariffs introduced, 1921 O
    See Common Market; European Economic Community; European Free Trade Association
  in France, Trianon tariff, 1810 H
    protection, 1891 N
    tariff war with Switzerland, 1893 N
      with Italy, 1898 L
    Franco-Canadian agreement, 1933 E
    Franco-Italian customs union, 1948 C
  in Germany, protectionist, 1879 G, 1902 M
    See also under Prussia *and main index under* Zollverein
  in New Zealand, protectionist, 1888 N
    favours Britain, 1903 N
  in Persia, discriminatory, 1902 L
  in Prussia, internal duties abolished, 1818 E
    treaty with Schwarzburg-Sonderhausen, 1819 K
    See also Zollverein
  in Russia, 1810 M
  in Siberia, tariff war with Austria, 1905 N
  in Sweden, protective, 1888 N
  in Switzerland, customs union with Liechtenstein, 1923 F
  in US, protectionist, 1816 O
    'Tariff of Abominations' (protectionist), 1828 E; revised, 1832 G
    Clay Tariff appeases S. Carolina, 1833 C
    New Whig Tariff (protective), 1842 N
    reciprocity with Canada, 1854 F
    Morrill Tariff, 1861 C
    as issue in presidential election, 1888 L
    Mackinley Tariff, 1890 K, 1892 L
      repealed, 1894 E
    Wilson-Gorman Tariff, 1894 H
    Dindley's Tariff (protective), 1897 G
    Payne-Aldrich Tariff, maintains protection, 1909 H
    reciprocity with Canada, 1911 D, G; annulled, 1911 J
    revised, 1913 E
    treaty with China, 1920 K
    protectionist tariff, 1922 J, O
    agricultural produce bill, defeated, 1926 F
    Smoot-Hawley Tariff (high duty), 1930 F, O
    Agricultural Adjustment tariff, 1933 O

president's power to reduce tariffs, 1934 F
Reciprocal Trade Agreements Act, 1958 J
See also under Treaties, Treaties of Commerce
Tarka the Otter (H. Williamson), 1927 U
Tarleton, Sir Banastre, B. general (1754–1833), 1780 H, 1781 A
Tartarescu, George, Rum. leader, 1933 M
Tartarin the Mountaineer (A. Daudet), 1885 U
Tartu, Estonia, peace of, 1920 K
Tarzan films, 1932 W
Task, The (W. Cowper), 1785 U
Task forces. *See* Commandos
Tasmania, proved to be an island, 1798 P
Tasso (Goethe), 1789 W
Taste of Honey, A (S. Delaney), 1959 W
Tati, Jacques, F. film actor, 1958 W
Tauroggen, Roumania convention of, 1812 M
Tawfiq Abul-Huda, Jordan. leader, 1955 E
Tawney, Richard Henry, B. historian (1880–1962), 1880 Z, 1926 R, 1931 O, 1958 Q, 1962 Z
Taxation:
in Britain: advertisements tax, repealed, 1853 O
capital gains tax, 1964 L, 1965 D
corporation tax, introduced, 1964 L
amended, 1965 F
customs duties, repealed, 1821 E, 1842 D, 1945 D
death duties, 1894 D
entertainment tax, doubled, 1942 D
reduced, 1948 W
abolished on living theatre, 1957 W
excise, on tea and spirits, reduced, 1784 F
excise scheme, Pitt's, 1786 F
imports surcharge, 1964 K
reduced, 1965 D
income tax, introduced, 1798 E
revived, 1842 D
Gladstone aims to abolish, 1874 B
standard rate raised to 7*s.* 6*d.* in £, 1939 J
10*s.* in £, 1941 D
PAYE, introduced, 1944 B
Schedule 'A' abolished, 1963 D
increased, 1964 L
land tax, reduced, 1767 B
newspaper, 1789 V, 1819 M
abolished, 1855 F, V
paper duties, repealed, 1861 O
purchase tax, 1940 G
profits tax, increased, 1960 D
speculative gains tax, 1962 D
Stamp duties, 1819 M
reduced, 1836 H
Surtax, starting-point of, raised, 1961 D
Window tax, abolished, 1851 G
revenue from direct exceeds that from indirect taxation, 1901 D
See also Rates
in France, reform of, 1780 N
duties on colonial imports, 1810 H
duties on wine, reduced, 1900 G
National Assembly withholds increases in, 1952 B
in Russia, poll tax, abolished, 1884 A
in US, Britain's taxation of American Colonies, 1764 E, 1765 E, 1766 C, 1767 E, 1768 G, 1769 E, 1770 D
customs duties, 1787 D
excise, 1794 N
Force Act enables collection of revenue, 1833 C
income tax, imposed, 1894 N
declared unconstitutional, 1895 E, 1916 A
net income taxed from business sources, 1912 C
federal income tax, 1913 B
surtax, 1935 H
Taxation, treatise on, 1817 O
Taxi, motor, 1903 P
Taylor, Elizabeth, B. film actress (b. 1932), 1963 W
Taylor, Zachary, Am. Whig (1784–1850), 12th president of US (1849–50), 1850 G; in Mexican War, 1846 E; inaugurated, 1849 C
Tchaikovsky, Peter Iljitch, R. musician (1840–93), 1840 Z, 1893 Z
ballet music, 1878 T, 1891 T
operas, 1864 T, 1876 T, 1880 T
overtures, 1864 T, 1876 T, 1880 T
piano concerto, 1875 T
symphonies, 1877 T, 1889 T, 1893 T
Tchesme, Turkey, battle, 1770 G
Tea: Boston Tea Party, 1773 M; production statistics, 1909 Y
Teaching. *See under* Education; Universities
Teaching machines, 1963 O
Teach-Ins, 1965 O
Technics and Civilization (L. Mumford), 1934 O
Technology:
history of, 1955 P
in Britain, professorship at Edinburgh University, 1855 O
Regent Street Polytechnic, 1882 O
agreement for pooling knowledge with US, 1940 L
increased spending on, 1956 O
Ministry of, 1964 O
in Ceylon, agreement with Russia, 1958 B
in Germany, Berlin School of Technology, 1884 O
in US, Massachusetts Institute of Technology, 1865 O
Teddington, Middlesex, England, National Physical Laboratory at, 1950 P
Tegner, Esias, Swe. author (1782–1846), 1822 U, 1825 U
Teheran, Iran:
Anglo-Persian agreement of, 1919 H
University, 1935 O
Conference of Allied leaders at, 1943 B, L
Teilhard de Chardin, Pierre, F. theologian (1881–1955), 1959 R
Tel Aviv, Israel, 1949 M
Telegraph:
invented, 1809 P
duplex, 1872 P
electric, 1833 P
first message transmitted in US, 1844 P
cross-Channel, 1846 P
London–Balaclava, 1855 P
trans-Atlantic, 1866 P
Morse, invented, 1832 P
optical, 1793 P
picture, 1930 P
water volta-meter, 1809 P
wireless, 1895 P
trans-Atlantic transmissions, 1901 P
Tel-el-Kebir, Egypt, battle, 1882 J
Telepathy and Clairvoyance (Teschner), 1921 R
Telephone, The: invented, 1876 P; automatic switchboard for, 1892 P; exchange, London's first, 1879 P; public, first, 1877 P; G.P.O. takes over B. system, 1912 O; Trans-Atlantic service, 1956 P; visual, 1956 P

Telephones, statistics of subscribers:
in Britain, 1910 Y, 1930 Y, 1940 Y, 1965 Y
in US, 1880 Y, 1940 Y
Telescopes:
Jodrell Bank radio telescope, 1957 P
Mount Wilson, 1910 P, 1918 P
Mullard Observatory, Cambridge, 1957 P
reflecting, 1789 P
See also Observatories
Television:
Baird demonstrates, 1926 P
colour, demonstrated, 1928 P
experiments with, 1953 P
Early Bird relays pictures, 1965 P
Eurovision network, 1954 P
Telstar relays pictures, 1962 P
Trans-Atlantic transmission, 1928 P
Television Services:
in Britain, BBC develops, 1932 O
BBC opens regular service, 1936 W
BBC service resumed, 1946 W
BBC2, alternative programme, 1964 W
Independent Television Authority, 1954 O
starts commercial programmes, 1955 W
cigarette advertising on, banned, 1965 W
Pilkington Committee's Report, 1962 W
Noble Committee's Report, 1963 O
statistics of viewers, 1946 W, 1959 Y, 1960 Y, 1965 Y
in Cuba, regular colour TV, 1959 W
in France, statistics of viewers, 1959 Y, 1960 Y
in Germany, regular service, 1935 W
statistics of viewers, 1960 Y
in Japan, regular colour TV, 1960 W
in S. Africa, decision against introducing TV, 1959 W
in US, Quiz scandal, 1959 W
confrontation of presidential candidates on, 1960 O
statistics of viewers, 1959 Y, 1960 Y
Telford, Thomas, B. engineer (1757–1834), 1802 P, 1805 P, 1819 P
Telstar, communications satellite, 1962 P
Temperance, 1869 J. *See also under* Prohibition
Temperatures:
bolometer for determining changes, 1881 P
very low, research into, 1933 P
Tempest, Marie, B. actress, 1864 Z, 1942 Z
Tempest, The (A. Ostrovsky), 1860 W
Temple, Frederick, B. churchman, Archbishop of Canterbury (1821–1902), 1860 R
Temple, Henry John, Viscount Palmerston, B. Whig-Liberal statesman (1784–1865), 1784 Z, 1865 Z; becomes foreign secretary, 1830 L, 1846 F; '*Civis Romanus Sum*' speech, 1850 F; resigns, 1851 M; forms ministry, 1855 B; resigns, following Orsini affair, 1858 B; forms ministry, 1859 F
Temple, Shirley, Am. film actress, 1932 W, 1936 W
Temple, William, B. churchman, Archbishop of Canterbury (1881–1944), 1881 Z, 1934 R, 1944 R, Z; appointed Archbishop of Canterbury, 1942 R
Templewood, Viscount. *See* Hoare, Samuel
Temporal power of Pope, attacked, 1859 O
Temps du mepris, Le (A. Malraux), 1935 U
Temps retrouvé, Le (M. Proust), 1927 U
Temptation of Pescara (K. Meyer), 1887 U
Tenant Right League, Ireland, 1850 F
Tender is the Night (S. Fitzgerald), 1934 U
Ténébreuse Affaire, Une (H. de Balzac), 1841 U
Tenedos, Isle, Asia Minor, battle off, 1913 A
Tennant, Charles, B. chemist (1768–1838), 1798 P
Tennant, Margot. *See* Asquith, M.
Tennessee, State, US: becomes US state, 1796 F; forbids teaching of evolution, 1925 O
Tennessee Valley Authority, 1933 E
Tenniel, Sir John, B. artist (1820–1914), 1820 Z, 1851 S, 1914 Z
Tennis, lawn, invented, 1874 X. *See entries* Lawn Tennis
Tennyson, Alfred, Lord Tennyson, B. poet (1809–1892), 1809 Z, 1827 U, 1830 U, 1832 U, 1842 U, 1850 U, 1855 U, 1859 U, 1892 Z
Tennyson, C. *See* Turner, Charles Tennyson
Tentation de St. Antoine, La (G. Flaubert), 1874 U
Tenzing, Norkey, Sherpa mountaineer (b. 1914), 1953 P
Teplitz, Czechoslovakia Treaty, 1813 J
Teppich des Lebens, Der (S. George), 1899 U
Tereshkova, Valentina, R. astronaut, first woman in space, 1963 P
Terre, La (E. Zola), 1888 U
Territorial Waters: limit of, fixed by Hague Convention, 1882 F; Iceland extends fishery limit, 1958 F, J; Indonesia extends, 1958 A; US, violated by Britain, 1811 L
Terrorism:
in Aden, 1965 J
in Algeria, 1953 L, M
in Angola, 1961 B
in Britain and Ireland, by Fenians, 1882 E, H, 1883 C
in British Guiana, 1963 D
in Cyprus, by EOKA, 1957 C
in Kenya, by Mau Mau, 1952 K, 1953 D, H, 1955 A
in US, by Ku-Klux-Klan, 1964 H, M, 1965 C
See also Atrocities; Massacres
Terry, Ellen, B. actress (1848–1928), 1848 Z, 1878 W, 1928 Z
Teruel, Spain, battles, 1937 M, 1938 B
Terylene, invention of, 1941 P
Teschen, Austria: Peace signed at, 1779 E; Agreement, between Czechoslovakia and Poland, 1920 G; ceded to Poland, 1938 K
Tesla, Nikola, Am. engineer (1856–1943), 1888 P
Tess of the D'Urbervilles (T. Hardy), 1891 U
Testament of Beauty, The (R. Bridges), 1929 U
Test ban treaty, 1963 H
Tetanus: bacillus discovered, 1884 P; is controlled by injections, 1915 P; treatment of, 1925 P
Tête des autres, La (M. Aymé), 1952 W
Te Tsung, Emperor of China (1875–1908), reforms under, 1898 F
Tewfik, Khedive of Egypt (1879–92), 1879 F, 1882 A; appoints Nationalist ministry, 1882 B
Tewfik Pasha, Grand Vizier of Persia, 1912 G
Texas, State, US: declares itself independent of Mexico, 1836 C, D; US treaty for annexation of, defeated, 1844 D; US Congress agrees to annexation, 1845 C; becomes a US state, 1845 M; US obtains, 1848 E; surrenders claim to New Mexico, 1850 H
Texel, Holland, River, 1795 A, 1797 E
Textiles Trade, British, 1772 Y, 1782 Y, 1812 Y, 1822 Y, 1832 Y, 1842 Y, 1852 Y, 1862 Y, 1872 Y, 1882 Y, 1892 Y, 1902 Y, 1912 Y, 1922 Y, 1932 Y
Teyte, Dame Maggie, B. prima donna (b. 1888), 1919 T
Thackeray, William Makepeace, B. novelist (1811–1863), 1811 Z, 1838 U, 1846 U, 1847 U, 1850 U, 1852 U, 1855 U, 1857 U, 1863 Z
edits *Cornhill*, 1860 V
Thailand: name changed from Siam, 1949 E; state of emergency in, 1957 C. *See also under* Siam

Thalaba, the Destroyer (R. Southey), 1801 U
Thallium, discovery of, 1861 P
Thames, River, England, tunnels under, 1843 P, 1890 P
Thames, River, Ontario, Canada, US victory at, 1813 K
Thanatopsis (W. C. Bryant), 1817 U
Thant, U., Burm. (b. 1909), plans for Congo, 1962 J; elected UN secretary, 1962 L
Thark (B. Travers), 1927 W
Thaw, The (I. Ehrenburg), 1955 W
Theatre of Cruelty, 1964 W
Thefts of works of art:
Cézanne paintings, 1961 S
Goya's *Wellington*, 1961 S, 1965 S
Mona Lisa, 1911 S
Theodorakis Mikis, Gk. musician, 1959 T
Theogony of Hesiod, illustrated edition, 1931 S
Theological Essays (F. D. Maurice), 1853 R
Theology and Politics (N. Micklem), 1941 R
Theoria motus corporum coelestium (K. F. Gauss), 1809 P
Théorie Analytique (P. Laplace), 1812 P
Théorie Analytique de la Chaleur (Fournier de Pescay), 1822 P
Théorie des fonctions analytiques (J. L. Lagrange), 1797 O
Théorie du pouvoir politique et religieux (L. de Bonald), 1796 O
Théorie mathématique de la Chaleur (S. D. Poisson), 1835 P
Theory and Practice of Socialism, The (J. Strachey), 1936 O
Theory of Beauty (E. F. Carritt), 1914 S
Theory of Chemical Proportions (J. J. Berzelius), 1814 P
Theory of Colours (Goethe), 1810 P
Theory of Linear Transformations (A. Cayley), 1845 P
Theory of Political Economy (W. S. Jevons), 1871 O
Theory of Sex (T. H. Morgan), 1928 O
Theosophical Society, founded, 1875 R
Theotokis, A., Greek premier, 1950 A
Therapeutic Research Council, British, 1941 P
There is No Armour (H. Spring), 1948 U
Thérèse Raquin (E. Zola), 1867 U
Thermidor (V. Sardou), 1891 W
Thermodynamics, second law of, 1850 P
Thermo-electricity, discovered, 1821 P
Thermomultiplier, used for discoveries in radiant heat, 1831 P
Thesiger, Wilfred, B. explorer (b. 1910), 1948 P
Thessaly, Greece: risings in, 1878 A; granted by Turkey to Greece, 1881 G; Turkish defeat at, 1879 E; Allies demand Greek withdrawal from, 1916 M
They Were Defeated (R. Macaulay), 1932 U
Thibault, Les (R. M. du Gard), 1922 U
Thibaut, Anton Friedrich Justus, G. jurist (1774–1840), 1798 O
Thibaut, Jacques, Antoine Anatole, F. novelist under pseudonym of 'Anatole France' (1844–1924), 1881 U, 1888 U, 1893 U, 1896 U, 1908 U
Thibaw, King of Burma, 1885 K
Thierry, Augustin, F. historian (1795–1856), 1795 Z, 1825 Q, 1840 Q, 1856 Z
Thiers, Louis Adolphe, F. statesman and historian (1797–1877), 1797 Z, 1823 Q, 1845 Q, 1873 E, 1877 Z; crushes Paris rising, 1834 D; becomes premier, 1836 B; resigns, 1836 J; becomes premier, 1840 B; resigns, 1840 K; holds Reform banquets, 1847 G; forms Third Party, 1863 L; becomes head of executive, 1871 B; elected President of France 1871 H
Thirlwall, Connor, B. churchman and historian (1797–1875), 1835 Q
Thirty-Nine Steps, The (J. Buchan), 1915 U
This Happy Breed (N. Coward), 1943 W
This Island Now (G. M. Carstairs), 1963 R
This Way to the Tomb (R. Duncan), 1945 W
Thoiry, France, Briand meets Stressmann at, 1926 J
Thomas, Charles Louis Ambroise, F. musician (1811–96), 1866 T
Thomas, Dylan Marlais, B. poet (1914–53), 1936 U, 1940 U, 1946 U, 1952 U, 1954 W
Thomas, James Henry, B. Trade-Union leader and Labour politician (1874–1949), 1874 Z, 1949 Z; is expelled from Labour Party, 1931 H; resigns over budget leakage, 1936 E
Thomas, John, Am. founder of Christadelphians (1805–71), 1844 R
Thomas, Sidney Gilchrist, B. metallurgist (1850–85), 1878 P
Thomas J. Wise in the Original Cloth (Carter and Pollard), 1948 Q
Thompson, Benjamin, Count Rumford, B. sentistic (1753–1814), 1798 P, 1799 P
Thompson, Dorothy, Am. journalist, 1894 Z
Thompson, Sir Edward Maunde, B. palaeographer (1840–1929), 1912 Q
Thompson, Francis, B. poet (1860–1907), 1860 Z, 1880 U, 1907 Z
Thompson, James Matthew, B. historian and theologian (1878–1956), 1911 R, 1943 Q
Thompson, Sir John Sparrow David, Canadian Conservative (1844–94), becomes premier, 1892 M; dies, 1894 M
Thompson, John Taliaferno, Am. gunsmith (1860–1940), 1920 P
Thompson, Joseph John, B. physicist (1856–1940), 1856 Z, 1903 P, 1906 P, 1913 P, 1940 Z
Thompson, Thomas, B. chemist (1773–1852), 1807 P
Thomson, William, lord Kelvin, B. scientist (1824–1907), 1824 Z, 1851 P, 1857 P, 1861 P, 1867 P, 1872 P, 1879 P, 1882 P, 1897 P, 1907 Z
Thorburn, Archibald, B. naturalist, 1915 P
Thoreau, Henry David, Am. author (1817–62), 1817 Z, 1854 U, 1862 Z
Thorkelin, Grim Jonsson, Dan. scholar (1752–1829), 1815 Q
Thorn, N. Poland, ceded to Prussia, 1790 C, 1793 E
Thorneycroft, Peter, B. Conservative politician (b. 1909), appointed Chancellor of Exchequer, 1957 A; resigns, 1958 A
Thornton, William, Am. architect (1759–1828), 1793 S
Thornton, William Thomas, B. author (1813–80), 1869 O
Thornycroft, Sir William Hamo, B. sculptor (1850–1925), 1899 S, 1927 S
Thorwaldsen, Bertel, Dan. sculptor (1770–1844), 1770 Z, 1797 S, 1811 S, 1819 S, 1820 S, 1844 Z
Those Barren Leaves (A. Huxley), 1925 U
Thoughts on Hunting (P. Beckford), 1781 X
Thoughts on the Cause of the Present Discontents (E. Burke), 1770 O
Thoughts on the Constitution (L. S. Amery), 1947 O
Thoughts on the Importance of the Manners of the Great to General Society (H. More), 1788 O
Thousand Days (A. Schlesinger), 1965 Q
Thrace, Greece: Greeks evacuate, 1922 K; frontier settled, 1913 J
Three-Cornered Hat (P. Alarcón), 1874 U

Three-dimensional films, 1953 W
Three Emperors' League, 1881 F, 1884 C
Three Men in a Boat (J. K. Jerome), 1889 U
Three Musketeers, The (A. Dumas), 1844 U
Three People (M. Gorki), 1900 U
Three Plays for Puritans (G. B. Shaw), 1900 U
Three Sisters (A. Chekhov), 1902 W
Three Soldiers (J. Dos Passos), 1921 U
Three Treatises on the Theory of Sex (S. Freud), 1905 R
Through the Looking-Glass (L. Carroll), 1871 U
Thunder Rock (R. Ardrey), 1940 W
Thurber, Charles, Am. inventor of typewriter (1803–86), 1843 P
Thurber, James, Am. humorist (b. 1894), 1894 Z, 1859 U
Thus Spake Zarathustra (F. Nietzsche), 1883 R
Thyroxine, 1915 P, 1928 P
Tibet: Anglo-Chinese convention on, 1906 H; Chinese Republic proclaimed in, 1912 D; Britain restrains China from sending expedition to, 1912 H; China offers regional autonomy to, 1950 E; China occupies, 1950 K; Tibet appeals to UN for restoration of independence, 1961 C
Tichborne claimant, 1874 O
Tieck, John Ludwig, G. author (1773–1854), 1773 Z, 1795 U, 1797 U, 1803 Q, 1854 Z
Tientsin, China: treaty, ends Anglo-Chinese War, 1858 F; Anglo-French troops take, 1860 H; commercial treaties, 1861 J, 1885 F; taken by international force, 1900 G; Japanese seize, 1937 G; Japanese blockade British concession at, 1939 F; falls to Communists, 1949 A
Tiepolo, Giovanni, It. artist (1692–1769), 1769 Z
Tieste (U. Foscolo), 1797 W
Tiflis, Georgia, Russia, sacked by Persian chief, 1783 K
Tight-rope walking, 1859 Q
Tikhivin, Russia, Russians recapture, 1941 M
Tilden, Samuel Jones, Am. Democrat (1814–86), 1876 L
Tilden, William, Am. lawn-tennis player, 1920 X
Tildy, Zoltan, Hung. leader of Smallholders Party, 1945 L, 1946 B, 1948 G
Tiller Girls, The, dancing troupe, 1908 W
Tillet, Ben, B. Trades Union leader (1860–1943), 1912 G
Tillich, Paul, Am. form. G., theologian (b. 1886), 1949 R, 1954 R
Tilsit, Russia: consequences of Treaty between Napoleon and Russia, for Britain, 1807 L; Treaty of 1807; violated, 1810 M, 1811 A; Russians take, 1945 A
Time and Freewill, Matter and Memory (H. Bergson), 1909 R
Time and the Conways (J. B. Priestley), 1937 W
Time for Decision, The (S. Welles), 1944 O
Time Machine, The (H. G. Wells), 1895 U
Time Must Have a Stop (A. Huxley), 1944 U
Time of Your Life, The (W. Saroyan), 1939 W
Time to Dance, A (C. Day Lewis), 1935 U
Timoshenko, Senyon, R. soldier (b. 1895), 1895 Z, 1941 L, 1942 G
Tin Drum, The (G. Grass), 1963 U
Tinned food, 1880 P, 1892 P
Tipperary, Ireland: rising in, 1848 G; captured by Nationalists, 1922 G
Tippett, Michael Kemp, B. musician (b. 1905), 1905 Z, 1940 T, 1955 T, 1962 T, 1963 T
Tippoo Sahib, ruler of Mysore (1782–99), 1782 M, 1783 D, 1784 C, 1789 M, 1791 E, 1792 B, 1799 E
Tiraboschi, Girolamo, It. author (1731–94), 1782 Q
Tirana, treaty between Italy and Albania, 1926 L
Tirannide, La (V. Alfieri), 1777 O
Tirard, Pierre Emanuel, F. politician (1827–93), 1889 B
Tirol, Austria, Austrians evacuate Southern, 1916 F
Tirpitz, Alfred von, G. minister of marine (1849–1930), 1849 Z, 1897 F, 1930 Z; expands navy, 1898 C; resigns, 1916 C
Tischendorf, Lobegott Friedrich Konstantin von, G. Biblical critic (1815–74), 1844 Q, 1859 Q
Tiso, Joseph, Czech. politician, 1939 C, 1947 D
Tissue culture, 1907 P
Tisza, Kálmán, Hung. statesman (1830–1902), 1875 C
Tisza, Stephen, Count, Hung. leader (1861–1918), elected president of Hungarian Chamber, 1912 E; resigns, 1917 E; assassinated, 1918 K
Titan (Jean Paul), 1800 U
Titanic disaster, 1912 P
Tithes, commutation of, in England, 1836 H, R
Titles, in Turkey, abolished, 1934 L
Tito, Josip, Yugos. leader (b. 1892), 1892 Z, 1945 L, 1955 L; Maclean's mission to, 1943 K; Yugoslav Communists give vote of confidence to, 1948 G; elected president, 1953 A; visits London, 1953 C; visits Greece, 1954 E; visits Delhi, 1954 M; meets Nasser, 1956 A; visits Moscow, 1956 F
Titulescu, Nicholas, Rum. leader, falls, 1937 M
Titusville, Pa., US, oil well at, 1859 P
Tizard, Sir Henry, B. scientist and administrator, 1885 Z, 1959 Z
Tobago, Island, West Indies: ceded to Britain, 1763 B; France captures, 1781 D; France recovers, 1783 J; British capture, 1803 F. *See also* Trinidad and Tobago
Tobias and the Angel (J. Bridie), 1952 W
Tobino, Mario, It. author, 1962 U
Tobruk, Libya: Rommel attacks, 1941 D
Rommel takes, 1942 F
British recapture, 1942 L
Tocqueville, Charles Alexis de, F. author (1805–59), 1805 Z, 1835 O, 1856 Q, 1859 Z
Todd, Garfield, Rhodesian politician (b. 1908), ousted from leadership of United Federal Party, 1958 B; forms United Rhodesian Party, 1958 D; founds Rhodesian New Africa Party, 1961 L
Togo (formerly Togoland), becomes an independent republic, 1960 D
Togoland, South-west Africa: German occupation, 1884 D; frontier with Gold Coast settled, 1886 G, 1899 L; British and French forces occupy, 1914 H; League of Nations mandate for, 1922 G; UN agrees on independence for, 1959 M; becomes an independent republic, as Togo, 1960 D
To Have or Have Not (E. Hemingway), 1937 U
Tojo, Hideki, Jap. general and premier, resigns, 1944 G; sentenced for war crimes, 1948 L
Tokio, Japan:
Conference to discuss extra-territorial concessions, 1886 E
population, 1881 Y, 1906 Y, 1950 Y, 1960 Y
population overtakes London's, 1960 Y
US air raids on, 1945 B
Tolentino, Italy: Treaty, between France and Papacy, 1797 B; Austrians defeat Murat at, 1815 E
To Let (J. Galsworthy), 1921 U
Tolkien, John Ronald Rouel, B. author (b. 1892), 1954 U
Toller, Ernst, G. revolutionary and dramatist, 1893 Z, 1939 Z
Tolpuddle Martyrs, 1834 C

Tolstoy, Leo, R. novelist and social reformer (1828–1910), 1828 Z, 1864 U, 1873 U, 1885 U, 1890 U, 1899 U, 1900 U, 1910 Z
Tom Brown's Schooldays (T. Hughes), 1857 U
Tompa, Mihály, Hung. poet (1817–68), 1854 U
Tonbridge, Kent, England, by-election, 1956 F
Tone, Theobald Wolfe, Ir. politician (1763–98), 1790 K
Tone poems. *See* Overtures, Symphonic Poems, etc.
Tonga Islands, S. Pacific, Britain annexes, 1899 L, 1900 E
Tonkin, Viet-Nam: French protectorate in, 1883 H; becomes part of French Union Indo-Chinese, 1887 N
Tono Bungay (H. G. Wells), 1909 U
Tooke, John Horne, B. politician and philologist (1736–1812), 1801 F
Tootal Company, Ltd., makes crease-resisting fabric, 1929 P
Topete, Juan Bauptista, Sp. naval officer and politician (1821–85), 1868 J
Tŏpffer, Rodolphe, Swi. author (1799–1846), 1838 U
Topolski, Felix, B. formerly Pol. artist (b. 1907), 1941 S
Torgau, E. Germany, juncture of US and Russian armies at, 1945 D
Tories. *See under* Political Parties
Tornadoes and typhoons:
in Hong Kong, 1960 F
in US Middle West, 1965 D
Toronto (formerly York Town), Canada, US force takes, 1813 D
Torpedoes: invented, 1777 P; Whitehead's, 1864 P; homing, 1945 A
Torrens, William Torrens McCullagh, B. politician (1813–94), 1867 O
Torres Vedras, Spain, Wellington holds line of, 1819 K
Torrington, Devon, England, by-election, 1958 C
Torsion balance invented, 1777 P
Torture, in Turkey, suppressed, 1856 B
Tosca, La (Sardou), 1887 W
Toscanini, Arturo, Am. formerly It. musician (1867–1957), 1867 Z, 1929 T, 1957 Z
Totem and Taboo (S. Freud), 1913 R
To the Finland Station (E. Wilson), 1941 O
To the Lighthouse (V. Woolf), 1927 U
To the Night (Novalis), 1800 U
Toulon, France, Bonaparte takes, 1793 M
Toulouse-Lautrec, Henri Marie Raymond de, F. artist (1864–1901), 1864 Z, 1891 S, 1892 S, 1900 S, 1901 Z
Tourcoing, N. France, battle, 1794 E
Tous les hommes sont mortels (S. de Beauvoir), 1946 U
Tovey, Sir Donald Francis, B. musicologist (1875–1940), 1935 T
Tower, The (W. B. Yeats), 1928 U
Town of the Prairie, A (W. Irving), 1832 U
Town planning:
in Britain, *County of London Plan*, 1943 O
Sharpe's plan for Greater London, 1944 O
Reith Committee on new towns, 1946 O
Holford's plan for St. Paul's precinct, London, 1955 S
New Towns Commission, 1961 O
in France, Haussmann rebuilds Paris, 1853 S
in Germany, model dwellings, 1853 O
Townshend, Charles, B. Tory politician (1725–67), 1766 G, 1767 E, J
Toxicologie générale (M. Orfila), 1814 P
Toynbee, Arnold Joseph, B. historian (b. 1889), 1889 Z, 1934 Q, 1952 O
Tractatus Logico-Philosophicus (Wittgenstein), 1922 R
Tractor, petrol-driven, 1898 P
Tracts for the Times, 1833 R
Trade, Council of, in Britain, 1786 N
Trades Unions:
Industrial Workers of the World, Detroit, 1909 O
World Conference, London, 1945 B
in Britain, forbidden by Combinations Act, 1800 O
permitted, with repeal of Combinations Acts, 1824 O
strike action prohibited, 1825 G
expansion of, 1825 O
Grand National Consolidated Union formed, 1834 A, C
legalised, 1871 F, O
National Agricultural Labourers Union, 1872 O
statistics of membership, 1892 Y, 1902 Y, 1912 Y, 1922 Y, 1932 Y
Taff Vale, judgment, 1901 G
peaceful picketing permitted, 1906 M
Osborne judgment rules levies illegal, 1909 O
TUC votes against Syndicalism, 1912 J
Act declares certain strikes and lock-outs illegal, 1927 G
repealed, 1946 B
Closed-shop dispute, 1946 H
TUC agrees to join National Economic Development Council, 1962 B
TUC signs statement of intent on productivity, prices and incomes, 1964 M
decision in Rookes *v.* Barnard, 1964 O
TUC sells *Daily Herald*, 1964 V
Royal Commission on, 1965 B
in France, government attempts to suppress, 1834 D
legalised, 1884 C
Congress adopts strike principle, 1895 A
in Germany, suppressed, 1933 E
in Italy, Confederazione Generale del Lavaro, 1906 O
non-Fascist, abolished, 1924 A
in US, General Trades Union, 1833 N
Knights of Labor, founded, 1869 O
excommunicated, 1885 O
stage Chicago riot, 1886 E
American Federation of Labor, 1881 O, 1886 O
statistics of membership, 1902 Y
Closed Shop outlawed, 1947 F
levies for political purposes prohibited, 1947 F
See also under Strikes
Trading Stamps, in Britain, campaign against, 1963 O
Trafalgar, Spain, battle of, 1805 K
Traffic in Towns (Buchanan Report), 1963 O
Traffic lights, in New York, 1918 P
Tragedy is Not Enough (K. Jaspers), 1953 R
Tragedy of Agis (G. Bessenyei), 1772 W
Traité d' Economique politique (J. B. Saye), 1803 O
Traité de Mécanique (S. D. Poisson), 1811 P
Traité des Propriétes projectives les figures (J. V. Poncelet), 1822 P
Traité élémentaire de chimie (A. L. Lavoisier), 1789 P
Traité medico-philosophique de l'aliénation mentale (P. Pinel), 1791 P
Traitors, The (A. Moorehead), 1952 O
Tram-road, iron, 1801 P
Trams, last London, 1952 P
Transatlantic cable, 1857 P, 1865 P
Transatlantic telephone service, 1956 P
Transcaucasia, Russia, Russian war with Persia over 1826 J
Transcendentalism, 1836 R, 1840 R
Transcendental Philosophy (J. G. Fichte), 1812 R

Transfer of Power in India (V. P. Menon), 1957 O
Transformer, electric, 1831 P
Trans-Iranian pipe-line, 1957 A
Transistor radio, invented, 1948 P
Transjordan: becomes independent, 1923 E; independence recognised, 1928 B, 1946 C; Arab Legion of, invades Palestine, 1948 E; is renamed Jordan, 1949 F. *See also* Jordan; Middle East
Transmutation of atoms, 1919 P, 1922 P
Transport industry, in Britain: nationalisation of, 1946 L; closed-shop dispute in, 1946 H; road transport denationalised, 1953 E
Transportation of Convicts:
  from Britain, 1823 G, 1834 C
    to Tasmania, suspended, 1853 N
  from France, 1851 O
Trans-Siberian Railway, 1891 G, 1901 P
Transvaal (or South African Republic), S. Africa: established, 1852 A; Pretorius organises, 1856 M; Britain annexes, 1877 D; Republic proclaimed, 1879 M, 1880 M; declares itself independent, 1880 K; Britain recognises independence, 1881 D; Kruger becomes president, 1883 D; status of, regulated, 1884 B; gold discovered in, 1885 P; communication with coast is blocked, 1887 F; relations with British S. Africa Company, 1889 K; Britain blocks coastal access, 1895 F; Jameson Raid into, 1895 M; franchise in, 1899 C, G; Britain annexes, 1900 K
Transylvania, now in Rumania and Russia: incorporated in Hungary, 1865 M; union with Russia proclaimed, 1918 L; Rumania annexes, 1919 A; Russian gains in, 1947 B
Travancore, India, Rajah of, attacked by Tippoo of Mysore, 1789 M
Traum, ein Leben, Der (F. Grillparzer), 1834 U
Travailleurs de la mer (V. Hugo), 1866 U
Traveller, The (O. Goldsmith), 1764 U
Travels in Arabia Deserta (C. M. Doughty), 1888 P
Travels in Asia Minor (R. Chandler), 1775 P
Travels in France (A. Young), 1792 O
Travels in the Interior of Africa (M. Park), 1799 P
Travels to Discover the Source of the Nile (J. Bruce), 1790 P
Travel-tours, 1841 W
Travers, Ben, B. dramatist (b. 1886), 1927 W
Travers, Morris William, B. chemist (1872–1947), 1898 P
Travis, Walter John, Am. golfer (1862–1927), 1904 X
Treason Trials:
  in Czechoslovakia, 1952 L
  in Ghana, 1963 M
  in South Africa, 1956 M, 1959 A, 1961 C, 1964 F
  in Turkey, 1960 K
  in US trials removed from Colonial courts to Westminster, 1769 G
Treasure Island (R. L. Stevenson), 1883 U
Treaties of Alliance, Leagues, etc.:
  Afghanistan with Persia, 1921 F
  Albania with Italy, 1927 L
  Armenia with Turkey (Alexandropol), 1920 M
  Austria with Britain and France, against Prussia and Russia, 1815 A
  Austria with Britain, Prussia and Russia, against France, 1815 C
  Austria with Britain and France, over Danubian Provinces, 1854 M
  Austria with France, 1812 C
  Austria with Germany, 1879 K
    joined by Italy, 1882 E
  Austria with Prussia, against France, 1792 B
  Austria with Prussia, against Russia, 1854 D
  Austria with Roumania, 1883 K
  Austria with Russia, against Turkey, 1781 B
  Austria with Serbia, 1881 F
  Austria with Turkey, 1771 G
  Balkan Alliance (Greece, Yugoslavia and Turkey), 1954
    dissolved, 1960 F
  Baltic States treaty of collaboration, 1934 J
  Bavaria with Austria (Reid), 1813 K
  Britain with Afghanistan, against Persia (Peshawar), 1855 C
  Britain with Egypt, 1899 A
    Egypt abrogates, 1951 K
  Britain with Egypt, to end occupation, 1936 H
    Egypt demands revision, 1945 J
    proposed British revision referred by Egypt to UN, 1947 A
  Britain with France (Entente Cordiale), 1904 D
  Britain with France, 1947 C
  Britain with France and Italy, 1915 D
  Britain with France and Turkey, 1854 C
  Britain with Holland, 1788 D
    joined by Prussia, 1788 H
  Britain with Germany, proposed, rejected, 1899 L, M
  Britain with Germany, negotiations for, founder, 1901 K
  Britain with Hyderabad, 1790 G
  Britain with Iraq, 1955 D
  Britain with Japan, negotiations for, 1901 G, K, M
    signed, 1902 A
    Franco-Russian declaration on, 1902 C
    renewed, 1905 H, 1911 G
  Britain with Jordan, 1948 D
    expires, 1957 C
  Britain with Libya, 1953 G
  Britain with Persia, against Russian interests in Near East, 1905 C
  Britain with Russia, against France, 1798 M
  Britain with Russia, talks founder, 1903 K
  Britain with Russia, 1907
    Russia denounces, 1918 A
  Britain with Russia, urged, 1939 D, G
    negotiations for, 1939 H
  Britain with Russia, 1942 E
    Russia threatens to annul, 1954 M
  Britain with Russia and Iran, 1942 A
  Britain with Sweden and Russia (Örebro), 1812 G, 1813 C
  Brussels, against armed attack in Europe, 1948 C
  Bulgaria with Austria-Hungary, 1913 F
  Bulgaria with Germany and Turkey, 1915 J
  China with Russia, 1896 F
  Czechoslovakia with Rumania, 1921 D
  Czechoslovakia with Yugoslavia, 1922 H
  Egypt with Saudi Arabia and Yemen, 1956 D
  Egypt with Syria, 1955 C
  European Defence Community (Paris), 1952 E
  France and Britain with Serbia, 1915 K
  France with Czechoslovakia, 1924 A
  France with Holland, 1785 L
  France with Prussia, against Britain, 1806 B
  France with Rumania, 1926 F
  France with Russia, 1808 K
  France with Russia, 1893 A, 1897 H
    extended, 1899 H
  France with Sardinia, 1859 A
  France with Spain (San Ildefonso), 1796 M
  France with Spain, against Portugal (Fontainebleau), 1807 K
  France with US, 1778 B

Fürstenbund, Die (League of German Princes), 1785 G
North German Confederation with Bavaria and Würtemberg, 1870 L
Germany with Austria, 1879 K
terms published, 1888 B
Germany with Italy ('Pact of Steel'), 1939 E
Germany with Russia (Re-insurance Treaty), 1887 F
terms published, 1896 K
lapses, 1890 F
Germany with Russia, negotiations founder, 1904 L
Germany with Turkey, 1914 H
Holland with US, 1778 J
Holy Alliance, between Austria, Prussia and Russia, 1815 J
Bavaria joins, 1816 H
Holland joins, 1816 H
Sweden joins, 1817 E
terms extended, 1833 K
Italy with France, 1902 L
Italy with Prussia, against Austria, 1866 D
Italy with Roumania, 1926 J
Little Entente, of Yugoslavia, Czechoslovakia and Roumania, 1920 H
London, between Allies, against separate peace, 1914 J
Japan a signatory to, 1915 K
North Atlantic, 1949 D. *See also under* NATO
Prussia with Baden, against France, 1866 H
Prussia with Bavaria, against France, 1866 H
Prussia with Hanover and Saxony (Three Kings' League), 1849 E
Hanover leaves, 1850 B
Prussia with Russia, against France (Kalisch), 1813 B
Prussia with Württemberg, against France, 1866 H
Quadruple Alliance, between Austria, Prussia, Russia and Britain, 1815 L
renewed, 1818 L
joined by Mehemet Ali, 1840 G, L
joined by France, 1841 G
Quadruple Alliance, between Britain, France, Spain and Portugal, 1834 D
Britain sends squadron to Portugal under terms of, 1846 E
Roumania with Poland, 1926 C
Roumania with Yugoslavia, 1921 F
Russia with Austria, 1787 A
Russia with Britain and Austria (St. Petersburg), 1794 J
Russia with Britain (St. Petersburg), 1805 D
Austria joins, 1805 H
Russia proposes defence alliance with Britain, 1939 D
Russia with Nationalist China, 1945 H
Russia with China, 1950 B
Russia with Czechoslovakia, for defeating Germany, 1943 M
Russia with Denmark, 1769 M, 1774 H, 1776 D
Russia with France (Tilsit), 1807 L
violated, 1810 M, 1811 A
Russia with Germany, attempt to renew, 1879 K
Russia with Germany, 1939 H
Russia with Japan, 1925 A
Russia with Latvia (Riga), 1920 H
Russia with Mongolia, 1920 L
Russia with Prussia, 1767 D, 1769 K
Russia with Turkey and Britain, 1799 A
Russia with Turkey, 1921 M, 1925 M
Serbia with Greece, Serbia refused aid under, 1915 K
Sweden with Allies, against Russia, 1855 L
Sweden with Russia (Abo), 1812 D
Switzerland with France, 1777 N
Teplitz, uniting Russia, Prussia and Austria against France, 1813 J
Three Emperors' League, of Germany, Russia and Austria-Hungary, 1873 K, 1881 F
renewed, 1884 C
Russia refuses extension, 1887 F
Transvaal with Orange Free State, 1896 C
Triple Alliance, of Britain, Holland and Prussia, 1788 H, L
Triple Alliance, of Germany, Austria and Italy, 1882 E
renewed, 1887 B, 1891 E, 1902 F, 1907 G
Italy denounces, 1915 E
naval convention of, 1913 L
Turkey with Afghanistan, 1923 B
Turkey with Russia (Unkiai-Skelessi), 1833 G
overthrown, 1841 G
US with Panama, 1926 G
Yugoslavia with Czechoslovakia and Roumania (Little Entente), 1920 H

Treaties of Arbitration in Disputes:
Britain with US, 1911 G
France with US, 1913 B
Germany with Lithuania, 1928 A
among Scandinavian States, 1930 F
Washington Treaty for inter-American arbitration, 1929 A

Treaties of Commerce, Trade Pacts, etc.:
Austria with Serbia, 1910 H
Bavaria with Württemberg, 1828 A
Belgium with Luxembourg, 1921 G
Belgium, Holland and Luxembourg (Benelux), 1958 B
Britain with Belgium, denounced, 1897 G
Britain with China, 1843 K, 1902 J
Britain with France (Eden Treaty), 1786 J
Britain with France (Cobden-Chevalier Treaty), 1860 A
Britain with France, 1872 L, 1959 D
Britain with Germany, denounced, 1897 G
Britain with Germany, 1924 M, 1933 D, 1959 A
Britain with India, 1935 A
Britain with Ireland, 1936 B
Britain with Japan, 1858 H, 1911 D
Britain with Madagascar, 1877 K
Britain with Persia, 1959 C
Britain with Russia, 1921 C, J, 1922 J
annulled, 1927 E
Britain with Russia, 1934 B, 1941 H, 1959 E
Britain with Scandinavian States, for economic co-operation, 1950 A
Britain with Siam, 1826 F
Britain with Spain, 1958 B, 1959 B
Britain with Zollverein, 1865 E
Canada with US, reciprocal, 1935 L
China with Ceylon, 1959 F
European Economic Community ('The Six' member states of the Common Market), Rome Treaty for, 1957 C
European Free Trade Association ('The Seven' member states of EFTA), 1959 L
Europe, Organization for Economic Co-operation and Development (OEC), 1960 M
Finland with Russia, 1854 G
France with Canada, 1922 M
France with Egypt, 1958 M
France with W. Germany, 1954 K, 1963 A

Treaties of Commerce, Trade Pacts, etc.—*contd.*
France with Italy, 1898 L
France with Madagascar, 1868 H
France with Prussia, 1862 H
France with Russia, 1857 F, 1893 F, 1957 B
France with US, 1778 B
Germany with Austria, 1892 B, 1904 G
Germany with Balkan States, 1893 N
Germany with Belgium, 1892 B, 1904 G
Germany with Estonia, 1923 F
Germany with Italy, 1892 B
Germany with Poland, 1935 L
Germany with Russia, 1894 B
unpopularity in Germany, 1894 K
Germany with Samoa, 1879 A
Germany with Sweden, 1904 G
Germany with Switzerland, 1892 B, 1904 G
Hungary with China, 1858 C
India with China, 1954 D
India with Pakistan, on Indus Waters development, 1960 J
Italy with Russia, 1921 M, 1922 E
Japan with powers, 1866 F
Japan with France, 1911 F
Oslo-Convention on Scandinavian economic co-operation, 1932 B
Pakistan with Russia, 1956 F
Pan-American reciprocity plan, rejected, 1889 K
Paris Treaty, embodying Schuman Plan, 1951 D
Prussia with Austria, 1953 B
Prussia with China, 1861 J
Prussia with Hanover, 1851 J
Prussia with Mecklenburg-Schwerin, 1826 M
Prussia with Poland, 1775 C
Prussia with US, 1785 J
Rome Treaty for Common Market, 1957 C
Russia with Austria, 1955 D
Russia with Cuba, 1962 A
Russia with Germany, 1939 H
Russia with Italy, 1961 F
Russia with Mongolian Republic, 1956 D
Russia with Poland, 1931 F
Russia with Sweden, 1922 C
Russia with US, 1935 G
Spain with Argentina, 1946 K
US with Britain. *See under* Lend Lease
US with China, 1920 K
US with Italy, 1948 B
US with Japan, 1911 B
US denounces, 1911 G
US with Russia, 1937 G
See also under Tariff Questions
Treaties—Conventions:
Austria with Germany, for Austrian independence, 1936 G
Balta-Liman, Russia with Turkey, 1849 E
Baltic, for maintaining status quo, 1908 H
Bloemfontein, for Orange Free State, 1854 B
Britain with Belgium, on Ruanda, 1921 C
Britain with China, on Tibet, 1906 H
Britain with Egypt, on Sudan, 1899 A
Britain with France, on Tripoli, 1899 C
Britain with Russia, on Persia, 1907 H
Britain with Turkey, 1938 E
Constantinople, declaring Suez Canal open to all nations, 1888 K
Drummond-Wolff, Britain with Egypt, 1887 E
Egypt with Sudan, over Nile, 1952 K
France with Belgium, 1920 H
France with Italy, over Tunis, 1896 J
France with Japan, on 'open door' in China, 1907 F
France with Spain, to break Portugal's allegiance to Britain, 1801 A
France with Spain, to enforce neutrality of Portugal, 1803 K
France with Syria, 1837 M
Genoa, Russia with Vatican, 1922 E
Helsinki, between Scandinavian States, 1962 C
London, defines the aggressor, 1933 G
London, naval, 1936 C, K
Mediterranean, Britain, Italy and Austria, 1887 B, C, E
Montreux, for Turkish sovereignty over Dardanelles, 1936 G
Montreux, abolishes Egyptian capitulations, 1937 E
Mozambique, denounced by S. Africa, 1922 D
Nicaragua, Honduras with Costa Rica, 1920 L
North Sea, for maintaining status quo, 1908 H
Preventing pollution of sea by oil, 1954 O
Russia with China, on Manchuria, 1896 J
Russia with Japan, on China, 1907 G
Sand River, establishes Transvaal, 1852 A
Straits, guarantees Ottoman independence, 1841 G
Treaties of Friendship:
Austria with Italy, 1930 B
Balkan, Entente, origins of, 1930 K
Britain with Eire, 1938 D
Britain with France (*Entente Cordiale*), 1904 D
Britain with France (Lausanne), 1932 F
Britain with Sikhs, 1809 D
Bulgaria with Turkey, 1929 C
Bulgaria with Yugoslavia (Treaty of Perpetual Peace), 1937 A
Burma with China, 1960 A
Central American States, 1887 N
Central American States (Washington), 1923 B
China with Mongolia, 1952 K
China with US, 1946 L
Egypt with Iraq, 1931 D
France with Lebanon, 1936 J
France with Russia, 1891 H
France with Syria, 1936 J
France with Yugoslavia, 1927 L
Germany with Russia (Berlin), 1926 D
Germany with Transvaal, 1885 A
Germany with Turkey, 1924 C
Greece with Turkey, 1938 D
Greece with Turkey and Yugoslavia, 1953 B
Greece with Yugoslavia, 1926 H, 1929 C
Iraq with Iran, 1929 H
Iraq with Transjordan, 1931 C
Italy with Ethiopia, 1928 H
Italy with Greece, 1928 J
Italy with Hungary, 1927 D
Japan with Korea, 1875 N
Malaya with Indonesia, 1959 D
Pan-American, 1924 E
Roumania with Yugoslavia, 1947 M
Russia with E. Germany, 1964 F
Russia with Poland, 1931 F
Russia with Yugoslavia, 1941 D
Russia denounces, 1949 J
Russia with Yugoslavia, 1955 E
Saudi Arabia with Persia, 1929 H
Saudi Arabia with Transjordan, 1933 G
Saudi Arabia with Turkey, 1929 H
Turkey with Greece, 1930 K
Turkey with Spain, 1959 D
US with Germany, 1923 M
US with Italy, 1949 B
Yugoslavia with Bulgaria, denounced, 1949 K

Yugoslavia with Poland, 1926 J
Yugoslavia with Roumania, denounced, 1949 K
Treaties of Mutual Assistance and Military Aid:
American Republics, 1947 J
Britain with Poland, 1939 H
Britain with Russia, 1941 G
Cuba with US, Cuba denounces, 1960 J
France with Belgium, Belgium denounces, 1936 K
France with Russia, 1935 E
Germany with Russia, 1905 G
Greece with Yugoslavia and Turkey, 1954 H
India with Indonesia, 1956 B
Persia with Turkey and Afghanistan, 1926 D
Russia with Czechoslovakia, 1935 E
Russia with Finland, 1948 D
Russia with Mongolia, 1936 D
South East Asia, 1954 J
United Arab Republic with Iraq, 1958 G
US with Japan, 1960 A
Japan ratifies, despite protests, 1960 F
US with S. Korea, 1953 H
US with Liberia, 1959 G
See also under Aid
Treaties of Peace:
Adrianople, ends Russo-Turkish War, 1829 J
Allies with Austria, note by Western powers to Russia on, 1952 J
Allies with Germany, Russia proposes Conference for, 1959 A
Amiens, between Britain and France, 1802 C
Ancór, between Peru and Chile, 1883 K
Basle, between France and Prussia, 1795 D
Bassein, between East India Company and Poona, 1802 M
Berlin, between Prussia and Denmark, 1850 G
Berlin, on Eastern Question, 1878 G
adjustment to, 1880 L
Turkey denounces, 1917 A
Berlin, Germany with Latvia, 1920 E
Bolivia with Chile, 1866 H
Brest-Litovsk, between Russia and Central Powers, 1918 C
Soviet government annuls, 1918 L
Britain with Ireland, 1921 M
Britain with Mysore, 1784 C
Bucharest, between Turkey and Russia, 1812 E
Bucharest, between Serbia and Bulgaria, 1886 C
Bulgaria with Turkey, 1913 J
Burma with Japan, 1954 L
Campo Formio, between France and Austria, 1797 K
Cherasco, between Sardinia and France, 1796 E
Constantinople, between Turkey and Russia, 1784 A
Constantinople, between Greece and Turkey, 1897 M
Dardanelles, between Britain and Turkey, 1809A
Estonia with Russia, 1920 B
Finland with Russia, 1940 C
Florence, between France and Naples, 1801 C
Fommenah, between Britain and Ashanti, 1874 B
Frankfurt, between France and Germany, 1871 E
Frederikshavn, between Russia and Sweden, 1810 A
France recognises, 1810 A
Germany with Russia, 1921 E
Ghent, Britain with US, 1814 M, 1815 A
Gramido, ends Portuguese Civil War, 1847 G
Greece with Turkey, 1913 L
Guadeloupe-Hidalgo, between US and Mexico, 1848 B
ratified, 1848 E
Hubertusburg, Prussia with Austria, 1763 B
India with Afghanistan, 1919 G
Jassy, between Russia and Turkey, 1792 A
Jaunaie, La, ends Vendéan revolt, 1795 B
Kutchuk-Kainardji, between Russia and Turkey, 1774 G
Lahore, Britain with Sikhs, 1846 L
Lausanne, between Greece, Turkey and the Allies, 1823 G
Lausanne, between Italy and Turkey, 1912 K
Leoben, between France and Austria, 1797 D
Lunéville, between Austria and France, 1801 B
Milan, between Sardinia and Austria, 1849 H
Montlucon, between France and Vendéans, 1800 A
Nanking, between Britain and China, 1842 H
confirmed, 1843 K
Neuilly, between Allies and Bulgaria, 1919 L
Nikolsburg, between Prussia and Austria, 1866 G
Paris, ends Seven Years War, 1763 B
Paris, between Allies and France, 1814 E, 1815 L
Paris, ends Crimean War, 1856 L
Turkey denounces, 1917 A
Paris, Britain with Persia, 1857 C
Paris, between Spain and US, 1898 M
Paris, Allies with Bulgaria, Finland, Hungary and Roumania, 1946 G, 1947 B
Peking, ends Boxer Rising, 1901 J
Portsmouth, between Russia and Japan, 1905 J
Posen, between Saxony and France, 1806 M
Prague, between Austria and Prussia, 1866 H
clause of annulled, 1878 K
Pressburg, between Austria and France, 1805 M
Prussia, Russia and Austria, with Saxony, 1815 E
Prussia with German States, 1866 H
Prussia with Saxony, 1866 K
Riga, between Russia and Poland, 1921 B
Russia with Afghanistan, 1921 B
Russia with Central Powers, 1918 E
Russia with Lithuania, 1920 G
Russia with Persia, 1921 B
St. Germain, Allies with Austria, 1919 J, 1920 G
Austria ratifies, 1919 K
Salbai, between East India Company and Mahrattas, 1782 E
San Francisco, Allies with Japan, 1951 C, J
San Stefano, between Russia and Turkey, 1878 C
Austria not reconciled to, 1878 C
Schönbrunn, between France and Prussia, 1805 M
Schönbrunn, between Austria and France, 1809 K
Sèvres, between Allies and Turkey, 1920 H
Shimonoseki, between China and Japan, 1895 D
Sistova, between Turkey and Austria, 1791 H
Tartu, between Russia and Poland, 1920 K
Teschen, ends War of Bavarian Succession, 1792 A
Tientsin, Britain with China, 1858 F
Tilsit, France with Prussia, 1807 G
Tilsit, France with Russia, 1807 G
Tolentino, between France and Papacy, 1797 B
Trianon, between Allies and Hungary, 1920 F
Turin, between France and Sardinia, 1860 C
Turkey with Afghanistan, 1921 C
Turkey with Serbia, 1914 C
Turkmanchai, between Persia and Russia, 1827 B
US with Austria, 1921 H
US with Germany, 1921 H
US with Hungary, 1921 H
US with Mexico, 1914 F, 1916 L
Valparaiso, between Bolivia and Chile, 1884 D
Vereeniging, ends Boer War, 1902 E
Verela, between Sweden and Russia, 1790 H
Versailles, between Britain and France, 1783 J

Treaties of Peace—*contd.*
Versailles, between Britain and Holland, 1784 C
Versailles, between France and Germany, 1871 B
Versailles, between Allies and Germany, 1919 F
Austria protests at, 1919 F
US Senate rejects, 1920 L
Mussolini champions revision of, 1930 E
Nazis in Germany denounce, 1930 J
Germany repudiates disarmament clauses of, 1935 C
Germany violates, 1936 C
Germany denounces, 1936 L
League Covenant is separated from, 1938 K
Vienna, between Allies and France, 1815 F
Austria violates, 1846 L
Vienna, between Denmark, Austria and Prussia, 1864 K
Villafranca, between Austria and France, 1859 G
treaty of Zurich confirms, 1859 L
Waitungi, Britain with Maoris, 1840 B
Yandaba, Britain with Burma, 1826 B
Zurich, confirms treaty of Villafranca between Austria and France, 1859 L

Other Treaties and International Agreements:
Adams-Onis, on Florida, 1819 B
Addis Ababa, Italy withdraws protectorate over Ethiopia, 1896 K
Afghanistan with Russia, 1926 G
Ankara, between France and Turkey, 1920 K
Aranjuez, Spain with France, for cession of Louisiana, 1801 A
Armed Neutrality of the North, 1800 M
Austria with France, secret, 1866 F
Badajoz, Spain with Portugal, 1801 F
Bardo, between France and Tunis, 1881 E
Barrier, between Austria and Holland (1715), abrogated, 1782 D
Britain with Austria and Italy, for status quo in Near East, 1887 M
Britain with China, on extra-territorial rights, 1943 A
Britain with Ethiopia, on Somaliland, 1897 E
Britain with France, on W. African colonial boundaries, 1882 E
Britain with Germany, on Portuguese Africa, 1898 H
Britain with Russia, on N.W. America, 1825 B
Britain with Russia, secret, on Bulgaria, 1878 E
Britain with Uganda, 1900 C
Britain with US, on W. Indian bases (1941), US relinquishes rights in, 1961 B
Calhoun's, for US annexation of Texas, 1844 D
Chaumont, for Allies not to make separate peace with Napoleon, 1814 C
Clayton-Bulwer, on Panama Canal, 1850 D
Corfu Pact, for union of Serbs, Croats and Slovenes, 1917 G
Elgin, between Britain and US, on Canada, 1854 F
Family Compact, between France and Spain, French obligations under, 1790 E
Fontainebleau, between Austria and Netherlands, 1785 L
France with Italy, over Florence and Rome, 1864 J
France with Italy, on Middle East, 1900 M
France with Prussia, for exchange of lands, 1796 H
France with Russia, military, 1892 H
France with Spain, on Morocco, 1904 K
Gandamak, between Britain and Afghanistan, 1879 E
Germany with Italy, military, 1888 A
Germany with Russia, military, 1873 E
Greece with Italy, on Dodecanese Isles, 1920 H
Greece with Turkey and Cyprus (1960), Makarios abrogates, 1964 D
Hague, The, for Britain to subsidise Allies, 1794 D
Hay-Pauncefoote, on Panama, 1901 L
infringement of, alleged, 1912 H
Hué, between Annam and France, 1884 F
Hyderabad, between Britain and the Nizam, 1798 J
Jay, US with Britain, on boundaries, 1794 L
Jeddah, on independence of Saudi Arabia, 1927 E
Kiel, between Denmark and Sweden, 1814 A, D
Lateran, for independence of Vatican City, 1929 B
Lausanne, for establishing world peace, 1924 H
Livadia, between Russia and China, on Ili Valley, 1879 J
Locarno, on mutual guarantees in Europe, 1925 M
Rome Pact endorses, 1933 G
Belgium is released from obligations under, 1937 D
London, between Britain, France and Russia, recognising Greek autonomy, 1827 G
London, for separation of Holland and Belgium, 1831 L
London, for Belgian independence, 1839 D
London, Schleswig-Holstein, 1850 H
London, guarantees integrity of Denmark, 1852 E
London, between France, Russia and Britain against a separate peace, 1914 J
Japan a signatory to, 1915 K
London, naval, 1936 C
Russia accedes to, 1936 K
Mackinnon, between British East Africa Company and Leopold II, 1890 E
Madrid, between France and Portugal, 1801 J
Mundoseer, between Britain and Indore, 1818 A
Nettuno, on Dalmatia, 1925 G
New States Treaty, 1920 H
Paris, for Western European Union, ratified, 1955 C, D
ratification provokes Russia to annul treaties with France and Britain, 1955 E
Peking, China with Britain and France, ratifying earlier treaties, 1860 K
Peking, Britain with China, 1925 A
Petropolis, Bolivar with Brazil, 1903 L
Pretoria, Britain with Boers, on independence of Transvaal, 1881 D
Rapallo, between Italy and Yugoslavia, 1920 L
Italy abrogates, 1924 J
Rapallo, Germany with Russia, 1922 D
Reichenbach, between Prussia and Austria, 1790 F
cession of Orsova, in defiance of, 1791 F
Reichenbach, Austria with Russia and Prussia, 1813 F
Russia with Afghanistan, neutrality, 1931 F
Russia with Poland, on Ukraine (Riga), 1921 C
St. Petersburg, Britain with the powers of the Armed Neutrality of the North, 1801 F
St. Petersburg, between China and Russia, 1881 B
San Ildefonso, between Spain and France, for sale of Louisiana, 1800 K
San Lorenzo, between US and Spain, 1795 K
Serbia with Austria, 1881 G
Spain with Peru, 1865 A
Straits Settlements federation, 1896 G
Test Ban, 1963 H
Tientsin, between France and China, on Annam, 1885 F
Tirana, between Italy and Albania, 1926 L
Ucciali, between Italy and Ethiopia, 1889 E
US with Japan, 1854 C
US with Panama, on Canal Zone, 1903 M

US with Panama, new canal treaty offered by US, 1964 M
US with Russia, on N.W. frontier, 1824 D
Valençay, between France and Spain, for restoration of Ferdinand VII, 1813 M
Vienna, Britain with France, US and Russia for restoring Austria's independence, 1955 E
Washington, fixing Oregon-Canadian frontier, 1846 F
Washington, to settle differences between US and Britain, 1871 E
Washington, on Pacific, 1921 M
Japan denounces, 1934 M
Washington, on submarine warfare and use of gas, 1922 B
Webster-Ashburton, on US–Canadian frontier, 1842 H
Windsor, Britain and Portugal, to prevent arms from passing from Delagoa Bay to Transvaal, 1899 K
See also under Pacts
Treaties, collection of, 1791 Q
Treatise of General Sociology (Pareto), 1916 R
Treatise on Differential and Integral Calculus (J. Bertrand), 1864 P
Treatise on Electricity and Magnetism, A (J. Clerk-Maxwell), 1879 P
Treatise on Magnetic Waves (W. and E. Weber), 1825 P
Treatise on Money (J. M. Keynes), 1930 O
Treatise on Radiography (M. Curie), 1910 P
Treatise on Representative Government (J. S. Mill), 1860 O
Treatise on Sound (Lord Rayleigh), 1877 P
Treatise on the Blood, Inflammation and Gunshot Wounds (J. Hunter), 1794 P
Treatise on the Coins of the Realm (Lord Liverpool), 1805 O
Treatise on Tolerance (Voltaire), 1763 R
Trebbia, The, Naples, Italy, battle, 1799 F
Trebizond, Turkey, Russians take, 1916 D
Tree, Sir Herbert Beerbohm, B. actor-manager, 1853 Z, 1912 Z
Treitschke, Heinrich von, G. historian (1834–96), 1834 Z, 1878 O, 1879 Q, 1896 Z
Trenchard, Hugh, Viscount Trenchard, B. Air-Marshal, 1873 Z, 1956 Z
Trent affair, 1861 L
Trenton, New Jersey, US, 1776 M
Trésaguet, P. M. J., F. engineer (1716–94), 1764 P
Trevelyan, Sir Charles Edward, B. administrator (1807–86), 1954 O
Trevelyan, Sir George Otto, B. author and Liberal politician (1838–1928), 1874 E
Trevelyan, George Macaulay, B. historian (1876–1962), 1876 Z, 1926 Q, 1930 Q, 1942 Q, 1962 Z
Treviranus, Gottfried Reinhold, G. naturalist (1776–1837), 1802 P
Trevithick, Richard, B. engineer (1771–1833), 1771 Z, 1800 P
Trevor-Roper, Hugh Redwald, B. historian (b. 1914), 1947 O
Trial, The (F. Kafka), 1925 U
Trials, notable:
in Britain, of CND Committee of a Hundred members for breaches of Secrets Acts, 1962 B
of Warren Hastings, 1788 B, 1795 D
of C. Keeler, for perjury, 1963 M
of Lonsdale and Blake, for espionage, 1961 O
of A. Orton, the Tichborne claimant, 1874 O
of T. Paine, 1792 M
of W. Vassall, for espionage, 1962 K
of O. Wilde, 1895 U
in Czechoslovakia, for treason, 1952 L
in Egypt, for espionage, 1957 F
in France, of de Lesseps, for corruption, 1892 L, 1893 C
of Louis XVI, 1792 M
in Germany, of Auschwitz prison camp officials, 1965 H
of Nazis in W. Germany, time limit for, extended, 1965 C. *See also* Tribunals, Allied
in Ghana, for treason, 1963 M
in Russia, for political offences, 1938 C
in South Africa, for treason, 1956 M, 1959 A, 1961 C, 1964 F
in Syria, for conspiracy, 1957 A
in Turkey, of members of Menderes' régime, 1960 K
in US, of Alger Hiss, 1950 A
Tribunals:
in Britain, Bank Rate, 1957 M
Lynski, 1948 L
Radcliffe, 1963 V
Allied, for war criminals:
German, Nuremberg, verdicts, 1946 J
Japanese, 1946 M, 1948 L
Trier, W. Germany, US troops near, 1944 J
Trieste, Italy: ceded by Austria to France, 1809 K; railway, from Vienna, 1853 P; Italian agitation for acquiring, 1878 N; loss of Austrian battleship in, 1917 M; established as free territory, 1947 B; administration of Zone A, to be handed to Italy, 1953 K; agreement for free territory to be divided into Italian and Yugoslav Zones, 1954 K
Trincomalee, Ceylon, surrendered by Holland to Britain, 1782 A
Trinidad, Island, W. Indies: Abercromby captures, 1797 B; Britain retains, 1801 K
Trinidad and Tobago, Islands, W. Indies, become independent within Commonwealth, 1962 H. *See also* Tobago
Triplepatte (T. Bernard), 1905 W
Tripoli, N. Africa: expeditions from, 1823 P; Italian interests in, 1900 M; Italian bombardment of, 1911 J; Italian victory in, 1911 J; Italy annexes, 1911 L; becomes autonomous under Italian suzerainty, 1912 K; pipe-line from Mosul, 1934 G; Eighth Army enters, 1943 A
Tripolitza, Morea, Greece, Greeks capture, 1821 K
Tristan da Cunha, eruption in, 1961 K
Tristram, Ernest William, B. art historian (1882–1952), 1945 S
Tristram Shandy (L. Sterne), 1767 U
Triumphant Democracy (A. Carnegie), 1886 O
Trocadero, Spain, French take, 1823 H
Troeltsch, Ernst, G. philosopher, 1912 R, 1922 R
Trois Villes, Les (E. Zola), 1894 U
Trolley-buses, 1938 P
Trollope, Anthony, B. novelist (1815–82), 1815 Z, 1855 U, 1857 U, 1864 U, 1867 U, 1882 Z
Trondheim, Norway, British expedition to, 1940 D
Trophées, Les (J. de Heredia), 1893 U
Tropical medicine, studies in, 1897 P
Tropic of Capricorn (H. Miller), 1962 U
Troppau, Austria, conference, 1820 K, L, M
Trotsky, Lev, R. politician (1877–1940), 1877 Z, 1903 H, 1940 Z; becomes premier, 1917 L; dismissed from chairmanship of Revolutionary Council, 1925 A; expelled from Politbureau, 1926 K; expelled from Communist Party, 1927 M;

Trotsky, Lev,—*contd.*
expelled from Russia, 1929 A, O; autobiography, 1930 O; biography of, 1954 Q, 1963 Q; *History*, by, 1933 O
Trovador, El (A. Garciá-Gutiérrez), 1836 U
Troy, excavations at, 1870 Q
Troyes, France, Parlement of Paris banished to, 1787 H
True Whig. *See* Political Parties
Truffant, François, F. film director (b. 1917), 1961 W, 1964 W
Truman, Harry S., Am. statesman, Democrat (b. 1884), 32nd president of US (1945–53), 1884 Z, 1952 P
succeeds to presidency, 1945 D
at Potsdam Conference, 1945 G
orders end of Lend-Lease, 1945 H
gives bill of credit to Britain, 1946 G
removes controls, 1946 L
Doctrine, of economic and military aid, 1947 C
vetoes Taft-Hartley Act, 1947 F
Four-point programme, 1949 A
signs Mutual Defense Assistance Act, 1949 K
orders development of hydrogen bomb, 1959 A
message to Congress on spending for Korean War, 1950 G
orders army to control railways, 1951 B
relieves MacArthur of command, 1951 D
urges compromise in Anglo-Iranian dispute, 1951 G
indicates retirement, 1952 C
orders seizure of steel industry, 1952 D
signs Foreign Aid bill, 1952 F
Trusts in US, Anti-Trust Laws, 1903 O, 1904 Y
Truter, Sir John Andreas, B. Cape of Good Hope judge and African explorer (*d.* 1826), 1802 P
Truth About the Peace Treaties, The (D. Lloyd George), 1938 O
Trypsin, 1930 P
Tsaldaris, Panyoti, Gk. moderate Royalist, 1932 K
Tsao Kun, president of China, 1924 K
Tschokke, Johann Henrich Daniel, G. author (1771–1848), 1830 U
Tshombe, Moise Congolese politician (b. 1918), leader of Conakat Party as premier of Katanga, 1960 G; imprisoned, 1961 F; ends Katanga secession, 1961 M; accepts UN plan on Katanga, 1963 A; resigns from premiership, 1963 F; becomes Congo premier, 1964 G; debarred from attending Cairo Conference, 1964 K; is dismissed, 1965 K
Tsingtao, China, Japanese take, 1938 A
Tsinan, China, Chinese-Japanese clashes at, 1928 E
TSR-2, military aircraft, contract cancelled, 1965 D
Tsushina Straits, Korea, Japanese victory at, 1905 E
Tuan Ch'i-Jui, Chinese premier, 1917 E, G
Tubbs, Ralph, B. architect (b. 1912), 1951 S
Tuberculosis, diagnosis of, 1907 P
Tube Investment, Ltd., high energy plant, 1956 P
Tubman, William V. S., Liberian president, True Whig (b. 1895), 1959 E; proposes conference of independent African states, 1959 G
Tucker, Abraham, B. philosopher (1705–74), 1765 R
Tucuman, Congress of, 1816 G
Tuke, William, B. chemist (1732–1822), 1792 O
Tumioja, Sakari, Finn., appointed mediator in Cyprus, 1964 C
Tugenbund, German patriotic organisation, formed, 1808 O
Tungsten, 1781 P, 1855 P
Tunis, Tunisia: accepts control by powers, 1869 N; Franco-Italian rivalry in, 1880 E; French occupation, 1881 C, D; Franco-Italian convention on, 1896 J; Allies take, 1943 E
Tunisia: French in, 1881 L; French control of, 1883 F; demands autonomy, 1952 A; independence is recognised, 1956 C; France's dispute with, 1958 B, D; clashes between French and Tunisians, 1961 G
Tunnels:
Channel, first proposed, 1882 O
Report on, 1963 J
Mont Cenis, 1871 P
New Croutown aqueduct, New York, 1893 P
railway, the first, 1826 P
St. Gotthard, 1882 P
Severn, 1886 P
Simplon, 1906 P
Thames railway, 1890 P
Turbine, gas, 1951 P; steam, 1884 P
Turf, Ruff's Guide to The, 1842 X
Turgeniev, Ivan, R. novelist (1818–83), 1818 Z, 1852 U, 1855 U, 1860 U, 1862 U, 1867 U, 1872 U, 1883 Z
Turgot, Anne Robert Jacques, F. economist and statesman (1727–81), 1765 O, 1774 H, J, 1775 J, 1776 A, E, 1781 Z, 1787 O
Turin, Italy: Suvorov occupies, 1799 D; Piazzo Vittorio Veneto in, 1818 S; supplanted as capital of Italy by Florence, 1864 J; Exhibition Hall, 1948 S
Turkestan, Russia: Russian control over, 1867 G
Turkey: Austria and Russia aim to maintain Ottoman Empire, 1804 L; integrity of Ottoman Empire guaranteed, 1833 K, 1856 C; financial collapse, 1874 N; reforms advocated, 1876 A, E, 1877 C; partition of Empire, proposed, 1895 H; Allies agree on, 1916 C; proclaimed a republic, 1922 L
Turner, Charles Tennyson, B. poet (1808–79), 1827 U
Turner, Joseph Mallord William, B. artist (1775–1851), 1775 Z, 1797 S, 1801 S, 1805 S, 1807 S, 1813 S, 1815 S, 1819 S, 1827 S, 1839 S, 1843 S, 1851 Z
Turner, Sharon, B. historian (1768–1847), 1799 Q
Turn of the Screw, The (H. James), 1898 U
Turn of the Tide, The (A. Bryant), 1957 Q
Turret-lathe, 1855 P
Tuscany, Italy: Grand Duchy, 1765 H; French occupy, 1799 C; is ceded to Parma, 1801 B; Napoleon annexes, 1808 E; Grand Duke flees, 1849 B; plebiscite supports union with Sardinia, 1860 K
Tushingham Rita, B. actress, 1965 W
Twain, Mark. *See* Clemens, Samuel Langhorne
Tweed, William Mancy, Am. political boss (1823–78), 1871 G
Tweedsmuir, lord. *See* Buchan, John
Twelve, The (A. Blok), 1918 U
Twenty-Five Years (Lord Grey of Falloden), 1925 Q
Twenty Thousand Leagues Under the Sea (J. Verne), 1869 U
Twenty Years' Crisis, The (E. H. Carr), 1939 U
Twilight of the Gods (R. Garnett), 1925 U
Twiss, Peter, B. test pilot (b. 1921), 1956 P
Two Cultures and the Sciences, The (C. P. Snow), 1959 U
Two Minutes' Silence, 1919 L
Two Tactics (Lenin), 1905 O
Tydings-McDuffie Act, for Philippines, 1934 C
Tyler, John, Am. Whig (1773–1841), president of US (1841), 1841 D
Tylor, Sir Edward Burnett, B. anthropologist (1832–1917), 1881 P

Typewriter, the:
forerunner of, 1843 P
Sholes's, 1873 P
Typhoid epidemics, 1963 C, 1964 E
Typhoons. *See* Tornadoes
Typography:
Gill's, 1927 S
Gothic, abandoned in Germany, 1941
Tyres:
balloon for tractors, 1932 P
pneumatic, 1888 P
Tyrol, Austrian, ceded to France, 1805 M; Germanisation of, 1926 B
Tytus, John, B. metallurgist, 1923 P
Tzara, Tristan, artist, 1916 S, 1931 U
Tzu-hsi, dowager empress of China, 1898 J

U

Ucciali, Ethiopia, treaty, 1889 E
Uddevalla, Sweden, convention between Denmark and Sweden, 1788 L
Ufa, Russia, Red Army takes, 1919 F
Uganda: Lugard occupies, 1890 M; East Africa Company hands over to Britain, 1893 C; becomes a British Protectorate, 1894 D; mutiny in, 1897 J; Britain regulates government, 1900 C; frontier with East Africa, 1907 M; attains full internal self-government, 1962 C; becomes independent within the Commonwealth, 1962 K
Ujiji, Africa, Stanley meets Livingstone at, 1871 L, P
Ukhrul, Burma, British take, 1944 G
Ukraine, Russia: Russia acquires Western Ukraine, 1793 E; republic proclaimed, 1917 L; Poland abandons claim to, 1921 C; Germans enter, 1941 G
Ulm, Bad-Württemburg, W. Germany, battle, 1805 K
Ulmanis, Karlis, Latvian dictator, 1934 E
Ulster, N. Ireland: rebellion in, 1797 C; exclusion from Government of Ireland Act, insisted upon, 1916 F; votes to accept Home Rule Bill, 1920 C. *See also* Ireland, Northern
Ulster Unionists. *See under* Political Parties
Ultima Thule (Longfellow), 1880 U
Ultra-high-frequency waves, 1955 P
Ultra-microscope, 1903 P
Ultra Royalists. *See under* Political Parties
Ultra-violet lamp, 1904 P
Ultra-violet rays, for sterilising water, 1912 P
Ulysses (J. Joyce), 1922 U
Umberto II, King of Italy (1946), 1946 E
leaves Italy, 1946 F
Unamuno y Jugo, Miguel de, Sp. poet, 1914 U
Uncle Tom's Cabin (H. Beecher-Stowe), 1852 U
Uncle Vanya (Chekhov), 1900 W
Unconscious, The (Jung), 1917 R
Underhill, Evelyn, B. religious author (1875–1941), 1875 Z, 1910 R
Under Milk Wood (D. Thomas), 1954 W
Under the Greenwood Tree (T. Hardy), 1872 U
Under the Red Robe (S. Weyman), 1894 U
Under Two Flags (Onida), 1867 U
Undine (F. Fowqué), 1811 U
Undset, Fru Sigrid, Da. Author (1882–1949), 1920 U, 1930 U
Unemployment (W. A. Appleton), 1923 O
Unemployment (W. Beveridge), 1909 O
Unemployment:
world, 1929 O
in Britain, 1817 F, 1919 Y, 1921 Y, 1932 Y
Hunger marches, 1922 K, L
legislation to ameliorate, 1925 G, 1934 E
Labour Party censure motion, 1933 D
means test, 1935 A, 1936 G
demonstrations, 1963 C
in France, national workshops for easing, 1848 B, F
in Germany, 1932 Y
commissioner for, 1932 O
four-year plan for, 1933 O
in Palestine, of Arabs, 1930 K
in USA, 1932 Y, 1958 O
Unfinished Novels:
Mystery of Edwin Drood (C. Dickens), 1870 U
Weir of Hermiston, The (R. L. Stevenson), 1896 U
Unicorn, The (I. Murdoch), 1963 U
Union Dead (R. Lowell), 1965 U
Union de la Gauche Socialiste. *See under* Political Parties
Union Générale des postes, 1874 O
Union Indo-Chinoise, S.E. Asia, 1887 N
Unionists. *See under* Political Parties
Union Now (C. K. Streit), 1939 O
Union of Soviet Socialist Republic (USSR), formally established, 1923 A. *See under* Russia
Union of Unions, Russian, 1909 E
Unitarians. *See under* Religious Denominations
Unitary Field Theory (Einstein), 1929 P
'Unité d'Habitation', near Marseilles, France, 1952 S
United Arab Republic (UAR):
formed by union of Egypt and Sudan, 1958 B
diplomatic relations with Jordan, 1959 H
with Britain, 1959 M
Syria secedes from, 1961 J
Syria and Iraq agree to federate with, 1963 D
United Irishmen, Society of, 1790 K
United Nations, The (UN):
preliminaries:
Bretton Woods monetary and financial conference, 1944 G
San Francisco Conference of, 1945 B, D
foundation of, 1945 K
charter is ratified, 1945 K
permanent headquarters for, 1946 M
Acheson Plan, to increase powers of, 1950 K, 1951 L
Apartheid Committee calls for sanctions against S. Africa, 1963 J
Atomic Energy Commission, 1946 M
suspends meetings, 1949 G
Balzan International Foundation Peace Prize awarded to, 1964 B
Educational, Scientific and Cultural Organisation (UNESCO) symposium on human rights, 1949 O
Food and Agricultural Organization, launches Freedom from Hunger Campaign, 1960 G
Forces, in Congo, 1960 G, H, 1961 J, 1962 M, 1963 A, 1964 F
in Cyprus, 1964 C, H, M
in Korea. *See under* Wars, Korean
in Middle East, occupies Gaza Strip, 1957 C
General Assembly, first session, in London, 1946 A
meets in New York, 1946 K
rules on Siam's return of territory to Indo-China, 1946 K
rejects S. Africa's proposal for incorporating S.W. Africa, 1946 M
bans Spain from activities, 1946 M
calls on Greece and Balkan countries to settle disputes, 1947 K
recognises Korea's claim to independence, 1947 L

United Nations—*contd.*
General Assembly—*contd.*
adopts convention on human rights, 1948 M
discusses alleged racial discrimination in S. Africa, 1949 E
votes for ultimate independence of Italy's former colonies, 1949 L
requires information on arms and forces, 1949 M
calls for recognition of China, 1949 M
revokes resolution on Spain, 1950 L
Acheson presents disarmament proposals to, 1951 L
adopts Indian armistice proposals for Korea, 1952 M
control of atomic energy proposed to, 1953 M
Greece proposes to lay Cyprus problem before, 1955 G, 1956 C
France leaves meeting on Algeria, 1955 K
withdraws inspection teams from Korea 1956E
censures Russia over Hungary, 1956 L
demands withdrawal of Soviet troops from Hungary, 1956 L
adopts Canadian resolution to send force to Middle East, 1956 L
calls on S. Africa to reconsider Apartheid, 1957 A
calls for peaceful solution of Cyprus problem, 1957 B
Elizabeth II addresses, 1957 K
adopts report on Hungary, 1957 J
meeting on Middle East, 1958 H
Khruschchev addresses, 1959 J, 1960 J
considers Apartheid in S. Africa, 1959 L
condemns all racial discrimination, 1959 L
resolves on independence for Togoland, 1959 M
Macmillan addresses, 1960 J
condemns S. African policies in S.W. Africa, 1961 D
calls for elections in Ruanda and Urundi, 1961 D
calls on Portugal to cease repression in Angola, 1961 F
resolution to treat Africa as a denuclearised zone, 1961 L
calls for independence of colonial peoples, 1961 L
requests Britain to suspend enforcement of new constitution in Rhodesia, 1962 K
demands end to nuclear tests, 1962 L
condemns repression in S. Africa, 1963 K
Pope Paul VI addresses, 1965 R
International Court of Justice, first decision by, 1949 D
Membership, changes in, since foundation,
Albania, 1955 M
Argentina, 1955 M
Bulgaria, 1955 M
Cambodia, 1955 M
Ceylon, 1955 M
China's admission rejected, 1958 J, 1961 M, 1962 K
Peking delegates attend as observers, 1950 L
Eire, 1955 M
Finland, 1955 M
Ghana, 1957 C
Hungary, 1955 M
Indonesia, 1950 J
withdraws, 1965 A
Israel, 1949 E
Italy, 1955 M
Japan, 1956 M
Jordan, 1955 M
Kuwait's admission vetoed, 1961 F
Laos, 1955 M
Libya, 1955 M
Mauritania, 1916 K
Mongolia, 1961 K
Nepal, 1955 M
Pakistan, 1947 J
Portugal, 1955 M
Roumania, 1955 M
S. Africa withdraws, 1955 L
resumes membership, 1958 G
Spain, excluded, 1945 F
elected, 1955 M
US participation approved by Senate, 1945 M
Yemen, The, 1947 J
Palestine, conciliatary commission for, 1951 J
mixed armistice commission for, Israel withdraws from, 1954 C
truce accepted, 1956 A
Relief and Rehabilitation Administration (UNRRA), 1943 O
Secretary General, T. Lie appointed, 1946 B
second term, 1950 F
D. Hammarskjold appointed, 1953 C
killed, 1961 J
U Thant as acting, 1961 J
elected, 1962 L
Security Council, Egypt refers revision of 1936 Treaty with Britain to, 1947 A
Palestine question referred to, 1947 D
appoints Trusteeship for Pacific Isles, 1947 D
calls for Indonesian cease fire, 1947 H
Kashmir problem referred to, 1947 M
orders truce in Palestine, 1948 G
Russia vetoes plan for ending Berlin blockade, 1948 K
calls for end of war in Burma, 1949 A
discusses Korea, 1950 H
Tibet appeals to, 1950 L
India complains to, over Pakistan, 1951 G
to supervise Sudan plebiscite, 1951 L
Greece elected to, 1951 M
Tunisia appeals to, 1952 A
proposal for supervised German elections rejected by Russia, 1952 D
Thailand complains her security is threatened, 1954 E
China appeals to, over Formosa, 1954 K
Vietnam appeals to, over actions of Viet Minh, 1955 D
Britain and France refer Suez dispute to, 1956 J, K
Hungary appeals to, 1956 L
considers Cyprus problems, 1957 M
Russia asks for action to end flights of military aircraft, 1958 D
Laos recognises, as sole arbiter, 1959 B
Dalai Lama appeals to, 1959 C, 1961 C
Lumumba appeals for aid, 1960 G
demands enquiry into Lumumba's death, 1961 B
supervises Cameroons plebiscite, 1961 B
orders ceasefire in Tunisia, 1961 G
votes for embargo on arms to S. Africa, 1963 M
Trusteeship, S. Africa refuses to place S.W. Africa under, 1947 A, 1950 M
for Pacific Isles, 1947 D
for Jerusalem, proposed, 1947 L
for Far East, China rejects proposal, 1951 A
for Ruanda Republic, 1961 A
Committee resolves to consider whether S. Rhodesia has obtained self-government, 1962 B

takes over administration of West New Guinea, 1962 K
asks Britain not to transfer Rhodesian Federation forces to S. Rhodesia, 1963 K
United Parties. *See under* Political Parties
United States of America (US):
Congress resolves on suppression of British authority, 1776 C
Congress passes Declaration of Independence, 1776 G
Confederation Articles of Perpetual Union, Congress adopts, 1777 L
Britain recognises independence, 1783 J
frontier treaty with Russia, over Alaska, 1824 D
frontier with Canada, defined, 1818 K, 1842 H
geology of, 1809 P
Western States, opening up of, 1902 O
United States Foreign Policy (W. Lippmann), 1943 O
Universe Around US, The (J. Jeans), 1929 P
Universities:
in Belgium, Ghent, 1816 O
in Britain, Robbins Report on, 1963 O
proposals for further foundations rejected by government, 1965 B
Cambridge, Churchill College, 1960 O
Girton College, 1869 O
Professorship of American history, 1943 O
Professorship of Experimental Physics, 1871 P
religious tests abolished, 1871 F, O
residence for women students (later Newnham College), 1871 O
University College, 1965 O
University extension lectures, 1870 O
Edinburgh, chair of technology, 1855 O
Kent, 1965 O
Leeds (formerly Yorkshire College), 1874 P
London, founded, 1836 O
science degrees at, 1860 O
established as a teaching university, 1898 O
moves to Bloomsbury, 1936 O
Bedford College, 1849 O
Imperial College of Science and Technology, 1850 O
Imperial Institute, 1893 O
King's College, 1830 O, 1853 R
London School of Economics and Political Science, 1895 O
School of Mines, 1850 O
School of Oriental and African Studies, 1916 O
University College, 1826 O
Warburg Institute, 1933 S
Manchester (Owen's College), 1851 O, 1880 O
North Staffordshire, 1949 O
Oxford, appoints Franks Commission, 1964 O
Balliol College under Jowett, 1870 O
Bampton Lectures, 1780 R
Keble College, 1870 O
Macmillan elected chancellor, 1960 C
music faculty, 1944 T
natural science honours school, 1850 O
Pitt Rivers Museum, 1874 Q
Professorship of modern history under Stubbs, 1866 Q
religious tests ended, 1871 F, O
Roosevelt honoured, at Harvard, 1941 O
Reading, 1926 O
Sussex, 1961 O, 1964 S
Wales, 1893 O
Warwick, 1965 O
in Czechoslovakia, Prague, 1882 O
in Europe, Cambridge Conference of European Vice-Chancellors, 1955 O
in France, clerical control, 1822 F
in Germany, placed under state supervision, 1819 J
women admitted, 1909 O
Berlin, 1810 O, 1818 R
Bonn, 1818 O
Göttingen, dismissals from, 1837 M
Munich, 1826 O
Strasburg, 1872 O
in Iran, Teheran, 1935 O
in Ireland, Gladstone's bill for, defeated, 1873 C
Dublin University College, 1854 O
in Norway, Christiania, 1811 O
in Spain, Madrid, closed by government, 1929 C
in Mexico, Mexico University City, 1950 S, 1952 S
in Rumania, Bucharest, 1864 O
in Russia, Odessa, 1865 O
in Switzerland, Zurich, 1832 O
in US, women awarded degrees, 1841 O
State colleges for science and technology, 1862 O
Alabama, desegregation crisis in, 1956 O
Brown, Rhode Island, 1764 O
Harvard, Carpenter Center for Visual Arts at, 1963 S
Johns Hopkins, 1876 O
Massachusetts Institute of Technology, 1865 O
Pennsylvania, archaeological expedition from, 1888 Q
Pittsburgh, scientific research at, 1955 P
Utah, 1954 P
Virginia, 1817 S
Yale, Beineche Library at, 1963 S
interprets Vinland Map, 1965 Q
Washington, Catholic University, 1889 O
in Yugoslavia, Belgrade, 1864 O
University Extension Lectures, 1850 O, 1870 O
Unkiar Skelessi, treaty, between Turkey and Russia, 1833 G
overthrown by Straits Convention, 1841 G
'Unknown Political Prisoner, The', sculpture competition, 1953 S
Unsettled Questions of Political Economy (J. S. Mill), 1844 O
Unsichtbare Loge, Die (Jean Paul), 1793 U
Unto Caesar (Vogt), 1938 R
Unto This Last (J. Ruskin), 1862 O
Untouchability, outlawed in India, 1947 E
Untouchables, in Bombay, disabilities removed, 1946 O
Unvanquished, The (W. Faulkner), 1938 U
Updike, John Hoyer, Am. author (b. 1932), 1960 U, 1963 U
Ur, discoveries at, 1927 Q
Ural Mountains, Russia, 1820 P
Ural Regional Council, orders execution of Nicholas II, 1918 G
Uranium, separation of, 1900 P
pile, 1944 P
Uranus, discovery of, 1781 P
Urea, synthesis of, 1828 P
Urey, Harold Clayton, Am. atomic scientist (b. 1893), 1893 Z, 1932 P, 1941 P
Uriburu, José, Argent. president, 1930 J
Urrutia, Manuel, Cuban premier, 1959 A
Uruguay: becomes independent of Brazil, 1825 H, 1828 H; Brazil's war with Argentina over, 1825 M
Urundi, S.E. Cen. Africa, UN calls for elections, 1961 D

Use of Poetry and the Use of Criticism (T. S. Eliot), 1933 U
Uses of Literary, The (R. Hoggart), 1957 U
Ustinov, Peter Alexander, B. dramatist (b. 1921), 1951 W
Usury, tract on, 1787 O
Utah, State, US: US obtains, 1848 E; becomes a US state, 1896 A, 1906 N
Utah, Utah, US, University, 1954 P
Uthwatt Report, 1942 O
Utilitarianism, 1802 O, 1862 O
Utilitarianism (J. S. Mill), 1862 O
Utilitarians, The (L. Stephen), 1900 O
Utility clothing, in Britain, 1941 O
Utrillo, Maurice, F. artist (1883–1955), 1908 S, 1923 S
U2 aircraft, US, incident, 1960 E
Utzon, Jørn, Swe. architect, 1956 S

V

Vaagno, near Trondheim, Norway, British commando raids on, 1941 M
Vaccination against smallpox, 1796 P
Vaccines:
for anthrax, 1881 P
for measles, 1963 P
for poliomyelitis (Salk's), 1955 P
Vacuum-cleaners, statistics, 1965 Y
Vaihinger, Hans, G. philosopher, 1911 R
Vailland, Auguste, F. anarchist, 1893 M
Vailland, Roger François, F. author (b. 1907), 1957 U
Valençay, France, treaty, 1813 M
Valencia, Spain, government moves to, 1936 L
Valency:
theory, 1916 P
wave mechanics of, 1927 P
Valentino, Rudolph, Am. film actor (*d.* 1926), 1926 W
Valera, Juan, Sp. novelist (1824–1905), 1848 U, 1879 U
Valera, Eamon de, Ir. statesman (b. 1882), 1919 D, 1922 A, C, 1933 A; proclamation of terms for amnesty to rebels, 1923 D; is arrested, 1923 H; resigns from Sinn Fein, 1926 C; founds Fianna Fail, 1926 C; agrees to take seat in Dail, 1927 H; elected premier of Irish Free State, 1932 C; founds Republican Army, 1933 G; is again premier, 1937 G; retains power, 1951 F; vote of confidence in, 1953 G; resigns premiership, 1959 F; becomes president of Eire, 1959 F
Valéry, Paul, F. author (1871–1945), 1871 Z, 1906 U, 1917 U, 1920 U, 1921 U, 1938 U, 1945 Z
Vallauris, France, pottery, 1946 S
Valmy, Marne, France, canonade, 1792 J
Valois, Dame Ninette de, B. ballerina (b. 1898), 1950 T
Valparaiso, Chile: Treaty, 1884 D; railway to, 1911 D
Valsarno, Italy. Austrian victory at, 1813 K
Valteline, Switzerland, France annexes, 1797 K
Value of world production, 1888 Y, 1929 Y
Valves, wireless, all-metal, 1933 P
Vancouver, George, B. naval officer and explorer (1758–98), 1790 P
Vancouver Island, British Columbia, Canada, Spain abandons claim to, 1790 K
Van der Noot, Henry, Du. patriot, 1787 A, 1789 K, 1790 C
Vane, Sutton, B. dramatist, 1923 W
Vanity Fair (W. M. Thackeray), 1847 U
Varennes, Meuse, France, Louis XVI stopped at, 1791 E
Vargas, Getúlio, Braz. leader (1883–1954), becomes president, 1930 K; given dictatorial powers, 1933 L; resigns, 1945 K
Variations of Animals and Plants under Domesticisation (C. Darwin), 1868 P
Variations, orchestral. *See under* Symphonic Suites
Varieties of Goodness (G. H. von Wright), 1963 R
Varieties of Religious Experience (W. James), 1902 R
Varna, Turkey, Russians occupy, 1828 K
Vassall, William, B. spy, 1962 K, L, 1963 D, V
Vatican, The: Pope allowed possession, of, 1871 E; Prussian legation at, 1882 D; relations with Italy, 1889 G; French ambassador to, recalled, 1904 E; independence of Vatican City, 1929 B, G. *See also under* Papacy
Vatican Council:
Pius IX calls, 1867 R; meets, 1869 R, 1870 R
John XXIII calls, 1959 R; preparations for, 1961 R; opens, 1962 R; approves principle of fixed Easter, 1963 K; approves use of vernacular liturgies, 1963 R; ends, 1964 J
Vatican Decrees, of Pius IX, refusal to accept leads to excommunication, 1871 R
Vatican Decrees, The (W. E. Gladstone), 1874 R
Vaughan, Herbert Alfred, B. cardinal (1832–1903), 1891 R, 1895 R
Vaughan Williams, Ralph, B. musician (1872–1958), 1872 Z, 1952 T, 1958 Z
as musical editor of *English Hymnal*, 1906 R
choral works, 1907 T, 1914 T
Fantasia, 1909 T
opera, 1951 T
Symphonies, 1910 T, 1914 T, 1922 T, 1943 T, 1953 T, 1958 T
Vaughan Williams, Ralph, The Works of (M. Kennedy), 1964 T
Vauxcelles, Louis, F. art critic, 1905 S
Vedic Concordance (M. Bloomfield), 1907 Q
Vedrenne, John E. (1867–1930), B. theatre manager, 1904 W
Veidt, Conrad, G. film actor (1893–1943), 1920 W
Velocipede, or fore-runner of bicycle, invented, 1779 P
See also Bicycle
Vendée, La, Poitou, France, Royalist revolt in, 1793 C, K, M
Venereal disease: cure for, 1909 P; in Britain, 1916 O, 1943 O
Venetia, Italy: restored to Austria, 1815 F; Prussia promises to restore to Italy, 1866 D; Austrian cession of, announced, 1866 G; plebiscites for union with Italy, 1866 K
Venezia Giulia, Yugoslavia, 1947 B
Venezuela: refuses allegiance to Joseph Bonaparte, 1810 D; independence proclaimed, 1811 G; Republic, falls, 1812 G; independence, proclamations of, 1813 G, 1818 L; forms, with New Granada, Colombia, 1819 M; independence guaranteed, 1821 F; leaves Colombia Union, 1830 J, 1831 L; boundary with British Guiana, 1899 K; blockaded by powers, 1902 M; blockade lifted, 1903 B; US severs diplomatic relations with, 1908 F; coffee production in, 1909 Y
Venice, Italy: Austria obtains, 1797 K; Republic proclaimed, 1848 C; submits to Austria, 1894 P, H; to remain an Austrian possession, 1859 G; Hitler meets Mussolini at, 1934 F; falls to Allies, 1945 D

Venizelos, Eleutherios, Greek statesman (1864–1942), 1935 C; as premier, 1910 K, 1915 C, 1916 K, 1924 A, 1928 E; resigns as premier, 1933 A; becomes premier, 1933 A
Venn, Henry, B. Evangelical divine (1725–97), 1763 R
Ventris, Michael, B. Minoan scholar (1922–56), 1952 Q
Vents (St. J. Perse), 1947 U
Venus, the planet:
  space research gives data on, 1962 P, 1963 P
  transit of, observations of, 1768 P, 1882 P
Venus de Milo, discovery of, 1820 S
Vera Cruz, Mexico: French troops occupy, 1838 L; Diaz occupies, 1912 K; US troops land at, 1914 D; withdraw from, 1914 J
Verdi, Giuseppe, It. musician (1813–1901), 1813 Z, 1844 T, 1847 T, 1851 T, 1853 T, 1862 T, 1867 T, 1871 T, 1874 T, 1887 T, 1893 T, 1901 Z
Verdun, Meuse, France: Austrian attack, 1792 J; battles, 1916 B, D, 1917 H; receives Congressional medal, 1922 F
Vereeniging, S. Africa, Peace of, 1902 E
Verela, Sweden, Treaty of, 1790 H
Vergennes, Charles Gravier, Comte de, F. statesman (1717–87), 1774 E, 1782 E, 1787 B
Verhaeren, Emile, Belg. author (1855–1916), 1883 U, 1902 U
Verlaine, Paul, F. author (1844–96), 1844 Z, 1866 U, 1869 U, 1874 U, 1881 U, 1884 U, 1888 U, 1896 Z
Vermont, State, US: becomes a US state, 1791 C; Fenians in, 1870 E; remains Republican, 1936 L
Verne, Jules, F. author (1828–1905), 1869 U, 1872 U
Verona, Italy: discoveries in, 1816 Q; Congress at, 1822 K, L, M; Fifth Army takes, 1945 D
Verranzano-Narrows Bridge, US, 1964 P
Versailles, France:
  Treaty ends War of American Independence, 1783 J, 1784 C
  Notables meet at, 1787 B
  Edict, for religious freedom for Protestants, 1787 R
  States General meet at, 1789 E
  March of women to, 1789 K
  Peace between France and Germany, 1871 B
  French Chamber is moved from, 1879 L
  Peace Conference, 1918 L, 1919 A
    Leage of Nations Covenant is laid before, 1919 B
    German delegates attend, 1919 D
    China leaves, 1919 D
    disposes of Germany's Colonies, 1919 E
    US delegates leave, 1919 M
    See also League of Nations
  Treaty of Peace, ending World War I:
    Austria protests at terms, 1919 F
    Germany signs, 1919 F
    US Senate rejects Shantung Clause, 1919 H
    US Senate virtually rejects treaty, 1919 L
    Clause 231, on Germany's war guilt, repudiated, 1927 J
    Mussolini champions revision, 1930 E
    denounced by Nazis, 1930 J
    Germany repudiates disarmament clauses, 1935 C
    Germany violates, 1936 C
    Germany denounces, 1936 L
    League Covenant is separated from Treaty, 1938 K
Verses and Sonnets (H. Belloc), 1895 U
Versuche über einzelne Theile der Theorie des Rechts, 1798 O
Vertebrate skulls, theory of, 1858 P
Verwoerd, Hendrik, S. Afr. Nationalist leader (b. 1869), becomes premier, 1958 J; attempted assassination, 1960 D; states S. Africa will leave Commonwealth, 1961 C
Vessels, steam, 1803 P, 1812 P, 1818 P. *See also under* Ships
Vestiges of the National History of Creation, The (R. Chambers), 1844 P
Vetus Testamentum Lebraicum cum variis lectionibus (B. Kennicott), 1776 Q
Viaud, Julien, F. author under pseudonym of 'Pierre Loti' (1850–1923), 1850 Z, 1886 U, 1912 U, 1923 Z
Viborg, Finland: manifesto, 1906 G; Russia takes, 1940 C
Vibrations, harmonic, analysis of, 1843 P
Vicar of Wakefield, The (O. Goldsmith), 1776 U
Vicenza, Italy, battle, 1848 F
Vices of the Political System of the United States, The (Madison), 1787 O
Vichy, France, French government at, breaks off relations with Britain, 1940 G
Vicksburg, Missouri, US, Confederate defeat at, 1863 G
Victor Emmanuel I, King of Sardinia (1802–5 and 1814–21), abdicates, 1821 C
Victor Emmanuel II, King of Sardinia (1849–61), King of Italy (1861–78), 1849 C, 1850 R, 1878 A; invades Papal States, 1860 J; proclaimed King of Italy, 1860 K, 1861 B
Victor Emmanuel III, King of Italy (1900–1943), 1904 D, 1943 G; abdicates, 1946 E
Victoria, Queen of Great Britain and Ireland (1837–1901), 1819 Z, 1837 F, 1895 F; Bedchamber Question, 1839 E; marriage, 1840 B; statute of, 1869 S; expenditure, enquiry into, 1872 C; proclaimed Empress of India, 1877 A; Golden Jubilee, 1887 F; Diamond Jubilee, 1897 W; Uitlanders petition to, 1899 C
Victoria, Lake, Cen. Africa, railway to, 1901 M
Victoria, Australia: is separated from New South Wales, 1850 H; proclaimed a British Colony, 1851 G
Victoria History of the Counties of England (ed. Doubleday), 1900 Q
Victoria Falls, Cen. Africa, discovered, 1855 P
Victorian Society, The, 1958 S
Victoria Nyanza, Lake, Cen. Africa, discovered, 1856 P
Victoria Regina (L. Housman), 1937 W
Victory (J. Conrad), 1915 U
Vidal, Gore, Am. author (b. 1925), 1964 U
Vidler, Alexander Roper, B. theologian (b. 1899), 1957 R, 1963 R
Vie de Jésus (E. Reman), 1863 R
Vie litteraire, La (A. France), 1888 U
Vie, Une (G. de Maupassant), 1883 U
Vienna, Austria:
  events:
    Pius VI visits, 1782 C
    Hungarian crown removed to, 1784 G
    Moreau advances on, 1800 M
    French capture, 1809 E
    Congress, 1814 L, 1815 F
    Treaty of Peace, 1815 F
    Conference at, under Metternich, 1820 E
    Ferdinard I flees from, 1848 E
    Note, on Eastern Question, 1853 G
    railway from, to Trieste, 1853 P
    Four Points, to Russia, 1854 H
    Austrian ultimatum to Russia on, 1855 M
    Peace Treaty of, 1864 K

Vienna, Austria—*contd.*
events—*contd.*
Treaty of, 1866 K
financial crisis in, 1873 E
strike in, 1918 A
Socialist riots and strikes in, 1927 G
Schuschnigg's *coup* in, 1935 K
Conference, on Danube basin, 1936 L
Communist Conference at, 1952 M
Treaty, restores Austria's independence, 1955 E
World Peace Council offices at, closed by government, 1957 B
places and institutions in:
aeronautical exhibition, 1888 P
Heinrichshof, 1861 S
Ringstrasse in, 1858 S
Votivkirche in, 1856 S
music in, 1887 T
population of, 1801 Y, 1841 Y, 1881 Y, 1906 Y
the theatre in, 1891 W
Vierge de Paris, La (P. J. Jouve), 1945 U
Viet Nam:
republic formed, 1945 J
France recognises as a free state within the Indo-Chinese Federation, 1946 L
Nationalists, under Bao Dai, recognised by France, 1949 L
state, established under Bao Dai, 1949 F
France transfers sovereignty to Republic, 1949 M
French evacuate N. Viet Nam, 1954 G
Communists evacuate S. Viet Nam, 1954 G
Republic proclaimed in S. Viet Nam, 1955 K
disturbances in, 1959 J
US military council in S. Viet Nam, 1962 B
martial law in S. Viet Nam, 1963 H
War in, 1964 H, M. *See also under* Wars
H. Davies attempts to open peace talks, 1965 G
Russia admits supplying arms to Hanoi, 1965 J
View from the Bridge, The (A. Miller), 1955 W
View of the Internal Evidence of the Christian Religion (S. Jenyns), 1776 R
View of the State of Europe in the Middle Ages, The (H. Hallam), 1818 Q
Vigevano, Italy, Peace, between Austria and Sardinia, 1848 H
Vigny, Alfred de, F. author (1797–1863), 1797 Z, 1826 U, 1835 U, 1864 U, 1863 Z
Világos, Hungary, Hungarians capitulate at, 1849 H
Vile Bodies (E. Waugh), 1930 U
Villafranca, Italy, Peace Treaty, Austria with France, 1859 G; confirmed by Treaty of Zurich, 1859 L
Village, The (T. Crabbe), 1783 U
Village trust, Bournville, 1900 O
Villari, Pasquale, It. historian (1827–1910), 1859 Q
Villèle, Jean Baptiste comte de, F. politician, Royalist (1773–1854), 1821 M, 1927 F, 1828 A
Villers-Bretonneux, France, British victory at, 1918 D
Villiers, George William Frederick, earl of Clarendon, B. foreign secretary (1800–70), 1868 M
Vilna, Lithuania: Germans take, 1915 J; Poles annex, 1920 K; recognised as Polish, 1923 C; Russia cedes to Lithuania, 1939 K
Vilna, River, Russia, Napoleon crosses, 1812 F
Vimiero, Portugal, Wellington's victory at, 1808 H
Vimy Ridge, France, Canadian troops take, 1917 D
Vincennes, Indiana, US, 1779 B
Vincent, Stenio, president of Haiti, 1930 B
Vindications of the Rights of Women (M. Wollstonecroft), 1792 O
Vindiciae Gallicae (J. MacKintosh), 1791 O
Vinegar Hill, Wexford, Ireland, rebels routed at, 1798 F
'Vingt, Les', artists, 1884 S
Vinland Map, 1965 Q
Vionville, France, falls to Prussians, 1870 H
Virginia, State, US: Colonial Assembly, 1765 E; dissolved, 1769 G; Provincial Committee of correspondence, 1773 C; Convention, 1776 E; Bill of Rights, 1776 F; legislature, 1798 M
Virginians, The (W. M. Thackeray), 1857 U
Virginibus Puerisque (R. L. Stevenson), 1881 U
Virgin Isles, US takes over, 1917 C
Vischer, Friedrich Theodor, G. philosopher (1807–1887), 1846 R
Visconti, Luchino, It. film director (b. 1900), 1960 W, 1963 W
Viscose, discovered, 1892 P
Vision of Judgment (R. Southey), 1814 U
Vision of Bernadette Soubirons, 1858 R
Vistula River, Poland, 1772 P
Vitamine, Funck coins term, 1912 P
Vitamins:
A, is isolated, 1931 P
A, crystalline, 1937 P
A, synthesis of, 1945 P
B, isolated, 1925 P
B.1, synthesis of, 1937 P
B.2, isolated, 1925 P
B12, composition of, 1955 P
C, pure, 1934 P
D, discovered, 1932 P
E, synthesis of, 1938 P
K, concentrate, 1937 P
Vitebsk, Russia, Germans trapped at, 1944 F
Vittoria, Spain, battle, 1813 F
Vivian Grey (B. Disraeli), 1826 U
Viviani, René, F. politician (1863–1925), 1914 F, 1915 K
Vivisection, royal commission on, 1912 O
Vladivostok, Russia: founded, 1860 G, O; British force lands, 1918 H
Vlakfontein, S. Africa, 1950 G
Vlaminck, Maurice, F. artist (1876–1958), 1908 S, 1947 S
Vocation of a Scholar (J. G. Fichte), 1794 R
Vogel, Sir Julius, premier of New Zealand (1835–99), 1875 K
Vogt, Ernst, Swi. theologian (b. 1903), 1938 R
Vogt, Hans, G. inventor of sound films, 1919 P
Vogüé, Eugène Melchior, comte de, F. author (1848–1910), 1886 U
Voices of Freedom (J. G. Whittier), 1846 U
Voices of the Night (H. W. Longfellow), 1839 U
Volcanoes, study of, 1774 P; eruption in Tristan da Cunha, 1961 K
Vol de Nuit (St. Exupéry), 1931 U
Volney, Constantin François, comte de, F. author (1757–1820), 1791 Q
Volta, Alessandro, comte, It. physicist (1745–1827), 1789 P, 1800 P, 1827 Z
Voltaic pile, 1798 P
Volta River Project, Ghana, 1961 M
Volta, Upper, Republic, becomes independent, 1960 G
Voltaire, François Marie Arouet de, F. philosopher (1694–1778), 1763 R, 1764 R, 1770 R, 1778 U, Z
Volturno, River, Italy, Germans retire from, 1943 K
Von deutscher Art und Kunst (Herder), 1773 U
Vor dem Sturm (T. Fontane), 1878 U
Voronezh, Russia, Russian victory at, 1943 A
Voroshilov, Kliment Efremovid, R. marshal (b. 1881), 1950 C, 1960 E
Vorovski, Vaslav, R. diplomat, 1923 E
Vortex motion theory, 1858 P
Vortex, The (N. Coward), 1924 W

Voss, Johann Heinrich, G. poet and translator (1751–1826), 1781 G, 1795 U, 1826 Z
Voss (P. White), 1957 U
Voyage au bout de la nuit (L. Céline), 1932 U
Voyage autour de ma chambre (X. de Maistre), 1794 U
Voyage aux régions équinoxiales (A. von Humboldt and A. Bonpland), 1807 P
Voyage de M. Perrichon, Le (E. Labiche), 1860 W
Voyage du jeune Anarcharsis en Grèce (J. Barthélney) 1787 Q
Voyage en Icarie (E. Cabet), 1842 O
Voyage of the Beagle (C. Darwin), 1839 P
Voyageur sans bagage (J. Anouilt), 1938 W
'V' particles, 1950 P
Vries, Hugo de, F. botanist, 1900 P
V2 rockets, 1942 P, 1944 J
Vyshinsky, Andrei Yanuarievich, R. marshal and diplomat (1883–1954), 1951 M
becomes foreign minister, 1949 C

W

Wackenroder, Wilhelm Heinrich, G. author (1773–1798), 1797 U
Waddell, Helen, B. author and translator (b. 1889), 1933 U
Waddington, William Henry, F. statesman (1826–94), 1878 F, 1879 B
Ward. *See under* Political Parties
Wage, Labour and Capital (K. Marx), 1848 O
Wages. *See* Prices, Wages and Incomes
Wagner, Adolph, G. economist (1835–1912), 1871 O
Wagner, Richard, G. musician (1813–83), 1813 Z, 1883 Z
Essay on Beethoven, 1870 T
Operas, 1840 T, 1842 T, 1843 T, 1845 T, 1850 T, 1851 T, 1855 T, 1859 T, 1865 T, 1868 T, 1869 T, 1870 T, 1874 T, 1876 T, 1882 T
text of *The Ring*, 1853 T
complete broadcast performance of *The Ring*, 1962 W
Wagner-Steagall Act in US, to finance housing, 1937 J
Wagram, Austria, battle, 1809 G
Wain, John Barrington, B. author (b. 1935), 1953 U
Waitangi, New Zealand, Treaty between Britain and Maoris, 1840 B
Waiting for Godot (S. Beckett), 1955 W
Waiting for Lefty (C. Odets), 1935 W
Waitz, Theodor, G. psychologist (1821–64), 1846 R
Wajda, Andrzej, R. film director, 1954 W, 1958 W
Wakatsuki, R., Jap. premier, 1927 D
Wakefield, Edward Gibbon, B. colonial statesman (1796–1862), 1796 Z, 1862 Z
Waksman, Selman A., Am. formerly R. microbiologist (b. 1888) 1943 P, 1949 P
Walcheren, Holland, British expedition to, fails, 1809 G, J
Waldeck Rousseau, René, F. Moderate Republican (1846–1904), 1899 F, 1902 F
Pardons Dreyfus, 1899 J
Walden, or Life in the Woods (H. D. Thoreau), 1854 U
Waldermar, Prince of Denmark, refuses to serve as King of Belgians, 1886 L
Waldorf, William, viscount Astor, B. newspaper owner (1848–1919), 1848 Z, 1919 Z
Wales:
education in, 1889 O
liquor licensing in, 1961 O
schism in, 1811 R
University of, 1893 O
Walfish Bay, South West Africa, Britain annexes, 1877 C
Walhalla, The, near Regensberg, W. Germany, 1830 S
Walker, Kenneth Macfarlane, B. surgeon and author (b. 1888), 1942 R
Wallace, Alfred Russell, B. naturalist (1823–1910), 1858 P
Wallace, Edgar, B. author and journalist (1875–1932), 1875 Z, 1928 U, 1932 Z
Wallace, Lewis, Am. soldier and author (1827–1905), 1880 U
Wallace Collection, Manchester Square, London, 1900 S
Wallachia, is united with Moldavia to form Roumania, 1861 M
Wallas, Graham, B. Socialist (1858–1932), 1858 Z, 1908 O, 1932 Z
Wallenstein (Schiller), 1799 W
Waller, Fred, Am. inventor of 'Cinerama', 1951 W
Wall-Painting, English Medieval (E. W. Tristram), 1945 S
Wall-paintings, 1842 S
Wallpapers, Morris's, 1861 S
Wall Street Crash, 1929 K, O
Walpole, Horace, 4th earl of Orford, B. author and wit (1717–97), 1763 S, 1765 U, 1771 S, 1797 Z
Walpole, Sir Hugh Seymour, B. author (1884–1941), 1911 U, 1922 U, 1930 U
Walter, John, B. founder of *The Times* (1739–1812), 1788 V
Walter, John, II, B. proprietor of *The Times* (1776–1847), 1814 V
Walter, Thomas Ustrick, Am. architect (1804–87), 1839 S, 1851 S
Walton, Sir William Turner, B. musician (b. 1902), 1902 Z, 1923 T, 1929 T, 1931 T, 1935 T, 1939 T, 1941 T, 1947 T, 1950 T, 1954 T, 1957 T, 1965 T
Waltz of the Toreadors, The (J. Anouilh), 1956 W
Wandering Jew, The (E. Sue), 1844 U
Wanderings of Oisin, The (W. B. Yeats), 1889 U
Wandsbeck Messenger, 1771 U
Wandsworth, Surrey, England, tram road at, 1801 P
Waning of the Middle Ages, The (J. Huizinga), 1919 Q
War and Peace (L. Tolstoy), 1864 U
War Artists, 1918 S, 1941 S
Warburg Institute, 1933 S
War correspondent, the first, 1808 V
War criminals, trial of:
in World War I, at Leipzig, 1921 A
in World War II, at Nuremberg, 1946 J
of Japanese, 1946 N, 1948 L
War debts (of World War I):
Balfour Note on, 1922 H
Hoover moratorium, 1931 F, H
Belgium to US, 1925 H
Britain to US, is funded, 1923 A, F
final payment, 1933 M
France, to US, Herrick defeated over, 1932 M
Germany, US Congress resolves against cancellation, 1932 M
Italy to US, agreement on, 1925 L
See also Reparations
Ward, Artemus. *See* Browne, C. F.
Ward, Mrs. Humphrey (Mary Augusta Arnold), B. novelist (1851–1920), 1851 Z, 1883 U, 1920 Z
Ward, James, B. philosopher and psychologist (1843–1925), 1899 R
Ward, Joseph, N. Zeal. United Party leader (1856–1930), 1919 H, 1928 L, 1930 E

Ward, Sir Leslie, B. cartoonist as 'Spy' (1851–1922), 1851 Z, 1922 Z
Ward, Lester, Frank, Am. sociologist and geologist (1841–1912), 1883 O
Ward, Stephen, B. osteopath (*d.* 1963), 1963 G
Warden, The (A. Trollope), 1855 U
Warmerdam, Am. pole-jumper, 1942 X
Warner Brothers, film company, 1929 W
War Office, British, reformed, 1870 F
War of the Worlds (H. G. Wells), 1898 U
War Raw Materials Department, German, 1914 O
Warren, Earl, Am. lawyer (b. 1891), 1891 Z, 1964 O
Warren, Robert Penn, Am. author (b. 1905), 1946 U
Wars:
American Civil, opens, 1861 D
ends, 1865 E
for campaign. *See under* Civil Wars
American War of Independence (1775–83):
opens, 1775 D
tract defending, 1776 O
Lafayette's volunteers for, 1777 D
French alliance with Americans, 1778 B
Britain declares war on France, 1778 B
Dutch alliance with America, 1778 J
Spain declares war on Britain, 1779 F
League of Armed Neutrality against Britain, 1780 C, 1781 E
Britain declares war on Holland, 1780 L
Rodney saves W. Indies, 1782 D
continuation of, deprecated, 1782 B
peace negotiations, 1782 E, L
armistice signed, 1783 B
Austria with Prussia, against Denmark, 1864 D, K
Austria against Sardinia, 1849 C, H
Balkan wars:
First, Turkey against Bulgaria, Serbia, Montenegro and Greece, 1912 K, L, M, 1913 C, E
Bulgaria renews, 1913 B
Second, Bulgaria against Serbia and Greece, 1913 F
Russia and Turkey declare against Bulgaria, 1913 G
Bavarian Succession, Prussia against Austria and Saxony, 1778 G, 1779 E
Bolivia against Paraguay (Chaco War), 1928 M, 1919 J, 1932 G
Brazil against Argentina, 1825 M, 1828 H
Britain against Afghanistan, 1838 K, 1840 C, 1841 C, 1842 A, K, 1919 E, G
Britain against Ashanti, 1873 D, 1874 B, 1896 A
Britain against Boers, in Natal, 1842 N
S. African War, opens, 1899 K
operations, 1899 K–M, 1900 passim, 1901 A, B
ends, 1902 E
casualties, 1902 E
Britain against Burma, 1824 B, E, 1826 B, 1852 D, M, 1853 F, 1885 K
Britain against China, 'Opium War', 1839 G, H, L, 1842 H
Second, 1856 K, L, 1857 F, M, 1858 F, 1860 H, J
Britain in India:
against Gurkhas, 1814 K
against Indore, 1804 D, L
against Mahrattas, 1782 E, 1802 K, 1803 H, 1817 L, 1818 F
against Nepalese, 1815 M
against Sikhs, 1834 E, 1845 M, 1846 A, B, C, 1848 C, 1849 A, B, C
against Sind, 1843 A
See also under Mutinies
Britain against Kaffirs, 1850 C, 1877 H
Britain against Maoris, 1860 C, 1861 C, 1865 J, 1868 F
Britain against Persia, 1856 L, 1857 C
Britain in Sudan, 1884 B, F, K
Britain against US, 1812 F, 1814 M
operations, 1813 D, E, F, J, K, L, M, 1814 G, J, 1815 A
burning of Washington, 1814 H
Britain against Zulus, 1877 D, 1879 A, H, J
Chaco. *See* Bolivia against Paraguay
Chile against Peru and Bolivia, 1836 L, 1880 N
China against India, 1959 H
Crimean War (1854–6):
Britain and France declare war on Russia, 1854 C
Greece promises neutrality, 1854 E
Austrian treaty with Turkey, for occupying Danubian provinces, 1854 F
Vienna Four Points, 1854 H
battle of the Alma, 1854 J
siege of Sebastapol opens, 1854 K
battle of Balaclava, 1854 K
Charge of Light Brigade, 1854 K
battle of Inkerman, 1854 L
Piedmont joins Allies against Russia, 1855 A
Russians capitulate at Sebastopol, 1855 J
British muddles and disasters, 1855 O
history of, 1863 Q
Cuba against Spain, 1878 B
France against Austria, 1859 E, F, G
France against China, 1860 H, J, 1885 C, F
France against King Dahomey in W. Africa, 1892 N
France in Indo-China, 1954 D, E, G
France against Madagascar, 1883 F
France in Morocco, 1844 H, J, 1925 D, H, 1926 F
France against Prussia (1870–1):
opens, 1870 G
French defeats, 1870 H
Belgian neutrality is guaranteed, 1870 H
Napoleon III capitulates at Sedan, 1870 J
siege of Paris opens, 1870 J
Strasbourg falls to Prussians, 1870 K
Paris capitulates, 1871 A
armistice signed, 1871 A
French revenge for, 1886 A
France against Spain, 1823 D, K
French and Indian (Seven Years), ends, 1763 B
French Revolutionary wars (1792–1801):
War of First Coalition: France declares war on Austria, 1792 D
France declares war on Prussia and Sardinia, 1792 G
battles of Longwy and Verdun, 1792 J
French check invaders at Valmy, 1792 J
battle of Jemappes, 1792 L
France declares war on Britain and Holland, 1793 B
First Coalition is formed, 1793 B
France declares war on Spain, 1793 C
US neutrality, 1793 D
French victory at Tourcoing, 1794 E
Austrian defeat at Fleurus, 1795 F
French invasion of Spain, 1794 F
Russia enters war against France, 1794 J
French troops reach Rhine, 1794 K
Prussia withdraws from war, 1794 K
French invade Holland, 1794 M
Spain signs peace with France, 1795 G
Prussia signs peace with France, 1795 D
Austrian defeat at Loano, 1795 L
Austria signs armistice with France, 1795 M

Bonaparte's Italian campaign, 1796 C, D, E, F, L, 1797 A, B
Jourdan's defeat at Würzburg, 1796 J
Spain declares war against Britain, 1796 K
British conquests in W. Indies, 1796 N
battle of Cape St. Vincent, 1797 B
Austria signs peace of Leoben with France, 1797 D
Peace of Campo Formio, 1797 K
US negotiations for preserving peace with France, 1797 K
French take Rome, 1798 B
Bonaparte conquers Egypt, 1798 G
Nelson's victory at battle of the Nile, 1788 H
Turkey declares war on France, 1798 J
French overrun Naples, 1798 M
Austria declares war on France, 1799 C
Siege of Acre, 1799 C, E
War of Second Coalition; coalition of Britain, Russia, Austria, Turkey, Portugal and Naples is formed by Pitt, 1798 F
Bonaparte leaves Egypt, 1799 H
Russia abandons coalition, 1799 K
Bonaparte reconquers Italy through battle of Marengo, 1800 F
Moreau advances on Vienna, 1800 M
Armed Neutrality of North, against Britain's right of search, 1800 M, 1801 C, F
Peace of Lunéville, 1801 B
Nelson's victory at Copenhagen, 1801 D
British take Cairo, 1801 F
Peace of Amiens, between Britain and France, 1801 K, 1802 C
Greek Independence, 1821 C, D, F, K, 1822 D, F, G, 1823 C, 1824 D, G, K, 1825 B, 1827 D, F, G, H, M
Greece with Turkey, 1878 B, 1897 D, E, M, 1921 F, G, H, 1922 G, H, K
Holland against Belgium, 1833 E
Holland in North Sumatra, 1873 D
Honduras with Nicaragua, 1907 B
India with Pakistan, over Kashmir, 1965 D, F
Pakistani troops cross cease-fire line, 1965 J
Indian troops invade Pakistan, 1965 J
Indian 'planes bomb Lahore, 1965 J
cease-fire, 1965 J
Indonesian War of Independence from Holland, opens, 1945 J
truce, 1948 A
is renewed, 1948 M
ends with Dutch transfer of sovereignty, 1949 M
Indonesia with Malaya, incidents, 1963 D
Malaysia breaks off relations with Indonesia, 1963 J
Indonesian landings in Malaya, 1964 J, K, 1965 A
Commonwealth troops move in, 1964 J
Italy with Austria, 1866 F
Italy with Ethiopia, 1896 C
Mussolini's war, 1935 K, L, 1936 E
Italy with Turkey, 1911 J, 1912 C, K
Japan with China. *See* Sino-Japanese War
Korea with China, 1894 G
Korean (1950–3):
opens, 1950 F
UN appoints force to assist S. Koreans, 1950 G
UN Security Council discusses, 1950 H
UN troops land, 1950 J
N. Koreans attack across Naktong River, 1950 J
UN force recapture Seoul, 1950 J
S. Koreans cross 38th parallel, 1950 K
massing of Chinese Communists in, 1950 L
UN troops forced to withdraw, 1950 L
emergency in US, following UN reverses, 1950 M
Chinese cross 38th parallel, 1950 M
Communists take Seoul, 1951 A
truce is urged, 1951 C
N. Korean offensive, 1951 E
attempts at armistice, 1951 F
Ridgway breaks off armistice talks, 1951 H
UN force takes Heartbreak Ridge, 1951 J
armistice talks resumed, 1951 K, M
allegations of killing prisoners of war, 1951 L
China accuses US of using germ warfare, 1952 C
Clark succeeds Ridgway as UN commander, 1952 D
Communists riot at Koje Prison Camp, 1952 E
UN air force bomb plants, 1952 F
UN adopts Indian proposals on armistice, 1952 M
China rejects, 1952 M
Eisenhower states principles of UN peace proposals, 1953 E
exchange of prisoners, 1953 D, F
armistice signed, 1953 G
withdrawal of all foreign troops from Korea, 1958 B
Latvia with Germany, 1919 L
Mexico with France, 1838 L, 1839 C
Napoleonic (1803–15):
Anglo-French hostilities renewed, 1803 E
neutrality of Spain and Portugal, 1803 K
Austro-Russian declaration on maintenance of Ottoman Empire, 1804 L
Spain declares war on Britain, 1804 M
Britain and Russia form 3rd Coalition against France, 1805 D
Austria joins Coalition, 1805 H
battle of Ulm, 1805 K
battle of Trafalgar, 1805 K
Napoleon's victory at Austerlitz, 1805 M
Austria signs Peace of Pressburg with France, 1805 M
end of Holy Roman Empire, 1806 H
Prussia declares war on France, 1806 K
Napoleon enters Warsaw, 1806 M
Russia and Prussia sign peace treaties with Napoleon at Tilsit, 1807 G
French invade Spain, 1808 B
Britain sends expedition to Portugal, 1808 H
battle of Corunna, 1809 A
Austria declares war on France, 1809 B
Wellington takes command in Peninsular, 1809 D
Napoleon defeat Austrians at Wagram, 1809 G
British expedition to Walcheren, 1809 G
Austria signs peace of Schönbrunn with France, 1809 K
Wellington holds lines of Torres Vedras, 1810 K
Wellington takes Cuidad Rodrigo, 1812 A
Napoleon invades Russia, 1812 F
Wellington enters Madrid, 1812 H
Napoleon enters Moscow, 1812 J
Napoleon retreats from Moscow, 1812 K
Prussia declares war on France, 1813 C
Wellington routs French at Vittoria, 1813 F
Austria declares war on France, 1813 H
Wellington enters France, 1813 K
Napoleon is defeated at battle of Leipzig, 1813 K
Allies offer peace proposals to Napoleon, 1813 L
Murat deserts Napoleon, 1814 A
Allies enter Paris, 1814 C
Napoleon is banished to Elba, 1814 D
Congress of Vienna opens, 1814 L
Napoleon's Hundred Days, 1815 C

Wars—*contd.*
Napoleonic (1813–15)—*contd.*
battle of Waterloo, 1815 F
Congress of Vienna closes, 1815 F
Allies re-enter Paris, 1815 G
Oranges (Spain with Portugal), 1801 C
Palestine, between Arabs and Jews, 1948 E
UN orders truce, 1948 G
See also main index under Middle East; Palestine
Paraguay against Argentina, Brazil and Uruguay (1865–70), 1865 C, 1870 C
Paraguay with Bolivia, 1933 E
Peninsular War. *See under* Napoleonic Wars, entries 1808–13
history of, 1828 Q
Peru with Columbia, 1932 J
Peru with Spain, 1866 A
Poland with Russia, 1920 D, G, H, K
Prussia with Denmark, 1848 E, H, 1850 G
Prussia with France, 1870 G–K, 1871 A, B
Russia with Finland, 1919 F;
1939 L, 1940 B, C
Russia with Japan, 1904 B, E, H, 1905 A, C, E, J
Russia with Persia, over Transcaucasia, 1826 J, 1828 B
Russia with Turkey, 1768 K, 1774 G, 1787 H,
1788 B, K, 1790 A, 1792 A
1806 K, 1809 E, 1810 N
1827 D, K, 1829 J
1853 K. *See also* Crimean War
1877 D, E, M, 1878 A
Sardinia with Austria, 1848 C, D, H
Saudi Arabia with the Yemen, 1934 F
Serbia with Bulgaria, 1885 L, 1886 C
Serbia with Turkey, 1876 F, 1877 B
Seven Years (or French and Indian) ends, 1763 B
Sino-Japanese, 1894 H, L, 1895 B, D, E, 1933 B, 1936 M, 1937 G, L, M, 1938 A, C, J, K, 1939 B, 1940 G
Japanese take Nanking, 1937 M
League pronounces Japan the aggressor, 1938 J
South Africa. *See* Britain against Boers
Spain against Moors, 1859 K, 1860 D
Spain against Portugal (War of the Oranges), 1801 C
Sweden against Denmark, 1809 C
Sweden against Russia, 1788 F, G
Turkey against Egypt, 1832 D, E, M
Russia supports Turkey, 1833 B
Turkey against Mehemet Ali, 1839 D, F, G
Turkey against Greece, 1828 B, 1897 D, E, M, 1921 F, G, H, 1922 G, H, K
Turkey against Russia. *See under* Russia
US against Spanish in Cuba, 1898 D, E, G, H, M, O
Uruguay against Argentina, 1839 B
Vietnam:
escalation of fighting between N. and S. Vietnamese, 1965 B
US aircraft bomb N. Vietnam, 1965 B, D
shot down by Russian 'planes, 1965 D
US marines land, 1965 C
demonstrations in Washington against war, 1965 D
Australian troops sent, 1965 D
S. Vietnam severs relations with France, 1965 F
US troops are authorised to take offensive, 1965 F
demonstrations in Britain against war, 1965 K
Ho Chi Minh rejects peace talks with US, 1965 K
World War I (1914–18):
Political events:
Austria-Hungary declares war on Serbia, 1914 G
on Russia, 1914 H
Germany declares war on Russia, 1914 H
on France, 1914 H
Britain declares war on Germany, 1914 H
Serbia and Montenegro declare war on Germany, 1914 H
France and Britain declare war on Austria, 1914 H
Russia declares war on Turkey, 1914 L
Britain and France declare war on Turkey, 1914 L
Italy declares war on Austria, 1915 E
on Turkey, 1915 H
Britain declares war on Bulgaria, 1915 K
Germany declares war on Portugal, 1916 C
Italy declares war on Germany, 1916 H
Turkey declares war on Russia, 1916 H
Roumania declares war on Austria, 1916 H
Bulgaria declares war on Roumania, 1916 J
Germany's peace note, 1916 M
President Wilson's peace note, 1916 M
Reichstag motion on peace talks, 1917 G
US declares war on Germany, 1917 D
on Austria, 1917 M
Cuba declares war on Germany, 1917 D
Brazil declares war on Germany, 1917 F
Greece severs connexion with Central Powers, 1917 F
China declares war on Germany and Austria, 1917 H
Soviets offer armistice, 1917 L, M
Peace of Brest-Litovsk, 1917 M
Roumania signs armistice with Central Powers, 1917 M
Ukraine signs peace with Central Powers, 1918 B
Roumania's peace treaty with Central Powers, 1918 E
Russia and US sever relations, 1918 H
Austro-Hungarian peace talk offer, 1918 J
Bulgaria signs armistice, 1918 J
Hindenburg's peace-offer, 1918 J
Germany and Austria make peace offer, 1918 K
agree to Wilson's terms, 1918 K
Turkey signs armistice, 1918 K
Allied armistice with Central Powers, 1918 L
Britain and France authorise resumption of relations with Germany, 1919 G
Wilson vetoes Knox peace resolution, 1920 E
Operations—Eastern Front:
Germany invades Belgium, 1914 H
battle of Mons, 1914 H
first battle of Marne, 1914 J
battle of Aisne, 1914 J
Antwerp surrenders, 1914 K
battle of Yser, 1914 K
first battle of Ypres, 1914 K
battle of Neuve Chapelle, 1915 C
second battle of Ypres, 1915 D
battle of St. Julien, 1915 D
Allies take Neuville, 1915 F
E. Cavell's execution, 1915 K
Haig succeeds French, 1915 M
battle of Verdun, 1916 B
Allies begin Somme offensive, 1916 G
tanks first used, 1916 J
German withdrawal, 1917 C
battle of Arras, 1917 D
battle of Vimy Ridge, 1917 D

Pétain becomes French C.-in-C., 1917 E
mutinies in French army, 1917 E
US troops land in France, 1917 F
third battle of Ypres (Passchendaele), 1917 G
second battle of Verdun, 1917 H
second battle of Somme, 1918 C
intensive German offensive, 1918 E
second battle of Marne, 1918 G
British offensive opens, 1918 H
Germans withdraw to Siegfried Line, 1918 J
British take Cambrai, 1918 K
Bruges is recaptured, 1918 K
Operations—Eastern Front:
Russians invade East Prussia, 1914 H
battle of Frankenau, 1914 H
German victory at Tannenberg, 1914 H
battle of Masurian Lakes, 1914 J
Russians invade Hungary, 1914 J
Russian break-through at Ivangorod, 1914 K
Germans take Lódź, 1914 M
second battle of Masuria, 1915 B
Russians evacuate East Prussia, 1915 B
German victory at Przemysl, 1915 F
Germans take Brest-Litovsk, 1915 H
Russians take Erzurum, 1916 B
Russians offensive checked, 1916 J
Kerensky's counter-attack, 1917 F
Russians break German line, 1917 G
armistice at Brest-Litovsk, 1917 M
Operations—Turkish Front:
Gallipoli landings, 1915 D
British defeat Turks at Kut-el-Amara, 1915 J
Allied landings at Salonika, 1915 K
battle of Cteisiphon, 1915 L
withdrawal of allies from Gallipoli, 1915 M
Turks take Kut-el-Amara, 1916 D
Arab revolt begins, 1916 F
Turks defeated at Gaza, 1917 C
British take Gaza and Jaffa, 1917 L
Australians occupy Jericho, 1918 B
collapse of Turkish army in Palestine, 1918 J
Allies take Beirut and Damascus, 1918 K
Operations—Italian Front:
Italians routed in Caporetto campaign, 1917 K
Operations—in Colonies:
Allied occupation of Togoland, 1914 H
Germans capitulate in New Guinea, 1914 J
de Wet's rebellion in S. Africa, 1914 K
S. Africans occupy Swakopmund, South West Africa, 1915 A
Botha occupies Windhoeck, 1915 E
Germans in South West Africa surrender, 1915 G
British take Dar-es-Salaam, 1916 J
German East Africa is cleared of German troops, 1917 M
Germans in N. Rhodesia surrender, 1918 L
Operations—at sea:
battle of Heligoland Bight, 1914 H
battle of Coronel, 1914 L
battle of Falkland Islands, 1914 M
Formidable sunk, 1915 A
Blücher sunk, 1915 A
S.S. *Lusitania* sunk, 1915 E
battle of Jutland, 1916 E
Hampshire sunk, 1916 F
Westfalen sunk, 1916 H
mutinies in German fleet, 1917 G
Breslau sunk, 1918 A
Zeebrugge raid, 1918 D
Germany mutiny at Kiel, 1918 L
Submarine warfare, German:
sinking without warning, 1915 A
sinkings of armed merchantmen, 1916 B
unrestricted warfare on neutrals, 1917 A
suspended, 1918 K
See also under Navies
Operations—in the air:
Zeppelin raids on London, first, 1915 F
on Paris, first, 1916 A
on English industrial areas, 1917 G
intensified, on London, 1917 J
See also under Air Forces
World War II (1939–45):
Political events:
Germany invades Poland, 1939 J
Britain and France declare war on Germany, 1939 J
Russia invades Poland, 1939 J
Russia invades Finland, 1939 L
Germany invades Norway and Denmark, 1940 D
Germany invades Holland and Belgium, 1940 E
Italy declares war on France and Britain, 1940 F
France signs armistice with Germany and Italy, 1940 F
Russia invades Roumania, 1940 F
Vichy government breaks off relations with Britain, 1940 G
Britain aids Greece, 1940 K, 1941 D
Allies invade Iran, 1941 J
Britain declares war on Finland, 1941 M
on Hungary, 1941 M
on Roumania, 1941 M
Germany invades Russia, 1941 F
Hungary declares war on Russia, 1941 F
Finland invades Karelia, 1941 F
Japanese bomb Pearl Harbor, 1941 M
Britain and US declare war on Japan, 1941 M
US declares war on Germany and Italy, 1941 M
Allies pledge not to make separate peace, 1942 A
Second Front demonstrations, 1942 G
Italy surrenders to Allies, 1943 J
Italy declares war on Germany, 1943 K
Russia declares war on Bulgaria, 1944 J
Hungary signs armistice, 1945 A
Egypt declares war on Germany, 1945 B
Germany capitulates, 1945 E
Japan capitulates, 1945 H, J
Russia decrees end of state of war with Germany, 1955 A
casualties, comparative, 1945 Y
See also under Conferences of Allied leaders
Early Campaigns:
fall of Poland, 1939 J
Russia's Finnish campaign, 1939 L, 1940 A, B
Germany's campaign in Norway and Denmark, 1940 D
Germany's campaign in Belgium, Holland and France, 1940 E
evacuation of Dunkirk, 1940 E
Germans enter Paris, 1940 F
Abyssinian campaign, 1940 H, 1941 A, D, E
British campaign in Greece, 1940 K, 1941 A, D
raids on Lofoten islands, 1941 M
St. Nazaire raid, 1942 C
Dieppe raid, 1942 H
North African Campaign:
British offensive under Wavell, 1940 M
German troops cross to N. Africa from Italy, 1941 B

Wars—*contd.*
World War II, (1939–45)—*contd.*
North African Campaign—*contd.*
German counter-offensive, 1941 C
British attack, 1941 L
British recapture Bardia, 1941 L
Benghazi, 1941 M
Rommel's offensive, 1942 A, E
British withdrawal, 1942 F
Rommel takes Tobruk, 1942 F
Eighth Army retreats to El Alamein, 1942 F
Alexander succeeds to C-in-C, 1942 H
Montgomery commands Eighth Army, 1942 H
battle of El Alamein, 1942 K
British take Tobruk, 1942 L
British re-occupy Benghazi, 1942 M
Eighth Army enters Tripoli, 1943 A
Eisenhower is appointed supreme allied commander, 1943 B
Montgomery breaks Mareth line, 1943 C
British and US armies link up, 1943 D
Von Arnim replaces Rommel, 1943 D
Allies take Tunis and Bizerta, 1943 E
German army in Tunisia surrenders, 1943 E
Italian Campaign:
Pantelleria surrenders to British, 1943 F
Allies land in Sicily, 1943 G
Allies occupy Palermo, 1943 G
Allies invade Italy, 1943 J
Italy surrenders, 1943 J
Naples falls, 1943 J
Italy declares war on Germany, 1943 K
Germans retire from Volturno River, 1943 K
Allies land at Nettuno and Anzio, 1944 A
Allies attack Monte Cassino, 1944 B, C, E
Allies attack Gustav line, 1944 E
Hitler line, 1944 E
Fifth Army enters Rome, 1944 F
Allies take Leghorn and Florence, 1944 G
Ravena, 1944 M
Eighth Army reaches Salerno, 1945 D
Bologna falls, 1945 D
Allies reach river Po, 1945 D
Fifth Army takes Genoa and Verona, 1945 D
death of Mussolini, 1945 D
surrender of German army in Italy, 1945 E
Liberation of Europe:
'D Day' landings in Normandy, 1944 F
Cherbourg falls, 1944 F
US troops break through at Avranches, 1944 H
Allies land in French Riviera, 1944 H
Paris is liberated, 1944 H
Antwerp is liberated, 1944 J
Brussels is liberated, 1944 J
US troops cross into Germany, 1944 J
British airborne forces land at Eindhoven and Arnhem, 1944 J
Canadians reach river Maas, 1944 K
Antwerp is re-opened, 1944 L
Strasbourg falls, 1944 L
'Battle of the Bulge' in Ardennes, 1944 M, 1945 A
Allies take Colmar, 1945 B
British reach river Rhine, 1945 B
Cologne falls, 1945 C
US take Osnabrück and Hanover, 1945 D
Allies enter Arnhem, 1945 D
Bremen surrenders, 1945 D
juncture of US and Russian forces at Torgau, 1945 D
Allies cross R. Elbe, 1945 D
death of Hitler, 1945 D
Allies enter Hamburg, 1945 D
Berlin surrenders, 1945 D
Jodl capitulates to Eisenhower, 1945 E
Russian Front:
Germany invades Russia, 1941 F
German offensives against Moscow, 1941 K, L, M
Timoshenko's counter-offensive, 1941 L
Leningrad is saved, 1941 M
Germans attack Kerch peninsula, 1942 E
German counter-offensive in Kharkov region, 1942 F
Germans take Rostov and overrun N. Caucasus, 1942 G
Germans reach Stalingrad, 1942 H
Russian counter-offensive from Stalingrad surrounds Germans, 1942 L
Germans withdraw from Caucasus, 1943 A
Russian victory at Voronezh, 1943 A
German defeat south-west of Stalingrad, 1943 A
Russians recapture Rostov and Kharkov, 1943 B
Russians evacuate Kharkov, 1943 L
German offensive at Kunsk, 1943 G
Russians recapture Orel, 1943 H
Kharkov, 1943 H
Russians cross R. Dnieper, 1943 J
Russians recapture Smolensk, 1943 J
Kiev, 1943 L
Russians relieve Leningrad, 1944 A
Russians force R. Dniester, 1944 C
Russians enter Roumania, 1944 D
Russians recapture Sebastopol, 1944 E
Russians encircle Germans at Vitebsk, 1944 F
Russian offensive against Finland, 1944 F
Russians recapture Minsk, 1944 G
Russians cross 'Curzon line', 1944 G
Russians take Brest-Litovsk, 1944 G
Russians enter Bucharest, 1944 H
Finnish cease-fire, 1944 J
Russians invade Yugoslavia, 1944 J
Belgrade is liberated, 1944 K
Russians invade Hungary, 1944 K
Russians surround Budapest, 1944 M
Russian offensive in Silesia, 1945 A
Russians take Warsaw and Cracow, 1945 A
Russians reach R. Oder, 1945 A
Russians cross Austrian frontier, 1945 C
Russians reach Berlin, 1945 D
juncture of Russian and US forces at Torgau, 1945 D
Berlin surrenders, 1945 E
von Keitel surrenders to Zhukov, 1945 E
Russians take Prague, 1945 E
Campaign in South East Asia:
Japanese invade Burma, 1942 A
Rangoon falls, 1942 C
Mandalay falls to Japanese, 1942 E
British operations in Burma, 1942 M
Wingate's commandoes in Burma Jungle, 1943 D
British offensive, 1944 B
Japanese advance on Imphal, 1944 C
British capture Ukhrul, 1944 G
North Burma is cleared of Japanese, 1944 M
Fourteenth Army launches offensive, 1945 A
enters Mandalay, 1945 C
enters Rangoon, 1945 E
Campaign in Far East:
Japanese bomb Pearl Harbor, 1941 M

Japanese invade Dutch East Indies, 1942 A
Japanese invade Java, 1942 B
Singapore falls, 1942 B
US force lands in Guadalcanal, 1942 H
Japanese are driven from Guadalcanal, 1943 A
US landings in Aleution Islands, 1943 E
in New Guinea, 1943 F
at Bouganville, 1943 L
US force occupies Makin, Gilbert Isles, 1943 L
US force recapture Solomon Isles, 1944 B
Allied landings in New Guinea, 1944 D
Siapan falls to US, 1944 F
US landings in Philippines, 1944 K
MacArthur enters Manila, 1945 B
air raids on Tokio, 1945 B
US force takes Okinawa, 1945 D
Russia invades Manchuria, 1945 H
US drops atomic bombs, 1945 H
Japan surrenders, 1945 H
Japan signs capitulation, 1945 J
War at Sea:
S.S. *Athenia* sunk, 1939 J
Courageous sunk, 1939 J
Royal Oak sunk, 1939 K
magnetic mines, 1939 L
Graf Spee scuttled, 1939 M
Altmark incident, 1940 B
Germany's intensified U-boat warfare, 1940 K
S.S. *Empress of Britain* sunk, 1940 K
Jervis Bay sunk, 1940 L
Southampton and *Illustrious* sunk, 1941 A
Italian cruisers sunk off Cape Matapan, 1941 C
Hood sunk, 1941 E
Bismarck sunk, 1941 E
Ark Royal sunk, 1941 L
Barham sunk, 1941 L
Prince of Wales and *Repulse* sunk, 1941 M
British losses in Bay of Bengal, 1942 D
convoys to Russia, 1942 F, J, M
convoys to Malta, 1942 F, H
Eagle and *Manchester* sunk, 1942 H
Scharnhorst sunk, 1943 M
Tirpitz sunk, 1944 L
Germans use homing-torpedoes, 1945 A
naval battle off Kynshu, 1945 D
naval losses, 1945 Y
losses of merchant shipping, 1939 Y, 1940 Y, 1941 Y, 1942 Y, 1943 Y, 1944 Y, 1945 Y
See also under Navies
War in the Air:
R.A.F. begins night bombing of Germany, 1940 G
Battle of Britain, 1940 G, H, J
'Blitz' begins in Britain, 1940 H
heavy raids on London, etc., 1940 J, L, 1941 E, 1943 A
raid on Coventry, 1941 D
German 'Baedeker' raids, 1942 D
R.A.F. raids Cologne, 1942 E
R.A.F. first 1000-bomber raid, 1942 F
R.A.F. bombs European railway system, 1943 C
heavy raids on Berlin, 1944 A, D
flying bombs on London, 1944 F
V2 rockets in England, 1944 J, 1945 L
atomic bombs on Japan, 1945 H
See also under Air Forces
War Production, 1939 Y, 1940 Y, 1941 Y, 1942 Y, 1943 Y, 1944 N, Y
Warsaw, Poland:
Russians enter, 1794 L
Prussians take, 1795 K
French take, 1806 L
Napoleon enters, 1806 M
Duchy of, established, 1807 G
Austrians occupy, 1809 D
Russians take, 1831 J
rising in, 1848 E
massacre by Russian troops, 1861 B
Conservatory, 1909 T
Germans advance towards, 1914 J
battle for, 1914 K
Germans enter, 1915 H
Russians defeated at, 1920 H
Germans reach, 1939 J
rising, 1944 H
falls to Russians, 1945 A
Communist Conference at, 1947 K
Communist Youth Congress at, 1955 H
Warships. *See under* Navies
Wartburg: Castle, frescoes at, 1854 S; Festival, 1817 K
Warton, Thomas, B. author (1728–90), 1774 U, 1784 S
Washburn, J., Am. atomic physicist, 1932 P
Washing-machines, electric, invented, 1869 P; statistics of ownership, 1965 Y
Washington, George, Am. soldier and statesman, Federalist (1732–99), first president of US (1789–97), 1785 S, 1799 Z; appointed C.-in-C. of American forces, 1775 F; as general, 1776 C, M, 1777 A, K, 1778 F, 1781 J; at Philadelphia Convention, 1787 E; inaugurated president, 1789 D; farewell address, 1796 J
Washington, D.C., US:
events:
is laid out, 1791 N
becomes seat of government, 1800 F, 1801 C
British burn, 1814 M
Treaty, fixes Oregon-Canada boundary, 1846 F
Peace convention, to attempt to preserve Union, 1861 B
Treaty between Britain and US, 1871 E
Conference on Samoa, 1887 F
Pan-American Conference, 1889 K
Treaty between US and Japan, 1911 B
Conference on disarmament, 1921 L, M, 1927 F
Treaty on Pacific, 1921 M
Treaty, on naval warfare, 1922 B
Treaty, to secure China's independence, 1922 B
Japan denounces, 1934 M
Canadian minister to, first appointed, 1926 L
Churchill visits, 1941 M
buildings and institutions in:
Capitol, 1793 S, 1851 S
Carnegie Institution, Dept. of Terrestrial Magnetism, 1944 P
Folger Library, 1932 Q
Catholic University, 1889 O
Lincoln Memorial, 1917 S
National Gallery of Art, 1937 S
Observatory observations from, 1877 P
White House, The, 1792 S
Washington, State, US, created a US state, 1889 B
Was Ist Das Deutsche Vaterland? (E. Arndt), 1813 U
Waste Land, The (T. S. Eliot), 1922 U
Waste-Makers, The (V. Packard), 1959 O
Waste, radio-active, disposal of, 1954 P, 1955 P, 1956 P
Watch, self-winding, 1922 P

Water:
compound nature of, discovered, 1784 P
electrolysed, 1932 P
sterilised by ultra-violet rays, 1912 P
Water-Babies, The (C. Kingsley), 1863 U
Water closet, Bramah's, 1778 P
Waterloo, battle of, 1815 F
Water skiing, 1958 X
Watkins, Henry George (Gino), B. explorer (1907–1930), 1927 P
Watkinson, Harold, Lord Watkinson, B. Conservative (b. 1910), dismissed from cabinet, 1962 G
Watson, Joshua, B. philanthropist (1771–1855), 1811 O
Watson, Richard, B. Methodist minister (1781–1833), 1796 R
Watson-Watt, Sir Robert, B. scientist (b. 1892), 1892 Z, 1935 P
Watson-Wentworth, Charles, Marquess of Rockingham, B. Tory premier (1730–82), 1765 G, 1766 G, 1782 C, G
Watt, James, B. engineer (1736–1819), 1765 P, 1775 P, 1785 P, 1807 P, 1819 Z
Watts, Sir George Frederick, B. artist (1817–1904), 1817 Z, 1904 Z
Waugh, Evelyn, B. novelist (1903–66), 1903 Z, 1930 U, 1945 U, 1952 U
Wavell, Archibald, Lord Wavell, B. soldier (1883–1950), 1883 Z, 1940 M, 1941 A, D, G
Waverley (W. Scott), 1814 U
Waverley Committee, on export of works of art, 1952 S
Waves, electrical, magnetic detection of, 1896 P
waves, radio, 1902 P, 1955 P. *See also under* Wireless
waves, ultra-high-frequency, 1955 P
Way of All Flesh, The (S. Butler), 1903 U
Way of an Eagle, The (E. M. Dell), 1912 U
Wealth (E. Cannan), 1914 O
Wealth of Nations, The (A. Smith), 1776 O
Weather: abnormally dry, 1959 Q; extreme cold, 1963 P
Weather forecasting. *See* Meteorology
Weaver, James Baird, Am. Populist (1833–1912), stands as presidential candidate, 1892 G, L
Webb, Sir Aston, B. architect (1849–1930), 1849 Z, 1905 S
Webb, Beatrice, Lady Passfield (nee Potter), B. Socialist and author (1858–1943), 1858 Z, 1894 O, 1897 O, 1913 V, 1926 O, 1935 O, 1943 Z
Webb, Clement Charles, John, B. philosopher (1865–1954), 1945 R
Webb, Mary Gladys, B. author (1881–1927), 1917 U, 1924 U
Webb, Sidney, Lord Passfield, B. Socialist and author (1859–1947), 1894 O, 1897 O, 1913 V, 1935 O
Weber, A., 1956 O
Weber, Carl Maria von, G. musician (1786–1826), 1786 Z, 1811 T, 1821 T, 1823 T, 1826 T, Z, 1838 W
Weber, Ernst Heinrich, G. anatomist (1795–1878), 1825 P
Weber, Max, G. economist (1864–1920), 1901 Q
Weber, Wilhelm Edward, G. physicist (1804–91), 1825 P, 1833 P
Webern, Anton, Aus. musician (1883–1945), 1924 T
Webster, Daniel, Am. lawyer and Diplomat (1782–1852), 1802 O, 1830 A, 1842 H
Webster, Noah, Am. lexicographer (1758–1843), 1828 Q
Wedekind, Franz, G. author (1864–1918), 1864 Z, 1891 U, 1907 W, 1918 Z
Wedgwood, Josiah, B. potter (1730–95), 1769 P, 1775 S, 1795 Z
Wedgwood, Thomas, B. photographer (1771–1805) 1802 P
Wegener, Anton, G. geographer, 1915 P
Wegscheider, Julius August Ludwig, G. theologian (1771–1849), 1815 R
Wei-hai-we, China: Japanese victory at, 1895 B; is leased to Britain, 1898 C; Britain restores to China, 1930 K
Weil, Kurt, G. musician (b. 1900), 1928 T
Weimar, Germany: Herder at, 1775 U; theatre at, under Goethe, 1791 W; German national assembly at, authorises signing of Versailles Treaty, 1919 F; Republican Constitution agreed at, 1919 G
Weinberger, Jaromir, Czech. musician (b. 1896), 1927 T, 1937 T
Weir of Hermiston, The (R. L. Stevenson), 1896 U
Weiss, Ernst, Hun. magician under pseudonym of 'Houdini' (d. 1936), 1936 Z
Weissenburg, W. Germany: French victory at, 1793 M; MacMahon defeated by Prussians at, 1870 H
Weissmuller, John, Am. swimming champion, 1927 X
Weizmann, Chaim, president of Israel (1874–1952), 1948 E, 1952 M
Welding, friction, 1963 P
Weldon, Walter, B. chemist (1832–85), 1870 P
Welensky, Sir Roy (Roland), Rhodesian (b. 1907), premier of Central African Federation, 1956 K
Welfare centre, infants', 1903 O
Welle, Congo, revolt in, 1905 B
Welles, Orson, Am. actor and director (b. 1915), 1941 W, 1943 W, 1949 W, 1952 W, 1958 W, 1962 W
Welles, Sumner, Am. statesman (1892–1961), 1892 Z, 1944 O, 1961 Z
Wellesley, Arthur, Duke of Wellington, B. soldier and Tory statesman (1769–1852), 1769 Z, 1809 D, 1814 C, 1828 D, 1832 E, 1852 A
in India, 1803 J, 1805 B
wins battle of Talavera, 1809 G
created duke, 1809 G
defeats soult at Oporto, 1809 E
wins battle of Vimiero, 1808 H
holds lines of Torres Vedras, 1810 K
defeats Marmont, 1812 G
enters Madrid, 1812 H
at Fuentes d'Onoro, 1811 E
wins battle of Vittoria, 1813 P
invades France, 1813 K
defeats Napoleon at Waterloo, 1815 F
at Verona Congress, 1822 K
becomes premier, 1828 A
duel with Winchilsea, 1829 C
resigns, 1830 L
Wellesley, Richard Colley, Marquess of Wellesley, B. and Tory (1760–1842), as governor-general of India, 1798 E
as foreign secretary, 1812 C
Wellington, Duke of. *See* Wellesley, Arthur
Wellington, New Zealand, supplants Auckland as capital, 1865 N
Wells, Herbert George, B. author (1866–1946), 1866 Z, 1895 U, 1897 U, 1898 U, 1905 U, 1909 U, 1910 U, 1911 U, 1920 Q, 1964 Z
Welsbach, C. A. von, G. inventor of gas mantle (1858–1929), 1886 P
Welwyn Garden City, Herts., England, 1920 O
Wembley, Middlesex, England: Cup Final at, 1923 X; Empire Exhibition at, 1924 W
Wenzel, Karl Friedrich, G. metallurgist (1740–93), 1777 P
Werfel, Franz, Czech. author (1890–1945), 1941 U

Werner, Abraham Gottlob, G. geologist (1750–1817), 1775 P
Werth, Alexander, B. author and journalist (b. 1901), 1964 Q
Wesker, Arnold, B. dramatist (b. 1932), 1959 W, 1960 W, 1962 W
Wesley, John, B. evangelist, founder of Methodism (1703–91), 1771 R; signs Methodist deed of declaration, 1784 R; *Sermons*, 1787 R
Wessex Poems (T. Hardy), 1898 U
West, Benjamin, B. artist (1738–1820), 1771 S, 1803 S
West Africa, British, Colony formed from lands of former African Company, 1821 E
West Africa, Archbishop of, expelled from Ghana, 1962 H
West Africa, French, re-organised, 1904 N
West Africa States, Union of, proposed, 1958 L
Westcott, Brooke Foss, B. churchman and New Testament Scholar (1825–1901), 1881 Q
Western Australia: representative government in, 1870 H; responsible government in, 1890 K
West Indian Island, sold by Denmark to US, 1916 H
West Indies: US trade with, closed down by Britain, 1805 N; Coffee production in, 1909 Y
West Indies Federation, British: federation in force, 1958 A; Jamaican referendum to secede from, 1961 J; federation ends, 1962 D; 'Little Eight' propose to form new federation, 1962 E
Westinghouse, George, Am. inventor (1846–1914), 1846 Z, 1868 P, 1888 P, 1914 Z
Westinghouse Company, US, 1920 W
West-östlicher Divan (Goethe), 1819 U
Westphalia, W. Germany, Kingdom of, under Jerome Bonaparte, 1807 H
West Point, New York, US, fort, plot to surrender, 1780 L
West Virginia, created a US state, 1863 F
Westward Ho! (C. Kingsley), 1854 U
Wet, Christian Rudolph de, Boer general (1854–1922), 1901 B; rebels, 1914 K, 1915 F, M
Wette, Wilhelm Martin Leberecht de, G. theologian (1780–1849), 1806 Q
Weyman, Stanley John, B. novelist (1855–1928), 1855 Z, 1894 U, 1928 Z
Weyprecht, Karl, Aus. explorer, 1873 P
Wharton, Edith (née Jones), Am. author (1862–1937), 1862 Z, 1905 U, 1911 U, 1913 U, 1937 Z
What is Philosophy? (Heidegger), 1929 R
Wheat:
international agreement, 1933 H, 1959 C
world shortage, 1946 G
See also under Corn Laws
Wheatstone, Sir Charles, B. inventor and maker of musical instruments (1802–75), 1829 T
Wheeler, Sir Charles, B. sculptor (b. 1892), 1924 S
Wheeler, Sir Mortimer, B. archaeologist (b. 1890), 1954 Q
Wheeler-Bennett, Sir John, B. historian (b. 1902), 1934 O, 1953 Q, 1958 Q
Whewell, William, B. moral philosopher (1774–1858), 1840 P, 1846 R
Whigs. *See under* Political Parties
Whinfield, J. R., Am. inventor of Terylene, 1941 P
Whipsnade, Beds., England, Zoo, 1931 O
Whispering Gallery, The (J. Lehmann), 1955 U
Whistler, James, Abbott McNeill, B. artist (1834–1903), 1863 S, 1871 S, 1886 S
libel action with Ruskin, 1878 S
Whistler, Reginald John (Rex), B. artist (1905–44), 1927 S, 1930 S, 1936 S, 1940 S, 1957 S
White, Edward, Am. Cosmonaut, walks in space, 1965 P
White, Sir George, B. soldier (1835–1911), Joubert defeats, 1899 K
White, Gilbert, B. naturalist (1720–93), 1789 P, 1793 Z
White, Patrick, B. author (b. 1912), 1957 U
White, Terrence, Hamburg, B. author (b. 1906), 1958 U
White, Theodore Harold, Am. author (b. 1915), 1962 O
White, William Hale, B. novelist under pseudonym of 'Mark Rutherford' (1829–1913), 1888 U, 1893 U
White Doe of Rylstone (W. Wordsworth), 1815 U
Whitehead, Alfred North, B. mathematician and philosopher (1861–1947), 1861 Z, 1910 R, 1925 P, 1933 P, 1947 Z
Whitehead, Sir Edgar Cuthbert, Rhodes, United Federal Party leader (b. 1905), 1958 B, 1962 M
Whitehead, Robert, B. inventor (1823–1905), 1864 P
White House Papers of Harry L. Hopkins, 1948 Q
White Lotus Society, China, 1774 N
Whiteman, Paul, Am. band-leader (b. 1890), 1920 W
White Monkey, The (J. Galsworthy), 1924 U
White Peacock, The (D. H. Lawrence), 1911 U
White Slave trade, Conference on, 1904 O
White Terror, in France, 1815 G
Whiting, John, B. dramatist (1917–63), 1961 W
Whitman, Walt, Am. poet (1819–92), 1819 Z, 1855 U, 1866 U, 1871 U, 1892 Z
Whitney, Eli, Am. inventor (1765–1825), 1765 Z, 1793 P, 1800 P
Whitney, John, B. dramatist, 1951 W
Whitsun Wedding, The (P. Larkin), 1964 U
Whittier, John Greenleaf, Am. poet (1807–92), 1846 U, 1862 U, 1890 U
Whittle, Sir Frank, B. aeronautical engineer (b. 1907). 1907 Z, 1937 P
Who's Afraid of Virginia Woolf? (E. Albee), 1962 W
Whose Body? (D. L. Sayers), 1923 U
Whymper, Edward, B. mountaineer (1840–1911), 1840 Z, 1865 X, 1911 Z
Whyte, William Hollingsworth, Jr., Am. author (b. 1917), 1956 O
Widowers' Houses (G. B. Shaw), 1892 W
Wieck, Dorothea, G. film actress, 1931 W
Wie die Alten den Tod gebildet (Lessing), 1769 U
Wieland, Christopher Martin, G. author (1733–1813), 1765 U, 1766 U, 1771 I, 1773 V, 1774 U, 1780 U
Wieland; or the Transformation (C. Brockden Brown), 1798 U
Wilberforce, Samuel, B. churchman (1805–73), 1852 R
Wilberforce, William, B. anti-slavery leader and philanthropist (1759–1833), 1797 R
Wild Duck, The (H. Ibsen), 1884 W
Wilde, Oscar O'Flahertie Willis, B. author (1856–1900), 1856 Z, 1882 S, 1891 U, 1892 W, 1893 W, 1895 U, 1898 U, 1905 U; trial, 1895 P; tomb of, 1911 S
Wilder, Billy, Am. film director (b. 1906), 1945 W, 1950 W, 1963 W
Wilder, Thornton Niven dramatist (b. 1897), 1927 W, 1938 W
Wilderness, The, Virginia, US battle, 1864 E
Wild life, African, conference for preservation, 1961 P
Wilhelmina, Princess of Orange, consort of William V, 1786 H, 1787 F
Wilhelmina, Queen of Netherlands (1890–1948), 1890 L, 1948 J, 1962 Z
Wilhelm Meister (Goethe), 1795 U
Wilhelm Meisters Wanderjahre (Goethe), 1821 U

Wilhemsthal, E. Africa, Smuts captures, 1916 F
Wilhelm Tell (F. Schiller), 1804 W
Wilkes, John, B. Radical (1727–97), 1763 D, L, 1764 A, B, 1768 C, E, 1769 A, B, 1782 E, 1787 Z; elected lord mayor of London, 1774 L
Wilkie, Sir David, B. artist (1785–1841), 1785 Z, 1800 S, 1841 Z
Wilkie, Wendell, Am. Republican (1892–1944), opposes Roosevelt in presidential election, 1940 L
Wilkins, Hugh Percival, B. astronomer (b. 1896), 1956 P
Wilkins, William, B. architect (1778–1839), 1832 S
Wilkinson, John, B. engineer (1728–1808), 1774 P
William IV, King of Great Britain and Ireland (1830–7), accession, 1830 F, 1834 X, 1837 F; forces Grey's resignation, 1832 E; agrees to create Whig peers, 1832 F; as King of Hanover, 1833 J
William I, King of Prussia (1861–71), emperor of Germany (1871–88), as regent, 1858 K; accession, 1861 A; proclaimed emperor at Versailles, 1871 A; death, 1888 C
William II, emperor of Germany (1888–1918), (b. 1859, *d.* 1941), 1888 K, 1900 K, 1910 L
accession, 1888 F
dismisses Bismarck, 1890 C
meets Alexander II at Narva, 1890 H
visits England, 1891 G, 1895 H, 1899 L, 1901 A
sends 'Kruger Telegram', 1896 A
visits Tangier, 1905 C
signs treaty of mutual aid with Russia, 1905 G
dismisses Holstein, 1906 D
meets Nicholas II, 1907 H
Daily Telegraph interview, 1908 K, L
speaks on Germany's place in the sun, 1911 H
Socialists attack, 1912 E
promises universal suffrage, 1917 D
abdicates, 1918 L
Holland refuses to surrender, 1920 A
William, Prince of Denmark (1856–1913), becomes King of Greece, 1863 C
William V, Prince of Orange (*d.* 1806), deposed from command of army, 1786 N; in England, 1795 J; restored, 1797 J; second restoration, 1813 L
William I of Holland (1772–40), as King of United Netherlands, 1828 G; accepts treaty of London on Belgian independence, 1839 D; abdicates, 1840 K
William III, King of Holland (1840–9), 1840 K, 1848 C
William Lovell (L. Tieck), 1795 U
William Shakespeare (R. W. Chambers), 1930 Q
Williams, David, B. dissenting minister (1738–1816), 1790 U
Williams, Emlyn, B. dramatist and actor (b. 1905), 1935 W, 1938 W
Williams, Eric Eustace, Trinid. politician (b. 1911), 1961 M
Williams, Raymond Henry, B. critic (b. 1921), 1961 O
Williams, Tennessee, Am. dramatist (b. 1914), 1944 W, 1947 W, 1954 W, 1956 W
Williamson, Henry, B. author (b. 1895), 1895 Z, 1927 U
Williamson, Malcolm, B. musician (b. 1933), 1965 T
Wills, Helen, A, lawn-tennis player, 1927 X
Willstätter, Richard, G. chemist (1872–1942), 1913 P
Wilmot, David, Am. politician (1814–65), introduces proviso on slavery, 1846 H
Wilson, Angus Frank Johnstone-, B. author (b. 1913), 1913 Z, 1952 U, 1956 U, 1958 U
Wilson, Charles Thomas Rees, B. inventor (1879–1956), 1903 P
Wilson, Charles, B. mail-train robber, escapes, 1964 H
Wilson, Sir Charles, B. soldier and archaeologist (1836–1905), 1886 Q
Wilson, Sir Charles Rivers, B. financier and civil servant (1831–1916), 1878 H
Wilson, Charles McMoran, Lord Moran, B. medical practitioner (b. 1882), 1945 O
Wilson, Colin Henry, B. author (b. 1931), 1956 R
Wilson, Daniel, F., son-in-law of Jules Grévy, scandals connected with, 1887 K, M
Wilson, Edmund, Am. author (b. 1895), 1941 O
Wilson, Horace Hayam, B. orientalist (1786–1860), 1819 Q
Wilson, James Harold, B. Labour Party leader (b. 1916), 1916 Z; resigns from Attlee's cabinet, 1951 D; unsuccessful candidate for leadership of Parliamentary Labour Party, 1960 K; defeated in election for deputy leadership, 1962 L; elected leader of Labour Party, 1963 B; forms ministry, 1964 K; states Rhodesian UDI would be open act of defiance, 1964 K; meets L. B. Johnson, 1964 M
Wilson, John, B. journalist (1785–1854), under pseudonym of 'Christopher North', 1817 V
Wilson, Richard, B. artist (1715–82), 1782 Z
Wilson, Sandy, B. composer (b. 1924), 1954 W
Wilson, William Lyne, Am. Confederate soldier and Democrat (1843–1900), 1894 H
Wilson, Woodrow, Am. statesman, Democrat (1856–1924), 27th president of US (1913–21), 1856 Z 1914 D, 1920 E, 1924 Z
nominated, 1912 G
wins presidential election, 1912 L
inaugurated, 1913 L
vetoes immigration bill, 1915 A
re-elected, 1916 L
declaration of war on Germany, 1917 B, C, D
propounds Fourteen Points, 1918 A
suggests peace terms, 1918 K
attends Versailles Peace Conference, 1918 M
presides at first League of Nations meeting, 1919 B
lays League Covenant before Peace Conference, 1919 B
vetoes Volstead Act on prohibition, 1919 K
vetoes Knox peace proposals, 1920 E
awarded Nobel Peace prize, 1920 M
Wimbledon, Surrey, England, All-England lawn tennis championships at, 1877 X
Winchilsea, Earl of. *See* Finch-Hatton, George
Winckelmann, Johann Joachim, G. archaeologist (1717–68), 1764 Q, 1767 Q
Winckler, Hugo, G. archaeologist (*d.* 1942), 1906 Q
Wind and the Rain, The (M. Hodge), 1933 W
Windhoek, South-west Africa, Botha occupies, 1915 E
Wind in the Willows (K. Grahame), 1908 E
Windischgratz, Prince Alfred, Aust. (1787–1862), 1848 F, K
Window in Thrums (J. M. Barrie), 1889 U
Windowless building, 1963 S
Window tax, abolished, 1851 G
Windsor, Berkshire, England:
Castle, royal apartments in, 1824 S
statue at, 1869 S
Treaty, between Britain and Portugal, 1899 K
Windsor, House of, British royal family adopt name, 1917 F
Windsor, duke of. *See under* Edward VIII
Wine-growers, French, aided, 1900 G
Wine industry, French, crisis in, 1906 N
Winesburg, Ohio (S. Anderson), 1919 T
Wingate, Orde Charles, B. soldier (1903–44), 1943 D

Wingate, Sir Reginald, B. soldier (1861–1953), 1899 L
Wingfield, Walter Clapton, B. inventor of Lawn Tennis (1833–1912), 1874 Y
Winnie the Pooh (A. A. Milne), 1926 U
Winnipeg, Manitoba, Canada: Riel's rebellion near, 1869 K; strike in, 1919 E
Winslow Boy, The (T. Rattigan), 1946 W
Winsor, Kathleen, Am. author, 1945 U
Winter Journey (C. Odets), 1952 W
Wireless:
first transmission of speech by, 1900 P
broadcasting by amateurs, 1919 W
medium wave broadcasts, 1921 P
2LO broadcasts in Britain, 1922 W
Conference on re-distribution of wave-lengths, 1948 P
licences issued in Britain, statistics, 1925 Y, 1930 Y, 1940 Y
See also under Broadcasting; B.B.C.
Wireless telegraphy: Marconi invents, 1895 P; trans-Atlantic messages, 1901 P
Wireless, waves, studies in, 1902 P
Wireless-valves, all-metal, 1933 P
Wirth, Karl Joseph, G. Centre Party leader (1879–1943), becomes Chancellor, 1921 E
Wisconsin, state, US: becomes a US state, 1848 E; adopts women's suffrage, 1912 L
Wise, Thomas, James, B. collector of manuscripts (1859–1937), 1948 Q
Wiseman, Nicholas Patrick Stephen, B. cardinal (1802-65), 1802 Z, 1865 Z
Witchcraft, legislation against, 1951 R
Within the Gates (O. Casey), 1934 W
Witos, Vincent, Pol. Peasants' Party leader, 1926 E
Witte, Sergei, Count, R. statesman (1849–1915), as finance minister, 1892 J, 1903 H; becomes premier, 1905 L; falls, 1906 E
Wittgenstein, Ludwig, B. philosopher (*d.* 1951), 1922 R, 1958 R
Wodehouse, John, Earl of Kimberley, B. Liberal (1826–1902), 1896 K
Wodehouse, Pelham Grenville, Am., formerly B., novelist (b. 1881), 1881 Z, 1925 U
Woëvre Plain, Belgium, French offensive near, 1916 M
Wöhler, Friedrich, G. chemist (1800–82), 1800 Z, 1827 P, 1828 P, 1862 P, 1882 Z
Wolf, Friedrich Augustus, G. philologist (1759–1824), 1795 Q, 1807 Q, 1824 Z
Wolf, Hugo, Aus. musician (1860–1903), 1860 Z, 1888 T, 1894 T, 1896 T, 1903 Z
Wolfe, Thomas, Am. author (1900–38), 1929 U
Wolfenden Report on homosexual offences and prostitution, 1957 J
Wolff, Sir Henry Drummond Charles, B. Conservative (1830–1908), 1880 E, 1887 E
Wolf-Ferrari, Ermanno, It. musician (b. 1876), 1911 T
Wolfram, Spanish exports to Germany, reduced, 1944 E
Wollaston, William Hyde, B. scientist (1766–1828), 1804 P
Wollstonecraft, Mary, B. political author (1759–1797), 1792 O
Wolseley, Garnet, Lord Wolseley, B. soldier (1833–1913), 1833 Z, 1874 B, 1882 J, 1913 Z
Wolverhampton, Staffs., England, riots in, 1874 B
Woman in White, The (W. Collins), 1860 U
Woman of No Importance A (O. Wilde), 1893 W
Women in Love (D. H. Lawrence), 1921 U
Women, achievements of:
first British magistrate, 1913 E
first British M.P., 1919 L
first High Court Judge, 1965 O
first Privy Councillor, 1929 O
first woman premier of Commonwealth, 1960 G
first woman member of US Congress, 1916 L
first woman state governor in US, 1925 A
first woman preacher in England, 1917 R
first woman to climb Matterhorn north wall, 1965 Z
first woman in space, 1963 P
Women, enfranchisement of:
advocated, 1869 O
in Australia, 1902 G
in Belgium, 1948 O
in Britain, bills for, rejected, 1912 C, 1914 E, 1915 A
Bow by-election, on issue of, 1912 L
gain vote at age of 30, 1918 O
first woman M.P., 1919 L
Lady Rhondda attempts to take seat in Lords, 1922 O
gain vote at age of 21, 1928 E
See also Suffragettes
in Denmark, 1915 F
in France, 1945 O
in Germany, 1919 O
in Italy, 1946 O
in New Zealand, 1893 O
in Norway, 1907 F
in South Africa, for white women, 1930 E
in Switzerland, inelegible to vote in federal elections, 1959 B
in Turkey, 1929 M, 1934 M
in US, in Wyoming, 1869 O
in Arizona, Kansas and Wisconsin, 1912 L
achieved by 19th Amendment, 1920 H
Women, equal pay for, proposed in Britain, 1946 L
Women, the ordination of, 1958 R, 1960 R, 1963 R
Women's clubs, 1892 O
Women Journalists, Society of, 1844 V
Women, Married, Property Acts, in Britain, 1882 O
Women's Institutes, 1915 P
Women's Social and Political Union, 1903 P
Women's Voluntary Service, 1938 O
Women, war work:
employed in British munitions factories, 1917 O
liability for military service (aged 20–30), 1941 M
Women, working conditions in factories, 1844 F, 1847 F, 1906 O
Wood, Charles Lindley, Viscount Halifax (1839–1934), 1894 R
Wood, Edward Frederick Lindley, Viscount Halifax, B. statesman, Conservative (1881–1959), as Lord Irwin, Viceroy of India, 1931 C; visits Hitler, 1937 L; becomes foreign secretary, 1938 B; meets Mussolini, 1939 A; as British ambassador in Washington, 1940 M
Wood, Ellen (Mrs. Henry Wood), B. author (1814–1887), 1861 U
Wood, Grant, Am. artist, 1929 S, 1930 S
Wood, Sir Henry Joseph, B. musician, conductor (1869–1944), 1869 Z, 1895 T, 1944 Z
Wood, Mrs. Henry. *See* Wood, Ellen
Wood, Matilda, B. musical hall artiste, under name of 'Marie Lloyd' (1870–1922), 1870 Z, 1922 Z
Woodcock, George, B. T.U.C. Secretary (b. 1904), 1960 J
Woodhead, Sir John Ackroys, B. administrator (b. 1881), 1938 A
Woodlanders, The (T. Hardy), 1887 U
Woodstock (W. Scott), 1826 U

Woodward, Robert Burns, Am. chemist (b. 1917), 1960 P
Wood-working machinery, 1793 P
Wool production, comparative statistics of, 1910 Y
Woolf, Virginia (née Stephen), B. author (1882–1941), 1882 Z, 1925 U, 1927 U, 1928 U, 1929 U, 1941 Z
Woollen goods, British exports, 1822 Y, 1832 Y, 1842 Y, 1852 Y, 1862 Y, 1872 Y, 1882 Y, 1892 Y, 1902 Y, 1912 Y, 1922 Y
Woolley, Sir Leonard, B. archaeologist (1880–1960), 1918 Q, 1927 Q, 1930 Q
Woolton, Lord. *See* Marquis, F. J.
Woomera, Australia, space rocket launched at, 1959 P
Wooton, Graham, B. author (b. 1897), 1963 O
Wordsworth, William, B. poet (1770–1850), 1770 Z, 1798 U, 1800 U, 1805 U, 1807 U, 1814 U, 1815 U, 1835 U, 1850 Z; appointed poet laureate, 1843 U
Worker-priest movement among French Roman Catholics, 1943 R, 1959 R, 1965 R
Workers' Educational Association, 1904 O
Workers' Party. *See under* Political Parties
Workhouse Donkey, The (J. Arden), 1963 W
Working Days (M. Jokai), 1846 U
Working Men's Association, London, 1836 F, 1838 O
Working Men's Association, international, 1864 O
Working men's club, 1847 R
Workmen's compensation, 1880 J, O, 1897 O
Workshops, national, Blanc proposes, 1839 O
in France, 1848 B
World, end of, predicted, 1831 R
World and the West, The (A. Toynbee), 1952 O
World Council of Churches: scheme for, 1946 R; founded, 1948 R; Delhi meeting of, attended by Roman Catholic observers, 1961 R
World Monetary Conference, London, 1933 F
World of Physics, The (A. Eddington), 1931 P
World Peace Council, in East Berlin, 1951 O
in Vienna, offices closed, 1957 B
World Population (A. Carr-Saunders), 1936 O
World Population and Resources (PEP Report), 1955 O
World Student Christian Federation, 1895 R
World War; Its Cause and Cure (L. Curtis), 1945 O
Wormell, Donald Ernest Wilson, B. ancient historian (b. 1908), 1957 Q
Wornum, George Grey, B. architect (1888–1957), 1933 S
Worship, freedom of. *See* Religious Toleration
Worth, France, Prussian victory at, 1870 H
Worthington, Henry Rossiter, Am. Hydraulic engineer (1817–80), 1841 P
Wouk, Herman, Am. author (b. 1915), 1951 U
Wrangell, Mount, Alaska, observatory, 1953 P
Wright, Frank Lloyd, Am. architect (1869–1959), 1869 Z, 1909 S, 1936 S, 1938 S, 1949 S, 1959 S, Z
Wright, Georg Henrik von, Fin. philosopher, 1963 R
Wright, Harold, B. economist, 1931 O
Wright, Orville, Am. aviator (1871–1948), 1871 Z, 1903 P, 1948 Z
Wright, Richard Robert, Am. author (b. 1878), 1954 O
Wright, Wilbur, Am. aviator (1867–1912), 1903 P
Writtle, Essex, England, first British broadcasting station at, 1920 W
Wrong Side of the Park, The (J. Mortimer), 1960 W
Wundt, Wilhelm Max, G. physiologist and philosopher (1832–1920), 1832 Z, 1874 R, 1900 R, 1920 Z
Wurmser, Dagobert Sigismond, Count of, Aus. general (1724–97), 1796 H
Württemberg, W. Germany: becomes a Kingdom, 1805 M; merged in N. German Confederation, 1870 L
Wuthering Heights (E. Bronte), 1847 U
Wyatt, Thomas Henry, B. architect (1807–80), 1852 S
Wyatville, Sir Jeffry, B. architect (1766–1840), 1824 S
Wylam, Staffs., England, colliery, 1813 P
Wyler, William, Am. film director (b. 1902), 1946 W, 1953 W
Wyndham, William, B. Whig (1750–1810), 1794 G
Wyndham, William, Lord Granville, B. Whig statesman (1759–1834), 1806 B, K, M, 1807 C
Wynne, Greville, B. businessman, arrested in Budapest on charge of espionage, 1962 L; released from Moscow imprisonment, on exchange, 1964 D
Wyoming, Penna, US: massacre by Indians, 1778 G; reprisals for, 1779 H
Wyoming, state, US: gold discovered, 1866 P; enfranchises women, 1869 O; becomes a US state, 1890 G; has first woman state governor, 1925 A
Wyszynski, Stefan, Pol. Cardinal, primate of Poland (b. 1901), arrested, 1953 J; released, 1956 K

X

X certificate films, 1951 W
Xenon, gas, discovered, 1903 P
Xerography, invented, 1946 P
Xi-particles, 1959 P
XLI Poems (E. E. Cummings), 1925 U
X-Ray crystallography, 1912 P, 1964 P
X-Rays:
invention of, 1895 P
diffraction of, 1915 P
XYZ Affairs, 1797 K, 1798 D

Y

Yachting, 1964 X
Yakub, Amir of Afghanistan, 1879 E, K
Yale University, New Haven, Conn., US, Beineche Library at, 1963 S
Hockey Rink, 1958 S
Yalta Conference of Allied leaders, 1945 B
Yandabu Treaty, between Britain and Burma, 1826 B
Yanggn, Korea, 1951 J
Yangtze Agreement, between Britain and Germany, 1900 K
Yangtze River, China, Japanese flotilla on, 1913 J
Yarmolinsky Report on US security precautions, 1955 O
Yarrow Revisited (W. Wordsworth), 1835 U
Year of the Lion, The (G. Hanley), 1953 U
Years With Ross, The (J. Thurber), 1959 U
Yeats, William Butler, Ir. poet (1865–1939), 1865 Z, 1889 U, 1895 U, 1901 U, 1928 U, 1939 Z
Yellow Book, The, 1894 S
Yellow Plush Papers (W. M. Thackeray), 1838 U
Yemen: Italian agreement with, 1926 J; Britain accused of plotting to overthrow regime, 1962 L; cease-fire in, 1964 L; signs cease-fire with United Arab Republic, 1965 H
Yonge, Charlotte Mary, B. author (1823–1901), 1823 Z, 1853 U, 1901 Z
York, England: Retreat, 1792 O; Social survey of, 1941 O
York, now Toronto, Canada, US forces take, 1813 D
York, duke of. *See* Frederick Augustus